British Qualifications 2020

50TH EDITION

A Complete Guide to Professional, Vocational & Academic Qualifications in the United Kingdom

KoganPage

LONDON NEW YORK NEW DELHI

Publisher's note

Every possible effort has been made to ensure that the information contained in this book is accurate at the time of going to press, and the publishers and authors cannot accept responsibility for any errors or omissions, however caused. No responsibility for loss or damage occasioned to any person acting, or refraining from action, as a result of the material in this publication can be accepted by the editor, the publisher or any of the authors.

First published in Great Britain in 1966

Fiftieth edition published in Great Britain and the United States in 2020 by Kogan Page Limited

2nd Floor, 45 Gee Street	122 W 27th St, 10th Floor	4737/23 Ansari Road
London EC1V 3RS	New York NY 10001	Daryaganj
United Kingdom	USA	New Delhi 110002
www.koganpage.com		India

© Kogan Page, 2020

British Library Cataloguing-in-Publication Data

A CIP record for this book is available from the British Library.

Paperback 978 0 7494 9740 8
Hardback 978 0 7494 9742 2
ebook 978 0 7494 9741 5
ISSN 0141-5972

Typeset by AMA DataSet Ltd, Preston
Print production managed by Jellyfish
Printed and bound by CPI Group (UK) Ltd, Croydon, CR0 4YY

British Qualifications
2020

PUBLISHER'S NOTE

This 50th edition of *British Qualifications* has been considerably revised and updated to reflect the many changes in degree, diploma and certificate courses and to take account of legislative reforms affecting the structure of higher and further education over the past year.

The editor and compilers are most grateful to the academic registrars and the secretaries of the many bodies they have contacted for information and advice. Without their cooperation, the revision and updating of *British Qualifications* would not have been possible.

CONTENTS

Contents

Contents

REFERENCES

Association of MBAs (AMBA) (annual) *AMBA – Financial Times Guide to Business Schools,* AMBA, London

Committee of Vice-Chancellors and Principals (CVCP) (annual) *University Entrance: The official guide*, CVCP, London

Department for Education and Skills (DfES) (2003) *The Future of Higher Education*, The Stationery Office, London [online] http://www.dfes.gov.uk/hegateway/strategy/hestrategy/foreword.shtml

DfES (2004) *Five-Year Strategy for Children and Learners*, DfES, London

Qualifications and Curriculum Authority (QCA) (2004) *New Thinking for Reform: A framework for achievement*, QCA, London (July)

HOW TO USE THIS BOOK

You may find these notes helpful when using the book.

Part 1 presents an overview of the further and higher educational systems currently in operation in the United Kingdom, including a discussion of the major reforms that have taken place over the past year and their impact.

Part 2 takes a look at the teaching establishments whose qualifications are listed in Part 4 of the book, offering an explanation of the different types of institution, their place in the overall system and the levels of qualification that they award.

Part 3 presents a detailed description of vocational qualifications awarded by many of the professional associations included in Part 5, including an explanation of validating, examining and awarding bodies.

Part 4 is a directory of qualifications awarded by universities in the United Kingdom (ordered by university name). There is a brief introduction detailing admission to degree courses, degree structure and the various categories of degree available.

Part 5 is a directory of qualifications awarded by professional, trade and specialist associations in the United Kingdom (ordered by profession / discipline), including certificates, diplomas, NVQs and SVQs. A short introduction explains the functions of professional associations and how to gain membership.

Part 6 describes various bodies involved in the accreditation of colleges in the independent sector of further and higher education.

Part 7 is a list of study associations and learned societies.

Also included (at the beginning of the book) is a list of all abbreviations and designatory letters used throughout *British Qualifications*.

INDEX OF ABBREVIATIONS AND DESIGNATORY LETTERS

AAB	Associate of the Association of Bookkeepers
AACB	Associate of the Association of Certified Bookkeepers
AACP	Associate of the Association of Computer Professionals
AAFC	Associate of the Association of Financial Controllers and Administrators
AASI	Associate of the Ambulance Service Institute
AIA	Association of International Accountants
AMSPAR	Associate of the Association of Medical Secretaries, Practice Managers, Administrators and Receptionists
AASW	Advanced Award in Social Work
AAT	Association of Accounting Technicians
ABC	Awarding Body Consortium
ABDO	Associate of the British Dispensing Opticians
ABE	Association of Business Executives
ABEng	Associate Member of the Association of Building Engineers
ABHA	Associate of the British Hypnotherapy Association
ABIAT	Associate Member of the British Institute of Architectural Technologists
ABIPP	Associate of the British Institute of Professional Photography
ABMA	Associate of the Business Management Association
ABPR	Association of British Picture Restorers
ABRSM	Associated Board of the Royal Schools of Music
ABSSG	Associate of the British Society of Scientific Glassblowers
ACA	Associate of the Institute of Chartered Accountants in England and Wales
ACA	Associate of the Institute of Chartered Accountants in Ireland
ACC	Accredited Clinical Coders
ACCA	Associate of the Association of Chartered Certified Accountants
ACCA	Association of Chartered Certified Accountants
ACE	Association for Conferences and Events
ACEA	Associate of the Institute of Cost and Executive Accountants
ACertCM	Archbishop of Canterbury's Certificate in Church Music
ACGI	Associate of City and Guilds of London Institute
ACIArb	Associate of the Chartered Institute of Arbitrators
ACIB	Associate of the Chartered Institute of Bankers
ACIBS	Associate of the Chartered Institute of Bankers in Scotland
ACIBSE	Associate of the Chartered Institution of Building Services Engineers
ACIH	Associate of the Chartered Institute of Housing
ACII	Associate of the Chartered Insurance Institute
ACILA	Associate of the Chartered Institute of Loss Adjusters
ACIM	Associate of the Chartered Institute of Marketing
ACIOB	Associate of the Chartered Institute of Building
ACIS	Associate of the Institute of Chartered Secretaries and Administrators
ACIT	Advanced Certificate in International Trade
ACLIP	Certified Affiliate of CILIP
ACMA	Associate of the Chartered Institute of Management Accountants
ACP	Association of Child Psychotherapists
ACP	Associate of the College of Preceptors
ACP	Association of Computer Professionals
ACPM	Associate of the Confederation of Professional Management

ACPP	Associate of the College of Pharmacy Practice
ACoT	Associate of the College of Teachers
ACYW	Associate of the Community and Youth Work Association
ADCE	Advanced Diploma in Childcare and Education
ADCM	Archbishop of Canterbury's Diploma in Church Music
ADE	Advanced Diploma in Education
ADI	Approved Driving Instructor
AECI	Association Member of the Institute of Employment Consultants
AEWVH	Association for the Education and Welfare of the Visually Handicapped
AFA	Associate of the Institute of Financial Accountants
AFBPsS	Associate Fellow of the British Psychological Society
AFCI	Associate of the Faculty of Commerce and Industry Ltd
AffBMA	Affiliate of the Business Management Association
AffIManf	Affiliate of the Institute of Manufacturing
AffIMI	Affiliate of the Institute of the Motor Industry
AffIMS	Affiliate of the Institute of Management Specialists
AffInstM	Affiliate of the Meat Training Council
AffIP	Affiliate of the Institute of Plumbing
AffProfBTM	Affiliate of Professional Business and Technical Management
AFIMA	Associate Fellow of the Institute of Mathematics and its Applications
AFISOL	Aerodrome Flight Information Service Officer's Licence
AFPC	Advanced Financial Planning Certificate
AFRCSEd	Associate Fellow of Royal College of Surgeons of Edinburgh
AGCL	Associate of the Guild of Cleaners and Launderers
AGI	Associate of the Greek Institute
AGSM	Associate of the Guildhall School of Music and Drama
AHCIMA	Associate of the Hotel and Catering International Management Association
AHFS	Associate of the Council of Health Fitness and Sports Therapists
AHRIM	Associate of the Institute of Health Record Information and Management
AIA	Associate of the Institute of Actuaries
AIA	Association of International Accountants
AIAgrE	Associate of the Institution of Agricultural Engineers
AIAT	Associate of the Institute of Asphalt Technology
AIBCM	Associate of the Institute of British Carriage and Automobile Manufacturers
AIBMS	Associate of the Institute of Biomedical Science
AICB	Associate of the Institute of Certified Bookkeepers
AIChor	Associate of the Benesh Institute of Choreology
AICHT	Associate of the International Council of Holistic Therapists
AICM(Cert)	Associate Member of the Institute of Credit Management
AICS	Associate of the Institution of Chartered Shipbrokers
AICSc	Associate of the Institute of Consumer Sciences Incorporating Home Economics
AIDTA	Associate of the International Dance Teachers' Association
AIE	Associate of the Institute of Electrolysis
AIEM	Associate of the Institute of Executives and Managers
AIExpE	Associate of the Institute of Explosive Engineers
AIFA	Associate of the Institute of Field Archaeologists
AIFBQ	Associate of the International Faculty of Business Qualifications
AIFireE	Associate of the Institution of Fire Engineers
AIFP	Associate of the British International Freight Association
AIGD	Associate of the Institute of Grocery Distribution
AIHort	Associate Member of the Institute of Horticulture
AIIMR	Associate of the Institute of Investment Management and Research

AIIRSM	Associate of the International Institute of Risk and Safety Management
AIL	Associate of the Institute of Linguists
AILAM	Associate of the Institute of Leisure and Amenity Management
AIMBM	Associate of the Institute of Maintenance and Building Management
AIMC	Associate of the Institute of Management Consultancy
AIMgt	Associate of the Institute of Management
AIMIS	Associate of the Institute for the Management of Information Systems
AIMM	Associate of the Institute of Massage and Movement
AInstAM	Associate of the Institute of Administrative Management
AInstBA	Associate of the Institute of Business Administration
AInstBCA	Associate of the Institute of Burial and Cremation Administration
AInstM	Associate of the Meat Training Council
AInstPkg	Associate of the Institute of Packaging
AInstPM	Associate of the Institute of Professional Managers and Administrators
AInstSMM	Associate of the Institute of Sales and Marketing Management
AInstTA	Associate of the Institute of Transport Administration
AInstTT	Associate Member of the Institute of Travel and Tourism
AIOC	Associate of the Institute of Carpenters
AIOFMS	Associate of the Institute of Financial and Management Studies
AIP	Associate of the Institute of Plumbing
AIQA	Associate of the Institute of Quality Assurance
AIS	Accredited Imaging Scientist
AISOB	Associate of the Incorporated Society of Organ Builders
AISTD	Associate of the Imperial Society of Teachers of Dancing
AISTDDip	Associate Diploma of the Imperial Society of Teachers of Dancing
AITSA	Associate of the Institute of Trading Standards Administration
AIVehE	Associate of the Institute of Vehicle Engineers
AIWSc	Associate Member of the Institute of Wood Science
ALCM	Associate of the London College of Music
ALI	Associate of the Landscape Institute
ALS	Associate of the Linnean Society of London
AMA	Associate of the Museums Association
AMABE	Associate Member of the Association of Business Executives
AMAE	Associate Member of the Academy of Experts
AMASI	Associate Member of the Architecture and Surveying Institute
AMBA	Association of MBAs
AMBA	Non-Teacher Associate Member of the British (Theatrical) Arts
AMBCS	Associate Member of the British Computer Society
AMBII	Associate Member of the British Institute of Innkeeping
AmCAM	Associate of the Communication Advertising and Marketing Education Foundation
AMCT	Associate of the Association of Corporate Treasurers
AMCTHCM	Associate Member of the Confederation of Tourism, Hotel and Catering Management
AMI	Association Montessori Internationale
AMIA	Affiliated Member of the Association of International Accountants
AMIAgrE	Associate Member of the Institution of Agricultural Engineers
AMIAP	Associate Member of the Institution of Analysts and Programmers
AMIAT	Associate Member of the Institute of Asphalt Technology
AMIBC	Associate Member of the Institute of Building Control
AMIBCM	Associate Member of the Institute of British Carriage and Automobile Manufacturers
AMIBF	Associate Member of the Institute of British Foundrymen

AMICE	Associate Member of the Institution of Civil Engineers
AMIChemE	Associate Member of the Institution of Chemical Engineers
AMIED	Associate Member of the Institution of Engineering Designers
AMIE	Associate Member of the Institution of Engineers
AMIEE	Associate Member of the Institution of Electrical Engineers
AMIEx	Associate Member of the Institute of Export
AMIHIE	Associate Member of the Institute of Highway Incorporated Engineers
AMIHT	Associate Member of the Institution of Highways and Transportation
AMIIE	Associate Member of the Institution of Incorporated Engineers
AMIIExE	Associate Member of the Institution of Incorporated Executive Engineers
AMIIHTM	Associate Member of the International Institute of Hospitality Tourism & Management
AMIISE	Associate Member of the International Institute of Social Economics
AMIM	Associate Member of the Institute of Materials
AMIManf	Member of the Institute of Manufacturing
AMIMechE	Associate Member of the Institution of Mechanical Engineers
AMIMechIE	Associate Member of the Institution of Mechanical Incorporated Engineers
AMIMI	Associate Member of the Institute of the Motor Industry
AMIMinE	Associate of the Institute of Mining Engineers
AMIMM	Associate Member of the Institution of Mining and Metallurgy
AMIMS	Associate Member of the Institute of Management Specialists
AMICE	Associate Member of the Institution of Engineers
AMInstE	Associate Member of the Institute of Energy
AMInstR	Associate Member of the Institute of Refrigeration
AMInstTA	Associate Member of the Institute of Transport Administration
AMIPlantE	Associate Member of the Institution of Plant Engineers
AMIPR	Associate Member of the Institute of Public Relations
AMIPRE	Associate Member of the Incorporated Practitioners in Radio and Electronics
AMIQ	Associate Member of the Institute of Quarrying
AMIQA	Associate Member of the Institute of Quality Assurance
AMIRTE	Associate Member of the Institute of Road Transport Engineers
AMISM	Associate Member of the Institute for Supervision & Management
AMIStrutE	Associate Member of the Institution of Structural Engineers
AMITD	Associate Member of the Institute of Training and Development
AMIVehE	Associate Member of the Institute of Vehicle Engineers
AMNI	Associate Member of the Nautical Institute
AMPA	Associate Member of the Master Photographers Association
AMProfBTM	Associate Member of Professional Business and Technical Management
AMRAeS	Associate Member of the Royal Aeronautical Society
AMRSH	Associate Member of the Royal Society for the Promotion of Health
AMS	Associate of the Institute of Management Services
AMS(Aff)	Affiliate of the Association of Medical Secretaries, Practice Managers, Administrators and Receptionists
AMSE	Associate Member of the Society of Engineers (Inc)
AMSPAR	Association of Medical Secretaries, Practice Managers, Administrators and Receptionists
AMusEd	Associate Diploma in Music Education
AMusLCM	Associate in Music of the London College of Music
AMusTCL	Associate in Music of Trinity College of Music
AMWES	Associate Member of the Women's Engineering Society
ANAEA	Associate of the National Association of Estate Agents
ANCA	Advanced National Certificate in Agriculture

AOP	Association of Photographers
AOR	Association of Reflexologists
APA	Accreditation of Prior Experience
APC	Assessment of Professional Competence
APCS	Associate of the Property Consultants Society
APMI	Associate of the Pensions Management Institute
APMP	Association for Project Management Professional
AQA	Assessment & Qualifications Alliance
ARAD	Associate of the Royal Academy of Dancing
ARAM	Associate of the Royal Academy of Music
ARB	Architects Registration Board
ARCM	Associate of Royal College of Music
ARCO	Associate of the Royal College of Organists
ARCS	Associate of the Royal College of Science
AREC	Associate of the Recruitment and Employment Confederation
ARELS	Association of Recognised English Language Services
ARELS-FELCO	Association of Recognised English Language Teaching Establishments in Britain
ARIBA	Associate of the Royal Institute of British Architects
ARICS	Associate of the Royal Institution of Chartered Surveyors
ARIPHH	Associate of the Royal Institute of Public Health and Hygiene
ARPS	Associate of the Royal Photographic Society
ARSC	Associate of the Royal Society of Chemistry
ARSCM	Associate of the Royal School of Church Music
ARSM	Associate of the Royal School of Mines
AS	Advanced Supplementary level
ASCA	Associate of the Institute of Company Accountants
ASCT	Associate of the Society of Claims Technicians
ASDC	Associate of the Society of Dyers and Colourists
ASE	Associate of the Society of Engineers (Inc)
ASI	Ambulance Service Institute
ASI	Architecture and Surveying Institute
ASIAffil	Affiliate of the Ambulance Service Institute
ASIS	Accredited Senior Imaging Scientist
ASLC	Advanced Secretarial Language Certificate
ASNN	Associate of the Society of Nursery Nursing
AssCI	Associate of the Institute of Commerce
AssociateCIPD	Associate of the Chartered Institute of Personnel and Development
AssociateIEEE	Associate of the Institution of Electrical and Electronics Engineers Incorporated
AssociateIIE	Associate of the Institution of Incorporated Engineers
AMIMechE	Associate of the Institution of Mechanical Engineers
AssocIPHE	Associate of the Institution of Public Health Engineers
AssocMIWM	Associate Member of the Institute of Wastes Management
AssocTechIIE	Associate Technician of the Institution of Incorporated Engineers
ASTA	Associate of the Swimming Teachers' Association
ASVA	Associate of the Incorporated Society of Valuers and Auctioneers
ATC	Art Teacher's Certificate
ATCL	Associate of Trinity College of Music
ATCLicence	Air Traffic Controller's Licence
ATCLTESOL	Associate Diploma in the Teaching of English to Speakers of Other Languages, Trinity College
ATD	Art Teacher's Diploma
ATI	Associate of the Textile Industry

ATII	Associate of the Chartered Institute of Taxation
ATPL	Airline Transport Pilot's Licence
ATSC	Associate in the Technology of Surface Coatings
ATT	Association of Taxation Technicians
ATT	Member of the Association of Taxation Technicians
ATTA	Association of Therapy Teachers Associate
ATTF	Association of Therapy Teachers Fellow
ATTM	Association of Therapy Teachers Member
AWeldI	Associate of the Welding Institute
BA	Bachelor of Arts
BA(Econ)	Bachelor of Arts in Economics & Social Studies
BA(Ed)	Bachelor of Arts (Education)
BA(Lan)	Bachelor of Languages
BA(Law)	Bachelor of Arts in Law
BA(Music)	Bachelor of Music
BABTAC	British Association of Beauty Therapy and Cosmetology Ltd
BAC	British Accreditation Council for Independent Further and Higher Education
BAC	British Association for Counselling
BAcc	Bachelor of Accountancy
BACP	British Association for Counselling Psychotherapy
BADA	British Antique Dealers' Association
BADN	British Association of Dental Nurses
BAE	British Association of Electrolysists Ltd
BAGMA	British Agricultural and Garden Machinery Association
BAgr	Bachelor of Agriculture
BAO	Bachelor of Obstetrics
BAP	British Association of Psychotherapists
BArch	Bachelor of Architecture
BASELT	British Association in State English Language Teaching
BBO	British Ballet Organisation
BChD	Bachelor of Dental Surgery
BChir	Bachelor of Surgery
BCL	Bachelor of Civil Law
BCom	Bachelor of Commerce
BCombStuds	Bachelor of Combined Studies
BComm	Bachelor of Communications
BCS	Bachelor of Combined Studies
BCS	British Computer Society
BD	Bachelor of Divinity
BDA	British Dietetic Association
BDes	Bachelor of Design
BDS	Bachelor of Dental Surgery
BEconSc	Bachelor of Economics
BECTU	Broadcasting, Entertainment, Cinematograph and Theatre Union
BEd	Bachelor of Education
BEng	Bachelor of Engineering
BEng and Man	Bachelor of Mechanical Engineering, Manufacture and Management
BER	Board for Engineers' Regulation
BFA	Bachelor of Fine Arts
BFin	Bachelor of Finance
BHA	British Hypnotherapy Association
BHI	British Horological Institute Ltd

BHS	British Horse Society
BHSAI	British Horse Society's Assistant Instructor's Certificate
BHSI	British Horse Society's Instructor's Certificate
BHSII	British Horse Society's Intermediate Instructor's Certificate
BHSIntSM	British Horse Society's Intermediate Stable Manager's Certificate
BHSSM	British Horse Society's Stable Manager's Certificate
BIA	Beauty Industry Authority
BIBA	Bachelor of International Business Administration
BIE	British Institute of Embalmers
BIFA	British International Freight Association
BIPP	British Institute of Professional Photography
BIS	British Interplanetary Society
BKSTS	British Kinematograph Sound and Television Society
BLD	Bachelor of Landscape Design
BLE	Bachelor of Land Economy
BLEng	Bi-Lingual Engineer
BLib	Bachelor of Librarianship
BLing	Bachelor of Linguistics
BLitt	Bachelor of Letters
BLS	Bachelor of Library Studies
BM	Bachelor of Medicine
BMA	British Medical Association
BM, BCh	Conjoint degree of Bachelor of Medicine, Bachelor of Surgery
BM, BS	Conjoint degree of Bachelor of Medicine, Bachelor of Surgery
BMedBiol	Bachelor of Medical Biology
BMedSci	Bachelor of Medical Sciences
BMedSci(Speech)	Bachelor of Medical Sciences (Speech)
BMet	Bachelor of Metallurgy
BMid	Bachelor of Midwifery
BMidwif	Bachelor of Midwifery
BMSc	Bachelor of Medical Sciences
BMus	Bachelor of Music
BN	Bachelor of Nursing
BNNursing	Bachelor of Nursing, Nursing Studies
BNSc	Bachelor of Nursing
BNurs	Bachelor of Nursing
BOptom	Bachelor of Optometry
BPA	Bachelor of Performing Arts
BPharm	Bachelor of Pharmacy
BPhil	Bachelor of Philosophy
BPhil(Ed)	Bachelor of Philosophy (Education)
BPL	Bachelor of Planning
BSc	Bachelor of Science
BSc(Archit)	Bachelor of Science (Architecture)
BSc(DentSci)	Bachelor of Science in Dental Science
BSc(Econ)	Bachelor of Science in Economics
BSc(MedSci)	Bachelor of Science (Medical Science)
BSc(Social Science)	Bachelor of Science (Social Science)
BSc(Town & Regional Planning)	Bachelor of Science (Town & Regional Planning)
BSc(VetSc)	Bachelor of Science (Veterinary Science)
BScAgr	Bachelor of Science in Agriculture

BScEng	Bachelor of Science in Engineering
BScFor	Bachelor of Science in Forestry
BScTech	Bachelor of Technical Science
BSocSc	Bachelor of Social Science
BSSc	Bachelor of Social Science
BSSG	British Society of Scientific Glassblowers
BSSG	Member of the British Society of Scientific Glassblowers
BTEC	Business and Technology Education Council
BTech	Bachelor of Technology
BTechEd	Bachelor of Technological Education
BTEC HC	Business and Technology Education Council Higher Certificate
BTEC HD	Business and Technology Education Council Higher Diploma
BTEC HNC	Business and Technology Education Council Higher National Certificate
BTEC HND	Business and Technology Education Council Higher National Diploma
BTechS	Bachelor of Technology Studies
BTh	Bachelor of Theology
BTheol	Bachelor of Theology
BTP	Bachelor of Town Planning
BVC	Bar Vocational Course
BVetMed	Bachelor of Veterinary Medicine
BVMS	Bachelor of Veterinary Medicine
BVM&S	Bachelor of Veterinary Medicine
BVSc	Bachelor of Veterinary Science
C&G	City and Guilds
CA	Member of the Institute of Chartered Accountants of Scotland
CAA	Civil Aviation Authority
CABE	Companion of the Association of Business Executives
CABS	Chartered Association of Business Schools
CACHE	Council for Awards in Children's Care and Education
CAE	Certificated Automotive Engineer
CAE	Companion of the Academy of Experts
CAM	Communication Advertising and Marketing Education Foundation
CAS	Certification of Accountancy Studies
CASS	Certificate of Applied Social Studies
CAT	Certificate for Accounting Technicians
CAT	College of Advanced Technology
CATS	Postgraduate Qualification by Credit Accumulation and Transfer
CBA	Companion of the British (Theatrical) Arts
CBS	The Chartered Banker Institute
CBIM	Companion of the British Institute of Management
CBiol	Chartered Biologist
CBLC	Certificate in Business Language Competence
CCETSW	Central Council for Education and Training in Social Work
CChem	Chartered Chemist
CCol	Chartered Colourist
CCST	Certificate of Completion of Specialist Training
CDBA	Certified Doctor of Business Administration
CDipAF	Certified Diploma in Accounting and Finance
CEE	Extended European Command Endorsement
CeFA	Certificate for Financial Advisers
CEM	Certificate in Executive Management
CeMAP	Certificate in Mortgage Advice and Practice

CEng	Chartered Engineer
CertAMed	Certificate in Aviation Medicine
CertArb	Certificate in Arboriculture
CertBibKnowl	Certificate of Bible Knowledge
CertCIH	Chartered Institute of Housing recognised Housing Qualification
CertCM	Certificate of Cash Management
CertDesRCA	Certificate of Designer of the Royal College of Art
CertEd	Certificate in Education
CertEPK	Certificate of Essential Pensions Knowledge
CertHE	Certificate of Higher Education
CertHSAP	Certificate in Health Services Administration Practice
CertHSM	Certificate in Health Services Management
CertMFS	Certificate in the Marketing of Financial Services
CertOccHyg	Certificate in Operational Competence in Comprehensive Occupational Hygiene
CertRP	Certificate in Recruitment Practice
CertTEL	Certificate in the Teaching of European Languages
CertTESOL	Certificate of Teaching of English to Speakers of Other Languages
CertTEYL	Certificate of Teaching of English to Young Learners
CertYCW	Certificate in Youth and Community Work
CETHV	Certificate of Education in Training as Health Visitor
CEYA	Council for Early Years Awards
CFS	Certificate in Financial Services
CFSP	Certificate in Financial Services Practice
CGeol	Chartered Geologist
CGLI	City & Guilds of London Institute
CHARM	Centre for Hazard and Risk Management
ChB	Bachelor of Surgery
CHD	Choral-Training Diploma
ChM	Master of Surgery
CHP	Certificate in Hypnosis and Psychology
CHRIM	Certified Member of the Institute of Health Record Information and Management
CIAgrE	Companion of the Institution of Agricultural Engineers
CIArb	Chartered Institute of Arbitrators
CIAT	Chartered Institute of Architectural Technologists
CIB	Chartered Institute of Bankers
CIBM	Corporate Member of the Institute of Builders' Merchants
CIBSE	Chartered Institution of Building Services Engineers
CIC	Construction Industry Council
CIEx	Companion of the Institute of Export
CIFE	Conference for Independent Further Education
CIH	Chartered Institute of Horticulture
CIH	Chartered Institute of Housing
CII	Chartered Insurance Institute
CILA	Chartered Institute of Loss Adjusters
CILEx	Chartered Institute of Legal Executives
CILIP	Chartered Institute of Library and Information Professionals
CILT	Chartered Institute of Logistics and Transport
CIM	Chartered Institute of Marketing
CIMA	Chartered Institute of Management Accountants
CIMediE	Companion of the Institution of Mechanical Engineers
CIMgt	Companion of the Institute of Management
CIOB	Chartered Institute of Building

CIP	Certificate of Institute Practice
CIPD	Chartered Institute of Personnel and Development
CIPFA	Chartered Institute of Public Finance & Accounting
CIPS	Chartered Institute of Purchasing and Supply
CISOB	Counsellor of the Incorporated Society of Organ Builders
CIT	Certificate in Information Technology
CIWEM	Chartered Institution of Water and Environmental Management
CL(ABDO)	Diploma in Contact Lens Practice of the Association of British Dispensing Opticians
CLAC	Commercial Language Assistant Certificate
CLAIT	Computer Literacy & Information Technology
CLC	Council for Licensed Conveyancers
CLE	Limited European Command Endorsement
ClinPsyD	Doctorate in Clinical Psychology
CMA	Certificate in Management Accountancy
CMathFIMA	Fellow of the Institute of Mathematics and its Applications
CMBA	Certified Master of Business Administration
CMBHI	Craft Member of the British Horological Institute
CMC	Certified Management Consultants
CMet	Chartered Meteorologist
CMIWSc	Certified Member of the Institute of Wood Science
CMS	Certificate in Management Studies
CNAA	Council for National Academic Awards
COA	Certificate of Accreditation
COBC	Certificate of Basic Competence
CoEA	Certificate of Educational Achievement
COES	Certificate of Educational Studies
CofE	Church of England
CofS	Church of Scotland
CompBCS	Companion of the British Computer Society
CompIAP	Companion of the Institution of Analysts and Programmers
CompIEE	Companion of the Institution of Electrical Engineers
CompIGasE	Companion of the Institution of Gas Engineers
CompIManf	Companion of the Institute of Manufacturing
CompIMS	Companion of the Institute of Management Specialists
CompIP	Companion of the Institute of Plumbing
CorporateIRRV	Corporate Member of the Institute of Revenues, Rating and Valuation
COSCA	Confederation of Scottish Counselling Agencies
CPA	Chartered Patent Agents
CPC	Certificate of Professional Competence, the Institute of Transport Administration
CPD	Continuing Professional Development
CPE	Common Professional Exam
CPEA	Certificate of Practice in Estate Agency
CIPFA	Member of Chartered Institute of Public Finance and Accountancy
CPhys	Chartered Physicist of the Institute of Physics
CPIM	Certificate in Production and Inventory Management
CPL	Commercial Pilot's Licence
CPM	Certified Professional Manager
CPP	Certificate of Pre-school Practice
CPR	Chartered Professional Review
CProfBTM	Companion of Professional Business and Technical Management
CPS	Certificate in Pastoral Studies and Applied Theology

CPSC	Certificate of Proficiency in Survival Craft
CPsychol	Chartered Psychologist, British Psychological Society
CPT	Continuing Professional Training
CPVE	Certificate of Pre-Vocational Training
CRAeS	Companion of the Royal Aeronautical Society
CRAH	Central Register of Advanced Hypnotherapists
CRCW	Church Related Community Workers
CRNCM	Companion of the Royal Northern College of Music
CSCT	Central School for Counselling Training
CSD	Chartered Society of Designers
CSE	Certificate of Secondary Education
CSM	Certificate in Safety Management
CSMGSM	Certificate in Stage Management (Guildhall School of Music and Drama)
CStat	Chartered Statistician
CSYS	Certificate of Sixth Year Studies
CTABRSM	Certificate of Teaching of the Associated Board of the Royal School of Music
CTextATI	Associate of the Textile Institute
CTextFTI	Fellow of the Textile Institute
CTHCM	Confederation of Tourism, Hotel and Catering Management
CVA	Certificated Value Analyst
CVM	Certificated Value Manager
CVT	Certified Vehicle Technologist
DA	Diploma in Anaesthesia
DAdmin	Doctor of Administration
DAES	Diploma in Advanced Educational Studies
DArch	Doctor of Architecture
DAvMed	Diploma in Aviation Medicine
DBA	Doctor of Business Administration
DBE	Diploma in Business Engineering
DBO	Diploma of the British Orthoptic Society
DBS	Diploma in Business Studies
DCC	Diploma of Chelsea College
DCDH	Diploma in Child Dental Health
DCE	Dangerous Cargo Endorsements
DCE	Diploma in Childcare and Education
DCG	Diploma in Careers Guidance
DCH	Diploma in Child Health
DChM	Diploma in Chiropodial Medicine, Institute of Chiropodists and Podiatrists
DCHT	Diploma in Community Health in Tropical Countries
DCL	Doctor of Civil Law
DCLF	Diploma in Contact Lens Fitting
DClinPsych	Doctor of Clinical Psychiatry
DCLP	Diploma in Contact Lens Practice
DCR(R)or(T)	Diploma of the College of Radiographers
DD	Doctor of Divinity
DDH(Birm)	Diploma in Dental Health, University of Birmingham
DDOrthRCPSGlas	Diploma in Dental Orthopaedics of the Royal College of Physicians and Surgeons of Glasgow
DDPHRCS(Eng)	Diploma in Dental Public Health, Royal College of Surgeons of England
DDS	Doctor of Dental Surgery
DDSc	Doctor of Dental Science
DDPH	Diploma in Dental Public Health

DEBA	Diploma in European Business Administration
DEdPsy	Doctor of Educational Psychiatry
DEM	Diploma in Executive Management
DEng	Doctor of Engineering
DES	Department of Education and Science (now the Department for Education)
DETR	Department of the Environment, Transport and the Regions
DFin	Doctor of Finance
DFSM	Diploma in Financial Services Management
DGA	Diamond Member of the Gemmological Association and Gem Testing Laboratory of Great Britain
DGDPRCSEng	Diploma in General Dental Practice, Royal College of Surgeons of England
DGM	Diploma in Geriatric Medicine
DGO	Diploma in Obstetrics and Gynaecology
DHC	Doctorate in Healthcare
DHE	Diploma in Horticulture, Royal Botanic Garden, Edinburgh
DHMSA	Diploma in the History of Medicine, Society of Apothecaries of London
DHP	Diploma in Hypnosis and Psychotherapy
DIA	Diploma of Industrial Administration
DIB	Diploma in International Business
DIC	Diploma of Membership of Imperial College of Science and Technology, University of London
DIH	Diploma in Industrial Health
DipABRSM	Diploma of the Associated Board of the Royal Schools of Music
DipAD	Diploma in Art and Design
DipAdvHYP	Diploma in Advanced Hypnotherapy
DipAE	Diploma in Adult Education
DipAgrComm	Diploma in Agricultural Communication
DipArb	Diploma in Arbitration
DipArb	Diploma in Arboriculture
DipArch	Diploma in Architecture
DipASE(CofP)	Graduate Level Specialist Diploma in Advanced Study in Education, College of Preceptors
DipASSc	Diploma in Arts and Social Sciences
DipAT	Diploma in Accounting Technology
DipAvMed	Diploma in Aviation Medicine
DipBA	Diploma in Business Administration
DipBldgCons	Diploma in Building Conservation
DipBMA	Diploma in Business Management
DipCAM	Diploma in the Communication Advertising and Marketing Education Foundation
DipCD	Diploma in Community Development
DipCHM	Diploma in Choir Training, Royal College of Organists
DipClinPath	Diploma in Clinical Pathology
DipCOT	Diploma of the College of Occupational Therapists
DipCP	Diploma of the College of Teachers
DipCT	Diploma in Corporate Treasury Management
DipDerm	Diploma in Dermatology
DipEd	Diploma in Education
DipEF	Diploma in Executive Finance
DipEH	Diploma in Environmental Health
DipEM	Diploma in Environmental Management
DipEMA	Diploma in Executive and Management Accountancy
DipEngLit	Diploma in English Literature

DipFD	Diploma in Funeral Directing, National Association of Funeral Directors
DipFS	Diploma in Financial Services
DipGAI	Diploma of the Guild of Architectural Ironmongers
DipGrTrans	Diploma in Greek Translation
DipGSM	Diploma of the Guildhall School of Music and Drama
DipHE	Diploma of Higher Education
DipHS	Diploma of the Heraldry Society
DipIEB	Diploma of the International Employee Benefits
DipISW	Diploma of the Institute of Social Welfare
DipLE	Diploma in Land Economy
DipLP	Diploma in Legal Practice
DipM	Postgraduate Diploma in Marketing
DipMedAc	Diploma in Medical Acupuncture
DipMetEng	Diploma in Meteorological Engineering
DipMFS	Diploma in the Marketing of Financial Services
DipMth	Diploma in Music Therapy
DipOccH	Diploma in Occupational Health
DipOccHyg	Diploma of Professional Competence in Comprehensive Occupational Hygiene
DipPDTC	Diploma in Professional Dancers Teaching Course
DipPharmMed	Diploma in Pharmaceutical Medicine
DipPhil	Diploma in Philosophy
DipProjMan	Diploma in Project Management
DipPropInv	Diploma in Property Investment
DipRAM	Diploma of the Royal Academy of Music
DipRCM	Diploma of the Royal College of Music
DipRMS	Diploma of the Royal Microscopical Society
DipSc	Diploma in Science
DipSM	Diploma in Safety Management
DipSurv	Diploma in Surveying
DipSW	Diploma in Social Work
DipTCL	Diploma of the Trinity College of Music, London
DipTCR	Diploma in Organ Teaching
DipTESOL	Diploma in Teaching of English to Speakers of Other Languages
DipTHP	Diploma in Therapeutic Hypnosis and Psychotherapy
DipTM	Diploma in Training Management, Institute of Personnel and Development
DipTransIoL	Diploma in Translation, Institute of Linguists
DipUniv	Diploma of the University
DipVen	Diploma in Venereology, Society of Apothecaries of London
DipWCF	Diploma of the Worshipful Company of Farriers
DIS	Diploma in Industrial Studies
DLang	Doctor of Language
DLit(t)	Doctor of Letters or Literature
DLO	Diploma of Laryngology and Otology
DLORCSEng	Diploma in Laryngology and Otology, Royal College of Surgeons of England
DLP	Diploma in Legal Practice
DM	Doctor of Medicine
DMedRehab	Diploma in Medical Rehabilitation
DMedSc	Doctor in Medical Science
DMet	Doctor of Metallurgy
DMJ(Clin) or DMJ(Path)	Diploma in Medical Jurisprudence (Clinical or Pathological), Society of Apothecaries of London
DMRD	Diploma in Medical Radio-Diagnosis

DMRT	Diploma in Radiotherapy
DMS	Diploma in Management Studies
DMU	Diploma in Medical Ultrasound
DMus	Doctor of Music
DMusCantuar	Archbishop of Canterbury's Doctorate in Music
DNSc	Doctor in Nursing Science
DO	Diploma in Ophthalmology
DO	Diploma in Osteopathy
DocEdPsy	Doctorate in Educational Psychology
DOpt	Diploma in Ophthalmic Optics
DOrth	Diploma in Orthoptics
DOrthRCSEdin	Diploma in Orthodontics, Royal College of Surgeons of Edinburgh
DOrthRCSEng	Diplomate in Orthodontics, Royal College of Surgeons of England
DP	Diploma in Psychotherapy
DPA	Diploma in Public Administration
DpBact	Diploma in Bacteriology
DPD(Dund)	Diploma in Public Dentistry, University of Dundee
DPH	Diploma in Public Health
DPharm	Diploma in Pharmacy
DPhil	Diploma in Philosophy
DPHRCSEng	Diploma in Dental Public Health, Royal College of Surgeons of England
DPM	Diploma in Psychological Medicine
DPodM	Diploma in Podiatric Medicine
DProf	Doctor of Professional Studies
DPS	Diploma in Professional Studies
DPSE	Diploma in Pastoral Studies and Applied Theology
DPsychol	Doctor of Psychology
DrAc	Doctor of Acupuncture
Dr(RCA)	Doctor of the Royal College of Art
DRCOG	Diploma of the Royal College of Obstetricians and Gynaecologists
DRDRCSEd	Diploma in Restorative Dentistry, Royal College of Surgeons of Edinburgh
DRE	Diploma in Remedial Electrolysis, Institute of Electrolysis
DRI	Diploma in Radionuclide Imaging
DRSAMD	Diploma in the Royal Scottish Academy of Music and Drama
DSA	Diploma in Secretarial Administration
DSc	Doctor of Science
DSc(Econ)	Doctor of Science (Economics) or in Economics
DSc(Eng)	Doctor of Science (Engineering)
DSc(Social)	Doctor of Science in the Social Sciences
DScEcon	Doctor in the Faculty of Economics and Social Studies
DSCh(Ox)	Diploma in Surgical Chiropody (Oxon), Oxford School of Chiropody and Podiatry
DScTech	Doctor of Technical Science
DSocSc	Doctor of Social Science
DSSc	Doctor of Social Science
DSTA	Diploma Member of the Swimming Teachers' Association
DTCD	Diploma in Tuberculosis and Chest Diseases
DTech	Doctor of Technology
DTI	Department of Trade and Industry
DTMH	Diploma in Tropical Medicine and Hygiene
DTM&H	Diploma in Tropical Medicine and Hygiene
DTp	Department of Transport
DUniv	Doctor of the University

DVetMed	Doctor of Veterinary Medicine
DVM	Doctor of Veterinary Medicine
DVM&S	Doctor of Veterinary Medicine and Surgery
DVS	Doctor of Veterinary Surgery
DVSc	Doctor of Veterinary Science
ECBL	European Certification Board for Logistics
ECDL	European Computer Driving Licence
ECG	Executive Group Committees (of the Board for Engineers Registration)
EDBA	Executive Diploma in Business Accounting
EdD	Doctor of Education
EDH	Efficient Deck Hand
EdPsyD	Doctor of Educational Psychology
EEAC	European Executive Assistant Certificate
EFB	English for Business
EFL	English as a Foreign Language
EHO	Environmental Health Officer
EIS	Educational Institute of Scotland
EITB	Engineering Industry Training Board
EMBA	European Master of Business Administration
EMBS	European Master of Business Sciences
EMFEC	East Midland Further Education Council
EN	Enrolled Nurse
EN(G)	Enrolled Nurse (General)
EN(M)	Enrolled Nurse (Mental)
EN(MH)	Enrolled Nurse (Mental Handicap)
ENB	English National Board
EngC	Engineering Council
EngD	Doctor of Engineering
EngTech	Engineering Technician
ENS	Electronic Navigational System
ESD	Executive Secretary's Diploma
ESOL	English for Speakers of Other Languages
ESSTL	Engineering Services Training Trust Ltd
EurIng	European Engineer
EuroBiol	European Biologist
FABE	Fellow of the Association of Business Executives
FACB	Fellow of the Association of Certified Bookkeepers
FACP	Fellow of the Association of Computer Professionals
FAE	Fellow of the Academy of Experts
FAFC	Fellow of the Association of Financial Controllers and Administrators
FAIA	Fellow of the Association of International Accountants
FAMS	Fellow of the Association of Medical Secretaries, Practice Managers, Administrators and Receptionists
FAPM	Fellow of the Association for Project Management
FASI	Fellow of the Ambulance Service Institute
FASI	Fellow of the Architecture and Surveying Institute
FASP	Fellow of the Association of Sales Personnel
FBA	Fellow of the British Academy
FBA	Fellow of the British (Theatrical) Arts
FBCS	Fellow of the British Computer Society
FBDO	Fellow of the Association of British Dispensing Opticians
FBDO(Hons)	Fellow of the Association of British Dispensing Opticians with Honours Diploma

FBDO(Hons)CL	Fellow of the Association of British Dispensing Opticians with Honours Diploma and Diploma in Contact Lens Practice
FBEI	Fellow of the Institution of Body Engineers
FBEng	Fellow of the Association of Building Engineers
FBHA	Fellow of the British Hypnotherapy Association
FBHI	Fellow of the British Horological Institute
FBHS	Fellow of the British Horse Society
FBID	Fellow of the British Institute of Interior Design
FBIDST	Fellow of the British Institute of Dental and Surgical Technologists
FBIE	Fellow of the British Institute of Embalmers
FBIPP	Fellow of the British Institute of Professional Photography
FBIS	Fellow of the British Interplanetary Society
FBMA	Fellow of the Business Management Association
FBPsS	Fellow of the British Psychological Society
FCA	Fellow of the Institute of Chartered Accountants in England and Wales
FCAM	Fellow of the Communication Advertising and Marketing Education Foundation
FCB	Fellow of the British Association of Communicators in Business Ltd
FCBSI	Fellow of the Chartered Building Societies Institute
FCCA	Fellow of the Association of Chartered Certified Accountants
FCEA	Fellow of the Institute of Cost and Executive Accountants
FCGI	Fellowship, City & Guilds
FChS	Fellow of the Society of Chiropodists and Podiatrists
FCI	Faculty of Commerce and Industry
FCI	Fellow of the Institute of Commerce
FCIArb	Fellow of the Chartered Institute of Arbitrators
FCIB	Fellow of the Chartered Institute of Bankers
FCIBS	Fellow of the Chartered Institute of Bankers in Scotland
FCIBSE	Fellow of the Chartered Institute of Building Services Engineers
FCIH	Fellow of the Chartered Institute of Housing
FCII	Fellow of the Chartered Insurance Institute
FCIJ	Fellow of the Chartered Institute of Journalists
FCILA	Fellow of the Chartered Institute of Loss Adjusters
FCIM	Fellow of the Chartered Institute of Marketing
FCIOB	Fellow of the Chartered Institute of Building
FCIPD	Fellow of the Chartered Institute of Personnel and Development
FCIPS	Fellow of the Chartered Institute of Procurement and Supply
FCIS	Fellow of the Institute of Chartered Secretaries and Administrators
FCIT	Fellow of the Chartered Institute of Transport
FCLIP	Chartered Fellow of CILIP (The Library and Information Assocation)
FCLS	First Certificate for Legal Secretaries
FCMA	Fellow of the Chartered Institute of Management Accountants
FCMA	Fellow of the Institute of Cost and Management Accountants
FCMC	Fellow Grade Certified Management Consultants
FCOphth	Fellow of the College of Ophthalmology
FCOptom	Fellow of the College of Optometrists
FCoT	Ordinary Fellow of the College of Teachers
FCPM	Fellow of the Confederation of Professional Management
FCPP	Fellow of the College of Pharmacy Practice (closed in 2010)
FCSP	Fellow of the Chartered Society of Physiotherapy
FCT	Fellow of the Association of Corporate Treasurers
FCoT	Fellow of the College of Teachers
FCTHCM	Fellow of the Confederation of Tourism, Hotel and Catering Management

FCYW	Fellow of the Community and Youth Work Association
FDSRCPSGlas	Fellow in Dental Surgery of the Royal College of Surgeons of Glasgow
FDSRCSEd	Fellow in Dental Surgery of the Royal College of Physicians and Surgeons of Edinburgh
FDSRCSEng	Fellow in Dental Surgery of the Royal College of Surgeons of England
FE	Further Education
FEANI	Fédération Européene d'Associations Nationales d'Ingénieurs
FECI	Fellow of the Institute of Employment Consultants
FEFC	Further Education Funding Council
FEIS	Fellow of the Educational Institute of Scotland
FFA	Fellow of the Faculty of Actuaries
FFA	Fellow of the Institute of Financial Accountants
FFARCSEng	Fellow of the Faculty of Anaesthetists of the Royal College of Surgeons in England
FFARCSIrel	Fellow of the Faculty of Anaesthetists of the Royal College of Surgeons in Ireland
FFAS	Fellow of the Faculty of Architects and Surveyors (Architects)
FFCA	Fellow of the Association of Financial Controllers and Administrators
FFCI	Fellow of the Faculty of Commerce and Industry
FFCS	Fellow of the Faculty of Secretaries
FFHom	Fellow of the Faculty of Homeopathy
FFPHM	Fellow of the Faculty of Public Health Medicine, Royal College of Physicians of London and Edinburgh and Royal College of Physicians and Surgeons of Glasgow
FFPHMIrel	Fellow of the Faculty of Public Health Medicine, Royal College of Physicians of Ireland
FFRRCSIrel	Fellow of the Faculty of Radiologists, Royal College of Surgeons in Ireland
FFS	Fellow of the Faculty of Architects and Surveyors (Surveyors)
FGA	Fellow of the Gemmological Association and Gem Testing Laboratory of Great Britain
FGCL	Fellow of the Guild of Cleaners and Launderers
FGI	Fellow of the Greek Institute
FGSM	Fellow of the Guildhall School of Music and Drama
FHCIMA	Fellow of the Hotel and Catering International Management Association
FHFS	Fellow of the Council of Health, Fitness and Sports Therapists
FHG	Fellow of the Institute of Heraldic and Genealogical Studies
FHRIM	Fellow of the Institute of Health Record Information and Management
FHS	Fellow of the Heraldry Society
FHSM	Fellow of the Institute of Health Services Management
FHT	Federation of Holistic Therapies
FIA	Fellow of the Institute of Actuaries
FIAB	Fellow of the International Association of Bookkeepers
FIAEA	Fellow of the Institute of Automotive Engineer Assessors
FIAgrE	Fellow of the Institution of Agricultural Engineers
FIAP	Fellow of the Institution of Analysts and Programmers
FIAT	Fellow of the Institute of Asphalt Technology
FIBA	Fellow of the Institution of Business Agents
FIBC	Fellow of the Institute of Building Control
FIBCM	Fellow of the Institute of British Carriage and Automobile Manufacturers
FIBCO	Fellow of the Institute of Building Control Officers
FIBE	Fellow of the Institution of British Engineers
FIBF	Fellow of the Institute of British Foundrymen
FIBiol	Fellow of the Institute of Biology
FIBM	Fellow of the Institute of Builders' Merchants

FIBMS	Fellow of the Institute of Biomedical Science
FIBMS	Fellow of the Institute of Medical Laboratory Sciences
FICA	Fellow of the Institute of Company Accountants
FICB	Fellow of the Institute of Certified Bookkeepers
FICE	Fellow of the Institution of Civil Engineers
FIChemE	Fellow of the Institution of Chemical Engineers
FIChor	Fellow of the Benesh Institute of Choreology
FICHT	Fellow of the International Council of Holistic Therapies
FICM	Fellow of the Institute of Credit Management
FICorr	Fellow of the Institute of Corrosion
FICS	Fellow of the Institute of Chartered Shipbrokers
FICW	Fellow of the Institute of Clerks of Works of Great Britain Incorporated
FIDTA	Fellow of the International Dance Teachers' Association
FIED	Fellow of the Institution of Engineering Designers
FIEE	Fellow of the Institution of Electrical Engineers
FIEM	Fellow of the Institute of Executives and Managers
FIEx	Fellow of the Institute of Export
FIExpE	Fellow of the Institute of Explosives Engineers
FIFBQ	Fellow of the International Faculty of Business Qualifications
FIFireE	Fellow of the Institution of Fire Engineers
FIFM	Fellow of the Institute of Fisheries Management
FIFST	Fellow of the Institute of Food Science and Technology
FIGasE	Fellow of the Institution of Gas Engineers
FIGD	Fellow of the Institute of Grocery Distribution
FIGeol	Fellow of the Institute of Geologists
FIHEc	Fellow of the Institute of Home Economics Ltd
FIHIE	Fellow of the Institute of Highway Incorporated Engineers
FIHort	Fellow of the Institute of Horticulture
FIHT	Fellow of the Institution of Highways and Transportation
FIIE	Fellow of the Institution of Incorporated Engineers
FIIHTM	Fellow of the International Institute of Hospitality Tourism & Management
FIIM	Fellow of the International Institute of Management
FIIMR	Fellow of the Institute of Investment Management and Research
FIIRSM	Fellow of the International Institute of Risk and Safety Management
FIISE	Fellow of the International Institute of Social Economics
FIISec	Fellow of the International Institute of Security
FIL	Fellow of the Institute of Linguists
FILAM	Fellow of the Institute of Leisure and Amenity Management
FILT	Fellow of the Institute of Logistics and Transport
FIM	Fellow of the Institute of Materials
FIMA	Fellow of the Institute of Mathematics and its Applications
FIManf	Fellow of the Institute of Manufacturing
FIMarE	Fellow of the Institute of Marine Engineers
FIMatM	Fellow of the Institute of Materials Management
FIMBM	Fellow of the Institute of Maintenance and Building Management
FIMechE	Fellow of the Institute of Mechanical Engineers
FIMechIE	Fellow of the Institute of Mechanical Incorporated Engineers
FIMF	Fellow of the Institute of Metal Finishing
FIMgt	Fellow of the Institute of Management
FIMI	Fellow of the Institute of the Motor Industry
FIMIS	Fellow of the Institute for the Management of Information Systems
FIMM	Fellow of the Institute of Massage and Movement

FIMM	Fellow of the Institution of Mining and Metallurgy
FIMM	International Federation of Manual Medicine
FIMS	Fellow of the Institute of Management Specialists
FIMunE	Fellow of the Institution of Municipal Engineers
FInstAEA	Fellow of the Institute of Automotive Engineer Assessors
FInstAM	Fellow of the Institute of Administrative Management
FInstBA	Fellow of the Institute of Business Administration
FInstBCA	Fellow of the Institute of Burial and Cremation Administration
FInstBOM	Fellow of the Institute Of Builders' Merchants
FInstBRM	Fellow of the Institute of Baths and Recreation Management
FInstCh	Fellow of the Institute of Chiropodists
FInstCM	Fellow of the Institute of Commercial Management
FInstD	Fellow of the Institute of Directors
FInstE	Fellow of the Institute of Energy
FInstLEx	Fellow of the Institute of Legal Executives
FInstMC	Fellow of the Institute of Measurement and Control
FInstNDT	Fellow of the British Institute of Non-Destructive Testing
FInstP	Fellow of the Institute of Physics
FInstPet	Fellow of the Institute of Petroleum
FInstPkg	Fellow of the Institute of Packaging
FInstPM	Fellow of the Institute of Professional Managers and Administrators
FInstPS	Fellow of the Institute of Purchasing and Supply
FInstR	Fellow of the Institute of Refrigeration
FInstSMM	Fellow of the Institute of Sales and Marketing Management
FInstTA	Fellow of the Institute of Transport Administration
FInstTT	Fellow of the Institute of Travel and Tourism
FInstWM	Fellow of the Institute of Wastes Management
FInstWM	Fellowship of the Institute of Wastes Management
FIntMC	Fellow of International Management Centre
FIOC	Fellow of the Institute of Carpenters
FIOM	Fellow of the Institute of Operations Management
FIOP	Fellow of the Institute of Plumbing
FIOP	Fellow of the Institute of Printing
FIOSH	Fellow of the Institution of Occupational Safety and Health
FIPA	Fellow of the Institute of Practitioners in Advertising
FIPD	Fellow of the Institute of Personnel Development
FIPI	Fellow of the Institute of Professional Investigators
FIPlantE	Fellow of the Institution of Plant Engineers
FIPR	Fellow of the Institute of Public Relations
FIQ	Fellow of the Institute of Quarrying
FIQA	Fellow of the Institute of Quality Assurance
FIR	Fellow of the Institute of Population Registration
FIRSE	Fellow of the Institution of Railway Signal Engineers
FIRTE	Fellow of the Institute of Road Transport Engineers
FIS	Fellow of the Institute of Statisticians
FISM	Fellow of the Institute for Supervision & Management
FISOB	Fellow of the Incorporated Society of Organ Builders
FISTC	Fellow of the Institute of Scientific and Technical Communicators
FISTD	Fellow of the Imperial Society of Teachers of Dancing
FIStrucE	Fellow of the Institution of Structural Engineers
FISW	Fellow of the Institute of Social Welfare
FIT	Foundation Insurance Test

FITD	Fellow of the Institute of Training and Development
FITSA	Fellow of the Institute of Trading Standards Administration
FIVehE	Fellow of the Institute of Vehicle Engineers
FIWM	Fellow of the Institute of Wastes Management
FLAW	Foreign Languages at Work
FLCM	Fellow of the London College of Music
FLCSP	Fellow of the London and Counties Society of Physiologists
FLI	Fellow of the Landscape Institute
FLIC	Foreign Languages for Industry and Commerce
FLS	Fellow of the Linnean Society of London
FMA	Fellow of the Museums Association
FMAAT	Fellow Member of the Association of Accounting Technicians
FMPA	Fellow of the Master Photographers Association
FMR	Fellow of the Association of Health Care Information and Medical Records Officers
FMS	Fellow of the Institute of Management Services
FMusEd	Fellowship in Music Education
FN	Fellow of the Nautical Society
FNAEA	Fellow of the National Association of Estate Agents
FNAEAHon	Honoured Fellow of the National Association of Estate Agents
FNCP	Fellow of the National Council of Psychotherapists
FNI	Fellow of the Nautical Institute
FNIMH	Fellow of the National Institute of Medical Herbalists
FPC	Financial Planning Certificate
FPC	Foundation for Psychotherapy and Counselling
FPCS	Fellow of the Property Consultants Society
FPMI	Fellow of the Pensions Management Institute
FPodS	Fellow of the Surgical Faculty of the College of Podiatrists
FProfBTM	Fellow of Professional Business and Technical Management
FRAeS	Fellow of the Royal Aeronautical Society
FRAS	Fellow of the Royal Astronomical Society
FRCA	Fellow of the Royal College of Anaesthetists
FRCGP	Fellow of the Royal College of General Practitioners
FRCM	Fellow of the Royal College of Music
FRCO	Fellow of the Royal College of Organists
FRCO(CHM)	Fellow of the Royal College of Organists (Choir-training Diploma)
FRCOG	Fellow of the Royal College of Obstetricians and Gynaecologists
FRCP	Fellow of the Royal College of Physicians of London
FRCPath	Fellow of the Royal College of Pathologists
FRCPEdin	Fellow of the Royal College of Physicians of Edinburgh
FRCPsych	Fellow of the Royal College of Psychiatrists
FRCR	Fellow of the Royal College of Radiologists
FRCS(Irel)	Fellow of the Royal College of Surgeons in Ireland
FRCSEd	Fellow of the Royal College of Surgeons of Edinburgh
FRCSEd(C/TH)	Fellow of the Royal College of Surgeons of Edinburgh, specialising in Cardiothoracic Surgery
FRCSEd(Orth)	Fellow of the Royal College of Surgeons of Edinburgh, specialising in Orthopaedic Surgery
FRCSEd(SN)	Fellow of the Royal College of Surgeons of Edinburgh, specialising in Surgical Neurology
FRCSEng	Fellow of the Royal College of Surgeons of England
FRCSEng(Oto)	Fellow of the Royal College of Surgeons of England, with Otolaryngology
FRCSGlasg	Fellow of the Royal College of Physicians and Surgeons of Glasgow

GDC	General Dental Council
GIBCM	Graduate of the Institute of British Carriage and Automobile Manufacturers
GIBiol	Graduate of the Institute of Biology
GIEM	Graduate of the Institute of Executives and Managers
GIMA	Graduate of the Institute of Mathematics and its Applications
GIMI	Graduate of the Institute of the Motor Industry
GInstP	Graduate of the Institute of Physics
GIntMC	Graduate of the International Management Centre
GIS	Graduate Imaging Scientist
GLCM	Graduate Diploma of the London College of Music
GMAT	Graduate Management Admissions Test
GMC	General Medical Council
GMDSS	Global Maritime Distress & Safety System
GMInstM	Graduate Member of the Meat Training Council
GMUS	Graduate Diploma in Music
GMusRNCM	Graduate in Music of the Royal Northern College of Music
GNSM	Graduate of the Northern School of Music
GNVQ	General National Vocational Qualifications
GradAES	Graduate of the Royal Aeronautical Society
GradBEng	Graduate Member of the Association of Building Engineers
GradBHI	Graduate of the British Horological Institute
GradDip	Graduate Diploma
GradIAP	Graduate of the Institution of Analysts and Programmers
GradIBE	Graduate of the Institution of British Engineers
GradIElecIE	Graduate of the Institution of Electrical and Electronics Incorporated Engineers
GradIIE	Graduate of the Institution of Incorporated Engineers
GradIISec	Graduate of the International Institute of Security
GradIManf	Graduate of the Institute Manufacturing
GradIMF	Graduate of the Institute of Metal Finishing
GradIMS	Graduate of the Institute of Management Specialists
GradInstNDT	Graduate of the British Institute of Non-Destructive Testing
GradInstP	Graduate of the Institute of Physics
GradInstPS	Graduate of the Institute of Purchasing and Supply
GradIOP	Graduate of the Institute of Printing
GradIPD	Graduate of the Institute of Personnel and Development
GradIS	Graduate of the Institute of Statisticians
GradISCA	Graduate of the Institute of Chartered Secretaries and Administrators
GradMechE	Graduate of the Institution of Mechanical Engineers
GradMIWM	Graduate Member of the Institute of Wastes Management
GradRNCM	Graduate of the Royal Northern College of Music
GradRSC	Graduate of the Royal Society of Chemistry
GradSMA	Graduate of the Society of Martial Arts
GradStat	Graduate Statistician
GraduateCIPD	Graduate of the Chartered Institute of Personnel and Development
GraduateIEIE	Graduate of the Institution of Electrical and Electronics Incorporated Engineers
GradWeldI	Graduate of the Welding Institute
GRC	General Readers Certificate
GRC	Grade Related Criteria
GRIC	Graduate Membership of the Royal Institute of Chemistry
GRSC	Graduate of the Royal Society of Chemistry
GRSM	Graduate Diploma of the Royal Manchester School of Music
GRSM(Hons)	Graduate of the Royal Schools of Music

GSMA	Graduate of the Society of Sales Management Administrators Ltd
GSNN	Graduate of the Society of Nursery Nursing
GTC	General Teaching Council
HABIA	Hairdressing and Beauty Industry Authority
HC	Higher Certificate
HCIMA	Hotel and Catering International Management Association
HD	Higher Diploma
HDCR (R) or (T)	Higher Award in Radiodiagnosis or Radiotherapy, College of Radiographers
HEFCE	Higher Education Funding Council for England
HFInstE	Honorary Fellow of the Institute of Energy
HNC	Higher National Certificate
HND	Higher National Diploma
HonASTA	Honorary Associate of the Swimming Teachers' Association
HonDrRCA	Honorary Doctorate of the Royal College of Art
HonFAE	Honorary Fellow of the Academy of Experts
HonFBID	Honorary Fellow of the British Institute of Interior Design
HonFBIPP	Honorary Fellow of the British Institute of Professional Photography
HonFCP	Charter Fellow of the College of Preceptors
HonFEIS	Honorary Fellow of the Educational Institute of Scotland
HonFHCIMA	Honorary Fellow of the Hotel, Catering and Institutional Management Association
HonFHS	Honorary Fellow of the Heraldry Society
HonFIEE	Honorary Fellow of the Institution of Electrical Engineers
HonFIExpE	Honorary Fellow of the Institute of Explosives Engineers
HonFIGasE	Honorary Fellow of the Institution of Gas Engineers
HonFIMarE	Honorary Fellow of the Institute of Marine Engineers
HonFIMechE	Honorary Fellow of the Institution of Mechanical Engineers
HonFIMM	Honorary Fellow of the Institution of Mining and Metallurgy
HonFInstE	Honorary Fellow of the Institute of Energy
HonFInstMC	Honorary Fellow of the Institute of Measurement and Control
HonFInstNDT	Honorary Fellow of the British Institute of Non-Destructive Testing
HonFIQA	Honorary Fellow of the Institute of Quality Assurance
HonFIRSE	Honorary Fellow of the Institution of Railway Signal Engineers
HonFIRTE	Honorary Fellow of the Institute of Road Transport Engineers
HonFPRI	Honorary Fellow of the Plastics and Rubber Institute
HonFRIN	Honorary Fellow of the Royal Institute of Navigation
HonFRINA	Honorary Fellow of the Royal Institution of Naval Architects
HonFRPS	Honorary Fellow of the Royal Photographic Society
HonFSE	Honorary Fellow of the Society of Engineers (Inc)
HonFSGT	Honorary Fellow of the Society of Glass Technology
HonFWeldI	Honorary Fellow of the Welding Institute
HonGSM	Honorary Member of the Guildhall School of Music and Drama
HonMIFM	Honorary Member of the Institute of Fisheries Management
HonMInstNDT	Honorary Member of the British Institute of Non-Destructive Testing
HonMRIN	Honorary Member of the Royal Institute of Navigation
HonMWES	Honorary Member of the Women's Engineering Society
HonRAM	Honorary Member of the Royal Academy of Music
HonRCM	Honorary Member of the Royal College of Music
HonRNCM	Honorary Member of the Royal Northern College of Music
HonRSCM	Honorary Member of the Royal School of Church Music
HSC	Higher School Certificate
HSE	Health & Safety Executive
HTB	Hairdressing Training Board

HTC	Higher Technical Certificate
IAAP	International Association for Analytic Psychology
IAB	International Association of Bookkeepers
IABC	International Association of Business Computing
IAC	Investment Advice Certificate
IAEA	Institute of Automotive Engineer Assessors
IAEA	Institute of Automotive Engineer Assessors
IAgrE	Institution of Agricultural Engineers
IAP	Institution of Analysts and Programmers
IAQ	Investment Administration Qualification
IAT	Institute of Asphalt Technology
IBA	Institute of Business Administration
IBC	Institute of Building Control
IBCA	Institute of Burial and Cremation Administration
IBE	Institution of British Engineers
IBF	Institute of British Foundrymen
IBMS	Institute of Biomedical Science
ICAEW	Institute of Chartered Accountants in England and Wales
ICAI	Institute of Chartered Accountants in Ireland
ICAS	Institute of Chartered Accountants of Scotland
ICB	Institute of Certified Bookkeepers
ICE	Institution of Civil Engineers
ICEA	Institute of Cost and Executive Accountants
ICG	Institute of Careers Guidance
IChemE	Institution of Chemical Engineers
ICIOB	Incorporated Member of the Chartered Institute of Building
ICM	Institute of Commercial Management
ICM	Institute of Complementary Medicine
ICM	Institute of Credit Management
ICM	The Institute of Commercial Management
ICMQ	International Capital Markets Qualification
ICSA	Institute of Chartered Secretaries and Administrators
ICSF	Intermediate Certificate of the Society of Floristry
IDA	Improvement and Development Agency
IDTA	International Dance Teachers' Association Ltd
IED	Institution of Engineering Designers
IEE	Institution of Electrical Engineers
IEM	Institute of Executives and Managers
IEng	Incorporated Engineer
IETTL	Insulation and Environmental Training Trust Ltd
IEx	Institute of Export
IExpE	Institute of Explosives Engineers
IFA	Institute of Field Archaeologists
IFA	Institute of Financial Accountants
IFA	Insurance Foundation Certificate
IFBQ	International Faculty of Business Qualifications
IFM	Institute of Fisheries Management
IAFoA	Institute and Faculty of Actuaries
IFST	Institute of Food Science and Technology (UK)
IHBC	International Health & Beauty Council
IHIE	Institute of Highway Incorporated Engineers
IHT	Institute of Highways and Transportation

ISTD	Imperial Society of Teachers of Dancing
IStructE	Institution of Structural Engineers
ITEC	International Therapy Examination Council
ITIL	IT Infrastructure Library
ITSA	Institute of Trading Standards Administration
IVehE	Institute of the Vehicle Engineers
IVM	Institute of Value Management
IWSc	Institute of Wood Science
JEB	Joint Examination Board
JET	Jewellery, Education and Training
JP	Justice of the Peace
LA	Library Association
LABAC	Licentiate Member of the Association of Business and Administrative Computing
LAE	Licentiate Automotive Engineer
LAEx	Legal Accounts Executive
LAMDA	London Academy of Music and Dramatic Art
LAMRTPI	Legal Associate Member of the Royal Town Planning Institute
LASI	Licentiate of the Ambulance Service Institute
LASI	Licentiate of the Architecture and Surveying Institute
LBEI	Licentiate of the Institution of Body Engineers
LBIDST	Licentiate of the British Institute of Dental and Surgical Technologists
LBIPP	Licentiate of the British Institute of Professional Photography
LCCI	London Chamber of Commerce and Industry
LCCIEB	London Chamber of Commerce and Industry Examinations Board
LCEA	Licentiate of the Association of Cost and Executive Accountants
LCFI	Licentiate of CFI International (Clothing and Footwear Institute)
LCGI	Licentiate, City & Guilds
LCIBSE	Licentiate of the Chartered Institution of Building Services Engineers
LCP	Licentiate of the College of Preceptors
LCSP	London and Counties Society of Physiologists
LCSP(Assoc)	Associate of the London and Counties Society of Physiologists
LCSP(BTh)	Member of the London and Counties Society of Physiologists (Beauty Therapy)
LCSP(Chir)	Member of the London and Counties Society of Physiologists (Chiropody)
LCSP(Phys)	Member of the London and Counties Society of Physiologists (Physical and Manipulative Therapy)
LCT	Licentiate of the College of Teachers
LDS	Licentiate in Dental Surgery
LDSRCPSGlas	Licentiate in Dental Surgery of the Royal College of Physicians and Surgeons of Glasgow
LDSRCSEd	Licentiate in Dental Surgery of the Royal College of Surgeons of Edinburgh
LDSRCSEng	Licentiate in Dental Surgery of the Royal College of Surgeons of England
LFA	Licentiate of the Institute of Financial Accountants
LFCI	Licentiate of the Faculty of Commerce and Industry
LFCS	Licentiate of the Faculty of Secretaries
LFS	Licentiate of the Faculty of Architects and Surveyors (Surveyors)
LGCL	Licentiate of the Guild of Cleaners and Launderers
LGSM	Licentiate of the Guildhall School of Music and Drama
LHCIMA	Licentiate of the Hotel and Catering International Management Association
LHG	Licentiate of the Institute of Heraldic and Genealogical Studies
LI	Landscape Institute
LIBOM	Licentiate of the Institute of Builders' Merchants
LicentiateCIPD	Licentiate of the Chartered Institute of Personnel and Development

LicIPD	Licentiate of the Institute of Personnel & Development
LicIQA	Licentiate of the Institute of Quality Assurance
LICW	Licentiate of the Institute of Clerks of Works of Great Britain Incorporated
LIDPM	Licentiate of the Institute of Data Processing Management (now IMIS, Institute for the Management of Information Systems)
LIEM	Licentiate of the Institute of Executives and Managers
LIIST	Licentiate of the International Institute of Sports Therapy
LILAM	Licentiate of the Institute of Leisure and Amenity Management
LIM	Licentiate of the Institute of Materials
LIMA	Licentiate of the Institute of Mathematics and its Applications
LIMF	Licentiate of the Institute of Metal Finishing
LIMIS	Licentiate of the Institute for the Management of Information Systems
LInstBCA	Licentiate of the Institute of Burial and Cremation Administration
LIOC	Licentiate of the Institute of Carpenters
LIR	Licentiate of the Institute of Population Registration
LISTD	Licentiate of the Imperial Society of Teachers of Dancing
LISTD(Dip)	Licentiate Diploma of the Imperial Society of Teachers of Dancing
LittD	Doctor of Letters
LIWM	Licentiate of the Institute of Wastes Management
LLB	Bachelor of Law
LLCM	Performers Diploma of Licentiateship in Speech, Drama and Public Speaking
LLCM(TD)	Licentiate of the London College of Music and Media (Teachers' Diploma)
LLD	Doctor of Law
LLM	Master of Law
LM	Licentiate in Midwifery
LMIFM	Licentiate Member of the Institute of Fisheries Management
LMInstE	Licentiate Member of the Institute of Energy
LMPA	Licentiate Member of the Master Photographers Association
LMRTPI	Legal Member of the Royal Town Planning Institute
LMSSALond	Licentiate in Medicine, Surgery and Obstetrics & Gynaecology, Society of Apothecaries of London
LMusEd	Licentiate Diploma in Music Education
LMusLCM	Licentiate in Music of the London College of Music
LMusTCL	Licentiate in Music, Trinity College of Music
LNCP	Licentiate of the National Council of Psychotherapists
LPC	Legal Practice Course
LRAD	Licentiate of the Royal Academy of Dancing
LRAM	Licentiate of the Royal Academy of Music
LRCPEdin	Conjoint Diplomas Licentiate of the Royal College of Physicians of Edinburgh
LRCPSGlasg	Conjoint Diplomas Licentiate of the Royal College of Physicians and Surgeons of Glasgow
LRCSEdin	Conjoint Diplomas Licentiate of the Royal College of Surgeons of Edinburgh
LRCSEng	Licentiate of the Royal College of Surgeons in England
LRPS	Licentiate of the Royal Photographic Society
LRSC	Licentiate of the Royal Society of Chemistry
LRSM	Licentiate Diploma of the Royal Schools of Music
LSBP	Licentiate of the Society of Business Practitioners
LSCP(Assoc)	Associate of the London and Counties Society of Physiologists
LTCL	Licentiate of Trinity College of Music
LTh	Licentiate in Theology
LTI	Licentiate of the Textile Industry
LTSC	Licentiate of the Oil and Colour Chemists' Association

LVT	Licentiate Vehicle Technologist
MA	Master of Arts
MA(Architectural)	Master of Arts (Architectural Studies)
MA(Econ)	Master of Arts in Economic and Social Studies
MA(Ed)	Master of Arts in Education
MA(LD)	Master of Arts (Landscape Design)
MA(MUS)	Master of Arts (Music)
MA(RCA)	Master of Arts, Royal College of Art
MA(SocSci)	Master of Arts (Social Science)
MA(Theol)	Master of Arts in Theology
MAAT	Member of the Association of Accounting Technicians
MABAC	Member of the Association of Business and Administrative Computing
MABE	Member of the Association of Business Executives
MAcc	Master of Accountancy
MACP	Member of the Association of Computer Professionals
MAE	Member of the Academy of Experts
MAgr	Master of Agriculture
MAgrSc	Master of Agricultural Science
MAMS	Member of the Association of Medical Secretaries, Practice Managers, Administrators and Receptionists
MAMSA	Managing & Marketing Sales Association Examination Board
MAnimSc	Master of Animal Science
MAO	Master of Obstetrics
MAP	Membership by Assessment of Performance
MAPM	Member of the Association for Project Management
MAppSci	Master of Applied Science
MAQ	Mortgage Advice Qualification
MArAd	Master of Archive Administration
MArb	Master of Arboriculture
MArch	Master of Architecture
MArt/RCA	Master of Arts, Royal College of Art
MasFCI	Master of the Faculty of Commerce and Industry
MASHAM	Management and Administration of Safety and Health at Mines
MASI	Member of the Architecture and Surveying Institute
MBA	Master of Business Administration
MBAE	Member of the British Association of Electrolysists
MB, BCh	Conjoint Degree of Bachelor of Medicine, Bachelor of Surgery
MB, BChir	Conjoint Degree of Bachelor of Medicine, Bachelor of Surgery
MB, BS	Conjoint Degree of Bachelor of Medicine, Bachelor of Surgery
MB, ChB	Conjoint Degree of Bachelor of Medicine, Bachelor of Surgery
MBChA	Member of the British Chiropody and Podiatry Association
MBCO	Member of the British College of Ophthalmic Opticians
MBCS	Member of the British Computer Society
MBEng	Member of the Association of Building Engineers
MBHA	Member of the British Hypnotherapy Association
MBHI	Member of the British Horological Institute
MBIAT	Member of the British Institute of Architectural Technologists
MBID	Member of the British Institute of Interior Design
MBIE	Member of the British Institute of Embalmers
MBII	Member of the British Institute of Innkeeping
MBioc	Master of Biochemistry
MBKS	Member of the British Kinematograph, Sound and Television Society

MBM	Master of Business Management
MBMA	Member of the Business Management Association
MBSc	Master in Business Science
MBSSG	Master of the British Society of Scientific Glassblowers
MCAM	Member of the Communication Advertising and Marketing Education Foundation
MCB	Mastership in Clinical Biochemistry
MCB	Member of the British Association of Communicators in Business
MCBDip	Member of the British Association of Communicators in Business who hold the Association's Certificate and Diploma
MCC	Master of Community Care
MCCDRCS(Eng)	Member of the Royal College of Surgeons of England, Clinical Community Dentistry
MCD	Master of Civic Design
MCDH	Master of Community Dental Health
MCGI	Membership, City & Guilds
MCGPIrel	Member of the Irish College of General Practitioners
MCh	Master of Surgery
MChD	Master of Dental Surgery
MChem	Master of Chemistry
MChemA	Master of Chemical Analysis
MChemPhys	Master of Chemical Physics
MChemPST	Master of Chemistry Polymer Science and Technology
MChir	Master of Surgery
MChOrth	Master of Orthopaedic Surgery
MChS	Member of the Society of Chiropodists and Podiatrists
MCIArb	Member of the Chartered Institute of Arbitrators
MCIBS	Member of the Chartered Institute of Bankers in Scotland
MCIBSE	Member of the Chartered Institution of Building Services Engineers
MCIH	Corporate Member of the Chartered Institute of Housing
MCIJ	Member of the Chartered Institute of Journalists
MCIM	Member of the Chartered Institute of Marketing
MCIOB	Member of the Chartered Institute of Building
MCIPD	Member of the Chartered Institute of Personnel and Development
MCIPS	Member of the Chartered Institute of Purchasing and Supply
MCIT	Member of the Chartered Institute of Transport
MCIWEM	Member of the Chartered Institution of Water and Environmental Management
MCLIP	Chartered Member of CILIP
MCom	Master of Commerce
MCommH	Master of Community Health
MComp	Master of Computer Science
MCOptom	Member of the College of Optometrists
MCoT	Member of the College of Teachers
MCPM	Member of the Confederation of Professional Management
MCPP	Member of the College of Pharmacy Practice
MCQ	Multiple Choice Question paper
MCSD	Member of the Chartered Society of Designers
MCSP	Member of the Chartered Society of Physiotherapy
MCT	Member of the Association of Corporate Treasurers
MCTHCM	Member of the Confederation of Tourism, Hotel and Catering Management
MCYW	Member of the Community and Youth Work Association
MD	Doctor of Medicine
MDA	Master of Defence Administration

MD; ChM	Conjoint Doctorate in Medicine, Doctorate in Surgery
MDCR	Management Diploma of the College of Radiographers
MDent	Master of Dental Science
MDes	Master of Design
MDes(RCA)	Master of Design, Royal College of Art
MDORCPSGlas	Membership of Dental Orthopaedics, Royal College of Physicians and Surgeons of Glasgow
MDra	Master of Drama
MDS	Master of Dental Surgery
MDSc	Master of Dental Science
MEBA	Master of European Business Administration
MECI	Member of the Institute of Employment Consultants
MEd	Master of Education
MEd(EdPsych)	Master of Education (Educational Psychology)
MEdStud	Master of Educational Studies
MEng	Master of Engineering
MEnv	Master of Environmental Studies
MEnvSci	Master of Environmental Science
MESc	Master of Earth Sciences
MFA	Master of Fine Art
MFC	Mastership in Food Control
MFCM	Member of the Faculty of Community Medicine
MFDO	Member of the Faculty of Dispensing Opticians
MFDS	Member of the Faculty of Dental Surgery
MFGDPEng	Membership in General Dental Practice, Royal College of Surgeons of England
MFHom	Member of the Faculty of Homeopathy
MFM	Master of Forensic Medicine
MFPHM	Member of the Faculty of Public Health Medicine, Royal College of Physicians of London and Edinburgh and Royal College of Physicians and Surgeons of Glasgow
MFPHMIrel	Member of the Faculty of Public Health Medicine, Royal College of Physicians of Ireland
MFTCom	Member of the Faculty of Teachers in Commerce
MGDSRCSEd	Membership in General Dental Surgery, Royal College of Surgeons of Edinburgh
MGDSRCSEng	Membership in General Dental Surgery, Royal College of Surgeons of England
MGeog	Master of Geography
MGeol	Master of Geology
MGeophys	Master of Geophysical Sciences
MHCIMA	Member of the Hotel and Catering International Management Association
MHM	Master of Health Management
MHort(RHS)	Master of Horticulture, Royal Horticultural Society
MHSM	Member of the Institute of Health Services Management
MIAB	Member of the International Association of Bookkeepers
MIAEA	Member of the Institute of Automotive Engineer Assessors
MIAgrE	Member of the Institution of Agricultural Engineers
MIAP	Member of the Institution of Analysts and Programmers
MIAT	Member of the Institute of Asphalt Technology
MIBC	Member of the Institute of Building Control
MIBCM	Member of the Institute British Carriage and Automobile Manufacturers
MIBCO	Member of the Institution of Building Control Officers
MIBE	Member of the Institution of British Engineers
MIBF	Member of the Institute of British Foundrymen

MIBiol	Member of the Institute of Biology
MIBM	Member of the Institute of Builders' Merchants
MICB	Member of the Institute of Certified Bookkeepers
MICE	Member of the Institute of Civil Engineers
MIChemE	Member of the Institution of Chemical Engineers
MICHT	Member of the International Council for Holistic Therapies
MICM	Member of the Institute of Credit Management
MICM(Grad)	Graduate Member of the Institute of Credit Management
MICorr	Member of the Institute of Corrosion
MICS	Member of the Institute of Chartered Shipbrokers
MICSc	Corporate Member of the Institute of Consumer Sciences Incorporating Home Economics
MICW	Member of the Institute of Clerks of Works of Great Britain Incorporated
MIDTA	Member of the International Dance Teachers' Association
MIED	Member of the Institution of Engineering Designers
MIEE	Member of the Institution of Electrical Engineers
MIEM	Member of the Institute of Executives and Managers
MIEx	Member of the Institute of Export
MIEx(Grad)	Graduate Member of the Institute of Export
MIExpE	Member of the Institute of Explosives Engineers
MIFA	Member of the Institute of Field Archaeologists
MIFireE	Member of the Institution of Fire Engineers
MIFM	Registered Member of the Institute of Fisheries Management
MIFST	Member of the Institute of Food Science and Technology
MIGasE	Member of the Institution of Gas Engineers
MIGD	Member of the Institute of Grocery Distribution
MIHEc	Member of the Institute of Home Economics
MIHIE	Member of the Institute of Highway Incorporated Engineers
MIHM	Member of the Institute of Healthcare Management
MIHort	Member of the Institute of Horticulture
MIHT	Member of the Institution of Highways and Transportation
MIIA	Member of the Institute of Internal Auditors
MIIE	Member of the Institution of Incorporated Engineers
MIIExE	Member of the Institution of Incorporated Executive Engineers
MIIHTM	Member of the International Institute of Hospitality Tourism & Management
MIIM	Member of the Institute of Industrial Managers
MIIM	Member of the International Institute of Management
MIIRSM	Member of the International Institute of Risk and Safety Management
MIISE	Member of the International Institute of Social Economics
MIISec	Member of the International Institute of Security
MIL	Member of the Institute of Linguists
MILAM	Member of the Institute of Leisure and Amenity Management
MILT	Member of the Institute of Logistics and Transport
MIM	Professional Member of the Institute of Materials
MIMA	Member of the Institute of Mathematics and its Applications
MIManf	Member of the Institute of Manufacturing
MIMarE	Member of the Institute of Marine Engineers
MIMatM	Member of the Institute of Materials Management
MIMBM	Member of the Institute of Maintenance and Building Management
MIMC	Member of the Institute of Management Consultancy
MIMechE	Member of the Institution of Mechanical Engineers
MIMechIE	Member of the Institution of Mechanical Incorporated Engineers

MIMF	Member of the Institute of Metal Finishing
MIMI	Member of the Institute of the Motor Industry
MIMinE	Member of the Institution of Mining Engineers
MIMIS	Member of the Institute for the Management of Information Systems (previously IDPM, the Institute of Data Processing Management)
MIMM	Member of the Institute of Massage and Movement
MIMM	Member of the Institution of Mining and Metallurgy
MIMS	Member of the Institute of Management Specialists
MInstAEA	Member of the Institute of Automotive Engineer Assessors
MInstAM	Member of the Institute of Administrative Management
MInstBA	Member of the Institute of Business Administration
MInstBCA	Member of the Institute of Burial and Cremation Administration
MInstBE	Member of the Institution of British Engineers
MInstBM	Member of the Institute of Builders' Merchants
MInstCF	Master Fitter of the National Institute of Carpet and Floorlayers
MInstChP	Member of the Institute of Chiropodists & Podiatrists
MInstCM	Member of the Institute of Commercial Management
MInstD	Member of the Institute of Directors
MInstE	Member of the Institute of Energy
MInstLEx	Member of the Institute of Legal Executives
MInstMC	Member of the Institute of Measurement and Control
MInstNDT	Member of the British Institute of Non-Destructive Testing
MInstP	Member of the Institute of Physics
MInstPet	Member of the Institute of Petroleum
MInstPkg	Member of the Institute of Packaging
MInstPkg(Dip)	Diploma Member of the Institute of Packaging
MInstPM	Member of the Institute of Professional Managers and Administrators
MInstPS	Corporate Member of the Institute of Purchasing and Supply
MInstPSA	Member of the Institute of Public Service Administrators
MInstR	Member of the Institute of Refrigeration
MInstSMM	Member of the Institute of Sales and Marketing Management
MInstTA	Member of the Institute of Transport Administration
MInstTT	Full Member of the Institute of Travel and Tourism
MInstWM	Member of the Institute of Wastes Management
MIOC	Member of the Institute of Carpenters
MIOFMS	Member of the Institute of Financial and Management Studies
MIOM	Member of the Institute of Operations Management
MIOP	Member of the Institute of Printing
MIOSH	Member of the Institution of Occupational Safety and Health
MIP	Member of the Institute of Plumbing
MIPA	Member of the Institute of Practitioners in Advertising
MIPD	Member of the Institute of Personnel and Development
MIPI	Member of the Institute of Professional Investigators
MIPlantE	Member of the Institution of Plant Engineers
MIPR	Member of the Institute of Public Relations
MIPRE	Member of the Incorporated Practitioners in Radio & Electronics
MIQ	Member of the Institute of Quarrying
MIQA	Member of the Institute of Quality Assurance
MIR	Member of the Institute of Population Registration
MIRRV	Member of the Institute of Revenue, Rating and Valuation
MIRSE	Member of the Institution of Railway Signal Engineers
MIRTE	Member of the Institute of Road Transport Engineering

MISM	Member of the Institute for Supervision & Management
MISOB	Member of the Incorporated Society of Organ Builders
MISTC	Member of the Institute of Scientific and Technical Communicators
MIStrucE	Member of the Institution of Structural Engineers
MISW	Member of the Institute of Social Welfare
MITAI	Member of the Institute of Traffic Accident Investigators
MITSA	Member of the Institute of Trading Standards Administration
MIVehE	Member of the Institute of Vehicle Engineers
MIWM	Member of the Institute of Wastes Management
MIWPC	Member of the Institute of Water Pollution Control
MJur	Master of Jurisprudence
MLA	Master of Landscape Architecture
MLang	Master of Languages
MLangEng	Master of Language Engineering
MLD	Master of Landscape Design
MLE	Master of Land Economy
MLI	Member of the Landscape Institute
MLing	Master of Languages
MLitt	Master of Letters
MLPM	Master of Landscape Planning and Management
MLS	Master of Library Science
MM	Master of Midwifery
MMA	Master of Management and Administration
MMAS	Master of Minimal Access Surgery
MMath	Master of Mathematics
MMedE	Master of Medical Education
MMedSci	Master of Medical Science
MMet	Master of Metallurgy
MML	Master of Modern Languages
MMS	Member of the Institute of Management Services
MMSc	Master of Medical Sciences
MMus	Master of Music
MMus(Comp)	Master of Music (Composition)
MMus(Perf)	Master of Music (Performance)
MMus, RCM	Master of Music, Royal College of Music
MMusArt	Master of Musical Arts
MN	Master of Nursing
MNAEA	Member of the National Association of Estate Agents
MNatSc	Master of Natural Science
MNCP	Member of the National Council of Psychotherapists
MNeuro	Master of Neuroscience
MNI	Member of the Nautical Institute
MNIMH	Member of the National Institute of Medical Herbalists
MNRHP	Full Member of the National Register of Hypnotherapists and Psychotherapists
MNRHP(Eqv)	Full Member (Equivalent) of the National Register of Hypnotherapists and Psychotherapists
MNTB	Merchant Navy Training Board
MObstG	Master of Obstetrics and Gynaecology
MOptom	Master of Optometry
MOrthRCSEng	Membership in Orthodontics, Royal College of Surgeons of England
MPA	Master of Public Administration
MPaedDenRCSEng	Membership in Paediatric Dentistry, Royal College of Surgeons of England

MPC	Master of Palliative Care
MPH	Master of Public Health
MPharm	Master of Pharmacy
MPharmSci	Master of Pharmaceutical Science
MPhil	Master of Philosophy
MPhil(Eng)	Master of Philosophy in Engineering
MPhys	Master of Physics
MPhysGeog	Master of Physical Geography
MPlan	Master of Planning
MPPS	Master of Public Policy Studies
MPRI	Member of the Plastics and Rubber Institute
MProf	Master of Professional Studies
MProfBTM	Member of the Professional Business and Technical Management
MPS	Member of the Pharmaceutical Society of Northern Ireland
MPsychMed	Master of Psychological Medicine
MPsychol	Master of Psychology
MQB	Mining Qualifications Board
MRad	Master of Radiology
MRad; MRad(D)	Master of Radiology (Radiodiagnosis) or (Radiotherapy)
MRAeS	Member of the Royal Aeronautical Society
MRCGP	Member of the Royal College of General Practitioners
MRCOG	Member of the Royal College of Obstetricians and Gynaecologists
MRCP	Member of the Royal College of Physicians of London
MRCP(UK)	Member of the Royal College of Physicians of the United Kingdom
MRCPath	Member of the Royal College of Pathologists
MRCPEdin	Member of the Royal College of Physicians of Edinburgh (superceded by MRCP(UK))
MRCPGlasg	Member of the Royal College of Physicians of Glasgow (superceded by MRCP(UK))
MRCPIrel	Member of the Royal College of Physicians of Ireland
MRCPsych	Member of the Royal College of Psychiatrists
MRCSEd	Member of the Royal College of Surgeons of Edinburgh
MRCSEng	Member of the Royal College of Surgeons of England
MRCVS	Member of the Royal College of Veterinary Surgeons
MRDRCS	Membership in Restorative Dentistry, Royal College of Surgeons of England
MREC	Member of the Recruitment and Employment Confederation
MREHIS	Member of the Royal Environmental Health Institute of Scotland
MRes	Master of Research
MRIN	Member of the Royal Institute of Navigation
MRINA	Member of the Royal Institution of Naval Architects
MRIPHH	Member of the Royal Institute of Public Health and Hygiene
MRPharmS	Member of the Pharmaceutical Society of Great Britain
MRSC	Member of the Royal Society of Chemistry
MRSH	Member of the Royal Society for the Promotion of Health
MRSS	Member of the Royal Statistical Society
MRTPI	Member of the Royal Town Planning Institute
MS	Master of Surgery
MSA	Marine Safety Agency
MSAPP	Member of the Society of Advanced Psychotherapy Practitioners
MSBP	Member of the Society of Business Practitioners
MSBT	Member of the Society of Teachers in Business Education
MSc	Master of Science

MSc(Econ)	Master of Science in Economics
MSc(Ed)	Master of Science in Education
MSc(Eng)	Master of Science in Engineering
MSc(Entr)	Master of Entrepreneurship
MSc(Mgt)	Master of Science in Management
MScD	Master of Dental Science
MScEcon	Master in Faculty of Economic and Social Studies
MSCi	Master of Natural Sciences
MScTech	Master of Technical Science
MSE	Member of Society of Engineers (Inc)
MSF	Member of the SMAE Institute
MSFA	Advanced Financial Planning Certificate
MSIAD	Member of the Society of Industrial Artists and Designers
MSMA	Member of the Society of Martial Arts
MSocSc	Master of Social Science
MSSc	Master of Social Science
MSSc	Master of Surgical Science
MSSCh	Member of the British Chiropody and Podiatry Association
MSSF	Member of the Society of Shoe Fitters
MSt	Master of Studies
MSTA	Member of the Swimming Teachers' Association
MSTI	Certificate of Insurance Work
MSurgDentRCSEng	Membership in Surgical Dentistry, Royal College of Surgeons of England
MSW	Master of Social Work
MTCP	Master of Town and Country Planning
MTD	Master of Transport Design
MTech	Master of Technology
MTh	Master of Theology
MTheol	Master of Theology
MTP	Master of Town Planning
MTPI	Master of Town Planning
MTropMed	Master of Tropical Medicine
MTropPaediatrics	Master of Tropical Paediatrics
MUniv	Master of University (Honorary)
MURP	Master of Urban and Regional Planning
MusB	Bachelor of Music
MusD	Doctor of Music
MVC	Management Verification Consortium
MVM	Master of Veterinary Medicine
MVSc	Master of Veterinary Science
MWeldI	Member of the Welding Institute
MWES	Member of the Women's Engineering Society
MYD	Member of the Youth Development Association
NACOS	National Approval Council for Security Systems
NAEA	National Association of Estate Agents
NAG	National Association of Goldsmiths
NAMCW	National Association for Maternal and Child Welfare
NC	National Certificate
NCA	National Certificate in Agriculture
NCC	National Computing Centre
NCC	Navigational Control Course
NCDT	National Council for Drama Training

NCTJ	National Council for the Training of Journalists
NCVQ	National Council for Vocational Qualifications
ND	Diploma in Naturopathy
NDD	National Diploma in Design
NDF	National Diploma in Forestry
NDH	National Diploma in Horticulture
NDSF	National Diploma of the Society of Floristry
NDT	National Diploma in the Science and Practice of Turfculture and Sports Ground Management
NEBOSH	National Examination Board in Occupational Safety and Health
NEBS	National Examining Board for Supervision & Management
NFTS	National Film and Television School
NICCEA	Northern Ireland Council for the Curriculum, Examinations and Assessment
NID	National Intermediate Diploma
NIM	Northern Institute of Massage
NNEB	National Nursery Examination Board
NRHP	National Register of Hypnotherapists and Psychotherapists
NRHP(Affil)	Affiliate of the National Register of Hypnotherapists and Psychotherapists
NRHP(Assoc)	Associate of the National Register of Hypnotherapists and Psychotherapists
N-SHAP	National School of Hypnosis and Psychotherapy
NTTG	National Textile Training Group
NUJ	National Union of Journalists
NVQ	National Vocational Qualification
NWRAC	North Western Regional Advisory Council for Further Education
OCCA	Oil and Colour Chemists' Association
OCR	Oxford, Cambridge & RSA Examinations
ODLQC	Open & Distance Learning Quality Council, formerly CACC, Council for Accreditation of Correspondence Colleges
ONC	Ordinary National Certificate
OND	Ordinary National Diploma
OSCE	Objective Structured Clinical Exam
PBTM	Professional Business and Technical Management
PCN	Personnel Certification in Non-Destructive Testing Ltd
PDP	Professional Development Programme
PESD	Private and Executive Secretary's Diploma, London Chamber of Commerce and Industry
PgC	Postgraduate Certificate
PGCE	Postgraduate Certificate in Education
PGCert	Postgraduate Certificate
PgD	Postgraduate Diploma
PGDip	Postgraduate Diploma
PGDip(Comp)	Postgraduate Diploma in Composition
PGDip(LCM)	Postgraduate Diploma of the London College of Music
PGDip(Perf)	Postgraduate Diploma in Performance
PGDip(RCM)	Postgraduate Diploma of the Royal College of Music
PGDipMin	Postgraduate Diploma in Ministry
PGDipMus	Postgraduate Diploma in Music
PhD	Doctor of Philosophy
PhD(RCA)	Doctor of Philosophy (Royal College of Art)
PIC	Professional Investment Certificate
PIFA	Practitioner of the Institute of Field Archaeologists
PIIA	Practitioner of the Institute of Internal Auditors

PInstNDT	Practitioner of the British Institute of Non-Destructive Testing
PJDip	Professional Jewellers' Diploma
PJGemDip	Professional Jewellers' Gemstone Diploma
PJManDip	Professional Jewellers' Management Diploma
PJValDip	Professional Jewellers' Valuation Diploma
PPL	Private Pilot's Licence
PPRNCM	Professional Performance Diploma of the Royal Northern College of Music
PQS	Professional Qualification Structure
PQSW	Post-Qualifying Award in Social Work
PRCA	Public Relations Consultants Association
PSC	Private Secretary's Certificate
PSD	Private Secretary's Diploma
PTA	Pianoforte Tuners' Association
PVM	Professional in Value Management
QC	Queen's Counsel
QCA	Qualifications and Curriculum Authority
QCG	Qualification in Careers Guidance
QDR	Qualified Dispute Resolver
QICA	Qualification in Computer Auditing
QIS	Qualified Imaging Scientist
QPA	Qualification in Pensions Administration
QPSPA	Qualification in Public Sector Pensions Administration
RA	Royal Academician
RAD	Royal Academy of Dancing
RADA	Royal Academy of Dramatic Art
RAM	Royal Academy of Music
RANA	Royal Animal Nursing Auxiliary
RAS	Royal Astronomical Society
RBS	Royal Ballet School
RC	Roman Catholic
RCM	Royal College of Midwives
RCN	Royal College of Nursing
RCSLT	Royal College of Speech and Language Therapists
RCVS	Royal College of Veterinary Surgeons
REA	Regional Examining Body
REC	Recruitment and Employment Confederation
Ret'dABID	Retired Associate of the British Institute of Interior Design
Ret'dFBID	Retired Fellow of the British Institute of Interior Design
Ret'dMBID	Retired Member of the British Institute of Interior Design
RGN	Registered General Nurse
RHS	Royal Horticultural Society
RHV	Registered Health Visitor
RIBA	Royal Institute of British Architects
RICS	Royal Institution of Chartered Surveyors
RINA	Royal Institution of Naval Architects
RJDip	Diploma for Retail Jewellers
RJGemDip	National Association of Goldsmiths Gemstone Diploma
RM	Registered Midwife
RMN	Registered Mental Nurse
RMS	Royal Microscopical Society
RNMH	Registered Nurse for the Mentally Handicapped
RP	Registered Plumber

RPS	Royal Photographic Society
RSA	Royal Society of Arts
RSBEI	Registered Student of the Institution of Body Engineers
RSC	Royal Society of Chemistry
RSCN	Registered Sick Children's Nurse
RSP	Registered Safety Practitioner
RTO	Recognised Training Organisation
RTPI	Royal Town Planning Institute
RWCMD	Royal Welsh College of Music and Drama
SA	Salvation Army Management
SBP	Society of Business Practitioners
SCAA	School Curriculum and Assessment Authority
ScD	Doctor of Science
SCE	Scottish Certificate of Education
SCLS	Second Certificate for Legal Secretaries
SCMT	Ship Captain's Medical Training
SCOTVEC	Scottish Vocational Education Council
SCPL	Senior Commercial Pilot's Licence
SE	Society of Engineers
SEE	Society of Environmental Engineers
SEFIC	Spoken English for Industry and Commerce
SenAWeldI	Senior Associate of the Welding Institute
SEng	Qualified Sales Engineer
SenMWeldI	Senior Member of the Welding Institute
SF	Society of Floristry Ltd
SFA	Securities and Futures Authority
SFInstE	Senior Fellow of the Institute of Energy
SG	Society of Genealogists
SGT	Society of Glass Technology
SHNC	Scottish Higher National Certificate
SHND	Scottish Higher National Diploma
SIEDip	Securities Industry Examination Diploma
SInstPet	Student of the Institute of Petroleum
SITO	Security Industry Training Organisation Ltd
SLC	Secretarial Language Certificate
SLD	Secretarial Language Diploma
SNC	Scottish National Certificate
SND	Scottish National Diploma
SNNEB	Scottish Nursery Nurses Examination Board
SPA	Screen Printing Association
SPRINT	Sport Play and Recreation Industries National Training Executive
SQA	Scottish Qualifications Authority
SRD	State Registered Dietician
SRN	State Registered Nurse
SSC	Secretarial Studies Certificate, London Chamber of Commerce and Industry
STA	Swimming Teachers' Association
STAT	Society of Teachers of the Alexander Technique
STL	Supporting Teaching and Learning Qualifications
StudentIEE	Student of the Institution of Electrical Engineers
StudentIIE	Student of the Institution of Incorporated Engineers
StudentIMechE	Student of the Institution of Mechanical Engineers
StudIAP	Student of the Institution of Analysts and Programmers

StudIManf	Student Member of the Institute of Manufacturing
StudIMS	Student of the Institute of Management Specialists
StudProfBTM	Student of the Professional Business and Technical Management
StudSE	Student of the Society of Engineers (Inc)
StudSElec	Student of the Society of Electroscience
StudWeldI	Student of the Welding Institute
SVQ	Scottish Vocational Qualification
TAE	The Academy of Experts
TC	Technician Certificate
TCA	Technician in Costing and Accounting
TCA	Technician of the Institute of Cost and Executive Accountants
TCert	Teacher's Certificate
TD	Technician Diploma
TDCR	Teacher's Diploma of the College of Radiographers
TechICorr	Technician of the Institute of Corrosion
TechMIWM	Technician Member of the Institute of Wastes Management
TechRICS	Technical Surveyor of the Royal Institution of Chartered Surveyors
TechRMS	Technological Qualification in Microscopy, Royal Microscopical Society
TechRTPI	Technical Member of the Royal Town Planning Institute
TechSP	Technician Safety Practitioner
TechWeldI	Technician of the Welding Institute
TEMOL	Training in Energy Management through Open Learning
TI	Textile Institute
TIMBM	Technician of the Institute of Maintenance and Building Management
TMBA	Teacher Member of the British (Theatrical) Arts
TnIMBM	Technicians of the Institute of Maintenance and Building Management
TOEFL	Test of English as a Foreign Language
TPP	Test of Professional Practice
TVM	Trainer in Value Management
UCAS	Universities and Colleges Admissions Service
UCL	University College London
UEB	United Examining Board
UKCC	United Kingdom Central Council
UKCP	United Kingdom Council for Psychotherapy
UMIST	University of Manchester Institute of Science and Technology
URC	United Reformed Church
VetMB	Bachelor of Veterinary Medicine
VTCT	Vocational Training Charitable Trust
WES	Women's Engineering Society
WJEC	Welsh Joint Education Committee
WMAC	West Midlands Advisory Council for Further Education
WSA	West of Scotland Agricultural College
YHAFHE	Yorkshire and Humberside Association for Further and Higher Education
ZSL	Zoological Society of London

Part 1

Introduction

INTRODUCTION

Since its first publication in 1970, *British Qualifications* has charted a number of fundamental changes in further and higher education provision in the UK. Major advances in technology and more flexible delivery and attendance patterns have created different types of learning opportunity, encouraging an ever more diverse student population to access education at all levels. The range of subjects delivered has grown beyond all recognition. New areas of research have been established and developed into major subject specialisms. Employers and professional bodies have collaborated to develop subject areas aligned to changing industry requirements. Flexibility and choice are the hallmarks of today's system, and anyone new to higher education may well be bewildered by the sheer variety of degree pathways available. The capacity to combine and mix modules and subjects has in fact grown beyond anything that could have been imagined in 1970.

Traditional boundaries between academic and vocational pathways continue to break down, and today most degrees have a vocational slant. Extended industry and professional placements, sponsored research projects, practitioner input and field-based assignments are common features in many degrees, and provide an important link into practice at the early stages of learning. Overall, in 20 years universities have doubled in size and the responsibilities they have taken on have expanded considerably. Collaboration between further education (FE) and higher education (HE) institutions has enabled a substantial amount of HE-level provision to be delivered in FE institutions. Clear progression routes have been established for some time. Considerable breadth of provision is now available in FE: not only has the sector grown to accommodate sub-degree provision, it has also continued to deliver a wide range of pre-and post-18 vocational qualifications, which include technical, occupational and professional awards.

Today, certain types of external qualification cross the boundaries between further and higher education. Several higher education institutions (HEIs) – particularly those that gained university status in the 1990s and in 2005 – deliver advanced professional qualifications and higher national diplomas or certificates from awarding bodies like Edexcel, OCR and SQA. At the same time there has been a significant shift towards FE's involvement in delivery of these types of qualification, and a greater input from private sector colleges.

EDUCATION REFORM

The Higher Education Act 2004 introduced in 2006/07 brought new student support and tuition fee arrangements. Following the Browne Review of 2010, universities are able to charge full-time UK and EU undergraduate students up to £9,000 a year as part of a reorganization of HE funding and student finance. You will find further authoritative, official information about universities and colleges in the UK at the Unistats website: unistats.ac.uk. The Unistats website enables you to compare data and information on UK university and college courses, as well as providing useful information on cost and financial support. Information on student finance and how to apply for it can be found at www.gov.uk/student-finance, and this site also gives information about university and higher education courses.

As well as implementing reforms, the further and higher education sectors contribute to UK economic performance and the delivery of the government's policies on HE. As part of this shared responsibility a great deal of effort is being made to increase access to and participation in education, particularly among individuals who have not had much involvement in the past. The general availability of modular study programmes and related credit recognition of units, and greater use of ICT and e-learning resources, have done a lot to create more flexible methods of delivery and attendance requirements in further and higher education.

Foundation degrees

Foundation degrees (FDs) were established to give people the intermediate technical and professional skills that are in demand from employers, and to provide more flexible and accessible ways of studying. They are a higher-level qualification awarded by universities. A foundation degree is the equivalent of two thirds of a full honours degree and is a fully flexible qualification allowing students to study part-time or full-time to fit their lifestyle. Unlike full degrees, there are no set entry requirements for foundation degrees. The qualification can be built up from a range of relevant learning experiences, to allow for extremely flexible and adaptable qualifications that can be tailored by employers to support their workforce and business development needs. They offer opportunities for employment and career advancement. Progression routes include links with associated professional qualifications and/or direct entry to the final year of a relevant Honours-level degree. FDs are offered by universities, colleges and other providers.

The first FDs in 2001 were studied by 4,000 students. In 2014–15, 2.3% of the higher education qualifications awarded were FDs. There are now hundreds of FD courses available, both full-and part-time.

- Information about FDs can be found on the UCAS website: www.ucas.com/ucas/under-graduate/getting-started/what-study/foundation-degrees
- Information, advice and guidance resources for work-based learners and their advisers are hosted by unionlearn at www.unionlearn.org.uk/higher-learning-work

Policy and regulation

The UK and Scottish parliaments and the Welsh and Northern Ireland assemblies set national priorities for further and higher education. Policy development, planning and implementation rest with the government departments responsible for each national education brief – the Department for Education (DfE, website: www.gov.uk/government/organisations/department-for-education), the Department for the Economy (DfENI, website: www.economy-ni.gov.uk) for Northern Ireland (covering further and higher education), the Scottish Government (www.gov.scot), and The Department for Education and Skills (DfES, website: http://gov.wales/topics/educationandskills) in Wales.

In England, delivery of FE is subject to external audit and public reporting by the Office for Standards in Education, Children's Services and Skills (Ofsted, website: www.gov.uk/government/organisations/ofsted).

In Scotland, the Scottish Funding Council (SFC, website: www.sfc.ac.uk) is the national, strategic body that is responsible for funding teaching and learning provision, research and other activities in Scotland's 26 colleges and 19 universities and higher education institutes. Inspection is carried out by Education Scotland (www.education.gov.scot).

DfES is responsible for planning, funding and promotion of all post-16 education in Wales. Estyn (the Welsh-language acronym for Her Majesty's Inspectorate for Education and Training in Wales, website: www.estyn.gov.uk) is the appointed authority for audit of the quality of provision and related areas.

The Department for the Economy (DfE) is responsible for planning and funding of further education provision in Northern Ireland. The Education and Training Inspectorate (ETI) (www.etini.gov.uk) undertakes inspection and audit on behalf of the Department.

QUALITY ASSURANCE

A degree of convergence exists in the quality assurance of qualifications at level 3 and below. England, Wales and Northern Ireland share a common qualifications system, and the regulators in each country (listed below) work together in regulating qualifications for use across the three countries. Scotland has a separate qualifications system, although there is close correlation across all four countries, particularly in the area of vocational qualifications.

The following four bodies are responsible for the accreditation and standards of external qualifications and for curriculum and assessment for ages 3–16:

- *England*: Office of the Qualifications and Examinations Regulator (Ofqual, website: www.gov.uk/government/organisations/ofqual);
- *Northern Ireland*: Council for Curriculum, Examinations and Assessment (CCEA*, website: http://ccea.org.uk);
- *Scotland*: Scottish Qualifications Authority (SQA**, website: www.sqa.org.uk);
- *Wales*: Qualifications Wales, which was established through the Qualifications Wales Act 2015 (website: http://qualificationswales.org) and is organised to focus on: recognising awarding bodies and approving and designating qualifications; regulating awarding bodies and reviewing qualifications already in existence; developing and commissioning new qualification requirements for Wales; and research to provide the evidence base for regulatory decision-making.

*CCEA is also an Awarding Body for qualifications in Northern Ireland, offering a diverse range of qualifications, such as GCSEs, including the GCSE Double Award specifications in vocational subjects, GCE A and AS levels, Entry Level Qualifications, and Online Language Assessment (OLA).

**SQA is also an Awarding Body that develops and validates SQA-branded qualifications including National Qualifications, Skills for Work, Scottish Baccalaureates, National Progression Awards and National Certificates, Higher National Certificates and Diplomas, Scottish Vocational Qualifications and Modern Apprenticeships, and Scottish Professional Development Awards. The Scottish Credit and Qualifications Framework (SCQF) is Scotland's national qualifications framework.

In HE the responsibility for standards and quality rests firmly with each institution. All institutions work with the independent Quality Assurance Agency for Higher Education (QAA) for England, Northern Ireland, Scotland and Wales. Institutional audits and subject-level reviews have been undertaken by QAA since 2001. It publishes its findings on its website (www.qaa.ac.uk) as publicly accessible information.

Given the current scale and diversity of degree provision in the HE sector, there has been a need to clarify what can reasonably be expected from undergraduate and postgraduate programmes. QAA has responded to this requirement and developed the Quality Code for HE providers (www.qaa.ac.uk/assuring-standards-and-quality/the-quality-code), and subject benchmark statements indicating the expected standards of degrees across a range of subjects.

QUALIFICATION FRAMEWORKS

In further response to the breadth and diversity of qualifications available, a number of national qualification frameworks have been introduced. The framework concept is closely associated with greater transparency and comparability between types of qualification, particularly between those that were traditionally classified as academic or vocational. The frameworks allow comparison with qualifications in different countries by grading them into levels based on the learning outcomes.

The framework for Higher Education Qualifications in England, Wales and Northern Ireland (FHEQ) applies to degrees, diplomas, certificates and other academic awards by higher education providers (see Figure 1.1). Further information can be found at www.qaa.ac.uk/assuring-standards-and-quality/the-quality-code/qualifications.

The Scottish Credit and Qualification Framework (SCQF) was developed by SQA, the Scottish Executive, QAA (Scottish Office) and Universities for Scotland. It provides an overview of all levels of national and higher qualifications provision in Scotland (see Figure 1.2). Further information and the database of courses can be found at http://scqf.org.uk

The Regulated Qualifications Framework was introduced in October 2015 (find more information at: https://ofqual.blog.gov.uk/2015/10/01/explaining-the-rqf).It is the new framework for recognizing and accrediting general and vocational qualifications in England and vocational qualifications in Northern Ireland. It is intended to act as a simple tool for describing qualifications. Ofqual regulates this framework, and more information can be found at https://www.gov.uk/ what-different-qualification-levels-mean and http://register.ofqual.gov.uk/, which is a searchable database of qualifications and organizations.

For current information about qualifications offered in Wales, please go to the Qualifications in Wales website, www.qiw.wales

The European Qualifications Framework (EQF) compares the level of qualifications across Europe to make it easier for employers and educational establishments to compare their value. More information can be found at the website of the European Commission: http://www.cedefop.europa.eu/en/events-and-projects/projects/european-qualifications-framework-eqf

Part 2

Teaching Establishments

INTRODUCTION

The statutory responsibility for the provision of education in the United Kingdom lies with the Department for Education (DfE) (www.gov.uk/government/organisations/department-for-education) in England, the Welsh Assembly Government's Department for Education and Skills (DfES) (http://gov.wales/topics/educationandskills), the Education Department of the Scottish Government (www.gov.scot/Topics/Education) and the Department of Education (DENI) (www.education-ni.gov.uk) and the Department for the Economy (DfENI) (www.economy-ni.gov.uk/), which is responsible for further and higher education, in Northern Ireland.

In the United Kingdom the statutory system of public education has three progressive stages: primary education (up to the age of 11 or 12), secondary education (up to age 16), and further education (post-16).

The Education and Skills Act 2008 introduced a new requirement that all young people in England must continue in education or training at least part-time until they are 18 years old, and this applies to any person born on or after 1 September 1997. The website https://www.ucas.com/further-education/post-16-qualifications gives useful information on the options available and the government website www.gov.uk/further-education-courses also gives information on courses and funding.

This section briefly describes further and higher provision and the main types of institution.

FURTHER AND HIGHER EDUCATION

'Higher education' (HE) is a term that broadly defines any course of study leading to a qualification at level 4 and above in the Regulated Qualifications Framework for England, Wales and Northern Ireland, and level 6 and above in the Scottish Credit and Qualifications Framework.

HE incorporates study towards a wide range of qualifications including Foundation, undergraduate and postgraduate degrees, certificates and diplomas awarded by individual universities and other higher education institutions (HEIs) with degree-awarding powers. It can also include study towards general, technical or occupationally-related diplomas and certificates awarded by the large unitary awarding bodies. Unitary awarding bodies are characterized by their breadth of provision, from NVQs and BTEC courses and A levels through to qualifications at level 5 and above in the national frameworks.

The other category that can be characterized as HE, includes post-experience education above level 4 (and level 7 in Scotland). This includes qualifications available from awarding bodies that represent a particular sector, occupation or technical/craft area, and professional institutions that are also approved as awarding bodies.

HE can take place in universities and HE colleges (which continue to provide the majority of undergraduate and postgraduate courses). It can also take place in colleges of further education (FE). A significant number of colleges deliver parts of, and in some cases entire, Foundation and undergraduate degree courses in agreement with a selected university partner that is responsible for quality assurance and final awards.

In general terms, FE is available for students who are over the age of 16 and still in full-time education, and for adults aged 19 and over. FE provision includes GCSEs, A levels and other types of general and vocational qualifications below level 4 (and level 6 in Scotland) in the National Qualifications Frameworks.

All qualifications are awarded by approved external awarding bodies that include AQA, City & Guilds, Edexcel, LCCI, OCR, OCN and SQA in Scotland. This also includes qualifications below level 4 (level 6 in Scotland) that have a craft or technical focus or are related to an occupation/ sector. At the time of writing, readers who want to find out more about approved qualifications below level 4 will find The Register of Regulated Qualifications website informative (https:// register.ofqual.gov.uk). It contains details of all regulated qualifications in England (Ofqual), Wales (Welsh Government) and Northern Ireland (Ofqual and CCEA).

FURTHER AND HIGHER EDUCATION INSTITUTIONS

England and Wales

There is a wide range of further and higher education establishments, including colleges with various titles. There are also a number of independent specialist establishments, like secretarial and correspondence colleges.

In 2016 there were 161 universities and colleges that were allowed to award degrees. All institutions that are recognized as having degree-awarding powers in the UK can be found on the government website (www.gov.uk/check-a-university-is-officially-recognised/recognised-bodies).

There were also over 600 colleges and other institutions that could not award degrees themselves, but provided courses leading to UK degrees. Institutions offering courses leading to a degree from a recognized body can be found at www.gov.uk/check-a-university-is-officially-recognised/listed-bodies. For general information on UK degrees visit www.gov.uk/recognised-uk-degrees.

Courses include those for first and second degrees, certain graduate-equivalent qualifications, and the examinations of the principal professional associations. These institutions also provide courses leading to important qualifications below degree level, such as Foundation degrees, Higher National Diplomas and Certificates, and Diplomas of Higher Education. Most FE colleges specialize in providing courses that lead to qualifications below degree level, such as A levels and BTEC qualifications. Some offer degree courses, including in many cases Foundation degrees.

Students aged 16–18 who have been ordinarily resident in the UK for three years and, while the UK is still part of the European Union, European Economic Area nationals normally have the right to attend a full-time course without paying tuition fees. More detailed information on tuition fees for international students can be found at www.ukcisa.org.uk. Colleges are free to determine fee levels for students who do not qualify for 'home fees'.

Further Education choices can be searched on www.gov.uk/government/statistical-data-sets/ fe-choices-performance-indicators and also http://findfe.com. The 2016 figures show there were 348 FE colleges in England (of which 94 were sixth-form colleges) 19 in Wales, 40 in Scotland and 6 in Northern Ireland.

Scotland

There are 26 FE colleges in Scotland that provide a broad mix of courses, many awarded by the Scottish Qualifications Authority (SQA). Most HE courses at or near degree level and beyond are provided by the 18 universities/HE institutions and The Open University in Scotland (www.universities-scotland.ac.uk; www.studyinscotland.org). These institutions offer a range of vocationally-oriented courses ranging from science, engineering and computing to health care, art and design, music and drama, and teacher training, as well as the more traditional 'academic' courses. The Scottish Funding Council funds all the universities and HE institutions in Scotland.

Northern Ireland

Responsibility for the FE sector in Northern Ireland rests with the Department for the Economy (DfENI) which directly funds colleges. There are six further and higher education colleges, offering a wide range of vocational and non-vocational courses for both full- and part-time students. Details can be found at www.anic.ac.uk

Queen's University Belfast and the University of Ulster receive Quality-related Research (QR) funding from the Department for the Economy. Many of the courses in both universities are designed to suit the needs of industry, commerce and the professions. Agricultural, horticultural and food colleges in Northern Ireland are administered through the Department of Agriculture, Environment and Rural Affairs (DAERA, website: www.daera-ni.gov.uk), which works with the College of Agriculture, Food and Rural Enterprise (CAFRE, website: www.cafre.ac.uk) to offer a range of further and higher education courses.

UNIVERSITIES AND HE COLLEGES

Universities are self-governing bodies, largely financed by the government through the Higher Education Funding Councils in the UK. They generally derive their rights and privileges from Royal Charter or Act of Parliament, and any amendment of their charters or statutes is made by the Crown acting through the Privy Council on the application of the universities themselves. The universities alone decide what degrees they award and the conditions on which they are awarded; they alone decide which students to admit and which staff to appoint. However, government policies have started to influence admission criteria, particularly in terms of widening access and participation in HE. Student fees set by universities are also subject to strict guidelines set by the government.

The Higher Education Funding Council (www.hefce.ac.uk) funds HE, research and related activities in English HE institutions and FE colleges. In 2016–17 it funded 132 HE institutions and 214 FE colleges.

Institutions receiving funding from Higher Education Funding Council for England

The schools and institutes of the University of London which receive funds directly from the HEFCE are marked *.

Anglia Ruskin University; Aston University; University of Bath; Bath Spa University; University of Bedfordshire; Birkbeck College, University of London*; University of Birmingham; Birmingham City University; University College Birmingham; Bishop Grosseteste University; University of Bolton; Arts University Bournemouth; Bournemouth University; University of Bradford; University of Brighton; University of Bristol; British School of Osteopathy; Brunel University; Buckinghamshire New University; University of Cambridge; Institute of Cancer Research*; Canterbury Christ Church University; University of Central Lancashire; University of Chester; University of Chichester; City University, London; Conservatoire for Dance and Drama; Courtauld Institute of Art*; Coventry University; Cranfield University; University for the Creative Arts; University of Cumbria; De Montfort University; University of Derby; University of Durham; University of East Anglia; University of East London; Edge Hill University; University of Essex; University of Exeter; Falmouth University; University of Gloucestershire; Goldsmiths' College, University of London*; University of Greenwich; Guildhall School of Music and Drama; Harper

Adams University; University of Hertfordshire; Heythrop College, University of London*; University of Huddersfield; University of Hull; Imperial College London; Keele University; University of Kent; King's College London*; Kingston University; University of Lancaster; University of Leeds; Leeds College of Art; Leeds Beckett University; Leeds Trinity University; University of Leicester; University of Lincoln; University of Liverpool; Liverpool Hope University; Liverpool Institute for Performing Arts; Liverpool John Moores University; Liverpool School of Tropical Medicine; University of the Arts, London; University of London; London Business School*; London School of Economics and Political Science*; London School of Hygiene and Tropical Medicine*; London Metropolitan University; London South Bank University; Loughborough University; University of Manchester; Manchester Metropolitan University; Middlesex University, London; National Film and Television School; University of Newcastle upon Tyne; Newman University; University of Northampton; University of Northumbria at Newcastle; Norwich University of the Arts; University of Nottingham; Nottingham Trent University; The Open University; University of Oxford; Oxford Brookes University; Plymouth University; Plymouth College of Art; University of Portsmouth; Queen Mary, University of London*; Ravensbourne; University of Reading; Roehampton University; Rose Bruford College; Royal Academy of Music*; Royal Agricultural University; Royal Central School of Speech and Drama*; Royal College of Art; Royal College of Music; Royal Holloway, University of London*; Royal Northern College of Music; Royal Veterinary College*; St George's, University of London*; University of St Mark and St John; St Mary's University, Twickenham; University of Salford; University of Sheffield; Sheffield Hallam University; School of Oriental and African Studies, University of London*; University of Southampton; Southampton Solent University; Staffordshire University; University Campus Suffolk; University of Sunderland; University of Surrey; University of Sussex; Teesside University; Trinity Laban Conservatoire of Music and Dance; University College London (including UCL Institute of Education)*; University of Warwick; University of the West of England, Bristol; University of West London; University of Westminster; University of Winchester; University of Wolverhampton; University of Worcester; Writtle College; University of York; York St John University.

(*Source*: Higher Education Funding Council for England)

Universities receiving funding from the Department for Employment and Learning in Northern Ireland

Queen's University Belfast; University of Ulster.

(*Source*: Higher Education Funding Council for England)

Higher Education Institutions receiving funding from the Scottish Funding Council

University of Aberdeen; Abertay University; University of Dundee; Edinburgh Napier University; University of Edinburgh; Glasgow Caledonian University; Glasgow School of Art; University of Glasgow; Heriot-Watt University; The Open University in Scotland; Queen Margaret University; Robert Gordon University; Royal Conservatoire of Scotland; SRUC; University of St Andrews; University of Stirling; University of Strathclyde; University of the Highlands and Islands; University of the West of Scotland. They also fund 25 colleges.

(*Source*: Scottish Funding Council, www.sfc.ac.uk/funding/funding.aspx)

Institutions receiving funding from the Higher Education Funding Council for Wales

Aberystwyth University; Bangor University; Cardiff University; Cardiff Metropolitan University; The Open University in Wales; University of South Wales; Swansea University; University of Wales; University of Wales Trinity Saint David; Wrexham Glyndwr University.

(*Source*: Higher Education Funding Council for Wales, www.hefcw.ac.uk)

OTHER HE ORGANIZATIONS

There are a number of other organizations involved in shaping the HE sector. You can find a full list of these organizations on the Universities UK website: www.universitiesuk.ac.uk

Part 3

Qualifications

INTRODUCTION

Definition of common terms

A number of terms are commonly used as synonyms for qualifications, for example 'examinations' and 'courses'. This can hide important differences of meaning and lead to confusion and mis-understanding. In some contexts, it may be important to make these differences explicit to guard against exaggerating or diminishing the level of achievement, which is an essential core of the concept of qualification. It is especially important to clarify the difference in meaning between 'examination', 'course' and 'qualification'.

Examination

An examination is a formal test or assessment. It can focus on one or more of the following: knowledge, understanding, skill or competence. An examination may be set as a written test, an oral test, an aural and oral test (e.g. a foreign language test) or a practical test. In the past, most forms of external assessment in FE were based on a model of examination dominated by the psychometric model, designed to discriminate between individuals – normative referencing – and took the form of written tests. There was considerable variation in different kinds of written examination, including essays, question and answer, and 'multiple response'. Today, largely as a result of the introduction of National Vocational Qualifications (NVQs), the purpose and format of many examinations have been reappraised, and criterion-referenced examinations that focus on achievement (and in the case of NVQs, competence) are increasingly common. Many forms of assessment are now an integral part of the learning process, with a formative as well as a summative function rather than a separate, terminal, summative function.

Course

A course implies an ordered sequence of teaching or learning over a period of time. A course is governed by regulations or requirements, frequently imposed by an external awarding body and sometimes by the institution providing the course. An important distinguishing feature between different courses is the length of time allocated to study: it can vary from a few days to several years. Some courses offer a terminal award on the basis of course completion, and these courses are set for a given period of time. Other 'set period' courses may prescribe examinations; these can include continuous assessment, terminal testing or a combination of both. In other courses, the programme of study may be accomplished at a faster or slower rate; such courses normally enjoin continuous assessment or a terminal examination, or both. Many courses require attendance at an institution, while distance learning, correspondence courses, and various forms of flexible learning courses are usually free of these requirements, although some may require occasional attendance for residential components or face-to-face tutoring. A successful examination result usually confers a qualification or an award.

Qualification

A qualification is normally a certificated endorsement, from a recognized awarding body, that a level or quality of accomplishment has been achieved by an individual. Qualifications are usually conferred on successful completion of an examination, although not all examinations necessarily offer qualifications. An examination may offer an award that is a part-qualification. For example, an NVQ candidate may acquire a unit of competence that is a part-qualification building towards a full statement of competence – an NVQ. A first-year student on an HND course may be required to pass all first-year examinations to be permitted to continue into the second year: in a sense that student is 'qualified' to continue the course but no qualification is awarded. Some award-bearing examinations may be fully recognized and certificated qualifications in themselves (e.g. a BTEC HNC) but only part-qualifications for a profession (e.g. chartered engineer).

Apparent anomalies do exist. Some professional bodies and trade associations award qualifications that are recognized within the profession or association but are not obtained by examination. They are usually awarded on the basis of experience, and payment of a fee, and denote membership or acceptance. When the body also offers an examination route to the same qualification, successful examinees are usually known as 'graduate members'.

There are a number of accreditation authorities that approve qualifications. There are also many specialist and general validating, examining and awarding bodies that are responsible for the design and assessment of qualifications.

ACCREDITING REGULATORY BODIES

England

Sector Skills Councils

Federation for Industry Sector Skills and Standards (FISSS)
Tel: 0300 303 4444 E-mail: info@fisss.org Website: www.fisss.org
The Federation for Industry Sector Skills and Standards, is an organization that supports the network of licensed UK Sector Skills Councils (SSCs). These are employer-led, independent organizations that cover specific work sectors across the UK (currently accounting for approximately 90 per cent of the UK workforce).With the influence granted by licences from the governments of England, Scotland, Wales and Northern Ireland, and with private and public funding, this independent network engages with the education and training supply-side such as universities, colleges, funders and qualifications bodies to increase productivity at all levels in the workforce. There are 20 Sector Skills Councils who work with over 550,000 employers to define skills needs and skills standards in their industry. There are also 19 National Skills Academies. Details of the Sector Skills Councils are listed in the following table.

Table 3.1

Cogent skills	**Creative & Cultural Skills**
Sector: Science industries	*Sector:* Craft, cultural heritage, design, literature, music, performing and visual arts
Tel: 01925 515 200	Tel: 020 7015 1800
E-mail: info@cogentskills.com	E-mail: info@ccskills.org.uk
Website: www.cogentskills.com	Website: www.ccskills.org.uk
Construction Skills	
Sector: Construction	**Creative Skillset**
Tel: 0344 994 4400	*Sector:* TV, film, radio, interactive media, animation, computer games, facilities, photo imaging, publishing, advertising and fashion and textiles
E-mail: call.centre@cskills.org	
Website: www.cskills.org	
	Tel: 020 7713 9800
	E-mail: info@creativeskillset.org
	Website: www.creativeskillset.org

continued

Table 3.1 *Continued*

Energy & Utility Skills
Sector: Gas, power, waste management and water industries
Tel: 0845 077 9922
E-mail: enquiries@euskills.co.uk
Website: www.euskills.co.uk

ecITB
Sector: Engineering
Tel: 01923 260000
E-mail: ecitb@ecitb.org.uk
Website: www.ecitb.org.uk

Financial Skills Partnership
Sector: Finance, accountancy and financial services
Tel: 0114 261 5800
E-mail: info@financialskillspartnership.org.uk
Website:
www.financialskillspartnership.org.uk

IMI The Institute of the Motor Industry
Sector: Retail motor industry
Tel: 01992 519039
E-mail: comms@theimi.org.uk
Website: www.theimi.org.uk

Instructus Group
Sector: Business and administration, customer service, enterprise and business support, human resources and recruitment, industrial relations, leadership and management, marketing and sales
Tel: 0207 091 9620
E-mail: info@skillscfa.org
Website: www.skillscfa.org

Lantra
Sector: Land management and production, animal health and welfare and environmental industries
Tel: 024 7669 6996
E-mail: connect@lantra.co.uk
Website: www.lantra.co.uk

National Skills Academy for Food and Drink
Sector: Food and drink manufacturing and associated supply chains
Tel: 0845 644 0558
E-mail: info@insafd.co.uk
Website: www.nsafd.co.uk

People 1st
Sector: Hospitality, leisure, passenger transport, travel and tourism and retail
Tel: 020 3074 1222
E-mail: info@people1st.co.uk
Website: www.people1st.co.uk

SEMTA
Sector: Science, engineering and manufacturing technologies
Tel: 0845 643 9001
E-mail: customerservices@semta.org.uk
Website: www.semta.org.uk

Skills Active
Sector: Sport, fitness, outdoors, playwork, caravans and hair and beauty
Tel: 0207 840 1900
E-mail: skills@skillsactive.com
Website: www.skillsactive.com

Skills for Care & Development
Sector: Social care, children, early years and young people's workforces in the UK
Tel: 01133 241 1240
E-mail:
sscinfo@skillsforcareanddevelopment.org.uk
Website:
www.skillsforcareanddevelopment.org.uk

Skills for Health
Sector: UK Health
Tel: 0117 922 1155
E-mail: office@skillsforhealth.org.uk
Website: www.skillsforhealth.org.uk

continued

Table 3.1 *Continued*

Skills for Justice	**Summit Skills**
Sector: Community Justice, Courts Services, Custodial Care, Fire and Rescue, Forensic Science, Policing and Law Enforcement and Prosecution Services	*Sector:* Building Services Engineering
	Tel: 0207 313 4890
	E-mail: enquiries@summitskills.org.uk
	Website: www.summitskills.org.uk
Tel: 0114 261 1499	**Tech Partnership**
E-mail: info@skillsforjustice.com	*Sector:* Software, internet and web, IT services, telecommunications and business change
Website: www.skillsforjustice.com	
Skills for Security	
Sector: Security	Tel: 020 7963 8920
Tel: 01905 744000	E-mail: info@thetechpartnership.com
E-mail: info@skillsforsecurity.org.uk	Website: www.thetechpartnership.com
Website: www.skillsforsecurity.org.uk	

In October 2013, in response to the Richard Review of Apprenticeships (2012), the government set out its plans to reform Apprenticeships in England by replacing the existing Apprenticeship frameworks with employer-defined standards, putting employers in control and giving them a high degree of freedom to develop these standards to best meet the needs of their occupations and sectors. To support this reform, they established 'trailblazers' – groups led by employers and professional bodies – to develop the first of these new Apprenticeship standards (www.gov.uk/government/publications/future-of-apprenticeships-in-england-guidance-for-trailblazers).

The Government plan to introduce new standards for all occupations by 2017. A number of new Apprenticeship standards have already been government approved with the number growing all the time. Information on the new standards can be found at www.apprenticeships.org.uk/standards. The Federation for Industry Sector Skills and Standards (http://fisss.org) is developing a series of practical tools and guides for employers and employer-led partnerships to support the development of a new Apprenticeship standard and the detail of the implementation requirements which go with it – assessment, training and governance. The Federation currently manages the following certification systems for apprenticeships: ACE (England), ACW (Wales), MA Online v1 (Scotland) and MA Online v2 (Scotland).

The National College for Teaching and Leadership

The National College for Teaching and Leadership (NCTL) is part of the Department for Education and is involved in the exam administration function. The NCTL can be found at www.gov.uk/nctl, General enquiries, Ministerial and Public Communications Division, Department for Education, Piccadilly Gate, Store Street, Manchester, M1 2WD; Tel: 0370 000 2288. Information about the administration of exams can be found at www.gov.uk/exams-administration-information-for-exam-centres. The Department for Education is also a useful source of information, www.gov.uk/government/organisations/department-for-education.

Standards and Testing Agency (STA)

The Standards and Testing Agency is responsible for the development and delivery of all statutory assessments from early years to the end of Key Stage 3; Standards and Testing Agency,

53–55 Butts Road, Earlsdon Park, Coventry, CV1 3BH; National Curriculum assessments helpline: 0300 303 3013; E-mail: assessments@education.gov.uk; Website: www.gov.uk/sta

Ofqual: Office of Qualifications and Examinations Regulation

Contact details for Ofqual are: Ofqual, Spring Place, HeraldAvenue, Coventry, CV5 6UB; Tel: 0300 303 3344; E-mail: public.enquiries@ofqual.gov.uk; Website: www.gov.uk/government/organisations/ ofqual. Vocational qualifications that are only provided in Northern Ireland are regulated by the Council for the Curriculum, Examinations and Assessment, 29 Clarendon Road, Clarendon Dock, Belfast BT1 3BG; Tel: 02890 261200; E-mail: info@ccea.org.uk; Website: http://ccea.org.uk/

Ofqual is the regulator of qualifications, examinations and tests in England and a wide range of vocational qualifications in both England and Northern Ireland. Ofqual also regulates the National Curriculum Assessments in England. It monitors organizations that deliver qualifications and assessments as set out in the Apprenticeship, Skills, Children and Learning Act (2009) and Education Act (2011). Ofqual's role is to ensure all learners get the results they deserve, standards are maintained, and qualifications are correctly valued and understood, now and in the future.

Ofqual is accountable to parliament rather than to government ministers and advises the Government on qualifications and assessment based on their research into these areas.

Scotland

Scottish Qualifications Authority (SQA)

Customer Contact Centre, Tel: 0345 279 1000; Fax: 0345 213 5000; E-mail: customer@sqa.org.uk; Website: www.sqa.org.uk

The Scottish Qualifications Authority (SQA) is the national accreditation and awarding body in Scotland. It is an executive non-departmental public body (NDPB) sponsored by the Scottish Government's Learning Directorate and is fully committed to working with other organizations, agencies and institutions in Scotland to help meet the Scottish Government's National Outcomes, strategies, policies and priorities.

SQA works in partnership with schools, colleges, universities and industry to provide high quality, flexible and relevant qualifications and assessments, embedding industry standards where appropriate. It strives to ensure that SQA qualifications are inclusive and accessible to all, that they provide clear progression pathways, facilitate lifelong learning and recognize candidate achievement. The National Qualifications have been designed to meet the aims, purposes and values of Curriculum for Excellence.

People take SQA qualifications at all stages of their lives – at school, at college, at work and in their leisure time. There are qualifications at all levels of attainment. SQA is responsible for three main types of qualification: units, courses and group awards. Most SQA-awarded qualifications are made up of a combination of units, which can also be used in their own right. Each unit represents approximately 40 hours of teaching with additional study. Units are achieved by passing an assessment.

National Courses

There are seven levels of National Courses – National 1–5, Higher, and Advanced Higher and there are at present four Scottish Baccalaureates, which are awarded at Pass and Distinction.

National Courses are designed to develop skills and knowledge in a specific subject area as well as skills for learning, skills for life and skills for work. Achieving a National Course shows that a learner has demonstrated the specified knowledge and skills in a particular subject at the defined national standard. Some of the new Awards cover work from across different subject areas, are shorter than traditional courses and recognize success at different levels of difficulty, meaning they are suitable for young people of all abilities.

Higher National Courses

Higher Courses provide progression from National 5 and lead on to Advanced Higher and are designed to develop skills and knowledge in a specific subject area. Offered by colleges, some universities and many other training centres, Higher National Certificates (HNCs) and Higher National Diplomas (HNDs) are specially designed to meet the needs of employers. HNCs are usually made up of 12 Higher National Unit credits (one credit represents roughly 40 hours of timetabled learning and 40 hours of self-guided learning and study) and usually take one year to complete; HNDs are made up of 30 credits and usually take two years to complete.

Advanced Higher National Courses

Advanced Higher awards are designed to meet the aims, purposes and values of Curriculum for Excellence, and provide progression from Higher Courses. These courses, which are designed to develop skills and knowledge in a specific subject area, are usually made up of three National Units and an external assessment by means of an examination and a project. Advanced Highers tend to be taken in the sixth year at school or college by students who have normally passed Highers.

Skills for Work

There are also Skills for Work Courses from National 3 to National 5. These are vocational courses for pupils in third and fourth year of secondary school and above. Normally pupils following the Skills for Work courses will spend some of their time at a local college or another training provider or with an employer. The courses are intended to provide progression pathways to further education, training and employment.

Skills for Work courses, National 3, 4 and 5 and Higher are designed to develop skills and knowledge in a broad vocational area, as well as an understanding of: the workplace skills and attitudes for employability, Core Skills, and other transferable skills. They involve a strong element of learning through involvement in practical activities which are directly related to a particular vocational area. National 3 is usually made up of three 40-hour units and National 4, 5 and Higher are usually made up of four 40-hour units.

Other SQA Courses

National Qualification Group Awards – National Certificates (NCs), Higher National Certificates and Diplomas (HNCs and HNDs) and National Progression Awards (NPAs) – are designed to be taken at college; Scottish Vocational Qualifications (SVQs), Professional Development Awards (PDAs), QCF (Qualifications and Credit Framework) registered Awards, Certificates and Diplomas and Functional Skills, and Customized Awards are designed for the workplace. A private company or training provider must become an 'approved centre' to deliver SQA qualifications, or work in partnership with a college or training provider. SQA also offer Modern Apprenticeships.

SQA Qualifications

Higher National Certificates (HNCs) and **Higher National Diplomas** (HNDs) are developed by SQA in partnership with FE colleges, universities, and industry and commerce. They are credible, flexible qualifications that are designed to deliver skills and knowledge to meet the needs of today's businesses. Some HNCs allow direct entry into the second year of a degree programme, and some HNDs allow direct entry to the third year. Higher National qualifications can also give you the knowledge and understanding required for Scottish Vocational Qualifications (SVQs).

National Progression Awards (NPAs) are designed to assess a defined set of skills and knowledge in specialist vocational areas. They are mainly used by colleges for short programmes of study.

National Certificates are primarily aimed at 16–18-year olds and adults in full-time education. They prepare candidates for employment or further study by developing a range of knowledge and skills.

Scottish Vocational Qualifications (SVQs) are based on job competence, and recognize the skills and knowledge people need in employment. SVQs can be attained in most occupations and are available for all types and levels of job. They are primarily delivered to candidates in full-time employment and in the workplace.

Professional Development Awards (PDAs) are qualifications for people who are already in a career and who wish to extend or broaden their skills. In some cases, they are designed for people wishing to enter employment. PDAs can be taken at college or the workplace.

Customized Awards are specially designed vocational qualifications at any level to meet an organization's need for skills and expertise and provide recognition and development opportunities for individuals. They can also help a company meet regulatory requirements and demonstrate the competence of its employees to external parties.

Scottish Credit and Qualifications Framework

The SQA is a partner in a 'credit' system called the Scottish Credit and Qualifications Framework (SCQF), which sets out the Scottish qualifications and how they relate to one another by making clear the credit value of each type of qualification available in Scotland. The framework has 12 levels, from Level 1 for very basic education to Level 12 for doctoral degrees.

More information about SQA and its qualifications can be found at its website: www.sqa.org.uk

Validating, examining and awarding bodies/organizations

A large number of external bodies provide qualifications recognized by accrediting and regulatory bodies. Not all qualifications are available across the entire FE sector: some colleges specialize in particular vocational areas while others are involved in more general adult education provision.

The Federation of Awarding Bodies (FAB) is a trade federation and membership organization for vocational awarding bodies. At the time of writing, there are around 120 Ofqual-recognized awarding bodies that are full members of FAB. It also has associate members. Find more information at www.awarding.org.uk.

It is important to contact the examining or awarding bodies directly to find which colleges deliver the qualifications desired. However, most colleges deliver courses leading to qualifications awarded by the sample selection of organizations listed below.

ABC Awards

Robins Wood House, Robins Wood Road, Aspley, Nottingham NG8 3NH; Tel: 0115 854 1620; Fax: 0115 854 1617; E-mail: centresupport@abcawards.co.uk; website: www.abcawards.co.uk

ABC Awards is a vocational awarding organization with accredited QCF qualifications in all sectors. It is a registered charity and part of the EMFEC Group. ABC has a portfolio of Ofqual regulated qualifications covering 16 industry sectors as well as functional skills and is designed for all ages and abilities post-14. ABC Awards' qualifications give learners the skills they need to find employment, progress within education and training or enhance their skills within their current job roles.

AQA

Stag Hill House, Guildford, Surrey GU2 7XJ; Tel: 0800 197 7162; Exams Office Support e-mail: eos@aqa.org.uk; website: www.aqa.org.uk

AQA is an independent education charity and the largest of the exam boards, currently setting and marking the papers for around half of all GCSEs and A-levels in England, Wales and Northern Ireland. AQA qualifications are internationally recognized and are taught in 30 countries around the world. As an awarding body, AQA offers a broad range of academic qualifications for 14–19-year olds including GCEs, GCSEs, AQA iGCSEs, the Extended Project Qualification and the AQA Baccalaureate.

ASDAN

Wainbrook House, Hudds Vale Road, St George, Bristol BS5 7HY; Tel: 0117 941 1126; e-mail: info@asdan.org.uk; website: www.asdan.org.uk

ASDAN is a curriculum development organization and awarding body, offering programmes and qualifications that explicitly grow skills for learning, for employment and for life. ASDAN is established as a registered charity for the 'advancement of education, by providing opportunities for all learners to develop their personal and social attributes and levels of achievement through ASDAN awards and resources, and the relief of poverty, where poverty inhibits such opportunities for learners'.

ASDAN qualifications contribute towards school/college performance measures and Ofsted requirements. ASDAN offers a range of nationally approved qualifications based around the development of personal, social and employability skills:

- Entry 1, 2 and 3 (Access) qualifications meet the needs of learners working below GCSE (Intermediate) level
- Levels 1 and 2 (Intermediate) qualifications are comparable to GCSEs
- Level 3 (Higher) qualifications are A/AS-level comparable
- Level 4 accreditation represents a Certificate of Higher Education

Ofqual, Qualifications Wales and CCEA approve ASDAN qualifications for pre-and post-16 provision. ASDAN qualifications sit within the Regulated Qualifications Framework (RQF) and the Qualifications and Credit Framework (QCF), and some have approval within the SCQF in Scotland. ASDAN also offers a wide choice of activity-based curriculum programmes that can be used in a variety of educational settings with learners working at a range of levels, offering imaginative ways of developing, recording and certificating young people's personal achievements. Through Customised Accreditation ASDAN also accredits programmes that are already being offered or has been written by another organization.

The following ASDAN qualifications are available:
- Qualifications in Personal Progress: Entry 1
- Personal and Social Development (PSD): Entry 1–3, Levels 1 and 2
- Employability: Entry 2 to Level 3
- Diplomas in Life Skills: Entry 1–3
- Event Volunteering Qualifications: Entry 3 to Level 3
- Wider Key Skills: Levels 1–4
- Certificate of Personal Effectiveness (CoPE): Levels 1–3
- Award of Personal Effectiveness (AoPE) Levels 1–3

City & Guilds

1 Giltspur Street, London EC1A 9DD; Tel: Customers: 0844 543 0000, Main switchboard: 0207 294 2468; e-mail: centresupport@cityandguilds.com; website: www.cityandguilds.com

City & Guilds is a leading vocational educational organization, offering hundreds of work-related qualifications worldwide. City & Guilds' qualifications, which span from basic skills to the highest level of professional achievement, are delivered in more than 80 countries across the world.

With over 130 years of experience, City & Guilds offers a wide range of vocational qualifications, apprenticeships and traineeships from agriculture to engineering; hairdressing to health and social care; IT to tourism; and photography to catering. They are developed with the help of industry experts and are workplace-relevant, so these qualifications equip people for doing a real job – benefiting them and their employer.

City & Guilds qualifications develop both knowledge and practical skills. They are available at nine levels, from Entry Level to Level 8, and are suitable for anyone, whether they are beginners or advanced in their career or area of study. Assessment is based on any combination of examination, projects or coursework. The organizations that offer City & Guilds qualifications include schools, colleges, training organizations, companies and adult education institutes. Depending on the organization, it is possible to study full-time, part-time or through distance learning.

City and Guilds offer the following qualifications: National Vocational Qualifications (NVQs) and Scottish Vocational Qualifications (SVQs), Functional Skills, Core Skills and Essential Skills, International Vocational Qualifications (IVQs), Single Subject Qualifications, International English Qualifications (IEQs), Institute of Leadership and Management (ILM) qualifications, Professional Recognition Awards, Tech Levels, TechBac, Apprenticeships and Traineeships.

Pearson (Edexcel, BTEC and LCCI)

190 High Holborn, London WC1V 7BH; website: https://qualifications.pearson.com, online contact form for students: http://qualifications.pearson.com/en/support/support-for-you/students/contact-us.html

Edexcel, of Pearson Education Limited, is the UK's largest awarding organization, offering academic and vocational qualifications and testing to schools, colleges, employers and other places of learning in the UK and internationally. Edexcel academic qualifications include GCSE,

GCE (A level) and International GCSE (Edexcel Certificate for UK state schools). Edexcel vocational qualifications include NVQ and BTEC from entry level to Higher National Diplomas.

Pearson acquired EDI, a leading provider of education and training qualifications and assessment services and the EDI qualifications have been rebranded as Pearson material. The qualifications selected from EDI have been redeveloped or reaccredited to be delivered through Pearson's brands including: Pearson Edexcel, Pearson BTEC and Pearson LCCI.

LCCI International Qualifications are widely used in South East Asia and over 100 countries around the world. LCCI International Qualifications, vocational qualifications available as single subjects or diplomas, cover the key areas of business, language and teaching.

NCFE

Q6, Quorum Business Park, Benton Lane, Newcastle upon Tyne NE12 8BT; Tel: 0191 239 8000; e-mail: service@ncfe.org.uk; website: www.ncfe.org.uk

NCFE is a national awarding organization and registered educational charity. It currently offers over 500 nationally accredited qualifications from Entry level up to and including level 4 as well as NVQs, Functional Skills, Apprenticeships and Traineeships. Further qualifications are constantly in development. The NCFE website has a qualifications finder search facility: www.ncfe.org.uk/qualification-search

OCR

1 Hills Road, Cambridge CB1 2EU;
General qualifications: Tel: 01223 553998; e-mail: general.qualifications@ocr.org.uk;
Vocational qualifications: Tel: 02476 851 509; e-mail: vocational. qualifications@ocr.org.uk; website: www.ocr.org.uk

OCR is a leading UK awarding body, committed to providing qualifications that engage learners of all ages at school, college, in work or through part-time learning programmes to achieve their full potential. OCR offers a wide range of general and vocational qualifications, from GCSEs, A levels and Diplomas to OCR Nationals, NVQs and specialist qualifications. You can find a full index of OCR qualifications at: www.ocr.org.uk/qualifications/index.aspx

WJEC

245 Western Avenue, Cardiff CF5 2YX; Tel: 029 2026 5000; e-mail: info@wjec.co.uk; website: www.wjec.co.uk

A registered charity with members from the 22 local authorities in Wales, WJEC is a leading awarding organization providing assessment, training and educational resources in England, Wales, Northern Ireland and elsewhere; WJEC CBAC Ltd is a company limited by guarantee, registered in England and Wales. WJEC offers the following major qualifications: GCSE; Entry Level (EL) and Advanced (A)/Advanced Supplementary (AS) levels and the Welsh Baccalaureate, which is available at different levels and incorporates GCSEs, A Levels and NVQs. In addition, WJEC provides Essential Skills Wales, Project and Extended Project, Pathways QCF, Principal Learning and Wider Key Skills qualifications. The reformed GCSE and GCE qualifications in England are provided via Eduqas, the new brand from WJEC (www.eduqas.co.uk).

Part 4

Qualifications Awarded or Validated by Universities

ADMISSION TO DEGREE COURSES

Higher Education Institutions (HEIs)

Most institutions have a general requirement for admission to a degree course; special requirements may be in force for particular courses. Requirements are usually expressed in terms of subjects passed at GCE A level and the Higher Grade of the SQC. UCAS is the clearing house for the universities and it handles applications for university courses (www. ucas.com).

All intending students who live in the UK may obtain information on application procedures from their schools or colleges, or directly from UCAS. The scheme covers all universities and all medical schools. UCAS also has specialist services: the UCAS Teacher Training (www.ucas.com/ucas/tea-cher-training), the UK Postgraduate Application and Statistical Service (www.ucas.com/ucas/post-graduate) and the UCAS Conservatoires (www. ucas.com/ucas/conservatoires). HEIs have specific schemes to encourage access and participation in higher education. These can include partnerships with further education colleges that run access to higher education courses.

The Open University

For admission to most first-degree courses, no formal educational qualifications are necessary. However, students who have successfully completed one or more years of full-time study at the higher education level (or its equivalent in part-time study) may be eligible for exemption from some credit requirements of the BA degree. The Open University handles its own admissions. See www.openuniversity.edu/study/admissions-applications/how-to-apply for further information.

Business schools

The degrees awarded by the various university business schools are postgraduate and therefore normally require an Honours degree as part of their entrance qualification.

AWARDS

The awards made by the universities may be separated into the following categories: first degrees; higher degrees; honorary degrees; first diplomas and certificates; higher diplomas and certificates.

First degrees

Nomenclature

Various names are given to first degrees at British universities. At most universities the first degree in Arts is the BA (Bachelor of Arts) and the first degree in Science is the BSc (Bachelor of Science), but at the universities of Oxford and Cambridge and at several new universities, the BA is the first degree gained by students in both arts and science. Although the first degree in most faculties in Scottish universities is a Bachelor's degree, the first degree in Arts in the four 'ancient' universities (Aberdeen, Edinburgh, Glasgow and St Andrews) and Dundee University is MA or Master of Arts. Heriot-Watt University also offers some 'first degree' MAs, but at Honours level only.

There are numerous variations on the bachelor theme, for example BSc (Econ) (Bachelor of Science in Economics), BCom (Bachelor of Commerce), BSocSc (Bachelor of Social Science), BEng (Bachelor of Engineering) and BTech (Bachelor of Technology). The first award in medicine is the joint degrees of MB, ChB (Bachelor of Medicine, Bachelor of Surgery), the designatory letters of which vary from university to university.

Structure of courses

First-degree courses vary considerably in structure, not only between one university and another but also between faculties in a single university. The degree examination is usually in two sections, Part I coming after one or two years of the course and Part II, 'finals, at the end of the course. The first-degree system at some Scottish universities differs substantially from that in English and Welsh universities (see *The Scottish first degree* section below).

First awards

- **BA, BEd, BEng, LLB, BSc, BBA, BMedSci:** with 1st Class, 2nd Class (Divisions 1 and 2), 3rd Class Honours or Pass; or unclassified with or without Distinction.
- **MEng:** awarded to students who successfully complete a course of study that is longer and more demanding than the BEng first degree course in engineering.
- **GMus (Graduate Diploma in Music):** awarded to those students who complete three years' approved full-time study (or equivalent) in music and who demonstrate competence in musical performance.
- **M.Ost (Master of Osteophathy):** M.Ost is an undergraduate degree of four years' full-time study.
- **DipHE (Diploma of Higher Education):** equivalent in standard and often similar in content to the first two years of an Honours degree course.
- **Certificates of Higher Education:** equivalent to the first year of an Honours degree course.

Bachelor degrees

These degrees, sometimes known as 'ordinary' or 'first' degrees, lead to qualifications such as Bachelor of Arts (BA), Bachelor of Science (BSc) or Bachelor of Medicine (MB). Each university decides the form and content of its own degree examinations. These vary from university to university.

The first-degree structure in all British universities is based on the honours degree. Successful candidates in honours degree examinations are placed in different classes according to their performance, first class being the highest. The other classes given vary from university to university, but the classification most often used is: Class I; Class II (Division 1); Class II (Division 2); Class III. Most graduates who go on to higher academic qualifications and those entering, for example, the higher grades in the Civil Service or research, normally have a good class honours degree.

You can find out more about recognized UK degrees at the Government website: www.gov.uk/recognised-uk-degrees.

Number of subjects studied

Excluding medicine and dentistry, the broad subject areas are Arts (or Humanities), Social Science, Pure Science and Applied Science. Most students study one main subject selected from one of these areas. It is possible to distinguish many types of degree course according to the number of subjects studied; these types are a variation on three main categories:

1. Honours course in one to three subjects with or without examinable subsidiary subjects.
2. Pass or ordinary courses in one to three subjects with or without examinable subsidiary subjects.
3. Common studies for pass and Honours in one to three subjects, with or without examinable subsidiary subjects.

Length of degree course

First-degree courses may be preceded by a preliminary or 'foundation' year, from which students with the appropriate entry qualifications may be exempted. At most universities Honours and pass courses in arts, social science, pure and applied science last three or four years, but courses in architecture, dentistry and veterinary medicine usually last five years, and complete qualifying courses in medicine up to six years. Courses in fine arts and pharmacy may last four years; four-year courses exist mainly in double Honours schools, especially when they involve foreign languages and a period of study abroad, and in the technological universities where some courses include a period of integrated industrial training (sandwich courses).

The Scottish first degree

Undergraduate Honours degrees in Scotland are usually four years in duration and are structured to ensure a great deal of flexibility during the first two years of study. Most students only confirm their major subject or subjects in the final two years of study, which usually allows the student to choose a variety of subjects. This is different from the English system of undergraduate education, which is normally three years in duration and is more specialized from the beginning. After three years of study, students can gain a Bachelor or Ordinary degree or obtain the Honours degree by studying for a further year.

The Medicine and Veterinary Medicine degrees and MA Fine Art degree all take five years. In several science and engineering subjects there are opportunities to study for a five-year MChem, MChemPhys, MEng or MPhys degree. These degrees entail in-depth study, often with a research focus, but are undergraduate degrees and not equivalent to postgraduate Master's.

Aegrotat degrees

Candidates who have followed a course for a degree but have been prevented from taking the examinations by illness may be awarded a degree certificate indicating that they were likely to have obtained the degree had they taken the examinations.

Note on listing of undergraduate courses

These listings are compiled from information provided by the universities and other institutions, and do not consistently include joint honours combinations, which may be available. Users should check the departmental website of the university to see if the subject(s) concerned are offered on a joint honours basis or on another combined subject course basis.

Higher degrees

These comprise:

- some Bachelor's degrees: BPhil, BLitt, etc;
- Master's degrees: MA, MSc, etc;
- Doctor of Philosophy: PhD or DPhil;
- Higher Doctorates: DLitt, DSc, etc.

At Oxford and Cambridge, the degree of MA is conferred on any BA of the university without any further course of study or examination after a specified number of years and on payment of a fee.

Candidates for a Master's degree at other universities (and at some for the degrees of BPhil, BLitt and BD, which are of equivalent standing) are normally required to have a first degree, although it need not have been obtained in the same university. Master's degrees are taken after one or two years' full-time study. The PhD requires at least two or more – usually three – years of full-time study.

In some universities and faculties students may be selected for a PhD course after an initial year's study or research common to both a PhD and a Master's degree. Candidates for a Master's degree are required either to prepare a thesis for presentation to examiners, who may afterwards question candidates on it orally, or to take written examination papers; they may be required to do both. All PhD students present a thesis; some may be required to take an examination paper as well. MPhil, MSc and similar degrees are usually awarded at the end of a one- or two-year course in a specific topic on the results of a written examination or a thesis. Higher doctorates are designated on a faculty basis, eg DLitt (Doctor of Letters) and DSc (Doctor of Science). Candidates are usually required to have at least a Master's degree of the awarding university. Senior doctorates are conferred on more mature and established people, usually on the basis of published contributions to knowledge.

Higher awards

- **MA, MBA, MEd, MSc:** for successful completion of an approved postgraduate course of full-time study of three trimesters duration (or the part-time equivalent).
- **MPhil, PhD:** for successful completion of approved programmes of supervised research.
- **DSc, DLitt, DTech:** for original and important contributions to knowledge and/or its applications.
- **Postgraduate Diploma:** awarded for the successful completion of an approved postgraduate course of study of 30 weeks' duration (or the part-time equivalent).
- **Postgraduate Certificate:** awarded for the successful completion of postgraduate/post-experience courses of 15 weeks' duration (or the part-time equivalent).
- **Postgraduate Certificate in Education (PGCE):** awarded on completion of a one-year full-time course; candidates must be British graduates or hold another recognized qualification.
- **Diploma in Professional Studies:** available in the fields of education and nursing, health visiting, midwifery and sports coaching. Students normally hold an initial professional qualification. A minimum of two years' experience is normally expected.

Foundation degrees

Foundation degrees were established to give people the intermediate technical and professional skills that are in demand from employers and to provide more flexible and accessible ways of studying. Increasing opportunities for employment and career advancement are priorities; Foundation degree content and assessment are therefore designed in consultation with employers. Additional progression routes include links with associated professional qualifications and/or direct entry to the final year of a relevant Honours-level degree. Provision is available across a range of FE colleges and a number of HEIs.

Diplomas and certificates of higher education

Courses for first diplomas and certificates are relatively simple in structure; they usually reach a level lower than that required for the award of a degree. There is usually a carefully defined course in a specialized or vocational subject, lasting one or two years, followed by all candidates. Most courses are full-time.

Postgraduate diplomas and certificates

Diplomas (e.g. in public health, social administration, medicine and technology) are awarded either on a full-time or, less often, part-time basis according to the subject and the university. Candidates must usually be graduates or hold equivalent qualifications. Diplomas are awarded after formal courses of instruction and success in written examinations. A Certificate or Diploma in Education is awarded to graduates training to become teachers after one year's full-time study and teaching practice.

Postgraduate courses

A number of courses for graduates or people with equivalent qualifications are offered in FE establishments. They include short specialist courses in management and business studies and secretarial courses for graduates.

Business schools

A Master of Business Administration (MBA) is an internationally recognized postgraduate qualification intended to prepare individuals for middle to senior general managerial positions. Most programmes contain as their core a number of subjects considered essential for understanding the operations of any enterprise. These are: accounting and finance, operations management, business policy, economics, human resource management, marketing, information systems and strategic planning.

Unlike any other Master's programme, the MBA is not only postgraduate, it is also strongly postexperience. A minimum of three years' (often more) work experience at an appropriate level of responsibility is generally expected of applicants. The requirement for a first degree (or equivalent) is sometimes waived for those holding an impressive track record of over five years at managerial level. Approximately one-third of MBA students have an engineering or information technology background. Many undertake the qualification to facilitate change from technical or specialist positions to more general ones.

The MBA was conceived originally in the United States at the beginning of the twentieth century.

Introduced in the United Kingdom in the late 1960s, it did not grow in popularity until the late 1980s. The popularity of this degree in the United Kingdom can be seen in the rapid expansion in the number of providers.

The Association of MBAs (AMBA) operates a system of accreditation. The accreditation process, which is internationally recognized for all MBA, DBA and Master's in Business and Management (MBM) programmes, measures individual MBA programmes against specific accreditation criteria.

Further information, including a list of accredited MBA programmes, can be obtained from the Association of MBAs, 25 Hosier Lane, London EC1A 9LQ; Tel: 020 7246 2686; e-mail: info@mbaworld.com; website: www.mbaworld.com.

The Chartered Association of Business Schools (CABS)

3rd Floor, 40 Queen Street, London EC4R 1DD; Tel: 020 7236 7678; website: www.associationofbusinessschools.org.

The CABS is the representative body for management and business education and all the United Kingdom's leading business schools and acts as a hub for sharing new ideas and developing best practice.

The CABS works broadly in three main areas: policy development, promotion and representation, and training and development. The CABS is able to provide general information about the wide range of courses and programmes provided by the United Kingdom's business schools.

UNIVERSITY OF ABERDEEN
www.abdn.ac.uk

Aberdeen Business School; www.abdn.ac.uk/business

MA Accountancy, MA Accountancy and Finance, MA Business Management, MA Economics, MA Finance, MA Financial Economics, MA/MBus International Business, MA Real Estate; MBA (Aberdeen), MBA (Global), MBA Energy Management, Executive MBA (London, Shanghai), MBA Finance; MSc Accounting and Finance, MSc Digital Marketing Leadership, MSc Finance and Investment Management, MSc Finance and Real Estate, MSc International Business and Finance, MSc International Business Management, MSc International Finance, MSc International Human Resource Management, MSc Law and Economics of Oil and Gas, MSc Marketing Management, MSc Petroleum, Energy Economics and Finance, MSc Real Estate (Commercial/International options); MRes Business Research;

PhDs in the areas of Accountancy and Finance, Business and Management, Real Estate and Economics

Arts and Social Sciences

School of Divinity, History & Philosophy; www.abdn.ac.uk/sdhp

BA Divinity, BA Theology; Certificate in Christian Studies; Diploma in Christian Studies; MA History, MA History of Art, MA Philosophy, MA Philosophy, Politics and Economics, MA Theology and Religious Studies; MLitt Art and Business, MLitt in Medieval and Early Modern Studies, MLitt Philosophy by Research, MLitt Modern History, MLitt Scandinavian Studies, MLitt Scottish Heritage (distance learning); MTh Biblical Studies, MTh Church History, MTh Ministry Studies, MTh Systematic Theology, MTh Theological Ethics; PhDs in the areas of divinity, history, history of art, philosophy, religious studies and Scandinavian studies.

School of Education; www.abdn.ac.uk/ education

BA in Childhood Practice, BA Professional Development; MA Education; MEd Autism and Learning, MEd Community Learning and Development, MEd Early Years, MEd Inclusive Practice, MEd Pastoral Care, Guidance and Pupil Support; MSc Leadership in Professional Contexts, MSc Person Centred Counselling; Professional Graduate Diploma in Education(PGDE); PGCert Gaelic Medium Education.

School of Language, Literature, Music and Visual Culture; www.abdn.ac.uk/sll

BMus Music, BMus Community Music, BMus Music Education; MA Celtic & Anglo-Saxon Studies, MA English, MA Film & Visual Culture, MA French Studies, MA French Studies (5 years), MA Gaelic Studies, MA German Studies (5 years), MA Language & Linguistics, MA Spanish & Latin American Studies (5 years); MLitt in Creative Writing, MLitt in Cultural and Creative Communication, MLitt in English Literary Studies, MLitt in Ethnology and Folklore, MLitt in Film and Visual Culture; MMus in Music, MMus in Sonic Arts, MMus in Vocal Arts; MSc Professional Communication, MSc TESOL (Teaching English as a Second or Other Language), MSc Translation Studies; PhDs, MPhils and Masters in all of the school€™s subject areas.

School of Law; www.abdn.ac.uk/law

LLB, LLB with Honours, Law with English Law, with options in French, German and Spanish languages, options in accountancy, economics, management studies and music, and options in Belgian law, French law, German law and Spanish law; online programmes in LL.M. Dispute Resolution, LL.M. International Trade Law, LL.M. International Trade Law and Treaty Negotiation with Professional Skills (Online and Summer School), LL.M. Oil and Gas Law with Dissertation, LL.M. Oil and Gas Law with Professional Skills (Online and Summer School); LL.M. Criminal Justice, LL.M. Human Rights, LL.M. Criminal Justice & Human Rights, LL.M. Human Rights & Criminal Justice, LL.M. International Law, LL.M. Public International Law, LL.M. Private International Law, LL.M. International Law and International Relations, LL.M. International Law and Strategic Studies, LL.M. International Commercial Law with Dissertation, LL.M. International Commercial Law with Professional Skills, LL.M International

Trade Law, LL.M. International Trade Law & Treaty Negotiation with Professional Skills, LL.M. Energy Law with Dissertation, LL.M. Energy Law with Professional Skills, LL.M. Oil & Gas Law with Dissertation, LL.M. Oil & Gas Law with Professional Skills, LL.M. Energy and Environmental Law with Dissertation, LL.M. Energy and Environmental Law with Professional Skills, LL.M Intellectual Property Law with Professional Skills, LL.M Intellectual property Law with Dissertation, LLM by research and PhDs

School of Social Science; www.abdn.ac.uk/ socsci/

MA Anthropology, MA Anthropology and Archaeology, MA Anthropology and English, MA Anthropology and Film and Visual Culture, MA Anthropology and French, MA Anthropology and French (5years), MA Anthropology and Gaelic Studies, MA Anthropology and Geography, MA Anthropology and German, MA Anthropology and German (5years), MA Anthropology and History, MA Anthropology and International Relations, MA Anthropology and Philosophy, MA Anthropology and Politics, MA Anthropology and Psychology, MA Anthropology and Sociology, MA Anthropology and Spanish & Latin American Studies (5 years), MA Anthropology and Theology and Religion, MA Politics and International relations, MA Philosophy, Politics and Economics, MA International Relations and Language & Linguistics, MA International Relations and Legal Studies, MA International Relations and Sociology, MA International Relations and Theology & Religion, MA Politics and Sociology, MA Politics and Theology & Religion, MA Sociology; Postgraduate courses in MLitt Museum Studies (Anthropology); MSc in People and Environment (Anthropology), MSc International Political Economy, MSc Energy Politics & Law, MSc in International Relations, MSc in International Relations & International Law, MSC in International Security, MSc Strategic Studies, MSc Strategic Studies and International Law, MSc in Strategic Studies & Management, MSc in Strategic Studies and Energy Security, MSc in Comparative European Society, MSc in Global Conflict & Peace Processes, MSc in Globalization, MSc in Policy Evaluation, MSc in Post-Conflict Justice & Peacebuilding, MSc in Religion & Society, MSc in Sex, Gender Violence, MSc in Sociology; MRes in Anthropology, MRes in Social Science

Life Sciences and Medicine

The School of Biological Science; www.abdn.ac.uk/biologicalsci

BSc Animal Behaviour, BSc Behavioural Biology, BSc Biological Sciences, BSc Biology, BSc Conservation Biology, BSc Ecology, BSc Environmental Science, BSc Marine Biology, BSc Plant and Soil Science, BSc Zoology; MSci Biological Sciences; Postgraduate courses in MSc Applied Marine and Fisheries Ecology, MSc Ecology and Conservation, MSc Environmental and Forest Management, MSc Environmental and Ecological Sciences, MSc Environmental Management, MSc Environmental Pollution and Remediation, MSc Environmental Science, MSc Marine Conservation, MSc Soil Science

The School of Medicine, Medical Sciences and Nutrition; www.abdn.ac.uk/smmsn/

Medicine (MBChB), BSc/MSci Medical Science, Dentistry(BDS); Postgraduate courses in MSc Biotechnology, Bioinformatics and Bio-business, MSc Cardiovascular Science and Diabetes, MSc Genetics, MSc Immunology and Immunotherapy, MSc Industrial Biotechnology, MSc Microbiology, MSc Molecular Medicine, MSc Reproductive and Developmental Biology, MSc Medical Sciences, MSc Clinical Pharmacology, MSc Drug Discovery and Development, MSc Stratified Medicine and Pharmacological Innovation, MRes Drug Discovery, Master of Public Health (MPH/Online), MSc Clinical Nutrition (Online), MSc Global Health and Management, MSc Health Psychology, MSc Human Nutrition, MSc Health Economics for Health Professionals (Online), MSc Clinical Education, MSc Physician Associate Studies, MSc Medical Imaging, MSc Medical Physics; PgCert Medical Research Skills, PgCert Research Methods for Health; PhD, MRes, MPhil, MD, ChM

The School of Psychology; www.abdn.ac.uk/psychology/

BSc Psychology, MA Psychology, MA Psychology with Counselling Skills, MA Psychology and Sociology, BSc/MA Psychology with French, MA Psychology with Gaelic, MA Psychology with German; Postgraduate degrees in MSc Foundations of Clinical Psychology, MSc Psychological Studies, PhD and MRes study

Physical Sciences

School of Engineering; www.abdn.ac.uk/engineering/

MEng Chemical Engineering, MEng Civil (and Structural) Engineering, MEng Electrical and Electronic Engineering, MEng Mechanical Engineering, MEng Petroleum Engineering; Postgraduate courses in MSc Advanced Chemical Engineering; MSc Advanced Mechanical Engineering, MSc Advanced Structural Engineering, MSc Decommissioning, MSc Offshore Structural Engineering, MSc Offshore Engineering, MSc Oil & Gas Engineering, MSc Oil & Gas Structural Engineering, MSc Petroleum Engineering, MSc Process Safety, MSc Project Management, MSc Renewable Energy Engineering, MSc Reservoir Engineering, MSc Safety and Reliability Engineering, MSc Safety and Reliability Engineering for Oil & Gas, MSc Subsea Engineering, MSc Global Subsea Engineering; PhD and MRes study

School of Geosciences; www.abdn.ac.uk/geosciences/

Archaeology

BSc/MA Archaeology, Postgraduate courses in MSc Archaeology, MSc Archaeology of the North, MSc Osteoarchaeology, PhD study

Geography and the Environment

BSc/MA Geography, Postgraduate courses in MSc Environmental Partnership Management, MSc Geographical Information Systems, MSc Land Economy (Rural Surveying), PhD and MRes study

Geology and Petroleum

BSc Geology and Petroleum, BSc Geology and Physics; MGeol Geology, MSc Geophysics, MSc Integrated Petroleum Geoscience, MSc Oil & Gas Enterprise Management, MSc Petroleum Data Management, MSc Reservoir Engineering, PhD and research study

The School of Natural and Computing Sciences; www.abdn.ac.uk/ncs

Chemistry

BSc Chemistry, BSc Environmental Chemistry, BSc Oil and Gas Chemistry, MChem Chemistry, MChem Environmental Chemistry, MChem Oil and Gas Chemistry; Postgraduate courses in MSc Environmental Analytical Chemistry, MSc Oil and Gas Chemistry, PhD study

Computing Science

BSc Computing Science, BSc Computing Science and Mathematics, BSc Computing Science and Physics, BSc Business Management and Information Systems;

MSci Computing Science with Industrial Placement; MEng Computing Science; MA Computing, MA Computing with Industrial Placement, MA Computing and Music, MA Business Management and Information Systems; LLB Law with Computing Science; Postgraduate courses in MSc Artificial Intelligence, MSc Information Technology, PhD study

Mathematical Sciences

BSc Computing Science, BSc Computing Science and Mathematics, BSc Computing Science and Physics, BSc Business Management and Information Systems; MSci Computing Science with Industrial Placement; MEng Computing Science; MA Computing, MA Computing with Industrial Placement, MA Computing and Music, MA Business Management and Information Systems; LLB Law with Computing Science; Postgraduate courses in MSc Artificial Intelligence, MSc Information Technology, PhD study

Mathematical Sciences

BSc Mathematics, BSc Applied Mathematics, BSc Mathematics and Physics, BSc Mathematics with French, BSc Mathematics with Gaelic, BSc Mathematics with German, BSc Mathematics with Spanish; MA Mathematics, MA Applied Mathematics, MA Mathematics and Philosophy, MA Business Management and Mathematics, MA French and Mathematics, MA German and Mathematics, MA Mathematics and Spanish and Latin American Studies, MA Economics with Mathematics, MA Mathematics with Gaelic. Postgraduate courses in MSc Financial Mathematics, MSc Mathematics of Computing, PhD study

Physics

BSc Physics, BSc Physical Sciences, BSc Geology and Physics, BSc Computing Science and Physics, BSc Mathematics and Physics, BSc Physics with Geology, BSc Physics with Philosophy; MA Philosophy and Physics, MA Natural Philosophy Postgraduate research PhDs

UNIVERSITY OF ABERTAY, DUNDEE
www.abertay.ac.uk

School of Design and Informatics; www.abertay.ac.uk/schools/school-ofdesign-and-informatics

BSc(Hons) Computer Games Technology, BA(Hons) Computer Arts, BSc(Hons) Computer Games Applications Development, BSc(Hons) Ethical Hacking, MSc Ethical Hacking and Cyber Security, BSc(Hons) Computing, Postgraduate courses, MSc Computer Games Technology, MProf Games Development.

School of Science, Engineering & Technology; www.abertay.ac.uk/studying/schools/set

BSc(Hons) Forensic Sciences, BSc(Hons) Biomedical Science, BSc(Hons) Fitness, Nutrition and Health, BSc(Hons) Food and Consumer Sciences, BSc(Hons) Food, Nutrition and Health.

Dundee Business School; www.abertay.ac.uk/studying/schools/dbs

BA(Hons) Business Management, BA(Hons) Marketing and Business, BA(Hons) Business and Human Resource Management, MSc/PGDip International Human Resource Management.

The School of Social & Health Sciences; www.abertay.ac.uk/studying/schools/shs

BA Accounting and Finance, BEng/MEng Civil and Environmental Engineering, BA(Hons) Criminology, BA(Hons) Games Design and Production, LLB(Hons) Law, BSc(Hons) Nursing (Mental Health Nursing), BSc(Hons) Physical Activity and Health, BSc(Hons) Psychology, BSc(Hons) Psychology and Counselling, BA(Hons) Social Science, BA(Hons) Sociology, BSc(Hons) Sport and Exercise, BSc(Hons) Sport and Exercise Science, BA(Hons) Sport and Management, BSc(Hons) Sports Development and Coaching, BSc(Hons) Strength and Conditioning; Postgraduate Taught Courses, MSc Counselling, MSc/MPhil/PhD Mental Health Counselling, MSc/MPhil/PhD Mental Health Nursing, Research Masters Degrees (MPhil or MbR) and Doctorates (PhD or DBA) in a range of subjects.

ABERYSTWYTH UNIVERSITY
www.aber.ac.uk

School of Art; www.aber.ac.uk/en/art

Art History (BA, 3 year), Creative Arts (BA, 3 year), Fine Art (BA, 3 year), Creative Writing and Fine Art (BA, 3 year), Education / Fine Art (BA, 3 year), Film and Television Studies / Fine Art (BA, 3 year), Fine Art / Art History (BA, 3 year), Fine Art / English Literature (BA, 3 year); Art History (MA, 1 year), Art and Art History (MA, 1 year), Fine Art (MA, 1 year); Art (PhD, 3 year).

Institute of Biological, Environmental & Rural Sciences; www.aber.ac.uk/en/ibers

Agriculture (BSc, 4 year), Agriculture (BSc, 3 year), Agriculture with Animal Science (BSc, 3 year), Agriculture with Animal Science (BSc, 4 year), Agriculture with Business Management (BSc, 3 year), Agriculture with Business Management (BSc, 4 year), Life Sciences (BSc, 4 year); Animal Science (MSc, 1 year), Biotechnology (MSc, 1 year), Environmental Management (MSc, 1 year), Equine Science (MSc, 1 year), Livestock Science (MSc, 1 year), Statistics for Computational Biology (MSc, 1 year), Biological Sciences (PhD, 3 year), Sport and Exercise Science (PhD, 3 year).

Dept of Computer Science; www.aber.ac.uk/en/cs

Artificial Intelligence and Robotics (BSc, 3 year), Artificial Intelligence and Robotics (BSc, 4 year), Business Information Technology (BSc, 3 year), Business Information Technology (includes foundation year) (BSc, 4 year), Computer Graphics, Vision and Games (BSc, 3 year), Computer Graphics, Vision and Games (BSc, 4 year), Computer Science (BSc, 3 year), Computer Science (BSc, 4 year), Computer Science and Artificial Intelligence (BSc, 3 year), Computer Science and Artificial Intelligence (BSc, 4 year), Data Science (BSc, 3 year), Data Science (BSc, 4 year), Robotics and Embedded Systems Engineering (BEng, 3 year), Robotics and Embedded Systems Engineering (BEng, 4 year), Software Engineering (BEng, 4 year), Space Science and Robotics (BSc, 3 year), Web Development (BSc, 3 year), Web Development (BSc, 4 year); Computer Science / Mathematics (BSc, 3 year), Computer Science / Physical Geography (BSc, 3 year), Computer Science / Physics (BSc, 3 year), Computer Science and Welsh (BSc, 4 year); Advanced Computer Science (MSc, 1 year), Advanced Computer Science (MSc, 2 year), Data Science (MSc, 1 year), Statistics for Computational Biology (MSc, 1 year), Computer Science (PhD, 3 year).

School of Education; www.aber.ac.uk/en/education

Childhood Studies (BA, 3 year), Education (BA, 3 year), Education / Drama and theatre Studies (BA, 3 year), Education / Fine Art (BA, 3 year), Education / History (BA, 3 year), English Literature / Education (BA, 3 year), Irish language and literature / Education (BA, 4 year), Mathematics / Education (BSc, 3 year), Media and Education (BA, 3 year), Psychology and Education (BSc, 3 year), Welsh / Education (BA, 3 year); Education (PhD, 3 year); Biology with Balanced Science (PGCE, 1 year), Chemistry with Balanced Science (PGCE, 1 year), Drama (PGCE, 1 year), English (PGCE, 1 year), French (PGCE, 1 year), Geography (PGCE, 1 year), German (PGCE, 1 year), History (PGCE, 1 year), Physics with Balanced Science (PGCE, 1 year), Primary (3-11) (PGCE, 1 year) Spanish (PGCE, 1 year).

Dept of English & Creative Writing; www.aber.ac.uk/en/english

Creative Writing (BA, 3 year), English Literature (BA, 3 year), English Literature and Creative Writing (BA, 3 year), Creative Writing and Drama and Theatre Studies (BA, 3 year), Creative Writing and Film and television Studies (BA, 3 year), Creative Writing and Fine Art (BA, 3 year), Creative Writing and French (BA, 4 year), Creative Writing and Scenography and Theatre Design (BA, 3 year), Creative Writing and Spanish (BA, 4 year), English Literature / Drama and theatre Studies (BA, 3 year), English Literature / Education (BA, 3 year), Film and television Studies / English Literature (BA, 3 year), Fine Art / English Literature (BA, 3 year), French / English Literature (BA, 4 year), History / English Literature (BA, 3 year), Human Geography / English Literature (BA, 3 year), Media and Creative Writing (BA, 3 year), Media and English Literature (BA, 3 year), Spanish / English Literature (BA, 3 year), Creative Writing (MA, 1 year), Literary Studies (MA, 1 year), Creative Writing (PhD, 3 year), English (PhD, 3 year).

Dept of Modern Languages; www.aber.ac.uk/en/modernlangs

French (BA, 4 year), Liberal Arts (BA, 3 year), Modern Languages (BA, 4 year), Spanish and Latin American Studies (BA, 4 year); Applied Translation (MA, 1 year), European Languages (PhD, 3 year).

Department of Geography & Earth Sciences; www.aber.ac.uk/en/dges/

Environmental Earth Science (BSc, 3 year), Environmental Science (BSc, 3 year), Geography (BSc, 3 year), Geography (with integrated year in industry) (BSc, 4 year), Geography (with integrated year studying abroad) (BSc, 4 year), Human Geography (BA, 3 year), Human Geography (with integrated year in industry) (BA, 4 year), Human Geography (with integrated year studying abroad) (BA, 4 year), Physical Geography (BSc, 3 year), Physical Geography (with integrated year in industry) (BSc, 4 year), Physical Geography (with integrated year studying abroad) (BSc, 4 year), Computer Science / Physical Geography (BSc, 3 year), Human Geography / English Literature (BA, 3 year), Physical Geography / Mathematics (BSc, 3 year); Practicing Human Geography (MA, 1 year), Environmental Change, Impact and Adaptation (MSc, 1 year), Remote Sensing and GIS (MSc, 1 year), Geography and Earth Sciences (Science) (PhD, 3 year).

Dept of History & Welsh History; www.aber.ac.uk/en/history

History (BA, 3 year), History (with integrated year studying abroad) (BA, 4 year), History and Welsh History (BA, 3 year), Liberal Arts (BA, 3 year), Medieval and Early Modern History (BA, 3 year), Modern and Contemporary History (BA, 3 year), Politics and Modern History (BA, 3 year); History and Heritage (MA, 1 year), History of Wales (MA, 1 year), Medieval Britain & Europe (MA, 1 year), Modern History (MA, 1 year), History (PhD, 3 year).

Information Management, Libraries and Archives; www.aber.ac.uk/en/imla

Information and Library Studies Single Honours (BSc); Archive Administration (MA), Digital Curation (MSc), Information and Library Studies (MA), Librarianship (PhD, 3 year).

Dept of International Politics; www.aber.ac.uk/en/interpol

International Politics (BA, 3 year), International Politics and Global Development (BA, 3 year), International Politics and Intelligence Studies (BA, 3 year), International Politics and Military History (BA, 3 year), International Politics and Strategic Studies (BA, 3 year), Politics (BA, 3 year), Politics and Modern History (BA, 3 year), Strategy, Intelligence and Security (BA, 3 year); International Politics (MA), International Politics MPhil; International Politics (PhD).

Dept of Law and Criminology; www.aber.ac.uk/en/lac

Business Law (LLB, 3 year), Criminal Law (LLB, 3 year), European Law (LLB, 3 year), Human Rights (LLB, 3 year), Law (LLB, 3 year), Law (LLB, 2 year), Law (BA, 3 year); Human Rights and Humanitarian Law (LLM, 1 year), International Commercial Law (LLM, 1 year), Law (LLM, 1 year), Law (MPhil, 1 year), Law (PhD, 3 year).

School of Business; www.aber.ac.uk/en/abs

Adventure Tourism Management (BSc, 3 year), Business Economics (BSc, 3 year), Business Finance (BSc, 3 year), Business and Management (BSc, 3 year), Tourism Management (BSc, 3 year), Business Economics (BSc, 3 year), Economics (BSc, 3 year), Marketing (BSc, 3 year) ; Business Administration (MBA, 1 year); Finance (MSc, 1 year), International Business Management (MSc, 1 year), International Business and Marketing (MSc, 1 year), International Finance (MSc, 1 year), Management and Finance (MSc, 1 year); Accounting (PhD, 3 year), Management and Business (PhD, 3 year).

Dept of Mathematics; www.aber.ac.uk/en/maths

Applied Mathematics / Pure Mathematics (BSc, 3 year), Applied Mathematics / Statistics (BSc, 3 year), Data Science (BSc, 3 year), Data Science (inc integrated year in industry) (BSc, 4 year), Financial Mathematics (BSc, 3 year), Mathematical and Theoretical Physics (BSc, 3 year), Mathematics (BSc, 3 year), Mathematics (includes foundation year) (BSc, 4 year), Pure Mathematics / Statistics (BSc, 3 year); Data Science (MSc, 1 year), Statistics for Computational Biology (MSc, 1 year), Mathematics (PhD, 3 year).

Dept of Physics; www.aber.ac.uk/en/phys

Astrophysics (BSc, 3 year), Astrophysics (BSc, 4 year), Engineering Physics (BEng, 3 year), Engineering Physics (with integrated year in industry) (BEng, 4 year), Mathematical and Theoretical Physics (BSc, 3 year), Physics (BSc, 3 year), Physics (BSc, 4 year), Physics (with integrated year in industry) (BSc, 4 year), Physics with Planetary and Space Physics (BSc, 3 year), Space Science and Robotics (BSc, 3 year); PhD study.

Dept of Psychology; www.aber.ac.uk/en/psychology

Psychology (BSc, 3 year), Psychology (with integrated year in industry) (BSc, 4 year), Psychology (with integrated year studying abroad) (BSc, 4 year), Psychology with Counselling (BSc, 3 year); Psychology (MPhil, 1 year), Psychology (PhD, 3 year).

Dept of Theatre, Film & Television Studies; www.aber.ac.uk/en/tfts

Drama and Theatre Studies (BA, 3 year), Film and Television Studies (BA, 3 year), Film-making (BA, 3 year), Media and Communication Studies (BA, 3 year), Scenography and Theatre Design (BA, 3 year), Writing for Broadcasting, Media and Performance (BA, 3 year); Theatre, Film and Television Studies (PhD, 3 year).

Dept of Welsh and Celtic Studies; ww.aber.ac.uk/en/cymraeg

Celtic Studies (BA, 4 year), Welsh (for Beginners) (BA, 4 year), Welsh and the Celtic Languages (BA, 3 year); Irish (MA, 1 year), Medieval Welsh Literature (MA, 1 year), Professional Translation Studies (MA, 1 year), Cymraeg (PhD, 3 year).

ANGLIA RUSKIN UNIVERSITY
www.aru.ac.uk

Economics, Finance and Law School; www.aru.ac.uk/business-and-law/economics-finance-and-law

Accounting and Finance – BSc(Hons), Banking and Finance – BSc(Hons), Business Administration (Top-Up) – BSc(Hons), Business Management and Finance – BSc(Hons), Economics – BSc(Hons), International Business Management – BSc(Hons), International Business Management (Accelerated) – BSc(Hons), International Business (Top-Up) – BSc(Hons), Accounting and Finance – MSc, Professional Doctorate in Business and Management – DBA; LLB(Hons) Law; LLM Advanced Legal Practice, LLM Digital Economy, LLM International Law, LLM International Business Law, LLM International Commercial Law, LLM Legal Practice (top-up), LLM Legal Practice PGDip; Research degrees MPhil/PhD Laws.

Faculty of Arts, Humanities and Social Sciences; aru.ac.uk/arts-humanities-and-social-sciences

Cambridge School of Art; aru.ac.uk/arts-humanities-and-social-sciences/cambridge-school-of-art

BA(Hons) Digital Media, BA(Hons) Fashion Design, BA(Hons) Fine Art, BA(Hons) Graphic Design, BA(Hons) Illustration, BA(Hons) Illustration and Animation, BA(Hons) Interior Design, BA(Hons) Photography; MA Children's Book Illustration, MA Graphic Design and Typography, MA Illustration and Book Arts, MA Printmaking; MPhil/PhD Art and Design, MPhil/PhD Children's Book Illustration, MPhil/ PhD Fine Art, MPhil/PhD Graphic Design and Typography.

Cambridge School of Creative Industries; aru.ac.uk/arts-humanities-and-social-sciences/creative-industries

BA(Hons) Computer Games Art, BA(Hons) Drama, BA(Hons) Drama and English Literature, BA(Hons) Drama and Film Studies, BA(Hons) Electronic Music, BA(Hons) Film and Television Production, BA(Hons) Film Studies, BA(Hons) Film Studies and Media Studies, BA(Hons) Journalism, BA(Hons) Media Studies, BA(Hons) Music, BA(Hons) Performing Arts, BA(Hons) Popular Music, BA(Hons) Professional Dance and Musical Theatre, BA(Hons) Writing and English Literature, BA(Hons) Writing and Film Studies; BSc(Hons) Audio and Music Technology, BSc(Hons) Computer Gaming Technology; MA Computer Games Development (Art), MA Creative Writing, MA Creative Writing and Publishing, MA Drama Therapy, MA Film and Television Production, MA Music Therapy, MA Publishing, MSc Computer Games Development (Computing), MSc Electronic and Electrical Engineering; PhD/MPhil Creative Writing, PhD/MPhil Dramatherapy, PhD/MPhil Film and Television Production, PhD/ MPhil Film Studies and Media Studies, PhD/MPhil Music Therapy, PhD/ MPhil Musicology, PhD/MPhil Publishing, PhD/ MPhil Theatre, Drama and Performance.

School of Humanities and Social Sciences; aru.ac.uk/arts-humanities-and-social-sciences/humanities-and-social-sciences

BA(Hons) Criminology, BA(Hons) Criminology and Policing, BA(Hons) Criminology and Sociology,

BA(Hons) English Language, BA(Hons) English Language and Linguistics, BA(Hons) English Literature, BA(Hons) History, BA(Hons) History and English Literature, BA(Hons) Philosophy, BA(Hons) Philosophy and English Literature, BSc(Hons) Policing and Criminal Justice, BA(Hons) Politics, BSc(Hons) Professional Policing, BA Psychosocial Studies, FdA Public Service, BA(Hons) Public Service, BA(Hons) Public Service (Top-up), BA(Hons) Sociology, BA(Hons) TESOL; MA Applied Linguistics and TESOL, MA Children's Literature, MA Contemporary Ethics, MA Contemporary Faith and Belief, MA Contemporary Policing, MA Criminology, MA English Literature, MA History, MA International Relations, MA Pastoral Care and Chaplaincy, MA Science Fiction and Fantasy, MA Sociology, MA Spirituality; MSc International Social Welfare and Social Policy; Postgraduate research in PhD/MPhil Criminology, PhD/MPhil Language and Intercultural Communication, PhD/MPhil English Language and Linguistics, PhD/MPhil English Literature, PhD/MPhil History, PhD/MPhil International Relations, PhD/MPhil Philosophy, PhD/MPhil Sociology, PhD/MPhil Theology, Professional Doctorate in Policing, Professional Doctorate in Practical Theology.

Faculty of Health, Education, Medicine and Social Care; aru.ac.uk/health-education-medicine-and-social-care

School of Allied Health; aru.ac.uk/health-education-medicine-and-social-care/allied-health

Applied Nutritional Science – BSc(Hons), Applied Nutritional Science with Foundation Year – BSc(Hons), Leadership and Management in Health and Social Care – FdSc, Management and Leadership in Health and Social Care (Top up) – BSc(Hons), Medical Science – BSc(Hons), Medical Science with Foundation Year – BSc(Hons), Operating Department Practice – BSc(Hons), Osteopathy – MOst, Osteopathy – BOst, Paramedic Science – BSc(Hons), Pharmaceutical Science – BSc(Hons), Pharmaceutical Science with Foundation Year – BSc(Hons), Public Health – BSc(Hons); Healthcare Management – MBA, Healthcare Management – MSc, Magnetic Resonance Imaging – MSc, Physician Associate – MSc, Public Health – MSc, Surgical Care Practice – MSc, Urology – Master of Surgery (MCh).

School of Education and Social Care; aru.ac.uk/health-education-medicine-and-social-care/education-and-social-care

Counselling and Psychotherapy (Top-Up) – BA(Hons), Counselling (Child and Young Person) – DipHE, Early Childhood Studies – BA(Hons), Early Years and Education – FdA, Education – BA(Hons), Primary Education Studies – BA(Hons), Primary Education Studies Accelerated – BA(Hons), Social Work – BA(Hons); Approved Mental Health Professional – PGCert, Early Childhood Education – MA, Education – MA, Educational Leadership and Management – MBA, Family Therapy and Systemic Practice – PGCert, Global Military Veteran and Family Studies – MSc, Higher Education – MA, Learning and Teaching (Higher Education) – PG Cert, Professional Social Work Practice – Step Up to Social Work – PGDip, Social Work – MA, Special Educational Needs and Disability – MA, Student Affairs in Higher Education – MA.

School of Medicine; aru.ac.uk/health-education-medicine-and-social-care/medicine

Advanced Clinical Practitioner Masters Degree Apprenticeship – MSc, Advanced Midwifery Practice – MSc, Advanced Practice (Clinical) – MSc, Approved Mental Health Professional – PG Cert, Child and Adolescent Mental Wellbeing – MSc – PG Cert – PG Dip, Children and Young People – MSc, Clinical Nursing – MSc, Community Specialist Practitioner (District Nursing) – PG Dip, Critical Care – PG Cert, Early Childhood Education – MA, Education – MA, Educational Leadership and Management – MBA, Emergency Care – PG Cert, Family Therapy and Systemic Practice – PG Cert, Global Military Veteran and Family Studies – MSc, Healthcare Management – MBA, Healthcare Management – MSc, Higher Education – MA, Learning and Teaching (Higher Education) – PG Cert, Magnetic Resonance Imaging – MSc, Medical and Healthcare Education – MSc, Medical and Healthcare Education – PG Cert, Mental Health – MSc, Pharmaceutical Science – MSc, Physician Associate – MSc, Professional Social Work Practice – Step Up to Social Work – PG Dip, Public Health – MSc, Simulation in Medical and Healthcare Education – PG Cert, Social Work – MA, Special Educational Needs and Disability – MA, Specialist Community Public Health Nursing (Health Visiting or School Nursing) – PG Dip, Student Affairs in Higher Education – MA,

Surgical Care Practice – MSc, Urology – Master of Surgery.

School of Nursing and Midwifery; aru.ac.uk/health-education-medicine-and-social-care/nursing-and-midwifery

Acute Care (Top-Up) – BSc(Hons), Assistant Practitioner (Nursing) – FdSc, Assistant Practitioner (Nursing) Higher Apprenticeship – FdSc, Child and Adolescent Mental Wellbeing (Top-up) – BSc(Hons), Children and Young People (Top-Up) – BSc(Hons), Community Specialist Practitioner (District Nursing) – BSc(Hons), International Nursing Studies – BSc(Hons), Mental Health (Top-Up) – BSBSc(Hons), BScHons, Midwifery – BSc(Hons), Nursing – Adult – BSc(Hons), Nursing – Child – BSc(Hons), Nursing – Mental Health – BSc(Hons), Nursing Associate Higher Apprenticeship – DipHE, Nursing Top-Up Degree Apprenticeship – BSc(Hons), Specialist Community Public Health Nursing (Health Visiting or School Nursing) (Top-Up) – BSc(Hons).

Faculty of Medical Science; www.anglia.ac.uk/medical-science

Facuty of Science and Engineering; aru.ac.uk/science-and-engineering

Animal Behaviour – BSc(Hons), Animal Behaviour with Foundation Year – BSc(Hons), Applied Computer Science – BSc(Hons), Architectural Technology – BSc(Hons), Architecture – BA(Hons), Artificial Intelligence – BSc(Hons), Audiology Top-up – BSc(Hons), Biomedical Science – BSc(Hons), Biomedical Science with Foundation Year – BSc(Hons), Bioscience – FdSc, Bioscience – BSc(Hons), Building Surveying – BSc(Hons), Building Surveying Chartered Surveyor Degree Apprenticeship – BSc(Hons), Civil Engineering – BEng(Hons), Civil Engineering – BSc(Hons), Civil Engineering – MEng(Hons), Civil Engineering Degree Apprenticeship – BSc(Hons), Coaching for Development in Football – BSc(Hons), Coaching for Performance in Football – BSc(Hons), Computer Networks – BSc(Hons), Computer Science – FdSc, Computer Science – BEng(Hons), Computing and Information Systems – BSc(Hons), Computing and Information Systems – FdSc, Construction Management – FdSc, Construction Management – BSc(Hons), Crime and Investigative Studies – FdSc, Crime and Investigative Studies – BSc(Hons), Crime and Investigative Studies with Foundation Year – BSc(Hons), Cyber Security – BSc(Hons), Digital and Technology Solutions Degree Apprenticeship –

BSc(Hons), Electronic Engineering – BEng(Hons), Forensic Science – BSc(Hons), Forensic Science with Foundation Year – BSc(Hons), Hearing Aid Audiology – FdSc, Hearing Sciences (Top-Up) – BSc(Hons), Integrated Engineering (Top-Up) – BEng(Hons), Marine Biology with Biodiversity and Conservation – BSc(Hons), Marine Biology with Biodiversity and Conservation – with Foundation Year – BSc(Hons), Mechanical Engineering – BEng(Hons), Mechanical Engineering – MEng(Hons), Medical Engineering – BEng(Hons), Ophthalmic Dispensing – BSc(Hons), Ophthalmic Dispensing Registerable Award – FdSc, Ophthalmic Dispensing with Foundation Year – BSc(Hons), Optometry – BOptom(Hons), Psychology – BSc(Hons), Psychology and Criminology – BSc(Hons), Psychology with Clinical Psychology – BSc(Hons), Quantity Surveying – BSc(Hons), Quantity Surveying Chartered Surveyor Degree Apprenticeship – BSc(Hons), Software Development – BSc(Hons), Sport and Exercise Science – BSc(Hons), Sport and Exercise Science with Foundation Year – BSc(Hons), Sport and Exercise Therapy – BSc(Hons), Sports Coaching and Physical Education – BSc(Hons), Sports Coaching and Physical Education with Foundation Year – BSc(Hons), Strength and Conditioning with Rehabilitation – BSc(Hons), Surveying – FdSc, Veterinary Nursing and Applied Animal Behaviour – BSc(Hons), Veterinary Nursing and Applied Animal Behaviour – FdSc, Zoology – BSc(Hons), Zoology with Foundation Year – BSc(Hons); Additive Manufacturing – MSc, Animal Behaviour Applications for Conservation – MSc, Applied Bioscience – MSc, Applied Positive Psychology – MSc, Applied Wildlife Conservation – MSc, Artificial Intelligence and Big Data – MSc, Artificial Intelligence with Cyber Security – MSc, Biomedical Science – MSc, Civil Engineering – MSc, Clinical Child Psychology – MSc, Cognitive and Clinical Neuroscience – MSc, Computer Science – MSc, Construction Management – MSc, Construction Project Management – MSc, Consumer Psychology – MSc, Cyber Security – MSc, Engineering Management – MSc, Forensic Science – MSc, Foundations in Clinical Psychology – MSc, Information and Communication Technology (Conversion) – MSc, Intelligent Systems and Machine Learning – MSc, Mechanical Engineering – MSc, Project Management – MSc, Psychology – MSc, Research Methods in Psychology – MSc, Sport and Exercise Science – MSc, Sustainability – MSc, Town Planning – MSc; Contact Lens Optician – PGCert; Audiology and Hearing Disability Research – MPhil – PhD, Biology – MPhil – PhD,

Biomedical Science – MPhil – PhD, Computing and Information Science – MPhil – PhD, Electronics – MPhil – PhD, Electronics and the Built Environment – MPhil – PhD, Forensic & Investigative Sciences – MPhil – PhD, Optometry and Vision Sciences – MPhil – PhD, Professional Doctorate in Science and Engineering – DProf, Psychology – MPhil – PhD, Sport and Exercise Sciences – MPhil – PhD, Sustainability – MPhil – PhD.

COLCHESTER INSTITUTE
www.colchester.ac.uk

Art and Design, Business and Management, Computer Games with 3D Modelling and Animation, Construction Management (Quantity Surveying), Construction Management (Site Management), Digital Film Production, Early Years, Education Studies, Engineering, Fashion and Textiles, Film Music and Soundtrack Production, Fine Art, Graphic Design and Digital Communication, Health and Social Care, IT Systems and Applications, Music Education, Musical Theatre, Person-Centred Counselling, Photography, Policing Practice, Popular Music, Sport Management.

ASHRIDGE
www.hult.edu/en/executive-education

Open programs in Coaching for Organization Consultants, HR Strategy and Impact, Advanced Management Program, Advanced Organization Design, Designing Operating Models, Leading Change and Organizational Development, Management Development Program, Senior Executive Program, Strategic Decisions, Team Coaching for Consultants, Translating Strategy into Action: Masters in Executive Coaching, Leadership Programs: Transformational Leader, The Leadership Experience, Leading Through Influence, Thriving in Leadership, Performance Through People, World Class Mentoring Program; Advanced Management Diploma; Strategies for Growth and innovation, Finance for Non Financial Managers, Digital Strategy Diploma; Coaching for Organization Consultants, Postgraduate Diploma in Organizational Supervision.

ASTON UNIVERSITY
www2.aston.ac.uk

Aston Business School;
www2.aston.ac.uk/aston-business-school/
Undergraduate courses in BSc Accounting and Finance, BSc Business Analytics, BSc Business and International Relations, BSc Business & Management, BSc Business & Politics, BSc Business Computing & IT, BSc Business Management & English Language Chartered Manager Degree Apprenticeship, BSc Economics, BSc Economics & Management, BSc Enterprise Development, BSc Finance, BSc Human Resource Management, BSc International Business & Economics, BSc International Business & Management, BSc International Business & Modern Languages (French / German / Spanish / Mandarin-Chinese), LLB Law, LLB Law with Management, BSc Marketing, BSc Mathematics with Economics; Postgraduate courses in Executive MBA/DBA, Executive Apprentice MBA, Management of Manufacturing MBA Degree Apprenticeship, International Pre-Masters, MSc Accounting & Finance, MSc Business Analytics, MSc Business & Management, MSc Business & Management (online), MSc Business Economics & Finance, MSc Business Psychology, MSci Design, Enterprise and Innovation, Doctor of Education Higher Education, MSc Entreprise Development, MSc Entrepreneurship, MSc Finance, MSc Global Operations and Service Management, MSc Human Resource Management, MSc Information Systems & Business Analysis, MSc International Accounting & Finance, MSc International Accounting & Finance (online), MSc International Business, MSc Investment

Analysis, MSc Strategic Marketing Management, MSc Strategy and International Business, MSc Supply Chain Management, MSc Work Psychology & Business, LLM: International Commercial Law; PhD in Management.

Aston Medical School; www2.aston.ac.uk/aston-medical-school/

Undergraduate: MBChB Medicine; Postgraduate: MCh Orthopaedics

School of Engineering & Applied Science; www2.aston.ac.uk/eas/

BSc Applied Chemistry, MEng Chemical Engineering, BEng Chemical Engineering, BSc Chemistry, BEng Civil Engineering, BSc Computer Science, BSc Computer Science with Business, BSc Computer Science and Mathematics, BSc Computer Science with Multimedia, BSc Construction Project Management, BSc Cybersecurity, BEng Design Engineering, Digital and Technology Solutions Degree Apprenticeship, Digital and Technology Solutions Specialist Degree Apprenticeship, MEng Electrical & Electronic Engineering, BEng Electrical & Electronic Engineering, MEng Electronic Engineering & Computer Science, BEng Electronic Engineering & Computer Science, Embedded Electronic Systems Design and Development Degree Apprenticeship, FdEng Engineering, Engineering Leadership and Management Executive Apprenticeship, BSc Industrial Product Design, BSc Business & Supply Chain Management, BSc Logistics and Operations Management, FdSc Logistics, BSc Logistics with Purchasing Management, Foundation Programme in Engineering and Applied Science, International Foundation Programme in Engineering and Applied Science, BSc Mathematics, BSc Mathematics with Computing, BSc Business & Maths (Joint honours), BSc Mathematics with Economics (Joint honours), MEng Mechanical Engineering, BEng Mechanical Engineering, FdEng Power Engineering, BSc Product Design & Management, BSc Quantity Surveying, BSc Transport Management, Transport Planning Degree Apprenticeship, MSc Artificial Intelligence, MSc Communication Systems and Wireless Networking, MSc Computer Science, MSci Design, Enterprise and Innovation, MSc Engineering Leadership & Management (Work-based learning), MSc Engineering Management, MSc Mechanical Engineering, MSc Photonic Integrated Circuits, Sensors and Networks (PIXNET), Postgraduate Engineers Degree Apprenticeship, MSc Product

Design, MSc Professional Engineering (Work-based learning), MSc Smart Telecom and Sensing networks (SMARTNET), MSc Supply Chain Leadership and Management (Work-based learning), MSc Supply Chain Management.

School of Languages and Social Sciences; www2.aston.ac.uk/lss

BSc Business and International Relations, BSc Business and Politics, BSc Business and Sociology, BSc Business Management and English Language, BSc Business, Management and Public Policy, BSc Chinese, BSc English Language, BSc English Language and Literature, BSc English Language and Sociology, BSc English Literature and International Relations, BSc English Literature and Modern Languages, BSc English Literature and Politics, BSc English Literature and Sociology, BSc French, BSc French and German, BSc French and Spanish, BSc German, BSc German and Spanish, BSc History Combinations, BSc Spanish, BSc Translation Studies and Modern Languages, BSc International Business and Modern Languages, BSc International Relations and English Language, BSc International Relations and Modern Languages, BSc International Relations and Social Policy, BSc International Relations and Sociology, BSc English Language and Modern Languages, BSc Politics and Economics, BSc Politics and English Language, BSc Politics and International Relations, BSc Politics and Social Policy, BSc Politics and Sociology, BSc Psychology and Sociology, BSc Sociology and Modern Languages, BSc Sociology and Social Policy, BSc Sociology, BSc TESOL Combinations; MA European Union and International Relations, Double MA in Europe & the World, Double MA in Governance and International Politics, MA in International Relations and Global Governance, Joint MA in Multilevel Governance & International Relations, MA in Forensic Linguistics, MA in Teaching English to Speakers of other Languages (TESOL), MA in TESOL and Translation Studies; Research degrees in the School of Languages and Social Sciences.

School of Life and Health Sciences; www2.aston.ac.uk/lhs

BSc Healthcare Science (Audiology), BSc Biochemistry, BSc Biological Sciences, MBiol Biological Sciences, BSc Biomedical Science, BEng/ MEng Biomedical Engineering, Healthcare Science Practitioner: Audiology Degree Apprenticeship, BSc Medical Bioscience, BSc Neuroscience, BSc Optometry/MOptom, BSc Optometry & Clinical Practice, MPharm Pharmacy,

BSc Psychology, BSc Psychology and Business, BSc Psychology and Marketing, BSc Psychology and Sociology, Advanced Hearing Therapy Practice – MSc, Clinical Science (Neurosensory Sciences) – MSc, Doctor of Hearing Therapy – Professional Doctorate, Regenerative Medicines Manufacturing – MSc, Stem Cells and Regenerative Medicine – MSc, Clinical Neurophysiology Practice – MSc, Neurophysiology – PgCert, Doctor of Optometry / Doctor of Ophthalmic Science – Professional Doctorate, Optometry / Ophthalmic Science – MSc, Overseas Pharmacists course (OSPAP) – Full time PgDip / MSc, Pharmacist Independent Prescribing – PgCert, Pharmacy (includes: MSc Pharmaceutical Sciences, MSc Drug Delivery, and MSc Pharmacokinetics) – MSc, Psychiatric Pharmacy Practice – MSc, Psychiatric Therapeutics by Distance Learning – PgCert, Cognitive Neuroscience – MSc, Health Psychology (online) – MSc, Health Psychology (on campus) – MSc; Doctor of Medicine – PhD.

BANGOR UNIVERSITY
www.bangor.ac.uk

College of Arts, Humanities and Business; www.bangor.ac.uk/arts-humanities-and-business/

Accounting and Banking BSc(Hons) (3 years), Accounting and Economics BSc(Hons) (3 years), Business BA, Business Economics BSc(Hons) (3 years), Business Studies BSc(Hons) (3 years), Financial Economics BSc(Hons) (3 years), Marketing BSc(Hons) (3 years), International Law LLB (3 years), Law (2-Year Degree Scheme) LLB(Hons) (2 years), Law LLB(Hons) (3 years), Business and Law BA(Hons) (3 years), English Law and French Law LLB (4 years), Law with Accounting and Finance LLB(Hons) (3 years), Law with Business Studies LLB(Hons) (3 years), Law with Chinese LLB(Hons) (4 years), Law with Creative Media Writing LLB(Hons) (3 years), Law with Criminology LLB(Hons) (3 years), Law with French (European Experience) LLB(Hons) (4 years), Law with German (European Experience) LLB(Hons) (4 years), Law with History LLB(Hons) (3 years), Law with Italian (European Experience) LLB (4 years), Law with Media Studies LLB(Hons) (3 years), Law with Philosophy and Religion LLB(Hons) (3 years), Law with Social Policy LLB(Hons) (3 years), Law with Spanish (European Experience) LLB(Hons) (4 years), Polisi Cymdeithasol a Chymraeg BA (Cydanrhydedd) (3 years), YGyfraith gydar Gymraeg (Law with Welsh) LLB(Hons) (3 years), Creative and Professional Writing BA(Hons) (3 years), Creative Studies BA(Hons) (3 years), Film Studies BA(Hons) (3 years), Film Studies with Game Design BA(Hons) (3 years), Media Studies BA(Hons) (3 years), Media Studies with Games Design BA(Hons) (3 years), Professional Writing with Game Design BA(Hons) (3 years), Cymraeg a Llenyddiaeth Saesneg BA (Cydanrhydedd) (3 years), English Language and English Literature BA (Joint Hons) (3 years), English Language with Creative Writing BA(Hons) (3 years), English Language with English Literature BA(Hons) (3 years), English Literature BA(Hons) (3 years), English Literature and Chinese BA (Joint Hons) (4 years), English Literature and Creative Writing BA(Hons) (3 years), English Literature and Criminology and Criminal Justice BA (Joint Hons) (3 years), English Literature and Film Studies BA (Joint Hons) (3 years), English Literature and Italian BA(Hons) (4 years), English Literature and Linguistics BA(Hons) (3 years), English Literature and Music BA (Joint Hons) (3 years), English Literature and Spanish BA (Joint Hons) (4 years), English Literature with CreativeWriting BA(Hons) (3 years), English Literature with English Language BA(Hons) (3 years), English Literature with Journalism BA(Hons) (3 years), English Literature with Theatre and Performance BA(Hons) (3 years), French and English Literature BA (Joint Hons) (4 years), French with Creative Writing BA(Hons) (4 years), German and English Literature BA (Joint Hons) (4 years), German with Creative Writing BA(Hons) (4 years), History and English Literature BA (Joint Hons) (3 years), Linguistics with English Literature BA(Hons) (3 years), Media Studies and English Literature BA(Hons) (3 years), Philosophy & Religion and English Literature BA (Joint Hons) (3 years), Sociology and English Literature BA (Joint Hons) (3 years), Spanish with Creative Writing BA(Hons) (4 years), Cymdeithaseg a Hanes BA (Cydanrhydedd) (3 years), Cymdeithaseg a Hanes Cymru BA (Cydanrhydedd) (3 years), Cymraeg a Hanes BA (Cydanrhydedd) (3 years), Film Studies and History BA (Joint Hons) (3 years), Hanes Cymru a Chymraeg BA (Cydanrhydedd) (3 years), Hanes gyda

Newyddiaduraeth BA(Hons) (3 years), Heritage, Archaeology and History BA(Hons) (3 years), History BA(Hons) (3 years), History MArts (4 years), History and Archaeology BA(Hons) (3 years), History and Criminology and Criminal Justice BA (Joint Hons) (3 years), History and Economics BA(Hons) (3 years), History and English Literature BA (Joint Hons) (3 years), History and French BA (Joint Hons) (4 years), History and German BA (Joint Hons) (4 years), History and Italian BA(Hons) (4 years), History and Music BA (Joint Hons) (3 years), History and Spanish BA (Joint Hons) (4 years), History with Archaeology BA(Hons) (3 years), History with Film Studies BA(Hons) (3 years), History with Journalism BA(Hons) (3 years), Medieval and Early Modern History BA(Hons) (3 years), Modern and Contemporary History BA(Hons) (3 years), Music and History and Welsh History BA (Joint Hons) (3 years), Philosophy & Religion and History BA (Joint Hons) (3 years), Philosophy & Religion and Welsh History BA (Joint Hons) (3 years), Polisi Cymdeithasol a Hanes BA (Cydanrhydedd) (3 years), Polisi Cymdeithasol a Hanes Cymru BA (Cydanrhydedd) (3 years), Social Policy and History BA(Hons) (3 years), Sociology and History BA (Joint Hons) (3 years), Welsh History and Archaeology BA (Joint Hons) (3 years), Welsh History and Film Studies BA (Joint Hons) (3 years), Welsh History and History BA (Joint Hons) (3 years), Welsh History and Music BA (Joint Hons) (3 years), Welsh History and Sociology BA (Joint Hons) (3 years), Welsh History with Archaeology BA (3 years), Welsh History with Film Studies (Joint Hons) (3 years), Bilingualism MArts (4 years), English Language BA(Hons) (3 years), English Language for TEFL BA(Hons) (3 years), English Language for TEFL MArts (4 years), International English Language for TEFL BA(Hons) (3 years), Linguistics BA(Hons) (3 years), Linguistics MArts (4 years), French BA(Hons) (4 years), German BA(Hons) (4 years), Spanish BA(Hons) (4 years), Creative Studies and Music BA (Joint Hons) (3 years), Cymraeg a Cherddoriaeth BA (Cydanrhydedd) (3 years), Electronic Engineering and Music BSc (Joint Hons) (3 years), English Literature and Music BA (Joint Hons) (3 years), History and Music BA (Joint Hons) (3 years), Media Studies and Music BA (Joint Hons) (3 years), Music BA(Hons) (3 years), Music BMus(Hons) (3 years), Music and Electronic Engineering BA (Joint Hons) (3 years), Music and French BA (Joint Hons) (4 years), Music and German BA (Joint Hons) (4 years), Music and History and Welsh History BA (Joint Hons) (3 years), Music and Italian BA(Hons) (4 years), Music and Spanish BA (Joint Hons) (4 years), Philosophy & Religion and Music BA (Joint Hons) (3 years), Welsh History and Music BA (Joint Hons) (3 years), Welsh History and Music BA (Joint Hons) (3 years), Philosophy & Religion and English Literature BA (Joint Hons) (3 years), Philosophy & Religion and French BA (Joint Hons) (4 years), Philosophy & Religion and German BA (Joint Hons) (4 years), Philosophy & Religion and History BA (Joint Hons) (3 years), Philosophy & Religion and Italian BA (Joint Hons) (4 years), Philosophy & Religion and Music BA (Joint Hons) (3 years), Philosophy & Religion and Spanish BA (Joint Hons) (4 years), Philosophy & Religion and Welsh BA (Joint Hons) (3 years), Philosophy & Religion and Welsh History BA (Joint Hons) (3 years), Philosophy and Religion BA(Hons) (3 years).

Postgraduate courses: Applied Linguistics for TEFL MA, Archaeology PhD/MPhil, Arthurian Literature MA/PgDip, Bilingualism MA, Bilingualism PhD/MPhil, Celtic Archaeology MA/PgDip, Composition and Sonic Art MMus/ PgDip, Creative and Critical Writing PhD/MPhil, Creative Practice MRes, Creative Writing MA/PgDip, English Literature MA/PgDip, English PhD/MPhil, Film Studies MRes, Filmmaking: Concept to Screen MA, Heritage PhD/, MPhil, History MA/PgDip, History PhD/MPhil, International Media and Management MSc, Language Acquisition and Development MSc, Linguistics MA, Linguistics PhD/MPhil, Literatures of Wales MA/ PgDip, MA European Languages and Cultures, MA in Translation Studies, Media MRes, Medieval Studies MA/PgDip, Medieval Studies MA/ PgDip, Music (MA by Research), Music (MMus by Research), Music (MPhil), Music (PhD), Music MA/ PgDip/ PgCert, Music with Education MA, Performance MMus/PgDip, Philosophy and Religion PhD/ MPhil, Professional Writing MRes, The Celt (MA), The Celts MA/PgDip, Welsh / Celtic Studies (MA/ Diploma), Welsh / Celtic Studies (MPhil/PhD), Welsh History MA/PgDip, Welsh History PhD/MPhil, Y Celtiaid MA/PgDip, Professional Writing, Film, Media, New Media, Journalism, Creative Studies, Drama, Professional Writing PhD/MPhil, Chinese Studies PhD/ MPhil, French and Francophone Studies PhD/MPhil, German Studies PhD/MPhil, Hispanic Studies PhD/ MPhil, Italian Studies PhD/MPhil, Translation Studies PhD/MPhil, Creative and Critical Writing PhD/ MPhil, English PhD/MPhil, Postgraduate Courses; Law and Banking LLM, Accounting and Banking MSc, Accounting and Finance MSc, Accounting MSc,

Banking and Finance (Chartered Banker) MA, Banking and Finance (Chartered Banker) MSc, Banking and Finance MBA, Banking and Finance MSc, Banking and Law MA, Banking and Law MBA, Business and Marketing MA, Business with Consumer Psychology MA, Business with Consumer Psychology MSc, Chartered Banker MBA, Comparative Criminology and Criminal Justice MA/PgDip/PgCert, Criminology and Criminal Justice PhD/MPhil, Criminology and Law MA, Criminology and Law MA, Criminology and Sociology MA/PgDip/PgCert, Criminology, Criminal Justice, Social Policy, Sociology MARes, Environmental Management MBA, Finance MBA, Finance MSc, Information Management MBA, International Business MBA, International Commercial and Business Law LLM, International Criminal Law and International Human Rights Law LLM, International Intellectual Property Law LLM, International Law LLM, International Marketing MBA, International Media and Management MSc, Investment Management MSc, Islamic Banking and Finance MBA, Islamic Banking and Finance MSc, Law and Banking LLM, Law and Criminology LLM, Law and Management MBA, Law LLM, Law LLM Res, Law of the Sea LLM, Law PhD/MPhil, Management and Finance MSc, Management MBA, Maritime Law LLM, Polisi a Chynllunio Ieithyddol MA, Procurement Law, Strategy and Practice by Distance Learning LLM, Public Procurement Law and Strategy LLM, Social Policy MA/PgDip/PgCert, Social Policy, Sociology MA, Sociology PhD/MPhil, Accounting, Banking, Economics, Finance, Management Studies and Marketing PhD/MPhil.

College of Human Sciences; www.bangor.ac.uk/ human-sciences/ index.php.en

Addysg Gynradd BA(Hons) with QTS (3 years), Astudiaethau Plentyndod ac Ieuenctid a Chymdeithaseg BA (Cydanrhydedd) (3 years), Astudiaethau Plentyndod ac Ieuenctid a Chymdeithaseg BA (Cydanrhydedd) (3 years), Astudiaethau Plentyndod ac Ieuenctid BA (Cydanrhydedd) (3 years), Childhood and Youth Studies BA(Hons) (3 years), Childhood and Youth Studies and Psychology BA (Joint Hons) (3 years), Childhood and Youth Studies and Social Policy BA (Joint Hons) (3 years), Childhood and Youth Studies and Sociology BA (Joint Hons) (3 years), Childhood and Youth Studies and Welsh BA(Hons) (3 years), Criminology and Criminal Justice and Psychology BA (Joint Hons) (3 years), English Language and Psychology BA (Joint Hons) (3 years), French with Psychology BA(Hons) (4 years), German with Psychology BA(Hons) (4 years), Linguistics and Psychology BA (Joint Hons) (3 years), Dylunio Cynnyrch BSc (Anrhydedd) (3 years), Health & Social Care and Social Policy BA(Hons) (3 years), Health and Social Care BA(Hons) (3 years), Health and Social Care MSocSci (4 years), Iechyd a Gofal Cymdeithasol BA (Anrhydedd) (3 years), Primary Education (Wales and beyond through the CaBan partnership) BA(Hons) with QTS (3 years), Product Design BSc(Hons) (3 years), Adult Nursing BN(Hons) (3 years), Biomedical Science BSc(Hons) (3 years), Children's Nursing BN(Hons) (3 years), Criminology and Criminal Justice and Psychology BA (Joint Hons) (3 years), Cymdeithaseg a Gofal Iechyd a Chymdeithasol BA (Cydanrhydedd) (3 years), Diagnostic Radiography BSc(Hons) (3 years), Health andWellbeing BSc(Hons) (3 years), Health Studies (International Students), Learning Disability Nursing BN(Hons) (3 years), Medical Biology BSc(Hons) (3 years), Medical Biology MBiol (4 years), Medical Sciences BMedSci(- Hons) (3 years), Mental Health Nursing BN(Hons) (3 years), Midwifery BM(Hons) (3 years), Nursing BN(Hons), Polisi Cymdeithasol a Gofal Iechyd a Chymdeithasol BA (Cydanrhydedd) (3 years), Social Policy and Psychology BA (Joint Hons) (3 years), Sociology and Psychology BA (Joint Hons) (3 years), Neuropsychology degree BSc (Intercalated) (1 years), Psychology degree BSc(Hons) (3 years), Psychology degree MSci (4 years), Psychology with Business degree BSc(Hons) (3 years), Psychology with Clinical and Health Psychology degree BSc(Hons) (3 years), Psychology with Clinical and Health Psychology degree MSci (4 years), Psychology with Forensic Psychology BSc(Hons) (3 years), Psychology with Neuropsychology degree BSc(Hons) (3 years), Adventure Sport Science MSci (4 years), Adventure Sport Science BSc(Hons) (3 years), Clinical Sports Science BSc (Intercalated) (1 years), Exercise, Behaviour Change and Disease Prevention BSc (Intercalated) (1 years), Sport and Exercise Psychology BSc(Hons), Sport Science (Outdoor Activities) BSc(Hons), Sport Science (Outdoor Activities) MSci, Sport Science (Outdoor Recreation) BSc Top-up Degree (1 years), Sport Science BSc(Hons), Sport Science MSci, Sport, Health and Exercise Science BSc(Hons), Sport, Health and Exercise Science MSci, Sport, Health and Physical Education BSc(Hons).

College of Environmental Sciences and Engineering; www.bangor.ac.uk/ environmental-sciences-and-engineering/

Applied Marine Biology BSc(Hons) (4 years), Applied Terrestrial and Marine Ecology (with placement year) BSc(Hons) (4 years), Applied Terrestrial and Marine Ecology BSc(Hons) (3 years), Biology BSc(Hons) (3 years), Biology MBiol (4 years), Biology with Biotechnology BSc(Hons) (3 years), Biology with Biotechnology MBiol (4 years), Conservation with Forestry (with placement year) BSc(Hons) (4 years), Conservation with Forestry BSc(Hons) (3 years), Environmental Conservation (with placement year) BSc(Hons) (4 years), Environmental Conservation BSc(Hons) (3 years), Environmental Science BSc(Hons) (3 years), Environmental Science (with placement year) BSc(Hons) (4 years), Environmental Science MEnvSci (4 years), Forestry (with placement year) BSc(Hons) (4 years), Forestry BSc(Hons) (3 years), Geography BA(Hons) (3 years), Geography (with placement year) BA(Hons) (4 years), Geography BSc(Hons) (3 years), Geography (with placement year) BSc(Hons) (4 years), Geography MGeog (4 years), Geography with Environmental Forestry (with placement year) BSc (4 years), Geography with Environmental Forestry BSc(Hons) (3 years), Geological Oceanography BSc(Hons) (3 years), Geological Oceanography MSci (4 years), Marine Biology and Oceanography BSc(Hons) (3 years), Marine Biology and Oceanography MSci (4 years), Marine Biology and Zoology BSc(Hons) (3 years), Marine Biology and Zoology MSci (4 years), Marine Biology BSc(Hons) (3 years), Marine Biology MSci (4 years), Marine Environmental Studies BSc(Hons) (3 years), Marine Geography BSc(Hons) (3 years), Marine Vertebrate Zoology BSc(Hons) (3 years), Marine Vertebrate Zoology MSci (4 years), Ocean and Geophysics BSc(Hons) (3 years), Ocean Science BSc(Hons) (3 years), Physical Geography and Oceanography BSc(Hons) (3 years), Physical Geography

and Oceanography BSc(Hons) (3 years), Physical Oceanography MSci (4 years), Zoology BSc(Hons) (3 years), Zoology MZool (4 years), Zoology with Animal Behaviour BSc(Hons) (3 years), Zoology with Animal Behaviour MZool (Animal Behaviour) (4 years), Zoology with Conservation BSc(Hons) (3 years), Zoology with Herpetology BSc(Hons) (3 years), Zoology with Herpetology MZool (Herpetology) (4 years), Zoology with Marine Zoology BSc(Hons) (3 years), Zoology with Marine Zoology MZool (Marine Zoology) (4 years), Zoology with Primatology BSc(Hons) (3 years), Zoology with Primatology MZool (Primatology) (4 years).

Postgraduate courses: Agriculture PhD/MPhil, Agriculture and Environment MRes, Agroforestry MSc, Agroforestry PhD/MPhil, Agroforestry and Food Security MSc by Distance Learning, Analytical Chemistry MSc, Applied Marine Geoscience MSc, Biological Sciences MScRes, Biological Sciences PhD/MPhil, Conservation PhD/MPhil, Conservation and Land Management MSc, Doctor of Agriculture and Environment DAgEnv, Environmental and Business Management MSc, Environmental Forestry MSc, Environmental Management MBA, Environmental Mircobiology and Biotechnology MSc by Research, Environmental Sciences MSc by Research, Forestry PhD/MPhil, Forestry MSc by Distance Learning, Tropical Forestry MSc by Distance Learning, Tropical Forestry (International Commonwealth Scholarship) MSc by Distance Learning, Forestry and Environmental Management degrees (TRANSFOR-M) MSc, Geography PhD/MPhil, Marine Biology MSc, Marine Environmental Protection MSc, Marine Renewable Energy MSc, Molecular Biology with Biotechnology MSc, Ocean Sciences MSc by Research, Ocean Sciences PhD/MPhil, Physical Oceanography MSc, Renewable Materials PhD/MPhil, Soil and Environmental Science PhD/MPhil, Sustainable Forest and Nature Management (SUFONAMA) (Erasmus Mundus course) MSc, Sustainable Tropical Forestry (SUTROFOR) (Erasmus Mundus course) MSc.

UNIVERSITY CAMPUS, BARNSLEY
universitycampus.barnsley.ac.uk

Animal Management Foundation Degree (FdSc), Business and Enterprise BA(Hons), Business Foundation Degree FdA, Professional Practice: Education Studies BA(Hons) Top-Up, Professional Practice: Supporting Young People, Children and Families

BA(Hons) Top-Up, Professional Practice : Early Childhood Studies BA(Hons) Top-up, Fine Art Practice BA(Hons), Fine Art Practice BA(Hons) Top-Up, Popular Music BA(Hons) (Performance and production Routes), Sport: Foundation Degree in

Coaching, Physical Education and Sports Development, Sport: Foundation Degree in Physical Activity, Health and Exercise, Sport, Physical Education and

Health BA/BSc(Hons) Top-Up, Games Design (Foundation Degree).

UNIVERSITY OF BATH
www.bath.ac.uk

Faculty of Engineering and Design;
www.bath.ac.uk/faculties/faculty-of-engineering-design/

Dept of Architecture & Civil Engineering; www.bath.ac.uk/departments/department-of-architecture-civil-engineering/

BSc(Hons) Architecture, BEng/MEng(Hons) Civil Engineering, MEng(Hons) Civil and Architectural Engineering
Postgraduate courses: MSc Architectural Engineering: Environmental Design, MSc Conservation of Historic Buildings, MSc in Civil Engineering: Innovative Structural Materials, MSc in Modern Building Design, PG Certificate in Professional Practice – RIBA Part 3.

Dept of Chemical Engineering; www.bath.ac.uk/ departments/department-of-chemical-engineering/

MEng/BEng Chemical Engineering, MEng Chemical Engineering with Environmental Engineering
Postgraduate courses: Environmental Engineering MSc, Sustainable Chemical Engineering MSc, MRes/PhD.

Dept of Electronic & Electrical Engineering; www.bath.ac.uk/departments/department-of-electronic-electrical-engineering/

BEng/MEng Computer Systems Engineering, BEng/MEng Electrical & Electronic Engineering, BEng/MEng Electrical Power Engineering, BEng/MEng Electronic Systems Engineering, MEng Integrated Mechanical and Electrical Engineering, MEng Robotics Engineering, BEng Electronic Engineering with Space Science & Technology
Postgraduate courses: MSc Electrical Power Systems, MSc Electronic Systems Design, MSc Mechatronics, MSc Robotics and Autonomous Systems, MSc Robotics and Autonomous Systems with three-month placement.

Dept of Mechanical Engineering; www.bath.ac.uk/departments/department-of-mechanical-engineering/

Aerospace Engineering MEng(Hons), Integrated Design Engineering MEng(Hons), Mechanical Engineering MEng(Hons), Mechanical Engineering with Manufacturing and Management MEng(Hons), Mechanical with Automotive Engineering MEng(Hons)
Postgraduate courses: MSc Automotive Engineering, MSc Engineering Business Management, MSc Engineering Design, MSc in Innovation and Technology Management.

Faculty of Humanities and Social Science;
www.bath.ac.uk/faculties/faculty-of-humanities-social-sciences/

Dept of Economics; www.bath.ac.uk/departments/department-of-economics/

BSc(Hons) Economics, BSc(Hons) Economics and Politics, BSc(Hons) Economics and Mathematics;
Postgraduate courses: MSc Applied Economics, MSc Applied economics (Banking and Financial Markets), MSc Applied Psychology and Economic Behaviour, MSc Economics, MSc Economics & Finance, MRes Economics, PhD Economics.

Dept of Education; www.bath.ac.uk/departments/department-of-education/

BA(Hons) Education with Psychology
Postgraduate courses: MA Education, MA English as a Medium of Instruction, MA International Education and Globalisation, MA Teaching English to Speakers of Other Languages (TESOL), MRes Education, EdD Doctor of Education, PhD Education.

Dept for Health; www.bath.ac.uk/health

BSc(Hons) Health and Exercise Science, BSc/MSci(Hons), Sport and Exercise Science, Foundation Degree and BSc(Hons) Sport (Sports Performance), Foundation Degree, Sports Management and Coaching BSc(Hons)
Postgraduate courses: MSc Research in Health Practice, PG Dip / MSc Sport and Exercise Medicine,

MSc Sports Physiotherapy, MRes Health and Well-being, MD Doctor of Medicine, PhD Health and Wellbeing, PhD Health, Professional Doctorate in Health.

Dept of Politics, Languages & International Studies; www.bath.ac.uk/departments/department-of-politics-languages-international-studies/

BSc(Hons) International Management and Modern Languages, BA(Hons) Language and Politics, BA(Hons) Modern Languages, BA(Hons) Modern Languages and European Studies, BSc(Hons) Politics with Economics, BSc(Hons) Politics and International Relations

Postgraduate courses: MA Contemporary European Studies ('Euromasters' and 'Euromasters with Trans-Atlantic track'), MA International Relations, MA International Relations and European Politics, MA International Security, MA Interpreting & Translating, MATranslation & Professional Language Skills, MA Translation with Business Interpreting (Chinese), MRes Politics and International Studies, MPhil/PhD.

Dept of Psychology; www.bath.ac.uk/departments/department-of-psychology/

BSc/MSci(Hons) Psychology

Postgraduate courses: MSc Applied Clinical Psychology, MSc Applied Forensic Psychology with Counselling, MSc Applied Psychology and Economic Behaviour, MSc Health Psychology, MRes Sustainable Futures, MRes Psychology, Doctorate in Clinical Psychology, MPhil/PhD Psychology.

Dept of Social & Policy Science; www.bath.ac.uk/departments/department-of-social-policy-sciences/

BSc(Hons) Criminology, BSc(Hons) Sociology, BSc(Hons) Social Policy, BSc(Hons) Social Sciences, BSc(Hons) Sociology and Social Policy, BSc(Hons) Social Work and Applied Social Studies, BSc(Hons) International Development with Economics

Postgraduate courses: MSc International Development, MSc International Development with Conflict and Humanitarian Action, MSc International Development with Economics, MSc International Development, Social Justice and Sustainability, MSc Humanitarianism, Conflict and Development, MSc Public Policy, MRes Advanced Quantitative Methods in Social Sciences, MRes European Social Policy, MRes Global Political Economy, MRes International Development, MRes Security, Conflict and Human Rights, MRes Social Policy, MRes Social Work, MRes Sociology, Social & Policy Sciences MPhil and PhD, Advanced Quantitative Methods in Social Sciences PhD, Global Political Economy PhD, Security, Conflict and Human Rights PhD, DPRP Professional Doctorate in Policy Research and Practice.

Faculty of Science; www.bath.ac.uk/faculties/faculty-of-science/

Dept of Biology & Biochemistry; www.bath.ac.uk/departments/department-of-biology-biochemistry/

Biochemistry BSc/MBiochem(Hons), Biology BSc/MBiol(Hons), Biomedical Sciences BSc/MBiomed(Hons)

Postgraduate courses: Molecular Biosciences (Bioinformatics) MSc, Molecular Biosciences (Biotechnology) MSc, Molecular Biosciences (Medical Biosciences) MSc, Molecular Biosciences (Microbiology) MSc, Biology & Biochemistry PhD.

Dept of Chemistry; www.bath.ac.uk/departments/department-of-chemistry/

Chemistry BSc(Hons), Chemistry for Drug Discovery BSc(Hons), Chemistry for Drug Discovery MChem(Hons), Chemistry MChem(Hons), Chemistry with Management BSc(Hons), Chemistry with Management MSci(Hons)

Postgraduate courses: MSc Drug Discovery, MRes and PhD.

Dept of Computer Science; www.bath.ac.uk/departments/department-of-computer-science/

Computer Science BSc(Hons), Computer Science MComp(Hons), Computer Science and Artificial Intelligence BSc(Hons), Computer Science and Artificial Intelligence MComp(Hons), Computer Science and Mathematics BSc(Hons), Computer Science and Mathematics MComp(Hons)

Postgraduate courses: MSc Computer Science, MSc Data Science, MSc Data Science and Statistics, MSc Human Computer Interaction, MSc Software Systems, MSc Machine Learning and Autonomous Systems, MRes and PhD, Accountable, Responsible and Transparent Artificial Intelligence / Computer Science.

Dept of Mathematical Sciences; www.bath.ac.uk/departments/department-of-mathematical-sciences/

Mathematical Sciences BSc(Hons), Mathematics BSc(Hons), Mathematics and Statistics BSc(Hons), Mathematics MMath(Hons), Statistics BSc(Hons)

Postgraduate courses: MSc Data Science and Statistics, MSc Modern Applications of Mathematics, PhD.

Natural Sciences; www.bath.ac.uk/topics/natural-sciences/

Natural Sciences BSc(Hons), Natural Sciences MSci(Hons).

Dept of Pharmacy & Pharmacology; www.bath.ac.uk/departments/department-of-pharmacy-pharmacology/

Pharmacology BSc(Hons), Pharmacology MPharmacol(Hons), Pharmacy MPharm(Hons), Pharmaceutical Sciences and Drug Development BSc(Hons), Pharmaceutical Sciences and Drug Development MSci(Hons); MSc, PhD study options.

Dept of Physics; www.bath.ac.uk/departments/department-of-physics/

Mathematics and Physics BSc(Hons), Mathematics and Physics MSci(Hons), Physics BSc(Hons), Physics MPhys(Hons), Physics with Astrophysics BSc(Hons), Physics with Astrophysics MPhys(Hons); PhD study.

School of Management ; www.bath.ac.uk/management

Accounting and Finance BSc(Hons), Business Administration BSc(Hons), International Management BSc(Hons), International Management and Modern Languages BSc(Hons), Management BSc(Hons), Management with Marketing BSc(Hons)

Postgraduate courses: MSc in Accounting & Finance, MSc in Business Analytics, MSc in Engineering Business Management, MSc in Entrepreneurship & Management, MSc in Finance, MSc in Finance with Banking, MSc in Finance with Risk Management, MSc in Human Resource Management & Consulting, MSc in Innovation & Technology Management, MSc in International Management, MSc in Management, MSc in Marketing, MSc in Operations, Logistics & Supply Chain Management, MSc in Sustainability & Management, MBA, PhD research.

BATH SPA UNIVERSITY
www.bathspa.ac.uk

Bath School of Art & Design; www.artbathspa.com

BA(Hons) Art & Design, BA(Hons) Ceramics, BA(Hons) Creative Arts, Practice BA(Hons) Digital Animation, BA(Hons) Fashion Design, BA(Hons) Fine Art, BA(Hons) Furniture and Product Design, BA(Hons) Graphic Arts, BA(Hons) Graphic Communication, BA(Hons) Interior Design, BA(Hons) Mised Media Textiles, BA(Hons) Photography, BA(Hons) Textile Design for Fashion and Interiors

Postgraduate courses: MA Art and Design, MA Design(Ceramics), MA Design (Fashion and Textiles), MA Curatorial Practice, MA Fine Art, MA Visual Communication.

Institute of Education; www.bathspa.ac.uk/schools/education

Undergraduate BA(Hons) degrees; Early Years Education, Education (Primary and Early Years), Education (Secondary), Education Studies, Educational Technology and Innovation, International Development and Education; Initial Teacher Training, Early Years Initial Teacher Training, PGCE Primary and Early Years, PGCE Primary and Early Years (part time), PGCE Secondary Art and Design, PGCE Secondary Computing, PGCE Secondary Design and Technology, PGCE Secondary Drama, PGCE Secondary English, PGCE Secondary Geography, PGCE Secondary History, PGCE Secondary Mathematics, PGCE Secondary Modern Languages, PGCE Secondary Music, PGCE Secondary Physical Education, PGCE Secondary Physical Education with EBacc, PGCE Secondary Religious Education, PGCE Secondary Science (Physics, Chemistry or Biology), Education (Early Childhood Studies), Education (Leadership and Management), Inclusive Education, National Award for Educational Needs Coordination (SENCO), Professional Doctorate in Education (EdD), Professional Practice, Professional Practice in Higher Education, TESOL; Postgraduate Masters Degrees; Professional Master's, Learning and Innovation, Education Studies, Education: International Education, PMP: Specific Learning Difficulties /Dyslexia/ PMP: Counselling and Psychotherapy, Professional Practice in HE, Education: Leadership and Management, Education: Early Years, Education: Learning Technology, TESOL, National Award for Special Educational Needs Coordination, Early Years Initial Teacher Training, Subject Knowledge Enhancement Courses Mathematics/Modern Languages/ Physics,

Foundation; Early Years, Education Studies for Teaching Assistants; PGCE (Primary (3-11)/ Middle Years (7-14)/Secondary (11-16); Range of Subjects), TESOL, International Education & Global Citizenship

School of Liberal Arts; www.bathspa.ac.uk/liberal-arts/

Undergraduate BA Degrees; Creative Computing, Creative Computing (Animation/Gaming/Web Technologies), Creative Media, Creative Writing, English Literature, Film and Screen Studies, Film, TV and Digital Production, History (Heritage and Public History), Journalism and Publishing, Media Communications, Philosophy and Ethics, Religion, Philosophy and Ethics, Study of Religions; Postgraduate Masters Degrees; Arts Management, Creative Computing, Creative Writing, Feature Filmmaking, Heritage Management, History, Literature, Scriptwriting, Travel and Nature Writing, Writing for Young People, MPhil/MRes/PhD study.

Bath Business School; www.bathspa.ac.uk/bath-business-school/

BA degrees in Business and Management, Business and Management (Accounting), Business and Management (Entrepreneurship), Business and Management (Fashion), Business and Management (Festivals and Events), Business and Management (Human Resource Management), Business and Management (International Business), Business and Management (Law), Business and Management (Marketing), Business and Management (Tourism Management); Postgraduate Masters degrees in Business and Management, Business and Management (Accounting), Business and Management (Entrepreneurship), Business and Management Extended, Business and Management (International Business), Business and Management (Marketing), Business and Management with Integrated Placement, Leadership (Senior Leader Degree Apprenticeship).

UNIVERSITY OF BEDFORDSHIRE
www.beds.ac.uk

Faculty of Creative Arts, Technologies & Science; www.beds.ac.uk/howtoapply/departments/cats

Art & Design

Advertising and Branding Design – BA(Hons), Animation – BA(Hons), Art and Design – BA(Hons), Contemporary Arts Practice – BA(Hons), Fashion Design – BA(Hons), Graphic Design – BA(Hons), Illustration – BA(Hons), Interior Architecture – BA(Hons), Interior Design – BA(Hons), Photography – BA(Hons), Photography and Video Art – BA(Hons) Postgraduate courses: Art and Design – MA.

Computer Science and Technology

Artificial Intelligence and Robotics – BSc(Hons), Automotive Engineering – BEng(Hons), Building Services and Sustainability – Foundation Degree, Building Technology – Foundation Degree of Science, Building Technology (Top Up) – BSc(Hons), Business Information Systems – BSc(Hons), Computer Animation and Visual Effects – BSc(Hons), Computer Games Development – BSc(Hons), Computer Networking – BSc(Hons), Computer Science – BSc(Hons), Computer Science and Robotics – BSc(Hons), Computer Science and Software Engineering – BSc(Hons), Computer Security and Forensics – BSc(Hons), Computer Systems Engineering – BEng(Hons), Computing and Data Science – BSc(Hons), Computing and Mathematics – BSc(Hons), Construction Management – Foundation Degree of Science, Construction Management (Top Up) – BSc(Hons), Cybersecurity – BSc(Hons), Electronic Engineering – BEng(Hons), Information and Data Systems – BSc(Hons), Information Technology – BSc(Hons), Interactive Digital Technologies – BSc(Hons), Mechanical Engineering – BEng(Hons), Mechanical Engineering (with Foundation year) – BEng(Hons), Network Management – Foundation Degree, Product Design – BSc(Hons), Software Engineering – BSc(Hons), Sustainable Construction – Foundation Degree, Telecommunications and Network Engineering – BEng(Hons).

Postgraduate; Applied Computing and Information Technology – MSc, Applied Computing and Information Technology (15 months) – MSc, Computer Networking – MSc, Computer Networking (15 month) – MSc, Computer Science – MSc, Computer Science (15 months) – MSc, Computer Security and Forensics – MSc, Cyber Security – MSc, Electronic Engineering – MSc, Electronic Engineering (22 months) – MSc, Sensors and Smart Cities – MSc, Software Engineering and Applications – MSc, Telecommunications Management – MSc.

Culture and Communications

BA(Hons) Broadcast Journalism, BA(Hons) Creative Industries and Business Management, BA(Hons) Creative Writing, BA(Hons) Creative Writing & Journalism, BA(Hons) English Literature, BA(Hons) English Language and Literature, BA(Hons) Education Studies and English, BA(Hons) English and Theatre Studies, BA(Hons) Journalism, BA(Hons) Journalism, Marketing and PR, BA(Hons) Media Communications, BA(Hons) Radio and Audio, BA(Hons) Sport Journalism, BA(Hons) Television Production, BA(Hons) Broadcast Television and Radio, BA(Hons) Journalism (with placement) UCMK, BA(Hons) Writing for Media
Postgraduate courses: MA International Journalism, MA Mass communications, MA English Literature, MA Television Production

Life Sciences

Food and Nutrition Science – BSc(Hons), Forensic Science – BSc(Hons), Biological Science – BSc(Hons), Biomedical Science – BSc(Hons), Biochemistry – BSc(Hons), Animal Science (Top Up) – BSc(Hons)
Postgraduate courses: MSc Biomedical Engineering, MSc Biotechnology, MSc Pharmacology, MSc Microbiology in Public Health, MSc Environmental Management.

Media and Performance

Film and Television Production – BA(Hons), Acting – BA(Hons), Dance and Professional Practice – BA(Hons), Film Production – BA(Hons), Media Make Up and Character Design Foundation Degree, Media Performance for Film, TV and Theatre – BA(Hons), Media Production – BA(Hons), Media Production – Foundation Degree, Media Production (Radio) – BA(Hons), Music Technology – BA(Hons), Music Technology – Foundation Degree, Performing Arts – BA(Hons), Theatre and Professional Practice – BA(Hons)
Postgraduate courses: Creative Digital Film Production – MA, Digital Film Technologies and Production – MA, Documentary – MA, Performing Before the Camera – Postgraduate Certificate, Screen Performance and Communications Techniques – MA, Dance Performance and Choreography – MA, Dance Science – MSc.

Psychology

Applied Psychology – BSc(Hons), Health Psychology – BSc(Hons), Psychology – BSc(Hons), Psychology and Crime – Foundation Degree, Psychology and Criminal Behaviour – Foundation Degree, Psychology and Criminal Behaviour – BSc(Hons), Psychology and Criminal Behaviour (Top up) – BA(Hons), Psychology and Criminology – BSc(Hons), Psychology, Counselling and Therapies – BSc(Hons).
Postgraduate courses: Applied Psychology (Conversion) – MSc, Forensic Psychology – MSc, Health Psychology – MSc.

Faculty of Education and Sport ; www.beds.ac.uk/howtoapply/departments/es

Education and English Language

Early Childhood Education – BA(Hons), Education Studies – BA(Hons), Education and TEFL – BA(Hons), Education with Psychology – BA(Hons), English Language Teaching – Certificate in English Language Teaching, English Language and Linguistics – BA(Hons), English Language and Teaching English as a Foreign Language – BA(Hons), English Literature and TEFL – BA(Hons), Special Needs and Inclusive Education – BA(Hons);
Postgraduate courses: Applied Linguistics – MA, Applied Linguistics (TEFL) – MA, Behavioural Issues in Schools – (PgCert), Difficulties in Literacy Development and Dyslexia – (PgCert), Early Years Education – BA(Hons), Education – MA, Education (Early Years) – MA, Education (Leadership) – MA, Education (National Award for Special Educational Needs Co-ordination) – (PgCert), Education (Practice) – MA, Education (Social Justice) – MA, Education (Special Educational Needs) – MA, English Language Teaching (Leadership and Management) – MA.

Sport Science and Physical Activity

Applied Personal Training and Specialist Exercise Instruction – BSc(Hons), Applied Sport Development and Management – BA(Hons), Applied Sport Science and Coaching – BSc(Hons), Applied Sport and Physical Education – BSc(Hons), Clinical Exercise Therapy – BSc(Hons), Exercise and Physical Activity for Health – BSc(Hons), Football Business – BA(Hons), Football Coaching – BA(Hons), Football Development – BA(Hons), Football Science – BSc(Hons), Football Studies – BA(Hons), Health, Nutrition and Exercise – BSc(Hons), Sport Development and Management – BA(Hons), Sport Rehabilitation and Training – BSc(Hons), Sport Science and Coaching – BSc(Hons), Sport Science and Personal Training – BSc(Hons), Sport and Exercise Science – BSc(Hons), Sport and Physical Education – BSc(Hons), Sport and Physical Education –

BA(Hons), Sports Science (Personal Training) – FD of Science, Sports Science (Sports Coaching) – FD of Science, Sports Studies – BA(Hons), Strength and Conditioning – BSc(Hons);
Postgraduate courses: Clinical Exercise Physiology - (PgDip), Clinical Exercise Physiology – MSc, Leadership and Management of Sport and Physical Activity – MA, Leadership and Management of Sport and Physical Activity – MSc, Physical Activity, Nutrition and Behaviour Change – MSc, Physical Education and Sport Pedagogy – MA, Sports Performance – MSc, Strength and Conditioning – MSc.

Teaching and Education

BA(Hons) Applied Early Years Studies, BA(Hons) Applied Education Studies, Applied Special Educational Needs and Disability, Early Years Studies,- Mathematics With Secondary Education (With QTS), PE Secondary, With QTS, Primary Education (With QTS), Primary Years Education, PGCE Primary, Early Years and PE, and Numerous Secondary Subjects, All With QTS, and PGCE Early Years Teaching With EYTS, and PGCE Early Years Birth To 5 With EYTS, Post Compulsory Education University Certificate of Continuing Professional Development in TESOL, Continuing Professional Development in Mathematics
Postgraduate Courses: PGCerts in a Variety of Subject Specialisms in Education, Primary and Secondary PGCerts, PGCerts in Post-Compulsory Education.

Faculty of Health and Social Science; www.beds.ac.uk/howtoapply/ departments/healthsciences

Sports Therapy and Rehabilitation

Occupational Therapy – BSc(Hons), Physiotherapy – BSc(Hons); Clinical Biomechanics – MSc, Health and Ageing – MSc.

Healthcare Practice

Health Care Practice (Top up) – BSc(Hons), Healthcare Practice – Foundation Degree of Science, Midwifery: Registered Midwife (2nd Registration) – BSc(Hons), Midwifery: Registered Midwife (3 Year) – BSc(Hons), Nursing Associate – Foundation Degree, Nursing Studies (Top up) – BSc(Hons), Nursing with Registered Nurse: Adult – BSc(Hons), Nursing with Registered Nurse: Child – BSc(Hons), Nursing with Registered Nurse: Mental Health – BSc(Hons), Operating Department Practice – BSc(Hons), Paramedic Science – BSc(Hons);

Postgraduate courses: Advanced Clinical Practice (Midwifery) – MSc, Advanced Clinical Practice (Nursing) – MSc, Advanced Clinical Practice (Paramedic Science) – MSc, Dental Education – Postgraduate Certificate, Dental Education – Postgraduate Diploma, Dental Education – MA, Dental Law and Ethics – Postgraduate Certificate, Dental Law and Ethics – Postgraduate Diploma, Dental Law and Ethics – MA, Medical Education – Postgraduate Certificate, Medical Education – Postgraduate Diploma, Medical Education – MA, Medical Simulation – Postgraduate Certificate, Nursing with Registration (Adult) – MSc, Nursing with Registration (Mental Health) – MSc, Public Health – MSc, Specialist Community Public Health Nursing (Health Visiting) – MSc, Specialist Community Public Health Nursing (Health Visiting) – Postgraduate Diploma, Specialist Community Public Health Nursing (School Nursing) – MSc, Specialist Community Public Health Nursing (School Nursing) – Postgraduate Diploma, Specialist Practitioner Community District Nursing – Postgraduate Diploma, Specialist Practitioner Community District Nursing – MSc.

Applied Social Studies

Child and Adolescent Studies – BA(Hons), Child and Family Studies – Foundation Degree, Criminology – BA(Hons), Criminology and Sociology – BA(Hons), Health and Social Care – BA(Hons), Health and Social Care Practice (Top up) – BA(Hons), Health and Social Care Practice – Foundation Degree of the Arts, Policing and Criminal Investigation – BA(Hons), Professional SocialWork Practice (UCMK) – BSc(Hons), Social Studies – BA(Hons), Social Work – BSc(Hons), Systemic Practice (Child Focused Practice) – Graduate Certificate, Systemic Practice (Families and Couples) – Graduate Certificate, Youth and Community Work – BA(Hons)
Postgraduate courses: Applied Social Work Practice: Children and Families – MA, Applied Social Work Practice: Leadership and Management – MA, Applied Social Work: Practice Education – MA, Childhood and Youth: Applied Perspectives – MA, Criminology – MA, Family and Systemic Psychotherapy – MSc, Intermediate Child Focused Systemic Practice – Postgraduate Certificate, Intermediate Systemic Practice with Families and Couples – Postgraduate Certificate, International Social Work and Social Development – MA, Professional Social Work Practice – Postgraduate Diploma, Social Work – MSc, Social Work Practice – Master of Professional

Social Work Practice, Systemic Leadership and Organisational Development – MSc.

University of Bedfordshire Business School; www.beds.ac.uk/howtoapply/departments/businessschool

Accounting BA(Hons), Accounting and Finance BSc(Hons), Business Economics BA(Hons), Business Information Systems BSc(Hons), Business Management BA(Hons), Business Management with Law BSc(Hons), Economics and Finance BSc(Hons), Aviation and Airport management – BSc(Hons), Hospitality and Tourism Management BA(Hons), Human Resource Management BSc(Hons), International Business BA(Hons), Law LLB(Hons), Law with Criminology LLB(Hons), Law with Financial Management LLB(Hons), Law with Psychology LLB(Hons), Marketing BA(Hons), Policing and Criminal Investigation BA(Hons), Public Relations in Practice (with placement) – BA(Hons), Advertising and Branding Design – BA(Hons), Advertising and Marketing Communications – BA(Hons), Event Management – BA(Hons), International Tourism Management – BA(Hons), International Tourism with Hospitality Management – BSc(Hons), Journalism, marketing and Public Relations – BA(Hons), Public Relations – BA(Hons).

Postgraduate courses: Accounting and Business Finance MSc, Business Administration (Finance) MBA, Business Administration (Marketing) MBA, Digital Marketing MSc, Events Management MSc, Financial Economics MSc, Financial Risk Management MSc, International Business Law LLM, International Business with Law MSc, International Commercial and Dispute Resolution Law LLM, International Oil and Gas Law LLM, International Tourism Planning and Management MSc, Management MSc, Marketing MSc, MBA, Purchasing, Logistics and Supply Chain Management MSc.

THE QUEEN'S UNIVERSITY OF BELFAST
www.qub.ac.uk

School of Arts, English and Languages ; www.qub.ac.uk/schools/ael/

Audio Engineering, Broadcast Production, Drama, Drama and English, English, English And Film Studies, English and French, English and History, English and Irish, English and Linguistics, English and Philosophy, English and Politics, English and Sociology, English and Spanish, English With Creative Writing, Film and Theatre Making, Film Studies and Production, French, French and History, French and International Studies, French and Irish, French and Politics, French and Portuguese, French and Spanish, Irish, Irish and History, Irish and Politics, Irish and Spanish, Mlba (Um) Liberal Arts, Music, Music and Audio Production, Music and Sound Design, Music Performance, Spanish, Spanish and Portuguese – BA, BMus, MLibArts, BSc.

School of Biological Sciences; www.qub.ac.uk/schools/schoolofbiologicalsciences

Agricultural Technology, Biochemistry, Biological Sciences, Environmental Management, Food Quality, Safety and Nutrition, Food Science and Food Security, Marine Biology, Microbiology, Zoology

Postgraduate; Microbes and Pathogen Biology, Ecosystem Biology and Sustainability; BSc(Hons), MSc, PhD, MPhil.

School of Chemistry and Chemical Engineering; www.ch.qub.ac.uk/schools/SchoolofChemistryandChemical Engineering

Chemical Engineering, Chemical Technology, Chemistry, Chemistry with French/Spanish, Medicinal Chemistry, BSc(Hons), MSci, BEng, MEng, MSc, PGDip, PhD, MSci.

School of Electronics, Electrical Engineering and Computer Science; www.qub.ac.uk/schools/eeecs

Business IT, Computing and IT, Computer Science, Electrical & Electronic Engineering, Software & Electronic Systems Engineering, Software Engineering; BEng, BSc, MEng, MSc, MPhil, PhD.

School of History and Anthropology, Philosophy and Politics; www.qub.ac.uk/schools/happ

Anthropology, Anthropology and English, Anthropology and French, Anthropology and History, Anthropology and Irish, Anthropology and Spanish, History, History and International Studies, History and Philosophy, History and Politics, History and Sociology, History and Spanish, International Politics and Conflict Studies, International Studies and Irish, International Studies and Politics, International Studies and Spanish, Philosophy, Philosophy and Politics, Politics, Politics and Spanish, Philosophy and Economics.

Postgraduate; History, Anthropology, Social Anthropology, Irish Studies; BA(Hons), GradDip, MA, MPhil, PhD

School of Law; www.qub.ac.uk/schools/SchoolofLaw/

Common and Civil Law (Major) with French, Common and Civil Law (Major) with Hispanic Studies, Law, Law (Major) and Politics, Law Senior Status;

Postgraduate; Human Rights, Human Rights & Criminal Justice, European Law and Governance, International Business and Law, Criminal Justice, Environmental Law and Governance, International Corporate Governance, Criminal Justice and Criminology; LlB, LlM, MSSc, MLSc, PGDip, MPhil, PhD, JD, MLaw

School of Mathematics and Physics; www.qub.ac.uk/schools/SchoolofMathematicsandPhysics

Applied Mathematics and Physics, Mathematics, Mathematics and Computer Science, Mathematics and Statistics & Op Research, Mathematics with Finance, Mathematics wth Extended Studies in Europe, Physics, Physics and Extended Studies in Europe, Physics with Astro-Physics, Physics with Medical Applications, Physics with Extended Studies in Europe, Theoretical Physics; BSc(Hons), GradDip, MSc, MSci, PhD

School of Mechanical and Aerospace Engineering; www.qub.ac.uk/schools/SchoolofMechanicalandAerospaceEngineering

Aerospace Engineering, Mechanical Engineering, Product Design Engineering; BEng, MEng, MSc, PhD

School of Medicine, Dentistry and Biomedical Sciences; www.qub.ac.uk/schools/mdbs

Medicine, Biomedical Science, Dentistry, Human Biology; BCh, BAO, BSc(Hons), BDS, DAO, MB, MD, MSc, MPH, PGDip/Cert

School of Natural and Built Environment; www.qub.ac.uk/schools/NBE/

Archaeology, Archaeology and History, Archaeology and Irish, Archaeology with French, Archaeology with Portuguese, Archaeology with Spanish, Archaeology-Palaeoecology, Archaeology-Palaeoecology and Geography, Architecture, Civil Engineering, Environmental and Civil Engineering, European Planning, Geography, Geography with a Language Planning, Environment and Development, Structural Engineering with Architecture; BA, BSc, MSci, BEng, MEng, MPlan

School of Nursing and Midwifery; www.qub.ac.uk/schools/SchoolofNursingandMidwifery

Adult Nursing, Health & Clinical Studies, Midwifery Sciences, Nursing Adult Nursing, Nursing Children's Nursing, Nursing Learning Disability Nursing, Nursing Mental Health Nursing; BSc(Hons), Diploma, MPhil, PhD, DNursing Practice

School of Pharmacy; www.qub.ac.uk/schools/SchoolofPharmacy

Pharmaceutical Biotechnology, Pharmaceutical Sciences, Pharmacy; MPharm, MSc, PGCert/Dip, MPhil

School of Psychology; www.qub.ac.uk/schools/psy/

Psychology; Atypical Child Development, Applied Psychology (Clinical Specialism), Psychology, Educational Child & Adolescent Psychology, Political Psychology, Politics, Clinical Psychology, Psychology of Childhood Adversity; BSc(Hons), MSc, DocClinPsych, PhD DocEducational

School of Social Sciences, Education and Social Work; www.qub.ac.uk/schools/ssesw

Criminology, Criminology and Social Policy, Criminology and Sociology, Social Policy and Sociology, Social Work, Social Work Relevant Degree Entry, Sociology; BA(Hons), BSW, MA, MSc, DChild, MRes

UNIVERSITY OF BIRMINGHAM
www.bham.ac.uk

College of Arts and Law; www.birmingham.ac.uk/university/colleges/artslaw/index.aspx

African Studies

African Studies BA, African Studies with Development BA, Anthropology and African Studies BA, Anthropology and History BA, Anthropology and Political Science BA, Archaeology and Anthropology BA

Postgraduate courses: Africa and Development MA, African Studies MA/Diploma, Social Research (African Studies) MA

American and Canadian Studies

American and Canadian Studies BA, American and Canadian Studies with year abroad BA

Archaeology

Ancient History BA, Archaeology & Ancient History and History BA, Archaeology and Ancient History BA, Archaeology and Anthropology BA

Postgraduate courses: Antiquity MA: Classical Archaeology pathway, Archaeology, Classical pathway: Antiquity MA, Cultural Archaeology MA / Diploma / Certificate, International Heritage Management MA, International Heritage Management MA (UK-US)

Classics

Ancient History BA, Anthropology and Classical Literature and Civilisation BA, Archaeology & Ancient History and History BA, Archaeology and Ancient History BA, Classical Literature & Civilisation and Philosophy BA, Classical Literature and Civilisation BA, Classics BA, English and Classical Literature & Civilisation BA

Postgraduate courses: Antiquity MA: Byzantine Studies pathway, Antiquity MA: Classics and Ancient History pathway, Antiquity MA: Egyptology pathway

Drama and Theatre Arts

Drama and English BA, Drama and Theatre Arts BA

English Literature

Drama and English BA, English and Classical Literature & Civilisation BA, English and Creative Writing BA, English and Film BA, English and History BA, English and History of Art BA, English and Philosophy BA, English BA, English Language and Literature BA, Modern Languages and English BA

Postgraduate courses: Creative Writing MA, Literature and Culture MA, Shakespeare and Creativity MA, Shakespeare and Education MA (on campus or by distance learning), Shakespeare and Theatre MA/Diploma/Distance learning, Shakespeare Studies MA

English Language and Applied Linguistics

English and Creative Writing BA, English Language and Linguistics BA, English Language and Literature BA, English Language BA, Modern Languages and English BA

Postgraduate courses: Applied Linguistics MA, Applied Linguistics MA (Distance Learning), Applied Linguistics PgCert (Distance Learning), Applied Linguistics with TESOL MA, Language, Culture and Communication MA, Teaching English to Speakers of Other Languages (TESOL) MA, Teaching English to Speakers of Other Languages (TESOL) MA (distance learning), Film and Creative Writing, Creative Writing MA, Film and Television: Research and Production MA, Heritage, International Heritage Management MA, International Heritage Management MA (UK-US), World Heritage Studies MA

History

Ancient and Medieval History BA, Ancient History BA, Anthropology and History BA, Archaeology & Ancient History and History BA, Archaeology and Ancient History BA, English and History BA, French Studies and History BA, German Studies and History BA, Hispanic Studies and History BA, History and History of Art BA, History and Philosophy BA, History and Political Science BA, History and Russian Studies BA, History and Theology BA, History BA, Modern Languages and History BA

Postgraduate courses: Contemporary History MA, Early Modern History MA, Global History MA, History of Warfare MA, Holocaust and Genocide MA/ Diploma/Certificate, Medieval Studies MA, Modern British Studies MA, Social Research (Economic and Social History) MA, West Midlands History MA

History of Art

English and History of Art BA, History and History of Art BA, History of Art BA, Modern Languages and History of Art BA

Postgraduate courses: Art History and Curating MA, History of Art MA

Law

Law LLB, Law with Business Studies LLB, Law with Criminology LLB, Law with French Law LLB, Law with German Law LLB, LLB for Graduates, LLB International Law and Globalisation

Postgraduate courses: Commercial Law LLM, Criminal Law and Criminal Justice LLM, General LLM, International Commercial Law LLM, International Law and Globalisation LLM, International Law LLM: Crime, Justice and Human Rights, International Law, Ethics and Politics MA, International Trade Law LLM, LLB for Graduates.

Modern Languages and Cultures

Chemistry with a Modern Language BSc, Chemistry with a Modern Language MSci, Economics with German BSc, Economics with Spanish BSc, French Studies and History BA, French Studies and Mathematics BA, German Studies and History BA, Hispanic Studies and History BA, History and Russian Studies BA, International Business with Language BSc, International Relations with French BA, International Relations with German BA, International Relations with Spanish BA, Law with French Law LLB, Law with German Law LLB, Modern Languages (University of Birmingham with The Open University pathway) BA, Modern Languages and English BA, Modern Languages and History BA, Modern Languages and History of Art BA, Modern Languages and Music BA, Modern Languages BA, Modern Languages with Business Management BA, Russian Studies and International Relations BA

Postgraduate courses: English-Chinese Interpreting with Translation MA, Holocaust and Genocide MA/Diploma/Certificate, Translation Studies MA

Music

Mathematics and Music BA, Modern Languages and Music BA, Music BMus

Postgraduate courses: Music MA: Choral Conducting pathway, Music MA: Electroacoustic composition/sonic art pathway, Music MA: Global Popular Musics pathway, Music MA: Instrumental/Vocal Composition pathway, Music MA: Mixed Composition pathway, Music MA: Musicology pathway, Music MA: Open Pathway with Performance, Music MA: Open

Pathway without Performance, Music MA: Performance pathway, Music MA: Performance Practice pathway

Philosophy

Classical Literature & Civilisation and Philosophy BA, English and Philosophy BA, History and Philosophy BA, Mathematics and Philosophy BA, Philosophy and Sociology BA, Philosophy BA, Philosophy, Religion and Ethics BA, Political Science and Philosophy BA, Political Science and Philosophy with Year Abroad BA

Postgraduate courses: Global Ethics and Justice MSc, International Law, Ethics and Politics MA, Philosophy MA, Philosophy of Health and Happiness MA, Philosophy of Mind and Cognitive Science MA, Philosophy of Religion and Ethics MA/Diploma

Theology and Religion

History and Theology BA, Philosophy, Religion and Ethics BA, Politics, Religion and Philosophy BA, Theology and Religion BA

Postgraduate courses: Holocaust and Genocide MA/Diploma/Certificate, Islamic Studies MA, Philosophy of Religion and Ethics MA/Diploma, Religion, Politics and Society, Theology and Religion MA

College of Medical and Dental Sciences; *www.birmingham.ac.uk/university/ colleges/mds/undergraduate/index.aspx*

Biomedical Materials Science BMedSc, Biomedical Science BSc, Dental Hygiene and Therapy BSc, Dental Surgery BDS, Medicine and Surgery MBChB, Medicine and Surgery MBChB Graduate Entry Course, Nursing BNurs, Nursing MNurs, Pharmacy MPharm (4 year), Pharmacy MPharm (5 year, integrated preregistration format), Clinical Anatomy BSc – Intercalated Degree, Clinical Science BMedSc – Intercalated Degree, Health Management and Leadership – Intercalated Degree, History of Medicine BMedSc – Intercalated Degree, International Health BMedSc – Intercalated Degree, Medical Sciences BMedSc – Intercalated Degree, Psychological Medicine BMedSc – Intercalated Degree, Public Health & Population Sciences BMedSc – Intercalated Degree

Postgraduate courses: Advanced Clinical Practice MSc, Advanced Critical Care Practitioner (ACCP) – Postgraduate Diploma, Advanced General Dental Practice MSc (Distance Learning), Advanced Practice in Healthcare (Global) MSc/PGDip/PGCert, Bioinformatics MSc/Diploma/Certificate, Biomedical Research: Cardiovascular Sciences MRes, Biomedical Research: Integrative and Translational MRes, Cancer

Sciences MRes, Clinical Health Research MRes, Clinical Neuropsychiatry MSc/Diploma, Clinical Oncology MSc/Diploma – Full-time, Clinical Oncology MSc/Diploma – Part-time, Clinical Research – Academic Clinical Fellows (ACF) Framework MRes/PGDip/PGCert, Dental Materials Science MSc/Diploma/Certificate, Functional and Clinical Anatomy MSc, Genomic Medicine MSc/Diploma/Certificate, Health Economics and Econometrics MSc/Diploma, Health Economics and Health Policy MSc/Diploma, Health Research Methods – MSc/Diploma/Certificate, Immunology and Immunotherapy MSc, Medicine and Surgery MBChB Graduate Entry Course, Multidisciplinary Healthcare Simulation – PGCert, Occupational Health MSc/Diploma/Certificate, Pharmaceutical Enterprise MSc/Diploma, Physician Associate Studies Diploma, Physician Associate Studies MSc, Physicians Assistant (Anaesthesia) Postgraduate Diploma, Practice Certificate in Independent Prescribing, Professional Doctorate in Pharmacy (DPharm), Public Health – Statement of Extra Accredited Learning (SEAL) MPH, Public Health (Health Technology Assessment) MPH/Diploma/Certificate, Public Health MPH/Diploma/Certificate, Respiratory Medicine – PGCert, Restorative Dentistry MSc/Diploma/Certificate Part-Time (Distance Learning), Trauma Science MSc; PhD and research Applied Health Research – PhD/MSc by Research, Biomedical Sciences – PhD/MSc by Research, Cancer and Genomic Sciences – PhD/MSc by Research, Cardiovascular Sciences – PhD/MSc by Research, Clinical Sciences – PhD/MSc by Research, Dentistry – PhD/MSc by Research, Immunology and Immunotherapy – PhD/MSc by Research, Inflammation and Ageing – PhD/MSc by Research, Metabolism and Systems Research – PhD/MSc by Research, Microbiology and Infection – PhD/MSc by Research, Nursing – PhD/MSc by Research, Pharmacy – PhD/MSc by Research

College of Life and Environmental Sciences; www.birmingham.ac.uk/university/colleges/les/index.aspx

Biosciences

Biochemistry (Genetics) BSc, Biochemistry BSc(Hons), Biochemistry MSci(Hons), Biochemistry with an International Year BSc(Hons), Biochemistry with Professional Placement MSci(Hons), Biochemistry with Study in Continental Europe BSc(Hons), Biological Sciences (Genetics) BSc, Biological Sciences (Zoology) BSc(Hons), Biological Sciences BSc(Hons), Biological Sciences MSci(Hons), Biological Sciences with an International Year BSc(Hons), Biological Sciences with Professional Placement MSci(Hons), Biological Sciences with Study in Continental Europe BSc(Hons), Human Biology BSc(Hons), Human Biology MSci(Hons), Human Biology with an International Year BSc(Hons), Human Biology with Professional Placement MSci(Hons), Medical Biochemistry BSc(Hons)

Postgraduate courses: Microbiology and Infection MSc, Molecular Biotechnology MSc, Toxicology MSc, Molecular and Cellular Biology MRes, Molecular Mechanistic Toxicology MRes, Biosciences PhD study

Earth Sciences (Geology)

Geology and Physical Geography BSc(Hons), Geology and Physical Geography MSci(Hons), Geology and Physical Geography with an International Year MSci(Hons), Geology BSc(Hons), Geology MSci(Hons), Geology with an International Year MSci(Hons), Palaeontology and Geology with an International Year MSci(Hons), Palaeontology and Geology BSc(Hons), Palaeontology and Geology MSci(Hons)

Postgraduate courses: Applied Meteorology and Climatology MSc, Health, Safety and Environment Management MSc/Diploma, Hydrogeology MSc, Micropalaeontology MSc, PhD study Earth Sciences

Environmental Science

Environmental Science BSc(Hons), Environmental Science MSci(Hons), Environmental Science with Professional Placement Abroad (Australasia) BSc(Hons), Environmental Science with Year Abroad BSc(Hons), Air Pollution Management and Control MSc/ Diploma, Applied Meteorology and Climatology MSc, Environmental Health MSc, Health, Safety and Environment Management MSc/Diploma, Hydrogeology MSc, Public and Environmental Health Sciences MSc, Atmospheric Sciences and Air Pollution PhD with Integrated Study, Environmental and Biological Nanoscience MRes and PhD study, Environmental Health and Risk Management PhD/MSc (Research), Geography and Environmental Sciences PhD, Environmental Risk Management Taught Programmes; Air Pollution Management and Control MSc/Diploma, Combined Taught/Research Programmes, Atmospheric Sciences and Air Pollution PhD with Integrated Study, Research Opportunities, Environmental Health and Risk Management PhD/MSc (Research)

Geography and Urban Planning

Geography and Urban and Regional Planning BSc(Hons), Geography BA(Hons), Geography BSc(Hons), Geography MSci(Hons), Geography with International Year MSci(Hons), Geography with Year Abroad BA(Hons), Geography with Year Abroad BSc(Hons), Geology and Physical Geography BSc(Hons), Geology and Physical Geography MSci(-Hons), Geology and Physical Geography with an International Year MSci(Hons)

Postgraduate courses: Applied Meteorology and Climatology MSc, Health, Safety and Environment Management MSc/Diploma, Hydrogeology MSc, Research in Human Geography MSc, River Environments and their Management MSc, Urban and Regional Planning (with RTPI accreditation) MSc/PG Diploma/Certificate, Research in Human Geography MRes and PhD, Geography and Environmental Sciences PhD, Geography PhD (Urban and Regional Studies)

Psychology (including Neuroscience)

Human Neuroscience BSc(Hons), Psychology and Psychological Practice MSci(Hons), Psychology and Psychological Research MSci(Hons), Psychology BSc(Hons), Psychology BSc with Integrated Foundation Year (Dubai)

Postgraduate courses: Brain Imaging and Cognitive Neuroscience MSc, Cognitive Behaviour Therapy High Intensity Postgraduate Diploma, Cognitive Behaviour Therapy Postgraduate Diploma, Compassion Focused Therapy Postgraduate Diploma, Computational Neuroscience and Cognitive Robotics MSc, Psychology MSc, Clinical Psychology MRes, Clinical Psychology Doctorate (ClinPsyD), Forensic Clinical Psychology Doctorate (ForenClinPsyD), Forensic Psychology Practice Doctorate (CPD route), Forensic Psychology Practice Doctorate (ForenPsyD), Psychology PhD/MSc (Research)

Sport, Exercise and Rehabilitation Sciences

Applied Golf Management Studies BSc(Hons), Physiotherapy BSc(Hons), Professional Golf Studies FdSc, Sport, Exercise and Health Sciences BSc(Hons), Sport, Physical Education and Coaching Science BSc(Hons)

Postgraduate courses: Advanced Certificate in Golf Coaching, Advanced Manipulative Physiotherapy MSc/Postgraduate Diploma, Clinical Health Research MRes, Exercise and Sports Medicine (Football) MSc/Postgraduate Diploma, Physical Education and Sport Pedagogy MSc, Physiotherapy (pre-registration) MSc, Sport Coaching PGDip/MSc, Clinical Health

Research MRes, Exercise and Sport Sciences MRes, Spinal Pain MRes and PhD study

College of Engineering and Physical Sciences; www.birmingham.ac.uk/university/colleges/eps/index.aspx

Aerospace Engineering

Aerospace Engineering BEng, Aerospace Engineering MEng

Chemical Engineering

Chemical Engineering (International Study) MEng, Chemical Engineering BEng, Chemical Engineering MEng, Chemical Engineering with Foundation Year, Chemical Engineering with Industrial Study BEng, Chemical Engineering with Industrial Study MEng, Chemical Engineering with International and Industrial Study MEng

Postgraduate courses: Advanced Chemical Engineering Masters/MSc/Diploma, Biochemical Engineering Masters/MSc/Diploma, Food Safety, Hygiene and Management Masters/MSc/PG Diploma/PG Certificate, Global Energy Technologies and Systems Masters/MSc, Industrial Project Management Masters/MSc/ Diploma/Certificate, PhD, Combined Taught/Research Programmes, Chemical Engineering PhD with Integrated Study, Chemical Engineering Science MRes, Formulation Engineering EngD, Hydrogen, Fuel Cells and their Applications MRes, PhD with Integrated Study in Fuel Cells and their Fuels, Research opportunities, Chemical Engineering PhD, Chemical Engineering PhD with Integrated Study, PhD with Integrated Study in Fuel Cells and their Fuels

Chemistry

Chemistry BSc, Chemistry MSci, Chemistry with a Modern Language BSc, Chemistry with a Modern Language MSci, Chemistry with Business Management BSc, Chemistry with Business Management MSci, Chemistry with Foundation Year, Chemistry with Industrial Experience MSci, Chemistry with Pharmacology BSc, Chemistry with Pharmacology MSci, Chemistry with Study Abroad MSci; Chemistry PhD/MSc

Civil Engineering

Civil and Railway Engineering BEng, Civil and Railway Engineering MEng, Civil Engineering BEng, Civil Engineering MEng, Civil Engineering with Industrial Experience MEng, Civil Engineering with International Study MEng, Engineering BEng, Engineering Foundation Year, Engineering MEng

Postgraduate courses: Advanced Engineering Management MSc: Construction Management, Civil Engineering and Management Masters/MSc/Diploma/Certificate, Civil Engineering Masters/MSc/Diploma, Geotechnical Engineering and Management Masters/MSc/Diploma/Certificate, Geotechnical Engineering Masters/MSc/Diploma/Certificate, Railway Safety and Control Systems MSc/Diploma/Certificate, Railway Systems Engineering and Integration Masters/MSc/Diploma/Certificate, Road Management and Engineering Masters/MSc/Diploma, Structural Engineering Masters/ MSc/Diploma, Railway Systems Integration MRes, Civil Engineering PhD/MPhil

Computer Science

Artificial Intelligence and Computer Science BSc, Artificial Intelligence and Computer Science BSc with a year in industry, Computer Science BSc, Computer Science BSc (Dubai Campus), Computer Science BSc with a year in industry, Computer Science BSc with Integrated Foundation Year (Dubai Campus), Computer Science MSci, Computer Science with an Industrial Year MSci, Computer Science with Digital Technology Partnership, Computer Science with Study Abroad BSc, Computer Science with Study Abroad MSci, Computer Science/Software Engineering MEng, Computer Science/Software Engineering MEng with a year in industry, Mathematics and Computer Science BSc, Mathematics and Computer Science MSci, Mathematics and Computer Science with Industrial Year BSc, Mathematics and Computer Science with Industrial Year MSci, Physical Sciences Foundation Year

Postgraduate courses: Advanced Computer Science Masters/MSc, Computational Neuroscience and Cognitive Robotics MSc, Computer Science Masters/MSc, Cyber Security Masters/MSc, Human Computer Interaction Masters/MSc, Natural Computation MRes, Cognitive Science (Computer Science) PhD, Computer Science PhD

Electronic, Electrical and Systems Engineering

Electrical and Railway Engineering BEng, Electrical and Railway Engineering MEng, Electronic and Electrical Engineering BEng, Electronic and Electrical Engineering MEng, Electronic and Electrical Engineering with Industrial Year BEng, Electronic and Electrical Engineering with Industrial Year MEng, Engineering BEng, Engineering Foundation Year, Engineering MEng, Mechatronics and Robotics Engineering BEng, Mechatronics and Robotics Engineering MEng

Postgraduate courses: Communications Engineering and Networks Masters/MSc, Electrical Power Systems Masters/MSc, Electrical Power Systems with Advanced Research Masters/MSc (Two Year), Electronic and Computer Engineering Masters/MSc, Railway Safety Control Systems MSc/Diploma/ Certificate, Railway Systems Engineering and Integration Masters/MSc/Diploma/Certificate, Electrical Power Systems with Advanced Research Masters/MSc (Two Year), Electrical Power Systems with Advanced Research Masters/MSc (Two Year), Electronic, Electrical and Systems Engineering PhD/MSc by Research

Materials Science and Engineering

Aerospace Engineering BEng, Aerospace Engineering MEng, Engineering Foundation Year, Materials Science and Engineering BEng, Materials Science and Engineering MEng, Materials Science and Engineering with Industrial Experience MEng, Mechanical and Materials Engineering BEng, Mechanical and Materials Engineering MEng, Metallurgy BEng, Nuclear Engineering MEng, Nuclear Science and Materials BSc

Mathematics

French Studies and Mathematics BA, Mathematics and Computer Science BSc, Mathematics and Computer Science MSci, Mathematics and Computer Science with Industrial Year BSc, Mathematics and Computer Science with Industrial Year MSci, Mathematics and Music BA, Mathematics and Philosophy BA, Mathematics BSc, Mathematics MSci, Mathematics with a Year in Industry BSc, Mathematics with an International Year BSc, Mathematics with Business Management BSc, Mathematics with Business Management MSci, Mathematics with Study in Continental Europe BSc, Physical Sciences Foundation Year, Theoretical Physics and Applied Mathematics BSc, Theoretical Physics and Applied Mathematics MSci

Postgraduate courses: Applied Mathematics MSc, Financial Engineering Masters/ MSc, Mathematical Finance MSc, Mathematics, Operational Research, Statistics and Econometrics (MORSE) Masters/MSc, Applied Mathematics MRes, Management Mathematics MRes, Pure Mathematics MRes, Applied Mathematics PhD, Management Mathematics PhD, Pure Mathematics PhD

Mechanical Engineering

Aerospace Engineering BEng, Aerospace Engineering MEng, Engineering BEng, Engineering Foundation

Year, Engineering MEng, Mechanical and Materials Engineering BEng, Mechanical and Materials Engineering MEng, Mechanical Engineering (Automotive) BEng, Mechanical Engineering (Automotive) MEng, Mechanical Engineering BEng, Mechanical Engineering MEng, Mechanical Engineering with Industrial Year MEng, Mechanical Engineering with Industrial Year BEng

Postgraduate courses: Advanced Engineering Management MSc, Advanced Engineering Management MSc: Operations Management, Advanced Engineering Management MSc: Project Management, Advanced Engineering Management MSc: Systems Management, Advanced Mechanical Engineering Masters/MSc, Mechanical Engineering PhD/MSc by Research

Nuclear Engineering

Nuclear Engineering MEng, Nuclear Science and Materials BSc

Physics and Astronomy

Nuclear Engineering MEng, Nuclear Science and Materials BSc, Physical Sciences Foundation Year, Physics (International Study) BSc, Physics (International Study) MSci, Physics and Astrophysics (International Study) BSc, Physics and Astrophysics BSc, Physics and Astrophysics MSci, Physics BSc, Physics MSci, Physics with Particle Physics and Cosmology BSc, Physics with Particle Physics and Cosmology MSci, Theoretical Physics and Applied Mathematics BSc, Theoretical Physics and Applied Mathematics MSci, Theoretical Physics BSc, Theoretical Physics MSci

Postgraduate courses: Nuclear Decommissioning and Waste Management MSc/PG Diploma, Physics and Technology of Nuclear Reactors Masters\MSc, PhD Translational Quantum Technology AQ, Physics and Astronomy PhD

College of Social Sciences (CoSS); www.birmingham.ac.uk/university/colleges/socsci/index.aspx

Business

Accounting and Finance (BSc), Business Management (BSc), Economics (BSc), International Business (BSc), Money Banking and Finance (BSc), Mathematical Economics and Statistics (BSc)

Postgraduate courses: Accounting and Finance MSc, Advanced Engineering Management MSc, Economics, Finance and Statistical MSc, Management MSc,

Marketing MSc, Online MSc, Graduate Diploma in Business Administration, MBA, PhD

Education

BA(Hons) Education, BA(Hons) Education and Sociology, BSc(Hons) Psychology in Education

Postgraduate Study in the Fields of Autism (Adults), Autism (Children), Autism Spectrum Disorders (Webautism), Bilingualism in Education, Character Education, Education for Health Professionals, Inclusion and Special Educational Needs (ISEN), International Studies in Education Language, Literacies and Dyslexia (LLD), Leadership of Educational Inclusion MA, Education Management of Special Education in Developing Countries, School Improvement and Educational Leadership, Severe, Profound and Multiple Learning Disabilities (SPMLD), Special Educational Needs Coordination (SENCO), Social, Emotional and Behavioural Difficulties (SEBD), Teachers of Children with Hearing Impairment, Teaching English as a Foreign Language (TEFL), Teaching Studies (Postgraduate Diploma), Vision Impairments: Mandatory and Non-Mandatory Qualification for Teachers of Children and Young People with a Vision Impairments; Postgraduate; Autism (Adults), Autism (Children), Autism Spectrum Disorders (Webautism), Bilingualism in Education, Character Education, Education for Health Professionals, Educational Leadership, Education of Learners with Multisensory Impairment (Deaf Blindness), Inclusion and Special Educational Needs, International Studies in Education, Language, Literacies and Dyslexia, Leadership of Educational Inclusion, MA Education, Management of Special Education in Developing Countries, School Improvement and Educational Leadership, Severe, Profound and Multiple Learning Difficulties, Special Educational Needs Coordination, Social, Emotional and Behavioural Difficulties, Teachers of Children with Hearing Impairment, Teaching English as a Foreign Language TEFL, Teaching Studies (Postgraduate Diploma), Visual Impairment: Mandatory and Non-Mandatory Qualification for Teachers of Children and Young People with a Visual Impairment, PhD

Government and Society

International Development and Politics, International Relations and Development BA, Political Science BA, Political Economy BA

Postgraduate courses: Global Cooperation and Security MSc, Political Psychology of International Relations MSc, International Development MSc, Environment, Development and Politics MSc, Conflict,

Statebuilding and Development MSc, Development Policy and Politics MSc, Poverty, Inequality and Development MSc, International Studies in Education (Education and Development) MA, Africa and Development MA, Conflict, Security and Development MSc/ GDip, Poverty, Inequality and Development MSc/Gdip, Masters in Public Administration (MPA), Political Science MA/PGDip, International Political Economy MA/PGDip, International Relations MA/PGDip, Diplomacy MA/PGDip, Global Cooperation and Security MSc, Political Psychology of International Relations MSc, International Security and Terrorism MA/PGDip, Public management MSc, Social Research (Local Government and Public Policy) MA/PGDip/PGCert

Social Policy

Policy, Politics and Economics BA, Social Work BA, Social Policy BA, Sociology BA, Criminology BA, Health Management and Leadership BMedSc – Intercalated Degree

Postgraduate courses: Health Care Policy and Management MSc/PGCert/PGDip, Migration, Superdiversity and Policy MA/PGDip/PGCert, Policy into Practice MA/PGDip/PGCert, Policy into Practice with Integrated Placement MA/PGDip, Social Policy MA, Social Research (Social Policy) MA, Social Research (Social Work and Professional Practice) MA/PGDip, Social Work MA, Specialist Social Work with Adults MA/PGDip/PGCert, Advanced Child Protection Studies MSc/PGDip/PGCert (online, distance learning)

UNIVERSITY COLLEGE BIRMINGHAM
www.ucb.ac.uk

Aesthetic Practitioner, Applied Health and Social Care Practice, Aviation and Airport Management, Bakery and Patisserie, Technology, Beauty Therapy Management, Business Enterprise, Chartered Manager Degree Apprenticeship, Childhood Education Studies, Childhood Studies, Culinary Arts Management, Digital Marketing, Early Childhood Studies, Events Management, Finance and Accounting, Food Development and Innovation, Food and Nutrition, Health and Social Care, Hospitality Business Management, Hospitality and Tourism Management, Hospitality with Events Management, Intensive English Course, International Foundation Diploma, International Hospitality and Tourism Management, International Tourism Business Management, International Tourism Management, Marketing Management, Marketing with Events Management, Nursing (Adult), Nursing (Adult) Degree Apprenticeship, Online Bridging, Physiotherapy, Professional Cookery, Public Health and Health Promotion, Spa Management, Specialist Hair and Media Make Up, Sport and Fitness Studies, Sports Management, Sports Massage and Remedial Therapy, Sports Therapy, Strength, Conditioning and Sports Nutrition, Summer Pre-Sessional English Course, Youth, Community And Families; Postgraduate; Aviation Management, Culinary Arts Management, Education and Learning, Enterprise Management, Finance and Accounting, Global Meetings and Events Management, Hospitality with Tourism Management, International Hospitality Management, International Tourism Management, Marketing Management for Events, Hospitality and Tourism, PGCE Primary Education QTS (Qualified Teacher Status), PGCE School Direct Pathway, Qualified Teacher Status (QTS) Assessment Only Route, Youth Work and Community Development; BA(Hons), BSc(Hons), FdA, Dip HE, FdSc, MA, MSc, PGCE, PGDip/Cert

BIRMINGHAM CITY UNIVERSITY
www.bcu.ac.uk

Faculty of Arts, Design andMedia; www.bcu.ac.uk/arts-design-and-media

Birmingham School of Architecture and Design; www.bcu.ac.uk/architecture-anddesign

BA(Hons) Architecture (RIBA Part 1 Exemption), BA(Hons) Architecture with a Foundation Year, BA(Hons) Design Management (Level 6 Top-up), BA(Hons) Interior Architecture and Design,BA(-Hons) Interior Architecture and Design with a Foundation Year, BA(Hons) Landscape Architecture, BA(Hons) Landscape Architecture with a Foundation Year, BA(Hons) Product and Furniture Design, BA(Hons) Product and Furniture Design with a Foundation Year

Postgraduate courses: PGDip Architectural Practice (RIBA Part 3 Exemption), MArch Architecture (RIBA Part 2 Exemption), PhD Art and Design, MA/PGDip/PGCert Conservation of the Historic Environment, MA Design and Visualisation, MA Design Management, MA Interior Architecture and Design, MA Landscape Architecture, MA Product and Furniture Design

Birmingham School of Art; www.bcu.ac.uk/art

BA(Hons) Art and Design, BA(Hons) Art and Design with a Foundation Year, BA(Hons)/HND Fine Art, BA(Hons) Fine Art with a Foundation Year

Postgraduate courses: MA Art and Design: Interdisciplinary Practices, MA Arts and Education Practices, MA Arts and Project Management, MA Contemporary Arts China, MA Fine Art, PhD Art and Design

Birmingham Conservatoire; www.bcu.ac.uk/conservatoire

BA(Hons) Acting, BA(Hons) Applied Theatre (Community and Education), BMus Jazz, BMus Music/Instrumental and Vocal Performance/Composition/Music Technology, BSc(Hons) Music Technology, BA(Hons) Stage Management

Postgraduate courses: MA/PGDip Acting, MMus/PGDip Choral Conducting, MMus/PGCert/PGDip Composition, MMus/PGCert/PGDip Experimental Performance, MMus/PGCert/PGDip Instrumental Performance, MMus/PGCert/PGDip Jazz, MMus/PGCert/PGDip Music Technology, MA Musicology,

MMus/PGDip Orchestral Performance (Strings), AdvPGDip Professional Performance, MA/PGDip Professional Voice Practice, MMus/PGCert/PGDip Vocal Performance, PhD Conservatoire Research Degree

School of English; www.bcu.ac.uk/english

BA (hons) Applied Linguistics, BA(Hons) English, BA(Hons) English and Creative Writing, BA(Hons) English and Drama, BA(Hons) English and Journalism, BA(Hons) English Language and Literature, BA(Hons) English Literature

Postgraduate course: MA Creative Writing, MA English Linguistics, PhD English Research Degree

School of Fashion and Textiles; www.bcu.ac.uk/fashion-and-textiles

BA(Hons) Costume Design and Practice, BA(Hons) Fashion Branding and Communication, BA(Hons) Fashion Business and Promotion, BA(Hons) Fashion Design, BA(Hons) Garment Technology, BA(Hons) Textile Design (Embroidery/Fibre Art/Knit and Weave/Print and Surface Design/Retail, Business and Marketing)

Postgraduate courses: MA Cosmetics Branding and Promotion, MA Fashion Design, MA Fashion Management, MA Fashion Promotion, MA Fashion Styling, MA Garment Technology, MA Luxury Brand Management, MA Textile and Surface Design, PhD Art and Design

School of Jewellery; www.bcu.ac.uk/jewellery

BSc(Hons) Gemmology and Jewellery Studies, BA(Hons) Horology, BA(Hons) International Jewellery Business, BA(Hons) Jewellery and Objects, HND Jewellery and Silversmithing, BA(Hons) Jewellery and Silversmithing – Design for Industry

Postgraduate courses: GradCert/MA Jewellery and Related Products, MA Luxury Jewellery Management

Birmingham School ofMedia; www.bcu.ac.uk/media

BA(Hons) Digital Marketing, BA(Hons) Fashion and Beauty Journalism, BA(Hons) Film and Screenwriting, BA(Hons) Film Business and Promotion, BA(Hons) Film Studies, BA(Hons) Filmmaking, BA(Hons) Journalism, BA(Hons)/HND Media and Communication, BA(Hons) Media Production,

BA(Hons) Music Industries, BA(Hons) Music Journalism, BA(Hons) Public Relations and Media, BA(Hons) Sports Journalism, BA(Hons) Video Game Design and Production, BSc(Hons) Video Game Development, BA(Hons) Video Game Digital Art

Postgraduate courses: Chartered Institute of Public Relations Professional Public Relations Certificate, Dip Chartered Institute of Public Relations Professional PR Diploma, MA/PGCert Data Journalism, MA Event, Festival and Exhibition Management, MA Feature Film Development, MA Film Distribution and Marketing, MA/MSc Future Media, MA Global Media Management, MA Media and Cultural Studies, MA Media Production, MA Multiplatform and Mobile Journalism, MA Public Relations, MA/MSc Video Game Development, MSc Video Game Enterprise, Production and Design, PhD Media and Cultural Studies

School of Visual Communication; www.bcu.ac.uk/visual-communication

BA(Hons) Design for Performance, Illustration, BA(Hons) Photography, BA(Hons) Visual Communication Graphic Communication

Postgraduate course: MA Visual Communication, PhD Art and Design

Faculty of Business, Law and Social Sciences; www.bcu.ac.uk/business-lawand-social-sciences

Birmingham City Business School; www.bcu.ac.uk/business-school

BSc(Hons) Accountancy, MAcc Accounting and Finance, BSc(Hons) Accounting and Finance, BA(Hons) Accounting and Finance, BA(Hons) Business, BA(Hons) Business (Marketing), BA(Hons) Business (Professional Practice), BSc(Hons) Business Accounting, BA(Hons) Business Administration (Top-up), HNC/HND Business and Management, BA(Hons) Business and Management, BA(Hons) Business Economics, BSc(Hons)/MFin Business Finance, BA(Hons) Business Management, BA(Hons) Business Management (Consultancy), BA(Hons) Business Management (Enterprise), BA(Hons) Business Management (Professional Practice), BA(Hons) Business Management (Supply Chain Management), BA(Hons) Economics, BA(Hons) Event, Venue and Experience Management, BSc(Hons)/MFin Finance and Investment, BA(Hons) Financial Economics, BA(Hons) Global Sport Management, BA(Hons) Human Resource Management, BA(Hons) International Business (Top-up), BA(Hons) International Marketing (Top-up), BA(Hons) Marketing, BA(Hons) Marketing (Advertising and Public Relations), BA(Hons) Marketing (Consumer Psychology), BA(Hons) Marketing (Digital), BA(Hons) Marketing (Professional Practice), BA(Hons) Marketing (Retailing).

Postgraduate courses: ACCA Course, MSc Accounting and Finance, MBA Executive Master of Business Administration, MSc Finance and Investment, MSc Insurance and Risk Management, MSc Internal Audit Management and Consultancy, MA/ PGDip International Human Resource Management, MBA International MBA, MSc Management and Entrepreneurship, MSc Management and Finance, MSc Management and International Business, MSc Management and Marketing, MSc/PGDip Multi-Unit Leadership and Strategy, MSc Organisation Risk Management, PhD Business Research Degree, Doctorate of Business Administration, PGCert Trade Management and Policy

School of Law; www.bcu.ac.uk/law

LLB Law, HND Law and Practice, LLB Law with American Legal Studies, LLB Law with Business, LLB Law with Criminology, HND Legal Studies

Postgraduate courses: LLM International Business Law, LLM International Human Rights, LLM International Law, LPC/LLM Legal Practice, LLM/PGDL/CPE Professional Law, PGDL/CPE Postgraduate Diploma in Law, PhD Law

School of Social Sciences; www.bcu.ac.uk/social-sciences

BA(Hons) Black Studies, BA(Hons) Black Studies in Criminal Justice, BA(Hons) Criminology, BA(Hons) Criminology and Security Studies, BA(Hons) Criminology, Policing and Investigation, BA(Hons) Professional Policing, BSc(Hons) Psychology, BSc(Hons) Psychology with Criminology, BSc(Hons) Psychology with Sociology, BA(Hons) Sociology, BA(Hons) Sociology and Criminology

Postgraduate courses: MA Criminology, MSc Forensic Psychology, MSc Health Psychology, MSc Psychology, MA Security Studies, PhD Social Sciences

Faculty of Health, Education and Life Sciences; www.bcu.ac.uk/healtheducation-and-life-sciences

School of Education and Social Work; www.bcu.ac.uk/education-and-socialwork

Initial Teacher Training

BA(Hons) Primary Education with QTS, PGCE Primary Education with Specialism in Mathematics with QTS, PGCE Post-Compulsory Education and Training, PGCE Primary and Early Years Education, PGCE Primary Education with Specialism in SEN with QTS, PGCE Secondary Art and Design, PGCE Secondary Computer Science, PGCE Secondary Drama, PGCE Secondary Design and Technology: Food, Textiles and Product Design, PGCE Secondary Geography, PGCE Secondary English, PGCE Secondary Mathematics, PGCE Secondary Music, PGCE Secondary Religious Education, PGCE Secondary Science: Biology, PGCE Secondary Science: Chemistry, PGCE Secondary Science: Physics, SKE Subject Knowledge Enhancement in Mathematics, SKE Subject Knowledge Enhancement in Chemistry, SKE Subject Knowledge Enhancement in Computer Science, SKE Subject Knowledge Enhancement in Design and Technology, SKE Subject Knowledge Enhancement in English, SKE Subject Knowledge Enhancement in RE

Education, Childhood and Youth

BA(Hons) Conductive Education, BA(Hons) Early Childhood Studies, FdA Early Years, BA(Hons) Education Studies, BA(Hons) Working with Children, Families and Young People, MA Education, MA Education (International Education), PhD Professional Doctorate in Education

Employability and Professional Development

MA Education (Special Needs Education), MA Education (Global Education Management), PGDip/MTL/MEL Teaching and Learning/Educational Leadership, MA Education (Childhood Studies), MA Education (Early Years Leadership)

School of Health Sciences; www.bcu.ac.uk/allied-and-public-health-professions

BSc(Hons) Biomedical Engineering, BSc(Hons) Biomedical Sciences, BSc(Hons) Diagnostic Radiography, BSc(Hons) Habilitation Work (Working with Children and Young People), Physical Education and School Sport, BSc(Hons) Radiotherapy, FdSc Rehabilitation Work (Visual Impairment), BSc(Hons) Speech and Language Therapy, BSc(Hons) Sport and Exercise Nutrition, BSc(Hons) Sport and Exercise Science, BSc(Hons) Sports Therapy

Postgraduate courses: MSc PhysiotPGDipherapy, MSc/PGDip/PGCert Public Health, MBA Healthcare Management

School of Nursing and Midwifery; www.bcu.ac.uk/nursing-and-midwifery

BSc/BSc(Hons) Applied Studies in Integrated Health and Social Care, BSc(Hons)/PGDip Community Health Nursing Specialist Practitioner – District Nursing, BSc(Hons) Midwifery, BSc(Hons) Nursing (Adult), BSc(Hons) Nursing (Child), BSc(Hons) Nursing (Learning Disability), BSc Specialist Community Public Health Nurse (Health Visitor/School Nurse), FdSc Health and Social Care, BSc(Hons) Nursing (Mental Health), FdSc Nursing Associate Higher Apprenticeship

Postgraduate courses: MSc Advanced Clinical Practice, MSc Advanced Practice, MSc/PGCert/PGDip Advancing Diabetes Care, MSc/PGDip/PGCert Safeguarding, MSc/PGCert/PGDip Transforming and Leading in Health Care, PhD Health

Top-Ups; Acute Care (Professional Practice) Top-up, Adult Acute Mental Health (Professional Practice) Top-up, Adult Critical Care (Professional Practice) Top-up, Burns and Plastic Surgery (Professional Practice) Top-up, Cancer and Haemato-oncology (Professional Practice) Top-up, Cardiac Care (Professional Practice) Top-up, Child, Adolescent and Young Adult Mental Health (Professional Practice) Top-up, Dementia and Frailty (Professional Practice) Top-up, Perioperative Practice (Professional Practice) Top-up, Tissue Viability (Professional Practice) Top-up

Faculty of Computing, Engineering and the Built Environment; www.bcu.ac.uk/computing-engineering-and-the-builtenvironment

School of the Built Environment; www.bcu.ac.uk/built-environment

BSc(Hons) Architectural Technology, BSc(Hons) Building Service Engineering, BSc(Hons) Building Surveying, BEng/MEng Civil Engineering, HNC Construction, BSc(Hons) Construction Management, BSc(Hons)/ MPlan Property Development and Planning, BSc(Hons) Quantity Surveying, BSc(Hons) Real Estate

Postgraduate courses: MSc Building Surveying with Facilities Management, MSc Construction Project Management, MA Planning Built Environments,

MSc/PGDip/PGCert Quantity Surveying, MSc Real Estate Management, PhD Planning Research Degree

School of Computing and Digital Technology; www.bcu.ac.uk/computing

BSc(Hons) Business Information Technology, BSc Computer and Data Science, BSc(Hons)/ MSci Computer Forensics, BSc(Hons)/MSci Computer Games Technology, BSc(Hons)/MSci Computer Networks, BSc(Hons)/MSci Computer Networks and Security, BSc(Hons)/MSci Computer Science, BSc Computing, BSc(Hons)/MSci Computing and Information Technology, BSc/MSci Cyber Security, BSc(Hons) Digital Media Computing

Postgraduate courses: MSc Advanced Computer Science, MSc/PGDip/PGCert Big Data Analytics, MSc Business Intelligence, MSc Cyber Security, MSc Data Networks and Security, MSc Enterprise Systems Management, MSc User Experience Design, PhD Computing Research Degree

School of Engineering; www.bcu.ac.uk/engineering

BEng(Hons)/MEng Automotive Engineering, BEng(Hons)/MEng Electronic Engineering, BEng(Hons)/MEng Manufacturing Engineering, BEng(Hons)/MEng Mechanical Engineering

Postgraduate courses: MSc Automotive Engineering, MSc International Logistics and Supply Chain Management, MSc International Project Management (Distance Learning), MSc Logistics and Supply Chain Management, MSc Mechanical Engineering, MSc Project Management, PhD Engineering Research Degree

---

BISHOP GROSSETESTE UNIVERSITY
www.bishopg.ac.uk

Undergraduate Courses in Archaeology and History, Applied Drama in the Community, Business, Business (Team Entrepreneurship), Drama, Early Childhood Studies, Education Studies, English, Geography, Health and Social Care, History, Primary Education with QTS, Psychology, Sociology, Special Educational Needs, Disability & Inclusion, Sport, TESOL and Linguistics, Theology & Ethics; PGCE Primary/Secondary, MA in Community Archaeology Education, Education with TESOL, English Literature, Health and Social Care Leadership, Heritage Education, Mathematics Education, Mental Health, Wellbeing and Resilience, Primary and Community Care, Professional Studies, Special Educational Needs & Disability, Social and Cultural History, Theology and Religious Studies, EdD (Doctor of Education), PhD Study

---

BLACKBURN COLLEGE
www.blackburn.ac.uk

Accounting BA(Hons) Top Up, BA(Hons) Retail Management (Top Up), Business BA(Hons) Top up, Business Foundation Degree FdA, Business with Human Resource Management with Industry Year BA(Hons), Business with Management BA(Hons), Business with Management with Foundation Entry BA(Hons), Care Leadership and Management Apprenticeship (Higher Level 5), Certificate in Education and Training, Introductory, Certificate in Education and Training, Preparatory, Certificate of Higher Education in Legal Studies, Chartered Legal Executive Apprenticeship, CIPD – Level 5 – Human Resource Consultant/Partner Apprenticeship, Coaching & Mentoring BA(Hons) Top Up, Commercial Procurement and Supply Apprenticeship (Level 4), Complementary and Integrative Health BSc(Hons) Top Up, Computing BSc(Hons) Top Up, Computing Foundation Degree FdSc, Construction and the Built Environment HNC, Contemporary Design for Interiors BA(Hons) Top Up, Contemporary Design for Interiors FdA, Contemporary Fashion BA(Hons) (Top Up), Contemporary Fashion Foundation Degree FdA, Contemporary Textiles BA(Hons) (Top Up), Contemporary Textiles Foundation Degree FdA, Control Engineering Apprenticeship BEng(Hons), Criminology & Criminal Justice Foundation Degree FdA, Criminology BA(Hons) Top Up, Disability Studies (Inclusive Practice) BA(Hons) Top Up, Disability Studies (Inclusive Practice) Foundation Degree FdA, Early Childhood Studies BA(Hons) Top Up,

Early Childhood Studies Foundation Degree FdA, Education Studies BA(Hons), Education Studies with Foundation Entry BA(Hons), Education Studies with Placement Year BA(Hons), Electrical and Electronic Engineering BEng(Hons), Electrical and Electronics Engineering (with Industry Year) BEng(Hons), Electrical and Electronics Engineering Apprenticeship BEng(Hons), Electrical and Electronics Engineering with Foundation Entry BEng(Hons), English Language, and Literary Studies BA(Hons), English Language and Literary Studies with Foundation Entry BA(Hons), Fine Art BA(Hons), Fine Art with Foundation Entry BA(Hons), General Engineering BEng(Hons), General Engineering with Foundation Entry BEng(Hons), General Engineering with Industry Year BEng(Hons), Graphic Communication BA(Hons), Graphic Communication with Foundation Entry BA(Hons), History and English Language BA(Hons), History and English Language with Foundation Entry BA(Hons), History and Literary Studies BA(Hons), History and Literary Studies with Foundation Entry BA(Hons), History and Politics BA(Hons), History and Politics with Foundation Entry BA(Hons), History and Sociology BA(Hons), History and Sociology with Foundation Entry BA(Hons), Hospitality Management BA(Hons) Top Up, Illustration and Animation with Foundation Entry BA(Hons), Law LLB(Hons), Law LLB(Hons) Accelerated Route, Law Masters LLM, LLB(Hons) Law – Part-Time Only, Mechanical Engineering (with Industry Year) BEng(Hons), Mechanical Engineering BEng(Hons), Mechanical Engineering with Foundation Entry BEng(Hons), PGCE (Education & Training) / CertEd (Education & Training), Photography BA(Hons) Top Up, Photography Foundation Degree FdA, Politics and English Language BA(Hons), Politics and English Language with Foundation Entry BA(Hons), Politics and Literary Studies BA(Hons), Politics and Literary Studies with Foundation Entry BA(Hons), Positive Practice with Children & Young People BA(Hons) Top Up, Positive Practice with Children & Young People Foundation Degree FdA, BA(Hons) Psychology, HNC/HND Public Services, Public Service Management BA(Hons) Top Up, Retail Management BA(Hons), Sociology and English Language BA(Hons), Sociology and English Language with Foundation Entry BA(Hons), Sociology and Literary Studies BA(Hons), Sociology and Literary Studies with Foundation Entry BA(Hons), Sports Coaching & Performance BSc(Hons) Top Up, Sports Coaching BSc(Hons) Top Up, Sports Coaching

Foundation Degree FdSc, Teaching & Learning Support (Primary) Foundation Degree BA(Hons), Mechanical Engineering (with Industry Year) BEng(Hons), Mechanical Engineering BEng(Hons), Mechanical Engineering Higher National Diploma (HND) Subject to validation PGCE (Education & Training) / CertEd (Education & Training), Photography BA(Hons) Top Up, Photography Foundation Degree FdA, Positive Practice with Children & Young People BA(Hons) Top Up, Positive Practice with Children & Young People Foundation Degree FdA, Public Service Management BA(Hons) Top Up, Sports Coaching & Performance BSc(Hons) Top Up, Sports Coaching BSc(Hons) Top Up (available from 2020 entry), Sports Coaching Foundation Degree FdSc, Teaching and Learning Support (Primary) Foundation Degree BA(Hons), Wellbeing and Social Care Practices BA(Hons) Top Up, Wellbeing and Social Care Practices Foundation Degree FdA, BEng(Hons) Control Engineering Apprenticeship, BEng(Hons) Electrical and Electronic Engineering Apprenticeship, Business with Management with Foundation Entry BA(Hons), Care Leadership and Management Apprenticeship (Higher Level 5), Chartered Legal Executive Apprenticeship, CIPD – Level 5 – Human Resource Consultant/Partner Apprenticeship, Education Studies with Foundation Entry BA(Hons), English Language and Literary Studies BA(Hons) – Subject to Validation, Fine Art with Foundation Entry BA(Hons), General Engineering (with Industry Year) BEng(Hons), Graphic Communication with Foundation Entry BA(Hons), History and English Language BA(Hons) – Subject to Validation, History and Literary Studies BA(Hons) – Subject to Validation, History and Politics BA(Hons), History and Sociology BA(Hons) – Subject to Validation, Illustration and Animation with Foundation Entry BA(Hons), Mechanical Engineering with Foundation Entry BEng(Hons), Politics and English Language BA(Hons) – Subject to Validation, Politics and Literary Studies BA(Hons) – Subject to Validation, Sociology and English Language BA(Hons) – Subject to Validation, Sociology and Literary Studies BA(Hons) – Subject to Validation, The Chartered Manager Degree Apprenticeship – BA(Hons) Business Management with Leadership, The Further Education Learning and Skills Teacher (PGCE/CertEd) (Level 5) Higher Level Apprenticeship, Wellbeing and Social Care Practices BA(Hons) Top Up, Wellbeing and Social Care Practices Foundation Degree FdA

BOURNEMOUTH UNIVERSITY
www.bournemouth.ac.uk

Faculty of Science & Technology; www1.bournemouth.ac.uk/about/ ourfaculties/faculty-science-technology

Department of Archaeology, Anthropology & Forensic Science

BSc(Hons) Anthropology, BA(Hons) and BSc(Hons) Archaeology, BA(Hons) Archaeology & Anthropology, BSc(Hons) Archaeological, Anthropological & Forensic Sciences, BSc(Hons) Forensic Biology, BSc(Hons) Forensic Investigation, BSc(Hons) Forensic Science

Postgraduate courses: MSc Biological Anthropology, MSc Forensic Anthropology, MSc Forensic Archaeology, MSc Forensic Toxicology by Research.

Department of Computing & Information Technology

BSc(Hons) Business Information Technology, BSc(Hons) Computing, BSc(Hons) Computer Networks, BSc(Hons) Cyber Security Management, BSc(Hons) Data Science and Analytics, BSc(Hons) Forensic Computing & Security, BSc(Hons) Information Technology Management, BSc(Hons) Software Engineering

Postgraduate courses: MSc Cyber Security and Human Factors, MSc Data Science and Artificial Intelligence, MSc Cyber Security & Human Factors, MSc Digital Health, MSc Digital Health and Artificial Intelligence, MSc Information Technology, MSc Internet of Things, MSc Internet of Things with Cyber Security, MSc Internet of Things with Data Analytics, MRes (Masters by Research)

Department of Computer Animation, Games & Visual Effects

BA(Hons) Computer Animation Art and Design, BA(Hons) Computer Animation Technical Arts, BSc(Hons) Games Software Engineering, BSc(Hons) Games Design, BA(Hons) Digital Creative Industries, BA(Hons) Visual Effects

Postgraduate courses: MA 3D Computer Animation, MA Digital Effects, MSc Computer Animation and Visual Effects

Department of Design & Engineering

BSC(Hons) Design Engineering, BEng(Hons) Engineering (part-time), MEng Engineering (part-time), BEng(Hons) Mechanical Engineering, MEng(Hons) Mechanical Engineering, MDes(Hons) Product Design, BSc(Hons) Product Design, BA(Hons) Product Design, BA(Hons) Product Design Futures

Postgraduate courses: MSc Design Management, MSc Engineering Project Management, MSc Mechanical Engineering Design

Department of Life & Environmental Sciences

BSc(Hons) Biological Sciences, BSc(Hons) Ecology & Wildlife Conservation, BSc(Hons) Environmental Science, BSc(Hons) Geography, BSc(Hons) Marine Ecology & Conservation (top-up)

Postgraduate courses: MSc Biodiversity Conservation, MSc Green Economy

Department of Psychology

BSc(Hons) Cyberpsychology, BSc(Hons) Psychology, BSc(Hons) Psychology with Forensic Investigation, BSc(Hons) Psychology with Counselling

Postgraduate courses: MA Political Psychology, MSc Clinical and Developmental Neuropsychology, MSc Forensic Anthropology and Archaeology, MSc Foundations of Clinical Psychology, MSc Health Psychology, MSc Hypnosis in Research, Medicine and Clinical Practice, MSc Internet of Things, MSc Investigative Forensic Psychology

All departments conduct applied sciences by research

The Faculty of Management ; www.bournemouth.ac.uk/about/ ourfaculties/faculty-management

Dept of Accounting, Finance & Economics

BA(Hons) Accounting & Business, BA(Hons) Accounting & Finance, MAccFin(Hons) Accounting & Finance, BA(Hons) Economics, BA(Hons) Finance & Business, BA(Hons) Finance & Economics

Postgraduate courses: MSc Corporate Governance, MSc Finance, MSc International Accounting and Finance, MSc International Finance and Economics, MSc Sustainable Economic Development and Emerging Markets

Dept of Business, Management and Marketing

BA(Hons) Business Studies, BA(Hons) Business Studies with Economics, BA(Hons) Business Studies with Enterprise, BA(Hons) Business Studies with Finance, BA(Hons) Business Studies with Human Resource Management, BA(Hons) Business Studies

with Marketing, BA(Hons) Business Studies with Operations & Project Management, BA(Hons) Global Business Management (online, part-time), BA(Hons) Global Business Management, BA(Hons) Business & Management (Top-up), BSc(Hons) Marketing
Postgraduate courses: Master of Business Administration, MSc Disaster Management, MSc Events Management, MSc Events Marketing, MSc Hotel and Food Services Management, MSc Innovation Management and Entrepreneurship, MSc International Management, MSc Management with Business Analytics, MSc Management with Human Resources, MSc Marketing & User Experience, MSc Marketing Management, MSc Marketing Management (Digital), MSc Marketing Management (Retail), MSc Organisational Project Management, MSc Sport Management, MSc Tourism Marketing Management

Dept of Sport

BSc(Hons) Sport Development & Coaching Sciences, BSc(Hons) Sports Management, BSc(Hons) Sports Therapy, BSc(Hons) Sports Psychology & Coaching Sciences
Postgraduate courses: MSc Sport Management

Dept of Tourism, Hospitality and Events

BA(Hons) Events Management, BA(Hons) International Hospitality Management, BA(Hons) Tourism Management, BA(Hons) International Tourism and Hospitality Management, BA(Hons) International Hospitality & Tourism Management (Top-up)
Postgraduate courses: MSc Disaster Management, MSc Events Management, MSc Events Marketing, MSc Hotel and Food Services Management, MSc International Hospitality and Tourism Management, MSc Tourism Management, MSc Tourism Marketing Management, PhD study

Faculty of Media & Communication; www.bournemouth.ac.uk/about/ ourfaculties/faculty-media-communication

Dept of Film, TV, Media and Music Production

BA(Hons) Film, BA(Hons) Film Production & Cinematography, BA(Hons) Media Production, BA(Hons) Music and Sound Production, BA(Hons) Photography, BA(Hons) Scriptwriting for Film and Television, BA(Hons) Television Production
Postgraduate courses: MA Cinematography for Film and Television, MA Creative Media Arts: Data and Innovation, MA Directing Film and Television, MA Post Production Editing, MA Producing Film and Television, MA Radio Production, MA Scriptwriting, MA Sound Design for Film and Television

School of History, Politics & Social Sciences

BA(Hons) History, BA(Hons) Politics, BA(Hons) Politics and Economics, BA(Hons) Sociology, BA(Hons) Sociology and Anthropology, BA(Hons) Sociology and Criminology

School of Media & Communication

BA(Hons) Communication & Media, BA(Hons) English, BA(Hons) Multimedia Journalism, MLit(Hons) English, BSc(Hons) Marketing, BA(Hons) Marketing Communications, BA(Hons) Marketing Communications with Advertising, BA(Hons) Marketing Communications with Digital Media, BA(Hons) Marketing Communications with Public Relations
Postgraduate courses: MA Advertising, MA Cinematography for Film and Television, MA Creative Writing and Publishing, MA Directing film and Television, MA English and Literary Media, MA International Political Communication, MA Marketing Communications, MA Marketing Communications Practice, MA Media and Communication, MA Media Management Practice, MA Multimedia Journalism, MA Political Psychology, MA Post Production Editing, MA Producing Film and Television, MA Radio Production, MA Scriptwriting, MA Sound Design for Film and Television

Dept. of Law

BA(Hons) Finance and Law, LLB(Hons) Law, LLB(Hons) Law with Politics, LLB(Hons) Law, Media & Creative Industries, Graduate Diploma/ CPE in Law, Postgraduate Certificate Intellectual Property, LLM Legal Practice, LPC Legal Practice, LLM Public International Law

Faculty of Health & Social Sciences; www1.bournemouth.ac.uk/about/ ourfaculties/faculty-health-social-sciences

Dept of Health and Social Care

BSc(Hons) Midwifery, BSc(Hons) Nutrition, BSc(Hons) Occupational Therapy, BSc(Hons) Physiotherapy, BSc(Hons) Operating Department Practice, BSc(Hons) Paramedic Science, BSc(Hons) Sports Therapy, BA(Hons) Social Work
Postgraduate courses: MSc Nutrition & Behaviour, MSc Public Health, PGDip Public Health with

Professional Registration as a Specialist Community Public Health Nurse (Health Visiting), MA Advanced Mental Health Practice, MA Advanced Practice, MA Leading & Developing Services, MA Social Work, PGDip/MA Social Work (Children & Families)

Medical Sciences

BSc(Hons) Biomedical Sciences, BSc(Hons) Medical Science, BSc(Hons) Adult Nursing, BSc(Hons) Children & Young People's Nursing, BSc(Hons) Mental Health Nursing, PGDip/MSc Advanced Clinical Practice, PGDip Adult Nursing PGDip Mental Health Nursing

---

UNIVERSITY OF BRADFORD
www.bradford.ac.uk

Faculty of Engineering & Informatics; www.bradford.ac.uk/ei/

School of Electrical Engineering and Computer Science

Computer Science; Business Computing, Computer Science, Computer Science for Cyber Security, Computer Science for Games, Software Engineering; Postgraduate; Big Data Science and Technology, Cyber Security, Internet of Things.
Electrical and Electronic Engineering; Engineering; Postgraduate; Electrical and Electronic Engineering, Personal, Mobile and Satellite Communications, Telecommunications Engineering and Entrepreneurship

School of Engineering

Chemical Engineering; Chemical Engineering; Postgraduate; Advanced Chemical and Petroleum Engineering
Civil and Structural Engineering; Civil and Structural Engineering; Postgraduate; Advanced Civil and Structural Engineering
Mechanical and Automotive Engineering; Mechanical Engineering; Postgraduate; Automotive Systems Engineering; Advanced Mechanical Engineering
Medical Engineering; Biomedical Engineering, Clinical Technology; Postgraduate; Advanced Biomedical Engineering, Medical Electronics Engineering Healthcare Technology

School of Media, Design and Technology

Games, Animation and VFX; Game Design and Development, Graphics for Games, Virtual and Augmented Reality. Film and Media; Animation, Film and TV Production, Film and Visual Effects Technology; Postgraduate; Filmmaking BEng(Hons), BSc(Hons), BA(Hons), FD, MEng, MPhil, MSc, PhD

Faculty of Health Studies; www.brad.ac.uk/health

Clinical Nursing Practice, Clinical Practice, Critical Care, Diagnostic Radiography, Midwifery Studies, Nursing (Adult/Child/Mental Health), Occupational Therapy, Paramedic Science, Physiotherapy, Public Health and Community Wellbeing; Postgraduate; Advanced Practice(Clinical Practitioner), Business Administration, Advanced Dementia Studies, Diversity Management, Leadership, Management and Change in Health and Social Care, Leading Service Improvement, Medical Imaging, Medical Imaging (Computed Tomography/Magnetic Resonance Imaging/Medical Image Reporting, Midwifery, Nursing Studies, Physiotherapy, Public Health (MPH)
AdvDip, BSc(Hons), CertHE, DipHE, FD, MSc, MPhil, PGDip/Cert, PhD, MPH

Faculty of Life Sciences; www.brad.ac.uk/life-sciences

Archaeological and Forensic Sciences; Archaeology, Forensic and Medical Sciences, Forensic Archaeology and Anthropology, Forensic Science; Postgraduate; Archaeological Sciences, Archaeology and Identity Forensic Archaeology and Crime Scene Investigation, Human Osteology & Palaeopathology, Landscape Archaeology and Digital Heritage; Chemistry and Biosciences; Chemistry, Chemistry (Analytical/Materials/Industrial), Mathematical and Computational Chemistry, Chemistry-Medicinal Chemistry, Healthcare Science (Life Sciences); Postgraduate; Analytical Sciences, Bioinformatics, Materials Chemistry, Medical Bioscience, Skin Science and Stem Cell Biology, Pharmacy and Medical Sciences; MPharm, Clinical Sciences BSc, MSc Courses in Pharmaceutical Technology, Cancer Pharmacology, Cancer Drug Discovery, and Drug Toxicology and Safety Pharmacology, Masters of Public Health, Postgraduate Diploma/MSc in Advanced Pharmacy Practice (Primary Care),

Clinical Pharmacy (Community), Clinical Pharmacy (Primary Care), and Clinical Pharmacy (Secondary Care), Professional Doctorate in Pharmacy (DPharm); Optometry and Vision Science; Optometry, Career Progression Programme; Professional Certificate in Glaucoma, PhD Research
BSc(Hons), MPhil, PhD, MChem, MPharm, CertHE, MSc, MSci(Hons), DPharm

Faculty of Management, Law and Social Sciences; www.bradford.ac.uk/mlss/

Management; Management and Business Analytics, Business and Management, Business Studies and Law, Marketing, International Business & Management, Economics, Finance and Business Analytics, Finance and Economics, Human Resource Management; Accounting and Finance; Postgraduate; European and International Business Management, Finance and Investment, Finance, Accounting and Management, Financial Management, Human Resource Management, International Business and Management, International Commercial Law, International Strategic Marketing, Logistics, Data Analytics and Supply Chain Management, Management, Marketing and Management, Innovation, Enterprise and The Circular Economy, Executive MBA, MBA; BA(Hons), BSc(Hons), DBA, LlB, LlM, GradDip(-Law), MBA, MRes, PhD, MSc, PGCert/Dip

School of Law
Law LLB, Law (Commercial/Criminal/Social Justice) LLB, Law with Business and Management;

Postgraduate: International Human Rights Law and Development LLM, International Legal Studies LLM, Natural Resources and Environmental Policy LLM, PhD

Faculty of Social Sciences; www.brad.ac.uk/acad/ssis

Economics; Economics and Finance for Development MSc
Peace Studies; MA/MSc: International, Relations, Politics and Security Studies BA(Hons), Politics, Peace and Development BA(Hons); Postgraduate; Advanced Practice in Peacebuilding and Conflict Resolution MA, International Development Management MA, International Relations and Security Studies MA, Peace, Conflict and Development MA, Peace, Resilience and Social Justice MA, Project Planning and Management MSc, Sustainable Development MSc
Psychology- Undergraduate: BSc(Hons) Psychology, Psychology with Counselling. Postgraduate: MSc Psycholgy, Psychology of Health and Wellbeing
Sociology & Criminology; BA(Hons) – Criminology and Criminal Behaviour, Sociology; Postgraduate: MA Sociology, Social Policy and Crime
Social Work & Social Care; BA(Hons) Social Work, Working With Children, Young People and Families; Postgraduate; MA – Mental Health Practice, Social Work BA(Hons), BSc(Hons), MA, MPhil, PhD, PGDip, MPA

BRADFORD COLLEGE
www.bradfordcollege.ac.uk

Accountancy, Business Management, Civil Engineering Project Management, Computer Networks and Systems Support, Computing and Information Systems, Computing, Construction Management, Counselling and Psychology in Community Settings, Education and Training, Early Years, Early Years Practice, Education Studies, Fashion, Film, Games and Digital Media, Graphic Design and Illustration, Health and Social Welfare, Hospitality and Travel Management, Interior Design, Law (Accountancy/Marketing/Social Welfare), Law and Legal Practice, Law, Make-Up Artistry, Management and Leadership, Media Make-Up with Special Effects, Music for the Creative Industries, Ophthalmic Dispensing, Performing Arts, Photography, Physical Activity, Health and Well-Being, Primary Education with QTS, Social Nutrition and Health, Social Work, Sport and Physical Activity, Sports Coaching, Supporting and Managing Learning in Education, Teaching and Learning in the Primary Phase with QTS, TESOL, Technical Production Arts for Film and Television, Textiles and Surface Design, Textiles Practice, Visual Arts, Youth and Community Development; Postgraduate; PGCE (Primary/Secondary), Education and Training, Education/Leadership & Management/Inclusive Practice/Early Childhood, Visual Arts Youth Work and Community Development; BSc(Hons), CertHE, DipHE, BA(Hons), LlB(Hons), BEngTech, MA, MEd, PGDipCert, MSc, PGCE, FD, LawPGDip, LlM

UNIVERSITY OF BRIGHTON
www.brighton.ac.uk

School of Applied Social Science; www.brighton.ac.uk/about-us/contact-us/academic-departments/school-ofapplied-social-science.aspx

Applied Psychology and Criminology BA(Hons), Applied Psychology and Sociology BA(Hons), Applied Psychology BSc(Hons), Criminology and Sociology BA(Hons), Criminology BA(Hons), Psychology with Counselling Studies BSc(Hons), Social Science BA(Hons), Social Work BSc(Hons), Sociology BA(Hons)

Postgraduate courses: Advanced Social Work and Management MSc, Advanced Social Work MSc, Approved Mental Health Practice PGDip, Community Psychology MA, Humanistic Psychotherapeutic Counselling PGDip, Professional Social Work Practice PGDip/PGCert, Psychodynamic Psychotherapeutic Counselling PGDip, Psychotherapy MSc, Social Research Methods (MSc/PGDip), Social Work MSc/PGDip

School of Architecture and Design; www.brighton.ac.uk/about-us/contact-us/academic-departments/school-ofarchitecture-and-design.aspx

Architecture BA(Hons), Interior Architecture BA(Hons), Product Design with Professional Experience BSc(Hons)

Postgraduate courses: Architectural and Urban Design MA (PGCert PGDip), Architecture Post Part 2 Professional Experience, Architecture Professional Practice Pre-Diploma, Architecture RIBA Part 2 MArch, Interior Design MA (PGCert PGDip), Management, Practice and Law in Architecture PGDip, Sustainable Design MA, Town Planning MSc (PGCert PGDip)

School of Art; www.brighton.ac.uk/aboutus/contact-us/academic-departments/school-of-art.aspx

3D Design and Craft BA(Hons), Fashion Communication with Business Studies BA(Hons), Fashion with Business Studies BA(Hons), Fine Art Painting BA(Hons), Fine Art Sculpture BA(Hons), Fine Art: Critical Practice BA(Hons), Fine Art: Printmaking BA(Hons), Graphic Design BA(Hons), Illustration BA(Hons), Textiles with Business Studies BA(Hons), Postgraduate courses: Arts and Design by Independent Project MA, Craft MA, Fine Art MA, Inclusive Arts Practice MA (PGCert PGDip), Sequential Design/Illustration MA, Textiles MA

Brighton Business School; www.brighton.ac.uk/bbs/index.aspx

Business and Management

Business BSc(Hons) top-up degree, Business Management BSc(Hons), Business Management with Economics and Placement Year BSc(Hons), Business Management with Economics BSc(Hons), Business Management with Finance and Placement Year BSc(Hons), Business Management with Finance BSc(Hons), Business Management with Human Resource Management and Placement Year BSc(Hons), Business Management with Human Resources BSc(Hons), Business Management with Marketing and Placement Year BSc(Hons), Business Management with Marketing BSc(Hons), Business Management with Placement Year BSc(Hons), International Business Management BSc(Hons)

Postgraduate courses: Human Resource Management MSc (PGCert PGDip), Human Resource Management PGDip, International Management MSc (PGCert PGDip), Management (Entrepreneurship) MSc (PGCert PGDip), Management (Human Resources) MSc (PGCert PGDip), Management MSc (PGCert PGDip), Brighton MBA (Full-time) MBA (PGCert PGDip)

Accounting, Finance and Economics

Accounting and Finance BSc(Hons), Economics BSc(Hons), Finance and Investment BSc(Hons)

Postgraduate courses: ACCA Professional Accountancy ACCA PROF, Accounting (ACCA) MSc (PGCert PGDip), Economics and Finance MSc (PGCert PGDip), Finance and Accounting MSc, Finance and Banking MSc, Finance and Investment MSc (PGCert PGDip), Finance and Risk Management MSc

Law

Law LLB(Hons), Law with Business LLB(Hons), Law with Criminology LLB(Hons)

Postgraduate courses: Law Conversion (LLM), Law CPE PGDip

Marketing

Marketing Management BSc(Hons), Marketing Management with Placement Year BSc(Hons)

Postgraduate courses: Marketing (Branding and Communications) MSc (PGCert PGDip), Marketing

(Digital Marketing) MSc (PGCert PGDip), Marketing (International Marketing) MSc (PGCert PGDip), Marketing (Social Marketing) MSc (PGCert PGDip), Marketing MSc (PGCert PGDip)

Tourism and events

International Event Management BSc(Hons), International Tourism Management BSc(Hons)

Logistics and Supply Chain Management

Logistics and Supply Chain Management MSc (PGCert PGDip)

Brighton and Sussex Medical School; www.bsms.ac.uk/index.aspx

Bachelor of Medicine Bachelor of Surgery (BM BS)
Postgraduate courses: Anaesthesia and Perioperative Medicine, Cardiology, Clinical Radiology, Clinical Education, Clinical Professional Studies, Dementia Studies, Diabetes in Primary Care, Global Health, Global Pharmacy, Healthcare Leadership and Commissioning, Internal Medicine, Medical Education, Medical Research, Paediatrics and Child Health, Physician Associate Studies, Psychiatry, Public Health, Simulation in Clinical Practice, Surgical Studies

School of Computing, Engineering and Mathematics www.brighton.ac.uk/ aboutus/contact-us/academic-departments/school-of-computing-engineering-andmathematics.aspx

Aeronautical Engineering BEng(Hons), Aeronautical Engineering BEng(Hons) (with integrated foundation year), Aeronautical Engineering BSc(Hons) top-up degree, Aeronautical Engineering MEng, Automotive Engineering BEng(Hons), Automotive Engineering BEng(Hons) (with integrated foundation year), Automotive Engineering BSc(Hons) top-up degree, Automotive Engineering MEng, Business Computing BSc(Hons), Business Computing with Cyber Security BSc(Hons), Computer Science (Games) BSc(Hons), Computer Science BSc(Hons), Computer Science with Artificial Intelligence BSc(Hons), Computer Science with Cyber Security BSc(Hons), Computing for Web and Mobile BSc(Hons), Digital Games Development BSc(Hons), Electrical and Electronic Engineering BEng(Hons), Electrical and Electronic Engineering BEng(Hons) (with integrated foundation year), Electrical and Electronic Engineering MEng, Electronic and Computer Engineering BEng(Hons), Electronic and Computer Engineering BEng(Hons) (with integrated foundation year), Electronic and Computer Engineering MEng, Electronic Engineering BSc(Hons) top-up degree, Mathematics BSc(Hons), Mathematics BSc(Hons) (with integrated foundation year), Mathematics for Data Science MMath, Mathematics MMath, Mathematics with Business BSc(Hons), Mathematics with Economics BSc(Hons), Mathematics with Finance BSc(Hons), Mechanical and Manufacturing Engineering BSc(Hons) top-up degree, Mechanical Engineering BEng(Hons), Mechanical Engineering BEng(Hons) (with integrated foundation year), Mechanical Engineering MEng, Software Engineering BSc(Hons)
Postgraduate courses: By Learning Objectives MSc (PGCert PGDip), Data Analytics MSc (PGCert PGDip), Information Security MSc (PGDip PGCert), User Experience Design MSc (PGCert PGDip)

School of Education www.brighton.ac.uk/ about-us/contact-us/ academicdepartments/school-of-education.aspx

Early Childhood Education and Care BA(Hons), Education BA(Hons), Professional Studies in Learning and Development BA(Hons), Working with Children and Young People BA(Hons), Primary Education (3-7 years) BA(Hons) with QTS, Primary Education (5-11 years) BA(Hons) with QTS, Primary English Education BA(Hons) with QTS, Primary Mathematics Education BA(Hons) with QTS, Secondary Mathematics Education BA(Hons) with QTS, Physical Education BA(Hons) with QTS
Postgraduate courses: (Secondary) Art and Design PGCE, (Secondary) Biology PGCE, (Secondary) Chemistry PGCE, (Secondary) English PGCE, (Secondary) Geography PGCE, (Secondary) Mathematics PGCE, (Secondary) Modern Foreign Languages PGCE, (Secondary) Physics PGCE, (Secondary) Physics with Mathematics PGCE, (Secondary) Religious Studies PGCE, Early Years Education PGCert with Early Years Teacher Status, Further Education and Training PGCE, Primary Education (3-7 years) PGCE (PROFGCE), Primary Education PGCE (PROFGCE), School Direct Tuition and School Direct Salaried, Subject Knowledge Enhancement for teacher training, Autism PGCert, Primary Mathematics Specialist Teacher PGCert, Specific Learning Difficulties (Dyslexia) PGCert, MA Education, Education MRes, Doctorate of Education (EdD), Postgraduate Teaching Apprenticeship

School of Environment and Technology; www.brighton.ac.uk/about-us/contact-us/academic-departments/school-ofenvironment-and-technology.aspx

Architectural Technology BSc(Hons), Building Surveying BSc(Hons), Civil Engineering (with integrated foundation year) BEng(Hons), Civil Engineering BEng(Hons), Civil Engineering MEng, Civil Engineering MEng (with integrated foundation year), Civil Engineering with Construction Management BEng(Hons), Civil Engineering with Construction Management MEng, Civil with Environmental Engineering BEng(Hons), Civil with Environmental Engineering MEng, Construction Management BSc(Hons), Earth and Ocean Science BSc(Hons), Environmental Management BSc(Hons), Environmental Sciences BSc(Hons), Geography BA(Hons), Geography BSc(Hons), Geography MGeog, Geography with Archaeology BSc(Hons), Geography with Remote Sensing and GIS BSc(Hons), Geology BSc(Hons), Physical Geography and Geology BSc(Hons), Project Management for Construction BSc(Hons), Quantity Surveying BSc(Hons).

Postgraduate courses: Civil Engineering MSc (PGCert PGDip), Construction Management MSc (PGCert PGDip), Earthquake and Structural Engineering MSc, Environmental Assessment and Management MSc (PGCert PGDip), Geographical Information Systems and Environmental Management MSc (PGDip), Project Management for Construction MSc (PGCert PGDip), Water and Environmental Management MSc (PGDip)

School of Health Sciences; www.brighton.ac.uk/about-us/contact-us/academic-departments/school-of-healthsciences.aspx

Clinical Practice BSc(Hons) top-up degree, Community Specialist Practice BSc(Hons), Health Studies BSc(Hons) top-up degree, Midwifery BSc(Hons), Nursing (Adult) BSc(Hons), Nursing (Child) BSc(Hons), Nursing (Mental Health) BSc(Hons), Occupational Therapy BSc(Hons), Paramedic Science BSc(Hons), Physiotherapy BSc(Hons), Podiatry BSc(Hons), Public Health BSc(Hons), Specialist Community Public Health Nursing BSc(Hons)

Postgraduate courses: Advanced Clinical Practice MSc (PGDip), Advanced Occupational Therapy MSc (PGCert PGDip), Advanced Physiotherapy MSc (PGCert PGDip), Advanced Podiatry MSc (PGCert PGDip), Clinical Practice (PGCert), Clinical Practice GradCert, Clinical Research MRes (PGCert PGDip), Community Specialist Practice MSc PGDip, European MSc in Occupational Therapy, Health and Education MSc (PGCert PGDip), Health and Management MSc (PGCert PGDip), Health MSc (PGCert PGDip), Health Promotion MSc (PGCert PGDip), Independent Prescribing, Musculoskeletal Physiotherapy MSc (PGCert PGDip), Occupational Therapy (Pre-Registration) MSc (PGCert PGDip), Physiotherapy (Pre-Registration) MSc (PGDip), Podiatry (Pre-Registration) MSc, Specialist Community Public Health Nursing MSc (PGCert PGDip), Transforming Practice for Health Professionals through Education (PGCert)

School of Humanities; www.brighton.ac.uk/about-us/contact-us/academicdepartments/school-of-humanities.aspx

Creative Writing BA(Hons), Critical History BA(Hons), English Language and Creative Writing BA(Hons), English Language and English Literature BA(Hons), English Language and Linguistics BA(Hons), English Language and Media BA(Hons), English Language BA(Hons), English Literature and Creative Writing BA(Hons), English Literature and Linguistics BA(Hons), English Literature BA(Hons), Fashion and Dress History BA(Hons), Globalisation: History, Politics, Culture BA(Hons), History of Art and Design BA(Hons), History, Literature and Culture BA(Hons), Humanities BA(Hons), Humanities: War, Conflict and Modernity BA(Hons), Linguistics BA(Hons), Media and English Literature BA(Hons), Philosophy, Politics and Ethics BA(Hons), Philosophy, Politics, Art BA(Hons), Visual Culture BA(Hons)

Postgraduate courses: Creative Writing MA (PGCert PGDip), Cultural and Critical Theory MA (PGCert PGDip), Cultural History, Memory and Identity MA (PGCert PGDip), Curating Collections and Heritage MA, Globalisation: Politics, Conflict and Human Rights MA (PGCert PGDip), History of Design and Material Culture MA, Language in Context MA, Making of Histories PGCert, Making of Histories PGDip, TESOL Diploma, TESOL MA, TESOL with ICT MA, War: History and Politics MA (PGCert PGDip)

School of Media; www.brighton.ac.uk/about-us/contact-us/academicdepartments/school-of-media.aspx

Animation BA(Hons), Digital Film BA(Hons), Design for Digital Media BA(Hons), Digital Music and Sound Arts BA(Hons), Film and Screen Studies

BA(Hons), Games Art and Design BA(Hons), Media and Environmental Communication BA(Hons), Media Production BA(Hons), Media Studies BA(Hons), Media Industry and Innovation BA(Hons), Music Business and Media BA(Hons), Moving Image BA(Hons), Photography BA(Hons)
Postgraduate courses: Digital Media Arts MA, Digital Media, Culture and Society MA, Digital Music and Sound Arts MA, Photography MA

School of Pharmacy and Biomolecular Sciences; www.brighton.ac.uk/about-us/contact-us/academic-departments/school-of-pharmacy-and-biomolecularsciences.aspx

Biological Sciences BSc(Hons), Biological Sciences BSc(Hons) (with integrated foundation year), Biological Sciences MSci, Biomedical Science BSc(Hons), Biomedical Science BSc(Hons) (with integrated foundation year), Biomedical Science MSci, Chemistry BSc(Hons), Chemistry BSc(Hons) (with integrated foundation year), Chemistry MChem, Ecology and Conservation BSc(Hons), Ecology and Conservation BSc(Hons) (with integrated foundation year), Ecology and Conservation MSci, Pharmaceutical and Chemical Sciences BSc(Hons), Pharmaceutical and Chemical Sciences BSc(Hons) (with foundation year), Pharmaceutical and Chemical Sciences MSci, Pharmacy MPharm, Pharmacy MPharm (with integrated foundation year)
Postgraduate courses: Biological Sciences MRes, Chemistry MRes (PGCert PGDip), Clinical Pharmacy MSc, Ecology and Conservation MRes (PGCert PGDip), General Pharmacy Practice PGDip (PGCert), Natural Sciences MRes, Non-Medical Prescribing for Pharmacists, Pharmaceutical and Biomedical Sciences MRes (PGCert PGDip), Pharmacy (OSPAP) MSc (PGDip), Pharmacy (OSPAP) PGDip

School of Sport and Service Management; www.brighton.ac.uk/about-us/contact-us/academic-departments/school-of-sportand-service-management.aspx

International Event Management BA(Hons) top-up degree, International Hospitality Management BA(Hons) top-up degree, International Tourism Management BA(Hons) top-up degree, Journalism BA(Hons), Physical Education BA(Hons), Physical Education BA(Hons) with QTS, Retail Management BA(Hons) top-up degree, Retail Marketing BA(Hons) top-up degree, Sport and Exercise Science BSc(Hons), Sport and Fitness BSc(Hons) top-up degree, Sport Business Management BSc(Hons), Sport Coaching and Development BA(Hons) top-up degree, Sport Coaching BSc(Hons), Sport Journalism BA(Hons), Sport Studies BA(Hons)
Postgraduate courses: (Secondary) Dance PGCE, (Secondary) Physical Education PGCE, Applied Exercise Physiology MSc (PGCert PGDip), Applied Sport Physiology MSc (PGCert PGDip), International Event Management MSc (PGCert PGDip), International Hospitality Management MSc (PGCert PGDip), International Tourism Management MSc (PGCert PGDip), Journalism MA (PGCert PGDip), Sport and International Development MA, Sport Business Management MSc, Sport Journalism MA (PGCert PGDip), Strength and Conditioning MSc, Tourism and International Development MSc (PGCert PGDip) MPhil/PhD study available in all departments

UNIVERSITY OF BRISTOL
www.bristol.ac.uk

Faculty of Arts; www.bristol.ac.uk/arts

School of Arts; www.bristol.ac.uk/school-of-arts

Department of Anthropology and Archaeology

BA Anthropology, MArts Anthropology with Innovation, BA Archaeology and Anthropology

Department of Filmand Television

BA Film and Television, BA Film and English, BA Film and French, BA Film and German, BA Film and Italian, BA Film and Portuguese, BA Film and Spanish, BA Theatre and Film, MArts Film and Television with Innovation
Postgraduate courses: MA in Film and Television, MA in Composition of Music for Film and Television

Department of Music

BA Music, BA Music and Czech, BA Music and French, BA Music and German, BA Music and Italian, BA Music and Portuguese, BA Music and Russian, MArts Music with Innovation
Postgraduate courses: MA in Music, MA in Composition of Music for Film and Television

Department of Philosophy

BA Philosophy, BA English and Philosophy (QV35), BSc Mathematics and Philosophy (VG51), MSci Mathematics and Philosophy (GV15), BSc Philosophy and Economics, BSc Philosophy and Economics with Study Abroad, Philosophy and French, BA Philosophy and German, BA Philosophy and Italian, BSc Philosophy and Politics, BA Philosophy and Portuguese, BA Philosophy and Russian, BA Philosophy and Spanish, BA Philosophy and Theology BSc Physics and Philosophy (FV35), MSci Physics and Philosophy (FVH5), BSc Sociology and Philosophy (LV35)

Department of Theatre

BA Theatre and Performance Studies, BA Theatre and English, BA Theatre and Film, BA Theatre and French, BA Theatre and German, BA Theatre and Italian, BA Theatre and Portuguese, BA Theatre and Spanish, MArts Theatre with Innovation

School of Humanities; www.bristol.ac.uk/ humanities

Department of Classics and Ancient History

BA Ancient History, BA Classical Studies, BA Classics

Department of English

BA English, BA English Literature and Community Engagement, BA English and Classical Studies, BA English and Philosophy, BA Film and English, BA Theatre and English, BA English and Czech, BA English and French, BA English and German, BA English and Italian, BA English and Portuguese, BA English and Russian, BA English and Spanish
Postgraduate course: MA in English Literature

Department of History

BA History, MArts History with Innovation, BA History and Czech, BA History and French, BA History and German, BA History and Italian, BA History and Portuguese, BA History and Russian, BA History and Spanish
Postgraduate course: MA in History, MA in Medieval Studies

Department of History of Art

BA History of Art, BA History of Art and French, BA History of Art and German, BA History of Art and Italian, BA History of Art and Portuguese, BA History of Art and Russian, BA History of Art and Spanish
Postgraduate course: MA in History of Art

Department of Religion and Theology

BA Religion and Theology, MArts Religion and Theology with Study Abroad, BA Philosophy nd Theology, BA Theology and Sociology
Postgraduate course: MA in Religion

School of Modern Languages; www.bristol.ac.uk/sml

BA Modern Languages, PG DIP/MA in Translation, MA in Chinese-English Translation, MA in Comparative Literatures and Cultures, MA in Black Humanities

Department of Czech

BA Czech and French, BA Czech and German, BA Czech and Italian, BA Czech and Portuguese, BA Czech and Russian, BA Czech and Spanish, BA English and Czech, BA History and Czech, BA Music and Czech

Department of French

BA French, BA Czech and French, BA English and French, BA Film and French, BA French and German, BA French and Italian, BA French and Portuguese, BA French and Russian, BA French and Spanish, BA History and French BA History of Art and French BA International Business Management and French, LLB Law and French, BA Music and French, BA Philosophy and French, BA Politics and French, BA Theatre and French

Department of German

BA German, BA Czech and German, BA English and German, BA Film and German, BA French and German, BA German and Italian, BA German and Portuguese, BA German and Russian, BA German and Spanish, BA History and German, BA History of Art and German, BA International Business Management and German, LLB Law and German, BA Music and German, BA Philosophy and German, BA Politics and German, BA Theatre and German.

Department of Hispanic, Portuguese and Latin American Studies

BA Hispanic Studies, BA Spanish, BA Spanish and Portuguese, BA Spanish and Russian, BA Hispanic Studies, BA Czech and Portuguese, BA English and Portuguese, BA Film and Portuguese, BA French and Portuguese, BA German and Portuguese, BA History and Portuguese, BA History of Art and Portuguese, BA Italian and Portuguese, BA Music and Portuguese, BA Philosophy and Portuguese, BA Politics and Portuguese, BA Russian and Portuguese, BA Spanish and Portuguese, BA Theatre and Portuguese, BA Spanish, BA Czech and Spanish, BA English and Spanish, BA Film and Spanish, BA French and

Spanish, BA German and Spanish, BA History and Spanish, BA History of Art and Spanish, BA International Business Management and Spanish, BA Italian and Spanish, LLB Law and Spanish, BA Music and Spanish, BA Philosophy and Spanish, BA Politics and Spanish, BA Spanish and Portuguese, BA Spanish and Russian, BA Theatre and Spanish

Department of Italian

BA Italian, BA Czech and Italian, BA English and Italian, BA Film and Italian, BA French and Italian, BA German and Italian, BA History and Italian, BA History of Art and Italian, BA Italian and Portuguese, BA Italian and Russian, BA Italian and Spanish, BA Music and Italian, BA Philosophy and Italian, BA Politics and Italian, BA Theatre and Italian

Postgraduate courses: BA Italian and Portuguese, BA Italian and Russian, BA Italian and Spanish

Department of Russian

BA Russian, BA Czech and Russian, BA English and Russian, BA French and Russian, BA German and Russian, BA History and Russian, BA Italian and Russian, BA Music and Russian, BA Philosophy and Russian, BA Politics and Russian, BA Russian and Portuguese, BA Spanish and Russian

Faculty of Biomedical Sciences; www.bristol.ac.uk/biomedical-sciences

School of Biochemistry; www.bristol.ac.uk/biochemistry

BSc Biochemistry, BSc Biochemistry with Medical Biochemistry, BSc Biochemistry with Molecular Biology and Biotechnology, MSci Biochemistry, MSci Biochemistry with Medical Biochemistry, MSci Biochemistry with Molecular Biology and Biotechnology

Postgraduate courses: MSc in Biomedical Sciences Research, MSc in Biophysics and Molecular Life Sciences

School of Cellular and MolecularMedicine; www.bristol.ac.uk/cellmolmed

BSc Cancer Biology and Immunology, BSc Cellular and Molecular Medicine, BSc Medical Microbiology, BSc Virology and immunology.

Postgraduate courses: MSc in Transfusion and Transplantation Sciences, MSc in Biomedical Sciences Research

School of Physiology, Pharmacology and Neuroscience; www.bristol.ac.uk/physpharm-neuro

BSc Neuroscience, MSci Neuroscience with Study in Industry, BSc Pharmacology, MSci Pharmacology with Study in Industry, BSc Physiological Science, MSci Physiological Science with Study in Industry

Postgraduate courses: MSc in Biomedical Sciences Research, MRes Systems Neuroscience

MRes Systems Neuroscience Elizabeth Blackwell Institute for Health Research; www.bristol.ac.uk/blackwell

Faculty of Engineering; www.bristol.ac.uk/engineering

School of Computer Science, Electrical and Electronic Engineering, and Engineering Mathematics; www.bristol.ac.uk/engineering/about/school-sceem

Department of Computer Science

BSc Computer Science, MEng Computer Science, MEng Computer Science with Innovation, BEng Computer Science and Electronics, MEng Computer Science and Electronics, BSc Mathematics and Computer Science, MEng Mathematics and Computer Science

Postgraduate courses: MSc Advanced Computing, MSc Advanced Computing – Creative Technology, MSc Advanced Computing – Machine Learning, Data Mining and High-Performance Computing, MSc Computer Science, PhD/MSc by research Computer Science, Neural Dynamics (Wellcome Trust)

Department of Electrical and Electronic Engineering

BEng Electrical and Electronic Engineering, MEng Electrical and Electronic Engineering, MEng Electrical and Electronic Engineering with Innovation, BEng Mechanical and Electrical Engineering, MEng Mechanical and Electrical Engineering, BEng Computer Science and Electronics, MEng Computer Science and Electronics.

Postgraduate courses: MSc in Communication Networks and Signal Processing, MSc in Image & Video Communications and Signal Processing, MSc in Optical Communications and Signal Processing, MSc in Wireless Communication Systems and Signal Processing, MSc in Advanced Microelectronics and Systems Engineering, MSc Biomedical Engineering, PhD Communication, PhD/MSc by research Electrical and Electronic Engineering

Department of Engineering Mathematics

BEng Engineering Mathematics, MEng Engineering Mathematics

Postgraduate courses: MSc in Engineering Mathematics, MSc in Robotics, PhD Engineering Mathematics and Neural Dynamics (Welcome Trust PhD)

School of Civil, Aerospace and Mechanical Engineering; www.bristol.ac.uk/engineering/about/school-came

Department of Aerospace Engineering

BEng Aerospace Engineering, MEng Aerospace Engineering

Postgraduate course: MSc Advanced Composites

Department of Civil Engineering

BEng Civil Engineering, MEng Civil Engineering

Postgraduate courses: MSc in Earthquake Engineering and Infrastructure Resilience, MSc Water and Environmental Management

Department of Mechanical Engineering

BEng in Mechanical Engineering, MEng in Mechanical Engineering, BEng Mechanical and Electrical Engineering, MEng Mechanical and Electrical Engineering

Postgraduate courses: MSc Nuclear Science and Engineering, MSc Advanced Composites, MSc Robotics

Faculty of Health Sciences; www.bristol.ac.uk/health-sciences

Bristol Dental School; www.bristol.ac.uk/dental

BDS Gateway to Dentistry, BDS Dentistry

Postgraduate courses: DDS Orthodontics Doctorate in Dental Surgery, MSc Dental Implantology, MSc Oral Medicine, Postgraduate Certificate Clinical Conscious Sedation and Anxiety Management, Postgraduate Certificate Clinical Oral Surgery, MSc/PGDip/PGCert Postgraduate Dental Studies

Bristol Medical School; www.bristol.ac.uk/medical-school

MB ChB Gateway to Medicine, MB ChB Medicine

Postgraduate courses: MRes Health Sciences Research, MSc Molecular Neuroscience, MSc Perfusion Science, MSc Reproduction and Development, MSc Stem Cells and Regeneration, MSc Translational Cardiovascular Medicine

Bristol Veterinary School; www.bristol.ac.uk/vetscience

BVSc Gateway to Veterinary Science, BVSc Veterinary Science, BVSc Veterinary Science: Accelerated Graduate Entry, BSc Veterinary Nursing and Bioveterinary Science, BSc Veterinary Nursing and Companion Animal Behaviour

Postgraduate course: MSc Global Wildlife Health and Conservation

Centre for Health Sciences Education; www.bristol.ac.uk/health-sciences/chse

BSc Applied Anatomy

Postgraduate course: PGDip/PGCert/MSc Teaching and Learning for Health Professionals

Faculty of Science; www.bristol.ac.uk/science

School of Chemistry

BSc Chemistry, MSci Chemistry, BSc Chemical Physics, MSci Chemical Physics

Postgraduate course: Chemistry PhD/MSc by Research Centres for Doctoral Training

School of Earth Sciences

BSc Environmental Geoscience, MSci Environmental Geoscience, BSc Geology, MSci Geology, BSc Geophysics, MSci Geophysics, BSc Palaeontology and Evolution, MSci Palaeontology and Evolution

Postgraduate courses: MSc Palaeobiology, MSc Volcanology

School of Geographical Sciences

BSc Geography, MSci Geography with Innovation, BSc Geography with Quantitative Research Methods

Postgraduate courses: MSc in Climate Change Science and Policy, MSc in Environmental Policy and Management, MSc in Human Geography: Society and Space, PhD in Geographical Sciences (Human Geography), PhD in Geographical Sciences (Physical Geography), MSc by Research in Geographical Sciences (Physical Geography)

School of Mathematics

Mathematics, BSc, Mathematics, MSci, Mathematics with Statistics, BSc, Mathematics with Statistics, MSci, Mathematics and Computer Science, BSc, Mathematics and Computer Science, MEng, Economics and Mathematics, BSc, Mathematics and Philosophy, BSc, Mathematics and Philosophy, MSci, Mathematics and Physics, BSc, Mathematics and Physics, MSci

Postgraduate course: MSc in Mathematical Sciences

School of Physics

MSci Physics, BSc Physics, MSci Physics with Astrophysics, BSc Physics with Astrophysics, MSci Physics with Innovation, MSci Physics and Philosophy, BSc Physics and Philosophy, MSci Theoretical Physics, MSci Chemical Physics, BSc Chemical Physics

Postgraduate courses: MSc Nanoscience and Functional Nanomaterials, MSc Nuclear Science and Engineering

Faculty of Life Sciences; www.bristol.ac.uk/life-science/

School of Biological Sciences

BSc Biology, BSc Zoology, MSci Biology, MSci Zoology, MSci Palaeontology and Evolution
Postgraduate course: MSc Palaeobiology, PhD/MSc by Research in Biological Sciences, GW4 Doctoral Training Partnership (DTP), South West Biosciences DTP, PhD in Complexity Sciences, PhD in Synthetic Biology

School of Experimental Psychology

BSc Psychology, MSci Psychology, MSci Psychology with Innovation
Postgraduate courses: MSc Experimental Psychology, MSc Clinical Neuropsychology, MSc in Applied Neuropsychology, Diploma in Applied Neuropsychology

Social Sciences and Law; www.bristol.ac.uk/fssl

School of Education; www.bristol.ac.uk/education

Education Studies, BSc, Psychology in Education, BSc
Postgraduate courses: MSc Education, Policy and International Development Leadership and Policy Learning, Technology and Society Mathematics Education Neuroscience and Education Teaching and Learning Inclusive Education, MSc Educational Research, MSc Psychology of Education, MSc Teaching English to Speakers of Other Languages

School for Policy Studies; www.bristol.ac.uk/sps

Childhood Studies
Childhood Studies, BSc, Childhood Studies with Management, BSc, Childhood Studies with Quantitative Research Methods, BSc, Childhood Studies with Quantitative Research Methods, MSci
Social Policy
Social Policy, BSc, Social Policy with Management, BSc, Social Policy and Politics, BSc, Social Policy and Sociology, BSc, Social Policy with Quantitative Research Methods, BSc, Social Policy with Criminology, BSc, Social Policy with Quantitative Research Methods, MSci
Criminology
Criminology, BSc

Postgraduate courses: MSc Disability Studies: Inclusive Theory and Research, MSc Nutrition, Physical Activity and Public Health, MSc Public Policy, MSc Policy Research, MSc Social Work Research, MRes Health and Wellbeing, MSc Social Work, MSc Advanced Social Work with Children and Families, Doctor of Educational Psychology (DEdPsy), PhD Social Policy, PhD Social Work, PhD Disability Studies, PhD Exercise, Nutrition and Health, PhD Health and Wellbeing (South West Doctoral Training Partnership interdisciplinary pathway)

School of Economics, Finance and Management

BSc Accounting and Finance, BSc Accounting and Management, BSc Economics and Accounting, BSc Economics, BSc Economics and Econometrics, BSc Economics and Finance, BSc Economics and Mathematics, BSc Economics and Politics, BSc Philosophy and Economics, BSc Management, BSc International Business Management
Postgraduate courses: MSc Accounting and Finance, MSc Economics, MSc Economics and Finance, MSc Finance and Investment, MSc Accounting, Finance and Management, MSc Economics, Accounting and Finance, MSc Economics, Finance and Management, MSc Management, MSc Management, MSc Management, MSc Management, MSc Social Science Research Methods, MSc Strategy, Change and Leadership, Graduate Diploma in Economics

School of Sociology, Politics and International Studies; www.bristol.ac.uk/spais

Politics and International Relations, BSc, Politics with Quantitative Research Methods, BSc, Politics with Quantitative Research Methods, MSci, Politics and Sociology, BSc, Social Policy and Politics, BSc, Politics and French, BA, Politics and German, BA, Politics and Italian, BA, Politics and Portuguese, BA, Politics and Russian, BA, Politics and Spanish, BA, Sociology, BSc, Sociology with Quantitative Research Methods, BSc, Sociology with Quantitative Research Methods, MSci, Social Policy and Sociology, BSc, Sociology and Philosophy, BSc, Theology and Sociology, BA
Postgraduate courses: MSc European and Global Governance, MSc Gender and International Relations, MSc International Relations, MSc International Security, LLM International Law and International Relations, MSc Social Science Research Methods, MSc Development and Security, MSc East Asian Development and the Global Economy, MSc International Development, MSc Contemporary Identities, MSc

Ethnicity and Multiculturalism, MSc Social and Cultural Theory, MSc Social Science Research Methods, MSc Sociology

University of Bristol Law School;
www.bristol.ac.uk/law/

LLB Law, LLB Law and French, LLB Law and German, LLB Law and Spanish

Postgraduate: LLM Commercial Law, LLM European Legal Studies, LLM General Legal Studies, LLM Health, Law and Society, LLM Human Rights Law, LLM International Commercial Law, LLM International Law, LLM International Law and International Relations, LLM Labour Law and Corporate Governance, LLM Law and Globalisation, LLM Public Law, MA Law, MSc Socio-Legal Studies, MRes Sustainable Futures

UNIVERSITY OF THE WEST OF ENGLAND, BRISTOL
www.uwe.ac.uk

Arts, Creative Industries and Education; www1.uwe.ac.uk/cahe

Arts and Cultural Industries; www1.uwe.ac.uk/cahe/ artsandculturalindustries.aspx

BA(Hons) Creative and Professional Writing, BA(Hons) English Literature, BA(Hons) English Language and Literature, BA(Hons) English and History, BA(Hons) English Language and Linguistics, BA(Hons) English Literature with Writing, BA(Hons) Film Studies, BA(Hons) History

Art and Design; www1.uwe.ac.uk/cahe/ artanddesign.aspx

BA(Hons) Drawing and Print, BA(Hons) Fashion Communication, BA(Hons) Fashion Textiles, BA(Hons) Fine Art, BA(Hons) Graphic Design, BA(Hons) Illustration, BA(Hons) Interior Design, BA(Hons Product Design, BSc(Hons) Product Design technology

Postgraduate courses: MRes Culture, MA/MFA Curating, MA/PGDip/PGCert Design, MA/PGDip/ PGCert Fine Art, MA/PGDip/PGCert Graphic Arts, MA/PGDip/PGCert Multi-Disciplinary Printmaking

Education and Childhood; www1.uwe.ac.uk/cahe/edu.aspx

BA(Hons) Early Childhood, BA(Hons) Education, BA(Hons) Education in Professional Practice, FdA Inclusive Practice, BSc(Hons) Mathematics with Qualified Teacher Status, BA(Hons) Primary Education (ITE), FdA Therapeutic Work with Children and Young People

Postgraduate courses: MA Education, ProfDoc Education, MA Education (Early Years), PGCE Primary Early Years Initial Teacher Education (3-7), PGCE Primary Initial Teacher Education (5-11), PGCE Secondary Initial Teacher Education Art and Design, PGCE Secondary Initial Teacher Education Biology with Science, PGCE Secondary Initial Teacher Education Business, PGCE Secondary Initial Teacher Education Chemistry with Science, PGCE Secondary Initial Teacher Education Computer Science, PGCE Secondary Initial Teacher Education English, PGCE Secondary Initial Teacher Education Geography, PGCE Secondary Initial Teacher Education History, PGCE Secondary Initial Teacher Education Mathematics, PGCE Secondary Initial Teacher Education Modern Languages, PGCE Secondary Initial Teacher Education Physics with Science

Film and Journalism; www1.uwe.ac.uk/ cahe/filmandjournalism.aspx

Drama, Acting and Music

BA(Hons) Drama, BA(Hons) Drama and Acting, BA(Hons) Music

Filmmaking, Animation and Photography

BA(Hons) Animation, BA(Hons) Filmmaking, BA(Hons) Film Studies, FdSc Games and Animation Production, BA(Hons) Photography

Postgraduate courses: MSc/PGDip/PGCert Animation, MA Contemporary Film Culture, MRes Culture, MA/PGDip/PGCert Documentary Production, MA/ PGDip/PGCert Photography, MA Virtual Reality, MA/PGDip/PGCert Wildlife Filmmaking

Journalism, Media and Public Relations

BA(Hons) Broadcast Journalism, BA(Hons) Journalism and Public Relations, BA(Hons) Media and Cultural Production, BA(Hons) Media Culture and Communication, BA(Hons) Media and Journalism

Postgraduate courses: MA/MFA Creative producing, MRes Culture, MA Documentary Production, MA Journalism, MA Radio Documentary

Business and Law; www1.uwe.ac.uk/bl/

Bristol Business School; www1.uwe.ac.uk/bl/bbs.aspx

Accounting and Finance
BA(Hons) Accounting, BA(Hons) Accounting and Finance, BA(Hons) Accounting and Management, BA(Hons) Banking and Finance, BA(Hons) Business Management with Accounting and Finance
Postgraduate courses: MSc/PGDip/PGCert Accounting and Finance, MSc Accounting and Financial Management (Fast Track route for qualified professionals), MSc/PGDip/PGCert Finance, MSc Financial Technology

Business Management
BA(Hons) Accounting and Management, BA(Hons) Business (Team Entrepreneurship), BA(Hons) Business and Events Management, BA(Hons) Business and Human Resource Management, BA(Hons) Business and Law, BA(Hons) Business and Management, BA(Hons) Business Management and Economics, BA(Hons) Business Management and Leadership, BA(Hons) Business Management with Accounting and Finance (Top Up), BA(Hons) Business Management with Law, BA(Hons) Business Management with Marketing, FdA Business with Management, BA(Hons) International Business, BA(Hons) International Business Management (Top Up), BA(Hons) Sports Business and Entrepreneurship
Postgraduate courses: MSc/PGDip/PGCert Business Management, DBA Doctor of Business Administration, PGCert Enterprise, MSc/PGDip/PGCert Events Management, MSc Financial Technology, MSc/PGDip/PGCert Human Resource Management, MSc/PGDip/PGCert Human Resource Management (International), MSc/PGDip/PGCert Innovation and Applied Entrepreneurship, MSc/PGDip/PGCert International Management, MBA Master of Business Administration (Executive) MBA, MSc Risk Management and Insurance

Economics
BA(Hons) Economics, BSc(Hons) Economics, BA Banking and Finance, BA(Hons) Business Management and Economics
Postgraduate courses: MSc/PGDip/PGCert Global Political Economy

Marketing
BA(Hons) Business and Events Management, BA(Hons) Business Management with Marketing, BA(Hons)Marketing, BA(Hons) Marketing Communication Management

Postgraduate courses: MSc/PGDip/PGCert Events Management, MSc/PGDip/PGCert Marketing, MSc/PGDip/PGCert marketing Communications, MSc Digital Marketing

Bristol Law School; www1.uwe.ac.uk/bl/bls.aspx
BA(Hons) Business and Law, BA(Hons) Business Management with Law, LLB(Hons) Commercial Law, BA(Hons) Criminology and Law, LLB(Hons) European and International Law, LLB(Hons) Law, LLB(Hons) Law with Business
Postgraduate courses: LLM Advanced Legal Practice (LPC LLM), LLM Bar Professional Training Studies/PGDip BPTC, LLM/PGDip/PGCert Commercial Law, LLM/PGDip/PGCert Environmental Law and Sustainable Development, LLM/PGDip/PGCert International Banking and Finance Law, LLM/PGDip/PGCert International Law, LLM/PGDip/PGCert International Trade and Economic Law, GDL Law, MSc Risk Management and Insurance

Environment and Technology; www1.uwe.ac.uk/et/

Architecture and the Built Environment; www1.uwe.ac.uk/et/abe.aspx

Architecture
BSc(Hons) Architectural Technology and Design, BSc(Hons) Architecture, BEng(Hons) Architecture and Environmental Engineering, BA(Hons) Architecture and Planning, BA(Hons) Interior Architecture
Postgraduate courses: MArch Architecture, MRes Architecture, Design and the Built Environment, MSc Facade Engineering, MA Urban Design, PGCert Professional Practice and Management in Architecture

Construction, Property and Surveying
BEng(Hons) Building Services Engineering, BSc(Hons) Building Surveying, BSc(Hons) Construction Project Management, BA(Hons)Property Development and Planning, BSc(Hons) Quantity Surveying and Commercial Management, BSc(Hons) Real Estate
Postgraduate courses: MSc/PGDip/PGCert Building Information Modelling (BIM) in Design Construction and Operations, MSc Building Services Engineering, MSc/Graduate Diploma Building Surveying, MSc/PGDip/PGCert Construction Project Management, MSc Facade Engineering, MSc/PGDip International Construction Law, Graduate Diploma/MSc Quantity Surveying, MSc/PGDip/PGCert Real Estate Finance

and Investment, MSc/PGDip/PGCert Real Estate Management

Product Design

BA(Hons) Graphic Design, BA(Hons) Interior Design, BA(Hons) Product Design, BSc(Hons) Product Design Technology

Postgraduate courses: MA/PGDip/PGCert Design, MA/PGDip/PGCert Graphic Arts

Computer Science and Creative Technologies; www1.uwe.ac.uk/et/csct.aspx

Audio and Music Technology

BSc(Hons) Audio and Music Technology, BSc(Hons) Creative Music Technology

Computer Science and Creative Technologies

BSc(Hons) Applied Computing, FdSc Applied Computing, BSc(Hons) Business Computing, BSc(Hons) Computer Science, BSc(Hons) Computing, BSc(Hons) Digital Media, BSc(Hons) Games Technology, BSc(Hons) Forensic Computing and Security, BSc(Hons) Information Technology, BSc(Hons) Information Technology Management for Business (ITMB), BSc(Hons) Software Engineering for Business

Postgraduate courses: MSc Commercial Games Development, MSc Creative Technology, MSc Cyber Security, MRes Data Science, MSc Financial Technology (FinTech), MSc/PGDip/PGCert Information Management, MSc/PGDip/PGCert Information Technology, MSc/PGDip/PGCert Software Engineering

Engineering Design and Mathematics; www1.uwe.ac.uk/et/edm.aspx

Engineering

BEng(Hons) Aerospace Engineering, MEng Aerospace Engineering, FdSc Aerospace Engineering Manufacturing, BEng(Hons) Aerospace Engineering with Pilot Studies, MEng Aerospace Engineering with Pilot Studies, BEng(Hons) Architecture and Environmental Engineering, BEng(Hons) Automotive Engineering, MEng Automotive Engineering, BEng(Hons) Civil and Environmental Engineering, BEng(Hons) Electronic and Computer Engineering, FdSc Electronic and Computer Engineering, BEng(Hons) Electronic Engineering, MEng Electronic Engineering, BSc(Hons) Engineering, BEng(Hons) Mechanical Engineering, FdSc Mechanical Engineering, MEng Mechanical Engineering, FdSc Mechatronics, BEng(Hons) Robotics, MEng Civil and Environmental Engineering

Postgraduate courses: MSc Civil Engineering, MRes Engineering, MSc Engineering Management, MSc/PGDip/PGCert Mechanical Engineering, MSc/PGDip/

PGCert Robotics, MSc Transport Engineering and Planning

Mathematics

BSc(Hons) Mathematics, MMath Mathematics, BSc(Hons) Mathematics and Statistics, BSc(Hons) Mathematics with Qualified Teacher Status

Geography and Environmental Management www1.uwe.ac.uk/et/gem

Geography and Environmental Management

BA(Hons) Geography, BSc(Hons) Geography, BA(Hons) Geography and Planning, BSc(Hons) Geology

Postgraduate courses: MRes Data Science, MSc/PGDip Environmental Consultancy, MSc/PGDip Environmental Health, MSc/PGDip/PGCert Environmental Management, MRes Geography and Environmental Management, MSc/PGDip/PGCert Public Health, MRes Social Research (Health and Wellbeing), MRes Social Research (Sustainable Futures), MSc/PGDip/PGCert Sustainable Development in Practice

Planning

BA(Hons) Architecture and Planning, BA(Hons) Geography and Planning, BA(Hons) Property Development and Planning, BSc(Hons) Urban Planning [text]Postgraduate courses: MSc Planning and Urban Leadership, MSc Planning Major Projects, MSc Transport Engineering and Planning, MSc/PGDip/PGCert Transport Planning, MSc/PGDip/PGCert Urban and Rural Planning, MSc/PGDip/PGCert Urban Planning, MSc/PGDip/PGCert Sustainable Development in Practice

Health and Applied Sciences; www1.uwe.ac.uk/hls/

Allied Health Professions; www1.uwe.ac.uk/hls/ahp.aspx

Health Professions

BSc(Hons) Diagnostic Radiography, Foundation Programme Health Professions, BSc(Hons) Optometry, BSc(Hons) Paramedic Science, DipHE Paramedic Science, BSc(Hons) Radiotherapy and Oncology

Postgraduate courses: MSc/PGDip/PGCert Advanced Practice, MSc/PGDip/PGCert Medical Ultrasound, MSc/PGDip/PGCert Nuclear Medicine, MSc Physician Associate Studies, MSc Rehabilitation

Physiotherapy, Occupational Therapy and Sports Rehabilitation

BSc(Hons) Occupational Therapy, BSc(Hons) Physiotherapy, BSc(Hons) Sport Rehabilitation

Postgraduate courses: MSc/PGDip/PGCert Advanced Practice, MSc Rehabilitation

Applied Sciences; www1.uwe.ac.uk/hls/as.aspx

Biosciences
BSc(Hons) Biological Sciences, MSci Biological Sciences, BSc(Hons) Biomedical Science, MSci Biomedical Science

Postgraduate courses: MRes Applied Sciences, PGDip Applied Science Communication, MSc/PGDip Biomedical Science, ProfDoc Biomedical Science, PGCert Practical Science Communication, MSc/PGDip Science Communication

Environmental Science
BSc(Hons) Biological Sciences, MSci Biological Sciences, MSci Environmental Health and Practice, BSc(Hons) Environmental Science, MSci Environmental Science, FdSc Integrated Wildlife Conservation, BSc(Hons) Public and Environmental Health, FdSc Public and Environmental Health, BSc(Hons) Wildlife Ecology and Conservation Science, MSci Wildlife Ecology and Conservation Science

Postgraduate courses: MSc/PGDip/PGCert Advanced Wildlife Conservation in Practice,

MRes Applied Sciences, PGDip Applied Science Communication, MSc/PGDip Environmental Health, PGCert Practical Science Communication, MSc/PGDip/PGCert Public Health, MSc/PGDip Science Communication, MSc Environmental Health Professional Practice

Forensic Science
BSc(Hons) Forensic Science, MSci Forensic Science

Health and Social Sciences; www.uwe.ac.uk/hls/hss.aspx

Philosophy and Politics
BA(Hons) Philosophy, BA(Hons) Politics and International Relations

Psychology, Sociology and Criminology
BA(Hons) Criminology, BA(Hons) Criminology and Law, BA(Hons) Criminology and Sociology, BSc(Hons) Criminology with Psychology, BSc(Hons) Psychology, BSc(Hons) Psychology with Criminology, BA(Hons) Sociology, BSc(Hons) Sociology with Psychology, FdA Therapeutic Work with Children and Young People

Postgraduate courses: ProfDoc Counselling Psychology, MSc/PGDip/PGCert Health Psychology, ProfDoc Health Psychology, MA Music Therapy, MSc/PGDip/PGCert Occupational Psychology, MRes Social Sciences, MSc/PGDip/PGCert Sport and Exercise Psychology

Social Work
BA(Hons) Early Childhood, BSc(Hons) Social Work, FdA Therapeutic Work with Children and Young People

Postgraduate courses: MSc/PGDip/PGCert Professional Development (Social Work), PGCert Approved Mental Health Practice

Nursing and Midwifery; www1.uwe.ac.uk/hls/nm.aspx

BA(Hons) Health and Social Care, FdSc Health and Social Care Practice, Foundation Programme Health Professions, BSc(Hons) Midwifery, BSc(Hons)/BSc Nursing (Adult Nursing), BSc(Hons) Nursing (Children's), BSc(Hons) Nursing (Learning Disabilities), BSc(Hons) Nursing (Mental Health), BSc(Hons) Public Health (Specialist Community Public Health Nursing), BSc(Hons) Specialist Practice (District Nursing)

Postgraduate courses: MSc/PGDip/PGCert Advanced Practice, MSc/PGDip/PGCert Public Health, PGDip Public Health (Specialist Community Public Health Nursing), MSc Specialist Practice (District Nursing)

BRUNEL UNIVERSITY
www.brunel.ac.uk

College of Engineering, Design and Physical Sciences; www.brunel.ac.uk/cedps

Aerospace Engineering; www.brunel.ac.uk/aerospace-engineering

Aerospace Engineering BEng(Hons), Aerospace Engineering MEng

Postgraduate courses: Aerospace Engineering MSc

Chemical Engineering; www.brunel.ac.uk/chemical-engineering

Chemical Engineering BEng(Hons), Chemical Engineering MEng

Postgraduate courses: Bioprocess Engineering MSc

Civil Engineering; www.brunel.ac.uk/civil-engineering

Civil Engineering BEng(Hons), Civil Engineering MEng, Civil Engineering with Sustainability BEng(Hons), Civil Engineering with Sustainability MEng, Flood and Coastal Engineering BSc (Top Up)
Postgraduate courses: Flood and Coastal Engineering MSc, Project and Infrastructure Management MSc, Structural Engineering MSc, Water Engineering MSc

Computer Science; www.brunel.ac.uk/computer-science

Business Computing BSc, Business Computing (eBusiness) BSc, Business Computing (Human Computer Interaction) BSc, Business Computing (Social Media) BSc, Computer Science BSc, Computer Science (Artificial Intelligence) BSc, Computer Science (Digital Media and Games) BSc, Computer Science (Network Computing) BSc, Computer Science (Software Engineering) BSc, Mathematics and Computing Foundation Year
Postgraduate courses: Data Science and Analytics MSc, Digital Service Design MSc, Information Systems Management MSc

Design; www.brunel.ac.uk/design

Industrial Design and Technology BA, Product Design BSc, Product Design Engineering BSc
Postgraduate courses: Design and Branding Strategy MA, Design Strategy and Innovation MA, Integrated Product Design MSc

Electronic and Electrical Engineering; www.brunel.ac.uk/electronic-and-electrical-engineering

Computer Systems Engineering BEng, Electronic and Electrical Engineering BEng/MEng, Engineering with Foundation Year, leading to -Aerospace Engineering BEng(Hons), Automotive Engineering BEng(Hons), Chemical Engineering BEng(Hons), Civil Engineering BEng(Hons), Civil Engineering with Sustainability BEng(Hons), Computer Systems Engineering BEng(Hons), Electronic and Communications Engineering BEng(Hons), Electronic and Computer Engineering BEng(Hons), Electronic and Electrical Engineering BEng(Hons), Mechanical Engineering BEng(Hons)
Postgraduate courses: Advanced Electronic and Electrical Engineering MSc, Computer Communication Networks MSc, Distributed Computing Systems Engineering MSc, Sustainable Electrical Power MSc, Wireless Communication Systems MSc

Mathematics; www.brunel.ac.uk/mathematics

Financial Mathematics BSc, Financial Mathematics MMath, Mathematics BSc, Mathematics MMath, Mathematics with Computer Science BSc, Mathematics and Statistics with Management BSc, Foundation year, leading to: Business Computing BSc (with the option to specialise in Business, eBusiness, Human Computer Interaction or Social Media), Computer Science BSc (with the option to specialise in Artificial Intelligence, Digital Media and Games, Network Computing or Software Engineering), Financial Mathematics BSc/MMath, Mathematics BSc/MMath, Mathematics with Computer Science BSc, Mathematics and Statistics with Management BSc (and Economics), BSc Economics, BSc Economics and Accounting, BSc Economics and Business Finance, BSc Economics and Management, BSc Finance and Accounting
Postgraduate courses: Financial Mathematics MSc, Statistics with Data Analytics MSc

Mechanical and Automotive Engineering; www.brunel.ac.uk/mechanical-engineering

Automotive Engineering BEng, Automotive Engineering MEng, Mechanical Engineering BEng, Mechanical Engineering MEng
Postgraduate courses: Advanced Engineering Design MSc, Advanced Manufacturing Systems MSc, Advanced Mechanical Engineering MSc, Automotive and Motorsport Engineering MSc, Biomedical Genetics and Tissue Engineering MSc, Biomedical, Biomechanics and Bioelectronics Engineering MSc, Building Services Engineering Management MSc, Building Services Engineering MSc, Building Services Engineering with Sustainable Energy MSc, Engineering Management MSc, Oil and Gas Engineering MSc, Renewable Energy Engineering MSc, Structural Integrity (Asset Reliability Management) MSc, Sustainable Energy – Technology and Management MSc

College of Business, Arts and Social Sciences; www.brunel.ac.uk/cbass

Anthropology; www.brunel.ac.uk/anthropology

Anthropology BSc, Anthropology and Sociology BSc
Postgraduate courses: Anthropology of Childhood, Youth and Education MSc, Anthropology of International Development and Humanitarian Assistance MSc, Children, Youth and International Development MA, Medical Anthropology MSc, Psychological and

Psychiatric Anthropology MSc, Social Anthropology MRes

Brunel Business School; www.brunel.ac.uk/business-school

Business and Management BSc, Business and Management (Accounting) BSc, Business and Management (Entrepreneurship & Innovation) BSc, Business and Management (Marketing) BSc, International Business BSc

Postgraduate courses: Accounting and Business Management MSc, Business Intelligence and Digital Marketing MSc, Corporate Brand Management MSc, Global Supply Chain Management MSc, Human Resource Management MSc, Human Resources and Employment Relations MSc, International Business MSc, Management MSc, Marketing MSc

Communication and Media Studies; www.brunel.ac.uk/communication-and-media-studies/homeold

Communication and Media Studies BSc

Postgraduate courses: Media and Communications MSc, Comedy Studies PhD

Creative Writing; www.brunel.ac.uk/creative-writing

Creative Writing BA, Theatre and Creative Writing BA

Postgraduate courses: Creative Writing MA, Contemporary Writing PhD, Creative Writing PhD

Economics and Finance; www.brunel.ac.uk/economics-and-finance

Accountancy BSc, Business and Finance BSc, Economics BSc, Economics and Accounting BSc, Economics and Business Finance BSc, Economics and Management BSc, Finance and Accounting BSc

Postgraduate courses: Banking and Finance MSc, Business Finance MSc, Finance and Accounting MSc, Finance and Investment MSc, Economics Integrated PhD, Economics and Finance PhD

Education; www.brunel.ac.uk/education

Education BA

Postgraduate courses: Education MA, PGCE in Primary Education, PGCE in Secondary Education (Science with Biology/Chemistry/Physics, English, Mathematics, Physical Education, Physics with Mathematics), Education Integrated PhD, Doctor of Education (EdD), Education PhD

Film and Television Studies; www.brunel.ac.uk/film-and-television-studies/homeold

Film Production and Theatre BA, Film and Television Studies BA, Film and Television Studies and English BA, Film Production BA

Postgraduate courses: Media and Public Relations MA, Screen Media (Film and TV) PhD

Games Design; www.brunel.ac.uk/games-design

Games Design BA, Games Design and Creative Writing BA

Postgraduate courses: Digital Games Theory and Design MA

Law; www.brunel.ac.uk/law

Law LLB, Law with Criminal Justice LLB, Law with International Arbitration and Commercial Law LLB

Postgraduate courses: International Commercial Law LLM, International Financial Regulation and Corporate Law LLM, International Human Rights Law LLM, International Intellectual Property Law LLM/PGCert, Master of Laws (LLM Law), Law, Policy and Practice MA, Law Integrated PhD, Law PhD

Music; www.brunel.ac.uk/music

Music BA

Postgraduate courses: Music PhD

Politics and History;

History BA, International Politics BSc, Politics and Economics BSc, Politics and History BSc, Politics and Sociology BSc, Politics BSc

Postgraduate courses: Intelligence Analysis PG Cert (Distance Learning), Intelligence and Security Studies (Distance Learning) MA, Intelligence and Security Studies MA, Military History MA, Public Affairs and Lobbying MSc

Sociology; www.brunel.ac.uk/sociology

Sociology (Media) BSc, Sociology BSc

Postgraduate courses: Media and Communications MSc, Sociology and Communication PhD

Theatre; www.brunel.ac.uk/theatre

Film Production and Theatre BA, Theatre BA, Theatre and Creative Writing BA, Theatre and English BA

Postgraduate courses: Theatre PhD

Global Challenges; www.brunel.ac.uk/global-challenges

Global Challenges (Global Innovation) BASc, Global Challenges (Planetary Health) BASc, Global

Challenges (Security) BASc, Global Challenges (Social Cohesion) BASc

College of Health and Life Sciences; www.brunel.ac.uk/chls

Biomedical Sciences; www.brunel.ac.uk/biomedical-sciences

Biomedical Sciences BSc, Biomedical Sciences (Biochemistry) BSc, Biomedical Sciences (Genetics) BSc, Biomedical Sciences (Human Health) BSc, Biomedical Sciences (Immunology) BSc

Postgraduate courses: Disease Mechanisms and Therapeutics MSc, Biosciences PhD, Environment and Health PhD, Synthetic Biology PhD

Environmental Sciences; www.brunel.ac.uk/environmental-sciences

Environmental Sciences BSc, Environmental Sciences MSci

Postgraduate courses: Environmental Management MSc, Sustainability, Entrepreneurship and Design MSc, Environment and Health PhD, Environmental Sciences PhD

Life Sciences; www.brunel.ac.uk/life-sciences

Life Sciences BSc

Occupational Therapy; www.brunel.ac.uk/occupational-therapy

Occupational Therapy BSc

Postgraduate courses: Advanced Clinical Practice PGCert/PGDip/MSc, Occupational Therapy (Pre-Registration) MSc, Occupational Therapy PhD

Physician Associate; www.brunel.ac.uk/physician-associate

Physician Associate MSc

Physiotherapy; www.brunel.ac.uk/physiotherapy

Physiotherapy BSc

Postgraduate courses: Advanced Clinical Practice PGCert/PGDip/MSc, Physiotherapy (Pre-Registration) MSc, Physiotherapy MSc/PhD

Psychology; www.brunel.ac.uk/psychology

Life Sciences BSc, Psychology BSc, Psychology (Sport, Health and Exercise) BSc

Postgraduate courses: Cognitive and Clinical Neuroscience MSc, Culture and Evolution MSc, Psychological Sciences (Conversion) MSc, Cognitive Neuroscience PhD, Culture and Evolution PhD, Psychology PhD

Public Health and Health Promotion; www.brunel.ac.uk/public-health-and-health-promotion

Public Health and Health Promotion MSc, Ageing Studies PhD, Environment and Health PhD, Health Economics PhD, Health Sciences PhD, Public Health and Health Promotion PhD, Welfare, Health and Wellbeing PhD, Youth and Community PhD

Social Work; www.brunel.ac.uk/social-work

Social Work MA, Social Work PhD, Youth and Community PhD

Specialist Community Public Health Nursing; www.brunel.ac.uk/specialist-community-public-health-nursing

Specialist Community Public Health Nursing BSc

Postgraduate courses: Specialist Community Public Health Nursing PGDip/MSc, Occupational Therapy PhD

Sport, Health and Exercise Sciences; www.brunel.ac.uk/sport-health-and-exercise-sciences

Life Sciences BSc, Physical Education and Youth Sport BSc, Sport, Health and Exercise Sciences BSc, Sport, Health and Exercise Sciences (Coaching) BSc, Sport, Health and Exercise Sciences (Human Performance) BSc, Sport, Health and Exercise Sciences (Sport Development) BSc, Sport, Health and Exercise Sciences with Business Studies BSc

Postgraduate courses: Sport and Exercise Psychology MSc, Sport, Health and Exercise Sciences MSc, Human performance, Exercise and Rehabilitation PhD, Sport, Health and Exercise Sciences PhD, Welfare, Health and Wellbeing PhD

UNIVERSITY OF BUCKINGHAM
www.buckingham.ac.uk

Business School; www.buckingham.ac.uk/business

BSc Accounting and Finance, BSc Operational Excellence Online, BSc Business and Management, BSc Marketing, BSc Business Enterprise

Postgraduate courses: MBA Business, MSc Accounting and Finance, MSc Entrepreneurial Consultancy & Practice, MSc Finance and Investment, MSc Financial Service Management, MSc Lean Enterprise, MSc Management in a Service Economy, MSc Strategic Marketing & Customer Experience Management

Computing; www.buckingham.ac.uk/computing

BSc Business and Management with Applied Computing, BSc Computing, BSc Computing with Accounting and Finance, BSc Computing with Business and Management, BSc Computing with Economics, BSc Economics with Applied Computing, BA International Relations with Applied Computing, BA Politics with Applied Computing, BSc Psychology with Applied Computing

Postgraduate courses: MSc in Applied Computing, MSc Applied Data Science, MSc in Computing (by Research), MSc in Innovative Computing, PhD Computing

Education; www.buckingham.ac.uk/education

Postgraduate courses: Independent PGCE, International PGCE, MA in Education, MA in Residential Education, MEd in Educational Leadership, National Award for SEN Coordination (NASENCO), Prep PGCE with Qualified Teacher Status, Primary PGCE with Qualified Teacher Status, Secondary PGCE with Qualified Teacher Status, Doctor of Education by Professional Record (EdD), Assessment Only (AO) Route to Qualified Teacher Status – Primary, Assessment Only (AO) Route to Qualified Teacher Status – Secondary, Preliminary PGCE, Qualified Teacher Status (QTS) Conversion Course – Primary, Qualified Teacher Status (QTS) Conversion Course – Secondary, TA to Teacher

School of Humanities and Social Sciences; www.buckingham.ac.uk/humanities

Centre for Security and Intelligence Studies

Postgraduate courses: PGCert in Law Enforcement, Security & Intelligence, MA in Security and Intelligence Studies, MA in Security, Intelligence and Diplomacy, MPhil/DPhil

Economics

BSc(Econ) Business Economics, BSc(Econ) Economics, BSc Economics, Business and Law, BSc Economics with Applied Computing, BSc Economics with English Language Studies, BSc Economics with French, BSc Economics with History, BSc Economics with Journalism, BSc Economics with Politics, BSc Economics with Spanish

Postgraduate courses: PhD Economics/International Studies

English

BA English Literature, BA English Literature with English Language Studies, BA English Literature with French, BA English Literature with History, BA English Literature with History of Art, BA English Literature with Journalism, BA English Literature with Psychology, BA English Literature with Spanish, BA English Studies, BA English Studies for Teaching, BA English Studies with Journalism

Postgraduate courses: MA in Biography, MA Dickens Studies by Research, MA English Literature by Research, MA Res/PhD Biography, PhD English Literature

History and History of Art

BA History of Art, BA History of Art and Heritage Management, BA History of Art with English Literature, BA History of Art with French, BA History of Art with History, BA History of Art with Journalism, BA History of Art with Spanish, BA History with Economics, BA History with English Literature, BA History with Journalism, BA History with Politics, BA History and Economics, BA History and Politics

Postgraduate courses: MA Biography, MA Decorative Arts and Historic Interiors, MA History of Art: Renaissance to Modernism, MA Military History, MA Modern War Studies and Contemporary Military History, MA The Art Market and the History of Collecting, MA The English Country House 1485-1945, MA Tudor History by Research, MA 20th-Century British History by Research, MA Western Architectural History by Research, PhDs by Research

Modern Foreign Languages

BA Modern Languages (French and Spanish) with Business and Management, BA Modern Languages (French and Spanish) with History of Art, BA

Modern Languages (French and Spanish) with Politics, BA Modern Languages (French and Spanish) with Journalism, BA Modern Languages (French and Spanish) with English language Studies

Institute of Sports Humanities

MA Leadership in Sport

Law School; www.buckingham.ac.uk/law

LLB Law, LLB Law and Professional Practice, LLB Law with Accounting & Finance, LLB Law with Business and Management, LLB Law with Economics, LLB Law with English Language Studies, LLB Law with French, LLB Law with Politics, LLB Law with Spanish

Postgraduate courses: LLM International and Commercial Law, PGCert Law Enforcement, Security and Intelligence, PGDip International and Commercial Law, LLM/PhD Law

Medical School; www.buckingham.ac.uk/medicine

MB ChB Medicine

Psychology; www.buckingham.ac.uk/psychology

BSc Psychology, BSc Psychology with Applied Computing, BSc Psychology with Business and Management, BSc Psychology with English Literature, BSc Psychology with French, BSc Psychology with Spanish

Postgraduate course: MSc Health Psychology, MSc/PhD Psychology by Research

---

BUCKINGHAMSHIRE NEW UNIVERSITY
www.bucks.ac.uk

School of Art Design & Performance; bucks.ac.uk/about-us/our-structure/schools-and-departments/school-of-art-design-and-performance

Department of Art & Design; bucks.ac.uk/about-us/our-structure/schools-and-departments/school-of-arts-and-creative-industries/art-and-design

BA(Hons) Costume Design and Making, BA(Hons) Creative Advertising, BA(Hons) Creative Brand Communications, BA(Hons) Fashion Design, BA(Hons) Fashion and Textiles, BA(Hons) Fashion Promotion and Communication, BA(Hons) Graphic Design, BA(Hons) Hair and Make-up for the Film Industry, BA(Hons) Illustration, BA(Hons) Interior and Spatial Design, BA(Hons) Photography, BA(Hons) Product Design, BA(Hons) Product Design: Interior Product, BSc(Hons) Product Design, BA(Hons) Textile Design

Postgraduate courses: MA Period Hair and Wig Design, MA Prosthetics and Sculpting, MA Screenwriting

Department of Performance and Dance; bucks.ac.uk/about-us/our-structure/schools-and-departments/school-of-art-design-and-performance/performance-and-dance

BA(Hons) Dance and Performance, BSc(Hons) Dance and Fitness, BA(Hons) Performing Arts (Film TV and Stage)

School of Aviation and Security; bucks.ac.uk/about-us/our-structure/schools-and-departments/school-of-aviation-and-security

Department of Aviation; bucks.ac.uk/about-us/our-structure/schools-and-departments/school-of-aviation-and-security/aviation

BSc(Hons) Air Transport with Commercial Pilot Training, BSc(Hons) Air Transport with Private Pilot Training, BSc(Hons) Air Transport with Helicopter Pilot Training, BA(Hons) Airline and Airport Management, BSc(Hons) Aviation Management for Professionals (Top-up)

Postgraduate courses: MSc Aviation Security, MSc International Aviation Regulation and Law

Department of Policing; bucks.ac.uk/about-us/our-structure/schools-and-departments/school-of-aviation-and-security/policing

BSc(Hons) Police Studies with Criminal Investigation

Department of Security & Resilience; bucks.ac.uk/about-us/our-structure/schools-and-departments/school-of-aviation-and-security/security-and-resilience

BA(Hons) Security Consultancy, BA(Hons) Organisational Security Management, BA(Hons) Protective

Security Management, BSc(Hons) Intelligence Analysis and Management
Postgraduate courses: MSc Organisational Resilience, MSc Aviation Security, MSc Critical Infrastructure Security

Department of Tourism and Events; bucks.ac.uk/about-us/our-structure/schools-and-departments/school-of-aviation-and-security/tourism-and-events
BA(Hons) Event and Festivals Management, BA(Hons) International Tourism Management with Air Travel

School of Business Law & Computing; bucks.ac.uk/about-us/our-structure/schools-and-departments/school-of-business-law-and-computing

Bucks Business School; bucks.ac.uk/about-us/our-structure/schools-and-departments/school-of-business-law-and-computing/bucks-business-school
BSc(Hons) Accounting and Finance, BA(Hons) Business and Finance, BA(Hons) Business and Human Resource Management, BA(Hons) Business Management, BSc(Hons) Business Management and Information Technology, BSc(Hons) Business and Psychology, BA(Hons) Marketing, BA(Hons) Marketing and Media Communications, BA(Hons) Sport Business Management, BA(Hons) Sport Marketing, BA(Hons) Sports Business and Coaching
Postgraduate courses: IMBA, MA Human Resource Management, MA Leadership and Management, PGCert Business Leadership

Department of Computing; bucks.ac.uk/about-us/our-structure/schools-and-departments/school-of-business-law-and-computing/computing
BSc(Hons) Artificial Intelligence, BSc(Hons) Computing, BSc(Hons) Computing and Web Development, BSc(Hons) Cyber Security, BSc(Hons) Games Development, BA(Hons) Independent Games Production, BSc(Hons) Software Engineering, FDSc Computing
Postgraduate courses: MSc Cyber Security

Department of Law; bucks.ac.uk/about-us/our-structure/schools-and-departments/school-of-business-law-and-computing/law
LLB(Hons) Business Law, LLB(Hons) Law, LLB(Hons) Law and Sociology

School of Media and Creative Industries; bucks.ac.uk/about-us/our-structure/schools-and-departments/school-of-media-and-creative-industries

Moving Image
BA(Hons) Animation, BA(Hons) Film Production, BA(Hons) Film and Television Production, BSc(Hons) Sound Design, BA(Hons) Visual Effects
Postgraduate courses: MA 3D Animation, MA Film Production

Music
BA(Hons) Audio and Music Production, BA(Hons) Music Business, BA(Hons) Music and Live Events Management, BA(Hons) Music Management and Studio Production, BA(Hons) Music Performance Management, BA(Hons) Music Production and Performance,
BSc(Hons) Music Technology, BA(Hons) Songwriting

School of Nursing and Allied Health; bucks.ac.uk/about-us/our-structure/schools-and-departments/school-of-nursing-and-allied-health
BSc(Hons) Nursing (Adult), BSc(Hons) Nursing (Children's), BSc(Hons) Nursing (Mental Health), BSc(Hons) Operating Department Practice, DipHE Operating Department Practice, FdSc Assistant Practitioner (Adult), FdSc Assistant Practitioner (Child), FdSc Assistant Practitioner (Mental Health), FdSc Assistant Practitioner (Community), FdSc Assistant Practitioner (Midwifery)
Postgraduate courses: MSc Nursing, PGDip Nursing (Adult), PGDip Nursing (Mental Health)

School of Health Care and Social Work; bucks.ac.uk/about-us/our-structure/schools-and-departments/school-of-health-care-and-social-work

Department of Health & Social Care; bucks.ac.uk/about-us/our-structure/schools-and-departments/school-of-health-care-and-social-work/health-and-social-care
BA(Hons) Public Health, BA(Hons) Professional Practice (Integrated Health and Social Care), FdA Health and Social Care

Department of Social Work; bucks.ac.uk/ about-us/our-structure/schools-and-departments/school-of-health-care-and-social-work/social-work

BSc(Hons) Social Work

Postgraduate courses: MSc Social Work, MSc Child Protection and Adult Safeguarding

Community Nursing Programme; bucks.ac.uk/CN

BSc(Hons) Specialist Community Public Health Nursing, BSc(Hons) Specialist Practitioner Qualification (Community Children's Nursing), BSc(Hons) Specialist Practitioner Qualification (District Nursing)

Postgraduate courses: PGDip Specialist Community Public Health Nursing, PGDip Specialist Practitioner Qualification (Community Children's Nursing), PGDip Specialist Practitioner Qualification (District Nursing), MSc (PG Diploma entry) Specialist Community Public Health Nursing, MSc (PG Diploma entry) Specialist Practitioner Qualification (Community Children's Nursing), MSc (PG Diploma entry) Specialist Practitioner Qualification (District Nursing)

School of Human & Social Sciences; bucks.ac.uk/about-us/our-structure/ schools-and-departments/school-of-human-and-social-sciences

Education & Early Years; bucks.ac.uk/ about-us/our-structure/schools-and-departments/school-of-human-and-social-sciences/education-and-early-years

BA(Hons) Early Childhood and Primary Education Studies, BA(Hons) Education Studies, BA(Hons) Professional Practice (Early Years), BA(Hons) Professional Practice (Primary Education and Education), FDA Early Years Practice, FDA Primary Education

Postgraduate courses: MA Education, PGCert Education

Human Performance & Sport; bucks.ac.uk/ about-us/our-structure/schools-and-departments/school-of-human-and-social-sciences/human-performance-and-sport

BSc(Hons) Football Development and Performance, BSc(Hons) Sport and Exercise Science, BA(Hons) Sport Development and Coaching, BSc(Hons) Sports Therapy, BA(Hons) Sports and Physical Education, BSc(Hons) Sports Psychology, BSc(Hons) Strength and Conditioning

Postgraduate courses: MSc Sports Therapy

Department of Psychology; bucks.ac.uk/ about-us/our-structure/schools-and-departments/school-of-human-and-social-sciences/psychology

BSc(Hons) Behavioural Sciences, BSc(Hons) Counselling Psychology, BSc(Hons) Criminological Psychology, BSc(Hons) Psychology, BSc(Hons) Psychology and Criminology, BSc(Hons) Sports Psychology

Postgraduate courses: MSc Applied Positive Psychology, MSc/PGDip Cognitive Behavioural Therapy, MSc Mental Health and Well-being in Education, MSc Psychosocial Interventions, MSc Psychology (Conversion)

Department of Social Sciences; bucks.ac.uk/about-us/our-structure/ schools-and-departments/school-of-human-and-social-sciences/social-sciences

BSc(Hons) Criminology, BSc(Hons) Criminology and Law, BSc(Hons) Health and Social Science

Postgraduate courses: MSc Criminology, Communities and Disorder

UNIVERSITY OF CAMBRIDGE
www.cam.ac.uk

Flexible undergraduate programmes www.undergraduate.study.cam.ac.uk/ courses

BA(Hons) Anglo-Saxon, Norse, and Celtic, BA(Hons) Archaeology, BA(Hons) Architecture, BA(Hons) Asian and Middle Eastern Studies, BA(Hons)/MEng Chemical Engineering, BA(Hons) Classics, BA(Hons) Computer Science, BA(Hons) Economics, BA(Hons) Education, MEng Engineering, BA(Hons) English, BA(Hons) Geography, BA(Hons) History, BA(Hons) History and Modern Languages, BA(Hons) History and Politics, BA(Hons) History of Art, BA(Hons) Human, Social, and Political Sciences, BA(Hons) Land Economy, BA(Hons) Law, BA(Hons) Linguistics, BA(Hons) Management Studies (Part II course), Manufacturing Engineering (Part II course), BA(Hons)/MMath Mathematics, MB/BChir Medicine, BA(Hons) Modern and Medieval Languages, BA(Hons) Music,

BA(Hons)/MSci Natural Sciences, BA(Hons) Philosophy, BA(Hons) Psychological and Behavioural Sciences, BA(Hons) Theology, Religion, and Philosophy of Religion, VetMB Veterinary Medicine

Postgraduate courses

School of Arts and Humanities; www.csah.cam.ac.uk

MPhil in Anglo-Saxon, Norse and Celtic, MPhil in Architecture, MPhil in Asian and Middle Eastern Studies, MPhil in Classics, MPhil in Divinity, MPhil in English, MPhil in Film and Screen Studies, MPhil in History of Art, MPhil in Music, MPhil in Philosophy, MPhil in Theoretical and Applied Linguistics, MPhil in European, Latin American and Comparative Literatures and Culture

School of Clinical Medicine; www.medschl.cam.ac.uk

MPhil in Biological Science (MRC Cognition and Brain Sciences Unit), PGCert in Clinical Medicine, MSt in Clinical Medicine (Intensive Care), MPhil in Clinical Science (Experimental Medicine), MPhil in Clinical Science (Rare Diseases), MPhil in Epidemiology, MPhil in Genomic Medicine, MSt in Genomic Medicine, PGDip in Genomic Medicine, PGCert in Genomic Medicine, MD (Doctor of Medicine), Postgraduate Certificate in Medical Education, MPhil in Medical Science (CIMR), MPhil in Medical Science (Clinical Biochemistry), MPhil in Medical Science (Clinical Neurosciences), MPhil in Medical Science (CRUKCI), MPhil in Medical Science (Medicine), MPhil in Medical Science (MRC Cancer Unit), MPhil in Medical Science (MRC Epidemiology Unit), MPhil in Medical Science (Obstetrics and Gynaecology), MPhil in Medical Science (Oncology), MPhil in Medical Science (Paediatrics), MPhil in Medical Science (Psychiatry), MPhil in Medical Science (Radiology), MPhil in Medical Science (Surgery), National Institutes of Health Oxford/Cambridge Programme, MPhil in Primary Care Research, MPhil in Public Health, MPhil in Translational Biomedical Research

School of Technology; www.tech.cam.ac.uk

MPhil in Advanced Chemical Engineering, MPhil in Advanced Computer Science, MPhil in Bioscience Enterprise, Master of Business Administration, Executive Master of Business Administration, MPhil in Chemical Engineering and Biotechnology, MSt in Construction Engineering, MPhil in Energy Technologies, MPhil in Engineering, MPhil in Engineering for Sustainable Development, Master of Finance, MPhil in Finance, MPhil in Industrial Systems, Manufacture, and Management, MPhil in Innovation, Strategy and Organisation, MSt in Interdisciplinary Design for the Built Environment, MPhil in Management, MPhil in Management Science and Operations, MPhil in Nuclear Energy, M.Res. Photonic Systems Development, MSt in Social Innovation, MSt in Sustainability Leadership, Postgraduate Certificate in Sustainable Business, MPhil in Technology Policy, PhD Degree in Chemical Engineering and Biotechnology, PhD Degree in Computer Science, PhD Degree in Engineering, Judge Business School PhD Programme

School of the Biological Sciences; www.bio.cam.ac.uk

MPhil in Basic and Translational Neuroscience, MPhil in Biological Science (Biochemistry), MPhil in Biological Science (Genetics), MPhil in Biological Science (MRC Laboratory of Molecular Biology), MPhil in Biological Science (MRC Mitochondrial Biology Unit), MPhil in Biological Science (Pathology), MPhil in Biological Science (Pharmacology), MPhil in Biological Science (Physiology, Development and Neuroscience), MPhil in Biological Science (Plant Sciences), MPhil in Biological Science (Psychology), MPhil in Biological Science (Sanger Institute), MPhil in Biological Science (Zoology), MPhil in Social and Developmental Psychology, Doctor of Veterinary Medicine, MPhil in Veterinary Science

School of the Humanities and Social Sciences; www.cshss.cam.ac.uk

MSt in Advanced Subject Teaching, MPhil in African Studies, MPhil in American History, MPhil in Applied Biological Anthropology, MSt in Applied Criminology and Police Management, MSt in Applied Criminology, Penology and Management, MPhil in Archaeological Research, MPhil in Archaeology, MPhil in Assyriology, MPhil in Biological Anthropology, Master of Corporate Law (MCL), MPhil in Criminological Research, MPhil in Criminology, MPhil in Development Studies, MPhil in Early Modern History, MPhil in Economic and Social History, MPhil in Economic Research, MPhil in Economics, Advanced Diploma in Economics, Doctor of Education, MPhil in Education (Arts, Creativity & Education), MPhil in Education (Child and Adolescent Psychotherapeutic Counselling), MPhil in Education (Critical Approaches to Children's Literature), MPhil in Education (Educational Leadership and School Improvement), MPhil in Education (Educational Research), MPhil in Education (Globalisation and International Development), MPhil in Education (Mathematics Education), MPhil in Education (Perspectives on Inclusive and Special Education), MPhil in Education (Politics, Development and Democratic Education), MPhil in Education (Primary Education), MPhil in Education (Psychology and Education), MPhil in Education (Research in Second Language Education), Master of Education (Researching Practice), Master of Education (Science Teacher Researchers and Practitioners), Postgraduate Advanced Certificate in Educational Studies, Postgraduate Certificate in Educational Studies, Postgraduate Diploma in Educational Studies, Postgraduate Award in Educational Studies, Educational Studies: Child and Adolescent Psychotherapeutic Counselling, Postgraduate Award in Educational Studies: Contemporary Issues in Music Education, Postgraduate Award in Educational Studies: Dialogic Teaching, Postgraduate Award in Educational Studies: Introduction to Child and Adolescent Psychotherapeutic Counselling, Postgraduate Certificate in Educational Studies: Teaching Advanced Mathematics, Postgraduate Award in Educational Studies: Understanding Shakespeare through Performance, MPhil in Egyptology, MPhil in Environmental Policy, MPhil in Finance and Economics, MPhil in Health, Medicine and Society, MPhil in Historical Studies, MSt in History, MPhil in History and Philosophy of Science and Medicine, MPhil in Human Evolutionary Studies, Postgraduate Diploma in International Law, MSt in International Relations, MPhil in International Relations and Politics, MPhil in Land Economy, MPhil in Land Economy Research, MPhil in Latin American Studies, Master of Law (LLM), MLitt in Law, Postgraduate Diploma in Legal Studies, MPhil in Medieval History, MPhil in Modern British History, MPhil in Modern European History, MPhil in Modern South Asian Studies, MPhil in Multi-disciplinary Gender Studies, MPhil in Planning, Growth and Regeneration, MPhil in Political Thought and Intellectual History, MPhil in Public Policy, MSt in Real Estate, MPhil in Real Estate Finance, MPhil in Social Anthropology, MRes in Social Anthropology, MPhil in Sociology (Political and Economic Sociology), MPhil in Sociology (The Sociology of Marginality and Exclusion), MPhil in Sociology (The Sociology of Media and Culture), MPhil in Sociology (The Sociology of Reproduction), MPhil in World History

School of the Physical Sciences; www.physsci.cam.ac.uk

MASt in Applied Mathematics, MPhil in Applied Mathematics and Theoretical Physics, MPhil in Astronomy, MASt in Astrophysics, MPhil in Chemistry, MPhil in Computational Biology, MPhil in Conservation Leadership, MPhil in Earth Sciences, MPhil in Geographical Research, MPhil in Geography, MASt in Materials Science, MPhil in Materials Science and Metallurgy, MASt in Mathematical Statistics, MPhil in Micro and Nanotechnology Enterprise, MASt in Physics, MPhil in Physics, MPhil in Polar Studies (Scott Polar Research Institute), MASt in Pure Mathematics, MPhil in Pure Mathematics and Mathematical Statistics, MPhil in Scientific Computing

CANTERBURY CHRIST CHURCH UNIVERSITY
www.canterbury.ac.uk

Faculty of Arts and Humanities; www.canterbury.ac.uk/arts-and-humanities

School of Humanities; www.canterbury.ac.uk/arts-and-humanities/school-of-humanities

American Studies BA, American Studies with Foundation Year BA, Archaeology BA, Archaeology with Foundation Year BA, Creative and Professional Writing BA, Creative and Professional Writing with Foundation Year BA, English Literature BA, English Literature with Foundation Year BA, History BA, History with Foundation Year BA, Medieval and Early Modern Studies BA, Medieval and Early Modern Studies with Foundation Year BA, Religion, Philosophy and Ethics BA, Religion, Philosophy and Ethics with Foundation Year BA, Theology BA, Theology with Foundation Year BA.

Postgraduate courses: American Studies by Research MA, Creative Writing MA, English Literature by Research MA, English Literature MA/MPhil/PhD, History by Research MA, History MPhil/PhD, Medieval and Early Modern Studies MA, Modern History MA, Theology and Religious Studies by Research MA, Theology and Religious Studies MPhil/PhD

School of Language Studies and Applied Linguistics; www.canterbury.ac.uk/arts-and-humanities/language-studies-and-applied-linguistics

English Language with Foundation Year BA, English Language BA

Postgraduate courses: Applied Linguistics MPhil/PhD, Teaching English to Speakers of Other Languages (TESOL) MA

School of Music and Performing Arts; www.canterbury.ac.uk/arts-and-humanities/music-and-performing-arts

Dance Education BA, Dance BA, Drama BA, Music Production BA, Music Production with Foundation Year BA, Music BA, Music with Foundation Year BA, Music: Commercial Music BA, Music: Commercial Music with Foundation Year BA, Music: Creative Music Technology BA, Music: Creative Music Technology with Foundation Year BA, Musical Theatre BA, Performing Arts BA, Performing Arts with Foundation Year BA, Theatre Technology and Production BA

Postgraduate courses: Arts and Cultural Management MA, Master of Music, Music MPhil/PhD

School of Media, Art and Design; www.canterbury.ac.uk/arts-and-humanities/media-art-and-design

Animation Production BA, Digital Media BA, Film Production BA, Film, Radio and Television BA, Games Design BA, Graphic Design BA, Illustration BA, Media and Communications BA, Multimedia Journalism BA, Photography BA, Public Relations and Media BA

Postgraduate course: Media, Art and Design by Research MA, Media and Communications MA, Public Relations MA/PGDip/PGCert

Faculty of Education; www.canterbury.ac.uk/education/faculty-of-education

Arts in Education BA, Childhood Studies BA, Counselling, Coaching and Mentoring BA, Early Childhood Education and Care BA(Hons), Early Childhood Studies BA, Education Studies BA, Human Development (Mind, Body, Spirit) BSc, Physical Education and Physical Activity BA, Physical Education and Sport & Exercise Science BA, Primary Education BA, Spanish with Secondary Education BA, Special Educational Needs and Inclusion Studies BA

Postgraduate courses: Career Management MA, Early Childhood Education with Early Years Teacher Status PGCE, Early Childhood Education MA, Education (Academic Practice) MA, Education and Training ProfGCE/Dip/Cert/Award, Education Doctorate, Education MA, Global and International Education MA, INSPIRE PGCE, Myth, Cosmology and the Sacred MA, National Award for SEN Co-ordination Postgraduate Certificate, PGCE 7-14 Years, PGCE Art and Design (Secondary), PGCE Computing (Secondary), PGCE English (Secondary), PGCE Further Education, PGCE Geography (Secondary), PGCE History (Secondary), PGCE Mathematics (Secondary), PGCE Modern Foreign Languages (Secondary), PGCE Music (Secondary), PGCE Physical Education (Secondary), PGCE Primary – Full-time, PGCE Primary Flexible Route, PGCE Primary with Mathematics Specialism, PGCE Religious Education (Secondary), PGCE Sciences (Secondary), PGCE Secondary, PGCE Teacher Enquiry (PGCE Top-up), Research in Guidance and Support MA, SEN Leadership MA, Special Needs and Inclusion MA, Specialist Assessment for a Specific Learning Difficulty: Dyslexia PG Cert, Transformational Leadership (Teach First) MA, Teaching English Diploma, Teaching Mathematics: Functional Skills/Numeracy, Diploma

Faculty of Health and Wellbeing; www.canterbury.ac.uk/health-and-wellbeing

School of Allied Health Professions; www.canterbury.ac.uk/health-and-wellbeing/allied-health-professions-public-health/allied-health-professions

BSc(Hons) Diagnostic Radiography, BSc(Hons) Operating Department Practice, BSc(Hons) Ophthalmic Dispensing, BSc(Hons) Paramedic Science, BSc(Hons) Physiotherapy, BSc(Hons) Public Health and Health Promotion, BSc(Hons) Speech and Language Therapy

Postgraduate courses: MSc Clinical Reporting, MSc Health and Wellbeing, MSc Medical Imaging, MSc Public Health

School of Nursing, Midwifery and Social Work; www.canterbury.ac.uk/health-and-wellbeing/nursing-midwifery-social-work/nursing-midwifery-and-social-work

BSc(Hons) Adult Nursing, BSc(Hons) Applied Practice (Health and Social Care), BSc(Hons) Child Nursing, BSc(Hons) Mental Health Nursing,

BSc(Hons) Midwifery, BA(Hons) Social Work, Foundation Degree in Health and Care (Nursing Associate)

Postgraduate courses: MA Social Work, MSc Nursing: Adult and Mental Health

Institute of Medical Sciences; www.canterbury.ac.uk/health-and-wellbeing/institute-of-medical-sciences/the-institute-of-medical-sciences

Postgraduate courses: MSc Physician Associate Studies, MCh in Surgery – Otorhinolaryngology, MCh in Surgery – Orthopaedics and Regenerative Medicine, MCh in Surgery – Urology, MCh in Surgery – Ophthalmology

Faculty of Social and Applied Sciences; www.canterbury.ac.uk/social-and-applied-sciences

The Business School; www.canterbury.ac.uk/social-and-applied-sciences/christ-church-business-school/christ-church-business-school

Accounting and Finance BSc, Accounting BSc, Advertising BSc, Business Management BSc, Business Studies BSc, Finance BSc, Human Resource Management BSc, International Business Management BSc, Logistics Management BSc, Management (Professional Practice) BSc, Marketing BSc, MBA Collaborative Leadership (Senior Leaders)

Postgraduate courses: Collaborative Transformation PGCert, Education Leadership and Management MBA, Leadership and Management in Healthcare MBA, Human Resource Management CIPD Advanced Diploma, Human Resource Management MA, International Business MSc, Management Studies MA/PgDip/PgCert, Master of Business Administration (MBA) MBA

School of Human and Life Sciences; www.canterbury.ac.uk/social-and-applied-sciences/human-and-life-sciences/human-and-life-sciences

Animal Science BSc, Biochemistry and Biological Chemistry BSc, Biology BSc, Biomolecular Science BSc, Chemistry for Drug Discovery BSc, Ecology, BSc, Environmental Science BSc, Events Management BSc, Geography BA, Geography BSc, Hospitality Management BSc, Human Biology BSc, Plant Science BSc, Sport and Exercise Psychology BSc, Sport and Exercise Science BSc, Sport Coaching Science BSc, Tourism Management BSc, Tourism Studies BA/BSc

Postgraduate courses: Applied Ecology and Environmental Management MSc, Applied Exercise and Health Science MSc, Biosciences by Research MSc, Cartography and Infographics by Research MSc, Ecology by Research MSc, Environmental Geography by Research MSc, Exercise and Health Science MSc, Geospatial Analysis by Research MSc, Human Geography by Research MSc, Sport and Exercise Sciences by Research MSc, Tourism and Event Management MSc, Tourism, Events and Leisure by Research MSc, Urban and Regional Studies by Research MSc

School of Law, Criminal Justice and Policing; www.canterbury.ac.uk/social-and-applied-sciences/law-criminal-justice-and-policing/school-of-law-criminal-justice-and-policing

Applied Criminology BSc, Applied Criminology with Forensic Investigation BSc, Forensic Investigation BSc, Law LLB, Law (with another subject) LLB, Law with Business LLB, Law with Finance LLB, Policing (Criminal Investigation) BSc, Policing (Criminal Psychology) BSc, Policing (Critical Incidents) BSc, Policing (Cybersecurity) BSc, Policing (Global Perspectives) BSc, Policing (In Service) BSc, Policing (Terrorism and Political Violence) BSc, Policing (Youth Justice) BSc, Policing BSc, Professional Policing BSc

Postgraduate courses: Applied Policing Practice MSc, Criminal Justice by Research MSc, Criminology by Research MSc, Digital Forensics and Cybersecurity by Research MSc, Forensic Investigation by Research MSc, Law by Research MSc, Law, Criminal Justice and Computing MSc by Research, Policing by Research MSc, Policing MSc

School of Psychology, Politics and Sociology; www.canterbury.ac.uk/social-and-applied-sciences/psychology-politics-and-sociology/psychology-politics-and-sociology

International Relations BSc, Politics BSc, Psychology (Sport and Exercise) BSc, Psychology BSc, Sociology and Social Policy BSc, Sociology BA/BSc

Postgraduate courses: Clinical Psychology DClinPsy/MSc, Cognitive Behavioural Therapy (High Intensity) PGDip, Cognitive Behavioural Therapy MSc, Forensic and Investigative Psychology MSc/PGCert, International Relations (Security Studies) MSc, Politics (Radical Political Theory) MSc, Politics and International Relations by Research MSc, Professional Practice: Psychological Perspectives PhD, Psychology

(Conversion Course) MSc, Psychology by Research MSc, Sociology by Research MSc, Sociology: Global Inequalities and Comparative Social Policy MSc

School of Engineering, Technology and Design; www.canterbury.ac.uk/social-and-applied-sciences/engineering-technology-and-design/school-of-engineering-technology-and-design

Biomedical Engineering MEng/BEng, Business Information Systems BSc, Chemical Engineering MEng/

BEng, Computer Forensics and Security BSc, Computer Science BSc, Computing BSc, Mechanical Engineering (Advanced Manufacture) MEng/BEng, Mechanical Engineering (Building Services) MEng/BEng, Mechanical Engineering (Systems) MEng/BEng, Mechanical Engineering BEng, Product Design Engineering MEng/BEng, Software Engineering BEng

Postgraduate courses: Computing by Research MSc

CARDIFF UNIVERSITY
www.cardiff.ac.uk

College of Arts, Humanities and Social Sciences; www.cardiff.ac.uk/colleges/arts-humanities-social-sciences

Business School; www.cardiff.ac.uk/business-school

Accounting and Finance

Accounting (BSc), Accounting and Finance (BSc)

Postgraduate courses: MSc in Accounting and Finance, MSc in Finance

Business Management

Business Management (BSc), Business Management (Human Resources) (BSc), Business Management (International Management) (BSc), Business Management (Logistics and Operations) (BSc), Business Management (Marketing) (BSc), Business Management with a European Language (French) (BSc), Business Management with a European Language (German) (BSc), Business Management with a European Language (Spanish) (BSc), Business Management with Welsh (BSc), Economics and Management Studies (BScEcon)

Postgraduate courses: MBA, MSc Business Strategy and Entrepreneurship, MSc Human Resource Management, MSc International Human Resource Management, MSc International Management, MSc Logistics and Operations Management, MSc Maritime Policy and Shipping Management, MSc in Public Leadership (Part-time), MSc Strategic Marketing, MSc Sustainable Supply Chain Management

Economics

Banking and Finance (BScEcon), Banking and Finance with a European Language (French) (BScEcon), Banking and Finance with a European Language (German) (BScEcon), Banking and Finance with a European Language (Spanish) (BScEcon), Business Economics (BScEcon), Business Economics with a European Language (French) (BScEcon), Business Economics with a European Language (German) (BScEcon), Business Economics with a European Language (Spanish) (BScEcon), Economics (BScEcon), Economics and Finance (BScEcon), Economics and Management Studies (BScEcon), Economics with a European Language (French) (BSc), Economics with a European Language (German) (BSc), Economics with a European Language (Spanish) (BSc)

Postgraduate courses: MSc in Financial Economics, MSc in International Economics, Banking and Finance

School of English, Communication and Philosophy; www.cardiff.ac.uk/english-communication-philosophy

English Language

BA English Language, BA English Language and Literature, BA English Language and Linguistics, BA English Language and French, BA English Language and German, BA English Language and Italian, BA English Language and Philosophy, BA English Language and Spanish, BA Welsh and English Language

English Literature

BA English language and Literature, BA English Literature, BA English Literature and Creative Writing, BA English Literature and Ancient History, BA English Literature and Archaeology, BA English Literature and History, BA English Literature and Philosophy, BA French and English Literature, BA German and English Literature, BA Italian and English Literature, BA Journalism, Media and English Language, BA Music and English Literature, BA

Religious Studies and English Literature, BA Spanish and English Literature, BA Welsh and English Literature

Philosophy

BA English Language and Philosophy, BA English Literature and Philosophy, BA French and Philosophy, BA Italian and Philosophy, BA Music and Philosophy, BA Philosophy, BA Philosophy and Ancient History, BA Philosophy and Archaeology, BA Philosophy and Economics, BA Philosophy and History, BA Philosophy and Politics, BA Religious Studies and Philosophy, BA Spanish and Philosophy, BA Welsh and Philosophy

Postgraduate courses

MA Applied Linguistics, MA Creative Writing, MA English Literature, MA Forensic Linguistics, MA Language and Linguistics, MA Language Communication Research, MA Philosophy

School of Geography and Planning; www.cardiff.ac.uk/geography-planning

Geography (Human) (BSc), Geography (Human) and Planning (BSc), Urban Planning and Development (BSc)

Postgraduate courses: City Futures (MSc), Eco-Cities (MSc), Environment and Development (MSc), Food Politics and Sustainability (MSc), International Planning and Development (MSc), International Planning and Urban Design (MSc), Planning Practice (PgCert), Social Science Research Methods (Environmental Planning) (MSc/PgDip), Spatial Planning and Development (MSc), Sustainability, Planning and Environmental Policy (MSc), Transport and Planning (MSc), Urban and Regional Development (MSc), Urban Design (MA)

School of History, Archaeology and Religion; www.cardiff.ac.uk/history-archaeology-religion

Ancient History

BA Ancient History, BA Ancient History and French, BA Ancient History and German, BA Ancient History and History, BA Ancient History and Italian, BA Ancient History and Spanish, BA Ancient and Medieval History, BA Archaeology and Ancient History, BA English Literature and Ancient History, BA Philosophy and Ancient History, BA Religious Studies and Ancient History

Archaeology and Conservation

BA Archaeology, BSc Archaeology, BA Archaeology and Ancient History, BA Archaeology and French, BA Archaeology and German, BA Archaeology and History, BA Archaeology and Italian, BA

Archaeology and Medieval History, BSc Conservation of Objects in Museums and Archaeology, BA English Literature and Archaeology, BA Philosophy and Archaeology, BA Religious Studies and Archaeology

Postgraduate courses: MA Archaeology, MSc Archaeological Science, MSc Care of Collections, MSc Conservation Practice, MSc Professional Conservation

History

BA Ancient History and History, BA Ancient and Medieval History, BA Archaeology and History, BA Archaeology and Medieval History, BA English Literature and History, BA History, BA History and Economics, BA History and French, BA History and German, BA History and Italian, BA History and Spanish, BA History with Welsh History, BA Music and History, BA Philosophy and History, BA Politics and Modern History, BA Religious Studies and History, BScEcon Sociology and History, BA History with Welsh History

Religious Studies and Theology

BA Religion and Theology, BA Religious Studies and Ancient History, BA Religious Studies and Archaeology, BA Religious Studies and English Literature, BA Religious Studies and German, BA Religious Studies and History, BA Religious Studies and Italian, BA Religious Studies and Music, BA Religious Studies and Philosophy, BA Religious Studies and Politics, BA Religious Studies and Spanish, BA Welsh and Religious Studies

Postgraduate courses: MA/PgDip Islam in Contemporary Britain, MTh/PgDip Theology, PgCert Theology, MTh/PgDip/PgCert Chaplaincy Studies, MTh in Chaplaincy Studies: Military Route

Journalism, Media and Culture; www.cardiff.ac.uk/journalism-media-cultural-studies

Journalism and Communications (BA), Media and Communications (BA), Media, Journalism and Culture (BA), Journalism, Communications and Politics (BA), Journalism, Media and English Literature (BA), Journalism, Media and Sociology (BA), Wlesh and Journalism (BA)

Postgraduate courses: Broadcast Journalism (MA), Computational and Data Journalism (MSc), Cultural and Creative Industries (MA), Digital Documentaries (MA), Digital Media and Society (MA), International Journalism (MA), International Public Relations and Global Communications Management (MA), Journalism, Media and Communications (MA), Magazine

Journalism (MA), Media Management (MBA), News Journalism (MA), Political Communication (MA), Science Communication (MSc)

School of Law and Politics; www.cardiff.ac.uk/law-politics

Law

LLB Law, LLB Law and Criminology, LLB Law and French, LLB Law and Politics, LLB Law and Sociology, LLB Law and Welsh

Postgraduate courses: LLM Canon Law, LLM European Legal Studies, LLM Governance and Devolution, LLM Human Rights Law, LLM Intellectual Property Law, LLM International Commercial Law, LLM Legal Aspects of Medical Practice, LLM Legal and Political Aspects of International Affairs, LLM Shipping Law, LLM Social Care Law, LLM Law, Graduate Diploma in Law

Politics and International Relations

French and Politics (BA), German and Politics (BA), International Relations (Bsc Econ), International Relations and Politics (BSc Econ), International Relations and Politics (with a Language) (BSc Econ), Italian and Politics (BA), Journalism, Communications and Politics (BA), Politics and Economics (BSc Econ), Politics and Modern History (BSc Econ), Politics and Philosophy (BA), Politics and Sociology (BSc Econ), Politics and Spanish (BA), Religious Studies and Politics (BA), Politics and Welsh (BA)

Postgraduate courses: Comparative Politics, Policy and Governance (PhD/MPhil), European Politics & Area Studies (PhD/MPhil), International Relations & Politics (PhD/MPhil), Political Theory (PhD/MPhil), Wales (PhD/MPhil)

School of Modern Languages; www.cardiff.ac.uk/modern-languages

Chinese

Chinese (BA), Modern Chinese (BA), Modern Languages and Translation (BA)

French

French (BA), French and Economics (BA), French and English Literature (BA), French and German (BA), French and Italian (BA), French and Japanese (BA), French and Music (BA), French and Philosophy (BA), French and Politics (BA), French and Portuguese (BA), French and Spanish (BA), Welsh and French (BA), Modern Languages and Translation (BA)

German

German (BA), German and Economics (BA), German and English Literature (BA), German and Italian (BA), German and Japanese (BA), German and Music (BA), German and Politics (BA), German and

Portuguese (BA), German and Spanish (BA), Modern Languages and Translation (BA)

Italian

Italian (BA), Italian and Economics (BA), Italian and English Literature (BA), Italian and Japanese (BA), Italian and Music (BA), Italian and Philosophy (BA), Italian and Politics (BA), Italian and Portuguese (BA), Italian and Spanish (BA), Modern Languages and Translation (BA)

Japanese

Business Studies and Japanese (BSc), French and Japanese (BA), German and Japanese (BA), International Relations and Politics (with a Language) (BSc Econ), Italian and Japanese (BA), Spanish and Japanese (BA), Modern Languages and Translation (BA)

Portuguese

French and Portuguese (BA), German and Portuguese (BA), Italian and Portuguese (BA), Portuguese and Spanish (BA), Modern Languages and Translation (BA)

Spanish

Spanish (BA), Spanish and Economics (BA), Spanish and English Literature (BA), Spanish and Japanese (BA), Spanish and Philosophy (BA), Welsh and Spanish (BA), Modern Languages and Translation (BA)

Translation

Translation (BA), Modern Languages and Translation (BA).

Postgraduate course

Global Cultures (MA), Translation Studies (MA)

School of Music; www.cardiff.ac.uk/music

BMus Music

Postgraduate course: MA in Music

School of Social Sciences; www.cardiff.ac.uk/social-sciences

Criminology

Criminology (BSc), Criminology and Sociology (BSc), Criminology and Social Policy (BSc), Law and Criminology (LLB)

Education

Education (BSc), Sociology and Education (BSc), Welsh and Education (BA)

Social policy

Criminology and Social Policy (BSc), Sociology and Social Policy (BSc)

Sociology

Criminology and Social Policy (BSc), Criminology and Sociology (BSc), Human and Social Sciences (BSc), Journalism Media and Sociology (BA), Law and Criminology (LLB), Law and Sociology (LLB), Politics and Sociology (BSc Econ), Social Analytics (BSc), Social Science (BSc), Sociology (BSc), Sociology and Education (BSc), Sociology and History (BSc Econ), Sociology and Social Policy (BSc)

Social Science
Social Science (BSc)

Human and Social Sciences
Human and Social Sciences (BSc)

Social Analytics
Social Analytics (BSc)

Postgraduate courses
MSc Childhood and Youth, MSc Crime, Safety and Justice, MSc Education, Policy and Society, PGCE Post-Compulsory Education and Training (PCET), MSc Science Communication, MSc Social and Public Policy, MSc Social Science, MSc Social Science Research Methods (SSRM), MA Social Work

School of Welsh; www.cardiff.ac.uk/welsh
BA Welsh, BA Welsh and the Professional Workplace
Postgraduate course: MA Welsh and Celtic Studies

College of Biomedical and Life Sciences; www.cardiff.ac.uk/colleges/biomedical-life-sciences

School of Biosciences; www.cardiff.ac.uk/biosciences
BSc Biological Sciences, BSc Biological Sciences (Zoology), BSc Biomedical Sciences, BSc Biochemistry, BSc Neuroscience, MBiol: Master's in Biological Sciences, MBiochem: Master's in Biochemistry, MBiomed: Master's in Biomedical Sciences, MNeuro: Master's in Neuroscience
Postgraduate course: Global Ecology and Conservation (MSc), Tissue Engineering (MSc/PgDip), MRes

School of Dentistry; www.cardiff.ac.uk/dentistry
Dental Hygiene (DipHE), Dental Surgery (BDS), Dental Therapy and Hygiene (BSc)
Postgraduate courses: Clinical Dentistry (MClinDent), Implantology (MSc/PgDip), Orthodontics (MScD), Oral Biology (MSc), Tissue Engineering (MSc)

School of Healthcare Sciences; www.cardiff.ac.uk/healthcare-sciences
Adult Nursing (BN), Children's Nursing (BN), Diagnostic Radiography and Imaging (BSc), Mental Health Nursing (BN), Midwifery (BMid), Occupational Therapy (BSc), Operating Department Practice (BSc), Physiotherapy (BSc), Radiotherapy and Oncology (BSc)
Postgraduate courses: Advanced Practice MSc/PgCert, Community Health Studies (SPQ) MSc/PgDip, Clinical Photography PgCert, Managing Care in Perioperative and Anaesthesia Practice MSc/PgDip/PgCert, Occupational Therapy (post-registration) MSc/PgDip, Physiotherapy MSc/PgDip, Radiographic Reporting PgDip/PgCert, Radiography MSc/PgDip, Specialist Community Public Health Nursing MSc/PgDip, Sport & Exercise Physiotherapy MSc/PgDip

School of Medicine; www.cardiff.ac.uk/medicine
Medical Pharmacology (BSc), Medicine (MBBCh)
Postgraduate courses: Advanced Surgical Practice MSc, Ageing Health and Disease MSc, Bioinformatics MSc, Bioinformatics and Genetic Epidemiology MSc, Clinical Dermatology MSc, Clinical Leadership and Leading Change in Cardiology MSc/PGDip, Critical Care MSc, Diabetes MSc/PgDip, Genetic and Genomic Counselling MSc, Medical Education MSc/PgDip/PgCert, Medical Toxicology MSc/PgDip/PgCert, Neonatal Medicine MSc/PgDip, Occupational Health (Policy and Practice) MSc, Pain Management MSc, Pain Management (Primary and Community Care) MSc/PgDip/PgCert, Palliative Medicine for Health Care Professionals MSc, Practical Dermatology MSc/PgDip, Psychiatry MSc, Public Health MPH, Therapeutics MSc/PgDip/PgCert, Wound Healing and Tissue Repair MSc

School of Optometry and Vision Sciences; www.cardiff.ac.uk/optometry-vision-sciences
BSc in Optometry
Postgraduate courses: MSc/Dip/PgCert Clinical Optometry, PGCert Eye Care Governance, PGCert Glaucoma, PGCert Therapeutic Prescribing for Optometrists

School of Pharmacy and Pharmaceutical Sciences; www.cardiff.ac.uk/pharmacy-pharmaceutical-sciences
Master of Pharmacy (MPharm)
Postgraduate courses: Drug Delivery and Microbiology (PhD/MPhil), Medicinal Chemistry (PhD/MPhil), Pharmacology and Physiology (PhD/MPhil), Pharmacy (PhD/MPhil), Pharmacy Practice and Clinical Pharmacy (PhD/MPhil)

School of Psychology; www.cardiff.ac.uk/psychology

Psychology BSc

Postgraduate courses: MSc Neuroimaging: Methods and Applications, MSc Children's Psychological Disorders, PgDip/PgCert Cognitive and Behavioural Therapies, MSc Social Science Research

College of Physical Sciences and Engineering; www.cardiff.ac.uk/colleges/physical-sciences-engineering

Welsh School of Architecture; www.cardiff.ac.uk/architecture

BSc Architectural Studies, MArch Master of Architecture

Postgraduate courses: PgDip in Architecture: Professional Practice (Part 3), MA Architectural Design, MA Urban Design, Master of Design Administration (MDA), MSc Advanced Building Performance Evaluation, MSc Computational Methods in Architecture, MSc in Environmental Design of Buildings, MSc Sustainable Building Conservation, MSc in Sustainable Mega Buildings

School of Chemistry; www.cardiff.ac.uk/chemistry

Chemistry (BSc), Chemistry (MChem)

MSc Advanced Chemistry, MSc Biological Chemistry, MSc Catalysis, MSc Medicinal Chemistry

School of Computer Science and Informatics; www.cardiff.ac.uk/computer-science

Applied Software Engineering (BSc), Computer Science (BSc)

Postgraduate courses: MSc Advanced Computer Science, MSc Artificial Intelligence, MSc Computing, MSc Computing and IT Management, MSc Cybersecurity, MSc Computational and Data Journalism, MSc Data Science and Analytics, MSc Software Engineering

School of Earth and Ocean Sciences; www.cardiff.ac.uk/earth-ocean-sciences

Environmental Geography (BSc), Environmental Geography (MESci), Exploration and Resource Geology (BSc), Exploration and Resource Geology (MESci), Environmental Geoscience (BSc), Environmental Geoscience (MESci), Geology (BSc), Geology (MESci), Marine Geography (BSc), Marine Geography (MESci)

Postgraduate courses: MSc Applied Environmental Geology

School of Engineering; www.cardiff.ac.uk/engineering

Architectural Engineering (BEng/MEng), Civil Engineering (BEng/MEng), Civil and Environmental Engineering (BEng/MEng), Electrical and Electronic Engineering (BEng/MEng), Integrated Engineering (BEng/MEng), Mechanical Engineering (BEng/MEng), Medical Engineering (BEng/MEng)

Postgraduate courses: MSc in Advanced Mechanical Engineering, MSc in Civil and Geoenvironmental Engineering, MSc in Civil and Water Engineering, MSc in Civil Engineering, MSc in Communication Technology and Entrepreneurship, MSc Compound Semiconductor Electronics, MSc in Electrical Energy Systems, MSc in Manufacturing Engineering, Innovation and Management, MSc in Structural Engineering, MSc in Sustainable Energy and Environment, MSc in Wireless and Microwave Communication Engineering

School of Mathematics; www.cardiff.ac.uk/mathematics

Financial Mathematics (BSc), Mathematics (BSc), Mathematics (MMath), Mathematics, Operational Research and Statistics (BSc), Mathematics and Music (BA)

Postgraduate courses: Data Science and Analytics (MSc), Mathematics (MSc), Operational Research and Applied Statistics (MSc), Operational Research, Applied Statistics and Financial Risk (MSc)

School of Physics and Astronomy; www.astro.cardiff.ac.uk

BSc Astrophysics, MPhys Astrophysics, BSc Physics, MPhys Physics, BSc Physics with Astronomy, MPhys Physics with Astronomy, Physics with Medical Physics (BSc)

Postgraduate courses: MSc Astrophysics, MSc Compound Semiconductor Physics, MSc Data Intensive Astrophysics, MSc Data Intensive Physics, MSc Physics

CARDIFF METROPOLITAN UNIVERSITY
www.cardiffmet.ac.uk

School of Art & Design;
www.cardiffmet.ac.uk/artanddesign

Animation BA(Hons), Architectural Design & Technology BSc(Hons), Artist Designer: Maker BA(Hons), Ceramics BA(Hons), Fashion Design BA(Hons), Fine Art BA(Hons), Graphic Communication BA(Hons), Illustration BA(Hons), Interior Design BA(Hons), Photography BA(Hons), Product Design BA/Bsc(Hons), Textiles BA(Hons)

Postgraduate courses: Ceramics & Maker MA/PgD/PgC, Creative Enterprise and Innovation MA/PgD/PgC, Fashion Design MA/PgD/PgC, Fine Art MFA, Global Design MDes/PgD/PgC, Illustration & Animation MA/PgD/PgC, MRes: Master of Research in Art and Design MRes/PgC, Product Design MSc/PgD/PgC

School of Education and Social Policy;
www.cardiffmet.ac.uk/education

Astudiaethau Addysg Gynradd (Dwyieithog) BA (Anrh), Astudiaethau Plentyndod Cynnar (gydag Statws Ymarferydd y Blynyddoedd Cynnar SYBC) (Dwyieithog) BA (Anrh), Creative Writing BA (Joint Hons), Creative Writing and Media BA(Hons), Drama BA (Joint Hons), Drama and Creative Writing BA(Hons), Drama and Media BA(Hons), Early Childhood Studies with Early Years Practitioner Status, BA(Hons), Education Studies & Drama BA(Hons), Education Studies & English BA(Hons), Education Studies and Social Policy BA(Hons), Education, Psychology and Special Educational Needs BA(Hons), English BA (Joint Hons), English & Creative Writing BA(Hons), English & Drama BA(Hons), English & Media BA(Hons), Health & Social Care BSc(Hons), Housing Studies BSc(Hons), Media BA (Joint Hons), Primary Education Studies BA(Hons), Primary Education Studies (with Qualified Teacher Status) BA(Hons), Social Work BSc(Hons), Teaching & Learning Studies BA(Hons), Youth & Community Work BA(Hons)

Postgraduate courses: Creative Writing MA/PgD/PgC, Cynradd – TAR, Education (with pathways) MA/PgD/PgC, English Literature MA/PgD/PgC, English Literature & Creative Writing MA/PgD/PgC, Post Compulsory Education & Training PGCE/PCE, Primary PGCE, Secondary PGCE, Specialist Journalism MA/PgD/PgC, TESOL MA, Uwchradd – TAR, Youth & Community Work PgD/Education: Youth & Community Work – MA

School of Sport and Health Sciences;
www.cardiffmet.ac.uk/sportandhealthsciences

Astudiaethau Chwaraeon ac Addysg Gorfforol (dwyieithog) BSc (Anrh), Biomedical Science BSc(Hons), Biomedical Sciences with Health, Exercise & Nutrition BSc(Hons), Dental Technology BSc(Hons), Environmental Health BSc(Hons), Food Science & Technology BSc(Hons), Foundation leading to BA/BSc Social Sciences, Foundation leading to BSc Health Sciences, Gweithgarwch Corfforol, Iechyd a Lles Dwyieithog BSc (Anrh), Healthcare Science BSc(Hons), Human Nutrition & Dietetics BSc(Hons), Nutrition BSc(Hons), Physical Activity, Health and Well-being (bilingual) BSc(Hons), Podiatry BSc(Hons), Psychology BSc(Hons), Speech and Language Therapy BSc(Hons)Sport & Exercise Science – BSc(Hons), Sport & Exercise Science (Intercalated) BSc(Hons), Sport and Physical Education Studies (bilingual) BSc(Hons), Sport Coaching BSc(Hons), Sport Conditioning, Rehabilitation & Massage BSc(Hons), Sport Development BSc(Hons), Sport Management BSc(Hons), Sport Media BSc(Hons), Sport Performance Analysis BSc(Hons), Sport Studies BSc(Hons), Sport, Physical Education & Health BSc(Hons), Sport, Physical Education & Health (Dance) BSc(Hons)

Postgraduate courses: Advanced Practice (with specialist pathways) MSc/PgD/PgC, Applied Public Health MSc/PgD/PgC, Biomedical Science MSc/PgD/PgC, Dental Technology MSc/PgD/PgC, Dietetics MSc/PgD, Food Science & Technology MSc/PgD/PgC, Food Technology for Industry MSc/PgD/PgC, Forensic Psychology Doctorate (D. Foren. Psy.), Forensic Psychology MSc/PgD/PgC, Forensic Psychology (Practitioner Programme) PgD, Health Psychology MSc/PgD/PgC, Master of Research (Biomedical Sciences) MRes/PgC, Master of Research (Health) MRes/PgC, Master of Research (Psychology) MRes/PgC, Nutrition for Sport and Exercise MSc/PgD/PgC, Occupational Safety, Health & Wellbeing MSc/PgD/PgC, Professional Practice (Sport Performance Analysis) MSc/PgD, Psychology of Applied Behaviour Change MSc/PgD/PgC, Sociology and Ethics of Sport MA/PgD/PgC, Sport & Exercise

Medicine MSc/PgD/PgC, Sport & Exercise Science MSc/PgD/PgC, Sport Broadcast MSc/PgD/PgC, Sport Coaching and Pedagogy MSc/PgD/PgC, Sport Management & Leadership MSc/PgD/PgC, Sport Performance Analysis MSc/PgD/PgC, Sport Psychology MSc/PgD/PgC, Sport Rehabilitation MSc/PgD/PgC, Strength & Conditioning MSc/PgD/PgC, Taught Doctorate in Sport Coaching DSC

School of Management;
www.cardiffmet.ac.uk/management

Accounting BA(Hons), Accounting & Economics BA(Hons), Accounting & Finance BA(Hons), Advertising and Marketing Management BA(Hons), Applied Entrepreneurship and Innovation Management BA(Hons), Aviation Management BA(Hons), Banking & Finance BSc(Hons), Brand and Marketing Management BA(Hons), Business & Management BA(Hons), Business & Management (Entrepreneurship) BA(Hons), Business & Management (Finance) BA(Hons), Business & Management (Human Resource Management) BA(Hons), Business & Management (International Trade) BA(Hons), Business & Management (Law) BA(Hons), Business & Management (Marketing) BA(Hons), Business & Management (Sustainability) BA(Hons), Business Economics BA(Hons), Digital Marketing Management BA(Hons), Economics BSc(Hons), Events Management BA(Hons), Fashion Buying and Brand Management BA(Hons), Fashion Marketing Management BA(Hons), Foundation Programme: Cardiff School of Management, Global Business Management (Top-Up) BA(Hons), International Accounting and Finance (Top-Up) BSc(Hons), International Banking and Finance (Top-Up) BSc(Hons), International Business Management BA(Hons), International Economics & Finance BSc/BScEcon(Hons), International Hospitality & Events Management BA(Hons), International Hospitality & Tourism Management BA(Hons), International Hospitality Management BA(Hons), International Tourism & Events Management BA(Hons), International Tourism Management BA(Hons), LLB Law(Hons), Marketing Management BA(Hons), PR and Marketing Management BA(Hons), Sales and Marketing Management BA(Hons)

Postgraduate courses: Accounting & Finance MSc, Banking & Finance MSc, CIM Certificate/Diploma in Professional Marketing, Digital Marketing Management MSc/PgD/PgC, Economics & Finance MSc, Entrepreneurship and Innovation Management MSc/PgD/PgC, Events Project Management MSc/PgD/PgC, Executive MBA, Fashion Marketing Management MSc/PgD/PgC, Financial Management MSc/PgD/PgC, Human Resource Management MSc/PgD/PgC, International Business Management MSc/PgD/PgC, International Hospitality and Tourism Management MSc/PgD/PgC, International Supply Chain and Logistics Management MSc, LLM International Business Masters of Laws, Strategic Marketing MSc/PgD/PgC, MBA Advanced Entry, MBA Master of Business Administration (MBA), Masters of Research in Management (MRes Management), Doctor of Management (DMan) (Taught Doctorate Degree), Project Management MSc, Production Engineering Management MSc, Strategic Marketing MSc/PgD/PgC, 20Twenty Sustainable Leadership & Management PgC

UNIVERSITY OF CENTRAL LANCASHIRE
www.uclan.ac.uk

Lancashire School of Business and Enterprise; www.uclan.ac.uk/schools/lancashire-school-business-enterprise/index.php

BA(Hons): Accounting and finance, advertising and marketing communications, business administration, accounting and financial studies, international tourism management, management in tourism, human resource management, global business management, international hospitality management, marketing, international business, business and management, economics, management in hospitality, business and marketing, event management, digital marketing, management in events, business management

Postgraduate courses: digital marketing communications, management coaching skills, management studies, management, marketing management, international hospitality and event management, international festivals and event management, internship in international tourism, hospitality and event management, human resource management/development, international business and management, human resource management, leadership skills, business management, business administration, international festivals and tourism management, accounting, accounting and finance, international hospitality and tourism management, public management; BA(Hons), BSc(Econ), MA, MSc, Cert, PGCert, PGDip, GradDip, MBA, DBA

Lancashire Law School; www.uclan.ac.uk/schools/lancashire-law-school/index.php

criminology and sociology, law, senior status, law with international studies, law with criminology, law with business, criminology and criminal justice
Postgraduate courses: financial and commercial law, law and international security, law, legal practice, international business law

Centre for Excellence in Learning and Teaching; www.uclan.ac.uk/schools/celt/index.php

education and history, education studies, education and sociology, education and psychology, education and deaf studies
Postgraduate courses: education; BA(Hons), BSc(Hons), MEd, PGDip, EdD

Faculty of Clinical and Biomedical Sciences; www.uclan.ac.uk/faculties/clinical-biomedical-sciences.php

School of Dentistry; www.uclan.ac.uk/schools/dentistry/index.php

clinical dental technology, dental hygiene and dental therapy, BSc(Hons), dentistry, BDS, dental studies (dental care professionals), BSc(Hons);
Postgraduate courses: prosthodontics, commissioning and dental advising, clinical periodontology, dental education, endodontology, mentoring in dental practice, clinical implantology, oral surgery; BSc(Hons), BDS, MSc, PGCert, PGDip

School of Medicine; www.uclan.ac.uk/schools/medicine/index.php

Physician associate studies MPAS(Hons), medicine (MBBS), medical sciences BSc(Hons)
Postgraduate courses: sports medicine, physician associate studies, musculoskeletal management, clinical studies, medical sciences, clinical practice, management and education, rural medicine/urgent care, medical education, hospitalist medicine; BSc(Hons), MPAS, MBBS, MSc, PGDip

School of Pharmacy and Biomedical Sciences; www.uclan.ac.uk/schools/pharmacy-biomedical-sciences/index.php

pharmacy, pharmacology, physiology and pharmacology, biomedical science, healthcare science, biomedical science; Postgraduate courses in cancer biology and therapy, advanced pharmacy practice, industrial pharmaceutics; MPharm, BSc(Hons), MSc

Faculty of Culture and the Creative Industries; www.uclan.ac.uk/faculties/culture-creative-industries.php

School of Art, Design and Fashion; www.uclan.ac.uk/schools/art-design-fashion/index.php

art and design, fine art, architectural studies, illustration, textile design, fashion design, interior design, fashion promotion, creative advertising, graphic design, architectural technology
Postgraduate courses: ceramics, fashion with lifestyle promotion, building conservation and adaptation, design, architecture, surface pattern and textiles, graphic design, product design, fashion design, fashion and lifestyle brand studies, fine art, children's book illustration, interior design, antiques (distance learning); BA(Hons), BSc(Hons), MA, PGCert, PGDip, MSc

School of Journalism, Media and Performance; www.uclan.ac.uk/schools/journalism-media-performance/index.php

film, media and popular culture, photography, acting, television production, games design, media production, publishing, journalism, animation, continuing drama production, sports journalism, film production, music theatre, music production and performance, theatre and performance, screenwriting with film, television and radio, web design and development, international journalism, dancer performance and teaching
Postgraduate courses in scriptwriting, film production, television production, games design, music, photography, publishing, animation, broadcast journalism, journalism, music industry management and promotion, dance and somatic wellbeing; BA(Hons), BSc(Hons), MA, PGCert, PGDip

School of Humanities and the Social Sciences; www.uclan.ac.uk/schools/humanities-social-sciences/index.php

English language and linguistics, politics, philosophy and society, film, media and popular culture, politics, liberal arts, sociology, English literature and creative writing, English literature and history, philosophy, English with a modern language, English language and creative writing, education and deaf studies, English language and literature, religion, culture and society, public services, British Sign Language and deaf studies, history, history and politics, English literature, transatlantic studies

Postgraduate courses in British Sign Language/ English interpreting and translation, history, religion, culture and society; BA(Hons), MA, PGDip, MRes

School of Language and Global Studies; www.uclan.ac.uk/schools/language-global-studies/index.php

european studies, teaching English to speakers of other languages and modern languages, English for international corporate communication with a modern foreign language, modern languages (Arabic, French, German, Japanese, Spanish or Italian) for international business, Asia Pacific studies, English for international corporate communication, business management and Chinese, intercultural business communication, international business communication, international business communication with a modern foreign language, middle eastern studies, modern languages (Arabic, Chinese, French, German, Japanese, Korean, Russian, Spanish and Italian)

Postgraduate courses in Asia Pacific studies, interpreting and translation, intercultural business communication, teaching English to speakers of other languages (TESOL), teaching English to speakers of other languages (TESOL) with applied linguistics, North Korean studies; BA(Hons), MA

Faculty of Health and Wellbeing; www.uclan.ac.uk/faculties/health-wellbeing.php

School of Community Health and Midwifery; www.uclan.ac.uk/schools/community-health-midwifery/index.php

community health practice, neonatal practice, counselling and psychotherapy studies, midwifery (direct entry programme), specialist community public health nurse – health visiting or school nursing or sexual health adviser, health and social care, sexual health studies, community specialist practitioner, midwifery for registered nurses

Postgraduate courses: practice teacher, nursing in general practice, supervision of counselling and psychotherapy, safeguarding in an international context, applied public health, health and social

care education, community specialist practitioner, sexual health studies, sustainability, health and wellbeing, safeguarding in an international context, primary care mental health practice, applied public health, midwifery, psychosexual therapy, integrative psychotherapy, cognitive behavioural psychotherapy, transforming integrated health and social care, community health practice; BSc(Hons), FCert, FDSC, FDA, PGDip, Cert, MSc, PGCert, MA

School of Health Sciences; www.uclan.ac.uk/schools/health-sciences/index.php

occupational therapy, professional practice, paramedic practice, paramedic science, physiotherapy, enhanced paramedic practice, sports therapy, operating department practice

Postgraduate courses: clinical research, football science and rehabilitation, compassionate leadership, health informatics, enhanced clinical practice, injection therapy, health, healthcare practice, occupational therapy, physiotherapy; BSc(Hons), DipHE, MSc, PGDip, PGCert, Cert, DProf

School of Nursing; www.uclan.ac.uk/schools/nursing/index.php

nursing, child and adolescent mental health, nursing (children), nursing (adult), nursing (mental health), psychosocial mental health care

Postgraduate courses: nursing, child and adolescent mental health, personality disorder, nursing (adult or mental health), personality disorder (practice development), conflict and violence minimisation, philosophy and mental health, investigating serious incidents; BSc(Hons), MSc, PGCert, PGDip, MA

School of Social Work, Care and Community; www.uclan.ac.uk/schools/social-work-care-community/index.php

children, schools and families, community and social care: policy and practice, community leadership, social work

Postgraduate courses: professional practice and mental health law, professional development and practice, doctor of professional practice, community social care policy and practice, community leadership, advanced community justice, contemporary practice with children and young people, specialist practice with adults, specialist child care practice, leadership and management in social work and social care, mental health practice including approved mental health professional training, safeguarding children, social policy, equality and community leadership, social work, social pedagogy leadership; BA(Hons), FDA, MA, PGDip, PGCert, DProf

School of Sport and Wellbeing; www.uclan.ac.uk/schools/sport-wellbeing/index.php

sports coaching and development, football coaching and development, sport and exercise science, outdoor adventure leadership, nutrition and exercise sciences, sports coaching, sport business management, strength and conditioning

Postgraduate courses: elite performance, nutrition and exercise sciences, elite coaching practice, sports leadership and professional development, sports business management, sports business marketing, sports coaching, sport and exercise science, physical education and school sport, strength and conditioning, food safety management, outdoor practice; BA(Hons), BSc(Hons), PGCert, PGDip, DProf, MRes, MA, MSc

Faculty of Science and Technology; www.uclan.ac.uk/faculties/science-technology.php

School of Engineering; www.uclan.ac.uk/schools/engineering/index.php

fire engineering, fire risk assessment, fire safety (engineering), fire safety (management), fire safety and risk management, robotics engineering, quantity surveying, construction project management, civil engineering, civil engineering and construction management, electrical and electronic engineering, electronic engineering, mechanical engineering, mechatronics and intelligent machines, motorsports engineering, nuclear engineering science, facilities management, computer aided engineering, energy engineering, oil and gas safety engineering, aerospace engineering, building services and sustainable engineering, fire and leadership studies, mechanical maintenance engineering, aerospace engineering with pilot studies, building surveying

Postgraduate courses: additive manufacturing, applied data science, design engineeering, intelligent maintenance engineering, maintenance engineering, fire safety engineering, mechatronics and intelligent machines, oil and gas engineering, nuclear safety, nuclear safety, security and safeguards, nuclear science and technology, nuclear security and safeguards, renewable energy engineering, fire scene investigation, fire and rescue service management,

mechanical engineering, project management, construction project management, building services, construction law and dispute resolution; MEng, BEng(Hons), BSc(Hons), MSc, PGDip, PGCert

School of Forensic and Applied Sciences; www.uclan.ac.uk/schools/forensic-applied-sciences/index.php

animal conservation, applied science, forensic science and molecular biology, archaeology, forensic science, environmental science, forensic science and criminal investigation, archaeology and anthropology, policing and criminal investigation, professional policing, geography, biology, forensic science and chemical analysis

Postgraduate courses: emergency management in high hazard industries, forensic science, financial investigation, criminal investigation, professional practice (early action), forensic anthropology, forensic toxicology, criminal justice, counter terrorism, DNA profiling, resource energy and environmental management, cybercrime investigation; MSci, BSc(Hons), FDSC, BA(Hons), MSc, PGDip, PGCert

School of Physical Sciences and Computing; www.uclan.ac.uk/schools/physical-sciences-computing/index.php

computer games development, cyber security, astrophysics, chemistry, physics with astrophysics, computing, physics, astronomy, forensic computing and security, computer networks and security, mathematics, computer science, software engineering

Postgraduate courses: user experience (ux) design, IT security, synthetic organic chemistry, child computer interaction, agile leadership, instrumental analysis, computing, nanoscience and nanotechnology, astrophysics, physics, mathematics; MComp, MPhys, BSc(Hons), MChem, MMath, FDSc, MSc, MRes, PGDip

School of Psychology; www.uclan.ac.uk/schools/psychology/index.php

psychology of child development, forensic psychology, psychology with psychotherapy counselling, cyberpsychology, psychology and criminology, clinical psychology, neuropsychology, neuroscience, psychology

Postgraduate courses: forensic psychology, psychology of child development, psychology conversion, applied clinical psychology; BSc(Hons), MSc

UNIVERSITY OF CHESTER
www1.chester.ac.uk

Faculty of Arts and Humanities; www1.chester.ac.uk/arts-and-humanities

Dept of Art and Design; www1.chester.ac.uk/departments/art-design

fashion design, fashion marketing and communication, fine art, graphic design, interior design, photography, product design
Postgraduate courses: arts and media, design, fine art; BA(Hons), MRes, MA

Dept of Media; www1.chester.ac.uk/departments/media

advertising, broadcast production and presenting, digital photography, film studies, journalism (single or combined), media, media studies, music journalism, radio production, sports journalism, television production
Postgraduate courses: broadcast media, journalism, radio production, television production; BA(Hons), MA, PGDip, PGCert

Dept of Performing Arts; www1.chester.ac.uk/departments/performing-arts

acting, dance, drama and theatre studies, music production, music production and performance, musical theatre, performing arts, popular music performance
Postgraduate courses: arts and media, dance, drama, popular music; BA(Hons), MA, PGDip, PGCert

Dept of English; www1.chester.ac.uk/english

creative writing, English, English language, English language and literature, English literature
Postgraduate courses: creative writing: writing and publishing fiction, English language and linguistics, nineteenth-century literature and culture; BA(Hons), MA, MRes, MPhil, PhD

Dept of History & Archaeology; www1.chester.ac.uk/departments/history-and-archaeology

archaeology (single or combined), history (single or combined)
Postgraduate courses: archaeology and heritage practice, archaeology of death and memory, history, military history, museums practice, past landscapes and environments, sustainable heritage practice, war, conflict and society; BA(Hons), MA, MRes

Institute of Gender Studies; www1.chester.ac.uk/igs

gender studies MRes

Dept of Modern Languages; www1.chester.ac.uk/departments/modern-languages

modern languages, Chinese, French (single or combined), German, Spanish (single or combined), Spanish, Portuguese and Latin American studies
Postgraduate courses: languages, cultures and translation, modern languages; BA(Hons), MA, MRes

Dept of Theology and Religious Studies; www1.chester.ac.uk/trs

philosophy, ethics and religion, religious studies, theology, theology and religious studies (single or combined)
Postgraduate courses: theology, religions studies; BA(Hons), MA, professional doctorate, MPhil, PhD

Chester Business School; www1.chester.ac.uk/chester-business-school/study/undergraduate

accounting and finance, business enterprise, business finance, business management, economics and business, events and business, events and festivals management, events management, global entrepreneurship and business management, international business management, international business management with a language (French/Spanish), international tourism management, international tourism management with a language (French/Spanish), law with business, marketing and advertising management, marketing management, physical activity and health, sport development, sport development and coaching
Postgraduate courses in creative industries management, digital marketing, health services management, international business, international finance, management, marketing management, business administration, sports coaching and development, sport management; BSc(Hons), MBus, BA(Hons), MSc, MBA

Faculty of Education and Children's Services; www1.chester.ac.uk/ education-and-childrens-services

childhood and youth professional studies, early childhood studies, early years – primary education (3-7) with QTS, education studies, primary education (3-11) with QTS, primary education (5-11) with QTS, primary education studies, school business leadership, special education needs and disabilities

Postgraduate courses: anglican church schools studies, autism spectrum condition, coaching and mentoring, creative practices in education, dyslexia research and practice, early childhood, early years practice with EYTS, primary (5-11 years), education in society, educational leadership, educational practice, SENCO – national award for SEN coordination, primary/early years (3-11 years), secondary, school direct initial teacher education, qualified teacher status (QTS) assessment only; BA(Hons), PGCE, MA, EdD

Faculty of Health and Social Care; www1.chester.ac.uk/departments/ health-and-social-care

adult nursing, children's nursing, health and social care, learning disability nursing, midwifery, nursing (mental health), return to practice (nursing)

Postgraduate courses: advanced practice, applied mental health practice, art therapy, cancer care, critical care, professional studies in health and social care, public health, endodontology, global health, integrated approaches to urgent care across community settings, maternal and women's reproductive health, non-medical prescribing, social work, specialist community public health nursing, specialist practice community; BSc, BN, BA, BSc(Hons), GDip, PGCert, PGDip, MSc, MEd, DProf, DrPH, MA

Faculty of Medicine, Dentistry and Life Sciences

Dept of Biological Sciences; www1.chester.ac.uk/departments/ biological-sciences

animal behaviour, animal behaviour & welfare, biology, bioveterinary science, forensic biology, marine biology, zoology

Postgraduate courses: animal behaviour, animal welfare, applied wildlife forensics, biological sciences, marine and coastal resource management, wildlife conservation, various research programmes; BSc(Hons), MSc, PGDip, PGCert

Dept of Clinical Sciences and Nutrition; www1.chester.ac.uk/departments/clinical-sciences-and-nutrition

food and nutrition sciences, food manufacturing with operations management, human nutrition, nutrition and exercise science, nutrition and dietetics

Postgraduate courses: cardiovascular health and rehabilitation, clinical sciences and nutrition, exercise and nutrition science, food integrity and innovation, food science and innovation, human nutrition, nutrition and dietetics, obesity and weight management, public health nutrition; BSc, MSc, MPhil, PhD

Chester Medical School; www1.chester.ac.uk/departments/ medical-school

biochemistry, biomedical science, biomedical science, biotechnology, cell and molecular biology, genetics and evolution, health and exercise science, immunology, medical genetics, medical science, microbiology, pharmacology

Postgraduate courses: biomedical science, cardiovascular disease, clinical bariatric practice, diabetes, doctor of medicine, exercise medicine, gastroenterology, haematology, infection and immunity, medical genetics, medical science, oncology, orthopaedics, physician associate studies, respiratory medicine, rural health, stem cell and regenerative medicine; BSc(Hons), MSc, MBA

Dept of Sport and Community Engagement; www1.chester.ac.uk/departments/sport-and-community-engagement

sports coaching and development; MA

Faculty of Science and Engineering; www1.chester.ac.uk/departments/ science-and-engineering

Dept of Computer Science; www1.chester.ac.uk/departments/ computer-science

applied computing, computer science, cybersecurity, games development, software engineering

Postgraduate courses: advanced computer science, cybersecurity (conversion), programme and project management; BSc, MComp, MSc, MRes, PhD

Dept of Chemical Engineering; www1.chester.ac.uk/departments/ chemical-engineering

chemical engineering; BEng/MEng.

Dept of Electronic and Electrical Engineering; www1.chester.ac.uk/departments/electronic-and-electrical-engineering

electronic and electrical engineering; BEng, MEng

Dept of Mathematics; www1.chester.ac.uk/departments/maths

applied science, mathematics; BSc(Hons), MSc, PGDip, PGCert, PhD, MPhil

Dept of Mechanical Engineering; www1.chester.ac.uk/departments/mechanical-engineering

mechanical engineering; BEng, MEng

Dept of Natural Sciences; www1.chester.ac.uk/departments/natural-sciences

applied science, physics, chemistry; BSc, MRes

Faculty of Social Science

Dept of Geography and International Development; www1.chester.ac.uk/departments/geography-and-international-development

geography (single or combined), international development studies, natural hazard management
Postgraduate courses: Flood Risk Assessment, Modelling and Engineering; BA(Hons), BSc(Hons), MA, MSc, PGCert, PGDip

Dept of Psychology; www1.chester.ac.uk/departments/psychology

psychology (single or combined), forensic psychology, applied psychology
Postgraduate courses: applied psychology, cognitive & behavioural therapies: high intensity training, family and child psychology, psychology; BSc(Hons), MSc, PGDip, PGCert, MRes, MPhil, PhD

Dept of Social and Political Science; www1.chester.ac.uk/departments/social-and-political-science

counselling skills, criminology (single or combined), economics, economics and business, international relations, politics (single or combined), sociology (single or combined); BA(Hons), BSc(Hons)
Postgraduate courses: clinical counselling, professional studies in counselling and psychotherapy, professional studies in psychological trauma

Dept of Law; www1.chester.ac.uk/departments/law

law, law with business, law with criminology, law with politics, contemporary legal studies; LLB, LLM

Institute of Policing; www1.chester.ac.uk/departments/policing

community policing and criminal investigation, professional policing, policing studies, policing, law and investigation

UNIVERSITY OF CHICHESTER
www.chi.ac.uk

Business School; www.chi.ac.uk/business-school

accounting and finance, business studies, business studies and event management, business studies and finance, business studies and human resource management, business studies and marketing, digital marketing, event management, event management and finance, human resource management, IT management for business, marketing, marketing and event management, tourism management; Postgraduate courses in data science and analytics, digital marketing, international business studies, leadership & management, MBA; BA(Hons), BSc(Hons), MA, MSc, PhD

Dept of Childhood, Social Work and Social Care; www.chi.ac.uk/department-childhood-social-work-social-care

early childhood studies, social work, adult social care, foundation early years; Postgraduate courses in advanced professional practice, social work; BA(Hons), MA, PhD

Dept of Computing; www.chi.ac.uk/computing

IT management for business, digital & technology solutions (software engineer/cyber security analyst), computing science, data science and analytics; BSc(Hons), MSc

Dept of Creative and Digital Technologies; www.chi.ac.uk/department-creative-digital-technologies

3D animation and visual effects, digital film production and screenwriting, media and communications, screen acting and creative technologies, screenwriting, sports media, esports, commercial music, digital film technologies, audio production and music technologies; Postgraduate courses in screen acting, composing for film, TV and games, film production, music industry innovation and enterprise; BA(Hons), BSc(Hons), MA

Dept of Dance; www.chi.ac.uk/department-dance

dance, dance performance, dance studies, dance science; Postgraduate courses in dance science, performance: dance (mapdance), dance and somatic practices (independent research), dance research, choreography and professional practices, choreography (independent research), dance: advanced practice, secondary dance; BA(Hons), MSci, MA, PGCE

Institute of Education; www.chi.ac.uk/institute-education

education, education and mathematics, education, special needs and disability, mathematics, mathematics and statistics, mathematics and teaching for KS2/3, primary teaching, primary teaching with early years, school direct – primary/secondary; Postgraduate courses in education, inclusive special education, national award for SENCO, workplace learning development, workplace learning development (send/mental health awareness in schools/growth mindsets); BSc, BA, PGCE, PGCiPP, MA

Dept of Engineering and Design; www.chi.ac.uk/engineering-and-design

science and engineering – integrated foundation year, electronic & electrical engineering, mechanical engineering, sports engineering, product design; BEng(Hons), BSc(Hons), BA(Hons), MEng

Dept of Fine Art; www.chi.ac.uk/fine-art

fine art; Postgraduate course in fine art; BA(Hons), MA, PGCE

Dept of Humanities; www.chi.ac.uk/humanities

creative writing, creative writing and English, drama and theatre, English literature, English literature and drama studies, history, medieval and early modern history, modern history, history and music, politics and contemporary history, politics, law, philosophy and ethics, LLB law, philosophy and ethics, religion, ethics and society, theology; Postgraduate courses in christian ministry, creative writing, cultural history, English literature, language and linguistics, public theology, schools chaplaincy, the history of Africa and the African diaspora; BA, BSc(Hons), MA, MRes, MPhil, PhD

Dept of Mathematics; www.chi.ac.uk/mathematics

education and mathematics, mathematics, mathematics & statistics, mathematics and teaching for KS2/3; BA, BSc(Hons)

Dept of Music; www.chi.ac.uk/department-music

acting for film, charity development, music, music performance, musical theatre (triple threat), musical theatre and cabaret performance, jazz performance, orchestral performance, performance, vocal performance, vocal teaching; Postgraduate courses in music performance, advanced performance; BA(Hons), BMus(Hons), MA

Dept of Psychology and Counselling; www.chi.ac.uk/department-psychology-and-counselling

psychology, humanistic counselling, counselling, counselling psychology, advanced applied psychology; BSc(Hons), Dip, BA(Hons), Cert, MSci

Institute of Sport; www.chi.ac.uk/chichester-institute-sport

community sport coaching, community sport coaching, football coaching and performance, outdoor and adventure education, physical education and sports coaching, physical education in the primary/secondary years, sport business & management, sport development & coaching, sport media, sport studies, sport and exercise psychology/science, sport science and coaching, sports therapy, dance science, sport and exercise science (performance sailing); Postgraduate courses in sport and exercise biomechanics, sport and exercise psychology (BPS stage 1), sport pedagogy and physical education, sports coaching science, sports performance analysis, sport and exercise physiology, strength and conditioning, applied sport and exercise nutrition, physical activity and public health, physiotherpay; BA, BSc(Hons), MSc, MSci, MA

Department of Theatre; www.chi.ac.uk/department-theatre

acting, drama and theatre, theatre, theatre (performance and production); Postgraduate courses in theatre, theatre collectives; BA(Hons), MA

CITY UNIVERSITY LONDON
www.city.ac.uk

Cass Business School; www.cass.city.ac.uk

accounting and finance, actuarial science, banking and international finance, business management, business management, digital innovation and entrepreneurship, business with finance, business with marketing, data analytics and actuarial science, finance, finance with actuarial science, international business, investment and financial risk management; Postgraduate courses in actuarial science, actuarial management, banking & international finance, business analytics, charity accounting & financial management, charity marketing & fundraising, corporate finance, energy, trade & finance, entrepreneurship, finance, financial mathematics, global finance, global supply chain management, grantmaking, philanthropy & social investment, innovation, creativity and leadership, insurance & risk management, international accounting & finance, international business, investment management, management, marketing strategy & innovation, mathematical trading & finance, medical leadership, NGO management, quantitative finance, real estate, real estate investment, shipping, trade & finance, voluntary sector management, business administration; BSc(Hons), MSc, PGCert, PGDip, MBA, EMBA

School of Arts & Social Sciences; www.city.ac.uk/arts-social-sciences

criminology, criminology and psychology, criminology and sociology, economics, economics with accounting, English, financial economics, history, history and politics, international political economy, international politics, international politics and sociology, journalism, media, communication and sociology, music, music, sound and technology, politics, psychology, sociology, sociology with psychology; Postgraduate courses in behavioural economics, broadcast journalism, business economics/international business economics, clinical, social and cognitive neuroscience, composition, creative writing and publishing, criminology and criminal justice, culture, policy and management, development

economics, diplomacy and foreign policy, economic evaluation in health care, economics, English, Erasmus Mundus masters: journalism, media and globalisation, financial economics, financial journalism, food policy, global political economy, health economics, interactive journalism, international communications and development, international journalism, international politics, international politics and human rights, international publishing, investigative journalism, magazine journalism, media and communications, newspaper journalism, organisational psychology, counselling psychology, publishing, research methods, research methods with psychology, sound practice and composition, television journalism; BSc(Hons), BA, MA, MSc, GCert

School of Health Sciences; www.city.ac.uk/health

speech and language science, midwifery, nursing: adult, nursing: child, nursing: mental health, optometry, radiography (diagnostic imaging), radiography (radiotherapy and oncology), speech and language therapy, health and social care; postgraduate courses in adult and mental health nursing (pre-registration), adult nursing, children's nursing, mental health nursing, speech and language therapy, midwifery, public health (school nursing, health visiting and district nursing), primary care; BSc(Hons), MSc, PGDip

School of Mathematics, Computer Science & Engineering; www.city.ac.uk/mathematics-computer-science-engineering

aeronautical engineering, biomedical engineering, civil engineering, computer science, computer science with cyber security, computer science with games technology, data science, electrical and electronic engineering, engineering, mathematics, mathematics and finance, mathematics with finance and economics, mechanical engineering; Postgraduate courses in advanced mechanical engineering, air safety management, air transport management, aircraft maintenance management, airport management, artificial intelligence, business systems analysis and design, civil engineering structures, civil engineering structures (nuclear power plants) computer games technology, construction management, cyber security, data science, energy and environmental technology and economics, human-computer interaction design, information science, internet of things with entrepreneurship, library science, maritime operations and management, project management, finance and risk, renewable energy and power systems management, software engineering, temporary works and construction method engineering; BSc(Hons), BEng(Hons), MEng, MSci, MSc

City Law School; www.city.ac.uk/law

LLB, LLB in legal practice (online); Postgraduate courses in international business law, law, LLM, maritime law (Greece/Dubai); LLB, LLM, MSc, MA, MInnov, MPhil, PhD

GUILDHALL SCHOOL OF MUSIC & DRAMA
www.gsmd.ac.uk

Department of Music; www.gsmd.ac.uk/music/

BMus(Hons) with principal study in strings, harp & guitar, wind, brass & percussion, keyboard, vocal studies, opera studies, historical performance, chamber music, composition, electronic music, jazz, music therapy; Postgraduate courses: Guildhall Artist Masters in performance, composition, orchestral artistry in association with London Symphony Orchestra, artist diploma (for strings, wind, brass, percussion, keyboard, vocal studies, opera studies, historical performance), MA in music therapy, MA in opera making & writing, PGCert performance teaching, MPhil/DMus, MPhil/PhD in music (including music therapy)

Department of Drama; www.gsmd.ac.uk/acting/

BA(Hons) acting, BA performance & creative enterprise; Postgraduate courses: MA acting, PGCert performance teaching

Department of Production Arts; www.gsmd.ac.uk/production.arts

BA(Hons) production arts, with pathways in stage management, costume supervision, design realisation (scenic art, scenic construction & props), and theatre technology, BA(Hons) video design for live performance; Postgraduate courses: MA collaborative theatre production & design, PGCert performance teaching

Creative Learning

BA(Hons) performance & creative enterprise, MMus leadership

REGENTS UNIVERSITY LONDON
www.regents.ac.uk

Business & Management; www.regents.ac.uk/about/subject-areas/business-management

Global Management (Enterprise & Innovation) – BA(Hons), Global Management (Enterprise & Innovation) with Integrated Foundation – BA(Hons), Global Management (Finance) – BA(Hons), Global Management (Finance) with Integrated Foundation – BA(Hons), Global Management (Leadership & Management) – BA(Hons), Global Management (Leadership & Management) with Integrated Foundation – BA(Hons), Global Management (Marketing) – BA(Hons), Global Management (Marketing) with Integrated Foundation – BA(Hons), International Business (French) – BA(Hons), International Business (German) – BA(Hons), International Business (Italian) – BA(Hons), International Business (Japanese) – BA(Hons), International Business (Mandarin Chinese) – BA(Hons), International Business (Russian) – BA(Hons)

Fashion & Design; www.regents.ac.uk/about/subject-areas/fashion-design

Fashion Design – BA(Hons), fashion design – BA(Hons) with integrated foundation, fashion design (marketing) – BA(Hons), fashion design (marketing) – BA(Hons) with integrated foundation, fashion marketing – BA(Hons), fashion marketing – BA(Hons) with integrated foundation, interior design

– BA(Hons), interior design – BA(Hons) with integrated foundation, graphic & digital design – BA(Hons) with integrated foundation, fashion design – BA(Hons), graphic & digital design – BA(Hons); international fashion marketing – MA

Film, Media & Performance; www.regents.ac.uk/about/subject-areas/film-media-performance

acting for stage & screen – BA(Hons), film & screen (film production/screenwriting & producing/TV & digital media) – BA(Hons); media & digital communications – MA

Liberal Arts & Humanities; www.regents.ac.uk/about/subject-areas/liberal-arts-humanities

Liberal Studies (Art History) – BA(Hons), Liberal Studies (Art History) with Integrated Foundation – BA(Hons), Liberal Studies (Business & Management) – BA(Hons), Liberal Studies (Business and Management) with Integrated Foundation – BA(Hons), Liberal Studies (English) – BA(Hons), Liberal Studies (English) with Integrated Foundation – BA(Hons), Liberal Studies (History) – BA(Hons), Liberal Studies (History) with Integrated Foundation – BA(Hons), Liberal Studies (International Relations) – BA(Hons), Liberal Studies (International Relations) with Integrated Foundation – BA(Hons), Liberal Studies (journalism) – BA(Hons), Liberal Studies (Journalism) with Integrated Foundation – BA(Hons), Liberal Studies (Media & Communications) – BA(Hons), Liberal Studies (Media & Communications) with Integrated Foundation – BA(Hons), Liberal Studies (Political Science) – BA(Hons), Liberal Studies (Political Science) with Integrated Foundation – BA(Hons), Liberal Studies (Psychology) – BA(Hons), Liberal Studies (Psychology) with Integrated Foundation – BA(Hons), Liberal Studies (Public Relations) – BA(Hons), Liberal Studies (Public Relations) with Integrated Foundation – BA(Hons); International Relations – MA

Psychotherapy & Psychology; www.regents.ac.uk/about/subject-areas/psychotherapy-psychology

Psychology – BSc(Hons); Counselling Psychology – DPsych, Existential Psychotherapy – Advanced Diploma, Integrative Psychotherapy – Advanced Diploma, Psychology – MSc, Psychotherapy & Counselling – Certificate, Psychotherapy & Counselling – MA

THE NORDOFF-ROBBINS MUSIC THERAPY CENTRE
www.nordoff-robbins.org.uk

Music Therapy, Music, Health, Society; MMusTherapy, PGDip, MPhil, PhD, DPsych

---

TRINITY LABAN CONSERVATOIRE OF MUSIC & DANCE
www.trinitylaban.ac.uk

Music; www.trinitylaban.ac.uk/study/music

BMus(Hons) in jazz, music education, performance/composition; Postgraduate courses: MA music education and performance, MA in music, master of music (MMus), MFA creative practice, postgraduate advanced diploma, postgraduate diploma; research degree programme: MPhil/PhD in dance/music/collaborative arts, the teaching musician – postgraduate certificate, diploma and MA

Musical Theatre; www.trinitylaban.ac.uk/study/musical-theatre

BA(Hons) musical theatre performance

Dance; www.trinitylaban.ac.uk/study/dance

BA(Hons) contemporary dance, dance science; Postgraduate courses: postgraduate diploma: community dance, MA/MFA dance performance (Transitions Dance Company), MA/MFA choreography, MA/MFA creative practice: transdisciplinary, MA/MFA creative practice: dance professional practice, MFA dance science, MSc dance science, MPhil/PhD in dance/music/collaborative arts

COVENTRY UNIVERSITY
www.coventry.ac.uk

Faculty of Arts and Humanities;
www.coventry.ac.uk/study-at-coventry/
faculties-and-schools/arts-and-
humanities/

School of Art and Design;
Architecture BSc(Hons), Automotive and Transport Design MDes/BA(Hons), Fashion BA(Hons), Fine Art BA(Hons), Fine Art and Illustration BA(Hons), Foundation Diploma in Art and Design, Games Art BA(Hons), Graphic Design BA(Hons), Illustration and Animation BA(Hons), Illustration and Graphic Design BA(Hons), Interior Architecture and Design BA(Hons), International Fashion Business BA(Hons), Product Design MDes/BA(Hons); Postgraduate courses: Architecture MArch, Automotive and Transport Design MA, Contemporary Arts Practice MA, Design and Transport MSc, Design Management MA, Graphic Design MA, Illustration and Animation MA, Industrial Product Design MSc, Interior Design MA, Painting MA, Photography and Collaboration MA

School of Humanities;
www.coventry.ac.uk/study-at-coventry/
faculties-and-schools/arts-and-
humanities/humanities/
Creative Writing BA(Hons), English BA(Hons), English and Creative Writing BA(Hons), English and Journalism BA(Hons), English Language BA(Hons), English Language and TEFL BA(Hons), English Literature BA(Hons), History BA(Hons), History and Politics BA(Hons), International Relations BA(Hons), Languages for Global Communication BA(Hons), Politics BA(Hons), Sociology BA(Hons), Sociology and Criminology BA(Hons); Postgraduate courses: Countering Organised Crime MA, Diplomacy, Law and Global Change MA, English Language Teaching and Applied Linguistics MA, International Policing MPA, International Relations MA, Professional Creative Writing MA, Terrorism, International Crime and Global Security MA

School of Media and Performing Arts;
www.coventry.ac.uk/study-at-coventry/
faculties-and-schools/arts-and-
humanities/media-and-performing-arts/
Digital Media BA(Hons), Journalism BA(Hons), Media and Communications BA(Hons), Media Production BA(Hons), Music BA(Hons), Music Technology BSc(Hons), Photography BA(Hons), Theatre and Professional Practice BA(Hons); Postgraduate courses: Automotive Journalism MA, Collaborative Theatre Making MA, Communication, Culture and Media MA, Global Journalism and Public Relations MA, 21st Century Media Practice MA

Coventry Business School;
www.coventry.ac.uk/study-at-coventry/
faculties-and-schools/coventry-
business-school/
Accountancy BA(Hons), Accounting and Finance BA(Hons), Advertising and Marketing BA(Hons), Business Administration BA(Hons), Business and Finance BA(Hons), Business and Human Resource Management BA(Hons), Business and Marketing BA(Hons), Business Economics BA(Hons), Business Law LLB(Hons), Business Management BA(Hons), Digital Marketing BA(Hons), Economics BA(Hons), Enterprise and Entrepreneurship BA(Hons), European Business Management BA(Hons), Event Management BA(Hons), Finance BSc(Hons), Finance and Investment BA(Hons), Financial Economics BA(Hons), International Business Management BA(Hons), International Law LLB(Hons), Law LLB(Hons), Marketing BA(Hons), Sport Management BA(Hons); Postgraduate courses: Accounting and Financial Management MSc, Advertising and Marketing MA, Banking and Finance MSc, Brand Management MA, Business Analytics MSc, Digital Marketing Management MSc, Enterprise and Entrepreneurship Education MA, Enterprise and Innovation MSc, Finance MSc, Financial Risk Management MSc, Global Entrepreneurship MA, Human Resource Development PgDip, Human Resource Management MA, International Business MSc, International Business Economics MSc, International Business Law LLM, International Business Management MSc, International Events Management MSc, International Human Resource Management MSc, International Law LLM, International Marketing Management MSc, Investment Management MSc, Law LLM, Leadership and Management MA, Masters in Business Administration (MBA), MBA (for the Cyber Security Management sector), MBA (for the Healthcare sector), MBA Sustainable Tourism, MBA with Artificial Intelligence specialism, MBA with

Marketing specialism, PgCert in Entrepreneurship, Professional Accountancy MSc, Project Management MSc, Sport Management MSc

Faculty of Engineering, Environment and Computing; www.coventry.ac.uk/study-at-coventry/faculties-and-schools/engineering-environment-and-computing/

School of Computing, Electronics and Mathematics; www.coventry.ac.uk/study-at-coventry/faculties-and-schools/engineering-environment-and-computing/computing-electronics-and-mathematics/

Computer Hardware and Software Engineering BEng(Hons), Computer Science MSci/BSc(Hons), Computing BSc(Hons), Electrical and Electronic Engineering MEng/BEng(Hons), Electronic Engineering BEng(Hons), Ethical Hacking and Cybersecurity MSci/BSc(Hons), Games Technology BSc(Hons), Information Technology for Business BSc(Hons), Mathematics BSc(Hons), Mathematics and Data Analytics MSci/BSc(Hons), Mathematics and Physics BSc(Hons), Mathematics and Statistics BSc(Hons), Multimedia Computing BSc(Hons), Physics MPhys/BSc(Hons); Postgraduate courses: Computer Science MSc, Cyber Security MSc, Data Science and Computational Intelligence MSc, Digital Technology for Business MSc, Digital Technology for Engineering MSc, Electrical Automotive Engineering MSc, Electrical and Electronic Engineering MSc, Embedded Systems Engineering MSc, Forensic Computing Msc, Management Information Systems MSc, Software Development MSc

School of Energy, Construction and Environment; www.coventry.ac.uk/study-at-coventry/faculties-and-schools/engineering-environment-and-computing/energy-construction-and-environment/

Architectural Technology BSc(Hons), Building Services Engineering BEng(Hons), Building Surveying BSc(Hons), Civil Engineering BEng/BSc/MEng(Hons), Civil and Environmental Engineering MEng/BEng, Civil and Structural Engineering MEng/BEng(Hons), Construction Management BSc(Hons), Disaster Management and Emergency Planning BSc(Hons), Geography BA/BSc(Hons), Geography and Natural Hazards BSc(Hons), International Disaster Management BSc(Hons), Oil, Gas and Energy Management BSc(Hons), Quantity Surveying and Commercial Management BSc(Hons); Postgraduate courses: Agroecology, Water and Food Sovereignty MSc, Civil Engineering MSc, Civil Engineering (Technical Route) MSc, Construction Management MSc, Construction Project and Cost Management MSc, Crowded Places and Public Safety Management MSc, Disaster Management and Resilience MSc, Emergency Management and Resilience MSc, Highways and Transportation Engineering MSc, Oil and Gas Engineering MSc, Oil and Gas Management MSc, Petroleum and Environmental Technology MSc, Sustainability and Environmental Management MSc

School of Mechanical, Aerospace and Automotive Engineering; www.coventry.ac.uk/study-at-coventry/faculties-and-schools/engineering-environment-and-computing/mechanical-aerospace-and-automotive-engineering/

Aerospace Systems Engineering BEng(Hons), Aerospace Technology BEng(Hons), Automotive Engineering MEng/BEng(Hons), Aviation Management BSc(Hons), Engineering BSc (Part Time), Engineering Business Management BEng(Hons) Top Up, Manufacturing Engineering MEng/BEng(Hons), Mechanical Engineering MEng/BEng(Hons), Motorsport Engineering MEng/BEng(Hons); Postgraduate courses: Aerospace Engineering MSc, Air Transport Management MSc, Automotive Engineering MSc, Control Engineering MSc, Engineering and Management MSc, Engineering Business Management MSc, Engineering Project Management MSc, Global Logistics MSc, Human Factors in Aviation MSc, Mechanical Engineering MSc, Production Engineering and Operations Management MSc, Renewable Energy Engineering MSc, Structural Engineering MSc, Supply Chain Management MSc, Systems and Control MSc

Faculty of Health and Life Sciences; www.coventry.ac.uk/study-at-coventry/faculties-and-schools/health-and-life-sciences/

School of Life Sciences; www.coventry.ac.uk/study-at-coventry/faculties-and-schools/health-and-life-sciences/life-sciences/

Analytical Chemistry and Forensic Science BSc(Hons), Biological and Forensic Sciences BSc(Hons), Biomedical Science/Applied Biomedical Science BSc(Hons), Food and Nutrition BSc(Hons),

Food Safety, Inspection and Control BSc(Hons), Human Biosciences BSc(Hons), Medical and Pharmacological Sciences BSc(Hons), Nutrition and Health BSc(Hons), Sport and Exercise Science BSc(Hons), Sports Therapy BSc(Hons); Postgraduate courses: Applied Sport and Exercise Science MSc, Biomedical Science MSc, Biotechnology MSc, Molecular Biology MSc, Pharmacology and Drug Discovery MSc, Science of Youth Coaching and Development MSc, Sports and Exercise Nutrition MSc, Strength and Conditioning MSc

School of Psychological, Social and Behavioural Sciences; www.coventry.ac.uk/study-at-coventry/faculties-and-schools/health-and-life-sciences/psychological-social-and-behavioural-sciences/

Childhood and Youth Studies BA(Hons), Criminology BA(Hons), Criminology and Law BA(Hons), Criminal Psychology BSc(Hons), Criminology and Psychology BA(Hons), Forensic Investigations BSc(Hons), Psychology BSc(Hons), Social Sciences BSc, Social Work BA(Hons), Sport and Exercise Psychology BSc(Hons); Postgraduate courses: Applied Psychology MSc, Business and Organisational Psychology MSc, Career Guidance (QCG) MA, Clinical Psychology Doctorate, Cognitive Behavioural Therapy PGDip/MSc, Forensic Psychology MSc, Forensic Psychology and Crime MSc, Fraud Investigation Management MSc, Health Psychology MSc, Mindfulness and Compassion MSc, Occupational Psychology MSc, Psychology MSc, Social Work MA

School of Nursing, Midwifery and Health; www.coventry.ac.uk/study-at-coventry/faculties-and-schools/health-and-life-sciences/nursing-midwifery-and-health/

Adult Nursing BSc(Hons), Children and Young People's Nursing BSc(Hons), Dietetics and Human Nutrition BSc(Hons), Learning Disabilities Nursing BSc(Hons), Mental Health Nursing BSc(Hons), Midwifery BSc(Hons), Occupational Therapy BSc(Hons), Operating Department Practice DipHE, Paramedic Science Foundation, Physiotherapy BSc(Hons); Postgraduate courses: Advanced Clinical Practice MSc, Advancing Physiotherapy Practice MSc, Global Healthcare Management MSc, Health Studies MSc, Manual Therapy MSc, Nursing Studies MSc, Public Health Nutrition MSc, Social and Therapeutic Horticulture MSc, Teenage and Young Adult Cancer Care PGCert

Coventry Law School; www.coventry.ac.uk/study-at-coventry/faculties-and-schools/coventry-law-school/

Business Law LLB(Hons), International Law LLB(Hons), Law LLB(Hons); Postgraduate courses: International Law LLM, Law LLM, International Business Law LLM

CRANFIELD UNIVERSITY
www.cranfield.ac.uk

Aerospace; www.cranfield.ac.uk/themes/aerospace/explore-aerospace-courses

Advanced Lightweight and Composite Structures MSc, Aerospace Computational Engineering MSc, Aerospace Dynamics MSc, Aerospace Vehicle Design MSc, Aircraft Design option in Aerospace Vehicle Design MSc, Aircraft Engineering MSc, Astronautics and Space Engineering MSc, Autonomous Vehicle Dynamics and Control MSc, Avionic Systems Design option in Aerospace Vehicle Design MSc, Computational and Software Techniques in Engineering MSc, Computational Fluid Dynamics MSc, Computer Aided Engineering option in Computational and Software Techniques in Engineering MSc, Computer and Machine Vision option in Computational and Software Techniques in Engineering MSc, Gas Turbine Technology option in Thermal Power MSc, Power, Propulsion and the Environment option in Thermal Power MSc, Pre-Master's in Engineering, Rotating Machinery, Engineering and Management option in Thermal Power MSc, Software Engineering for Technical Computing option in Computational and Software Techniques in Engineering MSc, Structural Design option in Aerospace Vehicle Design MSc, Thermal Power MSc, Aerospace Propulsion option in Thermal Power MSc/MSc by Research

Defence and Security; www.cranfield.ac.uk/themes/defence-and-security

Counterterrorism MSc, Counterterrorism Risk Management and Resilience MSc, Cyber Defence and

Information Assurance MSc, Cyberspace Operations MSc, Defence Acquisition Management MSc, Defence and Security (Engineering/Leadership and Management/Technology) MSc, Defence Leadership MSc, Defence Simulation and Modelling MSc, Digital Forensics MSc, Explosives Ordnance Engineering MSc, Forensic Archaeology and Anthropology MSc, Forensic Ballistics MSc, Forensic Engineering and Science MSc, Forensic Explosive and Explosion Investigation MSc, Forensic Investigation MSc, Forensic Investigation of Heritage Crime MSc, Guided Weapon Systems MSc, Gun Systems Design MSc, Information Capability Management MSc, Military Aerospace and Airworthiness MSc, Military Electronic Systems Engineering MSc, Military Operational Research MSc, Military Vehicle Technology MSc, Programme and Project Management (Defence) MSc, Systems Engineering for Defence Capability MSc, Vehicle and Weapon Engineering (USA)

Energy and Power; www.cranfield.ac.uk/themes/energy-and-power

Advanced Chemical Engineering MSc, Advanced Mechanical Engineering MSc, Energy Informatics MSc, Energy Systems and Thermal Processes MSc, Offshore and Ocean Technology with Offshore Materials Engineering MSc, Offshore Engineering MSc, Process Systems Engineering MSc, Renewable Energy MSc, MBA Energy

Environment and Agrifood; www.cranfield.ac.uk/themes/environment-and-agrifood

Applied Bioinformatics MSc, Food Systems and Management MSc, Future Food Sustainability MSc, Geographical Information Management MSc, Land Reclamation and Restoration MSc, Environmental Management for Business MSc, Environmental Engineering MSc

Manufacturing; www.cranfield.ac.uk/themes/manufacturing

Advanced Materials MSc, Aerospace Manufacturing MSc, Aerospace Materials MSc, Cyber-Secure Manufacturing MSc, Engineering and Management of Manufacturing Systems MSc, Global Product Development and Management MSc, Management and Information Systems MSc, Maintenance Engineering and Asset Management MSc, Manufacturing Technology and Management MSc, Metal Additive Manufacturing MSc, Operations Excellence MSc, Through-life System Sustainment MSc, Welding Engineering MSc, Pre-Masters in Engineering

Transport Systems; www.cranfield.ac.uk/themes/transport-systems

Advanced Motorsport Engineering MSc, Air Transport Management MSc, Air Transport Management MSc (Executive), Airport Planning and Management MSc, Advanced Motorsports Mechatronics MSc, Airworthiness MSc, Automotive Engineering MSc, Automotive Mechatronics MSc, Connected and Autonomous Vehicle Engineering (Automotive) MSc, Safety and Accident Investigation – Air Transport MSc, Safety and Accident Investigation – Marine Transport PgCert, Safety and Accident Investigation – Rail Transport PgCert, Safety and Human Factors in Aviation MSc

Water; www.cranfield.ac.uk/themes/water

Environmental Water Management MSc, Water and Sanitation for Development MSc, Water and Wastewater Engineering MSc

School of Management; www.cranfield.ac.uk/som

Finance and Management MSc, Investment Management MSc, Logistics and Supply Chain Management MSc, Logistics and Supply Chain Management MSc (Executive), Management MSc, Management & Corporate Sustainability MSc, Management and Entrepreneurship MSc, Management and Leadership MSc, Procurement and Supply Chain Management MSc, Strategic Marketing MSc; MBA Full-time, Executive MBA, Executive MBA Human Capital, MBA Energy, MBA Defence, Executive MBA Defence Export, MBA Events

UNIVERSITY FOR THE CREATIVE ARTS
www.uca.ac.uk (at Canterbury, Epsom, Farnham, Maidstone and Rochester)

BA(Hons) Acting, BA(Hons) Acting & Performance, BA(Hons) Advertising, BA(Hons) Animation, BA(Hons) Architecture (ARB/RIBA Part 1), BA(Hons) Business Innovation and Management (top up), BA(Hons) Business Management, BA(Hons) Ceramics and Glass, BA(Hons) Computer Animation Arts, BA(Hons) Creative Arts, BA(Hons) Creative Computing, BA(Hons) Creative Writing, BA(Hons)

Drawing, BA(Hons) Event and Promotion Management, BA(Hons) Fashion, BA(Hons) Fashion Atelier, BA(Hons) Fashion Design, BA(Hons) Fashion Journalism, BA(Hons) Fashion Management & Marketing, BA(Hons) Fashion Media & Promotion, BA(Hons) Fashion Photography, BA(Hons) Fashion Promotion & Imaging, BA(Hons) Fashion Textiles, BA(Hons) Film and Digital Art, BA(Hons) Film Production, BA(Hons) Fine Art, BA(Hons) Games Arts, BA(Hons) Games Design, BA(Hons) Games Technology, BA(Hons) Garden Design, BA(Hons) Graphic Design, BA(Hons) Hand Embroidery, BA(Hons) HR Management, BA(Hons) Illustration, BA(Hons) Illustration & Animation, BSc(Hons) Industrial Design, BA(Hons) Interior Architecture & Design, BA(Hons) Interior Design, BA(Hons) International Buying and Merchandising, BA(Hons) Jewellery and Silversmithing, BA(Hons) Journalism & Media Production, BA(Hons) Make-up and Hair Design, BA(Hons) Marketing, BA(Hons) Moving Image, BA(Hons) Music, BA/BSc(Hons) Music Composition & Technology, BA(Hons) Music Marketing and Communications, BA(Hons) Painting, BA(Hons) Photography, BA(Hons) Supply Chain and Logistics Management, BA(Hons) Television Production, BA(Hons) Television and Media Production, BA(Hons) Textile Design, BA(Hons) Theatre Design, BA(Hons) Visual Communications

Postgraduate courses: MA Animation, MA Architecture, MArch Master of Architecture (ARB/RIBA Part 2), Professional Practice in Architecture (ARB/RIBA Part 3), MA Ceramics, MA Creative Business Management, MA Creative Direction for Fashion, MA Creative Marketing and Advertising, MA Creative Education, MA Design, Innovation & Brand Management, MA Digital Media, MA Fashion Business and Management, MA Fashion Design, MA Fashion Marketing and Communication, MA Fashion Photography, MA Filmmaking, MA Filmmaking: Documentary, MA Fine Art, MA Games Design, MA Glass, MA Global Media Management, MA Graphic Design, MA Illustration, MA Interior Design, MSc International Financial Management for the Creative Industries, MA International Jewellery Management, MBA International Master of Business Administration, MA International Music Management, MA Jewellery, MA Luxury Brand Management, MA Media Communication, MA Metalwork, MA Photography, MFA Photography, MA Printed Textiles for Fashion & Interiors, MA Product Design, MA Textiles, MA Visual Communication

UNIVERSITY OF CUMBRIA
www.cumbria.ac.uk

Department of Business, Law, Policing and Social Sciences; www.cumbria.ac.uk/study/academic-departments/business-law-policing-and-social-sciences/

BA(Hons) Business Management, BA(Hons) Business Management with Entrepreneurship, BA(Hons) Business Management with Human Resources Management, BA(Hons) Business Management with Marketing, BA(Hons) Business, Accounting and Finance, BSc(Hons) Criminology, BSc(Hons) Criminology with Applied Psychology, BSc(Hons) Criminology with Forensic Investigation, BSc(Hons) Criminology with Law, BSc(Hons) Criminology with Policing and Investigation, BA(Hons) Global Business Management (Top-Up), BA(Hons) International Business Management, LLB(Hons) Law, BSc(Hons) Professional Policing, BSc(Hons) Security, Intelligence and Investigative Practice

Postgraduate courses: MSc Applied Forensic Psychology, MSc Applied Social Science, MSc Finance and Accounting & PgD target award, MSc International Management, PgC Interpersonal Violence and Abuse Studies, MSc Legal and Criminological Psychology, MBA Masters of Business Administration, MSc Psychological Research Methods, MBA Public Health Management, MSc Strategic Policing, PgC Sustainable Leadership

Department of Health, Psychology and Social Studies; www.cumbria.ac.uk/study/academic-departments/health-psychology-and-social-studies/

BSc(Hons) Applied Psychology, BSc(Hons) Occupational Therapy, BSc(Hons) Physiotherapy, BSc(Hons) Psychology, BA(Hons) Social Work, BA(Hons) Working with Children and Families, BA(Hons) Youth Work and Community Development

Postgraduate courses: PgD Advanced Practice of Cognitive Behavioural Therapy, PgC Digital Health, MSc Occupational Therapy (Pre-Registration), MSc Physiotherapy (Pre-registration), MA Social Work,

MA Working with Children, Adolescents and Families, MA Youth Work and Community Development

Institute of the Arts; www.cumbria.ac.uk/study/academic-departments/institute-of-the-arts/

BA(Hons) Acting, Dip HE Creative Writing, BA(Hons) Creative Writing, BA(Hons) Dance, Dip HE English Literature, BA(Hons) English Literature, BA(Hons) Film and Television, BA(Hons) Fine Art, BA(Hons) Games Design, BA(Hons) Graphic Design, BA(Hons) History and Heritage, BA(Hons) Illustration, BA(Hons) Musical Theatre, BA(Hons) Performing Arts, BA(Hons) Photography, BA(Hons) Wildlife Media

Postgraduate courses: MA Arts and Cultural Leadership and Management, MA Contemporary Fine Art, MA Creative Practice, MA Creative Writing, MA Literature, Romanticisim and the English Lake District, MA Photography

Institute of Education; www.cumbria.ac.uk/study/academic-departments/institute-of-education/

BA(Hons) Education Studies, Dip HE Education Studies, BA(Hons) Primary Education (3-11) with QTS, BA(Hons) Primary Education: Inclusion with SEND (with QTS), BA(Hons) Teaching and Learning PGCE courses: PGCE General Primary with QTS (5 - 11 years), PGCE General Primary with QTS – Mathematics specialism (PGCE), PGCE General Primary with QTS – Modern Foreign Languages specialism, PGCE General Primary with QTS – Physical Education specialism, PGCE Lower Primary with QTS (3-7 year olds), PGCE Postgraduate Certificate in Education (non-QTS), PGCE Secondary Education with QTS: Art and Design, PGCE Secondary Education with QTS: Biology, PGCE Secondary Education with QTS: Chemistry, PGCE Secondary Education with QTS: Computer Science and ICT, PGCE Secondary Education with QTS: Design and Technology, PGCE Secondary Education with QTS: English, PGCE Secondary Education with QTS: Geography, PGCE Secondary Education with QTS: History, PGCE Secondary Education with QTS: Mathematics, PGCE Secondary Education with QTS: Modern Foreign Languages, PGCE Secondary Education with QTS: Music, PGCE Secondary Education with QTS: Physical Education, PGCE Secondary Education with QTS: Physics, PGCE Secondary Education with QTS: Religious Education

Postgraduate courses: MA Education Professional Practice (with pathways), PgC Learning and Teaching for Higher Education, NPQ Middle Leadership (Now Recruiting for January 2017), PgC National Award for SEN Coordination, QTS Direct (Assessment Only), NPQ Senior Leadership, SKE Subject Knowledge Enhancement: Computing (8 weeks), SKE Subject Knowledge Enhancement: Mathematics (28 weeks)

Department of Medical and Sport Sciences; www.cumbria.ac.uk/study/academic-departments/medical-and-sport-sciences/

BSc Biomedical Sciences, BSc(Hons) Diagnostic Radiotherapy, BSc(Hons) Healthcare Science, BSc(Hons) Sport Rehabilitation, BSc(Hons) Sport and Exercise Science, BA(Hons) Sport Coaching and Physical Education, BA(Hons) Sport Coaching and Development

Postgraduate courses: PGCE General Primary with QTS (5-11 years) – Physical Education specialism, PGCE Secondary Education with QTS: Physical Education (11-16 years), MSc/PgC/PgD Medical Imaging, MSc/PgC/PgD Medical Imaging: Ultrasound, MSc/PgC/PgD Medical Imaging: Magnetic Resonance Imaging

Department of Nursing, Health and Professional Practice; www.cumbria.ac.uk/study/academic-departments/nursing-health-and-professional-practice/

BSc(Hons) Midwifery, BSc(Hons) Nursing (Adult), BSc(Hons) Nursing (Child), BSc(Hons) Nursing (Learning Disabilty), BSc(Hons) Nursing (Mental Health), BSc(Hons) Practice Development: Developing Paramedic Practice, DipHE Paramedic Practice, ILM Level 5 certificate in Coaching and Mentoring, BSc(Hons) Management and Leadership in Health and Social Care programme, BSc Practice Management, DipHE Practice Management, ILM Executive Coaching and Mentoring Level 7 certificate, MSc Management and Leadership in Health and Social Care programme, BSc(Hons) Nursing Practice, BSc(Hons) Practice Development with pathways, UAD Practice Development with pathways, DipHE Practice Development, MSc Practice Development with pathways, PG Cert Practice Development with pathways, PG Dip Practice Development, BSc(Hons) Community Specialist Practice Top-up (District Nursing), BSc(Hons) Community Specialist Practice Top-up (General Practice Nursing), BSc(Hons) Practice Management, Dip HE Practice Management

Postgraduate courses: Graduate Diploma Practice Development: Developing Paramedic Practice, MSc Practice Development: Enhancing Paramedic Practice, MA Counselling and Psychotherapy, PgDip Counselling and Psychotherapy, MSc Advanced Practice (Clinical), PGc Advanced Practice (Clinical), Postgraduate Diploma Community Specialist Practice (District Nursing), Postgraduate Diploma Community Specialist Practice (General Practice Nursing), Graduate Diploma Community Specialist Practice (District Nursing), Graduate Diploma Community Specialist Practice (General Practice Nursing)

Department of Science, Natural Resources and Outdoor Studies; www.cumbria.ac.uk/study/academic-departments/science-natural-resources-and-outdoor-studies/

BSc(Hons) Animal Conservation Science, BSc(Hons) Biology (Microbiology), BSc(Hons) Biomedical Sciences, BSc(Hons) Conservation Biology, BSc(Hons) Forensic and Investigative Science, BSc(Hons) Forest Management, FDSc Forestry, BSc(Hons) Geography, BSc(Hons) Marine and Freshwater Conservation, BSc(Hons) Outdoor Adventure and Environment, FDA Outdoor Education, BA(Hons) Outdoor Leadership, BSc(Hons) Woodland Ecology and Conservation, BSc(Hons) Zoology

Postgraduate courses: MSc Ecosystem Services Evaluation, MA Outdoor and Experiential Learning

DE MONTFORT UNIVERSITY
www.dmu.ac.uk

Leicester Castle Business School; www.lcbs.ac.uk

Accounting and Business Management BA(Hons), Accounting and Economics BA(Hons), Accounting and Finance BA(Hons), Advertising and Marketing Communications BA(Hons), Business and Entrepreneurship and Innovation BA(Hons), Business and Globalisation BA(Hons), Business and Management BA(Hons), Business and Marketing BA(Hons), Business Management and Economics BA, Business Management and Finance BA, Business Management and Human Resource Management BA, Economics BA/BSc(Hons), Economics and Finance BSc(Hons), Economics and International Relations BA(Hons), Economics and Politics BA(Hons), Global Finance BSc(Hons), Human Resource Management BA(Hons), International Marketing and Business BA(Hons), International Relations BA(Hons), Marketing BA(Hons), Politics BA(Hons), Public Administration and Management BA(Hons)

Postgraduate courses: Advertising and Public Relations Management MSc, Air Transport Management MSc, Business Economics and Business Finance MSc, Business Economics and International Relations MSc, Business Economics and Marketing MSc, Business Economics and Risk management MSc, Business Management in the Creative Industries MSc, Business Management in Sport MSc, Business of Motorsport MA, Creative Enterprise MSc, Diplomacy and World Order MA, Forensic Accounting MSc, Global

Policy MA, Human Resource Management (CIPD) MA/PG DIp, Intercultural Business Communication MSc, International Banking and Finance MSc, International Business and Finance MSc, International Business and Human Resource Management MSc, International Business and Management MSc, International Business and Marketing MSc, International Finance and Investment MSc, International Relations MA, Marketing Management MSc, Professional ACCA Course, Project Management MSc, Risk Management MSc, Strategic and Digital Marketing MSc, Urban Studies MA; Doctor of Business Administration DBA, Executive MBA, Master of Business Administration MBA (Global), MBA for Engineers

Leicester Media School; www.dmu.ac.uk/about-dmu/schools-and-departments/leicester-media-school/

Animation BA(Hons), Animation Visual Effects BA(Hons), Broadcast Journalism BA(Hons), Communication Arts BA(Hons), Film Studies BA(Hons), Film Studies BA(Hons) (Joint Honours), Film Studies with Languages BA(Hons), Media and Communication BA(Hons), Media and Communication with Languages BA(Hons), Media BA(Hons) (Joint Honours), Media Production BSc(Hons), Visual Effects BSc(Hons), Game Art BA(Hons) (Skillset accredited), Graphic Design BA(Hons), Graphic Design and Illustration BA(Hons), Graphic Design (Interactive) BA(Hons), Graphic Design and e-Media Foundation Degree (FdA), Journalism BA(Hons) (NCTJaccredited), Journalism BA(Hons) BA(Hons) (Joint Honours), Audio and Recording Technology BSc(Hons), Creative Music Technology BA(Hons), Music Technology BSc(Hons), Music, Technology and Performance BA(Hons), Creative Sound Technology FdSc, Graphic Design and e-Media Foundation Degree FdA

Postgraduate courses: Independent Study MA, International Film Production MA, Investigative Journalism MA

School of Computer Science and Informatics; www.dmu.ac.uk/about-dmu/schools-and-departments/school-of-computer-science-and-informatics/

Computing BSc(Hons), Computing HND, Foundation Year in Computing, Computer Security BSc(Hons), Computer Science BSc(Hons), Forensic Computing BSc(Hons), Software Engineering BSc(Hons), Computer Games Programming BSc(Hons), Intelligent Systems BSc(Hons), Intelligent Systems MComp, Business Information Systems BSc(Hons), Computing for Business BSc(Hons), Information and Communication Technology BSc(Hons), Mathematics BSc(Hons)

Postgraduate courses: Cyber Security MSc, Cyber Technology MSc, Software Engineering MSc, Forensic Computing for Practitioners MSc/PG Dip/PG Cert, Professional Practice in Digital Forensics and Security MSc, Intelligent Systems MSc, Intelligent Systems and Robotics MSc, Business Intelligence Systems and Data Mining MSc, Computing MSc, Data Analytics MSc, Information Systems Management MSc

School of Engineering and Sustainable Development; www.dmu.ac.uk/about-dmu/schools-and-departments/school-of-engineering-and-sustainable-development/

Engineering Year Zero (Foundation year), Electrical and Electronic Engineering BEng/MEng(Hons), Mechanical Engineering BEng(Hons), Mechanical Engineering (Integrated Masters), Mechatronics BEng(Hons), Mechatronics (Integrated Masters), Physics BSc/MPhys(Hons)

Postgraduate courses: Electronic Engineering MSc, Engineering Management MSc, Mechanical Engineering MSc, Mechatronics MSc, Energy and Sustainable Building Design MSc, Energy and Sustainable Development MSc

Leicester De Montfort Law School; www.dmu.ac.uk/about-dmu/schools-and-departments/leicester-de-montfort-law-school/

LLB Law(Hons), LLB Business Law(Hons), LLB Law and Criminal Justice(Hons), LLB Law, Human Rights and Social Justice(Hons), BA Business Management and Law (Joint Hons), BA Law and Economics (Joint Hons)

Postgraduate courses: LLM Business Law, LLM Employment Law and Practice, LLM Environmental Law and Practice, LLM Food Law, LLM International Business Law, LLM International Human Rights, LLM Medical Law and Ethics, LLM Sports Law and Practice

Leicester School of Architecture; www.dmu.ac.uk/about-dmu/schools-and-departments/leicester-school-of-architecture/

Architecture BA(Hons), Architectural Technology BSc(Hons)

Postgraduate courses: Architecture March, Architectural Practice PG Dip, Architectural Design MA, Architecture and Sustainability MSc

School of Visual and Performance Arts, www.dmu.ac.uk/about-dmu/schools-and-departments/school-of-visual-and-performing-arts/

Dance BA(Hons), Dance BA (Joint Honours)(Hons), Drama Studies BA(Hons), Drama Studies (Joint Honours) BA(Hons), Performing Arts BA(Hons), Art and Design (Foundation Studies) BTEC Diploma, Fine Art BA(Hons), Photography and Video BA(Hons), Arts and Festivals Management BA(Hons), Arts and Festivals Management (Joint Honours) BA(Hons)

Postgraduate courses: Arts MA, Cultural Events Management MSc, Digital Arts MA, Fine Art MA, Performance Practices MA, Performance Practices MFA

School of Design; www.dmu.ac.uk/about-dmu/schools-and-departments/school-of-design/

Design Crafts BA(Hons), Design Products MDes(Hons), Digital Design BA(Hons), Interior Design BA(Hons), Interior Design MDes(Hons), Product Design BA(Hons), Product Design BSc(Hons), Product and Furniture Design BA(Hons), Contour Fashion BA(Hons), Contour Fashion Communication BA(Hons), Fashion Buying with Design BA(Hons),

Fashion Buying with Garment Technology BA(Hons), Fashion Buying with Marketing BA(Hons), Fashion Buying with Merchandising BA(Hons), Fashion Design BA(Hons), Fashion Textile Design BA(Hons), Footwear Design BA(Hons), Textile Design BA(Hons) Postgraduate courses: Design MA, Design Innovation MA, Design Management and Entrepreneurship MA, Digital Design MA, Fashion and Textiles MA, Fashion Management with Marketing MA, Interior Design MA, Product Design MA, Textile Design, Technology and Innovation MSc

School of Humanities; www.dmu.ac.uk/about-dmu/schools-and-departments/school-of-humanities/

Creative Writing (Joint Honours) BA(Hons), English BA(Hons), English (Joint Honours) BA(Hons), English with Languages BA(Hons), English Language (Joint Honours) BA(Hons), English Language with Languages BA(Hons), English Language with TESOL BA(Hons), History BA(Hons), History (Joint Honours) BA(Hons), History with Languages BA(Hons) Postgraduate courses: English MA, English Language Teaching MA, History MA, Photographic History MA, Sports History and Culture MA, Management, Law and Humanities of Sport MA, Humanities research degree MPhil/PhD

Institute of Creative Technologies; www.ioct.dmu.ac.uk

IOCT Masters in Creative Technologies

School of Allied Health Sciences; www.dmu.ac.uk/about-dmu/schools-and-departments/school-of-allied-health-sciences/

Biomedical Science BSc(Hons), Health and Wellbeing in Society BSc(Hons), Speech and Language Therapy BSc(Hons), Medical Science B Med Sci(Hons) Postgraduate courses: Advanced Biomedical Science MSc/PG Dip/PG Cert, Master's by Research MA/MSc, Physician Associate Studies MSc

School of Applied Social Sciences; www.dmu.ac.uk/about-dmu/schools-and-departments/school-of-applied-social-sciences/

Criminology and Criminal Justice BA(Hons), Criminology and Criminal Justice with Psychology BA(Hons), Criminal Investigation with Policing BA(Hons), Education Studies BA(Hons), Education Studies with French BA(Hons), Education Studies with Mandarin BA(Hons), Education Studies with Psychology BA(Hons), Policing BA(Hons), Psychology BSc(Hons), Psychology with Criminology BSc(Hons), Psychology with Education Studies BSc(Hons), Psychology with Health Studies BSc(Hons), Social Work BA(Hons), Youth Work and Community Development BA(Hons) Postgraduate courses: Education Practice MA, Health and Community Development Studies, Health Psychology MSc, Master's in Research (Applied Health Studies) MRes, Psychological Well-being MSc, Social Work MA, Youth and Community Development Studies MA, Youth Work and Community Development PQ, Youth Work, Health and Community Development PQ MA/PGDip

School of Nursing and Midwifery; www.dmu.ac.uk/about-dmu/schools-and-departments/the-leicester-school-of-nursing-and-midwifery/

Health and Professional Practice BSc(Hons), Learning Beyond Registration Professional, Midwifery (Pre-registration Midwifery) BSc(Hons), Non-medical Prescribing BSc, Nursing with Registration (Adult) BSc(Hons), Nursing with Registration (Child) BSc(Hons), Nursing with Registration (Mental Health) BSc(Hons), Nursing with Registration (Learning Disability) BSc(Hons) Postgraduate courses: Non-medical Prescribing PG Cert, Specialist Community Public Health Nursing MSc/PG Dip/PG Cert

Leicester School of Pharmacy; www.dmu.ac.uk/about-dmu/schools-and-departments/leicester-school-of-pharmacy/

Pharmaceutical and Cosmetic Science BSc(Hons), Forensic Science BSc(Hons), Pharmacy MPharm(Hons) Postgraduate courses: Clinical Pharmacy MSc/PG Dip/PG Cert, Medical Leadership and Advanced Professional Skills MSc, Pharmaceutical Biotechnology MSc/PG Dip/PG Cert, Pharmaceutical Quality by Design MSc/PG Dip/PG Cert, Practice Certificate in Independent Prescribing for Pharmacists PG Cert, Quality by Design for the Pharmaceutical Industry MSc/PG Dip/PG Cert with professional qualification

UNIVERSITY OF DERBY
www.derby.ac.uk

College of Arts, Humanities and Education; www.derby.ac.uk/colleges/ahe

School of Arts; www.derby.ac.uk/departments/arts

Animation BA(Hons), Animation MDes, CGI and Visual Effects BA(Hons), Creative Art and Design Practice FdA/BA(Hons) Top-Up, Costume and Set Design BA(Hons), Creative Expressive Therapies BA(Hons), Dance BA(Hons), Fashion Design and Marketing BA(Hons), Fashion Design BA(Hons), Film and Television Studies (Joint Honours), Film Production BA(Hons), Fine Art BA(Hons), Graphic Design BA(Hons), Graphic Design MDes, Illustration BA(Hons), Illustration MDes, Interior Design BA(Hons), Media and Communcation BA(Hons), Media Production BA(Hons), Media Studies (Joint Honours), Music Production BSc(Hons), Popular Music BA(Hons), Popular Music Performance (Joint Honours), Photography (Professional and Applied) BA(Hons), Photography BA(Hons), Photography (Joint Honours), Product Design BA(Hons), Product Design Engineering BSc(Hons),Textile Design BA(Hons), Technical Theatre BA(Hons), Theatre Studies BA(Hons), Theatre (Joint Honours), Year Zero – Arts,

Postgraduate courses: MA Applied Theatre and Education, MA Fashion and Textiles, MA Film and Photography, MA Fine Art, MA Music Production, MA Visual Communication, MA Writing for Performance, MA Dance and Contemporary Circus

Humanities and Journalism; www.derby.ac.uk/departments/humanities

English, Creative Writing and Publishing

Creative & Professional Writing (Joint Honours), Creative & Professional Writing BA(Hons), Creative & Professional Writing BA(Hons) with Foundation Year, English (Joint Honours), English BA(Hons), English BA(Hons) with Foundation Year, English Integrated Masters (MLit), English Language (Joint Honours), English Literature and Language with Foundation Year with optional TESOL pathway BA(Hons), English Literature and Language with optional TESOL pathway BA(Hons), English with Foundation Year BA(Hons), Publishing (Joint Honours), Writing and Publishing BA(Hons), Writing and Publishing with Foundation Year BA(Hons)

Postgraduate courses: Creative Writing MA, Publishing MA

History

American Studies (Joint Honours), History (Joint Honours), History BA(Hons), History BA(Hons) with Foundation Year, History Integrated Masters (MHist);

Postgraduate courses: Public History and Heritage MA

Journalism

Football Journalism BA(Hons), Football Journalism with Foundation Year BA(Hons), Journalism (Joint Honours), Journalism BA(Hons), Journalism BA(Hons) with Foundation Year, Magazine Journalism BA(Hons), Magazine Journalism with Foundation Year BA(Hons), Specialist Sports Journalism BA(Hons), Specialist Sports Journalism with Foundation Year BA(Hons)

Institute of Education; www.derby.ac.uk/departments/education

BA(Hons) Child and Youth Studies, BA(Hons) Child and Youth Studies with Foundation Year, BA(Hons) Early Childhood Studies, BA(Hons) Early Childhood Studies with Foundation Year, Early Childhood Studies (Joint Honours), MEdu Education with Qualified Teacher Status Integrated Masters, BEd(-Hons) Primary Education with Qualified Teacher Status, BA(Hons) Education Studies with optional pathway in SEND/TESOL, BA(Hons) Education Studies with Foundation Year, Education Studies (Top-Up), BA(Hons) Special Educational Needs and Disability, BA(Hons) Special Educational Needs and Disability with Foundation Year

Postgraduate courses: MA Careers Education and Coaching, MA Childhood, MA Inclusion and SEND, MA/MPhil/PhD Education, MA Education: Early Years, MA Education: Teaching English to Speakers of Other Languages (TESOL), MA Education: Leadership Coaching and Mentoring, MA Education: Leadership and Management, MA Education: Lifelong Learning, MA Education: Primary Mathematics, MA Education: Special Educational Needs and Disabilities, National Award for SEN Co-ordination: Leading Effective, Inclusive Practice in SEN PG Cert, PGCE Primary with Qualified Teacher Status, PGCE Primary (School Direct) with Qualified Teacher Status, PGCE Post-14 (Education and Training),

PGDE Post-14 (Education and Training), Assessment Only Route to Qualified Teacher Status (QTS)

College of Business, Law and Social Sciences; www.derby.ac.uk/colleges/blss

Derby Business School; www.derby.ac.uk/departments/derby-business-school/

Accounting (Joint honours), Accounting and Finance BA(Hons), Accounting and Finance Integrated Masters MAccFin, Applied Business management BA(Hons), Business Accounting and Finance BA(Hons), Economics and Finance BSc(Hons), Economics BA(Hons), Finance with Foundation Year BSc(Hons), Human Resource Management (Joint honours), Logistics and Supply Chain Management BSc(Hons), Logistics Management BSc (Top-Up Hons), Marketing (Consumer Psychology) BSc(Hons), Marketing (Digital) BSc(Hons), Marketing (Management) BA(Hons), Marketing (PR and Advertising) BA(Hons), Marketing (Joint honours)

Derby Management School; www.derby.ac.uk/departments/derby-management-school/

MSc Accounting and Finance, MBA Global and Global Finance, MBA Block Delivery, MSc International Business, MSc International Business & Finance, MSc International Business & HRM, MSc International Business & Marketing, MSc Marketing Management, MSc Supply Chain Improvement, PG Dip Human Resource Management (CIPD accredited), MSc Human Resource Management (Top Up), Doctorate in Business Administration (DBA)

Derby Law School; www.derby.ac.uk/departments/derby-law-school/

Law with Foundation Year BA(Hons), LLB(Hons), Law (Joint Honours), Law – LLB(Hons) with Criminology

Postgraduate courses: LLM (including specialist pathways), LLM Legal Practice

Department of Criminology and Social Sciences; www.derby.ac.uk/departments/criminology-social-sciences/

Criminal Psychology BSc(Hons), Criminal Psychology BSc(Hons) with Foundation Year, Criminology (Joint Honours), Criminology BSc(Hons), Criminology BSc(Hons) with Foundation Year, International Relations and Diplomacy (Joint Honours), International Relations and Diplomacy (with optional year in The Hague) BA(Hons), Politics (Joint Honours), Professional Policing BA(Hons), Policing and Investigations BA(Hons), Sociology (Joint Honours), Sociology BA(Hons), Sociology BA(Hons) with Foundation Year

Postgraduate courses: Criminal Investigation MSc, Criminal Justice and Criminology MSc, Financial Investigation and Digital Intelligence MSc, Forensic and Criminal Psychology MSc, Intelligence, Security, Disaster Management MSc, Police Leadership, Strategy and Organisation MSc, Understanding Radicalisation PG Cert, Social and Political Studies MA, Social Science and Humanities MRes

International Policing and Justice Institute; www.derby.ac.uk/business-services/research-and-expertise/international-policing-and-justice-institute/

BA(Hons) Policing, LLB(Hons) with Criminology, BSc(Hons) Criminology, BSc(Hons) Criminal Psychology, BSc(Hons) Global Security, BSc(Hons) Intelligence, BSc(Hons) Policing, Global Security and Intelligence, Diploma in Policing, Certificate of Knowledge in Policing, FdSc Criminal Justice (Forensic Criminology), FdSc Criminal Justice (Security), FdA Criminal Justice (Human Rights), FdA Criminal Justice (Policing), BSc(Hons) Computer Forensic Investigation, BSc(Hons) Forensic Science, BSc(Hons) Forensic Science with Criminology, BSc(Hons) Forensic Science with Psychology

Postgraduate courses: MSc Police Leadership, Strategy and Organisation, Master of Business Administration (MBA Global & MBA Global Finance), MBA (Online), MSc Criminal Investigation, MSc Digital Forensics and Computer Security, MRes (Forensic Science), PG Cert Understanding Radicalisation

Centre for Contemporary Hospitality and Tourism; www.derby.ac.uk/departments/contemporary-hospitality-tourism/

Event Management BA(Hons), Event Management FdA, International Hospitality Management BA(Hons), International Hospitality Management FdA, International Spa Management BSc(Hons), International Spa Management FdSc, International Tourism Management BA(Hons), International Tourism Management FdA, Professional Culinary Arts (FdA), Professional Culinary Arts BA(Hons)

College of Engineering and Technology; www.derby.ac.uk/colleges/engineering-technology

School of Electronics, Computing and Mathematics; www.derby.ac.uk/departments/electronics-computing-mathematics/

Analytics (Joint Honours), Broadcast Engineering and Live Event Technology BSc(Hons), Computer Games Modelling and Animation BA(Hons), Computer Games Programming, Computer Network Engineering BEng(Hons), Computer Networks and Security BSc(Hons), Computer Science BSc(Hons), Computing FdSc, Cyber Security BSc(Hons), Digital Forensics and Security BSc(Hons), Electrical and Electronic Engineering BSc/BEng(Hons), Electrical and Electronic Engineering FdEng, Information Technology BSc(Hons), Mathematics (Joint Honours), Mathematics BSc(Hons), Mathematics and Computer Science BSc(Hons), Sound, Light and Live Event Technology BSc(Hons)

Postgraduate courses: Advanced Computer Networks MSc, Audio Engineering MSc, Big Data Analytics MSc, Control and Instrumentation MSc, Cyber Security MSc, Information Technology MSc, Mobile App Development MSc, Electronics, Computing or Mathematics MPhil or PhD

School of Mechanical Engineering and the Built Environment; www.derby.ac.uk/departments/mechanical-engineering/

Architectural Design (Joint Honours), Architectural Technology and Practice BSc(Hons), Civil Engineering BSc/BEng(Hons), Construction Management and Property Development BSc(Hons), Engineering Management (Top Up) BEng(Hons), Interior Architecture and Venue Design BA(Hons), Interior Design BA(Hons), Manufacturing and Production Engineering BEng(Hons), Mechanical Engineering BEng/MEng, Mechanical and Manufacturing Engineering BEng(Hons), Mechanical and Manufacturing Engineering FdSc, Motorsport Engineering BEng(Hons), Motorsport Engineering MEng, Product Design BA(Hons), Product Design Engineering BSc(Hons), Property Development (Joint Honours), Quantity Surveying and Commercial Management BSc(Hons), University Diploma in CAD and BIM (Architecture)

Postgraduate courses: Advanced Materials and Additive Manufacturing MSc, Building Information Management and Project Collaboration MSc, Civil Engineering and Construction Management MSc, Mechanical Engineering and Manufacturing Engineering MSc, Professional Engineering MSc, Strategic Engineering Management MSc, Sustainable Architecture and Healthy Buildings MSc, Mechanical Engineering and the Built Environment MPhil or PhD

School of Allied Health and Social Care; www.derby.ac.uk/departments/health-social-care/

BA(Hons) Applied Social Work, BSc(Hons) Child and Family Health and Wellbeing, BSc(Hons) Counselling and Psychotherapy Principles and Practices, BA(Hons)Creative Expressive Therapies with Foundation Year, Dance and Movement Studies Joint Honours, BSc(Hons) Diagnostic Radiography, BA(Hons) Health and Social Care, BSc(Hons) Occupational Therapy, Systemic Thinking and Practice University Advanced Diploma, BA(Hons) Youth Work and Community Development

College of Life and Natural Sciences; www.derby.ac.uk/colleges/science/

School of Human Sciences; www.derby.ac.uk/departments/human-sciences/

BSc(Hons) Adventure Sport and Coaching Science, BSc(Hons) Biomedical Health, MSci Biomedical Health, BSc(Hons) Forensic Science, BSc(Hons) Forensic Science with Criminology, BSc(Hons) Forensic Science with Psychology, BSc(Hons) Human Biology, BA(Hons) Outdoor Leadership and Management, BSc(Hons) Performance Analysis and Coaching Science, BSc(Hons) Physical Activity, Nutrition and Health, BSc(Hons) Psychology, Psychology (Joint Honours), BA(Hons) Sport and Education, BSc(Hons) Sport and Exercise Science, Ba(Hons) Sport Coaching and Development, BA(Hons) Sport Management, BSc(Hons) Sport Therapy and Rehabilitation, BSc(Hons) Strength, Conditioning and Rehabilitation

Postgraduate courses: MSc Biomedical Health, MSc Biological Sciences, MRes Forensic Science, MSc Applied Sport and Exercise Science, MRes Sport and Exercise, MSc Health Psychology, MRes Psychology, MSc Applied Developmental Psychology, MSc Behaviour Change

School of Environmental Sciences; www.derby.ac.uk/departments/environmental-sciences/

BSc(Hons) Biology, Biology (Joint Honours), BSc(Hons) Zoology, Zoology (Joint Honours), BSc(Hons) Forensic Science, BSc(Hons) Forensic

Science with Criminology, BSc(Hons) Forensic Science with Psychology, BSc(Hons) Geography, Geography (Joint Honours), Geography and Environmental Hazards BSc(Hons), Global Development (Joint Honours), BSc(Hons) Geology, Geology (Joint Honours), BSc(Hons) Geology and Environmental Hazards

Postgraduate courses: MSc Applied Acoustics, MSc Conservation Biology, MSc Environmental Assessment and Control, MSc Applied Petroleum Geoscience, Institution of Acoustics Diploma in Acoustics and Noise Control

UNIVERSITY CENTRE DONCASTER
www.don.ac.uk/university-centre-doncaster

Art, Design and Media
HND in Creative Media Production (Sound Media/ Games Development/Motion Graphics/Visual Effects), BA(Hons) in English Literature, BA(Hons) Fine Art and Crafts, BA(Hons) in Games Design and Animation (Top Up), BA(Hons) Graphic Design, BA(Hons)/FdA Illustration and Concept Art
Postgraduate courses: MA in Literature and Digital Culture

Early Years
FdA Children's Learning and Development on Campus, BA(Hons) Early Childhood Studies, FdA/ BA(Hons) Supporting Children with Special Educational Needs and Disability
Postgraduate courses: MA in Early Childhood Studies, MA in Education Studies (Primary/Secondary/SEND)

Foundation for Counselling and Relationship Studies
BA(Hons) Contemporary Relational Counselling, BA(Hons) Counselling Solutions (Top Up)
Postgraduate courses: MA in Contemporary Relationship Studies, MSc Contemoporary Psychosexual Therapy

Humanities and Social Sciences
BA(Hons) Applied Social Science, BA(Hons) Criminal Justice, BA(Hons) English, BA(Hons) Psychology in the Community, HND/HNC Health and Social Care

Postgraduate course: MA in Literature and Digital Culture

Leadership and Management
BA(Hons) Business Management, BA(Hons) International Football Business Management
Postgraduate courses: MBA Masters in Business Administration, Postgraduate Diploma in Human Resource Management, MSc in Human Resource Management

Music and Performing Arts
FdA Live Performance Technology, FdA Performing Arts in the Community (Dance, Drama, Music), BA(Hons) Creative Music Technology, BA(Hons) Performing Arts in the Community Top Up (Dance, Drama, Music)

Sports
BA(Hons) Physical Education and Sports Coaching, BSc(Hons) Sport Science and Coaching in Football, BSc(Hons) Sport, Fitness and Exercise Science, BSc(Hons) Sport, Exercise and Health Sciences (Top Up)

Teacher Education and Professional Studies
BA(Hons) Education and Advancing Professional Practice
Postgraduate courses: MEd in Advancing Professional Practice, Professional Graduate / Postgraduate Certificate in Education (PgCE / PGCE), Certificate in Education (Cert Ed)

UNIVERSITY OF DUNDEE
www.dundee.ac.uk

Duncan of Jordanstone College of Art & Design; www.dundee.ac.uk/djcad
Animation BDes, Art & Design (General Foundation) BA / BDes, Art & Philosophy BA(Hons), Digital Interaction Design BSc(Hons), Fine Art BA(Hons), Graphic Design BDes(Hons), Illustration

BDes(Hons), Interior & Environmental Design BDes(Hons), Jewellery & Metal Design BDes(Hons), Product Design BSc(Hons), Textile Design BDes(Hons)
Postgraduate courses: Animation & VFX MSc, Art & Humanities MFA, Comics & Graphic Novels MLitt/

MDes, Design for Business MSc, Forensic Art & Facial Identification MSc, Medical Art MSc, Product Design MSc

School of Business; www.dundee.ac.uk/business/

Accountancy BAcc(Hons), Accountancy (without Honours) BAcc, Accountancy and Mathematics BSc(Hons), Business Economics with Marketing BSc(Hons), Business Economics with Marketing MA(Hons), Business Economics with Marketing and European Studies MA(Hons), Business Economics with Marketing and Geography MA(Hons), Business Economics with Marketing and History MA(Hons), Business Economics with Marketing and Mathematics MA(Hons), Business Economics with Marketing and Politics MA(Hons), Business Economics with Marketing with French MA(Hons), Business Economics with Marketing with German MA(Hons), Business Economics with Marketing with Spanish MA(Hons), Business Management BSc(Hons), Economics MA(Hons), Economics BSc(Hons), Economics and History MA(Hons), Economics and International Relations MA(Hons), Economics and Politics MA(Hons), Economics with French MA(Hons), Economics with German MA(Hons), Economics with Spanish MA(Hons), Finance BFin, Financial Economics BSc(Hons), Financial Economics MA(Hons), Financial Economics with French MA(Hons), Financial Economics with German MA(Hons), Financial Economics with Spanish MA(Hons), International Business BSc(Hons), International Business MA(Hons), International Business and International Relations MA(Hons), International Business with French BSc(Hons), International Business with French MA(Hons), International Business with German BSc(Hons), International Business with German MA(Hons), International Business with Marketing BSc(Hons), International Business with Marketing MA(Hons), International Business with Spanish BSc(Hons), International Business with Spanish MA(Hons), International Finance BIFin

Postgraduate courses: Accountancy MSc, Accounting & Finance MRes, Accounting & Finance MSc, Accounting, Management and Strategy MSc, Digital and Social Media Marketing MSc, Finance MSc, International Accounting MSc, International Banking MSc, International Banking and Finance MSc, International Banking, Finance and Investment Management MSc, International Banking, Finance, Risk and Regulation MSc, International Business MSc, International Business and Banking MSc, International Business and Entrepreneurship MSc, International Business and Finance MSc, International Business and Human Resource Management MSc, International Business and Investment MSc, International Business and Management MSc, International Business and Marketing MSc, International Business and Strategy MSc, International Business, Accounting and Finance MSc, International Business, Banking and Finance MSc, International Business, Marketing and Human Resource Management MSc, International Finance MFin, International Finance and Investment Management MFin, International Finance, Risk and Regulation MFin, International Marketing MSc, International Marketing and Branding MSc, International Marketing and Finance MSc, International Marketing and Management MSc, Islamic Banking and Finance MSc, Islamic Banking, Finance, and International Business MSc, Islamic Finance MSc, Management MSc, Management and Entrepreneurship MSc, Management and Finance MSc, Management and International Human Resource Management MSc, Management and Marketing MSc, Management, Strategy and Leadership MSc, Professional Accountancy MSc

School of Dentistry; dentistry.dundee.ac.uk

Bachelor of Dental Surgery, BSc in Oral Health Sciences

Postgraduate courses: Dental Public Health MDPH, Endodontics MDSc, Forensic Dentistry MSc & MFOdont, Prosthodontics MDSc

School of Education & Social Work; www.dundee.ac.uk/esw

Childhood Practice/Childhood Studies BA, Community Education BA (Honours), Education (Primary) MA (Honours), Primary Education PGDE, Secondary Education – Chemistry/Dual Qualification/English/Home Economics/Mathematics/Physics PGDE, Social Work BA (Honours), Teaching Qualification Further Education Cert

Postgraduate courses: Advanced Social Work Studies MSc, Community Learning and Development MSc, Education (including IB Certificate) MEd, Education (Leading Learning and Teaching) MEd, Education (Inclusion and Learner Support) MEd, Education (Nursery/Early Education) MEd, Education (International Education) MEd, Education (Educational Leadership) MEd, Education (Primary) PGDE, Education (Secondary) with Supported Induction Route (Chemistry/Computing/Home Economics/Mathematics/Physics) PDGE, Secondary Education Chemistry/DualQualification/English/Home Economics/

Mathematics/Physics PGDE, Educational Psychology MSc, Social Work MSc, Teaching in Higher Education PGCert

School of Humanities; www.dundee.ac.uk/humanities

Art and Philosophy BA(Hons), English and Creative Writing MA(Hons), English and European Studies MA(Hons), English and Film Studies MA(Hons), English and History MA(Hons), European Studies MA(Hons), European Studies and European Languages & Culture MA(Hons), European Studies and Economics MA(Hons), European Studies and English MA(Hons), European Studies and Geography MA(Hons), European Studies and History MA(Hons), European Studies and International Relations MA(Hons), European Studies and Philosophy MA(Hons), European Studies and Psychology MA, European Studies with French MA(Hons), European Studies with German MA(Hons), European Studies with Spanish MA(Hons), Geography and History MA(Hons), History MA(Hons), History and International Relations MA(Hons), History and Philosophy MA(Hons), History and Politics MA(Hons), History and Psychology MA(Hons), History with French MA(Hons), History with German MA(Hons), History with Spanish MA(Hons), History and European Languages MA(Hons), Languages MA, BSc, Philosophy MA(Hons), Philosophy and Film MA(Hons), Scottish Historical Studies MA(Hons), Scottish Historical Studies with French MA(Hons), Scottish Historical Studies with German MA(Hons), Scottish Historical Studies with Spanish MA(Hons)

Postgraduate courses: Archives and Records Management MLitt/MSc, Comics & Graphic Novels MDes, Comics & Graphic Novels MLitt, Creative Writing Practice and Study MLitt, Crime Writing and Forensic Investigation MLitt, English Studies MLitt, Family and Local History MLitt, Film Studies MLitt, History MRes, History MLitt, Humanities MLitt, Philosophy MLitt, Philosophy and Literature MLitt, Records Management PGCert, Science Fiction MLitt, Scottish History (by distance learning) MLitt

School of Life Sciences; www.lifesci.dundee.ac.uk

Biochemistry BSc(Hons), Biological and Biomedical Sciences BSc(Hons), Biological Chemistry and Drug Discovery BSc(Hons), Biological Chemistry and Drug Discovery (with a year in industry) BSc, Biological Sciences BSc(Hons), Biological Sciences (with a year in industry) BSc(Hons), Biomedical Sciences BSc(Hons), Biomedical Sciences (with a year in industry) BSc(Hons), Microbiology BSc(Hons), Molecular Biology BSc(Hons), Molecular Genetics BSc(Hons), Neuroscience BSc(Hons), Pharmacology BSc(Hons), Physiological Sciences BSc(Hons)

School of Medicine; medicine.dundee.ac.uk

Medicine MBChB, Intercalated degree BMSc(Hons)

Postgraduate courses: Cancer Biology MRes, Clinical Audit and Research for Healthcare Professionals PGCert, Diabetes Care, Education & Management MSc, Human Clinical Embryology and Assisted Conception MSc, Medical Education MMEd, Motion Analysis MSc, Orthopaedic and Rehabilitation Technology MSc, Orthopaedic Science MSc, Orthopaedic Surgery MCh Orth, Palliative Care Research MPH, Psychological Therapy in Primary Care MSc, Public Health MPH, Quality Diabetes Care MSc/PGDip/PGCert

School of Nursing and Health Sciences; nursing-health.dundee.ac.uk

Adult Nursing BSc, Child Nursing BSc, Health Studies BSc, Infection: Prevention and Control BSc, Mental Health Nursing BSc, Midwifery BSc, Nursing BSc, Nursing & Health BSc

Postgraduate courses: Advanced Practice MSc, Health Studies MSc, Infection Prevention and Control MSc, Nursing MSc, Nursing and Health MSc, Leadership in Healthcare MSc, Quality Improvement and Patient Safety MSc

School of Science and Engineering; www.dundee.ac.uk/scienceengineering

Anatomical Sciences BSc(Hons), Applied Computing BSc(Hons), Applied Computing: Human Computer Interaction BSc, Applied Physics BSc(Hons), Biomedical Engineering BEng(Hons), Civil Engineering BEng / MEng(Hons), Computing Science BSc(Hons), Forensic Anthropology BSc(Hons), Mathematical Biology BSc(Hons), Mathematical Biology MSci, Mathematics MMath, Mathematics BSc(Hons), Mathematics and Astrophysics BSc(Hons), Mathematics and Economics BSc, Mathematics and Financial Economics BSc, Mathematics and Physics MSci, Mathematics and Physics BSc, Mathematics and Psychology BSc, Mechanical Engineering BEng(Hons), Mechanical Engineering with Renewables BEng, Physics MSci, Physics BSc(Hons), Physics BSc / MSci(Hons), Physics with Astrophysics BSc(Hons), Physics with Renewable Energy Science MSci, Physics with Renewable Energy Science BSc

Postgraduate courses: Anatomy & Advanced Forensic Anthropology MSc, Applied Computing MSc, Applied Computing with Work Placement MSc, Applied Mathematics MSc, Biomedical Engineering MSc, Civil Engineering MSc, Computing MSc, Computing with International Business MSc, Computing with International Business with Work Placement MSc, Computing with Work Placement MSc, Data Engineering MSc, Data Science PGCert, Data Science MSc, Data Science (part time) MSc, Design for Healthcare and Assistive Technologies MSc, Forensic Anthropology MSc, Forensic Archaeology and Anthropology MSc, Forensic Art & Facial Identification MSc, Geotechnical Engineering MSc, Human Anatomy MSc, Industrial Engineering and International Finance MSc, Industrial Engineering and Management MSc, Information Technology & International Business MSc, Marine Hydrodynamics and Ocean Engineering MSc, Mathematical Biology MSc, Mathematics PGDip, Mathematics for the Financial Sector MSc, Medical Art MSc, Medical Imaging MSc, Renewable Energy and Environmental Modelling MSc, Structural Engineering and Concrete Materials MSc

School of Social Sciences; www.dundee.ac.uk/social-sciences

Architecture MArch(Hons), Architecture (RIBA Part II) MArch, Architecture Studies MArch, English and Psychology MA(Hons), Environmental Science BSc(Hons), Environmental Science (with Dundee & Angus College) BSc(Hons), Environmental Science and Geography MA(Hons), Environmental Sustainability MA(Hons), Environmental Sustainability and Geography MA(Hons), European Politics MA(Hons), European Politics with French MA(Hons), European Politics with German MA(Hons), European Politics with Spanish MA(Hons), Geography BSc(Hons), Geography MA(Hons), Geography and Economics MA(Hons), Geography and Environmental Science BSc(Hons), Geography and History MA(Hons), Geography and Planning MA(Hons), Geography and Politics MA(Hons), Geography and Psychology MA(Hons), Geography with French MA(Hons), Geography with German MA(Hons), Geography with Spanish MA(Hons), Geopolitics MA(Hons), International Business and Environmental Sustainability MA(Hons), International Relations and European Languages MA(Hons), International Relations and Politics MA(Hons), Law LLB, Law – Accelerated LLB, Law with Energy Law LLB, Law with French LLB, Law with German LLB, Law with Spanish LLB, Law (Scots and English Dual Qualifying) LLB, Law (Scots and English Dual Qualifying) with Energy

Law LLB, Law (Scots) LLB, Law (Scots) – Accelerated LLB, Law (Scots) with Energy Law LLB, Law (Scots) with French LLB, Law (Scots) with German LLB, Law (Scots) with Spanish LLB, Politics MA(Hons), Politics and European languages MA(Hons), Politics and Psychology MA(Hons), Politics with French MA(Hons), Politics with German MA(Hons), Politics with Spanish MA(Hons), Psychology MA/BSc(Hons), Psychology with French BSc(Hons), Psychology with French MA(Hons), Psychology with German BSc(Hons), Psychology with German MA(Hons), Psychology with Spanish BSc(Hons), Psychology with Spanish MA(Hons), Urban Planning MA(Hons)

Postgraduate courses: Augmentative & Alternative Communication MSc, Comparative & European Private International Law LLM, Corporate & Commercial Law LLM, Developmental Psychology MSc, Energy Finance MSc, Environmental Law LLM, Healthcare Law and Ethics LLM, Human Rights and Conflict MSc, International and European Electricity Markets LLM, International Commercial Law LLM, International Criminal Justice & Human Rights LLM, International Energy Dispute Resolution and Avoidance LLM, International Energy Law and Policy LLM, International Energy Studies and Energy Economics MSc, International Energy Studies and Energy Finance MSc, International Energy Studies and Energy Policy MSc, International Energy Studies and Oil and Gas Economics MSc, International Energy Studies and the Environment MSc, International Law & Security LLM, International Mineral Law and Policy LLM, International Mineral Resources Management MSc/MBA, International Natural Resources Law and Policy LLM, International Oil and Gas Management MSc, International Oil and Gas Law and Policy (LLM), International Oil and Gas Management MSc/MBA, International Petroleum Taxation and Finance LLM, International Relations MSc, Law (General) LLM, Law, Banking and Finance LLM, Managing in the Energy Industries MSc, Professional Legal Practice PGDip, Psychological Research Methods MSc, Psychology of Language MSc, Social Research Methods MSc, Spatial Planning with Environmental Assessment MSc, Spatial Planning with Geographic Information Systems MSc, Spatial Planning with Marine Spatial Planning MSc, Spatial Planning with Sustainable Urban Design MSc, Spatial Planning with Urban Conservation MSc, Sustainability MSc, Sustainability and the Transition to a Low Carbon Economy MSc, Sustainability and Water Security MSc, Sustainability: Climate Change and the Green Economy MSc, The Low Carbon Just Transition LLM

DURHAM UNIVERSITY
www.dur.ac.uk

Department of Anthropology;
www.dur.ac.uk/anthropology
Anthropology BA(Hons), Anthropology BSc(Hons), Health & Human Sciences BSc(Hons), BA(Hons) Anthropology and Archaeology, BA(Hons) Anthropology and Sociology
Postgraduate courses: Socio-Cultural Anthropology MA, MA Research Methods (Anthropology), Sustainability, Culture and Development MSc, Medical Anthropology MSc, Energy and Society MSc

School of Applied Social Sciences;
www.dur.ac.uk/sociology
BA Criminology, BA Sociology, BA Anthropology and Sociology, BA Education Studies with Sociology
Postgraduate courses: MSc Criminology and Criminal Justice, MA Social Research Methods (Criminology), MA Social Research Methods (Sociology), MA Social Research Methods (Social Policy), Master of Social Work, MA Social Research Methods (Social Work), MA Social Research Methods

Department of Archaeology;
www.dur.ac.uk/archaeology
BA Archaeology, BSc Archaeology, BA Archaeology and Ancient Civilisations, BA Archaeology of the Historic World, BA Anthropology and Archaeology, BA Ancient History and Archaeology, BA Combined Honours (Archaeology)
Postgraduate courses: MA Archaeology, MSc Bioarchaeology, MSc Human Bioarchaeology and Paleopathology, MA International Cultural Heritage Management, MA Museum and Artefact Studies, MA in the Conservation of Archaeological and Museum Objects

Department of Biosciences;
www.dur.ac.uk/biosciences
BSc Biological Sciences, MBiol Biosciences; Postgraduate opportunities on website

Business School; www.dur.ac.uk/business
BSc Accounting and Finance, BA Accounting and Management, BSc Finance, Business and Management (BA), Marketing and Management (BA), BA Economics, BA Economics with Management, BA Economics with French, BA Economics and Politics, BA Philosophy, Politics and Economics
Postgraduate courses: Master of Business Administration, MSc Accounting, MSc Economics, MSc Environmental and Natural Resource Economics, MSc Experimental Economics, MSc Public Economics, MSc Finance, MSc Finance (Accounting and Finance), MSc Finance (Corporate and International Finance), MSc Finance (Economics and Finance), MSc Finance (Finance and Investment), MSc Finance (International Banking and Finance), MSc Finance (International Money, Finance and Investment), MSc Islamic Finance, MSc Islamic Finance and Management, MSc Management, MSc Management (Entrepreneurship), MSc Management (Finance), MSc Management (Human Resource Management), MSc Management (International Business), MSc Management (Supply Chain Logistics), Part-time MA Management, MSc Marketing

Department of Chemistry; www.dur.ac.uk/chemistry
BSc Chemistry, MChem Chemistry; Postgraduate courses: various research degrees

Department of Classics and Ancient History; www.dur.ac.uk/classics
BA in Ancient History, BA in Classical Civilisation, BA in Classics, Ancient History and Archaeology, BA in Ancient, Medieval and Modern History
Postgraduate courses: MA in Classics, MA in Ancient Philosophy, MA in Greece, Rome and the Near East

Department of Earth Sciences;
www.dur.ac.uk/earth.sciences
BSc Geology, BSc Environmental Geoscience, BSc Geophysics with Geology, MSci Earth Sciences, BSc Geoscience, MSci Earth Sciences, BSc Geoscience; Postgraduate courses: various research degrees

School of Education; www.dur.ac.uk/education
BA(Hons) Education Studies, BA(Hons) Primary Education;
Postgraduate courses: MA Education, MA Education International, MA Intercultural Communication and Education, MA Research Methods, Postgraduate Certificate in the Practice of Education

School of Engineering and Computing Sciences; www.dur.ac.uk/ecs
MEng Computer Science, BSc Computer Science, MEng General Engineering, BEng General Engineering;

Postgraduate courses: MSc Advanced Mechanical Engineering, MSc in Business Analytics, MSc Civil Engineering, MSc Electronic and Electrical Engineering, MSc New and Renewable Energy, MSc in Scientific Computing and Data Analysis (MISCADA)

English Language Centre; www.dur.ac.uk/ englishlanguage.centre

Postgraduate courses: MA TESOL, MA Applied Linguistics for TESOL

Department of English Studies; www.dur.ac.uk/english.studies

BA English Literature, BA English Literature and History, BA English Literature and Philosophy; Postgraduate courses: MA in English Literary Studies, MA in Medieval and Renaissance Literary Studies, MA in Romantic and Victorian Literary Studies, MA in Twentieth and Twenty-First Century Literary Studies, MA in Studies in Poetry, MA in Creative Writing

Department of Geography; www.dur.ac.uk/ geography

BA Geography, BSc Geography; Postgraduate courses: Risk Masters MA/MSc, MA in Geography (Research Methods)

School of Government & International Affairs; www.dur.ac.uk/sgia

BA Politics, BA International Relations, BA Economics & Politics, BA Philosophy & Politics, BA Philosophy, Politics and Economics, BA Combined Honours in Social Sciences; Postgraduate courses: MSc Conflict Prevention and Peacebuilding, MSc Defence, Development and Diplomacy, MSc Global Politics, MA Politics and International Relations, MA Research Methods, MA International Relations, MA International Relations (Europe), MA International Relations (East Asia), MA International Relations (Middle East)

Department of History; www.dur.ac.uk/ history

BA History, BA Ancient, Medieval and Modern History, BA English Literature and History, BA Modern European Languages and History; Postgraduate courses: MA in Social & Economic History (Research Methods), MA in History

Durham Law School; www.dur.ac.uk/law

Law LLB; Postgraduate courses: LLM Corporate Law, LLM European Trade and Commercial Law, LLM International Trade and Commercial Law, LLM International Law and Governance

Department of Mathematical Sciences; www.dur.ac.uk/mathematical.sciences

Mathematics BSc, Mathematics MMath; Postgraduate courses: MSc in Mathematical Sciences, MSc in Particles, Strings and Cosmology, various research degrees

School of Modern Languages & Cultures; www.dur.ac.uk/mlac

BA Modern Languages and Cultures, BA in Modern Languages and History, BA in Chinese Studies, BA in Japanese Studies, BA Liberal Arts, BA in Visual Arts and Film; Postgraduate courses: MA in Languages, Literatures and Cultures, MA in Translation Studies, MA in Visual Culture, various research degrees

Department of Music; www.dur.ac.uk/ music

Music BA; Postgraduate course: Music MA

Department of Natural Sciences; www.dur.ac.uk/natural.sciences

BSc Natural Sciences, MSci Natural Sciences

Department of Philosophy; www.dur.ac.uk/ philosophy

BA Philosophy, BA Philosophy and Politics, BA Philosophy and Psychology, BA Philosophy and Theology, BA English Literature and Philosophy, BA Music and Philosophy, BA Philosophy, Politics and Economics (PPE), BA Education Studies – Philosophy; Postgraduate courses: Graduate Diploma in Philosophy, Philosophy (MA)

Department of Physics; www.dur.ac.uk/ physics

BSc Physics, MPhys Physics, MPhys Physics and Astronomy, MPhys Theoretical Physics, BSc Natural Sciences, MSc Natural Sciences; Postgraduate courses: MSc Particles, Strings and Cosmology, various research degrees

Department of Psychology; www.dur.ac.uk/psychology

BSc(Hons) Behavioural Science, BSc(Hons) in Psychology; Postgraduate courses: MSc Behavioural Science, MSc Cognitive Neuroscience, MSc Developmental Psychopathology, MA Research Methods

Department of Theology and Religion; www.dur.ac.uk/theology.religion/

BA Theology and Religion, BA Philosophy and Theology, BA Religion, Society and Culture;

Postgraduate courses: MA in Biblical Studies, MA in Christian Theology, MA in Christian Theology (Anglican Studies), MA in Christian Theology (Catholic Studies), MA in Religion and Society, MA in Theology and Religion, Graduate Diploma

---

CRANMER HALL, ST JOHN'S COLLEGE
www.cranmerhall.com

Certificate in Theology, Ministry and Mission, Diploma in Theology, Ministry and Mission, BA in Theology, Ministry and Mission, BA(Hons) Theology; Postgraduate courses: MA in Theology and Ministry, MA in Consultancy for Mission and Ministry, MA in Digital Theology, Doctor of Theology and Ministry (DThM)

NEW COLLEGE DURHAM
www.newdur.ac.uk

Art & Design
FdA Visual Arts, BA(Hons) top-up Design, BA(Hons) top-up Visual Arts

Business & Management
BA(Hons) top-up Management, FdA Business & Management, FdA Event Management

Computing
BSc(Hons) top-up Computing with Networking, BSc(Hons) top-up Business Computing, FdSc Computing with Networking, FdSc Cyber Security, FdSc Business Computing, FdSc Software Development

Counselling
FdA Counselling, BA(Hons) top-up Counselling Studies

Early Years
FdA Childhood Studies & Professional Practice, BA(Hons) top-up Early Childhood Studies

Education
FdA Supporting Learning & Teaching

Graphic Design & Media
FdA Film & Media Production, FdA Graphic Design

Health & Care
FdSc Applied Health & Social Care (Adults), BSc(Hons) top-up Health & Social Care

Housing
FdA Housing & Community Studies

Music
FdA Roots and Popular Music, BA(Hons) top-up Popular Music

Public Services
FdA Public & Community Services

Sport
BA(Hons) top-up Sport & Exercise Development

Tourism, Hospitality & Events
FdA Tourism Management

ROYAL ACADEMY OF DANCE
www.rad.org.uk

Ballet Education, Ballet/Dance Teaching Studies, Benesh, Dance Education, Movement Notation; BA(Hons), Dip/CertHE, MTeach(Dance), Licenciate, PGCE

UNIVERSITY OF EAST ANGLIA
www.uea.ac.uk

School of Art, Media and American Studies; www.uea.ac.uk/web/ama

BA American and English Literature, BA American History, BA American Literature with Creative Writing, BA American Studies, BA American Studies (3 Years), BA Archaeology, Anthropology and Art History, BA Film and Television Studies, BA Film Studies and English Literature, BA History and Film Studies, BA History and History of Art, BA History of Art, BA History of Art and Literature, BA History of Art with Gallery and Museum Studies, BA Media Studies

Postgraduate courses: MA American Studies, MA Comics Studies, MA Cultural Heritage and Museum Studies, MA Film Studies, MA Film, Television and Creative Practice, MA History of Art, MA The Arts of Africa, Oceania and the Americas

School of Biological Sciences; www.uea.ac.uk/web/biological-sciences

BSc Biochemistry, BSc Biological Science (with Education), BSc/MSci Biological Sciences, BSc Biomedicine, BSc Ecology and Conservation, BSc Molecular Biology and Genetics; Postgraduate courses in: Graduate Diploma Ecology, MSc Applied Ecology and Conservation, MSc Molecular Medicine, MSc Plant Genetics and Crop Improvement

School of Chemistry; www.uea.ac.uk/web/chemistry

BSc Chemical Physics, BSc Chemistry, BSc Chemistry (with Education), BSc Physics, BSc Physics (with Education), MChem Chemical Physics, MChem Chemistry, MPhys Physics

Postgraduate courses: MSc Advanced Organic Chemistry

School of Computing Sciences; www.uea.ac.uk/web/computing

BEng Computer Systems Engineering, BSc Business Information Systems, BSc Computer Graphics, Imaging and Multimedia, BSc Computing Science, BSc Computing Science (with Education), MComp Computing Science

Postgraduate courses: MSc Advanced Computing Science, MSc Computing Science, MSc Cyber Security, MSc Data Science

School of Economics; www.uea.ac.uk/web/economics

BSc Business Economics, BSc Business Finance and Economics, BSc Economics, BSc Economics and Finance, BSc Economics with Accountancy, BA Philosophy, Politics and Economics, BSc Politics and Economics

Postgraduate courses: MSc Behavioural and Experimental Economics, MSc Competition Economics and Policy, MSc Economics, MSc Finance and Economics

School of Education and Lifelong Learning; www.uea.ac.uk/web/education

BA Education, BSc Physical Activity and Health, BSc Physical Education, BSc Physical Education, Sport and Health, BSc Sports Development

Postgraduate courses: MSc Education Leadership and Management, MA Education: Learning, Pedagogy and Assessment, MA Educational Practice and Research (Part Time), MA Mathematics Education, MA Second Language Education, MA Teaching English to Speakers of Other Languages (TESOL), PGCE Physics with Mathematics, PGCE Primary (General Class Teacher with Mathematics Specialism), PGCE Primary (Key Stage 2 with Primary Languages French/German/Spanish), PGCE Primary (Specialising in Foundation Stage and Key Stage 1/ Key Stage 1 and Key Stage 2/Key Stage 2), PGCE Secondary English, PGCE Secondary Geography, PGCE Secondary History, PGCE Secondary Mathematics, PGCE Secondary Modern Foreign Languages, PGCE Secondary Physical Education, PGCE Secondary Science (Specialising in Biology/Chemistry/Physics), MRes Social Science Research Methods

School of Environmental Sciences; www.uea.ac.uk/web/environmental-sciences

BA/BSc Geography, BSc Climate Change, BSc/MSci Environmental Sciences, BSc Environmental Sciences (with Education), BSc Environmental Sciences and International Development, BSc Geography (with Education), BSc/MSci Geology with Geography, BSc/MSci Geophysics, BSc/MSci Meteorology and Oceanography;

Postgraduate courses: MSc Applied Ecology – International Programme, MSc Climate Change, MSc Environmental Assessment and Management, MSc Environmental Sciences

School of Health Sciences; www.uea.ac.uk/web/health-sciences

BSc Adult Nursing, BSc Mental Health Nursing, BSc Midwifery, BSc Occupational Therapy, Dip HE Operating Department Practice, BSc Paramedic Science, BSc Physiotherapy, BSc Speech and Language Therapy

Postgraduate courses: MSc Nursing – Preregistration, MSc Advanced Professional Practice, MSc/PDIP Clinical Research, MSc Occupational Therapy, MSc Physiotherapy

School of History; www.uea.ac.uk/web/history

BA History, BA History and Politics, BA Modern History

Postgraduate courses: MA Early Modern History, MA Landscape History, MA Medieval History, MA Modern History

Interdisciplinary Institute for the Humanities; www.uea.ac.uk/web/humanities

BA American Studies (with a Foundation Year), BA English Literature (with a Foundation Year), BA Film and Television Studies (with a Foundation Year), BA History (with a Foundation Year), BA History of Art (with a Foundation Year), BA Intercultural Communication with Business Management (with a Foundation Year), BA Philosophy (with a Foundation Year), BA Politics (with a Foundation Year)

Postgraduate courses: MA Creative Entrepreneurship, MA Gender Studies

School of International Development; www.uea.ac.uk/web/international-development

BA Geography and International Development, BA International Development, BA International Development with Anthropology, BA International Development with Economics, BA International Development with Politics, BA Media and International Development, BSc International Development and the Environment, BA Media and International Development

Postgraduate courses: MA Agriculture and Rural Development, MA Conflict, Governance and International Development, MA Development Practice, MA Education and Development, MA Gender Analysis in International Development, MA Globalisation, Business and Sustainable Development, MA International Development, MA International Social Development, MA Media and International Development, MSc Climate Change and International Development, MSc Development Economics, MSc Environment and International Development, MSc Impact Evaluation for International Development

School of Law; www.uea.ac.uk/web/law

LLB Law, LLB Law with American Law, LLB Law with European Legal Systems

Postgraduate courses: Graduate Diploma in Legal Studies, LLM Information Technology and Intellectual Property Law, LLM International Commercial and Business Law, LLM International Commercial and Competition Law, LLM International Commercial Dispute Resolution, LLM International Trade Law, LLM Master of Laws, LLM Media Law, Policy and Practice, PG Certificate Employment Law (Part Time)

School of Literature, Drama and Creative Writing; www.uea.ac.uk/web/literature

BA American and English Literature, BA Culture, Literature and Politics, BA Drama, BA Drama and Creative Writing, BA English and American Literature, BA English Literature, BA English Literature and Drama, BA English Literature with Creative Writing, BA Film Studies and English Literature, BA History of Art and Literature, BA Literature and History, BA Scriptwriting and Performance

Postgraduate courses: MA Biography and Creative Non-Fiction, MA Creative Writing Poetry, MA Creative Writing Prose Fiction, MA Creative Writing Scriptwriting, MA Literary Translation, MA Medieval and Early Modern Textual Cultures 1381 – 1688, MA Modern and Contemporary Writing, MA Theatre Directing: Text and Production

School of Mathematics; www.uea.ac.uk/web/mathematics

BEng Energy Engineering, BEng Energy Engineering with Environmental Management, BEng Engineering, BSc Mathematics, BSc Mathematics (with Education)

Postgraduate courses: MA Mathematics Education, MEng Energy Engineering, MEng Engineering, MMath Master of Mathematics, MSc Energy Engineering with Environmental Management

School of Natural Sciences; www.uea.ac.uk/web/natural-sciences

BSc Natural Sciences; Postgraduate course: MNatSci Natural Sciences

Norwich Business School; www.uea.ac.uk/web/norwich-business-school

BSc Accounting and Finance, BSc Accounting and Management, BSc Business Analytics and Management, BSc Business Finance and Management, BSc Business Management, BA Business and Human Resource Management, BA International Business Management, BSc Marketing and Management
Postgraduate courses: MSc Accounting and Finance, MSc Banking and Finance, MSc Brand Leadership, MSc Business Management, MSc Enterprise and Business Creation, MSc Finance and Management, MSc Human Resource Management, MSc International Accounting and Financial Management, MSc Investment and Financial Management, MSc Management, MSc Marketing, MSc Marketing and Management, MSc Operations and Logistics Management

Norwich Medical School; www.uea.ac.uk/web/medicine

Postgraduate courses: MBBS Medicine, MclinEd/PDIP Clinical Education, MRes Clinical Science, MS/PDIP Oncoplastic Breast Surgery, MSc/PDIP Health Economics, MSc Physician Associate Studies, PG Certificate Clinical Education (Part Time)

School of Pharmacy; www.uea.ac.uk/web/pharmacy

BSc/MSci Pharmacology and Drug Discovery; Postgraduate courses: MPharm Pharmacy, MSc Natural Product Drug Discovery, PG Diploma Pharmacy Practice

School of Politics, Philosophy and Language and Communication Studies; www.uea.ac.uk/web/ppl

BA Broadcast and Multimedia Journalism, BA Culture, Literature and Politics, BA English Literature and Philosophy, BA Intercultural Communication with Business Management, BA International Relations, BA International Relations and Modern History, BA International Relations and Modern Languages, BA International Relations and Politics, BA Modern Language (3 Year Option with a Semester Abroad), BA Modern Language(s) with Management Studies, BA Modern Languages (Double Honours with a Year Abroad), BA Philosophy, BA Philosophy and History, BA Philosophy and Politics, BA Politics, BA Politics and Digital Cultures, BA Politics and Media Studies, BA Society, Culture and Media, BA Translation and Interpreting with Modern Languages (Double Honours with a Year Abroad), BA Translation, Media and Modern Language (3 Year Option with a Semester Abroad), BA Translation, Media and Modern Languages (Double Honours with a Year Abroad)
Postgraduate courses: MA Broadcast and Digital Journalism International, MA Broadcast and Digital Journalism UK, MA International Relations, MA International Security, MA Media and Cultural Politics, MA Media, Culture and Society, MA Philosophy and Literature, MA Public Policy and Public Management, MRes Philosophy

School of Psychology; www.uea.ac.uk/web/psychology

BSc/MSci Cognitive Psychology, BSc Computational Psychology, BSc/MSci Developmental Psychology, BSc Psychology, BSc/MSci Social Psychology
Postgraduate courses: MRes Social Science Research Methods, MSc Cognitive Neuroscience, MSc Developmental Science, MSc Social Psychology

School of Social Work; www.uea.ac.uk/web/socialwork

BA Social Work; Postgraduate course: MA Social Work

CITY COLLEGE NORWICH
www.ccn.ac.uk

BSc(Hons) Professional Aviation Engineering Practice, BSc(Hons) Applied Sport, Health and Exercise, BA(Hons) Psychology with Sociology, BA(Hons) Leadership in the Public Sector, BA(Hons) Integrated Health and Social Care Top Up, BA(Hons) English and Social Sciences, BA(Hons) English, BA(Hons) Childhood Studies, BA(Hons) Business Management

EASTON & OTLEY COLLEGE
www.eastonotley.ac.uk

BA(Hons) Crime, Terrorism and Global Security, BSc(Hons) Agriculture (Top-Up), BSc(Hons) Animal Science and Welfare (Top-Up), BSc(Hons) Landbased Sciences (Ecology/Equine) (Top-Up), BSc(Hons) Zoology, BSc Sports Coaching Science (Top-Up), FdSc Agricultural Management, FdSc Animal Science & Welfare, FdSc Equine Science & Welfare, FdSc Football Development & Coaching, FdSc Health, Fitness, Strength & Conditioning (subject to approval), FdSc Sports Coaching Science, FdSc Wildlife & Conservation

EDGE HILL UNIVERSITY
www.edgehill.ac.uk

Faculty of Arts and Sciences; www.edgehill.ac.uk/fas

Department of Biology; www.edgehill.ac.uk/biology
BSc(Hons) Biology, BSc(Hons) Biomedical Science, BSc(Hons) Biotechnology, BSc(Hons) Ecology and Conservation, BSc(Hons) Food Science, BSc(Hons) Genetics, BSc(Hons) Human Biology, BSc(Hons) Plant Science
Postgraduate course: MRes Biology, MSc Conservation Management

Business School; www.edgehill.ac.uk/business
BSc(Hons) Accountancy, BSc(Hons) Business and Economics, BSc(Hons) Business and Management, BSc(Hons) Business and Management with Accounting and Finance, BSc(Hons) Business and Management with Human Resource Management, BSc(Hons) Business and Management with Leisure and Tourism, BSc(Hons) Business and Management with Logistics and Supply Chain Management, BSc(Hons) Business and Management with Marketing, BSc(Hons) Business Innovation and Enterprise, BSc(Hons) International Business, BSc(Hons) Marketing, BSc(Hons) Marketing with Advertising, BSc(Hons) Marketing with Digital Communications
Postgraduate courses: PGCert Employment, Enterprise and Entrepreneurship Developmentm MSc Leadership and Management Development, Master of Business Administration, Master of Business Administration (Finance), Master of Business Administration (Human Resource Management), Master of Business Administration (Information Technology), Master of Business Administration (Marketing), MSc Psychology in Business, MA Marketing Communications and Branding

Department of Computer Science; www.edgehill.ac.uk/computerscience
BSc(Hons) Computer Engineering, BSc(Hons) Computer Science, BSc(Hons) Computer Science and Mathematics, BSc(Hons) Computing, BSc(Hons) Computing (Games Programming), BSc(Hons) Computing (Networking, Security and Forensics), BSc(Hons) Data Science, BSc(Hons) Information Technology Management for Business, BSc(Hons) Robotics and Artificial Intelligence, BSc(Hons) Software Engineering, BSc(Hons) Systems Automation, BSc(Hons) Web Design and Development, MComp Business Information Systems, MComp Computer Security and Networks, MComp Computing, MComp Software Application Development, MComp Web Design and Development
Postgraduate courses: MSc Advanced Computer Networking, MSc/PGCert Big Data Analytics, MSc Computing, MSc Cyber Security, MSc Games Programming and Visual Computing, MSc Information Security and IT Management, MBA Master of Business Administration (Information Technology), MRes Masters by Research

English, History and Creative Writing; www.edgehill.ac.uk/englishhistorycreativewriting
English
BA(Hons) English, BA(Hons) English Language, BA(Hons) English Literature, BA(Hons) English and Film Studies, BA(Hons) English Language with Creative Writing, BA(Hons) English Literature and History, BA(Hons) English Literature with Creative Writing, BA(Hons) English with Creative Writing
Postgraduate courses: MA English, MA Popular Culture

History

BA(Hons) History, BA(Hons) History with Politics, BA(Hons) English Literature and History, BA(Hons) Politics and History

Postgraduate courses: MA History and Culture, MA Popular Culture

Creative Writing

BA(Hons) Creative Writing, BA(Hons) Creative Writing and Drama, BA(Hons), BA(Hons) Creative Writing and English Literature, Creative Writing and Film Studies

Postgraduate course: MA Creative Writing

Department of Geography;
www.edgehill.ac.uk/geography

BSc(Hons) Geoenvironmental Hazards, BA(Hons) Geography, BSc(Hons) Geography, BSc(Hons) Geology with Physical Geography, BSc(Hons) Physical Geography and Geology

Department of Law and Criminology;
www.edgehill.ac.uk/law

LLB(Hons) Law, LLB(Hons) Law with Criminology, LLB(Hons) Law with Politics, BA(Hons) Childhood & Youth Studies and Criminology, BA(Hons) Criminology, BA(Hons) Criminology and Law, BA(Hons) Criminology and Psychology, BA(Hons) Criminology and Sociology, BA(Hons) Politics and Criminology, BSc(Hons) Psychology and Criminology, BSc(Hons) Professional Policing, BA(Hons) Policing, BA(Hons) History and Politics, BA(Hons) Politics and Sociology

Department of Media;
www.edgehill.ac.uk/media

BA(Hons) Animation, BA(Hons) Film Studies, BA(Hons) Film Studies with Film Production, BA(Hons) Film and Television Production, BA(Hons) Media, Film and Television, BA(Hons) Media, Music and Sound, BA(Hons) Television Production Management

Postgraduate courses: MA Film and Media

Department of Performing Arts;
www.edgehill.ac.uk/performingarts

BA(Hons) Creative Writing and Drama, BA(Hons) Dance, BA(Hons) Dance and Drama, BA(Hons) Drama, BA(Hons) Drama and English Literature, BA(Hons) Drama & Film Studies, BA(Hons) Music Production, BA(Hons) Musical Theatre

Department of Psychology;
www.edgehill.ac.uk/psychology

BSc(Hons) Psychology, BSc(Hons) Educational Psychology, BSc(Hons) Sport and Exercise Psychology,

BSc(Hons) Psychology and Criminology, BA(Hons) Criminology and Psychology

Postgraduate course: MSc Psychology (Conversion), MSc Psychology in Business, MRes Research, PhD (Psychology)

Department of Sport and Physical Activity;
www.edgehill.ac.uk/sport

BA(Hons) Physical Education and School Sport, BSc(Hons) Sport and Exercise Psychology, BSc/MSci(Hons) Sport and Exercise Science, BA/MSci(-Hons) Sports Coaching and Development, BA(Hons) Sports Development and Management, BA(Hons) Sports Management and Coaching, BSc/MSci(Hons) Sports Therapy

Postgraduate course: MSc Sport, Physical Activity and Mental Health

Faculty of Education;
www.edgehill.ac.uk/education

Early Years Unit; www.edgehill.ac.uk/education/earlyyears-education

BA(Hons) Early Years Education with QTS, PGCE Early Years Education with QTS, FdA Early Years Education and Leadership, BA(Hons) Early Years Leadership, BA(Hons) Early Years Practice

Primary Education Unit;
www.edgehill.ac.uk/education/children-education-communities

BA(Hons) Children and Young People's Learning and Development, BA(Hons) Teaching, Learning and Child Development, BA(Hons) Working with Children 5-11, BA(Hons) Primary Education with QTS, BA(Hons) Primary Education with QTS (School-Based Route)

Postgraduate courses: PGCE Primary Education with QTS, PGCE Primary Mathematics Specialist with QTS

Professional Learning Unit;
www.edgehill.ac.uk/education/professional-learning

Postgraduate courses: Dyslexia Alternative Pathway CPD (Online), PGCert/MA Specialist Primary Mathematics Practice, PGCert SpLD (Dyslexia) with AMBDA/ATS, Postgraduate Certificate Education (Dyscalculia), Postgraduate Certificate Education (Inclusion and SEN), MA Educational Enquiry and Professional Learning, National Award Special Educational Needs Coordination

Secondary and Further Education Unit; www.edgehill.ac.uk/education/secondary-and-further-education

BA(Hons) Education, BA(Hons) Education and English, BA(Hons) Education and History, BA(Hons) Education and Religion, BA(Hons) Education and Sociology, BA(Hons) Religion, BA(Hons) Secondary English Education with QTS, BSc(Hons) Secondary Mathematics Education with QTS, BA(Hons) Secondary Religious Education with QTS

Postgraduate course: PGCE Further Education and Training, PGCE Secondary Computer Science and Information Technology Education (Age Phase 11-16) with QTS, PGCE Secondary English (Age Phase 11-16) with QTS, PGCE Secondary Geography (Age Phase 11-16) with QTS, PGCE Secondary History (Age Phase 11-16) with QTS, PGCE Secondary Mathematics (Age Phase 11-16) with QTS, PGCE Secondary Physical Education (Age Phase 11-16) with QTS, PGCE Secondary Religious Education (Age Phase 11-16) with QTS, PGCE Secondary Science (Biology) (Age Phase 11-16) with QTS

Faculty of Health and Social Care; www.edgehill.ac.uk/health

Nursing; www.edgehill.ac.uk/health/nursing

BSc(Hons) Nursing (Adult), BSc(Hons) Nursing (Child), BSc(Hons) Nursing (Learning Disabilities), BSc (Hons Nursing (Mental Health), MNSW Adult Nursing and Social Work, MNSW Children's Nursing and Social Work, MNSW Learning Disabilities Nursing and Social Work, MNSW Mental Health Nursing and Social Work, MSci Nursing

Midwifery; www.edgehill.ac.uk/health/midwifery

BSc(Hons) Pre-Registration Midwifery

Operating Department Practice; www.edgehill.ac.uk/health/odp

BSc(Hons) Operating Department Practice

Paramedic Practice; www.edgehill.ac.uk/health/paramedic

BSc(Hons) Paramedic Practice, BSc Clinical and Professional Paramedic Practice

Applied Health and Social Care; www.edgehill.ac.uk/health/ahsc

BSc(Hons) Child and Adolescent Mental Health and Wellbeing, BSc(Hons) Child Health and Wellbeing, BA(Hons) Counselling and Psychotherapy, BSc(Hons) Critical Approaches to Counselling and psychotherapy, BSc(Hons) Global Public Health, BSc(Hons) Health and Social Care Leadership and Management, BA(Hons) Health and Social Wellbeing, BSc(Hons) Nutrition and Health, MSci Nutrition, BSc(Hons) Psychosocial Analysis of Offending Behaviour, BSc(Hons) Integrated Children and Young People's Practice

Postgraduate courses: MSc Child and Adolescent Mental Health and Wellbeing, MHealth Res Master of Health Research, MSc Leadership Development, MSc Public Health Nutrition

Social Work; www.edgehill.ac.uk/health/socialwork

BA(Hons) Social Work, MNSW Adult Nursing and Social Work, MNSW Children's Nursing and Social Work, MNSW Learning Disabilities Nursing and Social Work, MNSW Mental Health Nursing and Social Work

Postgraduate course: MA Social Work

THE UNIVERSITY OF EDINBURGH
www.ed.ac.uk

School of Biological Sciences; www.ed.ac.uk/biology

Biological Sciences (BSc), Biological Sciences (Biochemistry) (BSc), Biological Sciences (Biotechnology) (BSc), Biological Sciences (Cell Biology) (BSc), Biological Sciences (Development, Regeneration and Stem Cells) (BSc), Biological Sciences (Ecology) (BSc), Biological Sciences (Evolutionary Biology) (BSc), Biological Sciences (Genetics) (BSc), Biological Sciences (Immunology) (BSc), Biological Sciences (Molecular Biology) (BSc), Biological Sciences (Molecular Genetics) (BSc), Biological Sciences (Plant Science) (BSc), Biological Sciences (Zoology) (BSc), Biological Sciences with Management

Postgraduate courses: Animal Breeding & Genetics MSc/PgDip, Biochemistry MSc/PgDip, Biodiversity & Taxonomy of Plants MSc/PgDip, Bioinformatics MSc, PgDip, Biotechnology MSc/PgDip, Drug Discovery &

Protein Biotechnology (Online Distance Learning) MSc/PgDip/PgCert/PgProfDev, Drug Discovery & Translational Biology MSc/PgDip, Evolutionary Genetics MSc/PgDip, Human Complex Trait Genetics MSc/PgDip, Next Generation Drug Discovery (Online Distance Learning) MSc/PgDip/PgCert/PgProfDev, Quantitative Genetics & Genome Analysis MSc/PgDip, Synthetic Biology & Biotechnology MSc/PgDip, Systems & Synthetic Biology MSc/PgDip

Business School; www.business-school.ed.ac.uk

MA Accounting and Business, MA Accounting and Finance, MA Business Management, MA Business with Decision Analytics, MA Business with Enterprise and Innovation, MA Business with Human Resource Management, MA Business with Marketing, MA Business with Strategic Economics, MA International Business, MA International Business with Arabic, MA International Business with Chinese, MA International Business with French, MA International Business with German, MA International Business with Italian, MA International Business with Japanese, MA International Business with Russian, MA International Business with Spanish, MA Business and Law, MA Business and Geography, MA Business and Economics, BSc Computer Science and Management Science, BSc Mathematics and Business, LLB Law and Business, LLB Law and Accountancy, MA Arabic and Business, MA Economics and Accounting, MA French and Business, MA German and Business, MA Italian and Business, MA Portuguese and Business, MA Psychology and Business, MA Russian Studies and Business, MA Spanish and Business

Postgraduate courses: MSc Accounting and Finance, MSc Banking and Risk, MSc Business Analytics, MSc Carbon Finance, MSc Entrepreneurship and Innovation, MSc Finance, MSc Finance, Technology and Policy, MSc Human Resource Management, MSc International Business and Emerging Markets, MSc International Human Resource Management, MSc Management, MSc Marketing, MSc Marketing and Business Analysis, Master of Business Administration

School of Chemistry; www.chem.ed.ac.uk

Chemical Physics (BSc), Chemical Physics (MChemPhys), Chemistry (BSc), Chemistry (MChem), Medicinal and Biological Chemistry (BSc), Medicinal and Biological Chemistry (MChem)

Postgraduate courses: Materials Chemistry MSc, Medicinal & Biological Chemistry MSc, MSc Sensors and Imaging Systems

School of Divinity; www.ed.ac.uk/divinity

Divinity (BD), Divinity and Classics (MA), Philosophy and Theology (MA), Religious Studies (MA), Religious Studies and English Literature (MA), Religious Studies and Scottish Literature (MA), Theology (MA)

Postgraduate courses: Biblical Studies MTh/MSc, Islam & Christian Muslim Relations MSc, Religious Studies MSc, Science & Religion MSc, Theology in History MTh/MSc, World Christianity MTh/MSc

School of Economics; www.ed.ac.uk/economics

Economics (MA), Economics and Accounting (MA), Economics and Economic History (MA), Economics and Mathematics (MA), Economics and Politics (MA), Economics and Sociology (MA), Economics and Statistics (MA), Economics with Environmental Studies (MA), Economics with Finance (MA), Economics with Management Science (MA)

Postgraduate courses: Economics MSc, Economics (Econometrics) MSc, Economics (Finance) MSc

Edinburgh College of Art; www.eca.ed.ac.uk

Acoustics and Music Technology (BSc), Animation (BA), Architectural History and Heritage (MA), Architecture (BA/MA), Fashion (BA), Film and Television (BA), Fine Art (MA), Graphic Design (BA), History of Art (MA), Illustration (BA), Interior Design (BA), Intermedia (BA), Jewellery and Silversmithing (BA), Landscape Architecture (MA), Music (BMus), Painting (BA), Performance Costume (BA), Photography (BA), Product Design (BA), Sculpture (BA), Textiles (BA)

Postgraduate courses: Acoustics & Music Technology MSc, Advanced Sustainable Design MSc, Animation Master of Fine Art, Architectural & Urban Design MSc, Architectural Conservation MSc, Architectural History PhD/MPhil, Architectural History & Theory MSc, Architectural Project Management (Online Distance Learning) MSc, Architecture, Master of (ARB/RIBA Part 2) MArch ARB Pt 2, Architecture by Design PhD, Art PhD/MPhil, Art, Space & Nature Master of Fine Art/MA, Collections and Curating Practices MSc by Research, Composition MMus, Composition for Screen MSc, Contemporary Art Practice Master of Fine Art/MA, Contemporary Art Theory MA, Creative Music Practice PhD, Cultural

Landscapes MSc, Cultural Studies MSc, Design MPhil/PhD, Design & Digital Media MSc, Design For Change MA, Design Informatics Master of Fine Art/MA, Digital Media & Culture MSc, Digital Media Design (Online Distance Learning) MSc, European Masters in Landscape Architecture European Masters, Fashion Master of Fine Art, Film Directing Master of Fine Art/MA, Glass Master of Fine Art/MA, Graphic Design Master of Fine Art/MA, History of Art MPhil/PhD/MSc, History of Art, Theory & Display MSc, Illustration Master of Fine Art/MA, Interdisciplinary Creative Practices MSc by Research, Interior Design MA, Jewellery Master of Fine Art, Landscape & Wellbeing MSc, Landscape Architecture MLA/MPhil/PhD, Material Practice MSc, Modern & Contemporary Art: History, Curating & Criticism MSc, Music PhD/MSc, Musical Composition PhD, Musicology MMus, Performance Costume Master of Fine Art, Sound Design MSc, Textiles Master of Fine Art, Urban Strategies & Design MSc

Edinburgh Medical School; www.ed.ac.uk/medicine-vet-medicine/edinburgh-medical-school

Medicine (MBChB), BSc Anatomy and Development, BSc Biomedical Sciences, BSc(Hons) in Medical Sciences, BSc in Oral Health Sciences, BSc Infectious Diseases, BSc Neuroscience, BSc Pharmacology, BSc Physiology, BSc Reproductive Biology, HCP-Med for healthcare professionals

Postgraduate courses: Advanced Clinical Practice (Online Learning) MVetSci/PgDip /PgCer/PgProfDev, Anatomical Sciences (Online Distance Learning) PgDip/PgCert/PgProfDev, Animal Biosciences MSc, Applied Animal Behaviour and Animal Welfare MSc, Applied Conservation Genetics with Wildlife Forensics (Online Learning) MSc/PgDip/PgCert/PgProfDev, Applied Poultry Science (Online Learning) MSc/PgDip/PgCert/PgProfDev, Biodiversity, Wildlife & Ecosystem Health (Online Distance Learning) MSc/PgCert/PgDip/PgProfDev, Clinical Animal Behaviour (Online Learning) MSc/PgDip/PgCert, Clinical Microbiology & Infectious Diseases (Online Distance Learning) MSc, Conservation Medicine (Online Learning) MVetSci/PgDip/PgCert/PgProfDev, Equine Science (Online Learning) MSc/PgDip/PgCert/PgProfDev, Food Safety (Online Learning) MSc/PgDip/PgCert/PgProfDev, Global Food Security and Nutrition (Online Learning) MSc/PgDip/PgCert/PgProfDev, Global Health & Infectious Diseases (Online Distance Learning) MSc/PgDip/PgCert/PgProfDev, Global Health Studies (Online Distance Learning) PgCert, Human Anatomy MSc, International Animal Health (Online Distance Learning) MSc/PgDip/PgCert/PgProfDev, International Animal Welfare, Ethics and Law (Online Learning) MSc/PgDip/PgCert/PgProfDev, Science Communication & Public Engagement (Online Distance Learning) MSc/PgCert/PgDip, Clinical Management of Pain (Online Distance Learning) MSc/PgDip/PgCert/PgProfDev, Clinical Ophthalmology (Online Distance Learning) ChM (Clinical Ophthalmology), General Surgery (Online Distance Learning) ChM (General Surgery), Imaging (Online Distance Learning) MSc/PgDip/PgCert/PgProfDev, Internal Medicine (Online Distance Learning) MSc/PgCert/PgDip, Neuroimaging for Research (Online Distance Learning) MSc/PgDip/PgCert/PgProfDev, One Health (Online Learning) MSc/PgDip/PgCert/PgProfDev, Oral Surgery MClinDent, Orthodontics MClinDent, Paediatric Dentistry MClinDent, Paediatric Emergency Medicine (Online Distance Learning) MSc/PgCert/PgDip, Patient Safety and Clinical Human Factors (Online Learning) MSc/PgCert/PgDip, Primary Care Ophthalmology (Online Distance Learning) MSc, Prosthodontics MClinDent, Stem Cells and Translational Neurology (Online Distance Learning) MSc/PgDip/PgCert/PgProfDev, Surgical Sciences (Online Distance Learning) MSc, Transfusion, Transplantation & Tissue Banking MSc, Trauma & Orthopaedics (Online Distance Learning) ChM (Trauma & Orthopaedics), Urology (Online Distance Learning) ChM (Urology), Vascular & Endovascular Surgery (Online Distance Learning) ChM (Vascular and Endovascular Surgery), Veterinary Epidemiology (Online Learning) MSc/PgCert/PgDip/PgProfDev, Veterinary Anaesthesia and Analgesia (Online Learning) MSc/PgDip/PgCert/PgProfDev, Clinical Education (Online Distance Learning) MSc/PgCert/PgDip, Clinical Trials (Online Distance Learning) MSc/PgCert/PgDip, Critical Care (Online Learning) MSc/PgCert/PgDip, Dental Sedation and Anxiety Management (Online Learning) PgCert, Family Medicine (Online Distance Learning) MFM, Global eHealth (Online Distance Learning) MSc/PgCert/PgDip/PgProfDev, Global Health Challenges (Online Distance Learning) PgCert/PgProfDev, Public Health MPH, Public Health (Online Distance Learning) MPH, Restorative Dentistry (Online Learning) MSc/PgCert/PgDip/PgProfDev

The Moray House School of Education; www.ed.ac.uk/education

Applied Sport Science (BSc), Childhood Practice (BA), Physical Education (MA), Primary Education with Gaelic (Fluent Speakers/Learners) (MA), Sport and Recreation Management (BSc)

Postgraduate courses: Academic Practice (PgCert), Dance Science & Education MSc/PgDip, Digital Education (Online Distance Learning) MSc/PgDip/PgCert, Education MSc, Inclusive Education MSc/PgDip/PgCert, Language Education MSc/PgDip, Learning for Sustainability MSc/PgDip/PgCert, Outdoor Education MSc/PgDip/PgCert, Outdoor Environmental & Sustainability Education MSc/PgDip/PgCert, Performance Psychology MSc/PgDip, Physical Activity for Health MSc/PgDip/PgCert, Professional Graduate Diploma in Education (Primary) PGDE, Professional Graduate Diploma in Education (Secondary) PGDE, Social Justice & Community Action (Online Distance Learning) MSc/PgDip/PgCert, Sport Policy/Management & International Development MSc, Strength & Conditioning MSc/PgDip, Teaching English to Speakers of Other Languages (TESOL) MSc/PgDip, Transformative Learning and Teaching MSc

School of Engineering; www.eng.ed.ac.uk

Chemical Engineering (BEng/MEng), Civil Engineering (BEng/MEng), Electrical and Mechanical Engineering (BEng/MEng), Electronics and Computer Science (BEng/MEng), Electronics and Electrical Engineering (BEng/MEng), Engineering (BEng/MEng), Mechanical Engineering (BEng/MEng), Structural and Fire Safety Engineering (BEng/MEng), Structural Engineering with Architecture (BEng/MEng)

Postgraduate courses: Advanced Chemical Engineering MSc, MSc Advanced Power Engineering, Electrical Power Engineering MSc, Electronics MSc, International Master of Science in Fire Safety Engineering MSc, Sensor & Imaging Systems MSc, Signal Processing & Communications MSc, Structural & Fire Safety Engineering MSc, Sustainable Energy Systems MS/PgDip

School of Geosciences; www.ed.ac.uk/geosciences

Ecological and Environmental Sciences (BSc), Environmental Geoscience (BSc), Geography (MA), Geography (BSc), Geology (BSc), Geology (MEarthSci), Geophysics (BSc), Geophysics and Geology (BSc), Geophysics and Meteorology (BSc)

Postgraduate courses: Applied Geoscience (Geoenergy) MSc, Carbon Innovation (Online Distance Learning) PgCert, Carbon Management MSc, Carbon Management (Online Distance Learning) MSc, Climate Change Management (Online Distance Learning) PgCert, Earth Observation & Geoinformation Management MSc, Ecological Economics MSc, Environment & Development MSc, Environment, Culture & Society MSc, Environmental Protection & Management MSc, Environmental Sustainability MSc, Food Security MSc, Geographical Information Science MSc, Geographical Information Science & Archaeology MSc, Managing Environmental Change MSc, Marine Systems & Policies MSc, Soils & Sustainability MSc, Sustainable Plant Health MSc

School of Health in Social Science; www.ed.ac.uk/health

Health, Science and Society (MA), Nursing Studies (BN)

Postgraduate courses: Advanced Nursing Practice MSc, Applied Psychology (Healthcare) For Children & Young People MSc, Mental Health in Children & Young People MSc, Mental Health in Children & Young People (Online Distance Learning) MSc, Clinical Psychology DClinPsychol, Counselling MCouns/PgCert/PgDip, Counselling (Interpersonal Dialogue) MCouns, Counselling Studies MSc, Psychological Therapies MSc, Psychology of Mental Health (Conversion) MSc

School of History, Classics and Archaeology; www.ed.ac.uk/history-classics-archaeology

Ancient and Medieval History (MA), Ancient History (MA), Ancient History and Classical Archaeology (MA), Ancient History and Greek (MA), Ancient History and Latin (MA), Ancient Mediterranean Civilisations (MA), Archaeology (MA), Archaeology and Ancient History (MA), Archaeology and Social Anthropology (MA), Classical and Middle East Studies (MA), Classical Archaeology and Greek (MA), Classical Archaeology and Latin (MA), Classical Studies (MA), Classics (MA), Classics and English Language (MA), Classics and Linguistics (MA), Economic History (MA), Greek Studies (MA), History (MA), History and Archaeology (MA), History and Classics (MA), History and Economics (MA), History and History of Art (MA), History and Politics (MA), History and Scottish History (MA), Latin Studies (MA)

Postgraduate courses: American History MSc, Ancient History MSc, Archaeology MSc, Classical Art & Archaeology MSc, Classics MSc, Contemporary History MSc, European Archaeology MSc, History MSc, History (Online Distance Learning) (TBC), Human Osteoarchaeology MSc, Intellectual History MSc, Late Antique, Islamic & Byzantine

Studies MSc, Medieval History MSc, Mediterranean Archaeology MSc, Scottish History MSc

School of Informatics; www.ed.ac.uk/informatics

Artificial Intelligence (BSc), Artificial Intelligence and Computer Science (BSc), Artificial Intelligence and Mathematics (BSc), Artificial Intelligence and Software Engineering (BEng), Cognitive Science (BSc), Computer Science (BSc), Computer Science (BEng), Computer Science and Electronics (BEng), Computer Science and Management Science (BSc), Computer Science and Mathematics (BSc), Computer Science and Physics (BSc), BSc(Hons) Data Science (Graduate Apprenticeship), Informatics (5-year undergraduate Masters Programme) (MInf), Software Engineering (BEng), Software Engineering with Management (BEng)

Postgraduate programmes: Advanced Design Informatics MSc, Artificial Intelligence MSc, Cognitive Science MSc, Computer Science MSc, Cyber Security, Privacy and Trust MSc, Data Science MSc, Design Informatics MSc, Informatics MSc

School of Law; www.law.ed.ac.uk

Law (Graduate Entry) (LLB), Law (Ordinary and Honours) (LLB), Law and Accountancy (LLB), Law and Business (LLB), Law and Celtic (LLB), Law and Economics (LLB), Law and French (LLB), Law and German (LLB), Law and History (LLB), Law and International Relations (LLB), Law and Politics (LLB), Law and Social Policy (LLB), Law and Sociology (LLB), Law and Spanish (LLB)

Postgraduate courses: Commercial Law LLM, Comparative & European Private Law LLM, Corporate Law LLM, Criminal Law & Criminal Justice LLM, Criminology & Criminal Justice MSc, European Law LLM, Global Crime, Justice & Security MSc, Global Environment & Climate Change Law LLM, Human Rights LLM, Information Technology Law (Online Distance Learning) LLM, Innovation, Technology & the Law LLM, Innovation, Technology & the Law (Online Distance Learning) LLM, Intellectual Property Law LLM, Intellectual Property Law (Online Distance Learning) LLM, International Banking Law & Finance LLM, International Commercial Law & Practice (Online Distance Learning) LLM, International Economic Law LLM, International Law LLM, Law LLM, Law (Online Distance Learning) LLM, Law (Online Distance Learning) PgCert, Medical Law & Ethics LLM, Medical Law & Ethics (Online Distance Learning) LLM

School of Literatures, Languages and Culture; www.ed.ac.uk/literatures-languages-cultures

Arabic (MA), Arabic and Ancient Greek/Business/Economics/French/History/Persian/Politics/Social Anthropology/Spanish (MA), Celtic (MA), Celtic and English Language/English Literature/French/Linguistics/Scandinavian Studies/Scottish Ethnology/Scottish History/Scottish Literature (MA), Chinese (MA), Chinese and Economics/French/German/History/History of Art/Linguistics/Russian Studies/Spanish (MA), English and Scottish Literature (MA), English Language and Literature (MA), English Literature (MA), French (MA), French and Business/Celtic/Chinese/Classics/English Language/English Literature/German/History/History of Art/Italian/Linguistics/Philosophy/Politics/Portuguese/Russian Studies/Scandinavian Studies/Scottish Literature/Social Policy/Spanish (MA), German (MA), German and Business/Celtic/Classics/Chinese/English Language/English Literature/French/History/History of Art/Italian/Linguistics/Philosophy/Politics/Portuguese/Russian Studies/Scandinavian Studies/Scottish Literature/Social Policy/Spanish (MA), Islamic Studies (MA), Italian (MA), Italian and Classics/English Language/English Literature/French/History/History of Art/Linguistics/Philosophy/Politics/Spanish (MA), Japanese (MA), Japanese and Linguistics (MA), Middle Eastern Studies (MA), Persian and Arabic/English Literature/Middle Eastern Studies/Social Anthropology (MA), Persian Studies (MA), Portuguese (MA), Portuguese and Arabic/Business/Chinese/Classics/English Language/English Literature/French/German/History/History of Art/Italian/Linguistics/Philosophy/Politics/Russian Studies/Scandinavian Studies/Scottish Literature (MA), Russian Studies (MA), Russian Studies and Chinese/Classics/English Language/English Literature/French/German/History/History of Art/Linguistics/Philosophy/Politics/Scandinavian Studies/Scottish Literature/Social Policy/Spanish (MA), Scandinavian Studies (Danish, Norwegian, Swedish) (MA), Scandinavian Studies and Celtic/Classics/English Language/English Literature/French/German/History/Linguistics/Philosophy/Politics/Scottish Literature/Scottish Ethnology/Social Policy/Spanish (MA), Scottish Ethnology (MA), Scottish Ethnology and Archaeology/Celtic/English Language/English Literature/Scandinavian Studies/Scottish History, Scottish Literature (MA), Scottish Literature and Scottish History (MA), Scottish Studies (MA), Spanish (MA), Spanish and Arabic/Business/Chinese/Classics/English

Language/English Literature/French/German/History/History of Art/Italian/Linguistics/Philosophy/Politics/Portuguese/Russian Studies/Scandinavian Studies/Scottish Literature (MA)

Postgraduate courses: Advanced Arabic MSc, Book History & Material Culture MSc, Celtic & Scottish Studies MSc, Chinese Society & Culture MSc, Chinese Studies MSc, Comparative Literature MSc, Creative Writing MSc, East Asian Relations MSc, Film Studies MSc, Film, Exhibition & Curation MSc, Islamic & Middle Eastern Studies MSc, Japanese Society & Culture MSc, Korean Studies MSc, Literature & Modernity: 1900 to the Present MSc, Literature & Society: Enlightenment, Romantic & Victorian MSc, Medieval Literatures & Cultures MSc, Middle Eastern Studies with Advanced Arabic MSc, Middle Eastern Studies with Arabic MSc, Persian Civilisation MSc, Playwriting MSc, Theatre & Performance Studies MSc, Translation Studies MSc, US Literature: Cultural Values from Revolution to Empire MSc,

School of Mathematics; www.maths.ed.ac.uk

Applied Mathematics (BSc), Mathematics (MA), Mathematics (BSc), Mathematics and Biology/Business/Music/Physics/Statistics (BSc), Mathematics with Management (BSc), Applied Mathematics (MMath), Mathematics (MMath)

Postgraduate courses: Computational Applied Mathematics MSc, Computational Mathematical Finance MSc/PgDip, Financial Mathematics MSc, Financial Modelling & Optimization MSc/PgDip, Operational Research MSc/PgDip, Operational Research with Computational Optimization MSc/PgDip, Operational Research with Data Science MSc, Operational Research with Risk MSc/PgDip, Statistics & Operational Research MSc, Statistics with Data Science MSc

School of Philosophy, Psychology and Language Sciences; www.ed.ac.uk/ppls

Cognitive Science (Humanities) (MA), Linguistics and English Language (MA), Philosophy (MA), Psychology (MA)

Postgraduate courses: Ancient Philosophy (MSc), Applied Linguistics (MSc), Developmental Cognitive Science (MSc), Developmental Linguistics (MSc), English Language (MSc), Epistemology, Ethics and Mind (MSc), Evolution of Language and Cognition (MSc), Human Cognitive Neuropsychology (MSc), Linguistics (MSc), Mind, Language and Embodied Cognition (MSc), Philosophy (MSc), Philosophy, Science and Religion (MSc), Phonetics (MSc),

Psychological Research (MSc), Psychology of Individual Differences (MSc), Psychology of Language MSc, Social Psychology MSc, Speech and Language Processing (MSc)

School of Physics and Astronomy; www.ph.ed.ac.uk

Astrophysics (MPhys), Astrophysics (BSc), Computational Physics (MPhys), Computational Physics (BSc), Mathematical Physics (MPhys), Mathematical Physics (BSc), Physics (BSc), Physics (MPhys), Physics with a Year Abroad (MPhys), Physics with Meteorology (BSc), Physics with Meteorology (MPhys), Theoretical Physics (BSc), Theoretical Physics (MPhys)

Postgraduate courses: Mathematical Physics MSc, Particle and Nuclear Physics MSc, Theoretical Physics MSc

School of Social and Political Science; www.sps.ed.ac.uk

Government, Policy and Society (MA), Government, Policy and Society with Quantitative Methods (MA), International Relations (MA), International Relations and International Law (MA), International Relations with Quantitative Methods (MA), Politics (MA), Politics, Philosophy and Economics (MA), Politics with Quantitative Methods (MA), Social Anthropology (MA), Social Anthropology and Politics/Social Policy/Development (MA), Social Policy and Economics/Law/Politics/Sociology (MA), Social Policy with Quantitative Methods (MA), Social Work (BSc), Sociology (MA), Sociology and Politics/Psychology/Social Anthropology (MA), Sociology with Quantitative Methods (MA), Sustainable Development (MA)

Postgraduate courses: Africa & International Development MSc, African Studies MSc, Comparative Public Policy MSc, Digital Society MSc, Energy, Society and Sustainability MSc, Global Crime, Justice and Security MSc, Global Environment, Politics & Society MSc, Global Health Policy MSc, Health Policy MSc, International & European Politics MSc, International Development MSc, International Political Theory MSc, International Relations MSc, International Relations of the Middle East MSc, International Relations of the Middle East with Arabic MSc, Management of Bioeconomy, Innovation & Governance MSc, Medical Anthropology MSc, Nationalism Studies MSc, Public Policy MSc, Science & Technology in Society MSc, Social Anthropology MSc, Social Research MSc/PgCert, Social Work, Master of MSW,

Sociology & Global Change MSc, LLM Human Rights

Royal (Dick) School of Veterinary Studies; www.ed.ac.uk/vet

BSc(Hons) Agricultural Economics, BSc(Hons) Agricultural Science – Animal Science, BSc(Hons) Agricultural Science – Crop and Soil Science, BSc(Hons) Agricultural Science – Global Agriculture and Food Security, Veterinary Medicine (5-year programme) (BVM&S); Veterinary Medicine (Graduate Entry Programme – 4-year programme) (BVM&S)

Postgraduate courses: Advanced Clinical Practice (Online Distance Learning) MVetSci/PgDip/PgCert/PgProfDev, Animal Bioscience MSc, Applied Animal Behaviour & Animal Welfare MSc, Applied Conservation Genetics with Wildlife Forensics MSc/Dip/ Cert, Applied Poultry Science MSc/Dip/Cert, Clinical Animal Behaviour (Online Distance Learning) MSc/PgDip/PgCert, Conservation Medicine (Online Distance Learning) MVetSci/PgDip/PgCert/PgProfDev, Equine Science (Online Distance Learning) MSc/PgDip/PgCert/PgProfDev, Food Safety MSc/Dip/Cert, Global Food Security and Nutrition MSc/Dip/Cert, International Animal Welfare, Ethics & Law (Online Distance Learning) PgProfDev, One Health (Online Distance Learning) MSc/PgDip/PgCert/PgProfDev, RCVS Certificate in Advanced Veterinary Practice (Online Distance Learning) PgProfDev, Veterinary Anaesthesia & Analgesia (Online Distance Learning) MSc/PgDip/PgCert, Veterinary Epidemiology (Online Distance Learning) MSc/PgCert/PgDip/PgProfDev

EDINBURGH NAPIER UNIVERSITY
www.napier.ac.uk

Film, Journalism & Media; www.napier.ac.uk/courses/study-areas/film-journalism-and-media

English & Film BA(Hons), Film BA(Hons), Journalism BA(Hons), Marketing with Digital Media BA(Hons), Mass Communications BA(Hons), Mass Communications, Advertising and Public Relations BA(Hons), Mass Communications and Media Ba(Hons), Photography BA(Hons), Television (advanced entry) BA(Hons)

Postgraduate courses: Advanced Film Practice MFA, Directing MFA, Film MA, International Journalism for Media Professionals MA, Journalism MA, Playwriting MFA, Photography MA/MFA, Publishing MSc, Screenwriting MA

Business and Management; www.napier.ac.uk/courses/study-areas/business-and-management

Business & Enterprise BA, Business & Enterprise in Sport BA(Hons), Business Information Technology BSc(Hons), Business Management BA/BA(Hons), Business Management with Entrepreneurship/Finance/Hospitality/HRM/Marketing BA/BA(Hons), Business Studies (Sandwich) BA(Hons), Human Resource Management with Organisational Psychology BA, International Business Management BA(Hons), International Business Management & Languages (French/German/Spanish) BA(Hons), Real Estate Surveying BSc(Hons)

Postgraduate courses: MBA (Leadership Practice), The Edinburgh Napier MBA, Executive MBA, MBA (various specialisms), Learning, Teaching and Assessment Practice in HE PgCert, Business Event Management MSc, Business Management MSc (various specialisms), International Business Management MSc, Intercultural Business Communication MSc, Real Estate Management & Investment MSc, Human Resource Management MSc, International Human Resource Management MSc, Leadership in Board Governance Certificate of Credit, Project and Programme Management (Executive Masters) MSc

Computing; www.napier.ac.uk/courses/browse-interests/computing

Business Information Technology BSc(Hons), Computer Systems and Networks BEng(Hons), Computing BEng/BEng(Hons), Computing BSc/BSc(Hons), Computing Science BSc/BSc(Hons), Computing & User Experience BSc/BSc(Hons), Cybersecurity and Forensics BEng(Hons), Digital Media and Interaction Design BSc(Hons), Digital Media and Interaction Design Global BSc(Hons), Games Development BSc/BSc(Hons), Information Technology Management BSc(Hons), Interactive Media Design BSc/BSc(Hons), Software Engineering BEng/BEng(Hons), Software Engineering MEng, Sound Design BSc(Hons), Web Design and Development BSc(Hons)

Postgraduate courses: Advanced Networking MSc/PGDip/PGCert, Advanced Security and Digital

Forensics MSc, Business Information Technology MSc, Computing MSc, Data Engineering MSc, Financial Technology MSc, Sound Design MSc, Advanced Security and Cybercrime MSc, Data Science MSc, Project and Programme Management MSc, Strategic ICT Leadership MSc

Criminology, Psychology and Sociology; www.napier.ac.uk/courses/study-areas/criminology-psychology-and-sociology

Criminology BA(Hons), Policing and Criminology BSc(Hons), Psychology BA(Hons)/BSc(Hons), Psychology with Sociology BA(Hons), Social Sciences BA(Hons)

Postgraduate courses: Applied Criminology and Forensic Psychology MSc, Blended and Online Education MSc/PgDip/PgCert, Career Development PgCert, Career Guidance & Development PGDip

Design & Photography; www.napier.ac.uk/courses/study-areas/design-and-photography

Architectural Technology BSc/BSc(Hons), Computing & User Experience BSc/BSc(Hons), Digital Media & Interaction Design BSc(Hons), Digital Media & Interaction Design Global BSc(Hons), Graphic Design BDes(Hons), Interior & Spatial Design BDes(Hons), Photography BA/BA(Hons), Product Design – BDes(Hons), Sound Design – BSc(Hons)

Postgraduate courses: Creative Advertising MSc, Design for Interactive Art Experiences MA/MFA, Heritage and Exhibition Design MA/MFA, Lighting Design MA/MFA, Motion Graphics MA/MFA, Product Design Making MA/MFA, Photography MA/MFA

Building & Surveying; www.napier.ac.uk/courses/study-areas/building-and-surveying

Architectural Technology BSc/BSc(Hons), Building Surveying BSc/BSc(Hons), Construction & Project Management BSc/BSc(Hons), Quantity Surveying BSc/BSc(Hons), Real Estate Surveying BSc/BSc(Hons)

Postgraduate courses: Architectural Technology & Building Performance MSc, Construction Project Management MSc, Environmental Sustainability MSc, Facilities Management MSc, Real Estate Management & Investment MSc

Engineering; www.napier.ac.uk/courses/study-areas/engineering

Civil Engineering BEng/BEng(Hons), Civil Engineering MEng, Civil & Transportation Engineering MEng, Electronic & Electrical Engineering BEng/BEng(Hons), Electronic & Electrical Engineering MEng, Energy & Environmental Engineering BEng/BEng(Hons), Engineering with Management BEng/BEng(Hons), Mechatronics BEng/BEng(Hons), Mechanical Engineering BEng/BEng(Hons), Mechanical Engineering MEng

Postgraduate courses: Advanced Materials Engineering MSc, Advanced Structural Engineering MSc, Automation & Control MSc, Business Management (Logistics & Supply Chains) MSc, Environmental Sustainability MSc, MBA (Logistics & Supply Chain Management), Renewable Energy MSc, Timber Architectural Design & Technology MSc, Transport Planning and Engineering MSc

Nursing & Midwifery; www.napier.ac.uk/courses/study-areas/nursing-and-midwifery

Nursing (Adult) BN, Nursing (Child Health) BN, Nursing (Learning Disabilities) BN, Nursing (Mental Health) BN, Nursing Studies BSc, Nursing Studies Global Online BSc, Midwifery BM, Care of People with Epilepsy Graduate Certificate, Neonatal Nursing Graduate Certificate, Sexual and Reproductive Health Graduate Certificate

Postgraduate courses: Advanced Practice MSc (named speciality), Health & Social Care MSc, Healthcare Management MSc, Masters in Midwifery MM, Masters in Nursing (Adult) MN, Masters in Nursing (Child Health) MN, Masters in Nursing (Learning Disability) MN, Masters in Nursing (Mental Health) MN

Biosciences; www.napier.ac.uk/courses/study-areas/biosciences

Animal & Conservation Biology BSc(Hons), Biological Science BSc(Hons), Biomedical Sciences BSc(Hons), Marine & Freshwater Biology BSc(Hons)

Postgraduate courses: Biomedical Science MSc, Drug Design & Biomedical Science MSc, Medical Biotechnology MSc, Pharmaceutical & Analytical Science MSc, Pharmaceutical Science MSc, Wildlife Biology & Conservation MSc, Ecotourism MSc

Sports and Exercise Sciences; www.napier.ac.uk/courses/study-areas/sport-and-exercise-sciences

Physical Activity and Health BSc(Hons), Sport & Exercise Science BSc(Hons), Sports Coaching BSc(Hons), Business & Enterprise in Sport BA(Hons)

Postgraduate courses: Clinical Exercise Science MSc, Sport Performance Enhancement MSc

Tourism, Hospitality, Festivals & Events Management; www.napier.ac.uk/study-areas/tourism-hospitality-festival-and-events-management

Business Management with Hospitality top-up BA, International Hospitality & Service Management BA(Hons), International Hospitality Management BA(Hons) & Joint Honours, International Tourism Management BA(Hons) & Joint Honours, International Tourism & Airline Management BA(Hons), International Festival & Event Management BA(Hons) & Joint Honours, Languages and Intercultural Communication BA(Hons)

Postgraduate courses: MBA (Events Management) MBA, MBA (Hospitality & Tourism Management) MBA, Business Event Management MSc, Business Management (Events) MSc, Business Management (Tourism & Hospitality) MSc, Ecotourism MSc, International Festival & Event Management MSc, International Heritage & Cultural Tourism Management MSc, International Hospitality Management MSc, International Marketing with Tourism & Events MSc, International Tourism Destination Management MSc, Marketing with Festival & Event Management – MSc

UNIVERSITY OF ESSEX
www.essex.ac.uk

School of Biological Sciences; www.essex.ac.uk/bs

BSc Biological Sciences, BSc Biochemistry, BSc Biomedical Science, BSc Genetics, BSc Genetics, BSc Marine Biology

Postgraduate courses: MSc Biotechnology, MSc Cancer Biology, MSc Tropical Marine Biology, MSc Molecular Medicine

School of Computer Science and Electronic Engineering; www.essex.ac.uk/csee

BSc Computer Science, BSc Computer Games, BEng Computer Networks, MSci Computer Science (integrated Masters), BSc Data Science and Analytics, BEng Robotic Engineering, BEng Computer Systems Engineering, BEng Computers with Electronics, BEng Electronic Engineering, BEng Communications Engineering, MEng Electronic Engineering (integrated Masters), MEng Communications Engineering (integrated Masters), BEng Mechatronic Systems, BEng Robotic Engineering

Postgraduate courses: MSc Advanced Computer Science, MSc Artificial Intelligence, MSc Big Data and Text Analytics, MSc Data Science, MSc Computer Engineering, MSc Computer Games, MSc Internet of Things, MSc Intelligent Systems and Robotics, MSc Computer Networks and Security, MSc Electronic Engineering, MSc Global Communication Systems, MSc Computational Finance, MSc Algorithmic Trading

East 15 Acting School; www.east15.ac.uk

BA Acting, BA Acting (International), BA Acting and Contemporary Theatre, BA Acting and Stage Combat, BA Creative Producing (Theatre and Short Film), BA Stage and Production Management, BA Acting and Community Theatre, BA Physical Theatre, BA World Performance, Certificate of Higher Education in Theatre Arts

Postgraduate courses: MA Acting, MA/MFA Acting (International), MA/MFA Theatre Directing, MA Theatre Practice

Department of Economics; www.essex.ac.uk/economics

BA/BSc Economics, BA/BSc Management Economics, BA/BSc International Economics, BA/BSc Financial Economics, BA Financial Economics and Accounting, BSc Economics with Mathematics, BSc Economics and Mathematics, BSc Economics with Computing, BA History and Economics, BSc Accounting with Economics, BA Philosophy, Politics and Economics, BA Economics and Politics, BA Political Economics, BA Economics with a Modern Language, BSc Economics with Psychology

Postgraduate courses: BA Business Economics, MRes Economics, MA Economics, MSc Economics, MSc Behavioural Economics, MSc Applied Economics and Data Analysis, MSc Computational Economics, Financial Markets and Policy, MSc Economics and Econometrics, MSc Economics with Data Analytics, MSc Economics with Professional Placement, MSc Economics, Computation and Game Theory, MA International Development, MSc International Economics, MSc Management Economics, MSc Money and Banking, MSc Financial Economics and Accounting, MSc Financial and Business Economics, MSc Financial Econometrics, MSc Financial Economics and Econometrics, Graduate Diploma Economics, MSc Quantitative International Development

Essex Business School; www.essex.ac.uk/ebs

BSc Accounting, BSc Accounting and Finance, BSc Accounting and Management, BSc Accounting with Economics, BA Business Economics, BSc Finance, MSc Finance and Data Analytics, BSc Finance and Management, BSc Finance and Mathematics, BA Financial Economics and Accounting, LLB Law with Finance, BSc Banking and Finance, BSc Marketing, BSc Management and Marketing, BSc Business Management, BBA Business Administration, BSc Tourism Management, BA Business Management and Modern Languages, BA Business Management with a Modern Language, BSc International Business and Entrepreneurship

Postgraduate courses: MSc Accounting, MSc Accounting and Finance, MSc Accounting and Financial Management, MA Advertising, Marketing and the Media, MSc Business Analytics, MSc International Accounting and Banking, MRes Accounting, MSc Computational Finance, MSc Finance, MRes Finance, MSc Banking and Finance, MSc Finance and Investment, MSc Finance and Management, MSc Financial Engineering and Risk Management, MSc International Finance, MSc Finance and Data Analytics, MSc Finance and Global Trading, MSc Management, The Essex MBA, The Essex Executive MBA, MA Management and Organisational Dynamics, MRes Management and Organisation, MSc Business Analytics, MSc Human Resource Management, MSc Global Project Management, MSc International Logistics and Supply Chain Management, MSc Entrepreneurship and Innovation, MSc International Business and Entrepreneurship, MSc International Marketing and Entrepreneurship, MSc Marketing and Brand Management, Postgraduate Diploma Management and Organisational Dynamics

Department of Government; www.essex.ac.uk/government

BA Politics, BA International Development, BA International Relations, BA Politics and International Relations, BA Political Economics, BA Political Theory and Public Policy, BA Philosophy, Politics and Economics, BA Economics and Politics, BA Politics with Human Rights, BA International Relations and Modern Languages, BA Sociology and Politics

Postgraduate courses: Graduate Diploma Politics, MA/MSc Political Science, MA Politics, MA/MSc

Conflict Resolution, MA United States Politics, MA/MSc Global and Comparative Politics, MA Ideology and Discourse Analysis, Ma International Development, MA/MSc International Relations, MA/MSc Political Economy, MA Political Theory, MA/MSc Public Opinion and Political Behaviour, MRes International Relations, MRes Political Economy, MRes Political Science, MSc Quantitative International Development

School of Health and Social Care; www.essex.ac.uk/hhs

BSc BSc Health Care Practice, Nursing (Mental Health), BSc Nursing (Adult), FdSc Oral Health Science, BSc Oral Health Science, BSc Occupational Therapy, BSc Physiotherapy, BA Social Work, BSc Speech and Language Therapy (TBC)

Postgraduate courses: Postgraduate Certificate Psychological Well-Being Practitioner, MSc Nursing (Adult) (pre-registration), MSc Nursing (Mental Health) (pre-registration), MSc Periodontology, MSc Advanced Periodontal Practice, MA Health and Organisational Research, MSc Health Care Practice, Postgraduate Diploma Health Care Practice, MSc Health Research, MSc Medical and Clinical Education, Postgraduate Diploma/Cert Medical and Clinical Education, Msc/Postgraduate Diploma/Cert Musculoskeletal Ultrasound Imaging, MA Professional Practice, MSc Occupational Therapy (Pre-Registration), MA Social Work, MSc Speech and Language Therapy (Pre-Registration)

Department of History; www.essex.ac.uk/history

BA Global Studies, BA History, BA Modern History, BA History and Literature, BA History with Film Studies, BA Philosophy and History, BA Art History and History, BA Modern History and Politics, BA Modern History and International Relations, BA History with Human Rights, BA History and Sociology, BA History and Criminology, BA History and Economics

Postgraduate course: MA History, Postgraduate Certificate History, MA War, Culture and Society

Department of Language and Linguistics; www.essex.ac.uk/langling

BA English Language and Linguistics, BA Linguistics, BA English Language and Literature, BA English Language and Sociology, BA English Language with Media Communication, BA Teaching English as a Foreign Language (TEFL), BA Language Studies (no year abroad), BA French/German/Italian/Portuguese/

145

Spanish and Modern Languages, MLang Modern Languages (Translation), BA Modern Languages and English Language, BA Modern Languages and Linguistics, BA Modern Languages and Teaching English as a Foreign Language, BA Modern Languages with Latin American Studies, BA Spanish, Portuguese and Brazilian Studies, BA International Relations and Modern Languages, BA European Studies and Modern Languages, BA Business Management with a Modern Language, BA Business Management and Modern Languages, LLB English and French Law, BA Art History and Modern Languages, BA Art History with Modern Languages

Postgraduate courses: MA Advanced Interpreting with Specialised Translation (Chinese-English), MRes Analysing Language Use, MA Applied Linguistics, MA Chinese-English Translation and Professional Practice, MA English Language and Linguistics, MRes Experimental Linguistics, MA/MRes Linguistics, MA Linguistic Studies, MA Psycholinguistics, MA Language in Society, MA Teaching English to Speakers of Other Languages (TESOL), Postgraduate Diploma Chinese-English Translation and Interpreting, MA Conference Interpreting and Translation (Chinese-English), MA Translation, Interpreting and Subtitling, MA Translation and Literature, MA Translation and Professional Practice

School of Law; www.essex.ac.uk/law

BA Global Studies with Human Rights, LLB Law, LLB Law with Business, LLB Law with Criminology, LLB Law with Finance, LLB Law with Human Rights, LLB Law with Politics, LLB Law with Philosophy, BA Philosophy and Law, BA Latin American Studies with Human Rights

Postgraduate courses: LLM Economic, Social and Cultural Rights, LLM International Human Rights Law, LLM International Humanitarian Law, LLM Economic, Social and Cultural Rights, LLM International Commercial and Business Law, LLM International Trade Law, LLM International Trade and Maritime Law, MA Theory and Practice of Human Rights, MA Human Rights and Cultural Diversity

Department of Literature, Film, and Theatre Studies; www.essex.ac.uk/lifts

BA Creative Producing (Theatre and Short Film), BA Creative Writing, BA English and Comparative Literature, BA Literature and Creative Writing, BA Film and Creative Writing, BA Drama, BA Drama and Literature, BA English Literature, BA English and United States Literature, BA Literature and Creative Writing, BA English Language and Literature, BA History and Literature, BA Liberal Arts, BA Literature and Sociology, BA Literature and Art History, BA Film Studies, BA Film Studies and Literature, BA American (United States) Studies, BA American (United States) Studies with Film, BA Film Studies and Art History, BA History with Film Studies, BA Multimedia Journalism, BA Journalism and Criminology/Economics/English Language/Liberal Arts/Literature/Modern Languages/Philosophy/Politics/Sociology, BA Journalism with Business Management/Human Rights

Postgraduate courses: MA Creative Writing, MA Literature, MA American Literatures, MA Film and Literature, MA Film Studies, MA Scriptwriting (Theatre and Digital Media), MA Theatre Practice, MA Translation and Literature, MA Wild Writing: Literature, Landscape and the Environment

Department of Mathematical Sciences; www.essex.ac.uk/maths

BSc Mathematics, BSc Mathematics and Statistics, BSc Actuarial Science, BSc Economics and/with Mathematics, BSc Finance and Mathematics, BSc Mathematics with Computing, BSc Data Science and Analytics, BSc Mathematics with Physics, BSc Statistics

Postgraduate courses: MSc Actuarial Science, PG Diploma Actuarial Science, MSc Data Science, MSc Mathematics, Graduate Diploma Mathematics, MSc Mathematics and Finance, PG Diploma Mathematics and Finance, MSc Statistics, MSc Statistics and Operational Research, PG Diploma Statistics and Operational Research

School of Philosophy and Art History; www.essex.ac.uk/depts/spah.aspx

BA Art History, BA Curatorial Studies, BA Philosophy and Art History, BA Art History and History, BA Art History with Modern Languages, BA Art History and Modern Languages, BA Film Studies and Art History, BA Literature and Art History, BA Philosophy, BA Philosophy, Religion and Ethics, BA Philosophy and Art History/History/Human Rights/Law/Literature/Politics/Sociology, BA Philosophy, Politics and Economics, LLB Law with Philosophy

Postgraduate courses: MA Art History and Theory, MA Curating, Graduate Diploma Art History and Theory, MA Philosophy

Department of Psychology; www.essex.ac.uk/psychology

BSc Cognitive Science, BA Psychology, BSc Psychology, BSc Psychology with Cognitive Neuroscience, BSc Psychology with Economics

Postgraduate courses: MSc Psychology, MSc Cognitive Neuroscience and Neuropsychology, MSc Research Methods in Psychology, MSc Sport and Exercise Psychology

Department of Psychosocial and Psychoanalytic Studies; www.essex.ac.uk/cps

FdA/BA Therapeutic Communication and Therapeutic Organisations, BA Childhood Studies, BA Psychosocial and Psychoanalytic Studies, BA Therapeutic Care, BA Sociology with Psychosocial Studies

Postgraduate courses: MA Psychoanalytic Studies, MA Jungian and Post-Jungian Studies, MA Psychodynamic Counselling, MA Refugee Care, PG Diploma/MA Management and Organisational Dynamics, Graduate Diploma Psychodynamic Approaches

Department of Sociology; www.essex.ac.uk/sociology

BA Sociology, BSc Sociology (Applied Quantitative Research), BSc Sociology with Data Science, BA Sociology with Counselling Skills, BA Sociology with Psychosocial Studies, BA Communications and Digital Culture, BA Sociology and Politics, BA Sociology with Human Rights, BA Sociology with Social Psychology, BA History and Sociology, BA Criminology, BA Sociology and Criminology, BA Criminology with Criminal Law, BA Criminology with Social Psychology, BA Criminology and American Studies, BA Criminology with Counselling Skills, BA Criminology with Criminal Law, BA Social Anthropology, BA Social Anthropology with Human Rights, BA Sociology with Psychosocial studies

Postgraduate courses: MA Sociology, MA Advertising, Marketing and the Media, MA Criminology, MSc Criminology and Socio-Legal Research, MA/MSc Migration Studies, MSc Organised Crime, Terrorism and Security, MA Sociological Research Methods, MSc Survey Methods for Social Research, MA Sociology and Management

School of Sport, Rehabilitation and Exercise Sciences; www.essex.ac.uk/sres

BSc Sports and Exercise Science, BSc Sports Performance and Coaching, BSc Sports Therapy

Postgraduate courses: MSc Physiotherapy (Pre-registration), MSc Sport and Exercise Science, MSc Sport and Exercise Psychology

WRITTLE COLLEGE
www.writtle.ac.uk

Agriculture

BSc(Hons) Agriculture, BSc(Hons) Agriculture (Arable Crop Management), BSc(Hons) Agriculture (Farm Livestock Production), BSc(Hons) Agriculture (Sustainable Environments), Diploma of Higher Education in Agriculture, Diploma of Higher Education in Agriculture (Arable Crop Management), Diploma of Higher Education in Agriculture (Farm Livestock Production), Diploma of Higher Education in Agriculture (Sustainable Environments), Certificate of Higher Education in Agriculture

Postgraduate course: MSc Crop Production (Agriculture)

Bioveterinary Science

MSci Bioveterinary Science, BSc(Hons) Bioveterinary Science, Certificate of Higher Education in Animal Bioscience

Canine Therapy

BSc(Hons) Canine Therapy, Diploma of Higher Education Canine Studies, Certificate of Higher Education in Canine Studies

Equine

BSc(Hons) Equine Behavioural Science, BSc(Hons) Equine Performance Science, BSc(Hons) Equine Performance and Business Management, BSc(Hons) Equine Sports Therapy and Rehabilitation, Diploma of Higher Education Equine Behavioural Science, Diploma of Higher Education Equine Performance and Business Management, Diploma of Higher Education Equine Sports Therapy and Rehabilitation, Certificate of Higher Education in Equine Studies, Certificate of Higher Education in Thoroughbred Stud Operations

Horticulture

BSc(Hons) Horticulture, BSc(Hons) Horticulture and International Business, BSc(Hons) Sustainable Food Production (Fresh Produce), Diploma of Higher

Education Horticulture, Certificate of Higher Education in Horticulture

Postgraduate courses: MSc Horticulture, MSc Crop Production (Horticulture), MSc Postharvest Technology, Postgraduate Certificate in Postharvest Technology

Landscape Architecture and Garden Design

BSc(Hons) Landscape Architecture, BSc(Hons) Landscape and Garden Design, Diploma of Higher Education in Garden Design, Diploma of Higher Education in Landscape Design, Certificate of Higher Education Landscape Studies

Postgraduate courses: MA Landscape Architecture, MA Garden Design, Master of Landscape Architecture, Postgraduate Diploma in Landscape Architecture

Postharvest Technology

Postgraduate courses: MSc Postharvest Technology, Postgraduate Certificate in Postharvest Technology

Sports, Performance

BSc(Hons) Sports and Exercise Performance, Foundation Degree (FdSc) Cycling Performance, Foundation Degree (FdSc) Sports Science with Aerial Performance, Foundation Degree (FdSc) Sports Science with Outdoor Activity Diploma of Higher Education Sports and Exercise Performance, Certificate of Higher Education in Cycling Studies, Certificate of Higher Education in Sports and Exercise Studies, Certificate of Higher Education in Sports Science Studies with Aerial Performance, Certificate of Higher Education in Sports Science Studies with Outdoor Activit

Veterinary Physiotherapy

MVetPhys Veterinary Physiotherapy, BSc(Hons) Animal Therapy, BSc(Hons) Canine Therapy, BSc(Hons) Equine Sports Therapy and Rehabilitation, Diploma of Higher Education Canine Studies, Certificate of Higher Education in Canine Studies

Postgraduate course: MSc Veterinary Physiotherapy

UNIVERSITY OF EXETER
www.exeter.ac.uk

Accounting and Finance;
www.exeter.ac.uk/undergraduate/courses-by-subject/

Accounting and Finance BSc, Accounting and Finance with European Study BSc, Accounting and Finance with Industrial Experience BSc, Accounting and Finance with International Study BSc, Applied Finance Degree Apprenticeship BSc

Postgraduate courses: Accounting and Finance MSc, Accounting and Taxation MSc

Anthropology; www.exeter.ac.uk

Anthropology BA, Anthropology with Study Abroad BA,

Arab and Islamic Studies;
www.exeter.ac.uk/undergraduate/courses-by-subject/

Arabic and Islamic Studies MA, Arabic, Middle East Studies BA

Postgraduate courses: Middle East Studies MA, Middle East Studies MRes

Archaeology; www.exeter.ac.uk

Archaeological Science BSc, Archaeological Science with Employment Experience/Abroad BSc, Archaeological Science with Study Abroad BSc, Archaeology BA, Archaeology with Employment Experience/ Employment Experience Abroad BA, Archaeology with Study Abroad BA, Archaeology and Anthropology BA, Archaeology and Anthropology with Employment Experience/Employment Experience Abroad BA, Archaeology and Anthropology with Study Abroad BA, Archaeology with Forensic Science BSc, Archaeology with Forensic Science with Employment Experience/Employment Experience Abroad BSc, Archaeology with Forensic Science with Study Abroad BSc

Postgraduate courses: Archaeology MA, Bioarchaeology MSc, Experimental Archaeology MA, Roman Archaeology MA

Art History & Visual Culture;
www.exeter.ac.uk/undergraduate/courses-by-subject/

Art History & Visual Culture BA, Art History & Visual Culture with Employment Experience / Employment Experience Abroad BA, Art History & Visual Culture with Study Abroad BA, Art History & Visual Culture and Classical Studies BA, Art History & Visual Culture and Classical Studies with Employment Experience / Employment Experience Abroad BA, Art History & Visual Culture and Classical Studies with Study Abroad BA, Art History & Visual Culture and Drama with Employment Experience /

Employment Experience Abroad BA, Art History & Visual Culture and English BA, Art History & Visual Culture and English with Employment Experience / Employment Experience Abroad BA, Art History & Visual Culture and English with Study Abroad BA, Art History & Visual Culture and History BA, Art History & Visual Culture and History with Employment Experience / Employment Experience Abroad BA, Art History & Visual Culture and History with Study Abroad BA, Art History & Visual Culture and Modern Languages BA, Art History & Visual Culture and Film & Television Studies BA, Art History & Visual Culture and Film & Television Studies with Study Abroad BA, Art History & Visual Culture and Film & Television Studies with Employment Experience / Employment Experience Abroad BA

Biosciences; www.exeter.ac.uk

Animal Behaviour BSc, Animal Behaviour MSci, Animal Behaviour with Professional Placement BSc, Animal Behaviour with Study Abroad BSc, Biochemistry BSc, Biochemistry MSci, Biochemistry with Industrial Experience BSc, Biochemistry with Study Abroad BSc, Biological and Medicinal Chemistry BSc, Biological and Medicinal Chemistry MSci, Biological and Medicinal Chemistry with Industrial Experience BSc, Biological and Medicinal Chemistry with Study Abroad BSc, Biological Sciences BSc, Biological Sciences MSci Biological Sciences with Professional Placement BSc, Biological Sciences with Study Abroad BSc, Conservation Biology and Ecology BSc, Conservation Biology and Ecology MSci, Conservation Biology and Ecology with Professional Placement BSc, Conservation Biology and Ecology with Study Abroad BSc, Evolutionary Biology BSc, Evolutionary Biology MSci, Evolutionary Biology with Professional Placement BSc, Evolutionary Biology with Study Abroad BSc, Human Sciences BSc, Human Sciences with Professional Placement BSc, Human Sciences with Study Abroad BSc, Marine Biology BSc, Marine Biology MSci, Marine Biology with Professional Placement BSc, Marine Biology with Study Abroad BSc, Zoology BSc, Zoology MSci, Zoology with Professional Placement BSc, Zoology with Study Abroad BSc

Postgraduate courses: Conservation and Biodiversity MSc, Conservation Science and Policy MSc, Evolutionary and Behavioural Ecology MSc, Food Security and Sustainable Agriculture MSc, Island Biodiversity and Conservation MSc

Business and Management; www.exeter.ac.uk/undergraduate/courses-by-subject/

Business and Management BSc, Business and Management with European Study BSc Business and Management with Industrial Experience BSc Business and Management with International Study, Marketing and Management BSc, Marketing and Management with European Study BSc, Marketing and Management with Industrial Experience BSc, Marketing and Management with International Study BSc Business BSc, Business with European Study BSc, Business with Industrial Experience BSc, Business with International Study BSc

Postgraduate courses: International Management MSc Management MSc, International Business MSc, Marketing MSc, Human Resource Management MSc/PgDip, International Tourism Management MSc, Management MRes, MBA – The Exeter MBA, Global Political Economy MRes, Entrepreneurship and Innovation Management MSc, Senior Leader Degree Apprenticeship

Classics and Ancient History; www.exeter.ac.uk/undergraduate/courses-by-subject/

Ancient History BA, Ancient History with Employment Experience/Employment Experience Abroad BA, Ancient History with Study Abroad BA, Classical Studies BA, Classical Studies with Employment Experience/Employment Experience Abroad BA, Classical Studies with Study Abroad BA, Classics BA, Classics with Employment Experience/Employment Experience Abroad BA, Classics with Study Abroad BA, Ancient History and Archaeology BA, Ancient History and Archaeology with Employment Experience/Employment Experience Abroad BA, Ancient History and Archaeology with Study Abroad BA, Classical Studies and English BA, Classical Studies and English with Employment Experience/Employment Experience Abroad BA, Classical Studies and English with Study Abroad BA, Classical Studies and Modern Languages BA, Classical Studies and Philosophy BA, Classical Studies and Philosophy with Employment Experience/Employment Experience Abroad BA, Classical Studies and Philosophy with Study Abroad BA, Classical Studies and Theology BA, Classical Studies and Theology with Employment Experience/Employment Experience Abroad BA, Classical Studies and Theology with Study Abroad BA

Postgraduate courses: Classics and Ancient History MA, Ancient Philosophy, Science & Medicine, Ancient Politics & Society, Classical Receptions, Cultural Histories & Material Exchanges, Literary Interactions

Climate Change; [possible link]
www.exeter.ac.uk/postgraduate/courses-
by-subject/

Postgraduate courses: Conservation Science and Policy MSc, Global Sustainability Solutions MSc, Sustainable Development MSc, Sustainable Futures MRes

Computer Science and IT;
www.exeter.ac.uk/undergraduate/courses-
by-subject/

Computer Science BSc, Computer Science MSci, Computer Science with Industrial Placement BSc, Computer Science and Mathematics BSc, Computer Science and Mathematics MSci, Computer Science and Mathematics with Industrial Placement BSc, Digital and Technology Solutions degree apprenticeship

Postgraduate courses: Advanced Computer Science MSc, Advanced Computer Science with Business MSc,

Data Science / Data Science and Analytics;
www.exeter.ac.uk/undergraduate/degrees/
datascience/

Data Science BSc, Data Science MSci, Mathematics and Data Science BSc, Mathematics and Data Science MSci

Postgraduate courses: Data Science MSc, Data Science with Business MSc, Applied Data Science and Statistics MSc, Data Science Degree Apprenticeship

Drama; www.exeter.ac.uk/undergraduate/

Drama BA, Drama with Employment Experience / Employment Experience Abroad BA, Drama with Study Abroad BA, Art History & Visual Culture and Drama BA, Art History & Visual Culture and Drama with Study Abroad BA

Postgraduate courses: Theatre Practice MA

Economics; www.exeter.ac.uk

Economics BSc, Economics with European Study BSc, Economics with Industrial Experience BSc, Economics with International Study BSc, Business Economics BSc, Business Economics with European Study BSc, Business Economics with Industrial Experience BSc, Business Economics with International Study BSc,

Economics with Econometrics BSc, Economics with Econometrics with European Study BSc, Economics with Econometrics with Industrial Experience BSc, Economics with Econometrics with International Study BSc, Economics and Finance BSc, Economics and Finance with European Study BSc, Economics and Finance with Industrial Experience BSc, Economics and Finance with International Study BSc, Economics and Politics BSc, Economics and Politics with European Study BSc, Economics and Politics with Industrial Experience BSc, Economics and Politics with International Study BSc

Postgraduate courses: Economics MSc, Economics and Econometrics MSc, Behavioural Economics and Finance MSc, Economics (Pathway to PhD) MRes, Economics MRes, Financial Economics MSc, Money, Banking and Finance MSc

Education; www.exeter.ac.uk

Postgraduate courses: Education MA, Creative Arts in Education MA, Education Leadership and Management MA, International Education MA, Language and Literacy in Education MA, Special Educational Needs MA, Technology, Creativity and Thinking in Education MA, Educational Research MSc, Med Teaching English to Speakers of Other Languages, Education DEdPsych – Professional Training

Engineering; www.exeter.ac.uk

Civil Engineering BEng, Civil Engineering MEng, Electronic Engineering BEng, Electronic Engineering MEng, Engineering BEng, Engineering MEng, Engineering and Entrepreneurship BEng, Engineering and Entrepreneurship MEng, Engineering and Management BEng, Engineering and Management Mechanical Engineering BEng, Mechanical Engineering MEng Mining Engineering BEng, Mining Engineering MEng, Renewable Energy Engineering BEng, Renewable Energy Engineering MEng, Renewable Energy Engineering with Industrial Experience MEng, Civil Engineering Degree Apprenticeship BEng

Postgraduate courses: Civil Engineering MSc, Civil Engineering with Management MSc, Engineering Business Management MSc, International Supply Chain Management MSc, Materials Engineering MSc, Materials Engineering with Management MSc, Mechanical Engineering MSc, Mechanical Engineering with Management MSc, Renewable Energy Engineering MSc, Structural Engineering MSc, Structural Engineering with Management MSc, Water Engineering MSc, Water Engineering with Management MSc

English; www.exeter.ac.uk/undergraduate/

English BA (Exeter), English with Employment Experience / Employment Experience Abroad BA (Exeter), English with Study Abroad BA (Exeter), English with Study in North America BA, English and Drama BA, English and Drama with Employment Experience /Employment Experience Abroad BA, English and Drama with Study Abroad BA, English and Film & Television Studies BA, English and Film & Television Studies with Employment Experience/Employment Experience Abroad BA, English and Film & Television Studies with Study Abroad BA, English and Modern Languages BA, English BA (Penryn), English with Study Abroad BA (Penryn), English and History BA, English and History with Study Abroad BA, English and History with Employment Experience / Employment Experience Abroad BA, English with Employment Experience / Employment Experience Abroad BA (Penryn) Postgraduate courses: Creative Writing MA, English Literary Studies MA, American and Atlantic Studies pathway, Criticism and Theory pathway, Enlightenment to Romanticism pathway, Film Studies pathway, Renaissance Studies pathway, Modern and Contemporary pathway, Victorian Studies pathway, World and Postcolonial Cultures pathway

Environmental Science www.exeter.ac.uk

Environmental Science BSc, Environmental Science with Professional Placement BSc, Environmental Science with Study Abroad BSc, Environmental Science MSci

Film Studies; www.exeter.ac.uk

Film & Television Studies BA, Film & Television Studies with Employment Experience / Employment Experience Abroad BA, Film & Television Studies with Study Abroad BA, Film & Television Studies and Modern Languages BA
Postgraduate course: International Film Business MA, Creativity: Innovation and Business Strategy MA

Finance; [possible link] www.exeter.ac.uk/undergraduate/courses-by-subject/

Postgraduate courses: Finance and Investment MSc, Finance and Management MSc, Financial Analysis and Fund Management MSc, Finance and Marketing MSc

Flexible Combined Honours; [possible link] www.exeter.ac.uk/undergraduate/courses-by-subject/

Flexible Combined Honours BA/BSc – Exeter, Flexible Combined Honours with Study Abroad BA/BSc – Exeter, Flexible Combined Honours with Work Abroad BA/BSc – Exeter, Flexible Combined Honours with UK Work Experience BA/BSc – Exeter, Flexible Combined Honours with Study and Work Abroad BA/BSc – Exeter, Flexible Combined Honours BA/BSc – Cornwall, Flexible Combined Honours with Study Abroad BA/BSc – Cornwall, Flexible Combined Honours with Work Abroad BA/BSc – Cornwall, Flexible Combined Honours with UK Work Experience BA/BSc – Cornwall, Flexible Combined Honours with Study and Work Abroad BA/BSc – Cornwall

Geography; www.exeter.ac.uk

Geography BA/BSc (Penryn), Geography with Professional Placement BA/BSc (Penryn), Geography with Study Abroad BA/BSc (Penryn), Geography BA (Exeter), Geography with European Study BA (Exeter), Geography with Study Abroad BA (Exeter), Geography with Professional Placement BA (Exeter), Geography BSc (Exeter), Geography with European Study BSc (Exeter), Geography with Study Abroad BSc (Exeter), Geography with Professional Placement BSc (Exeter), Geography with Applied Geographical Information Systems (GIS) BSc, Geography with Applied Geographical Information Systems (GIS) with European Study BSc, Geography with Applied Geographical Information Systems (GIS) with Study Abroad BSc, Geography with Applied GIS with Professional Placement BSc, Geography and Geology BSc, Geography and Geology with Study Abroad BSc, Geography and Geology with Professional Placement BSc, Politics and Geography BA (Penryn), Politics and Geography with Study Abroad BA (Penryn)
Postgraduate courses: Global Sustainability Solutions MSc, Sustainable Development MSc, Critical Human Geographies MRes, Sustainable Futures MRes,

Geology; www.exeter.ac.uk

Applied Geology BSc, Applied Geology MGeol, Engineering Geology and Geotechnics BSc, Engineering Geology and Geotechnics MGeol, Geography and Geology BSc, Geography and Geology with Professional Placement BSc, Geography and Geology with Study Abroad BSc, Geology BSc, Geology MGeol

Postgraduate courses: Applied Geotechnics MSc/ PgDip, Mining Geology MSc, Exploration Geology MSc, Geotechnical Engineering MSc

Healthcare and Medicine; [possible link] www.exeter.ac.uk/undergraduate/courses-by-subject/

Clinical Education MSc, Environment and Human Health MSc, Healthcare Leadership and Management MSc, Health Research Methods MSc, Extreme Medicine MSc, Genomic Medicine MSc, Clinical Pharmacy MSc, Practice Certificate in Independent Prescribing, Genomic Medicine Online PGCert, Advanced Clinical Practice MSc

History; www.exeter.ac.uk/undergraduate/

History BA (Exeter), History with Employment Experience / Employment Experience Abroad BA (Exeter), History with Study Abroad BA (Exeter), History and Ancient History BA, History and Ancient History with Employment Experience / Employment Experience Abroad BA, History and Ancient History with Study Abroad BA, History and Archaeology BA, History and Archaeology with Employment Experience / Employment Experience Abroad BA, History and Archaeology with Study Abroad BA, History and Modern Languages BA History BA (Penryn), History with Study Abroad BA (Penryn), History and International Relations BA (Penryn), History and International Relations with Study Abroad BA (Penryn), History and Politics BA (Penryn), History and Politics with Study Abroad BA (Penryn), History with Employment Experience / Employment Experience Abroad BA (Penryn), History and International Relations with Employment Experience / Employment Experience Abroad BA (Penryn), History and Politics with Employment Experience / Employment Experience Abroad BA (Penryn)
Postgraduate courses: Economic and Social History MRes, History MA, Medieval Studies MA, International Heritage Management and Consultancy MA/ MRes/PGDip/PGCert

Human Sciences; www.exeter.ac.uk

Human Sciences BSc, Human Sciences with Professional Placement BSc, Human Sciences with Study Abroad BSc

Law; www.exeter.ac.uk

Liberal Arts BA, Liberal Arts with Employment Experience / Employment Experience Abroad BA (Exeter), Liberal Arts with Study Abroad BA

Mathematics; www.exeter.ac.uk

Mathematical Sciences BSc, Mathematical Sciences (Ecology and Evolution) MSci, Mathematical Sciences (Energy Systems and Control) MSci, Mathematical Sciences (Environmental Science) MSci, Mathematics BSc, Mathematics MMath, Mathematics with International Study MMath, Mathematics with Professional Experience MMath, Mathematics (Climate Science) MSci, Mathematics (Geophysical and Astrophysical Fluid Dynamics) MSci, Mathematics (Mathematical Biology) MSci, Mathematics with Accounting BSc, Mathematics with Economics BSc, Mathematics with Finance BSc, Mathematics with Management BSc, Mathematics and Physics BSc, Mathematics with Accounting MSci, Mathematics with Economics MSci, Mathematics with Finance MSci, Mathematics with Management MSci
Postgraduate courses: Advanced Mathematics MSc, Financial Mathematics MSc, Mathematical Modelling (Fluid Dynamics) MSc, Mathematical Modelling (Biology and Medicine) MSc, Mathematical Modelling (Climate Science) MSc

Medical Imaging (Radiography); www.exeter.ac.uk/undergraduate/courses-by-subject/

Medical Imaging (Diagnostic Radiography) BSc

Medical Sciences; www.exeter.ac.uk

Medical Sciences BSc, Medical Sciences with Professional Training Year BSc, Sport and Exercise Medical Sciences BSc, Sport and Exercise Medical Sciences with Professional Training Year BSc, Medical Sciences (Environment and Human Health) MSci, Medical Sciences (Human Genomics) MSci

Medicine; www.exeter.ac.uk

Medicine BMBS

Mining Engineering; www.exeter.ac.uk

Mining Engineering BEng, Mining Engineering MEng, Mining Engineering with Study Abroad in Minerals Engineering BEng
Postgraduate courses: Mining Engineering MSc/ PgDip, Surveying and Land/Environmental Management MSc/PgDip, Mining Lifecycle (Professional) PgCert, Mining Engineering (Professional) MSc Minerals Processing MSc, Minerals Processing (Professional) MSc/PgCert, Tunnel Engineering MSc, Mining Environmental Management MSc

Modern Languages; www.exeter.ac.uk

Modern Languages BA, Chinese, French, German, Italian, Portuguese, Russian, Spanish, Modern

Languages and Arabic BA, Modern Languages and Latin BA

Postgraduate courses: Translation Studies MA, Global Literatures and Cultures MA

Natural Sciences; www.exeter.ac.uk
Natural Sciences BSc, Natural Sciences MSci

Neuroscience; [possible link] www.exeter.ac.uk/undergraduate/courses-by-subject/
Neuroscience BSc, Neuroscience With Professional Training Year BSc

Nursing; [possible link] www.exeter.ac.uk/undergraduate/courses-by-subject/
Nursing MSci

Philosophy; www.exeter.ac.uk
Philosophy BA, Philosophy with Study Abroad BA, Philosophy and History BA, Philosophy and History with Study Abroad BA, Philosophy and Modern Languages BA, Philosophy and Politics BA, Philosophy and Politics with Study Abroad BA, Philosophy and Sociology BA, Philosophy and Sociology with Study Abroad BA, Philosophy and Theology BA, Philosophy and Theology with Study Abroad BA, Philosophy Combined Honours

Physics and Astronomy; www.exeter.ac.uk
Physics BSc, Physics MPhys, Physics with Astrophysics BSc, Physics with Astrophysics MPhys,

Politics and International Relations; www.exeter.ac.uk/undergraduate/courses-by-subject/
International Relations BA, International Relations with Study Abroad BA, Politics BA, Politics with Study Abroad BA, Politics, Philosophy and Economics BA, Politics, Philosophy and Economics with Study Abroad BA, Politics and International Relations BSc (Exeter), Politics and International Relations with Study Abroad BSc (Exeter), Politics Combined Honours, International Relations and Modern Languages BA, Politics and Modern Languages BA, Politics and Sociology BA, Politics and Sociology with Study Abroad BA, Politics and English BA (Penryn), Politics and English BA with Study Abroad (Penryn), Politics and Geography BA (Penryn), Politics and Geography BA with Study Abroad (Penryn) Politics and International Relations BA (Penryn), Politics and International Relations with Study Abroad BA (Penryn), International Relations BA (Penryn), International Relations with Study

Abroad BA (Penryn), Politics and International Relations (Cornwall)

Postgraduate courses: Applied Security Strategy MA, Conflict, Security and Development MA, European Politics MA, Global Governance MSc, International Relations MA, MPA – see Public Administration Masters, Public Administration Masters (MPA), Public Administration Masters (MPA) with Applied Study, Political Thought MA, Politics and International Relations of the Middle East MA, Policy Analytics MSc, Politics MRes, Security – see MA Applied Security Strategy, Security Conflict and Human Rights MRes, Advanced Quantitative Methods (AQM) In Social Sciences MRes MA Food Studies (strangely) is listed on the website under Politics and International Relations

Programmes for International Students; [possible link] www.exeter.ac.uk/postgraduate/courses-by-subject/
Graduate Diploma in Finance Graduate Diploma in Management

Psychology; www.exeter.ac.uk
Applied Psychology (Clinical) MSci, Psychology BSc, Psychology with Sport and Exercise Science BSc

Postgraduate courses: Animal Behaviour MSc, Psychological Research Methods MSc, Social and Organisational Psychology MSc

Renewable Energy Engineering; www.exeter.ac.uk/undergraduate/courses-by-subject/
Renewable Energy Engineering BEng, Renewable Energy Engineering MEng, Renewable Energy BSc, Renewable Energy Engineering with Industrial Experience MEng

Sociology, Criminology, Philosophy and Anthropology www.exeter.ac.uk/undergraduate/courses-by-subject/
Criminology BSc, Criminology with Study Abroad BSc, Sociology BA, Sociology with Study Abroad BA, Sociology BSc, Sociology with Study Abroad BSc, Sociology and Anthropology BA, Sociology and Anthropology with Study Abroad BA, Sociology and Criminology BSc, Sociology and Criminology with Study Abroad BSc, Sociology Combined Honours, Sociology and Modern Languages BA

Postgraduate courses: Anthrozoology MA, Cultural Sociology MA, Philosophy MA, Philosophy and Sociology of Science MA, Science and Technology Studies MRes, Sociology MA, Food Studies MA (strangely) is listed on the website under Sociology

**Sport and Health Sciences;
www.exeter.ac.uk/undergraduate/courses-
by-subject/**

Exercise and Sport Sciences BSc, Exercise and Sport
Sciences MSci, Human Biosciences BSc, Nutrition BSc
Postgraduate courses: Health and Wellbeing MRes,
Paediatric Exercise and Health MSc, Sport and Health
Sciences MSc

Theology and Religion; www.exeter.ac.uk

Theology and Religion BA, Theology and Religion
with Study Abroad BA, Theology and Religion with
Employment Experience / Employment Experience
Abroad BA (Exeter)
Postgraduate course: Theology MA

**INTO: Programmes for International
Students; www.exeter.ac.uk/
undergraduate/degrees/foundation**

Foundation, International Year One

UNIVERSITY OF ST MARK & ST JOHN
www.marjon.ac.uk

**Faculty of Education, Enterprise & Culture;
www.marjon.ac.uk/courses/our-faculties/
faculty-of-education-social- sciences**

BA(Hons) Childhood Practice, BA(Hons) Criminol-
ogy, BA(Hons) Early Childhood Studies – Progres-
sion, FdA Early Years, BA(Hons) Education Studies,
BSc(Hons) Forensic Criminology, BSc(Hons) Global
Education, FdA Learning and Teaching, BA(Hons)
Outdoor Adventure Education, BA(Hons) Perform-
ing Arts Education, BEd(Hons) Physical Education –
Secondary Ed (with QTS), BEd(Hons) Primary
Education (with QTS), BA(Hons) Primary Education,
BEd(Hons) Primary Education – Early Years (with
QTS), BEd Primary Education – Physical Education
(with QTS), BSc(Hons) Psychology, BSc(Hons) Psy-
chotherapy & Counselling, BA(Hons) Social Sciences,
BA(Hons) Sociology, BA(Hons) Special Educational
Needs & Disability Studies, BA(Hons) Theology,
BA(Hons) Youth and Community Work
Postgraduate courses: MA Literature for Children
and Young Adults, MA Education, MRes Outdoor
Education or Outdoor Learning, Postgraduate
Diploma in Early Years with Initial Teacher Training,
PGCE in Secondary Education with Art and Design,
PGCE Primary, PGCE Secondary Education with
Drama, PGCE Secondary Education with English,
PGCE Secondary Education with Geography, PGCE
Secondary Education with Media Studies, PGCE
Secondary Education with Modern Foreign Lan-
guages, PGCE Secondary Education with Physical
Education, PGCE Secondary Education with Psy-
chology, PGCE Secondary Education with Religious
Education (RE), Postgraduate Certificate in Coaching
& Mentoring, MSc Psychology, School Direct, MA
Social Policy, MRes Social Science, MSc Sport &
Exercise Psychology, PG Dip/MA Youth and Com-
munity Work

**Faculty of Sport, Health and Wellbeing;
www.marjon.ac.uk/courses/our-faculties/
faculty-of- sport-health-sciences/**

BSc(Hons) Exercise Physiology, BA(Hons) Football
Development & Coaching, BSc(Hons) Human Bios-
ciences, MOst Master of Osteopathic Medicine
(Undergraduate Pre-registration Master), BSc(Hons)
Nutrition, BA(Hons) Outdoor Adventure Education,
BA(Hons) Physical Education (non QTS), BEd(Hons)
Physical Education – Secondary Ed (with QTS),
BSc(Hons) Rehabilitation in Sport and Exercise –
Progression, BSc(Hons) Rehabilitation in Sport and
Exercise, BSc(Hons) Sport & Exercise Psychology,
BSc(Hons) Sport and Exercise Science, BA(Hons)
Sport Coaching, BA(Hons) Sport Development –
Coaching and School Sport, BA(Hons) Sport Devel-
opment – Progression, BA(Hons) Sport Development
– Sport Management, BA(Hons) Sport Development,
FdA Sport Development and Coaching, BSc(Hons)
Sport, Physical Activity and Health, BSc(Hons)
Sports Therapy – Progression, BSc(Hons) Sports
Therapy, BSc(Hons) Strength and Conditioning –
Progression, BSc(Hons) Strength and Conditioning
Postgraduate courses: MRes Outdoor Education or
Outdoor Learning, MRes Sport and Exercise Medi-
cine, MRes Sport and Exercise Science, MRes Sport
and Health Sciences, MRes Sport Development,
MRes Sport Management, PGCE Secondary Educa-
tion with Physical Education, Master of Public Health
(MPH), MSc Sport & Exercise Psychology, MSc Sport
Rehabilitation (Pre-Registration)

FALMOUTH UNIVERSITY
www.falmouth.ac.uk

Academy of Music and Theatre Arts; www.falmouth.ac.uk/departments/academy-of-musictheatre-arts

Acting BA(Hons), Creative Music Technology BA(Hons), Dance & Choreography BA(Hons), Music BA(Hons), Music, Theatre & Entertainment Management BA(Hons), Musical Theatre BA(Hons), Popular Music BA(Hons), Technical Theatre Arts BA(Hons), Theatre & Performance BA(Hons)

Postgraduate course: Creative Events Management MA/PgDip (online)

Falmouth School; of Entrepreneurship www.falmouth.ac.uk/departments/school-of-entrepreneurship

Business & Marketing BSc(Hons), Business & Entrepreneurship Bsc(Hons), Business & Management BSc(Hons), Creative Events Management BA(Hons), Sustainable Festival Management BA(Hons), Sustainable Tourism Management BA(Hons)

Postgraduate courses: Business Finance Innovation MA, Creative Education MA, Launchpad (with MA Entrepreneurship)

Falmouth School of Art; www.falmouth.ac.uk/departments/school-of-art

Drawing BA(Hons), Fine Art BA(Hons), Illustration BA(Hons)

Postgraduate course: Illustration: Authorial Practice MA, Illustration MA/PgDip (online)

Fashion & Textiles Institute; www.falmouth.ac.uk/departments/fashion-textiles

Costume Design for Film & Television BA(Hons), Fashion Design BA(Hons), Fashion Marketing BA(Hons), Fashion Photography BA(Hons), Sportswear Design BA(Hons), Textile Design BA(Hons)

Postgraduate course: Postgraduate Certificate in Higher Education (PGCHE) (online)

Games Academy; www.falmouth.ac.uk/departments/games-academy

Computing for Games BSc(Hons), Creative Robotics Bsc(Hons), Creative Virtual Reality BA(Hons) Game Art BA(Hons), Game Development BA(Hons), Immersive Computing BSc(Hons), Web Development BSc(Hons)

Postgraduate courses: Creative App Development MA/PgDip (online), Game Art MA, Game Design MA

Institute of Photography; www.falmouth.ac.uk/departments/photography

Commercial Photography BA(Hons), Marine & Natural History Photography BA(Hons), Photography BA(Hons), Photography BA(Hons) (Top Up) (online), Press & Editorial Photography BA(Hons)

Postgraduate course: Photography MA/PgDip (online)

School of Architecture, Design & Interiors; www.falmouth.ac.uk/departments/architecture-design-interiors

Architecture BA(Hons), Interior Design BA(Hons), Sustainable Product Design BA(Hons)

School of Communication Design; www.falmouth.ac.uk/departments/communication-design

Creative Advertising BA(Hons), Graphic Design BA(Hons), Marketing & Communications BA(Hons)

Postgraduate courses: Advertising Strategy & Planning MA/PgDip (online), Communication Design MA, Creative Advertising MA, Graphic Design MA/PgDip (online)

School of Film & Television; www.falmouth.ac.uk/departments/school-of-filmtelevision

Animation & Visual Effects BA(Hons), Costume Design for Film & Television BA(Hons), Film BA(Hons), Post-production for Film & Television BA(Hons), Television BA(Hons)

Postgraduate course: Film & Television MA

School of Writing & Journalism; www.falmouth.ac.uk/departments/writing-journalism

Creative Writing BA(Hons), English with Creative Writing BA(Hons), Journalism BA(Hons), Journalism and Creative Writing BA(Hons), Publishing & Communications BA(Hons), Sports Journalism BA(Hons)

Postgraduate courses: Professional Writing MA, Writing for Script & Screen MA/PgDip (online)

UNIVERSITY OF GLASGOW
www.gla.ac.uk

Accounting and Finance; www.gla.ac.uk/subjects/accountingfinance

Accountancy & Finance [BAcc], Accounting & Mathematics [BSc], Accounting & Statistics [BSc], Finance & Mathematics [BSc], Finance & Statistics [BSc]

Postgraduate courses: Corporate Governance & Accountability [MSc], Financial Modelling [MSc], International Accounting & Financial Management [MAcc], International Corporate Finance & Banking [MSc], International Finance [MFin], International Financial Analysis [MSc]

Archaeology; www.gla.ac.uk/subjects/archaeology

Archaeology (Bsc/MA/MA(SocSci))

Postgraduate courses: Ancient Cultures [MSc], Archaeology [MSc], Conflict Archaeology & Heritage [MSc/PgDip], Material Culture & Artefact Studies [MSc/PgDip], Museum Studies: Artefacts & Material Culture [MSc], Museum Studies: Collecting & Collections [MSc], Museum Studies: Theory & Practice [MSc]

Biodiversity, Animal Health and ComparativeMedicine; www.gla.ac.uk/subjects/bahcm

Postgraduate courses: Animal Welfare Science, Ethics & Law [MSc], Conservation Management of African Ecosystems [MSc], Ecology & Environmental Biology [MRes], Epidemiology of Infectious Diseases & Antimicrobial Resistance [MSc], Quantitative Methods in Biodiversity, Conservation and Epidemiology

Business; www.gla.ac.uk/subjects/business

Accountancy & Finance [BAcc], Accounting & Mathematics [BSc], Accounting & Statistics [BSc], Business & Management [BSc/MA/LLB/MA(SocSci)], Business Economics [MA(SocSci)], Economics [BAcc/BSc/MA/LLB/MA(SocSci)], Finance & Mathematics [BSc], Finance & Statistics [BSc]

Postgraduate courses: Aerospace Engineering & Management [MSc], Asset Pricing & Investment [MSc], Biotechnology and Management [MSc/PgDip], Civil Engineering & Management [MSc], Corporate Governance & Accountability [MSc], Creative Industries and Cultural Policy [MSc], Development Studies [MSc], Economic Development [MSc], Economics [MRes], Economics, Banking & Finance [MSc], Electronics & Electrical Engineering & Management [MSc], Environment & Sustainable Development [MSc], Finance & Economic Development [MSc], Finance & Management [MSc], Financial Economics [MSc], Financial Forecasting & Investment [MSc], Financial Modelling [MSc], Financial Risk Management [MSc], Geomatics & Management [MSc], Global Markets, Local Creativities (Erasmus Mundus International Master) [IntM], International Accounting & Financial Management [MAcc], International Banking & Finance [MSc], International Business [MSc], International Corporate Finance & Banking [MSc], International Finance [MFin], International Financial Analysis [MSc], International Human Resource Management & Development [MSc], International Management & Design Innovation [MSc], International Real Estate & Management [MSc], International Strategic Marketing [MSc], Investment Banking & Finance [MSc], Investment Fund Management [MSc], Management [MSc], Management [MRes], Management & Sustainable Tourism [MSc], Management with Enterprise & Business Growth [MSc], Management with Human Resources [MSc], Management with International Finance [MSc], MBA (Master of Business Administration) [MBA], Mechanical Engineering & Management [MSc], Media Management [MSc], Public Policy & Management [MSc], Quantitative Finance [MSc]

Cancer Sciences; www.gla.ac.uk/subjects/cancersciences

Postgraduate courses: Advanced Lymphoedema Management [PgCert], Cancer Research & Precision Oncology [MSc], Molecular Pathology [MSc/PgDip/PgCert: Blended learning

Cardiovascular and Medical Sciences; www.gla.ac.uk/subjects/cms

Biomedical Engineering [BEng/MEng]

Postgraduate courses: Applied Neuropsychology [MSc(MedSci)/PgDip], Cardiovascular Sciences [MSc(MedSci)], Clinical Pharmacology [MSc(MedSci)], Clinical Trials & Precision Medicine [MSc], Diabetes [MSc(MedSci)], Precision Medicine [MSc], Sport & Exercise Science & Medicine [MSc], Sport & Exercise Science & Medicine [MSc/PgDip/PgCert: Online distance learning], Translational Medicine [MRes]

Celtic and Gaelic; www.gla.ac.uk/subjects/celticgaelic
Celtic Civilisation [MA/MA(SocSci)], Celtic Studies [MA], Gaelic [MA]
Postgraduate courses: Ancient Cultures [MSc], Celtic Studies [MLitt]

Central and East European Studies; www.gla.ac.uk/subjects/cees
Central & East European Studies [MA/MA(SocSci)], Quantitative Methods [MA(SocSci)], Russian [MA]
Postgraduate courses: Central & East European, Russian & Eurasian Studies (Erasmus Mundus International Master) [IntM], Global Security [MRes], Global Security [MSc], Russian, East European & Eurasian Studies [MRes], Russian, East European & Eurasian Studies [MSc]

Chemistry; www.gla.ac.uk/subjects/chemistry
Chemical Physics [BSc/MSci], Chemistry [BSc/MSci], Chemistry with Medicinal Chemistry [BSc/MSci]
Postgraduate courses: Chemistry [MSc], Chemistry with Medicinal Chemistry [MSc], Industrial Heterogeneous Catalysis [MRes]

Classics; www.gla.ac.uk/subjects/classics
Ancient History [MA], Classics (Classical Civilisation) [MA/MA(SocSci)], Greek [MA], Latin [MA]
Postgraduate courses: Ancestral Studies [MSc] & Classics Ancient History [MSc]

Comparative Literature; www.gla.ac.uk/subjects/comparativeliterature
Comparative Literature [MA]
Postgraduate courses: Comparative Literature [MLitt], English Literature: American Modern Literature [MLitt], Translation Studies [MSc/PgDip/PgCert]

Computing Science; www.gla.ac.uk/subjects/computing
Computing Science [BSc/MA/MA(SocSci)/MSci], Computing Science (in partnership with SIT), Digital Media & Information Studies [MA], Electronic & Software Engineering [BSc/BEng/MEng], Software Engineering [BSc/MSci], Software Engineering (Graduate Apprenticeship) [BSc]
Postgraduate courses: Bioinformatics [MSc/PgDip/PgCert], Computer Systems Engineering [MSc], Computing Science [MSc], Data Analytics [MSc], Data Analytics [MSc/PgDip/PgCert: Online distance learning], Data Science [MSc], Information Security [MSc], Information Technology [MSc], IT Cyber Security [MSc], Security, Intelligence & Strategic Studies (Erasmus Mundus International Master) [IntM], Software Development [MSc]

Creative Writing; www.gla.ac.uk/subjects/creativewriting
Postgraduate courses: Creative Writing [MLitt],Creative Writing [MLitt: online distance learning]

Dentistry; www.gla.ac.uk/schools/dental/
Dentistry [BDS]
Postgraduate courses: Endodontics [MSc(DentSci)], Oral & Maxillofacial Surgery [MSc(DentSci)], Oral Sciences [MSc]

Economic and Social History; www.gla.ac.uk/subjects/economicsocialhistory
Economic & Social History [MA/MA(SocSci)], Quantitative Methods [MA(SocSci)]
Postgraduate courses: Global Economy [MSc], Global Markets, Local Creativities (Erasmus Mundus International Master) [IntM], History [MSc/PgDip], History (with an emphasis on the History of Medicine) [MSc]

Economics; www.gla.ac.uk/subjects/economics
Business Economics [MA(SocSci)], Economics [BAcc/BSc/MA/LLB/MA(SocSci)]
Postgraduate courses: Asset Pricing & Investment[MSc], Development Studies [MSc], Economic Development [MSc], Economics [MRes], Economics, Banking & Finance [MSc], Environment & Sustainable Development [MSc], Finance & Economic Development [MSc], Finance & Management [MSc], Financial Economics [MSc], Financial Forecasting & Investment [MSc], Financial Risk Management [MSc], Global Markets, Local Creativities (Erasmus Mundus International Master) [IntM], International Banking & Finance [MSc], Investment Banking & Finance [MSc], Investment Fund Management [MSc], Quantitative Finance [MSc]

Education; www.gla.ac.uk/subjects/education
Childhood Practice [BA], Community Development [BA], Education With Primary Teaching Qualification [MEduc], Primary Education with Teaching Qualification (Dumfries Campus) [MA], Technological Education [BTechEd]
Postgraduate courses: Academic Practice [MEd: Online distance learning available], Adult & Continuing Education [MSc], Adult Education for Social Change (Erasmus Mundus International Master)

[IntM], Adult Education, Community Development & Youth Work [MEd/ PgDip], Advanced Educational Leadership [PgCert: Online distance learning], Assessment in Education [MSc: Online distance learning], Childhood Practice [MEd/PgDip], Children's Literature & Literacies [MEd], Children's Literature, Media & Culture (Erasmus Mundus International Master) [IntM], Education [MSc: Online distance learning], Education (Primary) [PGDE], Education (Secondary) [PGDE], Education Policies for Global Development (Erasmus Mundus International Master) [IntM],Education, Public Policy & Equity [MSc], Educational Leadership [MEd], Educational Studies [MEd], Educational Studies [MSc], Educational Studies for Adult, Youth & Community Contexts [MSc], Enhanced Practice in Education (Dumfries Campus) [MSc], Health-Professions Education / Health Professions Education (with Research) [MSc/MSc(Research)/PgDip/PgCert: Online distance learning], Inclusive Education: Research, Policy & Practice [PgDip/PgCert: online distance learning available], In Headship [PgDip], Inclusive Education: Research, Policy & Practice [MEd], Inclusive Education: Research, Policy & Practice [PgDip/PgCert: Online distance learning available], Into Headship [PgCert], Middle Leadership & Management in Schools [PgCert], Museum Education [MSc], Museum Education [MSc: online distance learning], Professional Practice with PGDE [MEd], Psychological Studies (conversion) [MSc], Religious Education by Distance Learning (CREDL) [Cert: Online distance learning], Teacher Leadership & Learning [PgCert], TESOL: Teaching of English to Speakers of Other Languages [MEd], TESOL: Teaching of English to Speakers of Other Languages [MSc]

Engineering; www.gla.ac.uk/subjects/engineering

Aeronautical Engineering [MEng/BEng], Aeronautical Engineering (in partnership with SIT), Aerospace Systems [BEng/MEng], Aerospace Systems (in partnership with SIT), Biomedical Engineering [BEng/MEng], Civil Engineering [BEng/MEng], Civil Engineering (jointly offered with SIT), Civil Engineering with Architecture [BEng/MEng[,Electronic & Software Engineering [BSc/BEng/MEng], Electronics & Electrical Engineering [BEng/MEng], Electronics & Electrical Engineering (in partnership with UESTC), Electronics & Electrical Engineering with Communication (in partnership with UESTC), Electronics with Music [BEng/MEng], Mechanical Design Engineering [BEng/MEng], Mechanical Design

Engineering (in partnership with SIT), Mechanical Engineering [BEng/MEng], Mechanical Engineering with Aeronautics [BEng/MEng], Mechatronics [BEng/MEng], Mechatronics (in partnership with SIT), Product Design Engineering [BEng/MEng]
Postgraduate courses: Aerospace Engineering [MSc], Aerospace Engineering & Management [MSc], Biomedical Engineering [MSc], Civil Engineering [MSc], Civil Engineering & Management [MSc], Computer Systems Engineering [MSc], Electronics & Electrical Engineering [MSc], Electronics & Electrical Engineering & Management [MSc], Electronics Manufacturing [MSc], Land & Hydrographic Surveying [MSc/PgDip/PgCert], Land & Hydrographic Surveying with Work Placement [MSc], Mechanical Engineering [MSc], Mechanical Engineering & Management [MSc], Mechatronics [MSc], Nanoscience and Nanotechnology [MSc], Product Design Engineering [MSc], Quantum Technology [MSc], Sensor & Imaging Systems [MSc], Structural Engineering [MSc], Sustainable Energy [MSc], Urban Transport [MSc]

English Language and Linguistics; www.gla.ac.uk/subjects/englishlanguage
English Language & Linguistics[MA]
Postgraduate courses: Applied Linguistics [MSc], English Language & English Linguistics [MSc], Speech, Language & Sociolinguistics [MSc], TESOL: Teaching of English to Speakers of Other Languages [Med], TESOL: Teaching of English to Speakers of Other Languages [MSc]

English Literature; www.gla.ac.uk/subjects/englishliterature
English Literature [MA]
Postgraduate courses: Creative Writing [MLitt], Creative Writing [MLitt: distance learning], English Literature [MLitt], English Literature: American Modern Literature [MLitt], English Literature: Fantasy [MLitt], English Literature: Medieval & Early Modern Literature & Culture [MLitt], English Literature: Modernities – Literature, Culture, Theory [MLitt], English Literature: Romantic Worlds [MLitt], English Literature: Victorian Literature [MLitt]

Filmand Television Studies; www.gla.ac.uk/subjects/filmtelevision
Film & Television Studies [MA]
Postgraduate courses: Creative Industries & Cultural Policy [MSc], Film & Television Studies [MLitt], Film Curation [MSc], Filmmaking & Media Arts [MSc], Media Management [MSc]

Geographical and Earth Sciences; www.gla.ac.uk/subjects/ges

Earth Science [BSc/MSci], Geography [BSc/MA/MA(SocSci)], Geology [BSc/MSci]

Postgraduate courses: Geoinformation Technology & Cartography [MSc/PgDip/PgCert], Geomatics & Management [MSc], Geospatial & Mapping Sciences [MSc/PgDip/PgCert], Human Geography: Spaces, Politics, Ecologies [MRes], Land & Hydrographic Surveying [MSc/PgDip/PgCert], Land & Hydrographic Surveying with Work Placement [MSc], Sustainable Water Environments [MSc]

Health and Wellbeing; www.gla.ac.uk/subjects/healthwellbeing

Postgraduate courses: Applied Neuropsychology [MSc(MedSci)/PgDip], Clinical Neuropsychology [MSc(MedSci)/PgDip], Clinical Psychology [DClinPsy], Developing & Evaluating Interventions [MSc/PgDip/PgCert/CPD], Global Health [MSc], Global Mental Health [MSc/PgDip/PgCert], Global Mental Health [MSc/PgDip/PgCert: Online distance learning], Global Mental Health with specialism in health promotion [MSc], Global Mental Health with specialism in health technology assessment [MSc], Global Mental Health with specialism in research methods [MSc], Health Services Management [MSc/PgDip/PgCert], Health Technology Assessment [MSc/PgDip/PgCert: Online distance learning], Leadership in Health & Social Care [PgCert: Online distance learning], One Health [MSc/PgDip/PgCert: Online distance learning], Pathology, Molecular [MSc/PgDip/PgCert: Blended learning], Population Health Sciences [MSc/PgDip/PgCert: Online distance learning], Primary Health Care [MSc/PgDip/PgCert], Public Health [MPH/PgDip/PgCert], Public Health [MPH/PgDip/PgCert: Online distance learning], Public Health (Data Science) [MPH], Public Health (Epidemiology) [MPH], Public Health (Health Economics) [MPH], Public Health (Health Promotion) [MPH], Sport & Exercise Science & Medicine [MSc]

History; www.gla.ac.uk/subjects/history

Ancient History [MA], History [MA/MA(SocSci)/], Scottish History [MA/MA(SocSci)]

Postgraduate courses: Early Modern History [MSc/PgDip], Gender History [MSc/PgDip], Global Security [MRes], Global Security [MSc], History [MSc/PgDip], History (with an emphasis on the History of Medicine) [MSc], Medieval History [MSc/PgDip], Modern History [MSc/PgDip], Scottish History [MSc/PgDip], Security, Intelligence & Strategic Studies (Erasmus Mundus International Master) [IntM], War Studies [MSc]

History of Art; www.gla.ac.uk/subjects/historyofart

History of Art [MA]

Postgraduate courses: Antiquities Trafficking & Art Crime [PgCert: Online distance learning], Art History: [MLitt], Art History: Collecting & Provenance in an International Context [MSc], Art History: Dress & Textile Histories [MLitt], Art History: Modern Material Artefacts [MSc], Art History: Technical Art History, Making & Meaning [MLitt], Curatorial Practice (Contemporary Art) (in conjunction with The Glasgow School of Art) [MLitt], Museum Studies: Artefacts & Material Culture [MSc], Museum Studies: Collecting & Collections [MSc], Museum Studies: Theory & Practice [MSc], Textile Conservation [MPhil]

Infection, Immunity and Inflammation; www.gla.ac.uk/subjects/iii

Immunology [BSc/MSci], Medicine [MBChB], Microbiology[BSc/MSci], Veterinary Biosciences [BSc/MSci], Veterinary Medicine & Surgery [BVMS]

Postgraduate courses: Bioinformatics [MSc/PgDip/PgCert], Immunology & Inflammatory Disease [MSc], Infection Biology (Microbiology specialism) [MSc], Infection Biology (Parasitology specialism) [MSc], Infection Biology (Virology specialism) [MSc],Infection Biology (with specialisms) [MSc], Infection Biology (with specialisms) [MSc]

Information Studies; www.gla.ac.uk/subjects/informationstudies

Digital Media & Information Studies [MA]

Postgraduate courses: Information Management & Preservation [MSc/PgDip/PgCert], Museum Studies: Artefacts & Material Culture [MSc], Museum Studies: Collecting & Collections [MSc], Museum Studies: Theory & Practice [MSc]

Law; www.gla.ac.uk/subjects/law

Common Law [LLB], Common Law (graduate entry)[LLB], Scots Law [LLB], Scots Law (graduate entry)[LLB]

Postgraduate courses: Corporate & Financial Law [LLM], Diploma in Professional Legal Practice [PgDip], Intellectual Property & the Digital Economy [LLM], International Commercial Law [LLM], International Competition Law & Policy [LLM], International Economic Law [LLM], International Law [LLM], International Law & Security [LLM], Law [LLM], Law [MRes], Socio-Legal Studies [MRes]

Life Sciences; www.gla.ac.uk/subjects/lifesciences

Anatomy [BSc/MSci], Biochemistry [BSc/MSci], Biomedical Engineering [BEng/MEng], Genetics [BSc/MSci], Human Biology [BSc/MSci], Human Biology & Nutrition [BSc], Immunology [BSc/MSci], Marine & Freshwater Biology [BSc/MSci], Microbiology [BSc/MSci], Molecular & Cellular Biology [BSc/MSci], Molecular & Cellular Biology (with Biotechnology) [BSc/MSci], Molecular & Cellular Biology (with Plant Science) [BSc/MSci], Neuroscience [BSc/MSci], Pharmacology [BSc/MSci], Physiology [BSc/MSci], Physiology & Sports Science [BSc/MSci], Physiology, Sports Science & Nutrition [BSc/MSci], Zoology [BSc/MSci]

Postgraduate courses: Bioinformatics [MSc/PgDip/PgCert], Biomedical Sciences [MSc], Biomedical Sciences [MRes], Biomedical Sciences (Integrative Mammalian Biology) [MRes], Human Anatomy [PgCert], Medical Visualisation & Human Anatomy [MSc], Sport & Exercise Science & Medicine [MSc/PgDip/PgCert: Online distance learning], Sport & Exercise Science & Medicine [MSc], Sports Nutrition [PgCert]

Management; www.gla.ac.uk/subjects/management

Accounting & Statistics [BSc], Business & Management [BSc/MA/LLB/MA(SocSci)], Business Economics [MA(SocSci)/]

Postgraduate courses: Aerospace Engineering & Management [MSc], Biotechnology & Management [MSc/PgDip], Civil Engineering & Management [MSc], Creative Industries and Cultural Policy [MSc], Electronics & Electrical Engineering & Management [MSc], Finance & Management [MSc], Geomatics & Management [MSc], International Business [MSc], International Human Resource Management & Development [MSc], International Management & Design Innovation [MSc], International Real Estate & Management [MSc], International Strategic Marketing [MSc], Management [MSc], Management [MRes], Management & Sustainable Tourism [MSc], Management with Enterprise & Business Growth [MSc], Management with Human Resources [MSc], Management with International Finance [MSc], MBA (Master of Business Administration) [MBA], Mechanical Engineering & Management [MSc], Media Management [MSc], Public Policy & Management [MSc]

Mathematics; www.gla.ac.uk/subjects/mathematics

Accounting & Mathematics [BSc], Finance & Mathematics [BSc], Mathematics [BSc/MA/MA(SocSci)/MSci]

Postgraduate courses: Data Analytics [MSc], Data Analytics [MSc/PgDip/PgCert: Online distance learning], Financial Modelling [MSc], Mathematics / Applied Mathematics[MSc]

Medicine; www.gla.ac.uk/subjects/medicine

Biomedical Engineering [BEng/MEng], Dentistry [BDS], Immunology [BSc/MSci], Medicine [MBChB], Nursing [BN], Nursing (jointly offered with SIT), Physiology, Sports Science & Nutrition [BSc/MSci]

Postgraduate courses: Child Health [PgCert], Clinical Anaesthesia [MSc/PgDip/PgCert: Online distance learning], Clinical Anaesthesia & Leadership [MSc/PgDip/PgCert: Online distance learning], Clinical Critical Care [MSc: Online distance learning] Clinical Genetics [MSc(MedSci)], Clinical Nutrition [MSc(MedSci)], Critical Care [MSc/PgDip/PgCert], Critical Care & Leadership [MSc: Online distance learning], Critical Care, Leadership & Management [MSc], Endodontics [MSc(DentSci)], Forensic Toxicology [MSc(MedSci)], Genetic and Genomic Counselling (with Work Placement) [MSc(MedSci)], Health Care, Advanced Practice in [MSc(MedSci)], Health-Professions Education / Health Professions Education (with Research) [MSc/ MSc(Research)/PgDip/PgCert: Online distance learning], Healthcare Chaplaincy [PgCert], Human Nutrition [MSc(MedSci)], Leadership in Health & Social Care [PgCert: Online distance learning], Lymphoedema Management, Advanced [PgCert], Medical Genetics & Genomics [MSc(MedSci)], Medical Physics [MSc], Nursing Science, Advanced [MSc], Oral & Maxillofacial Surgery [MSc(DentSci)], Oral Sciences [MSc], Pathology, Molecular [MSc/PgDip/PgCert: Blended learning], Sports Nutrition [PgCert], Trauma Management [MSc/PgDip/PgCert: Online distance learning]

Modern Languages and Cultures; www.gla.ac.uk/subjects/modernlanguages

Comparative Literature [MA], French [MA], German [MA], Italian [MA], Portuguese [MA], Russian [MA], Spanish [MA]

Postgraduate courses: Comparative Literature [MLitt], South European Studies (Erasmus Mundus International Master) [IntM], Translation Studies [MSc/PgDip/PgCert]

Molecular, Cell and Systems Biology; www.gla.ac.uk/subjects/mcsb

Postgraduate courses: Biotechnology [MSc], Biotechnology & Management [MSc/PgDip], Food Security [MSc], Stem Cell Engineering for Regenerative Medicine [MSc]

Music; www.gla.ac.uk/subjects/music

Electronics with Music [BEng/MEng], Music [MA], Music [BMus]

Postgraduate courses: Composition & Creative Practice [MMus], Historically Informed Performance Practice (in conjunction with the Royal Conservatoire of Scotland)) [MA], Music Industries [MSc], Musicology [MMus], Sound Design & Audiovisual Practice [MSc]

Neuroscience and Psychology; www.gla.ac.uk/subjects/neurosciencepsychology

Neuroscience [BSc/MSci], Psychology [BSc/MA/MA(SocSci)]

Postgraduate courses: Applied Neuropsychology [MSc(MedSci)/PgDip], Brain Sciences [MSc], Clinical Neuropsychology [MSc(MedSci) /PgDip], Clinical Neuropsychology Knowledge & Practice [MSc(MedSci)], Clinical Neuropsychology Practice [PgCert], Psychological Science (conversion) [MSc], Psychological Science, Research Methods of [MSc], Psychological Studies (conversion) [MSc]

Nursing and Health Care; www.gla.ac.uk/subjects/nursing

Nursing [BN], Nursing (jointly offered with SIT)

Postgraduate courses: Advanced Nursing Science [MSc], Advanced Practice in Health Care [MSc(MedSci)], Leadership in Health & Social Care [PgCert: Online distance learning]

Parasitology; www.gla.ac.uk/subjects/parasitology

Bioinformatics [MSc/PgDip/PgCert], Infection Biology (Microbiology specialism) [MSc], Infection Biology (Parasitology specialism) [MSc], Infection Biology (Virology specialism) [MSc], Infection Biology (with specialisms) [MSc]

Philosophy; www.gla.ac.uk/subjects/philosophy

Philosophy [BSc/MA/MA(SocSci)]

Postgraduate courses: Philosophy [MSc], Philosophy (Conversion) [MSc], Philosophy of Mind & Psychology [MSc]

Physics and Astronomy; www.gla.ac.uk/subjects/physics

Astronomy [BSc/MSci], Chemical Physics [BSc/MSci], Physics / Theoretical Physics [BSc/MSci], Physics with Astrophysics [BSc/MSci]

Postgraduate courses: Astrophysics [MSc], Physics: Advanced Materials [MSc], Physics: Energy & the Environment [MSc], Physics: Nuclear Technology [MSc], Quantum Technology [MSc], Sensor & Imaging Systems [MSc], Sustainable Energy [MSc], Theoretical Physics [MSc]

Politics and International Relations; www.gla.ac.uk/subjects/politics

International Relations [LLB/MA(SocSci)], Politics [MA/LLB/MA(SocSci)], Quantitative Methods [MA(SocSci)]

Postgraduate courses: Chinese Studies [MSc], Global Security [MRes], Global Security [MSc], Human Rights & International Politics [MRes], Human Rights & International Politics [MSc], International Relations [MRes], International Relations [MSc], Political Communication [MRes], Political Communication [MSc/PgDip], Security, Intelligence & Strategic Studies (Erasmus Mundus International Master) [IntM], South European Studies (Erasmus Mundus International Master) [IntM], Transnational Crime, Justice & Security [MSc]

Psychology; www.gla.ac.uk/subjects/psychology

Psychology [BSc/MA/MA(SocSci)]

Postgraduate courses: Brain Sciences [MSc], Clinical Neuropsychology [MSc(MedSci)/PgDip], Philosophy of Mind & Psychology [MSc], Psychological Science (conversion) [MSc], Psychological Science, Research Methods of [MSc], Psychological Studies (conversion) [MSc], Psychology (conversion) [MSc: Online distance learning]

Scottish Literature; www.gla.ac.uk/subjects/scottishliterature

Scottish Literature [MA]

Sociology; www.gla.ac.uk/subjects/sociology

Sociology [MA/MA(SocSci)]

Postgraduate courses: Antiquities Trafficking & Art Crime [PgCert: Online distance learning], Criminology [MRes], Criminology & Criminal Justice [MSc], Equality & Human Rights [MRes], Equality & Human Rights [MSc], Global Health [MSc], Global Migrations & Social Justice [MRes], Global Migrations & Social Justice [MSc], Media, Communications

& International Journalism [MSc], Sociology [MSc], Sociology & Research Methods [MRes], Transnational Crime, Justice & Security [MSc]

Statistics; www.gla.ac.uk/subjects/statistics

Accounting & Statistics [BSc], Finance & Statistics [BSc], Statistics [BSc/MSci]

Postgraduate courses: Advanced Statistics [MRes], Biostatistics [MSc], Data Analytics [MSc], Data Analytics [MSc/PgDip/PgCert: Online distance learning], Environmental Statistics [MSc], Financial Modelling [MSc], Statistics [MSc]

Theatre Studies; www.gla.ac.uk/subjects/theatre

Theatre Studies [MA]

Postgraduate courses: Playwriting & Dramaturgy [MLitt], Theatre & Performance Practices [MLitt], Theatre Studies [MLitt]

Theology and Religious Studies; www.gla.ac.uk/subjects/theology

Theology & Religious Studies [BD/BD(Min)/MA]

Postgraduate courses: Ancient Cultures [MSc], Church History & Theology [MTh/PgDip/PgCert], Ministry, Theology & Practice [MTh], Religious Education by Distance Learning (CREDL) [PgCert: Online distance learning]

Translation Studies; www.gla.ac.uk/subjects/translationstudies

Postgraduate courses: Translation Studies [MSc/PgDip/PgCert]

Urban Studies; www.gla.ac.uk/subjects/urbanstudies

Health & Social Sector Leadership (Dumfries Campus) [MA], Quantitative Methods [MA(SocSci)],Social & Public Policy [MA/LLB/MA(SocSci)]

Postgraduate courses: City Planning [MSc], City Planning & Real Estate Development [MSc], International Real Estate & Management [MSc], Public & Urban Policy [MSc/ PgDip], Public Policy & Management [MSc], Public Policy Research [MRes], Real Estate [PgCert], Real Estate [MSc], Spatial Planning [PgCert], Urban Analytics [MSc],Urban Research [MRes], Urban Studies [PgCert], Urban Transport [MSc]

VeterinaryMedicine; www.gla.ac.uk/subjects/veterinary

Veterinary Biosciences [BSc/MSci], Veterinary Medicine & Surgery [BVMS]

Postgraduate courses: Advanced Practice in Veterinary Nursing [MSc/PgDip/PgCert: Online distance learning], One Health [MSc/PgDip/PgCert: Online distance learning]

GLASGOW CALEDONIAN UNIVERSITY
www.gcu.ac.uk

School of Engineering and Built Environment; www.gcu.ac.uk/ebe

3D Animation and Visualisation BSc(Hons), Audio Technology BSc(Hons), Building Services Engineering BEng(Hons), Building Surveying BSc(Hons), Building Surveying Pathway BSc(Hons), Computer Games (Art and Animation) BSc(Hons), Computer Games (Design) BSc(Hons), Computer Games (Software Development) BSc(Hons), Computer Networking BEng(Hons), Computer-Aided Mechanical Engineering BEng(Hons), Computer-Aided Mechanical Engineering MEng Computer-Aided Mechanical Engineering Pathway MEng, Computing BSc(Hons), Construction Management BSc(Hons), Construction Management Pathway BSc(Hons), Cyber Security and Networks BSc(Hons), Cyber Security and Networks Pathway BSc(Hons), Digital Design BSc(Hons), Digital Security and Forensics BSc(Hons), Electrical Power Engineering MEng, Electrical Power Engineering BEng(Hons), Electrical Power Engineering Pathway MEng, Electrical and Electronic Engineering BEng(Hons), Electrical and Electronic Engineering MEng, Electrical and Electronic Engineering Pathway MEng, Environmental Civil Engineering BSc(Hons), Environmental Management BSc(Hons), Fire Risk Engineering BEng(Hons), Forensic Investigation BSc(Hons), Health and Safety Management BSc, Health, Safety and Environmental Management BSc(Hons), IT Management for Business BSc(Hons), Mechanical Systems Engineering MEng, Mechanical Systems Engineering BEng(Hons), Mechanical and Power Plant Systems MEng, Mechanical and Power Plant Systems BEng(Hons), Networked Systems Engineering BEng(Hons), Quantity Surveying BSc(Hons), Quantity Surveying Pathway BSc(Hons), Real Estate BSc(Hons), Software Development for Business BSc(Hons)

Postgraduate courses: 3D Design for Virtual Environments MSc, Advanced Internetwork Engineering MSc, Big Data Technologies MSc, Building Services Engineering MSc, Climate Justice MSc, Electrical and Electronic Engineering MSc, Electrical Power Engineering MSc, Environmental Management (Waste, Energy, Water, Oil and Gas) MSc, International Project Management (Energy, Construction Management, Oil and Gas) MSc, Mechanical Engineering MSc, Quantity Surveying MSc

Glasgow School for Business and Society; www.gcu.ac.uk/gsbs

Accountancy BA(Hons), Accountancy Pathway BA/BA(Hons), Bachelor of Laws LLB(Hons) Bachelor of Laws Fast-track LLB, Business Management BA(Hons), Fashion Design with Business BA(Hons), Finance, Investment and Risk BA(Hons), Finance, Investment and Risk Pathway BA(Hons), International Business BA(Hons), International Business and Human Resource Management BA(Hons), International Business and Human Resource Management Pathway BA(Hons), International Business and Tourism Management BA(Hons), International Business with Language BA(Hons), International Events Management BA(Hons), International Events Management Pathway BA(Hons), International Fashion Branding BA(Hons), International Fashion Business BA(Hons), International Marketing BA(Hons), International Sports Management BA(Hons), International Supply Chain Management BA(Hons), International Tourism and Events Management BA(Hons), International Tourism and Events Management Pathway BA(Hons), Media and Communication BA(Hons), Multimedia Journalism BA(Hons), Risk Management BA(Hons), Risk Management Pathway BA(Hons), Social Sciences BA(Hons)

Postgraduate courses: Accounting, Finance and Regulation MSc/Msc(Fast-track), Association of Chartered Certified Accountants (ACCA) CPD, Doctorate of Business Administration DBA, Global Master of Business Administration (MBA) MBA, Health History MSc/PgD/PgC, Human Resource Management MSc, International Banking, Finance and Risk Management MSc, International Business Management MSc, International Economic and Social Justice MSc, International Fashion Marketing MSc, International Human Resource Management MSc, International Operations and Supply Chain Management MSc, International Tourism and Events Management MSc, Marketing MSc, Multimedia Journalism MA, Risk

Management MSc, Social Innovation MSc Television Fiction Writing MA,

School of Health and Life Sciences; www.gcu.ac.uk/hls

Applied Biomedical Science/Biomedical Science BSc(Hons), Applied Psychology BSc(Hons), COSCA Counselling Skills Certificate, Cell and Molecular Biology BSc(Hons), Cell and Molecular Biology Pathway BSc(Hons), Diagnostic Imaging BSc(Hons), Food Bioscience BSc(Hons), Food Bioscience Pathway BSc/BSc(Hons), Human Nutrition and Dietetics BSc(Hons), Microbiology BSc(Hons), Microbiology Pathway BSc(Hons), Nursing Studies (Adult) BSc, Nursing Studies (Adult) BSc(Hons), Nursing Studies (Child) BSc, Nursing Studies (Child) BSc(Hons), Nursing Studies (Dual Registration Learning Disability/Child) BSc(Hons), Nursing Studies (Learning Disability) BSc, Nursing Studies (Learning Disability) BSc(Hons), Nursing Studies (Mental Health) BSc, Nursing Studies (Mental Health) BSc(Hons), Occupational Therapy BSc(Hons), Optometry BSc(Hons), Oral Health Science BSc, Orthoptics BSc Pharmacology Pathway BSc(Hons), Pharmacology Pathway BSc(Hons), Physiotherapy BSc(Hons), Podiatry BSc(Hons), Professional Studies in Nursing BSc, Professional Studies in Nursing BSc(Hons), Radiotherapy and Oncology BSc(Hons), Social Work BA(Hons)

Postgraduate courses: Advanced Practice MSc, Advanced Practice in District Nursing with Specialist Practitioner Qualification PgD, Biomedical Science MSc, Biomolecular and Biomedical Sciences MSc, Clinical Microbiology MSc, Counselling Psychology DPsych, Diabetes Care and Management MSc, Diagnostic Imaging MSc, Doctor of Physiotherapy (Pre-registration)DPT, Education in Academic and Practice Settings PgC, Food Bioscience MSc, Forensic Psychology MSc, Health Psychology DPsych, Investigative Ophthalmology and Vision Research MSc, Master of Public Health MPH, Medical Ultrasound MSc, Nursing Studies Adult (Pre-registration) MSc, Nursing: Advancing Professional Practice MSc, Occupational Therapy (pre-registration) MSc, Pharmacology MSc, Physiotherapy MSc, Physiotherapy (Pre-registration) MSc, Psychology (Conversion) Graduate Diploma, Social Work MSc, Sports and Exercise Psychology DPsych, Theory of Podiatric Surgery MSc

GCU London; www.gculondon.ac.uk

Postgraduate courses: Fashion Business Creation MSc, Fashion and Lifestyle Marketing MSc, Fire

Risk Engineering BEng(Hons), Global MBA Masters of Business Administration (with additional pathways in Public Health or Insurance) MBA, Global Marketing MSc, Insurance and Sustainable Risk Management MSc, International Banking, Finance and Risk Management MSc, International Business, Trade and Diplomacy MSc, International Diplomacy and the Digital State MSc International Management and Business Development MSc, International Project Management (Construction) MSc, International Security and Diplomacy MSc, Luxury Brand Management MBA, Luxury Brand Marketing MSc, Public Health MSc, Quantity Surveying MSc, Risk Management MSc

THE GLASGOW SCHOOL OF ART
www.gsa.ac.uk

BSc(Hons) Immersive Systems Design, BArch/BArch(Hons)/ DipArch Architecture, BA(Hons) Communication Design, BEng/MEng Engineering with Architecture, BA(Hons) Fashion Design, BA(Hons) Fine Art BA(Hons) Interaction Design, BA(Hons) Interior Design, BDes/MEDes Product Design, BEng(Hons) /MEng Product Design Engineering, BA(Hons) Sculpture & Environmental Art, BA(Hons) Silversmithing and Jewellery Design, BDes(Hons) Sound for the Moving Image, BA(Hons) Textile Design

Postgraduate courses: MArch in Architectural Studies, MLitt Art Writing, MDes Communication Design, MLitt Curatorial Practice (Contemporary Art), MDes in Design Innovation and Citizenship, MDes in Design Innovation and Collaborative Creativity, MDes in Design Innovation and Environmental Design, MDes in Design Innovation and Interaction Design, MDes in Design Innovation and Service Design, MDes in Design Innovation and Transformation Design, MSc in Environmental Architecture, MDes Fashion + Textiles, MLitt Fine Art Practice, MDes in Graphics/Illustration/Photography, MSc Heritage Visualisation, MDes in Interior Design, MSc International Management and Design Innovation, MFA Master of Fine Art, Master of Research, MSc Medical Visualisation and Human Anatomy, PG Certificate Higher Education in Learning and Teaching in the Creative Disciplines PGCert Supervisory Practices in the Creative Disciplines MSc Product Design Engineering, MSc Serious Games and Virtual Reality, MDes Sound for the Moving Image

UNIVERSITY OF GLOUCESTERSHIRE
www.glos.ac.uk

School of Art and Design; www.glos.ac.uk/academic-schools/art-and-design

Advertising BA(Hons), Animation BA(Hons), Fashion Design BA(Hons), Fine Art BA(Hons), Graphic Design BA(Hons), Illustration BA(Hons), Interior Design BA(Hons), Landscape Architecture BA(Hons), Photography BA(Hons), Photography: Editorial and Advertising BA(Hons), Photojournalism and Documentary Photography BA(Hons), Product Design BA(Hons), Visual Communication (Level 6) BA(Hons)

Postgraduate courses: Fine Art PGCert/PGDip/MA, Illustration MA, Landscape Architecture PGDip/MA, Landscape Architecture (with conversion year) MA, MDes Creative Advertising MDes Graphic Design Photography PGCert/PGDip/MA

School of Business and Technology www.glos.ac.uk/academic-schools/business

Accounting and Business Management BA(Hons), Accounting and Finance BA(Hons), Advertising BA(Hons), Business and Marketing Management BA(Hons), Business Management BA(Hons), Business Management and Strategy (Level 6) BA(Hons), Computer and Cyber Forensics BSc(Hons), Computer Games Design BSc(Hons), Computer Games Programming BSc(Hons), Computing BSc(Hons), Computing (Level 6) BSc(Hons), Cyber and Computer Security BSc(Hons), Digital Media and Web Technologies BSc(Hons), Events Management BA(Hons), Hotel, Resort and Tourism Management BA(Hons), International Business Management BA(Hons), Law LLB, Marketing BA(Hons),

Marketing, Advertising and Branding BA(Hons), Sports Business Management BA(Hons),
Postgraduate courses. Accounting and Finance MSc, Accounting and Finance (Masters Stage) MSc, Computing (Masters Stage) MSC Masters Stage, Cyber Security (MSc) MSc, Finance PGCert/PGDip/MSc, Game Development MSc, International Business MSc, Marketing PGCert/PGDip/MSc, MBA Business Administration MBA, MBA Business Administration (Masters stage) MBA Top Human Resource Management PGDip/MSc, Human Resource Management (Masters Stage) MSc, Intermediate Human Resource Management Certificate of Professional Studies

School of Education; www.glos.ac.uk/academic-schools/education

Early Childhood Studies BA(Hons), Education BA(Hons), Education, Inclusion and Special Educational Needs BA(Hons), Primary – general (FS/KS1, ages 3-7) BEd(Hons), Primary – general (KS1/KS2, ages 5-11) BEd(Hons), Primary – general (maths) (KS1/KS2, ages 5-11) BEd(Hons), Working With Children, Young People And Families Level 4 Cert HE
Postgraduate courses: Academic Practice PGCert, Early Years PGCert, Education MA, Inclusive Education National Award for Special Educational Needs Co-ordination PGCert, Teacher Training PGCE (Primary) PGCE Primary, Teacher Training PGCE (Secondary) PGCE

School of Engineering Technologies; www.glos.ac.uk/engineering

Industrial Control Engineering BEng(Hons), Industrial Control Engineering MEng, Industrial Systems Engineering BEng(Hons), Industrial Systems Engineering MEng, Integrated Engineering (Level 6) Bachelor of Engineering Level 6, Mechatronics Engineering BEng(Hons), Mechatronics Engineering MEng
Postgraduate courses: Industrial Control Engineering MSc, Industrial Sustainable Energy MSc, Industrial Systems Engineering MSc, Mechatronics Engineering MSc

School of Health and Social Care; www.glos.ac.uk/academic- schools/health-and- social-care

BSc(Hons) Physiotherapy, Health and Social Care CertHE, Nursing (Adult) BSc(Hons), Nursing (Mental Health) BSc(Hons), Paramedic Science BSc(Hons), Paramedic Science (Level 6) BSc(Hons), Social Work BSc(Hons), Social Work (Yeovil College University Centre), Working With Children, Young People And Families Level 4 Cert HE
Postgraduate courses: Advanced Clinical Practice (MSc) PGCert/PGDip/MSc, Advanced Professional Practice (MSc) MSc, Social Work PGCert/PGDip/MA

School of Law; www.glos.ac.uk/academicschools/law

Law LLB(Hons), Law with Business LLB(Hons)
Postgraduate course: Legal Research (PGCert/PGDip/LLM Legal Research)

School of Liberal and Performing Arts; www.glos.ac.uk/academic-schools/liberaland- performing-arts

Creative Writing BA(Hons), Dance BA(Hons), Drama and Performance Practice BA(Hons), English BA(Hons), English and Creative Writing BA(Hons), English Literature and Creative Writing BA(Hons), History BA(Hons), Performing Arts BA(Hons), Religion, Philosophy and Ethics BA(Hons)
Postgraduate courses: Creative and Critical Writing PGCert/PGDip/MA

School of Media; www.glos.ac.uk/academic-schools/media

Animation BA(Hons), Creative Music Technology BA(Hons), Film and Television Production (Level 6) BA(Hons), Film Production BA(Hons), Journalism BA(Hons), Magazine Journalism and Production, Media Production BA(Hons), Music Business BA(Hons), Popular Music BA(Hons), Sports Journalism BA(Hons), Television Production BA(Hons)
Postgraduate courses: Animation MA, Communications, PR and the Media MA, Creative Music Practice MA, Film Making MA

School of Natural and Social Sciences; www.glos.ac.uk/academic- schools/natural-and- social- sciences

Animal Biology BSc(Hons), Applied Social Sciences (Level 6) BSc(Hons), Biology BSc(Hons), Criminology BSc(Hons), Criminology and Criminal Justice (Level 6) BSc(Hons), Criminology and Psychology BSc(Hons), Criminology and Sociology BSc(Hons), Ecology and Environmental Science BSc(Hons), Geography(Hons), Geography BSc(Hons), Human Geography BA(Hons), International Relations BA(Hons), Professional Policing BSc(Hons), Psychology BSc(Hons), Sociology BA(Hons)
Postgraduate courses: Applied Ecology PGCert/PGDip/MSc, Conservation GIS PGCert, Criminology PGCert/PGDip/MSc, Forensic Psychology Psychology MSc, Public Protection PGCert

**School of Sport and Exercise;
www.glos.ac.uk/academic- schools/sport-
and- exercise/**

Applied Sport and Exercise Studies (Level 6) BSc(Hons), BSc(Hons) Physiotherapy, Exercise, Fitness and Health Foundation Degree, Physical Education BSc(Hons), Physical Education and Coaching BSc(Hons), Sport and Exercise Sciences BSc(Hons), Sport Business Management BA(Hons), Sports

Business and Coaching BSc(Hons), Sports Coaching BSc(Hons), Sports Strength and Conditioning BSc(Hons), Sports Therapy BSc(Hons)

Postgraduate courses: Professional Practice in Physical Education and School Sport PGCert/PGDip/MA, Professional Practice in Sports Coaching PGCert/PGDip/MSc, Sports Performance Analysis MSc, Sports Strength and Conditioning PGCert/PGDip/MSc, Sports Therapy MSc

---

GLYNDWR UNIVERSITY
www.glyndwr.ac.uk

Faculty of Arts, Science and Technology and incorporates Applied Science, Computing and Engineering www.glyndwr.ac.uk/en/Faculties/FacultyofArtsScienceandTechnology/

Applied Art

BA(Hons) Applied Arts
Postgraduate courses: MA Art Practice, MA Design Practice, PGDip Advanced Professional Practice

Design Communication & Digital Art

MDes Animation, BA(Hons) Animation, MDes Comics, BA(Hons) Comic MDes Children's Books, BA(Hons) Children's Books, MDes Game Art, BA(Hons) Game Art, MDes Graphic Design, BA(Hons) Graphic Design, MDes Illustration, BA(Hons) Illustration, Graphic Novels and Children's Publishing, MDes Photography & Film, BA(Hons) Photography & Film, MDes Visual Effects, BA(Hons) Visual Effects.

Fine Art

MFA Fine Art, BA(Hons) Fine Art

Creative Media Technology

BSc(Hons) Live Sound, BSc(Hons) Music Technology, BSc(Hons) Professional Sound and Video, BA(Hons) Radio Production, BA(Hons) Sound Design, BSc(Hons) Sound Technology, BSc(Hons) Television Production and Technology

Creative Writing

BA(Hons) Creative Writing, BA(Hons) Creative Writing & English, BA(Hons) Social and Cultural History & Creative Writing

English

BA(Hons) Creative Writing & English, BA(Hons) Social and Cultural History & English

History

BA(Hons) Social and Cultural History, BA(Hons) Social and Cultural History & Creative Writing, BA(Hons) Social and Cultural History & English

Theatre

BA(Hons) Theatre, Television and Performance

School of Applied Science, Computing and Engineering; www.glyndwr.ac.uk/en/Faculties/FacultyofArtsScienceandTechnology/

Aeronautical and Mechanical Engineering

BEng(Hons) Aeronautical and Mechanical Engineering, BEng(Hons) Aircraft Maintenance (top-up year)
Postgraduate courses: MSc Aeronautical Engineering MSc Unmanned Aircraft System Technology

Automotive

BEng(Hons) Automotive Engineering
Postgraduate course: MSc Automotive Engineering

Building studies

BSc(Hons) Architectural Design Technology, BSc Civil Engineering Studies (top-up) BSc(Hons) Construction Management

Computing

BSc(Hons) Computing, BSc(Hons) Computer Science, BSc(Hons) Computer Game Design and Enterprise, MComp Computer Game Development, BSc(Hons) Computer Game Development, BSc(Hons) Computer Network and Security, BSc(Hons) Cyber Security
Postgraduate courses: MSc Computer Game Development, MSc Computer Networking, MSc Computer Science, MSc Computing, MSc Cyber Security

Electrical and Electronic Engineering

BEng(Hons) Electrical and Electronic Engineering
Postgraduate course: MSc Engineering (Electrical & Electronic)

Housing

BSc(Hons) Housing Studies (top-up)

Industrial Engineering

BEng(Hons) Industrial Engineering (top-up year), FdEng Industrial Engineering,

Postgraduate courses: MSc Composite Material Engineering, MSc Mechanical Manufacturing, MSc Mechatronics Engineering

Renewable and Sustainable Engineering

Eng(Hons) Renewable and Sustainable Engineering

Postgraduate course: MSc Renewable Engineering and Sustainable Energy

Science and Environment

BSc(Hons) Forensic Science

Postgraduate courses: MRes Analytical & Forensic Chemistry, MRes Forensic Anthropology & Bioarchaeology

North Wales Business School; www.glyndwr.ac.uk/en/Faculties/ NorthWalesBusinessSchool/

Business

BA(Hons) Business

Postgraduate courses: MA Human Resource Management, MBA Master of Business, Executive MBA

Finance

BA(Hons) Accounting and Finance, FdA/BA(Hons) Applied Business Management, FdA Business, BA(Hons) Business, BSc(Hons) Financial Technology Management, BA(Hons) Hospitality, Tourism and Event Management, BA(Hons) Human Resource Management, BA(Hons) Marketing

Postgraduate courses: MA Human Resource Management, MBA Master of Business Administration, CIM Digital Diploma in Professional Marketing Online (100% online delivery): MBA, MBA Human Resource Management, MBA Marketing, MBA Finance, MBA Project Management, MBA Entrepreneurship, MBA Healthcare Management BA(Hons) Accounting and Finance, BSc(Hons) Financial Technology Management

Hospitality, Leisure and Tourism

BA(Hons) Hospitality Tourism and Event Management

Marketing

BA(Hons) Marketing

Faculty of Social and Life Sciences; www.glyndwr.ac.uk/en/Faculties/ FacultyofSocialandLifeSciences/

Animal Studies and Equine Science

FdSc Applied Animal Behaviour, Welfare and Conservation, BSc(Hons) Animal Behaviour, Welfare and Conservation (Top-Up), BSc(Hons) Animal Behaviour, Welfare and Conservation Science, BSc(Hons) Equine Science and Welfare Management

Biomedical Sciences

Postgraduate courses: MRes Applied Clinical Research, MRes Applied Biomedical Sciences Research, MSc Biomedical Science

Complementary Medicine

BSc(Hons) Complementary Therapies for Healthcare, BSc(Hons) Sports Injury Rehabilitation

Childhood Studies

BA(Hons) Education and Childhood Studies, BA(Hons) Families and Childhood Studies, FdA Early Childhood Practice, FdA Early Childhood Practice (Early Years Practitioner), BA(Hons) Childhood, Welfare & Education Top-up

Education

BA(Hons) Primary Education with QTS (Franchise with St Mary's Twickenham), BA(Hons) Education (ALN/SEN), BA(Hons) Education Studies (top-up)

Postgraduate courses: Primary PGCE (Franchise with St Mary's, Twickenham), MA Education, Professional Graduate Certificate in Education, MA Play, Policy and Practice

Counselling

Diploma of Higher Education in Counselling BSc(Hons) Counselling Adults (top up), BSc(Hons) Counselling Children and Young People (top up)

Health Care Studies

Dip HE Health and Social Wellbeing, BSc(Hons) Mental Health and Wellbeing, BSc(Hons) Public Health and Wellbeing

Nursing pre-registration

BN(Hons) Registered Nurse (Adult)

Nursing post-registration

BSc(Hons) Community Specialist Practice (District Nursing), BSc(Hons) Leadership and Healthcare Management, BSc(Hons) Primary Healthcare (top-up), BSc(Hons) Specialist Community Public Health Nursing (Health Visiting), BSc(Hons) Specialist Community Public Health Nursing (School Nursing)

Postgraduate courses: MSc Advanced Clinical Practice, MSc Health & Social Care (Community Specialist Practice), MSc Health Sciences, MSc Primary Healthcare, MSc Specialist Community Public Health Nursing

Occupational Therapy

BSc(Hons) Occupational Therapy

Physiotherapy

BSc(Hons) Physiotherapy

Psychology

BSc(Hons) Psychology

Public Services
Postgraduate course: MA Public Service Leadership

Criminal Justice
BA(Hons) Criminology and Criminal Justice, BA(Hons) Professional Policing
Postgraduate course: MA Criminology and Criminal Justice

Social Care
BA(Hons) Social Work, FdA Therapeutic Child Care, BA(Hons) Therapeutic Child Care (top-up year)

Youth and Community
BA(Hons) Youth and Community Work (JNC)
Postgraduate courses: MA Youth & Community (JNC), MA Youth & Community Studies

Sport
BSc(Hons) Football Coaching and the Performance Specialist, BSc(Hons) Sports Coaching for Participation and Performance Development, BSc(Hons) Sport, Health and Performance Science
Postgraduate course: MRes Sport, Exercise and Health Science

UNIVERSITY OF GREENWICH
www.gre.ac.uk

Law www.gre.ac.uk/ach/study/law/ programmes

Faculty of Architecture, Computing and Humanities; www.gre.ac.uk/ach

Animation, BA(Hons), Architecture, BA(Hons), Building Studies, HNC (LSEC Bexley Campus), Business Computing, BSc(Hons), Business Information Technology (Extended), BSc(Hons), Business Information Technology, BSc(Hons), Computer Science, BSc(Hons), Computer Security and Forensics, BSc(Hons), Computer Systems and Networking, BSc(Hons), Computing, BSc(Hons) (Extended), Computing, BSc(Hons), Construction Management, BSc(Hons), Creative Writing and English Literature, BA(Hons), Creative Writing, BA(Hons), Criminology (Extended), BA(Hons), Criminology and Criminal Psychology (Extended), BSc(Hons), Criminology and Criminal Psychology, BSc(Hons), Criminology, BA(Hons), Digital Arts Practice, BA(Hons), Digital Film Production, BSc(Hons), Digital Media Design and Development, BSc(Hons) Drama and English Literature, BA(Hons), Drama, BA(Hons), English Language and English Language Teaching (ELT), BA(Hons), English Language and Literature, BA(Hons), English Literature with Creative Writing, BA(Hons), English Literature, BA(Hons), Film and Television Production, BA(Hons), Film Studies, BA(Hons), Financial Mathematics, BSc(Hons), Games Design and Development, BSc(Hons), Garden Design, BA(Hons), Graphic and Digital Design, BA(Hons), Graphic and Digital Design, HND, History and English, BA(Hons), History and Politics, BA(Hons), History and Sociology, BA(Hons), History, BA(Hons), Landscape Architecture, BA(Hons), Languages and International Relations, BA(Hons), Law (Extended), LLB Hons, Law Senior Status, LLB Hons, Law, LLB Hons, Mathematics and Computing, BSc(Hons), Mathematics with Business, BSc(Hons), Mathematics with Economics, BSc(Hons), Mathematics, BSc(Hons), Mathematics, BSc(Hons) (Extended), Media and Communications, BA(Hons), Occupational Safety, Health and Environment, BSc(Hons) (Top-up), Photography (Top-up), BA(Hons) (North Kent College), Politics and International Relations, BA(Hons), Professional Dance and Musical Theatre, BA(Hons), Quantity Surveying, BSc(Hons), Sociology (Extended), BA(Hons), Sociology and Criminology, BSc(Hons), Sociology and Psychology, BSc(Hons), Sociology, BA(Hons), Software Engineering, BEng Hons, Sound Design, BA(Hons), Statistics and Operational Research, BSc(Hons)

Postgraduate courses: Applied Social Policy and Practice, MA, Architectural Practice, PGDip (ARB/ RIBA Part 3 Exemption), Architecture Part 2, MArch, Architecture, Landscape and Urbanism, MSc, Big Data and Business Intelligence, MSc, Computer Forensics and Cyber Security, MSc, Computer Science, MSc, Computer Systems and Network Engineering, MSc, Computing and Information Systems, MSc, Construction Management and Economics, MSc, Construction Project Management, MSc, Criminology and Criminal Psychology, MSc, Digital Arts, MA English: Literary London, MA, Enterprise Systems and Database Administration, MSc, Facilities Management (Distance Learning), MSc, Film Production MSc, Information Systems Management, MSc, International and Commercial Law, LLM, International Criminology, MA, International Maritime Policy, MA, Landscape Architecture, MA,

Landscape Architecture, MLA, Management of Business Information Technology, MSc, Mathematics, MMath, Media and Creative Cultures, MA, Occupational Hygiene, MSc/PGDip, Operational Cyber Security, MSc, Project Management – International (Distance Learning), MSc, Project Management – International, MSc, Real Estate (Distance Learning), MSc, Real Estate Development and Investment, MSc, Safety, Health and Environment, PGDip/MSc, Second Language Learning and Teaching, MA, Software Engineering, MSc, Spatial Data Science, MSc, Sustainable Building Design and Engineering, MSc, Web Design and Content Planning, MA

Faculty of Education and Health;
www.gre.ac.uk/eduhea

Adult Nursing, BSc(Hons), Assistant Health and Social Care Practitioner, FdS, Childhood and Youth Studies (Extended), BA(Hons), Childhood and Youth Studies, BA(Hons), Children's Nursing, BSc(Hons), Early Years, BA(Hons), Early Years, BA(Hons) (Topup), Education Studies, BA(Hons), FdA Community Sport, Health and Social Care, BA(Hons) (Top-up), Health and Wellbeing (Extended), BSc(Hons), Health and Wellbeing, BSc(Hons), Language and Literacy Education (2-Year Accelerated Degree), BA(Hons), Learning Disabilities Nursing, BSc(Hons), Mathematics Education (2-Year Accelerated Degree), BA(Hons), Mental Health Nursing, BSc(Hons), Mental Health Work, BSc(Hons) (Top-up), Midwifery, BSc(Hons), Paramedic Science, BSc(Hons), Physical Education and Sport (Extended), BA(Hons), Physical Education and Sport, BA(Hons), Primary Education (2-Year Accelerated Degree), BA(Hons), Primary Education with Qualified Teacher Status (QTS), BA(Hons), Psychology with Counselling, BSc(Hons), Psychology, BSc(Hons), Public Health (Extended), BSc(Hons), Public Health, BSc(Hons), School Direct Training Programmes (Early Years), School Direct Training Programmes (Primary), Sexual Health, BSc(Hons) (Top up), Social Work, BA(Hons), Specialist Community Public Health (Health Visiting and School Nursing), BSc(Hons) (Top-up), Specialist Practitioner (District Nursing), BSc(Hons) (Top up), Speech and Language Therapy, BSc(Hons)

Postgraduate courses: Advanced Clinical Practice, MSc, Child and Adolescent Psychology, MSc, Doctorate in Education, EdD, Early Years Teacher Status (Professional), PGCE, Early Years Teacher Status, PGCE, Education and Training, MPhil/PhD, Education, MA, Education, MPhil/PhD, Health and Social Care Research, MPhil/PhD, Healthcare Practice, MA, Higher Education, PGCert, Lifelong Learning Sector (ESOL and Literacy), PCE, Lifelong Learning Sector (ESOL and Literacy), PGCE, Lifelong Learning Sector (ESOL), PCE, Lifelong Learning Sector (ESOL), PGCE, Lifelong Learning Sector (Literacy), PCE, Lifelong Learning Sector (Literacy), PGCE Nursing (Adult Nursing), MSc, Lifelong Learning Sector (Numeracy), PCE, Lifelong Learning Sector (Numeracy), PGCE, Lifelong Learning Sector, PCE, Lifelong Learning Sector, PGCE, Nursing (Children's Nursing), MSc, Nursing (Mental Health Nursing), MSc, Nursing, PGDip (Adult Nursing), Nursing, PGDip (Mental Health Nursing), Primary Education, PGCE, Primary Mathematics (Subject Specialist), PGCE, Primary Professional Development, PGCert, Professional Certificate in Education/ProfGCE (Bromley), Psychology, MPhil/PhD, Psychology, MSc (Conversion Degree), Psychology, MSc by Research, School Direct Training Programme (Secondary), PGCE, Secondary Education Mathematics, PGCE, Secondary Education Modern Languages (French), PGCE, Secondary Education Physical Education, PGCE, Secondary Education Science with Biology, PGCE, Secondary Education Science with Chemistry, PGCE, Secondary Education Science with Physics, PGCE, Secondary Musicians in Education, PGCE, Social Work, MA, Specialist Practitioner (District Nursing), PGDip, Specialist Community Public Health Nursing (Health Visiting and School Nursing), PGDip, Sport and Exercise Psychology, MSc, Therapeutic Counselling, MSc

Primary Education www.gre.ac.uk/eduhea/ study/pe/programmes

Department of Secondary, LLTE and PE and Sport www.gre.ac.uk/eduhea/study/ slltepes/programmes

Faculty of Engineering and Science;
www.gre.ac.uk/engsci

Applied Biomedical Science, BSc(Hons), Applied Bioscience Technology, Foundation Degree, Biology (Extended), BSc(Hons), Biology, BSc(Hons), Biomedical Science (Extended), BSc(Hons), Biomedical Science, BSc(Hons), Building Services Engineering, FdE (RSME), Business Administration (Extended), BA(Hons), Business Administration with Accounting and Finance, BA(Hons), Business Administration with Marketing, BA(Hons), Business Administration, BA(Hons), Business Administration, FdA, Chemical Engineering (Extended), BEng Hons, Chemical

Engineering, BEng Hons, Chemistry (Extended), BSc(Hons), Chemistry BSc(Hons), (Degree Apprenticeship), Chemistry FdSc, (Higher Apprenticeship), Chemistry HNC, (Higher Apprenticeship), Chemistry, BSc(Hons), Chemistry, HNC, Civil Engineering (Extended), BEng Hons, Civil Engineering, BEng Hons, Civil Engineering, FdSc (RSME), Computer Engineering (Extended), BEng Hons, Computer Engineering, BEng Hons, Construction Management, FdSc (RSME), Cybernetics (Extended), BEng Hons, Cybernetics, BEng Hons, Design, Innovation and Entrepreneurship (Extended), BEng Hons, Design, Innovation and Entrepreneurship, BEng Hons, Digital and Technology Solutions BSc(Hons), (Degree Apprenticeship), Electrical and Electronic Engineering (Extended), BEng Hons, Electrical and Electronic Engineering, BEng Hons, Electrical and Electronic Engineering, Foundation Degree, Electrical Engineering, FdE (RSME), Engineering Management (Extended), BEng Hons, Engineering Management, BEng Hons, Engineering Technology, BEng Hons, Environmental Science, BSc(Hons), Forensic Science (Extended), BSc(Hons), Forensic Science with Criminology (Extended), BSc(Hons), Forensic Science with Criminology, BSc(Hons), Forensic Science, BSc(Hons), Geography, BSc(Hons), Human Nutrition (Extended), BSc(Hons), Human Nutrition, BSc(Hons), Industrial Engineering (Extended), BEng Hons, Industrial Engineering, BEng Hons, Information Technology Management for Business, BSc(Hons), Mechanical Engineering (Extended), BEng Hons, Mechanical Engineering, BEng Hons, Mechanical Engineering, Foundation Degree, Natural Sciences (Extended) BSc, Natural Sciences, BSc(Hons), Pharmaceutical Sciences (Extended), BSc(Hons), Pharmaceutical Sciences BSc(Hons), (Degree Apprenticeship), Pharmaceutical Sciences FdSc, (Higher Apprenticeship), Pharmaceutical Sciences, BSc(Hons), Pharmacology and Physiology (with Integrated Foundation Year), BSc(Hons), Pharmacology and Physiology, BSc(Hons), Sports Science (Extended), BSc(Hons), Sports Science with Coaching (Extended), BSc(Hons), Sports Science with Coaching, BSc(Hons), Sports Science with Professional Football Coaching (Extended), BSc(Hons), Sports Science with Professional Football Coaching, BSc(Hons), Sports Science, BSc(Hons)

Postgraduate courses: Agricultural and Food Sciences – Research, MPhil/PhD, Agriculture for Sustainable Development, MSc, Applied Plant Science, MSc, Biology, MBiol, Biomedical Sciences (Online), MSc/PGDip/PGCert, Biotechnology, MSc, Chemical Engineering, MEng, Chemistry, MChem, Civil Engineering, MEng, Civil Engineering, MSc, Computer Engineering, MEng, Cybernetics, MEng, Design, Innovation and Entrepreneurship, MEng, Development Studies – Research, MPhil/PhD, Electrical and Electronic Engineering, MEng, Electrical and Electronic Engineering, MSc, Electrical Power Engineering, MSc, Engineering – Research, MPhil/PhD, Engineering Management, MEng, Engineering Management, MSc, Engineering, MSc by Research, Environmental Conservation, PGDip/MSc, Food Innovation, MSc, Food Safety and Quality Management e-learning, MSc/PGDip/PGCert, Food Safety and Quality Management, PGDip/MSc, Formulation Science, MSc, Future Intelligent Technologies, MSc, General Pharmacy Practice, PGCert/PGDip/MSc, Global Oil and Gas Management, MSc, Global Shipping Management, MSc, Independent/Supplementary Prescribing, PGCert, Industrial Engineering, MEng, Mechanical and Manufacturing Engineering, MSc, Mechanical Engineering, MEng, Medicines Management, PGCert/PGDip/MSc, Natural Resources, MSc by Research, Pharmaceutical Biotechnology, MSc, Pharmaceutical Sciences, MSc/PGDip, Pharmacy MPharm, Science MSc by Research, Strength and Conditioning MSc, Sustainable Environmental Management MSc, Water, Waste and Environmental Engineering MSc

GRIMSBY INSTITUTE/UNIVERSITY CENTRE
www.grimsby.ac.uk

Animal Care
FdSc Animal Management
Business
BA(Hons) Business Management with Accounting, BA(Hons) Business Management with Marketing, BA(Hons) Business Management with Organisational Behaviour, Level 7 Award, Certificate, Diploma in Strategic Management and Leadership
Community Studies
BA(Hons) Childhood and Youth Studies Top Up, BA(Hons) Criminology, FdA Children, Young People and Families

Computing

BSc(Hons) Computing Technologies Top Up FdSc Computing Technologies

Creative Arts, Performance & Music

BA(Hons) Design, BA(Hons) Human Scale Prop-Making, BA(Hons) Music Production, BA(Hons) Performing Arts Top Up, BA(Hons) Popular Music Performance, BA(Hons) Special Effects Make-up Design and Prosthetics, FdA Performing Arts

Early Years

BA(Hons) Early Childhood Studies (Top Up), FdEd Early Childhood Studies

Education

FdEd Primary Education Studies (subject to revalidation) In-Service Certificate in Education, Professional Graduate Certificate in Education and Postgraduate Certificate in Education (Teaching in the Education, Training and Skills Sector), Level3 Award in Education and Training (C&G 6502), Pre-Service Certificate in Education, Professional Graduate Certificate in Education and Postgraduate Certificate in Education (Teaching in the Education, Training and Skills Sector)

Engineering & Construction

HNC Construction, HNC Electrical and Electronic Engineering, HNC Mechanical Engineering, HND Construction, HND Construction Top Up, HND

Electrical and Electronic Engineering, HND Engineering (General Engineering)

Health & Social Care

BA(Hons) Counselling Top Up, BA(Hons) Counselling Theory Top Up, BSc(Hons) Psychology, BSc(Hons) Health and Social Care Top Up, BSc(Hons) Nursing (Adult)–a University of Hull course delivered at the University Centre Grimsby, FdA Counselling Studies, FdSc Community Mental Health, FdSc Health and Social Care, FdSc Mental Health Studies (Clinical), FdSc Professional Healthcare Studies

Postgraduate

Level 7 Award, Certificate, Diploma in Strategic Management and Leadership

Media & Writing

BA(Hons) Independent Game Design (Game Art), BA(Hons) Independent Game Design (Game Development), BA(Hons) Photography Top Up, BA(Hons) Professional and Creative Writing, BA(Hons) TV Production Top Up, FdA Photography, FdA TV Production

Sport

FdSc Football Coaching and Youth Development

Tourism and Events

BA(Hons) Tourism and Business Management Top-up, FdA Events Management, FdA Tourism Management

HARPER ADAMS UNIVERSITY
www.harper-adams.ac.uk

Agriculture

BSc(Hons) Agriculture, FdSc Agriculture, BSc(Hons)Agriculture with Animal Science, BSc(Hons) Agriculture with Crop Management, BSc(Hons) Agriculture with Farm Business Management, BSc(Hons) Agriculture with Mechanisation, FdSc Agriculture with Mechanisation

Animal Sciences

BSc(Hons)/BSc Animal Behaviour and Welfare (Clinical),BSc(Hons)/BSc Animal Behaviour and Welfare(-Non-clinical), BSc(Hons) Animal Health and Welfare, FdSc Animal Management and Welfare, BSc(Hons) Animal Production Science, BSc(Hons) Bioveterinary Science, MSci Bioveterinary Science

Applied Biology

BSc/BSc(Hons) Applied Biology, BSc/BSc(Hons) Applied Biology with Biotechnology

Business and Agri-food

BSc(Hons) Agri-business, FdSc Agri-business, BSc Agri-business, BSc(Hons) Agri-food Marketing with Business, FdSc Agri-food Marketing with Business, Bsc Agri-food Marketing with Business, BSc(Hons) Business Management with Marketing, FdSc Business Management with Marketing, BSc Business Management with Marketing

Countryside, Environment, Wildlife and Geography

BSc(Hons) Countryside and Environmental Management, BSc(Hons) Countryside Management, FdSc Countryside Management, BSc(Hons) Geography and Environmental Management, BSc(Hons) Wildlife Conservation and Environmental Management

Engineering

BEng(Hons) Agricultural Engineering, MEng Agricultural Engineering, BEng(Hons) Automotive Engineering (Off-Highway), MEng Automotive Engineering(Off-Highway), BEng(Hons) Mechanical

Engineering, MEng Mechanical Engineering, BSc(Hons) Product Support Engineering

Food, Technology and Innovation

BSc(Hons) Food and Consumer Studies, BSc Food and Consumer Studies, BSc(Hons) Food Manufacture with Marketing, BSc(Hons) Food Technology and Product Development, BSc(Hons) Food Technology with Nutrition

Rural Estate, Property and Land Management

BSc(Hons) Real Estate, BSc(Hons) Rural Enterpriseand Land Management (REALM), BSc(Hons) Rural Property Management

Veterinary Nursing

BSc/BSc(Hons) Veterinary Nursing, BSc/BSc(Hons)- Veterinary Nursing with Companion Animal Behaviour, BSc(Hons) Veterinary Nursing with Small Animal Rehabilitation

Vetrinary Physiotherapy

BSc(Hons) Veterinary Physiotherapy

Zoology

BSc(Hons) Applied Zoology, BSc(Hons) Zoology with Entomology, BSc(Hons) Zoology with Environmental Management

Postgraduate courses

Grad Cert/PgC/ PgD/MSc Advanced Veterinary Nursing PgC Agricultural Law, PgC/PgD/MSc Agricultural Sciences and Production Systems, PgC/PgD/ MSc/MRes Agroecology, PgC/PgD/MSc/MRes Applied Mechatronic Engineering, PgC/PgD/MSc/ MRes Conservation and Forest Protection, PgD/MSc Ecological Applications, PgC/PgD/MSc Engineering Business Management, PgC/PgD/MSc/MRes Entomology, PgC Equine Medicine, PgC Exotic Animal Practice PgC Feline Practice PgC/PgD/MSc/MRes Food Industry Management, PgC/PgD/MSc/MRes Forestry Management, PgC/PgD/MSc/MRes Integrated Pest Management, PgC/PgD/MSc International Agri-Business and Food Chain Management, MRes Master of Research, PgC Plant Health and Biosecurity, PgC/PgD/MSc/MRes Plant Pathology, PgC Renewable Energy PgC/PgD/MSc/MRes Ruminant Nutrition, MProf/MSc Rural Estate and Land Management, PgC/PgD Rural Property Management, PgC Small Animal Cardiology Studies, PgC Small Animal Dentistry and Oral Surgery, PgC Small Animal Dermatology, PgC Small Animal Diagnostic Imaging, PgC Small Animal Emergency Medicine and Surgery, PgC Small Animal Endoscopy and Endosurgery, PgC Small Animal Medicine, PgC Small Animal Ophthalmology, PgC Small Animal Practice, PgC Small Animal Surgery, PgC State Veterinary Medicine, PgC/PgD/MSc Veterinary Pharmacy, PgD/MSc Veterinary Physiotherapy

ASKHAM BRYAN COLLEGE
www.askham-bryan.ac.uk

Agriculture

BSc/BSc(Hons) Agricultural Management (Top Up) BSc/BSc(Hons) Agriculture, BSc/BSc(Hons) Applied Agriculture, Extended Foundation Degree Animal Management, Agriculture or Equine Foundation Degree (FdSc) Agriculture

Animal Management

BSc/BSc(Hons) Animal Conservation (Top Up) BSc/BSc(Hons) Animal Management, BSc/BSc(Hons) Animal Management and Science, BSc/BSc(Hons) Canine and Feline Behaviour and Welfare (Top Up) BSc/BSc(Hons) Zoo Management, Extended Foundation Degree Animal Management Foundation Degree (FdSc) Canine and Feline Training and Behaviour, Foundation Degree Management of Animal Collections with Conservation

Postgraduate courses: MSc in Applied Animal Behaviour and Welfare, MSc in Zoo Management and Conservation

Arboriculture

Foundation Degree Arboriculture with Urban Forestry

Countryside and the Environment

BSc/BSc(Hons) Countryside Management, (Top Up)

Equine

BSc/BSc(Hons) Equine Science, BSc/BSc(Hons) Equine Science and Management, Foundation Degree (FdSc) Equine Science and Management, Extended Foundation Degree Animal Management, Agriculture or Equine

Horticulture

BSc/BSc(Hons) Applied Horticulture (Top Up)

Sport

Foundation Degree (FdSc) Sport (Coaching and Fitness)

Veterinary Nursing

BSc(Hons) Veterinary Nursing (Top Up), Foundation Degree (FdSc) Veterinary Nursing

HERIOT-WATT UNIVERSITY
www.hw.ac.uk

School of Energy, Geoscience, Infrastructure and Society;

Architectural Engineering

Architectural Engineering BEng(Hons), Architectural Engineering MEng, Architectural Engineering with International Studies MEng, Architecture BA(Hons)

Biology

Biological Sciences BSc(Hons), Biological Sciences(-Cell and Molecular Biology) BSc(Hons), Biological Sciences (Human Health) BSc(Hons), Biological Sciences (Microbiology) BSc(Hons), Marine Biology BSc(Hons)

Civil Engineering and Structural Engineering

Civil Engineering BEng(Hons), Civil Engineering BEng(Hons)/MEng, Civil Engineering MEng, Civil Engineering Construction Management BEng(Hons), Civil Engineering with International Studies MEng, Structural Engineering BEng(Hons), Structural Engineering MEng, Structural Engineering with Architectural Design BEng(Hons), Structural Engineering with Architectural Design MEng, Structural Engineering with International Studies MEng

Postgraduate courses: Advanced Structural Engineering MSc, Civil Engineering (distance learning only) MSc/Diploma, Civil Engineering and Construction Management MSc/Diploma, Civil Engineering with Industry Placement (2 years) MSc, Safety and Risk Management (distance learning only) MSc/Diploma, Safety, Risk and Reliability Engineering (distance learning only) MSc/Diploma, Water and Environmental Management MSc/Diploma

Construction Management and Surveying

Civil Engineering Construction Management BEng, Construction Project Management BSc(Hons), Quantity Surveying BSc(Hons)

Postgraduate courses: Civil Engineering and Construction Management MSc, Commercial Management and Quantity Surveying MSc/Diploma, MSc Commercial Management and Quantity Surveying with Industry Placement (2 years) MSc, Construction Project Management MSc/Diploma, Construction Project Management with Industry Placement (2 years) MSc

Energy and Renewables

Postgraduate courses: Energy MSc/Diploma, Marine Biodiversity and Biotechnology MSc, Marine Renewable Energy MSc, Marine Resource Development and Protection MSc, Renewable Energy Development (RED) MSc/Diploma, Renewable Energy Engineering MSc/Diploma/Certificate

Food Science, Health and Nutrition

Biotechnology MSc/Diploma, Food and Beverage Science MSc/Diploma/Certificate, Food Science and Nutrition MSc/Diploma/Certificate, Food Science, Safety and Health MSc/Diploma/Certificate, Human Health and Disease MSc/Diploma

Geoscience

Postgraduate courses: Applied Petroleum Geoscience MSc, Reservoir Evaluation and Management MSc, Subsurface Energy Systems MSc

Marine, Environment and Climate Change

Postgraduate courses: Climate Change: Managing the Marine Environment MSc/Diploma/Certificate, Integrative Marine Science MSc/Diploma, Marine Biodiversity and Biotechnology MSc/Diploma/Certificate, Marine Planning for Sustainable Development MSc/Diploma, Marine Renewable Energy MSc/Diploma, Marine Resource Development and Protection MSc/Diploma/Certificate, Renewable Energy Development (RED) MSc

Petroleum Engineering

Petroleum Engineering BEng(Hons)/MEng

Postgraduate course: Mature Field Management MSc, Petroleum Engineering MSc, Reservoir Evaluation and Management MSc

Real Estate

Real Estate Management and Finance BA/MA(Hons)

Postgraduate courses: Real Estate and Planning MSc/Diploma, Real Estate Investment and Finance MSc/Diploma, Real Estate Management and Development MSc/Diploma

Urban Studies

Geography BSc(Hons) Geography, Society and Environment MA(Hons), Urban Planning and Property Development BSc(Hons)

Postgraduate courses: Building Services Engineering MSc/Diploma, Commercial Interiors Management and Practice MSc, Facilities Management MSc, Interior Architecture and Design MA, Real Estate and Planning MSc, Sustainable Urban Management MSc/Diploma, Urban and Regional Planning MSc/Diploma, Urban Strategies and Design MSc/Diploma

School of Engineering and Physical Sciences

Chemistry

Chemistry MChem, Chemistry BSc(Hons), Chemistry and Professional Education BSc(Hons), Chemistry with a European Language MChem, Chemistry with a Year in Australia MChem, Chemistry with a Year in Europe MChem, Chemistry with a Year in North America MChem, Chemistry with Biochemistry BSc(Hons), Chemistry with Biochemistry MChem, Chemistry with Computational Chemistry BSc(Hons), Chemistry with Computational Chemistry MChem, Chemistry with Industrial Experience MChem, Chemistry with Materials BSc(Hons), Chemistry with Materials and Nanoscience MChem, Chemistry with Pharmaceutical Chemistry BSc(Hons), Chemistry with Pharmaceutical Chemistry MChem, Professional Education (Primary) with specialism in Primary Science (STEM) BSc(Hons)

Chemical Engineering

Brewing and Distilling Bsc(Hons), Chemical Engineering BEng(Hons), Chemical Engineering MEng, Chemical Engineering BEng(Hons)/MEng, Chemical Engineering and Diploma in Industrial Training BEng(Hons), Chemical Engineering and Diploma in Industrial Training MEng, Chemical Engineering with Energy Engineering MEng, Chemical Engineering with Energy Engineering with Diploma in Industrial Training MEng with DIT, Chemical Engineering with Oil and Gas Technology MEng, Chemical Engineering with Oil and Gas Technology with Diploma in Industrial Training MEng with DIT, Professional Education (Secondary) with Engineering Technologies BSc(Hons)

Electrical, Electronic and Computer Engineering

Computing and Electronics BEng(Hons), Computing and Electronics MEng, Electrical and Electronic Engineering BEng(Hons), Electrical and Electronic Engineering MEng, Professional Education (Secondary) with Engineering Technologies BSc(Hons), Robotics, Autonomous and Interactive Systems BEng(Hons), Robotics, Autonomous and Interactive Systems MEng

Postgraduate courses: Human Robot Interaction MSc, Human Robot Interaction (2 years) MSc, Robotics MSc, Smart Systems Integration (Erasmus Mundus), MSc, Telecommunications MSc

Mechanical Engineering

Automotive Engineering BEng(Hons), Mechanical Engineering BEng(Hons)/MEng, Mechanical Engineering and Energy Engineering BEng(Hons)/MEng, Professional Education (Secondary) with Engineering Technologies BSc(Hons)

Postgraduate courses: Advanced Mechanical Engineering MSc/Diploma, Energy MSc/Diploma, Renewable Energy Engineering MSc/Diploma

Physics

Chemical Physics BSc(Hons)/MPhys, Engineering Physics BSc(Hons)/MPhys, Mathematical Physics BSc(Hons)/MPhys, Physics BSc(Hons)/MPhys, Physics and Professional Education BSc(Hons)

Postgraduate courses: Photonics and Optoelectronic Devices, MSc

School of Mathematical and Computer Sciences

Actuarial Mathematics and Statistics

Actuarial Science BSc(Hons), Actuarial Science and Diploma in Industrial Training BSc(Hons), Financial Mathematics BSc(Hons), Statistical Data Science BSc(Hons)

Postgraduate courses: Actuarial Management MSc, Actuarial Science MSc, Actuarial Science and Management MSc, Financial Mathematics MSc, Stochastic Modelling and Computational Data Science MSc

Computer Science

Computer Science BSc(Hons), Computer Science (Artificial Intelligence) BSc(Hons), Computer Science (Data Science) BSc(Hons), Computer Science (Data Science) and Diploma in Industrial Training BSc(Hons), Computer Science (Games Programming) BSc(Hons), Computer Science (Software Engineering) BSc(Hons), Computer Science and Diploma in Industrial Training BSc(Hons),Computer Systems BSc(Hons), Computer Systems (Computer Games Programming) BSc(Hons), Computer Systems (Games Programming) BSc(Hons), Computer Systems and Diploma in Industrial Training BSc(Hons), Information Systems BSc(Hons), Information Systems (Interaction Design) BSc(Hons), Information Systems (Internet Systems) BSc(Hons), Information Systems (Management) BSc(Hons), Information Systems and Diploma in Industrial Training BSc(Hons),Software Engineering MEng

Postgraduate courses: Artificial Intelligence MSc/Diploma, Artificial Intelligence (2 years) MSc, Artificial Intelligence with Speech and Multimodal Interaction MSc/Diploma, Business Information Management MSc/Diploma, Computational Mathematics MSc, Computer Systems Management MSc/Diploma, Computing (2 years) MSc, Data Science MSc/Diploma, Data Science (2 years) MSc, Games Design and Development MDes, Information Technology

(Business) MSc/Diploma, Information Technology (Software Systems) MSc/Diploma, Network Security MSc/Diploma, Software Engineering MSc/Diploma, Sports Data Science MSc

Mathematics

Mathematics BSc, Mathematics MMath, Mathematical, Statistical and Actuarial Sciences BSc(Hons),-Mathematical, Statistical and Actuarial Sciences and Diploma in Industrial Training BSc(Hons), Mathematics and Computer Science BSc(Hons), Mathematics with Computer Science BSc(Hons), Mathematics with Finance BSc(Hons) Mathematics with Finance and Diploma in Industrial Training BSc,(Hons) Mathematics with French BSc(Hons), Mathematics with German BSc(Hons), Mathematics with Spanish BSc(Hons), Mathematics with Physics BSc(Hons) Mathematics with Statistics BSc(Hons)

Postgraduate courses: Applied Mathematical Sciences MSc/Diploma, Applied Mathematical Sciences (2 years) MSc, Applied Mathematical Sciences Climate Change Modelling MSc/Diploma, Applied Mathematical Sciences Climate Change Modelling MSc/Diploma

School of Social Sciences

Accountancy and Finance

Accountancy and Finance BA/MA(Hons), Accountancy and Finance MA(Hons), Accounting and Business Finance MA, Business and Finance BA/MA(Hons), Business and Finance MA(Hons), Finance MA(Hons)

Postgraduate courses: International Accounting and Finance MSc, International Accounting and Management MSc, Strategy and International Management Accounting MSc, Finance MSc, Finance and Management MSc, International Accounting and Finance MSc, International Banking and Finance MSc, International Finance and Corporate Accountability MSc, Investment Management MSc, Islamic Banking and Finance MSc, Real Estate Investment and Finance MSc

Business Management

Bachelor of Business Administration BBA(Hons), Business and Finance BA/MA(Hons), Fashion Marketing and Retailing BA(Hons), International Business Management BA/MA(Hons), International Business Management MA(Hons), International Business Management with Economics MA(Hons), International Business Management with Enterprise MA(Hons), International Business Management with Human Resource Management MA(Hons), International Business Management with Marketing

MA(Hons), International Business Management with Operations Management MA(Hons), International Business Management with Year Abroad MA(Hons), Psychology with Management Bsc(Hons)

Postgraduate courses: Business Psychology MSc/Diploma, Finance and Management MSc, International Business Management with Finance MSc, International Business Management with HRM MSc, International Business Management with Industry Placement MSc, International Business Management with Logistics MSc, International Business Management with Marketing MSc, International Business Management with Performance Management MSc, International Business Management with Project Management MSc, International Business Management with Sustainability MSc, International Business Management with Tourism MSc, International Fashion Marketing MSc, International Marketing MSc, International Marketing with Consumer Psychology MSc, International Marketing with Digital Marketing MSc, Marketing MSc, Cultural Heritage Management with Tourism MSc, Business Strategy, Leadership and Change MSc, European Master in Strategic Project Management (MSPME) MSc, International Master in Industrial Management (IMIM) MSc, Lean Six Sigma for Operational Excellence MSc, Management and Leadership in Sports Business MSc, Management and Leadership in Sports Performance MSc, Managing Business Performance MSc, Managing Innovation MSc, Operations Management MSc, Strategic Project Management MSc, Logistics and Supply Chain Management MSc, Logistics and Supply Chain Management with Business Analytics MSc, Logistics and Supply Chain Management with Business Performance MSc, Logistics and Supply Chain Management with Lean Six Sigma MSc, Logistics with Green and Sustainable Supply Chain Management MSc, Master of Business Administration MBA, MBA with Specialism in Finance MBA, MBA with Specialism in Marketing MBA, MBA with Specialism in Strategic Planning MBA, Strategic Project Management MSc

Economics

Economics MA(Hons), Economics and Accountancy MA(Hons), Economics and Business Management MA(Hons), Economics and Finance MA(Hons), Economics and Marketing MA(Hons)

Postgraduate courses: MSc Economics, Banking and Finance, MSc Energy and Economics, MSc International Finance and Economic Development MSc

Interpreting and Translating

Chinese English Interpreting and Translating (2 Years) MSc, Chinese English Translating (2 Years) MSc, Interpreting MSc, Interpreting and Translating MSc, Sign Language Interpreting (EUMASLI) MSc, Translating MSc, Translating for Business MSc, Translating for Business with Entrepreneurship MSc, Translating with Entrepreneurship MSc

Languages and Intercultural Studies

Applied Languages and Translating (French/German)MA(Hons), Applied Languages and Translating(French/Spanish) MA(Hons), Applied Languages and Translating (German/ Spanish) MA(Hons), British Sign Language (Interpreting, Translating and Applied Language Studies) MA(Hons), Languages(Interpreting and Translating) (French/German)-MA(Hons), Languages (Interpreting and Translating)(French/Spanish) MA(Hons), Languages (Interpreting and Translating) (German/Spanish) MA(Hons),Languages (Interpreting and Translating) (French/British Sign Language) MA(Hons), Languages (Interpreting and Translating) (German/British Sign Language)MA(Hons), Languages (Interpreting and Translating) (Spanish/British Sign Language)MA(Hons), French and Applied Language Studies MA(Hons), German and Applied Language Studies MA(Hons), Spanish and Applied Language Studies MA(Hons), International Business Management and Languages: Chinese as Main Language MA(Hons),International Business Management and Languages: French as Main Language MA(Hons), International Business Management and Languages: German as Main Language MA(Hons), International Business Management and Languages: Spanish as Main Language MA(Hons)

Psychology

Psychology BSc(Hons), Psychology with Management BSc(Hons)

School of Textiles and Design

Design for Textiles (Fashion, Interior, Art) BA(Hons), Fashion BA(Hons), Fashion Communication BA(Hons), Fashion Marketing and Retailing BA(Hons), Fashion Technology BSc(Hons), Interior Design BA(Hons)

Postgraduate courses: Fashion and Textiles Management MSc, Interior Architecture and Design MA, International Fashion Marketing MSc, Knitwear (Design, Heritage and Production) MA

Edinburgh Business School; www.ebsglobal.net

Postgraduate courses: MBA, DBA, MSc Financial Management, MSc Marketing

---

UNIVERSITY OF HERTFORDSHIRE
www.herts.ac.uk

Hertfordshire Business School; www.herts.ac.uk/apply/schools-of-study/business

BA(Hons) Accounting, BA(Hons) Accounting & Finance, BA(Hons) Business Administration, BA(Hons) Business Economics, BA(Hons) Business Studies, BA(Hons) Economics, BA(Hons) Event Management, BA(Hons) Finance, BA(Hons) Human Resource Management, BA(Hons) IT Management for Business (ITMB), BA(Hons) International Business, BA(Hons) International Management (Dual Award), BA(Hons) International Tourism Management, BA(Hons) Management, BA(Hons) Marketing, BA(Hons) Tourism Management, BA(Hons) Business and Accounting, BA(Hons) Business and Finance, BA(Hons) Business Studies with Information Systems, BA(Hons) Business Studies with Logistics, BA(Hons) Business Studies with Leadership and Management BA(Hons) Business and Event Management, BA(Hons) Business and Marketing, BA(Hons) Business and Human Resources, BA(Hons) Business and Tourism, BA(Hons) Accounting and Economics, BA(Hons) Event Management and Marketing, BA(Hons) Event Management and Tourism, BA(Hons) Finance and Economics, BA(Hons) Marketing and Advertising, BA(Hons)-Marketing with Digital Communications

Postgraduate courses: MSc Accounting & Financial Management, MSc Business Analysis and Consultancy, MSc Business and Organisational Strategy, MSc Finance and Investment Management, MSc Global Business (Dual Award), MA Human Resource Management, MSc International Business, MSc International Tourism, Hospitality and Event Management, MSc Management, MSc Marketing, MBA Master of Business Administration, MSc Project Management

School of Creative Arts; www.herts.ac.uk/apply/schools-of-study/creative-arts

Digital Animation

BA(Hons) 2D Animation and Character for Digital Media, BA(Hons) 3D Computer Animation and Modelling, BA(Hons) 3D Games Art & Design, BA(Hons) Visual Effects for Film and Television

Design and Crafts

BA(Hons) Architecture, BA(Hons) Design Crafts (Ceramics and Glass), BA(Hons) Design Crafts (Jewellery), BA(Hons) Design Crafts (Textiles), BA(Hons) Fashion and Fashion Business, BA(Hons) Fashion Design, BA(Hons) Graphic Design, BA(Hons) Illustration, BA(Hons) Interior Architecture and Design, BA(Hons) Product and Industrial Design

Postgraduate courses: MA Fashion, MA Graphic Design, MA Graphic Design (Online), MA Illustration, MA Illustration (Online), MArch Architecture and Urbanism, MA Interior Architecture & Design, MA Product Design

Film and Media

BA(Hons) Digital Media Design, BA(Hons) Film and Television (Production), BA(Hons) Model Design (Model Effects), BA(Hons) Model Design (Special Effects), BA(Hons) Model Design (Character and Creative Effects)

Postgraduate courses: MA Animation, MA Digital Media Arts, MA Film & TV Production, MA Games Art & Design

Music

BSc(Hons) Audio Recording and Production, BSc(Hons) Live Sound and Lighting Technology, BSc(Hons) Music and Sound Design Technology, BSc(Hons) Music Composition and Technology, BSc(Hons) Music Composition and Technology for Film and Games, BSc(Hons) Music Industry Management, BSc(Hons) Music Production, BSc(Hons) Songwriting and Music Production

Postgraduate courses: MSc Music and Sound for Film & Games, MSc Music and Sound Technology (Audio Engineering), MSc Music and Sound Technology (Audio Programming), MA Creative Music Production

Therapies

Postgraduate course: MA Art Therapy

Visual Arts

BA(Hons) Fine Art, BA(Hons) Photography
Postgraduate courses: MA Fine Art, Contemporary Crafts, MA Contemporary Textiles, MA Photography

School of Education; www.herts.ac.uk/apply/schools-of-study/education

BEd(Hons) Primary Education with QTS, BA(Hons) Early Childhood Education, Foundation degree in Early Years, BA(Hons) Education Studies, BA(Hons) Education Studies with Learning and Teaching, BA(Hons)Education Studies with Special Educational Needs Mathematics Specialist Teacher programme, Doctorate in Education (EdD), PhD in Education

School of Engineering and Computer Science www.herts.ac.uk/study/schools-of-study/engineering-and-computer-science

Aerospace Engineering

BEng(Hons) Aerospace Engineering, MEng(Hons) Aerospace Engineering, BEng(Hons) Aerospace Engineering with Space Technology, MEng(Hons) Aerospace Engineering with Space Technology, BEng(Hons) Aerospace Systems Engineering, MEng(Hons) Aerospace Systems Engineering, BEng(Hons) Aerospace Systems Engineering with Pilot Studies, MEng(Hons) Aerospace Systems Engineering with Pilot Studies, BSc Aerospace Technology with Management, BSc Aerospace Technology with Pilot Studies

Postgraduate course: MSc Aerospace Engineering

Automotive Engineering

BEng(Hons) Automotive Engineering, MEng(Hons) Automotive Engineering, BEng(Hons) Automotive Engineering with Motorsport, MEng(Hons) Automotive Engineering with Motorsport, BSc(Hons) Automotive Technology with Management, BSc(Hons) Motorsport Technology

Postgraduate course: MSc Automotive Engineering

Civil Engineering

BEng(Hons) Civil Engineering, MEng(Hons) Civil Engineering

Computer Science

MEng Computer Science, BSc(Hons) Computer Science, BSc(Hons) Computer Science (Artificial Intelligence), BSc(Hons) Computer Science (Networks),BSc(Hons) Computer Science (Software Engineering), BSc(Hons) Computer Technology and Networks, BSc(Hons) Information Technology

Postgraduate courses: MSc Artificial Intelligence and Robotics, MSc Advanced Computer Science, MSc Computer Science, MSc Computer Networks and Systems Security, MSc Cyber Security, MSc Data Science and Analytics

Electrical and Electronic Engineering

BEng(Hons) Electrical and Electronic Engineering, MEng(Hons) Electrical and Electronic Engineering Postgraduate courses: MSc Communications and Information Engineering, MSc Electronics Engineering, MSc Power Electronics and Control

Manufacturing and Operations Management

Postgraduate course: MSc Manufacturing Management

Mechanical Engineering

BEng(Hons) Mechanical Engineering, MEng(Hons) Mechanical Engineering, BEng(Hons) Mechanical Engineering and Mechatronics, MEng(Hons) Mechanical Engineering and Mechatronics, BSc(Hons) Engineering with Management Postgraduate course: MSc Mechanical Engineering

School of Health and Social Work; www.herts.ac.uk/apply/schools-of-study/ health-and-social-work

Diagnostic radiography

BSc(Hons) Diagnostic Radiography and Imaging, BSc(Hons) Radiotherapy and Oncology Postgraduate courses: Medical Imaging and Radiation Sciences Diagnostic Imaging MSc, Medical Imaging and Radiation Sciences Image Interpretation MSc, Medical Imaging and Radiation Sciences Radiotherapy and Oncology MSc, Medical Imaging and Radiation Sciences Diagnostic Ultrasound MSc

Dietetics and nutrition

Nutrition (BSc(Hons)), Dietetics (BSc(Hons))Postgraduate course: MSc Dietetics (Advanced Practice)

Health visiting

BSc(Hons) Specialist Community Nursing (Community Children's Nursing), BSc(Hons) Specialist Community Nursing (Community District Nursing),BSc(Hons) Specialist Community Nursing (General Practice Nursing), BSc(Hons) Specialist Community Public Health Nursing (Health Visiting), BSc(Hons)Specialist Community Public Health Nursing (School Nursing) Postgraduate courses: MSc/PgDip Specialist Community Nursing (Community Children's Nursing), MSc/PgDip Specialist Community Nursing (Community District Nursing), MSc/PgDip Specialist Community Nursing (General Practice Nursing), MSc/PgDip Specialist Community Public Health Nursing (Health Visiting), MSc/PgDip Specialist Community Public Health Nursing (School Nursing)

Midwifery

Midwifery BSc(Hons), Midwifery Shortened (BSc(Hons)), Midwifery and Women's Health (BSc)

Postgraduate courses: Master of Midwifery (Masters), Midwifery and Women's Health (MSc)

Nursing

Adult Nursing Bsc(Hons), Children's Nursing BSc(Hons), Learning Disability Nursing BSc(Hons),- Mental Health Nursing BSc(Hons), Contemporary Nursing BSc(Hons)

Postgraduate courses: MSc Adult Nursing, Mental Health Recovery and Social Inclusion MSc/PgDip/ PgCert (Online), Contemporary Nursing (MSc)

Radiotherapy

Radiotherapy and Oncology BSc(Hons)Postgraduate courses: Medical Imaging and Radiation Sciences Diagnostic Imaging (MSc/PgD/PgC),Medical Imaging and Radiation Sciences Image Interpretation (MSc/PgD/PgC), Medical Imaging and Radiation Sciences Oncological Sciences (MSc/PgD/PgC), Medical Imaging and Radiation Sciences Ultrasound (MSc/PgD/PgC)

Paramedic sciences

Paramedic Science BSc(Hons) Postgraduate course: Paramedic Science (MSc)

Physiotherapy

Physiotherapy BSc(Hons) Postgraduate courses: Advanced Physiotherapy(-Neuromusculoskeletal) (MSc/PgD), Advanced Physiotherapy(MSc/PgD/PgC)

Social work

Social Work BSc/BSc(Hons) Postgraduate course: Social Work MSc

School of Humanities; www.herts.ac.uk/ apply/schools-of-study/humanities

American Studies

BA(Hons) English Literature and American Studies, BA(Hons) History and American Studies, BA(Hons) Politics & International Relations and American Studies

Creative Writing

BA(Hons) English Language and Creative Writing, BA(Hons) English Literature and Creative Writing, BA(Hons) History and Creative Writing, BA(Hons) Journalism, BA(Hons) Journalism and Creative Writing, BA(Hons) Media and Creative Writing, BA(Hons) Philosophy and Creative Writing Postgraduate course: MA Creative Writing

English Language & Linguistics

BA(Hons) English Language and Linguistics, BA(Hons) English Language and Applied Linguistics, BA(Hons) English Language with English Language Teaching, English Language (with various joint options)

Postgraduate course: MA Teaching English to Speakers of Other Languages

English Language Teaching

BA(Hons) English Language with English Language Teaching

Postgraduate course: MA Teaching English to Speakers of Other Languages

English Literature

BA(Hons) English Literature, BA(Hons) English Literature (with various joint options)

Postgraduate course: MA Literature and Culture

Film

BA(Hons) English Language with Film, BA(Hons) English Literature with Film, BA(Hons) History with Film, BA(Hons) Philosophy with Film, BA(Hons) Mass Communications

Postgraduate course: MA Global Film and Television (Online)

History

History BA(Hons), BA(Hons) History and American Studies, BA(Hons) History and Creative Writing, BA(Hons) History and English Language, BA(Hons) History with Film, BA(Hons) History and English Literature, BA(Hons) History with French, German, Japanese, Mandarin or Spanish, BA(Hons) History and Journalism, BA(Hons) History and Philosophy, BA(Hons) History with Religious Studies

Journalism

BA(Hons) Mass Communications, BA(Hons) Journalism, BA(Hons) Journalism and Creative Writing, BA(Hons) Journalism and Media, BA(Hons) English Language and Journalism, BA(Hons) English Literature and Journalism, BA(Hons) History and Journalism, BA(Hons) Media, BA(Hons) Philosophy and Journalism, BA(Hons) Politics & International Relations and Journalism

Postgraduate course: MA Journalism & Media Communications

Media

BA(Hons) Media, BA(Hons) Media (with various joint options)

Philosophy

BA(Hons) Philosophy, BA(Hons) Philosophy (with various joint options)

Politics & International Relations

BA(Hons) Politics and International Relations, BA(Hons) Politics and International Relations (with various joint options)

Religious Studies

BA(Hons) English Literature with Religious Studies, BA(Hons) History with Religious Studies, BA(Hons) Philosophy, Religion and Ethics

Philosophy with Religious Studies School of Law, Criminology and Political Science

Accelerated (Two-Year) LLB(Hons), LLB(Hons) Law, LLB(Hons) Criminal Justice, BA(Hons) Criminal Justice and Criminology, BA(Hons) Politics and International Relations

Postgraduate courses: LLM Business Law, LLM Energy Law and the Environment, LLM Governance, Risk Management and Compliance, LLM International Financial Law, LLM International Human Rights Law, LLM International Law, LLM Intellectual Property and Data Protection Law, LLM International Commercial Law, LLM International Development Law, LLM IT Law and Policy, LLM Master of Laws

School of Life and Medical Sciences; www.herts.ac.uk/apply/schools-of-study/life-and-medical- sciences

Biosciences

Applied Plant and Animal Biology (BSc(Hons)), Biochemistry (BSc(Hons)), Biological Sciences (BSc(Hons)), Biomedical Science (BSc(Hons)), Molecular Biology (BSc(Hons)), Pharmacology (BSc(Hons))

Postgraduate courses: Biotechnology (MSc/PgD/PgC), Molecular Biology (MSc/PgD/PgC), Pharmacology(MSc/PgD/PgC), Pharmacovigilance (MSc/PgD/PgC)

Dietetics and Nutrition

Nutrition (BSc(Hons)), Dietetics (BSc(Hons))

Geography, Environment and Agriculture

Applied Plant and Animal Biology (BSc(Hons)), Geography (BSc(Hons)), Human Geography (BSc(Hons)), Physical Geography (BScHonours), Environmental Management and Ecology(BSc(Hons))

Postgraduate courses: Environmental Management(MSc/PgD/PgC/AIEMA), Environmental Management for Agriculture (MSc), Sustainable Planning(MSc), Sustainable Planning and Environmental Management (MSc), Sustainable Planning and Transport(MSc), Water and Environmental Management(MSc/PgD/PgC/AIEMA)

Optometry

Postgraduate course: Optometry (Masters in Optometry MOptom)

Pharmacy

Pharmacy courses MPharm

Postgraduate courses: MSc/PgD/PgC Pharmacy Practice, MSc Advancing Clinical Pharmacy Practice, MSc Advancing Clinical Pharmacy Practice with extended placement, PgDip Pharmacy (Overseas Pharmacists Assessment Programme), MSc in Regulatory Affairs with TOPRA

Pharmacology

Pharmacology (BSc(Hons))

Postgraduate course: MSc Pharmacology

Pharmaceutical Science

Pharmaceutical Science BSc(Hons)

Postgraduate course: Regulatory Science (MRegSci)

Postgraduate medicine

Postgraduate courses: MSc Cardiology and Stroke, MSc Clinical Dermatology, MSc Public Health(online), MSc Health and Medical Simulation, MSc Health and Medical Education, MSc Clinical Skin Integrity and Wound Management, MSc Physician Associate Studies

Psychology

BSc Psychology

Postgraduate courses: Business Psychology (MSc),Occupational Psychology (MSc), Psychology Conversion Course (MSc), Research in Clinical Psychology (MSc), Doctorate in Clinical Psychology (DClinPsy)

Public Health

Postgraduate course: Master of Public Health (Online)

Sports, health and exercise

Physical Activity and Sports Development (BSc(Hons)), Sport and Exercise Science (BSc(Hons)), Sports Business Management (BSc(Hons)), Sports Coaching (BSc(Hons)) Sports Studies (BSc/BSc(Hons)), Sports Therapy (BSc/BSc(Hons))

School of Physics, Astronomy and Mathematics; www.herts.ac.uk/apply/schools-of-study/physics-astronomy-and mathematics

Physics

BSc(Hons) Physics

Postgraduate course: MPhys Physics

Astrophysics

BSc(Hons) Astrophysics, BSc(Hons) Astrophysics with Science Education

Postgraduate course: MPhys Astrophysics

Mathematics

BSc(Hons) Mathematics, BSc(Hons) Financial Mathematics

HERTFORDSHIRE REGIONAL COLLEGE
www.hrc.ac.uk

Access to higher education courses in the following areas: 3D dimensional design, art & design, business with HRM/accounting/information systems/ marketing computing technologies, fine art practice, graphic design, visual merchandising

---

NORTH HERTFORDSHIRE COLLEGE
www.nhc.ac.uk

Foundation and extended degrees and other courses covering the following subjects: accounting/information systems/ computing technology, business/with HRM, creative enterprises-fashion & textile, early years, marketing, sports studies, business with HRM/accounting/information systems/marketing

---

OAKLANDS COLLEGE
www.oaklands.ac.uk

HNC/HND Courses

HNC Civil Engineering Studies (Part-time), HNC in Construction and the Built Environment, HND Electrical and Electronic Engineering, HNC Engineering (Mechanical), HNC/HND Art and Design, HNC Electrical and Electronic Engineering, HND Engineering (Mechanical)

Foundation Degrees

Foundation Degree in Business Management, Foundation Degree in Business Management with Accounting, Foundation Degree in Business Management with Law, Foundation Degree in Business Management with Marketing, Foundation Degree in Early Years (part-time), Foundation Degree in Media Production

Extended Degrees

Extended Degree in Science – Subjects Allied to Medicine (Initial Year), Extended Degree in Science – Biological Science (Initial Year), Extended Degrees in Engineering (Initial Year)

WEST HERTS COLLEGE
www.westherts.ac.uk

Foundation degrees covering the following subjects: Accounting, Business Management, Computing Technologies, HND courses covering the following subjects: Computing, Creative Media Production, Graphic Design, Health and Social Care, Hospitality & Event, Management, Music, Performing Arts, Public Services, Travel and Tourism

---

THE UNIVERSITY OF HUDDERSFIELD
www.hud.ac.uk

A to D

Accountancy and Finance BA(Hons), Accountancy BA(Hons), Accountancy with Financial Services BA(Hons), Advertising and Marketing Communications BA(Hons), Air Transport and Logistics Management BSc(Hons), Animation BA(Hons), Applied Computing (Top-up) BSc(Hons), Applied English Language Studies BA(Hons), Technology BSc(Hons), Architecture/Architecture(International) (RIBA Part 1) BA(Hons), Automotive and Motorsport Engineering BEng(Hons), Automotive and Motorsport Engineering MEng, Behavioural Sciences BSc(Hons), Biochemistry BSc(Hons), Biochemistry with Research Placement BSc(Hons), Biological Sciences BSc(Hons), Biology (Biomedical & Molecular) (Top-Up) BSc(Hons), Biology (Molecular and Cellular) BSc(Hons), Biology (Molecular and Cellular) with Research Placement BSc(Hons), Biomedicine BSc(Hons), Broadcast Journalism BA(Hons), Business Accounting(Top-up) BA(Hons), Business Administration and Management (Top-up) BA(Hons), Business and Human Resource Management BA(Hons), Business and Marketing BA(Hons), Business Data Analytics BSc(Hons), Business Economics BSc(Hons), Business Law LLB(Hons), Business Management and Leadership BA(Hons), Business Management BA(Hons), Business Management Professional BA(Hons) (Chartered Manager Degree Apprenticeship), Business Management with Finance BA(Hons), Business with Financial Services BA(Hons), Business with Supply Chain Management BA(Hons), Business with Supply Chain Management Professional BA(Hons) (Chartered Manager Degree Apprenticeship), Certificate in Management Studies (CMS), Cervical Screening (H), Chemical Engineering and Chemistry BSc(Hons), Chemical Engineering BEng(Hons), Chemical Engineering MEng, Chemistry BSc(Hons), Chemistry MChem, Chemistry with Chemical Engineering BSc(Hons),Chemistry with Forensic Science BSc(Hons), Chemistry with Industrial Experience MChem, Childhood Studies BA(Hons), Computer Games Design BA(Hons), Computing Science MSci, Computer Science with Cyber Security BSc(Hons), Computing Science with Games Programming BSc(Hons), Computer Systems Engineering BEng(Hons), Computing BSc(Hons), Computing in Business BA(Hons), Computing MComp, Contemporary Art and Illustration BA(Hons), Contemporary Art BA(Hons), Continuing Professional Development for Pharmacy Technicians, Costume with Textiles BA(Hons), Creative Media and Production BA(Hons), Creative Music Production BA(Hons), Criminology BSc(Hons), Criminology with Law BSc(Hons), Critical Care CPS, Digital and Social Media Marketing BA(Hons), Drama and English Language BA(Hons), Drama and English Literature BA(Hons),Drama BA(Hons), Drama with Creative Writing BA(Hons)

Postgraduate courses: Accounting and Finance MA, Accounting and Finance MSc, Acute Care PgCert, Advanced Architectural Design MA, Advanced Clinical Practice MSc, Advanced Project Management in Construction MSc, Analytical Bioscience MSc, Analytical Chemistry MSc, Master of Architecture/ Architecture(International) (RIBA Part 2), Artificial Intelligence MSc, Assessment and Examination of the Newborn, Assessment and Supported Year in Employment (ASYE), Assessment, Care and Management of Acute/Critical Illness or Injury, Automotive Engineering MSc, Banking and Finance MSc,

Behavioural Economics and Decision Science MSc, Business Intelligence and Analytics MSc, Career Guidance and Development MA, Career Guidance and Development Postgraduate Diploma, Computing MSc, Creative Pattern Cutting MA, Criminology and Evidence-Based Policing MSc, Criminology and International Security MSc, Data Analytics MSc, Digital Marketing MSc, Digital Media MA, Drug Discovery and Business Strategy MSc

E to I

Early Early Childhood and Education BA(Hons), Years BA(Hons), Economics and Politics BSc(Hons), Economics BSc(Hons), Economics with Financial Services BSc(Hons), Education and Professional Development BA/BA(Hons), Education BA(Hons), Education Human Resource Development and Training BA(Hons),Electronic and Communication Engineering BEng(Hons), Electronic and Electrical Engineering MEng/BEng(Hons), Electronic Engineering and Computer Systems BEng(Hons), Electronic Engineering BEng(Hons), Electronic Engineering MEng, Energy Engineering BEng(Hons), Energy Engineering MEng, English Language and Linguistics BA(Hons), English Language and Literature BA(Hons), English Language and Politics BA(Hons), English Language and Sociology BA(Hons), English Language BA(Hons), English Language with a Modern Language BA(Hons), English Language with Creative Writing BA(Hons), English Literature and History BA(Hons), English Literature BA(Hons),English Literature with a Modern Language BA(Hons), English Literature with Creative Writing BA(Hons), Events Management BA(Hons), Exercise Science BSc(Hons), Fashion Brand Marketing BA(Hons), Fashion Creative Direction BA(Hons), Fashion Design with Digital Technology BA(Hons), Fashion Design (Fashion Design with Marketing BA(Hons), Fashion Design with Textiles) BA(Hons),- Film Studies and Drama BA(Hons), Film Studies and English Literature BA(Hons), Film Studies and History BA(Hons), Film Studies BA(Hons), Forensic and Analytical Science BSc(Hons), Forensic and Analytical Science MSci, Forensic and Analytical Science with Industrial Experience MSci, Geography BSc(Hons), Global Marketing (Top-up) BA(Hons), Graphic Design and Animation BA(Hons), Graphic Design BA(Hons), Health and Social Care BSc(Hons), Health and Social Care BSc(Hons), International Events and Tourism Management BA(Hons), International Fashion Buying Management BA(Hons), International Politics BSc(Hons), International Trade and Investment (Top up)BA(Hons)

Postgraduate courses: Early Years Initial Teacher Training (EYTS) -Graduate Employment Route PT Economics MSc, Education MA, Electronic and Automotive Engineering MSc, Electronic and Communication Engineering MSc, Electronic Engineering MSc, Engineering Control Systems and Instrumentation MSc, Engineering Management MSc, English Language and Applied Linguistics MA, Fashion Textile Practices MA, Finance MSc, Fintech MSc, Forensic and Analytical Science MSc, Forensic Mental Health MSc, Forensic Science (Forensic Anthropology) MSc, Forensic Science (Forensic Biology) MSc, Forensic Science(Forensic Entomology) MSc, Forensic Science (Forensic Toxicology) MSc, Graphic Design MA, Health Professional Education PgCert, Health Service Research MSc Health Studies MSc, Higher Education MA, Human Resource Management MA, Human Resource Management PgDip, Information Systems Management MSc, International Business MSc, International Business with Entrepreneurship MSc, International Business with Event Studies MSc, International Business with Humanitarian Challenges MSc, International Business with Marketing MSc, International Business with Project Management MSc, International Business with Tourism and Hospitality MSc, International Fashion Design Management MSc, International Relations MA, Internet of Things MSc, Investigative Psychology MSc

J to N

Journalism BA(Hons), Law LLB(Hons), Law with Criminology LLB(Hons),Learning Support BA(Hons), Lifelong Learning CertEd pre-service/in-service, Linguistics and Criminology BA(Hons), Linguistics BA(Hons), Logistics and Supply Chain Management BSc(Hons), Marketing BA(Hons), Marketing with Public Relations BA(Hons), Mathematics BSc(Hons), Mechanical Engineering (Top-up) BEng(Hons), Mechanical Engineering BEng(Hons), Mechanical Engineering MEng, Media and Popular Culture BA(Hons), Media Studies BA(Hons), Media, Promotional Culture and Advertising BA(Hons), Medical Biochemistry BSc(Hons), Medical Biology BSc(Hons),Medical Genetics BSc(Hons), Midwifery Studies BSc(Hons), Music and Sound for Image BA(Hons),Music BMus(Hons), Music Journalism BA(Hons),Music Performance BMus(Hons), Music Technology and Audio Systems BSc(Hons), Nursing (Adult) BSc(Hons), Nursing(Child) BSc(Hons), Nursing (Learning Disability)BSc(Hons), Nursing (Mental Health) BSc(Hons),Nursing Studies (Top-up) (Distance Learning)BSc(Hons)

Postgraduate courses:Leadership and Management PgCert, Leadership, Communication and Humanitarian Challenges MSc, Lifelong Learning PGCE pre-service/in-service LLM in Law and Global Governance, Logistics and Supply Chain Management MSc, Long Term Conditions PgCert, Management MSc, Management with Communication MSc, Management with Entrepreneurship MSc, Management with Event Studies MSc, Management with Human Resource Management MSc, Management with International Business MSc, Management with Leadership MSc, Management with Marketing MSc, Management with Tourism and Hospitality MSc, Marketing MSc, Marketing with Brand Management MSc, Marketing with Events Studies MSc, Master of Business Administration (MBA), Master of Podiatric Surgery, Master of Public Health, Mechanical Engineering Design MSc, Mechanical Engineering MSc, Music Performance Postgraduate Diploma, Nursing (Adult) MSc, Nursing (Child) MSc, Nursing (Learning Disability) MSc, Nursing (Mental Health) MSc

O to S

Occupational Therapy BSc(Hons), Operating Department Practice BSc(Hons), Optometry BSc(Hons), Paramedic Practice (Top-up) (Distance Learning) BSc(Hons), Perioperative Studies (Top up)(Distance Learning) BSc(Hons), Pharmaceutical Chemistry BSc(Hons), Pharmaceutical Chemistry MSci, Pharmacology BSc(Hons), Pharmacy MPharm, Photography BA(Hons), Physical Geography BSc(Hons), Physiotherapy BSc(Hons), Podiatry BSc(Hons), Policing and Investigation BSc(Hons),Politics and Criminology BSc(Hons), Politics BSc(Hons), Politics with Sociology BSc(Hons), Popular Music BMus(Hons), Primary and Early Years Education with QTS BA(Hons), Primary Education Studies (Non QTS Accelerated Degree) BA(Hons), Product Design BA/BSc(Hons), Psychology BSc(Hons), Psychology with Counselling BSc(Hons), Psychology with Criminology BSc(Hons), Science Extended Degree leading to a BSc(Hons) Degree, Social Work MSc, Social Work MSci, Sociology and Criminology BSc(Hons), Sociology and Geography BSc(Hons) Sociology and Psychology BSc(Hons), Sociology BSc(Hons), Sociology with Social Policy BSc(Hons), Software Engineering BSc(Hons), Software Engineering MEng, Sonic Arts and Composition BMus(Hons), Sound Engineering and Music Production BSc(Hons), Special Educational Needs, Disabilities and Inclusion BA(Hons), Sport and Exercise Nutrition MSci, Sport Exercise and Nutrition BSc(Hons), Sport Science BSc(Hons), Sport, Exercise and Nutrition BSc(Hons), Sports

Journalism BA(Hons), Supply Chain Management BSc(Hons),Supply Chain Management with Logistics (Top-up)BSc(Hons), Supporting Learning and Assessment in Practice (Distance Learning)
Postgraduate courses: Oil and Gas Engineering with Management MSc, Paramedic Science (Pre-Registration) MSc, Participatory Culture and Social Media MA, Pharmaceutical and Analytical Science MSc, Pharmaceutical Formulation and Business Strategy MSc, Pharmacy Practice with Community Placement MSc, Pharmacy Practice with Hospital Placement MSc, Pharmacy Practice with Research Project MSc, Podiatry MSc, Postgraduate Certificate in Career Leadership, Postgraduate Certificate Special Educational Needs Coordination, Primary Education 3-7 PGCE with QTS, Primary Education PGCE with QTS, Professional Practice and Management in Architecture (RIBA Part 3) PgCert, Project Management and Operations Management MSc, Psychology MSc, School Direct (Primary/Secondary) PGCE with QTS, Secondary Art and Design PGCE with QTS, Secondary Computing PGCE with QTS, Secondary Design and Technology PGCE with QTS, Secondary Drama PGCE with QTS, Secondary English PGCE with QTS, Secondary Geography PGCE with QTS, Secondary History PGCE with QTS, Secondary Mathematics PGCE with QTS, Secondary Modern Languages PGCE with QTS, Secondary Music PGCE with QTS, Secondary Physical Education PGCE with QTS, Secondary Religious Education PGCE with QTS, Secondary Science with Biology PGCE with QTS, Secondary Science with Chemistry PGCE with QTS, Secondary Science with Physics PGCE with QTS, Senior Leader Master's Degree Apprenticeship, Master of Business Administration (MBA), Social Work MSc Sport and Exercise Nutrition MSc, Strategic Communication and Leadership MSc, Strategic Communication, Leadership and Sustainability MSc, Strategic Human Resource Management MSc, Supply Chain Management with Humanitarian Challenges MSc, Sustainable Business Leadership MSc, Sustainable Supply Chain Management MSc

T to Y

TESOL (Top-up) BA(Hons), TESOL and Education BA(Hons), TESOL and Younger Learners (Top-up) BA(Hons), Textile Practice BSc(Hons), Transport and Logistics Management BSc(Hons), Travel and Tourism Management BA(Hons), Web Design BSc(Hons), Web Programming BSc(Hons), Web Programming with Cyber Security BSc(Hons), Youth and Community Studies (Top up)BA(Hons), Youth and Community Work BA(Hons),Youth and Community Work

In-Service BA(Hons)Postgraduate courses: Teaching English to Speakers of Other Languages MA, Teaching in Lifelong Learning (Top-up) MA, Theory of

Podiatric Surgery MSc, Tissue Viability and Wound Management (Distance Learning) (Masters)

UNIVERSITY OF HULL
www.hull.ac.uk

Faculty of Arts, Cultures and Education; www.hull.ac.uk/Faculties/face.aspx

School of Arts

Drama

BA(Hons) Drama and Theatre Practice BA(Hons) Drama and English, BA(Hons) Drama and Film Studies, BA(Hons) Music, Theatre and Performance Postgraduate course: MA in Theatre Making

English

BA(Hons) Creative Writing and English, BA(Hons)Creative Writing and Film Studies, BA(Hons) Drama and English, BA(Hons) English, BA(Hons) English and American Literature and Culture, BA(Hons)English and Film Studies

Postgraduate course: MA in English (Creative Writing and English Literature), MA in Creative Writing (Online)

Film and Digital Media

BA(Hons) Creative Writing and Film Studies, BA(Hons) Digital Design BA(Hons) Drama and Film Studies, BA(Hons) English and Film Studies, BA(Hons) Film Studies, BA(Hons) Game and Entertainment Design, BA(Hons) Media Studies

Postgraduate course: MA in Digital Media

Music

BA(Hons) Creative Music Technology, BA(Hons) Music, BA(Hons) Music (Popular), BA(Hons) Music, Theatre and Performance BMus Music

Postgraduate course: MMus in Music (Musicology, Composition, Performance, Technology)

School of Education and Social Sciences

Criminology

BA(Hons) Criminology, BA(Hons) Criminology and Sociology, BA(Hons) Criminology with Forensic Science, BA(Hons) Criminology with Law, BA(Hons)Criminology with Psychology, LLB Law with Criminology, BSc(Hons) Psychology with Criminology Postgraduate course: MA in Criminal Justice and Crime Control

Education, Teaching and Childhood Studies

BA(Hons) Early Childhood Studies, BA(Hons) Education Studies, BA(Hons) Early Childhood Education

and Care (1 year top-up), BA(Hons) TESOL and Education Studies FdEd Early Childhood Studies, BA(Hons) Learning and Teaching (Primary QTS) (top-up), BA(Hons) Primary Teaching, BA(Hons) Working with Children, Young People and Families, BEd Education and Early Years (1 year top-up)

Postgraduate courses: MA in Education, MA in Education and Digital Technologies, MA in Education and Early Childhood, MA in Education and Leadership, MA in Education, Inclusion and Special Needs, MA in Pedagogy and Practice

Sociology and Social Sciences

BA(Hons) Criminology and Sociology, BA(Hons) Sociology

Postgraduate courses: MSc in Social Research

School of Histories, Languages and Cultures

American Studies

BA(Hons) American Studies, BA(Hons) English and American Literature and Culture

History

BA(Hons) History, BA(Hons) History and Politics Postgraduate courses: MA in History

Languages

BA(Hons) American Studies with a Modern Language, BA(Hons) Chinese and French (Dual Languages),BA(Hons) Chinese and German (Dual Languages), BA(Hons) Chinese and Italian (Dual Languages), BA(Hons) Chinese and Spanish (Dual Languages), BA(Hons) Chinese Studies, BA(Hons)Combined Three Languages, BA(Hons) Digital Design with a Modern Language, BA(Hons) Drama with a Modern Language, BA(Hons) Dual Languages, BA(Hons) English Language, Linguistics and Cultures, BA(Hons) English with a Modern Language, BA(Hons) Film Studies with a Modern Language, BA(Hons) French and German (Dual Languages), BA(Hons) French and Italian (Dual Languages), BA(Hons) French and Spanish (Dual Languages), BA(Hons) French Studies, BA(Hons)-Game and Entertainment Design with a Modern Language, BA(Hons) German and Italian (Dual Languages), BA(Hons) German and Spanish (Dual Languages), BA(Hons) German Studies,

BA(Hons)History with a Modern Language, BA(Hons) Italian and Spanish (Dual Languages), BA(Hons) Italian Studies, LLB Law with a Modern Language, BA(Hons) Music with a Modern Language, BA(Hons) Spanish and Latin American Studies

Postgraduate courses: MA in TESOL, MA in Translation Studies

Philosophy

BA(Hons) Philosophy, BA(Hons) Philosophy and Politics, BA(Hons) Philosophy, Politics and Economics

Faculty of Business, Law and Politics; www.hull.ac.uk/Faculties/fblp.aspx

Hull University Business School

Accounting and Finance

BSc(Hons) Accounting, BSc(Hons) Accounting and Financial Management, BA(Hons) Business Management and Accounting, BA(Hons) Business Management and Financial Management

Postgraduate courses: MSc in Accounting and Finance, MSc in Finance and Investment, MSc in Financial Management, MSc in Professional Accounting

Business and Management

BA(Hons) Business Management, BA(Hons) Business Management and Accounting, BA(Hons) Business Management and Financial Management, BA(Hons) Business Management and Marketing, BA(Hons) Business Management and Supply Chain, BA(Hons) Business Management with Entrepreneurship, BA(Hons) Business Management with Human Resource Management, BA(Hons)Business Management with ICT, BA(Hons) Business Management with Sustainability, BA(Hons) International Business, BA(Hons) Marketing and Management, LLB Law with Business Management

Postgraduate courses: Hull Executive MBA (EMBA),MSc in Business Management, MSc in Business Management (with Internship), MSc in Economics and Business, MSc in Human Resource Management, MSc in International Business

Economics and Business Economics

BA(Hons) Philosophy, Politics and Economics

Postgraduate course: MSc in Economics and Business

Marketing

BA(Hons) Marketing, and Management BA(Hons) Business Management and Marketing, BA(Hons) Marketing

Postgraduate courses: MSc in Advertising and Marketing, MSc in Marketing Management

Logistics and Supply Chain Management

BA(Hons) Business Management and Supply Chain Management BSc(Hons) Logistics and Supply Chain Management

Postgraduate course: MSc in Logistics and Supply Chain Management

School of Law and Politics

Law

BA(Hons) Criminology with Law, LLB Law, LLB Law (Senior Status) LLB Law with Business Management, LLB Law with Criminology, LLB Law with Legislative Studies, LLB Law with Politics

Postgraduate course: LLM in International Law(Conflict, Security and Human Rights)

Politics and International Relations

BA(Hons) British Politics and Legislative Studies, BA(Hons) History and Politics, LLB Law with Legislative Studies, LLB Law with Politics, BA(Hons)Philosophy and Politics, BA(Hons) Philosophy, Politics and Economics, BA(Hons) Politics, BA(Hons)Politics and International Relations, BA(Hons) War and Security Studies

Postgraduate courses: MA in International Politics, MA in Strategy and International Security

Faculty of Health Sciences; www.hull.ac.uk/Faculties/fhs.aspx

Hull York Medical School

Hull MBBS, BSc Biomedical Sciences

Postgraduate courses: PgCert/PgDip/Msc in Health Professions Education, MSc Clinical Anatomy, MSc Clinical Anatomy and Education, MSc in Human Anatomy and Evolution, MSc in Pharmacology and Drug Development, MSc in Physician Associate Studies

School of Health and Social Work

Health, Nursing and Midwifery

BSc(Hons) Gastroenterology Care, BSc(Hons) Midwifery, BSc(Hons) Midwifery (Short Programme), BSc(Hons) Nursing (Adult), BSc(Hons)Nursing (Child), BSc(Hons) Nursing (Learning Disability),BSc(Hons) Nursing (Mental Health),BSc(Hons) Nursing Studies, BSc(Hons) Operating Department Practice, BSc(Hons) Paramedic Science, BSc(Hons) Physiotherapy

Postgraduate courses: MSc in Advanced Practice, MSc in Colonoscopy, MSc in Dementia, MSc in Gastroenterology Care, MSc in Health Studies, MSc in Leadership in Health and Social Care, PGCert Educator in Practice, PGCert Practice Teacher, PGCert/PGDip Cognitive Behavioural Therapy (Secondary Care), Postgraduate Diploma in Midwifery(-Short Programme)

Social Work, Youth and Community Development
BA(Hons) Social Work
Postgraduate course: MA in Social Work

School of Life Sciences

Biomedical Sciences
BSc(Hons) Biomedical Science, BSc(Hons) Forensic Science
Postgraduate courses: MSc in Biomedical Sciences

Psychology
BSc(Hons) Criminology with Psychology, BSc(Hons)Psychology, BSc(Hons) Psychology with Criminology Postgraduate courses: MSc in Clinical Applications of Psychology

Sport, Health and Exercise Sciences
BSc(Hons) Physiotherapy, BSc(Hons) Sport and Exercise Nutrition, BSc(Hons) Sport and Exercise Science, BSc(Hons) /MSci Sport Rehabilitation, BSc(Hons) Sports Coaching and Performance Science
Postgraduate courses: MSc in Cancer Rehabilitation, MSc in Cardiovascular Rehabilitation, MSc in Clinical Exercise Physiology

Faculty of Science and Engineering

School of Engineering and Computer Science

Chemical Engineering
BEng/MEng Chemical Engineering,
Postgraduate courses: MSc in Energy Engineering, MSc in Engineering Management

Electrical and Electronic Engineering
BEng/MEng Electrical and Electronic Engineering, BEng/MEng Mechatronics and Robotics
Postgraduate courses: MSc in Electrical and Electronic Engineering, MSc in Energy Engineering, MSc in Engineering Management

Computer Science
BSc(Hons)/MEng Computer Science, BSc(Hons)/MEng Computer Science for Games Development, BSc(Hons)/MEng Computer Science (Software Engineering), BEng/MEng Mechatronics and Robotics
Postgraduate courses: MSc in Advanced Computer Science, MSc in Computer Science (Security and Distributed Computing), MSc in Computer Science(Software Engineering), MSc in Computer Science for Games Development, MSc in Engineering Management

Mechanical Engineering
BEng/MEng Mechanical and Medical Engineering, BEng Mechanical Engineering,
Postgraduate courses: MSc in Energy Engineering, MSc in Engineering Management, MSc in Mechanical Engineering

Medical and Biomedical Engineering
BEng/MEng Biomedical Engineering, BEng/MEng Mechanical and Medical Engineering
Postgraduate courses: MSc in Biomedical Engineering, MSc in Public Engagement and Science Communication

School of Environmental Sciences

Biological and Environmental Science
BSc(Hons) Biology, BSc(Hons) Environmental Science, BSc(Hons) Marine Biology, BSc(Hons) Zoology
Postgraduate courses: MSc in Environmental Change, Management and Monitoring, MSc in Marine Environmental Management

Geography and Geology
BA(Hons) Geography, BSc(Hons) Geography, BSc(Hons) Geology, BSc(Hons) Geology with Physical Geography, BA(Hons) Human Geography, BSc(Hons) Physical Geography
Postgraduate course: MSc in Renewable Energy

School of Mathematics and Physical Sciences; www.hull.ac.uk/Faculties/fse/mp.aspx

Chemistry
BSc(Hons) /MBiochem Biochemistry, BSc(Hons) Chemistry (top-up) (part-time), BSc(Hons)/MChem Chemistry, BSc(Hons)/MChem Chemistry (Forensic and Analytical Science), BSc(Hons) Safety and Environmental Management (with NEBOSH) (part-time), National Diploma in Environmental Management (part-time), National Diploma Safety and Environmental Management (with NEBOSH) (part-time), Safety and Environmental Management(with NEBOSH) (part-time)Postgraduate courses: MSc in Analytical and Forensic Chemistry, Msc in Biochemistry, Msc in Chemistry, MSc/MRes Environmental Management(in partnership with NEBOSH), MSc/MRes in Occupational Health and Safety Management (in partnership with NEBOSH), MSc/MRes in Occupational Health, Safety and Environmental Management(in partnership with NEBOSH)

Mathematics
BSc(Hons) Mathematics
Postgraduate courses: MSc in Mathematics

Physics and Astrophysics
BSc(Hons)/MPhys Physics, BSc(Hons)/MPhys Physics with Astrophysics, BSc(Hons) MPhys Theoretical Physics

BISHOP BURTON COLLEGE
www.bishopburton.ac.uk

FdSc Sport, Exercise Science and Health, FdSc Animal Management and Behaviour, FdSc Applied Canine Behaviour and Training, FdA Design, FdA Fashion and Clothing Design, FdSc Agriculture, FdSc Agriculture (Farm Business Administration), FdSc Agriculture (Precision Crop Technology), FdSc Ecology and Environmental Management, FdSc Equine Therapy and Rehabilitation, FdSc Equine Sports Science and Coaching, FdSc Business Management for the Equine Industry, FdA Floristry Design, FdA Criminology, and Criminal Justice HNC Agriculture BSc(Hons) Agricultural Resource Management(Top Up), BSc Applied Animal Behaviour and Training, BSc Bioveterinary Science, BSc Animal Behaviour and Welfare (Top Up), BSc Canine Behaviour Management (Top Up), BA Design (Top Up), BA Fashion, Design and Manufacture (Top Up), HNC/HND in Business, HNC/HND in Travel and Tourism Management, BSc Ecology and Environmental Management (Top Up), BSc Sport, Exercise Science and Health, FdSc Wildlife and Conservation Management, BSc Wildlife and Conservation Management (Top Up), BSc(Hons) Equine Therapy and Rehabilitation, BSc(Hons) Equine Sports Science and Coaching, BSc(Hons) Equine Science, BSc(Hons) Business Management for the Equine Industry, BA Floristry Design (Top Up), HND Horticulture (Garden Design), Higher National Certificate (HNC) in Agriculture (Livestock or Crop Production), HNC in Animal Management, HNC Sport, BA Contemporary Criminology (Top Up), Certificate in Education, Professional Graduate Certificate in Education and Postgraduate Certificate in Education, City and Guilds Level 5 Diploma in Education and Training, BA(Hons) Education and Professional Development Postgraduate courses: MSc Applied Animal Behaviour and Training, MSc Animal Behaviour and Welfare

DONCASTER COLLEGE
www.don.ac.uk

Art, Design and Media
FdA Illustration and Concept Art, HND in Creative Media Production – Computer Games Design/Animation, HND Creative Media Production – Motion Graphics, HND Creative Media Production Sound Media, HND Creative Media Production – Visual Effects, BA(Hons) Fine Art and Crafts, BA(Hons)-Games Design and Animation (Top Up), BA(Hons)-Graphic Design, BA(Hons) Graphic Design (distance learning), BA(Hons) Illustration and Concept Art Postgraduate courses: MA in Creative Industries: Practice, Business and Innovation, MA in Creative Pattern Cutting

Early Years
FdA Children's Learning and Development FdA Supporting Children with Special Educational Needs and Disability, BA(Hons) Supporting Children with Special Educational Needs and Disability (top up – distance learning), BA(Hons) Early Childhood Studies, BA(Hons) Early Childhood Studies(top up), BA(Hons) Early Childhood Studies (top up) Northern Ireland, BA(Hons) Early Childhood Studies (top up- distance learning)
Postgraduate courses: MA in Early Childhood Studies, MA in Early Childhood Studies (Distance Learning), MA in Education Studies (Primary/Secondary/SEND), MA in Supporting Children with Special Educational Needs and Disabilities

Education
HNC in Health and Social Care, HND in Health and Social Care, HND Social and Community Work, FdSc Professional Practice in Health and Social Care, BA(Hons) Education and Advancing Professional Practice

Foundation for Counselling and Relationship Studies
BA(Hons) Contemporary Relational Counselling, BA(Hons) Counselling Solutions (Top Up)
Postgraduate courses: MA in Contemporary Relationship Studies, MSc in Contemporary Psychosexual Therapy, CPD Programme

Hospitality and Catering
Professional Culinary Arts Diploma Level 4
Humanities and Social Sciences
BA(Hons) Applied Social Science, BA(Hons) Criminal Justice, BA(Hons) English, BA(Hons) Psychology in the Community
Postgraduate courses: MA in Literature and Digital Culture
Leadership and Management
BA(Hons) Business Management, BA(Hons) International Football Business Management Postgraduate courses: MBA Masters in Business Administration, Postgraduate Diploma in Human Resource Management, MSc in Human Resource Management
Music and Performing Arts
FdA Live Performance Technology, FdA Performing Arts in the Community (Dance, Drama, Music),BA(Hons) Creative Music Technology, BA(Hons)Performing Arts in the Community Top Up (Dance, Drama, Music)

Sports
BA(Hons) Physical Education and Sports Coaching, BSc(Hons) Sport Science and Coaching in Football(-Distance Learning), BSc(Hons) Sports, Fitness and Exercise Science, BSc(Hons) Sports, Exercise and Health Science (Top Up)

Advanced Technologies
HNC Construction, HND Construction, HND Construction(one year conversion), HNC Electrical/Electronic Engineering, HND Electrical/Electronic Engineering (top-up), HND Engineering (General Engineering), HNC Mechanical Engineering, HND Engineering (Mechanical Engineering), HND Mechanical Engineering (one year conversion)

Teacher Education and Professional Development
Postgraduate courses: MEd in Advancing Professional Practice, Professional Graduate/Postgraduate Certificate in Education (PgCE/PGCE), Certificate in Education (Cert Ed)

IMPERIAL COLLEGE, LONDON
www.imperial.ac.uk

Department of Aeronautics; www.imperial.ac.uk/aeronautics
MEng Aeronautical Engineering, MEng Aeronautics with Spacecraft Engineering
Postgraduate courses: MSc Advanced Aeronautical Engineering, MSc Advanced Computational Methods for Aeronautics, Flow Management and Fluid-Structure Interaction, MSc Composites: the Science, Technology and Engineering Application of Advanced Composites, MRes Fluid Dynamics Across Scales

Department of Bioengineering; www.imperial.ac.uk/bioengineering
MEng Biomedical Engineering, MEng Molecular Bioengineering
Postgraduate courses: MRes Bioengineering, MSc Biomedical Engineering, MSc Human and Biological Robotics, MRes Medical Device Design and Entrepreneurship, MRes Neurotechnology

Department of Biomedical Science
BSc Medical Biosciences, BSc Medical Biosciences with Management

Imperial College Business School; www.imperial.ac.uk/business-school
Postgraduate courses: MSc Business Analytics, MSc Climate Change, Management and Finance (delivered in partnership with the Grantham Institute),MSc Economics and Strategy for Business, MSc Finance, MSc Finance and Accounting, MSc Financial Technology, MSc Innovation, Entrepreneurship and Management, MSc International Health Management, MSc International Management, MSc Investment and Wealth Management, MSc Management, MBA, MBA (Executive), MBA (Global Online), MBA (Weekend), MSc Risk Management and Financial Engineering, MSc Strategic Marketing

Department of Chemical Engineering; www.imperial.ac.uk/chemical-engineering
MEng Chemical Engineering, MEng Chemical with Nuclear Engineering
Postgraduate courses: MSc Advanced Chemical Engineering, MSc Advanced Chemical Engineering with Biotechnology, MSc Advanced Chemical Engineering with Process Systems Engineering, MSc Advanced Chemical Engineering with Structured Product Engineering, MRes Molecular Science and Engineering (delivered by the Institute for Molecular Science and Engineering)

Department of Chemistry; www.imperial.ac.uk/chemistry

BSc Chemistry, MSCi Chemistry, MSCi Chemistry with French for Science, MSCi Chemistry with German for Science, BSc Chemistry with Management, MSCi Chemistry with Medicinal Chemistry, MSCi Chemistry with Molecular Physics, MSCi Chemistry with Research Abroad, MSCi Chemistry with Spanish for Science

Postgraduate courses: MRes Advanced Molecular Synthesis, MRes Bioimaging Sciences, MRes Catalysis: Chemistry and Engineering, MRes Chemical Biology and Bio-Entrepreneurship MRes Drug Discovery and Development: Multidisciplinary Science for Next Generation Therapeutics, MRes Green Chemistry, Energy and the Environment, MRes Nanomaterials, MRes Plant Chemical Biology: Multidisciplinary Research for Next Generation Agri-Sciences

Department of Civil and Environmental Engineering; www.imperial.ac.uk/civil-engineering

MEng Civil Engineering

Postgraduate courses: MSc Advanced Materials for Sustainable Infrastructure, MSc Concrete Structures, Earthquake Engineering, MSc Engineering Fluid Mechanics for the Offshore, Coastal and Built Environments, MSc Environmental Engineering, MSc Environmental Engineering and Business Management, MSc General Structural Engineering, MSc Hydrology and Business Management, MSc Hydrology and Water Resources Management, MSc Soil Mechanics, MSc Soil Mechanics and Business Management, MSc Soil Mechanics and Engineering Seismology, MSc Soil Mechanics and Environmental Geotechnics, MSc Structural Steel Design, MSc Transport, MSc Transport and Business Management

Department of Computing; www.imperial.ac.uk/computing

MEng Computing (Artificial Intelligence), and Machine Learning BEng Computing, MEng Computing (International Programme of Study), MEng Computing (Management and Finance), MEng Computing, MEng Computing (Security and Reliability), MEng Computing (Software Engineering), MEng Computing (Visual Computing and Robotics), BEng Mathematics and Computer Science, MEng Mathematics and Computer Science

Postgraduate courses: MSc Advanced Computing, MSc Artificial Intelligence, MSc Computing (Artificial and Machine Learning) MSc Computing (Management and Finance), MSc Computing (Security and Reliability), MSc Computing (Software Engineering), MSc Computing (Visual Computing and Robotics), MSc Computing Science

Dyson School of Design Engineering; www.imperial.ac.uk/design-engineering

MEng Design Engineering

Postgraduate courses: MA/MSc Global Innovation Design, MA/MSc Innovation Design Engineering

Department of Earth Science and Engineering; www.imperial.ac.uk/earth-science

BSc Earth and Planetary Science, MSci Earth and Planetary Science, BSc Geology, MSci Geology, BSc Geophysics, MSci Geophysics

Postgraduate courses: MSc Applied Computational Science and Engineering, MSc Metals and Energy Finance, MSc Petroleum Engineering, MSc Petroleum Geoscience

Department of Electrical and Electronic Engineering; www.imperial.ac.uk/electrical-engineering

BEng Electrical and Electronic Engineering, MEng Electrical and Electronic Engineering, MEng Electrical and Electronic Engineering with Management, BEng Electronic and Information Engineering, MEng Electronic and Information Engineering

Postgraduate courses: MSc Analogue and Digital Integrated Circuit Design, MSc Communications and Signal Processing, MSc Control Systems, MSc Future Power Networks

Centre for Environment Policy; www.imperial.ac.uk/environmental-policy

Postgraduate courses: MSc Environmental Technology

Department of Life Sciences; www.imperial.ac.uk/life-sciences

BSc Biochemistry, BSc Biochemistry with French for Science, BSc Biochemistry with German for Science, BSc Biochemistry with Management, BSc Biochemistry with Spanish for Science, BSc Biological Sciences, BSc Biological Sciences with French for Science, BSc Biological Sciences with German for Science, BSc Biological Sciences with Management, BSc Biological Sciences with Spanish for Science, BSc Biotechnology, BSc Biotechnology with French for Science, BSc Biotechnology with German for Science, BSc Biotechnology with Management, BSc

Biotechnology with Spanish for Science, BSc Ecology and Environmental Biology, BSc Microbiology
Postgraduate courses: MSc Applied Biosciences and Biotechnology, MSc Bioinformatics and Theoretical Systems Biology, MRes Biosystematics, MRes Computational Methods in Ecology and Evolution MSc Computational Methods in Ecology and Evolution, MSc Conservation Science, MSc Ecological Applications, MSc Ecology, Evolution and Conservation, MRes Ecology, Evolution and Conservation Research, MRes Ecosystem and Environmental Change, MRes Molecular and Cellular Biosciences, MRes Molecular Plant and Microbial Sciences, MRes Structural Molecular Biology, MRes Systems and Synthetic Biology, MSc Taxonomy, Biodiversity and Evolution MRes Tropical Forest Ecology

Department of Materials;
www.imperial.ac.uk/materials

MEng Biomaterials and Tissue Engineering, BEng Materials Science and Engineering, MEng Materials Science and Engineering, BEng Materials with Management, MEng Materials with Nuclear Engineering
Postgraduate courses: MSc Advanced Materials Science and Engineering

Department of Mathematics;
www.imperial.ac.uk/mathematics

BSc Mathematics, MSci Mathematics, BSc Mathematics (Pure Mathematics), BSc Mathematics with Applied Mathematics/Mathematical Physics, BSc Mathematics with Mathematical Computation, BSc Mathematics with Statistics, BSc Mathematics with Statistics for Finance, BSc Mathematics, Optimisation and Statistics
Postgraduate courses: MSc Applied Mathematics, MSc Mathematics and Finance, MSc Pure Mathematics, MSc Statistics

Department of Mechanical Engineering;
www.imperial.ac.uk/mechanical-engineering

MEng Mechanical Engineering, MEng Mechanical with Nuclear Engineering
Postgraduate courses: MSc Advanced Mechanical Engineering, MSc Sustainable Energy Futures (delivered by Energy Futures Lab)

Department of Medicine;
www.imperial.ac.uk/medicine/departments

MBBS Medicine (Lee Kong Chian School of Medicine, Singapore), MBBS/BSc Medicine

Postgraduate courses: MBBS Medicine (Graduate entry), MBBS/PhD Intercalated PhD option for Medical Students, MSc/PGCert/PGDip Allergy, MRes Bacterial Pathogenesis and Infection, MRes/PGCert Clinical Research PGDip Digital Health Leadership, MRes Experimental Neuroscience, MSc Human Molecular Genetics, PGCert/MSc Immunology, MRes Molecular Basis of Human Disease, MSc Molecular Biology and Pathology of Viruses, MSc Molecular Medicine, PGCert/PGDip MSc Paediatrics and Child Health, MSc Translational Neuroscience

National Heart and Lung Institute;
www.imperial.ac.uk/nhli

Postgraduate courses: MSc Applied Genomics, MSc Cardiorespiratory Nursing, PGCert/PGDip/MSc Cardiovascular and Respiratory Healthcare, PGCert/MSc Genes, Drugs and Stem Cells – Novel Therapies, PGCert/PGDip/Msc Genomic Medicine, MSc Medical Ultrasound, PGCert/Msc Innovations in Cardiological Science, PGCert/PGDip/MSc Preventive Cardiology, MRes Respiratory and Cardiovascular Science

Department of Physics;
www.imperial.ac.uk/physics

BSc Physics, MSci Physics, BSc Physics and Music Performance, BSc Physics with Theoretical Physics, MSci Physics with Theoretical Physics
Postgraduate courses: MRes Controlled Quantum Dynamics, MSc Optics and Photonics, MRes Photonics, MSc Physics, MSc Physics with Extended Research, MSc Physics with Nanophotonics, MSc Physics with Quantum Physics, MRes Plastic Electronic Materials, MSc Quantum Fields and Fundamental Forces, MSc Security and Resilience: Science and Technology

School of Public Health;
www.imperial.ac.uk/school-public-health

Postgraduate courses: MSc Epidemiology, MRes Epidemiology, Evolution and Control of Infectious Diseases, MPH Public Health, MPH Global Master of Public Health

Science Communication Unit

Postgraduate courses: MSc Science Communication, MSc Science Media Production

Student Recruitment and Outreach

PGCE INSPIRE teacher training programme

Department of Surgery and Cancer; www.imperial.ac.uk/department-surgery-cancer

Postgraduate courses: MRes Anaesthetics, Pain Medicine and Intensive Care, MRes Biomedical Research, MRes Cancer Biology, MRes Cancer Informatics, MRes Data Science, MSc Health Data Analytics and Machine Learning, PGCert/PGDip/MSc Health Policy (delivered by the Institute of Global Health Innovation), MSc Healthcare and Design (delivered by the Institute of Global Health Innovation), MRes Medical Robotics and Image-Guided Intervention(delivered by the Institute of Global Health, MRes Microbiome in Health and Disease (delivered by the Institute of Global Health Innovation), PGCert/PGDip/MSc Patient Safety (delivered by the Institute of Global Health Innovation), PGCert/MSc Reproductive and Developmental Biology, PGDip/MEd Surgical Education, PGCert/PGDip/MSc Surgical Innovation

KEELE UNIVERSITY
www.keele.ac.uk

A to D

BA(Hons) Accounting and Business Management, BA(Hons) Accounting and Finance, BSc(Hons) Accounting and Mathematics, BA(Hons) Accounting, Finance and International Business, BSc(Hons) Adult Nursing, BSc(Hons) Astrophysics and Chemistry, BSc(Hons)Astrophysics and Computer Science, BSc(Hons)Astrophysics and Education, BSc(Hons) Astrophysics and Environmental Science, BSc(Hons) Astrophysics and Forensic Science, BSc(Hons) Astrophysics and Geology, BSc(Hons) Astrophysics and Human Geography, BSc(Hons) Astrophysics and Mathematics, BSc(Hons) Astrophysics and Medicinal Chemistry, BSc(Hons)Astrophysics and Physical Geography, BSc(Hons)Biochemistry, BSc(Hons) Biochemistry and Biology, BSc(Hons) Biochemistry and Chemistry, BSc(Hons)Biochemistry and Human Biology, BSc(Hons) Biochemistry and Medicinal Chemistry, BSc(Hons) Biochemistry and Neuroscience, BSc(Hons) Biology, BSc(Hons) Biology and Chemistry, BSc(Hons) Biology and Computer Science, BSc(Hons) Biology and Education, BSc(Hons) Biology and Environmental Science, BSc(Hons) Biology and Forensic Science, BSc(Hons) Biology and Geology, BSc(Hons) Biology and Human Geography, BSc(Hons) Biology and Mathematics, BSc(Hons)Biology and Physical Geography, BSc(Hons) Biology and Psychology, BSc(Hons) Biomedical Science, BA(Hons) Business and Human Resource Management, BA(Hons) Business Management and Computer Science, BA(Hons) Business Management and Economics, BA(Hons) Business Management and Finance, BA(Hons) Business Management and Psychology, BSc(Hons) Chemistry, MChem Chemistry: (Master of Chemistry), BSc(Hons) Chemistry and Environmental Science, BSc(Hons) Chemistry and Forensic Science, BSc(Hons) Chemistry and Geology, BSc(Hons) Chemistry and Human Biology, BSc(Hons) Chemistry and Mathematics, BSc(Hons)Chemistry and Neuroscience, BSc(Hons) Chemistry and Physics, BSc(Hons) Chemistry with Medicinal Chemistry, MChem Chemistry with Medicinal Chemistry (Master of Chemistry with Medicinal Chemistry), BSc(Hons) Children's Nursing, BSc(Hons) Clinical Practice, BSc(Hons) Computer Science, BSc(Hons) Computer Science and Forensic Science, BSc(Hons) Computer Science and Geology, BSc(Hons) Computer Science and Mathematics, BSc(Hons) Computer Science and Music Technology, BSc(Hons) Computer Science and Neuroscience, BSc(Hons) Computer Science and Physics, MComp Computer Science with Integrated Master's, BA(Hons) Criminology, BA(Hons) Criminology and History, BSc(Hons) Criminology and History, BSc(Hons) Criminology and Psychology, BA(Hons) Criminology and Sociology

Postgraduate courses: MSc Accounting and Financial Management, MSc Adult Nursing MSc/PgCert/PgDip Advanced Clinical Practice MSc Advanced Computer Science, PgCert Advanced Critical Care Practitioner PgCert Advanced Practice in Computed Tomographic Colongraphy, MSc/PgCert/PgDip Advancing Professional Practice (Nursing), MSc Analytical Science for Industry PgCert Applied Clinical Anatomy, MSc Applied Social and Political Psychology, MSc (IBMS accreditation)/PgCert/PgDip Biomedical Blood Science, MSc/PgDip Biomedical Engineering, Pre-MSc/GradDip Biomedical Science (Graduate Diploma), MSc (seeking IBMS Accreditation)/PgCert/PgDip Biomedical Science (Medical Microbiology), MSc/PgDip Cell and Tissue Engineering, MA/PgDip Child Care Law and Practice, MSc

Child Development, MSc/PgCert/PgDip Clinical Pharmacy Graduate Certificate Clinical Practice MSc Cognitive Psychology, MA Creative Music Technology, MA Creative Writing, MA/PgCert/PgDip Criminology and Criminal Justice, PgCert Critical Care Practice

E to I

BA(Hons) Economics, BA(Hons) Economics and Finance, BA(Hons) Economics and Mathematics, BA(Hons) Economics and Politics, BA(Hons) Education, BA(Hons) Education and English Literature, BA(Hons) Education and History, BSc(Hons) Education and Human Biology, BSc(Hons) Education and Mathematics, BA(Hons) Education and Music, BA(Hons) Education and Philosophy, BSc(Hons)Education and Physics, BA(Hons) Education and Sociology, BA(Hons) English and American Literature, BA(Hons) English Literature, BA(Hons) English Literature and Creative Writing, BA(Hons) English Literature and Film Studies, BA(Hons) English Literature and History, BA(Hons) English Literature and Music, BA(Hons) English Literature and Philosophy, BA(Hons) English Literature and Psychology, BA(Hons) or BSc(Hons) Environment and Sustainability, BSc(Hons) Environmental Science, BSc(Hons) Environmental Science and Biology, BSc(Hons)Environmental Science and Human Geography, BSc(Hons) Environmental Science and Medicinal Chemistry, BSc(Hons) Environmental Science and Physical Geography, BSc(Hons) Environmental Science and Physics, BA(Hons) Film Studies, BA(Hons) Film Studies and Creative Writing, BA(Hons) Film Studies and Media, BA(Hons) Film Studies and Music Technology, MSci Forensic and Analytical Investigation–Integrated Master's BSc(Hons) Forensic Science, BSc(Hons)Forensic Science and Criminology, BSc(Hons) Forensic Science and Human Biology, BSc(Hons) Forensic Science and Neuroscience, BSc(Hons) Forensic Science and Physics, BSc(Hons) Forensic Science and Psychology, BA(Hons) or BSc(Hons) Geography, BSc(Hons) Geology, BSc(Hons) Geology and Human Geography, BSc(Hons) Geology and Physical Geography, BSc(Hons) Geology and Physics, MGeol Geology with Integrated Master's, BSc(Hons) Health and Wellbeing BA(Hons) History, BA(Hons) History and Human Geography, BA(Hons) History and International Relations, BA(Hons) History and Politics, BSc(Hons) History and Psychology, BSc(Hons) Combined Human Biology, BSc(Hons) Human Biology and Mathematics, BSc(Hons) Human Biology and Medicinal Chemistry, BSc(Hons) Human Biology and Psychology, BA(Hons) Human Geography, BSc(Hons) Human Geography and Mathematics, BSc(Hons) Human Geography and Physics, BA(Hons) Human Geography and Politics, BA(Hons)Human Geography and Sociology, BSc(Hons) Human Resource Management and Psychology, BA(Hons) International Business and International Relations, BA(Hons) International Business and Marketing, BA(Hons) International Business Management, BA(Hons) International Governance and Public Policy, BA(Hons) International Relations, BA(Hons) International Relations and Politics

Postgraduate courses: MA Education, MA English Literatures, MSc Environmental Sustainability and Green Technology, MSc/MA Geographical and Environmental Research MSc Geoscience Research, MA Global Media and Culture, MA Global Media and Management, MHPE/PgCert/PgDip Health Professions Education: Accreditation and Assessment MSc/PgCert/PgDip Health Sciences MA/PgDip (APA) Higher Education Practice (Keele staff only), MA History, MA Human Resource Management, MA Human Rights, Globalisation and Justice, MRes Humanities MRes, Certificate in Independent Prescribing (including the professional Independent Prescribing Preparatory Certificate) Independent Prescribing, MSc International Business, LLM International Law, LLM International Law (and Business), LLM International Law (and Human Rights), LLM International Law (and Politics), LLM International Law (and the Environment)

J to N

LLB(Hons) Law, LLB(Hons) Law with Business, LLB(Hons)Law with Criminology, LLB(Hons) Law with Politics, BSc(Hons) Learning Disability Nursing, BA(Hons)Liberal Arts, MLib Arts Liberal Arts with Integrated Masters, BA(Hons) Management, BA(Hons) Marketing and Business Management, BA(Hons) Marketing and Media, BSc(Hons) Marketing and Psychology, BSc(Hons) Mathematics, BSc(Hons) Mathematics and Music, BSc(Hons) Mathematics and Philosophy, BSc(Hons)Mathematics and Physical Geography, BSc(Hons) Mathematics and Physics, BSc(Hons) Mathematics and Psychology, MMath Mathematics with Integrated Master's, BA(Hons) Media and Music Technology, BA(Hons) Media and Sociology, BA(Hons) Media, Communications and Creative Practice, BSc(Hons)Medicinal Chemistry and Biology, BSc(Hons) Medicinal Chemistry and Forensic Science, BSc(Hons)Medicinal

Chemistry and Geology, BSc(Hons) Medicinal Chemistry and Mathematics, BSc(Hons) Medicinal Chemistry and Neuroscience, BSc(Hons) Medicinal Chemistry and Physics, MB ChB Medicine, BSc(Hons) Mental Health Nursing, BSc(Hons) Midwifery, BA(Hons) Music and Music Technology, BA(Hons) Music Technology BSc(Hons) Music Technology and Psychology, BSc(Hons) Natural Sciences, MSci Integrated Master's Natural Sciences, with Integrated Master's BSc(Hons) Neuroscience, BSc(Hons) Neuroscience and Psychology, BSc(Hons) Nursing(Adult Nursing)

Postgraduate courses: LLM/PgCert/PgDip/CPD Law and Society, PgCert Learning and Teaching in Higher Education(With NMC Registered Teacher Status) MSc Management, MBA MBA Senior Leader Degree Apprenticeship, PgCert (Certificate has 2 pathways)/ PgDip/MA Medical Education, MA Medical Education (Intercalated), MSc Medical Engineering Design, MA/PgCert/PgDip Medical Ethics and Law, MA/ PgDip/PgCert Medical Ethics and Palliative Care, MMedSci Medical Science (Anatomical Sciences), PgCert Medical Science (Leadership and Management), MA Music, MSc/PgCert/PgDip Neurological Rehabilitation, MSc/PgCert/PgDip Neuromusculoskeletal Healthcare

O to U

BSc(Hons) Pharmaceutical Science, Technology and Business, MPharm(Hons) Pharmacy, MPharm (only available to international students) Pharmacy with Integrated Training Year, BA(Hons) Philosophy, BA(Hons) Philosophy and Politics, BSc(Hons) Philosophy and Psychology, BSc(Hons) Physical Geography, BSc(Hons) Physical Geography and Physics, BSc(Hons) Physics, BSc(Hons) Physics with

Astrophysics, MSci Physiotherapy, BA(Hons) Politics, BSc(Hons) Psychology, BSc(Hons) Psychology (Single Honours)with Placement Year, BSc(Hons) Psychology and Sociology, BSc(Hons) Psychology with Counselling, BSc(Hons) Radiography (Diagnostic Imaging),BSc(Hons) Rehabilitation and Exercise Science, BA(Hons) Social Work, BA(Hons) Sociology, BSc(Hons) Specialist Community Nursing: District Nursing Pathway, BSc Specialist Community Public Health Nursing: Health Visiting Pathway, BSc(Hons) Specialist Community Public Health Nursing: School Nursing Pathway, BVetMS Veterinary Medicine and Surgery

Postgraduate courses: MSc/PgCert/PgDip Pain Science and Management, PGCE/ProfGCE Academic AwardMSc Pharmaceutical Development with Business Management, Doctorate Pharmacy (DPharm), MSc Pharmacy (Professional MSc), MRes Philosophy, MSc Physician Associate Studies, MSc/PgCert/PgDip Physiotherapy (Part-Time), MSc Physiotherapy (Pre-registration), MSc/PgCert/PgDip Physiotherapy–Advanced, MSc Physiotherapy–Advanced(Cardiorespiratory), MSc Physiotherapy–Advanced(Neurology), Modular Practice Education (Social Work), Pre-Master's (international students), Msc/PgDip Rheumatology Practice MA/PgCert/PgDip Safeguarding Adults: Law, Policy Practice MRes, Social Science Research Methods MRes, MA (incorporating the professional qualification in Social Work) Social Work PgDip Specialist Community Nursing-District Nursing Pathway, MSc/PgDip Specialist Community Nursing-Health Visiting Pathway, MSc/PgDip Specialist Community Public Health Nursing-School Nursing Pathway, Postgraduate module Teaching and Learning in Geoscience Education

UNIVERSITY OF KENT
www.kent.ac.uk

American Studies

American Studies BA(Hons), American Studies (History)BA(Hons), American Studies (Latin America)-BA(Hons), American Studies (Literature) BA(Hons)
Postgraduate course: American Studies MA

Anthropology and Conservation

Anthropology BSc(Hons), Biological Anthropology BSc(Hons), Cultural Studies and Social Anthropology BA(Hons), Environmental Social Sciences BA(Hons),History and Social Anthropology BA(Hons), Human Geography BSc(Hons), Law and Social

Anthropology LLB(Hons), Social Anthropology BA(Hons), Social Anthropology and Politics BA(Hons), Social Anthropology and Social Policy BA(Hons), Social Anthropology with French BA(Hons), Social Anthropology with German BA(Hons), Social Anthropology with Spanish BA(Hons), Sociology and Social Anthropology BA(Hons), Wildlife Conservation BSc(Hons)

Postgraduate courses: Biological Anthropology MSc, Conservation and International Wildlife Trade MSc, Conservation and Primate Behaviour MSc,

Conservation and Rural Development MSc, Conservation and Tourism MSc, Conservation Biology MSc, Conservation Project Management MSc, Environmental Anthropology MA/MSc, Environmental Social Science MSc, Ethnobotany MSc, Forensic Osteology and Field Recovery Methods MSc, Social Anthropology MA, Social Anthropology and Conflict MA, Social Anthropology of Europe MA, Social Anthropology with Visual Ethnography MA

Archaeology, Ancient History and Classics

Ancient History BA(Hons), Ancient, Medieval and Modern History BA(Hons), Asian Studies and Classical & Archaeological Studies BA(Hons), Classical and Archaeological Studies BA(Hons), Classical & Archaeological Studies and Comparative Literature BA(Hons), Classical and Archaeological Studies and Film BA(Hons), Classical and Archaeological Studies and Italian BA(Hons), Classical and Archaeological Studies and Philosophy BA(Hons), Classical Studies BA(Hons)

Architecture

Architecture BA(Hons) ARB/RIBA Part 1, Architecture MArch ARB/RIBA Part 2

Postgraduate courses: Architectural Conservation MSc, Architectural Practice PDip, Architectural Visualisation MA, Architecture and the Sustainable Environment MSc, Architecture and Urban Design MA, Architecture– ARB/RIBA Part 2 MArch, Bio Digital Architecture MSc

Arts

Art History BA(Hons), Art History and Classical & Archaeological Studies BA(Hons), Art History and English and American Literature BA(Hons), Art History and Film BA(Hons), Art History and French BA(Hons), Art History and Hispanic Studies BA(Hons), Art History and History BA(Hons), Art History and Media Studies BA(Hons), Digital Arts BA(Hons), Digital Arts MArt, Drama and Media Studies BA(Hons), Drama and Theatre and Art History BA(Hons), Film and Media Studies BA(Hons), Liberal Arts BA(Hons), Media Studies BA(Hons), Multimedia Technology and Design BSc(Hons), Philosophy and Art History BA(Hons),Photography (top-up) BA(Hons)

Postgraduate courses: Advanced Communications Engineering (RF Technology and Telecommunications)MSc, Advanced Communications Engineering(Wireless Systems and Networks) MSc, Advanced Electronic Systems Engineering MSc, Architectural Visualisation MA, Computer Animation MSc, Creative Producing MA, Curating MA, Digital Visual Effects MSc, Film MA, Film with Practice MA,

History and Philosophy of Art MA, History of Art MA, Information Security and Biometrics MSc, Theatre Making MA

Biosciences

Biochemistry BSc(Hons),Biology BSc(Hons), Biomedical Engineering BEng(Hons), Biomedical Science BSc(Hons)

Postgraduate courses: Biomedicine MSc, Biotechnology and Bioengineering MSc, Biotechnology and Business MSc, Cancer Biology and Therapeutics MSc, Conservation Biology MSc, Infectious Diseases MSc, Reproductive Medicine: Science and Ethics MSc, Advanced and Specialist Healthcare MSc, Analysis and Intervention in Intellectual and Developmental Disabilities PDip/MSc, Autism Studies PCert/PDip/MA, Biomedicine MSc, Biotechnology and Bioengineering MSc, Biotechnology and Business MSc, Cancer Biology and Therapeutics MSc, Infectious Diseases MSc, Intellectual and Developmental Disabilities PCert/PDip/MA, Intellectual and Developmental Disabilities and Forensic Issues MA, Intellectual and Developmental Disabilities (Distance Learning) PCert/PDip/MA, Reproductive Medicine: Science and Ethics MSc

Business, Accounting, Finance and Marketing

Accounting and Finance BSc(Hons),Accounting and Finance and Economics BSc(Hons), Business and Management BA(Hons), Business (top-up) BA(Hons), Chartered Manager BSc(Hons), Economics and Management BA(Hons), English Language and Linguistics and Management BA(Hons), Finance and Investment BSc(Hons), French and Management BA(Hons), German and Management BA(Hons), Hispanic Studies and Management BA(Hons), International Business BSc(Hons), Italian and Management BA(Hons), Law and Accounting and Finance LLB(Hons), Law and Management LLB(Hons), Management BSc(Hons), Marketing BSc(Hons), Mathematics and Accounting and Finance BA(Hons), Philosophy and Management BA(Hons)

Postgraduate courses: Business Analytics MSc, Conservation Project Management MSc, Digital Marketing and Analytics MSc, Healthcare Management MSc, Human Resource Management MSc, International Business and Management MSc, International Business and Management with a Foreign Language MSc, Logistics and Supply Chain Management MSc, Management MSc, Marketing MSc, Organisational and Business Psychology MSc/PDip/PCert, The Kent MBA, Finance(Finance and Management) MSc, Finance (Finance, Investment and Risk) MSc, Finance (Financial Markets)MSc, Finance (Financial Markets)

[HKBU Dual Award] MSc, Finance (International Banking and Finance) MSc

Computing

Business Information Technology BSc(Hons), Computer Science BSc(Hons), Computer Science (Artificial Intelligence) BSc(Hons), Computer Science for Health BSc(Hons), Computer Science (Networks) BSc(Hons),Computing BSc(Hons), Computing (Consultancy)BSc(Hons),Software Engineering BSc(Hons)
Postgraduate courses: Advanced Computer Science MSc, Advanced Computer Science (Computational Intelligence) MSc, Computer Animation MSc, Computer Science MSc, Cyber Security MSc, Networks and Security MSc

Criminology

Criminal Justice and Criminology BA(Hons), Criminology BA(Hons), Criminology and Cultural Studies BA(Hons), Criminology and Social Policy BA(Hons),Criminology and Sociology BA(Hons), Criminology with Quantitative Research BA(Hons), Law and Criminology LLB(Hons)
Postgraduate course: Criminology MA

Cultural Studies

Criminology and Cultural Studies BA(Hons), Cultural Studies and Comparative Literature BA(Hons), Cultural Studies and Media BA(Hons), Cultural Studies and Media and Journalism BA(Hons), Cultural Studies and Social Anthropology BA(Hons), Film and Cultural Studies BA(Hons)

Digital Arts

Digital Arts BA(Hons), Digital Arts MArt, Multimedia Technology and Design BSc(Hons)

Drama and Theatre

Comparative Literature and Drama BA(Hons), Drama and English and American Literature BA(Hons), Drama and English Language and Linguistics BA(Hons), Drama and Theatre BA(Hons),Drama and Theatre and Art History BA(Hons), Film and Drama BA(Hons), History and Drama BA(Hons)

Economics

Accounting and Finance and Economics BSc(Hons),Economics BSc(Hons), Economics and Management BA(Hons), Economics and Politics BA(Hons), Economics with Econometrics BSc(Hons), Financial Economics BSc(Hons), Financial Economics with Econometrics BSc(Hons), Law and Economics BSc(Hons), Sociology and Economics BA(Hons), Sociology with Quantitative Research BA(Hons)
Postgraduate courses: Development Economics MSc, Economics MSc, Economics and Econometrics MSc, Economics Conversion Programme MSc, Finance

Economics MSc, International Finance and Economics MSc Quantitative Finance and Econometrics MSc

Education

Postgraduate courses: Higher Education PCert/PDip/MA

Engineering and Electronics

Biomedical Engineering BEng(Hons), Computer Systems Engineering BEng(Hons), Computer Systems Engineering MEng, Electronic and Communications Engineering BEng(Hons), Electronic and Communications Engineering MEng, Electronic and Computer Systems (top-up) BEng(Hons),Mechanical Engineering BEng(Hons)
Postgraduate courses: Advanced Communications Engineering (RF Technology and Telecommunications)MSc, Advanced Communications Engineering(Wireless Systems and Networks) MSc, Advanced Electronic Systems Engineering MSc, Architectural Visualisation MA, Computer Animation MSc, Digital Visual Effects MSc, Information Security and Biometrics MSc

English Literature and Comparative Literature

Asian Studies and Comparative Literature BA(Hons),Asian Studies and English and American Literature BA(Hons), Classical & Archaeological Studies and Comparative Literature BA(Hons), Comparative Literature BA(Hons), Comparative Literature and Drama BA(Hons), Comparative Literature and English Language and Linguistics BA(Hons), Comparative Literature and English Literature BA(Hons), Comparative Literature and Film BA(Hons), Comparative Literature and French with a Year Abroad BA(Hons),Comparative Literature and German with a Year Abroad BA(Hons), Comparative Literature and Hispanic Studies BA(Hons), Comparative Literature and Italian with a Year Abroad BA(Hons), Contemporary Literature BA(Hons), Cultural Studies and Comparative Literature BA(Hons), Drama and English and American Literature BA(Hons), English, American and Postcolonial Literature and Film BA(Hons), English and American Literature BA(Hons), English and American Literature and Film BA(Hons), English and American Literature and French BA(Hons), English and American Literature and Journalism BA(Hons), English and American Literature and Philosophy BA(Hons), English and American Literature and Religious Studies BA(Hons), English and American Literature and Sociology BA(Hons),English and American Literature with an Approved Year Abroad BA(Hons)
Postgraduate courses: Comparative Literature MA, Critical Theory MA, European Culture MA, French

and Comparative Literature MA, Applied Linguistics with TESOL (Teaching English to Speakers of Other Languages) MA, Creative Writing MA, Critical Theory MA, Dickens and Victorian Culture MA, Eighteenth-Century Studies MA, English and American Literature MA, Language and Literature MA, Linguistics MA, Medieval and Early Modern Studies MA, Postcolonial Studies MA, The Contemporary MA

Film

Classical and Archaeological Studies and Film BA(Hons), Comparative Literature and Film BA(Hons), English, American and Postcolonial Literature and Film BA(Hons), English and American Literature and Film BA(Hons), Film BA(Hons), Film and Cultural Studies BA(Hons), Film and Drama BA(Hons), Film and Philosophy BA(Hons), History and Film BA(Hons)

Health and Social Care

Autism Studies BSc(Hons)/DipHE/Cert/GDip, Health and Social Care BA(Hons), Positive Behaviour Support Diploma/BSc(Hons)/Cert/DipHE/GDip Social Work BA(Hons)

Postgraduate course: Advanced Child Protection PCert/PDip/MA

History

Ancient History BA(Hons), Ancient, Medieval and Modern History BA(Hons),Asian Studies and Classical & Archaeological Studies BA(Hons), Classical and Archaeological Studies BA(Hons), Classical & Archaeological Studies and Comparative Literature BA(Hons), Classical and Archaeological Studies and Film BA(Hons), Classical and Archaeological Studies and Italian BA(Hons), Classical and Archaeological Studies and Philosophy BA(Hons), Classical Studies BA(Hons), French and History BA(Hons), German and History BA(Hons), Hispanic Studies and History BA(Hons), History BA(Hons), History and Drama BA(Hons), History and English, American and Postcolonial Literatures BA(Hons),History and English and American Literature BA(Hons), History and English Language and Linguistics BA(Hons), History and Film BA(Hons), History and Italian BA(Hons), History and Philosophy BA(Hons), History and Politics BA(Hons), History and Religious Studies BA(Hons), History and Social Anthropology BA(Hons), Law and History LLB(Hons)

Postgraduate courses: Ancient History MA, Archaeology MA, First World War Studies MA, Heritage Management MA, History and Philosophy of Art MA, History of Medicine and Health MA, Imperial History MA, International Heritage and Law MA,

Medieval and Early Modern Studies MA, Modern History MA, Roman History and Archaeology MA, War, Media and Society MA

Journalism

Cultural Studies and Media and Journalism BA(Hons), Cultural Studies and Media with Journalism BA(Hons), English and American Literature and Journalism BA(Hons), Journalism BA(Hons)

Postgraduate courses: International Multimedia Journalism MA, Multimedia Journalism MA

Languages and Linguistics

Art History and French BA(Hons), Asian Studies and Classical & Archaeological Studies BA(Hons), Asian Studies and Comparative Literature BA(Hons), Asian Studies and English and American Literature BA(Hons), Asian Studies and English Language and Linguistics BA(Hons), Asian Studies and French BA(Hons),Asian Studies and German BA(Hons), Asian Studies and Philosophy BA(Hons), Asian Studies and Religious Studies BA(Hons), Classical and Archaeological Studies and Italian BA(Hons), Comparative Literature and English Language and Linguistics BA(Hons), Comparative Literature and French with a Year Abroad BA(Hons), Comparative Literature and German with a Year Abroad BA(Hons), Comparative Literature and Hispanic Studies BA(Hons), Comparative Literature and Italian with a Year Abroad BA(Hons), Drama and English Language and Linguistics BA(Hons), English and American Literature and French BA(Hons), English Language and Linguistics BA(Hons), English Language and Linguistics and French BA(Hons), English Language and Linguistics and German BA(Hons), English Language and Linguistics and Hispanic Studies BA(Hons), English Language and Linguistics and Italian BA(Hons), English Language and Linguistics and Management BA(Hons), English Literature and English Language and Linguistics BA(Hons), European Studies (Combined Languages) BA(Hons), European Studies (French) BA(Hons), European Studies (German) BA(Hons), European Studies (Italian) BA(Hons), European Studies (Spanish) BA(Hons), French BA(Hons), French and German BA(Hons), French and Hispanic Studies BA(Hons), French and History BA(Hons), French and Italian BA(Hons), French and Management BA(Hons), French and Philosophy BA(Hons), German BA(Hons), German and Hispanic Studies BA(Hons), German and Italian BA(Hons), German and History BA(Hons), German and Management BA(Hons), German and Philosophy BA(Hons), Hispanic Studies BA(Hons), Hispanic Studies and

English and American Literature BA(Hons), Hispanic Studies and History BA(Hons), Hispanic Studies and Management BA(Hons), History and English Language and Linguistics BA(Hons), History and Italian BA(Hons), Italian BA(Hons), Italian and Hispanic Studies BA(Hons), Italian and Management BA(Hons), Philosophy and English Language and Linguistics BA(Hons)

Law

English and French Law LLB(Hons), European Legal Studies LLB(Hons), European Legal Studies with German LLB(Hons), European Legal Studies with Italian LLB(Hons), European Legal Studies with Spanish LLB(Hons), International Legal Studies with a Year Abroad LLB(Hons), Law LLB(Hons), Law and Accounting and Finance LLB(Hons), Law and Criminology LLB(Hons), Law and Economics LLB(Hons), Law and English Literature BA(Hons), Law and History LLB(Hons), Law and Management LLB(Hons), Law and Philosophy LLB(Hons), Law and Politics LLB(Hons), Law and Social Anthropology LLB(Hons), Law and Sociology LLB(Hons), Law Certificate LLB(Hons), Law (Senior Status)LLB(-Hons), Law with a Language (French)LLB(Hons), Law with a Language (German)LLB(Hons), Law with a Language (Spanish)LLB(Hons), Law with Quantitative Research LLB(Hons)

Postgraduate courses: Criminology MA Human Rights Law LLM, International Law LLM, Law Certificate LLB Two Year Master's in Criminology MA

Liberal Arts

Liberal Arts BA(Hons)

Mathematics, Statistics and Actuarial Sciences

Actuarial Science BSc(Hons), Financial Mathematics BSc(Hons), Mathematics BSc(Hons), Mathematics MMath, Mathematics and Accounting and Finance BA(Hons), Mathematics and Statistics BSc(Hons), Mathematics with Secondary Education (QTS) BSc(Hons)

Postgraduate courses: Actuarial Science PDip, Applied Actuarial Science MSc, International Master's in Mathematics and its Applications MSc, Mathematics and its Applications MSc, Statistical Data Science MSc, Statistics with an Industrial Placement MSc, Statistics with Finance MSc

Music

Music Business and Production BA(Hons), Music, Performance and Production BA(Hons), Music Technology and Audio Production BSc(Hons)

Pharmacy

Pharmacology and Physiology BSc(Hons), Pharmacy MPharm

Postgraduate courses: General Pharmacy Practice PCert/ PDip/MSc, Independent/Supplementary Prescribing PCert, Medicines Optimisation PCert/PDip/MSc

Philosophy

Asian Studies and Philosophy BA(Hons), Classical and Archaeological Studies and Philosophy BA(Hons), English and American Literature and Philosophy BA(Hons), Film and Philosophy BA(Hons), French and Philosophy BA(Hons), German and Philosophy BA(Hons), History and Philosophy BA(Hons), Law and Philosophy BA(Hons), Philosophy BA(Hons), Philosophy and Art History BA(Hons), Philosophy and English Language and Linguistics BA(Hons), Philosophy and Management BA(Hons), Philosophy and Politics BA(Hons), Philosophy and Religious Studies BA(Hons), Philosophy and Sociology BA(Hons)

Postgraduate courses: Medical Humanities MA, Philosophy MA

Physical Sciences

Astronomy, Space Science and Astrophysics BSc(Hons), Astronomy, Space Science and Astrophysics MPhys, Chemistry BSc(Hons), Chemistry MChem, Forensic Science BSc(Hons), Forensic Science MSci, Physics BSc(Hons), Physics MPhys, Physics with Astrophysics BSc(Hons), Physics with Astrophysics MPhys

Postgraduate courses: Forensic Science MSc, Physics (Euromasters) MSc

Politics and International Relations

Economics and Politics BA(Hons), History and Politics BA(Hons), Law and Politics LLB(Hons), Philosophy and Politics BA(Hons), Politics BA(Hons), Politics and International Relations BA(Hons), Politics and International Relations(Bi-diploma) BA(Hons), Politics and International Relations with a Language BA(Hons), Politics and International Relations with Quantitative Research BA(Hons), Social Anthropology and Politics BA(Hons), Social Policy and Politics BA(Hons), Sociology and Politics BA(Hons), War and Conflict BA(Hons)

Postgraduate courses: EU External Relations MA, EU International Relations and Diplomacy PDip/MA, International Conflict Analysis PDip/MA, International Conflict and Security MA, International Development MA, International Migration MA, International Political Economy MA, International Relations PDip/MA, International Relations with International

Law PDip/MA, Peace and Conflict Studies (International Joint Award) MA, Political Strategy and Communication MA, Security and Terrorism PDip/MA

Psychology

Business Psychology BSc(Hons), Psychology BSc(Hons), Psychology with Clinical Psychology BSc(Hons), Psychology with Forensic Psychology BSc(Hons), Social Psychology BSc(Hons)

Postgraduate courses: Cognitive Psychology/Neuropsychology MSc, Developmental Psychology MSc, Forensic Psychology MSc, Organisational Psychology PCert/PDip/MSc, Political Psychology MSc, Social and Applied Psychology MSc

Religious Studies

Asian Studies and Religious Studies BA(Hons), English and American Literature and Religious Studies BA(Hons), Global Philosophies BA(Hons), History and Religious Studies BA(Hons), Philosophy and Religious Studies BA(Hons), Religious Studies BA(Hons)

Postgraduate course: Religion MA

Sociology and Social Policy

Criminology and Social Policy BA(Hons), English and American Literature and Sociology BA(Hons),- Law and Sociology LLB(Hons), Philosophy and Sociology BA(Hons), Positive Behaviour Support GDip, Social Anthropology and Social Policy BA(Hons), Social Policy BA(Hons), Social Policy and Politics BA(Hons), Social Policy and Sociology BA(Hons),Social Policy with Quantitative Research BA(Hons),Social Sciences BSc(Hons), Sociology BA(Hons),Sociology and Economics BA(Hons), Sociology and Politics BA(Hons), Sociology and Social Anthropology BA(Hons), Sociology with Quantitative Research BA(Hons)

Postgraduate courses: Analysis and Intervention in Intellectual and Developmental Disabilities PDip/MSc, Applied Behaviour Analysis PCert/PDip/MSc, Autism Studies PCert/PDip/MA, Intellectual and Developmental Disabilities PCert/PDip/MA, Intellectual and Developmental Disabilities and Forensic Issues MSc, Political Sociology MA, Positive Behaviour Support PDip/MSc, Social Work MA, Sociology MA

Sports and Exercise Sciences

Sport and Exercise for Health BSc(Hons), Sport and Exercise Science BSc(Hons), Sport Management BA(Hons), Sports Therapy and Rehabilitation BSc(Hons)

Postgraduate course: Sport and Exercise Science MSc

KINGSTON UNIVERSITY
www.kingston.ac.uk

Kingston School of Art; fada.kingston.ac.uk

Architecture BA(Hons), Creative and Cultural Industries: Art Direction BA(Hons), Creative and Cultural Industries: Curation, Exhibition and Events BA(Hons), Creative and Cultural Industries: Design Marketing BA(Hons), Creative Writing and Film Cultures BA(Hons), Drama and Film Cultures BA(Hons), Fashion BA(Hons), Filmmaking BA(Hons), Fine Art BA(Hons), Fine Art & Art History BA(Hons), Graphic Design BA(Hons), Historic Building Conservation FdSc and BSc(Hons), Illustration Animation BA(Hons), Interior Design BA(Hons), Photography BA(Hons), Product & Furniture Design BA(Hons)

Postgraduate courses: Aesthetics and Art Theory MA, Architecture (ARB/RIBA Part 2) MArch, Art Market & Appraisal (Professional Practice) MA, Communication Design: Graphic Design MA, Communication Design: Illustration MA, Computer Animation MA, Curating Contemporary Design(in partnership with the Design Museum) MA, Experimental Film MA, Fashion MA, Fine Art MFA, Graduate Diploma Creative Practice, Historic Building Conservation MSc, Landscape Architecture MLA (LI accredited),Landscape Architecture PgDip (LI accredited), Landscape and Urbanism MA, Managing in the Creative Economy MA, Museum and Gallery Studies MA, Photography MA, Product & Furniture Design MA, Professional Practice Architecture (ARB/RIBA Part 3 exemption) PgDip, Project Management for Creative Practitioners MSc, Sustainable Design MA

Faculty of Business and Social Sciences; fass.kingston.ac.uk

Business Economics BSc(Hons), Creative and Professional Writing BA(Hons), Creative Writing and Film Cultures BA(Hons), Criminology BSc(Hons) Criminology and Forensic Psychology BSc(Hons), Criminology and International Relations BSc(Hons), Criminology and Sociology BSc(Hons), Dance BA(Hons),

Dance and Drama BA(Hons), Drama BA(Hons), Drama and Creative Writing BA(Hons), Drama and English BA(Hons), Drama and Theatre Arts BA(Hons), English and Creative Writing BA(Hons), Economics BSc(Hons),English Language & Linguistics BA(Hons), English Literature BA(Hons), Financial Economics BSc(Hons), Forensic Psychology BSc(Hons), Global Politics and International Relations BA(Hons), History BA(Hons), Human Rights and Criminology BA(Hons), Human Rights and Sociology BA(Hons), Human Rights and Social Justice BA(Hons), Human Rights and Sociology BA(Hons), International Law LLB(Hons), International Relations BSc(Hons), Journalism BA(Hons), Journalism and Media BA(Hons), Law LLB(Hons), Media Skills BA(Hons), Media & Communication BA(Hons),Music Technology BA(Hons), Politics & International Relations BA(Hons), Popular Music BA(Hons), Psychology with Sociology BSc(Hons), Psychology with Criminology BSc(Hons), Psychology with Sociology BSc(Hons),Publishing BA(Hons), Sociology BSc(Hons),Sociology and International Relations BSc(Hons)

Postgraduate courses: Aesthetics and Art Theory MA, Applied Linguistics for TESOL MA, Behavioural Decision Science MSc, Child Psychology MSc, Clinical Applications of Psychology MSc, Composing for Film and Television MMus, Contemporary European Philosophy MA, Creative Writing and Publishing MA, Creative Writing Distance Learning MA, Creative Writing MA, Creative Writing MFA, Criminology MA, Criminology with Forensic Psychology MA, Development and International Economics MA, English Literature MA, Film Studies MA, Financial Economics MA, Forensic Psychology MSc, Gender Without Borders MA, General Law LLM, History MA, Human Rights MA, International Conflict MSc, International Politics and Economics MA, International Relations MSc, Journalism PgDip/MA, Literature and Philosophy MA, Magazine Journalism MA, Media and Communication MA, Modern European Philosophy MA, Music Education MA, Music MA, Music Performance MMus, Philosophy and Contemporary Critical Theory MA, Philosophy MPhil Stud, Political Economy MA, Production of Popular Music MMus, Psychology MSc, Publishing MA, Terrorism and Political Violence MSc

Kingston Business School; business.kingston.ac.uk

Accounting & Finance with Business Experience BSc(Hons), Business Finance BA(Hons), Business Management with Business Experience BSc(Hons) and choice of specialisms, Business Psychology BSc(Hons), Digital Business BSc(Hons), Entrepreneurship and Innovation Management BSc(Hons), Human Resource Management BA(Hons), International Business with Business Experience BSc(Hons), Marketing Management BA(Hons), Marketing & Advertising with Business Experience BSc(Hons), Real Estate Management with Business Experience BSc(Hons)

Postgraduate courses: Accounting and Finance MSc, Banking and Finance MSc Behavioural Decision Science MSc, Business and Management MRes, Creative Industries & the Creative Economy MA, Finance MSc, Financial and Business Management MSc, Human Resource Management MSc, Innovation Management & Entrepreneurship MSc, International Business Management MSc, International Business Management with Entrepreneurship MSc, International Business Management with Marketing MSc, International Business Management with Project Management MSc, International Human Resource Management MSc, Investment and Financial Risk Management MSc, Leadership and Management in Health PgCert/PgDip/MSc top-up/MSc, Logistics and Supply Chain Management MSc, Marketing and Strategy MSc, Marketing Communications and Advertising MSc, Marketing & Brand Management MSc, Master of Business Administration MBA, Occupational and Business Psychology MSc, Public Relations and Corporate Communications MA, Real Estate MSc

Faculty of Health, Social Care and Education www.healthcare.ac.uk

Adult Nursing BSc(Hons), Children's Nursing BSc(Hons), Early Years FdA, Early Years: Education & Leadership in Practice BA(Hons) top up, Early Years: Leadership & Management FdA, Early Years: Teaching & Learning BA(Hons) top-up, Healthcare Practice DipHE and BSc(Hons), Healthcare Practice FdSc, Learning Disability Nursing BSc(Hons), Mental Health Nursing BSc(Hons), Midwifery/Registered Midwife BSc(Hons), Midwifery/Registered Midwife for Registered Nurses BSc(Hons), Occupational Therapy BSc(Hons), Paramedic Practice BSc(Hons),Paramedic Science BSc(Hons), Physical Education, Sport and Activity (PESA) FdA, Physiotherapy BSc(Hons), Primary Teaching leading to Qualified Teacher Status BA(Hons), Radiography, Diagnostic BSc(Hons), Radiography, Therapeutic BSc(Hons),Social Work BA(Hons), Special Educational Needs Inclusive

Practice FdA, Working with Children and Young People : Social Pedagogy BA(Hons)

Postgraduate courses: Adult Nursing PgDip, Advanced Social Work MA, Applied Exercise for Health PgCert/PgDip/MSc, Children's Nursing PgDip, Clinical Leadership MSc, Clinical Research MClinRes Early Years Teacher Birth to 5 leading to Early Years Teacher Status (EYTS) PGCE, Education MRes, Healthcare Practice, PgCert/PgDip/MSc, Leadership and Management in Social Care PgCert, Learning Disability Nursing MSc, Mental Health Nursing MSc, Midwifery/Registered Midwife PgDip, Midwifery/Registered Midwife for Registered Nurses PgDip, Physiotherapy MSc, Practice Education PgCert, Primary Teaching leading to Qualified Teacher Status (QTS) PGCE, Professional Education and Training PgCert/PgDip/MA, Radiography: Breast Evaluation PgCert/PgDip/MSc, Radiography: Medical Imaging PgCert/PgDip/MSc, Radiography: Medical Imaging (Mammography) PgCert/PgDip/MSc, Radiography: Oncology Practice PgCert/PgDip/MSc, Rehabilitation PgCert/PgDip/MSc, Secondary Teaching leading to Qualified Teacher Status(QTS) PGCE, Master of Social Work MSW

Faculty of Science, Engineering and Computing; sec.kingston.ac.uk

Aerospace Engineering, Astronautics & Space Technology MEng/BEng(Hons), Aerospace Engineering MEng/BEng(Hons), Aircraft Engineering BEng(Hons), Aircraft Engineering BEng(Hons) top-up, Aviation Engineering BEng(Hons), Aviation Operations with Commercial Pilot Training BSc(Hons), Biochemistry BSc(Hons), Biological Sciences BSc(Hons), Biological Sciences (Genetics and Molecular Biology)BSc(Hons), Biological Sciences (Human Biology)BSc(Hons), Biological Sciences (Medical Biology) BSc(Hons), Biomedical Science BSc(Hons), Building Surveying BSc(Hons), Chemistry BSc(Hons), Chemistry MChem(Hons), Civil and Infrastructure Engineering BEng(Hons), Computer Games Programming BSc(Hons) Computer Science BSc(Hons), Computing and Mathematics foundation year, Construction Management BSc(Hons), Cyber Security & Computer Forensics BSc(Hons), Digital Media Technology BSc(Hons), Engineering Foundation with pathways in Aerospace, Civil, Mechanical Engineering, Environmental Science BSc(Hons), Environmental Science with Hazards & Disaster Management BSc(Hons), Environmental Management BSc(Hons), Forensic Science BSc(Hons), Geography BSc(Hons), Human Geography BA(Hons), International Foundation Year (delivered by Study Group), Mathematics BSc(Hons), Mechanical Engineering MEng/BEng(Hons), Nutrition (Exercise and Health) BSc(Hons),Nutrition (Human Nutrition) BSc(Hons), Pharmaceutical Science BSc(Hons), Pharmaceutical Science MPharmSci(Hons), Pharmaceutical Science with Regulatory Affairs BSc(Hons), Pharmaceutical & Chemical Sciences FdSc, Pharmacology BSc(Hons), Pharmacy MPharm(Hons), Quantity Surveying Consultancy BSc(Hons), Science foundation year, Sport Coaching FdSc, Sport Science BSc(Hons), Sport Science (Coaching)BSc(Hons),Sport & Exercise Science FdSc

Postgraduate courses: Advanced Industrial & Manufacturing Systems MSc, Advanced Product Design Engineering & Manufacturing MSc, Aerospace Engineering MSc, Aerospace Systems MSc, Analytical Chemistry MSc, Biomedical Science with Management Studies MSc, Biomedical Science (Haematology/Medical Microbiology) MSc, Building Surveying MSc, Cancer Biology MSc, Computer Animation MA, Environmental Management MSc, Environmental Management (Energy) MSc, Forensic Analysis MSc, Game Development (Design) MA, Game Development (Programming) MSc, Geographical Information Systems & Science MSc, Information Systems MSc, International Enterprise Information Management MSc, IT & Strategic Innovation MSc, Management in Construction MSc, Management in Construction (Civil Engineering) MSc, Mechanical Engineering MSc, Mechatronic Systems MSc, Network & Information Security MSc, Network & Information Security with Management Studies MSc, Networking & Data Communications MSc, Networking & Data Communications with Management Studies MSc, Pharmaceutical Analysis MSc, Pharmaceutical Analysis with Management Studies MSc, Pharmaceutical Science MSc, Pharmaceutical Science with Management Studies MSc, Pharmacy Practice (Overseas Pharmacists Assessment Programme) PgDip/MSc top-up, Professional Engineering MSc, Quantity Surveying MSc, Renewable Energy Engineering MSc, Software Engineering MSc, Software Engineering with Management Studies MSc, Structural Design & Construction Management MSc, Structural Design & Construction Management with Sustainability MSc Technology (Maritime Operations) MSc, User Experience Design MSc

LANCASTER UNIVERSITY
www.lancaster.ac.uk

Faculty of Arts and Social Sciences; www.lancaster.ac.uk/arts-and-socialsciences

Department of English Literature and Creative Writing; www.lancaster.ac.uk/english-literature-and-creative-writing

English Literature BA(Hons), English Literature and History BA(Hons), English Literature and Linguistics BA(Hons), English Literature and Philosophy BA(Hons), English Literature and Religious Studies BA(Hons), English Literature with Creative Writing BA(Hons), English Literature, Creative Writing and Practice BA(Hons)]

Postgraduate courses: MA in English Literary Research, MA in English Literary Studies, MA in English Literary Studies with Creative Writing

Department of History; www.lancaster.ac.uk/history

History BA(Hons), History and International Relations BA(Hons), History and Philosophy BA(Hons), History and Politics BA(Hons), History and Religious Studies BA(Hons), History, Philosophy and Politics BA(Hons), Medieval and Early Modern Studies BA(Hons)

Postgraduate course: MA Digital Humanities, MA History, MA International and Military History

Lancashire Institute for the Contemporary Arts; www.lancaster.ac.uk/lica

Architecture BA(Hons), Design BA(Hons), Drama, Theatre and Performance BA(Hons), Film Studies BA(Hons), Film and Creative Writing BA(Hons), Film and English Literature BA(Hons), Film and Philosophy BA(Hons), Film and Sociology BA(Hons), Film and Theatre BA(Hons), Film, Media and Cultural Studies BA(Hons), Fine Art BA(Hons), Fine Art and Creative Writing BA(Hons), Fine Art and Film BA(Hons), Fine Art and Theatre BA(Hons), Marketing and Design BSc(Hons), Theatre and Creative Writing BA(Hons), Theatre and English Literature BA(Hons)

Postgraduate courses: Architecture MArch, Arts Management MA, Design Management MA

Department of Languages and Cultures; www.lancaster.ac.uk/languages-andcultures

French Studies BA(Hons), French Studies and Computing BSc(Hons), French Studies and English Literature BA(Hons), French Studies and Film BA(Hons), French Studies and Geography BA(Hons), French Studies and German Studies BA(Hons), French Studies and History BA(Hons), French Studies and Linguistics BA(Hons), French Studies and Mathematics BA(Hons), French Studies and Philosophy BA(Hons), French Studies and Politics BA(Hons), French Studies and Spanish Studies BA(Hons), French Studies and Theatre BA(Hons), French Studies with Chinese BA(Hons), French Studies with Italian BA(Hons), German Studies BA(Hons), German Studies and Computing BSc(Hons), German Studies and English Literature BA(Hons), German Studies and Film BA(Hons), German Studies and Geography BA(Hons), German Studies and History BA(Hons), German Studies and Linguistics BA(Hons), German Studies and Mathematics BA(Hons), German Studies and Philosophy BA(Hons), German Studies and Politics BA(Hons), German Studies and Spanish Studies BA(Hons), German Studies and Theatre BA(Hons), German Studies with Chinese BA(Hons), German Studies with Italian BA(Hons), Linguistics with Chinese BA(Hons), Management Studies and European Languages BA(Hons), Modern Languages BA(Hons), Modern Languages and Cultures MLang(Hons), Spanish Studies BA(Hons), Spanish Studies and Computing BSc(Hons), Spanish Studies and English Literature BA(Hons), Spanish Studies and Film BA(Hons), Spanish Studies and Geography BA(Hons), Spanish Studies and History BA(Hons), Spanish Studies and Linguistics BA(Hons), Spanish Studies and Mathematics BA(Hons), Spanish Studies and Philosophy BA(Hons), Spanish Studies and Politics BA(Hons), Spanish Studies and Theatre BA(Hons), Spanish Studies with Chinese BA(Hons), Spanish Studies with Italian BA(Hons)

Postgraduate courses: MA in Translation, MA in Languages and Cultures, European Languages and Cultures MPhil/PhD

Law School; www.lancaster.ac.uk/law

Law LLB(Hons), Law with Criminology LLB(Hons), Law with Politics LLB(Hons), Law (Clinical Learning) LLB(Hons), Law (International Law) LLB(Hons), Criminology BA(Hons), Criminology and French Studies BA(Hons), Criminology and Law BA(Hons), Criminology and Psychology BA(Hons), Criminology and Sociology BA(Hons)

Postgraduate courses: LLM Law, PGDip Law, LLM International Business and Corporate Law, LLM International Human Rights Law, LLM International Human Rights and Terrorism Law, LLM International Law, LLM Criminology and Criminal Justice, MA Criminology and Criminal Justice, MSc Criminal Justice and Social Research Methods, MSc Criminology and Social Research Methods

Department of Linguistics and English Language; www.lancaster.ac.uk/linguistics

English Language BA(Hons), English Language (Study Abroad) BA(Hons), English Language and Creative Writing BA(Hons), English Language and French Studies BA(Hons), English Language and German Studies BA(Hons), English Language and Linguistics BA(Hons), English Language and Literature BA(Hons), English Language and Spanish Studies BA(Hons), English Language in the Media BA(Hons), English Language in the Media (Study Abroad) BA(Hons), English Language with Chinese BA(Hons), English Literature and Linguistics BA(Hons), Linguistics BA(Hons), Linguistics and Philosophy BA(Hons), Linguistics and Psychology BA(Hons), Linguistics with Chinese BA(Hons)

Postgraduate courses: Applied Linguistics and TESOL MA, Discourse Studies MA, English Language (Distance) MA, English Language and Literary Studies MA, Intercultural Communication MA, Language Testing (Distance) MA, Language and Linguistics MA, Language Testing (Distance) MA, Teaching English to Speakers of Other Languages(-TESOL) (by Distance) MA

Department of Politics, Philosophy and Religion; www.lancaster.ac.uk/ppr

Ethics, Philosophy and Religion BA(Hons), International Relations BA(Hons), International Relations and Religious Diversity BA(Hons), Peace Studies and International Relations BA(Hons), Philosophy BA(Hons), Philosophy and Politics BA(Hons), Philosophy and Religious Studies BA(Hons), Philosophy with Chinese BA(Hons), Philosophy, Politics and Economics BA(Hons), Politics BA(Hons), Politics and International Relations BA(Hons), Politics and Religious Studies BA(Hons), Politics and Sociology BA(Hons), Politics with Chinese BA(Hons), Politics, International Relations and Management BSc(Hons), Religious Studies BA(Hons), Religious Studies and Sociology BA(Hons), Religious Studies with Chinese BA(Hons)

Postgraduate courses: Conflict, Development and Security Conflict Resolution and Peace Studies, MA Diplomacy and Foreign Policy, MA Diplomacy and International Law LLM/MA Diplomacy and International Law (Distance Learning) LLM Diplomacy and International Law (Distance Learning) MA Diplomacy and International Relations (Distance Learning), MA Diplomacy and Religion, MA International Law and International Relations LLM International Relations, MA Politics, MA Philosophy MA/PgCert, Philosophy and Religion MA, Politics, Philosophy and Religion, MA Politics and Philosophy MA Religion and Conflict MA MRes International Relations, Politics, Philosophy and Management, MSc Politics, Philosophy and Religion MA Politics and Philosophy MA PGCert Philosophy, Quakerism in the Modern World (Distance Learning), Religion and Conflict, MA Religious Studies, MA/PGCert Religious Studies (Distance Learning), PgCert

Department of Sociology; www.lancaster.ac.uk/sociology

Social Work BA(Hons), Sociology BA(Hons)

Postgraduate courses: Environment, Culture and Society MA, Gender and Womens Studies MA, Gender and Womens Studies and English MA, Gender and Womens Studies and Sociology MA, Media and Cultural Studies MA, Social Research MA, Social Work MA, Sociology MA

Faculty of Health and Medicine; www.lancaster.ac.uk/fhm

Biochemistry BSc(Hons), Biochemistry MSci(Hons), Biology BSc(Hons), Biology MSci(Hons), Biology with Psychology BSc(Hons), Biology with Entrepreneurship BSc(Hons), Biomedical Science BSc(Hons), Biomedicine BSc(Hons), Biomedicine MSci(Hons), Medicine and Surgery MBChB, Sports and Exercise Science BSc(Hons), Zoology BSc(Hons)

Postgraduate courses: Ageing MSc, Biomedicine MSc, Clinical Research MSc, Global Health: translational research and quantitative skills MRes, Health Economics and Policy MSc, Medical Education MSc

Management School;
www.lancaster.ac.uk/lums

Accounting and Finance BSc(Hons), Accounting and Management BSc(Hons), Accounting, Finance and Mathematics BSc(Hons), Advertising and Marketing BA(Hons), logy with Entrepreneurship BSc(Hons), Business Analytics BSc(Hons), Business Economics (Industry) BSc(Hons), Business Management BSc(Hons), Economics BA(Hons)/BSc(Hons), Economics and International Relations BA(Hons), Economics and Mathematics BSc(Hons), Economics and Politics BA(Hons), Finance BSc(Hons), Finance and Economics BSc(Hons), Financial Mathematics BSc(Hons), Financial Mathematics MSci(Hons), International Business Management(France/Germany/ Italy/Mexico/Spain) BSc(Hons), International Management BSc(Hons), Management and Entrepreneurship BSc(Hons), Management and French Studies BA(Hons), Management and German Studies BA(Hons), Management and Spanish Studies BA(Hons), Management and Human Resources BSc(Hons), Management and Information Technology BSc(Hons), Management, Politics and International Relations BSc(Hons), Marketing BSc(Hons), Marketing Management BSc(Hons), Marketing and Design BSc(Hons), Marketing with Psychology BSc(Hons), Mathematics, Operational Research, Statistics and Economics (MORSE) BSc(Hons), Philosophy, Politics and Economics BA(Hons), Politics, International Relations and Management BSc(Hons) Postgraduate courses: MSc Accounting & Financial Management, MSc Advanced Financial Analysis (including CFA training), MSc/MRes Advanced Marketing Management, Business Administration MBA, MSc Business Analytics, MSc E-Business & Innovation, MSc Economics, MSc Entrepreneurship and Innovation MSc Finance, MBA Full-time MBA, MSc Human Resource Management, MA Human Resources and Consulting, MSc/MRes Information Technology, Management & Organisational Change MSc International Business MSc International Business Strategy, MSc Logistics and Supply Chain Management, MSc Management, MRes Management Science, Marketing MSc, MSc Marketing Analytics, MSc Money, Banking and Finance, MSc Politics, Philosophy and Management, MSc Project Management, MSc Quantitative Finance

Faculty of Science and Technology;
www.lancaster.ac.uk/sci-tech

Biology and Biological Sciences

Biology BSc(Hons), Biology MSci(Hons), Biochemistry BSc(Hons), Biochemistry MSci(Hons), Biology with Psychology BSc(Hons), Biochemistry with Genetics BSc(Hons), Biomedical Science BSc(Hons), Biomedicine BSc(Hons), Biomedicine: MSci(Hons),Biology with Entrepreneurship BSc(Hons), Zoology BSc(Hons)

Chemistry

Chemistry BSc(Hons), Chemistry MChem(Hons)

Computing and Communications

Computer Science BSc(Hons), Computer Science and Mathematics BSc(Hons), Computer Science and Mathematics MSci(Hons), Management and Information Technology BSc(Hons), Software Engineering BSc(Hons)

Ecology and Conservation

Ecology and Conservation BSc(Hons)

Engineering

Engineering BEng(Hons), Engineering MEng(Hons), Chemical Engineering BEng(Hons), Chemical Engineering MEng(Hons), Electronic and Electrical Engineering BEng(Hons), Electronic and Electrical Engineering MEng(Hons), Mechanical Engineering BEng(Hons), Mechanical Engineering MEng(Hons), Mechatronics BEng(Hons), Mechatronics MEng(Hons), Nuclear Engineering BEng(Hons), Nuclear Engineering MEng(Hons)

Environmental and Earth Sciences

Earth and Environmental Science BSc(Hons), Earth and Environmental Science MSci(Hons), Environmental Science BSc(Hons), Environmental Science MSci(Hons)

Geography

Geography BA(Hons), Geography BSc(Hons), Geography MArts(Hons), Geography MSci(Hons), Geography and Economics BA(Hons), Human Geography BA(Hons), Physical Geography BSc(Hons), Physical Geography MSci(Hons)

Mathematics and Statistics

Mathematics BSc(Hons), Mathematics MSci(Hons), Mathematics and Philosophy BA(Hons), Mathematics with Statistics BSc(Hons), Mathematics with Statistics MSci(Hons), Mathematics, Operational Research, Statistics and Economics (MORSE) BSc(Hons), Theoretical Physics with Mathematics BSc(Hons), Theoretical Physics with Mathematics MSci(Hons), Financial Mathematics BSc(Hons), Financial Mathematics MSci(Hons)

Natural Sciences

Natural Sciences BSc(Hons), Natural Sciences MSci(Hons)

Physics

Physics BSc(Hons), Physics MPhys(Hons), Physics with Particle Physics and Cosmology BSc(Hons), Physics with Particle Physics and Cosmology MPhys(Hons), Physics, Astrophysics and Cosmology BSc(Hons), Physics, Astrophysics and Cosmology MPhys(Hons), Theoretical Physics BSc(Hons), Theoretical Physics MPhys(Hons), Theoretical Physics with Mathematics BSc(Hons), Theoretical Physics with Mathematics MSci(Hons)

Psychology

Psychology BA(Hons), Psychology BSc(Hons), Psychology MPsych(Hons), Psychology and French Studies BA(Hons), Psychology and Spanish Studies BA(Hons)

Postgraduate courses

Computer Science MSc, Conservation and Biodiversity MSc, Cyber Security MSc, Data Science MSc, Developmental Disorders MSc, Developmental Psychology MSc, Electronic Engineering MSc, Engineering Project Management MSc, Environment and Development MSc, Environment and Development MA, Environment, Culture and Society MA, Environmental Management MSc, Flood and Coastal Risk Management MSc, Food Security (Distance Learning) MSc Mechanical Engineering MSc, Mechanical Engineering with Project Management MSc, Psychological Research Methods MSc, Psychology of Advertising MSc, Quantitative Finance MSc, Statistics MSc, Statistics and Operational Research (STOR-i) MRes, Sustainable Water Management MSc, Volcanology and Geological Hazards MSc

---

BLACKPOOL AND THE FYLDE COLLEGE
www.blackpool.ac.uk

Accounting and Finance

Accounting Level 4 Higher Apprenticeship (AAT)

Administration

Business Administration Level 4 Higher Apprenticeship (OCR), Human Resource Management Level 5 Diploma (CIPD)

Architecture and Advanced Construction

Construction and the Built Environment HNC (Edexcel)

Automotive and Motorsport

Automotive Engineering and Technology (Automotive) BEng(Hons), Automotive Engineering and Technology (Automotive) FdA, Automotive Engineering and Technology (Motorsport) BEng(Hons), Automotive Engineering and Technology (Motorsport) FdA, Automotive Engineering and Technology with Foundation Year (Automotive) FdA, Automotive Engineering and Technology with Foundation Year (Motorsport) FdA

Building and Construction

Civil Engineering HNC (Edexcel)

Business and Project Management

Business and Financial Management BA(Hons), Business and Financial Management FdA, Human Resource Management Level 5 Intermediate Diploma (CIPD), Management FdA, Management and Leadership Level 5 Higher Apprenticeship (OCR), Management in the Workplace BA(Hons), Project Management BSc(Hons), Project Management FdA, Project Management Level 4 Higher Apprenticeship (EAL)

Child Development and Wellbeing

Early Childhood Studies BA(Hons), Early Childhood Studies Level 5 FdA, Family Support and Wellbeing BA(Hons), Family Support and Wellbeing FdA, Youth Studies FdA

Computing-Digital Media and ICT

Computer Science and Digital Technologies FdA, Computing HNC, Digital and Technology Solutions (Cyber Security Analyst) Apprenticeship, Digital and Technology Solutions (Network Engineer) Apprenticeship, Digital and Technology Solutions (Software Engineering) Apprenticeship, Network Engineering (Cyber Security) BSc(Hons), Network Engineering (Cyber Security) FdA, Network Engineering (Systems Administration) BSc(Hons), Network Engineering (Systems Administration) FdA, Software Engineering (App Development) BSc(Hons) Software Engineering (Game Development) BSc(Hons),Web Technologies and Digital Media FdA

Creative Arts, Design and Crafts

Fashion Design (Contemporary Costume) BA(Hons), Fashion Design BA(Hons), Fine Art Professional Practice BA(Hons), Graphic Design BA(Hons), Photography BA(Hons)

Criminology and Criminal Justice
Criminology and Criminal Justice BA(Hons), Criminology and Criminal Justice FdA

Engineering
Aerospace Engineering Degree Apprenticeship Electrical and Electronic Engineering HNC (Edexcel), Engineering (Aerospace) BEng(Hons), Engineering (Mechanical) BEng(Hons), Engineering (Mechatronics) BEng(Hons), General Engineering HNC (Edexcel), Mechanical Engineering HNC (Edexcel)

Health and Medical Professions
Health and Social Care BA(Hons) Topup, Health and Social Care FdA

Hospitality and Catering
Hospitality and Events Management BA(Hons), Hospitality and Events Management FdA

Learning Support
Teaching and Learning Support BA(Hons), Teaching and Learning Support FdA

Media Production, Film and Television
English: Language, Literature and Writing BA(Hons), Filmmaking BA(Hons)

Performing Arts and Music
Musical Theatre BA(Hons)

Public Services
Public Services BA(Hons) Topup, Public Services FdA

Science
Human Biosciences BSc(Hons), Top up Human Biosciences FdA, Marine Biology FdA, Marine Biology and Coastal Zone Management BSc(Hons), Materials Science Degree Apprenticeship

Sport, Leisure and Recreation
Physical Activity, Health and Nutrition BSc(Hons), Physical Activity, Health and Nutrition FdA, Sports Coaching and Performance Science BSc(Hons), Sports Coaching and Performance Science FdA

Teacher Training
Post Graduate Certificate in Education Level 7 PGCE

Travel and Tourism
Tourism Management BA(Hons) Top-up, Tourism Management FdA

UNIVERSITY OF LEEDS
www.leeds.ac.uk

Faculty of Arts, Humanities and Cultures; www.leeds.ac.uk/info/130500/faculties

Faculty of Arts; www.leeds.ac.uk/arts

BA Arabic and Islamic Studies, BA Arabic and Middle Eastern Studies UG, BA Asia Pacific Studies, BA Asia Pacific Studies (International), BA Biomedical and Health Care Ethics, BA Chinese (Modern), BA Classical Civilisation, BA Chinese and East Asian Religions and Cultures, BA East Asian Religions and Cultures, BA English Language and Literature, BA English Literature, BA English Literature and Theatre Studies, BA French, BA German, BA History, BA International History and Politics, BA Islamic Studies, BA Italian, BA Japanese, BA Languages and Cultures, BA Liberal Arts, BA Linguistics and Phonetics, BA Middle Eastern Studies, BA Philosophy, BA Philosophy, Ethics and Religion, BA Russian, BA Spanish, BA Thai Studies, BA Theatre and Performance with Enterprise, BA Theology and Religious Studies, various joint honours options
Postgraduate courses: MA American Literature and Culture PGT, MA Applied and Professional Ethics (Distance Learning) MA Applied Translation Studies, MA Arabic/English Translation, MA Audiovisual Translation Studies, MA Biomedical and Healthcare Ethics, MA Biomedical and Healthcare Ethics (Distance Learning) MA Business and Public Service Interpreting and Translation Studies, MA Chinese and Management, MA Conference Interpreting and Translation Studies, MA Creative Writing and Critical Life, MA East Asian Cultures and Societies, MA East Asian Cultures and Societies (Language Pathway), MA English Literature, MA English Literature (Modern and Contemporary pathway), MA English Literature (Renaissance pathway), MA English Literature (Romantic pathway), MA English Literature (Victorian pathway), MA History of Health, Medicine and Society, MA History of Science, Technology and Medicine, MA in Social and Cultural History, MA Linguistics, MA Linguistics and English Language Teaching, MA Medieval History, MA Medieval Studies, MA Middle Eastern and Islamic Studies, MA Modern History, MA Philosophy, MA Philosophy of Religion and Ethics, MA Postcolonial Literary and Cultural Studies, MA Professional Language and Intercultural Studies, MA Race and Resistance, MA Religion and Public Life, MA Religious Studies and Global Development, MA Theology and Religious

Studies, MA War and Strategy, MA Writing Identities: Critical and Creative Practices, MRes Biomedical and Healthcare Ethics, MRes Classics, MRes East Asian Studies, ND Language for Engineering, ND Language for Science, ND Language for Science: Engineering, ND Language for Science: General Science, PGCert Philosophy of Religion and Ethics, PGCert Theology and Religious Studies, PGDip Applied and Professional Ethics (Online), PGDip Applied Translation Studies, PGDip Biomedical and Health Care Ethics, PGDip Biomedical and Health Care Ethics (Online), PGDip Business and Public Service Interpreting, PGDip Conference Interpreting, PGDip Philosophy of Religion and Ethics, PGDip Theology and Religious Studies

School of Media and Communication; www.media.leeds.ac.uk

BA Communication and Media, BA Digital Media, BA Film, Photography and Media, BA Journalism
Postgraduate courses: MA Communication and Media, MA Film, Photography and Media, MA International Communication, MA International Journalism, MA Media Industries, MA New Media, MA Political Communication, MA Promotional Media

School of Design; www.design.leeds.ac.uk

BA Art and Design, BA Fashion Design, BA Fashion Marketing, BA Fashion Technology, BA Graphic and Communication Design, BA Textile Design
Postgraduate courses: MA Advertising and Design, MA Design, MA Fashion, Enterprise and Society, MA Global Fashion Management, MSc Textiles

School of Fine Art, History of Art and Cultural Studies; www.fine-art.leeds.ac.uk

BA Cultural and Media Studies, BA Fine Art, BA Fine Art with Contemporary Cultural Theory, BA Fine Art with History of Art, BA History of Art, BA History of Art with Cultural Studies
Postgraduate courses: MA Art Gallery and Museum Studies, MA Arts Management and Heritage Studies, MA Critical and Cultural Theory MA Curating Science, MA Fine Art (MAFA), MA Social History of Art

School of Music; www.music.leeds.ac.uk

BA Music, BMus Music (Performance), BA Music with Enterprise, BSc Music, Multimedia and Electronics BSc, BA Music and Psychology, MArts/BA Music and Music Psychology
Postgraduate courses: MA Applied Psychology of Music, MA Critical and Applied Musicology, MMus

Critical and Experimental Composition, MA Electronic and Computer Music, MA Music and Management, MMus Performance, MA/PGCert/PGDip Music and Wellbeing, PGDip Performance, Graduate Diploma in Music

School of Performance and Cultural Industries; www.pci.leeds.ac.uk

BA Theatre and Performance, BA Theatre and Performance with Enterprise
Postgraduate courses: MA Applied Theatre and Intervention, MA Culture, Creativity and Entrepreneurship, MA Performance Design, MA Writing for Performance and Publication, MA/PGDip/PGCert Audiences, Engagement, Participation, PGCert Arts Fundraising and Philanthropy, PGCert Developing Teachers' Research and Practice in Drama

Faculty of Biological Sciences; www.fbs.leeds.ac.uk

BSc Biochemistry, MBiol Biochemistry, BSc Biological Sciences, MBiol Biological Sciences, BSc Biology, MBiol Biology, BSc Biotechnology with Enterprise, MBiol Biotechnology with Enterprise, BSc Ecology and Conservation Biology, MBiol Ecology and Conservation Biology, BSc Genetics, MBiol Genetics, BSc Human Physiology, MBiol Human Physiology, BSc Medical Biochemistry, MBiol Medical Biochemistry, BSc Medical Microbiology, BSc Medical Sciences, MBiol Medical Sciences, BSc Microbiology, MBiol Microbiology, BSc Natural Sciences, BSc Neuroscience, MBiol Neuroscience, BSc Pharmacology, MBiol Pharmacology, BSc Sport and Exercise Sciences, MSci Sport and Exercise Sciences, BSc Sports Science and Physiology, MSci Sports Science and Physiology, BSc Zoology, MBiol Zoology
Postgraduate courses: MSc Biodiversity and Conservation, MSc Biodiversity and Conservation with African Field Course, MRes Biodiversity and Conservation, MRes Biodiversity and Conservation with African Field Course, MSc Biopharmaceutical Development, MSc Bioscience, MSc Infection, Immunity and Human Disease, MNatSc BSc Natural Sciences, MSc Plant Science and Biotechnology, MSc Precision Medicine: Genomics & Analytics, MSc Sport and Exercise Medicine

Faculty of Business; www.business.leeds.ac.uk

BSc Accounting and Finance, BSc Banking and Finance, BSc Business Economics, BSc Business Management and Mathematics, BSc Economics, BSc

Economics and Finance, BSc Economics and Management, BSc Economics and Mathematics, BSc Financial Mathematics, BA Human Resource Management, BSc International Business, BSc International Business and Finance, BSc International Business and Marketing, BA Management, BA Management and the Human Resource, BA Management with Marketing, various joint honours options

Postgraduate courses: Master of Business Administration, MSc Accounting and Finance, MSc Actuarial Finance, MSc Banking and International Finance, MSc Finance and Investment, MSc Financial Mathematics, MSc Financial Risk Management, MSc Economics, MSc Economics and Finance, MSc Business Analytics and Decision Sciences, MSc Business Psychology (also available part-time), MSc Enterprise and Enterpreneurship MSc Global Strategy and Innovation Management, MSc Global Supply Chain Management, MSc Information Systems and Information Management, MSc Management, MSc Management Consulting, MSc Organizational Psychology, MA Human Resource Management (available part-time), MSc International Business, MA Advertising and Marketing, MSc Consumer Analytics and Marketing Strategy, MA Corporate Communications, Marketing and Public Relations, MSc International Marketing Management

Faculty of Education, Social Sciences and Law; *www.essl.leeds.ac.uk*

School of Education; www.education.leeds.ac.uk

BA Childhood Studies, BA Education, BA Teaching English to Speakers of Other Languages (TESOL), BSc Psychology with Education

Postgraduate courses: MA Childhood Studies, MA Education, MA International Education Leadership and Policy, MA Digital Education MA Leadership and Digital Education, MA Special Educational Needs, PGCert Provision for Children with Developmental Disorders, MA/PGDip Deaf Education (Teacher of the Deaf), MA Teaching English to Speakers of Other Languages (TESOL), MEd Teaching English to Speakers of Other Languages (TESOL), MA TESOL Studies, MA Teaching English to Speakers of Other Languages (China), MA Teaching English to Speakers of Other Languages and Information and Communications Technology, MA Teaching English to Speakers of Other Languages for Young Learners, MA Teaching English to Speakers of Other Languages (Teacher Education)

School of Sociology and Social Policy; www.sociology.leeds.ac.uk

BA Sociology, BA Social Policy, BA Social Policy and Crime, BA Social Policy with Enterprise, BA Social Policy and Sociology, BA Sociology and International Relations, various joint honours options

Postgraduate courses: MA Disability Studies, MA Gender Studies, MSc Inequalities and Social Science, MPA Public Administration, MA Social and Political Thought, MA Social and Public Policy, MA Social Research, MA Society, Culture and Media

School of Politics and International Studies; www.polis.leeds.ac.uk

BA Economics and Politics, BA International Development, BA International Relations, BA Politics

Postgraduate courses: MA Conflict, Development and Security, MA Global Development, MA Global Governance and Diplomacy, MA International Relations, MA International Relations and Politics of the Middle East, MSc Political Science, MA Security, Terrorism and Insurgency

School of Law; www.law.leeds.ac.uk

LLB Law, LLB Law with European Legal Studies, LLB Law with International Legal Studies, LLB Law with French Law, LLB Law with German Law, LLB Law with Hispanic Law, BA Criminal Justice and Criminology

Postgraduate courses: LLM Criminal Justice and Criminal Law, MSc Criminal Justice and Criminology, LLM Intellectual Property Law, LLM International Banking and Finance Law, LLM International Business Law, LLM International Corporate Law, LLM International Human Rights Law, LLM International Law, LLM International Trade Law, LLB Law (graduate programme), LLM Law and Social Justice, MSc Law and Finance, MSc Security, Conflict and Justice

Faculty of Engineering; *www.engineering.leeds.ac.uk*

School of Chemical and Process Engineering; www.engineering.leeds.ac.uk/ info/20135/ school_of_chemical_and_ process_engineering

Aviation Technology and Management BSc, Aviation Technology with Pilot Studies BSc, Aviation Technology with Pilot Studies and Management BEng, Chemical Engineering MEng/BEng, Chemical and Energy Engineering MEng/BEng, Chemical and

Materials Engineering MEng/BEng, Chemical and Nuclear Engineering MEng/BEng, Petroleum Engineering MEng/BEng

Postgraduate courses: Advanced Chemical Engineering MSc, Chemical Process Engineering MSc, Energy and Environment MSc, Materials Science and Engineering MSc, Petroleum Production Engineering MSc

School of Civil Engineering; www.engineering.leeds.ac.uk/info/20131/ schoolofcivil-engineering

Architectural Engineering MEng/BEng, Architecture MEng/BEng, Civil Engineering MEng/BEng, Civil and Environmental Engineering MEng/BEng, Civil and Structural Engineering MEng/ BEng, Civil Engineering with Project Management MEng/BEng, Civil Engineering with Transport MEng/BEng

Postgraduate courses: Advanced Concrete Technology MSc (Eng), Advanced Concrete Technology PGDip, Engineering Project Management MSc (Eng), Environmental Engineering and Project Management MSc (Eng), Geotechnical Engineering MSc(Eng), International Construction Management and Engineering MSc (Eng), Railway Engineering with Project Management MSc(Eng), Structural Engineering MSc (Eng), Transport Infrastructure: Design and Construction MSc(Eng), Water, Sanitation and Health Engineering MSc (Eng), Engineering Management MSc/PGCert (online)

School of Computing; www.engineering.leeds.ac.uk/info/20132/ school_of_computing

Computer Science MEng/BSc, Computer Science (Digital & Technology Solutions) BSc, Computer Science with Artificial Intelligence MEng/BSc, Computer Science with High-Performance Graphics and Games Engineering MEng/BSc, Computer Science with Mathematics MSci/BSc, Electronics and Computer Engineering MEng/BEng

Postgraduate courses: Advanced Computer Science MSc, Advanced Computer Science (Cloud Computing) MSc, Advanced Computer Science (Data Analytics) MSc, Advanced Computer Science (Artificial Intelligence) MSc, High-Performance Graphics and Games Engineering MSc, Mathematics and Computer Science MSc

School of Electronic and Electrical Engineering; www.engineering.leeds.ac.uk/info/20133/ school_of_electronic_and_ electrical_engineering

Electronic and Communications Engineering MEng/BEng, Electronics and Computer Engineering MEng/BEng, Electronic and Electrical Engineering MEng/BEng, Electronic Engineering MEng Electronics and Renewable Energy Systems MEng/Mechatronics and Robotics MEng/BEng, Music Multimedia and Electronics BSc

Postgraduate courses: Communications and Signal Processing MSc (Eng), Digital Communications Networks MSc (Eng), Electrical Engineering and Renewable Energy Systems MSc (Eng), Electronic and Electrical Engineering MSc (Eng), Embedded Systems Engineering MSc (Eng), Engineering, Technology and Business Management MSc (Eng), Mechatronics and Robotics MSc (Eng), Engineering Management MSc/PGCert (online)

School of Mechanical Engineering; www.engineering.leeds.ac.uk/info/20134/ school_of_mechanical_engineering

Aeronautical and Aerospace Engineering MEng/BEng, Automotive Engineering MEng/BEng, Mechanical Engineering MEng/BEng, Mechatronics and Robotics MEng/BEng, Medical Engineering MEng/BEng, Product Design MDes/BSc

Postgraduate courses: Advanced Mechanical Engineering MSc(Eng), Aerospace Engineering MSc, Automotive Engineering MSc(Eng), Mechatronics and Robotics MSc(Eng), Medical Engineering MSc(Eng), Joint European Master in Tribology of Surface and Interfaces, Engineering Management MSc/PGCert (online)

Faculty of Environment ; www.environment.leeds.ac.uk

BSc Geography and Geology, Bsc Geology, MGeol Geology, Bsc Geophysics, MGeol Geophysics, BSc Geological Sciences, MGeol Geological Sciences, BSc Geophysical Sciences, MGeophys Geophysical Sciences, BSc Environmental Science, MEnv Environmental Science, BSc Geography, BSc Meteorology and Climate Science, MEnv Meteorology and Climate Science, BSc Geography with Environmental Mathematics, BA Geography, BA Geography with Transport Studies, BA Geography Joint Honours Courses, BA Environment and Business, MEnv Environment and Business, BSc Sustainability and Environmental

Management, MEnv Sustainability and Environmental Management

Postgraduate courses: MSc Engineering Geology, MSc Exploration Geophysics, MSc Structural Geology with Geophysics, MRes Climate and Atmospheric Science, MSc Geographical Information Systems (GIS), MSc Geographical Information Science (GIS) (Online distance learning), MSc River Basin Dynamics and Management with GIS, MSc Climate Change and Environmental Policy, MSc Ecological Economics, MSc Environment and Development, MSc Environment and Development with Integrated International Fieldwork, MSc Sustainability and Business, MSc Sustainability and Consultancy, MSc Sustainable Food Systems, MSc Sustainability in Transport, MSc Sustainable Cities, MSc Mathematical Modelling for Transport, Railway Operations, Management and Policy MSc, MSc Transport Economics, MSc Transport Planning, MSc (Eng) Transport Planning and Engineering, MSc Transport Planning and the Environment

Faculty of Mathematics and Physical Sciences; www.maps.leeds.ac.uk

BSc Actuarial Mathematics, BSc Chemistry, BSc/MChem Chemistry Chemistry and Mathematics BSc/MChem, BSc Food Science and Nutrition, BSc Food Science, MSci Food Science, BSc Mathematics and Music, BSc Mathematics and Philosophy, BSc Mathematics and Statistics, BSc/MMath Mathematics and Statistics, BSc Mathematics, BSc/MMath Mathematics, BSc Medicinal Chemistry, BSc/MChem Medicinal Chemistry, BSc Nutrition MSci Nutrition, BSc Physics with Astrophysics, MPhys Physics with Astrophysics, BSc Physics, MPhys Physics, BSc Theoretical Physics, MPhys Theoretical Physics

Postgraduate courses: MSc Chemical Biology and Drug Design, MSc Chemistry, MSc Polymers, Colorants and Fine Chemicals, MSc Food Quality and Innovation, MSc Food Science, MSc Food Science (Food Biotechnology), MSc Food Science and Nutrition, MSc Nutrition, MSc Atmosphere-Ocean Dynamics, MSc Data Science and Analytics, MSc Mathematics, MSc Mathematics and Computer Science, MSc Medical Statistics, MSc Statistics, MSc Statistics with Applications to Finance, MSc Financial Mathematics, MSc Actuarial Finance, MSc Physics, MSc Physics and Business Management

Faculty of Medicine and Health; medicinehealth.leeds.ac.uk/

BA Social Work MBChB Medicine and Surgery, BSc Midwifery, BSc Nursing (Adult), BSc Nursing (Child), BSc Nursing (Mental Health), BSc Psychology, MPsyc/BSc Advanced Psychology, MChD/BChD Dental Surgery, Bsc Oral Science, BSc Dental Hygiene and Dental Therapy

Postgraduate courses: MA Psychotherapy and Counselling, MA Social Work, MPH Public Health (International), MPH Public Health- Health Management, Planning and Policy (International), MPH Public Health- Health Management, Planning and Policy (International), MSc Advanced Clinical Practice, MEd/PGCert Clinical Education, MSc Diagnostic Imaging, MSc Health Data Analytics, MSc Health Informatics, PGCert Health Research, MSc International Health, MSc Medical Education, MSc Medical Imaging, MRes Medicine, MSc Molecular Medicine, MSc/PGDip Pharmacy Practice, MSc/PGCert Pharmacy Practice with Prescribing, MSc Physician Associate Studies, MSc Systemic Family Therapy, ND Systemic Practice (Foundation), ND Systemic Practice (Intermediate), PGCert Cardiac Device and Rhythm Management, PGCert Clinical Assessment, PGCert Echocardiography, PGCert Health Informatics (Part Time-12 months), PGCert Public Health (International), PGCert Public Health-Health Management, Planning and Policy (International), PGCert Systemic Practice, PGDip Clinical Embryology (Distance Learning), PGDip Health Informatics, PGDip Pharmacy Practice, PGDip Pharmacy Practice with Prescribing, PGDip Public Health (International), PGDip Public Health-Health Management, Planning and Policy (International), MClinDent Advanced Dental Practice, MSc Clinical Dentistry (Implant Dentistry), MSc Clinical dentistry (Restorative Dentistry), MSc Dental Public Health, MSc Digital Dentistry, MSc Oral Surgery, MSc Paediatric Dentistry, MSc Cognitive Development and Disorders, MSc Psychological Approaches to Health

---

COLLEGE OF THE RESURRECTION
college.mirfield.org.uk

BA(Hons) in Theological Studies

Postgraduate courses: MA/PGDip in Ministry & Theology, MA in Liturgy

LEEDS ARTS UNIVERSITY
www.leeds-art.ac.uk

BA(Hons) Animation, BA(Hons) Comic & Concept Art, BA(Hons) Creative Advertising, BA(Hons) Creative Writing, BA(Hons) Fashion Branding With Communication, BA(Hons) Fashion Design, BA(Hons) Fashion Photography, BA(Hons) Filmmaking, BA(Hons) Fine Art, BA(Hons) Graphic Design, BA(Hons) Illustration, BA(Hons) Photography, BMus(Hons) Popular Music Performance, BA(Hons) Textile Design, BA(Hons) Visual Communication Postgraduate courses: MA Creative Practice, MA Curation Practices, MA Fine Art, MA Graphic Design, MA Photography

LEEDS COLLEGE OF MUSIC
www.lcm.ac.uk

BA(Hons) Acting, BA(Hons) Actor Musician, BA(Hons) Music (Business), BA(Hons) Music (Classical), BA(Hons) Music (Film Music), BA(Hons) Music (Folk), BA(Hons) Music (Jazz), BA(Hons) Music (Popular), BA(Hons) Music (Production), BA(Hons) Music (Songwriting), BA(Hons) Musical Theatre, FdA Music Production Postgraduate course: MMus/PGDip Creative Musician

LEEDS TRINITY UNIVERSITY
www.leedstrinity.ac.uk

Undergraduate degrees in the following subjects

Business
Accounting and Business, Business and Economics, Business and Enterprise, Business and Management, Business and Marketing, Economics, International Business

Childhood and Education
Early Childhood Studies, Education and Religious Studies, Education Studies, Working with Children, Young People and Families

Computer Science
Computer Science

Criminology and Sociology
Criminology, Criminology and Sociology, Criminology with Police Studies, Psychology and Criminology, Psychology and Sociology, Professional Policing, Sociology

English
Creative and Professional Writing, English and Creative Writing, English and Film, English and Media, English Language and Linguistics, English Literature

Health and Nutrition
Exercise, Health and Nutrition, Health and Social Care

Humanities
Philosophy, Ethics and Religion, Theology and Religious Studies

Journalism
Broadcast Journalism, Journalism, Journalism and Creative Media, Sports Journalism

Law
Criminology and Law, Law(LLB)

Media and Film
Digital Marketing, Film, Digital Media (Game Art and Design), Digital Media (Visual Effects and Virtual Reality), Media, Photography, Television Production

Primary Education
Primary Education (Early Years 3-7) with QTS, Primary Education (Later Years 5-11) with QTS

Psychology
Counselling, Psychology, Forensic Psychology Health Psychology, Psychology, Psychology and Business, Psychology and Child Development, Sport Psychology

Sport and Physical Education
Physical Education Physical Education and Sports Coaching, Secondary Education, Physical Education and Sport (2 years), Sport and Exercise Sciences, Sport and Exercise Sciences (Sports Nutrition), Sport Therapy and Rehabilitation, Sports Coaching, Strength and Conditioning

Postgraduate degrees in the following subjects: International Business, MBA, Family Support MA/PGCert/PGDip Education, Creative Writing Health and Wellbeing, Mental Health in Children and Young

People, Journalism, PGCE Business, PGCE Computer Science with ICT, PGCE English, PGCE Geography, PGCE History, PGCE Mathematics, PGCE Modern Foreign Languages (MFL), PGCE Religious Education, PGCE Science with Biology, PGCE Science with Chemistry, PGCE Science with Physics

NORTHERN SCHOOL OF CONTEMPORARY DANCE
www.nscd.ac.uk

BA(Hons) Dance (Contemporary)
Postgraduate courses: MA Dance & Creative Enterprise, MA Contemporary Dance Performance (PAS), MA Contemporary Dance Performance (Verve), PGDip Arts Learning & Teaching in Higher Education, CertHE Contemporary Dance

YORK ST JOHN UNIVERSITY
www.yorksj.ac.uk

Art and Design
Animation BA(Hons), Computer Science BSc(Hons), Fine Art BA(Hons), Furniture Design BA(Hons), Games Design BA(Hons), Games Development BSc(Hons) Graphic Design BA(Hons), Illustration BA(Hons), Interior Design BA(Hons), Photography BA(Hons), Product Design BA(Hons, Software Engineering BSc(Hons)
Postgraduate course: Fine Arts MA/PgDip/PgCert

Business
Accounting & Finance BA(Hons), Business and Economics BA(Hons), Business Information Management BA(Hons), Business Information Technology BA(Hons), Business Studies BA(Hons), Business Management BA(Hons), Business Management & Finance BA(Hons), Business Management & HR Management BA(Hons), Digital Marketing and Data Analysis BA(Hons), Economics & Finance BSc(Hons), Economics and Geography BA(Hons), Events and Experience Management BA(Hons), Events and International Hospitality Management BA(Hons), Events Management BA(Hons), Fashion Marketing BA(Hons), Financial and Investment Management BSc(Hons), Human Resource Management BA(Hons), International Business BA(Hons), International Business Management BA(Hons), International Tourism and Hospitality Management BA(Hons), Management & Entrepreneurship BA(Hons), Marketing BA(Hons), Marketing and Events Management BA(Hons), Marketing and International Hospitality Management BA(Hons), Marketing Management BA(Hons), Politics, Philosophy and Economics BA(Hons), Sports Business Management BA(Hons), Sports Management BA(Hons), Tourism Management BA(Hons), Tourism and Destination Management BA(Hons), Tourism and Events Management BA(Hons)

Postgraduate courses: Conversion MBA (online), Human Resource Management MSc, International Business MSc, International Fashion Marketing MSc, Leadership & Management MSc, Marketing MSc, Masters of Business Administration MBA

Computing
Computer Science BSc(Hons), Games Design BA(Hons), Games Development BSc(Hons), Software Engineering BSc(Hons)

Health Sciences
Biochemistry BSc(Hons), Biology BSc(Hons), Biomedical Science BSc(Hons), Occupational Therapy BSc(Hons), Physiotherapy BSc(Hons)

Humanities
Creative Writing BA(Hons), English Literature BA(Hons), Environmental Geography BSc(Hons), Film Studies BA(Hons), Geography BSc(Hons), History BA(Hons), Human Geography BA(Hons), Human Geography with American Studies BA(Hons), Human Geography with History BA(Hons), Human Geography with Media Studies BA(Hons), Media BA(Hons), Politics BA(Hons), Politics & History BA(Hons), Politics, Philosophy & Ethics BA(Hons), War Studies BA(Hons), American Studies & Film Studies BA(Hons), American Studies & History BA(Hons), Creative Writing & English Language BA(Hons), Creative Writing & English Literature BA(Hons), Creative Writing & Media BA(Hons), Education Studies and English Literature BA(Hons), English Literature & English Language BA(Hons), English Literature and Film Studies BA(Hons), English Literature and Media BA(Hons), Film Studies and Media BA(Hons), Politics & War Studies BA(Hons)
Postgraduate courses: Contemporary Literature MA, Creative Writing MA, International History MA

Languages and Linguistics

British Sign Language & Deaf Studies BA(Hons), British Sign Language & Educational Linguistics BA(Hons), British Sign Language, English Language & Linguistics BA(Hons), Educational Linguistics BA(Hons), Education Studies and English Language BA(Hons), English Language & Linguistics BA(Hons), English Language, Linguistics & TESOL BA(Hons), Japanese & Intercultural Communication BA(Hons), Japanese & TESOL BA(Hons), Japanese, English Language & Linguistics BA(Hons), Japanese, Intercultural & Contemporary Communication BA(Hons), Japanese, TESOL & Linguistics BA(Hons), Korean, TESOL & Linguistics BA(Hons), Language & Communication Studies BA(Hons), Languages & Linguistics Degrees with Foundation Year

Postgraduate courses: Applied Linguistics: TESOL MA, Language & Social Justice MA

Media and Production

Film Studies BA(Hons), Media BA(Hons), Media Production BA(Hons), Media Production: Film and Television BA(Hons), Media Production: Journalism BA(Hons), Media & Film Studies BA(Hons)

Performance

Acting BA(Hons), Digital Music BA(Hons), Drama & Dance BA(Hons), Drama: Education & Community BA(Hons), Drama & Theatre BA(Hons), Music BA(Hons), Music Composition BA(Hons), Music: Education & Community BA(Hons), Music: Performance BA(Hons), Music Production BA(Hons), Music Production & Creative Business BA(Hons)

Postgraduate courses: Applied Theatre Community Music MA, Music Composition MA Music Production MA, Theatre & Performance MA/PgDip/PgCert

Psychology and Counselling

Counselling, Coaching and Mentoring BA(Hons), Psychology BSc(Hons), Psychology with Child Development BSc(Hons), Psychology with Counselling BSc(Hons)

Postgraduate courses: Counselling MA/PGDip, Criminal Justice MA

Religion and Philosophy

Christian Theology BA(Hons), Religion, Philosophy & Ethics BA(Hons), Religious Studies BA(Hons), Theology & Religious Studies BA(Hons)

Postgraduate course: Contemporary Religion MA, Religion in Society MA

Social Sciences

Sociology BA(Hons), Criminology BA(Hons), Sociology with Criminology BA(Hons), Police Studies BA(Hons), Criminology with Police Studies BA(Hons), Sociology with Police Studies BA(Hons), Data Science BSc(Hons), Degree in Professional Policing BA(Hons), Law LLB(Hons), Mathematics BSc(Hons), Social Sciences Degrees with Foundation Year BA(Hons)

Postgraduate courses: Occupational Therapy (preregistration) MSc, Physiotherapy (Pre-registration) MSc, Leadership in Health & Social Care MSc, Professional Health & Social Care MSc, Promoting Health in Long Term Conditions MSc

Sport

Sport & Exercise Science BSc(Hons), Sport & Exercise Therapy BSc(Hons), Physical Education & Sports Coaching BA(Hons)

Education

Children, Young People & Families BA(Hons), Children, Young People & Families with British Sign Language (BA Hons), Children, Young People & Families with Special Educational Needs & Inclusion BA(Hons), Children, Young People & Families and Education Studies BA(Hons), Early Childhood Studies BA(Hons), Education Studies BA(Hons), Primary Education 3-7 years BA(Hons), Primary Education 5-11 years BA(Hons), Education Studies with Spanish BA(Hons), Education Studies with Special Educational Needs & Inclusion BA(Hons), Education Studies & Sociology BA(Hons)

Postgraduate courses: Primary Education PGCE, Secondary Education RE PGCE, Secondary Education (School Direct) PGCE, Education MA, Education: Early Childhood MA, Education: Mentoring MA, Education: Post-compulsory Education MA, Education: Research-engaged Setting MA, Educational Leadership & Management MA, SEN Coordination: Leading Effective, Inclusive Practice in SEN PGCE (National Award), Special Educational Needs & Inclusion MA

LEEDS BECKETT UNIVERSITY
www.leedsbeckett.ac.uk

Faculty of Arts, Environment & Technology; www.leedsbeckett.ac.uk/aet

The Leeds School of Art, Architecture & Design; www.leedsbeckett.ac.uk/aet/#artarchitecture- design

architecture, architectural professional practice, art & design, fashion, fashion marketing, fine art, interior architecture & design, urban design, graphic art & design, landscape architecture, product design, urban design

School of Built Environment & Engineering; www.leedsbeckett.ac.uk/aet/#builtenvironment- engineering

building/engineering studies/services engineering, civil engineering/& construction, construction/commercial/ management, strategic/project management, facilities management, architectural technology, building/quantity surveying, environmental engineering & construction, health & neighbourhood planning, housing/strategy, housing, regeneration & urban management, planning law & practice, strategic project management, project management/construction, town & regional planning, UK planning law & dispute practice, sustainable urban planning

School of Computing, Creative Technology & Engineering; www.leedsbeckett.ac.uk/aet/#computing-creative-technology

advanced engineering management, business information technology/intelligence, computer forensics/& security, computer science computing/systems engineering, computer sustainable engineering, creative media/technology, digital forensics & security/journalism/ photography, electrical & electronic engineering, engineering robotics & automation, food engineering, games design, information management/systems, web applications development, mathematics & computer science, mobile device applications, information & technology/management, broadcast media technologies, computer animation/& special effects & visual effects, sustainable computing/technology, creative technology, 3D visualisation & interactive environments, networking systems engineering

School of Cultural Studies & Humanities; www.leedsbeckett.ac.uk/as/cs

English/& history/media/creative writing, English literature, history, media, communication & cultures, English contemporary literature, social history; BA(Hons), BSc(Hons), DipHE, FdAA, GradCert, MPhil, MRes, MSc, PGDip

School of Film, Music & Performing Arts; www.leedsbeckett.ac.uk/aet/#filmmusic-performingarts

music performance/production/technology, dance, audio engineering, performance, music for moving image, sound & music for interactive games, sound design, pop music & culture, documentary film making

Northern Film School

animation, film making, film & TV

Faculty of Business and Law; www.leedsbeckett.ac.uk/fbl

Leeds Business School; www.leedsbeckett.ac.uk/fbl/leeds_business_school

business analytics/finance/marketing, business management development, business studies/administration/ economics, business & management/HRM/ management studies, action by facilitation, corporate governance/communications, executive leadership/ business coaching, entrepreneurship & business, HRM, international HRM, international business/ communications/business law/trade & finance/banking & investment/leadership/marketing, journalism, leadership & change, management, marketing, marketing & advertising management, PR & communication/ journalism/strategic communication, retail marketing management, strategic & digital marketing, supply chain management & logistics, MBA (Executive/Graduate)

Leeds Law School; www.leedsbeckett.ac.uk/lbs/law

law, legal practice, international business law, law & finance/international business/management; BA(Hons), HND, LlB(Hons), LlM, MA, MSc, PGDip/ Cert, MBA, DBA

Faculty of Health & Social Sciences; *www.leedsbeckett.ac.uk/hss*

Social Sciences & Psychology

play work, youth work & community development, young people, communities and society, criminology, criminology & psychology, psychology, psychology & society, social psychology, social work, sociology, therapeutic counselling, young people, communities and society, youth work & community development,- Postgraduate; advanced social work practice, art psychotherapy practice, criminology, interdisciplinary psychology, interpersonal & counselling skills, mental health practice, psychological therapies, psychology, psychotherapy, youth work & community development, community & youth studies

Health

environmental health, toxicological sciences, nutrition adult nursing, biomedical sciences (human biology/microbiology/molecular biology), dietetics, environmental health, health and community care, mental health nursing, nutrition, nutritional health, physiotherapy, safety, health & environmental management, speech & language therapy, sports and exercise therapy, support work; Postgraduate; acoustics, advanced practice, advanced social work practice, applied biomedical sciences research, chaplaincy in health & social care, community & youth studies, community specialist practitioner – district nursing, dietetics, eating disorders, environmental health, health and community care, health and safety, mental health practice, microbiology and biotechnology, nutrition in practice, occupational therapy, physiotherapy, play therapy, practice based play therapy, public health, health promotion, social work, specialist community public health nursing – health visiting/occupational health nursing/school nursing, therapeutic play skills, toxicological sciences

Short Courses and CP; BA(Hons), BSc(Hons), CertHE, MA, MSc, PGDip/Cert, Prof Dip, DipHE, FdAA, GradCert, MPhil, MRes, PGDip, MBioms

Carnegie Faculty; *www.leedsbeckett.ac.uk/carnegie*

childhood and early years, higher and further education, childhood studies, education studies, internationalisation inclusion training in intellectual disability for educators in Europe, partnerships with schools playwork researchers, childhood outdoor & adventurous activities, psychology, strength & coordination, PE, leisure, sport & culture, PE with outdoor education, sport & exercise science, sport & business management/development/management/coaching/studies, sport physical activity & health, sport & exercise medication, psychology of sport & exercise, international/event management, sport event management, sport & exercise/biomedicine/nutrition/physiology/health/psychology/science/therapy, sport, law & society, conference & exhibition management, entertainment management, managing cultural & major events, event sponsorship and fundraising; BA(Hons), BSc(Hons), FdSc, PGCE, PGCert/Dip, MA, PhD, Prof DocEd

UNIVERSITY OF LEICESTER
www.le.ac.uk

Department of American Studies; www2.le.ac.uk/departments/americanstudies

BA American Studies

School of Archaeology and Ancient History; www2.le.ac.uk/departments/archaeology

BA Archaeology, BSc Archaeology, BA Ancient History and Archaeology, BA Ancient History
Postgraduate courses: MA Archaeology, MA Archaeology and Heritage, MA Classical Mediterranean, MA The Graeco-Roman World

School of Arts; www2.le.ac.uk/departments/arts
English

BA English, BA English and American Studies, BA English and History, BA French and English, BA Italian and English, BA Spanish and English, BA Film Studies and English, BA History of Art and English
Postgraduate courses: MA in Applied Linguistics and TESOL, MA Creative Writing, MA English Language and Linguistics, MA English Studies, MA Modern Literature/Modern Literature and Creative Writing, MA TESOL, MA Victorian Studies, Postgraduate Certificate in Teaching English for Academic Purposes (TEAP) PGCert (by distance learning)

History of Art and Film

BA History of Art, BA History of Art and English, BA Film Studies, BA Film Studies and English, BA Film and Media Studies

Postgraduate courses: MA in Film and Film Cultures

Modern Languages

BA French and Italian, BA French and Spanish, BA Italian and Spanish, BA French and English, BA Italian and English, BA Spanish and English, BA Modern Languages with Translation, BA Modern Languages and Translation BA European Studies, BA Modern Language Studies, BA Modern Languages with Film Studies, BA Modern Languages with Management

Postgraduate course: Translation Studies MA

School of Biological Sciences; www2.le.ac.uk/departments/ biologicalsciences

Molecular and Cell Biology

BSc/MBiolSci Biological Sciences (Biochemistry), BSc/MBiolSci Biological Sciences (Biochemistry), BSc/MBiolSci Biological Sciences (Microbiology),BSc/MBiolSci Biological Sciences (Neuroscience), BSc Medical Biochemistry, BSc Medical Physiology

Postgraduate courses: MSc Bioinformatics, MSc Cancer Cell and Molecular Biology

Genetics

BSc Biological Sciences (Genetics), BSc Medical Genetics

Postgraduate courses: MSc Molecular Genetics, MSc Bioinformatics, MSc/PGCert Molecular Pathology and Therapeutics of Cancer

Infection, Immunity & Inflammation

BSc Biological Sciences, BSc Biological Sciences (Microbiology), BSc Medical Microbiology

Postgraduate courses: MSc Infection and Immunity, MSc Chronic Disease and Immunity

Neuroscience, Psychology and Behaviour

Postgraduate courses: MSc Psychological Research Methods, MSc Occupational Psychology (DL), MSc Psychology of Work (DL)

School of Business; www2.le.ac.uk/ departments/business

Accounting and Finance

BSc Accounting, BSc Accounting and Finance, Major in Accounting and Finance, Minor in Accounting and Finance

Postgraduate courses: MSc Accounting and Finance, MSc Management, Finance and Accounting, MSc Banking and International Finance, MSc Business

Analysis and Finance, MSc Finance, MSc Financial Risk Management

Economics

BSc Economics, BSc Economics and Accounting, BSc Economics and Business, BSc Economics and Econometrics, BSc Financial Economics and Banking, BSc Financial Economics and Econometrics

Postgraduate courses: MSc Economics, MSc Financial Economics, MSc Forecasting and Economic Analysis

Management and Marketing

BA Management Studies, BA Management Studies (Finance), BA Management Studies (Marketing), BA Management Studies (Organisation Studies), BA Management Studies and Economics, BA Human Resource Management, BA Marketing, Major in Human Resource Management, Major in Management Studies, Minor in Entrepreneurship, Minor in Human Resource Management, Minor in Management Studies, Minor in Marketing

Postgraduate courses: MSc Healthcare Management, MSc Human Resource Management and Training, MSc International Management, MSc Management, MSc International Marketing, MSc Marketing, MSc Marketing for the Creative Industries, MSc Marketing for Places and Tourism, MSc Entrepreneurship, MSc Innovation Management in Organisations

Department of Chemistry; www2.le.ac.uk/ departments/chemistry

BSc Chemistry, BSc Pharmaceutical Chemistry, BSc Chemistry with Forensic Science, MChem Chemistry, MChem Pharmaceutical Chemistry, MChem Chemistry with Forensic Science

Postgraduate courses: MSc Chemical Research (Biological Chemistry) MSc Chemical Research (Green Chemistry) MSc Chemical Research (Physical Chemistry) MSc Forensic Science and Criminal Justice

Department of Criminology; www2.le.ac.uk/departments/criminology

BSc Criminology, Major in Criminology, Minor in Criminal Justice, Minor in Criminal Behaviour

Postgraduate courses: MSc Criminology, MSc Criminology in Practice, Terrorism, MSc Security and Policing, Crime, MSc Justice and Psychology

School of Education; www2.le.ac.uk/ departments/education

Postgraduate courses: PGCE Primary (University-led), PGCE Primary (School Direct), PGCE Secondary (University-led), PGCE Secondary (School Direct), MEd Master of Education, International Education (with Specialist Routes)MA, MSc Educational

Leadership(Distance Learning), PGCert Learning Technologies (Distance Learning)

Department of Engineering;
www2.le.ac.uk/departments/engineering

BEng/MEng General Engineering, BEng/MEng Aerospace Engineering, BEng/MEng Engineering, BEng/MEng Mechanical Engineering

Postgraduate courses: MSc Advanced Electrical and Electronic Engineering, MSc Advanced Engineering, MSc Advanced Materials Engineering MSc Advanced Electrical and Electronic Engineering with Management, MSc Advanced Mechanical Engineering, MSc Embedded Systems and Control Engineering, MSc Information and Communications Engineering, Master of Engineering Management (MEM)

Centre for English Local History;
www2.le.ac.uk/centres/
elh?uol_r=948a87cd

Postgraduate course: MA History (Local History)

School of Geography, Geology and the Environment; www2.le.ac.uk/
departments/geoggeolenv

Geography

BA Geography, BA Human Geography BSc Geography, BSc Physical Geography, BSc Geography with Foundation Year

Postgraduate courses: MSc

Geology

BSc/MGeol Geology, BSc/MGeol Applied and Environmental Geology, BSc/MGeol Geology with Geophysics, BSc/MGeol Geology with Palaeontology, BSc Geology with Foundation Year

Department of Health Sciences;
www2.le.ac.uk/departments/
healthsciences

Postgraduate courses: MSc Medical Statistics, MSc/PGDip/PGCert Quality and Safety in Healthcare, MRes/PGCert Applied Health Research, Diabetes MSc/PGDip/PGCert (Distance Learning)

Department of History; www2.le.ac.uk/
departments/history

BA History, BA Contemporary History, BA History and Politics, BA International Relations and History, BA History and American Studies, BA English and History, BA History and Archaeology, Ancient History and Classical Archaeology BA, BA Ancient History and History

Postgraduate courses: MA History, MA History (Local History), MA History (Urban History), MA History (Holocaust and Genocide Studies), MA Urban Conservation, MRes History

Department of Informatics;
www2.le.ac.uk/departments/informatics

BSc Computer Science, MComp Computer Science, BA/BSc Creative Computing, BSc Data Science, BSc Software Engineering

Postgraduate courses: MSc Advanced Computer Science, MSc Advanced Computational Methods, MSc Advanced Distributed Systems, MSc Advanced Software Engineering, MSc Cloud Computing, MSc Human Technology Interaction, MSc Agile Software Engineering Techniques, MSc Software Engineering for Financial Services, MSc Web Applications and Services

Leicester Law School; www2.le.ac.uk/
departments/law

LLB Law, LLB Law (JD Pathway), LLB Law (Graduate Entry), LLB English and French Law (Matrise), LLB Law with Criminology, LLB Law with a Modern Language, LLB Law with Politics

Postgraduate courses: LLM International Commercial Law, LLM International Human Rights Law, LLM International Law, LLM Public International Law, LLM Law

Department of Mathematics;
www2.le.ac.uk/departments/mathematics

BSc Mathematics, MMath Mathematics, BSc Mathematics with Foundation Year, BSc Mathematics and Artificial Intelligence, BSc Mathematics and Actuarial Science, Major in Mathematics

Postgraduate courses: MSc Applied Computation and Numerical Modelling, MSc Financial Mathematics and Computation, MSc Data Analysis in Business Intelligence programme, MSc/PGDip Actuarial Science with Data Analysis

Department of Media and Communication;
www2.le.ac.uk/departments/media

BA Media and Communication, BA Media and Society, BA Film and Media Studies, BA Journalism, BA Journalism with Creative Writing

Postgraduate courses: MA Digital Media and Society, MA Global Media and Communication, MA Mass Communications MA Media and Advertising, MA Media, Culture and Society, MA Media, Gender and Social Justice, MA Media and Public Relations

Department of Medical and Social Care Education; www2.le.ac.uk/departments/msce

MBChB Medicine, BSc(Hons) Operating Department Practice, BSc Perioperative Practice

Department of Museum Studies; www2.le.ac.uk/departments/museumstudies

MA/MSc/PGDip Museum Studies, MA/PGDip Art Museum and Gallery Studies

Department of Physics and Astronomy; www2.le.ac.uk/departments/physics

BSc Physics, MPhys Physics, BSc Physics with Astrophysics, MPhys Physics with Astrophysics, BSc Physics with Space Science, MPhys Physics with Space Science

Postgraduate courses: MSc Applied Computation and Numerical Modelling, MSc/PGDip Space Exploration Systems

Department of Politics and International Relations; www2.le.ac.uk/departments/politics

BA Politics, BA International Relations, BA International Relations and History, BA Politics and Economics, BA Politics and Sociology, BA History and Politics, BA Politics and International Relations, LLB Law with Politics

Postgraduate courses: MA Diplomatic Studies (Distance Learning), MA Human Rights and Global Ethics, MA International Relations and World Order, MA Intelligence and Security Studies MA Politics of Conflict and Violence (Distance Learning), Security, Conflict and International Development (Distance Learning)

School of Psychology; www2.le.ac.uk/departments/psychology

BSc Psychology, BSc Psychology with Cognitive Neuroscience, BSc Applied Psychology

Postgraduate courses: MSc in Psychological Research Methods, MSc Occupational Psychology, MSc/PGDip Psychology of Work

Department of Sociology; www2.le.ac.uk/departments/sociology

BA Sociology

Postgraduate courses: MA Contemporary Sociology, MSc Social Research, MA Media, Culture and Society

---

NEWMAN UNIVERSITY
www.newman.ac.uk

Accounting and Finance BA(Hons), Applied Social Science BA(Hons), BA(Hons) Education Studies, BSc(Hons) Sport and Exercise Science full-time top up, Business Management BA(Hons), Computer Science BSc(Hons), Counselling Studies and Working with Children, Young People and Families BA(Hons), Criminology BA(Hons), BA(Hons) Drama, Theatre and Applied Performance, Early Childhood Education and Care BA(Hons), English BA(Hons), English and Creative Writing BA(Hons), Forensic Psychology BSc(Hons), Health and Social Care BSc(Hons), History BA(Hons), Law LLB(Hons), Liberal Arts BA(Hons), Mathematics BSc(Hons), Mathematics with opt-in route to QTS BSc(Hons), Physical Education and Sport BA(Hons), Primary Education (3-7) With QTS BA(Hons), Primary Education (5-11) With QTS BA(Hons), Psychology BSc(Hons), Psychology and Childhood Studies BSc(Hons), Psychology and Counselling Studies BSc(Hons), Psychology with Sport BSc(Hons), Sport Coaching and Performance BSc(Hons), Sport Coaching Science (Tournament Golf) BSc(Hons), Sport Development with Coaching BA(Hons) Studies in Primary Education BA(Hons), Theology and Philosophy BA(Hons), Working with Children, Young People and Families BA(Hons), Working with Children, Young People and Families/International Social Work (Dual Award) BA(Hons), Youth and Community Work BA(Hons)

Postgraduate courses: Clinical Applications of Psychology MSc/PGDip/PGCert, Contemporary Christian Theology MA/PGDip/PGCert, Education MA/PGCert (Catholic School Leadership), Education MA/PGCert (Early Childhood Education and Care), Education MA/PGCert (Higher Education), Education MA/PGCert (Inclusion and Special Educational Needs and Disability), Education MA/PGCert (Leadership and Management), Education MA/PGCert (Learning and Teaching), Education MA/PGCert (Mentoring and Coaching), Education MA/PGCert (Research in Education), Education MA/PGCert (Safeguarding), National Award for SEN Coordination PGCert, Professional and Academic Learning in Education PGCert

UNIVERSITY OF LINCOLN
www.lincoln.ac.uk

College of Arts; www.lincoln.ac.uk/ home/collegeofarts

Lincoln School of Architecture and the Built Environment; www.lincoln.ac.uk/home/abe

BSc(Hons) Architectural Science and Technology, BA(Hons) Architecture, BArch(Hons) Bachelor of Architecture with Honours, BSc(Hons) Construction Science and Management

Postgraduate courses: MSc Architecture March International Construction Science and Management, MArch Master of Architecture, PGDip Professional Practice and Management in Architecture PGDip

Lincoln School of Design; www.lincoln.ac.uk/home/lsd

BA(Hons) Creative Advertising, BA(Hons) Design for Exhibition and Museums, BA(Hons) Fashion, BA(Hons) Graphic Design, BA(Hons) Illustration, BA(Hons) Interior Architecture and Design, BA(Hons) Product Design

Postgraduate courses: MA Design, MA Interior Architecture and Design

Lincoln School of Film & Media; www.lincoln.ac.uk/home/fm

Animation and Visual Effects BA(Hons), Film and Television Studies BA(Hons), Film Production BA(Hons), Media Production BA(Hons), Media Studies BA(Hons), Photography BA(Hons), Sound and Music production BA(Hons)

Postgraduate courses: MA Film Production, MA Media & Cultural Studies MA by Research, Photography, MA Studies in Media and Culture

Lincoln School of English and Journalism; www.lincoln.ac.uk/home/ej

BA(Hons) Communication and Public Relations, BA(Hons) Creative Writing, BA(Hons) English, BA(Hons) English and Creative Writing, BA(Hons) English and History, BA(Hons) English and Journalism, BA(Hons) Journalism, BA(Hons) Journalism and Creative Writing, BA(Hons) Journalism and Public Relations, BA(Hons) Journalism Studies, BA(Hons) Magazine Journalism, BA(Hons) Sports Journalism

Postgraduate courses: MA 21st Century Literature, MA Creative Writing Creative Writing and Publishing MA, MA English Studies, MA International Journalism, MA Journalism, MA Journalism (Arts), MA Journalism (Digital), MA Journalism (Science and Environment), MA Journalism (Sports), MA Journalism (War and International Human Rights), MA Public Relations

School of Fine & Performing Arts; www.lincoln.ac.uk/home/fpa

BA(Hons)Dance, BA(Hons) Drama and English, BA(Hons) Drama and Theatre, BA(Hons) Fine Art, BA(Hons) Music, BA(Hons)Technical Theatre and Stage Management

Postgraduate courses: MA Fine Art, MA Music, MA Theatre, MA Theatre for Young Audiences

School of History and Heritage; www.lincoln.ac.uk/home/hh

American Studies BA(Hons), Art History and History BA(Hons), Classical Studies BA(Hons), Conservation of Cultural Heritage BA(Hons), English and History BA(Hons), History BA(Hons), Philosophy BA(Hons)

Postgraduate courses: MA Conservation of Cultural Heritage, MA Conservation Studies Graduate Diploma, MA Historical Studies, MA History, MA Medieval Studies

Medieval Studies MA College of Science; www.lincoln.ac.uk/home/ collegeofscience

School of Chemistry; www.lincoln.ac.uk/home/chemistry

BSc(Hons)Chemistry, MChem Chemistry, BSc(Hons) Chemistry for Drug Discovery and Development, MChem Chemistry for Drug Discovery and Development, BSc(Hons) Chemistry with Education, MChem Chemistry with Education, BSc(Hons) Chemistry with Mathematics, MChem Chemistry with Mathematics, BSc(Hons) Forensic Chemistry, MChem Forensic Chemistry, BSc(Hons) Forensic Science

Postgraduate courses: MSc Analytical Sciences, MSc Forensic Science, MSc Forensic Toxicology, MSc Nanoscience

School of Computer Science; www.lincoln.ac.uk/home/socs

BSc(Hons) Computer Science, MComp Computer Science, BSc(Hons) Games Computing, MComp Games Computing

Postgraduate courses: MSc Computer Science, MSc Games Development and Design, MSc Innovation in Intelligence, Surveillance and Reconnaissance, MSc Intelligence Systems, MSc Intelligent Vision, MSc Robotics and Autonomous Systems

School of Engineering; www.lincoln.ac.uk/home/engineering

BEng(Hons) Automation Engineering, BEng/MEng(Hons) Electrical Engineering (Control Systems), BEng/MEng(Hons) Electrical Engineering (Electronics), BEng/MEng(Hons) Electrical Engineering (Power and Energy), BEng/MEng(Hons) Integrated Engineering, BEng/MEng(Hons) Mechanical Engineering, BEng/MEng(Hons) Mechanical Engineering (Control Systems), BEng/MEng(Hons) Mechanical Engineering (Power and Energy)
Postgraduate courses: MSc Engineering Management, MSc Mechanical Engineering

School of Geography; www.lincoln.ac.uk/home/geography

BA/BSc(Hons) Geography

School of Life Sciences; www.lincoln.ac.uk/home/lifesciences

BSc(Hons) Animal Behaviour and Welfare, MBio Animal Behaviour and Welfare, BSc(Hons) Biochemistry, MBio Biochemistry, BSc(Hons) Biology, MBio Biology, BSc(Hons) Biomedical Science, MBio Biomedical Science, BSc(Hons) Bioveterinary Science, MBio Bioveterinary Science, BSc(Hons) Ecology and Conservation, MBio Ecology and Conservation, BSc(Hons) Zoology, MBio Zoology
Postgraduate courses: MSc Biotechnology, MSc Clinical Animal Behaviour, MSc Microbial Biotechnology, MSc Microbiology

School of Mathematics and Physics; www.lincoln.ac.uk/home/smp

BSc(Hons) Mathematics, MMath Mathematics, BSc(Hons) Mathematics and Computer Science, BSc(Hons) Mathematics and Physics, MMath Mathematics and Physics, BSc(Hons) Mathematics with Philosophy, BSc(Hons) Physics, MPhys Physics, BSc(Hons) Physics with Philosophy, MPhys Physics with Philosophy
Postgraduate course: MSc Physics

School of Pharmacy; www.lincoln.ac.uk/home/lsp

BSc(Hons) Pharmaceutical Science, MPharm Pharmacy

National Centre for Food Manufacturing; www.lincoln.ac.uk/home/holbeach/apprenticeships

Level 7 Senior Leader Master's Degree Apprenticeships (option: MSc in Strategic Leadership in the Food and Drink Industry), Level 6 Degree Apprenticeships, Level 5 Higher Apprenticeships, Level 2 and 3 Apprenticeships and Advanced Apprenticeships

College of Social Science; www.lincoln.ac.uk/home/collegeofsocialscience

School of Education; www.lincoln.ac.uk/home/education

BA(Hons) Education, BSc(Hons) Education and Psychology
Postgraduate courses: MA Education, PGCE Postgraduate Certificate in Education (Primary), PGCE Postgraduate Certificate in Education (Secondary)

School of Health and Social Care; www.lincoln.ac.uk/home/shsc

BA(Hons) Applied Social Science, BSc(Hons) Health and Social Care, BSc(Hons) Midwifery, BSc(Hons) Nursing with Registered Nurse (Adult), BSc(Hons) Nursing with Registered Nurse (Children's Nursing), BSc(Hons), BSc(Hons) Nursing with Registered Nurse (Mental Health) Paramedic Science
Postgraduate courses: MSc Interprofessional Practice (Approved Mental Health Professional) PG Cert Nursing (Pre-registration-Adult), MSc Nursing (Pre-registration-Child), MSc Nursing (Pre-registration-Mental Health), MSc Occupational Therapy (pre-registration), MSc Physiotherapy (pre-registration), Postgraduate Certificate in Non-Medical PG Cert Prescribing/Practice Certificate in Independent Prescribing (Level 7, Level M), MSc Social Work, MSc Social Work Advanced Professional Practice

Lincoln Law School; www.lincoln.ac.uk/home/law

LLB(Hons) Law, LLB(Hons) Law and, LLB(Hons) Law for Business
Postgraduate courses: LLM Conflict and Disaster Law, MA Criminology and Criminal Justice, LLM International Corporate and Commercial Law, LLM International Law

School of Psychology; www.lincoln.ac.uk/home/psychology

BSc(Hons) Psychology, BSc(Hons) Psychology with Clinical Psychology, BSc(Hons) Psychology with Forensic Psychology

Postgraduate courses: MSc Developmental Psychology, MSc Forensic Psychology, MSc Psychological Research Methods, DclinPsy Psychology

School of Social & Political Sciences; www.lincoln.ac.uk/home/socialsciences

BA(Hons) Criminology, BA(Hons) Criminology and Social Policy, BA(Hons) Criminology and Sociology, BA(Hons) International Relations, BA(Hons) International Relations and Politics, BA(Hons) International Relations and Social Policy, BA(Hons) Politics, BA(Hons) Politics and Social Policy, BA(Hons) Politics and Sociology, BA(Hons) Social Policy, BA(Hons) Social Policy and Sociology, BA(Hons) Sociology

Postgraduate courses: MA Gender Studies, MA International Relations, MA Politics

School of Sport and Exercise Science; www.lincoln.ac.uk/home/sport

BSc(Hons) Health and Exercise Science, BSc(Hons) Physical Education and Sport, BSc(Hons) Sport and Exercise Science, BSc(Hons) Sport and Exercise Therapy, BSc(Hons) Sport Development and Coaching, BSc(Hons) Strength and Conditioning in Sport

Postgraduate courses: MSc Sport Science, MSc Sports Therapy

Lincoln International Business School; www.lincoln.ac.uk/home/lbs

BA(Hons) Accountancy and Finance, BA(Hons)Advertising and Marketing, (MFin) Banking and Finance, BSc(Hons) Banking and Finance, BA(Hons) Business and Enterprise Development, BA(Hons) Business and Finance, BA(Hons) Business and Management (with Professional Practice, BA(Hons) Business and Marketing (with Professional Practice), BA(Hons) Business Economics, BA(Hons) Business Management, BSc(Hons) Business Psychology, BA(Hons) Business Studies (with Professional Practice), BSc(Hons) Economics, (MEcon) Economics and Finance, BSc(Hons) Economics and Finance, BSc(Hons) Engineering Management, BSc(Hons) Events Management, BSc Human Resource Management (Open), BA(Hons) International Business Management, BA(Hons) International Tourism Management, FdSc Logistics Management, BSc(Hons) Logistics Management (Open), BA(Hons) Marketing Management, BA(Hons) Sports Business Management

Postgraduate courses: MSc Accounting, MSc Accounting and Finance, MSc Crisis and Disaster Management, MA Culture and Heritage Management, MSc Events Management, MSc Fashion Management, MSc Finance, MSc Governance, MSc Human Resource Management Full Time, MSc Human Resource Management Part Time, MSc International Business, MSc International Business Economics, MSc International Investment Banking, MSc International Tourism Management, MBA Leadership, MSc Logistics and Global Operations, MSc Management, MSc Management and International Relations, MSc Marketing, MSc Marketing with Luxury Brands, MBA Master of Business Administration (Full-time), MSc Project Management, MSc Tourism and Marketing

---

EAST RIDING COLLEGE
www.eastridingcollege.ac.uk

BA(Hons) Contemporary Media, Design and Production, BA(Hons) Education and Professional Development, BA(Hons) in Early Childhood Policy and Practice (Top-up), BA(Hons) Social Science, BA(Hons) Top Up in Public Service Management, BSc(Hons) Sports, Coaching and Health Sciences (Top-up), Foundation Degree in Computing, Foundation Degree in Early Childhood Studies Foundation Degree in Learning Support Foundation Degree in Public Services Management, Foundation Degree in Sport, Exercise and Health Sciences, ILM Level Seven NVQ Diploma in Strategic Management and Leadership, In-Service Certificate in Education (Lifelong Learning) and Professional Graduate Certificate in Education (Lifelong Learning), Masters in Education, Pre-Service Certificate in Education (Lifelong Learning), Pre-Service Professional Graduate Certificate in Education (PGCE)

HULL COLLEGE
www.hull-college.ac.uk

BA(Hons) Architecture, BA(Hons) Dance, BA(Hons) Fashion, BA(Hons) Film-Making and Creative Media Production, BA(Hons) Fine Art, BA(Hons) Games Design, BA(Hons) Graphic Design, BA(Hons) Illustration, BA(Hons) Journalism and Digital Media, BA(Hons) Music Performance, BA(Hons) Music Production, BA(Hons) Musical Theatre, BA(Hons) Photography, BA(Hons) Technical and Theatre Production, BA(Hons) Textiles, Foundation Degree Digital Design and Development, BA(Hons) Digital Design and Development, Foundation Degree Sound Design for Games and Media, Foundation Degree Sound Design for Games and Media, Foundation Degree Performing Arts, FdA Performing Arts, MA Creative Practice, MArch Architecture, BA(Hons) Applied Social Science, BA(Hons) Business and Management, BA(Hons) Business and Management (Top Up), BA(Hons) Criminology (Top Up), BA(Hons) Health and Social Care, BA(Hons) Young Children's Learning and Development, BEng(Hons) Engineering Technology, BSc(Hons) Computing, BSc(Hons) Construction Management (Top-Up), BEng(Hons) Engineering Technology, BSc(Hons) Sport and Health Sciences, Foundation Degree Business and Management, Foundation Degree Young Children's Learning and Development, Foundation Degree Criminology, Foundation Degree Travel and Tourism Management, Professional Graduate Certificate in Education (In-Service), Professional Graduate Certificate in Education (Pre-Service)

NORTH LINDSEY COLLEGE
www.northlindsey.ac.uk

Business, Education and Professional Development
BA(Hons) English and History Studies, BA(Hons) Business Studies, BA(Hons) Business and Management, FdA Management, Professional and Post Graduate Certificate in Education (PGCE), Certificate in Education (Cert. Ed.) FdA Children, Learning and Development (Early Childhood), FdA Children, Learning and Development (Learning Support), FdA Children Learning and Development (SEND), BA(Hons) Children, Learning and Development, MA Educational Research Practice

Engineering and Technology
FdSc Animal Welfare Science, FdEng Materials Engineering, FdEng Integrated Engineering Manufacturing FdEng Integrated Engineering (Mechanical)
Health, Life and Social Sciences
BA(Hons) Counselling, BA(Hons) Social Science, BSc(Hons) Sport, Exercise and Coaching Science, FdSc(Hons) Sport, Exercise and Coaching Science, FdA Counselling, FdSc Professional Practice in Health and Social Care

UNIVERSITY OF LIVERPOOL
www.liv.ac.uk

Department of Archaeology, Classics and Egyptology; www.liverpool.ac.uk/archaeology-classics-and-egyptology
Ancient History BA(Hons), Archaeology BA(Hons), Archaeology BSc(Hons), Archaeology of Ancient Civilisations BA(Hons), Classical Studies BA(Hons), Classics BA(Hons), Egyptology BA(Hons), Evolutionary Anthropology BSc(Hons)
Postgraduate courses: Archaeology MA, Archaeology MSc, Classics and Ancient History MA, Egyptology MA, Palaeoanthropology MSc

Department of Architecture; www.liverpool.ac.uk/architecture
Architecture BA(Hons), Architecture (Design Studies) BA
Postgraduate courses: Master of Architecture March

Department of Chemistry; www.liverpool.ac.uk/chemistry
Chemical Sciences BSc(Hons), Chemistry BSc(Hons), Chemistry for Sustainable Energy MChem Chemistry MChem, Chemistry with a Year in Industry BSc(Hons), Chemistry with Research in Industry MChem, Medicinal Chemistry BSc(Hons), Medicinal Chemistry with Pharmacology MChem
Postgraduate course: Advanced Chemical Sciences MSc

Department of Communication and Media; www.liverpool.ac.uk/communication-andmedia
Communication and Media BA, Game Design Studies BA

Postgraduate courses: Arts: Communication and Media MRes, Media and Communication: Digital Culture and Communication pathway MA, Media and Communication: Media and Politics pathway MA, Strategic Communication MSc (Based in London campus)

Department of Computer Science; www.liverpool.ac.uk/computer-science

Computer Science BSc(Hons), Computer Science MEng(Hons), Computer Science with Software Development BSc(Hons), Financial Computing BSc(Hons), Mathematics and Computer Science BSc (Joint Honours)

Postgraduate courses: Advanced Computer Science MSc, Advanced Computer Science with Internet Economics MSc, Big Data and High Performance Computing MSc, Computer Science MSc

Department of Dental Sciences; www.liverpool.ac.uk/study/ undergraduate/courses/departments/ index.php?department=dental-sciences

Dental Surgery BDS, Dental Dental Therapy BSc(Hons)

Postgraduate courses: Endodontics DDSc, Orthodontics DDSc, Paediatric Dentistry DDSc

Department of Earth Sciences; www.liverpool.ac.uk/earth-ocean-andecological-sciences

Earth Sciences entry route leading to BSc(Hons), Geology (North America) MESci(Hons), Geology and Geophysics MESci(Hons), Geology and Physical Geography BSc(Hons), Geology and Physical Geography MESci(Hons), Geology BSc(Hons), Geology MESci(Hons), Geophysics (Geology) BSc(Hons), Geophysics (North America) MESci(Hons), Geophysics (Physics) BSc(Hons)

Postgraduate course: Petroleum Reservoir Geoscience MSc

Department of Ecology and Marine Biology; www.liverpool.ac.uk/ecology

Marine Biology BSc(Hons), Marine Biology MMarBiol(Hons), Marine Biology with Oceanography BSc(Hons)

Postgraduate courses: Conservation and Resource Management MRes, Conservation and Resource Management MSc

Department of Electrical Engineering and Electronics; www.liverpool.ac.uk/ electrical-engineering-and-electronics

Avionic Systems BEng(Hons), Avionic Systems MEng(Hons), Computer Science and Electronic Engineering BEng(Hons), Computer Science and Electronic Engineering MEng(Hons), Electrical and Electronic Engineering BEng(Hons), Electrical and Electronic Engineering MEng(Hons), Mechatronics and Robotic Systems BEng(Hons), Mechatronics and Robotic Systems MEng(Hons)

Postgraduate courses: Energy and Power Systems MSc (Eng), Microelectronic Systems MSc (Eng), Telecommunications and Wireless Systems MSc (Eng)

Department of Engineering; www.liv.ac.uk/ engineering

Aerospace Engineering BEng(Hons), Aerospace Engineering MEng(Hons), Aerospace Engineering with Pilot Studies BEng(Hons), Aerospace Engineering with Pilot Studies MEng(Hons), Architectural Engineering BEng(Hons), Architectural Engineering MEng(Hons), Civil and Structural Engineering MEng(Hons), Civil Engineering BEng(Hons), Civil Engineering MEng(Hons), Engineering BEng(Hons), Engineering MEng(Hons), Industrial Design BEng, Industrial Design MEng, Mechanical Engineering BEng(Hons), Mechanical Engineering MEng(Hons)

Postgraduate courses: Advanced Aerospace Engineering MSc (Eng), Advanced Manufacturing Systems and Technology MSc (Eng), Advanced Mechanical Engineering MSc (Eng), Biomedical Engineering MSc (Eng), Advanced Transdisciplinary Design MSc(Eng), Product Design and Management MSc(Eng), Sustainable Civil and Structural Engineering MSc (Eng)

Department of English; www.liverpool.ac.uk/english

English BA(Hons), English Language BA(Hons), English Literature BA(Hons)

Postgraduate courses: Applied Linguistics MA, Arts: English MRes, English MA, English: Modern and Contemporary Literature MA, English: Renaissance and Eighteenth-Century Literature MA, English: Science Fiction Studies MA, English: Victorian Literature MA, Teaching English to Speakers of Other Languages (TESOL) MA

Department of Geography; www.liverpool.ac.uk/geography

Environmental Science BSc(Hons), Geography BA(Hons), Geography BSc(Hons), Geography and Planning BA(Hons), Geology and Physical Geography BSc, Geology and Physical Geography MESci, Geography and Oceanography BSc(Hons)

Postgraduate courses: Contemporary Human Geography (Research Methods) MA, Environment and Climate Change MSc, Environmental Sciences MSc, Geographic Data Science MSc

Department of Health Sciences; www.liv.ac.uk/healthsciences

Diagnostic Radiography BSc(Hons), Nursing BN(Hons), Occupational Therapy BSc(Hons), Orthoptics BSc(Hons), Physiotherapy BSc(Hons), Therapeutic Radiography and Oncology BSc(Hons)

Postgraduate courses: Advanced Practice in Healthcare MSc/PGDip/PGCert, Nursing MSc/PGDip/PGCert, Radiotherapy MSc, Radiotherapy PGDip

Department of History; www.liverpool.ac.uk/history

History BA(Hons)

Postgraduate courses: Archives MRes, Archives and Records Management MARM, Archives and Records Management (International Pathway) MARMI, History MRes, History: Cultural History MA, History: Eighteenth-Century Worlds MA, History: Medieval and Renaissance Studies MA, History: Twentieth-Century History MA, International Slavery Studies MA

Department of Irish Studies; www.liverpool.ac.uk/irish-studies

Irish Studies BA(Hons)

Postgraduate courses: Irish Studies MRes, Irish Studies MA/PGDip

Department of Law; www.liverpool.ac.uk/law

Law LLB(Hons), Law with Accounting and Finance LLB(Hons), Law with Criminology LLB(Hons)

Postgraduate courses: LLB Law for Graduates, International Economic Law LLM/PGDip/PGCert, International Human Rights Law LLM/PGDip/PGCert, Law, Medicine and Healthcare LLM/PGDip/PGCert, LLM (General) LLM/PGDip/PGCert

Department of Life Sciences; www.liverpool.ac.uk/life-sciences

Anatomy and Human Biology BSc(Hons), Biochemistry BSc(Hons), Biological and Medical Sciences BSc(Hons), Biological Sciences BSc(Hons), Biological Sciences MBiolSci, Bioveterinary Science BSc(Hons), Genetics BSc(Hons), Human Physiology BSc(Hons), Microbiology BSc(Hons), Pharmacology BSc(Hons), Tropical Disease Biology BSc(Hons), Zoology BSc(Hons)

Postgraduate courses: Advanced Biological Sciences MSc, Advanced Biological Sciences MRes

Management School; www.liverpool.ac.uk/management

Accounting and Finance BA(Hons), Business Economics BA(Hons), Business Management BA(Hons), Economics BSc(Hons), Finance BSc(Hons), International Business BA(Hons), Marketing BA(Hons)

Postgraduate courses: Accounting MSc (Based in London campus), Accounting and Finance MSc, Business Analytics and Big Data MSc, Economics MSc, Entrepreneurship MSc, Finance and Investment Management MSc (Based in London campus), Finance MSc, Football Industries MBA, Human Resource Management MSc (CIPD Accredited) MSc, International Accounting MSc (Based in London campus), International Business MSc, Management MRes, Marketing MSc, Master in Management MIM, MBA (The Liverpool MBA) on campus MBA, Occupational and Organisational Psychology MSc, Operations and Supply Chain Management MSc, Project Management MSc, Sports Business and Management MSc, Thoroughbred Horseracing Industries MBA

Department of Mathematical Sciences; www.liverpool.ac.uk/mathematicalsciences

Actuarial Mathematics BSc(Hons), French and Mathematics BA (Joint Hons), Mathematical Physics MMath, Mathematical Sciences entry route leading to BSc(Hons), Mathematics and Business Studies BSc (Joint Hons), Mathematics and Economics BSc(Hons), Mathematics and Music Technology BSc(Hons), Mathematics and Statistics BSc(Hons), Mathematics BSc(Hons), Mathematics MMath, Mathematics with Finance BSc(Hons), Mathematics with Languages BSc(Hons), Physics and Mathematics BSc (Joint Hons), Theoretical Physics MPhys

Postgraduate courses: Financial Mathematics MSc/PGDip/PGCert, Mathematical Sciences MSc/PGDip/PGCert

Department of Medicine; www.liverpool.ac.uk/medicine

Foundation to Health and Veterinary Studies, Medicine-Medicine and Surgery MBChB

Postgraduate courses: Medicine and Surgery MBChB (Graduate Entry), Master of Public Health MPH, Medical Education PGCert/PGDip/MSc, Physician Associate Studies PGDip, Master of Public Health MPH (Based in London campus), Renal Transplantation Science PGCert/PGDip/MSc (Online)

Department of Modern Languages and Cultures; www.liverpool.ac.uk/modernlanguages-and-cultures

Basque (Honours Select), Catalan (Honours select), Chinese (Honours Select), French BA(Hons), German BA(Hons), Hispanic Studies BA(Hons), Italian (Honours Select), Italian BA(Hons), Modern European Languages BA(Hons), Modern Language Studies BA (Joint Hons), Portuguese (Honours Select), Spanish (Honours Select)

Postgraduate courses: Basque Studies-Modern Languages and Cultures MRes, Catalan Studies-Modern Languages and Cultures MRes, Chinese Studies-Modern Languages and Cultures MRes, Film Studies-Modern Languages and Cultures MRes, French Studies-Modern Languages and Cultures MRes, German Studies-Modern Languages and Cultures MRes, Hispanic Studies-Modern Languages and Cultures MRes, Italian Studies-Modern Languages and Cultures MRes, Latin American Studies MRes, Modern Languages and Cultures MRes, Portuguese Studies-Modern Languages and Cultures MRes, Spanish Studies-Modern Languages and Cultures MRes

Department of Music; www.liverpool.ac.uk/music

Music and Popular Music BA(Hons), Music and Technology BA(Hons), Music BA(Hons), Popular Music BA(Hons)

Postgraduate courses: Arts: Music MRes, Classical Music Industry MA, Music Industry Studies MA, Performance MMus

Department of Ocean Sciences; www.liverpool.ac.uk/earth-ocean-andecological-sciences

Earth Sciences entry route leading to BSc(Hons), Geography and Oceanography BSc(Hons), Marine Biology with Oceanography BSc(Hons), Mathematics with Ocean and Climate Sciences BSc(Hons), Ocean Sciences BSc(Hons), Ocean Sciences MOSci(Hons)

Postgraduate course: MSc Marine Planning & Management, Sea Level: From Coast to Global Ocean MSc

Department of Philosophy; www.liverpool.ac.uk/philosophy

Mathematics and Philosophy BA (Joint Hons), Philosophy BA(Honours), Philosophy, Politics and Economics BA

Postgraduate courses: Art, Aesthetics and Cultural Institutions MA, Arts: Philosophy MRes, Philosophy MA

Department of Physics; www.liverpool.ac.uk/physics

Astrophysics MPhys, Physical Sciences entry route leading to BSc(Hons), Physics BSc(Hons), Physics MPhys, Physics with Astronomy BSc(Hons), Physics with Medical Applications BSc(Hons), Physics with Nuclear Science BSc(Hons)

Postgraduate courses: Nuclear Science and Technology MSc, Radiometrics: Instrumentation and Modelling MSc

Department of Planning; www.liverpool.ac.uk/geography-andplanning

Environment and Planning BA(Hons), Geography and Planning BA(Hons), Town and Regional Planning MPlan, Urban Planning BA(Hons)

Postgraduate courses: Environmental Assessment and Management MSc, Marine Planning and Management MSc, Town and Regional Planning M/CD, Town and Regional Planning MA, Urban Design and Property Development MSc (Based in London campus), Urban Planning MSc (Based in London campus)

Department of Politics; www.liverpool.ac.uk/politics

International Politics and Policy BA(Hons), Politics BA(Hons)

Postgraduate courses: International Relations and Security MA, International Relations and Security MRes

Department of Psychology; www.liverpool.ac.uk/psychology

Psychology BSc(Hons), Psychology BSc(Hons) (2+2 programme with Foundation Element), Psychology MPsycholSci(Hons)

Postgraduate courses: Doctor of Clinical Psychology DClinPsychol, Investigative and Forensic Psychology MSc/PGDip/PGCert, Research Methods in Psychology MSc/PGDip/PGCert

Department of Sociology, Social Policy and Criminology; www.liverpool.ac.uk/ sociology-social-policy-and-criminology

Criminology and Security BA(Hons), Criminology BA(Hons), Criminology with Social Policy BA(Hons), Criminology with Sociology BA(Hons), Social Policy BA (Honours Select), Sociology BA(Hons), Sociology with Criminology BA(Hons), Sociology with Social Policy BA(Hons)

Postgraduate courses: Criminological Research MRes, Social Research MRes, Social Research Methods MA

Department of Veterinary Science; www.liverpool.ac.uk/veterinary-science

Veterinary Conservation Medicine Intercalated Honours BSc, Foundation to Health and Veterinary Studies, Veterinary Science BVSc

Postgraduate courses: Bovine Reproduction DBR, Certificate in Advanced Veterinary Practice (CertAVP), Veterinary Business Management PGCert, (VBM) Veterinary Physiotherapy MSc/PGDip, Veterinary Professional Studies MSc /PGDip/PGCert, Veterinary Science MSc

---

LIVERPOOL HOPE UNIVERSITY
www.hope.ac.uk

Business School; www.hope.ac.uk/ businessschool

BA Accounting & Finance, BA Business Management, BA Marketing

Postgraduate courses: Educational Leadership MBA International MBA

Disability and Education; www.hope.ac.uk/ disabilityandeducation

BA Disability Studies in Education, BA Special Educational Needs

Postgraduate courses: MA Disability Studies, MA Special Educational Needs (Interdisciplinary Studies)

Drama, Dance and Performance Studies; www.hope.ac.uk/creativeperformingarts/

BA Creative and Performing Arts, BA Dance, BA Drama and Theatre Studies

Early Childhood; www.hope.ac.uk/ earlychildhood

BA Early Childhood

Postgraduate course: MA Developmental Psychology (Interdisciplinary Studies), MA Early Childhood (Interdisciplinary Studies)

Education Studies; www.hope.ac.uk/ educationstudies

BA Education

Postgraduate courses: MA Education, MA International Education, MA & MEd Professional Practice

English; www.hope.ac.uk/english

BA English Language, BA English Literature

Postgraduate courses: MA English Literature

Fine and Applied Art; www.hope.ac.uk/ creativeperformingarts

BA Art and Design History, BA Design, BA Fine Art, BA Graphic Design

Geography and Environmental Science; www.hope.ac.uk/geography

BSc Biogeography, BSc Environmental Change and Tourism, BSc Environmental Geography, BSc Environmental Science, BSc Geography, BSc Physical Geography, BSc Tourism, BA Tourism Management

Postgraduate course: MSc Ecology and Environmental Management

Health Sciences; www.hope.ac.uk/ healthsciences

BSc Clinical Nutrition, BSc Nutrition, BSc Sport and Exercise Science, BSc Sport and Physical Education, BSc Sport Psychology, BSc Sport Rehabilitation

Postgraduate courses: Sport and Exercise Science (MRes)

History and Politics; www.hope.ac.uk/ historyandpolitics

BA History, BA International Relations, BA Politics, BA Politics and International Relations

Postgraduate courses: MA History

Law; www.hope.ac.uk/law

LLB Law (Qualifying Law Degree), BA Law

Mathematics and Computer Science; www.hope.ac.uk/ mathematicsandcomputerscience

BSc Computer Science, BEng Electronic and Computer Engineering, MEng Electronic and Computer Engineering, BSc Mathematics, MMath Mathematics, BEng Robotics, MEng Robotics

Postgraduate courses: MSc Advanced Computer Science, MSc Computer Science, MSc Data Science, MSc Mathematical Informatics (Dual International Masters), MSc Robotics Engineering

Media and Communication; www.hope.ac.uk/ mediaandcommunication

BA Media and Communication, BA Creative Writing, BA Film and Visual Culture
Postgraduate courses: MA Film, Media and Society

Music; www.hope.ac.uk/ creativeperformingarts/

BA Music, BA Popular Music

Psychology; www.hope.ac.uk/psychology

BSc Psychology, BSc Sport Psychology
Postgraduate courses: MSc Cognitive Neuroscience and Neuroimaging, MSc Psychology

Social Science; www.hope.ac.uk/ socialsciences

BA Applied Social Sciences, BA Criminology, BA Sociology
Postgraduate courses: MA Criminology, MA Sociology

Social Work, Care and Justice; www.hope.ac.uk/socialworkcareandjustice

BA Childhood and Youth, BA Health and Wellbeing, BA Health and Social Care, BA Social Policy, BA Social Work
Postgraduate courses: MA Social Policy, MA Social Work, MA Youth and Community Work

School of Teacher Education; www.hope.ac.uk/teachereducation

BA Primary Education (QTS)
Postgraduate courses: PGCE Early Years (QTS), PGCE Primary (QTS), PGCE Secondary (QTS), PGDE in FE MA/MEd Professional Practice, Education Doctorate EdD, School Direct

Theology, Philosophy and Religion; www.hope.ac.uk/theology

BA Christian Theology, BA Philosophy and Ethics, BA Philosophy, Ethics and Religion, BA Religious Studies, BA Theology, BA Theology and Religious Studies
Postgraduate courses: MA African Christianity, MA, MA Bible and Pastoral Contexts, MA/MEd Christian Education and Leadership, PG Cert Biblical Studies

LIVERPOOL JOHN MOORES UNIVERSITY
www.ljmu.ac.uk

Faculty of Arts, Professional and Social Studies; www.ljmu.ac.uk/about-us/ faculties/faculty-of-arts-professionaland- social-studies

Liverpool School of Art and Design; www.ljmu.ac.uk/about-us/faculties/ faculty-of-arts-professional-and- socialstudies/liverpool-school-of-art-and- design

Architecture BA(Hons), Fashion: Design and Communication BA(Hons), Fine Art BA(Hons), Graphic Design and Illustration BA(Hons), History of Art and Museum Studies BA(Hons), Interior Architecture BA(Hons)
Postgraduate courses: Architecture MArch, Art in Science MA, Exhibition Studies MA, Fashion Innovation and Realisation MA, Fine Art MA, Graphic Design and Illustration MA, Urban Design MA

Liverpool Screen School; www.ljmu.ac.uk/ about-us/faculties/faculty-of- artsprofessional-and-social-studies/ liverpoolscreen-school

Creative Writing BA(Hons), Creative Writing and Film Studies BA(Hons), Drama BA(Hons), Drama and Creative Writing BA(Hons), Drama and English Literature BA(Hons), English Literature and Creative Writing BA(Hons), Film Studies BA(Hons), Journalism BA(Hons), Media Production BA(Hons), Sports Journalism BA(Hons)
Postgraduate courses: Cities, Culture and Creativity MA, Creative Technology MA, Documentary MA, Film MA, Immersive Arts MA, International Journalism MA, International News Journalism MA, Musical Theatre MA, Screenwriting MA, Writing MA

School of Justice Studies; www.ljmu.ac.uk/about-us/faculties/faculty-of-arts-professional-and-social-studies/school-of-justice-studies/courses

Criminal Justice BA(Hons), Criminology BA(Hons), Criminology and Psychology BSc(Hons), Forensic Psychology and Criminal Justice BSc(Hons), Law and Criminal Justice LLB(Hons), Policing Studies BA(Hons), Policing Studies FDA, Policing Studies and Cybercrime BSc(Hons), Policing Studies and Forensics BSc(Hons), Professional Policing BA(Hons), Professional Policing Practice BSc(Hons)

Postgraduate courses: Counter-Terrorism Studies MSc, Criminal Justice MA, Criminology and Social Policy MA, Diplomacy and Security Studies MSc, Evidence Informed Practice MA/PgDip/PgCert, Intelligence and Security Studies MSc, International and Transnational Policing MSc, Policing and Criminal Investigation MSc, Policing and Cybercrime MSc, Policing and Law Enforcement Leadership MSc, Security and Terrorism Law MA, Security Management MSc, Security Studies MSc, Terrorism, Policing and Security MSc

School of Humanities and Social Science; www.ljmu.ac.uk/about-us/faculties/faculty-of-arts-professional-and-socialstudies/school-of-humanities-and-socialscience

Criminology and Sociology BA(Hons), English Literature BA(Hons), English, Media and Cultural Studies BA(Hons), History BA(Hons), History and English Literature BA(Hons), International Relations and Politics BA(Hons), Media, Culture, Communication BA(Hons), Sociology BA(Hons)

Postgraduate courses: English Literature MA, International Relations MA, Mass Communications MA

School of Law; www.ljmu.ac.uk/about-us/faculties/faculty-of-arts-professional-andsocial-studies/school-of-law

Law LLB(Hons), Law and Business BA(Hons)

Postgraduate courses: Global Crime, Justice and Security LLM, International Business Corporate and Finance Law LLM, International Corporate Law and Management LLM/MSc, Legal Practice Course LPC/LLM/PgDip, Legal Practice (LPC BPTC Conversion) LLM, Master of Laws LLM, Qualifying Law LLM

Faculty of Education, Health and Community; www.ljmu.ac.uk/about-us/faculties/faculty-of-education-healthand-community

School of Education; www.ljmu.ac.uk/about-us/faculties/faculty-of-educationhealth-and-community/school-ofeducation

Early Childhood Studies BA(Hons), Education Studies BA(Hons), Education Studies and Early Years BA(Hons), Education Studies and Inclusion BA(Hons), Learning, Development and Support BA(Hons), Primary Education with recommendation for Qualified Teacher Status (QTS) BA(Hons)

Postgraduate courses: Art and Design: Secondary with Qualified Teacher Status (QTS) PGDE, Biology: Secondary with Qualified Teacher Status (QTS) PGDE, Chemistry: Secondary with Qualified Teacher Status (QTS) PGDE, Computer Science: Secondary with Qualified Teacher Status (QTS) PGDE, Design and Technology: Secondary PGDE with QTS, Digital Literacies and Learning PgDip, Education Practice MA, Geography: Secondary with Qualified Teacher Status (QTS) PGDE, History: Secondary with Qualified Teacher Status (QTS) PGDE, Leadership in Education MA, Mathematics: Secondary with Qualified Teacher Status (QTS) PGDE, Media Studies: Secondary with Qualified Teacher Status (QTS) PGDE, Modern Foreign Languages: Secondary with Qualified Teacher Status (QTS) PGDE, Performing Arts (Dance): Secondary with Qualified Teacher Status (QTS) PGDE, Performing Arts (Drama): Secondary with Qualified Teacher Status (QTS) PGDE, PGDE Primary Key Stage 1/2 (5-11 years) with Qualified Teacher Status (QTS) PGDE, Physical Education: Secondary with Qualified Teacher Status (QTS) PGDE, Physics: Secondary with Qualified Teacher Status (QTS) PGDE, Physics with Mathematics: Secondary with Qualified Teacher Status (QTS) PGDE, Primary Foundation Stage/Key Stage 1 (3-7 years) with QTS PGDE, Primary with Mathematics Specialism (5-11 years) with QTS PGDE, Primary with Physical Education Specialism (5-11 years) and QTS PGDE, Religious Education: Secondary with Qualified Teacher Status (QTS) PGDE, School Direct Initial Teacher Training (salaried) with QTS PGCert, School Direct Primary Initial Teacher Training with QTS, School Direct Secondary Initial Teacher Training with QTS, Special Educational Needs Co-ordinator (SENCO) PGCert, Teaching Learners with a Visual Impairment (QTVI) PgDip

School of Nursing and Allied Health; www.ljmu.ac.uk/about-us/faculties/faculty-of-education-health-andcommunity/school-of-nursing-and-alliedhealth

Adult Nursing BSc(Hons), Child Nursing BSc(Hons), Mental Health Nursing BSc(Hons) with Registered Nurse Status, Midwifery BA(Hons) with Registered Midwife Status, Nursing (International) Top Up Degree BSc(Hons), Paramedicine BSc(Hons), Paramedic Science BSc(Hons)

Postgraduate courses: Advanced Healthcare Practice (Clinical) MSc, Advanced Paediatric and Neonatal Practice MSc, Counselling and Psychotherapy Practice MA, Improving Access to Psychological Therapies in Primary Care PGCert, Nursing MA, Nursing Clinical Education MA, Nursing Mental Health MA, Paramedicine MSc, Social Work MA, Specialist Community Practitioner (District Nursing) PgDip, Specialist Community Public Health Nursing PgDip, Specialist Practitioner: Community Children's Nursing PgDip

School of Sport Studies, Leisure and Nutrition; www.ljmu.ac.uk/about-us/faculties/faculty-of-education-healthand-community/school-of-sport-studiesleisure-and-nutrition

Disability Sport Coaching and Development Foundation Degree, Nutrition BSc(Hons), Physical Education BA(Hons), Sport and Nutrition for Health BSc(Hons), Sport Coaching BSc(Hons), Sport Development BA(Hons)

Postgraduate courses: MA Dance Practices, Public Health Nutrition MSc, Sport Coaching MSc

Faculty of Science; www.ljmu.ac.uk/about-us/faculties/faculty-of-science

School of Natural Sciences and Psychology; www.ljmu.ac.uk/about-us/faculties/faculty-of-science/school-of-naturalsciences-and-psychology

Animal Behaviour BSc(Hons), Biology BSc(Hons), Forensic Anthropology BSc(Hons), Geography BSc(Hons), Psychology BSc(Hons), Wildlife Conservation BSc(Hons), Zoology BSc(Hons)

Postgraduate courses: Brain and Behaviour MSc, Environmental Science and Drone Applications MSc, Forensic Anthropology MSc, Health Psychology MSc, Positive Psychology and Wellbeing MSc, Primate Behaviour and Conservation MSc, Professional Doctorate in Health Psychology DHealthPsych, Wildlife Conservation and Drone Applications MSc

School of Pharmacy and Biomolecular Sciences; www.ljmu.ac.uk/about-us/faculties/faculty-of-science/school-ofpharmacy-and-biomolecular-sciences

Biochemistry BSc(Hons), Biomedical Science BSc(Hons), Biotechnology BSc(Hons), Chemistry BSc(Hons), Forensic Science BSc(Hons), Pharmaceutical Science BSc(Hons), Pharmacy MPharm

Postgraduate courses: Clinical Pharmacy for Primary and Interface Care PGCert/PGDip/MSc, Clinical Pharmacy for Secondary and Tertiary Care PGCert/PGDip/MSc, Cosmetic Science MSc, Drug Discovery and Design PGCert/PGDip/MSc, Forensic Bioscience MSc, Industrial Biotechnology MSc, Pharmaceutical Manufacture and Quality Control PGCert/PGDip/MSc

School of Sport and Exercise Sciences; www.ljmu.ac.uk/about-us/faculties/faculty-of-science/school-of-sportandexercise-sciences

Science and Football BSc(Hons) Sport and Exercise Science BSc(Hons), Sport Psychology BSc(Hons)

Postgraduate courses: Clinical Exercise Physiology MSc, Exercise Physiology MSc, Professional Doctorate in Applied Sport and Exercise Science DSportExSci, Professional Doctorate in Sport and Exercise Psychology DSportExPsy, Sport and Clinical Biomechanics MSc, Sport Nutrition MSc, Sport Psychology MSc, Strength and Conditioning MSc

Faculty of Engineering and Technology; www.ljmu.ac.uk/about-us/faculties/faculty-of-engineering-and-technology

Department of Applied Mathematics; www.ljmu.ac.uk/about-us/faculties/faculty-of-engineering-and-technology/department-of-applied-mathematics

Mathematics BSc(Hons), Mathematics with Finance BSc(Hons)

Department of the Built Environment; www.ljmu.ac.uk/about-us/faculties/faculty-of-engineering-and-technology/department-of-the-built-environment

Architectural Engineering BEng/MEng(Hons), Architectural Technology BSc(Hons), Building Services Engineering BEng/ MEng(Hons), Building Services Engineering Project Management BSc(Hons), Building Surveying BSc(Hons), Construction and Property

HNC, Construction Engineering BEng(Hons), Construction Management BSc(Hons), Quantity Surveying BSc(Hons), Real Estate BSc(Hons)

Postgraduate courses: Commercial Building Surveying MSc,Construction Project Management MSc, Project Management MSc, Quantity Surveying and Commercial Management MSc, Real Estate MSc

Department of Civil Engineering; www.ljmu.ac.uk/about-us/faculties/ faculty-of-engineering-and-technology/ department-of-civil-engineering

Civil and Environmental Engineering MEng(Hons), Civil and Offshore Engineering MEng(Hons), Civil and Structural Engineering MEng(Hons), Civil and Transportation Engineering MEng(Hons), Civil Engineering BEng/MEng(Hons) Civil Engineering and Architecture MEng(Hons), Civil Engineering and Construction Management MEng(Hons)

Postgraduate course: Civil Engineering MSc, Water, Energy and the Environment MSc

Department of Computer Science; www.ljmu.ac.uk/about-us/faculties/ faculty-of-engineering-and-technology/ department-of-computer-science

Computer Forensics BSc(Hons), Computer Games Development BSc(Hons), Computer Networks BSc(Hons), Computer Science BSc(Hons), Computer Security MComp/ BSc(Hons), Computer Studies BSc(Hons), Data Science BSc(Hons), Digital and Technology Solutions BSc(Hons), Multimedia Computing BSc(Hons), Software Engineering BSc(Hons)

Postgraduate courses: Computing and Information Systems MSc, Cyber Security MSc

Department of Electronics and Electrical Engineering www.ljmu.ac.uk/about-us/ faculties/faculty-ofengineering-and- technology/departmentof-electronics- and-electrical-engineering

Audio and Music Production BSc(Hons), Computing and Smart Devices BSc(Hons), Control and Automation Engineering BEng(Hons), Electrical and Electronic Engineering BEng/MEng(Hons), Electrical Power Engineering BEng(Hons), Electronic Engineering BEng(Hons), Mechatronics and Autonomous Systems BEng/MEng(Hons), Product Design Engineering BSc(Hons), Video Production and Streaming BSc(Hons)

Postgraduate courses: Audio Forensics and Restoration MSc, Electrical Power and Control Engineering MSc, Embedded Systems and IC Design MSc, Sensors, Data and Management MSc, Wireless Communications MSc

Department of Maritime and Mechanical Engineering; www.ljmu.ac.uk/about-us/ faculties/faculty-of-engineering- andtechnology/department-of-maritime- andmechanical-engineering

Marine and Mechanical Engineering BEng/MEng(Hons), Maritime Business and Management BSc(Hons), Mechanical Engineering BEng/MEng(Hons), Mechanical Engineering with Management BEng/ MEng(Hons), Nautical Science BSc(Hons)

Postgraduate courses: Drone Technology and Applications MSc, International Transport, Trade and Logistics MSc, Logistics and Supply Chain Management MSc, Marine and Offshore Engineering MSc, Maritime Operations Management MSc, Port Management MSc, Unmanned Aircraft Systems Design MSc

Liverpool Business School; www.ljmu.ac.uk/about-us/faculties/ liverpool-business-school

Accounting and Finance BSc(Hons), Business and Human Resource Management BA(Hons), Business and Public Relations BA(Hons), Business Management BA(Hons), Business Management Practice (Chartered Manager Degree Apprenticeship) BA(Hons), Business with Finance BA(Hons), Business with International Business Management BA(Hons), Business with Marketing BA(Hons), Events BA(Hons), Human Resource Management BA(Hons), International Tourism Management BA(Hons), Marketing BA(Hons), Sport Business BA(Hons)

Postgraduate courses: Digital Marketing MSc, Doctorate in Business Administration DBA, Entrepreneurship MSc, Financial Management MSc, Human Resource Management MA, International Business and Management MSc, International Events Management MSc, International Human Resource Management MSc, International Public Relations MSc, International Tourism Management MSc, Leadership and Management Practice MSc, Management MSc, Management and Digital Business MSc, MBA, Public Relations MSc

UNIVERSITY OF THE ARTS LONDON
www.arts.ac.uk

Camberwell College of Arts; www.arts.ac.uk/camberwell

BA(Hons) Fine Art Painting, BA(Hons) Fine Art Drawing, BA(Hons) Fine Art Photography, BA(Hons) Fine Art Sculpture, BA(Hons) Graphic Design, BA(Hons) Illustration, BA(Hons) Interior and Spatial Design

Postgraduate courses: MA Designer Maker, MA Fine Art Drawing, MA Fine Art Painting, MA Fine Art Printmaking, MA Graphic Design Communication, MA Illustration, Graduate Diploma Illustration

Central Saint Martins; www.arts.ac.uk/csm

BA(Hons) Acting – Drama Centre London, BA(Hons) Architecture, BA(Hons) Ceramic Design, BA(Hons) Culture, Criticism and Curation, BA(Hons) Fashion: Fashion Design with Knitwear, BA(Hons) Fashion: Fashion Design with Marketing, BA(Hons) Fashion: Fashion Design Menswear, BA(Hons) Fashion: Fashion Design Womenswear, BA(Hons) Fashion: Fashion Print, BA(Hons) Fashion Communication: Fashion Communication and Promotion, BA(Hons) Fashion Communication: Fashion History and Theory, BA(Hons) Fashion Communication: Fashion Journalism, BA(Hons) Fine Art, BA(Hons) Graphic Communication Design, BA(Hons) Jewellery Design, BA(Hons) Performance: Design and Practice, BA(Hons) Product Design, BA(Hons) Textile Design

Postgraduate courses: Central Saint Martins Birkbeck MBA, Graduate Diploma in Fashion, MA Acting – Drama Centre London, MA Applied Imagination in the Creative Industries, M Arch Architecture, MA Art and Science, MA Arts and Cultural Enterprise, MA Biodesign MA Character Animation, MA Cities, MA Contemporary Photography; Practices and Philosophies, MA Culture, Criticism and Curation, MA Design (Ceramics/Furniture/Jewellery), MA Directing, MA Dramatic Writing, MA Fashion, MA Fashion Communication, MA Fine Art, MA Graphic Communication Design, MA Industrial Design, MA Innovation Management, MA Material Futures, MA Narrative Environments, MA Performance Design and Practice, MA Photography, MA Screen: Acting – Drama Centre London, MA Screen: Directing – Drama Centre London, MRes Art: Exhibition Studies, MRes Art: Moving Image, MRes Art: Theory and Philosophy

Chelsea College of Arts; www.arts.ac.uk/chelsea

BA(Hons) Fine Art, BA(Hons) Graphic Design Communication, BA(Hons) Interior Design, BA(Hons) Product and Furniture Design, BA(Hons) Textile Design

Postgraduate courses: MA Curating & Collections, MA Fine Art, MA Interior and Spatial Design, MA Textile Design, Graduate Diploma Fine Art, Graduate Diploma Graphic Design, Graduate Diploma Interior Design, Graduate Diploma Textile Design

London College of Communication; www.arts.ac.uk/lcc

Preparation for Design, Media and Screen (Certificate in Higher Education), BA(Hons) Advertising, BA(Hons) Animation, BA(Hons) Contemporary Media Cultures, BA(Hons) Design for Art Direction, BA(Hons) Design for Branded Spaces, BA(Hons) Design Management, BA(Hons) Film Practice, BA(Hons) Film and Screen Studies, BA(Hons) Film and Television, BA(Hons) Games Design, BA(Hons) Graphic and Media Design, BA(Hons) Graphic Branding and Identity, BA(Hons) Illustration and Visual Media, BA(Hons) Interaction Design Arts, BA(Hons) Journalism, BA(Hons) Magazine Journalism and Publishing, BA(Hons) Media Communications, BA(Hons) Photography, BA(Hons) Photojournalism and Documentary Photography, BA(Hons) Public Relations, BA(Hons) Sound Arts and Design, BA(Hons) Television and Live Events Production, BA(Hons) User Experience Design, BA(Hons) Virtual Reality

Postgraduate courses: Graduate Diploma Photography, MA 3D Computer Animation, MA Advertising, MA Animation, MA Arts and Lifestyle Journalism, MA Data Journalism, MA Data Visualisation, MA Design for Art Direction, MA Design Management MA Design Histories and Futures, MA Design for Social Innovation and Sustainable Futures, MA Documentary Film, MA Film, MA Games Design, MA Graphic Branding and Identity, MA Graphic Media Design, MA Illustration and Visual Media, MA Interaction Design Communication, MA Media, Communications and Critical Practice, MA Photography, MA Photojournalism and Documentary Photography, MA Photojournalism and Documentary Photography (Part Time/ Online Mode), MA

Public Relations, MA Publishing, MA Screenwriting, MA Service Design, MA Sound Arts, MA Television, MA User Experience Design, MA Virtual Reality, MA Visual Effects, Postgraduate Certificate Design for Visual Communication, Postgraduate Diploma Design for Visual Communication

London College of Fashion;
www.arts.ac.uk/fashion

International Preparation for Fashion (Certificate in Higher Education), BA(Hons) 3D Effects for Performance and Fashion, BA(Hons) Bespoke Tailoring, BA(Hons) Cordwainers Fashion Bags and Accessories: Product Design and Innovation, BA(Hons) Cordwainers Footwear: Product Design and Innovation, BA(Hons) Costume for Performance, BA(Hons) Creative Direction for Fashion, BA(Hons) Fashion Buying and Merchandising, BA(Hons) Fashion Contour, BA(Hons) Fashion Design and Development, BA(Hons) Fashion Design Technology: Menswear, BA(Hons) Fashion Design Technology: Womenswear, BA(Hons) Fashion Imaging and Illustration, BA(Hons) Fashion Jewellery, BA(Hons) Fashion Journalism, BSc(Hons) Fashion Management, BA(Hons) Fashion Marketing, BA(Hons) Fashion Pattern Cutting, BA(Hons) Fashion Photography, BA(Hons) Fashion Public Relations and Communication, BA(Hons) Fashion Sportswear, BA(Hons) Fashion Styling and Production, BA(Hons) Fashion Textiles: Embroidery, BA(Hons) Fashion Textiles: Knit, BA(Hons) Fashion Textiles: Print, BA(Hons)

Fashion Visual Merchandising and Branding, BA(Hons) Hair and Make-up for Fashion, BA(Hons) Hair, Make-up and Prosthetics for Performance, BSc(Hons) Psychology of Fashion, MA Fashion Media Practice and Criticism, MSc Cosmetic Science, MSc Strategic Fashion Management

Postgraduate courses: MBA (Fashion), Graduate Diploma Fashion Management, Graduate Diploma Fashion Design Technology, LCF MBA, MA Costume Design for Performance, MA Fashion Artefact, MA Fashion Cultures: History and Culture, MA Fashion Curation, MA Fashion Design Management, MA Fashion Design Technology Menswear, MA Fashion Design Technology Womenswear, MA Fashion Entrepreneurship and Innovation, MA Fashion Futures, MA Fashion Journalism, MA Fashion Media Production, MA Fashion Photography, MA Fashion Retail Management, MA Footwear, MA Pattern and Garment Technology, MA Strategic Fashion Marketing, MSc Applied Psychology in Fashion, Postgraduate Certificate Fashion: Buying and Merchandising, Postgraduate Certificate Fashion: Fashion Visual Merchandising

Wimbledon College of Arts;
www.arts.ac.uk/wimbledon

BA(Hons) Acting and Performance, BA(Hons) Contemporary Theatre and Performance, BA(Hons) Costume for Theatre and Screen, BA(Hons) Production Arts for Screen, BA(Hons) Theatre DesignPostgraduate: MA Theatre Design

LONDON CONTEMPORARY DANCE SCHOOL
www.theplace.org.uk

BA(Hons) in Contemporary Dance

Postgraduate courses: PGDip/MA in Contemporary Dance, PGDip/MA in Developing Artistic Practice

LONDON METROPOLITAN UNIVERSITY
www.londonmet.ac.uk

Guildhall School of Business and Law;
www.londonmet.ac.uk/schools/businessand-law

Accounting and Finance BA(Hons), Accounting and Finance (Extended Degree) BA(Hons), Advertising, Marketing Communications and Public Relations BA(Hons), Airline, Airport and Aviation Management BSc(Hons), Banking and Finance BSc(Hons),

Banking and Finance (with Integrated Professional Training) BSc(Hons), Business Economics BA(Hons), Business Management BA(Hons), Business Management (Extended Degree) BA(Hons), Business Management and Marketing BA(Hons), Business Studies BA(Hons), CICM Diploma in Credit Management Level 3 Diploma, CICM Diploma in Credit Management Level 5 Diploma, CIM Certificate in

Professional Marketing Certificate, CIM Diploma in Professional Marketing Diploma, Commercial Law LLB(Hons), Digital Business Management BSc(Hons), Economics BSc(Hons), Economics and Finance BSc(Hons), Events Management BA(Hons), Fashion Marketing and Business Management BA(Hons), Financial Mathematics BSc(Hons), Human Resource Management Int Dip PD, International Business Management BSc(Hons), International Business Management (Top-Up) BSc(Hons), Law BA(Hons), Law (with International Relations) LLB(Hons), LLB (Criminal Law)(Hons), LLB Law(Hons), Marketing BA(Hons), Music Business BA(Hons), Tourism and Travel Management BA(Hons), Translation BA(Hons) Postgraduate courses: Aviation Management in the Digital Age MSc, Common Professional Exam GDL, Conference Interpreting MA, Corporate Social Responsibility and Sustainability Adv Dip Pro Dev, Corporate Social Responsibility and Sustainability MSc, Employment Law and Practice Adv Dip Pro Dev Human Resource Management MA, Human Resource Management PG Dip, International Trade and Finance MSc, Interpreting MA, Legal Practice LLM, Legal Practice Course PG Dip, LLM Legal Practice LLM, Management and Strategic Leadership (Top-Up) MA, Maritime Law (Top-Up) (Distance Learning) LLM, Marketing MA, Master of Business Administration MBA, Master of Business Administration (Architecture) MBA, Master of Business Administration (Arts Management) #MBA, Master of Business Administration (Business Psychology) MBA, Master of Business Administration (Cyber Security) MBA, Master of Business Administration (Data Analytics) MBA, Master of Business Administration (Islamic Finance) MBA, MBA (Top Up) MBA, Media and Entertainment Law LLM, Media and Entertainment Law PG Dip, Teaching Languages (Arabic) MA, Teaching Languages (English) MA, Translation MA

School of Computing and Digital Media; www.londonmet.ac.uk/schools/computing-and-digital-media

Beauty Marketing and Journalism BA(Hons), Business Computer Systems (Top Up) BSc(Hons), Business Information Technology BSc(Hons), Computer Networking and Infrastructure Security BEng(Hons), Computer Networking and Cyber Security BSc(Hons), Computer Science BSc(Hons), Computer Systems Engineering and Robotics BEng(Hons), Computing BSc(Hons), Computing Extended Degree BSc(Hons), Computing, Technology and Mathematics Extended Degree BSc(Hons), Creative Music Technologies BA(Hons), Cyber Security and Forensic Computing (Top-up) BSc(Hons), Digital Forensics and Cyber Security BSc(Hons), Digital Media BA(Hons), Electronics and Internet of Things BEng(Hons), Fashion Marketing and Journalism BA(Hons), Film and Television Production BA(Hons), Film and Television Studies BA(Hons), Games Animation, Modelling and Effects BSc(Hons), Games Programming BSc(Hons), Journalism BA(Hons), Journalism FdA, Journalism, Film and Television Studies BA(Hons), Mathematical Sciences BSc(Hons), Mathematics BSc(Hons), Mathematics Extended Degree BSc(Hons), Mathematics and Computer Science BSc(Hons), Media and Communications BSc(Hons), Media and Communications Extended Degree (including Foundation Year) BSc(Hons), Media and Marketing BA(Hons), Media and Public Relations BA(Hons), Media with Arabic BA(Hons), Media with French BA(Hons), Media with Languages BA(Hons), Media with Spanish BA(Hons), Media, Communications and Journalism BSc(Hons), Multimedia Journalism BA(Hons), Music Technology and Production BSc(Hons), Photojournalism BA(Hons), Software Engineering (Top-up) BEng(Hons)

Postgraduate courses: Computer Networking and Cyber Security MSc, Data Analytics MSc, Digital Media MA, Information Technology (Distance Learning) MSc

School of Human Sciences; www.londonmet.ac.uk/schools/humansciences

Biochemistry BSc(Hons), Biochemistry Extended Degree BSc(Hons), Biological Science BSc(Hons), Biological Sciences Extended Degree BSc(Hons), Biology of Infectious Disease BSc(Hons), Biomedical Science BSc(Hons), Biomedical Science Extended Degree BSc(Hons), Biomedical Science leading to MD BSc(Hons), Biotechnology BSc(Hons), Biotechnology Extended Degree BSc(Hons), Chemistry BSc(Hons), Chemistry Extended Degree BSc(Hons), Dietetics BSc(Hons), Dietetics and Nutrition BSc(Hons), Forensic Science BSc(Hons), Forensic Science Extended Degree BSc(Hons), Herbal Medicinal Science (Top-Up) BSc(Hons), Human Nutrition BSc(Hons), Human Nutrition Extended Degree BSc(Hons), Medical Bioscience BSc(Hons), Medical Bioscience Extended Degree BSc(Hons), Medical Sciences BSc(Hons), Medicinal Chemistry and Drug Discovery BSc(Hons), Natural Sciences (Biology)

BSc(Hons), Natural Sciences (Chemistry) BSc(Hons), Pharmaceutical Science BSc(Hons), Pharmaceutical Science Extended Degree BSc(Hons), Pharmacology BSc(Hons), Pharmacology Extended Degree BSc(Hons), Public Health and Health Promotion (Top-up) BSc(Hons), Sciences Extended Degree (Biology, Chemistry, Health, Psychology) BSc(Hons), Sport and Exercise Performance Analysis BSc(Hons), Sport and Exercise Science BSc(Hons), Sport Psychology, Coaching and Physical Education BSc(Hons), Sports and Dance Therapy BSc(Hons), Sports Therapy BSc(Hons), Sports Therapy Extended Degree BSc(Hons), Toxicology BSc(Hons)

Postgraduate courses: Biomedical Science MSc, Biomedical Studies (Distance Learning) MSc, Blood Science MSc, Blood Science (Distance Learning) MSc, Cancer Immunotherapy MSc, Cancer Pharmacology MSc, Dietetics and Nutrition MSc, Food Science MSc, Human Nutrition (Public Health / Sports) MSc, Medical Genomics MSc, Pharmaceutical Science and Drug Delivery Systems MSc, Sports Therapy MSc

School of Social Professions; www.londonmet.ac.uk/schools/ socialprofessions

Community Development and Leadership BSc(Hons), Community Development and Youth Extended Degree BSc(Hons), Creative Writing and English Literature Extended Degree BA(Hons), Early Childhood Studies BA(Hons), Early Childhood Studies FdA, Early Childhood Studies Extended Degree (including Foundation Year) BA(Hons), Education and Social Policy BA(Hons), Education BA(Hons), Education: Early Years and Primary FdA, Education Studies and English Literature BA(Hons), Education Studies Extended Degree (including Foundation Year) BA(Hons), Health and Social Care BSc(Hons), Master of Public Administration (MPA) MA, Montessori Early Childhood Practice FdA, Primary Education BA(Hons), Public Health BSc(Hons), Social Work BSc(Hons), Wellbeing in Later Life (Top-Up) BA(Hons), Working with Older People FdA, Youth Studies BSc(Hons)

Postgraduate courses: Early Childhood Studies MA, Education MA, English Language Teaching (Distance Learning) MA, Health and Social Care Management and Policy MSc, Learning and Teaching in Higher Education MA, Master of Public Administration (MPA) MA, PGCE Early Childhood (Employment based), PGCE Early Years (3-7), PGCE Early Years (3-7)(ILTTA), PGCE Early Years (3-7) (Train to Teach North London), PGCE Early Years (3-7) (ILTTA), PGCE Early Years (3-7) (Princess May), PGCE Primary (5-11) (ILTTA), PGCE Primary (5-11) (Train to Teach North London), PGCE Primary (5-11) (Princess May), PGCE Primary (5-11),PGCE Primary (5-11) (ILTTA), PGCE Primary (5-11) (Train to Teach North London), PGCE Primary (Viridis), PGCE Secondary English with Drama, PGCE Secondary English with Media, PGCE Secondary English with Media (ILTTA), PGCE Secondary English with Media (Aylward Academy), PGCE Secondary English with Media (Crest), PGCE Secondary Mathematics, PGCE Secondary Mathematics (Crest), PGCE Secondary Mathematics, PGCE Secondary Mathematics (ILTTA), PGCE Secondary Mathematics (Train to Teach North London), PGCE Secondary Modern Languages, PGCE Secondary Modern Languages (Crest), PGCE Secondary Modern Languages (ILTTA), PGCE Secondary Modern Languages (Train to Teach North London), PGCE Secondary Science with Biology, PGCE Secondary Science with Biology (Crest), PGCE Secondary Science with Biology (ILTTA), PGCE Secondary Science with Biology (Train to Teach North London), PGCE Secondary Science with Chemistry, PGCE Secondary Science with Chemistry (Crest), PGCE Secondary Science with Chemistry (ILTTA), PGCE Secondary Science with Chemistry (Train to Teach North London), PGCE Secondary Science with Physics, PGCE Secondary Science with Physics (Crest), PGCE Secondary Science with Physics (ILTTA), PGCE Secondary Science with Physics(Train to Teach North London), Social Work MSc, Teaching MA

School of Social Sciences; www.londonmet.ac.uk/schools/ socialsciences

Counselling and Coaching BSc(Hons), Criminology BSc(Hons), Criminology and International Security BA(Hons), Criminology and Law BA(Hons), Criminology and Policing BSc(Hons), Criminology and Psychology BSc(Hons), Criminology and Sociology BSc(Hons), Criminology and Youth Studies BSc(Hons), Diplomacy and International Relations BA(Hons), International Relations BA(Hons), International Relations and Law BA(Hons), International Relations and Politics BA(Hons), International Relations and Politics Extended Degree BA(Hons), International Relations with Arabic BA(Hons), International Relations with French BA(Hons), International Relations with Languages BA(Hons), International

Relations with Spanish BA(Hons), International Relations, Peace and Conflict Studies BA(Hons), Police Studies, Procedure and Investigation BSc(Hons), Politics BA(Hons), Psychology BSc(Hons), Psychology and Sociology BSc(Hons), Psychology Extended Degree BSc(Hons), Social Sciences and Humanities Extended Degree BA(Hons), Society, Politics and Policy BA(Hons), Sociology BSc(Hons), Sociology and Social Policy BA(Hons)

Postgraduate courses: Addiction and Mental Health MSc, Child and Adolescent Mental Health MSc, Counselling Psychology Prof Doc, Crime, Violence and Prevention MSc, Criminology MSc, Human Rights and International Conflict MA, International Relations MA, Organised Crime and Global Security MA, Peace, Conflict and Diplomacy MA, Policing, Security and Community Safety Prof Doc, Political Violence and Radicalisation Studies MSc, Psychology for Graduates (by Distance Learning) Uni Cert, Psychology MSc, Psychology of Mental Health MSc, Safeguarding and Security MA, Woman and Child Abuse MA

The Sir John Cass School of Art, Architecture and Design; www.londonmet.ac.uk/schools/the-cass

Architecture BA(Hons), Art and Design Extended Degree BA(Hons), Creative Writing and English Literature BA(Hons), Design for Publishing BA(Hons), Design Studio Practice BA(Hons), English Literature BA(Hons), Fashion BA(Hons), Fashion Accessories and Jewellery BA(Hons), Fashion Photography BA(Hons), Fashion Textiles BA(Hons), Fine Art BA(Hons), Furniture FdA, Furniture and Product Design BA(Hons), Graphic Design BA(Hons), Illustration and Animation BA(Hons), Interior Architecture and Design BA(Hons), Interior Design BA(Hons), Interior Design and Decoration BA(Hons), Painting BA(Hons), Photography BA(Hons), Retail Design BA(Hons), Textile Design BA(Hons), Textiles BA(Hons), Theatre and Film BA(Hons), Theatre and Performance Practice BA(Hons)

Postgraduate courses: Architectural History, Research and Writing MA, Architecture MA, Architecture: Professional Practice in Architecture RIBA3 PGCert, Creative, Digital and Professional Writing MA, Design for Cultural Commons MA, Environmental, Sustainable and Regeneration Design MA, Master of Fine Arts MFA, Furniture Design MA, Interior Design MA, MArch Architecture RIBA2, Product Design MA, Textile Design MA

THE LONDON SCHOOL OF OSTEOPATHY
www.lso.ac.uk

MOst Osteopathy; BOst Osteopathy

LONDON SOUTH BANK UNIVERSITY
www.lsbu.ac.uk

School of Applied Sciences; www.lsbu.ac.uk/schools/applied-sciences

Food Sciences

BSc(Hons) Baking Science and Technology, BSc(Hons) Baking Science and Technology (Management), BSc(Hons) Baking Science and Technology (New Product Development), BSc(Hons) Baking Science and Technology (Nutrition), BSc(Hons) Human Nutrition, FdSc Baking Science and Technology, FdSc Baking Science and Technology (Management), FdSc Baking Science and Technology (New Product Development), FdSc Baking Science and Technology (Nutrition)

Human Sciences

BSc(Hons) Bioscience, BSc(Hons) Forensic Science, BSc(Hons) Sport and Exercise Science, BSc(Hons) Sports Coaching and Analysis, Extended Degree Programme Science, HND Applied Biology

Psychology

BSc(Hons) Psychological Counselling, BSc(Hons) Psychology, BSc(Hons) Psychology (Addiction Psychology), BSc(Hons) Psychology (Child Development), BSc(Hons) Psychology (Clinical Psychology),

BSc(Hons) Psychology (Forensic Psychology), BSc(Hons) Psychology (Sport Psychology), BSc(Hons) Psychology with Criminology, Extended Degree Programme Science

Postgraduate courses: MRes Psychology, MSc Addiction Psychology and Counselling, MSc Psychology, MSc/PgCert Mental Health and Clinical Psychology

School of Arts and Creative Industries; www.lsbu.ac.uk/schools/arts-and-creative-industries

BA(Hons) Animation, BA(Hons) Creative Advertising with Marketing, BA(Hons) Drama and Applied Theatre, BA(Hons) Drama and Performance, BA(Hons) Fashion Promotion with Marketing, BA(Hons) Film Practice, BA(Hons) Film Studies, BA(Hons) International Relations with Journalism, BA(Hons) Journalism, BA(Hons) Media Production, BA(Hons) Photography, BA(Hons) Politics with Journalism, BA/BSc(Hons) Game Design and Development, BA/BSc(Hons) Music and Sound Design, BSc(Hons) Criminology with Journalism

Postgraduate courses: MA Creative Performance Practice, MA Editing and Post Production (EPP), MRes Arts and Creative Industries

School of the Built Environment and Architecture; www.lsbu.ac.uk/schools/the-built-environment-and-architecture

Architecture

BA(Hons) Architectural Assistant Apprenticeship – Architecture, BA(Hons) Architecture, MArch Architect Apprenticeship – Architecture, MArch Architecture

Postgraduate courses: MSc Architecture, MSc Digital Architecture and Robotic Construction, Professional Practice Part 3 RIBA

Civil and Building Services Engineering

Institute of Acoustics Certificate of Competence, BEng(Hons) Building Service Engineering Site Management Apprenticeship, BEng(Hons) Building Services Design Engineering Apprenticeship, BEng(Hons) Building Services Engineering, BEng(Hons) Civil Engineer Apprenticeship Degree – Civil Engineering, BEng(Hons) Civil Engineering, BSc(Hons) Civil Engineering, BSc(Hons) Civil Engineering Site Management Apprenticeship, BTEC HNC Civil Engineering, BTEC HNC Construction Site Engineering Technician Apprenticeship, BTEC HND Building Services Engineering, HNC Building Services Engineering Technician Apprenticeship, IOA Acoustics and Noise Control

Postgraduate courses: MSc Building Services Engineering, MSc Civil and Structural Engineering, MSc Civil Engineering, MSc Environmental and Architectural Acoustics, MSc Structural Engineering

Construction, Property and Surveying

BSc(Hons) Architectural Engineering, BSc(Hons) Architectural Technology, BSc(Hons) Building Surveying, BSc(Hons) Chartered Surveying Degree Apprenticeship – Building Surveying, BSc(Hons) Chartered Surveying Degree Apprenticeship – Quantity Surveying, BSc(Hons) Commercial Management (Quantity Surveying), BSc(Hons) Construction Management, BSc(Hons) Quantity Surveying, BTEC HNC Construction, Extended Degree Programme Built Environment

Postgraduate courses: MSc Construction Project Management, PgDip/MSc Quantity Surveying, PgDip/MSc/Top-up to MSc Building Surveying, PgDip/MSc/Top-up to MSc Real Estate

School of Business; www.lsbu.ac.uk/schools/business

Accounting, Finance and Economics

BA(Hons) Accounting and Finance, BSc(Hons) Economics, BSc(Hons) Economics with Accounting, BSc(Hons) Economics with Finance, CertHE Accounting and Finance, Foundation Course Business

Postgraduate courses: MBA Master of Business Administration (International Management), MSc Corporate Governance with Graduate ICSA, MSc International Accounting and Finance, MSc International Finance, Top-up MSc Corporate Governance (Fast Track for ICSA Graduates)

Business and Enterprise

International Diploma Programme, BA(Hons) Business Management, BA(Hons) Business Management with Accounting, BA(Hons) Business Management with Enterprise and Entrepreneurship, BA(Hons) Business Management with Finance, BA(Hons) Business Management with Human Resources, BA(Hons) Business Management with Law, BA(Hons) Business Management with Marketing, BA(Hons) Business Management with Project Management, BA(Hons) Chartered Manager Apprenticeship – Business Management with Business Practice, BA(Hons) International Business Management Top-up, BA(Hons) Lewisham and Greenwich NHS Trust – Chartered Manager Apprenticeship, Foundation Course Business

Postgraduate courses: MBA Master of Business Administration (International Management), MSc Business Project Management, MSc International Business Management, MSc International Business

Management (with internship), MSc International Business Management with Finance, MSc International Business Management with HRM, MSc International Business Management with Marketing, MSc International Business Management with Project Management

Management, Marketing and People

BA(Hons) Digital Marketer Degree Apprenticeship – Digital Marketing, BA(Hons) Marketing, BA(Hons) Marketing with Advertising and Digital Communications, BA(Hons) Marketing with Enterprise and Entrepreneurship, CIPD Certificate Human Resource Practice, CertHE Associate Project Manager Apprenticeship – Associate Project Manager, Foundation Course Business

Postgraduate courses: MBA Master of Business Administration (International Management), MSc International Human Resource Management, (IGS/ Carlos III), MSc International Marketing, MSc Marketing, PgCert Leadership and Management: Homelessness and Housing, PgDip/MSc Human Resource Management

School of Engineering; www.lsbu.ac.uk/schools/ engineering

Chemical and Petroleum Engineering

BEng(Hons) Chemical and Process Engineering, BEng(Hons) Petroleum Engineering, BTEC HND Chemical Engineering, MEng(Hons) Chemical and Process Engineering, MEng(Hons) Petroleum Engineering

Postgraduate courses: MSc Chemical Engineering and Process Management, MSc Petroleum Engineering

Computer Science and Informatics

Digital & Technology Solutions Professional Apprenticeship – Business Analyst Pathway, Digital & Technology Solutions Professional Apprenticeship – Cyber Security Analyst, Digital & Technology Solutions Professional Apprenticeship – Data Analyst, Digital & Technology Solutions Professional Apprenticeship – IT Consultant Pathway, Digital & Technology Solutions Professional Apprenticeship – Network Engineer Pathway, Digital & Technology Solutions Professional Apprenticeship – Software Engineer Pathway, BSc(Hons) Business Information Technology, BSc(Hons) Computer Science (Top-up), BSc(Hons) Data Science, Foundation Year Computing

Postgraduate courses: MSc Data Science, Top-up Course to BSc Applied Computing, Top-up Course to BSc Business Information Technology, Top-up Course to BSc Information Technology

Electrical and Electronic Engineering

BEng(Hons) Computer Engineering, BEng(Hons) Computer Systems and Networks Engineering, BEng(Hons) Electrical and Electronic Engineering, BEng(Hons) Electrical Engineering and Power Electronics, BEng(Hons) Embedded Electronic Systems Design and Development Engineer Apprenticeship – Electrical and Electronic Engineering, BEng(Hons) Power Engineering (Electrical), BEng(Hons) Power Engineering (Mechanical), BTEC HND Electrical and Electronic Engineering, MEng(Hons) Computer Engineering, MEng(Hons) Computer Systems and Networks Engineering, MEng(Hons) Electrical and Electronic Engineering, MEng(Hons) Electrical Engineering and Power Electronics, MEng(Hons) Power Engineer Integrated Degree Apprenticeship – Power Engineering (Electrical Engineering), MEng(Hons) Power Engineer Integrated Degree Apprenticeship – Power Engineering (Mechanical Engineering), MEng(Hons) Power Engineer Integrated Degree Apprenticeship – Power Engineering (Transmission and Distribution), MEng(Hons) Power Engineering (Electrical)

Postgraduate courses: MRes General Engineering, MRes Master of Research in Electrical and Electronic Engineering, MSc Electrical and Electronic Engineering

Mechanical Engineering and Design

BEng(Hons) Advanced Vehicle Engineering, BEng(Hons) Mechanical Engineering, BSc(Hons) Engineering Product Design, BSc(Hons) Product Design, Extended Degree Programme Engineering, MEng(Hons) Advanced Vehicle Engineering, MEng(Hons) Mechanical Engineering, MEng(Hons) Power Engineering (Mechanical)

Postgraduate courses: MSc Mechanical Engineering, Top-up to BEng Mechanical Engineering and Design

School of Health and Social Care; www.lsbu.ac.uk/schools/health-andsocial-care

Adult Nursing and Midwifery

Continuous Personal and Professional Development CPPD/CPD Health and Social Care, Health and Social Care – Foundation Year, BSc(Hons) Adult Nursing, BSc(Hons) Midwifery (3 year), BSc(Hons) Midwifery (Shortened Course), FdSc Healthcare Assistant Practitioner Apprentice – Foundation Degree in Health

Postgraduate courses: Professional Doctorate in Health and Social Care, MSc Nursing (Neuroscience Care), PgCert Older People's Care, PgCert/PgDip/

MSc Palliative and End of Life Care, PgCert/PgDip/ MSc Perinatal Mental Health, PgDip Adult Nursing, PgDip/MSc Mental Health Advanced Nurse Practitioner, PgDip/Top up to MSc Advanced Clinical Practice

Allied Health Sciences

Continuous Personal and Professional Development CPPD/CPD Health and Social Care, Conversion course for Supplementary Prescribers, Health and Social Care – Foundation Year, BSc(Hons) Diagnostic Radiography, BSc(Hons) Occupational Therapy, BSc(Hons) Operating Department Practice, BSc(Hons) Physiotherapy, BSc(Hons) Radiographic Studies, BSc(Hons) Sport Rehabilitation, BSc(Hons) Therapeutic Radiography, DipHE Diagnostic Imaging, DipHE Radiotherapy Practice, FdSc Healthcare Assistant Practitioner Apprentice – Foundation Degree in Health, Integrated Masters Chiropractic, Integrated Masters Physiotherapy, Integrated Masters Sport Rehabilitation

Postgraduate courses: GradCert/PgCert Non-Medical Prescribing, Professional Doctorate in Health and Social Care, MSc (Pre-Registration) Physiotherapy, PgCert Breast Imaging, PgCert/PgDip/ MSc Diagnostic Imaging, Leading Social Change MA, Systems Change: Collaborative Communities PGCert, PgCert/ PgDip/MSc Radiographic Reporting, PgCert/PgDip/ MSc Radiotherapy and Oncology, PgCert/Top up to PgDip/Top up to MSc Advancing Practice in Occupational Therapy, PgDip/MSc Occupational Therapy (pre-registration mode), PgDip/MSc (Top-up)/MSc Therapeutic Radiography, PgDip/Top up to MSc Advanced Clinical Practice

Children???s Nursing

Continuous Personal and Professional Development CPPD/CPD Health and Social Care, Health and Social Care – Foundation Year, BSc(Hons) Children???s Nursing, BSc(Hons)/PgDip Children???s Nursing – Second registration programme, FdSc Healthcare Assistant Practitioner Apprentice – Foundation Degree in Health

Postgraduate courses: Professional Doctorate in Health and Social Care, MSc Children???s Nursing, PgDip Children???s Nursing, PgDip/MSc Children???s Advanced Nurse Practitioner, PgDip/MSc Professional Practice: Children???s Nursing, PgDip/ Top up to MSc Advanced Clinical Practice

Institute of Vocational Learning

Continuous Personal and Professional Development CPPD/CPD Health and Social Care, 60 Credits Award: 50 credits at Level 3 and 10 credits at Level 4 University Certificate of Competence Mental

Health and Learning Disabilities Nursing, Health and Social Care – Foundation Year

Postgraduate courses: Leading Social Change MA, PgDip/MSc Learning Disability Nursing, PgDip/MSc Health Nursing, PgCert/ PgDip/MSc Perinatal Mental Health, PGCert Systems Change: Collaborative Communities, PgDip/ Top up to MSc Advanced Clinical Practice

Primary and Social Care

Continuous Personal and Professional Development CPPD/CPD Health and Social Care, Health and Social Care – Foundation Year, BA(Hons) Social Work, BSc(Hons) Health Visiting (Specialist Community Public Health Nursing), BSc(Hons) School Nursing (Specialist Community Public Health Nursing), FdSc Healthcare Assistant Practitioner Apprentice – Foundation Degree in Health, Grad Cert / BSc(Hons) Workplace Health Management

Postgraduate courses: Professional Doctorate in Health and Social Care, MA Social Work, Leading Social Change MA, PgCert/PgDip/Msc Leadership and Service Improvement, PgDip Health Visiting (Specialist Community Public Health Nursing), PgDip/Top up to MSc Advanced Clinical Practice, PGCert Systems Change: Collaborative Communities

School of Law and Social Sciences; www.lsbu.ac.uk/schools/law-and-socialsciences

Centre for Education and School Partnerships

Continuing Professional Development – Education, BA(Hons) Education Studies, BA(Hons) Education Studies (work-based), BA(Hons) Education Studies – Top Up

Postgraduate courses: EdD Professional Doctorate in Education, MA Education (Autism), MA Education – Special Educational Needs and Disability (SEND), PGCE Primary, PGCE School Direct, PgCert Education Autism, PgCert National Award for Special Educational Needs Coordinator(SENCO)

Law

LLB(Hons) Business Law, LLB(Hons) Criminal Law, LLB(Hons) Law, LLB(Hons) Law with Criminology, PgDip / LLM Law Conversion Course: incorporating the CPE

Postgraduate courses: LLM Crime and Litigation, LLM International Commercial Law, LLM International Human Rights and Development

Social Sciences

BA(Hons) History BA(Hons) History with Politics, BA(Hons) International Relations, BA(Hons) International Relations with Journalism, BA(Hons)

International Relations with Politics, BA(Hons) Politics, BA(Hons) Politics with Journalism, BSc(Hons) Criminology, BSc(Hons) Criminology with Journalism, BSc(Hons) Criminology with Law, BSc(Hons) Criminology with Psychology, BSc(Hons) Sociology, BSc(Hons) Sociology with Criminology

Postgraduate courses: MSc Development Studies, MSc Refugee Studies,MSc/PgDip Education for Sustainability

Urban, Environment and Leisure Studies

Chartered Town Planner Apprenticeships, BA(Hons) Events and Entertainment Management, BA(Hons) Human Geography, BA(Hons) Tourism and Hospitality Management, BA(Hons) Urban and Environmental Planning

Postgraduate courses: CertHE Senior Housing/Property Management Apprenticeship – Housing Management, MA Hospitality Leadership in Universities and the Public Sector, MA Urban Design and Planning, MSc International Tourism and Hospitality Management, PgDip/MA Town and Country Planning, MRes Planning Studies and Tourism, Hospitality and Events

UNIVERSITY OF EAST LONDON
www.uel.ac.uk

School of Architecture, Computing and Engineering; www.uel.ac.uk/schools/ace

Architecture and Design

BSc(Hons) Architectural Design Technology (Accredited by CIAT), BSc(Hons) Architecture (ARB/RIBA Part 1), BA(Hons) Interior Design

Postgraduate courses: MArch Architecture (ARB/RIBA Part 2), MRes Architecture (Reading the Neoliberal City), MA Architecture and Urbanism, MA Interior Design, PGDip Landscape Architecture, MA Professional Landscape Architecture

Computer Science and Informatics

BSc(Hons) Applied Computing (Top-up), BSc(Hons) Computer Science, BSc(Hons) Computer Science with Education and Qualified Status, BSc(Hons) Computing for Business, BSc(Hons) Cyber Security Networks

Postgraduate courses: MSc Big Data Technologies, MSc Computer Science, MSc Computing and Information Technology, MSc Data Science, MSc Information Security and Digital Forensics, Prof Doc Data Science, Prof Doc Information Security

Civil and Structural Engineering

BEng(Hons) Civil Engineering, MEng Civil Engineering (Integrated Master's), BSc(Hons) Civil Engineering, FdSc Civil Engineering and Construction Management, BSc(Hons) Construction Management, BSc(Hons) Surveying and Mapping Sciences

Postgraduate courses: MSc Civil Engineering, MSc Structural Engineering, PGDip Civil Engineering, PGDip Structural Engineering, MSc Construction Engineering Management

Mechanical Engineering

BEng(Hons) Design Engineering, BEng(Hons) Engineering Management, BEng(Hons) General Engineering, BEng(Hons) Mechanical Engineering, MEng Mechanical Engineering (Integrated Master's)

Surveying and Construction

BSc(Hons) Construction Management, BSc(Hons) Surveying and Mapping Sciences

Postgraduate courses: MSc Construction Engineering Management, MSc Civil Engineering, MSc Structural Engineering, PGDip Civil Engineering, PGDip Structural Engineering

School of Arts and Digital Industries; www.uel.ac.uk/schools/adi

Art and Design

BA(Hons) Animation, BA(Hons) Fine Art, BA(Hons) Graphic Design, BA(Hons) Illustration, BA(Hons) Photography, BSc(Hons) Product Design, Prof Doc Fine Art (DFA)

Postgraduate course: MA Fine Art

Fashion

BA(Hons) Fashion Design, BA(Hons) Fashion Journalism, BA(Hons) Fashion Marketing, BA(Hons) Fashion Textiles

Postgraduate courses: MFA Fashion, MA International Fashion Business

Humanities and Creative Industries

BA(Hons) Advertising, BA(Hons) Creative and Professional Writing, BA(Hons) Creative Enterprise Top-up, BA(Hons) Fashion Journalism, BA(Hons) Film, BA(Hons) Journalism, BA(Hons) Sports Journalism

Media and Screen subjects

BSc(Hons) Computer Game Development, BA(Hons) Computer Games Design: Story Development, BA(Hons) Film, BA(Hons) Media and Communication

Performing Arts

BA(Hons) Dance: Urban Practice, BA(Hons) Drama, Applied Theatre and Performance, BA(Hons) Music Journalism BA(Hons) Music Performance and Production, BA(Hons) Hons Performing Arts

Postgraduate courses

MA Acting, MFA Acting, MA Contemporary Performance Practices, MA Theatre Directing, MFA Theatre Directing

Cass School of Education and Communities; www.uel.ac.uk/schools/cass

Early Childhood

BA(Hons) Social and Community Work, BA(Hons) Special Education, BA(Hons) Primary Education with QTS, BA(Hons) Early Childhood Studies, FdA Montessori Pedagogy

Postgraduate course: MA Early Leadership and Practice

Education

BA(Hons) (Education Studies)

Postgraduate courses: MA Education, MA Leadership in Education

English Language Teaching

Postgraduate course: MA English Language Teaching

Social Work

BA(Hons) Social Work, BA(Hons) Social and Community Work

Postgraduate courses: MA Post Qualifying Professional Practice, MA Social Work

Special Educational Needs

BA(Hons) Special Education

Postgraduate courses: MA/PgDip/PgCert Special and Additional Learning Needs, MA Special Educational Needs, PGCE Primary with SEN (Inclusion), PGCE Primary with SEN (Special Schools) PGCert Autism Spectrum Conditions and Learning, PGCert Special Educational Needs Coordination, PGCert Understanding and Supporting Behaviour

Teacher Training

Postgraduate courses: PGCE iPGCE, PGCE Non-Qualified Teacher Status (QTS), PGCE Post-compulsory Education and Training (PCET), PGCE Primary (5-11), PGCE Primary with Early Years (3-7), PGCE Primary with English, PGCE Primary with English as an Additional Language, PGCE Primary with Humanities and Religious Education, PGCE Primary with ICT and Computing, PGCE Primary with Mathematics, PGCE Primary with Music, PGCE Primary with Physical Education, PGCE Primary with Science, PGCE Secondary Biology, PGCE Secondary Chemistry, PGCE Secondary Community Languages, PGCE Secondary Computing, PGCE Secondary Design and Technology, PGCE Secondary Drama, PGCE Secondary English, PGCE Secondary Modern Languages (French), PGCE Secondary Modern Languages (French with German), PGCE Secondary Modern Languages (French with Italian), PGCE Secondary Modern Languages (French with Spanish), PGCE Secondary Geography, PGCE Secondary Modern Languages (German with French), PGCE Secondary Mathematics, PGCE Secondary Music, PGCE Secondary Physical Education, PGCE Secondary Physics, PGCE Secondary Physics with Mathematics, PGCE Secondary Religious Education, PGCE Secondary Modern Languages (Spanish with French)

Youth and Community

Postgraduate course: MA Youth and Community Work

School of Health, Sport and Bioscience; www.uel.ac.uk/schools/health-sport-andbioscience

Applied Sport and Exercise Sciences

FdSc Community Sports Management (West Ham United Foundation), BSc(Hons) Sport and Exercise Science, BSc(Hons) Sport and Exercise Science (with Foundation year), BSc(Hons) Sport Physical Education and Development, BSc(Hons) Sport, Physical Education and Development (with Foundation Year, BSc(Hons) Sports Coaching, BA(Hons) Sports Journalism, BSc(Hons) Sports Therapy

Postgraduate courses: MSc Applied Sport and Exercise Sciences (with specialism), MSc Sports Management, MRes Sport and Exercise Science

Bioscience

BSc(Hons) Biochemistry, BSc(Hons) Biomedical Science, BSc(Hons) Chemistry, BSc(Hons) Medical Physiology, BSc(Hons) Pharmaceutical Science, BSc(Hons) Pharmacology

Postgraduate courses: MSc Biomedical Science (with specialism), MRes Bioscience, MSc Pharmaceutical Science (with specialism)

Health

BSc(Hons) Nursing (Adult), BSc(Hons) Public Health, BSc(Hons) Public Health and Health Promotion, BSc(Hons) Public Health and Health Services Management

Postgraduate courses: MRes Health Science, MSc Public Health

Physiotherapy and Podiatry

BSc(Hons) Physiotherapy, BSc(Hons) Podiatry

Postgraduate course: PGCert Musculoskeletal Ultrasonography

School of Psychology; www.uel.ac.uk/schools/psychology

BSc(Hons) Business Psychology, BSc(Hons) Child Psychology, BSc(Hons) Clinical and Community Psychology, BSc(Hons) Counselling, BSc(Hons) Forensic Psychology, BSc(Hons) Psychology

Postgraduate courses: MSc Applied Positive Psychology and Coaching Psychology, MSc Business Psychology, PGDip Career Coaching, MSc Career Coaching, MSc Clinical and Community Psychology MA Counselling and Psychotherapy, PGDip Counselling and Psychotherapy, Msc Humanitarian Intervention, PGDip Integrative Counselling and Coaching, MSc Integrative Counselling and Coaching, MSc Occupational and Organisational Psychology, MSc Psychology

Royal Docks School of Business and Law; www.uel.ac.uk/schools/royal-docks

Accounting, Finance and Economics

BA(Hons) Accounting and Finance, MAccFin Accounting and Finance, BSc(Hons) Economics

Postgraduate courses: MSc Finance and Risk, MSc Professional Accounting

Business

BA(Hons) Advertising, BA(Hons) Business Management, BA(Hons) Business Management, BSc(Hons) Human Resource Management, BSc(Hons) Marketing

Postgraduate courses: MA Human Resource Management, MA International Fashion Business, MBA Master of Business Administration, MSc International Business Management, MSc Oil and Gas Management

Criminology

BA(Hons) Criminology and Criminal Justice, BA(Hons) Criminology and Law, BA(Hons) Criminology and Psychology, BSc(Hons) Policing Studies Top-Up, BA/MSc(Hons) Professional BA(Hons) Sociology with Criminology

Law

LLB(Hons) Business Law, BA(Hons) Criminology and Law, LLB(Hons) Law, LLB(Hons) Law with Criminology, LLB(Hons) Law with International Relations

Postgraduate courses: LLM (Business and Financial Law), LLM Energy and Natural Resources Law, LLM General Law, LLM Human Rights Advocacy, LLM International Law and Legal Practice, LLM Transitional Justice and Conflict

Tourism, Hospitality and Events

BA(Hons) Events Management, BA(Hons) Hospitality Management, BA(Hons) Tourism Management

School of Social Sciences; www.uel.ac.uk/schools/social-sciences

Global Studies

BA(Hons) Politics and International Relations, BA(Hons) International Development, BA(Hons) International Development with NGO Management

Postgraduate courses: MA Conflict, Displacement, and Human Security, MA Refugee Studies, MSc International and Comparative Public Policy, MSc International Relations, MSc NGO and Development Management

Sociology

BA(Hons) Sociology, BA(Hons) Sociology with Criminology

Postgraduate courses: PGCert Narrative Research via Distance Learning

Psychosocial

BA(Hons) Psychosocial Theory and Practice

UNIVERSITY OF WEST LONDON
www.uwl.ac.uk

London School of Film, Media and Design; www.uwl.ac.uk/academic-schools/filmmedia-design

BA(Hons) Advertising and Public Relations, BA(Hons) Broadcast and Digital Journalism, BA(Hons) Journalism, BA(Hons) English and Media and Communications, BA(Hons) English and Film, BA(Hons) English and Creative Writing, BA(Hons) Fashion Branding and Marketing, BA(Hons) Fashion Buying and Management, BA(Hons) Fashion and Textiles, BA(Hons) Fashion Promotion and Imaging, BA(Hons) Film Production, BA(Hons) Graphic Design (Visual Communication and Illustration), BA(Hons) Media and Communications, BA(Hons) Media Production, BA(Hons) Photography, BA(Hons) Commercial Photography, FdA Photography, BA(Hons) Radio and Digital Media, BA(Hons) Visual Effects, BA(Hons) Games, Design and Animation, BA(Hons) Content, Media and Film Production, BA(Hons) Interior Design

Postgraduate courses: MA Advertising, Branding & Communication, MA Creative Communications Entrepreneurship, MA Creative Fashion Entrepreneurship, MA Creative Media Entrepreneurship

The Claude Littner Business School; www.uwl.ac.uk/academic-schools/business

BA(Hons) Accounting and Finance, BSc(Hons) Business Economics, BA(Hons) Business Studies, BA(Hons) Business Studies with Entrepreneurship, BA(Hons) Business Studies with Finance, BA(Hons) Business Studies with Human Resource Management, BA(Hons) Business Studies with Marketing, BA(Hons) Finance and Management, BSc(Hons) Human Resource Management, BA(Hons) International Business Management, BSc(Hons) Marketing and Social Media, BSc(Hons) Social Media Marketing
Postgraduate courses: MSc Digital Marketing, MSc Finance and Accounting, MSc Finance and Risk Management, MA/PGDip Human Resource Management, MSc International Business Management, MSc International Marketing, MBA Masters in Business Administration

School of Computing and Engineering; www.uwl.ac.uk/academic-schools/computing

BEng(Hons) Civil and Environmental Engineering, BEng(Hons) Electrical and Electronic Engineering, BSc(Hons) Applied Sound Engineering, BSc(Hons) Architectural Design and Technology, BSc(Hons) Building Surveying, BSc(Hons) Computer Games Technology, BSc(Hons) Computer Science, BSc(Hons) Computing and Information Systems (part-time only), BSc(Hons) Construction Project Management, BSc(Hons) Creative Computing, BSc(Hons) Cyber Security, BSc(Hons) Information Technology, BSc(Hons) Information Technology Management for Business (ITMB), BSc(Hons) Mathematics and Statistics, BSc(Hons) Mobile Computing, FdEng Civil and Environmental Engineering (part-time only), FdSc Architectural Design and Technology (part-time only), FdSc Building Surveying, FdSc Computing and Information Systems (part-time only), FdSc Construction Project Management (part-time only)
Postgraduate courses: MSc Applied Project Management, MSc Civil Engineering, MSc Civil and Environmental Engineering, MSc Construction Project Management, MSc/PgDip Cyber Security, MSc Digital Audio Engineering, MSc Health Informatics, MSc Information Systems, MSc Software Engineering

London Geller College of Hospitality and Tourism; www.uwl.ac.uk/academicschools/hospitality-tourism

BA(Hons) Airline and Airport Management, BSc(Hons) Aviation management with Commercial Pilot Licence, BSc(Hons) Culinary Arts Management, BA(Hons) Event Management, BA(Hons) Event Management with Hospitality, BA(Hons) Event Management with Tourism, BA(Hons) Food and Professional Cookery (top-up), BA(Hons) Hospitality Management, BA(Hons) Hospitality Management and Food Studies, BA(Hons) International Hotel Management, BA(Hons) Leisure Management, BSc(Hons) Nutrition and Food Management, BA(Hons) Strategic Transport Management, BA(Hons) Travel and Tourism Management, FdA Airline and Airport Management, FdA Event Management, FdA Event Management with Hospitality, FdA Event Management with Tourism, FdA Hospitality Management, FdA Hospitality Management and Food Studies, FdA International Hotel Management, FdA Travel and Tourism Management
Postgraduate courses: MA International Tourism and Aviation Management, MSc Air Transport Operations and Management, MA Food Business Management, MA Luxury Hospitality Management, MA Luxury Hospitality Management with Internship, MPhil Hospitality

School of Law and Criminology; www.uwl.ac.uk/academic-schools/law

BA(Hons) Criminology, BA(Hons) Criminology with Law, BA(Hons) Criminology with Psychology, BA(Hons) Criminology, Policing and Forensics, BA(Hons) Applied Sociology, BA(Hons) International Relations with Sociology, BA(Hons) Politics with Sociology, LLB(Hons) Law
Postgraduate courses: MA Criminology, MA Criminology and Global Security, MA Criminology and Global Crime, MA/LLM International Criminal Justice, PgDip Legal Practice (LPC Stage 1 and 2), LLM Legal Practice, LLM International Business and Commercial Law, LLM International Banking and Finance Law, LLM International Studies in Intellectual Property Law

London College of Music; www.uwl.ac.uk/academic-schools/music

BA(Hons) Acting, BA(Hons) Acting, Writing and Directing, BA(Hons) Actor Musicianship, BA(Hons) Electronic Music Production, BA(Hons) Live Sound Production, BA(Hons) Music Management, BA(Hons) Music Mixing and Mastering, BA(Hons)

Music Recording and Production, BA(Hons) Music Technology – Audio Post Production, BA(Hons) Music Technology (Top-up), BA(Hons) Music Technology and Radio Broadcasting, BA(Hons) Music Technology and Video Production, BA(Hons) Music Technology Specialist, BA(Hons) Music Technology with Composition, BA(Hons) Music Technology with Performance, BA(Hons) Music Technology with Popular Music Performance, BA(Hons) Musical Theatre, BA(Hons) Text and Performance, BA(Hons) Theatre Production (Design and Management), BA(Hons) Voice in Performance, BMus(Hons) Composition, BMus(Hons) Songwriting and Recording, BMus(Hons) Film Composition, BMus(Hons) Music Performance, BMus(Hons) Music Performance and Recording, BMus(Hons) Music Performance and Music Management, BMus(Hons) Music Performance with Technology, BSc(Hons) Applied Sound Engineering, DipHE Music Technology

Postgraduate courses: MA Advanced Music Technology, MA Music Industry Management and Artist Development, MA Record Production, MMus Composition (Electronic Music, Concert Music or Film and Television), MMus Performance, MMus Popular Music Performance, PGDip Performance

College of Nursing, Midwifery and Healthcare; www.uwl.ac.uk/academicschools/nursing-midwifery

BNursing(Hons) Adult Nursing, BNursing(Hons) Children's Nursing, BSc(Hons) Health Promotion and Public Health, BSc(Hons) Midwifery (pre-/post-registration), BNursing(Hons) Nursing (Learning Disabilities), BNursing(Hons) Nursing (Mental Health), BSc(Hons) Operating Department Practice, BSc(Hons) Professional Practice (Top-up)

Postgraduate courses: MSc Advanced Practice, MSc Advanced Clinical Practice, MSc Improvement Science, MSc Infection Prevention and Control, MSc Nursing (top-up), MSc Person-Centred Health and Social Care, MSc Public Health and Wellbeing, PGCert Strategic Workforce Planning, PGCert/PGDip/MSc Professional Practice, PGCert/PGDip/MSc Psychosocial Interventions for Psychosis, PGDip Nursing (Adult), PGDip Nursing (Learning Disabilities), PGDip Nursing (Mental Health), PGDip/MSc Management Studies (Health and Social Care), MSci Nursing (Adult and Mental Health), MSci Nursing (Children's Nursing and Mental Health), MSci Nursing (Learning Disabilities and Mental Health)

School of Human and Social Sciences; www.uwl.ac.uk/academic-schools/psychology

BA(Hons) Community Development, BA(Hons) Early Years Education, BA(Hons) Education Studies, BSc(Hons) Policing, BA(Hons) Politics and International Relations, BA(Hons) Public Services, BSc(Hons) Forensic Science, BSc(Hons) Psychology, BSc(Hons) Psychology with Applied Forensic Investigation, BSc(Hons) Psychology with Counselling Theory, BSc(Hons) Psychology with Criminology, BSc(Hons) Psychology with Foundation, BSc(Hons) Psychology with Substance Use and Misuse Studies, BSc(Hons) Social Work, BSc(Hons) Substance Use and Misuse Studies (Top-up), BSc Nutritional Therapy, FdSc Nutritional Therapeutics

Postgraduate courses: MSc Dementia Care, MSc Health Psychology, MSc Psychology Conversion

UNIVERSITY OF LONDON; BIRKBECK
www.bbk.ac.uk

School of Arts; www.bbk.ac.uk/arts

Department of English and Humanities; www.bbk.ac.uk/english

Arts and Humanities (BA), Creative Writing (BA), English (BA), Theatre and Drama Studies (BA), Theatre Studies and English (BA),

Postgraduate courses: Contemporary Literature and Culture (MA), Creative Producing (MA), Creative Writing (MA), Cultural and Critical Studies (MA), Humanities and Cultural Studies (MRes), Medical Humanities (MA/PGDip/PGCert), Medical Leadership (MSc/PGDip/PGCert), Medieval Literature and Culture (MA), Modern and Contemporary Literature (MA), Renaissance Studies (MA), Romantic Studies (MA/PGDip/PGCert), Screenwriting (MA/PGCert), Shakespeare and Contemporary Performance (MA), Text and Performance (MA), Text and Performance (with RADA) (MA), Theatre Directing (MFA), Victorian Studies (MA)

Department of Cultures and Languages; www.bbk.ac.uk/languages

BA French Studies, BA German Studies, BA Spanish and Latin American Studies (Spanish or Portuguese pathways), BA Modern Languages (with two of French, German, Japanese, Portuguese or Spanish), BA Linguistics and Languages (with one of French/German/Japanese/Portugues/Spanish), BA Language and Management/Management and Language (with one of French/German/Japanese/Portuguese/Spanish), BA Language and History/History and Language (with one of French/German/Japanese/Portuguese/Spanish), BA Language and Film/Media, BA Language English, BA Language and Global Politics, BA Language and International law, BA Language and Journalism, BA language and Politics,

Postgraduate courses: Comparative Literature, Cultures and Thought (MA), French Studies (GradDip), German Studies (GradDip), Iberian and Latin American Studies (GradCert), International Foundation Programme for Postgraduate Study (GradDip), Japanese Cultural Studies (MA), Language Teaching (MA), Politics with [Language] (Intensive) (MRes), Spanish, Portuguese and Latin American Cultural Studies (MA), Teaching English to Speakers of Other Languages (TESOL) (MA), World Cinema (MA)

Department of History of Art; www.bbk.ac.uk/art-history

History of Art (CertHE), BA History of Art, BA History of Art with Curating, BA History of Art with Film, BA History of Art with History, History of Art and Architecture (GradCert)

Postgraduate courses: MA History of Art, MA History of Art with History and Theory of Photography

Department of Film, Media and Cultural Studies; www.bbk.ac.uk/culture

Arts and Media Management (Foundation Degree), BA Film and Media, BA Journalism and Media, BA Media and Culture, BA Global Cinemas and Screen Arts

Postgraduate courses: Arts Policy and Management (MA/PGDip/PGCert), Digital Media Culture (MA), Digital Media Design (MA), Digital Media Management (MA), Film, Television and Screen Media (MA), Film Programming and Curating (MA), Journalism (MA/PGCert), Investigative Reporting (MA), Screenwriting (MA/PGCert), Digital Media Management (PGCert), Web Design and Development (PGCert)

School of Business, Economics and Informatics; www.bbk.ac.uk/business

Department of Economics, Mathematics and Statistics; www.bbk.ac.uk/ems

BSc Economic and Social Policy, BSc Economics, BSc Economics and Business, BSc Financial Economics, BSc Financial Economics with Accounting, BSc Mathematics, BSc Mathematics and Accounting, BSc Mathematics and Economics, BSc Mathematics and Management, BSc Mathematics and Statistics, BSc Statistics and Economics

Postgraduate courses: MSc Applied Statistics, MSc Applied Statistics and Financial Modelling, MSc Economics, MSc Finance, MSc Finance (with advanced pathways), MSc Financial Economics, MSc Financial Risk Management, MSc Mathematical Finance, MSc Mathematics, MSc Mathematics and Financial Modelling, PGCert in Econometrics

Department of Computer Science and Information Systems; www.dcs.bbk.ac.uk

BSc in Computing, BSc in Data Science, BSc in Digital and Technology Solutions Degree Apprenticeship (Software Engineering), BSc in Information Systems and Management, FdSc in Computing/Information Technology/Web Development, CertHE in Information Technology, CertHE in Web Design Technologies

Postgraduate courses: MSc in Computer Science, MSc in Data Science, MSc in Information Technology, PGCert in Cloud and Data Technologies, MSc in Advanced Computing Technologies, MSc in Computing for the Financial Services, MSc in Data Analytics, MSc in Information and Web Technologies, MSc in Information Systems and Management

Department of Management; www.bbk.ac.uk/management

Accounting (BSc), Accounting and Management (BA), Accounting with Finance (BSc), Accounting and management with Finance (BSc), Applied Accounting and Business (BSc), Business (BSc), Funeral Management (CertHE), Management (BA), Management (CertHE), Management (Foundation Degree), Management and Accounting (Foundation Degree), Management for Personal Assistants (CertHE), Marketing (BSc), Professional Studies (BSc Top-Up)

Postgraduate courses: Accounting and Financial Management (MSc), Business Innovation (PGCert), Business Innovation with E-Business (MSc), Business Innovation with Entrepreneurship and Innovation Management (MSc), Business Innovation with

International Technology Management (MSc), Corporate Governance and Business Ethics (MSc), Corporate Responsibility & Sustainability (MSc), Creative Industries (Management) (MSc), Creative Industries (PGCert), International Business (MSc), International Business and Development (MSc), International Management (MSc), International Marketing (MSc), Investment Management (MSc), Management (MRes/MSc/PGCert/PGDip), Management with Business Innovation (MSc), Management with Business Strategy and the Environment (MSc), Management with Corporate Governance and Business Ethics (MSc), Management with Creative Industries (MSc), Management with Human Resource Management (MSc), Management with International Business (MSc), Management with International Business and Development (MSc), Management with Marketing (MSc), Management with Sport Management (MSc), Marketing (MSc), Marketing Communications (MSc), Sport Governance (PGCert), Sport Management (MSc/PGCert), Sport Management and Marketing (MSc), Sport Management and the Business of Football (MSc), Sport Management, Governance and Policy (MSc), Sport Marketing (MSc)

Department of Organisational Psychology; www.bbk.ac.uk/orgpsych
Business Psychology (BSc)
Postgraduate courses: Career Management and Coaching (MSc), Coaching (PGCert), Human Resource Development and Consultancy (MSc), Human Resource Management (MSc), Management Consultancy and Organisational Change (MSc), Medical Leadership (MSc), Organizational Psychology (MSc)

School of Law; www.bbk.ac.uk/law

Department of Criminology; www.bbk.ac.uk/law/departments/department-of-criminology
Criminology (CertHE), Criminology and Criminal Justice (BSc)
Postgraduate courses: Criminal Law and Criminal Justice (MA/LLM), Global Criminology (MSc)

Department of Law; www.bbk.ac.uk/law/departments/department-of-law
Legal Method (CertHE)
Law (LLB)
Language and/with International Law (French, German, Japanese, Portuguese, Spanish) (BA)

Postgraduate courses: Constitutional Politics, Law and Theory (LLM), Criminal Law and Criminal Justice (MA/LLM), Human Rights (LLM/MA), International Economic Law (Finance or Justice and Development Pathway) (Intensive) (LLM), International Economic Law, Justice and Development (Evening) (LLM), Law General (LLM), Law, Democracy, and Human Welfare: Global Perspectives (Intensive) (LLM), Qualifying Law Degree (LLM)

School of Science; www.bbk.ac.uk/science

Department of Biological Sciences
Biomedicine (BSc), Structural Molecular Biology (BSc), Laboratory Science (Foundation Degree/Higher Apprenticeship), Life Sciences for Subjects Allied to Medicine (CertHE), Physics and Mathematics (CertHE)
Postgraduate courses: Analytical Bioscience (MSc/PGDip), Analytical Chemistry (MSc/PGDip), Biobusiness (MSc), Bioinformatics with Systems Biology (MRes/MSc), Chemical Research (MRes), Microbiology (MRes/MSc), Principles of Protein Structure (PGCert), Protein Crystallography (PGCert), Structural Biology (MRes), Structural Molecular Biology (MSc), Techniques in Structural Molecular Biology (PGCert)

Department of Earth and Planetary Sciences; www.bbk.ac.uk/geology
Earth History and Palaeontology (CertHE), Earth Sciences (BSc), Environmental Geology (BSc), Environmental Geology (GradCert), Geology (BSc), Geology (CertHE/GradCert), Mineralogy and Volcanology (CertHE), Planetary Science with Astronomy (BSc/CertHE)
Postgraduate courses: Environmental Geology (GradCert), Geology (GradCert), Planetary Sciences (GradCert)

Department of Psychological Sciences; www.bbk.ac.uk/psychology
Business Psychology (BSc), Psychodynamic Counselling and Organisational Dynamics (CertHE), Psychology (BSc), Psychology for Education (BA), Psychology for Education Professionals (Foundation Degree), Applied Psychology (CertHE), Counselling and Counselling Skills (CertHE), Psychology (CertHE)
Postgraduate courses: Cognition and Computation (MA), Cognition and Computation (MSc), Cognitive Neuroscience and Neuropsychology (MSc/MA),

Developmental Sciences (MA/MSc), Educational Neuroscience (MA/MSc), Functional Neuroimaging (MRes), Psychoanalytic Studies (MA), Psychodynamic Counselling & Psychotherapy with Children and Adolescents (MSc), Psychodynamic Counselling and Psychotherapy (MSc), Psychodynamics of Human Development (MSc/PGDip), Psychological Research Methods (MSc), Psychology (MRes/MSc/PGDip), Psychosocial Studies (MA/GradCert)

School of Social Sciences, History and Philosophy; www.bbk.ac.uk/sshp

Department of Applied Linguistics and Communication; www.bbk.ac.uk/linguistics

CertHE Higher Education Introductory Studies, CertHE Introduction to History, CertHE Introduction to Geography, CertHE Introduction to Politics, CertHE Introduction to Social Sciences, CertHE Linguistics and Language, BA Linguistics and Language, BA Intercultural Communication, BA Intercultural Communication and/with Language

Postgraduate courses: GradCert Linguistic Studies, IPGCert Intercultural Communication, PGDip Intercultural Communication, MA Applied Linguistics and Communication, MA Intercultural Communication for Business and Professions, MA Language Teaching, MA TESOL (Teaching English to Speakers of Other Languages)

Department of Geography; www.bbk.ac.uk/geography

Community Development and Public Policy (BSc), Community Leadership (CertHE), Development and Globalisation (BSc), Development Studies (CertHE), Environmental Management (BSc), Geography (BSc), Human Geography (BA), Introduction to Social Sciences (CertHE), Social Anthropology (CertHE), Social Sciences (BSc)

Postgraduate courses: Children, Youth and International Development (MSc), Climate Change (MSc/PGDip/PGCert), Environment and Sustainability (MSc/PGDip), Geographic Information Science (MSc/PGDip/PGCert), Geography (MSc/PGDip/PGCert), Global Environmental Politics and Policy (MSc), International Development (MSc/PGDip/PGCert), International Development and Social Anthropology (MSc/PGDip), Social and Cultural Geography (MA), War and Humanitarianism (MSc)

Department of History, Classics and Archaeology; www.bbk.ac.uk/history

BA Archaeology, BA Classics/BA Classical Studies, BA Contemporary History and Politics, BA History, BA History and Archaeology, BA History and International Relations

Postgraduate courses: MA Archaeological Practice, MA Classical Archaeology, MA Classical Civilisation/MA Classics, MA Contemporary History and Politics, MA Early Modern History, MA European History, MA Gender, Sexuality and Culture, MSc Gender, Sexuality and Society, MA Global History: Empires, States and Cultures, MA Historical Research, MA History of Ideas, MA History of Science and Medicine, MA History of the British Isles, MA Medieval History, MA Public Histories, MRes History, MSc War and Humanitarianism, GradCert in History

Department of Philosophy; www.bbk.ac.uk/philosophy

CertHE Philosophy, BA Philosophy

Postgraduate course: PGCert/PGDip/MA/MRes Philosophy

Department of Politics; www.bbk.ac.uk/politics

International Studies (CertHE), Politics (CertHE), Global Politics and International Relations (BA), Politics (BA), Politics, Philosophy and History (BA)

Postgraduate courses: European Politics and Policy (MSc), Global Governance and Emerging Powers (MSc), Global Politics (MRes/MSc), Government, Policy and Politics (MSc), International Security and Global Governance (MSc), Middle East in Global Politics: Islam, Conflict and Development (MSc), Nationalism and Ethnic Conflict (MSc), Politics (MRes), Politics of Population, Migration and Ecology (MSc), Public Policy and Management (MRes/MSc), Social and Political Theory (MSc), Social Research (MSc/PGCert/PGDip)

Department of Psychosocial Studies; www.bbk.ac.uk/psychosocial

Counselling and Counselling Skills (CertHE), Psychodynamic Counselling and Organisational Dynamics (CertHE), Psychosocial Studies (BA), Psychosocial Studies and Principles of Psychodynamic Counselling (BA)

Postgraduate courses: Culture, Diaspora, Ethnicity (PGDip), Culture, Diaspora, Ethnicity (PGCert/MA), Education, Power and Social Change (MSc/PGCert/PGDip), Psychoanalytic Studies (MA),

Psychodynamic Counselling & Psychotherapy with Children and Adolescents (MSc), Psychodynamic Counselling and Psychotherapy (MSc), Psychodynamics of Human Development (PGDip/MSc),

Psychosocial Studies (GradCert), Psychosocial Studies (MA), Social Research and Psychosocial Studies (MRes)

UNIVERSITY OF LONDON; COURTAULD INSTITUTE OF ART
www.courtauld.ac.uk

BA History of Art
Postgraduate courses: GradDip in the History of Art, MA History of Art, MA Curating the Art Museum,

MA Buddhist Art: History and Conservation, PGDip in the Conservation of Easel Paintings, MA Conservation of Wall Painting

UNIVERSITY OF LONDON; GOLDSMITHS
www.goldsmiths.ac.uk

Department of Anthropology; www.gold.ac.uk/anthropology

BA(Hons) Anthropology, BA(Hons) Anthropology & Media, BA(Hons) Anthropology & Sociology, BA(Hons) Anthropology & Visual Practice, BA(Hons) Digital Anthropology, BA(Hons) History & Anthropology, BA(Hons) Politics, Philosophy & Economics, BA Religion
Postgraduate courses: MA Anthropology & Cultural Politics, MA in Anthropology & Museum Practice, MA Applied Anthropology & Community & Youth Work, MA in Applied Anthropology & Community Arts, MA Applied Anthropology & Community Development, MA Migration & Mobility, MA in Social Anthropology, MA in Visual Anthropology, MRes in Anthropology, MRes in Visual Anthropology

Department of Art; www.gold.ac.uk/art

BA(Hons) Fine Art, BA(Hons) Fine Art & History of Art, BSc(Hons) Digital Arts Computing
Postgraduate courses: MA in Artists Film & Moving Image, MFA in Curating, MFA in Fine Art

Department of Computing; www.gold.ac.uk/computing

BSc(Hons) Business Computing & Entrepreneurship, BSc(Hons) Computer Science, BSc(Hons) Creative Computing, BSc(Hons) Digital Arts Computing, BMus/BSc(Hons) Electronic Music, Computing and Technology, BSc(Hons) Games Programming
Postgraduate courses: MA in Computational Arts, MSc Computational Cognitive Neuroscience, MA in Computer Games Art & Design, MSc Computer Games Programming, MA in Creative & Cultural Entrepreneurship: Computing Pathway, MSc Data Science, MA/MSc/MRes Digital Journalism, MA Independent Games and Playable Experience Design, MSc User Experience Engineering, MA/MSc Virtual and Augmented Reality

Confucius Institute for Dance and Performance; www.gold.ac.uk/confucius-institute

BA(Hons) International Relations & Chinese, BA(Hons) Sociology & Chinese

Department of Design; www.gold.ac.uk/design

BA(Hons) Design
Postgraduate courses: MA in Design: Expanded Practice, PGCE (Secondary): Design and Technology, MPhil and PhD in Design, Graduate Diploma in Design

Department of Educational Studies; www.gold.ac.uk/educational-studies

BA(Hons) Education, Culture & Society
Postgraduate courses: MA Arts & Learning, MA Children's Literature, MA Children's Literature: Children's Illustration, MA Creative Writing and Education, MA Education: Culture, Language & Identity, MA Multilingualism, Linguistics & Education, PGCE (Primary with Mathematics), PGCE (Primary with Modern Languages), PGCE (Primary), PGCE (Secondary): Art & Design, PGCE (Secondary) Standard Programme, PGCE (Secondary): Design and Technology, PGCE (Secondary): Drama, PGCE (Secondary): English, PGCE (Secondary): Mathematics, PGCE (Secondary): Media Studies with

English, PGCE (Secondary): Modern Languages, PGCE (Secondary): Part-time Programme, PGCE (Secondary): Science Education (Biology, Chemistry or Physics)

Department of English and Comparative]Literature; www.gold.ac.uk/ecl

BA(Hons) English, BA(Hons) English & American Literature, BA(Hons) English & Comparative Literature, BA(Hons) English & Drama/Drama & English, BA(Hons) English & History, BA(Hons) English Language & Literature, BA(Hons) English with Creative Writing, BA(Hons) Media & English
Postgraduate courses: MA Black British Writing, MA Children's Literature, MA Creative & Life Writing, MA Creative Writing and Education, MA Literary Studies, MA Literary Studies: Pathway in American Literature & Culture, MA Literary Studies: Pathway in Comparative Literature & Criticism, MA in Literary Studies: Pathway in Literature of the Caribbean and its Diasporas, MA in Literary Studies: Pathway in Critical Theory, MA in Literary Studies: Pathway in Modern Literature, MA in Literary Studies: Pathway in Romantic & Victorian Literature & Culture, MA in Literary Studies: Pathway in Shakespeare: Early & Modern, MA in Multilingualism, Linguistics & Education, MA in Sociocultural Linguistics, MA in Translation

English Language Centre; www.gold.ac.uk/ english-language-centre

Postgraduate courses: Graduate Diploma in Creative & Cultural Industries, Graduate Diploma in Design, Graduate Diploma in Media, Culture & Social Sciences, Graduate Diploma in Music

Department of History; www.gold.ac.uk/ history

BA(Hons) English & History, BA(Hons) History, BA(Hons) History & Anthropology, BA(Hons) History & Politics, BA History & Journalism
Postgraduate courses: MA Black British History, MA History, MA Queer History, MRes History

Institute for Creative and Cultural Entrepreneurship (ICCE); www.gold.ac.uk/ icce

BA(Hons) Arts Management
Postgraduate courses: MA Arts Administration & Cultural Policy, MA Arts Administration & Cultural Policy: Music Pathway, MA Creative & Cultural Entrepreneurship, MA Creative & Cultural Entrepreneurship: Computing Pathway, MA in Creative & Cultural Entrepreneurship: Design Pathway, MA

Creative & Cultural Entrepreneurship: Fashion Pathway, MA Creative & Cultural Entrepreneurship: Leadership Pathway, MA Creative & Cultural Entrepreneurship: Media & Communications Pathway, MA Creative & Cultural Entrepreneurship: Music Pathway, MA Creative & Cultural Entrepreneurship: Theatre & Performance Pathway, MA Cultural Policy, Relations & Diplomacy, MA in Events and Experience Management, MA Luxury Brand Management, MA in Social Entrepreneurship, MA Tourism & Cultural Policy, MA Translation, PGCert in Museums & Galleries Entrepreneurship, Graduate Diploma in Creative & Cultural Industries

Institute of Management Studies; www.gold.ac.uk/institute-managementstudies

BA(Hons) Economics, BA(Hons) Economics with Marketing, BSc(Hons) Economics with Econometrics, BSc(Hons) Management with Economics, BSc(Hons) Management with Entrepreneurship, BSc(Hons) Management with Marketing, BSc(Hons) Marketing, BSc(Hons) Psychology with Management, BA Promotional Media
Postgraduate courses: MSc Consumer Behaviour, Management of Innovation, MSc MSc Marketing & Technology, MSc Occupational Psychology, PGCert in Coaching

Department ofMedia and Communications; www.gold.ac.uk/ mediacommunications

BA(Hons) Anthropology and Media, BA History and Journalism, BA(Hons) Journalism, BA(Hons) Media & Communications, BA(Hons) Media & English, BA(Hons) Media & Sociology, BA Promotional Media
Postgraduate courses: MA Brands, Communication & Culture, MA Children's Literature: Children's Illustration, MA Creative & Cultural Entrepreneurship: Media & Communications Pathway, MA Cultural Studies, MA Culturedustry, MA Digital Media: MA Film & Screen Studies, MA Filmmaking, MA Filmmaking (Cinematography), MA Filmmaking (Directing Fiction), MA Filmmaking (Editing), MA Filmmaking (Producing), MA Filmmaking (Screen Documentary), MA Filmmaking (Sound Recording, Post-Production & Design), MA Gender, Media & Culture, MA Global Media & Transnational Communications, MA Journalism, MA Media & Communications, MA Photography: The Image & Electronic Arts, MA Political Communications, MA Postcolonial Culture & Global Policy, MA Promotional Media: Public Relations, Advertising & Marketing, MA Race,

Media & Social Justice, MA Radio, MA Script Writing, MA Television Journalism, MA/ MSc Digital Journalism, MRes, MRes Media & Communications

Department of Music; www.gold.ac.uk/music

BMus(Hons) Music, BMus(Hons) Popular Music, BMus/BSc(Hons) Electronic Music, Computing and Technology

Postgraduate courses: MA Arts Administration & Cultural Policy: Music Pathway, MA Creative & Cultural Entrepreneurship: Music Pathway, MA Music, MA Music (Contemporary Music Studies), MA Music (Ethnomusicology), MA Music (General), MA Music (Musicology), MA Music (Popular Music Research), MMus Composition, MMus Creative Practice, MMus Performance, MMus Popular Music, MMus Sonic Arts, Graduate Diploma in Music

Department of Politics and International Relations; www.gold.ac.uk/politics-and-international-relations

BA(Hons) Economics, Politics & Public Policy, BA(Hons) History & Politics, BA(Hons) International Relations, BA(Hons) International Relations & Chinese, BA(Hons) Politics, BA(Hons) Politics & International Relations, BA(Hons) Politics, Philosophy & Economics, BA(Hons) Sociology & Politics

Postgraduate courses: MA Art & Politics, MA Global Political Economy, MA International Relations, MA in Politics, Development and the Global South

Department of Psychology; www.gold.ac.uk/psychology

BSc(Hons) Psychology, BSc(Hons) Psychology with Clinical Psychology, BSc(Hons) Psychology with Cognitive Neuroscience, BSc(Hons) Psychology with Forensic Psychology, BSc(Hons) Psychology with Management

Postgraduate courses: MRes Research Methods in Psychology, MSc in Cognitive & Clinical Neuroscience, MSc Computational Cognitive Neuroscience, MSc Forensic Psychology, MSc Foundations in Clinical Psychology & Health Services, MSc Mind & Brain, MSc Psychology of Social Relations, MSc Psychology of the Arts, Neuroaesthetics & Creativity

Department of Social, Therapeutic and Community Studies (STACS); www.gold.ac.uk/stacs

BA(Hons) Applied Social Science, Community Development & Youth Work, BA(Hons) Psychosocial Studies, BA(Hons) Social Work

Postgraduate courses: Graduate Certificate in Humanistic & Psychodynamic Counselling, MA Applied Anthropology & Community & Youth Work, MA Anthropology & Community Arts, MA Anthropology & Community Development, MA Psychotherapy, MA Counselling, MA Movement Psychotherapy, MA Professional Leadership for Social Work (qualified Social Workers), MA in Social Work, MA in Understanding Domestic Violence & Sexual Abuse, MSc/ PGDip in Cognitive Behavioural Therapy

Department of Sociology; www.gold.ac.uk/sociology

BA(Hons) Anthropology & Sociology, BA(Hons) Criminology, BA(Hons) Media & Sociology, BA(Hons) Sociology, BA(Hons) Sociology & Chinese, BA(Hons) Sociology & Politics, BA(Hons) Sociology with Criminology

Postgraduate courses: MA Brands, Communication & Culture, MA Cities & Society, MA Critical & Creative Analysis, MA Gender, Media & Culture, MA Human Rights, Culture & Social Justice, MA Photography & Urban Cultures, MA Race, Media & Social Justice, MSc Social Research, MA Visual Sociology

Department of Theatre and Performance; www.gold.ac.uk/theatre-performance

BA(Hons) Drama & Theatre Arts, BA(Hons) Drama: Comedy and Satire, BA(Hons) Drama: Musical Theatre, BA(Hons) Drama: Performance, Politics and Society, BA(Hons) English & Drama/ Drama & English

Postgraduate courses: MA in Applied Theatre: Drama Educational, Community & Social Contexts, MA Black British Writing, MA Creative & Cultural Entrepreneurship: Theatre & Performance Pathway, MA Dramaturgy and Writing for Performance, MA Musical Theatre, MA Performance & Culture: Interdisciplinary Perspectives, MA Performance Making, MA World Theatres

Department of Visual Cultures; www.gold.ac.uk/visual-cultures

BA(Hons) Curating, BA(Hons) Fine Art & History of Art, BA(Hons) History of Art

Postgraduate courses: Graduate Diploma Contemporary Art History, MA Art Theory, MA Research Architecture, MRes Curatorial/Knowledge, MRes Visual Cultures

UNIVERSITY OF LONDON; INSTITUTE IN PARIS
www.ulip.lon.ac.uk

BA French Studies, BA French Studies with Business, BA French Studies with History, BA French Studies & International Relations, BA International Politics Paris, BA International Politics & French

Postgraduate courses: LLM (Master of Laws) in Paris – QMUL, MA International Relations (Paris) – QMUL, MA Urban History and Culture, Sorbonne Law School – Queen Mary University of London Double LLM

UNIVERSITY OF LONDON; INSTITUTE OF EDUCATION
www.ioe.ac.uk

Undergraduate courses
Education Studies BA, Psychology with Education BSc, Social Sciences BSc, Social Sciences with Quantitative Methods BSc

Postgraduate courses
Culture, Communication and Media
Applied Linguistics MA, Art and Design in Education MA, Digital Media: Critical Studies MA, Digital Media: Education MA, Digital Media: Production MA, Education and Technology MA, English Education MA, Museums and Galleries in Education MA, Music Education MA, Teaching English to Speakers of Other Languages (TESOL) In-Service MA, Teaching of English to Speakers of Other Languages (TESOL) Pre-Service MA
Curriculum, Pedagogy and Assessment
Advanced Educational Practice Grad Dip, Development Education and Global Learning MA, Education MA, Educational Assessment MA, Mathematics Education MA, Science Education MA, Teaching MTeach
Education Practice and Society
Comparative Education MA, Education and International Development MA, Education, Gender and International Development MA, Education, Health Promotion and International Development MA, Educational Planning, Economics and International Development MA, Philosophy of Education MA, Policy Studies in Education MA, Social Justice and Education MA, Sociology of Education MA Social Justice and Education MA, Sociology of Education MA
Learning and Leadership
Applied Educational Leadership MA, Early Years Education MA, Educational Leadership (International) MBA, Primary Education (4-12) MA, Reading

Recovery and Literacy Leadership MA, Social Science Research Methods PG Dip
Psychology and Human Development
Child Development MSc, Developmental and Educational Psychology MSc, Education (Psychology) MA, Educational Neuroscience MA/MSc, Habilitation and Disabilities of Sight (Children and Young People) Grad Dip, National Award for Special Educational Needs Co-ordination PG Cert, Psychology Grad Cert, Psychology of Education MSc, Special and Inclusive Education MA, Specific Learning Difficulties (Dyslexia) MA, Speech, Language and Communication Needs in Schools: Advanced Practice MSc
Social Science
Social Policy and Social Research MSc, Social Research Methods MSc, Sociology of Childhood and Children's Rights MA

Teacher training
University-led
PGCE Early years: Initial Teacher Training (Employment/ Mainstream Pathway), PGCE Primary (including EYFS/KS1 or Specialist Mathematics), PGCE Secondary (Art and Design/Biology/Business Education/ Chemistry/Citizenship/Computing and ICT/ English/English with Drama/Geography/History/ Languages/Mathematics/Music/Physics/Physics with Mathematics/Psychology/Religious Education/ Social Science), PGCE Post-Compulsory (Education)
School Direct (Salaried or Tuition Fee)
PGCE Primary, PGCE Primary Mathematics Specialist, PGCE Secondary (Art and Design/Biology/Business Education/Chemistry/Citizenship/Computing and ICT/Economics/English/English with Drama/ Geography/History/Languages/Mathematics/Music/ Physics/Physics with Mathematics/Psychology/Religious Education/Social Science)

UNIVERSITY OF LONDON; KING'S COLLEGE LONDON
www.kcl.ac.uk

Arts, Culture and Media; www.kcl.ac.uk/study/subject-areas/artsculture-and-media/index.aspx

Comparative Literature with Film Studies BA, Digital Culture BA, English with Film Studies BA, Film Studies BA, French with Film Studies with a year abroad BA, German & Music with a year abroad BA, German with Film Studies with a year abroad BA, Liberal Arts BA, Music BMus, Spanish with Film Studies with a year abroad BA

Postgraduate courses: Advanced Musical Studies PG Cert, Arts & Cultural Management MA, Big Data in Culture & Society MA, Christianity & the Arts MA, Classical Art & Archaeology MA, Cultural & Creative Industries MA, Digital Asset & Media Management MA, Digital Culture & Society MA, Digital Curation MA, Digital Humanities MA, Film Studies MA (Film & Philosophy pathway available), Global Media Industries MA, Music MMus (Composition or Musicology and Ethnomusicology), Shakespeare Studies MA, Theatre & Performance Studies MA, The Classical World & its Reception MA

Biomedical and Life Sciences; www.kcl.ac.uk/study/subject-areas/biomedical-and-life-sciences/index.aspx

Anatomy, Developmental & Human Biology BSc, Biochemistry BSc/MSci, Biomedical Science BSc, Chemistry with Biomedicine BSc/MSci, Health & Social Medicine BSc, Medical Physiology BSc, Molecular Genetics BSc, Molecular Genetics MSci, Neuroscience BSc, Neuroscience MSci, Nutrition BSc, Pharmacology BSc, Pharmacology & Molecular Genetics BSc, Sport & Exercise Medical Sciences BSc

Postgraduate courses: Aerospace Medicine MSc / PG Dip, Biomedical and Molecular Sciences Research MSc/ MRes, Cardiovascular Research MSc, MPhil / PhD, Global Air Pollution & Health: and Science MSc, Genomic Medicine MSc/ PG Dip / PG Cert, Healthcare Technologies MSc/MRes, Human and Applied Physiology MSc, Immunology MSc, Medical Engineering and Physics MSc, Medical Humanities MSc, Microbiome in Health & Disease MSc, Molecular Biophysics for Medical Sciences MRes, Nutrition, MSc PGCE Biology, Regenerative Dentistry MSc, Space Physiology and Health MSc, Stem Cell & Regenerative Therapies: From Bench to Market MSc, Tissue Engineering & Innovation Technology MRes, Translational Cancer Medicine MRes, Women & Children's Health MSc

Chemistry; www.kcl.ac.uk/study/subject-areas/chemistry/index.aspx

Chemistry BSc, Chemistry MSci, Chemistry with Biomedicine BSc, Chemistry with Biomedicine MSci

Computer Science; www.kcl.ac.uk/study/subject-areas/computer-science/index.aspx

Computer Science BSc, Computer Science MSci, Computer Science with Intelligent Systems BSc, Computer Science with Management BSc, Computer Science with Robotics BSc

Postgraduate courses: Advanced Computing MSc, Advanced Software Engineering MSc, Advanced Artifical Intelligence MSc, Big Data in Culture & Society MA, Computational Finance MSc, Computing & Security MSc, Cyber Security MSc, Data Science MSc, Postgraduate Certificate in Education (Computer Science) PGCE, Robotics MSc, Urban Informatics MSc, Web Intelligence MSc

Conflict and Security; www.kcl.ac.uk/study/subject-areas/conflict-and-security/index.aspx

History and International Relations BA, International Relations BA, War Studies BA, War Studies & History BA, War Studies & Philosophy BA

Postgraduate courses: Arms Control & International Security MA / PG Dip / PG Cert, Conflict Resolution in Divided Societies MA, Conflict, Security & Development MA, Geopolitics, Territory & Security MA, History of War MA, Intelligence & International Security MA, International Affairs MA with pathways in Cyber Security or Espionage & Surveillance MA/PGDip/PGCert, International Conflict Studies MA, International Peace & Security MA, International Relations & Contemporary War MA, International Relations MA, National Security Studies MA, Non-Proliferation & International Security MA, Science & International Security MA, Security, Leadership & Society MSc/PGDip, South Asia & Global Security MA, Strategic Communications MA, Terrorism, Security & Society MA, War & Psychiatry MSc, in the Modern World MA, War Studies MA

Dental Training and Science; www.kcl.ac.uk/study/subject-areas/ dental-training-and-science/index.aspx

Postgraduate courses: Advanced Minimum Intervention Dentistry MSc, Aesthetic Dentistry MSc, Conscious Sedation for Dentistry PG Dip, Dental Cone Beam CT Radiological Interpretation PG Cert, Dental Public Health MSc, Endodontics MSc, Endodontics PG Dip, Endodontology MClinDent, Fixed & Removable Prosthodontics MClinDent, Maxillofacial & Craniofacial Technology MSc, Maxillofacial Prosthetic Rehabilitation MSc, Microbiome in Health & Disease MSc, Operative Dentistry PG Dip, Orthodontics MSc, Paediatric Dentistry MSc, Periodontology MClinDent, Prosthodontics MClinDent, Regenerative Dentistry MSc, Special Care Dentistry MSc, Tissue Engineering & Innovation Technology MRes

Dentistry; www.kcl.ac.uk/study/subject-areas/dentistry/index.aspx

Dentistry BDS, Dentistry Entry Programme for Medical Graduates BDS, Dentistry Graduate/Professional Entry Programme BDS, Enhanced Support Dentistry Programme BDS

Education Management and Policy; www.kcl.ac.uk/study/subject-areas/ education-management-and-policy/ index.aspx

Postgraduate courses: Applied Linguistics and English Language Teaching MA, Child & Adolescent Mental Health MSc, Child Studies MA, Education MA, Education in Arts & Cultural Settings MA, Education Management MA, Education, Policy & Society MA, International Child Studies MA, Mathematics Education MA, PGCE (Biology/Chemistry/Computing/English/Geography/Latin with Classics/Mathematics/Modern Foreign Languages/Physics with Mathematics/Physics/Religious Education), Teaching English to Speakers of Other Languages (TESOL) MA

Engineering; www.kcl.ac.uk/study/subject-areas/engineering/index.aspx

Biomedical Engineering BEng/MEng, Computer Science with Robotics BSc, Electronic Engineering BEng/MEng, Electronic & Information Engineering BEng/MEng, Electronic Engineering with Management BEng/MEng, General Engineeing BEng/MEng Postgraduate courses: Artificial Intelligence MSc, Data Science MSc, Electronic Engineering with Management MSc, Engineering with Management MSc, Healthcare Technologies MSc/MRes, Medical Engineering & Physics MSc, Mobile & Personal Communications MSc, Robotics MSc, Telecommunications & Internet Technology MSc

Finance; www.kcl.ac.uk/study/subject-areas/finance/index.aspx

Accounting & Finance BSc

Postgraduate courses: Accounting, & Financial Management MSc, Banking & Finance MSc, Computational Finance MSc, Digital Marketing MSc, MSc in International Marketing MSc, Finance Analytics MSc, Finance (Asset Pricing) MSc, Finance (Corporate Finance) MSc, Financial Mathematics MSc

Geography and the Environment; www.kcl.ac.uk/study/subject-areas/ geography-and-the-environment/ index.aspx

Geography BA/BSc, Liberal Arts BA

Postgraduate courses: Climate Change: Environment, Science & Policy MSc, Disasters, Adaptation & Development MA/MSc, Environment & Development MA/MSc, Environment, Politics & Globalisation MA/MSc, Environmental Monitoring, Modelling & Management MSc, Geography MA/MSc, Geopolitics, Territory & Security MA, Global Air Quality: Management and Science MSc, Risk Analysis MA/MSc, Sustainable Cities MA/MSc, Tourism, Environment & Development MA / MSc, Water: Science & Governance MSc

History and Classics; www.kcl.ac.uk/study/ subject-areas/history-and-classics/ index.aspx

Ancient History BA, Classical Archaeology BA, Classical Studies and Comparative Literature BA, Classical Studies and French with a year abroad BA, Classical Studies BA, Classical Studies with English BA, Classics (Greek & Latin) BA, French & History with a year abroad BA, German & History with a year abroad BA, Liberal Arts BA, History BA, History & Iberian Studies (Spanish or Portuguese) with a year abroad BA, History and International Relations BA, Liberal Arts BA, War Studies & History BA

Postgraduate courses: Ancient History MA, Classical Art & Archaeology MA, Classical Studies Grad Dip, Classics MA, Contemporary British History MA, Early Modern History MA, Eighteenth-Century Studies MA, Medieval History MA, Medieval Studies MA, Modern History MA, Politics & Contemporary History MA, Postgraduate Certificate in Education (Latin with Classics), Science, Technology &

Medicine in History MA, The Classical World & Its Reception MA, World History & Cultures MA

Imaging Sciences; www.kcl.ac.uk/study/subject-areas/imaging-sciences/index.aspx

Biomedical Engineering BEng/MEng
Postgraduate courses: Healthcare Technologies MSc/MRes, Medical Engineering & Physics MSc, Medical Ultrasound MSc/PG Dip/PG Cert, Neuroimaging MSc, Nuclear Medicine: Science & Practice MSc/PG Dip/PG Cert, Radio Pharmaceutics and PET Radiochemistry MSc, Specialist Ultrasound Practice PG Cert, Ultrasound in Emergency and Critical Care PGCert, Vascular Ultrasound MSc/PG Dip/PG Cert

International Affairs and Development; www.kcl.ac.uk/study/subject-areas/international-affairs-and-development/index.aspx

Geography BA/BSc, Global Health & Social Medicine BA/BSc, International Development BA
Postgraduate courses: China & Globalisation MSc, Conflict, Security & Development MA, Contemporary India MA, Disasters, Adaptation & Development MA/MSc, Emerging Economies & Inclusive Development MSc, Emerging Economies & International Development MSc, Environment, Politics & Globalisation MA/MSc, & Development MA/MSc, Eurasian Political Economy & Energy MSc, Geography MA/MSc, Geopolitics, Territory & Security MA, Global Affairs MSc, Global Ethics & Human Values MA, Global Health & Social Justice MSc, Global Health with Conflict & Security MSc, Global Health Disasters & Adaptation MSc, Global Health with Global Surgery MSc, Global Health with Health Professions MSc, Mental Health MSc, History of War MA, Intelligence & International Security MA, International Conflict Studies MA, International Peace & Security MA, International Political Economy MA, International Relations & Contemporary War MA, International Relations MA, Latin American Development MSc, Leadership & Development MSc/PG Dip, Middle Eastern Studies MA, Political Economy of Emerging Markets MSc, Political Economy of the Middle East MA, Russia in Global Systems MSc, Russian Politics & Society MSc, Security, Leadership & Society MSc / PG Dip, South Asia & Global Security MA, Sustainable Cities MA/ MSc, Tourism, Environment & Development MA/ MSc, War Studies MA, Water: Science & Governance MSc

Languages and Literature; www.kcl.ac.uk/study/subject-areas/languages-and-literature/index.aspx

Classical Studies & Comparative Literature BA, Classical Studies & French with a year abroad BA, Classical Studies with English BA, Comparative Literature BA, Comparative Literature with Film Studies BA, English BA, English Language & Linguistics BA, English with Film Studies BA, European Studies (French/German/Spanish pathways) with a year abroad BA, French & German with a year abroad BA, French & History with a year abroad BA, French & Management with a year abroad BA, French & Philosophy with a year abroad BA, French & Spanish with a year abroad BA, French (four year) with a year abroad BA, French (three year) BA, French with English with a year abroad BA, French with Film Studies with a year abroad BA, German & History with a year abroad BA, German & Management with a year abroad BA, German & Music with a year abroad BA, German & Philosophy with a year abroad BA, German & Portuguese with a year abroad BA, German & Spanish with a year abroad BA, German with a year abroad BA, German with English with a year abroad BA, German with Film Studies with a year abroad BA, History and Iberian Studies (Spanish or Portuguese) with a year abroad BA, Liberal Arts BA, Philosophy & Spanish with a year abroad BA, Portuguese & French with a year abroad BA, Portuguese & Management with a year abroad BA, Spanish & Latin American Studies with a year abroad BA, Spanish & Management with a year abroad BA, Spanish & Philosophy with a year abroad BA, Spanish & Portuguese with a year abroad BA, Spanish with English with a year abroad BA, Spanish with Film Studies with a year abroad BA
Postgraduate courses: Ancient History MA, Applied Linguistics & English Language Teaching MA, Classical Art & Archaeology MA, Classical Studies Grad Dip, Classics MA, Comparative Literature MA, Contemporary Literature, Culture & Theory MA, Critical Methodologies MA, Early Modern English Literature: Text & Transmission MA, Eighteenth Century Studies MA, European Studies MA, Language & Cultural Diversity MA, Medical Humanities MSc, Medieval Studies MA, Modern Languages, Literature & Culture MA, Modern Literature & Culture MA, PGCE (English), PGCE (Latin with Classics), PGCE (Modern Foreign Languages), Shakespeare Studies MA, Teaching English to Speakers of Other Languages (TESOL) MA, The Classical

World & Its Reception MA, Theatre & Performance Studies MA

Law; www.kcl.ac.uk/study/subject-areas/law/index.aspx

Law LLB, English Law & French Law LLB and Maitrise en droit (with Universit Paris 2, Panthon-Assas), English Law & German Law LLB and MLLP or Certificate in Rechtswissenschaften (with Humboldt University of Berlin), English Law & Hong Kong Law LLB and JD (with Chinese University of Hong Kong), English Law & Spanish Law LLB and Grado en Derecho (with Universitat Pompeu Fabra), Politics, Philosophy & Law LLB

Postgraduate courses: Competition Law LLM, Construction Law & Dispute Resolution MSc, Economics for Competition Law MA/PGDip, EU Compeition Law MA/PGDip, European Law LLM, European Union Law MA/PGDip, Global Ethics & Human Values MA, Intellectual Property & Information Law LLM, International Business Law LLM, International Corporate & Commercial Law LLM, International Dispute Resolution LLM, International Financial & Commercial Law LLM/PGDip/PGCert, International Financial Law LLM, International Tax LLM, Master of Laws LLM, Medical Ethics & Law MA, Medical Law MA, Mental Health & Law MSc, Public Procurement Regulation in the EU & in its Global Context MA/PGDip, Transnational Law LLM, UK, EU & US Copyright Law MA/PGDip

Management; www.kcl.ac.uk/study/subject-areas/management/index.aspx

Accounting & Finance BSc, Business Management BSc, Computer Science with Management BSc, Computer Science with Management and a year abroad BSc, Computer Science with Management and a year in industry BSc, Economics & Management BSc, Electronic Engineering with Management BEng/MEng, French & Management with a year abroad BA, German & Management with a year abroad BA, International Management BSc

Postgraduate courses: Accounting, Accountability & Financial Management MSc, Digital Marketing MSc, Management MSc, Human Resource Management & Organisational Analysis MSc, International Management MSc, International Marketing MSc, Organisational Psychiatry & Psychology MSc, Public Policy & Management MSc

Mathematics; www.kcl.ac.uk/study/subject-areas/mathematics/index.aspx

Mathematics & Philosophy BSc, Mathematics BSc/MSci, Mathematics with Management & Finance BSc, Mathematics with Statistics BSc

Postgraduate courses: Complex Systems Modelling – From Biomedical and Natural to Economic and Social Sciences MSc, Financial Mathematics MSc, Mathematics Grad Dip, Mathematics MSc, Non-Equilibrium Systems: Theoretical Modelling, Simulation and Data-Driven Analysis MSc, Postgraduate Certificate in Education (Mathematics), Postgraduate Certificate in Education (Physics with Mathematics), Theoretical Physics MSc

Medicine; www.kcl.ac.uk/study/subject-areas/medicine/index.aspx

Medicine MBBS, Medicine MBBS: Extended Medical Degree Programme, Medicine MBBS: Graduate and Professional Entry Programme, Medicine MBBS: Maxfax Entry Programme

Nursing andMidwifery; www.kcl.ac.uk/study/subject-areas/nursing-and-midwifery/index.aspx

Midwifery with Registration as a Midwife BSc, Nursing Studies (for qualified healthcare professionals) BSc, Nursing with Registration as a Children's Nurse BSc, Nursing with Registration as a Mental Health Nurse BSc, Nursing with Registration as an Adult Nurse BSc, Specialist Community Public Health Nursing (Health Visiting/ School Nursing) BSc

Postgraduate courses: Advanced Clinical Practice MSc/PGDip/PGCert, Advanced Critical Care Practice PGDip, Advanced Practice: Leadership MSc/PGDip/PGCert, Clinical Nursing MSc, Clinical Research MRes, Maternal and Newborn Healthcare MSc/PGDip/PGCert, Midwifery MSc, Nursing MSc, Nursing with Registration as a Children's Nurse MSc, Nursing with Registration as a Mental Health Nurse MSc, Nursing with Registration as an Adult Nurse MSc, Palliative Care MSc/PGDip/PGCert, Specialist Community Public Health Nursing/Health Visiting/ School Nursing MSc/PGDip

Pharmacy, pharmacology and forensic science; www.kcl.ac.uk/study/subject-areas/pharmacy-pharmacology-and-forensic-science/index.aspx

Pharmacology & Molecular Genetics BSc, Pharmacology BSc, Pharmacology iBSc, Pharmacology MSci, Pharmacy MPharm, Analytical Toxicology MSc,

Biopharmaceuticals MSc, Clinical Pharmacology MSc/PG Dip/PG Cert, Clinically Enhanced Pharmacy Independent Prescribing PGCert, Drug Development Science MSc/PG Dip/PG Cert, Drug Discovery Skills MSc, Forensic Science MSc/MRes, Pharmaceutical Analysis & Quality Control MSc, Pharmaceutical Technology MSc, Pharmacology MSc/MRes, Pharmacy Practice Prescribing MSc/PG Dip/PG Cert, Radiopharmaceutics & PET Radiochemistry MSc, Translational Medicine MRes

Philosophy and religion; www.kcl.ac.uk/study/subject-areas/philosophy-and-religion/index.aspx

French & Philosophy with a year abroad BA, German & Philosophy with a year abroad BA, Liberal Arts BA, Mathematics & Philosophy with a year abroad BA, Philosophy BA, Philosophy & Spanish with a year abroad BA, Philosophy, Politics & Economics (PPE) BA, Physics & Philosophy BSc, Physics & Philosophy with a year abroad BSc, Politics, Philosophy & Law LLB, Religion, Philosophy & Ethics BA, Religion, Politics & Society BA, Theology, Religion and Culture BA, War Studies & Philosophy BA

Postgraduate courses: Bioethics & Society MSc, Christianity & the Arts MA, Critical Methodologies MA, Global Ethics & Human Values MA, Global Health & Social Justice MSc, History of Philosophy MA, Jewish Studies MA, Mental Health, Ethics & Law MSc, PGCE (Religious education), Philosophy MA, Philosophy of Medicine and Psychiatry MA, Philosophy of Psychology MA, Systematic Theology MA, Theology & Religious Studies Grad Dip

Physics; www.kcl.ac.uk/study/subject-areas/physics/index.aspx

Physics BSc/MSci, Physics with Astrophysics & Cosmology BSc/MSci, Physics with Biophysics BSc/MSci, Physics & Philosophy BSc/MSci, Physics with a year abroad BSc, Physics & Philosophy with a year abroad BSc, Physics with Theoretical Physics BSc/MSci

Postgraduate courses: Medical Engineering & Physics MSc, PGCE (Physics), PGCE (Physics with mathematics), Physics MSc, Physics Grad Dip, Theoretical Physics MSc

Policy and society; www.kcl.ac.uk/study/subject-areas/policy-and-society/index.aspx

Global Health & Social Medicine BA/BSc, Social Sciences BA

Postgraduate courses: Ageing & Society MSc, Bioethics & Society MSc, Child & Adolescent Mental Health MSc, Child Studies MA, China & Globalisation MSc, Climate Change: Environment, Science & Policy MSc, Conflict Resolution in Divided Societies MA, Conflict, Security & Development MA, Dental Public Health MSc, Emerging Economies & Inclusive Development MSc, Emerging Economies & International Development MSc, Environment, Politics & Globalisation MA/MSc, Gerontology MSc, Global Health & Social Justice MSc, Global Health with Global Surgery MSc, Global Health with Health Professions Education MSc, Global Health with Conflict & Security MSc, Global Health with Disasters & Adaptation MSc, Global Mental Health MSc, International Child Studies MA, International Programme in Addiction Studies MSc, Medical Humanities MSc, Medicine, Health and Public Policy MSc, Mental Health, Ethics and Law MSc, Public Policy & Ageing MA/PG Dip/ PG Cert, Public Policy & Management MSc, Public Policy MA

Politics and economics; www.kcl.ac.uk/study/subject-areas/politics-and-economics/index.aspx

Economics & Management BA, Economics BSc, European Politics BA, European Studies with a year abroad (French, German or Spanish pathway) BA, Liberal Arts BA, Philosophy, Politics & Economics (PPE) BA, Political Economy BA/BSc, Politics BA/BSc, Religion, Politics and Society BA

Postgraduate courses: China & Globalisation MSc, Conflict Resolution in Divided Societies MA, Contemporary India MA, Double Master's in Asian and European Affairs MA, Emerging Economies & Inclusive Development MSc, Emerging Economies & International Development MSc, Eurasian Political Economy & Energy MSc, European Studies MA, Intelligence & International Security MA, International Political Economy MA, Political Economy MA, Political Economy of Emerging Markets MSc, Political Economy of the Middle East MA, Politics & Contemporary History MA, Public Policy MA, Russia in Global Systems MSc, Russian Politics & Society MSc

Psychiatry, psychology and neuroscience; www.kcl.ac.uk/study/subject-areas/psychiatry-psychology-and-neuroscience/index.aspx

Neuroscience BSc/iBSc/MSci, Neuroscience & Psychology BSc, Psychology BSc/iBSc

Postgraduate courses: Addiction Studies MSc, Affective Disorders MSc, Applied Neuroscience MSc/PGDip/PGCert, Applied Statistical Modelling & Health Informatics PGCert, CBT Informed & Carer Supportive Practice in Psychosis Grad Cert/Grad Dip, Child & Adolescent Mental Health MSc, Clinical Neurodevelopmental Sciences MSc, Clinical Neuropsychiatry MSc, Clinical Neuroscience MSc, Cognitive Behavioural Therapies PG Dip, Cognitive Behavioural Therapy for Psychosis PGDip/PGCert, Developmental Psychology & Psychopathology MSc, Early Intervention in Psychosis MSc, Family Therapy MSc/Grad Cert, Forensic Mental Health MScGenes, Environment & Development in Psychology & Psychiatry MSc, Global Mental Health MSc, Health Psychology MSc, International Programme in Addiction Studies MSc Distance Learning, Mental Health Studies MSc, Mental Health, Ethics & Law MSc, Neuroimaging MSc, Neuroscience MSc, Organisational Psychiatry & Psychology MSc, Psychiatric Research MSc/PG Cert, Psychology & Neuroscience of Mental Health MSc/PG Dip/PG Cert Distance Learning, War & Psychiatry MSc

Public health; www.kcl.ac.uk/study/subject-areas/public-health/index.aspx

Postgraduate courses: Dental Public Health MSc, Global Air Pollution & Health: Management & Science MSc, Global Health MSc (with Global Surgery, Health Professions, Disasters & Adaptation and Conflict & Security pathways), Global Health and Social Justice MSc/PG Dip/PG Cert, Palliative Care MSc/PG Dip/PG Cert, Public Health MPH (with Environmental Health, Primary Care or Allied Health pathways), Public Health MSc/PGDip/PGCert – 100% online, Women & Children's Health MSc

Specialist training formedical professionals; www.kcl.ac.uk/study/subject-areas/specialist-training-for-medical-professionals/index.aspx

Postgraduate courses: Advanced Medical Training PGCert, Advanced Musculoskeletal Physiotherapy MSc/PGDip, Advanced Paediatrics MSc, Aerospace Medicine MSc/PG Dip, Cardiovascular Research MSc, Clinical Dermatology MSc, Clinical Education MA/PGDip/PGCert, Dental Public Health MSc, Dentistry BDS (Entry programme for Medical Graduates), Dietetics MSc/PG Dip, Genomic Medicine MSc/PG Dip/PG Cert, Global Health MSc/PG Dip/PG Cert, Maxillofacial Prosthetic Rehabilitation MSc, Medical Ultrasound MSc/PG Dip/PG Cert, Nuclear Medicine: Science & Practice MSc/PG Dip/PG Cert, Nutrition MSc, Palliative Care MSc/PG Dip/PG Cert, Physiotherapy (pre-registration) MSc, Radiopharmaceutics & PET Radiochemistry MSc, Rheumatology MSc/PG Dip, Specialist Ultrasound Practice PG Cert, Translational Cancer Medicine MRes, Ultrasound in Emergency and Critical Care PGCert, Ultrasound MSc/PG Dip/PG Cert, Women & Children's Health MSc

Teaching; www.kcl.ac.uk/study/subject-areas/teaching/index.aspx

Postgraduate courses: Biology PGCE, Chemistry PGCE, Computing PGCE, English PGCE, Geography PGCE, Latin with Classics PGCE, Mathematics PGCE, Modern Foreign Languages PGCE, Physics PGCE, Physics with Mathematics PGCE, Postgraduate Certificate in Education (PGCE), Religious Education PGCE, Science Education MA, Teaching English to Speakers of Other Languages (TESOL) MA

Therapeutic health; www.kcl.ac.uk/study/subject-areas/therapeutic-health/index.aspx

Nutrition BSc, Nutrition & Dietetics BSc, Physiology iBSc, Physiotherapy BSc Sport & Exercise Medical Sciences BSc

UNIVERSITY OF LONDON; LONDON SCHOOL OF ECONOMICS & POLITICAL SCIENCE
www.lse.ac.uk

Department of Accounting; www.lse.ac.uk/accounting

BSc/Dip Accounting and Finance

Postgraduate courses: MSc Accounting, Organisations and Institutions, MSc Accounting and Finance, MSc Law and Accounting

Department of Anthropology; www.lse.ac.uk/anthropology

BA/BSc Social Anthropology, BA Anthropology and Law

Postgraduate courses: MSc Social Anthropology, MSc Social Anthropology (Religion in the Contemporary World), MSc Anthropology and Development, MSc Anthropology and Development Management, MSc China in Comparative Perspective

Department of Economics; www.lse.ac.uk/economics

BSc Economics, BSc Econometrics and Mathematical Economics, BSc Economics with Economic History

Postgraduate courses: MSc Economics, MSc Econometrics and Mathematical Economics

Department of Economic History; www.lse.ac.uk/Economic-History

BSc Economic History, BSc Economic History with Economics, BSc Economics and Economic History, BSc Economic History and Geography

Postgraduate courses: MSc Economic History, MSc Economic History (Research), Erasmus Mundus MA Global Studies: A European Perspective, MSc Political Economy of Late Development, MSc Quantitative Economic History

Department of Finance; www.lse.ac.uk/finance

BSc Finance

Postgraduate courses: MSc Finance, MSc Finance and Economics, MSc Finance and Private Equity, MSc Risk and Finance

Department of Gender Studies; www.lse.ac.uk/Gender

Postgraduate courses: MSc Gender, MSc Gender (Research), MSc Gender (Sexuality), MSc Gender, Development and Globalisation, MSc Gender, Media and Culture, MSc Gender, Policy and Inequalities, MSc Women, Peace and Security, MSc Social Research Methods (Gender)

Department of Geography and Environment; www.lse.ac.uk/geography-and-environment

BA Geography, BSc Geography with Economics, BSc Environment and Development, BSc Environmental Policy with Economics

Postgraduate courses: MSc Environment and Development, MSc Environmental Economics and Climate Change, MSc Environmental Policy and Regulation, MSc Human Geography and Urban Studies (Research), MSc Local Economic Development, MSc Real Estate Economics and Finance, MSc Regional and Urban Planning Studies, MSc Urbanisation and Development, Double Master's Degree in Urban Policy

Department of Government; www.lse.ac.uk/government

BSc Politics, BSc Politics and Economics, BSc Politics and History, BSc Politics andInternational Relations, BSc Politics and Philosophy

Postgraduate courses: MSc Comparative Politics, MSc Conflict Studies, MSc Global Politics, MSc Public Policy and Administration, MSc Political Science and Political Economy, MSc Political Theory, MSc Regulation

Department of Health Policy; www.lse.ac.uk/health-policy

Postgraduate courses: MSc Global Health, MSc Health Policy, Planning, and Financing (HPPF), MSc International Health Policy (IHP-HP), MSc International Health Policy (Health Economics) (IHP-HE), MSc Evaluation of Health Care Interventions and Outcomes, MSc Health Economics, Outcomes and Management in Cardiovascular Sciences, MSc, Health Economics, Policy, and Management

Department of International Development; www.lse.ac.uk/international-development

Postgraduate courses: MSc African Development, MSc Development Management, MSc Development Studies, MSc International Development and Humanitarian Emergencies, MSc Health and International Development

Department of International History; www.lse.ac.uk/international-history

BA History, BSc International Relations and History

Postgraduate courses: MSc Empires, Colonialism and Globalisation, MSc History of International Relations, MSc Theory and History of International Relations, LSE-Columbia University Double MSc in International and World History, LSE-Peking University Double MSc in International Affairs

Department of International Relations; www.lse.ac.uk/international-relations

BSc International Relations

Postgraduate courses: MSc in International Relations, MSc in International Political Economy, Sciences Po-LSE Double Degree in Affaires Internationales and IR/IPE, MSc International Relations Theory

Department of Law; www.lse.ac.uk/collections/law

LLB Bachelor of Laws

Postgraduate courses: LLM Master of Laws, LLM, MSc Law and Accounting

Department of Management; www.lse.ac.uk/management

BSc Management

Postgraduate courses: Global Master's in Management, Master's in Management, MSc Economics and Management, MSc Human Resources and Organisations, MSc Management and Strategy, MSc Management of Information Systems and Digital Innovation, MSc Marketing, MSc Social Innovation and Entrepreneurship

Department of Mathematics; www.lse.ac.uk/maths

BSc Financial Mathematics and Statistics, BSc Mathematics and/with Economics

Postgraduate courses: MSc Applicable Mathematics, MSc Financial Mathematics, MSc Operations Research & Analytics

Department of Media and Communications; www.lse.ac.uk/media-and-communications

Postgraduate courses: MSc Global Media and Communications (with Year 2 in either University of Southern California, Fudan University or University of Cape Town), MSc Media and Communications, MSc Media and Communications (Research track), MSc Media and Communications (Data and Society), MSc Media and Communications (Governance), MSc Media, Communication and Development, MSc Politics and Communication, MSc in Strategic Communications

Department of Methodology; www.lse.ac.uk/methodology

Postgraduate courses: MSc Applied Social Data Science, MSc Social Research Methods

Department of Philosophy, Logic and Scientific Method; www.lse.ac.uk/philosophy

BSc Philosophy & Economics, BSc Philosophy, Logic & Scientific Method, BSc Philosophy, Politics & Economics, BSc Politics & Philosophy

Postgraduate courses: MSc Economics & Philosophy, MSc Philosophy & Public Policy, MSc Philosophy of Science, MSc Philosophy of the Social Sciences

Department of Psychological and Behavioural Science; www.lse.ac.uk/DPBS

BSc Psychological & Behavioural Science

Postgraduate courses: MSc Organisational and Social Psychology, MSc Psychology of Economic Life, MSc Social and Cultural Psychology, MSc Social and Public Communication, MSc Behavioural Science

Department of Social Policy; www.lse.ac.uk/social-policy

BSc Criminology, BSc International Social and Public Policy, BSc International Social and Public Policy and Economics, BSc International Social and Public Policy with Politics

Postgraduate courses: Masters of Public Administration (MPA), MSc Criminal Justice Policy, MSc International Social and Public Policy, MSc Social Research Methods

Department of Sociology; www.lse.ac.uk/sociology

BSc Sociology

Postgraduate courses: MSc Sociology, MSc City Design and Social Science, MSc Culture and Society, MSc Economy, Risk and Society, MSc Human Rights, MSc Human Rights and Politics, MSc Inequalities and Social Science, MSc International Migration and Public Policy

Department of Statistics; www.lse.ac.uk/statistics

BSc Actuarial Science, BSc Business Mathematics and Statistics, BSc Financial Mathematics and Statistics

Postgraduate courses: MSc Statistics, MSc Quantitative Methods for Risk Management, MSc Data Science, LSE-Fudan Double Master's Financial Statistics and Chinese Economy

UNIVERSITY OF LONDON; LONDON SCHOOL OF JEWISH STUDIES
www.lsjs.ac.uk

BA(Hons) Jewish Education

Postgraduate courses: MA Jewish Education, Religion (Jewish Studies pathway)

UNIVERSITY OF LONDON; QUEEN MARY
www.qmul.ac.uk

Faculty of Humanities and Social Sciences; www.qmul.ac.uk/about/hss

School of Business and Management; www.busman.qmul.ac.uk

BSc Accounting and Management, BSc Business Management, BSc Business with Law, BSc Marketing and Management

Postgraduate courses: Accounting and Finance MSc, Accounting and Management MSc, Business Analytics MSc, Creative Industries and Arts Organisation MA, Development and International Business MSc, Entrepreneurship and Innovation MSc, Heritage Management MA, Innovation and Enterprise MRes, International Business and Politics MRes/MSc, International Business MRes/MSc, International Financial Management MRes/MSc, International Human Resource Management MRes/MSc, Management MSc, Management (Paris) Msc, Marketing MSc, Public Services MRes, Work and Organisation MRes

School of Economics and Finance; www.econ.qmul.ac.uk

Economics BSc(Hons), Economics and Finance BSc(Hons), Economics and International Finance BSc(Hons), Economics, Finance and Management BSc(Hons), Economics and Politics BSc(Hons), Economics, Statistics and Mathematics BSc(Hons), Finance BSc(Hons)

Postgraduate courses: Accounting and Finance MSc, Banking and Finance MSc, Behavioural Finance MSc, Business Finance MSc, Corporate Finance MSc, Economics MSc, Finance MSc, Finance and Econometrics MSc, Investment and Finance MSc, Investment Banking MSc, Law and Economics LLM, Law and Finance MSc, Mathematical Finance MSc, Wealth Management MSc

School of English and Drama; www.sed.qmul.ac.uk

BA(Hons) Drama, BA(Hons) Drama and English, BA(Hons) Drama and Film Studies, BA(Hons) English, BA(Hons) English and Drama, BA(Hons) English with Creative Writing, BA(Hons) English and History, BA(Hons) English and Film Studies, BA(Hons) English and French, BA(Hons) English and German, BA(Hons) English and Hispanic Studies, BA(Hons) English and Russian, BA(Hons) English Literature and Linguistics

Postgraduate courses: MA Live Art with Live Art Development Agency, MA Theatre and Performance, MSc Creative Arts and Mental Health, MA English Literature

School of Languages, Linguistics and Film; www.sllf.qmul.ac.uk

Comparative Literature and Film BA, Comparative Literature and Linguistics BA, Comparative Literature BA, English Language BA, English Language and Linguistics BA, English Literature and Linguistics BA, Film Studies and Drama BA, Film Studies and English BA, Film Studies and French BA, Film Studies and German BA, Film Studies and Hispanic Studies BA, Film Studies and Russian BA, Film Studies BA, French and Comparative Literature BA, French and German BA, French and Hispanic Studies BA, French and Linguistics BA, French and Portuguese BA, French and Russian BA, French BA, French with Business Management BA, German and Comparative Literature BA, German and Hispanic Studies BA, German and Linguistics BA, German and Russian BA, German BA, German with Business Management BA, Catalan BA, Hispanic Studies and Comparative Literature BA, Hispanic Studies and Linguistics BA, Portuguese BA, Hispanic Studies and Russian BA, Hispanic Studies BA, Hispanic Studies with Business Management BA, History and Comparative Literature BA, Linguistics BA, Russian and Comparative Literature BA, Russian and Linguistics BA, Russian BA, Russian with Business Management BA, Spanish and Latin American Studies BA

Postgraduate courses: Anglo-German Cultural Relations MA, Applied Linguistics for English Language Teaching MA/PGCert/PGDip, Comparative Literature and Culture MA, Film Studies MA, Linguistics MA, MRes in Linguistics (1 year full time)

School of Geography; www.geog.qmul.ac.uk

Geography BA/BSc, Human Geography BA, Geography with Business Management BSc, Environmental Science BSc, Environmental Science with Business Management BSc

Postgraduate courses: Cities and Cultures MA/MRes, Development and Global Health MA, Development and International Business MSc, Environmental Science by Research MSc, Geography MA/MSc/

MRes, Global Development Futures MA/MRes, Global Health Geographies MA/MRes

School of History; www.history.qmul.ac.uk

BA History, BA Medieval History, BA Modern and Contemporary History, BA Cultural History, BA Intellectual History, BA World History, BA English and History. BA History and Comparative Literature, BA History and Politics

Postgraduate courses: MA History of Political Thought and Intellectual History, MA Urban History and Culture

School of Law; www.law.qmul.ac.uk

LLB Law, LLB Law Senior Status, LLB Global Law, LLB English and European Law, LLB Law and Politics, LLB Law with Business, LLB English and French Law

Postgraduate courses: LLM Art, Business and Law, LLM Banking and Finance Law, LLM Commercial and Corporate Law, LLM Comparative and International Dispute Resolution, LLM Competition Law, LLM/MRes Criminal Justice, LLM Energy and Natural Resources Law, LLM Environmental Law, LLM European Law, LLM Human Rights Law, LLM Immigration Law, LLM Insurance Law, LLM /PGCert Intellectual Property Law, LLM International Business Law, PGDip International Dispute Resolution (Arbitration), LLM/MRes International Economic Law, PGDip International Finance Law, LLM International Shipping Law, PGDip Language and the Law, LLM/PGDip/PGCert Law and Economics, MSc/PGDip/PGCert Law and Finance, LLM/PGDip Laws, LLM Legal Theory, MSc Management of Intellectual Property, LLM Law, LLM Paris, LLM/MRes Public International Law, LLM/MA Regulation and Compliance, LLM Law, LLM/PGDip/PGCert Technology, Media and Telecommunications Law, PGCert Trade Mark Law and Practice, Master of Laws

School of Politics and International Relations; www.politics.qmul.ac.uk

BA(Hons) International Relations, BA(Hons) Politics and International Relations, BA(Hons) Politics with Business Management, BA(Hons) Politics, BSc(Econ)(Hons) Economics and Politics

Postgraduate courses: MSc International Business and Politics, MSc International Public Policy, MA/MRes/PGCert/PGDip International Relations, MRes/MSc Public Policy

Faculty of Medicine and Dentistry; www.smd.qmul.ac.uk

Barts and the London School of Medicine and Dentistry; www.smd.qmul.ac.uk

Undergraduate degrees

MBBS Medicine, BDS Dentistry, BSc Oral Health, BSc Global Health, BSc Pharmacology and Innovative Therapeutics, BSc Neuroscience

Medicine postgraduate degrees

Aesthetic Medicine MSc/PGCert/PGDip, Biomedical Science (Medical Microbiology) MSc, Burn Care MSc/PGCert, Cancer and Clinical Oncology MSc/PGDip, Cancer and Molecular and Cellular Biology MSc/PGDip, Cancer and Molecular Pathology and Genomics MSc/PGDip, Cancer and Therapeutics MSc/PGDip, Clinical Dermatology PgDip, Clinical Drug Development MSc/PGDip, Clinical Endocrinology MSc/PgDip, Clinical Microbiology MSc/PGDip, Creative Arts and Mental Health MSc/ PGDip, Critical Care MSc, Cultural and Global Perspectives in Mental Health Care MSc/PGDip, Education for Clinical Contexts MA, Endocrinology and Diabetes MSc/PgDip, Forensic Medical Sciences MSc, Gastroenterology MSc/PGDip, Genomic Medicine MSc, Global Health, Law and Governance MSc, Global Public Health and Policy MSc, Health Systems and Global Policy MSc, Healthcare Research Methods MSc/PGDip, Inflammation: Cellular and Vascular Aspects MRes, International Primary Healthcare MSc, Mental Health and Law MSc/PGDip, Mental Health: Psychological Therapies MSc/PGDip, Migration, Culture and Global Health MSc, Orthopaedic Trauma Science MSc, Physician Associate Studies MSc, Podiatric Sports Medicine PGCert, Professional Doctorate Intercultural Psychoanalytical Psychotherapy, Reconstructive Microsurgery MSc, Regenerative Medicine MSc, Sports and Exercise Medicine MSc/PGDip (Medics), Sports and Exercise Medicine MSc/PGDip (Physio), Surgical Skills and Sciences MSc, Trauma Sciences (Military and Humanitarian) MScg, Trauma Sciences MSc

Dentistry postgraduate degrees

Advanced Oral Biology MSc, Craniofacial Trauma Reconstruction MSc, Dental Materials MSc, Dental Public Health MSc, Dental Science for Clinical Practice MSc, Dental Technology MSc, Endodontic Practice MSc, Experimental Oral Pathology (Oral Sciences) MSc, Minimally Invasive Dentistry MSc, Oral Biology MSc, Oral Medicine MClinDent, Oral Surgery MClinDent, Orthodontics DClinDent,

Paediatric Dentistry DClinDent, Periodontology DClinDent, Prosthodontics DClinDent

Faculty of Science and Engineering; www.qmul.ac.uk/about/se

School of Biological and Chemical Sciences; www.sbcs.qmul.ac.uk

BSc(Hons) Biochemistry with a Year in Industry/Research, BSc/MSci(Hons) Biochemistry, BSc(Hons) Biology, BSc(Hons) Biomedical Sciences, BSc(Hons) Chemistry with a Year in Industry/Research, BSc/MSci(Hons) Chemistry, BSc(Hons) Genetics, BSc(Hons) Medical Genetics, BSc(Hons) Neuroscience, BSc/MSci(Hons) Pharmaceutical Chemistry, BSc(Hons) Pharmacology and Innovative Therapeutics, BSc(Hons) Psychology, BSc(Hons) Zoology
Postgraduate courses: MSc Aquatic Ecology by Research, MSc Bioinformatics, MRes Biomedical Sciences, MSc Chemical Research, MSc Ecological and Evolutionary Genomics, MSc/PGCert Ecology and Evolutionary Biology, MSc/PGCert Freshwater and Marine Ecology, MSc Plant and Fungal Taxonomy Diversity and Conservation

School of Electronic Engineering and Computer Science; www.eecs.qmul.ac.uk

BEng/MEng Electrical and Electronic Engineering, BEng Electronic Engineering, BSc (Eng) Creative Computing, BSc (Eng) IT Management for Business (ITMB), BSc Computer Science, BSc Computer Science with Accounting, BSc Computer Science with Business Management, BSc Computer Science with Mathematics, BSc Computer Science with Multimedia, BSc Software Engineering for Business, MEng/BEng Computer Systems Engineering, MEng/BEng Electronic Engineering and Telecommunications
Postgraduate courses in the following subjects: Advanced Electronic and Electrical Engineering, Artificial Intelligence, Big Data Science, Computer Science, Computer Science by Research, Computing and Information Systems, Electronic Engineering by Research, Internet of Things (Data), Machine Learning for Visual Data Analytics, Media and Arts Technology by Research, Sound and Music Computing, Telecommunication and Wireless Systems

School of Engineering and Materials Science; www.sems.qmul.ac.uk

MEng/BEng Aerospace Engineering, BSc(Hons)/MSci(Hons) Biomaterials for Biomedical Sciences, BSc/MSci Biomedical Engineering, MEng/BEng Chemical Engineering, MEng/BEng Dental Materials, MEng/BEng Design, Innovation and Creative Engineering, MEng/ BEng Materials and Design, MEng/BEng Materials Science and Engineering, MEng/BEng Mechanical Engineering, MEng/BEng Robotics Engineering, MEng/BEng Sustainable Energy Engineering
Postgraduate courses: MSc Advanced Mechanical Engineering, MSc Advanced Robotics, MSc Aerospace Engineering, MSc Biomaterials, MSc Biomedical Engineering, MSc Biomedical Engineering (conversion programme), MSc Biomedical Engineering with Biomaterials and Tissue Engineering, MSc Biomedical Engineering with Imaging and Instrumentation, MSc Computer Aided Engineering, MSc Dental Materials, MSc/MRes Materials Research, MSc Mechanical Engineering (conversion programme), MSc Polymer Science and Nanotechnology, MSc Regenerative Medicine, MSc Sustainable Energy Engineering (conversion programme), MSc Sustainable Energy Systems

School of Mathematical Sciences; www.maths.qmul.ac.uk

BSc/MSci Mathematics, BSc Pure Mathematics, BSc/MSci Mathematics and Statistics, BSc Mathematics, Statistics and Financial Economics, BSc Mathematics with Management, BSc Mathematics with Management, BSc Mathematics with Actuarial Science, BSc Mathematics with Finance and Accounting, MSci Financial Mathematics
Postgraduate courses: MSc Mathematics, MSc Mathematical Finance, MSc Financial Computing, MSc Business Analytics, MSc Data Analytics

School of Physics and Astronomy; www.ph.qmul.ac.uk

BSc/MSci Physics, BSc/MSci Astrophysics, BSc/MSci Physics with Astrophysics, BSc/MSci Theoretical Physics, BSc/MSci Physics with Particle Physics, BSc Physics with Management
Postgraduate courses: MSc Condensed Matter Physics, MSc Particle Physics, MSc Theoretical Physics, MSc (EuroMasters), PGCert Astronomy and Astrophysics

UNIVERSITY OF LONDON; ROYAL HOLLOWAY
www.rhul.ac.uk

School of Biological Sciences; www.royalholloway.ac.uk/biologicalsciences

Biochemistry BSc, Biology BSc, Biomedical Sciences BSc, Ecology and Conservation BSc, Medical Biochemistry BSc, Molecular Biology BSc, Zoology BSc

Department of Classics; www.royalholloway.ac.uk/classics

Ancient History BA, Ancient and Medieval History BA, Ancient History and Philosophy BA, Ancient History with Philosophy BA, Classical Archaeology and Ancient History BA, Classical Studies BA, Classical Studies and Comparative Literature and Culture BA, Classical Studies and Drama BA, Classical Studies and Philosophy BA, Classical Studies with Philosophy BA, Classics BA, Classics and Philosophy BA, Classics with Philosophy BA, Greek BA, Latin BA

Postgraduate courses: Ancient History MA, Classical Art and Archaeology MA, Classical Reception by Research MRes, Classics MA, Rhetoric MRes

Department of Computer Science; www.royalholloway.ac.uk/computerscience

Computer Science BSc/MSci, Artificial Intelligence BSc/MSci, Information Security BSc/MSci, Software Engineering BSc/MSci, Computer Science and Mathematics BSc, Digital Media Culture & Technology BA/BSc

Postgraduate courses: Artificial Intelligence MSc, Computational Finance MSc, Data Science and Analytics MSc, Distributed and Networked Systems MSc, Machine Learning MSc, The Internet of Things MSc

Department of Drama, Theatre and Dance; www.royalholloway.ac.uk/dramaandtheatre

Drama and Creative Writing BA, Drama and Dance BA, Drama and Music BA, Drama and Philosophy BA, Drama and Theatre Studies BA, Drama with Film BA, Drama and Philosophy BA, Drama with Philosophy BA, English and Drama BA, Modern Languages and Drama BA, English and Drama BA, Modern Languages and Drama BA

Postgraduate courses: Contemporary Performance Practices MA, Playwriting MA, Research in Drama, Theatre and Dance MA, Theatre Directing MA

Department of Earth Sciences; www.royalholloway.ac.uk/earthsciences

Digital Geosciences BSc, Environmental Geology BSc/MSci, Geology BSc, Geoscience MSci, Petroleum Geology BSc

Postgraduate courses: Earth Sciences by Research MSc, Environmental Diagnosis and Management MSc, Petroleum Geoscience MSc, Petroleum Geoscience (By Distance Learning) MSc

Department of Economics; www.royalholloway.ac.uk/economics

Economics BSc (Econ), Economics and Management BSc, Economics and Mathematics BSc, Economics with French BSc (Econ), Economics with German BSc (Econ), Economics with Italian BSc (Econ), Economics with Music BSc (Econ), Economics and Econometrics BSc (Econ), Economics and Management BSc, Economics and Corporate Finance BSc (Econ)/MSci, Economics and Business Economics BSc (Econ), Economics with Political Studies BSc (Econ), Economics with Spanish BSc (Econ), Economics, Politics and International Relations BSc, Finance and Mathematics BSc, Financial and Business Economics BSc (Econ), Politics, Philosophy and Economics BA

Postgraduate courses: Computational Finance MSc, Corporate Finance MSc, Economics MSc, Finance MSc

Department of Electronic Engineering; www.royalholloway.ac.uk/electronicengineering

Electronic Engineering BEng/MEng, Computer Systems Engineering BEng/MEng

Postgraduate course: Engineering Management MSc, Immersive Technology MSc, Project Management MSc, Research Electronic Engineering MSc

Department of English; www.royalholloway.ac.uk/english

American Literature and Creative Writing BA, Comparative Literature and Culture and English BA, English BA, English and American Literature BA, English and Classical Studies BA, English and Creative Writing BA, English and Drama BA, English and Film Studies BA, English and History BA,

English and Latin BA, English and Philosophy BA, English with Philosophy BA

Postgraduate courses: Creative Writing MA, English Literature MA, Medieval Studies MA, Shakespeare MA, Victorian Literature, Art and Culture MA

Department of Geography; www.royalholloway.ac.uk/geography

Geography BA/BSc, Human Geography BA, Physical Geography BSc

Postgraduate courses: Cultural Geography (Research) MA by Research, Geopolitics and Security MSc, Practising Sustainable Development MSc, Quaternary Science MSc, Sustainability and Management MSc

Department of History; www.royalholloway.ac.uk/history

Ancient History BA, Ancient History and Philosophy BA, Ancient History with Philosophy BA, Ancient and Medieval History BA, Classical Archaeology and Ancient History BA, English and History BA, History BA, History and Music BA, History and Philosophy BA, History, Politics and International Relations BA, History of Art and Visual Culture and Comparative Literature and Culture BA, Modern and Contemporary History BA

Postgraduate courses: Crusader Studies MA, History MA, History: Hellenic Studies MA, Holocaust Studies MA, slamic and West Asian Studies MA, Late Antique and Byzantine Studies MA, Medieval Studies MA, Public History MA

School of Law; www.royalholloway.ac.uk/criminologyandsociology

Criminology and Psychology BSc, Criminology and Sociology BSc, Law LLB, Law (Senior Status) LLB, Law with Criminology LLB Law with International Relations LLB, Law with Politics LLB, Law with Sociology LLB

Postgraduate courses: Consumption, Culture and Marketing MA, Forensic Psychology MSc, Policing and Security Studies MSc, Terrorism and Counter-Terrorism Studies MSc

School of Management; www.royalholloway.ac.uk/management

Accounting and Finance BSc, Business and Management BSc, Financial and Business Economics BSc (Econ), Management with Accounting BSc, Management with Corporate Responsibility BSc, Management with Digital Innovation BSc, Management with Entrepreneurship BSc, Management with Human Resources BSc, Management with International

Business BSc, Management with Marketing BSc, Management with Mathematics BSc

Postgraduate courses: Accounting and Financial Management MSc, Business Information Systems MSc, Consumption, Culture and Marketing MA Digital Innovation and Analytics MSc, Entrepreneurship and Innovation MSc, International Accounting MSc, International Human Resource Management MSc, International Management MBA/MSc, International Management (Marketing) MSc, International Supply Chain Management MSc, Managing Digital Innovation MSc, Marketing MA, MBA (Year in Business) MBA

Department of Mathematics; www.royalholloway.ac.uk/mathematics

Mathematical Studies BSc, Mathematics BSc/MSci, Mathematics and Management BSc, Mathematics and Music BA, Mathematics and Physics BSc/MSci, Mathematics with French BSc, Mathematics with German BSc, Mathematics with Italian BSc, Mathematics with Management BSc, Mathematics with Philosophy BSc, Mathematics with Spanish BSc, Mathematics with Statistics BSc

Postgraduate courses: Mathematics for Applications MSc, Mathematics of Cryptography and Communications MSc

Department of Media Arts; www.royalholloway.ac.uk/mediaarts

Digital Media Culture & Technology BA/BSc, Film Studies BA, Film Studies with Philosophy BA, Film, Television and Digital Production BA, Video Games Art and Design BA

Postgraduate courses: Documentary by Practice MA, Immersive Storytelling MA, Immersive Technology MSc, International Television Industries MA, Media Management MA, Producing Film and Television MA, Screenwriting for Television and Film (in Retreat) MA

School of Modern Languages, Literatures and Cultures; www.royalholloway.ac.uk/mllc

Comparative Literature and Culture BA, Comparative Literature and Culture and Drama BA, Comparative Literature and Culture and English BA, Comparative Literature and Culture and Philosophy BA, Comparative Literature and Culture with History of Art and Visual Culture BA, Comparative Literature and Culture with International Film BA, Comparative Literature and Culture with Philosophy BA, European and International Studies (French) BA,

European and International Studies (German) BA, European and International Studies (Italian) BA, European and International Studies (Spanish) BA, History of Art and Visual Culture & Comparative Literature and Culture BA, Liberal Arts BA, Modern Languages BA, Modern Languages and Classical Studies BA, Modern Languages and Comparative Literature and Culture BA, Modern Languages and Drama BA, Modern Languages and English BA, Modern Languages and Greek BA, Modern Languages and History BA, Modern Languages and History of Art and Visual Culture BA, Modern Languages and Latin BA, Modern Languages and Management BA, Modern Languages and Music BA, Modern Languages and Philosophy BA, Modern Languages and Translation Studies BA, Modern Languages with History of Art and Visual Culture BA, Modern Languages with International Film BA, Modern Languages with International Relations BA, Modern Languages with Mathematics BA, Modern Languages with Music BA, Modern Languages with Philosophy BA, Modern Languages with Translation Studies BA, Translation Studies BA, Translation Studies and Comparative Literature and Culture BA, Translation Studies and History of Art and Visual Culture BA, Translation Studies with History of Art and Visual Culture BA, Translation Studies with International Film BA

Department of Music; www.royalholloway.ac.uk/music
Music BMus, Music and English BA, Music and Philosophy BA, Music with French BA, Music with German BA, Music with Italian BA, Music with Philosophy BA, Music with Political Studies BA, Music with Spanish BA
Postgraduate courses: Advanced Musical Studies MMus, Music Performance PG Dip

Department of Philosophy; www.royalholloway.ac.uk/philosophy
Philosophy BA

Postgraduate courses: European Philosophy MA, Modern Philosophy MA, Political Philosophy MA, Philosophy by Research MA

Department of Physics; www.royalholloway.ac.uk/physics
Astrophysics BSc/MSci, Physics BSc/MSci, Physics with Music BSc, Physics with Particle Physics BSc/MSci, Physics with Philosophy BSc, Theoretical Physics BSc/MSci
Postgraduate courses: Physics (Euromasters) MSc, Physics by Research MSc

Department of Politics and International Relations; www.royalholloway.ac.uk/politicsandir
International Relations BA, Politics BA, Politics and International Relations BA, Politics and International Relations and Philosophy BA, Politics with Philosophy BA, Politics, Philosophy and Economics BA
Postgraduate courses: Elections, Campaigns and Democracy MSc, Geopolitics and Security MSc, International Public Policy MSc, International Relations MSc, International Security MSc, Islamic and West Asian Studies MA, Media, Power and Public Affairs MSc, Politics of Development MA

Department of Psychology; www.royalholloway.ac.uk/psychology
Applied Psychology BSc, Psychology BSc/MSci, Psychology, Clinical and Cognitive Neuroscience BSc, Psychology, Clinical Psychology and Mental Health BSc, Psychology, Development and Developmental Disorders BSc
Postgraduate courses: Applied Social Psychology MSc, Clinical Psychology MSc, Forensic Psychology MSc, Cognitive Behavioural Therapy MSc/PGDip/PGCert

Department of Social Work; www.royalholloway.ac.uk/socialwork
Postgraduate courses: Advanced Practice MSc, Social Work MSc, Social Work (Step up to Social Work) PG Dip

UNIVERSITY OF LONDON; ROYAL VETERINARY COLLEGE
www.rvc.ac.uk

BSc Biological Sciences, BSc Biological Sciences (Animal Behaviour, Welfare and Ethics), BSc Biological Sciences or BSc Bioveterinary Sciences with a Certificate in Work-Based Learning and Research, BSc Bioveterinary Sciences, BSc Veterinary Nursing, BVetMed Bachelor of Veterinary Medicine, FdSc Veterinary Nursing, Graduate Diploma in Equine Locomotor Research, Graduate Diploma Veterinary

Nursing, Intercalated BSc Bioveterinary Science, Intercalated BSc Comparative Pathology, MSci Applied Biological Research, MSci Applied Bioveterinary Research, MSci Biological Sciences, MSci Bioveterinary Sciences, MSci Wild Animal Biology Postgraduate courses: GradDip in Equine Locomotor Research, GradDip in Veterinary Nursing, MSc Wild

Animal Biology, MSc Wild Animal Health, MSc/Cert Intensive Livestock Health and Production, MSc/Dip/Cert Livestock Health and Production, MSc/Dip/Cert Veterinary Education, MSc/Dip/Cert Veterinary Epidemiology and Public Health, MSc/PGDip One Health (Infectious Diseases), MSc/PGDip Veterinary Epidemiology, PGCert in Veterinary Clinical Studies

UNIVERSITY OF LONDON; SCHOOL OF ORIENTAL AND AFRICAN STUDIES
www.soas.ac.uk

Department of Anthropology and Sociology; www.soas.ac.uk/anthropology
BA Social Anthropology, various joint options
Postgraduate courses: MA Anthropological Research Methods, MA Anthropological Research Methods and Intensive Language, MA Anthropological Research Methods and Nepali, MA Anthropology of Food, MA Anthropology of Media, MA Anthropology of Media with Intensive Language, MA Anthropology of Travel and Tourism, MA Medical Anthropology, MA Medical Anthropology and Intensive Language, MA Migration and Diaspora Studies and Intensive Language, MA Museums, Heritage and Material Culture Studies, MA Social Anthropology, MA Social Anthropology Programme with Intensive Language, MA Social Anthropology of Development, MA in Migration and Diaspora Studies
Postgraduate: Research degrees – Anthropology and Sociology, MA Anthropology of Food, MA Anthropology of Food and Intensive Language, MA Medical Anthropology, MA Medical Anthropology and Intensive Language, MA Migration and Diaspora Studies, MA Migration and Diaspora Studies and Intensive Language, MA Museums, Heritage and Material Culture Studies, MA Social Anthropology, MA Social Anthropology Programme with Intensive Language, MA Social Anthropology of Development, MA Social Anthropology of Development and Intensive Language, MRes Social Anthropology, MRes Social Anthropology and Intensive Language

Centre for English Studies; www.soas.ac.uk/english-studies
BA English, BA Creative Arts various joint options

Department of History of Art and Archaeology; www.soas.ac.uk/art
BA Creative Arts, BA History of Art, BA History of Art (Asia, Africa and Europe), BA History of Art and Archaeology, various joint options
Postgraduate courses: MA Arts of Asia and Africa, MA Contemporary Art and Art Theory of Asia and Africa, MA Critical Media and Cultural Studies, MA Global Creative and Cultural Industries, MA History of Art and Archaeology of East Asia, MA History of Art and Archaeology of East Asia and Intensive Language, MA History of Art and Architecture of the Islamic Middle East, MA History of Art and Architecture of the Islamic Middle East and Intensive Language, MA History of Art and/or Archaeology, MA Museums, Heritage and Material Culture Studies, MA Religious Arts of Asia, PGDip/PGCert Asian Art

Department of Music; www.soas.ac.uk/music
BA Creative Arts, BA Music, BA in Global Popular Music, various joint options
Postgraduate courses: MA Global Creative and Cultural Industries, MA Music in Development, MMus Ethnomusicology, MMus Performance, MPhil/PhD in Music

Department of Development Studies; www.soas.ac.uk/development
BA Development Studies, various joint options
Postgraduate courses: MSc Development Studies, MSc Development Studies (Central Asia Pathway), MSc Development Studies (Contemporary India Pathway), MSc Development Studies (Palestine Pathway), MSc Environment, Politics and Development, MSc Globalisation and Development, MSc Humanitarianism, Aid & Conflict, MSc Labour, Activism and Development, MSc Migration Mobility and Development, MSc Research for International Development,

MSc Violence, Conflict & Development, MSc Violence, Conflict & Development (Palestine Pathway), MPhil/PhD in Development Studies, MPhil/PhD in International Development

Department of East Asian Languages and Cultures; www.soas.ac.uk/east-asia

BA Chinese (Modern and Classical), BA Chinese Studies, BA Japanese, BA Japanese Studies, BA Korean, BA Korean Studies, various joint options
Postgraduate courses: MA and Intensive Language (Japanese), MA and Intensive Language (Korean), MA Advanced Chinese Studies, MA Chinese Studies, MA Chinese Studies (Literature Pathway), MA Japanese Studies, MA Japanese Studies (Dual Degree Programme), MA Japanese Studies (Literature Pathway) (not running 2019/20), MA Japanese Studies and Intensive Language, MA Korean Studies, MA Korean Studies (Literature Pathway), MA Korean Studies and Intensive Language, MA Sinology, MA Taiwan Studies, Research Degrees (MPhil/PhD) in Chinese and Inner Asian Studies, Research Degrees (MPhil/PhD) in Japanese and Korean Studies

Department of Economics; www.soas.ac.uk/economics

BSc Development Economics, BSc Economics, various joint options
Postgraduate courses: MSc Development Economics, MSc Economics, MSc Economics and Environment, MSc Global Economic Governance and Policy, MSc International Finance and Development, MSc Political Economy of Development, MSc Research for International Development, MPhil/PhD in Development Economics, MPhil/PhD in Economics, MPhil/PhD in International Development, PGDip in Economics

School of Finance and Management; www.soas.ac.uk/finance-andmanagement

BSc Accounting and Finance, BSc International Management (China), BSc International Management (Japan and Korea), BSc International Management (Japan), BSc International Management (Korea), BSc International Management (Middle East and North Africa), BSc Management, BA International Management and South East Asian Studies
Postgraduate courses: MSc Finance and Financial Law, MSc International Management (China), MSc International Management (Japan), MSc International Management (Middle East and North Africa), MSc Public Financial Management, MSc Public Policy and Management, MSc in Finance, MSc Finance (Banking), MSc Finance (Economic Policy), MSc Finance (Financial Sector Management), MSc Finance (Quantitative Finance), MSc Finance and Financial Law, MSc International Business Administration, MSc Public Financial Management, MSc in Public Policy and Management, Research Degrees in Finance and Management

Department of History; www.soas.ac.uk/history

BA Ancient Near Eastern Studies, BA Global Liberal Arts, BA History, various joint options
Postgraduate courses: MA Ancient Near Eastern Languages, MA History, MA History and Intensive Language

Department of History, Religions and Philosophies; www.soas.ac.uk/religions-andphilosophies

BA Ancient Near Eastern Studies, BA Global Liberal Arts, BA History, BA Religion, Culture and Society, BA World Philosophies, various joint options
Postgraduate courses: MA Ancient Near Eastern Languages, MA Buddhist Studies, MA History, MA History and Intensive Language, MA Islamic Intellectual History, MA Islamic Intellectual History and Intensive Language, MA Religion in Global Politics, MA Religions of Asia and Africa, MA Religions of Asia and Africa and Intensive Language, MA Traditions of Yoga and Meditation, MA Muslim Minorities in a Global Context, Research Degrees: History, Research Degrees: Religions and Philosophies

Centre for Development, Environment and Policy; www.soas.ac.uk/cedep

Postgraduate courses: PGCert/PGDip/MSc Climate Change and Development, PGCert/PGDip/MSc Sustainable Development, MPhil/PhD in Development, Environment & Policy

Centre for Gender Studies; www.soas.ac.uk/genderstudies

Postgraduate courses: MA Gender Studies, MA Gender Studies and Law, MA Gender and Sexuality, MA Gender and Sexuality with special reference to the Middle East, MA in Gender Studies with special reference to the Middle East, MPhil/PhD in Gender Studies

Centre for Global Media and Communications; www.soas.ac.uk/ globalmedia-and-communications

Postgraduate courses: MA Global Digital Cultures, MA International Journalisms, MA Media in Development, MA in Global Media and Postnational Communication, Research Degrees: Media Studies

Centre for International Studies and Diplomacy; www.soas.ac.uk/cisd

Postgraduate courses: MA/PGDip International Studies and Diplomacy, MSc Global Energy and Climate Policy, MA Global Diplomacy (Online), MA Global Diplomacy: MENA (Online), MA Global Diplomacy: South Asia (Online), MA Global Security and Strategy (Online), MSc Global Corporations and Policy (Online), MSc Global Energy and Climate Policy (Online), MSc Global Public Policy (Online), PhD/MPhil in Global Studies

School of Languages, Cultures and Linguistics; www.soas.ac.uk/languages-cultures-linguistics

BA African Studies, BA Arabic, BA Arabic and (a language), BA Arabic and Islamic Studies, BA Middle Eastern Studies, BA South Asian Studies, BA South Asian Studies (Sanskrit Pathway), BA South East Asian Studies, various joint options
Postgraduate courses: MA and Intensive Language (Arabic), MA and Intensive Language (South East Asian Language), MA African Studies, MA African Studies (Literature Pathway), MA African Studies and Intensive Swahili, MA Comparative Literature (Africa/Asia), MA Iranian Studies, MA Iranian Studies and Intensive Persian, MA Islamic Studies, MA Israeli Studies, MA Language Documentation and Description, MA Linguistics, MA Linguistics and Intensive Language, MA Near and Middle Eastern Studies, MA Near and Middle Eastern Studies and Intensive Languages, MA Pacific Asian Studies, MA Palestine Studies, MA Palestine Studies and Intensive

Language, MA Postcolonial Studies, MA South Asian Area Studies, MA South Asian Studies and Intensive Language, MA South East Asian Studies, MA South East Asian Studies & Intensive Language, MA Translation, MA Turkish Studies, MA Turkish Studies and Intensive Language, MA in Cultural Studies, MA and Intensive Language (Swahili), Research Degrees (MPhil/PhD) in African Studies, Research Degrees (MPhil/PhD) in Cultural, Literary and Postcolonial Studies, Research Degrees (MPhil/PhD) in Linguistics, Research Degrees (MPhil/PhD) in Near and Middle Eastern Studies, Research Degrees (MPhil/PhD) in South Asian Studies, Research Degrees (MPhil/PhD) in South East Asian Studies, Research Degrees (MPhil/PhD) in Translation Studies

School of Law; www.soas.ac.uk/law

LLB Single Honours, Senior Status LLB, various joint options
Postgraduate courses: LLM (Master of Laws), LLM in Environmental Law and Sustainable Development, LLM in Human Rights, Conflict and Justice, LLM in International Commercial and Economic Law, LLM in International Law, LLM in Islamic Law, LLM in Law and Gender, LLM in Law, Development and Globalisation, MA Legal Studies (General Programme), MA in Environmental Law and Sustainable Development, MA Human Rights Law, MA in International Law, MA in Islamic Law, MRes Law

Department of Politics and International Studies; www.soas.ac.uk/politics

BA International Relations, BA Politics, BA Politics and International Relations, various joint options
Postgraduate courses: MSc African Politics, MSc Asian Politics, MSc Comparative Political Thought, MSc International Politics, MSc Middle East Politics, MSc Politics of China, MSc Politics of Conflict, Rights & Justice, MSc State, Society and Development, PhD Politics and International Studies

UNIVERSITY OF LONDON; THE SCHOOL OF PHARMACY
www.pharmacy.ac.uk

Master of Pharmacy (MPharm)
Postgraduate courses: MRes in Drug Sciences; MSc in Pharmaceutics, MSc Drug Discovery and Development; MSc Drug Discovery and Pharma Management; MSc in Medicinal Natural Products and

Phytochemistry; MSc in Pharmaceutical Formulation and Entrepreneurship; MSc Experimental Pharmacology and Therapeutics (jointly with the UCL Division of Biosciences) and an MSc Clinical Pharmacy, International Practice and Policy

UNIVERSITY OF LONDON; UNIVERSITY COLLEGE LONDON (UCL)
www.ucl.ac.uk

Anthropology

BSc Anthropology, Medical Anthropology IBSc
Postgraduate courses: MRes Anthropology, MSc Anthropology, Environment and Development, MSc Biosocial Medical Anthropology, MA Creative and Collaborative Enterprise, MSc Digital Anthropology, MA Ethnographic and Documentary Film (Practical), MSc Human Evolution and Behaviour, MA Material and Visual Culture, MSc Medical Anthropology, MA Public Diplomacy and Cultural Anthropology, MSc Social and Cultural Anthropology

Applied Medical Sciences

BSc/MSci Applied Medical Sciences

Archaeology

MA in Archaeology, MA in Archaeology and Heritage of Asia, MA Archaeology and Heritage of Egypt and the Middle East, MA in Artefact Studies, MA in Cultural Heritage Studies, MA in Managing Archaeological Sites, MA in Mediterranean Archaeology, MA in Museum Studies, MA in Principles of Conservation, MA in Public Archaeology, MA in Research Methods for Archaeology, MSc in Archaeological Science: Technology and Materials, MSc in Bioarchaeology and Forensic Anthropology, MSc in Computational Archaeology: GIS, Data Science and Complexity, MSc in Conservation for Archaeology and Museums (2 years), MSc in Environmental Archaeology, MSc in Palaeoanthropology and Palaeolithic Archaeology (joint degree with UCL Anthropology)

Architecture

BSc/MSci Architecture, MEng Engineering and Architectural Design, BSc Architectural and Interdisciplinary Studies
Postgraduate courses: PGCert Advanced Architectural Research, MRes Architectural Computation, MSc Architectural Computation, MArch Architectural Design, MA Architectural History, MArch (ARB/RIBA Part 2) Architecture, MRes Architecture and Digital Theory, MA Architecture and Historic Urban Environments, Bio-Integrated Design MArch/MSc, MArch Design for Manufacture, MArch Design for Performance and Interaction, Landscape Architecture MA/MLA, MA Situated Practice, MRes Space Syntax: Architecture and Cities, MSc Space Syntax: Architecture and Cities, MArch Urban Design

Arts and Sciences

BASc Arts and Sciences

Biochemical Engineering and Bioprocessing

BSc Bioprocessing of New Medicines (Science and Engineering)

Biochemistry and Biotechnology

BSc/MSci Biochemistry, BSc Biotechnology
Postgraduate courses: MSc Biochemical Engineering, MRes Synthetic Biology

Biological/Biomedical Sciences

BSc/MSci Biological Sciences, BSc Biomedical Sciences
Postgraduate courses: MRes Biodiversity, Evolution and Conservation, MSc Biomedical Sciences, MRes Biosciences, MSc Experimental Pharmacology and Therapeutics, MSc Genetics of Human Disease, MSc Neuroscience

Cancer

BSc Cancer Biomedicine
Postgraduate course: MSc/PGDip/PGCert Cancer

Chemical Engineering

BEng/MEng Engineering (Chemical)
Postgraduate courses: MSc Chemical Process Engineering, MSc Global Management of Natural Resources, MSc Sustainable Energy Systems

Chemistry

BSc Chemistry, MSci Chemistry, BSc Chemical Physics, MSci Chemical Physics, BSc Medicinal Chemistry, MSci Medicinal Chemistry, BSc Chemistry with Mathematics, MSci Chemistry with Mathematics, BSc Chemistry with a European Language, MSci Chemistry with a European Language, BSc Chemistry with Management Studies, MSci Chemistry with Management Studies, MSci Chemistry (International Programme)
Postgraduate courses: MSc Applied Analytical Chemistry, MSc Chemical Research, MSc Materials for Energy and Environment, MSc Molecular Modelling, MRes Molecular Modelling and Materials Science, MRes Organic Chemistry: Drug Discovery

Child Health

Postgraduate courses: MSc/PGDip/PGCert Cell and Gene Therapy, MSc/PGDip/PGCert Child and Adolescent Mental Health, MSc/PGDip/PGCert Infancy and Early Childhood Development, MSc/PGDip/PGCert Paediatrics and Child Health, MSc Paediatrics and Child Health with Clinical Practice, MSc/PGDip Paediatric Neuropsychology, MSc/PGDip/PGCert Physiotherapy, MSc Personalised Medicine and Novel Therapies

Civil and Environmental Engineering

BEng/MEng Engineering (Civil)

Postgraduate courses: Civil Engineering MSc, Civil Engineering Graduate Diploma, Earthquake Engineering with Disaster Management MSc, Engineering for International Development MSc, Environmental Systems Engineering MSc, Geospatial Sciences MSc routes, Spatio-Temporal Analytics and Big Data Mining MSc, Transport MSc routes, Urban Railways MSc, Urban Sustainability and Resilience MRes, Banking and Digital Finance MSc, Urban Sustainability and Resilience MRes EngD, Civil, Environmental and Geomatic Engineering MPhil/PhD

Classical World

BA Ancient World, BA Classics, BA Greek with Latin, BA Latin with Greek, various joint degree options

Postgraduate courses: MA Classics, MA Reception of the Classical World

Computer Science

BSc/MEng Computer Science, MEng Mathematical Computation

Postgraduate courses: MSc Computational Finance, MSc Computational Statistics and Machine Learning, MRes Computational Statistics and Machine Learning, MSc Computer Graphics, Vision and Imaging, MSc Computer Science, MSc Data Science, International Data Science and Machine Learning MSc, Disability, Design and Innovation MSc, MSc Financial Risk Management, MSc Information Security, MSc Machine Learning, MSc Robotics and Computation, MSc Software Systems Engineering, MRes Virtual Reality, Robotics MRes, Computer Science MPhil/PhD, CDT Cybersecurity

Dentistry

Postgraduate courses: PGCert Advanced Aesthetic Dentistry, MSc Conservative Dentistry, MSc Dental Hygiene, PGCert Dental Sedation and Pain Management, PGDip Endodontic Practice, MSc Endodontics, MClinDent Endodontology, MClinDent Endodontology (Advanced Training), PGDip Implant Dentistry, MSc Oral Medicine, MClinDent Oral Surgery, MClinDent Oral Surgery (Advanced Training), MSc Oral and Maxillofacial Surgery, MClinDent Orthodontics, MClin-Dent Orthodontics (Advanced Training), MSc/DDent Paediatric Dentistry, MSc/MClinDent Periodontology, MClinDent Prosthodontics, MClinDent Prosthodontics (Advanced Training), MSc Restorative Dental Practice, MSc Special Care Dentistry, PGCert Special Care Dentistry, MSc Sports Dentistry

Development Planning

Postgraduate courses: MSc Building and Urban Design in Development, MSc Development Administration and Planning, MSc Environment and Sustainable Development, MSc Social Development Practice, MSc Urban Development Planning, MSc Urban Economic Development

Ear Institute

Postgraduate courses: MSc Advanced Audiology, MSc Audiological Science, MSc Audiological Science with Clinical Practice, MSc Otology and Audiology, MRes in Brain Sciences (SenSyT pathway)

Earth Sciences

BSc/MSci Earth Sciences, MSci Earth Sciences (International Programme), BSc Environmental Geoscience, BSc/MSci Geology, BSc/MSci Geophysics, BSc Natural Science

Postgraduate courses: MSc Geophysical Hazards, MSc Geoscience, PGCert Natural Hazards, PGCert Natural Hazards for Insurers, MSc Global Management of Natural Resources, MRes/PGCert Risk and Disaster Reduction, Msc Planetary Science

Economics

BSc Economics, various joint options

Postgraduate courses: MSc Economics, MSc Finance

Education

BA Education Studies, BSc Psychology with Education, BSc Social Sciences, BSc Social Sciences with Quantitative Methods, BSc Sociology

Postgraduate courses: Grad Dip Advanced Educational Practice, Applied Educational Leadership, MA Art and Design in Education, Child Development MSc, MA Comparative Education, MA Development Education and Global Learning, MSc Developmental and Educational Psychology, MA Digital Media: Critical Studies/Education/Production, Culture and Education, MA Early Years Education, MA Education, MA Education and International Development, MA Education and Technology, MA Education, Gender and International Development, MA Education, Health Promotion and International Development, Educational Planning, Economics and International Development MA, Engineering and Education MSc, MA English Education, Habilitation and Disabilities of Sight (Children and Young People) Grad Dip, MA Mathematics Education, MA Museums and Galleries in Education, MA Music Education, National Award for Special Educational Needs Co-ordination PG Cert, MA Philosophy of Education, Policy Studies in Education MA, MA Primary Education 4-12, Psychology of Education MSc, Reading Recovery and Literacy Leadership MA, Social Justice and Education MA, Social Policy and Social Research (with Systematic Reviews) MSc, Social Policy and Social Research MSc, Social Research

Methods MSc, Social Science Research Methods PG Dip, Sociology of Childhood and Children's Rights MA, Sociology of Education MA, Special and Inclusive Education MA, Specific Learning Difficulties (Dyslexia) MA, Speech, Language and Communication Needs in Schools: Advanced Practice MSc, Teaching English to Speakers of Other Languages (TESOL) In-Service, Teaching English to Speakers of Other Languages (TESOL) Pre-Service MA, Educational Neuroscience MA/MSc

Electronic and Electrical Engineering

BEng/MEng Engineering (Electronic and Electrical) Postgraduate courses: Integrated Machine Learning Systems MSc, Internet Engineering MSc, Nanotechnology MSc/PG Dip, Telecommunications MSc, Telecommunications with Business MSc, Wireless and Optical Communications MSc, Telecommunications MRes, Telecommunications MSc (IGDP)

Energy

Postgraduate courses: Energy Systems and Data Analytics MSc, MSc Economics and Policy of Energy and the Environment, MRes Energy Demand Studies, MPhil/PhD in Energy

English

BA English, BA Modern Language and English, BA Latin and English, BA Greek and English Postgraduate courses: MA in English: Issues in Modern Culture, MA in English Linguistics, MA Medieval and Renaissance Studies, MA Early Modern Studies, MPhil/PhD in English Language and Literature

European Languages, Culture and Society

BA Comparative Literature, BA Language with Film Studies, BA Dutch, BA French, BA French and an Asian or African Language, BA German, BA German and History, BA Icelandic, BA Italian, BA Italian Studies and History of Art: UCL – Venice Double Degree, BA Italian Studies: UCL – Venice Double Degree, BA Language and Culture, BA Modern Language Plus, BA Modern Languages, BA Scandinavian Studies, BA Scandinavian Studies and History, BA Spanish and Latin American Studies, BA Viking and Old Norse Studies, various combined degrees
Postgraduate courses: MA Comparative Literature MA, MA European Culture and Thought: Culture, MA Gender, Society and Representation, MA Health Humanities, MA Language, Culture and History, MA/MSc Translation Studies

European Social and Political Studies

BA European Social and Political Studies, International Social and Political Studies BA

Fine Art

BA/BFA Fine Art
Postgraduate courses: MA/MFA Fine Art, MPhil/PhD Fine Art

Geography

BA/BSc Geography, BSc Geography and Economics, BA Human Geography with Quantitative Methods Postgraduate courses: MSc Aquatic Conservation, Ecology and Restoration, MSc Climate Change, MSc Conservation, MSc Environment, Politics and Society, MSc Environmental Mapping, MSc Environmental Modelling, MSc Geospatial Analysis, MSc Global Migration, MSc Remote Sensing, and Environmental Mapping

Hebrew and Jewish Studies

BA Ancient Languages, BA Hebrew and Jewish Studies, BA History (Central and East European) and Jewish Studies, Modern Languages Plus Postgraduate course: MA Jewish Studies

History

BA Ancient History, BA History, BA History with a European Language
Postgraduate courses: MA Ancient History, MA Chinese Health and Humanity, MA European History, MA History, MA Late Antique and Byzantine Studies, MA Medieval and Renaissance Studies, MA Transnational Studies

History of Art

BA History of Art, BA History of Art with Material Studies
Postgraduate course: MA/MPhil/PhD History of Art

History, Politics and Economics

BA History, Politics and Economics

Human Sciences

BSc Human Sciences, MSci Human Sciences and Evolution

Infection and Immunity

BSc Infection and Immunity
Postgraduate course: MSc Infection and Immunity

Information Studies and Information Management for Business

BSc/MSci Information Management for Business Postgraduate courses: MA Archives and Records, Management, MA/MSc Digital Humanities, MSc Information Science, MRes Information Studies, MA Library and Information Studies, MA Publishing

Law

LLB Bachelor of Law (UCL) and Bachelor of Law (HKU), LLB English and German Law Dual Degree, LLB Law, LLB Law with French Law, LLB Law with German Law, LLB Law with Hispanic Law, Law with Another Legal System (Australia, Singapore, Hong

Kong), LLB Bachelor of Laws (UCL) and LLB Bachelor of Laws (HKU), LLB Dual Degree English and German Law with Universitt zu Kln, Dual LLB/ Juris Doctor (JD) with Columbia University, New York

Postgraduate course: LLM Law

Linguistics

BA Linguistics BA Linguistics International Programme, BSc Experimental Linguistics

Postgraduate courses: MA Linguistics (conversion programme), MA Linguistics with a specialisation in Phonology, MA Linguistics with a specialisation in Syntax, MSc Language Sciences with specialisation in Language Development, MSc Language Sciences with specialisation in Linguistics with Neuroscience, MSc Language Sciences with specialisation in Neuroscience and Communication, MSc Language Sciences with specialisation in Sign Language and Deaf Studies, MSc Language Sciences with specialisation in Speech and Hearing Sciences

Management

BSc/MSci Management Sciences

Postgraduate courses: MBA Business Administration, MSc Business Analytics (with specialisation in Management Science), MSc Entrepreneurship, MSc Finance, MSc Management

Mathematics

BSc/MSci Mathematics

Postgraduate courses: MSc Financial Mathematics, MSc Mathematical Modelling, MPhil/PhD in Mathematics

Mechanical Engineering

BEng/MEng Engineering (Mechanical with Business Finance), BEng/MEng Engineering (Mechanical)

Postgraduate courses: MSc Biomaterials and Tissue Engineering, MSc Engineering with Finance, MSc Engineering with Innovation and Entrepreneurship, MSc Marine Engineering, MSc Mechanical Engineering, MSc Naval Architecture, MSc Power Systems Engineering

Medical Physics and Biomedical Engineering

BEng/MEng Engineering (Biomedical), MSci Medical, Physics, BSc Physics with Medical Physics

Postgraduate courses: MRes Medical Physics and Biomedical Engineering, MSc/PGDip Physics and Engineering in Medicine by Distance Learning, PG Dip/MSc Physics and Engineering in Medicine, MRes Medical Imaging

Medicine

Nutrition and Medical Sciences BSc, iBSc in Clinical Sciences, BSc/MSci Applied Medical Sciences

Postgraduate courses: MSc Advanced Biomedical Imaging, MSc Clinical and Public Health Nutrition, MSc Drug Design, MRes Drug Design, MSc Eating Disorders and Clinical Nutrition, MSc/MRes Human Tissue Repair, MSc Precision Medicine

Centre for Multidisciplinary and Intercultural Inquiry

Single or combined honours degrees with BA Language and Culture, BA Comparative Literature, Dutch, French, German, Italian, Scandinavian Studies, Spanish, Portuguese and Latin American Studies, SELCS Language with Film Studies BA

Postgraduate courses: MA Comparative Literature, MA Early Modern Studies, MA European Culture and Thought: Culture, MA European Culture and Thought: Thought, MA European Studies: European Society, MA European Studies: Modern European Studies, MA Film Studies, MA Gender, Society and Representation, MA Health Humanities, Language, Culture & History, MSc, Specialised Translation (Audiovisual), MSc Specialised Translation (Scientific, Technical and Medical), MSc Specialised Translation (with Interpreting), MA Translation: Research, MA Translation: Translation Studies, MA Translation: Translation and Culture

Natural Sciences

BSc/MSci Natural Sciences

Neuroscience

BSc/MSci Neuroscience

Postgraduate courses: MSc Advanced Neuroimaging, MSc in Applied Paediatric Neuropsychology, MSc in Audiological Science, MSc in Advanced Audiology, MSc Brain and Mind Sciences, MSc in Cell and Gene Therapy, MSc in Child and Adolescent Mental Health, MSc Clinical Neurology, MSc Clinical Neuroscience, MSc in Clinical Paediatric Neuropsychology, MSc in Cognitive and Decision Sciences, MSc/MRes in Cognitive Neuroscience, MSc Dementia: (Neuroscience), MRes in Developmental Neuroscience and Psychopathology, MRes Neuromuscular Disease, MSc Neuromuscular Disease, MSc in Genetics of Human Disease (includes module in Neurogenetics), MSc in Language Sciences, MA in Linguistics, MA Linguistics with a specialisation in Phonology, MA Linguistics with a specialisation in Pragmatics, MA Linguistics with a specialisation in Semantics, MA Linguistics with a specialisation in Syntax, MSc in Medical Image Computing, MSci in Medical Physics, MSc Neurology for Clinical Trainees, MSc/MRes in Neuromuscular Disease, MSc in Neuroscience, MSci in Neuroscience (4 year programme for BSc Neuroscience students), MSc in Neuroscience, Language and Communication, MSc

Otology and Audiology, MSc in Physics and Engineering for Medicine, MSc in Psychoanalytic Developmental Psychology, MSc Research Methods in Psychology, MRes Speech, Language and Cognition, MSc in Social Cognition: Research and Applications, MSc/MRes/Diploma/PG Certificate in Stroke Medicine, MSc in Theoretical Psychoanalytical Studies

Nutrition

Ophthalmology

Postgraduate courses: Ophthalmology, MSc Bioscience Entrepreneurship, MSc Investigative Ophthalmology and Vision Science, MSc Advanced Clinical Optometry and Ophthalmology, MSc Clinical Ophthalmic Practice, MSc Sensory Systems, Technologies and Therapies, MRes Advanced Clinical Practice in Ophthalmology, MSc Degree Apprenticeship

Pharmacology

BSc/MSci Pharmacology

Pharmacy

MPharm Pharmacy

Postgraduate courses: MSc Clinical Pharmacy, International Practice and Policy, MSc Drug Discovery and Development, MSc Drug Discovery and Pharma Management, MSc in Experimental Pharmacology and Therapeutics MSc Medicinal Natural Products and Phytochemistry, MSc Pharmaceutical Formulation and Entrepreneurship, MSc Pharmaceutics

Philosophy

BA Philosophy, BA Philosophy and Economics, BA Philosophy and Greek, BA Philosophy and History of Art

Postgraduate course: MA Philosophy

Physics and Astrophysics

BSc/MSci Astrophysics, BSc/MSci Physics, BSc/MSci Theoretical Physics

Postgraduate courses: MSc Astrophysics, MSc Biological Physics, MSc Nanotechnology, MSc Physics, MSc Planetary Science, MSc Quantum Technologies, MSc Scientific Computing

Political Science and Politics

BSc Philosophy, Politics and Economics, BSc Politics and International Relations

Postgraduate courses: Executive Master of Public Administration (EMPA), MSc Democracy and Comparative Politics, MSc European Politics and Policy, MSc Global Governance and Ethics, MA Human Rights, MSc International Public Policy, MA Legal and Political Theory, MPA Public Administration and Management, MSc Public Policy, MSc Security Studies

Population Health

BSc Population Health

Postgraduate courses: Cardiovascular Science MSc, Advanced Physiotherapy: Cardiorespiratory MSc, Advanced Physiotherapy: Neurophysiotherapy MSc, Applied Paediatric Neuropsychology MSc, Cell and Gene Therapy MSc, Child Health MRes, Child and Adolescent Mental Health MSc, Clinical Paediatric Neuropsychology MSc, Infancy and Early Childhood Development MSc, Paediatrics and Child Health with Clinical Practice MSc, Paediatrics and Child Health: Advanced Paediatrics MSc, Paediatrics and Child Health: Community Child Health MSc, Paediatrics and Child Health: Global Child Health MSc, Paediatrics and Child Health: Intensive Care MSc, Paediatrics and Child Health: Molecular and Genomic Paediatrics MSc, Personalised Medicine and Novel Therapies MSc, Physiotherapy Studies: Cardiorespiratory MSc, Physiotherapy Studies: Neurophysiotherapy MSc, Physiotherapy Studies: Paediatrics MSc, Clinical Trials MSc, Dental Public Health MSc, Health Psychology MSc, Health and Society: Social Epidemiology MSc, Population Health MSc, Applied Infectious Disease Epidemiology MSc, Global Health and Development MSc, Global Health and Development: tropEd programme MSc, Health Economics and Decision Science MSc, Health Data Science MSc, Health Data Analytics MSc, Health Informatics MSc, Prenatal Genetics and Fetal Medicine MSc, Reproductive Science and Women's Health MSc, Reproductive Science and Women's Health MRes, Women's Health MSc, Cardiovascular Science MPhil/PhD, Lifelong Health PhD, British Heart Foundation Cardiovascular Biomedicine PhD, Child Health MD(Res), Child Health PhD, Clinical Trials and Methodology MPhil/PhD, Epidemiology and Public Health MD(Res), Epidemiology and Public Health MPhil/PhD, Primary Care and Population Health MPhil/PhD, Global Health MPhil/PhD, Global Health and Infection MD(Res), Health Informatics MPhil/PhD, Women's Health MD(Res), Women's Health MPhil/PhD

Project Management for Construction

BSc Project Management for Construction

Postgraduate courses: MSc Construction Economics and Management MSc Digital Innovation in Built Asset Management, MSc Infrastructure Investment and Finance, MSc Project and Enterprise Management, MSc Strategic Management of Projects, MPhil/PhD Construction and Project Management

Psychology and Language Sciences

BA Linguistics, BA Linguistics (International Programme), BSc Experimental Linguistics, BSc Psychology, MSci Psychology Integrated, BSc Psychology for Medics, BSc Psychology and Language Sciences, MSci Psychology and Language Sciences

Postgraduate courses: Brain Sciences MRes, Cognitive Behavioural Therapy for Children and Young People, MSc/PGDip/PGCert Cognitive Behavioural Therapy for people with psychosis, PGDip Developmental Neuroscience and Psychopathology, MRes Developmental Psychology and Clinical Practice, MSc Low Intensity Cognitive Behavioural Interventions, PGCert Psychoanalytic Developmental Psychology, MSc Theoretical Psychoanalytical Studies, MSc Behaviour Change, MSc Cognitive and Decision Sciences, MSc Cognitive Neuroscience, MRes Social Cognition, MSc Speech, Language and Cognition, MRes Cognitive Behavioural Therapy for Children and Young People, MSc/PGDip/PGCert Developmental Neuroscience and Psychopathology, MRes Developmental Psychology and Clinical Practice, MSc Psychoanalytic Developmental Psychology, MSc Applied Research in Human Communication Disorders, PGCert/MRes Language Sciences (Language Development), MSc Language Sciences (Neuroscience, Language and Communication), MSc Language Sciences (Sign Language and Deaf Studies), MSc Language Sciences (Speech Sciences), MSc Linguistics (conversion programme), MA Linguistics with specialisation in Phonology, MA Linguistics with specialisation in Pragmatics, MA (will not run in 2020/21) Linguistics with specialisation in Syntax, MA Speech, Language and Cognition, MRes Applied Research in Human Communication Disorders, PGCert/MRes Speech and Language Sciences, MSc Cognitive Neuroscience, MRes Developmental Neuroscience and Psychopathology, MRes Language Sciences (Neuroscience, Language and Communication), MSc Industrial/Organisational and Business Psychology, MSc Behaviour Change, MSc Human-Computer Interaction, MSc/PGDip/PGCert Psychological Sciences, MSc Clinical Mental Health Sciences, MSc Mental Health Sciences Research

Slavonic and Eastern European Studies

Politics, Sociology and East European Studies BA, Politics, Sociology and East European Studies with a Year Abroad BA, Economics and Business with East European Studies BA, Economics and Business with East European Studies with a Year Abroad BA, History, Politics and Economics BA, Russian and History BA, German and History BA (Joint Honours with the School of European Languages, Culture and Society), History (Central and East European) and Jewish Studies BA, Scandinavian Studies and History BA, Bulgarian and East European Studies BA, Czech (and Slovak) and East European Studies BA, Finnish and East European Studies BA, Hungarian and East European Studies BA, Polish and East European Studies BA, Romanian and East European Studies BA, Russian Studies BA, Russian and History BA, Russian with an East European Language BA, Serbian/Croatian and East European Studies BA, Slovak (with Czech) and East European Studies BA, Ukrainian and East European Studies BA, Modern Languages BA

Postgraduate courses: Political Analysis (Russia and Eastern Europe) MA, Political Sociology (Russia and Eastern Europe) MA, Russian and Post-Soviet Politics MA, Comparative Business Economics MA, Comparative Economics and Policy MA, Central and South-East European Studies MA, Russian Studies MA, Russian and East European Literature and Culture MA, History (SSEES) MA, IMESS (International Masters in Economy, State and Society), East European Studies MRes, Politics and Economics of Eastern Europe MRes, MPhil/PhD, Slavonic and East European Studies MPhil/PhD

Science and Technology Studies

BSc History and Philosophy of Science, Sociology and Politics of Science BSc, Natural Sciences BSc and MSci

Postgraduate courses: MSc/PGDip/PGCert History and Philosophy of Science, MSc/PGDip/PGCert, Science, Technology and Society

Security and Crime Science

BSc Security and Crime Science, BSc Professional Policing

Postgraduate courses: MSc Countering Organised Crime and Terrorism, MSc Crime Science, MSc Crime and Forensic Science, MSc Policing, PGCert Security and Crime Science

Social Sciences

BSc Social Sciences, BSc Social Sciences with Quantitative Methods, BSc Sociology

Postgraduate courses: Social Policy and Social Research (with Systematic Reviews) MSc, Social Policy and Social Research MSc, Social Research Methods MSc, Sociology of Childhood and Children's Rights MA, Social Science MPhil/PhD

Space and Climate Physics

Postgraduate courses: MSc Space Science and Engineering: Space Science, MSc Space Science and Engineering: Space Technology, MSc Systems Engineering Management, MSc Technology Management, MSc in Management of Complex Projects, MSc in Space Risks and Disaster Reduction

Statistical Science

BSc (Econ) Economics and Statistics, MSci Statistical Science (International Programme), BSc Statistics, BSc Statistics and Management for Business, BSc Statistics, Economics and Finance, BSc Statistics, Economics and a Language

Postgraduate courses: MSc Data Science, MSc Statistics, MSc Statistics (Medical Statistics)

Surgery and Interventional Science

Medical Innovation & Enterprise, BSc Sports & Exercise, Medical Sciences BSc, Medical Sciences & Engineering BSc/MSci, Medical Innovation & Enterprise MSci

Postgraduate courses: MS Advanced Minimally-Invasive Surgery, MSc Burns, Plastic and Reconstructive Surgery, MSc Musculoskeletal Science, MSc Nanotechnology and Regenerative Medicine, Orthopaedics MSc, Pain Management MSc, MSc Performing Arts Medicine, MSc Perioperative Medicine, MSc Physical Therapy in Musculoskeletal Healthcare and Rehabilitation, MSc Rehabilitation Engineering and Assistive Technologies, MSc Sports Medicine, Exercise and Health, MSc Surgical and Interventional Sciences

The Americas

BA History and Politics of the Americas

Postgraduate courses: MA Caribbean and Latin American Studies, MSc Globalisation and Latin American Development, MSc International Relations of the Americas, MSc Latin American Politics, MA Latin American Studies, MA United States Studies: History and Politics

Urban Planning, Design and Real Estate

BSc Planning and Real Estate, BSc Urban Planning, Design and Management, BSc Urban Studies

Postgraduate courses: MSc Spatial Planning, MSc International Planning, MSc/Dip Urban Regeneration, MSc/Dip International Real Estate and Planning, MSc/Dip Sustainable Urbanism, MSc/Dip Urban Design and City Planning, MSc Infrastructure Planning Appraisal and Development, MSc Housing and City Planning, MSc Transport and City Planning, MPlan City Planning, MRes Inter-disciplinary Urban Design, MSc Smart Cities and Urban Analytics (RTPI Pathway)

UNIVERSITY OF LOUGHBOROUGH
www.lboro.ac.uk

Department of Aeronautical and Automotive Engineering; www.lboro.ac.uk/departments/aae

BEng/MEng(Hons) Aeronautical Engineering, BEng/MEng(Hons) Automotive Engineering

Postgraduate courses: MSc Automotive Systems Engineering, PGCert Aeronautical and Automotive Engineering Short Courses for Industry, PGCert Automotive Engineering

School of Architecture, Building and Civil Engineering; www.lboro.ac.uk/departments/abce

Architecture BArch(Hons), Architectual Engineering & Design Management BSc(Hons) 2019 entry only, Urban Planning BSc(Hons), Urban Planning MPlan(-Hons), Architectural Engineering BEng(Hons), Architectural Engineering MEng(Hons), Civil Engineering MEng(Hons), Civil Engineering BEng(Hons), Civil Engineering with an International Foundation Year, Commercial Management and Quantity Surveying BSc(Hons), Construction Engineering Management BSc(Hons)

Postgraduate courses: Construction Management MSc Construction Project Management MSc Construction Project Management with Building Information Modelling MSc Low Energy Building Services Engineering MSc Water Management for Development MSc Sustainable Design and Construction MSc

School of the Arts, English and Drama; www.lboro.ac.uk/departments/aed

English BA(Hons), English Literature BA(Hons), English with Digital Humanities BA(Hons), English with Creative Writing BA(Hons), English and Sport Science BA(Hons), English with Business Studies BA(Hons) BA(Hons) Fine art, BA(Hons) Graphic Communication and Illustration, BA(Hons) Publishing and English, BA(Hons) Textiles: Innovation and Design

Postgraduate courses: MA Graphic Design and Visualisation, MA Creative Writing,

School of Business and Economics; www.lboro.ac.uk/departments/sbe

BSc Accounting and Financial Management, BSc Finance and Management, BSc Business Analytics,

BSc International Business, BSc Management, BSc Marketing and Management, BSc Economics, BSc Business Economics and Finance, BSc Economics and Management

Postgraduate courses: MSc Management, MSc International Business, MSc International Management (Joint programme, based in London), MSc Marketing, MSc Finance and Management, MSc Finance, MSc Finance and Investment, MSc Corporate Finance, MSc Economics and Finance, MSc Banking and Finance, MSc Economics and Business Strategy, MSc Economics and International Business, MSc Business Analytics, MSc Information Management and Business Technology, MSc Human Resource Management, MSc Employment Relations and HRM, MSc Work Psychology, MSc Business Psychology

Department of Chemical Engineering; www.lboro.ac.uk/departments/chemical

BEng/MEng Chemical Engineering
Postgraduate courses: MSc Advanced Chemical Engineering with IT and Management

Department of Chemistry; www.lboro.ac.uk/departments/chemistry

BSc/MChem(Hons) Chemistry, BSc/MChem(Hons) Medicinal and Pharmaceutical Chemistry, BSc/MSci(-Hons) Natural Sciences
Postgraduate courses: MSc/PGDip/PGCert Analytical Chemistry, MSc/PGDip/PGCert Analytical and Pharmaceutical Science, MSc/PGDip/PGCert Pharmaceutical Science and Medicinal Chemistry
Department of Computer Science; www.lboro.ac.uk/departments/compsci
BSc/MSci Computer Science, BSc/MSci Computer Science, BSc/MSci Computer Science and Artificial Intelligence, BSc/MSci Computing and Management, BSc/MSci Computer Science and Mathematics, BSc/MSci Information Technology for Management
Postgraduate courses: MSc Advanced Computer Science

Design School; www.lboro.ac.uk/departments/design-school

BA(Hons) Industrial Design & Technology, BSc(Hons) Product Design & Technology, BSc(Hons) User Centred Design
Postgraduate courses: MSc/PGDip/PGCert Ergonomics & Human Factors, MSc/PGDip/PGCert Human Factors in Transport, MSc/PGDip/PGCert Human Factors for Inclusive Design, MSc/PGDip/PGCert Ergonomics in Health & Community Care, MSc/PGDip/PGCert Human Factors & Ergonomics

for Patient Safety, MA User Experience Design, MA Integrated Industrial Design

Department of Geography; www.lboro.ac.uk/departments/geography

BA/BSc(Hons) Geography, BSc(Hons) Geography and Management, BSc(Hons) Geography and Sport Science, BSc(Hons) Geography with Economics
Postgraduate courses: Childhood, Youth and Social Policy MA MSc Environmental Monitoring for Management, MSc International Financial and Political Relations, MSc Globalization and Cities

Department of Materials; www.lboro.ac.uk/departments/materials

BEng/MEng(Hons) Materials Science and Engineering, BEng/MEng(Hons) Automotive Materials, BEng/MEng(Hons) Biomaterials Engineering, BEng/MEng(Hons) Bioengineering
Postgraduate courses: MSc/PGDip/PGCert Materials Science and Technology, MSc/PGDip/PGCert Polymer Science and Technology

Department of Mathematical Sciences; www.lboro.ac.uk/departments/maths

BSc/MMath(Hons) Mathematics, BSc(Hons) Mathematics and Accounting and Financial Management, BSc(Hons) Mathematics with Economics, BSc(Hons) Mathematics and Sport Science, BSc(Hons) Mathematics with Statistics, BSc(Hons) Financial Mathematics
Postgraduate courses: MSc Industrial Mathematical Modelling, MSc Mathematical Finance

Department of Mechanical, Electrical and Manufacturing Engineering; www.lboro.ac.uk/departments/meme

BEng/MEng(Hons) Electronic and Computer Systems Engineering, BEng/MEng(Hons) Electronic and Electrical Engineering, BSc(Hons) Engineering Management, BEng/MEng(Hons) Manufacturing Engineering, BEng/MEng(Hons) Mechanical Engineering, BEng/MEng(Hons) Product Design Engineering, BEng/MEng(Hons) Robotics, Mechatronics and Control Engineering, BSc(Hons) Sports Technology
Postgraduate courses: MSc Advanced Manufacturing Engineering and Management, MSc Electronic and Electrical Engineering, MSc Engineering Design, MSc Mechanical Engineering, MSc Mobile Communications, MSc Renewable Energy Systems Technology (Distance Learning), MSc Renewable Energy Systems Technology, European Masters in Renewable Energy MSc Systems Engineering MSc Telecommunications Engineering

Department of Physics; www.lboro.ac.uk/departments/physics

BSc/MPhys(Hons) Physics, BSc/MPhys(Hons) Engineering Physics, BSc/MPhys(Hons) Physics and Mathematics, BSc/MPhys(Hons) Physics with Theoretical Physics

Postgraduate courses: MSc Advanced Physics, MSc Physics of Materials

Department of Politics, History and International Relations; www.lboro.ac.uk/departments/phir

BA(Hons) History, BA(Hons) History and International Relations, BA(Hons) History and Politics, BA(Hons) International Relations, BA(Hons) Politics, BA(Hons) Politics and International Relations, BA(Hons) Politics with Economics, BA(Hons) Politics with History, BA(Hons) Politics, Philosophy and Economics

Postgraduate: MA Security

Department of Social Policy Studies www.lboro.ac.uk/subjects/social-policy-studies/

BSc(Hons) Communication and Media Studies, Criminology and Social Policy BSc(Hons) Criminology and Sociology BSc(Hons) Sociology BSc(Hons) Sociology and Media BSc(Hons) MA Childhood, Youth and Social Policy MA Digital Media and Society, MSc Social Science Research (Social Policy)

School of Sport, Exercise and Health Sciences; www.lboro.ac.uk/departments/ssehs

Sport and Exercise Science BSc(Hons) Sport, Coaching and Physical Education BSc(Hons) Sport Management BSc(Hons) Sport and Exercise Science (Intercalated) Biochemistry BSc(Hons) Biochemistry MSci(Hons) Biological Sciences BSc(Hons) Biological Sciences MSci(Hons) Human Biology BSc(Hons) Natural Sciences BSc(Hons) Natural Sciences MSci(Hons) Business Psychology BSc(Hons) Psychology BSc(Hons) Psychology with Communication BSc(Hons) Psychology with Criminology BSc(Hons) Sport and Exercise Psychology BSc(Hons); Postgraduate: Exercise As Medicine MSc Exercise Physiology MSc Musculoskeletal Sport Science and Health MSc Physical Education with Qualified Teacher Status MSc/PGCE Social Science Research (Sport and Exercise Science) MSc Sport and Exercise Nutrition MSc Sport and Exercise Psychology MSc Sport Biomechanics MSc Sport Management MSc Sport Management, Politics and International Development MSc Strength and Conditioning MSc

Department of Teacher Education; www.lboro.ac.uk/departments/teachereducation

Postgraduate courses: Mathematics PGCE/MSc with QTS, Physical Education PGCE/MSc with QTS

Loughborough University in London; www.lborolondon.ac.uk

Postgraduate courses: Cyber Security and Big Data MSc, Design and Culture MA, Design Innovation MA/MSc/MRes, Design Innovation Management MSc, Digital Creative Media MSc, MSc Digital Marketing, Diplomacy and International Governance MRes, Diplomacy, Business and Trade MSc, Diplomacy, Statecraft and Foreign Policy MSc, Entrepreneurial Design Management MSc, Entrepreneurship and Innovation Management MSc, Entrepreneurship and Innovation MRes, Entrepreneurship, Finance and Innovation MSc, Global Communication and Development MA, International Management and Emerging Economies MSc, International Management MSc, Management and Work in a Global Context MSc, Managing Innovation in Creative Organisations MSc, Media and Creative Industries MA/MRes, MSc Risk, Governance and International Management Security, Peace-Building and Diplomacy MSc, Sport Analytics and Technologies MSc Sport Business and Innovation MSc, Sport Business and Leadership MSc, MSc Sport Marketing

UNIVERSITY OF MANCHESTER
www.manchester.ac.uk

Faculty of Biology, Medicine and Health; www.bmh.manchester.ac.uk

Adult Nursing BNurs, Anatomical Sciences BSc, Anatomical Sciences MSci, Anatomical Sciences with a Modern Language BSc, Anatomical Sciences with Industrial/Professional Experience BSc, Biochemistry BSc, Biochemistry MSci, Biochemistry with a Modern Language BSc, Biochemistry with Industrial/Professional Experience BSc, Biology BSc, Biology MSci, Biology with a Modern Language BSc,

Biology with Industrial/Professional Experience BSc, Biology with Science & Society BSc, Biology with Science and Society with Industrial/Professional Experience BSc, Biomedical Sciences BSc, Biomedical Sciences MSci, Biomedical Sciences with a Modern Language BSc, Biomedical Sciences with Industrial/Professional Experience BSc, Biotechnology BSc, Biotechnology MSci, Biotechnology with Industrial/Professional Experience BSc, Cell Biology BSc, Cell Biology MSci, Cell Biology with a Modern Language BSc, Cell Biology with Industrial/Professional Experience BSc, Children's Nursing BNurs, Cognitive Neuroscience and Psychology BSc, Cognitive Neuroscience and Psychology MSci, Cognitive Neuroscience and Psychology with Industrial/Professional Experience BSc, Dentistry (first-year entry) BDS, Dentistry (pre-dental entry) BDS, Developmental Biology BSc, Developmental Biology MSci, Developmental Biology with a Modern Language BSc, Developmental Biology with Industrial/Professional Experience BSc, Genetics BSc, Genetics MSci, Genetics with a Modern Language BSc, Genetics with Industrial/Professional Experience BSc, Healthcare Science (Audiology) BSc, Immunology BSc, Immunology MSci, Immunology with a Modern Language BSc, Immunology with Industrial/Professional Experience BSc, Life Sciences BSc, Life Sciences with a Modern Language BSc, Life Sciences with Industrial/Professional Experience BSc, Medical Biochemistry MSci, Medical Biochemistry with Industrial/Professional Experience BSc, Medical Physiology BSc, Medical Physiology MSci, Medical Physiology with a Modern Language BSc, Medical Physiology with Industrial/Professional Experience BSc, Medicine (6 years including foundation year) MBChB, Medicine MBChB, Mental Health Nursing BNurs, Microbiology BSc, Microbiology MSci, Microbiology with a Modern Language BSc, Microbiology with Industrial/Professional Experience BSc, Midwifery BMidwif, Molecular Biology BSc, Molecular Biology MSci, Molecular Biology with a Modern Language BSc, Molecular Biology with Industrial/Professional Experience BSc, Neuroscience BSc, Neuroscience MSci, Neuroscience with a Modern Language BSc, Neuroscience with Industrial/Professional Experience BSc, Optometry BSc, Oral Health Science BSc, Pharmacology and Physiology BSc, Pharmacology and Physiology with Industrial/Professional Experience BSc, Pharmacology BSc, Pharmacology MSci, Pharmacology with a Modern Language BSc, Pharmacology with Industrial/Professional Experience BSc, Pharmacy MPharm, Pharmacy with a Foundation Year MPharm, Plant Science BSc, Plant Science MSci, Plant Science with a Modern Language BSc, Plant Science with Industrial/Professional Experience BSc, Psychology BSc, Speech and Language Therapy BSc, Speech and Language Therapy MSpchLangTher, Zoology BSc, Zoology MSci, Zoology with a Modern Language BSc, Zoology with Industrial/Professional Experience BSc

Faculty of Science and Engineering; www.se.manchester.ac.uk

School of Chemical Engineering and Analytical Science; www.ceas.manchester.ac.uk

BEng/MEng Chemical Engineering, MEng Chemical, Engineering (Energy and Environment), MEng Chemical, Engineering with Industrial Experience, MEng, Chemical Engineering with Study in Europe Postgraduate courses: MSc Advanced Chemical, Engineering, MSc Advanced Process Integration, and Design

School of Chemistry; www.chemistry.manchester.ac.uk

BSc/MChem Chemistry, BSc/MChem Chemistry with Medicinal Chemistry, MChem Chemistry with International Study, MChem Chemistry with Industrial Experience, MSc Chemistry,

School of Computer Science; www.cs.manchester.ac.uk

Artificial Intelligence BSc, Artificial Intelligence MEng, Artificial Intelligence with Industrial Experience BSc, Artificial Intelligence with Industrial Experience MEng, Computer Science and Mathematics BSc, Computer Science and Mathematics with Industrial Experience BSc, Computer Science BSc, Computer Science (Human Computer Interaction) BSc, Computer Science (Human Computer Interaction) MEng, Computer Science (Human Computer Interaction) with Industrial Experience BSc, Computer Science (Human Computer Interaction) with Industrial Experience MEng, Computer Science MEng, Computer Science with Industrial Experience BSc, Computer Science with Industrial Experience MEng, Computer Systems Engineering BEng, Computer Systems Engineering MEng, Computer Systems Engineering with Industrial Experience BEng, Computer Systems Engineering with Industrial Experience MEng, Science with an Integrated Foundation Year BSc/MSc, Software Engineering BSc, Software Engineering MEng, Software Engineering with Industrial Experience BSc, Software Engineering with Industrial Experience MEng

Postgraduate courses: ACS: Advanced Web Technologies MSc, ACS: Artificial Intelligence MSc, ACS: Computer Security MSc, ACS: Data and Knowledge Management MSc, ACS: Digital Biology MSc, ACS: Semantic Technologies MSc, ACS: Software Engineering MSc, Advanced Computer Science MSc

School of Earth and Environmental Sciences; www.sees.manchester.ac.uk

BSc Environmental Science, BSc/MEarthSci Earth and Planetary Sciences

Postgraduate courses: MSc Petroleum Geoscience, Petroleum Geoscience for Reservoir Development and Production, MSc Pollution and Environmental Control

School of Electrical and Electronic Engineering; www.eee.manchester.ac.uk

BEng/MEng Electrical and Electronic Engineering, BEng/MEng Electronic Engineering, BEng/MEng Mechatronic Engineering

Postgraduate courses: MSc Advanced Control and Systems Engineering, MSc Electrical Power Systems Engineering, MSc Communications and Signal Processing, MSc Advanced Electrical Power Systems Engineering, MSc Renewable Energy and Clean Technology

School of Materials; www.materials.manchester.ac.uk

Engineering with an Integrated Foundation Year BEng/MEng, Fashion Buying and Merchandising BSc, Fashion Management BSc, Fashion Marketing BSc, Fashion Technology BSc, Materials Science and Engineering BSc, Materials Science and Engineering MEng, Materials Science and Engineering with Biomaterials MEng, Materials Science and Engineering with Corrosion MEng, Materials Science and Engineering with Metallurgy MEng, Materials Science and Engineering with Nanomaterials MEng, Materials Science and Engineering with Polymers MEng, Materials Science and Engineering with Textiles Technology MEng

Postgraduate courses: Advanced Engineering Materials MSc, Biomaterials MSc, Corrosion Control Engineering MSc, International Fashion Marketing MSc, International Fashion Retailing (Business Process Improvement) MSc, International Fashion Retailing MSc, International Fashion Retailing (Multichannel Marketing) MSc, Nanomaterials MSc, Polymer Materials Science and Engineering MSc

School of Mathematics; www.maths.manchester.ac.uk

Actuarial Science and Mathematics BSc, Computer Science and Mathematics BSc, Computer Science and Mathematics with Industrial Experience BSc, Mathematics and Philosophy BSc, Mathematics and Physics BSc, Mathematics and Physics MMath & Phys, Mathematics and Statistics BSc, Mathematics and Statistics MMath, Mathematics BSc, Mathematics MMath, Mathematics with a Modern Language BSc, Mathematics with Finance BSc, Mathematics with Financial Mathematics BSc, Mathematics with Financial Mathematics MMath

Postgraduate courses: MSc Actuarial Science, MSc Applied Mathematics, MSc Mathematical Finance, MSc Pure Mathematics and Mathematical Logic, MSc Statistics

School of Mechanical, Aerospace and Civil Engineering; www.mace.manchester.ac.uk

BEng/MEng Aerospace Engineering, MEng Aerospace Engineering with Management, BEng/MEng Civil Engineering, MEng Civil Engineering with Industrial Experience, MEng Civil Engineering (Enterprise), MEng Civil and Structural Engineering, BEng/ MEng Mechanical Engineering, MEng Mechanical Engineering, MEng Mechanical Engineering with Industrial Experience, BEng/MEng Mechanical Engineering with Management

Postgraduate courses: MSc Adv. Manufacturing Tech. and Systems Management, MSc Aerospace Engineering, MSc Commercial Project Management, MSc Construction Project Management, MSc Engineering Project Management, MSc Management of Projects, MSc Mechanical Engineering Design, MSc Reliability Engineering and Asset Management, MSc Renewable Energy and Clean Technology, MSc Structural Engineering, MSc Thermal Power and Fluid Engineering

School of Physics and Astronomy; www.physics.manchester.ac.uk

BSc/MMath & Phys Mathematics and Physics, BSc/MPhys Physics, BSc/MPhys Physics with Astrophysics, BSc/MPhys Physics with Philosophy, BSc/MPhys Physics with Theoretical Physics

Postgraduate courses: MSc Nuclear Science and Technology

Faculty of Humanities; www.humanities.manchester.ac.uk

Alliance Manchester Business School; www.mbs.ac.uk

BSc(Hons) Accounting, BSc(Hons) IT Management for Business, BSc(Hons) Accounting with Industrial/

Professional Experience, BSc Business Accounting with Industrial/Professional Experience, BSc(Hons) IT Management for Business, BSc(Hons) IT Management for Business with Industrial Experience, BSc(Hons) International Business, Finance and Economics, BSc(Hons) International Business, Finance and Economics with Industrial/Professional Experience, BSc(Hons) International Management, BSc(Hons) International Management with American Business Studies, BSc(Hons) Management, BSc(Hons) Management with Industrial/Professional Experience, BSc(Hons) Management (Accounting and Finance), BSc(Hons) Management (Accounting and Finance) with Industrial/Professional Experience, BSc(Hons) Management (Human Resources), BSc(Hons) Management (Human Resources) with Industrial/Professional Experience, BSc(Hons) Management (Innovation, Strategy and Entrepreneurship), BSc(Hons) Management (Innovation, Strategy and Entrepreneurship) with Industrial/Professional Experience, BSc(Hons) Management (International Business Economics), BSc(Hons) Management (International Business Economics) with Industrial/Professional Experience, BSc(Hons) Management (Marketing), BSc(Hons) Management (Marketing) with Industrial/Professional Experience

Postgraduate courses: MSc Accounting, MSc Accounting and Finance, MSc Finance, MSc Human Resource Management and Industrial Relations, MSc Innovation Management and Entrepreneurship, MEnt Master of Enterprise, MSc International Business and Management (Management), MSc Business Analysis and Strategic Management, MSc Management, MSc Management Practice (available only through apprenticeship levy funding), MSc Marketing, MSc Operations, Project and Supply Chain Management, MSc Business Analytics: Operational Research and Risk Analysis, MSc International Human Resource Management and Comparative Industrial Relations, MSc Business Psychology, MSc Organisational Psychology, MSc Quantitative Finance

School of Arts, Languages and Cultures; www.alc.manchester.ac.uk

BA American Studies, BA Ancient History and Archaeology/History, BA Ancient History, BA Arabic and a Modern European Language, BA Arabic Studies, BA Archaeology and Anthropology/History, BA Archaeology, BA Art History and English Literature/History, BA Chinese and Japanese/Linguistics, BA Chinese Studies, BA Classical Studies, BA Classics, BA Drama and English Literature/Film Studies, BA Drama, BA East Asian Studies, BA English Language and Arabic/Chinese/English Literature/ French/German/Italian/Japanese/Portuguese/ Russian/Spanish, BA English Language, BA English Literature and a Modern Language (French/German/ Italian/Spanish), BA English Literature and American Studies/History, BA English Literature, BA English Literature with Creative Writing, BA Film Studies and Arabic/Archaeology/Chinese/East Asian Studies/ English Language/English Literature/French/German/ History/History of Art/Italian/Japanese/Linguistics/ Middle Eastern Studies/Portuguese/Russian/ Spanish, BA French and Chinese/German/Italian/ Japanese/Linguistics/Portuguese/Russian/Spanish, BA French Studies, BA German and Chinese/Italian/ Japanese/Linguistics/Portuguese/Russian/Spanish, BA German Studies, BA History and American Studies/Arabic/French/German/Italian/Portuguese/ Russian/Sociology/Spanish, BA History, BA History of Art, BSc International Disaster Management & Humanitarian Response, BA Italian and Chinese, BA Italian and Japanese/Linguistics/Portuguese/Russian/ Spanish, BA Italian Studies, BA Japanese Studies, BA Latin and English Literature/Italian/Linguistics/Spanish, BA Latin with French, BA Linguistics and Arabic/ Japanese/Portuguese/Russian/Social Anthropology/ Sociology/Spanish), BA Linguistics, BA Middle Eastern Studies, BA Modern History with Economics, BA Modern Language and Business & Management (Arabic/Chinese/French/German/Italian/Japanese/ Portuguese/Russian/Spanish), BA Music and Drama, MusB Music, BA Politics and Arabic/Chinese/French/ German/Italian/Japanese/Modern History/Portuguese/ Russian/Spanish, BA Portuguese and Chinese/ Japanese, BA Religion and Anthropology, BA Religions and Theology, BA Russian and Chinese/ Japanese/Portuguese/Spanish, BA Russian Studies, BA Spanish and Chinese/Japanese/Portuguese, BA Spanish, Portuguese and Latin American Studies, BA Theological Studies in Philosophy and Ethics, BA World Literatures

Postgraduate courses: Art Gallery and Museum Studies MA Arts Management, Policy and Practice MA Classics and Ancient History MA Composition (Electroacoustic Music and Interactive Media) MusM Composition (Instrumental and Vocal music) MusM Conference Interpreting MA/PGDip Creative Writing MA Disaster Management (Resilience, Response and Relief) MSc Egyptology MA English Literature and American Studies MA Film Studies MA Gender, Sexuality and Culture MA Global Health MSc

Heritage Studies MA/PGDip History MA History of Science, Technology and Medicine MSc Humanitarian Practice MSc Humanitarianism and Conflict Response MA Intercultural Communication MA International Disaster Management MSc Linguistics MA Medieval and Early Modern Studies MA Modern and Contemporary Literature MA Modern Languages and Cultures MA Music (Ethnomusicology) MusM Music (Musicology) MusM Playwriting MA Religions and Theology MA Screenwriting MA Translation and Interpreting Studies MA

School of Environment, Education and Development; www.seed.manchester.ac.uk

BA Architecture, BSc Education, BSc Educational Psychology, BA Environmental Management, BA/BSc Geography, BA/ BSc Geography with International Study/ Professional Placement, BA Management, Leadership and Leisure, MPlan Master of Planning, MPRE Master of Planning with Real Estate, BSc Environmental Management, BSc Planning and Real Estate, BSc Planning and Real Estate with Professional Placement, Planning MSc

Postgraduate courses: MA Architecture and Urbanism, MArch Architecture, MSc Development Economics and Policy, MSc Development Finance, MA Digital Technologies, Communication and Education, MA Education (International), MA Educational Leadership, MA Intercultural Communication, MEd Psychology of Education, MSc Research Methods with Education, TESOL MA, PD Counselling Psychology, PhD Education, DEdChPsy Educational and Child Psychology, MSc Environmental Governance, MSc Environmental Impact Assessment & Management, MSc Environmental Monitoring, Modelling and Reconstruction, MSc Geographical Information Science, MSc Global Urban Development and Planning, MSc Human Resource Development (International Development), MSc ICTs for Development, MSc International Development: Development Management, MSc International Development: Environment Climate Change and Development, MSc International Development: Globalisation, Trade and Industry, MSc International Development, MSc International Development: Politics, Governance and Development Policy, MSc International Development: Poverty Conflict and Reconstruction, MSc International Development: Poverty, Inequality and Development, MSc International Development: Public Policy and Management, MSc Management and Implementation of Development Projects, MSc Management and Information Systems: Change and Development, MSc Organisational Change and Development, Research Methods with International Development MSc, PGCE Primary, PGCE Primary School Direct 5-11, PGCE Sec Sch Dir: Geography (Cheadle & Marple College), PGCE Sec Sch Dir: History (Cheadle & Marple College), PGCE Secondary Business Education, PGCE Secondary Chemistry, PGCE Secondary Economics and Business Education, PGCE Secondary English, PGCE Secondary French, PGCE Secondary (Geography), PGCE Secondary German, PGCE Secondary (History), PGCE Secondary Mathematics, PGCE Secondary Physics, PGCE Secondary Physics with Maths, PGCE Secondary School Direct (English), PGCE Secondary School Direct (Mathematics), PGCE Secondary School Direct Science: Biology (11- 16 or 11-18), PGCE Secondary School Direct Science: Chemistry (11-16 or 11-18), PGCE Secondary School Direct Science: Physics (11-16 or 11-18), PGCE Secondary Science Biology, PGCE Secondary Spanish, Planning MSc, PGCE Secondary School Direct (French), PGCE Secondary School Direct (German), PGCE Secondary School Direct (Physics with Maths), PGCE Secondary School Direct (Spanish), MEd Psychology of Education

School of Law; www.law.manchester.ac.uk

LLB Law, LLB Law with Criminology, LLB Law with Politics,

Postgraduate courses: LLM Corporate Governance, MRes Criminology (Social Statistics), LLM/MA/PGDip Healthcare Ethics and Law, PGCert Healthcare Ethics, PGCert Healthcare Law, LLM Intellectual Property Law, LLM International Business and Commercial Law, LLM International Financial Law, LLM International Trade Transactions, LLM Law, LLM Public International Law, LLM/MA Security and International Law, LLM Transnational Dispute Resolution, PhD Bioethics and Medical Jurisprudence, MPhil Law, PhD Law

School of Social Sciences; www.socialsciences.manchester.ac.uk

Accounting and Finance BAEcon, Criminology and Quantitative Methods BASS, Criminology BA, Criminology with International Study BA, Development Studies and Social Statistics BA, Development Studies BAEcon, Economics and Finance BAEcon, Economics and Philosophy BAEcon, Economics and Politics BAEcon, Economics and Social Statistics BA, Economics and Sociology BAEcon, Economics BAEcon, Economics BSc, Finance BAEcon, Law LLB, Law with Criminology and International Study LLB, Law with Criminology LLB, Law with International Study

LLB, Law with Politics and International Study LLB, Law with Politics LLB, Philosophy and Criminology BASS, Philosophy and Politics BASS, Philosophy and Quantitative Methods BASS, Philosophy BA, Politics and Arabic BA, Politics and Chinese BA, Politics and Criminology BASS, BASS3 years, Politics and French BA, Politics and German BA, Politics and International Relations BSocSc, Politics and Italian BA, Politics and Japanese BA, Politics and Portuguese BA, Politics and Quantitative Methods BASS, Politics and Russian BA, Politics and Social Anthropology BASS, Politics and Sociology BASS, Politics and Spanish BA, Politics, Philosophy and Economics BA, Social Anthropology and Criminology BASS, Social Anthropology and Quantitative Methods BASS, Social Anthropology and Sociology BASS, Social Anthropology BSocSc, Sociology and Criminology BASS, Sociology and Philosophy BASS, Sociology and Quantitative Methods BASS, Sociology Postgraduate courses: Anthropological Research MA, Corporate Governance LLM, Criminology MA, Criminology MRes, Criminology PGDip, Criminology (Social Statistics) MRes, Data Science MSc, Economics MA, Economics MSc, Financial Economics MSc, Healthcare Ethics and Law (Distance Learning) LLM, Healthcare Ethics and Law (Distance Learning) MA, Healthcare Ethics and Law (Distance Learning) PGDip, Healthcare Ethics and Law (Intercalated) MSc, Healthcare Ethics and Law LLM, Healthcare Ethics and Law MA, Healthcare Ethics and Law Postgraduate Diploma PGDip, Healthcare Ethics (Distance Learning) PGCert, Healthcare Ethics Postgraduate Certificate PGCert, Healthcare Law (Distance Learning) PGCert, Healthcare Law Postgraduate Certificate PGCert, Human Rights – Law/Political Science Pathway (Research Route) MA, Human Rights – Law/Political Science Pathway (Standard Route) MA, Human Rights – Political Science (Research Route) MA, Human Rights – Political Science (Standard Route) MA, Intellectual Property Law LLM, International Business and Commercial Law LLM, International Financial Law LLM, International Political Economy (Research) MA, International Political Economy (Standard) MA, International Relations (Research) MA, International Relations (Standard) MA, International Trade Transactions LLM, Law LLM, Peace and Conflict Studies MA, Philosophy MA, Political Economy (Research Route) MA, Political Economy (Standard Route) MA, Political Science – Democracy and Elections (Research Route) MA, Political Science – Democracy and Elections (Standard Route) MA, Political Science – European Politics & Policy Pathway (Research Route) MA, Political Science – European Politics & Policy Pathway (Standard Route) MA, Political Science – Governance and Public Policy Pathway (Research Route) MA, Political Science – Governance and Public Policy Pathway (Standard Route) MA, Political Science – Philosophy and Political Theory MA, Political Science – Political Theory Pathway (Research Route) MA, Political Science – Political Theory Pathway (Standard Route) MA, Politics MA, Public International Law LLM, Security and International Law LLM, Security and International Law MA, Social Anthropology MA, Social Research Methods and Statistics MSc, Sociological Research MSc, Sociology MA, Transnational Dispute Resolution LLM, Visual Anthropology MA

MANCHESTER METROPOLITAN UNIVERSITY
www.mmu.ac.uk

Faculty of Arts and Humanities; www.mmu.ac.uk/artshumanities

Manchester School of Art;
www.art.mmu.ac.uk

Foundation Diploma in Art and Design, BA Acting, BA Animation, BA Architecture, BA Art History, BA, Art History and Curating, BA Drama and Contemporary, Performance, BA Fashion, BA Fashion Art, Direction, BA Filmmaking, BA Fine Art, BA Fine Art, and Art History, BA Fine Art and Curating, BA, Graphic Design, BA Illustration with Animation, BA, Interior Design, BA Music and Sound for Media, BA, Photography, BA Product design, BA Product, Designs and Craft, BA Textiles in Practice

Postgraduate courses: MA/MFA Animation, MA/, MFA Architecture MArch, MA Architecture & Urbanism MA, MA/MFA Contemporary Curating, MA/MFA Design: Craft MA/MFA Design: Embroidery, MA/MFA, Design: Fashion, MA/MFA Design: Fashion Art Direction, MA/MFA Design: Graphic Design & Art Direction, MA/MFA Design: Illustration, MA/MFA Design: Interior Design, MA/MFA Design: Product & Furniture, MA/MFA Design: Textile Practice, MA/MFA Design: Textiles for

Fashion, MA/MFA Filmmaking, MA/MFA Fine Art, MA/MFA Landscape Architecture MLA, MA/MFA Photography, MA Music & Sound for Media, MA/MFA Painting

Humanities, Languages and Social Science; www.mmu.ac.uk/hlss

English

BA(Hons) English, BA(Hons) English and American, Literature, BA(Hons) Creative Writing, BA(Hons) English and American Literature, BA(Hons), English and Creative Writing, BA(Hons) English and Film, BA(Hons) Film and Media Studies, BA(Hons) English and Multimedia Journalism, BA(Hons) English and History, BA(Hons), English and Philosophy, BA(Hons) English and, Politics, BA(Hons) English and Linguistics, BA(Hons), English and French, BA(Hons) English and Spanish, BA(Hons) English with a minor route language, BA(Hons) English/ Teaching English to Speakers of Other Languages (TESOL)

Postgraduate courses: MA English Studies, MA/MFA Creative Writing

History, Politics and Philosophy

BA(Hons) American History, BA(Hons) Ancient and Medieval History, BA(Hons) Ancient History, BA(Hons) Ethics, Religion & Philosophy, BA(Hons) History, BA(Hons) Politics, BA(Hons) International Relations, BA(Hons) History / International Relations, BA(Hons) History / Philosophy, BA(Hons) English / History, BA(Hons) Philosophy / Politics, BA(Hons) International Relations / Philosophy, BA(Hons) English / Philosophy, BA(Hons) English / Politics, BA(Hons) History / Politics, BA(Hons) History / International Relations, BA(Hons) Philosophy / Politics, BA(Hons) International Relations / Philosophy, BA(Hons) Economics / Politics, BA(Hons) International Relations / French, BA(Hons) International Relations / Philosophy, BA(Hons) International Relations / Spanish, BA(Hons) International Relations with a minor route language, BA(Hons) War and Society, BSc(Hons) Medieval and Early Modern History

Postgraduate courses: MA Creative Writing, MFA, Creative Writing, MA English Studies, MA History, MA International Relations and Global Communications, MA European Philosophy, Master of Public, Administration

Sociology

BA(Hons) Sociology, BSc(Hons) Sociology with Quantitative Methods, BA(Hons) Criminology, BA(Hons) Sociology and Criminology, BSc(Hons)

Criminology and Sociology with Quantitative Methods, BSc(Hons) Criminology with Quantitative Methods

Postgraduate courses: MA Applied Criminology, MSc Urban Policy and Analytics, MSc Applied Quantitative Methods

Languages, Linguistics and TESOL

BA(Hons) French with Modern Standard Arabic, BA(Hons) Spanish with Modern Standard Arabic, English Literature or Multimedia Journalism, BA(Hons) English with Modern Standard Arabic, BA(Hons) Multimedia Journalism with Modern Standard Arabic, BA(Hons) Linguistics with Modern Standard Arabic, BA(Hons) Teaching English to Speakers of other Languages with Modern Standard Arabic, BA(Hons) Business with Modern Standard Arabic, BA(Hons) International Business with Modern Standard Arabic, BA(Hons) International Relations with Modern Standard Arabic, BA(Hons) French Studies, BA(Hons) French with German, BA(Hons) French with Italian, BA(Hons) French and Spanish, BA(Hons) French with Modern Standard Arabic, BA(Hons) French with Mandarin Chinese, BA(Hons) French with Japanese, BA(Hons) English / French, BA(Hons) Multimedia Journalism with French, BA(Hons) Teaching English to Speakers of other Languages / French, BA(Hons) Linguistics / French, BA(Hons) Business / French, BA(Hons) International Business / French, BA(Hons) International Relations / French, BA(Hons) French with German, BA(Hons) Spanish with German, BA(Hons) English with German, BA(Hons) Multimedia Journalism with German, BA(Hons) Teaching English to Speakers of other Languages with German, BA(Hons) Linguistics with German, BA(Hons) Business with German, BA(Hons) International Business with German, BA(Hons) International Relations with German, BA(Hons) French with Italian, BA(Hons) Spanish with Italian, BA(Hons) English with Italian, BA(Hons) Multimedia Journalism with Italian, BA(Hons) Teaching English to Speakers of other Languages with Italian, BA(Hons) Linguistics with Italian, BA(Hons) Business with Italian, BA(Hons) International Business with Italian, BA(Hons) International Relations with Italian, BA(Hons) French with Japanese, BA(Hons) Spanish with Japanese, BA(Hons) English with Japanese, BA(Hons) Multimedia Journalism with Japanese, BA(Hons) Linguistics with Japanese, BA(Hons) Teaching English to Speakers of other Languages with Japanese, BA(Hons) Business with Japanese, BA(Hons)

International Business with Japanese, BA(Hons) International Relations with Japanese, BA(Hons) Linguistics, BA(Hons) Linguistics / French, BA(Hons) Linguistics / Spanish, BA(Hons) Linguistics with Modern Standard Arabic, BA(Hons) Linguistics with Mandarin Chinese, BA(Hons) Linguistics with German, BA(Hons) Linguistics with Italian, BA(Hons) Linguistics with Japanese, BA(Hons) English / Linguistics, BA(Hons) Teaching English to Speakers of Other Languages and Linguistics, BA(Hons) French with Mandarin Chinese, BA(Hons) Spanish with Mandarin Chinese, BA(Hons) English with Mandarin Chinese, BA(Hons) Multimedia Journalism with Mandarin Chinese, BA(Hons) Linguistics with Mandarin Chinese, BA(Hons) Teaching English to Speakers of other Languages with Mandarin Chinese, BA(Hons) Business with Mandarin Chinese, BA(Hons) International Business with Mandarin Chinese, BA(Hons) International Relations with Mandarin Chinese, BA(Hons) Spanish Studies, BA(Hons) French and Spanish, BA(Hons) Spanish with German, BA(Hons) Spanish with Italian BA(Hons) Spanish with Modern Standard Arabic, BA(Hons) Spanish with Mandarin Chinese, BA(Hons) Spanish with Japanese, English Literature or Multimedia Journalism, BA(Hons) English / Spanish, BA(Hons) Multimedia Journalism with Spanish, BA(Hons) Linguistics / Spanish, BA(Hons) Teaching English to Speakers of other Languages / Spanish, BA(Hons) Business / Spanish, BA(Hons) International Business / Spanish, BA(Hons) International Relations / Spanish, BA(Hons) Teaching English to Speakers of other Languages / French, BA(Hons) Teaching English to Speakers of other Languages / Spanish, BA(Hons) Teaching English to Speakers of other Languages with German, BA(Hons) Teaching English to Speakers of other Languages with Italian, BA(Hons) Teaching English to Speakers of other Languages with Modern Standard Arabic, BA(Hons) Teaching English to Speakers of other Languages with Mandarin Chinese, BA(Hons) Teaching English to Speakers of other Languages with Japanese, BA(Hons) English / Teaching English to Speakers of Other Languages, BA(Hons) Teaching English to Speakers of Other Languages and Linguistics

Postgraduate courses: MA Teaching English to Speakers of Other Languages (TESOL) and Applied Linguistics, MA Linguistics and English Studies, MA Linguistics and English Language

Journalism, Information and Communications

BA(Hons) Multimedia Journalism, BSc(Hons) Digital Media and Communications, BA(Hons) English and Multimedia Journalism, BA(Hons) Multimedia Journalism with a minor route language

Postgraduate courses: MA Library and Information Management, MA Multimedia Journalism

Manchester Fashion Institute; fashioninstitute.mmu.ac.uk

Fashion Design and Technology: BA(Hons) Womenswear, BA(Hons) Fashion Design and Technology: Menswear, BA(Hons) Fashion Design and Technology: Sportswear, BA(Hons) Fashion Promotion, BA(Hons) Fashion Buying and Merchandising, BA(Hons) Fashion Business and Management, BA(Hons) Fashion, BA(Hons) Fashion Art Direction, BA International Fashion (Top Up)

Postgraduate courses: MA International Fashion Business: MA/ MSc Fashion and Business, MA Fashion Buying and Merchandising Management, MA/MFA Design: Fashion Art Direction, MA/MFA Design: Fashion

Faculty of Business and Law; www.mmu.ac.uk/business-and-law

Business School; www.mmu.ac.uk/business-school

International Hospitality Businesss Management (Foundation Year), Tourism Management (Foundation Year), BA(Hons) Accounting and Finance, BA(Hons) Banking and Finance, BA/BSc(Hons) Economics, BA(Hons) Economics and Banking, BA(Hons) Economics and Finance (Joint Honours), BA(Hons) Economics / International Business, BA(Hons) Economics / Politics, BA(Hons) Business / Economics, BA(Hons) Sustainable Performance Management (CIMA), BA(Hons) Accounting (top-up), BA(Hons) Business Management, M.Bus(Hons) Business, BA(Hons) Business Management with Law, BA(Hons) International Business Management, BA(Hons) Business Management Professional (Degree Apprenticeship), BA(Hons) Business / Economics, BA(Hons) Business Enterprise / Human Resource Management, BA(Hons) Business Enterprise / Marketing, BA(Hons) International Business / Marketing, BA(Hons) Business (top-up), Business Management (Foundation Year), International Business Management (Foundation Year), BA(Hons) Business and Human Resource Management, BA(Hons) Business and Marketing, BA(Hons)

Business Psychology, BSc(Hons) Business Technology, BSc(Hons) Digital & Technology Solutions (Degree Apprenticeship), BA(Hons) Human Resource Management, Human Resource Management (Foundation Year), BA(Hons) Business Psychology BA(Hons) Advertising and Brand Management, BA(Hons) Marketing Management, BA(Hons) Public Relations and Marketing, BA(Hons) Business Management Professional in Retail (Degree Apprenticeship), BA(Hons) Sports Marketing Management, BA(Hons) Business / Marketing, BA(Hons) Business Enterprise / Marketing, BA(Hons) International Business / Marketing, Marketing Management (Foundation Year), BA(Hons) Marketing, BA(Hons) Business and Marketing, BA(Hons) Advertising and Brand Communications, BSc(Hons) Digital Marketer Degree Apprenticeship, Marketing (Foundation Year), BA(Hons) Sports Management, BA(Hons) Sports Marketing Management, Sports Management (Foundation Year), BSc(Hons) Sports Business Management, BSc(Hons) Sports Marketing Management, Sports Business Management (Foundation Year), Sports Marketing Management (Foundation Year), BA(Hons) Events Management, BA(Hons) Tourism Management, BA(Hons) Hospitality Business Management, BA(Hons) Business Management Professional in Hospitality (Degree Apprenticeship), Events, Hospitality and Tourism degrees (Foundation Year), BA(Hons) International Tourism Management, BA(Hons) International Hospitality Businesss Management, BA(Hons) International Tourism Management (Foundation Year), International Hospitality Businesss Management (Foundation Year)
Postgraduate courses: ACCA Professional Stage, MSc Accounting and Finance, MSc Accounting and Finance (Online Advanced Standing), MSc Banking and Finance, MSc Finance and Business, MSc Financial Planning and Business Management, MSc Finance and Strategy, MSc Financial Technology (FinTech), MSc Strategic Business Management (CIMA), BA(Hons) Sustainable Performance Management (CIMA), MSc Behavioural and Economic Science, MSc Economic and Financial Analysis, MSc International Business Management, MSc Management, MSc Place Management and Leadership, MSc Sport Business, Management and Policy, MSc Sport Business, Management and Policy, Master of Sport Directorship, MBA Master of Business Administration (MBA), CIPD Level 5 Certificate in Human Resource Management, MSc Human Resource Management with CIPD, MSc Human Resource Management with CIPD, MSc International Human Resource Management with CIPD, MSc International Human Resource Management, MSc Business Analytics, MSc Logistics and Supply Chain Management, MSc Project Management, MSc Digital Marketing, MSc Digital Marketing Communications, MSc Marketing, MSc Marketing (Creative Advertising), MSc Marketing (Sport), MSc Public Relations, MSc Crowd Safety and Risk Analysis, MSc International Events Management, MSc International Tourism and Hospitality Management

Law School; www.mmu.ac.uk/law
LLB(Hons) Law
Postgraduate courses: Graduate Diploma in Law, Bar Professional Training Course LLM in Legal Practice at the Bar (combined BPTC/LLM), Legal Practice Course, LLM in Legal Practice with LPC (combined LPC/LLM), Master of Laws (LLM), Top-up LLM in Legal Practice Accelerated

Faculty of Education; www.mmu.ac.uk/education
BA(Hons) Early Years and Childhood Studies,BA(Hons) Education Studies, BSc(Hons) Educational Psychology, BA(Hons) Primary Education with Mathematics with QTS, BA(Hons) Primary Education with QTS, BSc(Hons) Secondary Mathematics Education with QTS
Postgraduate courses: MA Autism Spectrum Conditions, MA Childhood and Youth Studies, MA Early Childhood Studies, MA Education, MA Education Studies, MA Educational Leadership, MA Educational Leadership and Management, MA Inclusive Education and Disability, MA Inclusive Education and Special Educational Needs and Disability (SEND), MA Leadership in Early Years, PgCert National Award for Special Educational Needs Coordination, MSc Science, Technology, Engineering, Mathematics (STEM) Education, MA Social Research, PgCert/PgDip/MA Specific Learning Difficulties

Faculty of Health, Psychology and Social Care; www.mmu.ac.uk/hpsc

Department of Health Professions; www.mmu.ac.uk/health-professions
BSc Nutritional Sciences, BSc Physiotherapy, BSc Speech and Language Therapy, BSc Nutritional Sciences, BSc Sport and Exercise Nutrition
Postgraduate courses: MSc Advanced Physiotherapy, MSc Physiotherapy (Pre-Registration), PgCert Advanced Stroke Practice, PgCert Simulation and Technology Enhanced Learning (STEL), PgCert

Simulation and Technology Enhanced Learning (STEL) in Healthcare, MSc/PgDip/PgCert Sport and Exercise Medicine, PgCert Dusphagia, MSc Speech and Language Therapy (Pre-Registration), MSc/PgDip Food Science and Innovation, MSc Human Nutrition, MSc/PgDip Sport Nutrition, MSc Occupational Safety, Health and Environment, MMed Masters in Medicine, MMed Masters in Medicine (Sport and Exercise Medicine), MMed Masters in Medicine (Emergency Medicine), MMed Masters in Medicine (Psychiatry), PgCert/PgDip/MSc Emergency Medicine

Department of Nursing; www.mmu.ac.uk/nursing

BSc Adult Nursing, BSc Community Health, BSc Mental Health Nursing, BSc(Hons) Specialist Community Public Health Nursing (Health Visiting or School Nursing)
Postgraduate course: PgDip Adult Nursing, MSc Adult Nursing (Pre-registration), MSc Mental Health Nursing (Pre-registration), PgDip Community Health, PgDip Specialist Community Public Health Nursing (Health Visiting or School Nursing)

Department of Psychology; www.mmu.ac.uk/psychology

BSc Forensic Psychology, BSc Psychology, BSc Psychology Foundation, BSc Psychology with Counselling and Psychotherapy
Postgraduate courses: MSc Clinical Skills in Integrative Psychotherapy, MSc Psychological Wellbeing in Clinical Practice, MSc/PgDip Psychology (Conversion), MSc Psychology by Research, MSc Childhood Development and Wellbeing in Practice, MSc Health Psychology, DProf Doctor of Psychological Therapies

Department of Social Care; www.mmu.ac.uk/social-care-and-socialwork

BA(Hons) Integrated Health and Social Care, BA(Hons) Integrated Health and Social Care (with foundation year), BA(Hons) Social Work
Postgraduate courses: MA Social Work

Faculty of Science and Engineering; www.mmu.ac.uk/science-engineering

Biology
MBiol/BSc(Hons) Biology, BSc(Hons) Animal Behaviour, BSc(Hons) Microbiology and Molecular Biology, BSc(Hons) Wildlife Biology, MBiol(Hons) / BSc(Hons) Zoology

Postgraduate courses: MSc Animal Behaviour, MSc Biological Recording, MSc Bird Conservation, MSc Conservation Biology, MSc Conservation Genetics, MSc Zoo Conservation Biology

Biomedical and Physiological Sciences
MBioMedSci(Hons) Biomedical Science, BSc(Hons) Biomedical Science, BSc(Hons) Human Biosciences, BSc(Hons) Human Physiology, BSc(Hons) Healthcare Science (Life Sciences), BSc(Hons) Healthcare Science (Physiological Sciences)
Postgraduate courses: MSc Biomedical Science, MSc Cellular Pathology, MSc Clinical Biochemistry, MSc Haematology and Transfusion Science, MSc Human Physiology, MSc Medical Microbiology

Chemistry
MChem/BSc(Hons) Pharmaceutical Chemistry, BSc(Hons) Medicinal and Biological Chemistry, BSc(Hons)/ MChem(Hons) Chemistry

Computing and Digital Technology
MComp Computer Science, BSc(Hons) Computer Science, BSc(Hons) Computing, BSc(Hons) Software Engineering, BSc(Hons) Computer Forensics and Security, BSc(Hons) Computer Games Technology, BSc(Hons) Computer Animation and Visual Effects, BSc(Hons) Software Development (Accelerated Degree)
Postgraduate courses: MSc Computing, MSc Data Science, MSc Data Analytics, MSc Advanced Computer Science, MSc Cyber Security, MSc Project Management (Cyber Security), MSc Project Management (Data Analytics)

Engineering
BEng/MEng(Hons) Mechanical Engineering, BEng/MEng(Hons) Electrical and Electronic Engineering, BSc(Hons) Product Design and Technology
Postgraduate courses: MSc Electronic Smart Systems Engineering, MSc Mechanical Smart Systems Engineering, MSc Project Management (Electronic Engineering), MSc Project Management (Mechanical Engineering), MSc Industrial Digitalisation

Environmental Science
BSc Environmental Science

Geography
MGeog(Hons) Geography, BSc(Hons) Geography, BSc(Hons) Human Geography, BSc(Hons) Physical Geography, BSc(Hons) Environmental Science

Mathematics
MMath(Hons) Mathematics, BSc(Hons) Mathematics

Science communication
Postgraduate course: MSc Science Communication

Sport and Exercise Sciences
BSc(Hons) Sport and Exercise Science, BSc(Hons) Sport, Physical Activity and Health, BSc(Hons) Sport Science and Human Physiology, BSc(Hons) Sport: Coaching and Development, BSc(Hons) Manchester City Community Football Coaching

---

MIDDLESEX UNIVERSITY
www.mdx.ac.uk

Faculty of Arts and Creative Industries

Professional Practice, Arts and Creative Industries (specialisation) BA(Hons), Fashion Communication and Styling BA(Hons), Music Business and Arts Management BA(Hons), Fashion Design BA(Hons), Professional Practice, Somatic Studies MA, Music BA(Hons), Advertising, Public Relations and Branding BA(Hons), Illustration BA(Hons), Television Production (Year 2 and Year 3 Entry) BA(Hons), Digital Media BA(Hons), Jazz BA(Hons), Film BA(Hons), Media and Cultural Studies (Year 3 Entry) BA(Hons), Fashion Communication and Styling BA(Hons), Fashion Textiles BA(Hons), Theatre Arts BA(Hons), Games Design BA/BSc(Hons), Animation BA(Hons), Photography BA(Hons), Interior Architecture BA(Hons), Music Business and Arts Management BA(Hons), Dance Practices BA(Hons), Creative Writing and Journalism BA(Hons), 3D Animation and Games BA(Hons), Fine Art BA(Hons), Graphic Design BA(Hons), Television and Digital Production BA(Hons), English BA(Hons), Interior Design BA(Hons)

Postgraduate: Printmaking MA, Fine Art MA, Media Management MSc, Arts Management MA, Novel Writing (Online Distance Learning) MA, Classical Music Business MA, Graphic Design MA, Interiors (Architecture and Design) MA, Creative Technology MA/MSc, Professional Practice, Dance Technique Pedagogy MA, Film MA, Fashion MA, Master of Philosophy MPhil and Doctor of Philosophy PhD, Children's Book Illustration and Graphic Novels MA, Creative Entrepreneurship (Media/Music) MA, Theatre Arts MA, Writing for Creative and Professional Practice MA/PGDip, Art and Design Research Degree

Faculty of Professional and Social Sciences

School of Law

Sociology BA(Hons), Sociology with Criminology BA(Hons), Sociology with Psychology BA(Hons), Criminology (Criminal Justice) BA(Hons), Criminology (Policing) BA(Hons), Criminology (Youth Justice) BA(Hons), Criminology BA(Hons), Criminology with Psychology BA(Hons), International Politics and Law BA(Hons), International Politics BA(Hons), International Politics, Economics and Law BA(Hons), Law BA(Hons), LLB Commercial Law, LLB European Law and Politics, LLB Law, LLB Law with Criminology, LLB Law with Human Rights, LLB Law with International Relations

Postgraduate: Comparative Drug and Alcohol Studies MA, Criminology MA, Criminology with Forensic Psychology MSc, Cybercrime and Digital Investigation MSc, Environmental Law and Justice MA, Global Governance and Sustainable Development MA, International Relations MA, Law MPhil/PhD, LLM Human Rights Law with Integrated Placement, LLM/PGDip/PGCert Commercial Law, LLM/PGDip/PGCert Employment Law, LLM/PGDip/PGCert European Law, LLM/PGDip/PGCert Human Rights Law, LLM/PGDip/PGCert International Business Law, LLM/PGDip/PGCert International Law, LLM/PGDip/PGCert International Minority Rights Law, LLM/PGDip/PGCert Law (General), Youth Justice, Community Safety and Applied Criminology MA

Business School

Business Management (Marketing) (Top-up) BA(Hons), International Business Admin (Final Year Entry) BA(Hons), Marketing BA(Hons), Banking and Finance BSc(Hons), Business Management (Finance) (Top-up) BA(Hons), International Tourism Management (Mandarin) BA(Hons), Business Management (Mandarin) BA(Hons), Business Management (Human Resource Management) BA(Hons), International Business and Trade (Top-up) BA(Hons), Business Accounting BSc(Hons), Banking and Finance BSc(Hons), Business Management (Marketing) BA(Hons), International Business BA(Hons), International Business Admin (Final Year Entry) BA(Hons), Financial Services (Top-up) BA(Hons), Business Management (Finance) BA(Hons), Business Management (Spanish) BA(Hons), International Tourism Management BSc(Hons), International Hospitality and Tourism Management (Top-up) BA(Hons), Business Management (Innovation and

Entrepreneurship) BA(Hons), International Business Administration (Top-up) BA(Hons), International Tourism Management (Spanish) BA(Hons), Business Management (Supply Chain) (Top-up) BA(Hons), Business Management (Innovation) (Top-up) BA(Hons), Human Resource Management BA(Hons) (CIPD Accredited), Business Management (Project Management) BA(Hons), Accounting and Finance BA(Hons), Business Management (Supply Chain & Logistics) BA(Hons), Business Management (Fast-Track) BA(Hons), Business Management (Marketing) (Top-up) BA(Hons), Marketing BA(Hons), Economics BSc(Hons)

Postgraduate: International Human Resource Management MA with Integrated Placement (15 months/24 months) (CIPD Accredited), International Hospitality and Events Management MSc/PGDip/PGCert, Management MSc/PGDip/PGCert, Professional Practice DProf (Business), Human Resource Practice MProf, Digital Marketing MSc/PGDip/PGCert, Professional Practice DProf (Business), Digital Marketing MSc with Integrated Placement (15 months/24 months), Global Supply Chain Management MSc/PG Dip/PG Cert, Global Supply Chain Management MSc with Integrated Placement (15 months/24 months), Financial Management MSc/PGCert/PGDip, Management MSc/PGDip/PGCert, Innovation Management and Entrepreneurship MSc/PG Dip/PG Cert Tourism MPhil/PhD, Investment and Finance MSc, Strategic Marketing MSc/PGDip/PGCert, Doctor of Business Administration DBA, Human Resource Practice MProf, Global Online MBA, Strategic Branding and Stakeholder Communication MA/PGDip/PGCert, International Business Management MA with Integrated Placement (15 months/24 months), Corporate and Marketing Communications MSc/PGDip/PGCert, International Business Management (Enhanced) MA, Transdisciplinary Practice MSc, International Tourism Management MSc, Strategic Marketing MSc with Integrated Placement (15 months/24 months), Master of Business Administration in Oil and Gas MBA, International Human Resource Management MA with Integrated Placement (15 months/24 months) (CIPD Accredited), Pharmaceutical Management MBA, Shipping and Logistics MBA, Management MSc with Integrated Placement (15 months/24 months), Master of Business Administration MBA, International Hospitality and Events Management MSc/PGDip/PGCert, International Human Resource Management MA/PGDip/PGCert (CIPD Accredited), Strategic Branding and Stakeholder Management MA with Integrated Placement (15 months/24 months), Corporate and Marketing Communications MSc with Integrated Placement (15 months/24 months), Human Resource Management and Development

Department of Adult, Child and Midwifery

Midwifery BSc(Hons), Professional Practice (Negotiated Specialism) BA/BSc/GradCert, Midwifery (Professional Practice) (Top-up) BSc(Hons), Midwifery with Professional Registration (Shortened Programme for Registered Adult Nurses) BSc(Hons), Mental Health Nursing (Professional Practice) (Top-up) BSc(Hons), Nursing (Adult) BSc(Hons), Nursing (Child) BSc(Hons), Nursing (Mental Health) BSc(Hons), Nursing (Professional Practice) (Top-up) BSc(Hons), Professional Practice (Negotiated Specialism) BA/BSc/GradCert

Postgraduate: Advanced Professional Practice (Negotiated Specialism) MA/MSc/PGCert, Neonatal Care GradCert/PGCert, Midwifery Studies MSc, Nursing (Mental Health) (Pre-registration programme) PGDip, Nursing Studies MSc / Nursing Studies (Advanced Nursing Practice) MSc, Primary Care Nursing PGDip

Department of Education

Early Childhood Studies BA(Hons), Education Studies BA(Hons)

Postgraduate: Leading Inclusive Education MA, Qualified Teacher Status – Assessment Only (Primary and Secondary), PGCE Primary Education with QTS, Novel Writing (Online Distance Learning) MA, Early Years Initial Teacher Training: Graduate Employment Based Route, Advanced Professional Practice (Negotiated Specialism) MA/MSc/PGCert, Higher Education MA, PGCE Secondary Education (Geography with Humanities), PGCE Secondary Education (History with Humanities) MA/PGDip/PGCert (CIPD Accredited), Early Years Initial Teacher Training: Graduate Entry Route, PGCE Secondary Education Drama with English, Childhood and Education in Diverse Societies MA, Advanced Professional Practice (Negotiated Specialism) MA/MSc/PGCert, Education MA, Higher Education MA, Leading Inclusive Education MA, PGCE Secondary Education Science with Chemistry, Higher Education PGCert, School Direct (QTS), PGCE Secondary Education Science with Physics, PGCE Secondary Education (Geography with Humanities), Translation (Business and Legal) MA/PGDip, Postgraduate Teacher Apprenticeship (with QTS) Primary or Secondary, Early Years Initial Teacher Training Assessment Only Route, PGCE Secondary Education (History with

Humanities), Teaching PGCert, Novel Writing (Online Distance Learning) MA, PGCE Secondary Education Mathematics, PGCE Primary Education with QTS

Department of Mental Health and Social Work

Social Work BA(Hons), Professional Practice (Negotiated Specialism) BA/BSc/GradCert, Nursing (Mental Health) BSc(Hons), Mental Health Nursing (Professional Practice) (Top-up) BSc(Hons)

Postgraduate: Advanced Professional Practice (Negotiated Specialism) MA/MSc/PGCert, Advanced Social Work Practice (Practice Education) PGCert, Advanced Social Work Practice MA/PGDip/PGCert, Social Work (Top-up) MA, Social Work MA, Social Work PGDip, Nursing (Mental Health) (Pre-registration programme) PGDip, Mental Health Studies (Top-up) MSc, Mental Health and Substance Use (Dual Diagnosis) MSc, Mental Health Studies MSc/PgDip, Healthcare Studies PGCert, Advanced Professional Practice (Negotiated Specialism) MA/MSc/PGCert

Faculty of Science and Technology

Department of Natural Sciences

Environmental Health (Apprenticeship) BSc (Honours), Public Health BSc, Occupational Safety and Health Management (Top-up) BSc(Hons), Biology (Environmental Biology) (Year 2 and Year 3 Entry) BSc(Hons), Medical Physiology BSc(Hons), Biology BSc/MScim Healthcare Science (Cardiac Physiology) (Degree Apprenticeship) BSc, Pharmaceutical Chemistry BSc/MSci, Biology (Environmental Biology) (Year 2 and Year 3 Entry) BSc(Hons), Environmental Health (Apprenticeship) BSc (Honours), Environmental Science BSc/MSci, Neuroscience BSc(Hons), Biology (Biotechnology) (Year 2 and Year 3 Entry) BSc(Hons), Environmental Health BSc(Hons), Healthcare Science (Neurophysiology) BSc(Hons), Biochemistry BSc(Hons), Healthcare Science (Cardiac Physiology) BSc(Hons), Biology (Molecular Biology) (Year 2 and Year 3 Entry) BSc(Hons), Biology (Year 2 and Year 3 Entry) BSc(Hons), Healthcare Science (Audiology) BSc(Hons), Nutrition BSc, Occupational Safety and Health Management (Top-up) BSc(Hons), Biomedical Engineering BEng/MEng

Postgraduate: Environmental Health MSc, Biodiversity, Evolution and Conservation in Action MSc/PGDip, Biomedical Science (Medical Microbiology) MSc/PGDip/PGCert, Biomedical Science (Clinical Biochemistry) MSc/PGDip/PGCert, Cancer Biomarkers and Therapeutics MSc/PGDip/PGCert, Cardiac Rhythm Management and Electrophysiology MSc/PGDip/PGCert, Biodiversity, Evolution and Conservation in Action MSc/PGDip, Evolutionary Behavioural Science MSc by Research, Occupational Health, Safety and Wellbeing Management MSc/PGDip, Sustainability and Environmental Management MSc, Clinical Physiology (Neurophysiology) MSc/PGDip, Cardiac Ultrasound MSc/PGDip/PGCert, Pharmaceutical Management MBA, Environmental Health MSc, Clinical Physiology (Cardiology) MSc/PGDip, Occupational Health and Safety and Environmental Management MSc/PGDip, Biomedical Science (Haematology and Transfusion Science) MSc/PGDip/PGCert, Biology and Biomedical Sciences MPhil/PhD, Applied Genomics MSc, Oncology MSc by Research, Public Health MSc/PGDip, Medical Biochemistry BSc/Clinical Biochemistry MSci

Department of Computer Science

Information Systems (Top-up) (Online Distance Learning) BSc, Professional Practice in Digital Technology (IT Consultancy) (Degree Apprenticeship) BSc, Computer Networks BSc, Computer Science BSc/MComp, Professional Practice in Digital Technology (Business Analytics) (Degree Apprenticeship) BSc, Computer Networks BSc, Professional Practice in Digital Technology (Network Engineering) Degree Apprenticeship BSc, Business Information Systems BSc/MComp, Information Systems (Top-up) (Online Distance Learning) BSc, Information Technology BSc/MComp, Computer Science BSc/MComp

Postgraduate: Engineering and Computing MSc by Research, Electronic Security and Digital Forensics MSc, Information Technology BSc/MComp, Mathematics with Computing BSc/MSci, Cyber Security and Pen Testing MSc with Integrated Placement (15 months/24 months), Cybercrime and Digital Investigation MSc, Visual Analytics MSc by Research, Cybercrime and Digital Investigation MSc, Electronic Security and Digital Forensics MSc, Cooperative Intelligent Transport Systems MSc, Computer Science MSc with Integrated Placement (15 months/24 months), Engineering and Computing MSc by Research, Ambient Assisted Living MSc by Research, Computer Science MSc, Data Science MSc by Research, Data Science MSc

Department of Design Engineering and Mathematics

Computer Systems Engineering BEng/MEng, Architectural Technology BSc(Hons), Robotics BEng/MEng, Product Design Engineering BEng/MEng,

Product Design BA Mathematics BSc/MMath, Computer Systems Engineering BEng/MEng, Electronic Engineering BEng/MEng, Design Engineering BEng/MEng, Robotics BEng/MEng, Product Design Engineering BEng/MEng

Postgraduate: Mechatronic Systems Engineering MSc, Applied Statistics MSc/PGDip, Operational Research MSc/PGDip, Robotics MSc/PGDip/PGCert, Engineering Management MSc with Integrated Placement (15 months/24 months), Financial Mathematics MSc/PGDip, Mechatronic Systems Engineering MSc

Department of Design Engineering and Mathematics

Mechatronics BEng/MEng, Mathematics BSc/MMath, Product Design BA, Product Design Engineering BEng/MEng, Architectural Technology BSc(Hons), Electronic Engineering BEng/MEng, Computer Communication and Networks (Year 2 and Year 3 Entry) BEng/MEng, Computer Systems Engineering BEng/MEng, Electronic Engineering BEng/MEng, Mechatronics BEng/MEng

Postgraduate: Engineering Management MSc, Operational Research MSc/PGDip, Mechatronic Systems Engineering MSc, Engineering Management MSc with Integrated Placement (15 months/24 months), Building Information Modelling Management and Integrated Digital Delivery MSc/PGDip/PGCert,

Applied Statistics MSc/PGDip, Financial Mathematics MSc/PGDip, Robotics MSc/PGDip/PGCert

Department of Psychology

Psychology BSc(Hons), Psychology with Counselling Skills BSc(Hons), Psychology with Criminology BSc(Hons), Psychology with Education BSc(Hons), Psychology with Neuroscience BSc(Hons)

Postgraduate: Applied Psychology MSc, Cognitive Neuroscience MSc by Research, Forensic Psychology MSc, Health Psychology MSc, Psychological Therapies and Interventions MSc/PGDip, Psychology Conversion MSc, Psychology, Health and Wellbeing MSc, Visual and Arts-based Methods MSc by Research

London Sport Institute

Sport and Exercise Rehabilitation BSc(Hons), Football Science (Top-up) BSc(Hons), Sport and Exercise Science BSc(Hons), Sport and Exercise Science (Physical Education and Coaching) BSc(Hons), Sport and Exercise Science (Strength and Conditioning) BSc(Hons)

Postgraduate: Strength and Conditioning MSc, Sport Performance Analysis MSc, Sport, Exercise and Physical Activity for Special Populations MSc, Sport Rehabilitation MSc/PGDip, Sport, Exercise and Physical Activity for Special Populations MSc, Sport and Exercise Psychology / Sport and Exercise Psychology (BPS Accredited) MSc

UNIVERSITY OF NEWCASTLE UPON TYNE
www.ncl.ac.uk

Accounting and Finance

Accounting and Finance BA/BSc(Hons), Mathematics and Accounting BSc(Hons), Business Accounting and Finance BA(Hons)

Postgraduate: Accounting, Finance and Strategic Investment MSc, Banking and Finance MSc, Banking and Finance MSc (London campus), Finance and Accounting MPhil, PhD, Finance and Accounting PhD (London campus), Finance and Economics (Research) MA, Finance MSc, International Economics and Finance MSc, International Financial Analysis MSc, Quantitative Finance and Risk Management MSc

Agri-Business Management

Agri-Business Management BSc(Hons), Food Business Management and Marketing BSc(Hons)

Agriculture

Agri-Business Management BSc(Hons), Agriculture BSc(Hons), Agriculture with Agronomy BSc(Hons), Agriculture with Animal Production Science BSc(Hons), Agriculture with Farm Business Management BSc(Hons), Applied Plant Science BSc(Hons)

Postgraduate courses: Agricultural and Environmental Science MSc, Agriculture MPhil, PhD, Animal Behaviour MRes, Animal Science MPhil, PhD, Biodiversity Conservation and Ecosystem Management MSc, Food and Rural Development Research MSc, Rural Studies MPhil, PhD, Sustainable Agriculture and Food Security MRes/MSc

Ancient History

Ancient History BA(Hons), Ancient History and Archaeology BA(Hons)

Animal Science

Animal Science BSc(Hons)

Postgraduate courses: Agricultural and Environmental Science MSc, Animal Behaviour MRes

Archaeology

Ancient History and Archaeology BA(Hons), Archaeology BA(Hons)/BSc(Hons), History and Archaeology BA(Hons), Combined Honours BA(Hons)

Postgraduate courses: Archaeology MA, Archaeology MLitt, Archaeology MPhil, PhD, Cultural Property Protection MLitt

Architecture

Architecture BA(Hons), Architecture and Urban Planning BA(Hons), Urban Planning BA(Hons), Master of Planning MPlan, Geography and Planning BA(Hons)

Postgraduate courses: Advanced Architectural Design (MSc), Architecture, Master of (MArch), Urban Energy Technology and Policy (MRes), Landscape Architecture Studies MA, Planning and Environment Research MA, Regional Development and Spatial Planning MA/PGDip, Spatial Planning PGDip, Urban Design MA/PGDip, Urban Planning MSc

Biochemistry

Biochemistry BSc(Hons), Biochemistry (Integrated Master??s) MSci Honours

Biology and Zoology

Applied Plant Science BSc(Hons), Biology BSc(Hons), Biology MBiol Honours, Biology (Cellular and Molecular Biology) BSc(Hons), Biology (Cellular and Molecular Biology) MBiol Honours, Biology (Ecology and Conservation) BSc(Hons), Biology (Ecology and Conservation) MBiol Honours, Biology and Psychology BSc Joint Honours, Dietetics MDiet Honours, Zoology BSc(Hons), Zoology MBiol Honours

Postgraduate courses: Biology MPhil, PhD Biotechnology and Biodesign MRes Computational Ecology MSc, Ecological Consultancy MSc, Ecology and Wildlife Conservation MSc Environmental Geoscience MRes Global Wildlife Science and Policy MSc, Industrial and Commercial Biotechnology MSc, Wildlife Management MSc

Biomedical and Biomolecular Sciences

Biochemistry BSc(Hons), Biochemistry (Integrated Master's) MSci Honours, Biomedical Genetics BSc(Hons), Biomedical Genetics (Integrated Master's) MSci Honours, Biomedical Sciences BSc(Hons), Biomedical Sciences (Integrated Master's) MSci Honours, Medical Science (Deferred Choice) BSc(Hons), Pharmacology BSc(Hons), Physiological Sciences BSc(Hons)

Postgraduate courses: Ageing and Health MRes, Clinical and Health Sciences with Ageing MSc/PGDip/PGCert, Clinical Research/Clinical Research (Ageing) MClinRes, PGDip/PGCert, Medical Sciences MSc, Musculoskeletal Ageing (CIMA) MRes, Systems Biology MRes, Cardiovascular Science in Health and Disease MRes, Cell Signalling in Health and Disease MRes, Clinical and Health Sciences with Clinical Research MSc/PGDip/PGCert, Clinical and Health Sciences with Molecular Pathology MSc/PGDip/PGCert, Clinical and Health Sciences MSc/PGDip/PGCert, Clinical and Health Sciences with Allergy PGCert, Clinical and Health Sciences with Therapeutics MSc/PGDip/PGCert, Clinical and Health Sciences with Ageing MSc/PGDip/PGCert, Clinical Research/Clinical Research (Ageing) MClinRes/PGDip/PGCert (E-learning), Clinical Research/Clinical Research (Leadership) MClinRes/PGDip/PGCert, Clinical Science (pathways in Medical Physics and Physiological Sciences) MSc, Diabetes MRes, Immunobiology MRes, Medical Sciences MRes/MSc, Medical Technology Innovation MRes, Mitochondrial Biology and Medicine MRes, Musculoskeletal Ageing (CIMA) MRes, Stem Cells and Regenerative Medicine MRes, Systems Biology MRes, Toxicology MRes, Translational Medicine and Therapeutics MRes, Transplantation MRes/PGCert, Biosciences MRes, Medical and Molecular Biosciences MRes, Medical Sciences MRes/MSc, Molecular Microbiology MRes, Systems Biology MRes, Biotechnology and Business Enterprise MRes, Industrial and Commercial Biotechnology MSc, Medical Technology Innovation MRes, Cancer MRes, Cancer Studies PGCert, Medical Sciences MSc, Oncology MSc/PGDip, Oncology for the Pharmaceutical Industry MSc/PGDip, Palliative Care MSc/PGDip, Stem Cells and Regenerative Medicine MRes, Medical Education MMedEd/PGDip/PGCert, Physician Associate Studies PGDip, Biofabrication and Bioprinting MRes Drug Delivery and Nanomedicine MRes Nanoscale Science and Technology MPhil, PhD

Business Management

Agri-Business Management BSc(Hons), Business Management BA(Hons), Economics and Business Management BA(Hons), Food Business Management and Marketing BSc(Hons), International Business Management BSc(Hons), International Marketing and Management BSc(Hons), Marketing and Management BSc(Hons)

Postgraduate courses: Accounting, Finance and Strategic Investment MSc, Advanced International Business Management and Marketing (Dual Award) MSc/MSc, Advanced International Business Management (Dual Award) MSc/MSc, Arts, Business and Creativity MA, Business and Humanities Graduate Diploma, Business and Humanities Graduate Diploma with Pre-Sessional English, Cross-Cultural Communication and International Management MA, E-Business (E-Marketing) MSc, E-Business (Information Systems) MSc, E-Business MSc, Employee Relations MA/PGDip/PGCert, Global Human Resource Management MSc, Human Resource Management MA, Innovation, Creativity and Entrepreneurship MSc, International Business Management MSc, International Human Resource Management MA, International Marketing MSc, Management and Business Studies (Research) MA/PGDip, Master of Business Administration MBA, Operations Management (Dual Award) MSc/MSc, Operations Management, Logistics and Accounting MSc, Operations, Logistics and Supply Chain Management MSc

Chemical Engineering

Chemical Engineering BEng Honours, Chemical Engineering MEng Honours, Chemical Engineering with Bioprocess Engineering MEng Honours, Chemical Engineering with Industry MEng Honours, Chemical Engineering with Process Control MEng Honours, Chemical Engineering with Sustainable Engineering MEng Honours

Postgraduate courses: Applied Process Control MSc/PGDip, Biotechnology and Biodesign MRes, Chemical Engineering MSc, Clean Technology MSc/PGDip, Materials Design and Engineering MSc Process Safety and Risk Management MSc Sustainable Chemical Engineering MSc/PGDip

Chemistry

Chemistry BSc/MChem Honours, Chemistry with Medicinal Chemistry BSc/MChem Honours

Postgraduate courses: Chemistry MSc, Drug Chemistry MSc

Civil Engineering

Civil Engineering BEng/MEng Honours, Civil and Structural Engineering BEng/MEng Honours

Postgraduate courses: Environmental Engineering MSc, Engineering Geology MSc, Geotechnical Engineering MSc, Structural Engineering MSc, Business and Humanities Graduate Diploma, Transport PGDip, Transport Planning and Business Management MSc, Transport Planning and Engineering MSc, Transport Planning and Intelligent Transport Systems (ITS) MSc, Transport Planning and Modelling MSc, Transport Planning and the Environment MSc, Flood Risk Management MSc, Hydrogeology and Water Management MSc, Hydroinformatics MSc, Hydroinformatics and Water Management (Euro Aquae) MSc, Hydrology and Climate Change MSc

Classics and Ancient History

Ancient History BA(Hons), Ancient History and Archaeology BA(Hons), Classical Studies BA(Hons), Classical Studies and English BA(Hons), Classics BA(Hons)

Postgraduate course: Classics and Ancient History MA/MPhil/PhD, Classics MLitt. Cultural Property Protection MLitt

Computing Science

Computer Science BSc/MComp Honours, Computer Science (Game Engineering) BSc/MComp Honours, Computer Science (Security and Resilience) BSc/MComp Honours, Computer Science (Software Engineering) BSc/MComp Honours

Postgraduate course: Advanced Computer Science MSc, Bioinformatics MSc, Cloud Computing for Big Data MRes/PGDip, Cloud Computing MSc, Computational Neuroscience and Neuroinformatics MSc, Computer Game Engineering MSc, Computer Science MSc, Computer Security and Resilience MSc, Computer Security and Resilience MSc, Data Science (with Specialisation in Statistics) MSc, PGDip, PGCert Data Science MSc, PGDip, PGCert Digital and Technology Solutions (Cyber Security Specialist) MSc (Specialist Integrated Degree Apprenticeship) Digital and Technology Solutions (Data Analytics Specialist) MSc (Specialist Integrated Degree Apprenticeship), Digital Civics MRes, E-Business (Information Systems) MSc, E-Business MSc, Synthetic Biology MSc

Dentistry

Dental Surgery BDS Honours, Oral and Dental Health Sciences BSc(Hons)

Postgraduate courses: Clinical Implant Dentistry PGDip, Conscious Sedation in Dentistry PGDip, Dentistry and Dental Sciences MPhil, PhD Orthodontics MSc, Restorative Dentistry MClinDent

Economics

Economics BSc(Hons), Economics and Business Management BA(Hons), Economics and Finance

BSc(Hons), Mathematics and Economics BSc Joint Honours, Politics and Economics BA(Hons)

Postgraduate course: International Economics and Finance MSc, Economics MPhil, PhD, Economics PhD (London campus), Finance and Economics (Research) MA

Education

Education BA(Hons)

Postgraduate courses: Applied Educational Psychology Doctor of (DAppEdPsy), Business and Humanities Graduate Diploma, Coaching and Mentoring for Teacher Development PGCert, Cross-Cultural Communication and Education MA, Education (Clinical) MPhil, PhD Education and Communication Integrated PhD Education Doctor of (EdD) Education MPhil, PhD Education Research MA, Education: International Perspectives (Development and Education) MA, Education: International Perspectives (Leadership and Management) MA, Education: International Perspectives (Teaching and Learning) MA, Education: International Perspectives (Technology in Education) MA, Educational Leadership PGCert, Educational Research and Innovation PGCert, International Development and Education with Cross Cultural Communication MA, International Development and Education MA, Medical Education MMedEd/PGDip/PGCert, Physician Associate Studies PGDip, Postgraduate Certificate in Education (PGCE) – School Direct, Postgraduate Certificate in Education (PGCE) Primary (with Qualified Teacher Status QTS), Postgraduate Certificate in Education (PGCE) Secondary (with Qualified Teacher Status QTS), Practitioner Enquiry MEd, Practitioner Enquiry (Leadership) Med

Electrical and Electronic Engineering

Automation and Control BEng/MEng Honours, Digital Electronics BEng/MEng Honours, Electrical and Electronic Engineering BEng/MEng Honours, Electrical Power Engineering BEng/MEng Honours, Electronic Communications BEng/MEng Honours, Electronics and Computer Engineering BEng/MEng Honours, Microelectronic Engineering BEng/MEng Honours

Postgraduate courses: Advanced Electrical Power Engineering MSc, Automation and Control MSc, Communications and Signal Processing MSc, Electrical and Electronic Engineering PhD, Electrical Power MSc, Electrical Power Engineering MSc, Embedded Systems and Internet of Things (ES-IoT) MSc, Microelectronics MSc, Power Distribution Engineering MSc/PGDip/PGCert, Smart Systems Engineering MSc

English Literature, Language and Linguistics

Classical Studies and English BA(Hons), Combined Honours BA(Hons), English Literature and History BA(Hons), English Language BA(Hons), English Language and Literature BA(Hons), English Literature BA(Hons), English Literature with Creative Writing BA(Hons), Linguistics BA(Hons), Linguistics with Chinese or Japanese BA(Hons), Linguistics with French BA(Hons), Linguistics with German BA(Hons), Linguistics with Spanish BA(Hons), Modern Languages and Linguistics BA(Hons)

Postgraduate courses: Creative Writing MA/PGCert/MPhil/PhD, Writing Poetry MA, English Language and/or Linguistics MLitt, English Literature MA/MLitt, English Literature MPhil, PhD Applied Linguistics and TESOL MA, Applied Linguistics Research MA, Clinical Linguistics and Evidence Based Practice (Research) MSc/PGDip, Cross-Cultural Communication and Applied Linguistics MA, English Language and/or Linguistics MLitt, Linguistics (with specialist pathways in English Language, Language Acquisition, and European Languages) MA, Sociolinguistics (Research) MA/PGDip

Environmental and Rural Studies

Countryside Management BSc(Hons), Environmental Science BSc(Hons), Environmental Sciences (Agricultural and Environmental Science) MEnvSci, Environmental Sciences (Clean Technology) MEnvSci Honours, Environmental Sciences (Ecosystem Management) MEnvSci Honours, Environmental Sciences (Environmental Geochemistry) MEnvSci Honours, Rural Studies BSc(Hons)

Postgraduate courses: Biodiversity Conservation and Ecosystem Management MSc, Computational Ecology MSc, Ecological Consultancy MSc, Ecology and Wildlife Conservation MSc, Environmental Consultancy MSc, Environmental Geoscience MRes, Environmental Science MPhil PhD, Global Wildlife Science and Policy MSc, Wildlife Management MSc, Geochemistry MPhil, PhD, Petroleum Geochemistry MSc

Exercise

Sport and Exercise Science BSc(Hons)

Film Studies

Combined Honours BA(Hons), Film and Media BA(Hons), Film Practices BA(Hons)

Postgraduate courses: Film Studies PhD/MLitt, Film: Theory and Practice MA

Fine Art

Fine Art BA(Hons)

Postgraduate course: Fine Art MFA, Fine Art MPhil, PhD

Genetics

Biomedical Genetics BSc(Hons), Biomedical Genetics (Integrated Master's) MSci Honours

Postgraduate courses: Genetics MPhil, PhD, MD Medical Genetics MRes, Mitochondrial Biology and Medicine MRes, Neuromuscular Diseases MRes, Stem Cells and Regenerative Medicine MRes

Geography

Geographic Information Science BSc(Hons), Geography BSc/BA(Hons), Geography and Planning BA(Hons), Physical Geography BSc(Hons), Surveying and Mapping Science BSc(Hons), Mapping and Geospatial Data Science MSci Honours, Physical Geography BSc(Hons)

Postgraduate courses: Environmental and Petroleum Geochemistry MSc, Environmental Consultancy MSc, Petroleum Geochemistry MSc, Business and Humanities Graduate Diploma, Human Geography Research MA, Local and Regional Development (Research) MA, Regional Development and Spatial Planning MA/PGDip

History

English Literature and History BA(Hons), History BA(Hons), History and Archaeology BA(Hons), Politics and History BA(Hons)

Postgraduate courses: British History MA, Classics and Ancient History MA/ MPhil/ PhD, Classics MLitt, Cultural Property Protection MLitt, European History MA, History MA/MLitt, History MLitt, History of Medicine MA

Journalism

Journalism, Media and Culture BA(Hons)

Postgraduate course: International Multimedia Journalism MA, Journalism and Public Relations PhD

Law

Law LLB Honours

Postgraduate courses: Business and Humanities Graduate Diploma, Environmental Law and Policy (Research) LLM, International Commercial Law LLM, International Law LLM, Law and Society (Legal Research) LLM, Law LLM, Law LLM (by research), MPhil, PhD

Linguistics

Linguistics BA(Hons), Linguistics with Chinese or Japanese BA(Hons), Linguistics with French/German/ Spanish BA(Hons), Modern languages and Linguistics BA(Hons)

Postgraduate courses: Applied Linguistics and TESOL MA, Applied Linguistics Research MA, Clinical Linguistics and Evidence Based Practice (Research) MSc, PGDip, Cross-Cultural Communication and Applied Linguistics MA, Educational and Applied Linguistics Integrated PhD, English Language and/or Linguistics MLitt, Linguistics (with specialist pathways in English Language and Language Acquisition) MA, Linguistics and English Language Integrated PhD, Linguistics, Applied Linguistics MPhil, PhD, Sociolinguistics (Research) MA, PGDip

Marine Sciences

Marine Biology BSc(Hons), Marine Zoology BSc(Hons)

Postgraduate courses: Environmental Geoscience MRes, International Marine Environmental Consultancy (IMEC) MSc, PGDip, Marine Ecosystems and Governance MRes, Marine Sciences MPhil, PhD

Marine Technology

Marine Technology with Marine Engineering BEng/ MEng Honours, Marine Technology with Naval Architecture BEng/MEng Honours, Marine Technology with Offshore Engineering BEng/MEng Honours, Marine Technology with Small Craft Technology BEng/MEng Honours

Postgraduate courses: Engineering and Science in the Marine Environment Integrated PhD Marine Engineering MSc, Marine Technology Education Consortium (MTEC) MSc/PGDip/PGCert, Marine Technology MPhil, PhD, Marine Technology MSc, Marine Transport Management MSc, Naval Architecture MSc, Offshore Engineering MSc, Pipeline Engineering MSc/PGDip/PGCert, Subsea Engineering and Management MSc, Technology in the Marine Environment MRes

Marketing

Food Business Management and Marketing BSc(Hons), International Marketing and Management BSc(Hons), Marketing BSc(Hons), Marketing and Management BSc(Hons), Nutrition with Food Marketing BSc(Hons)

Postgraduate courses: Advanced International Business Management and Marketing (Dual Award) MSc/ MSc, Business and Humanities Graduate Diploma Business and Humanities Graduate Diploma with Pre-Sessional English, Cross-Cultural Communication and International Marketing MA, E-Business (E-

Marketing) MSc, International Marketing MSc, International Marketing MSc (London campus), Marketing MPhil, PhD

Mathematics and Statistics

Mathematics and Accounting BSc(Hons), Mathematics and Economics BSc(Hons), Mathematical Sciences with Foundation Year BSc(Hons), Mathematics BSc/MMath Honours, Mathematics and Statistics BSc/MMath Honours, Mathematics with Business BSc(Hons), Mathematics with Finance BSc(Hons), Statistics BSc(Hons), Psychology and Mathematics BSc Joint Honours
Postgraduate: Data Science (with Specialisation in Statistics) MSc, PGDip, PGCert Data Science MSc, PGDip, PGCert Digital and Technology Solutions (Cyber Security Specialist) MSc (Specialist Integrated Degree Apprenticeship) Digital and Technology Solutions (Data Analytics Specialist) MSc (Specialist Integrated Degree Apprenticeship) Mathematics MPhil, PhD, Statistics MPhil, PhD

Mechanical and Systems Engineering

Mechanical Design and Manufacturing Engineering BEng/MEng Honours, Mechanical Engineering BEng/MEng Honours, Mechanical Engineering with Biomedical Engineering MEng Honours, Mechanical Engineering with Mechatronics MEng Honours, Mechanical Engineering with Energy MEng Honours, Sustainable Transport Engineering MEng Honours
Postgraduate courses: Renewable Energy, Enterprise and Management (REEM) MSc/PGDip/PGCert, Renewable Energy Flexible Training Programme (REFLEX) MSc/PGDip/PGCert, Urban Energy Technology and Policy MRes, Energy and Sustainability MSc Energy MPhil, PhD, Biomedical Engineering MSc, Design and Manufacturing Engineering MSc, Digital and Technology Solutions (Cyber Security Specialist) MSc (Specialist Integrated Degree Apprenticeship), Mechanical and Systems Engineering MPhil, PhD, Mechanical Engineering MSc, Mechatronics MSc, Rail and Logistics MSc/PGDip/PGCert, Smart Systems Engineering MSc, Sustainable Transport Engineering MSc

Media, Communication and Cultural Studies

Film and Media BA(Hons), Film Practices BA(Hons), Journalism, Media and Culture BA(Hons), Media, Communication and Cultural Studies BA(Hons)
Postgraduate courses: Creative Arts Practice MA, Cross-Cultural Communication and Media Studies MA, Cultural Property Protection MLitt, Media and Cultural Studies MPhil, PhD, Media and Journalism MA, Media and Public Relations MA, Media and Society (Research) MA, Digital Media PhD

Medicine

Medicine and Surgery MB BS Honours, Medical Science (Deferred Choice) BSc, Medicine and Surgery (Accelerated Programme) MB BS
Postgraduate courses: Cardiovascular Science in Health and Disease MRes, Clinical and Health Sciences with Clinical Research MSc/PGDip/PGCert, Clinical and Health Sciences with Molecular Pathology MSc/PGDip/PGCert, Clinical and Health Sciences MSc/PGDip/PGCert, Clinical and Health Sciences with Allergy PGCert, Clinical and Health Sciences with Surgery PGCert, Clinical and Health Sciences with Therapeutics MSc/PGDip/PGCert, Clinical and Health Sciences with Ageing MSc/PGDip/PGCert, Clinical Leadership PGCert, Clinical Research/Clinical Research (Ageing) MClinRes/PGDip/PGCert (E-learning), Clinical Research/Clinical Research (Leadership) MClinRes/PGDip/PGCert, Medicine and Surgery MPhil, PhD, MD, Neuromuscular Diseases MRes, Physician Associate Studies PGDip, Translational Medicine and Therapeutics MRes, Transplantation MRes, Epidemiology MRes, Health Services Research MSc/PGDip, Public Health MPH/PGDip, Public Health and Health Services Research MSc/PGDip/PGCert, Social Science and Health Research MSc, Cancer MPhil, PhD, MD, Cancer MRes, Cancer Studies PGCert, Medical Sciences MSc, Oncology for the Pharmaceutical Industry MSc, PGDip, PGCert, Oncology MSc, PGDip, PGCert, Palliative Care MSc, PGDip, PGCert, Regenerative Medicine and Stem Cells MRes, Global Public Health MSc, PGDip, Public Health, Epidemiology and Health Services Research MPhil, PhD, MD

Modern Languages

Chinese Studies OR Japanese Studies BA(Hons), Modern Languages BA(Hons), Modern Languages and Business Studies BA(Hons), Modern Languages and Linguistics BA(Hons), Modern Languages, Translation and Interpreting; Spanish, Portuguese and Latin American Studies BA(Hons)
Postgraduate courses: Chinese Studies MLitt, French MLitt, German MLitt, Japanese Studies MLitt, Latin American Interdisciplinary Studies MA, Latin American Studies MLitt, Modern Languages MPhil, PhD, Portuguese MLitt, Professional Translation for European Languages MA, Spanish MLitt

Music

Contemporary and Popular Music BA(Hons), Folk and Traditional Music BA(Hons), Music BA/BMus Honours

Postgraduate courses: Music Graduate Diploma, Music MLitt/MMus/PhD

Nutrition and Food

Dietetics MDiet Honours, Food and Human Nutrition BSc(Hons), Food Business Management and Marketing BSc(Hons), Nutrition and Psychology BSc Joint Honours, Nutrition with Food Marketing BSc(Hons), Psychology and Nutrition BSc Joint Honours

Postgraduate courses: Security MRes/MSc, Biosciences MPhil, PhD, MD, Food and Human Nutrition MPhil, PhD, Food and Rural Development Research MSc, Food and Society MPhil, PhD, Food Packaging PGCert, Sustainable Agriculture and Food Security MRes, Sustainable Agriculture and Food Security MSc

Pharmacology

Pharmacology BSc(Hons)

Pharmacy

Pharmacy MPharm Honours

Postgraduate courses: Drug Delivery and Nanomedicine MRes, Pharmacy MPhil, PhD, MD, Toxicology MRes

Philosophy

Philosophy BA(Hons)

Postgraduate course: Philosophy MLitt/PhD/MPhil

Physics

Physics BSc/MPhys Honours, Physics with Astrophysics BSc(Hons)/ MPhys Hons, Theoretical Physics BSc/MPhys Honours

Postgraduate course: Physics MRes/PhD/MPhil

Physiological Sciences

Physiological Sciences BSc(Hons)

Politics

Government and European Union Studies BA(Hons), International Relations Politics BA(Hons), Politics and Economics BA(Hons), Politics and History BA(Hons), Politics and Sociology BA(Hons)

Postgraduate courses: Cross-Cultural Communication and International Relations MA, Cultural Property Protection MLitt, European Union Studies MA, International Politics (Global Justice and Ethics) MA, International Politics (Globalisation, Poverty and Development) MA, International Development and Education MA, International, Political Economy MA,

International Politics (Critical Geopolitics) MA, International Relations MA, Politics (Research) MA, Politics MPhil, PhD, World Politics and Popular Culture MA

Psychology

Psychology BSc(Hons), Psychology and Biology BSc Joint Honours, Psychology and Mathematics BSc Joint Honours, Psychology and Nutrition BSc Joint Honours, Psychology and Sport and Exercise Science BSc Joint Honours

Postgraduate courses: Animal Behaviour MRes, Applied Educational Psychology Doctor of (DAppEdPsy), Clinical Psychology Doctor of (DClinPsy), Cognitive Behavioural Therapy for Anxiety Disorders PGCert, Cognitive Behavioural Therapy PGDip, Evolution and Human Behaviour MRes, Forensic Psychology MSc, Forensic Psychology Practice PGDip, Foundations in Clinical Psychology MSc, Low Intensity Psychological Therapies PGCert, Neuroscience MRes, Psychology MPhil, PhD

Sociology

Sociology BA(Hons), Politics and Sociology BA(Hons)

Postgraduate courses: Sociology and Social Research MA, Sociology MA, Sociology MPhil, PhD

Speech and Language Sciences

Speech and Language Sciences MSc, Honours, Speech and Language Therapy BSc(Hons)

Postgraduate course: Clinical Linguistics and Evidence Based Practice (Research) MSc/PGDip, Language Pathology MSc, Phonetics and Phonology Integrated PhD, Speech and Language Sciences MPhil, PhD

Sport and Exercise Science

Psychology and Sport and Exercise Science BSc Joint Honours, Sport and Exercise Science BSc(Hons)

Surveying and Mapping Science

Geospatial Surveying and Mapping BEng Honours, Mapping and geospatial data Science MSci Honours/ BSC Honours

Postgraduate course: Master of Planning MPlan Honours

TESOL, Cross-Cultural Communication, Translating and Intrepreting

Postgraduate courses: Applied Linguistics and TESOL MA, Cross-Cultural Communication and Applied Linguistics MA, Cross-Cultural Communication and Education MA, Cross-Cultural Communication and Media Studies MA, Cross-Cultural

Communication and International Marketing MA, Cross-Cultural Communication and International Relations MA, Cross-Cultural Communication and International Management MA, Cross-Cultural Communication MA, Educational and Applied Linguistics Integrated PhD, International Development and Education with Cross Cultural Communication MA, Interpreting MA, Professional Translation for

European Languages MA, Translating and Interpreting MA, Translating MA, Translation Studies MA, Translation Studies MLitt

Zoology
Marine Zoology BSc(Hons), Zoology BSc/MBiol Honours

UNIVERSITY OF NORTHAMPTON
www.northampton.ac.uk

Advertising and Marketing
Advertising (Joint Honours) BA/BSc(Hons), Advertising & Digital Marketing BA(Hons), Marketing (Joint Honours) BA/BSc(Hons), Marketing and Advertising (Joint Honours) BA, Marketing and Business (Joint Honours) BA(Hons), Marketing and Events Management (Joint Honours) BA(Hons), Marketing and Management (Joint Honours) BA(Hons), Marketing Management (Top-Up) BA(Hons), Marketing Management BSc(Hons), Psychology and Marketing (Joint Honours) BA(Hons)
Postgraduate: International Marketing Strategy MSc

Art and Design
Architectural Technology BSc(Hons), Fine Art BA(Hons), Fine Art Painting and Drawing BA(Hons), Graphic Communication BA(Hons), Illustration BA(Hons), Interior Architecture & Spatial Design BA(Hons), Product Design BSc(Hons), Product Design HND
Postgraduate: Fine Art MA

Biological Sciences
Biology BSc(Hons), Biomedical Science BSc(Hons), Human Bioscience BSc(Hons), Infection Control (University Certificate)
Postgraduate: Molecular Bioscience MSc

Business Studies & Entrepreneurship
Business (Joint Honours) BA/BSc(Hons), Business and Accounting (Joint Honours) BA(Hons), Business and Business Entrepreneurship (Joint Honours) BA(Hons), Business and Management (Top-Up) BA(Hons), Business Entrepreneurship (Joint Honours) BA/BSc(Hons), Business Entrepreneurship (Top-up) BA(Hons), Business Entrepreneurship BA(Hons), Business Entrepreneurship FdA, Business HND, Business Studies BA(Hons), International Business BA(Hons), International Business Communications (Top-Up) BA(Hons), Marketing and

Business (Joint Honours) BA(Hons), Psychology and Business (Joint Honours) BA(Hons), Sports Studies and Business (Joint Honours) BA(Hons)
Postgraduate: Business Analytics MSc, Social Innovation MA

Computing
Business Computing (Systems) BSc(Hons), Business Computing (Web Design) BSc(Hons), Business Computing (Web Design) HND, Computing (Computer Networks Engineering) BEng(Hons), Computing (Computer Networks Engineering) BEng(Hons) / MEng, Computing (Computer Systems Engineering) BEng(Hons), Computing (Computer Systems Engineering) BEng / MEng, Computing (Graphics and Visualisation) BSc(Hons), Computing (Mobile Computing) BSc(Hons), Computing (Software Engineering) BSc(Hons), Computing (Web Technology and Security) BSc(Hons), Computing (Web Technology and Security) BSc(Hons), Computing BSc(Hons), Games Art BA(Hons), Games Design BA(Hons), Games Programming BSc(Hons)
Postgraduate: Computing (Software Engineering) MSc, Computing (Web Technology and Security) MSc, Computing MSc, Computing (Computer Networks Engineering) MSc

Economics, Accounting and Finance
Accounting (Joint Honours) BA/BSc(Hons), Accounting and Finance BSc(Hons), Banking and Financial Planning BSc(Hons), Business and Accounting (Joint Honours) BA(Hons), Economics (Joint Honours) BA/BSc(Hons), Economics and Accounting (Joint Honours) BA/BSc(Hons), Economics and Business (Joint Honours) BA/BSc(Hons), Economics BSc(Hons), International Accounting (Top-Up) BSc(Hons), International Banking and Finance (Top-Up) BSc(Hons)

Postgraduate: Accounting and Finance (Top-up) MSc, Accounting and Finance MSc, Economics MSc, International Banking and Finance MSc

Education

Applied Social Care and Education Studies Joint Honours BA/BSc(Hons), Childhood and Youth BA(Hons), Early Childhood Studies (top-up) BA(Hons), Early Childhood Studies BA(Hons), Education Studies (Joint Honours) BA/BSc(Hons), Education Studies BA(Hons), International Education (Top-Up) BA(Hons), Learning and Teaching (top-up) BA(Hons), Psychology and Education Studies Joint Honours BA(Hons), Special Educational Needs and Inclusion BA(Hons), Sports Studies and Education Studies (Joint Honours)

Postgraduate: Education (Early Years Pathway) MA, Education (English Language Teaching) MA, Education (Leadership and Management) MA, Education (Mathematics Pathway) MA, Education MA, PGCE Top-up Primary/Early Years/Secondary, Postgraduate Certificate in Digital Leadership, Postgraduate Certificate Primary Mathematics, Postgraduate Certificate Secondary Mathematics Specialist Teacher Programme, Postgraduate Diploma in Specific Learning Difficulties and Inclusion, Pre-sessional English Programme (PEP) – Research Degrees, Special Educational Needs and Inclusion (Autism Pathway) MA, Special Educational Needs and Inclusion MA, The National Award for SEN Co-ordination PGCert

Engineering

Electrical and Electronic Engineering BEng(Hons) / MEng, Electromechanical Engineering BEng(Hons) / MEng, Engineering (top-up) BSc(Hons), Engineering BSc(Hons), Mechanical Engineering BEng(Hons) / MEng, Non-Destructive Testing (top-up) BSc(Hons)

Postgraduate: Advanced Industrial Practice (Non-Destructive Testing) MSc, Engineering MSc, Lift Engineering MSc

English

English (Joint Honours) BA(Hons), English and Drama Joint Honours BA(Hons), English and Education Studies (Joint Honours) BA(Hons), English BA(Hons), Multimedia Journalism and English (Joint Honours) BA(Hons), Psychology and English (Joint Honours) BA(Hons)

Postgraduate: English – Contemporary Literature MA

Environmental Sciences

Environmental Science BSc(Hons), Geography (Human Geography) BSc(Hons), Geography (Physical Geography) BSc(Hons), Geography BSc(Hons), Human Geography (Joint Honours) BA/BSc(Hons), Wastes Management (Top-up) BSc(Hons)

Postgraduate: Advanced Industrial Practice (Wastes Management) MSc, Managing Waste and Environmental Resources MSc

Events, Tourism and Hospitality

Events Management (Joint Honours) BA/BSc, Events Management and Business Entrepreneurship (Joint Honours) BA(Hons), Events Management BA(Hons), International Tourism Management (Joint Honours) BA/BSc(Hons), International Tourism Management (Top-Up) BA(Hons), International Tourism Management and Events Management (Joint Honours) BA(Hons), International Tourism Management BA(Hons), Live Event Production (Top-up) BA(Hons), Marketing and Events Management (Joint Honours) BA(Hons), Travel and Tourism Management HND

Postgraduate: International Hotel Management MA, International Special Events Management MSc, International Tourism Development MA

Fashion

Fashion (Textiles for Fashion) BA(Hons), Fashion BA(Hons), Fashion Marketing BA(Hons), Fashion Promotion and Communication BA(Hons), Footwear and Accessories BA(Hons), Leather for Fashion BA(Hons)

History, International Relations and Politics

History (Joint Honours) BA/BSc(Hons), History and Education Studies (Joint Honours) BA(Hons), History and English (Joint Honours) BA(Hons), History BA(Hons), International Development and Economics (Joint Honours) BA/BSc(Hons), International Development and Human Geography (Joint Honours) BA(Hons), International Development (Joint Honours) BA/BSc(Hons), International Development BA(Hons), International Politics (Joint Honours) BA/BSc(Hons), International Relations and Politics BA(Hons)

Postgraduate: History MA, International Relations MA

Human Resource Management

Human Resource Management (Joint Honours) BA/BSc(Hons), Human Resource Management (Top-Up) BA(Hons), Human Resource Management (Top-Up) MA, Human Resource Management and Business (Joint Honours) BA(Hons), Human Resource Management BA(Hons)

Postgraduate: Human Resource Management MA, Human Resource Management PGDip

Journalism and Media

Creative Film, Television and Digital Media Production (Joint Honours) BA/BSc(Hons), Creative Film, Television and Digital Media Production and Multimedia Journalism (Joint Honours) BA(Hons), Creative Film, Television and Digital Media Production BA(Hons), Film and Screen Studies (Joint Honours) BA(Hons), Multimedia Journalism (Joint Honours) BA/BSc(Hons), Multimedia Journalism and English (Joint Honours) BA(Hons), Multimedia Journalism BA(Hons), Multimedia Sports Journalism BA(Hons), Photography (Top-Up) BA(Hons), Photography BA(Hons)

Law

Law (Joint Honours) BA/BSc(Hons), Law (two-year intensive) LLB(Hons), Law and Business (Joint Honours) BA(Hons), Law and Criminology (Joint Honours) BA(Hons), Law LLB(Hons), Psychology and Law (Joint Honours) BA(Hons)

Postgraduate: Transnational Rights and Security LLM, Multinational Corporate Law LLM

Leather

Leather Technology BSc(Hons), Leather Science, Marketing and Business, Leather Technology Top-Up BSc(Hons)

Postgraduate: PGCert in Leather Finishing – Automotive, PGCert in Leather Technology (Professional), Leather Technology PhD, Leather Technology (Professional) MSc, PGDip in Leather Technology (Professional)

Management and Logistics

International Logistics and Trade Finance (Top-Up) BA(Hons), Management (Joint Honours) BA(Hons), Management (two-year intensive) BA(Hons), Management and Business Entrepreneurship (Joint Honours) BA(Hons), Management and International Tourism, Marketing and Management (Joint Honours) BA(Hons), Sports Studies and Management (Joint Honours)

Postgraduate: Corporate Governance and Leadership MSc, International Business Management MSc, Logistics and Supply Chain Management MSc, Project Management MSc, Strategic Technology Management MSc

MBA

Postgraduate: Doctor of Business Administration DBA, Executive Master of Business Administration MBA, Executive Master of Business Administration Top-Up MBA, Master of Business Administration (with Work Placement) MBA, Master of Business Administration MBA

Nursing and Midwifery

Adult Nursing BSc(Hons), Children and Young People's Nursing BSc(Hons), Dental Nursing FdSc, Learning Disability Nursing BSc(Hons), Mental Health Nursing BSc(Hons), Midwifery BSc(Hons), Specialist Community Public Health Nursing (SCPHN) Top-up BSc(Hons)

Postgraduate: Specialist Community Public Health Nursing (SCPHN) (Top Up) MSc, Specialist Community Public Health Nursing PGDip

Performing Arts

Acting & Creative Practice BA(Hons), Acting BA(Hons), Drama (Joint Honours) BA/BSc(Hons), Drama BA(Hons), Popular Music (Joint Honours) BA/BSc(Hons), Popular Music BA(Hons), Psychology and Drama (Joint Honours) BA(Hons)

Policing and Criminology

Applied Criminal Justice Studies (Top-Up) BA(Hons), Criminal and Corporate Investigation BA(Hons), Criminology (Joint Honours) BA/BSc(Hons), Criminology BA(Hons), Professional Policing BA(Hons), Psychology and Criminology (Joint Honours) BA(Hons), Sociology and Criminology (Joint Honours) BA(Hons)

Psychology, Counselling and Sociology

Psychology (Counselling) BSc(Hons), Psychology (Developmental and Educational) BSc(Hons), Psychology (Joint Honours) BA/BSc(Hons), Psychology and Business (Joint Honours) BA(Hons), Psychology and Criminology (Joint Honours) BA(Hons), Psychology and Drama (Joint Honours) BA(Hons), Psychology and Education Studies Joint Honours BA(Hons), Psychology and English (Joint Honours) BA(Hons), Psychology and Law (Joint Honours) BA(Hons), Psychology and Marketing (Joint Honours) BA(Hons), Psychology BSc(Hons), Sociology (Joint Honours) BA/BSc(Hons), Sociology and Criminology (Joint Honours) BA(Hons), Sociology and Psychology (Joint Honours), Sociology BA(Hons), Sports Studies and Psychology (Joint Honours) BA(Hons)

Postgraduate: Child and Adolescent Mental Health (CAMH) MSc, Counselling Children and Young People MSc, Counselling MSc, Psychology MSc, Public Sociology MSc

Public and Professional Healthcare

Health Studies (Joint Honours) BA/BSc(Hons), Occupational Therapy BSc(Hons), Paramedic Science BSc(Hons), Podiatry BSc(Hons), Professional Practice (Top-Up) BSc(Hons)

Postgraduate: Advanced Clinical Practice MSc, Advanced Occupational Therapy MSc, Advancing Practice MSc, Doctor of Professional Practice in Health and Social Care, Postgraduate Certificate in Practice Education, Public Health MSc

Social Work and Social Care

Applied Social Care (Joint Honours) BA/BSc(Hons), Applied Social Care and Education Studies Joint Honours BA/BSc(Hons), Applied Social Care and Health Studies (Joint Honours) BA(Hons), Health and Social Care (Top-up) BSc(Hons), Health and Social Care FdSc, Health Studies (Joint Honours) BA/BSc(Hons), Social Care and Community Practice BA(Hons), Social Work BA(Hons)

Postgraduate: Social Work MA

Sport and Exercise

Sport and Exercise Science BSc(Hons), Sport Coaching BSc(Hons), Sport Development and Physical Education BA(Hons), Sport Rehabilitation and Conditioning BSc(Hons), Sports Studies (Joint Honours) BA/BSc, Sports Studies and Business (Joint Honours) BA(Hons), Sports Studies and Education Studies (Joint Honours), Sports Studies and Management (Joint Honours), Sports Studies and Psychology (Joint Honours) BA(Hons)

Postgraduate: Sport MSc/MA Strength and Conditioning MSc

Teacher Training

Primary Education 5-11 (QTS) BA(Hons)

Postgraduate: Early Years Teacher Status (0-5), PGCE QTS Primary Education (School Direct Route), Primary Education (5-11) (QTS) PGCE

UNIVERSITY OF NORTHUMBRIA AT NEWCASTLE
www.northumbria.ac.uk

Department of Applied Sciences; www.northumbria.ac.uk/about-us/academic-departments/applied-sciences

Biology BSc(Hons), Biomedical Science BSc(Hons), Chemistry BSc(Hons), Chemistry MChem, Criminology and Forensic Science BSc(Hons), Food Science and Nutrition BSc(Hons), Forensic Science BSc(Hons), Medicine Pathway Programme

Postgraduate courses: Biotechnology MSc, Forensic Science MSc, Microbiology MSc, Nutritional Science MSc

Department of Architecture and Built Environment; www.northumbria.ac.uk/about-us/academic-departments/architecture-and-built-environment

Architecture BA(Hons) / MArch, Building Surveying BSc(Hons), Interior Architecture BA(Hons), Quantity Surveying Bsc, Real Estate BSc(Hons), Building Surveying BSc(Hons) Degree Apprenticeship, Quantity Surveying BSc(Hons) Degree Apprenticeship, Real Estate BSc(Hons) Degree Apprenticeship

Postgraduate courses: Architecture MArch, Interior Architecture Postgraduate Certificate, Real Estate (International) MSc, Real Estate MSc, Surveying (Building Surveying) MSc, Surveying (Quantity Surveying) MSc, Surveying (Real Estate) MSc

Department of Arts; www.northumbria.ac.uk/about-us/academic-departments/arts

Animation BA(Hons), Drama BA(Hons), Film and Television Studies BA(Hons), Film and TV Production BA(Hons), Fine Art BA(Hons)

Postgraduate courses: Animation MA, Arts MRes, Conservation of Fine Art MA, Creative and Cultural Industries Management MA, Master of Fine Art (MFA), Preventive Conservation MA, Theatre and Performance MA

Department of Computer and Information Sciences; www.northumbria.ac.uk/aboutus/academic-departments/computer-andinformation-sciences

Computer and Digital Forensics BSc(Hons)/MComp, Computer Networks and Cyber Security BSc(Hons)/MComp, Computer Science BSc(Hons)/MComp, Computer Science with Artificial Intelligence BSc(Hons)/MComp, Computer Science with Games Development BSc(Hons)/MComp, Computer Science with Web Development BSc(Hons)/MComp, Information Technology Management for Business BSc(Hons)

Postgraduate courses: Advanced Computer Science MSc, Computer Network Technology MSc,

Computer Science MSc, Computing and Information Technology MSc, Computing and Information Technology MSc (London Campus), Computing and Information Technology with Advanced Practice (London Campus)) MSc, Cyber Security MSc (London Campus), Cyber Security MSc Part-time (London Campus), Cyber Security with Advanced Practice MSc (London Campus), Information Science (Data Analytics) MSc, Information Science MSc – Library Management, Web and Mobile Development Technologies (Part-time) MSc, Information Security Management MSc (London)

Department of Geography and Environmental Sciences;
www.northumbria.ac.uk/about-us/
academic-departments/geography

Environmental Science BSc(Hons), Geography BA/BSc(Hons), Human Geography (MGeog), Physical Geography MGeog/BSc(Hons)

Postgraduate courses: Disaster Management and Sustainable Development MSc, Environmental Health MSc, Environmental Monitoring, Modelling and Reconstruction MSc, Safety, Health and Environmental Management MSc

Department of Humanities;
www.northumbria.ac.uk/about-us/
academic-departments/humanities

American Studies BA(Hons), English Language and Literature BA(Hons), English Language Studies BA(Hons), English Literature and American Studies BA(Hons), English Literature and Creative Writing BA(Hons), English Literature and History BA(Hons), English Literature BA(Hons), History and American Studies BA(Hons), History and Politics BA(Hons), History BA(Hons), Music BA(Hons)

Postgraduate courses: Applied Linguistics for TESOL MA, Creative Writing MA, English Literature MA, English Literature MRes, History MA, History MRes, TESOL MA

Department of Mathematics, Physics and Electrical Engineering;
www.northumbria.ac.uk/about-us/
academic-departments/
mathematicsphysics-and-electrical-
engineering

Electrical and Electronic Engineering BEng/MEng(Hons), Electronic Design Engineering Top Up BEng, Mathematics BSc/MMath(Hons), Mobile Communications Engineering (top-up award) BEng(Hons),

Physics BSc(Hons), Physics MPhys(Hons), Physics with Astrophysics BSc/MPhys(Hons)

Postgraduate courses: Electrical Power Engineering MSc, Microelectronic and Communications Engineering MSc, Statistics MSc

Department of Mechanical and Construction Engineering;
www.northumbria.ac.uk/about-us/
academic-departments/mechanical-
andconstruction-engineering

Automotive Engineering BEng/MEng(Hons), Civil Engineering BEng/MEng(Hons), Construction Engineering Management BSc(Hons), Mechanical and Architectural Engineering BEng(Hons), Mechanical and Automotive Engineering BEng/MEng(Hons), Mechanical Engineering BEng/MEng(Hons)

Postgraduate courses: Construction Project Management with BIM MSc, Engineering Management MSc, International Project Management (London) MSc, Mechanical Engineering MSc, Pipeline Integrity Management MSc/PGDip, Professional Practice in Project Management MSc Part-time (London Campus), Programme and Project Management (London) MSc, Project Management MSc, Project Management with Advanced Practice (London) MSc, Renewable and Sustainable Energy Technologies MSc

Newcastle Business School;
www.northumbria.ac.uk/about-us/
academic-departments/
newcastlebusiness-school

Accounting and Finance BA(Hons), Accounting BA(Hons), Business (top up award) BA(Hons), Business (with Law) BA(Hons), Business and Finance (top up award) BA(Hons), Business and International Management (top up award) BA(Hons), Business and Management MBus, Business and Marketing (top up award) BA(Hons), Business Enterprise, Creation and Management BA(Hons) (London Campus), Business Leadership and Management Practice BA(Hons) Degree Apprenticeship, Business Management BA(Hons), Business Top-up BA(Hons) (London Campus), Business with Accounting BA(Hons), Business with Economics BA(Hons), Business with Entrepreneurship BA(Hons), Business with Financial Management BA(Hons), Business with Human Resource Management BA(Hons), Business with International Management BA(Hons), Business with Logistics and Supply Chain Management BA(Hons), Business with Management BA(Hons), Business with Marketing Management BA(Hons), Business with Tourism Management BA(Hons), Entrepreneurial

Business Management BA(Hons), Finance and Investment Management BA(Hons), Human Resource Management BA(Hons), International Banking and Finance (Completion award) BA(Hons), International Business Management BA(Hons), International Business Management with French BA(Hons), International Business Management with Spanish BA(Hons), International Hospitality and Tourism Management (Top- Up) BA(Hons), Leadership and Management BA(Hons), Logistics and Supply Management BA(Hons), Marketing Management BA(Hons), Risk and Compliance BSc(Hons), Tourism and Events Management BA(Hons)

Postgraduate courses: Business Graduate Certificate, Business with Business Analytics MSc, Business with Entrepreneurship MSc, Business with Entrepreneurship with Advanced Practice (London) MSc, Business with Financial Management MSc, Business with Financial Management with Advanced Practice MSc, Business with Hospitality and Tourism Management MSc, Business with Human Resource Management MSc, Business with Human Resource Management with Advanced Practice (London Campus) MSc, Business with International Management and Finance MSc, Business with International Management and Marketing MSc, Business with International Management MSc, Business with International Management with Advanced Practice MSc, Business with Logistics and Supply Chain Management MSc, Business with Management and Finance MSc, Business with Management and Marketing MSc, Business with Management MSc, Business with Marketing Management MSc, Business with Marketing Management with Advanced Practice MSc, Coaching MA/PGCert/PGDip, Digital Marketing MSc, Entrepreneurship MSc, Finance MSc, Forensic Accounting MSc/PGCert, Global Logistics, Operations and Supply Chain Management MSc, Human Resource Management and Development MA, International Business Management MSc, International Finance and Investment MSc, International Financial Management MSc, Leadership and Management MSc, Marketing MSc, MBA, MSc Business with Management and Finance, MSc Digital Marketing with Advanced Practice (London Campus), Multidisciplinary Innovation MA MSc, Professional Accounting (with Professional Study Preparation) MSc, Senior Leader Master's Degree Apprenticeship – MBA, Senior Leader Master's Degree Apprenticeship – Strategic Leadership in Public Services MSc, Senior Leader Master's Degree Apprenticeship – Strategic Leadership MSc

Northumbria Law School; www.northumbria.ac.uk/about-us/academic-departments/northumbria-lawschool

Law LLB(Hons), M Law, Solicitor Apprenticeship Degree (LLB Hons)

Postgraduate courses: Advanced Legal Practice LLM, Data Protection Law and Information Governance Postgraduate Certificate, Employment Law in Practice Postgraduate Certificate/Diploma/LLM, Information Rights Law and Practice Postgraduate Certificate, Law (Cyber Law) LLM, International Commercial Law LLM, Law (International Finance) LLM, Law (Space Law) LLM, Legal Practice Postgraduate Diploma, LLM in Bar Professional Training, LLM in Legal Practice, Professional Practice in Mental Health Law Postgraduate Certificate

Northumbria School of Design; www.northumbria.ac.uk/about-us/academic-departments/northumbriaschool-of-design

3D Design BA(Hons), Design for Industry BA(Hons), Fashion BA(Hons), Fashion Communication BA(Hons), Fashion Design and Marketing BA(Hons), Graphic Design BA(Hons), Interaction Design BA(Hons), Interior Design BA(Hons)

Postgraduate courses: Communication Design MA, Design MA, Design Management MA, Design Management MA (London Campus), Design MRes, Luxury Brand Management MA, MA Luxury Brand Management with Advanced Practice, Multidisciplinary Innovation MA MSc

Department of Nursing,Midwifery & Health; www.northumbria.ac.uk/aboutus/academic-departments/nursingmidwifery-health

Midwifery Studies BSc(Hons), Nursing Degree Apprenticeship 18 Month Programme, Nursing Science BSc(Hons), Nursing Studies/Registered Nurse Adult BSc(Hons), Nursing Studies/Registered Nurse Child BSc(Hons), Nursing Studies/Registered Nurse Learning Disabilities BSc(Hons), Nursing Studies/Registered Nurse Mental Health BSc(Hons), Operating Department Practice Diploma of Higher Education

Postgraduate courses: Healthcare Professional Practice MRes, Nursing Leadership MSc, Nursing MSc, Professional Non-Surgical Aesthetic Practice MSc/PGCert

Department of Primary Education

Education Leadership in Learning (Teach First) MA

Department of Psychology; www.northumbria.ac.uk/about-us/academic-departments/psychology

Psychology BSc(Hons), Psychology with Criminology BSc(Hons)

Postgraduate courses: Health Psychology MSc, Occupational and Organisational Psychology MSc, Psychology MRes, Psychology MSc, Sport and Exercise Psychology MSc

Department of Social Sciences; www.northumbria.ac.uk/about-us/academic-departments/social-scienceslanguages

Bachelor of Arts(Hons) Mass Communication (Top-up) (KAPLAN), Criminology and Sociology BSc(Hons), Criminology BSc(Hons), Film and Media Foundation Year BA(Hons), International Relations and Politics BA(Hons), Journalism and English Literature BA(Hons), Journalism BA(Hons), Mass Communication (Completion Award) BA(Hons), Mass Communication BA(Hons), Mass Communication with Advertising BA(Hons), Mass Communication with Business BA(Hons), Mass Communication with Public Relations BA(Hons), Media and Journalism BA(Hons), Professional Policing BSc(Hons), Sociology BSc(Hons)

Postgraduate courses: Criminology and Criminal Justice MA, International Development MSc, International Relations, Conflict and Security MA, Social Sciences MRes

Department of SocialWork, Education & Community Wellbeing; www.northumbria.ac.uk/about-us/academic-departments/social-workeducation-community-wellbeing

Childhood and Early Years Studies (Top-up) BA(Hons) (KAPLAN), Childhood and Early Years Studies BA(Hons), Guidance and Counselling BA(Hons), Integrated Health and Social Care BSc(Hons), Occupational Therapy BSc(Hons), Primary Education BA(Hons), Social Work BSc(Hons)

Postgraduate courses: Autism MA, Education MA, Healthcare Management MSc, Master of Education, Master of Public Health, Occupational Therapy (Pre-Registration) MSc, Primary Education PGCE, Secondary Art, Craft and Design PGCE, Social Work MA, Special and Inclusive Education (National Award for Special Educational Needs Co-ordinators) PGCert, Teaching Pupils with Dyslexia within an Education and Training Setting PGCert

Department of Sport, Exercise and Rehabilitation; www.northumbria.ac.uk/about-us/academic-departments/sportexercise-and-rehabilitation

Applied Sport and Exercise Science BSc(Hons), Applied Sport Science with Coaching BSc(Hons), Physiotherapy BSc(Hons), Sport Coaching BSc(Hons), Sport Development BA(Hons), Sport Management BSc(Hons), Sport, Exercise and Nutrition BSc(Hons)

Postgraduate courses: Clinical Exercise Physiology MSc, Exercise Science MRes, International Sport Management MSc, Physiotherapy (Pre-registration) MSc, Strength and Conditioning MSc

UNIVERSITY OF NOTTINGHAM
www.nottingham.ac.uk

Faculty of Arts; www.nottingham.ac.uk/arts

American and Canadian Studies

American and Canadian Literature, History and Culture BA, American and Canadian Literature, History and Culture (International Study) BA, Film and Television Studies and American Studies BA, American Studies and English BA, American Studies and History BA, American Studies and Latin American Studies BA, Politics and American Studies BA

Postgraduate courses: American Studies MA, American and Canadian Studies MRes, Comparative Literature MA, Languages and Intercultural Studies MA

Classics and Archaeology

Archaeology BA, Archaeology BSc, Historical Archaeology BA, Ancient History BA, Classical Civilisation BA

Postgraduate courses: Archaeological Science MRes (by Research), Archaeology

Classics BA, Classical Civilisation BA, Latin BA

Postgraduate courses: Classics MA

Cultural, Media and Visual Studies

Film and Television Studies BA, International Media and Communications Studies BA, French/German/Portuguese/Spanish and International Media and Communications Studies, Film and Television Studies and American Studies BA, History of Art BA, History of Art BA with English/History/ Archaeology Postgraduate courses: Art History MA, Critical Theory and Cultural Studies MA, Critical Theory and Politics MA, Cultural Industries and Entrepreneurship MSc, International Media and Communication Studies MA, Film, Television and Screen Industries MA, Visual Culture MA

English

English BA, English Language and Literature BA, English with Creative Writing BA, English and French BA, English and German BA, English and Hispanic Studies BA, English and History BA, English and Philosophy BA, American Studies and English Joint Honours BA, Classics and English BA, History of Art and English BA

Postgraduate courses: Applied Linguistics MA, Applied Linguistics and English Language Teaching MA, Applied Linguistics and English Language Teaching by Web-based Distance Learning MA, Applied Linguistics by Web based Distance Learning MA, Communication and Entrepreneurship MSc, Creative Writing MA, English Literature MA, English Studies MA, English Studies by Web-based Distance Learning MA, Health Communication by Web-based Distance Learning MA, Literary Linguistics MA, Literary Linguistics by Web-based Distance Learning MA, Modern English Language by Web-based Distance Learning MA, Viking and Anglo-Saxon Studies MA, Professional Communication by Web-based Distance Learning MA/PGCert/PGDip

Department of Modern Languages and Cultures

French Studies, Russian Studies, German, Hispanic Studies, Combinations with French, German, Portuguese, Russian, Serbian/Croatian, and Spanish, French and Contemporary Chinese Studies, German and Contemporary Chinese Studies, Russian and Contemporary Chinese Studies, Spanish and Contemporary Chinese Studies, Modern Languages, American Studies and Latin American Studies, English, English and French, English and German, English and Hispanic Studies, International Media and Communications Studies, French and International Media and Communications Studies, German and International Media and Communications Studies, Portuguese and International Media and Communications Studies, Spanish and International

Media and Communications Studies, History, French and History, German and History, Russian and History, Hispanic Studies and History, History and East European Cultural Studies, History and Contemporary Chinese Studies, Modern European Studies, Philosophy, French and Philosophy, Politics, French and Politics, German and Politics, Hispanic Studies and Politics, Modern European Studies

History

History BA, Ancient History and History BA, History and History of Art BA, History and Politics BA, History with Contemporary Chinese Studies BA, History and East European Cultural Studies BA, English and History BA, American Studies and History BA, Archaeology and History BA, French and History BA, German and History BA, Hispanic Studies and History BA, Russian and History BA, Modern European Studies BA

Postgraduate course: History MA

Music

Music BA, Music and Music Technology BA, Music and Philosophy BA

Postgraduate courses: Music MA, Music MRes, Music Composition MPhil/PhD, Musicology MPhil/Phd, Music Performance MPhil/PhD

Philosophy

Philosophy and Theology BA, Philosophy BA, Philosophy, Politics and Economics BA

Postgraduate courses: Philosophy MA

Theology and Religious Studies

Theology and Religious Studies BA, Biblical Studies and Theology BA, Religion, Culture and Ethics BA, Religion, Philosophy and Ethics BA, Philosophy and Theology BA

Postgraduate courses: Church History (distance learning) MA, Systematic and Philosophical Theology (distance learning) MA

Philosophy

Philosophy BA, Classical Civilisation and Philosophy BA, Economics and Philosophy BA, English and Philosophy BA, French and Philosophy BA, Music and Philosophy BA, Physics and Philosophy BSc, Philosophy, Politics and Economics BA, Philosophy and Psychology BA, Religion, Philosophy and Ethics BA, Philosophy and Theology BA

Faculty of Engineering; www.nottingham.ac.uk/engineering

Architecture and Built Environment

MEng Architecture and Environmental Design, BArch Bachelor of Architecture, MArch Architecture (ARB/RIBA Part 2), MArch Architecture with

Collaborative Practice Research (ARB/RIBA Part 2), BEng Architectural Environment Engineering, BEng Architectural Environment Engineering (with industrial year), MEng Architectural Environment Engineering, MEng Architectural Environment Engineering (with industrial year)

Postgraduate courses: Architecture Design MArch, Architecture Design and Build MArch, Building Performance Engineering MSc, Architecture and Sustainable Design MArch, Professional Pratice in Architecture PGCert ARB/RIBA Part 3, Renewable Energy and Architecture MSc, Sustainable Building Technology MSc, Sustainable Building Technology Collaborative MSc, Sustainable Energy and Entrepreneurship MSc, Sustainable Urban Design March

Chemical and Environmental Engineering

BEng/MEng Chemical Engineering, BEng/MEng Environmental Engineering, BEng/MEng Chemical with Environmental Engineering

Postgraduate courses: Chemical Engineering MSc, Environmental Engineering MSc, Energy Process Systems Engineering MSc, Food Process Engineering MSc, Chemical Engineering PhD, Environmental Engineering PhD

Civil Engineering

Civil Engineering BEng/MEng

Postgraduate courses: Civil Engineering MSc, Civil Engineering: Structural Engineering MSc, Transportation Infrastructure Engineering: Sustainable Highways / Sustainable Railways MSc, Engineering Surveying MSc

Electrical and Electronic Engineering

Electrical and Electronic Engineering BEng/MEng, Electrical Engineering BEng/MEng, Electronic Engineering BEng/MEng, Electronic and Computer Engineering BEng/MEng

Postgraduate courses: Advanced Electrical and Electronic Engineering with Extended Research MSc, Electrical Engineering MSc, Electrical and Electronic Engineering MSc, Electrical and Electronic Engineering and Entrepreneurship MSc, Electrical Engineering for Sustainable and Renewable Energy MSc, Electronic Communications and Computer Engineering MSc, Power Electronics and Drives MSc, Sustainable Transportation and Electrical Power Systems, MSc, Sustainable Energy Engineering MSc

Mechanical, Materials and Manufacturing Engineering

Manufacturing Engineering BEng/MEng, Mechanical Engineering BEng/MEng, Product Design and Manufacture BEng/MEng, Aerospace Engineering BEng/MEng

Postgraduate courses: Advanced Materials MSc, Applied Ergonomics MSc/PGCert, Human Factors and Ergonomics MSc, Bioengineering MSc, Mechanical Engineering MSc, Bioengineering: Biomaterials and Biomechanics MSc, Additive Manufacturing and 3D Printing MSc, Aerospace Technologies MSc, Human Factors and Ergonomics MSc, Applied Ergonomics MSc/PGCert, Usability and Human Computer Interaction PGCert

Medicine and Health Sciences; www.nottingham.ac.uk/mhs

Applied Psychology

Postgraduate courses: Clinical Psychology DClinPsy, Forensic Psychology – Full Programme DForenPsy, Forensic Psychology – top-up programme DForenPsy, Health Psychology MSc, Management Psychology MSc, Management Psychology PGDip, Mental Health Research MSc, Occupational Psychology MSc, Rehabilitation Psychology MSc, Work and Organisational Psychology MSc, Work and Organisational Psychology PGDip, Workplace Health and Wellbeing MSc (Distance eLearning)

Medical Physiology and Therapeutics

Medical Physiology and Therapeutics BSc
Postgraduate courses:

Medicine

Medicine BMBS, Medical Physiology and Therapeutics, Cancer Sciences BSc/MSci

Postgraduate courses: Assisted Reproduction Technology MMedSci, Oncology MSc, Applied Sport and Exercise Medicine MSc, Cancer Immunology and Biotechnology MSc, Health Psychology MSc, Management Psychology MSc, Master of Public Health MPH, Medical Education MMedSci, Mental Health Research and Practice MSc, Occupational Psychology MSc, Rehabilitation Psychology MSc, Sports and Exercise Medicine MSc, Stem Cell Technology and Regenerative Medicine MSc, Work and Organisational Psychology MSc, Work and Organisational Psychology PGDip, Workplace Health and Wellbeing MSc (Distance eLearning), Immunology MRes, Immunology PhD, Molecular Pathology, Bioinformatics and Diagnostics MRes, Clinical Microbiology MSc (Distance), Clinical and Molecular Microbiology MSc, Cancer Immunology and Biotechnology MSc, Mental Health: Research and Practice MSc, Public Health (Global Health) MPH, Physician Associate Studies MSc, Forensic and Criminological Psychology MSc (by research), Stem Cell Technology MSc, Virology MRes/ PhD, Ruminant Population Health PhD

Health Sciences

Midwifery BSc(Hons), Nursing (Adult) BSc, Nursing (Child) BSc, Nursing (Mental Health) BSc, Nursing (Graduate Entry) Adult MSc, Nursing (Graduate Entry) Child MSc, Nursing (Graduate Entry) Mental Health MSc, Graduate Entry Nursing – Learning Disability, Physiotherapy BSc, Sport Rehabilitation BSc

Postgraduate courses: Advanced Clinical Practice MSc, Advanced Clinical Skills PGCert, Advanced Nursing MSc, Cognitive Behavioural Therapy MSc, Cognitive Behavioural Therapy PGDip, Graduate Entry Nursing – Adult MSc, Graduate Entry Nursing – Child Branch MSc, Graduate Entry Nursing – Mental Health MSc, Health Communication (MA), Quality and Patient Safety Improvement MSc, Quality and Patient Safety Improvement PGCert, Quality and Patient Safety Improvement PGDip, Midwifery Studies, Maternal and Newborn Health MSc, Midwifery MSc, Midwifery PGDip, Physiotherapy MSc, Physiotherapy PGDip, Physiotherapy PGCert

Sport and Exercise Science

Sport and Exercise Science BSc

Veterinary Medicine and Science

Veterinary Medicine and Surgery – BVM BVS with BVMed Sci

Postgraduate courses: Veterinary Education PGCert, Veterinary Medicine and Surgery PGCert, Veterinary Physiotherapy MSc/PGDip

Life Sciences

Biochemistry

Biochemistry BSc, Biochemistry MSci, Biochemistry and Biological Chemistry BSc, Biochemistry and Biological Chemistry MSci, Biochemistry and Genetics BSc, Biochemistry and Genetics MSci, Biochemistry and Molecular Medicine BSc, Biochemistry and Molecular Medicine MSci

Postgraduate course: Biological Photography and Imaging MSc

Biology, Genetics and Zoology

Biology BSc, Biology MSci, Zoology BSc, Zoology MSci, Genetics MSci, Genetics BSc

Postgraduate courses: Biological Photography and Imaging MSc, Sythetic Biology MRes

Biosciences

Agriculture BSc, Integrated Agricultural Business Management BSc, Agricultural and Crop Science BSc, Agricultural and Livestock Science BSc, International Agricultural Science BSc, Animal Science BSc/ MSci, Biotechnology BSc/MSci, Environmental Science BSc, Environmental Science MSci, International Environmental Science BSc, International Environmental Science MSci, Environmental Biology BSc/MSci, Microbiology BSc, Consumer Behaviour – Food and Nutrition BSc/ MSci, Nutrition BSc/MSci, Nutrition and Dietetics MNutr, Plant Science BSc/MSci, Food Science and Nutrition MSci, Food Science BSc, Food Science and Nutrition BSc, Food Science MSci Postgraduate courses: Advanced Dietetic Practice MSc, Advanced Dietetic Practice PGDip, Advanced Dietetic Practice PGCert, Agrifood MSc, Agrifood PGDip, Agrifood PGCert, Animal Nutrition MSc, Animal Nutrition PGDip, Applied Biopharmaceutical Biotechnology and Entrepreneurship (ABBE) MSc, Biotechnology MSc, Applied Biomolecular Technology MSc, Industrial Physical Biochemistry MRes, Brewing Science MSc, Brewing Science and Practice MSc, Brewing Science PGDip, Brewing Science MRes, Brewing: Principles and Practice (ELearning) PGCert, Clinical Nutrition MSc, Clinical Nutrition PGDip, Crop Improvement MSc, Crop Improvement PGDip, Food Production Management MSc, Food Production Management PGDip, Food Science and Engineering MRes, Nutritional Sciences MSc, Sensory Science MRes, Sensory Science PGCert

Chemistry

Chemistry BSc, Chemistry with a Year in Industry MSci, Chemistry MSci, Medicinal and Biological Chemistry BSc, Chemistry with an International Study Year MSci, Medicinal and Biological Chemistry MSci, Medicinal and Biological Chemistry with an Assessed Year in Industry MSci, Chemistry and Molecular Physics BSc, Chemistry and Molecular Physics MSci, Biochemistry and Biological Chemistry BSc(Hons), Biochemistry and Biological Chemistry MSci Hons

Postgraduate courses: Green and Sustainable Chemistry MSc, Chemistry MSc (by Research)

Computer Science

Computer Science BSc, Computer Science MSci, Computer Science including International Year MSci, Computer Science With Year in Industry BSc, Computer Science with Artificial Intelligence BSc, Computer Science with Artificial Intelligence MSci, Computer Science with Artificial Intelligence including International Year MSci, Computer Science and Artificial Intelligence with Year in Industry BSc

Postgraduate courses: Computer Science MSc, Human Computer Interaction MSc, MSc Computer science with Artificial Intelligence MSc, Data Science

Mathematical Sciences

Statistics BSc, Mathematics (International Study) BSc, Mathematics MMath, Mathematics and Economics BSc, Mathematics BSc, Financial Mathematics BSc, BSc Natural Sciences, MSci Natural Sciences

Postgraduate courses: Financial and Computational Mathematics MSc, Gravity, Particles and Fields MSc, Mathematical Medicine and Biology MSc, Pure Mathematics MSc, Scientific Computation MSc, Statistics MSc, Statistics and Applied Probability MSc

Neuroscience

Neuroscience BSc, Neuroscience MSci

Pharmacy

Pharmaceutical Sciences (with a Year in Industry) MSci, Pharmacy MPharm

Postgraduate course: Drug Discovery and Pharmaceutical Sciences MSc, MRes Pharmacy, Drug Discovery and Pharmaceutical Sciences with industrial training MSc

Physics and Astronomy

Physics BSc, Physics MSci, Mathematical Physics BSc, Mathematical Physics MSci, Physics with Astronomy BSc, Physics with Astronomy MSci, Physics with European Language BSc, Physics with European Language MSci, Physics with Medical Physics BSc, Physics with Medical Physics MSci, Physics with Nanoscience BSc, Physics with Nanoscience MSci, Physics with Theoretical Astrophysics BSc, Physics with Theoretical Astrophysics MSci, Physics with Theoretical Physics BSc, Physics with Theoretical Physics MSci, Physics and Philosophy BSc, Physics with a Year in Industry BSc, Physics with a Year in Industry MSci

Postgraduate courses: Physics MRes/PhD, Gravity, Particles and Fields MSc, Machine Learning in Science MSc

Psychology

Psychology BSc, Psychology MSci, Psychology and Cognitive Neuroscience BSc, Liberal Arts BA

Postgraduate courses: Applied Educational Psychology Doctorate DAppEdPsy, Psychology (Conversion Course) PGDip, Psychology (Conversion) MSc, Psychology Research Methods MSc, Cognitive Neuroscience MSc, Computational Neuroscience, Cognition and AI MSc, Developmental Disorders MSc

Faculty of Social Sciences

Business

Accountancy BSc, Finance, Accounting and Management BSc, International Management BSc, Industrial Economics BSc, Industrial Economics with Insurance BSc, Management BSc

Postgraduate courses: Accounting and Finance MSc, Banking and Finance MSc, Business and Management MSc, Entrepreneurship, Innovation and Management MSc, Finance and Investment MSc, Human Resource Management and Organisation MSc, Industrial Engineering and Operations Management MSc, Information Systems and Operations Management MSc, International Business MSc, Logistics and Supply Chain Management MSc, Management MSc, Marketing MSc, Master of Business Administration – General MBA, Master of Business Administration (Executive) MBA, Master of Business Administration (Executive) – Healthcare MBA, Master of Business Administration – Singapore MBA, Risk Management MSc, Supply Chain and Operations Management MSc, Sustainable Business MSc, Business Analytics MSc, International Tourism Management and Marketing MSc

Economics

Economics BA/BSc, Economics and Econometrics BSc, Economics and International Economics BSc, Economics with French BA, Economics with German BA, Economics with Hispanic Studies BA, Economics and Philosophy BA, Philosophy, Politics and Economics BA, Mathematics and Economics BSc, Politics and Economics BA

Postgraduate courses: Economics MSc, Economics of Monetary and Financial Policy MSc, Economic Development and Policy Analysis MSc, Behavioural Economics MSc, Economics and Development Economics MSc, Economics and Econometrics MSc, Economics and Financial Economics MSc, Economics and International Economics MSc, Economics GDip

Education

Education BA, Education MArts, Humanistic Counselling Practice BA

Postgraduate courses: Education MA, Education (Flexible) MA, Educational Leadership and Management MA, Educational Leadership and Management (by distance learning) MA, International Student Advice and Support PGCert, Learning, Technology and Education MA, Learning, Technology and Education (online) MA, Mentoring and Coaching Teachers PGCert, Person-Centred Experiential Counselling and Psychotherapy Practice MA, Special and Inclusive Education MA, Special and Inclusive Education (online) MA, Teaching Chinese to Speakers of Other Languages (TCSOL) MA, Teaching English to Speakers of Other Languages (TESOL) MA, Teaching English for Academic Purposes (TEAP) by distance learning MA, Teaching English to Speakers of Other Languages (TESOL) by

Webbased Distance Learning MA, PGCE Postgraduate Certificate in Primary Education, Trauma Studies MA, PGCE Postgraduate Certificate in Secondary Education, PGCE (International) Postgraduate Certificate in Education PGCEi

Geography

Geography BA, Geography BSc, Environmental Geoscience BSc, Geography with Business BA

Postgraduate courses: Environmental Leadership and Management MSc

Law

Law BA, Law LLB, Law with French and French Law BA, Law with German and German Law BA, Law with Spanish and Spanish Law BA

Study abroad options: Law with American Law LLB/BA, Law with Australian Law LLB/BA, Law with Canadian Law LLB/BA, Law with Chinese Law LLB/BA, Law with European Law LLB/BA, Law with New Zealand Law LLB/BA, Law with South-East Asian Law LLB/BA

Postgraduate courses: Master of Laws LLM, Criminal Justice LLM, Environmental Law LLM, European Law LLM, Human Rights Law LLM, International Commercial Law LLM, International Criminal Justice and Armed Conflict LLM, International Law and Development LLM, International Law LLM, Public International Law LLM, Social Science Research (Socio-Legal Studies) MA, Public Procurement Law and Policy LLM/PGDip/PGCert

Politics and International Relations

Politics and International Relations BA, Politics and American Studies BA, Politics and Economics BA, French and Politics BA, German and Politics BA, History and Politics BA, International Relations and Asian Studies BA, Philosophy, Politics and Economics BA

Postgraduate courses: Asian and International Studies MA, Slavery and Liberation MA/PGDip/PGCert, Diplomacy MA, International Relations MA, Governance and Political Development MA, Politics and Contemporary History MA, International Security and Terrorism MA, Social Science Research (Political Science and International Relations) MA

Sociology and Social Policy

Criminology BA, Criminology and Social Policy BA, Criminology and Sociology BA, Social Work BA, Sociology BA, Sociology and Social Policy BA

Postgraduate courses: Criminology MA, Criminology PGDip, Global Citizenship, Identities and Human Rights MA, Global Citizenship, Identities and Human Rights PGDip, International Social Policy MA, Master of Public Administration MPA, Master of Public Administration PGDip, Public Policy MA, Public, Policy PGDip, Social Work MA, Social Science, Research (Social Policy and Social Work) MA, Social, Science Research (Sociology) MA

NOTTINGHAM TRENT UNIVERSITY
www.ntu.ac.uk

School of Animal, Rural and Environmental Sciences; www.ntu.ac.uk/ares

Animal Biology BSc(Hons), Ecology and Conservation BSc(Hons), Environmental Science BSc(Hons), Equine Behaviour, Health and Welfare, BSc(Hons), Equine Sports Science BSc(Hons), Food Science and Technology BSc(Hons), Geography MGeog, Geography BSc(Hons), Geography (Physical) BSc(Hons), Horticulture (final year top-up) BSc(Hons), Veterinary Nursing (final year top up) BSc(Hons), Wildlife Conservation BSc(Hons), Wildlife Conservation and Management (final year top-up) BSc(Hons), Zoo Biology BSc(Hons)

Postgraduate courses: MSc/MRes Animal Health and Welfare, MSc/MRes Biodiversity Conservation, MSc/MRes Endangered Species Recovery and Conservation, MRes Equine Health and Welfare, MRes Equine

Performance, MSc Equine Performance, Health and Welfare, MSc/MRes Global Food Security and Development

School of Architecture, Design and the Built Environment; www.ntu.ac.uk/adbe

Architectural Design

BArch(Hons) Architecture (ARB/RIBA Part 1), BA(Hons) Interior Architecture and Design, BSc(Hons) Architectural Technology

Postgraduate courses: MArch Architecture, MA Interior Architecture and Design, Professional Certificate in Architecture MSc, Digital Architecture and Construction

Civil Engineering

BEng(Hons) Civil Engineering, BSc(Hons) Civil Engineering, MEng(Hons) Civil Engineering Design and Construction

Postgraduate courses: MSc Civil Engineering, MSc Structural Engineering with Management, MSc Structural Engineering with Materials

Construction Management and Quantity Surveying

BSc(Hons) Construction Management, BSc(Hons) Quantity Surveying and Commercial Management, Level 6 Chartered Surveyor (Degree Apprenticeship), Studying BSc(Hons) Quantity Surveying and Commercial Management

Postgraduate courses: MSc Construction Management, MSc Project Management (Construction), MSc Quantity Surveying

Property Management and Development

BSc(Hons) Building Surveying, BSc(Hons) Property Development and Planning, BSc(Hons) Property Finance and Investment, BSc(Hons) Real Estate

Postgraduate courses: MSc Building Surveying, MSc Real Estate, MSc International Real Estate Investment and Finance MSc, Corporate Real Estate

Product Design

BA(Hons) Product Design, BSc(Hons) Product Design, BA(Hons) Furniture and Product Design

Postgraduate courses: MA Design: Products and Furniture, MSc Design: Products and Technology

School of Art & Design; www.ntu.ac.uk/art

BArch(Hons) Architecture, BA(Hons) Animation, BA(Hons) Costume Design and Making, BA(Hons) Decorative Arts, BA(Hons) Design for Film and Television, BA(Hons) Fashion Communication and Promotion, BA(Hons) Fashion Design, BA(Hons) Fashion Knitwear Design and Knitted Textiles, BA(Hons) Fashion Management, BA(Hons) Fashion Marketing and Branding, BA(Hons) Filmmaking, BA(Hons) Fine Art, BA(Hons) Furniture and Product Design, BA(Hons) Graphic Design, BA(Hons) Interior Architecture and Design, BA(Hons) International Fashion Business (one year top-up), BA(Hons) Photography, BA(Hons) Product Design, BA(Hons) Textile Design, BA(Hons) Theatre Design, BSc(Hons) Product Design Postgraduate courses: MA Fashion Knitwear Design, MA Branding and Identity, MA Commercial Photography, MA Culture, Style and Fashion, MA Fashion Marketing, MA Fashion Marketing, MA Fashion Communications, MA Fashion Design, MA Graphic Design, MA Illustration, MA International Fashion Management, MA Luxury Fashion Brand Management, MA Animation, MA Photography, MA Textile Design Innovation, MFA Fine Art, MFA Fine Art

School of Arts and Humanities; www.ntu.ac.uk/hum

BA(Hons) Broadcast Journalism, BA(Hons) Journalism, BA(Hons) English, BA(Hons) History, BA(Hons) Creative Writing, BA(Hons) Media Production, BA(Hons) Media Communications and Culture various joint options in Humanities and Modern Languages

Postgraduate courses: MA/PGDip Broadcast Journalism, MA/PGDip News Journalism, MA/PGDip Documentary Journalism, MA/PGDip Magazine Journalism, MA Creative Writing, MA English Language Teaching, MA History, MA Holocaust and Genocide (by research), MA Linguistics (by research), MA Media and Globalisation, MA Philosophy (by research), MATESOL (Teaching English to Speakers of Other Languages), MA/ PGDip/ PGCert Museum and Heritage Development, MA International Development, MRes English Literary Research

Nottingham Business School; www.ntu.ac.uk/nbs

BA(Hons) Accounting and Finance, BA(Hons) Business, BA(Hons) Business Management and Accounting and Finance, BA(Hons) Business Management and Economics, BA(Hons) Business Management and Entrepreneurship, BA(Hons) Business Management and Human Resources, BA(Hons) Business Management and Marketing, BA(Hons) Economics, BA(Hons) Economics with Business, BA(Hons) Economics with International Finance and Banking, BA(Hons) International Business, BA(Hons) International Business (with French), BA(Hons) International Business (with Spanish), BA(Hons) Marketing, BA(Hons) Business Management (1 Year In-Company), BA(Hons) Business Management (2 Year In-Company), BA(Hons) Management and Leadership, Chartered Manager Degree Apprenticeship

Postgraduate courses: MSc Branding and Advertising, MSc Digital Marketing, MSc Economics, MSc Economics and Investment Banking, MSc Entrepreneurship, MSc Finance, MSc Finance and Accounting, MSc Finance and Investment Banking, MSc Human resource Management (full-time), MSc International Business, MSc Management, MSc Management and Finance, MSc Management and Global Supply Chain Management, MSc Management and International Business, MSc Management and Marketing, MSc Marketing, MSc Project Management, MSc Management and Business Analytics

Nottingham Institute of Education; www.ntu.ac.uk/edu

BA(Hons) Primary Education, BA(Hons) Childhood (Psychology), BA(Hons) Childhood (Special Educational Needs and Inclusion), BA(Hons) Childhood (Learning and Development), BA(Hons) Early Years, BA(Hons) Education, BA(Hons) Education (Early Years), BA(Hons) Education (Psychology), BA(Hons) Education (Special Educational Needs and Inclusion), BA(Hons) Education Policy and Practice, BA(Hons) Youth Studies

Postgraduate course: MA Education, various teacher training options

Nottingham Law School; www.ntu.ac.uk/nls

LLB(Hons) Law (Full-time), LLB(Hons) Law (Sandwich), LLB(Hons) Business Law, LLB(Hons) / LLM European Law, LLB(Hons) International Law, LLB(Hons) Law with Business, LLB(Hons) Law with Criminology, LLB(Hons) Law with Psychology, LLB(Hons) Law (Distance Learning), LLB(Hons) Law (Flexible Learning), LLB(Hons) Law Senior Status Postgraduate courses: Master of Law (LLM) courses in the following areas: Corporate and Insolvency Law, General Law, Health Law and Ethics, Human Rights and Justice, Intellectual Property Law, International Financial Law, International Trade and Commercial Law, Oil, Gas and Mining Law, Sports Law, Legal Practice

School of Science and Technology; www.ntu.ac.uk/sat

Engineering

MEng(Hons) Biomedical Engineering, BEng(Hons) Biomedical Engineering, MEng(Hons) Electronic Engineering, BEng(Hons) Electronic Engineering, MEng(Hons) Sport Engineering, BEng(Hons) Sport Engineering, MEng(Hons) Mechanical Engineering, BEng(Hons) Mechanical Engineering

Biosciences

BSc(Hons) Biological Sciences, BSc(Hons) Biomedical Science, BSc(Hons) Biochemistry, MBiol Biochemistry, BSc(Hons) Microbiology, MBiol Microbiology, BSc(Hons) Pharmacology, MBiol Pharmacology

Postgraduate courses: MSc Biomedical Science, MSc Biotechnology, MSc Molecular Cell Biology, MSc Pharmacology, MSc Neuropharmacology, MSc Molecular Microbiology, MRes Biotechnology, MRes Cancer Biology, MRes Cell Biology, MRes Molecular Biology, MRes Molecular Microbiology, MRes Neuropharmacology, MRes Pharmacology

Chemistry

BSc(Hons) Chemistry, BSc(Hons) Medicinal Chemistry, MChem Chemistry

Postgraduate courses: MSc Chemistry/Chemistry (Professional Practice), MRes Chemistry, MRes Advanced Materials Engineering, MRes Analytical Chemistry, MRes Pharmaceutical Analysis, MRes Pharmaceutical and Medicinal Science, MSc Forensic Science

Computing and Technology

BSc(Hons) Computer Science, BSc(Hons) Computer Science (Games Technology), BSc(Hons) Software Engineering, BSc(Hons) Computer Systems Engineering, BSc(Hons) Computer Systems (Networks), BSc(Hons) Computer Systems (Forensic and Security), BSc(Hons) Computing, BSc(Hons) Digital Media Technology, BSc(Hons) Information Systems, BSc(Hons) Information and Communications Technology, BSc(Hons) Data Science, BSc(Hons) Computer Science and Mathematics, MComp(Hons) Computer Science, MComp(Hons) Computer Systems Engineering

Postgraduate courses: MSc Computer Science, MSc Computing Systems, MSc Computer Games Systems, MSc IT Security, MSc Cloud and Enterprise Computing, MSc Interactive Media Engineering, MSc Engineering (Cybernetics and Communications), MSc Engineering (Electronics), MSc Engineering Management, MSc Data Analytics for Business, MRes Computer Science, MRes Electronic Systems

Forensics

BSc(Hons) Forensic Science, FdSc Forensic Science

Mathematics

BSc(Hons) Mathematics, BSc(Hons) Financial Mathematics, BSc(Hons) Computer Science and Mathematics, BSc(Hons) Sport Science and Mathematics, BSc(Hons) Physics and Mathematics, BSc(Hons) Data Science, MMath(Hons) Mathematics

Postgraduate courses: MRes Mathematical Sciences, MSc Data Analytics for Business

Physics

BSc(Hons) Physics, BSc(Hons) Physic with Nuclear Technology, BSc(Hons) Physics with Astrophysics, BSc(Hons) Physics and Mathematics, MSci Physics

Postgraduate course: MRes Medical and Materials Imaging

Sport Science

BSc(Hons) Sport Science and Management, BSc(Hons) Sport and Exercise Science, BSc(Hons) Coaching and Sport Science, BSc(Hons) Exercise, Nutrition and Health

Postgraduate courses: MRes Sport Science, MRes Exercise Physiology, MRes Performance Nutrition, MRes Performance Analysis, MRes Biomechanics, MRes Sport and Exercise Psychology

School of Social Sciences; www.ntu.ac.uk/soc

BA(Hons) Criminology, BA(Hons) Health and Social Care, BA(Hons) International Relations, BA(Hons) Politics, BA(Hons) Policing, BA(Hons) Politics and International Relations, BSc(Hons) Psychology (British Psychological Society accredited), BSc(Hons) Psychology with Criminology (British Psychological Society accredited), BSc(Hons) Psychology with Sociology (British Psychological Society accredited), BA(Hons) Sociology, BA(Hons) Social Work, BA(Hons) Youth Justice, BA(Hons) Youth Studies

Postgraduate courses: MSc/ PGDip Psychology, MSc Applied Child Psychology, MRes/ MSc Psychological Research Methods, MSc Forensic Mental Health, MSc Forensic Psychology, MSc Cyberpsychology, MSc Psychology in Clinical Practice, MSc Psychological Wellbeing and Mental Health, MA Criminology, MA Sociology, MA Politics, MA International Relations, Online MA International Relations (Distance learning), MA Public Health, PG Cert/ MA Career Development

THE OPEN UNIVERSITY
www.open.ac.uk

Arts & Humanities

BA (Honours) Arts and Humanities, BA (Honours) Arts and Humanities (Philosophy), BA (Honours) Arts and Humanities (Religious Studies), BA (Honours) Criminology and Law, Bachelor of Laws (Honours) (LLB), Bachelor of Laws (Honours) (graduate entry), BA (Honours) Philosophy and Psychological Studies, BA (Honours) Politics, Philosophy and Economics, BA (Honours) Religion, Philosophy and Ethics, BA (Honours) Arts and Humanities (Music), BA (Honours) Classical Studies, BA (Honours) Music, BA (Honours) Arts and Humanities (Classical Studies), BA (Honours) Music, BA (Honours) Arts and Humanities (Creative Writing), BA (Honours) Social Sciences (Religious Studies), BA (Honours) Arts and Humanities (English Language), BA (Honours) Arts and Humanities (English Literature), BA (Honours) Arts and Humanities (History), BSc (Honours) Combined STEM BSc (Honours) Computing & IT and Design, BSc (Honours) Computing & IT and a second subject, BA/BSc (Honours) Design and Innovation, BA (Honours) English Language and Literature, BA (Honours) English Literature, BA (Honours) English Literature and Creative Writing, BA (Honours) History, BA (Honours) History and Politics, BA(Honours) International Studies, (Honours) Language Studies, BA (Honours) Arts and Humanities (French), BA (Honours) Arts and Humanities (German), BA (Honours) Arts and Humanities (Spanish), BA (Honours) Language Studies with English and French, BA (Honours) Language Studies with English and German, BA (Honours) Language Studies with English and Spanish, BA (Honours) Language Studies with French and German, BA (Honours) Language Studies with French and Spanish, BA (Honours) Language Studies with German and Spanish, BA/BSc(honours) Open Degree, BA (Honours) Arts and Humanities (Art History), BA (Honours) Childhood and Youth Studies

Business & Management

BA (Honours) Business Management, BA (Honours) Business Management (Economics), BA (Honours) Business Management (Leadership Practice), BA (Honours) BSc (Honours) Computing & IT and Business, BSc (Honours) Computing & IT and a second subject, BA (Honours) Business Management (Innovation and Enterprise), BSc (Honours) Combined STEM, BA (Honours) Business Management (Accounting), BA (Honours) Business Management (Marketing)

Computing & IT

BSc (Honours) Computing and IT, BSc (Honours) Computing and IT (Communications and Networking), BSc (Honours) Computing and IT (Communications and Software), BSc (Honours) Computing and IT (Software), Top-up BSc (Honours) Computing and IT Practice, BSc (Honours) Combined STEM, (Honours) Computing & IT and Psychology, BSc (Honours) Computing & IT and a second subject, BSc (Honours) Data Science, BA/BSc (Honours) Open degree

Design

BSc (Honours) Computing & IT and Design, BA/BSc (Honours) Design and Innovation, BSc (Honours)

Computing & IT and a second subject BSc (Honours) Combined STEM, BA/BSc (Honours) Open degree

Education, Childhood & Youth

BA (Honours) Childhood and Youth Studies, BA (Honours) Early Childhood, Top-up BA (Honours) Early Childhood, BA (Honours) Health and Social Care, BSc (Honours) Sport, Fitness and Coaching, BA (Honours) Education Studies (Primary), BSc (Honours) Mathematics and its Learning BA/BSc (Honours) Open degree

Engineering

Bachelor of Engineering (Honours), Top-up Bachelor of Engineering (Honours), BSc (Honours) Combined STEM, BA/BSc (Honours) Design and Innovation

Environment & Development

BSc (Honours) Combined STEM, BSc (Honours) Environmental Science, BSc (Honours) Environmental Science (Environmental Management), BA (Honours) Environmental Studies, BSc (Honours) Geography and Environmental Science, BA/BSc (Honours) Design and Innovation BA/BSc (Honours) Open degree

Health & Social Care

BA (Honours) Health and Social Care, BSc (Honours) Health Sciences, BSc (Honours) Healthcare and Health Science, BSc (Honours) Adult Nursing, BSc (Honours) Psychology with Counselling, BA (Honours) Childhood and Youth Studies, BSc (Honours) Mental Health Nursing, BA (Honours) Social Work (England), BA (Honours) Social Work (Scotland), BA (Honours) Social Work (Scotland) (graduate entry), BA (Honours) Social Work (Wales), BA (Honours) Education Studies (Primary), BA/BSc (Honours) Open degree

Health & Wellbeing

BSc (Honours) Sport, Fitness and Coaching, BSc (Honours) Health Sciences, BA (Honours) Health and Social Care, BSc (Honours) Healthcare and Health Science, BSc (Honours) Mental Health Nursing, BSc (Honours) Combined STEM, BA/BSc (Honours) Open degree

Languages

BA (Honours) Arts and Humanities, BA (Honours) Arts and Humanities (English Language), BA (Honours) Arts and Humanities (English Literature), BA (Honours) English Language and Literature, BA (Honours) Language Studies, BA (Honours) Language Studies with English and French, BA (Honours) Language Studies with English and German, BA (Honours) Language Studies with English and Spanish, BA (Honours) Language Studies with French and German, BA (Honours) Language Studies with French and Spanish, BA (Honours) Language Studies with German and Spanish, BA (Honours) Arts and Humanities (French), BA (Honours) Arts and Humanities (German), BA (Honours) Arts and Humanities (Spanish), BA (Honours) English Literature, BA (Honours) English Literature and Creative Writing, BA (Honours) Classical Studies, BA/BSc (Honours) Open degree

Law

Bachelor of Laws (Honours) (LLB), Bachelor of Laws (Honours) (graduate entry), BA (Honours) Criminology and Law

Mathematics & Statistics

BSc (Honours) Mathematics and Statistics, BSc (Honours) Computing & IT and Mathematics, BSc (Honours) Computing & IT and a second subject, BSc (Honours) Economics and Mathematical Sciences, BSc (Honours) Mathematics, BSc (Honours) Mathematics and Physics, BSc (Honours) Mathematics and its Learning, BSc (Honours) Data Science, BSc (Honours) Computing & IT and Statistics, BSc (Honours) Combined STEM

Medical Sciences

BSc (Honours) Health Sciences, BSc (Honours) Combined STEM, BA/BSc (Honours) Open degree

Nursing & Healthcare Practice

BSc (Honours) Nursing Practice, BSc (Honours) Health Sciences, BA (Honours) Health and Social Care, BSc (Honours) Healthcare and Health Science, BSc (Honours) Adult Nursing, BSc (Honours) Mental Health Nursing, BA (Honours) Social Work (England), BA (Honours) Social Work (Scotland), BA (Honours) Social Work (Scotland) (graduate entry), BA (Honours) Social Work (Wales), BA/BSc (Honours) Open degree

Psychology & Counselling

BSc (Honours) Combined STEM, BSc (Honours) Computing & IT and Psychology, BSc (Honours) Computing & IT and a second subject, BA (Honours) Criminology and Psychology, BA (Honours) Philosophy and Psychological Studies, BSc (Honours) Psychology, BSc (Honours) Psychology with Counselling, BA (Honours) Social Sciences (Psychology), BSc (Honours) Forensic Psychology, BSc (Honours) Social Psychology, BA (Honours) Childhood and Youth Studies, BA/BSc (Honours) Open degree

Science

BSc (Honours) Geography and Environmental Science, BSc (Honours) Health Sciences, BSc (Honours) Healthcare and Health Science, BSc (Honours) Combined STEM, BSc (Honours) Natural Sciences, BSc (Honours) Natural Sciences (Chemistry), BSc (Honours) Natural Sciences (Environmental Science), BSc (Honours) Natural Sciences (Physics), BSc (Honours) Mathematics and Physics, BSc (Honours) Environmental Science, BSc (Honours) Environmental Science (Environmental Management), BSc (Honours) Natural Sciences (Astronomy and Planetary Science), BSc (Honours) Natural Sciences (Biology), BSc (Honours) Natural Sciences (Earth Sciences), BA (Honours) Environmental Studies, BSc (Honours) Sport, Fitness and Coaching, BA/BSc (Honours) Open degree

Social Sciences

BA (Honours) Social Sciences, BA (Honours) Social Sciences (Economics), BA (Honours) Business Management (Economics), BSc (Honours) Economics and Mathematical Sciences, BA(Honours) International Studies, BA (Honours) Politics, Philosophy and Economics, BSc (Honours) Combined STEM, BSc(Hons)) Computing & IT and Psychology, BSc (Honours) Computing & IT and a second subject, BA (Honours) Criminology and Psychology, BA (Honours) Environmental Studies, BSc (Honours) Forensic Psychology, BSc (Honours) Geography and Environmental Science, BA (Honours) History and Politics, BA (Honours) Philosophy and Psychological Studies, BSc (Honours) Psychology, BSc (Honours) Psychology with Counselling, BA(Honours) Criminology, BSc (Honours) Social Psychology, BA (Honours) Childhood and Youth Studies, BA (Honours) Social Sciences (Criminology), BA (Honours) Social Sciences (Geography), BA (Honours) Social Sciences (Politics), BA (Honours) Social Sciences (Psychology), BA (Honours) Social Sciences (Religious Studies), BA (Honours) Social Sciences (Sociology), BA (Honours) Criminology and Law, BA (Honours) Criminology and Sociology, BA (Honours) Economics, Bachelor of Laws (Honours) (LLB), Bachelor of Laws (Honours) (graduate entry), BA/BSc (Honours) Open degree

Postgraduate courses

Masters Degrees in: Advanced Clinical Practice, Art History, Childhood and Youth, Classical Studies, Computing, Creative Writing, Crime and Justice, Development Management, Education, Engineering, English, Environmental Management, Finance, Forensic Psychological Studies, History, Human Resource Management, MA/MSc Open, Mathematics, MBA (Master of Business Administration), MBA (Technology Management), Mental Health Science, Philosophy, Psychology, Science, Social Work, Space Science and Technology, Systems Thinking in Practice, Technology Management, Translation

PG Diplomas in: Advanced Clinical Practice Business Administration, Childhood and Youth Studies, Computing, Development Management, Engineering, Environmental Management, Finance, Human Resource Management, Humanities, Mathematics, Mental Health Science, Online and Distance Education, Professional Studies in Education, Social Work, Space Science and Technology, Systems Thinking in Practice, Technology Management, Translation

PG Certificates in: Business Administration Childhood and Youth Studies, Computing, Conflict and Development, Development Management, Environmental Management, Finance, Human Resource Management, Human Rights and Development Management, Humanities, Mathematics, Non-Medical Prescribing, Online and Distance Education, Professional Studies in Education, Social and Psychological Inquiry, Space Science, Systems Thinking in Practice, Technology Management, Translation

UNIVERSITY OF OXFORD
www.ox.ac.uk

Division of Humanities; www.ox.ac.uk/divisions/humanities

Rothermere American Institute; www.rai.ox.ac.uk

English and American studies/US history/politics/literature; MSt

Faculty of Classics; www.classics.ox.ac.uk

BA(Hons), MPhil, MSt and DPhil degrees in the following areas: classics, classics and English/modern languages/ oriental studies, classical archaeology and ancient history, ancient and modern history, Greek and/or Roman history, Greek and/or Latin languages and literature, ancient history, classical languages and literature

Ruskin School of Drawing and Fine Art; www.ruskin-sc.ox.ac.uk

BFA, MFA DPhil in the following areas: fine art

Faculty of English, Language & Literature; www.english.ox.ac.uk

BA(Hons), DPhil, MLitt, MPhil, MSt degrees in the following areas: English language and literature (650-1550; 1550-1700; 1600-1830; 1800-1914; 1900-present day), English & modern languages/classics/history

History of Art Department; www.hoa.ox.ac.uk

BA(Hons), DPhil, MLitt and MSt degrees in the following areas: history of art, topics include gothic: artistic originality and the transmission of style in medieval art, image and thought, media and modernity: art and mass culture, 1880–2000, the apparatus of art history, theories of vision: the eye and the gaze, women, art and culture in early modern Europe

Faculty of History; www.history.ox.ac.uk

BA(Hons), DPhil, MPhil, MSc, MSt and MLetters degrees in the following areas: history of the British Isles, general history, historical methods, British history, general history, ancient and modern history, history and economics, history and English, history and modern languages, history and politics; Postgraduate studies include; British and European history, from 1500 to the present, economic and social history, global and imperial history, history of art and visual culture, history of science, medicine and technology, late antique and Byzantine studies, medieval history, medieval studies, modern south Asian studies, US history

Faculty of Linguistics, Philology and Phonetics; www.ling-phil.ox.ac.uk

BA, MPhil, PhD and MSt degrees in the following areas: modern languages and linguistics, psychology, philosophy and linguistics, Graduate Courses; general linguistics and comparative philology, general linguistics and comparative philology, comparative philology and general linguistics

Faculty of Medieval & Modern Languages; www.mod-langs.ox.ac.uk

BA(Hons), DPhil, MPhil and MSt degrees in the following areas: Arabic, Czech (with Slovak, modern Greek, classics, French, German, Hebrew, history, Italian, linguistics, Persian, philosophy, Polish, Portuguese, Russian, Spanish, Turkish; Graduate Taught Courses; modern languages, Slavonic studies, Yiddish studies, women's studies, film aesthetics, medieval studies, MSt in comparative literature and critical translation

Faculty ofMusic; www.music.ox.ac.uk

BMus, DPhil, MA(Hons), MPhil, MSt and MLitt degrees in the following areas: chamber music, choral studies/conducting performance, composition & analysis, dance music, musicology, ethnomusicology, historical musicology, jazz, musical history/theory, the motet in the 14/15th centuries, orchestration, music analysis & criticism, performance & interpretation, psychology of music, theory & analysis, source studies, technology of composition, south Western music theory; Masters; composition, ethnomusicology, musicology, performance, psychology of music

Faculty of Oriental Studies; www.orinst.ox.ac.uk

BA(Hons), DPhil, MPhil and MSt degrees in the following areas: Arabic, Aramaic with Syriac, Armenian, Asia & Near Asian studies, bible interpretation, Buddhist studies, Chinese studies, classic & oriental studies, Classical Armenian studies, Classical Hebrew studies, Classical Indian religion, Coptic, Cuneiform studies, Eastern Christian studies, eastern Christianity, Egyptology, Egyptology & ancient Near East, European & Middle East languages, Hebrew & Jewish studies, Hindi & Urdu, Hindi and Urdu, Islamic art and archaeology, Islamic studies and history, Islamic world, Japanese studies, Jewish studies, Jewish studies in the Graeco-Roman period, Judaism and Christianity in the Graeco-Roman World, Korean, Korean studies, Medieval Arabic thought, Modern Chinese studies, Modern Jewish studies, Modern Middle Eastern studies, Modern South Asian studies, Old Iranian, Oriental studies, Ottoman Turkish studies, Pali, Pali and Prakrit, Persian, Sanskrit, Syriac studies, theology & oriental studies, Tibetan and Himalayan studies, Traditional East Asia, Turkish

Faculty of Philosophy; www.philosophy.ox.ac.uk

BA(Hons), BPhil, MPhil and PhD degrees in the following areas: philosophy and modern languages; philosophy and theology; physics and philosophy; mathematics and philosophy; psychology, philosophy and linguistics; computer science and philosophy early modern philosophy, knowledge and reality, ethics: philosophy of mind, philosophy of science and social science, philosophy of religion, the philosophy of logic and language, aesthetics, medieval philosophy: Aquinas/Duns Scotus and Ockham, the philosophy of Kant, post-Kantian philosophy, theory of politics, Plato, Republic, Aristotle, Frege, Russell and Wittgenstein, formal logic, philosophy of physics, philosophy of mathematics, philosophy of science, philosophy of cognitive science, the philosophy and economics of the environment, philosophical logic, Plato, Latin philosophy, jurisprudence

Faculty of Theology;
www.theology.ox.ac.uk

BA(Hons), BTh, MTh, MSt, MLitt, MPhil, DPhil, PGDip/Cert degrees in the following areas: theology & religion/oriental studies, philosophy & theology, applied theology, theology in applied theology, sociology of religion, pastoral psychology, science and faith in the modern world, the use of the bible, Christian spirituality, liturgy and worship, Christian ethics, mission in the modern world, inter-faith dialogue, ecclesiology in an ecumenical context, Old Testament, New Testament, biblical interpretation, Christian ethics, philosophical theology, science & religion, modern/Reformation/scholastic/patristic theology, ecclesiastical history, the study of religions, issues in theology, Judaism and Christianity in the Graeco-Roman world

Division of Mathematical, Physical and Life Sciences; www.ox.ac.uk/divisions/mpls

Dept of Chemistry; www.chem.ox.ac.uk

DPhil, MChem, MSc degrees in the following areas: chemical biology, inorganic chemistry, organic chemistry, physical chemistry, mathematical techniques, molecular biochemistry/& chemical biology, organic chemistry/reactions/synthesis, organometallic chemistry, physical & theoretical chemistry, quantum mechanics, reaction mechanisms, solid state chemistry, spectroscopy, theoretical chemistry, thermodynamics

Dept of Computer Science;
www.cs.ox.ac.uk

BA(Hons), MSc, DPhil, PhD degrees in the following areas: computer science, mathematics/ & computer science, modelling & scientific computing, mathematics & foundations of computer science & philosophy, software engineering, software & systems security

Dept of Engineering Science;
www.eng.ox.ac.uk

DPhil, MEng, MSc, EngD degrees in the following areas: engineering science, autonomous intelligent machines and systems, gas turbines aerodynamics, synthetic biology, renewable energy marine uk DPhil, MEng, MSc, EngD degrees in the following areas: engineering science, autonomous intelligent machines and systems, gas turbines aerodynamics, synthetic biology, renewable energy marine structures; research in engineering science, automotive engineering, aerothermal engineering, micromechanics and materials modelling, mechanical performance and integrity, advanced structures, biotechnics, hydraulics, sustainable energy, environmental engineering, bioprocesses, process systems, chemical engineering, production engineering, optoelectronics, microelectronics, communications, power electronics, machine vision and robotics, machine learning, multivariable control, nonlinear and predictive control, medical imaging and informatics, cellular engineering and therapy, dynamic systems, chaos, optimization and mathematical models, autonomous intelligent machines and systems CDT, gas turbines aerodynamics CDT

Life Science Interface; Doctoral Training Centre; www.lsi.ox.ac.uk

DPhil degrees in the following areas; biological systems, biological experimental techniques, biological physics, organic chemistry, molecular genetics & cell biology, mathematical biology, medicinal chemistry, programming, bioinformatics, statistical data systems, structural biology

Division of Materials;
www.materials.ox.ac.uk

DPhil, MEng, MSc, MS, MEm degrees in the following areas: materials science, materials structures & mechanical properties of metals, electrical/mechanical properties, nanoelectronics, materials economics, non-metallic materials, composites, polymers, packaging/superconducting/semiconducting materials, structural & nuclear materials, device materials, nanomaterials, process & manufacturing, characterisation, computational nuclear modelling

Mathematical Institute;
www.maths.ox.ac.uk

BA(Hons), DPhil, MCF, MFoCS, MS, MSc, MMath degrees in the following areas: mathematics, mathematics and statistics/philosophy/computer science/theoretical physics; Research Areas; algebra, combinatorics, functional analysis, geometry, history of mathematics, logic, mathematical and computational finance, mathematical physics, number theory, numerical analysis, industrial and applied mathematics, nonlinear partial differential equations, stochastic analysis, topology, mathematical biology

Dept of Physics; www.physics.ox.ac.uk

BA(Hons), DPhil, MPhys, MPhysPhil degrees in the following areas: physics, atmospheric oceanic & planetary physics, astrophysics, condensed matter physics, cosmology, general relativity, quantum theory, sub-atomic physics, particle physics, physics, atomic & laser/theoretical physics, physics & philosophy

Dept of Plant Science; www.plants.ox.ac.uk/plants

DPhil, MRes, MSc degrees in the following areas: biochemistry & systems biology, biological science, cell biology/physiology, cell & development biology, comparative developmental genetics, ecology, evolution & systematics, plant science

Dept of Statistics; www.stats.ox.ac.uk

BA(Hons), DPhil, MMath, MSc, PGDip degrees in the following areas: applied statistics, mathematics & statistics, applied probability & research in statistics

Dept of Zoology; www.zoo.ox.ac.uk

DPhil, MRes, MSc degrees in the following areas: animal behaviour/welfare, ageing biology, biological science, infectious disease, ecology & conservation, evolution & development, food science, molecular biology & bioinformatics, indigenous biology, ornithology, integrative bioscience, wildlife conservation

Biological Science; www.biologyy.ox.ac.uk

organisms, cells & genes, ecology, qualitative methods, evolution, adaptation to the environment, cell & developmental biology, animal behaviour, disease, plants

Division of Medical Sciences; www.ox.ac.uk/divisions/ medical_science

Dept of Biochemistry; www.bioch.ox.ac.uk

DPhil, MBiochem, MSc, PhD degrees in the following areas: biochemistry, molecular & cellular biology, structural chromosome and developmental biology, infection, immunity and translational medicine, neuroscience, integrative systems biology, life sciences interface systems approaches to biomedical science e biochemistry, biomedical imaging, synthetic biology, iological chemistry and biophysical chemistry, organic chemistry and maths & statistics, macromolecular structure and function, bioenergetics and

metabolism, genetics and molecular biology, cell biology, molecular immunology, plant molecular biology, neuropharmacology, membrane transport, glycobiology, human disease, bionanotechnology, systems biology and signalling to the nucleus, biochemistry, medical sciences, chromosome & developmental biology, structural biology, infection, immunity and translational medicine

Nuffield Dept of Clinical Medicine; www.ndm.ox.ac.uk

PhD, MSc degrees in the following areas: cancer biology, genetic medicine, immunology & infectious diseases, protein science & structural biology, physiology, cellular & molecular biology, tropical medicine & global health

Dept of Clinical Neurosciences; www.ndcn.ox.ac.uk

DPhil, MSc degrees in the following areas: medicine, medical sciences, sleep medicine, MRT physics/analysis, biomedical sciences, experimental psychology, clinical neurology, functional MRI of the brain, anaesthesia

Dept of Experimental Psychology; www.psy.ox.ac.uk

BA(Hons), DPhil, MSc degrees: experimental psychology, psychology, philosophy & linguistics, psychological research;

Radcliffe Department of Medicine

Division of Cardiovascular Medicine, Oxford Centre for Diabetes, Endocrinology and Metabolism, MRC Weatherall Institute of Molecular Medicine, Nuffield Division of Clinical Laboratory Sciences, The Oxford Acute Vascular Imaging Centre, Centre for the Advancement of Sustainable Medical Innovation Investigative Medicine Division

Nuffield Dept of Obstetrics & Gynaecology; www.obs-gyn.ox.ac.uk

obstetrics & gynaecology, clinical embryology; MSc, DPhil

Dept of Oncology; www.oncology.ox.ac.uk

oncology, radiation biology, experimental therapeutics, medical oncology, radiation oncology & radiobiology; DPhil, MRes, MSc

Department of Orthopaedics, Rheumatology andMusculoskeletal Sciences; www.ndorms.ox.ac.uk

orthopaedics, rheumatology, musculoskeletal sciences, translational medicine & medical technology, immunology; MSc, DPhil

Dept of Paediatrics;
www.paediatrics.ox.ac.uk
medicine, paediatric infection and immunity, paediatric infectious diseases, international child health, paediatric endocrinology and diabetes, paediatric haematology, neonatology, paediatric gastroenterology and nutrition, HIV infection and immune control, molecular infectious diseases, developmental immunology, paediatric neuroimaging and pain, vaccinology; PhD, MSc, DPhil

Sir William Dunn School of Pathology;
www.path.ox.ac.uk
bacteriology and virology, cell biology, infection, immunology & molecular medicine, microbiology and molecular biology; DPhil

Dept of Pharmacology;
www.pharm.ox.ac.uk
pharmacology, cardiovascular/autonomic in vivo/ systems neuroscience, drug discovery/medicinal chemistry, cell signalling, molecular neuroscience and disease, cellular neuroscience, experimental therapeutics, practical drug therapy, medical chemistry for cancer; MSc, DPhil

Dept of Physiology, Anatomy and Genetics;
www.dpag.ox.ac.uk
functional genomics, cell physiology, development cell biology,neuroscience, cardiac science; BA, MPhil, MSc, DPhil

Nuffield Department of Population Health;
www.ndph.ox.ac.uk
global health science, population technology, population health, ethics & law, medical sociology, population pathology, integrated population health, global health, preventive medicine; DPhil, MSc

Nuffield Dept of Primary Health Sciences;
www.phc.ox.ac.uk
evidence-based health care, health research, primary healthcare, behavioural medicine, evidence-based medicine, health service economics and organisation, chronic kidney disease, clinical trials, tobacco addiction, diabetes and long-term conditions, health, heart failure research, hypertension, infectious diseases research; DPhil, MSc

Dept of Psychiatry;
www.psychiatry.ox.ac.uk
experimental psychology, eating disorders, suicide, child & adolescent psychiatry, clinical psychopharmacology, bipolar research, experimental psychopathology & cognitive therapies, forensic psychiatry, neural correlates of gene function, neurobiology and experimental therapeutics, neurobiology of ageing, autism, eating disorders, human brain activity, cognitive approaches to psychosis, cognitive health and neuroscience clinical trials, mindfulness, perinatal psychopathology and offspring development, psychological medicine, psychopharmacology and emotion, social psychiatry, translational neurobiology of psychosis, translational neuroimaging, translational neuroscience & dementia MSc, DPhil, MRCPsych

Nuffield Dept of Surgical Science;
www.surgery.ox.ac.uk
surgical science, endovascular neurosurgery, integrated immunology, surgical science and practice; DPhil, MCh, MS, MSc

Division of Social Sciences;
www.socsci.ox.ac.uk

School of Anthropology and Museum Ethnography; www.anthro.ox.ac.uk
anthropology, archaeology & anthropology, human science, medical anthropology, cognitive & evolutionary anthropology, visual material & museum anthropology, migration studies; BA, BSc, DPhil, MPhil, MSc

Pitt Rivers Museum; www.prm.ox.ac.uk
visual, material & museum anthropology, material culture, visual anthropology, art and aesthetics, sensory anthropology, ethnographic photography and film, and museum anthropology; DPhil, MPhil, MSc

School of Archaeology; www.arch.ox.ac.uk
archaeology & anthropology, bioarchaeology, Eurasian prehistory, classical archaeology & ancient history, historical & classical chronology, materials & technology, chronology, Eurasian prehistory, Palaeolithic archaeological science; BA(Hons), DPhil, MLitt, MSc, MSt

SAID Business School; www.sbs.ox.ac.uk
law and finance, major programme management, MBA economics and management, management studies, executive MBA, financial economics, strategic management, financial strategy, global business, organisational leadership, strategy and innovation, cyber risk for managers, finance, high performance leadership, performing leaders, private equity, real estate, women transforming leadership; BA, Dip, MBA, Exec MBA, MSc

Dept of Economics; www.economics.ox.ac.uk

economics, macroeconomics, microeconomics, quantitative economics, British economic history since 1870, command & transitional economies, comparative demographic systems, econometrics, economics of developing countries, economics of industry, finance, game theory, international economics, labour economics & industrial relations, mathematical methods, microeconomic theory, money & banking, philosophy & economics of the environment, public economics, advanced econometrics, advanced macroeconomics, advanced microeconomics, behavioural economics, development economics, economic history, financial economics, industrial organisation, international trade, labour economics, public economics, theory based empirical analysis; BA(Hons), DPhil, MEng, MSc, MPhil

Dept of Education; www.education.ox.ac.uk

applied linguistics, education (comparative & international education/higher education/learning & technology/ children & education/research), learning and teaching/in HE, PGCE (numerous secondary subjects, Schools Direct), teaching English in university setting; DPhil, MSc, PGCE, PGDip

School of Geography & the Environment; www.geog.ox.ac.uk

geographical research, space, place and society, earth system dynamics, biogeography, biodiversity and conservation, climate change and variability, climate change impacts and adaptation, complexity, contemporary urban life, island life, cultural spaces: geographies of affective experience, desert landscapes and dynamics, environmental change & management, environmental geography, European integration, forensic geography, geographies of finance, geographies of nature, geopolitics in the margin, heritage science & conservation, post-Soviet Russia in transition, quaternary period: natural & human systems, transport & mobilities, geography & the environment, conservation/environmental change & management, nature, society & environmental governance, water science, policy & management; BA(Hons), BCL, Dip, DPhil, MJur, MLitt, MPhil, MSc, MSt, PGDip

School of Interdisciplinary Area Studies; www.area-studies.ox.ac.uk

African studies, Latin American studies, contemporary Chinese studies, contemporary India, modern Japanese studies, Middle East studies, Russian and East European studies, MBA, MSc, MPhil, DPhil

Dept of International Development; www.qeh.ox.ac.

international development, development studies, economics for development, global governance and diplomacy, migration studies;MPhil, MSc, DPhil

Oxford Internet Institute; www.oil.ox.ac.uk

social science of the internet, information, communication & the social sciences; DPhil, MSc

Faculty of Law; www.law.ox.ac.uk

law, jurisprudence, jurisprudence with senior status, law with law studies in Europe, legal studies, Postgraduate; civil law, magister juris, criminology and criminal justice, law and finance, taxation, international human rights law, intellectual property law and practice BA(Hons), BCL, Dip. DPhil, MJur, MLitt, MPhil, MSc, MSt, PGDip, MJur

Oxford Martin School; www.oxfordmartin.ox.ac.uk

research in health & medicine, energy & environment, technology & society, ethics & governance

Oxford-Man Institute of Quantitative Finance; www.oxford-man.ox.ac.uk

data analysis and patterns in data, decision making under uncertainty and asset allocation, efficient markets, risk premia and market anomalies, electronic trading, numerical methods and high performance computing in finance, pensions, investments and hedge fund industry, stability of financial systems

Dept of Politics & International Relations; www.politics.ox.ac.uk

history and politics, international relations, politics (political theory/European politics & society), political/ political theory research, philosophy, politics and economics; BA(Hons), DPhil, MLitt, MPhil, MSc

Dept of Social Policy & Intervention; www.spi.ox.ac.uk

comparative social policy, evidence-based social intervention and policy evaluation, social policy or social intervention, social policy, social intervention BA, MPhil, MSc

Dept of Sociology; www.sociology.ox.ac.uk

sociology, history & politics, human sciences, philosophy, politics & economics, sociology and demography; BA(Hons), DPhil, MPhil, MSc

OXFORD BROOKES UNIVERSITY
www.brookes.ac.uk

Business School; www.brookes.ac.uk/OBBS

BSc(Hons) Accounting and Finance, BSc(Hons) Accounting and Economics, BSc(Hons) Business and Finance, BSc(Hons) Economics, Finance and International Business, BA(Hons) Economics, Politics and International Relations, BA(Hons) Business and Management, BA(Hons) International Business Management, BA(Hons) Business, Enterprise and Entrepreneurship, BA(Hons) Business and Marketing Management, BA(Hons) Marketing Management, BA(Hons) Marketing Communications Management, BA(Hons) Marketing and Events Management, BA(Hons) Events Management, BSc/BA(Hons) Business Management, BA(Hons) Business Management and Geography, BA(Hons) Business Management and International Relations, BSc/BA(Hons) Business Management and Sport, Coaching and Physical Education, BSc(Hons) Applied Accounting, Fd(A) Events Management, Fd(A) Business and Enterprise, Fd(A) Business and Management Practice, BA(Hons) Business and Marketing Management (Top-up), BA(Hons) International Business Management (Top-up), BA(Hons) Business and Management (Top-up)

Postgraduate courses in the following subjects: MSc Accounting and Finance, MSc Finance, MSc International Business Economics, MSc Business Management, MSc Business Management and Corporate Social Responsibility, MSc Business Management and Human Resource Management, MSc Business and Marketing Management, MSc Business Management and Digital Strategy, MSc Business Management and Entrepreneurship, MSc Business Management and Finance, MSc Business and Supply Chain Management, MSc Entrepreneurship and Innovation, MSc Human Resource Management, MSc International Management, MSc International Human Resource Management, MSc International Management (Human Resource Management), MSc International Management and International Relations, MSc Marketing, MSc Marketing and Brand Management, MSc International Luxury Marketing, MSc Digital Marketing, MSc Marketing Communications Management, MSc International Events Management, MSc International Events Marketing, MSc International Hospitality, Events and Tourism Management, MSc International Hotel and Tourism Management, MSc International Tourism Management, The Oxford Brookes Global MBA, MA Human Resource Management, Postgraduate Diploma in Human Resource Management, MA Human Resource Management – A fast-track MA for Postgraduate Diploma holders, Doctor of Coaching and Mentoring (DCM), Postgraduate Certificate, Diploma and MA Coaching and Mentoring Practice, Global MBA, MSc Applied Accounting

Department of Biological and Medical Sciences; www.brookes.ac.uk/bms

Undergraduate degrees in the following subjects:, Animal Biology and Conservation BSc(Hons), Biological Sciences BSc(Hons), Biological Sciences (Genetics and Genomics) BSc(Hons), Biological Sciences (Human Biosciences) BSc(Hons), Biological Sciences (Zoology) BSc(Hons), MBiol (Biological Sciences) MBiol, Biomedical Science BSc(Hons), Equine Science BSc(Hons), Equine Science and Thoroughbred Management BSc(Hons), Life Sciences Foundation FdSc, Medical Science BSc(Hons)

Postgraduate courses in the following subjects: MSc/PgDip/ PGCert Conservation Ecology, MSc/ PgDip/ PGCert Medical Genetics and Genomics

Department of English and Modern Languages; www.brookes.ac.uk/englishlanguages

Undergraduate degrees in the following subjects: Applied Languages BA(Hons), English Literature BA(Hons), Literature with Creative Writing BA(Hons), Japanese Studies BA(Hons), Humanities FdA

Postgraduate courses in the following subjects: MA International Business and Intercultural Communication, Creative Writing MA, English Literature MA

Department of Nursing and Midwifery www.brookes.ac.uk/osnm/

Undergraduate degrees in the following subjects: Adult Nursing BSc, Children's Nursing BSc, Mental Health Nursing BSc, Midwifery BSc, Health Sciences Open Award BSc

Postgraduate courses in the following subjects: Adult Nursing MSc, Children's Nursing MSc, Health Sciences Open Award MSc, Mental Health Nursing MSc, Midwifery MSc, Adult and Mental Health Nursing MSci, Mental Health and Child Nursing MSci

317

Department of Psychology, Health and Professional Development; www.brookes.ac.uk/phpd

Undergraduate degrees in the following subjects: Health Sciences Open Award, Operating Department Practice BSc, Paramedic BSc, Psychology BSc

Postgraduate courses in the following subjects: Psychology MSc, MSc/ PGDip/ PGCert Management in Health and Social Care, MSc/ PGDip/ PGCert Health Sciences Open Award, PGDip/ PGCert/ MPH Public Health, PGDip/ PGCert/ MPH Global Public Health Leadership

Department of Social Sciences; www.brookes.ac.uk/social-sciences

Foundation in Humanities FdA, Anthropology BSc(Hons), Biological Anthropology BSc(Hons), Social Anthropology BA(Hons), Geography BSc(Hons), International Relations BA/ BSc(Hons), International Relations and Politics BA(Hons), Politics BA(Hons), Sociology BA(Hons), PGDip in Anthropology, MA International Relations, MA International Relations (Distance Learning), MA International Security, MRes Primatology and Conservation, MSc Primate Conservation, Research Degrees

Department of Sport, Health Sciences and Social Work; www.brookes.ac.uk/shssw

Undergraduate degrees in the following subjects: BSc Physical Activity and Health Promotion, BSc Sport and Exercise Science, BSc Sport, Coaching and Physical Education, BSc Top-up Applied Sports Science, FdSc Sports Coaching, Fitness and Rehabilitation, FdSc Sports Science with Sports Coaching Education, BSc Nutrition, BSc Occupational Therapy, BA Social Work, BSc Physiotherapy

Postgraduate courses in the following subjects: MSc Applied Sport and Exercise Nutrition, MSc Applied Human Nutrition, MSc Ocupational Therapy (pre-registration), MA/ PGDip Social Work, MSc Physiotherapy (pre registration)

School of Architecture; www.architecture.brookes.ac.uk

Undergraduate degrees in the following subjects: Architecture BA(Hons), Interior Architecture BA(Hons) Design BA(Hons)

Postgraduate courses in the following subjects: Architecture MArch/ PGDip, International Architectural Regeneration and Development MA / PGDip / PGCert, Sustainable Architecture: Evaluation and Design MA / PGDip / PGCert, Development and Emergency Practice, MA / PGDip / PGCert, Humanitarian Action and Peacebuilding, MA / PGDip / PGCert, Shelter after Disaster PGCert

School of Arts; www.brookes.ac.uk/schoolof-arts

FdA Art & Design, BA Fine Art, BA Graphic Design, BA Photography, BSc Digital Media, BA Film, BA Music, BA Media, Journalism & Publishing

Postgraduate courses in the following subjects: MA Publishing Media, MA Digital Publishing, MA Publishing Studies, MFA Fine Art, MA Sound Arts, MSc Digital Media Production, MA Film Studies: Popular Cinema, MA Music, MA Sound Arts

School of Education; www.brookes.ac.uk/education

Foundation in Humanities FdA, Early Childhood Studies BA(Hons), Education Studies BA(Hons), Education Studies – SEN, Disabilities and Inclusion BA(Hons), English Language and Linguistics BA(Hons), Primary Teacher Education BA(Hons)

Postgraduate courses in the following subjects: MA Education, Doctor of Education, PGCE Primary (3–7 and 5–11), PGCE Secondary (School Direct), PGCE – Post-compulsory, Research Degrees

School of Engineering, Computing and Mathematics; www.brookes.ac.uk/ecm

Engineering Foundation FdEng, Foundation Degree in Motorsports Engineering FdEng, Electrical and Electronic Engineering FdEng, Mechanical Engineering FdEng, Motorsports – Performance and Automotive Technology FdEng, Electro-Mechanical Engineering BEng(Hons), Mechanical Engineering BEng(Hons), MEng, Mechanical Engineering BSc(Hons) single, Motorsport Engineering BEng(Hons), MEng, Motorsport Technology BSc(Hons) single, Robotic Engineering BEng or MEng, Electronic Engineering (Top-up), BSc(Hons) single, Automotive Engineering with Electric Vehicles MSc, Computing FdSc, Computer Science BSc(Hons), Computer Science for Cyber Security BSc(Hons) single, Robotics BSc(Hons) single, Information Technology Management for Business BSc(Hons) single, Mathematics BSc(Hons)

Postgraduate courses in the following subjects: Data Analytics MSc, Data Analytics for Government MSc, Automotive Engineering BEng(Hons), MEng, Computer Science MSc, PGDip, PGCert, Computer Science for Cyber Security MSc, PGDip, PGCert, Computing MSc, PGDip, PGCert, Data Analytics MSc, Software Engineering MSc, PGDip, PGCert,

Mechanical Engineering MSc, Motorsport Engineering MSc, Racing Engine Systems MSc

School of History, Philosophy and Culture; www.brookes.ac.uk/hpc

FdA in Humanities, Communication, Media and Culture BA(Hons), Criminology BSc(Hons), History BA(Hons), History of Art BA(Hons), Philosophy BA(Hons)

Postgraduate courses in the following subjects: MA History, MA History of Medicine, Research Degrees

School of Law; www.brookes.ac.uk/schoolof-law

LLB Law, LLB International transfer

Postgraduate courses in the following subjects: PGDip Law, LLM International Law, LLM International Human Rights Law, LLM Commercial Law and International Trade, LLM Legal Practice, Research Degrees

School of the Built Environment; be.brookes.ac.uk

FdSc Built Environment, Construction Project Management BSc, Quantity Surveying and Commercial Management BSc, Planning and Property Development BA, Urban Design, Planning and Development BA, Real Estate Management BSc, Planning and Property Development BA

Postgraduate courses in the following subjects: Building Information Modelling and Management MSc, Construction Project Management MSc, Infrastructure and Sustainable Development MSc, Project Management in the Built Environment MSc, Quantity Surveying and Commercial Management MSC, Environmental Assessment and Management MSc, Historic Conversion MSc, Infrastructure and Sustainable Development MSc, Spatial Planning MSc, Urban Design MSc, Real Estate MSc, Real Estate Investment Finance MSc

The Oxford School of Hospitality Management; www.brookes.ac.uk/hospitality

BSc(Hons) International Hospitality Management

Postgraduate courses in the following subjects: MSc International Hospitality, Events and Tourism Management, MSc International Hotel and Tourism Management, MSc International Tourism Management

---

UNIVERSITY OF PLYMOUTH
www.plymouth.ac.uk

Plymouth Institute of Education; www.plymouth.ac.uk/schools/education

CertEd Certificate in Education (incorporating the Diploma in Education and Training) (Full-time), BA(Hons) Early Childhood Studies (Full-time), BA(Hons) Education (Full-time), BA(Hons) Education with Foundation (Full-time), BEd(Hons) Primary (FS/KS1 with QTS) (Full-time), BEd(Hons) Primary (KS1/KS2 with QTS) (Full-time), BEd(Hons) Primary (Special Educational Needs with QTS) (Full-time)

Postgraduate courses: MA Education (Full-time, Part-time route available), PgCert Education: Autism (Part-time), PGCE (incorporating the Diploma in Education and Training) (Part-time), PGCE (incorporating the Diploma in Education and Training) (Full-time), PGCE Primary (Full-time), PGCE Primary (Early Years) (Full-time), PGCE Secondary (Art & Design) (Full-time), PGCE Secondary (Drama) (Full-time), PGCE Secondary (English) (Full-time), PGCE Secondary (Geography) (Full-time), PGCE Secondary (History) (Full-time), PGCE Secondary (Mathematics) (Full-time), PGCE Secondary (Music) (Full-time), PGCE Secondary (Science with Biology) (Full-time), PGCE Secondary (Science with Chemistry) (Full-time), PGCE Secondary (Science with Physics) (Full-time), PgCert The National Award for Special Educational Needs Coordination (Part-time)

Plymouth University Peninsula Dental School; www.plymouth.ac.uk/schools/peninsula-school-of-dentistry

BDS Dental Surgery, BSc(Hons) Dental Therapy and Hygiene

Postgraduate courses: MSc Minor Oral Surgery, MSc Periodontology, MSc Restorative Dentistry

Plymouth University Peninsula Medical School; www.plymouth.ac.uk/schools/peninsula-school-of-medicine

BMBS Bachelor of Medicine, Bachelor of Surgery, BSc(Hons) Diagnostic Radiography

Postgraduate courses: MClinEd Clinical Education, MClinEd Clinical Education, PgCert Clinical Education, MSc Clinical Sciences (Blended learning), MSc Healthcare Management, Leadership and Innovation,

MSc Physician Associate Studies, MSc Global Health, MSc Healthcare Improvement and Patient Safety, Research Masters (ResM), Master of Philosophy (MPhil), Doctor of Philosophy (PhD) and Doctor of Medicine (MD) programmes, PgDip Simulation and Patient Safety

School of Art, Design and Architecture; www.plymouth.ac.uk/schools/school-ofart-design-and-architecture

BA(Hons) 3D Design, BA(Hons) 3D Design – Designer Maker/Product Designer/Spatial and Interior Designer, BA(Hons)/MArch Architecture, BA/BSc(Hons) Digital Media Design, BA/BSc(Hons) Digital Design Innovation BA(Hons), Documentary Photography, BA(Hons) Film & Television Production, BA(Hons) Fine Art, BA(Hons) Game Arts and Design, BA(Hons) Graphic Communication with Typography, BA(Hons) Illustration, BA(Hons) Creative Media, BA/BSc(Hons) Internet Design, BA(Hons) Media Arts, BA(Hons) Photography, BA(Hons) English with Publishing, BSc(Hons) Architectural Engineering, BSc(Hons)

Postgraduate courses: MA Architecture, MA Contemporary Art Practice, MA Design, MA Publishing, MArch Architecture, MRes Digital Art and Technology, MSc High Performance Buildings, ResM Art, Design and Architecture, MA Smart Urban Futures, MA Illustration, MA Integrated Design Innovation, Mphil/PhD and ResM in Environmental Building, Mphil/PhD and ResM in Design Thinking, Mphil/PhD and ResM in Architecture

School of Biological and Marine Sciences; www.plymouth.ac.uk/schools/school-ofbiological-and-marine-sciences

BSc(Hons) Animal Behaviour and Welfare, BSc(Hons) Animal Conservation Science, BSc(Hons) Biological Sciences, BSc(Hons) Biosciences, BSc(Hons) Conservation Biology, BSc(Hons) Marine Biology, BSc(Hons) Marine Biology and Coastal Ecology, BSc Marine Biology and Oceanography, BSc(Hons) Ocean Science, BSc(Hons) Ocean Exploration and Surveying, BSc(Hons) Ocean Science and Marine Conservation, BSc(Hons) Oceanography and Coastal Processes

Postgraduate courses: MRes Applied Marine Science, MRes Marine Biology, MRes Marine Renewable Energy, MSc Applied Marine Science, MSc Hydrography, MSc Marine Renewable Energy, MSc Sustainable Aquaculture Systems, MSc Zoo Conservation Biology, MSci(Hons) Ocean Science, ResM Biological Sciences, MSc Marine Conservation

School of Biomedical Sciences www.plymouth.ac.uk/schools/biomedicalsciences

BSc(Hons) Biomedical Science, BSc(Hons) Health and Fitness, BSc(Hons) Healthcare Science (Life Sciences), BSc(Hons) Healthcare Science (Physiological Sciences), BSc(Hons) Human Biosciences, BSc(Hons) Nutrition, Exercise and Health BSc Medical Physiology

Postgraduate courses: MSc Biomedical Science, PgDip Biomedical Science, MSc Clinical Cardiac Science, MPhil/PhD Biomedical Sciences, ResM Biomedical Sciences, MPhil/PhD Dental Studies, ResM Dental Studies, MPhil/PhD Medical Studies, ResM Medical Studies, MD Medicine

School of Computing, Electronics and Mathematics; www.plymouth.ac.uk/schools/school-of-computing-electronics-and-mathematics

BEng(Hons) Electrical and Electronic Engineering, MEng(Hons) Electrical and Electronic Engineering, BEng(Hons) Electrical and Electronic Engineering with Foundation Year, BEng(Hons) Robotics, BSc(Hons) Computer and Information Security, BSc(Hons) Computer Science, MSci(Hons) Computer Science, BSc(Hons) Computing & Games Development, BSc(Hons) Computing, BSc(Hons) Data Modelling and Analytics, BSc(Hons) Electrical and Electronic Engineering, BSc(Hons) Mathematics, BSc(Hons) Mathematics and Statistics, BSc(Hons) Mathematics with Education, BSc(Hons) Mathematics with Finance, BSc(Hons) Mathematics with Foundation Year, BSc(Hons) Mathematics with High Performance Computing, BSc(Hons) Mathematics with Theoretical Physics, BSc(Hons) Robotics

Postgraduate courses: MEng(Hons) Robotics, MRes Robotics, MEng(Hons) Robotics, MRes Robotics, MSc Data Science and Business Analytics, MSc Electrical and Electronic Engineering, MSc Robotics, MSci(Hons) Computer Science, MSc Cyber Security

School of Engineering; www.plymouth.ac.uk/schools/school-ofengineering

BEng/MEng(Hons) Civil and Coastal Engineering, BEng/MEng(Hons) Civil Engineering, BEng/MEng(Hons) Marine Technology, BEng/MEng(Hons) Mechanical Engineering, BEng/MEng(Hons) Mechanical Engineering with Composites, FdSc/HNC Mechanical Design and Manufacture, BSc(Hons) Navigation and Maritime Science, FdSc Navigation and Maritime Science, FdSc/HNC

Manufacturing and Mechatronic Engineering, FdSc Mechanical Engineering

Postgraduate courses: MSc Advanced Engineering Design, MSc Civil Engineering, MSc Coastal Engineering, MSc Autonomous Systems, MPhil/PhD Civil Engineering

School of Geography, Earth and Environmental Sciences; www.plymouth.ac.uk/schools/school-ofgeography-earth-and-environmentalsciences

BA(Hons) Geography, BA(Hons) Geography with International Relations, BSc(Hons) Applied Geology, BSc(Hons) Chemistry, BSc(Hons) Chemistry with Foundation Year, BSc(Hons) Environmental Management and Sustainability, BSc(Hons) Environmental Science, BSc(Hons) Environmental Science with Foundation Year, BSc(Hons) Geography, BSc(Hons) Geography with Ocean Science, BSc(Hons) Geology, BSc(Hons) Geology with Ocean Science, BSc(Hons) BSc(Hons) Physical Geography and Geology MChem Analytical Chemistry, MRes Sustainable Environmental Management, MSc Analytical Chemistry, MSc Environmental Consultancy, MSc Planning, MSc Sustainable Environmental Management, MSc Human Geography Research

School of Health Professions; www.plymouth.ac.uk/schools/school-ofhealth-professions

BA(Hons) Social Work, BSc(Hons) Dietetics, BSc(Hons) Occupational Therapy, BSc(Hons) Optometry, BSc(Hons) Paramedic, BSc(Hons) Physiotherapy, BSc(Hons) Podiatry

Postgraduate courses: MA Social Work, MClinRes Clinical Research, MSc Advanced Professional Practice (Health and Social Care Professions), MSc Advanced Professional Practice in Dietetics, MSc Advanced Professional Practice in Neurological Rehabilitation, MSc Advanced Professional Practice in Occupational Therapy, MSc Advanced Professional Practice in Paediatric Dietetics, MSc Advanced Professional Practice in Physiotherapy, MSc Human Nutrition, MSc Occupational Therapy (Pre-Registration), MSc Pre-Hospital Critical Care/Retrieval and Transfer

School of Humanities and Performing Arts; www.plymouth.ac.uk/schools/hpa

BA(Hons) Acting, BA(Hons) Anthropology, BA(Hons) Art History, BSc(Hons) Computing, Audio and Music Technology, BA(Hons) Creative and Professional Writing BA(Hons) Dance, BA(Hons) Directing BA(Hons) Drama and Theatre Practice BA(Hons) English, BA(Hons) English and Creative Writing, BA(Hons) English with History, BA(Hons) English with Publishing, BA(Hons) Fine Art and Art History, BA(Hons) History, BA(Hons) History with English, BA(Hons) History with International Relations, BA(Hons) History with Politics, BA(Hons) Music

Postgraduate courses: MA Archival Practice, MA Creative Writing, MA English Literature, MA English Literature, MA History, MA Performance Training, MFA Performance Training, MRes English, ResM Art History, ResM Computer Music, ResM Dance, ResM History, ResM Theatre and Performance, MPhil/PhD Art History, PhD Creative Writing, MPhil/PhD English, MPhil/PhD History, MPhil/PhD Music, MPhil/PhD Performing Arts

School of Law, Criminology and Government; www.plymouth.ac.uk/schools/law-criminology-government

BSc(Hons) Criminology and Criminal Justice Studies, BSc(Hons) Criminology and Criminal Justice Studies with International Relations, BSc(Hons) Criminology and Criminal Justice Studies with Law, BSc(Hons) Criminology and Criminal Justice Studies with Psychology, BSc(Hons) Criminology and Criminal Justice Studies with Sociology, BSc(Hons) International Relations, BSc(Hons) International Relations with Law, BSc(Hons) International Relations with Politics, BSc(Hons) Law with Business, BSc(Hons) Law with Criminology and Criminal Justice Studies, BSc(Hons) Police and Criminal Justice Studies, BSc(Hons) Politics with International Relations, BSc(Hons) Politics with Law, BSc(Hons) Sociology, GradDip Law, LLB(Hons) Law, LLB(Hons) Law with Criminology and Criminal Justice Studies

Postgraduate courses: MA International Relations: Global Security and Development, MSc Criminology

School of Nursing and Midwifery; www.plymouth.ac.uk/schools/school-ofnursing-and-midwifery

BSc(Hons) Critical Care (Intercalated), BSc(Hons) Critical Care, MNurs(Hons) Nursing (Adult Health and Child Health) BSc(Hons) Nursing (Adult), MNurs(Hons) Nursing (Child Health and Mental Health) BSc(Hons) Nursing (Child Health), BSc(Hons) Nursing (Mental Health), BSc(Hons) Pre-Registration Midwifery, BSc(Hons) Professional Development in Advancing Practice, BSc(Hons) Professional Development in Community and

Primary Care, BSc(Hons) Professional Development in Critical Care, BSc(Hons) Professional Development in End of Life Care, BSc(Hons) Professional Development in Health and Social Care, BSc(Hons) Professional Development in Long Term Conditions, BSc(Hons) Professional Development in Mental Health, BSc(Hons) Professional Development in Neonatal Care, BSc(Hons) Professional Development in Nursing, BSc(Hons) Urgent and Emergency Care (Intercalated), BSc(Hons) Urgent and Emergency Care

Postgraduate courses: MSc Advanced Critical Care Practitioner, MSc Advanced Neonatal Nurse Practitioner, MSc Advanced Professional Practice (Clinical Practitioner), MSc Advanced Professional Practice (Community and Primary Care Practitioner), MSc Advanced Professional Practice (Mental Health Practitioner), MSc Advanced Professional Practice (Nursing and Midwifery Professions), MSc Contemporary Healthcare (Education), MSc Pre-registration Nursing (Adult Health), MSc Pre-registration Nursing (Child Health), MSc Pre-registration Nursing (Mental Health) MSc Surgical Care Practitioner (Abdominal, Pelvic and General Surgery), MSc Surgical Care Practitioner (Cardiothoracic Surgery), MSc Surgical Care Practitioner (Trauma and Orthopaedic Surgery), PgDip Advanced Critical Care Practitioner, PgDip Surgical Care Practitioner (Abdominal, Pelvic and General Surgery), PgDip Surgical Care Practitioner (Cardiothoracic Surgery), PgDip Surgical Care Practitioner (Trauma and Orthopaedic Surgery)

School of Psychology; www.plymouth.ac.uk/schools/psychology

BSc(Hons) Psychological Studies, BSc(Hons) Psychology, BSc(Hons) Psychology with Criminology and Criminal Justice Studies, BSc(Hons) Psychology with Human Biology, BSc(Hons) Psychology with Sociology, MPsych(Hons) Advanced Psychology, MPsych(Hons) Clinical Psychology (Full-time)

Postgraduate courses: MSc Psychology, MSc Clinical Psychology, PgCert Clinical Psychology, PgDip Clinical Psychology

SOUTH DEVON COLLEGE
www.southdevon.ac.uk

FdSc Adventure Leadership, FdSc Animal Science, BSc(Hons) Applied Animal Science, FdA Applied Arts*, FdSc Biosciences, HNC Business, FdA Business & Management, BA(Hons) Child Development and Education, FdSc/HNC Civil and Coastal Engineering, BSc(Hons) Civil Engineering, BSc(Hons) Coaching (Outdoor Leadership), BSc(Hons) Coaching (Sports Performance and Development), FdSc Community Health and Wellbeing, FdSc Computing, FdA Creative Digital Design*, FdSc Criminology and Psychology, BSc(Hons) Digital and Technology Solutions, FdA Digital Marketing, BTEC Diploma in Education and Training, FdA Early Years Care and Education, BA(Hons) Education, Development and Society, FdSc/HNC Electronics and Robotic Control Engineering, HNC Enhanced Care Work, BSc(Hons) Enhanced Integrated Care, FdA Fashion with Textiles, FdA Film and Photography, FdA Games and Interactive Design, FdSc Healthcare Practice, FdA History with English, FdA Illustration Arts, FdSc Law, BA(Hons) Leadership and Management, FdSc/ HNC Manufacturing and Mechatronic Engineering, FdSc Marine Technologies, FdA Professional Practice in Construction Operations Management, FdSc Psychology with Sociology, FdSc Sports Coaching and Fitness, FdSc Sustainable Construction and the Built Environment, FdA Teaching and Learning, FdA Tourism, Hospitality and Events Management, FdA Working with Children, Young People and Families*, FdSc Yacht Operations * Subject to Approval

TRURO & PENWITH COLLEGE
www.trurocollege.ac.uk

BA(Hons) Applied Media, BA(Hons) Business, Enterprise and Leadership, BA(Hons) Education and Training, BA(Hons) Human Behavioural Studies, BA(Hons) Silversmithing and Jewellery, BSc(Hons) Applied Computing Technologies, BSc(Hons) Applied Social Science, BSc(Hons) Applied Sport and Health Science, BSc(Hons) Archaeology, FDA Business, Certificate in Education Full/ Part-Time, FDA Childhood Education, FDA Children and Young Peoples Workforce, FDA Computer Games Design and Production, FDA English Studies, FDA Film, Media and Photography, FDA History, Heritage and Archaeology, FDA Silversmithing and Jewellery, FDSc Archaeology, FDSc Biomedical Studies, FDSc Community Studies (Development and Youth Work), FDSc Computer Technology, FDSc Cyber Technology FDSc Exercise, Health and Fitness, FDSc Health and Nutrition, FDSc Health & Social Care, FDSc Law, FDSc Public Services, FDSc Sports Coaching, FDSc Sports Coaching, FDSc Sports Rehabilitation, HNC Applied Psychology, HNC Applied Psychology,

HNC Art and Design, HNC Business, HNC Children and Young Peoples Workforce, HNC Children and Young Peoples Workforce, HNC Computer Games Design and Production, HNC Cyber Security, HNC Hospitality Management, HND Applied Biology, HND Applied Psychology, HND Applied Psychology, HND Art and Design, HND Hospitality Management, Postgraduate Certificate in Education

UNIVERSITY OF PORTSMOUTH
www.port.ac.uk

Faculty of Creative and Cultural Industries; www.port.ac.uk/faculty-ofcreative-and-cultural-industries

Portsmouth School of Architecture and Surveying;

Architecture BA(Hons), Building Surveying (Degree Apprenticeship) BSc(Hons), Building Surveying BSc(Hons) Interior Architecture and Design BA(Hons) Property Development BSc(Hons), Quantity Surveying (Degree Apprenticeship) BSc(Hons), Quantity Surveying BSc(Hons)

Postgraduate courses: Architecture MArch, Architecture Degree Apprenticeship MArch, Building Information Management MSc, Building Information Management PgCert, Creative Industries MRes Final Examination in Professional Practice (Part 3) Architecture, Historic Building Conservation MSc, Interior Design MA Quantity Surveying MSc, Real Estate Management MSc, Sustainable Cities MA, Technology MRes, Architecture and Surveying MPhil and PhD

Fashion, Photography, Graphic Arts and Design

Fashion and Textile Design BA(Hons), Graphic Design BA(Hons), Illustration BA(Hons), Photography BA(Hons), Creative Media and Technology HND

Postgraduate courses: Creative Industries MRes Data Visualisation Design MA, Fashion and Textiles MA, Graphic Design MA, Illustration MA, Photography MA, Art, Design and Performance MPhil and PhD

Computer Games, Animation and Digital Technologies

Animation BA(Hons), Computer Animation and Visual Effects BSc(Hons), Computer Games Enterprise BSc(Hons), Computer Games Technology

BSc(Hons), Creative Media Technologies BSc(Hons), Creative Technologies and Enterprise (Learning at Work) BA(Hons)/BSc(Hons), Digital Media BSc(Hons), Virtual and Augmented Reality BSc(Hons)

Postgraduate courses: Computer Animation MSc, Computer Games Technology MSc, Creative Industries MRes, Creative Technologies MSc, Professional Studies (Learning at Work) MA/MSc, Computing and Creative Technologies MPhil and PhD

Film & Television Courses

Film Industries BA(Hons), Film Production BA(Hons), Television and Broadcasting BSc(Hons), Creative Media and Technology

Postgraduate courses: Creative Industries MRes, Creative Professional Development PGCert, Film and Television MSc, Film, Media and Communication MPhil and PhD, Media and Communication MA

Media and Journalism

Journalism BA(Hons), Journalism with Media Studies BA(Hons), Media and Digital Practice BA(Hons), Media Studies BA(Hons), HND Creative Media and Technology

Postgraduate courses: Creative Industries MRes, Creative Writing MA, Digital Media MSc, Film and Television MSc, Media and Communication MA, Film, Media and Communication MPhil and PhD

Drama, Music and Creative Arts

Creative Music Technology Top-up BA(Hons), Drama and Performance BA(Hons), Musical Theatre BA(Hons), Music and Sound Technology BSc(Hons)

Postgraduate courses: Creative Industries MRes, Music Technology MSc, Art, Design and Performance MPhil and PhD

English and Creative Writing

Creative Writing BA(Hons), English and Creative Writing BA(Hons), Film Industries BA(Hons), English Language and Linguistics BA(Hons), English Language and Linguistics with Literature BA(Hons), English Literature BA(Hons), English Literature with History BA(Hons), English Literature with Media Studies BA(Hons) Film Industries and Creative Writing

Postgraduate courses: Creative Writing MA, Creative Industries MRes Humanities and Social Sciences MRes, PGCE courses PGCE, Film, Media and Communication MPhil and PhD, Victorian Gothic History Literature and Culture MA

Faculty of Humanities and Social Sciences; www.port.ac.uk/faculty-ofhumanities-and-social-sciences

Childhood, Youth Studies and Education

Further Education and Training CertEd, Childhood and Youth Studies BA(Hons), Childhood and Youth Studies with Criminology, BA(Hons),Childhood and Youth Studies with Psychology BA(Hons), Early Childhood Studies BA(Hons), Early Childhood Studies with Psychology BA(Hons), Early Years Care and Education FDA, Education Studies (Top-Up) BA(Hons), Further Education and Training CertEd, Learning Support FDA

Postgraduate courses: Education Studies MA, Educational Leadership and Management PgDip, Educational Leadership and Management PgCert, Educational Leadership and Management MSc, Early Years Initial Teacher Training GradCert, MRes Humanities and Social Sciences MRes, PGCE Computer Science, PGCE English, PGCE Geography, PGCE Mathematics, PGCE Modern Foreign Languages, PGCE Science, Education and Sociology MPhil and PhD

Languages

Applied Languages BA(Hons), Modern Languages BA(Hons)

Postgraduate courses: Applied Linguistics and TESOL MA Humanities and Social Sciences MRes Masters of French Language Double Diploma PGCE PGCE courses PGCE Translation Studies MA Languages and Applied Linguistics MPhil and PhD

History, Politics and International Relations

History BA(Hons), History with Politics BA(Hons), History with Sociology BA(Hons), International Relations and Languages BA(Hons), International Relations with History BA(Hons), International Relations with International Development Studies BA(Hons) International Relations BA(Hons), International Relations and Politics BA(Hons), Politics BA(Hons), Sociology BSc(Hons), Sociology and Criminology BSc(Hons), Sociology with Media Studies BSc(Hons) Sociology with Psychology BSc(Hons)

Postgraduate courses: Conservation Architecture MA, Humanities and Social Sciences MRes, International Business and Management MSc, International Development Studies MSc/PgDip/PgCert International Relations MA, Naval History MA PGCE courses PGCE, Area Studies, History and Politics MPhil and PhD, Victorian Gothic History Literature and Culture MA

Portsmouth Business School; www.port.ac.uk/portsmouth-businessschool

Accounting, Economics and Finance

Accountancy and Financial Management (Top-up) BA(Hons), Accounting with Finance BA(Hons), Economics BSc (Econ)(Hons), Economics and Management BA(Hons), Economics, Finance and Banking BSc (Econ)(Hons), Financial Management BA(Hons)

Postgraduate courses: Accounting and Finance MSc, Corporate Finance MSc, Economics, Finance and Banking MSc, Finance MSc Forensic Accounting MSc, International Finance and Banking MSc, Accounting, Economics and Finance, MPhil and PhD opportunities

Business Management and Marketing

Business and Human Resource Management BA(Hons) – An EPAS accredited programme, Business and Management BA(Hons) – An EPAS accredited programme, Business and Management FDA, Business and Supply Chain Management BSc(Hons) Business HND, Business with Business Communication (Top-up) BA(Hons), Business Management and Entrepreneurship BA(Hons) – An EPAS accredited programme, Chartered Manager Degree Apprenticeship (Business, Leadership and Management) BA(Hons), Digital Marketing BA(Hons), Finance with Business Communication (Top-up) BA(Hons), International Business BA(Hons) – An EPAS accredited programme, Leadership, Business and Management (Top-up) BA(Hons), Marketing BA(Hons) – An EPAS accredited programme, Project Manager Degree Apprenticeship, (Project Management) BSc(Hons)

Postgraduate courses: Business and Management MSc – An EPAS accredited programme, Business and Management MPhil and PhD, Digital Business Management MSc, Digital Marketing MA, Global MBA, Human Resource Management MSc/PgDip, Human Resource Development and Training Management PgDip, Human Resource Development (Top-up) MSc, Human Resource Management (Top-up) MSc, International Human Resource Management MSc, Innovation Management and Entrepreneurship MSc, International Business and Management MSc, Leadership and Management (Top-up) MSc, Marketing MA, Project Management MSc, Risk, Crisis and Resilience Management MSc, Strategic Leadership MBA, Strategic Leadership (Degree Apprenticeship) MBA

Law

Law with Business LLB(Hons), Law with Criminology LLB(Hons), Law with International Relations LLB(Hons)

Postgraduate courses: Corporate Governance and Law/Grad ICSA LLM, Counter Fraud and Counter Corruption MSc, Crime Science MSc, Criminal Justice MSc, Criminal Psychology MSc, Criminology MSc, Cybercrime MSc, Dispute Resolution LLM/PgCert, Forensic Accounting MSc, Forensic Information Technology MSc, Forensic Psychology MSc, Forensic Psychology Practice PgDip, Humanities and Social Sciences MRes, Intelligence MSc, International Criminal Justice MSc, Law LLM, Law and Legaltech LLM, Policing, Policy and Leadership MSc, Professional Studies (Learning at Work) MA/MSc, Science MRes, Security Management MSc, Victimology MSc, Law and Criminology MPhil and PhD

Faculty of Science; www.port.ac.uk/ faculty-of-science

School of Biological Sciences

Biochemistry BSc(Hons), Biology BSc(Hons), Marine Biology BSc(Hons)

Postgraduate courses: Applied Aquatic Biology MSc, Applied Science (Learning at Work) MA/MSc, Biotechnology MSc, Medical Biotechnology MSc, PGCE courses PGCE, Professional Studies (Learning at Work) MA/MSc, Science MRes Biological Sciences MPhil and PhD

Earth Sciences

Engineering Geology and Geotechnics BEng(Hons), Environmental Science BSc(Hons), Geology BSc(Hons), Palaeontology BSc(Hons)

Postgraduate courses: Applied Science (Learning at Work) MA/MSc, Coastal and Marine Resource Management MSc Crisis and Disaster Management MSc, MSc Engineering Geology MSc, Environmental Geology and Contamination MSc, Geological and Environmental Hazards MSc, Geographical Information Systems MSc, Professional Studies (Learning at Work) MA/MSc, Science MRes Earth and Environmental Sciences MPhil and PhD

Geography and Environmental Science

Environmental Management BSc(Hons), Environmental Science BSc(Hons), Geography BA(Hons), Geography BSc(Hons), Marine Environmental Science BSc(Hons)

Postgraduate courses: Applied Science (Learning at Work) MA/MSc Civil Engineering with Environmental Engineering MSc Coastal and Marine Resource Management MSc, Crisis and Disaster Management MSc, Engineering Geology MSc, Environmental Geology and Contamination MSc, Geographical Information Systems MSc, Geological and Environmental Hazards MSc, Maritime Studies (Learning at Work) MSc, PGCE courses PGCE, Professional Studies (Learning at Work) MA/MSc, Science MRes, Earth and Environmental Sciences MPhil and PhD

Healthcare and Social Care

Advanced Dental Nursing BSc(Hons), Advanced Dental Nursing DipHE, Advancing Professional Practice (Top-up) BSc(Hons), Biomedical Science BSc(Hons), Dental Hygiene and Dental Therapy BSc(Hons), Dental Hygiene BSc(Hons), Dental Nursing CertHE, Diagnostic Radiography and Medical Imaging BSc(Hons), Nursing (Adult) BN(Hons), Nursing (Mental Health) BN(Hons), Operating Department Practice BSc(Hons), Optometry MOptom, Paramedic Science BSc(Hons), Pharmaceutical Science (Top-Up) BSc(Hons), Pharmacology BSc(Hons), Pharmacy MPharm(Hons), Social Work BSc(Hons)

Postgraduate courses: Applied Science (Learning at Work) MA/MSc, Health Psychology MSc, Humanities and Social Sciences MRes, Occupational Health and Safety Management (Distance Learning) PgCert, Occupational Health and Safety Management (Learning at Work) MA/MSc, Occupational Health, Safety and Environmental Management (Learning at Work) MSc, Physician Associate Studies MSc, Prescribing and Therapeutics PgCert, Professional Studies (Learning at Work) MA/MSc, Psychology and Learning Disability MSc, Science MRes, Social Work MSc

Approved, Health Sciences and Social Work MPhil and PhD

Criminology and Forensic Studies

Counter Fraud and Criminal Justice Studies (Distance Learning) BSc(Hons), Crime and Criminology (Distance Learning) BSc(Hons), Criminology and Criminal Justice BSc(Hons), Criminology and Cybercrime BSc(Hons), Criminology and Forensic Studies BSc(Hons), Criminology with Psychology BSc(Hons), Policing and Investigation (Distance Learning) BSc(Hons), Risk and Security Management (Distance Learning) BSc(Hons), Sociology and Criminology BSc(Hons)

Postgraduate courses: Corporate Governance and Law/Grad ICSA LLM, Counter Fraud and Counter Corruption MSc, Crime Science MSc, Criminal Justice MSc, Criminal Psychology MSc, Criminology MSc, Cybercrime MSc, Dispute Resolution LLM/PgCert, Forensic Accounting MSc, Forensic Information, Technology MSc, Forensic Psychology MSc, Forensic Psychology Practice PgDip, Intelligence MSc, International Criminal Justice MSc, Law LLM, Policing, Policy and Leadership MSc, Professional Studies (Learning at Work) MA/MSc, Security Management MSc, Victimology MSc, Humanities and Social Sciences MRes Law and Criminology MPhil and PhD Science MRes, Professional Doctorate in Criminal Justice DCrimJ, Professional Doctorate in Security Risk, Management DSyRM

Psychology

Forensic Psychology BSc(Hons), Psychology BSc(Hons)

Postgraduate courses: Criminal Psychology MSc Forensic Psychology MSc, Forensic Psychology Practice PgDip, Health Psychology MSc, Professional Studies (Learning at Work) MA/MSc, Science MRes, Psychology and Learning Disability MSc, Sport and Exercise Psychology MSc, Psychology MPhil and PhD

Sport Science

Exercise and Fitness Management BSc(Hons), Sport and Exercise Psychology BSc(Hons), Sport and Exercise Science BSc(Hons), Sports Management and Coaching HND, Sports Management and Development BSc(Hons)

Postgraduate courses: Clinical Exercise Science MSc, Human and Applied Physiology MSc, Science MRes, Clinical Exercise Science PgCert, Clinical Exercise Science PgDip, Physical Activity, Exercise and Health MSc, Sport and Exercise Psychology MSc, Sports

Management MSc, Sports Performance MSc, Sport and Exercise Science MPhil and PhD, Professional Doctorate in Sport and Exercise Psychology

Faculty of Technology; www.port.ac.uk/ faculty-of-technology

School of Computing

Business Information Systems BSc(Hons), Computer Networks BSc(Hons), Computer Science BSc(Hons), Computer Science MEng, Computing and Information Systems (Distance Learning Top-Up) BSc(Hons), Computing BSc(Hons), Computing HND, Cyber Security and Forensic Computing BSc(Hons), Data Science and Analytics BSc(Hons) Software Engineering BSc(Hons)

Postgraduate courses: Applied Computing (Learning at Work) MA/MSc, Business and Computer Studies (Learning at Work) MA/MSc, Computer Network Administration and Management MSc, Data Analytics MSc, Forensic Information Technology MSc, Geographical Information Systems MSc, Information Systems MSc, Law and LegalTech LLM, PGCE courses PGCE, Professional Studies (Learning at Work) MA/MSc, Technology MRes, Computing and Creative Technologies MPhil and PhD

Engineering

Civil Engineering (Degree Apprenticeship) BEng(Hons), Civil Engineering BEng(Hons), Civil Engineering MEng, Construction Engineering Management BEng(Hons), Electronic Engineering (Top-Up) (Degree Apprenticeship) BEng(Hons) Electronic Engineering BEng(Hons), Electronic Engineering MEng, Electronic Systems Engineering (Distance Learning) (Top-up) (2 or 3 Year) BEng(Hons), Engineering and Technology with Foundation Year BEng(Hons), Industrial Design BSc(Hons), Innovation Engineering BEng(Hons), Innovation Engineering MEng, Mechanical and Manufacturing Engineering BEng(Hons), Mechanical Engineering BEng(Hons), Mechanical Engineering HNC, Mechanical Engineering MEng, Petroleum Engineering BEng(Hons), Petroleum Engineering MEng, Product Design and Innovation BSc(Hons)

Postgraduate courses: Advanced Manufacturing Technology MSc, Civil Engineering MSc, Civil Engineering with Environmental Engineering MSc, Civil Engineering with Structural Engineering MSc, Construction Project Management MSc, Electronic Engineering MSc, Energy and Power Systems Management MSc, Engineering (Learning at Work) MA/MSc, Engineering and Management (Learning at

Work) MA/MSc, Engineering Competence (Distance Learning) (Degree Apprenticeship) PgDip, Engineering Geology MSc, Engineering Management MSc, Engineering Project Management (Learning at Work) MA/MSc, Maritime Studies (Learning at Work) MSc, Mechanical Engineering MSc, Petroleum and Gas Engineering MSc, Quantity Surveying MSc, Technology MRes, Engineering MPhil and PhD

Mathematics and Physics

Mathematics BSc(Hons), Mathematics MMath, Mathematics for Finance and Management BSc(Hons), Mathematics with Statistics BSc(Hons), Physics BSc(Hons), Physics MPhys(Hons), Physics, Astrophysics and Cosmology BSc(Hons), Physics, Astrophysics and Cosmology MPhys(Hons)

Postgraduate course: PGCE courses, Professional Studies (Learning at Work) MA/MSc, Science MRes, Technology MRes, Mathematics and Physics MPhil and PhD opportunities

---

QUEEN MARGARET UNIVERSITY
www.qmu.ac.uk

BA/ BA(Hons) Accounting and Finance, BA Acting, BA(Hons) Acting for Stage and Screen, BA(Hons) Business Management, BA(Hons) Business Management (Graduate Apprenticeship) BA(Hons) Business Management with Enterprise, BA(Hons) Business Management with Finance, BA(Hons) Business Management with Marketing, BA(Hons) Costume Design and Construction, BSc(Hons) Diagnostic Radiography, MDiet Dietetics, BA/BA(Hons) Drama, BA(Hons) Drama, Theatre and Performance, BA(Hons) Education Studies, BA(Hons) Education Studies (Primary), BA(Hons) Events and Festival Management, BA(Hons) Film and Media, Diploma in Higher Education Hearing Aid Audiology, BA(Hons) International Hospitality and Tourism Management, Certificate of Higher Education in Mammography, BA/ BA(Hons) Marketing Management, BA/ BA(Hons) Media and Communications, BA Musical Theatre, BSc(Hons) Nursing, BSc(Hons) Nutrition, BSc(Hons) Nutrition, BSc(Hons) Occupational Therapy, BSc(Hons) Physical Activity, Health and Wellbeing, BSc(Hons) Physiotherapy, BSc(Hons) Podiatry, BSc(Hons) Psychology, BSc(Hons) Psychology and Sociology, BA/BA(Hons) Public Relations and Marketing Communications, BA(Hons) Public Relations and Media, BA(Hons) Public Relations, Marketing and Events, BSc(Hons) Public Sociology, BSc(Hons) Speech and Language Therapy, BA(Hons) Theatre and Film, BSc(Hons) Therapeutic Radiography

Postgraduate courses: MSc Accounting and Finance with CIMA, PgDip/ MSc in Advancing Practice in Community Health and Wellbeing (Advancing Practice in Healthcare Framework), PgCert/ PgDip/ MSc Advancing Practice in Health (Advancing Practice in Healthcare Framework), PgDip/ MSc in Advancing Practice in Medical Imaging (Advancing Practice in Health Framework), PgDip/ MSc in Advancing Practice in Physiotherapy (Advancing Practice in Healthcare Framework), PgDip/ MSc in Advancing Practice in Podiatry (Advancing Practice in Healthcare Framework), MA Applied Arts and Social Practice, PgCert Applied Social Development, MSc Art Psychotherapy (International), PgCert Arts Management, MA Arts, Festival and Cultural Management, PgDip/MSc Audiology (Pre-Registration), MSc/ PgDip BSL/ English Interpreting (post-Registration), CIPR Professional Public Relations Diploma, CIPR Specialist Diploma (Digital Communications/ Internal Communication/ Public Affairs), MSc Cognitive Behavioural Therapy, PgCert Collaborative Working: Education and Therapy, Professional Doctorate in Cultural Leadership, MSc Diagnostic Radiography (Pre-Registration), PgDip/MSc Dietetics, MSc Digital Campaigning and Content Creation, MSc PgDip/ PgCert Dispute Resolution, MSc Gastronomy, MSc Global Health, PgCert Health in Fragile and Conflict-Affected States, PGDE Home Economics Secondary, MSc International Management and Leadership, MSc International Marketing, MSc Mammography, MSc Media, Management and the Creative Industries, MSc Musculoskeletal Medicine, MSc Music Therapy, PgDip/MSc Occupational Therapy (Post-Registration), MSc Occupational Therapy (Pre-Registration), MSc/ PgDip/PgCert Person-Centred Practice, PgDip Person-Centred Practice (District Nursing), PgDip Person-Centred Practice (Health Visiting), MSc/ PgDip/ PgCert Person-Centred Practice (Mental Health and Wellbeing), MSc/ PgDip Person-Centred Practice (Palliative Care), MSc/PgDip Person-Centred Practice (Public Health and Wellbeing), PgDip

Person-Centred Practice (School Nursing), PhD, PgDip/MSc Physiotherapy (Pre-Registration), MSc Play Therapy, PgCert Professional and Higher Education, Professional Doctorate, MSc Public Sociology, PgDip/ MSc Radiotherapy and Oncology (Pre-Registration), Master of Research, MSc Sexual and Reproductive Health, MSc Social Development and Health, PgDip/MSc Speech and Language Therapy (Pre-Registration), MA Stage Management, MSc Strategic Communication and Public Relations, MSc Theory of Podiatric Surgery

UNIVERSITY OF READING
www.reading.ac.uk

School of Agriculture, Policy and Development; www.reading.ac.uk/apd

BSc Agriculture, BSc Animal Science, BSc Consumer Behaviour and Marketing, BSc Food Marketing and Business Economics, BSc Environmental Management, BSc International Development

Postgraduate courses in the following subjects: Agriculture and Development, Applied International Development, Climate Change and Development, Communication for Development, Environment and Development, Agricultural Economics, Food Economics and Marketing, Research Agricultural and Food Economics, MSc Development Finance, MSc Consumer Behaviour Research Agriculture, Ecology and Environment, MSc by Research in Animal Science, MSc Agriculture and Development

Department of Archaeology; www.reading.ac.uk/archaeology

BA Archaeology, BA Archaeological Science, BA Archaeology and Ancient History, BA Archaeology and Classical Studies, BA Archaeology and History BA Archaeology and Anthropology, BSc Geography and Archaeology BA Museum Studies and Archaeology

Postgraduate courses: MA Archaeology MSc Professional Human Osteoarchaeology

School of Architecture; www.reading.ac.uk/architecture

BSc Architecture

School of Art; www.reading.ac.uk/fineart

BA Art, BA Fine Art, BA Art and English Literature, BA Art and Film, BA Art and Film and Theatre, BA Art and History of Art, BA Art and Philosophy, BA Art and Psychology, BA Art and Theatre BA Art and Creative Writing

Postgraduate courses: MFA/ MA Fine Art, MA Creative Enterprise: Art pathway, MA Creative Enterprise (Film Pathway), MA Book Design, MA Creative Enterprise (Communication Design Pathway) MA Graphic Communication: General Pathway, MA Graphic Communication: Book Design Pathway, MA Graphic Communication: Information Design, MA Graphic Communication: Typeface Design, MA by Research Typography and Graphic Communication, MRes Typeface Design

School of Biological Sciences; www.reading.ac.uk/biologicalsciences

BSc Biochemistry, BSc Biological Sciences, BSc Biomedical Sciences, BME Undergraduate courses, BEng/MEng Biomedical Engineering, BSc Ecology and Wildlife Conservation, BSc Microbiology, BSc Zoology

Postgraduate courses: MSc by Research Entomology, MSc by Research Biomedicine, MSc Molecular Medicine, MSc Plant Diversity, MSc Species Identification and Survey Skills

School of the Built Environment; www.reading.ac.uk/built-environment

BSc Architecture, BEng(Hons) Architectural Engineering, BSc Building Surveying, BSc Construction Management, BSc Construction Management and Surveying, BSc Quantity Surveying MEng(Hons) Architectural Engineering

Postgraduate courses: MSc Construction Cost Management, MSc Construction Management, MSc Construction Management & International Development, MSc Design and Management of Sustainable Built Environments, MSc Information Management for Design, MSc Construction and Operation, MSc Project Management Project Management, MSc Renewable Energy: Technology and Sustainability

Department of Chemistry; www.reading.ac.uk/chemistry

MChem Chemistry, BSc Chemistry, BSc Chemistry with Cosmetic Science, BSc Pharmaceutical Chemistry

Postgraduate course: MSc in Chemical Research PhD Programmes

Department of Classics; www.reading.ac.uk/classics

BA Ancient History, BA Classical Studies, BA Classics, BA Ancient History and Archaeology, BA Ancient History and History, BA Archaeology and Classical Studies, BA Classical Studies and English Literature, BA Classical Studies and Medieval Studies, BA Italian and Classical Studies, BA Museum and Classical Studies, BA Philosophy and Classical Studies
Postgraduate courses: MA Classics and Ancient History, MA City of Rome

Department of Computer Science; www.reading.ac.uk/dcs - computerscience.aspx

BSc Computer Science, BSc Mathematics with Computer Science
Postgraduate course: MSc Advanced Computer Science

Department of Economics; www.reading.ac.uk/economics

BSc Economics, BSc Business Economics, BSc Economics and Econometrics, BSc Economics and Finance, BSc Mathematics and Economics, BA Politics and Economics, BA Philosophy, Politics and Economics, BA International Relations and Economics, BSc Geography and Economics, BA History and Economics, BA French and Economics, BA German and Economics BA Italian and Economics BA Spanish and Economics
Postgraduate courses: MSc Economics, MSc Business Economics, MSc Economics and Finance, MA Public Policy

Institute of Education; www.reading.ac.uk/education

Primary Education (QTS) BA Children's Development and Learning, BA Education Studies
Postgraduate courses: MA Education, MA Education (Early Years), MA Education (English Language Teaching), MA Education (Inclusive Education), MA Education (Leadership and Management), MA Education (Music Education), PGCert Special Education Needs Coordinator (SENCO), various PGCE Options

Department of English Language and Applied Linguistics; www.reading.ac.uk/english-language-and-applied-linguistics

BA English Language and Linguistics, BA English Language and Literature, BA French Studies and English Language, BA German Studies and English,
BA Italian Studies and English Language, BA Spanish Studies and English Language
Postgraduate courses: MA in Applied Linguistics, MA in TESOL

English Literature; www.reading.ac.uk/english-literature

BA Art and Creative Writing, BA Creative Writing and Film, BA Creative Writing and Film & Theatre, BA Creative Writing and Theatre, BA English and Comparative Literature, BA English Literature, BA English Literature with Creative Writing, BA English Language and Literature, BA English Literature with Foundation, BA Art and English Literature, BA Classical Studies and English Literature, BA History and English Literature, BA English Literature and Film and Theatre, BA English Literature and Film, BA English Literature and German, BA English Literature and International Relations, BA English Literature and Italian, BA English Literature and Politics, BA English Literature and Theatre, BA English Literature with French, BA French and English Literature, BA Philosophy and English Literature, BA Spanish and English Literature
Postgraduate: MA English, MRes Children's Literature

Department of Film, Theatre & Television; www.reading.ac.uk/ftt

BA Film, BA Theatre, BA Film and Theatre, BA English Literature and Film & Theatre, BA English Literature and Theatre, BA English Literature and Film, BA Creative Writing and Film, BA Creative Writing and Film & Theatre, BA Creative Writing and Theatre, BA Art and Film & Theatre, BA Art and Theatre, BA Art and Film
Postgraduate courses: MA Creative Enterprise, Film/Theatre pathways

Food and Nutritional Sciences; www.reading.ac.uk/food

BSc Food Science, BSc Food Technology with Bioprocessing, BSc Nutrition and Food Science, BSc Nutrition with Food Consumer Sciences, BSc Food Science with Business, BSc Nutrition
Postgraduate courses: MSc Food Science, MSc Nutrition and Food Science, MSc Food Technology – Quality Assurance, MSc Sustainable Food Quality for Health

Department of Geography and Environmental Science; www.reading.ac.uk/ geographyandenvironmentalscience

BSc Environmental Science, MEnvSci Environmental Science, BSc Geography and Economics, BSc Human and Physical Geography, BSc Human Geography, BSc Physical Geography, BSc Geography and Archaeology

Postgraduate courses: MSc Environmental Management, MSc Environmental Pollution

Graduate Institute of Political and International Studies; www.reading.ac.uk/ spirs/about/spirs-gipis.aspx

BA Politics and International Relations, BA War, Peace and International Relations, BA English Literature and International Relations, BA English Literature and Politics, BA French and International Relations, BA German and International Relations, BA History and International Relations, BA History and Politics, BA Italian and International Relations, BA Philosophy and International Relations, BA Philosophy and Politics, BA Philosophy, Politics and Economics, BA Spanish and International Relations

Department of Health Sciences; www.reading.ac.uk/ready-to-study/study/ subject-area/healthcare-ug

BSc Biomedical Sciences, BSc Nutrition and Food Science, BSc Nutrition with Food Consumer Sciences, BSc Psychology with Neuroscience, MEng Biomedical Engineering, MPharm Pharmacy, MSci Applied Psychology (Clinical)

Henley Business School; www.henley.reading.ac.uk

BA Accounting and Business, BSc Accounting and Finance, BA Accounting and Management, BA Accounting (Beijing Institute of Technology), BA Business and Management, BA Entrepreneurship, BA Entrepreneurship and Management, BA International Business and Management, BA International Management and Business Administration with French, BA International Management and Business Administration with German, BA International Management and Business Administration with Italian, BA International Management and Business Administration with Spanish, BSc International Business and Finance, BSc Management with Information Technology, BSc Finance and Investment Banking, BSc Finance and Management with the University of Venice, BSc Economics and Finance, BSc Mathematics with Finance and Investment Banking, BSc Real Estate, BSc Investment and Finance in Property, BSc Real Estate with MSc/Dip Urban Planning & Development

Postgraduate courses: MSc Accounting and Financial Management, MSc Accounting and International Management, MSc Accounting and Finance, MSc Management, MSc Management (International Business), MSc Management (International Business and Finance), MSc International Human Resource Management, MSc Entrepreneurship (Leadership), MSc Entrepreneurship (Financing), MSc Entrepreneurship (Creative Industries), MSc Marketing (Digital Marketing), MSc Marketing (International Marketing), MSc Marketing (Consumer Marketing), Doctor of Business Administration (DBA), Executive MBA (EMBA), Flexible Executive MBA, Henley MA Leadership, Henley MSc in Coaching & Behavioural Change, MSc Finance and Financial Technology (FinTech), MSc Finance, MSc Capital Markets, Regulation and Compliance, MSc Corporate Finance, MSc Financial Engineering, MSc Financial Risk Management, MSc International Shipping and Finance, MSc Investment Management, MSc Behavioural Finance, MSc Economics and Finance, MSc Business Technology Consulting, MSc Information Management & Digital Business – Digital Innovation, MSc Information Management & Digital Business – Business Service Design, MSc Information Management & Digital Business – Big Data in Business, MSc Information Management & Digital Business – Digital Health and Data Analytics, MSc Management, MSc Management (International Business), MSc Management (International Business and Finance), MSc International Human Resource Management, MSc Real Estate, MSc Real Estate Finance, MSc Spatial Planning and Development (full and part-time), MSc Rural Land and Business Management (full and part-time), MSc Real Estate (Flexible), MSc Real Estate Investment and Finance (Flexible), IPF Certificate, IPF Diploma & MSc Real, Estate Investment and Finance (IPF Entry Route)

Department of History; www.reading.ac.uk/history

BA History, BA Ancient History and History, BA Archaeology and History, BA History and Economics, BA History and English Literature, BA History and International Relations, BA History and Philosophy, BA History and Politics, BA French and History, BA German and History, BA Italian and

History, BA Spanish and History BA Classical Studies and Medieval Studies

Postgraduate courses: MA History, MRes Medieval Studies

School of Law; www.reading.ac.uk/law

LLB Law, LLB Law with Legal Studies in Europe

Postgraduate courses: M Advanced Legal Studies, LLM International Law, LLM International Commercial Law, Graduate Diploma in Law and Legal Practice Course MRes (Law), MRes (Law and Society), MA (Res) Legal History

Department of Mathematics and Statistics; www.reading.ac.uk/maths-and-stats

BSc Mathematics, MMath Mathematics, BSc Computational Mathematics, BSc Mathematics with Computer Science, BSc Mathematics and Economics, BSc Mathematics with Finance and Investment Banking, BSc Mathematics and Meteorology, MMath Mathematics and Meteorology, BSc Mathematics and Psychology, BSc Mathematics and Statistics

Postgraduate course: MSc in Financial Engineering

Department of Meteorology; www.met.reading.ac.uk

BSc/MMet Meteorology and Climate, BSc Physics of the Environment, BSc Mathematics and Meteorology, MMath Mathematics and Meteorology

Postgraduate courses: MSc Atmosphere, Oceans and Climate (MSc AOC), MSc Applied Meteorology MSc Applied Meteorology and Climate with Management

Department of Modern Languages and European Studies; www.reading.ac.uk/modern-languages-and-european-studies

French BA, French and Economics BA, French and English Literature BA, French and German BA, French and History BA, French and International Relations BA, French and Italian BA, French and Management BA, French Studies and English Language BA, French Studies and Comparative Literature BA International Management and Business Administration with French BA, German BA, German and Economics BA, German and English Literature BA, German Studies and Comparative Literature BA German Studies and English Language BA, German and History BA, German and International Relations BA, German and Italian BA, German and Management BA, International Management and Business Administration with German BA, Italian BA, Italian and Classical Studies BA, Italian and Economics BA, Italian and English Literature BA, Italian Studies and English Language BA, Italian

Studies and Comparative Literature BA Italian and History BA, Italian and International Relations BA, Italian and Management BA, International Management and Business Administration with Italian BA, Spanish BA, Spanish and French BA, Spanish and German BA, Spanish and Italian BA, Spanish and Economics BA, Spanish and English Literature BA, Spanish Studies and Comparative Literature BA Spanish and History BA, Spanish and Management Studies BA, Spanish and International Relations BA, Spanish Studies and English Language BA, International Management and Business Administration with Spanish BA

Postgraduate: PhD study

School of Pharmacy; www.reading.ac.uk/pharmacy

MPharm Pharmacy

Postgraduate courses: Non-Medical Prescribing, PGCert/PGDip in Pharmacy Practice, PGCert/PGDip in Pharmacy Practice Details, MSc Advancing Healthcare Practice, MSc by Research in Pharmacy Practice, PhD

Department of Philosophy; www.reading.ac.uk/Phil

BA Ethics, Value and Philosophy, BA Philosophy, BA Philosophy and Classical Studies, BA Philosophy and English Literature, BA Philosophy and International Relations, BA Philosophy and Politics, BA Philosophy, Politics and Economics, BA Psychology and Philosophy, BA Art and Philosophy, BA History and Philosophy

Postgraduate course: MRes Philosophy

Department of Politics and International Relations; www.reading.ac.uk/spirs

BA Politics and International Relations, BA War, Peace and International Relations, BA English Literature and International Relations, BA English Literature and Politics, BA French and International Relations, BA German and International Relations, BA History and International Relations, BA History and Politics, BA Italian and International Relations, BA Philosophy and International Relations, BA Philosophy and Politics, BA Philosophy, Politics and Economics, BA Spanish and International Relations

Postgraduate courses: MA International Relations, MA Diplomacy, MA International Security Studies, MA Strategic Studies, MA Public Policy, MRes Politics and International Relations

School of Psychology and Clinical Language Sciences; www.reading.ac.uk/psychology/

BSc Psychology, BSc Language Sciences & Psychology, MSci Speech & Language Therapy, BSc Psychology with Neuroscience, MSci Applied Psychology (Clinical), BSc Mathematics and Psychology, BA Psychology and Philosophy, BA Art and Psychology

Postgraduate courses: MSc Theory and Practice in Clinical Psychology MSc Cognitive Neuroscience, MSc Language Sciences, MSc Research Methods in Psychology, MSc Speech and Language Therapy, MSc Psychology Conversion

ROBERT GORDON UNIVERSITY
www.rgu.ac.uk

Aberdeen Business School; www.rgu.ac.uk/about/schools-anddepartments/aberdeen-business-school

Graduate Apprenticeship in BA(Hons) Accounting, BA(Hons) Accounting and Finance, BA(Hons) Accounting and Management, BA(Hons) Business Management, BA(Hons) International Business Management, BA(Hons) Management Degree, BA(Hons) Management with Human Resource Management, BA(Hons) Management with Marketing, Graduate Apprenticeship in BA(Hons) Business Management: Financial Services

Postgraduate Courses: PgCert Accelerator Development, MSc / PgCert/ PgDip Accounting and Finance, PgCert/ PgDip/ MSc Business with HR Management, PgCert/ PgDip/ MSc Business with Marketing Management, PgCert/ PgDip/ MSc Business with Strategic Risk Management, PGCert/ PgDip/ MSc Business and Management, BA(Hons) Business Management, PGCert/ PgDip/ MSc Business Innovation and Entrepreneurship, BA(Hons) Business Management, PgCert/ PgDip/ MSc Business Leadership and Management, PgCert/ PgDip/ MSc International Business Management, MSc / PgCert/ PgDip Energy Management, MSc / PgCert/ PgDip Financial Management, MSc / PgCert/ PgDip Health Safety and Risk Management, MSc Human Resource Management, Master of Business Administration, MBA Oil and Gas Management, MSc Oil and Gas Accounting and Finance, PgCert/ PgDip/ MSc Procurement and Supply Chain Management, MSc / PgCert/ PgDip Project Management, MSc Quality Management, Doctor of Business Administration DBA

School of Applied Social Studies; www.rgu.ac.uk/about/schools-anddepartments/school-of-applied-socialstudies

PgCert Mental Health Officer Award, BA(Hons) Social Work – Blended Learning, BA(Hons) Applied Social Sciences, BA Residential Child Care, Graduate Certificate Practice Learning Qualification – Social Services, PgCert/ PgDip/ MSc Social Work, BA(Hons) Social Work, PgCert/ PgDip/ MSc Applied Psychology

School of Computing Science and Digital Media; www.rgu.ac.uk/about/schools-and-departments/school-of-computingscience-and-digital-media

Graduate Apprenticeship in BSc(Hons) IT: Software Development, PgCert/ PgDip/ MSc Information Technology with Cyber Security, Graduate Apprenticeship in BSc(Hons) IT: Management for Business, PgCert/ PgDip/ MSc Cyber Security, Graduate Apprenticeship in BSc(Hons) Data Science, PgCert/ PgDip/ MSc Information Technology with Business Intelligence, PgCert/ PgDip/ MSc Information Technology with Network Management, BSc(Hons) Computing – Application Software Development, PgCert/ PgDip/ MSc Data Science, BSc(Hons) Cyber Security, BSc(Hons) Digital Media, PgCert/ PgDip/ MSc Information Technology, BSc(Hons) Computer Network Management and Design, MSci Computing Science, PgCert/ PgDip/ MSc IT for the Oil and Gas Industry, BSc(Hons) Computer Science

School of Creative and Cultural Business; www.rgu.ac.uk/about/schools-anddepartments/school-of-creative-andcultural-business

DInfSc Doctor of Information Science, PgCert/ PgDip/ MSc International Tourism and Hospitality Management, PgCert/ PgDip/ MSc Information and Library Studies, BA(Hons) Journalism, Events Management BA(Hons), PgCert/ PgDip/ MSc Digital Marketing, PgCert/ PgDip/ MSc Corporate Communications and Public Affairs, PgCert/ PgDip/ MSc Fashion Management, BA(Hons) Digital Marketing, PgCert/ PgDip/ MSc Journalism, BA(Hons) International Hospitality

Management, PgCert/ PgDip/ MSc Business Analytics, BA(Hons) Media, BA(Hons) International Tourism Management, PgCert/ PgDip/ MSc International Marketing Management, BA(Hons) Fashion Management, BA(Hons) Public Relations

School of Engineering; www.rgu.ac.uk/ about/schools-and-departments/ schoolof-engineering

BEng(Hons) Mechanical and Electrical Engineering, BSc (Eng) Mechanical Engineering, PgCert/ PgDip/ MSc Petroleum Production Engineering, BEng(Hons) Mechanical Engineering, PgCert/ PgDip/ MSc Oil and Gas Engineering, MEng Mechanical and Offshore Engineering, BEng(Hons)/ MEng Electronic and Biomedical Technology, PgCert/ PgDip/ MSc Asset Integrity Management, MEng Electronic and Electrical Engineering, BSc (Eng) Electronic and Electrical Engineering, PgCert/ PgDip/ MSc Drilling and Well Engineering, PgCert/ PgDip/ MSc Subsea Engineering, BEng(Hons)/ MEng Mechanical and Biomedical Technology, Graduate Apprenticeship in BEng(Hons) Engineering: Instrumentation, Measurement and Control, PgCert/ PgDip / MSc Solar Energy Systems, MEng Mechanical Engineering, Graduate Apprenticeship in BEng(Hons) Engineering: Design and Manufacture, MEng Mechanical and Electrical Engineering, BEng(Hons) Electronic and Electrical Engineering, BEng(Hons) Mechanical and Offshore Engineering, PgCert/ PgDip/ MSc Biomedical Technology, PgCert/ PgDip/ MSc Engineering

Gray's School of Art; www.rgu.ac.uk/ about/schools-and-departments/gray-s-school-of-art

PgCert/ PgDip/ MA Jewellery, BA(Hons) Three Dimensional Design, PgCert/ PgDip/ MA Product Design, BA(Hons) Painting, PgCert/ PgDip/ MA Fine Art, BA(Hons) Fashion and Textile Design, PgCert/ PgDip/ MA Communication Design, BA(Hons) Contemporary Art Practice – Moving Image, Photography, Printmaking, Sculpture, PgCert/ PgDip/ MA Fashion & Textiles, BA Photography, PgCert/ PgDip/ MA Curatorial Studies, BA(Hons) Communication Design: Graphic Design, Illustration, Photography

School of Health Sciences; www.rgu.ac.uk/ about/schools-and-departments/ schoolof-health-sciences

PgCert/ PgDip/ MSc Physiotherapy – Pre-registration, PgCert/ PgDip/ MSc Health Professionals and Sports Scientists CPD Framework, BSc(Hons) Applied Sport and Exercise Science, MOccTh

Occupational Therapy, MDRad Diagnostic Radiography, BSc(Hons) Sport Coaching, PgCert/ PgDip/ MSc Strategic Service Planning and Delivery in Health and Social Care, MDiet Dietetics, PgCert Diagnostic Image Reporting, DPT Doctorate of Physiotherapy, MPhys Physiotherapy, PgCert/ PgDip/ MSc Public Health and Health Promotion

The Law School; www.rgu.ac.uk/about/ schools-and-departments/the-law-school

LLM Law and International Commercial Law, LLM Law, PgDip Professional Legal Practice, LLM Law and Dispute Resolution, LLB(Hons) Law, MSc/ LLM Oil, Gas and Renewable Energy Law, DipHE/ LLB Law – Online Learning, LLM Law and International Law, PgCert/ PgDip/ LLM/ MSc Construction Law and Arbitration, BA(Hons) Law and Management, LLM Law and Energy Law

School of Nursing and Midwifery; www.rgu.ac.uk/about/schools-anddepartments/school-of-nursing-andmidwifery

BSc Occupational Health, PgCert/ PgDip/ MSc Advancing Nursing Practice, BMidwifery Midwifery, BSc/ DipHE/ CertHE Paramedic Practice: Remote & Hazardous Environments, BN Nursing – Adult, BN(Hons) Nursing – Adult, BN Nursing – Mental Health, BN Nursing – Children and Young People, BSc(Hons) Nursing Studies – For Overseas Qualified Nurses

School of Pharmacy and Life Sciences; www.rgu.ac.uk

PgCert/ PgDip/ MSc Advanced Pharmacy Practice, PgCert/ PgDip/ MSc Clinical Pharmacy Service Development, PgCert/ PgDip/ MSc Analytical Science – Environmental Analysis, BSc(Hons) Biomedical Science, PgCert/ PgDip/ MSc Analytical Science – Food Analysis, Authenticity and Safety, BSc(Hons) Forensic and Analytical Science, MPharm Pharmacy, PgCert/ PgDip/ MSc Analytical Science – Drug Analysis and Toxicology, BSc(Hons) Applied Biomedical Science, BSc(Hons) Food, Nutrition and Human Health, PgCert/ PgDip/ MSc Clinical Pharmacy Practice, PgCert/ PgDip/ MSc Pharmaceutical Science, BSc(Hons) Applied Bioscience

The Scott Sutherland School of Architecture and Built Environment; www.rgu.ac.uk/ about/schools-and-departments/thescott-sutherland-school-of-architectureand-built-environment
BSc(Hons) Surveying – Quantity, Master of Architecture Part 2 RIBA/ARB, Graduate Apprenticeship in BSc(Hons) Construction and the Built Environment, BSc/ Master of Architecture, PgCert/ PgDip/ MSc Architectural Design Innovation, PgCert/ PgDip/ MSc Construction Project Management, BSc(Hons) Architectural Technology, BSc(Hons) Construction Management, BSc(Hons) Surveying – Building

ROEHAMPTON UNIVERSITY
www.roehampton.ac.uk

Business School; www.roehampton.ac.uk/ business
Undergraduate degrees in the following subjects: Accounting, Business Management, Business Management and Economics, Business Management and Entrepreneurship, Business Management and Finance, Business Management and Marketing, Human Resource Management, International Business, Marketing, Marketing Communications
Postgraduate degrees in the following subjects: Global Business Management, Global Financial Management, Global Human Resources Management, Global Marketing, Master of Business Administration

Dance; www.roehampton.ac.uk/dance
Undergraduate degrees in the following subject: Dance, Diverse Dance Styles
Postgraduate degrees in the following subjects: Choreography, Choreography and Performance (MRes), Choreomundus: International Master in Dance Knowledge, Practice and Heritage, Dance Anthropology, Dance Philosophy and History, Dance Politics and Sociology, Dance Embodied Practice

Drama, Theatre and Performance; www.roehampton.ac.uk/drama-theatreand-performance
Undergraduate degrees in the following subjects: Drama, Theatre and Performance Studies, Theatre Practices and Production
Postgraduate degrees in the following subject: London's Theatre and Performance: Viewing, Making, Writing

Education; www.roehampton.ac.uk/ education
Undergraduate degrees in the following subjects: Early Childhood Studies, Education Studies, Primary Education (QTS), Sport Coaching, Sports Coaching Practice

Postgraduate degrees in the following subjects: Early Childhood Studies, Education Leadership and Management, Education Studies subjects: Educational Practice, National Award for SEN Coordinators, PGCE Primary, PGCE Primary – general (with Mathematics), PGCE Secondary, School Direct – Primary and Secondary, Social Research Methods, Sounds of Intent

English and Creative Writing; www.roehampton.ac.uk/english-andcreative-writing
Undergraduate degrees in the following subjects: Creative Writing, English Literature, English Literature and History
Postgraduate degrees in the following subjects: Children's Literature, Children's Literature (Distance Learning), Creative Writing, Creative Writing (specialist pathway), Publishing

Humanities; www.roehampton.ac.uk/ humanities
Undergraduate degrees in the following subjects: Ancient History, Classical Civilisation, History, Ministerial Theology (FdA/BTh), Ministerial Theology (Graduate Diploma), English and History, History and Philosophy, Philosophy, Religion and Ethics, Religion, Theology and Culture
Postgraduate degrees in the following subjects: Christian Ministry, Theology and Religious Studies Classics and Ancient History, Cold War History, History (MA), History (MRes), Practical Theology (DTh), Theology and Religious Studies

Life Sciences; www.roehampton.ac.uk/ lifesciences
Undergraduate degrees in the following subjects: Adult Nursing, Anthropology, Biological Sciences, Biomedical Science, Nutrition and Health, Social Anthropology, Sport and Exercise Sciences, Sport Psychology, Zoology

Postgraduate degrees in the following subjects: Anthropology of Health, Biomechanics, Cell Biomedicine (MRes), Clinical Neuroscience, Clinical Nutrition, Nutrition and Metabolic Disorders (MRes), Primate Biology, Behaviour and Conservation, Psychology of Sport and Exercise (BPS Accredited), Sport and Exercise Nutrition Sport and Exercise Physiology, Sport and Exercise Science

Media, Culture and Language; www.roehampton.ac.uk/media-cultureand-language

Undergraduate degrees in the following subjects: Computer Science, Digital Media, English Language and Linguistics, Film, Journalism, Media, Culture and Identity, Photography

Postgraduate degrees in the following subjects: TESOL, Audiovisual Translation, Film and Screen Cultures, Intercultural Communication in the Creative Industries, Journalism, Media Communication and Culture, Specialised Translation

Psychology; www.roehampton.ac.uk/psychology

Undergraduate degrees in the following subjects: Psychology, Psychology and Counselling, Psychology and Criminology Therapeutic Psychology

Postgraduate degrees in the following subjects: Art Psychotherapy, Attachment Studies, Counselling Psychology (HCPC approved and BPS accredited), Dance Movement Psychotherapy, Dramatherapy, Forensic Psychology Integrative Counselling and Psychotherapy, Integrative Counselling and Psychotherapy for Children, Adolescents and Families Music Therapy, Play Therapy

Social Sciences; www.roehampton.ac.uk/social-sciences

Undergraduate degrees in the following subjects: Criminology, LLB(Hons) Law, LLB(Hons) Law and Criminology, Sociology

Postgraduate degrees in the following subjects: Erasmus Mundus Human Rights Policy and Practice, Global Criminology, Human Rights and International Relations, LLM Human Rights and Legal Practice

THE ROYAL ACADEMY OF DANCE
www.rad.org.uk

BA(Hons) Ballet Education, BA(Hons) Dance Education, Certificate in Ballet Teaching Studies, Certificate of Higher Education: Dance Education, Diploma in Dance Teaching Studies, Diploma of Higher Education: Dance Education, Licentiate of the Royal Academy of Dance, MA in Education (Dance Teaching), PGCE: Dance Teaching (with QTS), Professional Dancers' Postgraduate Teaching Certificate, Professional Dancers' Teaching Diploma

ROYAL ACADEMY OF DRAMATIC ART
www.rada.ac.uk

BA(Hons) in Acting, Foundation Course in Acting, MA in Text and Performance, MA Theatre Lab, Foundation Degree (FdA) in Technical Theatre and Stage Management, BA(Hons) in Technical Theatre & Stage Management (Progression Year), Postgraduate Diploma in Theatre Costume

ROYAL AGRICULTURAL UNIVERSITY
www.rau.ac.uk

BSc(Hons) Agricultural Management (Top-up), BSc(Hons) Agriculture, FdSc Agriculture and Farm Management, FdSc Animal Science, BSc(Hons) Applied Equine Science and Business, BSc(Hons) Applied Farm Management, BSc(Hons) Bloodstock and Performance Horse Management, FdSc British Wildlife Conservation, FdSc Business and Enterprise, BSc(Hons) Countryside Management (Top-up), FdSc Environmental Conservation and Heritage Management, BSc(Hons) Equine Studies (Top-up), BSc(Hons)

International Business Management, BSc(Hons) International Business Management (Food and Agribusiness), BSc(Hons) International Equine and Agricultural Business Management, BSc(Hons) Real Estate, Diploma in Real Estate Valuation, BSc(Hons) Rural Land Management, BSc(Hons) Wildlife and Countryside Management (Top Up)

Postgraduate courses: MBA Advanced Farm Management, MSc Agricultural Technology and Innovation, MSc Business Management, MSc Food Safety and Quality Management, Graduate Certificate in Agriculture, Graduate Diploma in Agriculture, MBA International Food and Agribusiness, MSc by Research Programme, MSc Real Estate, MSc Rural Estate Management, MSc Sustainable Agriculture and Food Security

---

ASKHAM BRYAN COLLEGE
www.askham-bryan.ac.uk

Agriculture
BSc/BSc(Hons) Agricultural Management (Top Up) BSc/BSc(Hons) Agriculture, BSc/BSc(Hons) Applied Agriculture, Extended Foundation Degree Animal Management, Agriculture or Equine Foundation Degree (FdSc) Agriculture,

Animal Management
BSc/BSc(Hons) Animal Conservation (Top Up) BSc/BSc(Hons) Animal Management, BSc/BSc(Hons) Animal Management and Science, BSc/BSc(Hons) Canine and Feline Behaviour and Welfare (Top Up) BSc/BSc(Hons) Zoo Management, Extended Foundation Degree Animal Management Foundation Degree (FdSc) Canine and Feline Training and Behaviour, Foundation Degree Management of Animal Collections with Conservation,

Postgraduate courses: MSc in Applied Animal Behaviour and Welfare, MSc in Zoo Management and Conservation

Arboriculture
Foundation Degree Arboriculture with Urban Forestry

Countryside and the Environment
BSc/BSc(Hons) Countryside Management, (Top Up)

Equine
BSc/BSc(Hons) Equine Science, BSc/BSc(Hons) Equine Science and Management, Foundation Degree (FdSc) Equine Science and Management, Extended Foundation Degree Animal Management, Agriculture or Equine

Horticulture
BSc/BSc(Hons) Applied Horticulture (Top Up)

Sport
Foundation Degree (FdSc) Sport (Coaching and Fitness)

Veterinary Nursing
BSc(Hons) Veterinary Nursing (Top Up), Foundation Degree (FdSc) Veterinary Nursing

---

ROYAL BALLET SCHOOL
www.royalballetschool.org.uk

Diploma of Dance Teaching, various training programmes for young dancers

---

ROYAL COLLEGE OF ART
www.rca.ac.uk

School of Architecture; www.rca.ac.uk/schools/school-of-architecture
Degrees in the following subjects: Architecture, City Design, Environmental Architecture, Interior Design, MRes RCA: Architecture Pathway

School of Arts & Humanities; www.rca.ac.uk/schools/school-of-artshumanities
Degrees in the following subjects: Ceramics & Glass, Contemporary Art Practice, Curating, Contemporary Art, Jewellery & Metal, Painting, Photography, Print,

Sculpture, V&A/RCA History of Design, Writing MRes RCA: Fine Art Pathway, MRes RCA: Fine Art and Humanities MPhil/PhD Arts & Humanities

School of Communication; www.rca.ac.uk/schools/school-of-communication

Degrees in the following subjects: Animation, Digital Direction, Information Experience Design, Visual Communication, MRes RCA: Communication Design Pathway

School of Design; www.rca.ac.uk/schools/school-of-design

Degrees in the following subjects: Design Products, Fashion Global Innovation Design, Innovation Design Engineering, Intelligent Mobility, MRes Healthcare & Design, Service Design, MRes RCA: Design Pathway, Service Design, Textiles MPhil/ PhD Design

ROYAL COLLEGE OF MUSIC
www.rcm.ac.uk

BMus(Hons) Bachelor of Music, BSc Physics and Music Performance
Postgraduate courses: Graduate Diploma in Vocal Performance, Master of Performance, Master of Composition, Master of Music, Master of Science in Performance Science, Master of Education

THE ROYAL COLLEGE OF ORGANISTS
www.rco.org.uk

Courses in playing, teaching and choral directing leading to the following qualifications: CertRCO, ARCO, FRCO, LTRCO, DipCHD

ROYAL CONSERVATOIRE OF SCOTLAND
www.rcs.ac.uk

BA Acting, BA(Hons) Contemporary Performance Practice, BA Filmmaking, Bachelor of Music (Honours), Bachelor of education (Music) with Honours, BA Musical Theatre, BA Performance in British Sign language and English, BA Production Arts and Design, BA Production technology and management, BA(Hons) Modern Ballet, Certificate in Ballet Teaching Studies, Certificate of Higher Education: Dance Education, Diploma in Dance Teaching Studies, Diploma of Higher Education: Dance Education, Licentiate of the Royal Academy of Dance
Postgraduate courses: MA Classical and Contemporary Text (Acting) or (Directing), MA Musical Theatre (Performance) or (Musical Directing) MMus/MA Music (Brass, Chamber Music, Composition, Conducting, Guitar and Harp, Historically Informed Performance Practice, Jazz, Keyboard, Opera, Piano Accompaniment, Piano for Dance, Repetiteurship, Scottish Music, Strings, Timpani and Percussion, Vocal Studies, Woodwind), MEd Learning and Teaching in the Performing Arts, MA Learning and Teaching (Gaelic Arts), PG Cert Learning Support and Administration in Higher Arts Education, PG Cert Learning and Teaching

ROYAL NORTHERN COLLEGE OF MUSIC
www.rncm.ac.uk

BA(Hons) Music, Bachelor of Music(Hons) Popular Music, Graduate Diploma of the Royal Northern College of Music; Postgraduate courses: Master of Music, Master of Performance, PG Dip Advanced Studies, Master of Philosophy and Doctor of Philosophy, Conducting, Postgraduate Diploma (International Artist), Hall/RNCM Strings Leadership Course, Northern Ballet / RNCM Postgraduate Diploma: Pianist for Ballet, PGCE in Music with Specialist Instrumental Teaching

UNIVERSITY OF ST ANDREWS
www.st-andrews.ac.uk

Ancient History

Ancient History MA(Hons), Ancient History & Archaeology MA(Hons), Classical Studies (Ancient History & Archaeology pathway), BA (International Hons), Gateway to Arts Pathway to MA(Hons), FE-HE Pathway to Arts Pathway to MA(Hons)
Postgraduate courses: Classics MLitt, Classics MPhil

Arabic

Postgraduate courses: Middle Eastern History MLitt, Middle Eastern Literary and Cultural Studies MLitt, Cultural Identity Studies MLitt

Archaeology

Ancient History & Archaeology MA(Hons), Mediaeval History & Archaeology MA(Hons), Classical Studies – Ancient History and Archaeology pathway BA (International Hons), Gateway to Arts Pathway to MA(Hons), FE-HE Pathway to Arts Pathway to MA(Hons)
Postgraduate courses: Art History MLitt, Museum and Gallery Studies MLitt, Classics MLitt, Classics MPhil, Anthropology, Art and Perception MRes, Mediaeval History MLitt, Mediaeval Studies MLitt, Scottish Historical Studies MLitt

Art History

Art History MA(Hons), Gateway to Arts Pathway to MA(Hons), Pathway to Arts Pathway to MA(Hons)
Postgraduate courses: Art History MLitt, History of Photography MLitt, Museum and Gallery Studies MLitt

Biology

Biology BSc(Hons), Biology MBiol(Hons), Animal Behaviour BSc(Hons), Biochemistry BSc(Hons), Biochemistry MBiochem(Hons), Cell Biology BSc(Hons), Ecology and Conservation BSc(Hons), Evolutionary Biology BSc(Hons), Marine Biology BSc(Hons), Marine Biology MMarBiol(Hons), Molecular Biology BSc(Hons), Neuroscience BSc(Hons), Sustainable Development BSc(Hons), Sustainable Development MA(Hons), Zoology BSc(Hons), FE-HE Pathway to Science Pathway to BSc(Hons)
Postgraduate courses: Animal Behaviour MSc, Marine Ecosystem Management MSc, Marine Mammal Science MSc, Sustainable Aquaculture – Distance Learning PGDip/MSc, Sustainable Aquaculture – Distance Learning PG Certificate, Sustainable Aquaculture Distance Learning modular

Chemistry

Chemistry BSc(Hons), Chemistry MChem(Hons), Chemical Sciences BSc(Hons), Chemistry with Medicinal Chemistry BSc(Hons), Chemistry with Medicinal Chemistry MChem(Hons), Materials Chemistry BSc(Hons), Materials Chemistry MChem(Hons), Sustainable Development BSc(Hons), Sustainable Development MA(Hons), FE-HE Pathway to Science Pathway to BSc(Hons)
Postgraduate courses: Catalysis MSc, Chemical Science MSc

Classics and Classical Studies

Classics MA(Hons), Classical Studies MA(Hons), Classical Studies BA (International Hons), Greek MA(Hons), Latin MA(Hons) Gateway to Arts Pathway to MA(Hons), FE-HE Pathway to Arts Pathway to MA(Hons)
Postgraduate courses: Classics MLitt, Classics MPhil

Comparative Literature

Joint honours only at undergraduate level
Postgraduate courses: Comparative Literature MLitt, Crossways in Cultural Narratives Erasmus Mundus MLitt, German and Comparative Literature MLitt

Computer Science

Computer Science BSc(Hons), Computer Science, MSci(Hons), Computer Science (Gateway) BSc(Hons), Computer Science (Gateway), MSci(Hons)

Postgraduate courses: Advanced Computer Science MSc, Advanced Systems Dependability MSc Erasmus Mundus, Artificial Intelligence MSc, Computing and Information Technology MSc, Data- Intensive Analysis MSc, Human Computer Interaction MSc, Information Technology MSc, Information Technology with Management MSc, Software Engineering MSc

Creative Writing

English MA(Hons), English BA (International Hons)
Postgraduate courses: Creative Writing MLitt

Divinity

Biblical Studies MA(Hons), Divinity BD(Hons), Hebrew MA (joint Hons), New Testament MA (joint Hons), Theological Studies MA(Hons), Theology MTheol(Hons), Gateway to Arts Pathway to MA(Hons), FE-HE-Pathway to Arts Pathway to BSc(Hons)
Postgraduate courses: Analytic and Exegetical Theology MLitt, Bible and the Contemporary World MLitt, Bible and the Contemporary World – Distance Learning PGDip/MLitt, Biblical Languages and Literature MLitt, Systematic and Historical Theology MLitt, Theology and the Arts MLitt, Sacred Music MLitt

Earth and Environmental Sciences

Earth Sciences MGeol(Hons), Environmental Earth Sciences BSc(Hons), Geology BSc(Hons), FE-HE Pathway to Science Pathway to BSc(Hons)
Postgraduate courses: Geochemistry MSc, Mineral Resources MSc

Economics and Finance

Economics BSc(Hons), Economics MA(Hons), Economics BA (International Hons), Financial Economics BSc(Hons), Financial Economics MA(Hons), Gateway to Arts Pathway to MA(Hons), FE-HE Pathway to Arts Pathway to MA(Hons), FE-HE Pathway to Science Pathway to BSc(Hons)
Postgraduate courses: Economics MSc, Finance and Economics MSc, Finance MSc

English

English MA(Hons), English BA (International Hons), Gateway to Arts Pathway to MA(Hons), FE-HE Pathway to Arts Pathway to MA(Hons)
Postgraduate courses: Creative Writing MLitt, Medieval English MLitt, Modern and Contemporary Literature and Culture MLitt, Playwriting and Screenwriting MLitt, Postcolonial and World Literatures MLitt, Romantic and Victorian Studies MLitt, Shakespeare and Renaissance Literary Culture MLitt, Women, Writing and Gender MLitt

Film Studies

Film Studies MA(Hons), Film Studies BA (International Hons), Gateway to Arts Pathway to MA(Hons), FE-HE Pathway to Arts Pathway to MA(Hons)
Postgraduate courses: Film Studies MLitt

French

French MA(Hons), Gateway to Arts Pathway to MA(Hons), FE-HE Pathway to Arts Pathway to MA(Hons)
Postgraduate courses: French Studies MLitt, Crossways in Cultural Narratives Erasmus Mundus MLitt, Cultural Identity Studies MLitt

Geography

Geography BSc(Hons), Geography MA(Hons), Gateway to Arts Pathway to MA(Hons), FE-HE Pathway to Arts Pathway to MA(Hons), FE-HE Pathway to Science Pathway to BSc(Hons)
Postgraduate courses: Sustainable Development MSc, Sustainable Development and Energy MSc, Sustainable Development and Environmental Economics MSc

German

German MA(Hons), Gateway to Arts Pathway to MA(Hons), FE-HE Pathway to Arts Pathway to MA(Hons)
Postgraduate courses: German Studies MLitt, German and Comparative Crossways in Cultural Narratives Literature MLitt, Erasmus Mundus MLitt, Cultural Identity Studies MLitt

Greek

Greek MA(Hons), Classical Studies (Greek and Latin pathway) BA (International Hons), Classics MA(Hons), Gateway to Arts Pathway to MA(Hons), FE-HE Pathway to Arts Pathway to MA(Hons)
Postgraduate courses: Classics MLitt, Classics MPhil

History

History MA(Hons), History BA (International Hons), Ancient History MA(Hons), Mediaeval History MA(Hons), Mediaeval History & Archaeology MA(Hons), Middle East Studies MA (joint Hons), Modern History MA(Hons), Scottish History MA(Hons), Gateway to Arts Pathway to MA(Hons), FE-HE Pathway to Arts Pathway to MA(Hons)
Postgraduate courses: Early Modern History MLitt, Economic and Social History Msc, Environmental History MLitt, History of Philosophy MLitt, Intellectual History MLitt, Iranian Studies MLitt, Legal and Constitutional Studies MLitt/PGDip, Mediaeval History MLitt, Mediaeval Studies MLitt, Middle Eastern History MLitt, Modern History MLitt, Reformation Studies MLitt, Scottish Historical Studies MLitt, The

Book. History and Techniques of Analysis MLitt, Transnational, Global and Spatial History MLitt

Interdisciplinary Studies

Sustainable Development BSc(Hons), Sustainable Development MA(Hons), Gateway to Arts Pathway to MA(Hons), FE-HE Pathway to Arts Pathway to MA(Hons), FE-HE Pathway to Science Pathway to BSc(Hons)

Postgraduate courses: Contemporary Studies MLitt, Conservation Studies MSc, Data-Intensive Analysis MSc, Digital Health Msc, Health Psychology MSc, Intellectual History MLitt, International Development Practice MSc, Global Social and Political Thought MLitt, Legal and Constitutional Studies PGDip/MLitt, Information Technology with Management MSc, Mediaeval Studies MLitt, Sustainable Development MSc, Sustainable Development and Energy MSc, Sustainable Development and Environmental Economics MSc, The Book: History and Techniques of Analysis MLitt

International Relations

International Relations MA(Hons), International Relations BA (International Hons), Gateway to Arts Pathway to MA(Hons), FE-HE Pathway to Arts Pathway to MA(Hons)

Postgraduate courses: International Political Theory MLitt, International Security Studies MLitt, Legal and Constitutional Studies MLitt, Middle East, Caucasus and Central Asian Security Studies MLitt, Strategic Studies MLitt, Terrorism and Political Violence MLitt, Terrorism and Political Violence – Distance Learning MLitt, International Relations MRes

Italian

Italian MA(Hons), Gateway to Arts Pathway to MA(Hons), FE-HE Pathway to Arts Pathway to MA(Hons)

Postgraduate courses: Italian Studies MLitt, Crossways in Cultural Narratives Erasmus Mundus MLitt, Cultural Identity Studies MLitt

Latin

Latin MA(Hons), Classics MA(Hons), Classical Studies (Greek and Latin pathway) BA (International Hons), Gateway to Arts Pathway to MA(Hons), FE-HE Pathway to Arts Pathway to MA(Hons)

Postgraduate courses: Classics MLitt, Classics MPhil

Management

Management BSc(Hons), Management MA(Hons), Management Science BSc(Hons), Gateway to Arts Pathway to MA(Hons), FE-HE Pathway to Arts Pathway to MA(Hons), FE-HE Pathway to Science Pathway to BSc(Hons)

Postgraduate courses: Banking and Finance MSc, Finance and Management MSc, Human Resource Management MLitt, Information Technology with Management MSc International Business MLitt, Management MLitt, Marketing MLitt

Marine Biology

Marine Biology BSc(Hons), Marine Biology MMarBiol(Hons), FE-HE Pathway to Science Pathway to BSc(Hons)

Postgraduate courses: Marine Ecosystem Management MSc, Marine Mammal Science MSc, Sustainable Aquaculture – Distance Learning PGDip/MSc, Sustainable Aquaculture – Distance Learning PG Certificate, Sustainable Aquaculture Distance Learning modular

Mathematics

Mathematics BSc(Hons), Mathematics MA(Hons), Mathematics MMath(Hons), Applied Mathematics MMath(Hons), Pure Mathematics MMath(Hons), Statistics BSc(Hons), Statistics MA(Hons), Statistics MMath(Hons), Gateway to Arts Pathway, FE-HE Pathway to Arts Pathway, FE-HE Pathway to Science Pathway

Postgraduate courses: Mathematics MSc, Applied Statistics and Datamining PGDip/MSc, Data-Intensive Analysis MSc, Statistics MSc

Mediaeval Studies

Postgraduate courses: Mediaeval Studies MLitt, Mediaeval History MLitt

Medicine

Medicine A100 (Scotland, England and No Preference routes) BSc(Hons), Medicine A990 (Canada route) BSc(Hons), Gateway to Medicine BSc(Hons), ScotGEM (2018 graduate entry programme) MBChB

Postgraduate courses: Health Psychology MSc

Middle East Studies

Postgraduate courses: Cultural Identity Studies MLitt, Middle Eastern Literary and Cultural Studies MLitt, Middle Eastern History MLitt Cultural Identity Studies MLitt Iranian Studies MLitt, Middle East, Caucasus and Central Asian Security Studies MLitt

Music

Postgraduate course: Sacred Music MLitt

Neuroscience

Neuroscience BSc(Hons), FE-HE Pathway to Science Pathway to BSc(Hons)

Postgraduate course: Neuroscience MRes

Persian

Postgraduate courses: Cultural Identity Studies MLitt, Iranian Studies MLitt, Middle East, Caucasus and Central Asian Security Studies MLitt, Middle

Eastern History MLitt, Middle Eastern Literary and Cultural Studies MLitt

Philosophy

Philosophy MA(Hons), Gateway to Arts Pathway to MA(Hons), FE-HE Pathway to Arts Pathway to MA(Hons)

Postgraduate courses: Conversion in Philosophy GradDip, Epistemology, Mind and Language MLitt, History of Philosophy MLitt, Logic and Metaphysics MLitt, Moral, Political and Legal Philosophy MLitt, Philosophy MLitt

Physics and Astronomy

Physics BSc(Hons), Physics MPhys(Hons), Astrophysics BSc(Hons), Astrophysics MPhys(Hons), Theoretical Physics MPhys(Hons), Physics and Astronomy (Gateway) BSc(Hons), Physics and Astronomy (Gateway) MPhys(Hons), International Physics and Astronomy (Gateway) BSc(Hons), International Physics and Astronomy (Gateway) MPhys(Hons), FE-HE Pathway to Science Pathway to BSc(Hons)

Postgraduate courses: Astrophysics MSc, Photonics and Optoelectronic Devices MSc

Psychology

Psychology BSc(Hons), Psychology MA(Hons), Gateway to Arts Pathway to MA(Hons), FE-HE Pathway to Arts Pathway to MA(Hons), FE-HE Pathway to Science Pathway to BSc(Hons)

Postgraduate courses: Evolutionary and Comparative Psychology: The Origins of the Mind MSc, Health Psychology MSc, Neuroscience MRes, Psychology (Conversion) MSc, Research Methods in Psychology MSc, The Psychology of Dementia Care PGCert

Russian

Russian MA(Hons), Gateway to Arts Pathway to MA(Hons), FE-HE Pathway to Arts Pathway to MA(Hons)

Postgraduate courses: Russian Studies MLitt, Cultural Identity Studies MLitt

Social Anthropology

Social Anthropology MA(Hons), Gateway to Arts Pathway, FE-HE Pathway to Arts Pathway

Postgraduate courses: Anthropology, Art and Perception MRes, Social Anthropology MRes, Social Anthropology and Amerindian Studies MRes, Social Anthropology with Pacific Studies MRes

Spanish

Spanish MA(Hons), Gateway to Arts Pathway to MA(Hons), FE-HE Pathway to Arts Pathway to MA(Hons)

Postgraduate courses: Spanish and Latin American Studies MLitt, Crossways in Cultural Narratives Erasmus Mundus MLitt, Cultural Identity Studies MLitt

Statistics

Statistics BSc(Hons), Statistics MA(Hons), Statistics MMath(Hons), Mathematics BSc(Hons), Mathematics MA(Hons), Mathematics MMath(Hons), Applied Mathematics MMath(Hons), Pure Mathematics MMath(Hons), Gateway to Arts Pathway to MA(Hons), FE-HE Pathway to Arts Pathway to MA(Hons), FE-HE Pathway to Science Pathway to BSc(Hons)

Postgraduate courses: Statistics MSc, Applied Statistics and Datamining PGDip/MSc, Data-Intensive Analysis MSc, Mathematics MSc

Sustainable Development

Sustainable Development BSc(Hons), Sustainable Development MA(Hons), Gateway to Arts Pathway to MA(Hons), FE-HE Pathway to Arts Pathway to MA(Hons), FE-HE Pathway to Science Pathway to MA(Hons)

Postgraduate courses: Sustainable Development MSc, Sustainable Development and Energy MSc

UNIVERSITY OF SALFORD
www.salford.ac.uk

School of Arts and Media;
www.salford.ac.uk/arts-media/courses

Art and Design

Foundation Year Art and Design Foundation Year, BA(Hons) Costume Design, BA(Hons) Fashion Design, BA(Hons) Fashion Image Making and Styling, BA(Hons) Film and TV Set Design, BA(hons) Fine Art, FdA Games Design (Taught at Salford City College), BA(Hons) Graphic Design, BA(Hons) Graphic Design (First year taught at Carmel College), FdA Graphic Design (Taught at Salford City College), BA(Hons) Interior Design, FdA Media Make-up For Fashion (Taught at Salford City College), BA(Hons) Photography, BA(Hons) Photography

Postgraduate courses: MA Contemporary Arts Practice with Industry Experience, MA Design for Communication with Industry Experience, MA

Socially Engaged Arts Practice with Community Experience

English and Creative Writing

BA(Hons) Drama and Creative Writing, BA(Hons) English and Creative Writing, BA(Hons) English and Drama, BA(Hons) English Language, BA(Hons) English Language and Creative Writing, BA(Hons) English Literature, BA(Hons) English Literature with English Language Postgraduate courses: MA/PgDip Creative Writing: Innovation and Experiment, MA/PgDip Literature, Culture and Modernity

Postgraduate courses: MA International Journalism for Digital Media, MA/PgDip News/Broadcast/Sport, MA Public Relations and Digital Communications Journalism: BA(Hons) Journalism (Broadcast), BA(Hons) Journalism (Multimedia), BA(Hons) Journalism with Public Relations

Media

BA(Hons) Animation, BA(Hons) Digital Media, BA(Hons) English and Film, BA(Hons) Film Production, BA(Hons) Film Studies, BSc(Hons) Games Design and production, FdA Media Production (Taught at Salford City College), BSc(Hons) Media Technology, BSc(Hons) Professional Broadcast Techniques (One year top-up), BA(Hons) Television and Radio

Postgraduate courses: MA/PgDip Media Production: Animation, MA/PgDip Media Production: Children's TV Production, MA/PgDip Media Production: Post-Production for TV, MA/PgDip Media Production: TV Documentary Production, MA/PgDip Media Production: TV Drama Production, MA Wildlife Documentary Production

Music

BA(Hons) Music: Creative Music Technology, BA(Hons) Music: Musical Arts, BA(Hons) Music: Popular Music and Recording, FdA Creative Music Postgraduate courses: MA Music

Performing Arts

BA(Hons) Comedy Writing & Performance, BA(Hons) Dance, BA(Hons) Media and Performance, BA(Hons) Technical Theatre (Production and Design), BA(Hons) Theatre and Performance Practice Postgraduate courses: MA Contemporary Performance Practice

Politics and History

BA(Hons) Contemporary History and Politics, BA(Hons) Contemporary Military and International History, BA(Hons) International Politics and Security, BA(Hons) International Relations and Politics, BA(Hons) Politics

Postgraduate courses: MA/PgDip Intelligence and Security Studies, MA/PgDip Terrorism and Security

School of the Built Environment; www.salford.ac.uk/built-environment

BSc(Hons) Architectural Design and Technology, BSc(Hons) Architecture, MArch Architecture, BSc(Hons) Architectural Engineering, BSc(Hons) Building Surveying, MSci(Hons) Building Surveying, BSc(Hons) Construction Project Management, BSc(Hons) Property and Real Estate, BSc(Hons) Quantity Surveying

Postgraduate courses: MSc BIM and Digital Built Environments, MSc/LLM Construction Law and Practice, MSc Building Surveying, MSc Construction Management, MSc Project Management in Construction, MSc Quantity Surveying, MSc Quantity Surveying (M&E), MSc Real Estate and Property Management

School of Computing, Science and Engineering; www.salford.ac.uk/computing-science-engineering

Acoustics, Audio and Video

BEng(Hons) / BEng Accoustical and Audio Engineering, BSc(Hons) Professional Sound and Video Technology

Postgraduate courses: MSc/PgDip Audio Acoustics, MSc/PgDip Environmental Acoustics, MSc/PgDip Audio Production

Aeronautical Engineering

BEng(Hons) Aeronautical Engineering, MEng(Hons) Aeronautical Engineering, BEng(Hons) Aeronautical Engineering with Foundation Year, BEng(Hons) Aircraft Engineering with Pilot Studies, MEng(Hons) Aircraft Engineering with Pilot Studies

Postgraduate courses: MSc/PgDip/PgCert Aerospace Engineering

Civil and Structural Engineering

BEng(Hons) Civil Engineering, BSc(Hons) Civil Engineering, MEng(Hons) Civil Engineering, BEng(Hons) Civil Engineering with Foundation Year, BEng(Hons) Civil and Architectural Engineering, MEng(Hons) Civil and Architectural Engineering Postgraduate courses: MSc/PgDip/PgCert Structural Engineering, MSc Transport Engineering and Planning

Computer Networking and Telecommunications

BSc(Hons) Computer Networks

Postgraduate courses: MSc/PgDip Data Telecommunication Networks

Computer Science

BSc(Hons) Computer Science, BSc(Hons) Computer Science with Professional Experience, BSc(Hons) Computer Science with Foundation Year, BSc(Hons) Computer Science with Web Development, BSc(Hons) Computer Science with Web Development and Professional Experience, BSc(Hons) Computer Science with Cyber Security, BSc(Hons) Computer Science with Cyber Security and Professional Experience, BSc(Hons) Computer Science with Data Analytics, BSc(Hons) Computer Science with Data Analytics and Professional Experience, BSc(Hons) Software Engineering, BSc(Hons) Software Engineering with Professional Experience

Postgraduate courses: MSc/PgDip Databases and Web-based Systems, MSc/PgDip Cyber Security, Threat Intelligence and Forensics, MSc/PgDip Data Science

Mathematics

BSc(Hons) Mathematics, BSc(Hons) Financial Mathematics

Mechanical Engineering

BEng(Hons) Mechanical Engineering, MEng(Hons) Mechanical Engineering, BEng(Hons) Mechanical Engineering with Foundation Year

Petroleum and Gas Engineering

BEng(Hons) Petroleum and Mechanical Engineering

Postgraduate courses: MSc/PgDip Gas Engineering and Management, MSc/PgDip/PgCert Industrial and Commercial Combustion Engineering, MSc/PgDip Petroleum and Gas Engineering

Physics

BSc(Hons) Physics, MPhys(Hons) Physics, BSc(Hons) Physics with Acoustics, MPhys(Hons) Physics with Acoustics, MPhys(Hons) Physics with Studies in North America, BSc(Hons) Pure and Applied Physics, BSc(Hons) Physics with Foundation Year

Postgraduate courses: MSc Renewable Energy Materials

Electronic Engineering

BEng(Hons) Electronic Engineering, BEng(Hons) Electronic Engineering with Foundation Year

Robotics and System Engineering

MSc/PgDip Advanced Control System, MSc/PgDip Robotics and Automation

School of Environment and Life Sciences; www.salford.ac.uk/environment-lifesciences/courses

BA(Hons) Archaeology and Geography with Professional Practice, BSc(Hons) Biochemistry, BSc(Hons) Biochemistry with Studies in the USA, BSc(Hons) Biology, Foundation Year Biology Foundation Year, BSc(Hons) Biology with Studies in the USA, BSc(Hons) Biomedical Science, BSc(Hons) Chemistry, BSc(Hons) Environmental Management, Foundation Year Environmental Management Foundation Year, BSc(Hons) Geography, BA(Hons) Geography, BSc(Hons) Human Biology and Infectious Diseases, BSc(Hons) Marine Biology, BSc(Hons) Medicinal Chemistry, BSc(Hons) Pharmaceutical Science, BSc(Hons) Wildlife and Practical Conservation, BSc(Hons) Wildlife Conservation with Zoo Biology, BSc(Hons) Zoology, BSc(Hons) Zoology with Marine Biology

Postgraduate courses: MSc Biomedical Science, MSc Biotechnology, MSc Drug Design and Discovery, MSc Environmental and Public Health, MSc Environmental Assessment and Management, MSc/PgDip/PgCert Environmental Modelling, MSc/PgDip/PgCert Geographical Information Systems, Msc/PgDip Molecular Parasitology and Vector Biology, MSc/PgDip Occupational Safety, Health and Wellbeing, MSc Safety, Health and Environment, MSc Science Communication and Future Media, MSc/PgDip Sustainability, MSc/PgDip/PgCert Wildlife Conservation

School of Health Sciences; www.salford.ac.uk/health-sciences

BSc(Hons) Diagnostic Radiography, BSc(Hons) Exercise, Nutrition and Health, BSc(Hons) Occupational Therapy, BSc(Hons) Physiotherapy, BSc(Hons) Podiatry, BSc(Hons) Prosthetics and Orthotics, BSc(Hons) Psychology, BSc(Hons) Psychology (First year taught at Salford City College), BSc(Hons) Psychology and Counselling, BSc(Hons) Psychology and Criminology, BSc(Hons) Psychology and Criminology (First year taught at Salford City College), BSc(Hons) Psychology of Sport, BSc(Hons) Public Health and Health Promotion, BSc(Hons) Public Health and Health Promotion with Placement, BSc(Hons) Sport Rehabilitation, FdSc Sports Coaching (Taught at Hopwood Hall College), BSc(Hons) Sports Science (Human Performance, Performance Analysis or Strength and Conditioning pathways)

Postgraduate courses: MSc/PgDip/PgCert Advanced Medical Imaging, MSc/PgDip/PgCert Advanced Occupational Therapy, MSc/PgDip/PgCert Advanced Physiotherapy, MSc/PgDip/PgCert Applied Psychology (Addictions), MSc Clinical Exercise Physiology, MSc/PgDip/PgCert Applied Psychology (Therapies), MSc/PgDip/PgCert Geriatric Medicine, MSc/PgDip/PgCert Media Psychology, MSc/PgDip Nuclear Medicine Imaging, MSc/PgDip/PgCert Occupational and

Vocational Rehabilitation, MSc/PgDip/PgCert Performance Analysis in Sport, MSc Pre-registration Masters Podiatry Programme, MSc/PgDip/PgCert Psychology of Coercive Control, MSc/PgDip/PgCert Public Health, PgCert Public Health (Block and Blend), MSc/PgDip/PgCert Sports Injury Rehabilitation, MSc/PgDip/PgCert Strength and Conditioning, MSc/PgDip/PgCert Trauma and Orthopaedics, MSc/PgDip/PgCert Trauma and Orthopaedics: Lower Limb, MSc/PgDip/PgCert Trauma and Orthopaedics: Spinal, MSc/PgDip/PgCert Ultrasound Imaging

School of Health and Society ; www.salford.ac.uk/health-and-society

Counselling and Psychotherapy

BSc(Hons) Counselling and Psychotherapy: Professional Practice, BSc(Hons) Criminology with Counselling
Postgraduate courses: MSc/PgDip/PgCert Advanced Counselling and Psychotherapy Studies, PgCert Cognitive Behaviour Therapy, MSc/PgDip/PgCert Cognitive Behavioural Psychotherapy, MSc/PgDip Counselling and Psychotherapy Studies (Professional Training)

Midwifery

BSc(Hons) Midwifery (156 weeks), BSc(Hons) Midwifery (Post RN)
Postgraduate courses: MSc/PgDip/PgCert Advanced Practice (Neonates), MSc/PgDip/PgCert Midwifery

Nursing

BSc(Hons) Integrated Practice in Learning Disabilities Nursing and Social Work, BSc(Hons) Nursing /RN Adult, BSc(Hons) Nursing /RN Children and Young People's, BSc(Hons) Nursing /RN Mental Health, BSc(Hons) Nursing Studies
Postgraduate courses: MSc/PgDip/PgCert Advanced Practice (Health and Social Care), MSc/PgDip/PgCert

Dementia

Care and the Enabling Environment, MSc/ PgDip/PgCert Diabetes Care, PgCert Gastrointestinal Disorders, MSc/PgDip/PgCert Leadership and Management for Healthcare Practice, MSc Leading Education for Health and Social Care Reform, PgCert

Leading Education in Practice

NMC Practice Teacher Award, MSc/PgDip/PgCert Military Veterans' Health and Wellbeing, Multi-professional Support of Learning and Assessment in Practice – Non-Credited, MSc/ PgDip/PgCert Nursing (Block and Blend), MA/RN Nursing/RN (Adult, Mental Health or Children & Young People), MSc/ PgDip/PgCert

Nursing

Research, Practice, Practice (Neuroscience), Education, International, Prof Doc Professional Doctorate (Health and Social Care), PgCert Simulation in Health and Social Care, PgCert

Work Based Learning

Using and Disseminating Evidence into Practice Social

Work and Social Policy

BSc(Hons) Social Policy, Foundation Year Social Sciences Foundation Year, BA(Hons) Social Work, BSc(Hons) Integrated Practice in Learning Disabilities Nursing and Social Work
Postgraduate courses: MSc/PgDip/PgCert Applied Social Work Practice, MA Social Pedagogy, MSc/ PgDip/PgCert Social Policy, MA Social Work

Sociology and Criminology

BSc(Hons) Criminology, BSc(Hons) Criminology and Sociology, BSc(Hons) Criminology with Counselling, BSc(Hons) Criminology with Security, BSc(Hons) Sociology
Postgraduate courses: MSc/PgCert/PgDip The Criminal Justice Process

Salford Business School; www.salford.ac.uk/business-school

BSc(Hons) Accounting and Finance, BSc(Hons) Business and Economics, FdSc Business and Events Management (Taught at Salford City College), BSc(Hons) Business and Financial Management, BSc Business and Financial Management (First Year taught at Salford City College), FdSc Business and Financial Management (Taught at Salford City College), FdSc Business and Hospitality Management (Taught at Salford City College), BSc(Hons) Business and Management, BSc(Hons) Business and Management (First year taught at Salford City College), FdSc Business and Management (Taught at Salford City College), FdSc Business and Marketing (Taught at Salford City College), Foundation Year Business Foundation Year, BSc(Hons) Business Information Technology, BSc(Hons) Business Management with Law, BSc(Hons) Business Management with Sport, LLB(Hons) Corporate Law, BSc(Hons) Human Resource Management, BSc(Hons) Human Resource Management (First year taught at Salford City College), Graduate Certificate Human Resource Management (HRM) with CIPD Intermediate Level Diploma, BSc(Hons) International Business, BSc(Hons) International Events Management, LLB(Hons) Law, LLB(Hons) Law (Media and Digital Industries), LLB(Hons) Law with Criminology,

LLB(Hons) Law with Management, BSc(Hons) Marketing, BSc(Hons) Marketing (First year taught at Salford City College)

Postgraduate courses: MSc/PgDip/PgCert Accounting and Finance, MSc/PgDip/PgCert Digital Marketing, MSc/PgDip/PgCert Financial Services Management, MSc/PgDip/PgCert Global Management, MSc/PgDip/PgCert Human Resource Management and Development, MSc/PgDip/PgCert Human Resource Management and Development – part time evening attendance, MSc/PgDip/PgCert Information Systems Management, MSc/PgDip/PgCert International Banking and Finance, MSc/PgDip/PgCert International Business, LLM/PgDip/PgCert International Business Law, MSc/PgDip/PgCert International Business with Law, LLM/PgDip/PgCert International Commercial Law, MSc/PgDip/PgCert International Corporate Finance, MSc/PgDip/PgCert International Events Management, Graduate Certificate International Management, MSc/PgDip/PgCert Islamic Banking and Finance, MSc/PgDip/PgCert Management, PgCert Management and Personal Development, MSc/PgDip/PgCert Marketing, MSc/PgDip/PgCert Procurement, Logistics and Supply Chain Management, MSc/PgDip/PgCert Project Management, MSc Risk and Crisis Management (Food Safety Assurance), MSc Sports Directorship, MBA The Salford MBA, MBA The Salford MBA Part-time Executive

RIVERSIDE COLLEGE, HALTON
www.riversidecollege.ac.uk

Sport Coaching and Sport Development, Sport Coaching, Counselling, Education, Health & Social Care; Dip, FD, FdSc, BSc(Hons), PCET

SCARBOROUGH TEC
www.scarboroughtec.ac.uk/about-scarborough-tec

Certificate in Education, Professional Graduate Certificate in Education, Postgraduate Certificate in Education (Teaching in the Lifelong Learning Sector)

UNIVERSITY OF SHEFFIELD
www.sheffield.ac.uk

Faculty of Arts and Humanities; www.sheffield.ac.uk/faculty/arts-andhumanities

Department of Archaeology
BA Archaeology, BSc Archaeology, BA Archaeology and History, BA Archaelogy and Modern Languages & Cultures, BA Classical and Historical Archaeology, BA Prehistoric Archaeology

Postgraduate courses: MA Aegean Archaeology, MA Archaeology, MA Archaeology of the Classical Mediterranean, MA Cultural Heritage Management, MA Cultural Materials, MSc Environmental Archaeology & Palaeoeconomy, MA Landscape Archaeology, MSc Osteoarchaeology, MSc Human Osteology & Funerary Archaeology, MSc Palaeoanthropology

School of English
BA (honours) English Language and guistics, BA (honours) English Language and Literature, BA (honours) English Literature, BA (honours) English and Theatre

Postgraduate courses: MA/PG Diploma Applied Linguistics with TESOL, MA Creative Writing, MA English Language and Linguistics, MA English Literature, MA Literature, Culture and Society 1700-1900, MA English Studies (online) MA Theatre and Performance Studies

Department of History
BA History BA Archaeology and History, BA English and History, BA History and Politics, BA History and Sociology, BA History and Philosophy, BA History & Modern Languages and Cultures

Postgraduate courses: MA Historical Research, MA Medieval History, MA Early Modern History, MA Modern History, MA American History, MA Global History

School of Languages and Cultures

Degree one, two or three languages as part of the BA Modern Languages and Cultures. Or a Dual degree where you combine one or two languages. Languages: French, German, Spanish, Russian, Dutch, Czech, Catalan, Italian, Portuguese, Luxembourgish. BA Modern Languages & Cultures, BA English and Modern Languages & Cultures, BA Linguistics and Modern Languages & Cultures, BA History and Modern Languages & Cultures, BA Philosophy and Modern Languages & Cultures, BA Business Management and Modern Languages & Cultures, BA Politics and Modern Languages & Cultures, BA Archaeology and Modern Languages & Cultures, BA Economics and Modern Languages & Cultures, BA Music and Modern Languages & Cultures

Postgraduate MA courses: MA Crossways in Cultural Narratives, MA Intercultural Communication, MA Communication and International Development, MA Multilingual Information Management, MA Screen Translation, MA Translation Studies, MA Modern Languages and Cultures

Department of Music

BMus Music, BA Music Education, BMus Music (part-time), BMus Music with foundation year, BA English and Music, BA History and Music, BA Music and Philosophy, BA Music and Modern Languages & Cultures, BA Music and Korean Studies, BMus with International Foundation Year

Postgraduate courses: MA Composition, MA Ethnomusicology, MA Music Management, MA Musicology, MA Music Performance Studies, MA Music Psychology in Education, Performance and Wellbeing (DL), MA Psychology of Music, MA Traditional and World Music distance learning

Department of Philosophy

BA Philosophy (Single Honours) BA Philosophy, Religion and Ethics, BA Economics and Philosophy, BA English and Philosophy, BA Philosophy and Modern Languages and Cultures, BA History and Philosophy, BA Linguistics and Philosophy, BSc Mathematics and Philosophy, BA Music and Philosophy, BSc/MPhys Physics with Philosophy, BA Politics and Philosophy

Postgraduate courses: MA Philosophy, MA Cognitive Studies, MA Political Theory

Faculty of Engineering; www.sheffield.ac.uk/faculty/engineering

Department of Aerospace Engineering; www.sheffield.ac.uk/aerospace

BEng/MEng Aerospace Engineering, BEng/MEng Aerospace Engineering with Private Pilot Instruction, BEng/MEng Aerospace Engineering with a Year in Industry, MEng Aerospace Engineering with a Year in North America, MEng Aerospace Engineering with a Foundation Year

Postgraduate courses: MSc Aerospace Engineering, MSc Advanced Aerospace Technologies

Department of Automatic Control and Systems Engineering; www.sheffield.ac.uk/acse

MEng/BEng Mechatronic and Robotic Engineering, MEng/BEng Mechatronic and Robotic Engineering with a Year in Industry, MEng/BEng Robotics with a Foundation Year, MEng/BEng Systems and Control Engineering, MEng/BEng Systems and Control Engineering with a Year in Industry, MEng/BEng Systems and Control Engineering (Engineering Management), MEng/BEng Computer Systems Engineering, MEng/BEng Computer Systems Engineering with a Year in Industry, MEng/BEng Foundation Year

Postgraduate courses: MSc Advanced Control and Systems Engineering, MSc Robotics, MSc Autonomous & Intelligent Systems, MRes in Control and Systems Engineering, MSc Advanced Manufacturing Technologies

Department of Bioengineering; www.sheffield.ac.uk/bioengineering

BEng/MEng Bioengineering, BEng/MEng Bioengineering with a Year in Industry, Bioengineering with a Foundation Year

Postgraduate course: MSc Computational Medicine

Department of Chemical and Biological Engineering; www.sheffield.ac.uk/cbe

BEng Chemical Engineering, BEng Chemical Engineering with Industrial Experience, MEng Chemical Engineering, MEng Chemical Engineering with a Year in Industry, MEng Chemical Engineering with Energy, MEng Chemical Engineering with Pharmaceutical Engineering, MEng Chemical Engineering with Biological Engineering, MEng Chemical Engineering with Nuclear Technology, MEng Chemical Engineering with a Year in Australasia, Chemical Engineering with Foundation Year

Postgraduate courses: MSc Biological and Bioprocess Engineering, MSc(Eng) Environmental and Energy Engineering, MSc(Eng)/PG Diploma Process Safety and Loss Prevention, MSc Biochemical Engineering with Industrial Management, MSc Energy Engineering with Industrial Management

Department of Civil and Structural Engineering; www.sheffield.ac.uk/civil

MEng Urban Engineering & Development, MEng Architectural Engineering, MEng Civil Engineering, MEng Civil & Structual Engineering, MEng Structural Engineering & Architecture

Postgraduate courses: MSc Architectural Engineering Design, MSc (Eng) Structural Engineering, MSc Civil Engineering, MSC Water Engineering

Department of Computer Science; www.sheffield.ac.uk/dcs

BSc/MComp Computer Science, BSc/MComp Artificial Intelligence and Computer Science, BEng/MEng Software Engineering, BSc/MComp Computer Science with a Year in Industry, BSc/MComp Artificial Intelligence and Computer Science with a Year in Industry, BEng/MEng Software Engineering with a Year in Industry, BSc or MComp Computer Science with a Foundation Year, BEng or MEng Software Engineering with a Foundation Year, MEng Engineering IPO, MEng Engineering with a Year in Industry

Postgraduate courses: MSc Data Analytics, MSc Cybersecurity and Artificial Intelligence, MSc (Eng) Advanced Software Engineering, MSc Advanced Computer Science, MSc Computer Science with Speech and Language Processing, MSc Software Systems and Internet Technology

Department of Electronic and Electrical Engineering; www.sheffield.ac.uk/eee

BEng/MEng Electrical and Electronic Engineering, BEng/MEng Electrical and Electronic Engineering with a Year in Industry, MEng Electrical and Electronic Engineering with a Modern Language

Postgraduate courses: MSc(Eng) Advanced Electrical Machines, Power Electronics and Drives, MSc(Eng) Data Communications, MSc(Eng) Electronic and Electrical Engineering, MSc(Eng) Semiconductor Photonics and Electronics, MSc(Eng) Wireless Communications

Department of Materials Science and Engineering; www.sheffield.ac.uk/materials

BEng/MEng Materials Science and Engineering, Materials Science and Engineering with Foundation Year, BEng Materials Science and Engineering (Year in Industry), BEng/MEng Biomaterials Science and Engineering, MEng Materials Science and Engineering (Research), MEng Metallurgy, MEng Materials Science with Nuclear Engineering

Postgraduate courses: MMEt Advanced Metallurgy Distance Learning, MSc Materials Science and Engineering, MSc Nuclear Science and Technology, MSc(Eng) Polymers and Polymer Composite Science and Engineering, MMet Advanced Metallurgy, MSc(Eng) Aerospace Materials, MSc Biomaterials and Regenerative Medicine, MSc Nanomaterials and Materials Science

Department of Mechanical Engineering; www.sheffield.ac.uk/mecheng

MEng/BEng Mechanical Engineering, MEng/BEng Mechanical Engineering with a Year in Industry, MEng Mechanical Engineering with French, MEng Mechanical Engineering with German, MEng Mechanical Engineering with Spanish, MEng Mechanical Engineering with a Year in North America, MEng Mechanical Engineering with Biomechanics, MEng Mechanical Engineering with Biomechanics with a Year in Industry, MEng Mechanical Engineering with a Semester in China, Mechanical Engineering with a Foundation Year

Postgraduate courses: MSc Advanced Mechanical Engineering, MSc Mechanical Engineering with Industrial Management, MSc(Res) Advanced Manufacturing Technologies, MSc(Res) Aerodynamics and Aerostructures, MSc(Res) Additive Manufacturing and Advanced Manufacturing Technologies

Faculty of Medicine, Dentistry & Health; www.sheffield.ac.uk/faculty/medicine-dentistry-health

The Medical School; www.sheffield.ac.uk/medicine

MBChb Medical degree, BSc Medical Sciences Research, BMedSci(Hons) Orthoptics

The School of Clinical Dentistry; www.sheffield.ac.uk/dentalschool

Bachelor of Dental Surgery, Diploma in Dental Hygiene and Dental Therapy, BSc Bio-dental Science and Technology, BMedSci Programme

Postgraduate courses: DClinDent in Restorative Dentistry, MSc in Dental Materials Science, Master in Dental Public Health, MSc in Dental Technology, DClinDent in Paediatric Dentistry, M/DClinDent in Orthodontics, MMedSci in Diagnostic Oral Pathology, MClinDent in International Dental Public Health

School of Health and Related Research; www.sheffield.ac.uk/scharr

Postgraduate courses (online): MSc/PgDip/PgCert International Health Management and Leadership, MPH/PgDip/PgCert Public Health, MSc, PgDip, PgCert International Health Technology Assessment, Pricing and Reimbursement, PgCert Cost-Effectiveness Modelling for Health Technology Assessment (Postgraduate certificate only)

Postgraduate courses (campus-based): MSc/PgDip/PgCert Clinical Research, MSc/PgDip/PgCert Health Economics and Decision Modelling, MSc/PgDip/PgCert Human Nutrition, MPH/PgDip/PgCert Public Health, MPH/PgDip/PgCert Public Health (Health Services Research), MPH/PgDip/PgCert Public Health (Management and Leadership), MPH in European Public Health

Department of Human Communication Sciences; www.sheffield.ac.uk/hcs

BSc Speech and Language Sciences, BMedSci Speech and Language Therapy, Advanced Certificate Language and Communication Impairment in Children (LACIC)

Postgraduate courses: MMedSci Speech and Language Therapy, MSc PG Certificate PG Diploma Speech Difficulties, MSc PG Certificate PG Diploma Language and Communication Impairment in Children, MSc PG Certificate PG Diploma Acquired Communication Disorders

Infection, Immunity & Cardiovascular Disease; www.sheffield.ac.uk/iicd

Postgraduate courses: MSc in Molecular Medicine, MRes Cardiovascular Medicine: From Molecules to Man, MA Medicine in Society, MSc Antimicrobial Resistance

Department of Neuroscience; www.sheffield.ac.uk/neuroscience

Postgraduate courses: MSc in Translational Neuropathology, MSc in Clinical Neurology, MSc in Translational Neuroscience, MSc in Neuroscience and Neurodegeneration (via distance learning), MSc in Genomic Medicine

The School of Nursing and Midwifery; www.sheffield.ac.uk/snm

BMedSci Health and Human Sciences (Full-Time or Part-Time), BMedSci Nursing (Adult), BMedSci Renal Nursing Care (Distance Learning)

Postgraduate courses: MMedSci Nursing Studies (Adult), MA Dementia Studies, MMEdSci Nursing Top Up, MMedSci Advanced Neonatal Nurse Practitioner, MMedSci Advanced Paediatric Nurse Practitioner, PG Cert in Long-Term Health Conditions, PG Cert in Neonatal Intensive Care, MMedSci Advanced General Practice Advanced Nurse Practitioner, MMed Sci Advanced Nursing Studies (online)

Department of Oncology & Metabolism; www.sheffield.ac.uk/oncology-metabolism

Postgraduate courses: MRes Musculoskeletal Ageing, MSc Reproductive and Developmental Medicine, MSc(Res) Translational Oncology, MMedSci/Postgraduate Diploma Vision & Strabismus (Distance Learning)

Science at Sheffield; www.sheffield.ac.uk/faculty/science

Department of Animal and Plant Sciences; www.sheffield.ac.uk/aps

BSc/MBiolSci Biology, BSc/MBiolSci Zoology, BSc/MBiolSci Ecology and Conservation Biology, BSc/MBiolSci Plant Sciences, BSc Biosciences Foundation Year, Biology with Foundation Year, BSc Environmental Science, MEnvSci Environmental Science

Postgraduate courses: MSc Biodiversity and Conservation, MSc Biological Sciences, MRes Ecology and Environment, MRes Evolution and Behaviour, MRes Plant and Microbial Biology, MSc Practical Entomology, MSc Sustainable Agricultural Technologies, MSc Science Communication

Department of Biomedical Science; www.sheffield.ac.uk/bms

BSc or MBiomedSci Biomedical Science, BSc Biomedical Science with a Year Abroad, BSc or MBiomedSci Biomedical Science with a Year in Industry, Biomedical Science with Foundation Year, BSc Biosciences Foundation Year

Postgraduate courses: MSc Biomedical Science, MSc Biomedical Science with Education, MSc Genomic Approaches to Drug Discovery, MSc Human Anatomy with Education, MSc Molecular and Cellular Basis of Human Disease, MSc Neuroscience, MSc

Stem Cell and Regenerative Medicine, MSc Science Communication

Department of Chemistry; www.sheffield.ac.uk/chemistry

BSc Chemistry, MChem Chemistry, MChem Chemistry with Study Abroad, BSc Chemistry with a Year in Industry, MChem Chemistry with a Year in Industry, BSc Chemistry with Biological and Medicinal Chemistry, MChem Chemistry with Biological and Medicinal Chemistry, BSc Chemistry with a Foundation Year

Postgraduate courses: MSc Chemistry, MSc(Res) Chemistry, MSc Polymers for Advanced Technologies

School of Mathematics and Statistics; www.sheffield.ac.uk/maths

BSc, MMath and Placement Year option in Mathematics, BSc, MMath and Placement Year option in Mathematics and Statistics, BA Accounting and Financial Management and Mathematics, BA Business Management and Mathematics, BSc Economics and Mathematics, BSc Mathematics and Philosophy, MMath Mathematics with French, German or Spanish, MMath Mathematics: Study abroad options, BSc Financial Mathematics

Postgraduate courses: MSc Mathematics, MSc Mathematical and Theoretical Physics, MSc Statistics, MSc Statistics with Financial Mathematics

Department of Molecular Biology & Biotechnology; www.sheffield.ac.uk/mbb

BSc Biochemistry, BSc Biochemistry Genetics, BSC Biochemistry Microbiology, BSc Medical Biochemistry, MBiolSci Biochemistry, MBiolSci Biochemistry Genetics, MBiolSci Biochemistry Microbiology, MBiolSci Medical Biochemistry, BSc Genetics, BSC Genetics Microbiology, BSc Medical Genetics, BSc Biochemistry Genetics, MBiolSci Genetics, MBiolSci Genetics Microbiology, MBiolSci Medical Genetics, MBiolSci Biochemistry Genetics, BSc Microbiology, BSc Medical Microbiology, BSc Biochemistry Microbiology, BSc Genetics Microbiology, MBiolSci Microbiology, MBiolSci Medical Microbiology, MBiolSci Biochemistry Microbiology, MBiolSci Genetics Microbiology, BSc Molecular Biology, MBiolSci Molecular Biology

Postgraduate courses: MSc Antimicrobial Resistance, MSc Human and Molecular Genetics, MSc Molecular Biology and Biotechnology, MSc Biological Imaging, MSc Science Communication

Department of Physics and Astronomy; www.sheffield.ac.uk/physics

BSc, MPhys, Year in Industry and Study Abroad in Physics, BSc, MPhys, Year in Industry and Study Abroad in Physics and Astrophysics, BSc, MPhys, Year in Industry and Study Abroad in Theoretical Physics, BSc and MPhys in Physics with Medical Physics, BSc and MPhys in Physics with Philosophy

Postgraduate courses: MSc Biological Imaging, MSc Mathematical and Theoretical Physics, MSc(Res) Particle Physics, MSc(Res) Quantum Photonics and Nanomaterials, MSc Solar Cell Technology

Department of Psychology; www.sheffield.ac.uk/psychology

BSc Psychology

Postgraduate courses: MSc Cognitive and Computational Neuroscience, MSc Cognitive Neuroscience and Human Neuro-imaging, MSc Systems Neuroscience, MSc Psychological Research Methods, MSc Psychological Research Methods with Advanced Statistics, MSc Psychological Research Methods with Data Science

Faculty of Social Sciences; www.sheffield.ac.uk/faculty/ socialsciences

School of Architecture; www.sheffield.ac.uk/architecture

BA Architecture, BA Architecture and Landscape, MEng Structural Engineering and Architecture

Postgraduate courses: MSc Digital Architecture and Design, MSc Sustainable Architecture Studies, MA Urban Design, MA Architectural Design

School of East Asian Studies; www.sheffield.ac.uk/seas

BA Chinese Studies, BA East Asian Studies, BA Japanese Studies, BA Korean Studies, BA Chinese Studies with Japanese, BA Chinese Studies and Business Management, BA Chinese Studies and History, BA Japanese Studies and History, BA Business Management and Japanese Studies, BA Linguistics and Japanese Studies, BA Korean Studies with Japanese, BA Music and Korean Studies

Postgraduate courses: MSc East Asian Business, MA Politics and Media in East Asia

Department of Economics; www.sheffield.ac.uk/economics

BA Economics, BSc Economics, BSc Economics with Finance, BA Accounting and Financial Management and Economics, BA Business Management and

Economics, BSc Economics and Mathematics, BA Economics and Philosophy, BA Economics and Politics, BA Economics and Modern Languages & Cultures
Postgraduate courses: MSc Economics, MSc Economics and Public Policy, MSc Economics and Health Economics, MSc Business Finance and Economics, MSc Finance, MSc Financial Economics, MSc Money, Banking and Finance, MSc International Finance and Economics

School of Law; www.sheffield.ac.uk/law
LLB Law, European and International LLB Law, LLB Law and Criminology, LLB Law (with French Law), LLB Law (with German Law), LLB Law (with Spanish Law), LLB Law (with Chinese Law), BA Criminology
Postgraduate courses: The Sheffield LLM, LLM Corporate and Commercial Law, LLM International Law and Global Justice, LLM Law (Doshisha), MA International Criminology, PG Certificate in International Criminology, MA Law, Legal Practice Course (MA in Legal Practice), Graduate Diploma in Law, PG Certificate in Investigation of Vulnerabilities Crime

Management School; www.sheffield.ac.uk/management
BA Accounting and Financial Management, BA Business Management, BA International Business Management with Study Abroad, BA Accounting and Financial Management and Economics, BA Accounting and Financial Management and Mathematics, BA Business Management and Economics, BA Business Management and Mathematics, BA Business Management and Modern Languages and Cultures, BA Business Management and Japanese Studies, BA Chinese Studies and Business Management
Postgraduate courses: MSc Accounting, Governance and Financial Management, MSc Creative and Cultural Industries Management, MSc Finance and Accounting, MSc Global Marketing Management, MSc Human Resource Management with CIPD Pathway, MSc Human Resource Management, MSc Information Systems Management, MSc International Management, MSc International Management and Marketing, MSc Logistics and Supply Chain Management, MSc Management, MSc Management (International Business), MSc Marketing Management Practice, MSc Occupational Psychology, MSc Work Psychology

Department of Politics and International Relations; www.sheffield.ac.uk/politics
BA Politics, BA International Relations and Politics, BA Economics and Politics, BA History and Politics, BA Politics and Philosophy, BA Politics and Sociology, BA Politics and Modern Languages & Cultures
Postgraduate courses: MA International Relations, MA Global Political Economy, MA Political Theory, MA Politics, Governance and Public Policy

Department of Sociological Studies; www.sheffield.ac.uk/socstudies
BA Sociology, BA Digital Media & Society, BA Sociology with Social Policy, BA Sociology with Criminology
Postgraduate courses: MA Sociology, MA Digital Media and Society, MSc International Social Change and Policy, MA Social Work, MA Advanced Professional Practice, Advanced Professional Practice (CPD)

Urban Studies and Planning; www.sheffield.ac.uk/usp
MPlan, BA Urban Studies, BA Geography and Planning
Postgraduate courses: MSc Real Estate, MSc Real Estate Planning & Development, MSc Urban and Regional Planning, MSc Cities and Global Development, MA Urban Design and Planning, MSc Applied GIS (Geographic Information Systems)

School of Education; www.sheffield.ac.uk/education
BA Education, Culture and Childhood, BA Education, Culture and Childhood with Foundation Year
Postgraduate courses: PGDE (Postgraduate Diploma in Education), MA Education, MA Education: Early Childhood, MA Globalising Education: Policy and Practice, MA Psychology and Education, MA Education: Language and Education, MSc (conversion) Psychology and Education, MA Education Teaching and Learning (Online)

Department of Geography; www.sheffield.ac.uk/geography
BA Geography, BSc Geography, MGeogSci Geography, BSc Environmental Science, MEnvSci Environmental Science, BA Geography and Planning
Postgraduate courses: MA International Development, MSc Environmental Change and International Development, MPH (Masters in Public Health) International Development, MSc Applied Geographical Information Systems (GIS), MSc(Res) Polar and Alpine Change

Information School www.sheffield.ac.uk/is

Postgraduate courses: MSc Data Science, MSc Health Informatics, MSc Information Management, MSc Information Systems, MSc Information Systems Management, MA Librarianship, MA Library and Information Services Management, MA Multilingual Information Management

Department of Journalism Studies; www.sheffield.ac.uk/journalism

BA Journalism Studies

Postgraduate courses: MA/PG Diploma Broadcast Journalism, MA Global Journalism, MA International Public and Political Communication, MA/PG Diploma Journalism, MA/PG Diploma Magazine Journalism, MSc Science Communication

Department of Landscape Architecture; www.sheffield.ac.uk/landscape

BA Landscape Architecture, BSc Landscape Architecture, BA Architecture and Landscape

Postgraduate courses: MA PG Diploma Landscape Architecture, MA PG Diploma Landscape Studies, MA PG Diploma Landscape Management

SHEFFIELD HALLAM UNIVERSITY
www.shu.ac.uk

Faculty of Science, Technology and Arts www.shu.ac.uk/about-us/academic-departments/faculty-of-science-technology-and-arts

Sheffield Institute of Arts www4.shu.ac.uk/sia/

BA (Honours) Animation, BSc (Honours) Architectural Technology, BSc (Honours) Architectural Technology (Part-time), BSc (Honours) Architecture, International Foundation Programme: Art, Design and Media BA (Honours) Fine Art, BA (Honours) Fine Art (parttime), BA (Honours) Creative Writing, BA (Honours) Fashion Design, BA (Honours) Fashion Management and Communication, BA (Honours) Digital Media Production, BA (Honours) Film and Media Production, BA (Honours) Games Design, BSc (Honours) Computer Science for Games, BA (Honours) Graphic Design BA (Honours) Illustration, BA (Honours) Interior Design, BA (Honours) Interior Architecture and Design with Foundation Year BA (Honours) Jewellery and Metalwork, BA(Hons)Journalism, BA(Hons) Sports Journalism BA (Honours) Media, BA(Hons) Public Relations, BA(Hons) Public Relations and Media, BA (Honours) Performance and Professional Practice (top up), BA (Honours) Performance for Stage and Screen, BA (Honours) Photography, BA (Honours) Product Design, BA (Honours) Product Design: Furniture

Postgraduate courses: MA/MFA Design (Fashion), MA/MFA Design (Graphics), MA/MFA Design (Illustration), MA/MFA Design (Interaction), MA/MFA Design (Interiors), MA/MFA Design (Jewellery and Metalwork), MA/MFA Design (Packaging), MA/MFA Design (Product), MA Fashion Management & Communication MA/MFA Fine Art, MA Animation and Digital Effects, MArt Animation, MA Arts and Cultural Management, MA Digital Media Managemnet, MA Multimedia Journalism, MA International Journalism, MA Sports Journalism, MA Filmmaking, MA Public Relations, MSc Games Software Development, MComp Computer Science for Games MArch Architecture, MSc Technical Architecture, MA Creative Writing MA Performance Practice

Department of Computing www.shu.ac.uk/about-us/academic-departments/computing

BSc (Honours) Computing Management (top-up), PGCE Secondary Computing, BSc (Honours) Business and ICT, BSc (Honours) Computer Security with Forensics, BSc (Honours) Cyber Security, BSc (Honours) Financial Technology BSc (Honours) Information Technology with Business Studies, BSc (Honours) Information Technology with Business Technologies (top up), BSc (Honours) Information Technology with Digital Media (top up), MEng Software Engineering, BSc (Honours) Information Technology with Networks (top up), BA (Honours) Animation, BSc (Honours) Computing, BEng (Honours) Software Engineering, BSc (Honours) Computer Networks, BSc (Honours) Computer and Information Security, BSc (Honours) Computer Science for Games, BA (Honours) Digital Media Production, BEng (Honours) Computer Systems Engineering, BA (Honours) Games Design, BSc (Honours) Computer Science

Postgraduate courses: MPhil/PhD Research Degrees' Materials and Engineering Research Institute, MPhil/ PhD Research Degrees – Cultural, Communication and Computing Research Institute, MComp Computer Science for Games, MSc Big Data Analytics, MSc Games Software Development, MSc Advanced Computer Networks, MSc Computing, MRes Computing (Enterprise Systems, Transformation and Innovation), MSc Information Systems Security, MA Animation and Digital Effects, MSc Computer and Network Engineering, MSc Information Technology Management

Department of Engineering and Mathematics

Engineering

PGCE Engineering, BEng (Honours) Mechanical Engineering top up, BEng (Honours) Food Engineering, BEng (Honours) Aerospace Engineering, BEng (Honours) Aerospace Manufacturing Engineering (top up), BEng (Honours) Automotive Engineering, BEng (Honours) Materials Engineering BEng (Honours) Chemical Engineering, BEng (Honours) Electrical and Electronic Engineering, BEng (Honours) Computer Systems Engineering, BEng (Honours) Mechanical Engineering, BSc (Honours) Physics, BEng (Honours) Software Engineering

Postgraduate courses: MEng Food Engineering, MEng Aerospace Engineering, MSc Telecommunication and Electronic Engineering, MSc Mechanical Engineering, MSc Electrical and Electronic Engineering, MEng Automotive Engineering, MEng Electrical and Electronic Engineering, MEng Chemical Engineering, MSc Automation, Control and Robotics, MSc Advanced Mechanical Engineering, MSc Computer and Network Engineering, MSc Advanced Engineering and Management, MBA Industrial Management, MSc Sports Engineering, BEng (Honours) Materials Engineering, MEng Mechanical Engineering, MEng Materials Engineering, MSc Advanced Engineering and Management, MSc Advanced Engineering, MEng Software Engineering, MPhil/ PhD Plasma Surface Engineering, MPhil/PhD Materials and Fluid Flow Modelling, MPhil/ PhD Ceramics, Glasses and Polymers, MPhil/ PhD Materials Science and Engineering, PGCE Secondary Engineering with Qualified Teacher Status

Mathematics

PGCE Secondary Mathematics, BSc (Honours) Mathematics with Education and Qualified Teacher Status, BSc (Honours) Mathematics, BSc (Honours) Physics

Department of Media Arts and Communication www.shu.ac.uk/about-us/academic-departments/media-arts-and-communication

Media Arts

BA (Honours) Journalism Public Relations (Full or Part-Time), BA (Honours) Public Relations and Media, BA (Honours) Public Relations, BA (Honours) Film and Media Production, BA (Honours) Animation, BA (Honours) Creative Writing, BA (Honours) Digital Marketing, BA (Honours) Fine Art, BA (Honours) Photography, BA (Honours) Journalism, BSc (Honours) Computer Science for Games, BA (Honours) Media, BA (Honours) Digital Media Production, BA (Honours) Games Design BA (Honours) Performance for Stage and Screen BA (Honours) Graphic Design BA (Honours) Esports

Postgraduate courses: MArt Animation, MArt Digital Media Production, MComp Computer Science for Games, MA Filmmaking, MSc Games Software Development, MA Games Design, MA Digital Media Management, MA Animation and Digital Effects, MA/MFA Fine Art PhD Media and Communications

Media, PR and Journalism

BA (Honours) Public Relations (Part-Time), BA (Honours) Media, BA (Honours) Journalism (Part-Time), BA (Honours) Public Relations and Media (Part-Time), BA (Honours) Public Relations and Media, BA (Honours) Public Relations, BA (Honours) Marketing Communications and Advertising, BA (Honours) Film and Media Production, BA (Honours) Photography, BA (Honours) Journalism, BA (Honours) Media, BA (Honours) Digital Media Production, BA (Honours) Games Design BA (Honours) Sports Journalism with Foundation Year

Postgraduate courses: MA International Journalism, MA Journalism, MA Arts and Cultural Management, MA Digital Media Management, MA Sports Journalism, MA Public Relations, MA Global Communication and Media, MA Multimedia Journalism

Faculty of Social Sciences and Humanities

Humanities

English

BA (Honours) Creative Writing, BA (Honours) English Literature, BA (Honours) English Language, BA (Honours) English, BA (Honours) English and History, MA English by Research, MA, Teaching English to Speakers of Other Languages (TESOL),

MA Teaching English to Speakers of Other Languages (TESOL), MA Creative Writing MA English by Research, PhD/ MPhil English

History

BA (Honours) History, MA History by Research MPhil/ PhD History, PGCE Secondary History with Qualified Teacher Status

Stage and Screen

BA (Honours) Performance and Professional Practice (top up), BA (Honours) Film Studies and Screenwriting, BA (Honours) Film and Media Production, BA (Honours) Performance for Stage and Screen, BA (Honours) Film Studies, MPhil/PhD Stage and Screen, BA (Honours), Film and TV Production

Law and Criminology

LLM International Sports Law in Practice, MPhil/ PhD Law and Criminology, LLMR Masters in Law by Research, BA (Honours) Forensic Accounting, LLB (Honours) Law with Criminology, LLB (Honours) Law, MSc Forensic Accounting, MA Applied Human Rights, MSc Forensic Psychology, LLM/PgDip/PgCert International Commercial Law, LLM Applied Human Rights, LLM Legal Professional Practice, MPhil/PhD Law and Criminology

Department of Psychology, Sociology and Politics www.shu.ac.uk/about-us/academic-departments/psychologysociology-and-politics

Psychology

BSc (Honours) Criminology and Psychology, BA (Honours) Education with Psychology and Counselling, BSc (Honours) Psychology, MSc Health Psychology, MSc Forensic Psychology, MSc Clinical Cognitive Neuroscience, MSc Psychology, MSc Developmental Psychology, MSc Psychology

Sociology

BA (Honours) Sociology, BA (Honours) Applied Social Science MRes Social Science, MSc Public Health, PhD Centre for Regional Economic and Social Research, PhD Sociology

Politics

BA (Honours) Politics MA International Relations and Global Crises, PhD Politics

Faculty of Development & Society ;

Natural & Built Environment

BSc (Honours) Architectural Technology, BSc (Honours) Architecture, MArch Architecture (2 years), MSc Technical Architecture, BSc (Honours) Building Surveying, BSc (Honours) Business Property

Management (1 year top-up), BSc (Honours) Construction Project Management, BSc (Honours) Quantity Surveying, BSc (Honours) Real Estate, MSc Building Surveying, MSc Construction Project Management, MSc Quantity Surveying, MSc Real Estate, BA (Honours) Human Geography, BSc (Honours) Environmental Science, BSc (Honours) Geography, MPhil Natural and Built Environment, MSc Environmental Management, MSc Geographical Information Systems, MSc Urban Planning, PhD Natural and Built Environment

Criminology & Community Justice; www.shu.ac.uk/prospectus/subject/law

BA (Honours) Criminology, BA (Honours) Criminology and Sociology, BA (Honours) Professional Policing, BSc (Honours) Criminology and Psychology, BSc (Honours) Criminology and Psychology with Foundation Year, MSc Criminology and Criminal Justice Practice

Education; www.shu.ac.uk/prospectus/subject/education-studies

BA (Honours) Early Years and Primary Education (3-7) with Qualified Teacher Status, BA (Honours) Education – Early Years (1 year top-up), BA (Honours) Education Studies, BA (Honours) Education and Learning Support (1 year top-up), BA (Honours) Education with Autism, Disability and Special Educational Needs, BA (Honours) Education with Psychology and Counselling, BA (Honours) International Education Management (1 year top-up), BA (Honours) Primary Education (5-11) with Qualified Teacher Status, BA (Honours) Teaching and Learning in Early Years and Primary Education (3-7) with Qualified Teacher Status, BA (Honours),Teaching and Learning in Primary Education (5-11) with Qualified Teacher Status (2 year top-up), BA (Honours) Teaching of English to Speakers of Other Languages (1 year top-up), BSc (Honours) Mathematics with Education and Qualified Teacher Status, BSc (Honours) Science with Education and Qualified Teacher Status, CertEd Post 16 and Further Education, MA Autism Spectrum, MA Education, MA Leadership in Learning (Teach First), MA Professional Practice in Education, MA Teaching English to Speakers of Other Languages, MPhil Education, PGCE Early Childhood Education and Care (0-5) with Early Years Teacher Status, PGCE Early Childhood Education and Care (0-5) with Early Years Teacher Status, PGCE Early Years and Primary Education (3-7) with Qualified Teacher Status, PGCE 16 and Further Education

PGCE Post 16 and Further Education (Special Education Needs), PGCE Primary Education (5-11) Physical Education Specialist with Qualified Teacher Status, PGCE Primary Education (5-11) with Qualified Teacher Status, PGCE Secondary Art and Design with Qualified Teacher Status, PGCE Secondary Business Education with Qualified Teacher Status, PGCE Secondary Citizenship with Qualified Teacher Status, PGCE Secondary Computing with Qualified Teacher Status, PGCE Secondary Design and Technology with Qualified Teacher Status, PGCE Secondary Design and Technology with Qualified Teacher Status (Food), PGCE Secondary Design and Technology with Qualified Teacher Status (Textiles), PGCE Secondary Engineering with Qualified Teacher Status, PGCE Secondary English with Qualified Teacher Status, PGCE Secondary Geography with Qualified Teacher Status, PGCE Secondary History with Qualified Teacher Status, PGCE Secondary Mathematics with Qualified Teacher Status, PGCE Secondary Modern Foreign Languages with Qualified Teacher Status, PGCE Secondary Physical Education with Qualified Teacher Status, PGCE Secondary Religious Education with Qualified Teacher Status, PGCE Secondary Science (Biology) with Qualified Teacher Status, PGCE Secondary Science (Chemistry) with Qualified Teacher Status, PGCE Secondary Science (Physics) with Qualified Teacher Status, PhD Education, PgCert Autism and Asperger Syndrome, PgCert Professional Practice in Digital Teaching and Learning, PgCert Special Educational Needs Co-Ordination (National Award for SEN Co-Ordination), PgCert Teaching in Higher Education

Geography and the Environment

BA (Honours) Human Geography, BSc (Honours) Environmental Science, BSc (Honours) Geography, MPhil Natural and Built Environment, MSc Environmental Management, MSc Geographical Information Systems, MSc Urban Planning, PhD Natural and Built Environment

History; www.shu.ac.uk/prospectus/subject/history

BA (Honours) English and History, BA (Honours) History, MA History by Research, MPhil History, PhD History

Faculty of Health & Wellbeing; www.shu.ac.uk/faculties/hwb

Sport and Physical Activity

BSc (Honours) Physical Activity, Sport and Health, BSc (Honours) Physical Education and School Sport, BSc (Honours) Sport Business Management, BSc (Honours) Sport Coaching, BSc (Honours) Sport Development with Coaching, BSc (Honours) Sport and Exercise Science, BSc (Honours) Sport and Exercise Technology, BSc (Honours) Sport and Exercise Technology with Foundation Year, MPhil Sport and Physical Activity, MSc Advanced Sport Coaching Practice, MSc Applied Sport and Exercise Science, MSc Sport Business Management, MSc Sport and Exercise Psychology, MSc Sports Engineering, MSc Strength and Conditioning Coaching, PhD Sport and Physical Activity, PgDip Advanced Sport Coaching Practice

Biosciences & Chemistry; www.shu.ac.uk/bio

BSc (Honours) Biochemistry, BSc (Honours) Biology, BSc (Honours) Biomedical Science, BSc (Honours) Chemistry, BSc (Honours) Human Biology, MPhil Biomolecular Sciences Research Centre, MRes Analytical Chemistry, MRes Biomedical Laboratory Science, MRes Cancer Biology, MRes Molecular Microbiology, MRes Pharmaceutical Analysis, MRes Pharmacology and Biotechnology, MSc Analytical Chemistry, MSc Analytical Chemistry, MSc Biomedical Laboratory Science, MSc Biomedical Laboratory Science, MSc Cancer Biology, MSc Molecular Microbiology, MSc Pharmaceutical Analysis, MSc Pharmacology and Biotechnology, PhD Biomolecular Sciences Research Centre, PgCert Mass Spectrometry

Radiography and Oncology

BSc (Honours) Radiotherapy and Oncology, MSc Advanced Clinical Practice Radiotherapy and Oncology, MSc Enhanced Radiotherapy and Oncology Practice, MSc Prostate Cancer Care, MSc Radiotherapy Planning Practice, MSc Supportive, Palliative and End of Life Care

Nursing & Midwifery; www.shu.ac.uk/faculties/lwb/departments/nursingmidwifery

BSc (Honours) Nursing (Learning Disability) and Social Work, BSc (Honours) Health Studies (Nursing) (1 year top-up), BSc (Honours) Midwifery, BSc (Honours) Nursing (Adult), BSc (Honours) Nursing (Child), BSc (Honours) Nursing (Mental Health), BSc (Honours) Specialist Community Public Health

Nursing (Health Visitor), BSc (Honours) Specialist Community Public Health Nursing (Health Visitor), BSc (Honours) Specialist Community Public Health Nursing (School Nurse), BSc (Honours) Specialist Practice District Nursing, MSc Advanced Clinical Practice, MSc Child, Adolescent and Family Mental Health, MSc Nursing (Adult), MSc Nursing (Child), MSc Nursing (Mental Health), MSc Nursing (Public Health), MSc Nursing Studies, MSc Perinatal Mental Health, MSc Specialist Practice District Nursing, PgDip Specialist Community Public Health Nursing (Health Visitor), PgDip Specialist Community Public Health Nursing (School Nursing), PgDip Specialist Practice District Nursing

Occupational Therapy; www.shu.ac.uk/occupational

BSc (Honours) Occupational Therapy, MSc Occupational Therapy (Pre-Registration), MSc Vocational Rehabilitation

Operating Department Practice; www.shu.ac.uk/odp

Operating Deptartment Practice

Paramedic Science

BSc(Hons) Paramedic Science

Physiotherapy;

BSc (Honours) Health Studies (Rehabilitation) (1 year top-up), BSc (Honours) Physiotherapy, MSc Advanced Clinical Practice Musculoskeletal Management, MSc Physiotherapy (Pre-Registration), MSc Specialist Physiotherapy Practice

Social Work; www.shu.ac.uk/socialwork

BA (Honours) Social Work, BA (Honours) Working with Children, Young People and Families (1 year top-up), FdA Working with Children, Young People and Families, MSW Social Work, PgCert Advanced Adult Social Work, PgCert Approved Mental Health Professional (AMHP)

Sheffield Business School; www.shu.ac.uk/sbs

Accounting, Banking & Finance;

BA (Honours) Accounting and Economics, BA (Honours) Accounting and Finance, BA (Honours) Accounting and Finance for International Business, BA (Honours) Business and Finance, BA (Honours) Forensic Accounting, BA (Honours) International Banking and Finance (1 year top-up), BSc (Honours) Accounting for Business, BSc (Honours) Financial Technology, BSc (Honours) Financial Trading and Investment Management, MSc Accounting and Finance, MSc Banking and Finance, MSc Finance and Investment, MSc Financial Management, MSc Forensic Accounting, MSc Wealth Management

Business & Management; www.shu.ac.uk/prospectus/subject/business-management

BA (Honours) Business Analytics, BA (Honours) Business Economics, BA (Honours) Business Management, BA (Honours) Business Studies, BA (Honours) Business and Enterprise Management, BA (Honours) Business and Finance, BA (Honours) Business and Financial Management, BA (Honours) Business and Human Resource Management, BA (Honours) Business and Management, BA (Honours) Business and Management with Law, BA (Honours) Business and Management with Psychology, BA (Honours) Business and Marketing, BA (Honours) International Business, BA (Honours) International Business with French, BA (Honours) International Business with German, BA (Honours) International Business with Spanish, DBA Business Administration, MBA Business Administration (Healthcare Leadership): Executive MBA Programme, MRes Business, MSc Branding and Consumer Behaviour, MSc Coaching and Mentoring, MSc Entrepreneurship, MSc Entrepreneurship (Design), MSc Human Resource Management, MSc International Business Management, MSc International Business Management (Work Experience), MSc International Business and Human Resource Management, MSc International Business and Marketing, MSc International Human Resource Management, PgCert Business Administration (Facilities Management), PgDip Professional Practice in Organisational and Regional Change Leadership

Languages; www.shu.ac.uk/prospectus/subject/languages/

BA (Honours) Languages with International Business (French), BA (Honours) Languages with International Business (German), BA (Honours) Languages with International Business (Spanish), BA (Honours) Languages with Teaching English to Speakers of Other Languages (French), BA (Honours) Languages with Teaching English to Speakers of Other Languages (German), BA (Honours) Languages with Teaching English to Speakers of Other Languages (Spanish), BA (Honours) Languages with Tourism (French), BA (Honours) Languages with Tourism (German), BA (Honours) Languages with Tourism (Spanish)

Tourism, Hospitality & Events Management;
www.shu.ac.uk/prospectus/subject/
tourism-hospitality-events

BA (Honours) International Tourism Management with French, BA (Honours) International Tourism Management with German, BA (Honours) International Tourism Management with Spanish, BSc (Honours) Airline and Airport Management, BSc (Honours) Events Management (Tourism) (1 year top-up), BSc (Honours) Food and Drink Entrepreneurship, BSc (Honours) International Hospitality Business Management, BSc (Honours) International Hospitality Business Management (Conference and Events) (1 year top-up), BSc (Honours) International Hospitality Business Management (Culinary Arts) (1 year top-up), BSc (Honours) International Hotel Management, BSc (Honours) International Tourism Management, BSc (Honours) International Tourism and Hospitality Business Management, MBA Business Administration (Hospitality Management): Executive MBA Programme, MSc Hospitality Management with Nutrition, MSc International Hospitality Management, MSc International Hospitality and Tourism Management, MSc International Tourism Management, MSc International Tourism and Aviation Management, BA (Honours) Esports, BA (Honours) Festival and Entertainment Management, BSc (Honours) Events Management, BSc (Honours) Events Management (Arts and Entertainment) (1 year top-up), BSc (Honours) Events Management (Experiential Marketing) (1 year top-up), BSc (Honours) Events and Leisure Management (1 year top-up), MSc International Events and Conference Management, MSc Strategic Events Marketing

UNIVERSITY OF SOUTH WALES
www.southwales.ac.uk

Faculty of Life Sciences and Education;
www.southwales.ac.uk/courses/faculty/
FLSE/?faculty_title=Faculty of Life
Sciences and Education

BA(Hons) Early Years Education and Practice (with Early Years Practitioner status), BA (Anrh) Astudiaethau Cynradd gyda SAC, BA(Hons) Counselling and Therapeutic Practice, BA(Hons) Creative and Therapeutic Arts, BA(Hons) Education BA(Hons) Primary Initial Teacher Education with QTS BBA(-Hons) Working with Children and Families, BSc(Hons) Acute and Critical Care, BSc(Hons) Childhood Development, BSc(Hons) Childhood Studies (Top Up), BSc(Hons) Community Health & Wellbeing (Top-Up), BSc(Hons) Community Health Studies (Specialist Practitioner Community Children's Nursing), BSc(Hons) Community Health Studies (Specialist Practitioner District Nursing) with integrated V100, BSc(Hons) Community Health Studies (Specialist Practitioner General Practice Nursing), BSc(Hons) Education for STEM (Science, Technology, Engineering and Mathematics) BSc(Hons) Football Coaching and Performance, BSc(Hons) Football Coaching, Development and Administration, BSc(Hons) Health and Social Care Management BSc(Hons) International Security and Risk Management BSc(Hons) Professional Policing BSc(Hons) Professional Practice (Health Care Studies), BSc(Hons) Professional Practice (Violence Reduction), BSc(Hons) Psychology, BSc(Hons) Psychology with Behaviour Analysis, BSc(Hons) Psychology with Counselling, BSc(Hons) Psychology with Criminology & Criminal Justice, BSc(Hons) Psychology with Developmental Disorders, BSc(Hons) Rugby Coaching and Performance, BSc(Hons) Social Work, BSc(Hons) Specialist Community Public Health Nursing (Health Visiting), BSc(Hons) Specialist Community Public Health Nursing (School Nursing), BSc(Hons) Sport and Exercise Psychology, BSc(Hons) Sport and Exercise Science, BSc(Hons) Sports Coaching and Development, BSc(Hons) Strength and Conditioning, Bachelor of Midwifery(Hons) Registered Midwife, Bachelor of Nursing(Hons)(Adult), Bachelor of Nursing(Hons)(Child Health), Bachelor of Nursing(Hons)(Learning Disabilities), Bachelor of Nursing(Hons)(Mental Health)

Postgraduate courses: MA Art Psychotherapy, MA CAMH (Child and Adolescent Mental Health), MA Consultative Supervision, MA Counselling Children and Young People, MA Education (Innovation in Learning and Teaching), MA Integrative Counselling and Psychotherapy, MA Leadership & Management (Education), MA Leadership in Sport, MA Music Therapy, MA SEN/ALN (Additional Learning Needs), MA SEN/ALN (Autism), MSc Advanced Clinical Practitioner, MSc Advanced Coaching in Strength and Conditioning MSc Advanced

Performance Football Coaching, MSc Advanced Practice, MSc Applied Health Economics, MSc Behaviour Analysis and Therapy, MSc Clinical Endodontics, MSc Clinical Psychiatry (Online Delivery) MSc Clinical Psychology, MSc Cognitive Behavioural Psychotherapy, MSc Community Health Studies (Children's Community Nursing), MSc Community Health Studies (District Nursing), MSc Community Health Studies (Practice Nursing), MSc Cosmetic Medicine (Online Delivery) MSc Dermatology in Clinical Practice, MSc Diabetes (Online Delivery), MSc Disaster Healthcare (Online Delivery), MSc Endocrinology (Online Delivery), MSc Gastroenterology (Online Delivery), MSc International Security and Risk Management (Online delivery), MSc Medical Education, MSc Obesity and Weight Management (Online Delivery), MSc Pain Management, MSc Play Therapy, MSc Preventative Cardiovascular Medicine (Online delivery), MSc Professional Practice, MSc Psychology by Research, MSc Public Health, MSc Renal Medicine (Online Delivery), MSc Respiratory Medicine (Online Delivery), MSc Rheumatology (Online Delivery), MSc Sexual and Reproductive Medicine, MSc Specialist Community Public Health Nursing (Health Visiting), MSc Specialist Community Public Health Nursing (School Nursing), MSc Sport, Health and Exercise Science, MSc Sports Coaching and Performance, MSc Sports and Exercise Medicine (Online delivery), MSc in Acute Medicine (Online Delivery)

Faculty of Creative Industries; www.southwales.ac.uk/courses/faculty/ FCI/?faculty_title=Faculty of Creative Industries

BA (Anrh) Theatr a Drama, BA(Hons) Advertising Design, BA(Hons) Animation (2D and Stop Motion), BA(hons) Cinema, BA(Hons) Computer Animation, BA(Hons) Computer Games Design, BA(Hons) Dance, BA(Hons) Documentary Photography, BA(Hons) Fashion Design, BA(Hons) Fashion Marketing and Retail Design, BA(Hons) Fashion Promotion, BA(Hons) Film, BA(Hons) Game Art, BA(Hons) Graphic Communication, BA(Hons) Illustration, BA(Hons) Interior Design, BA(Hons) Journalism, BA(Hons) Media Production, BA(Hons) Media, Culture and Journalism, BA(Hons) Music Business, BA(Hons) Performance and Media, BA(Hons) Photography, BA(Hons) Photojournalism, BA(Hons) Popular and Commercial Music, BA(Hons) Sports Journalism, BA(Hons) TV and Film Set Design, BA(Hons) Theatre and Drama, BA(Hons) Visual

Effects and Motion Graphics, BSc(Hons) Creative Industries (Popular Music Technology) (Top-Up) Postgraduate courses: MA Animation, MA Arts Practice (Art, Health and Wellbeing), MA Arts Practice (Fine Art), MA Documentary Photography, MA Drama, MA Film, MA Film (Documentary), MA Film (Directing), MA Film (Production Management), MA Film (Visual Effects) MA Games Enterprise, MA Graphic Communication, MA Songwriting and Production, MSc Music Engineering and Production

Faculty of Computing, Engineering and Science

BEng(Hons) Aeronautical Engineering, BEng(Hons) Aeronautical Engineering (Including Foundation Year), BEng(Hons) Automotive Engineering BEng(Hons) Civil Engineering, BEng(Hons) Electrical and Electronic Engineering, BEng(Hons) Electrical and Electronic Engineering (Including Foundation Year), BEng(Hons) Mechanical Engineering, BSc(Hons) Aircraft Maintenance Engineering BSc(Hons) Aircraft Maintenance Engineering (Top-Up), BSc(Hons) Aircraft Maintenance Systems and Management, BSc(Hons) Analytical and Forensic Science (Top Up), BSc(Hons) Applied Cyber Security, BSc(Hons) Biology, BSc(Hons) Chemistry, BSc(Hons) Civil Engineering BSc(Hons) Civil Engineering (Including Foundation Year), BSc(Hons) Computer Applications Development, BSc(Hons) Computer Forensics, BSc(Hons) Computer Games Development, BSc(Hons) Computer Science, BSc(Hons) Computer Security BSc(Hons) Construction Project Management, BSc(Hons) Electrical and Electronic Engineering (Top Up), BSc(Hons) Forensic Investigation, BSc(Hons) Forensic Science, BSc(Hons) Forensic Science with Criminology, BSc(Hons) Geography, BSc(Hons) Geology, BSc(Hons) Geology and Physical Geography, BSc(Hons) Human Biology, BSc(Hons) Information Communication Technology, BSc(Hons) International Wildlife Biology, BSc(Hons) Lighting Design and Technology, BSc(Hons) Mathematics, BSc(Hons) Mechanical Engineering, BSc(Hons) Medical Sciences, BSc(Hons) Medicinal and Biological Chemistry, BSc(Hons) Natural History, BSc(Hons) Pharmaceutical Science, BSc(Hons) Quantity Surveying and Commercial Management, BSc(Hons) Sound and Live Event Production, MComp Computer Applications Development, MComp Computer Games Development, MComp Computer Science, MComp Information Communication Technology, MEng Aeronautical Engineering, MEng Automotive

Engineering, MEng Civil Engineering, MEng Electrical and Electronic Engineering, MEng Mechanical Engineering, MGeog Geography, MMath Mathematics, MSci Chemistry, MSci Forensic Biology, MSci Forensic Investigation, MSci Forensic Science, MSci Forensic Science with Criminology, MSci Pharmaceutical Science

Postgraduate courses: MRes Applied Sciences, MSc Advanced Applied Field Geoscience, MSc Aeronautical Engineering, MSc Analytical and Forensic Science, MSc Artificial Intelligence, MSc Aviation Engineering and Management, MSc Civil Engineering and Environmental Management, MSc Civil and Structural Engineering, MSc Computer Forensics, MSc Computer Systems Security, MSc Computing and Information Systems, MSc Construction Project Management, MSc Cyber Security, MSc Data Science, MSc Electronics and Information Technology, MSc Mechanical Engineering, MSc Mobile and Satellite Communications (with internship), MSc Pharmaceutical Chemistry, MSc Professional Engineering, MSc Renewable Energy and Resource Management, MSc Safety, Health and Environmental Management, MSc Wildlife and Conservation Management, Postgraduate Diploma Medical Sciences

Faculty of Business and Society ; www.southwales.ac.uk/courses/faculty/ FBS/?faculty_title=Faculty of Business and Society

BA(Hons) Accounting and Finance, BA(Hons) Accounting and Management, BA(Hons) Business, BA(Hons) Business Studies (Top Up), BA(Hons) Business and Accounting (Top Up), BA(Hons) Business and Finance (Top Up), BA(Hons) Business and Human Resource Management (Top Up), BA(Hons) Business and Management, BA(Hons) Business and Management (Event Management), BA(Hons) Business and Marketing (Top Up) BA(Hons) Business and Supply Chain Management (Top Up), BA(Hons) English, BA(Hons) English and Creative Writing, BA(Hons) Forensic Accounting, BA(Hons) History, BA(Hons) Hotel and Hospitality Management, BA(Hons) Human Resource Management, BA(Hons) International Business (Top Up), BA(Hons) International Business and Management, BA(Hons) Logistics and Supply Chain Management, BA(Hons) Marketing, BA(Hons) Public Services, BA(Hons) Sports Law and Business BA(Hons) Youth and Community Work, BA(Hons) Youth and Community Work (Youth Justice), BSc(Hons) Banking, Finance and Investment (Top Up), BSc(Hons) Criminology & Criminal Justice and Youth Justice, BSc(Hons) Criminology and Criminal Justice, BSc(Hons) Criminology and Criminal Justice and Sociology, BSc(Hons) Criminology and Criminal Justice with Psychology, BSc(Hons) Sociology, Certificate in Business Accounting, Chartered Institute of Procurement and Supply (CIPS) Diploma in Procurement and Supply, Chartered Institute of Procurement and Supply (CIPS) Professional Diploma in Procurement and Supply, Institute of Chartered Accountants in England and Wales (ICAEW), LLB(Hons) Law, LLB(Hons) Law Accelerated Route, LLB(Hons) Law with Criminology and Criminal Justice, LLB(Hons) Legal Practice (Exempting)

Postgraduate courses: Association of Chartered Certified Accountants (ACCA), LLM Laws, LLM Legal Practice MA Buddhist Studies, MA English by Research, MA History by Research, MBA (Master of Business Administration), MBA (Master of Business Administration) Global, MSc Crime and Justice, MSc Engineering Management, MSc Finance and Investment, MSc Forensic Audit and Accounting, MSc Global Governance, MSc Health and Public Service Management, MSc Human Resource Management, MSc International Business and Enterprise, MSc International Human Resource Management, MSc International Logistics and Supply Chain Management, MSc Leadership and Management, MSc Leadership in Healthcare (Online Delivery), MSc Management, MSc Marketing, MSc Project Management, MSc Public Relations, MSc Strategic Digital Marketing, MSc Strategic Leadership (Health and Social Care), MSc Strategic Procurement Management, MSc Working with Adult and Young Offenders Postgraduate Diploma Leadership in Healthcare (Online Delivery)

UNIVERSITY OF SOUTHAMPTON
www.soton.ac.uk

Accounting and Finance

BSc Accounting and Economics, BSc Accounting and Finance, BSc Accounting and Finance with placement year, BSc Economics and Actuarial Science, BSc Economics and Finance, BSc Finance, BSc Finance with Placement Year BSc Mathematics with Actuarial Science, BSc Mathematics with Finance

Postgraduate courses: MSc Accounting and Finance, MSc Accounting and Management, MSc Finance, MSc Finance and Econometrics, MSc Finance and Economics, MSc in Operational Research and Finance, MSc International Banking and Financial Studies, MSc International Financial Markets, MSc/ PG Dip in Actuarial Science

Acoustical Engineering

BEng/MEng(Hons) Acoustical Engineering, BSc(Hons) Acoustics with Music, MEng Mechanical Engineering and Acoustical Engineering

Postgraduate course: MSc Acoustical Engineering

Aeronautics and Astronautics

BEng(Hons) Aeronautics & Astronautics MEng Aeronautics & Astronautics MEng Aeronautics & Astronautics / Aerodynamics, MEng Aeronautics & Astronautics / Airvehicle Systems Design, MEng Aeronautics & Astronautics / Computational Engineering and Design, MEng Aeronautics & Astronautics / Engineering Management, MEng Aeronautics & Astronautics / Materials and Structures, MEng Aeronautics & Astronautics / Semester Abroad, MEng Aeronautics & Astronautics / Spacecraft Engineering

Postgraduate courses: MSc Aerodynamics and Computation, MSc Race Car Aerodynamics, MSc Space Systems Engineering, MSc Unmanned Aircraft Systems Design

Ageing and Gerontology

Postgraduate courses: MSc Gerontology, MSc Gerontology (Distance Learning), MSc Gerontology (Research), MSc Global Ageing and Policy (Distance Learning), PG Cert Gerontology, PG Cert Gerontology (Distance Learning), PG Cert Global Ageing and Policy (Distance Learning), PG Dip Gerontology (Distance Learning), PG Dip Global Ageing and Policy (Distance Learning)

Anthropology

BA Archaeology and Anthropology, BA Archaeology and Anthropology (with a Year Abroad), BSc Sociology with Anthropology

Archaeology

BA Ancient History and Archaeology, BA Ancient History and Archaeology with Year Abroad, BA Archaeology, BA Archaeology (with a Year Abroad), BA Archaeology and Anthropology, BA Archaeology and Anthropology (with a Year Abroad), BA Archaeology and History, BA Archaeology and History (with a Year Abroad), BSc Archaeology, BSc Archaeology (with a Year Abroad), MArc Archaeology Integrated Master, MSci Archaeology

Postgraduate courses: MA/ MSc Maritime Archaeology, MSc Archaeology, MSc Archaeology (Bioarchaeology), MSc Archaeology (Higher Archaeological Practice), MSc Archaeology (Palaeoanthropology), MSc Business and Heritage Management

Astronomy

MPhys Astrophysics (with a Year Abroad), MPhys Physics with Astronomy

Audiology

BSc Audiology

Postgraduate courses: MSc Audiology and MSc Audiology (with Clinical Placement)

Biochemistry

BSc Biochemistry, MBiochem Master of Biochemistry, MSci Chemistry and Biochemistry

Biology

BSc Biology, MSci Biology, MSci Biology and Marine Biology

Postgraduate courses: MRes Evolution: From the Galapagos to the 21st Century MRes Wildlife Conservation MSc Neurosciences

Biomedical Engineering

MEng Biomedical Electronic Engineering with Industrial Studies

Postgraduate course: MSc Biomedical Engineering

Biomedical Sciences

BEng Biomedical Electronic Engineering, BSc Biomedical Sciences, MBioSci Master of Biomedical Sciences, MEng Biomedical Electronic Engineering

Business

BSc Business Analytics, BSc Business Analytics with placement year, BSc Business Entrepreneurship, BSc Business Entrepreneurship with placement year, BSc Business Management, BSc Business Management and Spanish, BSc Business Management with placement year

Postgraduate courses: Master of Business Administration (full-time), MSc Business Analytics and

Finance, MSc Business Strategy and Innovation Management, MSc Cyber Security Risk Management, MSc Digital Business MSc Entrepreneurship and Management, MSc Human Resource Management, MSc International Management, MSc Knowledge and Information Systems Management, MSc Marketing Management, MSc Project Management, MSc Risk and Finance, MSc Risk Management, MSc Supply Chain Management and Logistics Part-time Master of Business Administration (MBA)

Chemistry

BSc Chemistry, MChem Chemistry, MChem Chemistry with Maths, MChem Chemistry with Medicinal Sciences MChem Chemistry with Research Project Abroad or Industry Experience, MChem Chemistry with Year-long Industry Experience, MSci Chemistry and Biochemistry

Postgraduate courses: MSc Advanced Chemical Engineering MSc Chemistry, MSc Chemistry by Research, MSc Electrochemistry and Battery Technologies, MSc Instrumental Analytical Chemistry, MSc Magnetic Resonance

Civil Engineering

BEng Civil Engineering, MEng Civil and Environmental Engineering, MEng Civil Engineering, MEng Civil Engineering and Architecture

Postgraduate courses: MSc Civil Engineering, MSc Civil Engineering with an Integrated Qualifying Year MSc Engineering in the Coastal Environment, MSc Transportation Planning & Engineering, MSc Transportation Planning and Engineering (Infrastructure), MSc Transportation Planning and Engineering (Operations), MSc Transportation Planning and Engineering (Behaviour)

Computer Science and Software Engineering

BEng Software Engineering, BSc Computer Science, BSc Mathematics with Computer Science, MEng Computer Science, MEng Computer Science with Artificial Intelligence, MEng Computer Science with Cyber Security, MEng Computer Science with Industrial Studies MEng Electrical Engineering with Industrial Studies MEng Software Engineering, MEng Software Engineering with Industrial Studies

Postgraduate courses: MSc Artificial Intelligence, MSc Computer Science, MSc Cyber Security, MSc Data Science, MSc Embedded Systems, MSc Internet of Things MSc Software Engineering

Criminology

BSc Criminal Justice and Social Policy BSc Criminology, BSc Criminology and Psychology BSc Sociology and Criminology

Postgraduate course: MSc Criminology

Demography

Postgraduate courses: MA Transnational Studies, MSc Applied Statistics MSc Data Analytics for Government, MSc Demography, MSc Global Health, MSc Social Research Methods with Applied Statistics PG Cert/PG Dip/MSc Official Statistics

Design

Postgraduate courses: MA Communication Design, MA Design Management, MA Global Advertising and Branding, MA Global Media Management, MA Luxury Brand Management

Ecology

BSc Ecology & Conservation, MSci Ecology and Conservation

Postgraduate courses: MRes Wildlife Conservation

Economics

BA Economics and Philosophy, BA Economics and Philosophy (with Year Abroad), BSc Accounting and Economics, BSc Economics, BSc Economics and Actuarial Science, BSc Economics and Finance, BSc Economics and Management Sciences, MMORSE (Mathematics, Operational Research, Statistics and Economics), BSc Politics and Economics, MEcon Master in Economics, MMORSE (Mathematics, Operational Research, Statistics and Economics)

Postgraduate courses: MSc Economics, MSc Finance and Econometrics, MSc Finance and Economics

Education Studies

BSc(Hons) Education, BSc(Hons) Education and Psychology

Postgraduate courses: SKE Computer Sciences Subject Knowledge Enhancement, SKE Mathematics Subject Knowledge Enhancement, SKE Science Subject Knowledge Enhancement, MA Applied Linguistics for Language Teaching MA ELT/TESOL Studies, MA English Language Teaching: Online (part time), MSc Education, MSc Education Management and Leadership, MSc Education online, MSc Education Practice and Innovation, PGCE English, PGCE FE Learning and Skills Sector, PGCE Geography, PGCE History, PGCE Information Technology and Computer Science (IT&CS), PGCE Mathematics, PGCE Modern Languages, PGCE Physical Education, PGCE Physics with Mathematics, PGCE Primary, PGCE Sciences, PGCE Secondary, PhD (Integrated) in Education, PhD Education, School Direct PGCE

Electrical and Electronic Engineering

BEng Electrical and Electronic Engineering, MEng Electrical and Electronic Engineering MEng Electrical Engineering with Industrial Studies MEng Electrical and Electronic Engineering with Industrial Studies

Electrical Engineering

BEng Electrical and Electronic Engineering, BEng Electrical Engineering, MEng Electrical and Electronic Engineering, MEng Electrical Engineering MEng Electrical Engineering with Industrial Studies

Postgraduate courses: EMECS European Masters in Embedded Computing Systems (2 years), MSc Energy and Sustainability with Electrical Power Engineering, MSc Micro and Nanotechnology (1 year full-time), MSc Microelectronics Systems Design, MSc Mobile Communications and Smart Networking, MSc System On Chip, MSc Systems, Control and Signal Processing

Electronic Engineering

BEng Aerospace Electronic Engineering, BEng Biomedical Electronic Engineering, BEng Electronic Engineering, MEng Aerospace Electronic Engineering, MEng Aerospace Electronic Engineering with Industrial Studies MEng Biomedical Electronic Engineering, MEng Electronic Engineering, MEng Electronic Engineering with Artificial Intelligence, MEng Electronic Engineering with Computer Systems MEng Electronic Engineering with Industrial Studies MEng Electronic Engineering with Mobile and Secure Systems, MEng Electronic Engineering with Nanotechnology, MEng Electronic Engineering with Photonics, MEng Electronic Engineering with Wireless Communications

Postgraduate courses: EMECS European Masters in Embedded Computing Systems (2 years), MSc Electronic Engineering, MSc Micro and Nanotechnology (1 year full-time), MSc Microelectronics Systems Design, MSc Mobile Communications and Smart Networking, MSc System On Chip, MSc Systems, Control and Signal Processing

English

BA English, BA English (with a Year Abroad) BA English and French, BA English and French, BA English and German, BA English and History, BA English and History with a year abroad, BA English and Music, BA English and Music (with Year Abroad) BA English and Spanish, BA English Literature, Language and Linguistics, BA English Literature, Language & Linguistics (with Year Abroad), BA English with Creative Writing BA Film and English, BA Film and English (with Year Abroad) BA Philosophy and English, BA Philosophy and English (with Year Abroad) MLang Languages and Contemporary European Studies (Integrated Masters in Languages)

Postgraduate courses: MA 20th and 21st Century Literature, MA Creative Writing, MA English Literary Studies, MA English Literary Studies, MA English Literary Studies (Eighteenth Century), MA English Literary Studies (Nineteenth Century), MA English Literary Studies (Postcolonial and World Literatures), MA English Literary Studies (Twentieth Century and Contemporary), MA Global Englishes, MA Global Literary Industries Management A Medieval and Renaissance Culture Master of Arts (MA) Jane Austen

Entrepreneurship

BSc Business Entrepreneurship, BSc Business Entrepreneurship with placement year

Environmental Engineering

MEng Civil and Environmental Engineering

Postgraduate courses: MSc Energy and Sustainability (Energy, Environment and Buildings), MSc Energy and Sustainability (Energy, Resources and Climate Change), MSc Engineering in the Coastal Environment, MSc Marine Technology, MSc Sustainable Energy Technologies

Environmental Science

BSc Environmental Management with Business, BSc(Hons) Environmental Science, MEnvSci(Hons) Environmental Science

Postgraduate courses: MSc Biodiversity and Conservation, MSc Environmental Monitoring and Assessment, MSc Environmental Pollution Control, MSc Integrated Environmental Studies, MSc Water Resources Management

Fashion

BA Fashion Design, BA(Hons) Fashion and Textile Design, BA(Hons) Fashion Marketing with Management

Postgraduate courses: MA Fashion Design, MA Fashion Management, MA Fashion Marketing and Branding

Film

BA Film and English, BA Film and English (with Year Abroad) BA Film and French, BA Film and German, BA Film and History, BA Film and History (with a Year Abroad) BA Film and Philosophy, BA Film and Spanish, BA Film Studies, BA Film Studies (with a Year Abroad) BA(Hons) Film and Philosophy (with a Year Abroad)

Postgraduate courses: MA Film and Cultural Management, MA Film Studies

Finance

BSc Accounting and Economics, BSc Accounting and Finance, BSc Accounting and Finance with Placement Year, BSc Economics and Actuarial Science, BSc Economics and Finance BSc Finance, BSc Finance with placement year BSc Mathematics with Actuarial Science BSc Mathematics with Finance

Fine Art

BA(Hons) Fine Art

Postgraduate courses: MA Contemporary Curation, MA Fine Art

French

BA Ancient History and French, BA English and French, BA Film and French, BA French, BA French, BA French and German, BA French and German (Linguistic Studies), BA French and Linguistics (4 years) BA French and Music, BA French and Philosophy, BA French and Portuguese, BA French and Spanish, BA French and Spanish (Linguistic Studies), BA Politics and French, BA French and History, BSc Business Management and French, BSc Management Sciences and French, BSc Mathematics with French, MLang French (Integrated Masters in Languages), MLang French and Linguistics (Integrated Masters in Languages), MLang French and German (Integrated Masters in Languages), MLang French and German Linguistic Studies (Integrated Masters in Languages), MLang French and Portuguese (Integrated Masters in Languages), MLang French and Spanish (Integrated Masters in Languages), MLang French and Spanish Linguistic Studies (Integrated Masters in Languages), MLang Languages and Contemporary European Studies (Integrated Masters in Languages), MSci Oceanography with French

Games Design and Art

BA(Hons) Games Design and Art

Geography

BA Geography, BSc Geography, BSc Geology with Physical Geography, BSc Oceanography with Physical Geography, BSc Population and Geography

Postgraduate courses: MSc Applied Geographical Information Systems and Remote Sensing MSc Engineering in the Coastal Environment, MSc Sustainability

Geology

BSc Geology, BSc Geology with Physical Geography, MSci Geology, MSci Geology with study abroad

Postgraduate courses: MRes Marine Geology and Geophysics

Geophysics

BSc Geophysical Sciences, BSc Geophysics with Foundation Year, BSc(Hons) Geophysics and Geology MSci Geophysics, MSci Geophysics and Geology MSci Geophysics with study abroad

Postgraduate courses: MRes Marine Geology and Geophysics

German

BA Ancient History and German, BA English and German, BA Film and German, BA French and German, BA French and German (Linguistic Studies), BA German, BA German and Linguistics, BA German and Music, BA German and Philosophy, BA German and Spanish, BA German and Spanish (Linguistic Studies), BA Politics and German, BA German and History, BSc Management Sciences and German, BSc Mathematics with German, BSc Business Management and German, MLang French and German (Integrated Masters in Languages), MLang French and German Linguistic Studies (Integrated Masters in Languages), MLang German (Integrated Masters in Languages), MLang German and Linguistics (Integrated Masters in Languages), MLang German and Spanish, MLang German and Spanish Linguistic Studies, MLang Languages and Contemporary European Studies (Integrated Masters in Languages)

Graphic Arts

BA(Hons) Graphic Arts

Healthcare

BSc(Hons) Clinical Practice, BSc(Hons) Healthcare Science (Cardiac Physiology)

Postgraduate courses: MRes Clinical and Health Research, MSc Advanced Clinical Practice (Advanced Allied Health Practitioner) MSc Advanced Clinical Practice (Advanced Critical Care Practitioner), MSc Advanced Clinical Practice (Advanced Neonatal Nurse Practitioner) MSc Advanced Clinical Practice (Advanced Nurse Practitioner) MSc Clinical Leadership in Cancer, Palliative and End of Life Care, MSc Health Sciences – Amputation & Prosthetic Rehabilitation, MSc Leadership and Management in Health and Social Care, MSc Midwifery with Advanced Standing (2 years) MSc Neonatology MSc Public Health, MSc Psychological Therapies and Mental Health, Postgraduate Certificate Low Intensity Cognitive Behavioural Therapy with IAPT PWP status

History

BA Ancient History, BA Ancient History and Archaeology, BA Ancient History and Archaeology with Year Abroad, BA Ancient History and French, BA Ancient History and German, BA Ancient History and History, BA Ancient History and History with Year Abroad, BA Ancient History and Philosophy, BA Ancient History and Philosophy with Year Abroad, BA Ancient History and Spanish, BA Ancient History with Year Abroad, BA Archaeology and History, BA Archaeology and History (with a Year Abroad), BA English and History, BA English and History with a year abroad, BA Film and History, BA Film and History (with a Year Abroad), BA History, BA History (with a Year Abroad), BA Modern History and Politics (with a Year Abroad), BA Philosophy and History, BA Philosophy and History (with Year Abroad), BA French and History, BA German and History, BA Modern History and Politics, BA Spanish and History

Postgraduate courses: MA Eighteenth-Century Studies, MA History, MA Jewish History and Culture, MA Medieval and Renaissance Culture, MA Transnational Studies

Language

BA Applied Linguistics and English Language BA English Literature, Language & Linguistics (with Year Abroad), BA English Literature, Language and Linguistics, BA Languages and Contemporary European Studies, BA Languages and Contemporary European Studies (English) (Non-native English speakers only), BA Modern Languages

Postgraduate courses: MA Applied Linguistics (Research Methodology), MA Applied Linguistics for Language Teaching, MA English Language Teaching, MA English Language Teaching: Online (part time – 2.5 years)

Law

BSc(Hons) Psychology with Law, LLB Accelerated Graduate Programme (2 years), LLB JD Accelerated Pathway Graduate Programme (2 years), LLB(Hons) Bachelor of Laws, LLB(Hons) European Legal Studies, LLB(Hons) International Legal Studies, LLB(Hons) Law with Psychology, LLB(Hons) Maritime Law

Postgraduate courses: LLM, LLM Commercial and Corporate Law, LLM Information Technology and Commerce, LLM Insurance Law, LLM International Business Law, LLM International Law, LLM Maritime Law

Linguistics

BA English Language and Linguistics, BA English Language and Linguistics with a Year Abroad (4 years) BA French and German (Linguistic Studies), BA French and Linguistics, BA French and Spanish (Linguistic studies), BA German and Linguistics, BA German and Spanish (Linguistic Studies), BA Spanish and Linguistics, MLang French and German Linguistic Studies, MLang French and linguistics, MLang French and Spanish Linguistic Studies, MLang German and Linguistics, MLang German and Spanish Linguistic Studies, MLang Spanish and Linguistics

Management and Management Sciences

BA Music and Business Management, BA Music and Business Management (with a Year Abroad), BA Music and Management Sciences, BA(Hons) Fashion Marketing with Management, BSc Business Management and French, BSc Economics and Management Sciences, BSc Management Sciences and French, BSc Management Sciences and German, BSc Management Sciences and Spanish, BSc Business Management and German

Postgraduate courses: MSc Business Analytics and Management Sciences, MSc Education Management and Leadership, MSc Leadership and Management in Health and Social Care

Marine Biology

BSc Marine Biology with Oceanography, BSc Biology and Marine Biology, BSc Marine Biology MSci Biology and Marine Biology, MSci Marine Biology, MSci Marine Biology with Oceanography (4 years) MSci Marine Biology with study abroad

Postgraduate courses: MSc Marine Technology MSc Maritime Engineering Science / Advanced Materials, MSc Maritime Engineering Science / Marine Engineering, MSc Maritime Engineering Science / Maritime Computational Fluid Dynamics, MSc Maritime Engineering Science / Naval Architecture, MSc Maritime Engineering Science / Offshore Engineering, MSc Maritime Engineering Science / Yacht and Small Craft

Marketing

BA(Hons) Fashion Marketing/Management, BSc Marketing, BSc Marketing with Placement Year, BSc Marketing with Study Abroad

Postgraduate courses: MA Fashion Marketing and Branding, MSc Digital Marketing, MSc Marketing Analytics, MSc Marketing Management

Mathematical Sciences

BA Philosophy and Mathematics, BA Philosophy and Mathematics (with Year Abroad), BSc Mathematical Sciences, BSc Mathematics, BSc Mathematics with Actuarial Science, BSc Mathematics with Computer Science, BSc Mathematics with Finance, BSc Mathematics with French, BSc Mathematics with German, BSc Mathematics with Spanish, BSc Mathematics with Statistics, BSc MORSE (Mathematics, Operational Research, Statistics and Economics), MChem Chemistry with Maths, MMath Mathematical Physics, MMath Mathematics, MMORSE (Mathematics, Operational Research, Statistics and Economics)

Postgraduate courses: MSc Data and Decision Analytics MSc in Operational Research, MSc in Operational Research and Finance, MSc in Statistics with

Applications in Medicine, MSc Operational Research and Statistics, MSc Statistics, MSc/PG Dip in Actuarial Science

Mechanical Engineering

BEng(Hons) Mechanical Engineering, MEng Mechanical Engineering, MEng Mechanical Engineering / Acoustical Engineering, MEng Mechanical Engineering / Advanced Materials, MEng Mechanical Engineering / Aerospace, MEng Mechanical Engineering / Automotive, MEng Mechanical Engineering / Biomedical Engineering, MEng Mechanical Engineering / Computational Engineering / Design, MEng Mechanical Engineering / Engineering Management, MEng Mechanical Engineering / Mechatronics, MEng Mechanical Engineering / Naval Engineering, MEng Mechanical Engineering / Sustainable Energy Systems

Postgraduate courses: MSc Biomedical Engineering, MSc Computational Engineering Design (Advanced Mechanical Engineering Science), MSc Engineering Materials (Advanced Mechanical Engineering Science), MSc Mechatronics (Advanced Mechanical Engineering Science), MSc Propulsion and Engine Systems Engineering (Advanced Mechanical Engineering Sciences), MSc Surface Engineering and Coatings (Advanced Mechanical Engineering Sciences)

Mechatronic Engineering

BEng Mechatronic Engineering, MEng Mechatronic Engineering

Medicine

Bachelor of Medicine, Bachelor of Surgery (BMBS) (International Transfer) Bachelor of Medicine BM(EU) BMBS Medicine (BM4, graduate entry), BMBS Medicine and BMedSc (BM5), BMBS Medicine and, BMedSc (BM6, widening participation) MChem Chemistry with Medicinal Sciences

Postgraduate courses: MSc Allergy, MSc Diabetes Best Practice, MSc Genomic Medicine, MSc in Statistics with Applications in Medicine, MSc Public Health

Midwifery

BSc(Hons) Midwifery, BSc(Hons) Midwifery with Advanced Standing

Postgraduate course: MSc Midwifery (preregistration)

Music

BA English and Music, BA English and Music (with Year Abroad), BA French and Music, BA German and Music, BA Music, BA Music (with a Year Abroad), BA Music and Business Management, BA Music and Business Management (with a Year Abroad), BA Philosophy and Music, BA Philosophy and Music (with Year Abroad), BSc(Hons) Acoustics with Music

Postgraduate course: MA International Music Management MMus Music (Performance, Composition, Musicology)

Natural Sciences

MSci Natural Sciences

Neurosciences

Master of Neuroscience

Postgraduate courses: MRes in Advanced Biological Sciences, Postgraduate Certificate Low Intensity Cognitive Behavioural Therapy with IAPT PWP status

Nursing

BSc(Hons) Public Health Practice: Specialist Community Public Health Nursing (SCPHN), MNurs Nursing (Adult and Child), MNurs Nursing (Adult and Mental Health), MNurs Nursing (Child and Mental Health)

Postgraduate courses: MSc Advanced Clinical Practice (Advanced Allied Health Practitioner) (5 years) MSc Advanced Clinical Practice (Advanced Critical Care Practitioner) MSc Advanced Clinical Practice (Advanced Nurse Practitioner), MSc Advanced Clinical Practice (Advanced Neonatal Nurse Practitioner), MSc Nursing Studies (Top-up for Postgraduate Diploma in Nursing or SCPHN), Postgraduate Diploma in Nursing – Adult (pre-registration), Postgraduate Diploma in Nursing – Child (pre-registration), Postgraduate Diploma in Nursing – Mental Health (pre-registration), Postgraduate Diploma in Public Health Practice: Specialist Community Public Health Nursing [SCPHN]

Occupational Therapy

BSc(Hons) Occupational Therapy

Oceanography

BSc Marine Biology with Oceanography, BSc Oceanography (single honours), BSc Oceanography with Physical Geography MSci Marine Biology with Oceanography MSci Oceanography, MSci Oceanography with French, MSci Oceanography with study abroad

Postgraduate courses: MRes Marine Geology and Geophysics, MRes Ocean Science, MSc Engineering in the Coastal Environment, MSc Marine Environment and Resources (2 years), MSc Oceanography

Optoelectronics

Postgraduate courses: MSc Optical Fibre and Photonic Engineering MSc Optical Fibre Technologies, MSc Photonics Technologies

Pharmacology

BSc Pharmacology

Philosophy

BA Ancient History and Philosophy, BA Ancient History and Philosophy with Year Abroad, BA Economics and Philosophy, BA Economics and Philosophy (with Year Abroad), BA Film and Philosophy, BA French and Philosophy, BA German and Philosophy, BA Philosophy, BA Philosophy, Ethics and Religion, BA Philosophy, Ethics and Religion with Year Abroad, BA Philosophy, Politics and Economics with Year Abroad, BA Philosophy (with Year Abroad), BA Philosophy and English, BA Philosophy and English (with Year Abroad), BA Philosophy and History, BA Philosophy and History (with Year Abroad), BA Philosophy and Mathematics, BA Philosophy and Mathematics (with Year Abroad), BA Philosophy and Music, BA Philosophy and Music (with Year Abroad), BA Philosophy and Politics, BA Philosophy and Politics (with Year Abroad), BA Philosophy and Sociology, BA Philosophy and Sociology (with Year Abroad), BA(Hons) Film and Philosophy with Year Abroad

Postgraduate course: MA Philosophy

Physics

BSc Physics MMath Mathematical Physics, MPhys Particle Physics with Research Year Abroad, MPhys Physics, MPhys Physics with a Year of Experimental Research, MPhys Physics with Industrial Placement, MPhys Physics with Mathematics, MPhys Physics with Nanotechnology, MPhys Physics with Photonics, MPhys Physics with Space Science

Physiotherapy

BSc(Hons) Physiotherapy

Postgraduate course: MSc Physiotherapy (pre-registration)

Podiatry

BSc(Hons) Podiatry

Politics and International Relations

BA Modern History and Politics (with a Year Abroad), BA Philosophy and Politics, BA Philosophy and Politics (with Year Abroad), BA Politics and French, BA Politics and German, BA Politics and Spanish and Latin American Studies, BA Modern History and Politics, BSc International Relations, BSc Politics, BSc Politics and Economics, BSc Politics and International Relations

Postgraduate courses: LLM International Business Law, MA Transnational Studies, Master of Public Administration MSc Governance and Policy (Research) MSc International Politics (Research), MSc International Security and Risk, PG Dip/MSc Governance and Policy, PG Dip/MSc International Politics

Psychology

BSc Criminology and Psychology, BSc(Hons) Education and Psychology, BSc(Hons) Psychology, BSc(Hons) Psychology with Law LLB(Hons) Law with Psychology

Postgraduate courses: MSc Foundations of Clinical Psychology, MSc Health Psychology, MSc Research Methods in Psychology, Postgraduate Certificate Low Intensity Cognitive Behavioural Therapy with IAPT PWP status, Postgraduate Diploma in CBT (Advanced level practice), Postgraduate Certificate in CBT (Advanced level practice), Postgraduate Certificate in CBT (Introductory level practice), Postgraduate Diploma CBT for Anxiety and Depression (IAPT)

Ship Science

BEng(Hons) Ship Science, MEng Ship Science

Sociology and Social Policy

BA Philosophy and Sociology, BA Philosophy and Sociology (with Year Abroad), BSc Criminal Justice and Social Policy BSc Population and Geography, BSc Sociology, BSc Sociology and Criminology, BSc Sociology and Social Policy, BSc Sociology with Anthropology

Postgraduate courses: MA Transnational Studies, MSc Data Analytics for Government MSc Public Health, MSc Sociology and Social Policy

Spanish, Portuguese and Latin American Studies

BA Ancient History and Spanish, BA English and Spanish, BA Film and Spanish, BA French and Portuguese, BA French and Spanish, BA French and Spanish (Linguistic Studies), BA German and Spanish, BA German and Spanish (Linguistic Studies), BA Politics and Spanish and Latin American Studies, BA Spanish, BA Spanish (Latin American Studies), BA Spanish and Linguistics BA Spanish and Portuguese Studies, BA Spanish and History, BSc Business Management and Spanish, BSc Management Sciences and Spanish, BSc Mathematics with Spanish, MLang French and Portuguese (Integrated Masters in Languages), MLang French and Spanish (Integrated Masters in Languages), MLang French and Spanish Linguistic Studies (Integrated Masters in Languages), MLang German and Spanish, MLang German and Spanish Linguistic Studies, MLang Languages and Contemporary European Studies (Integrated Masters in Languages), MLang Spanish (Integrated Masters in Languages), MLang Spanish and Latin American Studies (Integrated Masters in Languages), MLang Spanish and Linguistics (Integrated Masters in Languages) MLang Spanish and Portuguese (Integrated Masters in Languages)

Textile
BA Textile Design
Postgraduate course: MA Textile Design

Zoology Science
BSc Zoology, MSci Zoology
Postgraduate course: MRes Wildlife Conservation

SOUTHAMPTON SOLENT UNIVERSITY
www.solent.ac.uk

www.solent.ac.uk/courses

BA(Hons) Architectural Design and Technology, BA(Hons) Architectural Design and Visualisation, HNC Architectural Technology, HNC Civil Engineering, BSc(Hons)/HNC Construction Management, BA(Hons) Interior Design, BSc(Hons) International Construction, Design and Sustainability (Top-up), MSc Sustainable Building Design, MSc Advanced Building Simulation, MSc Architectural Project Management

Art and Design

BA(Hons) Animation, BA(Hons) Body Art, MA Critical Creative Practice, BA(Hons) Digital Animation, BA(Hons) Fine Art, BA(Hons) Graphic Design, BA(Hons) Graphic Design (Top-up), BA(Hons) Illustration, BA(Hons) Interior Design Decoration, BA(Hons) Interior Design Decoration (Top-up), BA(Hons) Photography, BA(Hons) Photography (Top-up), BA(Hons) Product Design, BA(Hons) Product Design (Top-up), BA(Hons) Special Effects, BA(Hons) Visual Arts (Top-up), BA(Hons) Visual Communication (Accelerated), MA Visual Communication

Business and Finance

BA(Hons) Accountancy and Finance, BSc(Hons) Accountancy and Finance (Top-up), BSc(Hons) Business Administration (Top-up), BA(Hons) Business Management, BA(Hons) Business (Professional Development), BA(Hons) Events Management, BA(Hons) Festival and Event Management, MBA Global Master of Business Administration, MA Human Resource Management, MSc International Business Management, MSc Management, Master's Degree Apprenticeship for Senior Leaders, Level 5 Operations and Departmental Manager Apprenticeship, MA Personnel and Development, PgD Personnel and Development, PGCert Professional Development Planning, MSc Project Management

Computing and Games

MSc Applied Computing, BSc(Hons) Business Information Technology, MSc Computer Engineering, BA(Hons) Computer Games (Art), BA(Hons) Computer Games (Design), BA(Hons) Computer Games Design (Top-up), BSc(Hons) Computer Games (Software Development), BSc(Hons) Computer Systems and Networks, BSc(Hons)Computing, MSc Cyber Security Engineering, BSc(Hons) Cyber Security Management, MSc Data Analytics Engineering, Digital and Technology Solutions Professional Degree Apprenticeship, BA(Hons) Digital Arts Top-Up, BSc(Hons) Digital Design and Web Development, MSc Digital Design, Foundation Year in Digital Arts, BSc(Hons) Information Technology Management, Level 4 Data Analyst Apprenticeship, Level 4 Network Engineer Apprenticeship, BSc(Hons) Software Engineering, BA(Hons) Virtual and Augmented Reality (Design), BSc(Hons) Web Design and Development

Engineering

MSc Applied Acoustics, BEng(Hons) Audio and Acoustic Engineering, BEng(Hons) Electronic Engineering, BSc(Hons) Engineering Design and Manufacture, HNC Engineering, BEng(Hons) Future Transport Engineering, BEng(Hons) Mechanical Engineering, BEng(Hons) Renewable Energy Engineering, Science and Engineering Foundation Year, MSc Superyacht Design, BEng(Hons) Yacht and Powercraft Design, BEng(Hons) Yacht Design and Production

English and Journalism

BA(Hons) English and Creative Writing, BA(Hons) English and Film, BA(Hons) English and Media, BA(Hons) English and Public Relations, BA(Hons) English, BA(Hons) Fashion Journalism, MA Journalism and Multimedia Communications, BA(Hons) Journalism, BA(Hons) Sport Journalism, MA Sports Broadcast Journalism

Fashion

BA(Hons) Beauty Promotion, MA Creative Direction for Fashion and Beauty, BA(Hons) Fashion, BA(Hons) Fashion Buying and Merchandising, BA(Hons) Fashion Graphics, BA(Hons) Fashion Management with Marketing, BA(Hons) Fashion Management with Marketing (Top-up), BA(Hons) Fashion Media, BA(Hons) Fashion Photography, BA(Hons) Fashion Photography (Top-up), BA(Hons)

Fashion Promotion and Communication, BA(Hons) Fashion Styling and Creative Direction, BA(Hons) Fashion Styling and Make-up for Media (Top-up), BA(Hons) Fashion (Top-up), BA(Hons) Make-up and Hair Design

BSc(Hons)

Adult Nursing Practice BSc(Hons), Applied Human Nutrition BSc(Hons), Biomedical Science BSc(Hons), Health, Nutrition and Exercise Science, Level 5 Healthcare Assistant Practitioner Apprenticeship, Level 5 Nursing Associate Apprenticeship, Level 6 Registered Nurse (Degree) Apprenticeship, MSci Mental Health and Psychological Wellbeing, BSc(Hons) Psychology, BSc(Hons) Psychology (Child Development and Education), BSc(Hons) Psychology (Counselling and Mental Health), BSc(Hons) Psychology (Forensic and Psychopathology), Social Sciences Foundation Year, BA(Hons) Social Work, BA(Hons) Sociology

Law and Criminology

BA(Hons) Criminal Investigation with Psychology, MSc Criminology and Criminal Justice, BA(Hons) Criminology and Psychology, BA(Hons) Criminology, Law and Criminology Foundation Year, LLB(Hons)

Maritime

MSc International Maritime Business, MSc International Shipping and Logistics, FdEng Marine Electrical and Electronic Engineering, BEng(Hons) Marine Engineering and Management (Top-up), FdEng Marine Engineering, FdSc Marine Operations, BSc(Hons) Maritime Business, BSc(Hons) Maritime Law and Business, BSc(Hons) Maritime Management Top-Up, BSc(Hons) Shipping and Port Management, MSc Shipping Operations

Marketing, Communications and Public Relations

MA Advertising and Multimedia Communications, CIM Certificate in Professional Marketing, CIM Diploma in Professional Marketing, CIM Foundation Certificate in Marketing, MA Creative Advertising, MA Creative Enterprise, BA(Hons) Creative Enterprise (Top-up), Foundation in Journalism, Advertising and Marketing, MA Luxury Brand Management, BA(Hons) Marketing, MSc Marketing, BSc(Hons) Marketing (Top-up), BA(Hons) Marketing with Advertising, BA(Hons) Marketing with Sport, BA(Hons) Public Relations and Communication, MA Public Relations and Multimedia Communications

Music and Performance

BA(Hons) Acting and Performance, MA Contemporary Music, BA(Hons) Digital Music, BA(Hons) Digital Music (Top-up), BA(Hons) Musical Theatre,

BA(Hons) Music Management, BA(Hons) Music Management (Top-Up), BA(Hons) Music Promotion, BSc(Hons) Music Technology (Top-Up), Performance Foundation Year, BA(Hons) Popular Music Journalism, BA(Hons) Popular Music Performance and Production, BA(Hons) Popular Music Performance, BA(Hons) Popular Music Performance (Top-up), BA(Hons) Popular Music Production, Popular Music Production Foundation Year, BA(Hons) Popular Music Production (Top-up), BA(Hons) Songwriting (Top-Up)

Sport and Fitness

BA(Hons) Adventure and Outdoor Management, BSc(Hons) Applied Sport Science, BSc(Hons) Fitness and Personal Training, BA(Hons) Football Business Management, Football Foundation Year, MSc Football Science, MSci Football Science, BA(Hons) Football Studies, BA(Hons) Health and Fitness Management, BA(Hons) Physical Education, BSc(Hons) Sport and Exercise Psychology, BSc(Hons) Sport and Exercise Therapy, BA(Hons) Sport Coaching and Physical Education (Top-up), BA(Hons) Sport Coaching and Sport Development, MA Sport Development and Management, PGCert Sport Development, Sport Foundation Year, Sport, Health and Exercise Science Foundation Year, BA(Hons) Sport Management, BSc(Hons) Sport Performance Coaching, MSc Sport Science and Performance Coaching, MA Youth Sport and Physical Education, PGCert Youth Sport and Physical Education

Travel and Tourism

Event and Tourism Foundation Year, BA(Hons) International Air Travel and Tourism Management, BSc(Hons) International Hospitality Management (Top-up), BA(Hons) International Tourism Management, BSc(Hons) International Travel and Tourism Management (Top-up)

TV, Film, Media Production and Technology

BSc(Hons) Audio Engineering, BA(Hons) Computer Generated Imagery, BA(Hons) Film and Television, BA(Hons) Film and Television (Top Up), BA(Hons) Film, BA(Hons) Film Production, MA Film Production, BA(Hons) Film Visual Effects, Foundation Year in Media, BSc(Hons) Live Sound Technology, MA Media Arts Management, BA(Hons) Media Production, BA(Hons) Media Production (Top-up), Media Technology Foundation Year, BA(Hons) Post Production for Film and Television, MA Post Production in Film and Television, BA(Hons) Post-Production (Top-up), BSc(Hons) Sound for Film, TV and Games, BA(Hons) Television Production, BA(Hons) Television Production (Top Up), BA(Hons) Television Studio Production, BA(Hons) Television Studio Production (Top Up)

STAFFORDSHIRE UNIVERSITY
www.staffs.ac.uk

Computing and Digital Technologies; www.staffs.ac.uk/about/departments/

Animation BA(Hons), AI and Robotics BSc(Hons), BSc(Hons) Computer Science, BSc(Hons) Computer Science (Cloud Technologies), BSc(Hons) Computer Science (Internet and Web Management), BSc(Hons) Computer Science (Network Computing), BSc(Hons) Computer Science (Software Development), Computer Science (Cyber Security) BSc(Hons), Advertising Film and Music Video Production BA(Hons), Experimental Film Production BA(Hons), Film Production and Interactive Technology BSc(Hons), Film, Television and Radio BA(Hons), Media (Film) Production BA(Hons), Post Production Technology BSc(Hons), Computer Gameplay Design and Production BSc(Hons), Computer Games Design BEng(Hons)/ BSc(Hons), Computer Games Design (Digital Institute London) BA(Hons), Computer Games Design and Programming BSc(Hons), Computer Games Development BSc(Hons), Computer Games Programming BSc(Hons), Games Studies BA(Hons), Virtual Reality Design BA(Hons), Games PR and Community Management BA(Hons), CGI and Visual Effects BSc(Hons), Concept Art for Games and film BA(Hons), Games Art BA(Hons), Sports Journalism BA(Hons), Music Business and Production BA(Hons), Music Production BA(Hons) Music Technology BSc(Hons), Sound Design BSc(Hons)

Postgraduate: Computer Science MSc, Computer Science MRes, Computer Science (Business Computing) MSc, Computer Science (Computer Networks and Security) MSc, Computer Science (Cyber Security) MSc, Computer Science (Software Engineering) MSc, Robotics and Smart Technologies MSc, Film, Media and Music MPhil / PhD, 3D Computer Games Design MSc, Journalism MA, Sports Broadcast Journalism MA, Journalism MPhil/PhD, Music Production MA, Music Technology MSc

CreativeArts and Engineering; www.staffs.ac.uk/about/departments/

3D Designer Maker BA(Hons), Art and Design BA(Hons), Cartoon and Comic Arts BA(Hons), Fine Art BA(Hons), Graphic Design BA(Hons), Illustration BA(Hons),Industrial Design: Product & Transport BA(Hons), Photography BA(Hons), Surface Pattern and Textile Design BA(Hons), Acting and Screen Performance BA(Hons), Acting and Theatre Arts BA(Hons), Aeronautical Engineering BEng(Hons)/ MEng, AI and Robotics BSc(Hons), Automotive and Motorsport Engineering BEng(Hons)/ MEng, Electrical and Electronic Engineering (Optional pathways in Electrical, Electronic & Telecommunications) BEng(Hons)/ MEng, Engineering Design BSc(Hons), General Engineering BEng(Hons), Mechanical Engineering BEng(Hons)/MEng, English Literature and Creative Writing BA(Hons), Fashion BA(Hons), Geography BA(Hons)

Postgraduate: Arts and Creative Technologies (By Negotiated Study) MA, Arts and Creative Technologies (By Negotiated Study) MA, Ceramic Design MA, Clinical Photography PgCert, Graphic Design for Health Care PgCert, Theatre Practice (By Negotiated Study) MA, Aeronautical Engineering MSc, Automotive Engineering MSc, Electrical Engineering and Renewable Energy Systems MSc, Electronic and Telecommunication Engineering MSc, Mechanical Engineering and Sustainable Energy Technologies MSc, Professional Engineering MSc, Robotics and Smart Technologies MSc, Continental Philosophy MA, Modern and Contemporary Writing MA

Health and Social Care; www.staffs.ac.uk/about/departments/

Health and Social Care BSc(Hons), Operating Department Practice BSc(Hons), Paramedic Science BSc(Hons), Midwifery Practice BSc(Hons), Nursing Practice (Adult) BSc(Hons), Nursing Practice (Child) BSc(Hons), Nursing Practice (Mental Health) BSc(Hons), Health and Social Care BSc(Hons), Social Welfare Law, Policy and Advice Practice BA(Hons), Social Work BA(Hons)

Postgraduate: Advanced Clinical Practice MSc, Advanced Forensic Practice (Custody Health Professional) MSc/ PgCert/ PgDip, Advanced Forensic Practice (Sexual Assault and Custody Health Professional) MSc/ PgDip, Advanced Forensic Practice (Sexual Assault Health Professional) MSc/ PgCert/ PgDip, Cognitive Behavioural Therapy MSc, Cognitive Behavioural Therapy PgDip, Master of Public Health MPH, Medical Education MSc, Health and Welfare Studies MPhil/PhD, Health Studies MPhil/ PhD, Healthcare Science Professional Doctorate, Advanced Clinical Practice MSc, Specialist Practice – District Nursing MSc, Health and Social Care (by negotiated study) MSc, Master of Public Health

MPH, Medical Education MSc, Health and Welfare Studies MPhil/PhD, Health Studies MPhil/PhD

Law, Policing and Forensics; www.staffs.ac.uk/about/departments/

Forensic Investigation BSc(Hons)/MSci, Forensic Science BSc(Hons)/MSci, Policing and Criminal Investigation BSc(Hons)/MSci, Professional Policing BSc(Hons), Criminal Justice with Offender Management BA(Hons), Law LLB(Hons), Law (Criminal Justice) LLB(Hons), Criminal Justice with Offender Management BA(Hons), Criminology BSc(Hons)/MSci

Postgraduate: Advanced Forensic Practice (Custody Health Professional) MSc/ PgCert/ PgDip, Advanced Forensic Practice (Sexual Assault and Custody Health Professional) MSc/ PgDip, Advanced Forensic Practice (Sexual Assault Health Professional) MSc/ PgCert/ PgDip, Applied Research MA/ MSc, Digital Forensic Investigation MSc, Forensic Science MSc, Legal Practice LLM/ PgDip, Law MPhil/ PhD, Criminology and Criminal Justice MSc, Sociology and Social Justice MA, Terrorism, Crime and Global Security MA, Transnational Organised Crime MA

Life Sciences and Education; www.staffs.ac.uk/about/departments/

Biological Science (optional pathways in Pre-Med, Genomics, Pharmacology, Ecology and Environmental Management) BSc(Hons)/MSci, Biomedical Science BSc(Hons)/MSci, Early Childhood Studies BA(Hons), Early Childhood Studies with Special Educational Needs and Disabilities BA(Hons), Education Studies BA(Hons), Education Studies with Special Educational Needs and Disabilities BA(Hons), Primary Education with Qualified Teacher Status (3-7) (5-11) BA(Hons), Forensic Psychology BSc(Hons), Psychology BSc(Hons), Psychology and Child Development BSc(Hons), Psychology and Counselling BSc(Hons), Psychology and Criminology BSc(Hons), Sport and Exercise Psychology BSc(Hons), Football Coaching and Performance BSc(Hons), Physical Education and Youth Sport Coaching BSc(Hons), Sport and Exercise Psychology BSc(Hons), Sport and Exercise Science (optional pathways in Strength and Conditioning) BSc(Hons), Sports Coaching BA(Hons), Sports Therapy BA(Hons)

Postgraduate: Applied Research MA/ MSc, Molecular Biology MSc, Biology MPhil/ PhD, Healthcare Science Professional Doctorate, Education Doctor of Education, Education MA, Higher and Professional Education PgCert, Secondary Physical Education PGCE, PGCE Primary (General), PGCE with PE Specialism, Secondary Art and Design PGCE, Secondary Biology PGCE, Secondary Business PGCE, Secondary Computer Science PGCE, Secondary Economics and Business Education PGCE, Secondary English PGCE, Secondary Geography PGCE, Secondary Mathematics PGCE, Education MPhil/ PhD, Applied Research MA/MSc, Cognitive Behavioural Therapy MSc/PgDip, Foundations of Clinical Psychology MSc, Health Psychology MSc, Psychology MSc, Psychotherapeutic Counselling MSc/PgDip, Clinical Psychology Professional Doctorate, Health Psychology Professional Doctorate, Psychology MPhil/ PhD, Applied Sport and Exercise Science MSc, Clinical Biomechanics MSc/PgCert, Sport and Exercise Psychology MSc, Sports Coaching MSc, Biomechanics MPhil/PhD, Sport and Exercise Psychology MPhil/PhD

School of Business, Leadership and Economics; www.staffs.ac.uk/about/departments/

Accounting and Finance BA(Hons), Business Management FdA, Business Management (Optional pathways in International Business Management) BA(Hons), Marketing Management BA(Hons), Professional Marketing CIM Diploma/ CIM Certificate, ESports BA(Hons), Events Management BA(Hons), Tourism Management BA(Hons), Visitor Attraction and Resort Management FdA

Postgraduate: Accounting and Finance MSc, Business Administration MBA, Business Administration DBA, Customer and Data Analytics MSc, Digital Marketing DMI Professional Diploma, Digital Marketing Management MSc, Human Resource Management MA/ PgCert, International Business Management MSc, ESports MA

UNIVERSITY OF STIRLING
www.stir.ac.uk

School of Arts and Humanities;
www.stir.ac.uk/arts-humanities/courses/
Digital Media BA(Hons), English Studies BA(Hons), Film and Media BA(Hons), French BA(Hons), Heritage and Tourism BA; BA(Hons), History BA(Hons), BA(Hons) International Management Studies with European Languages and Society Journalism Studies BA(Hons), Law BA, Law LLB, LLB Law: Accelerated Graduate Modern Languages BA(Hons), Philosophy BA(Hons), Politics BA(Hons), Politics (International Politics) BA(Hons), Politics, Philosophy and Economics BA(Hons), Religion BA(Hons), Scottish History BA(Hons), Spanish and Latin American Studies BA(Hons)

Postgraduate courses: Creative Writing (MLitt), MSc Digital Media and Society Doctor of Diplomacy (DDipl), English Language and Linguistics (MLitt), Environment, Heritage and Policy (MSc), Environmental Policy and Governance (LLM/MSc), Gender Studies (Applied) (MSc/MLitt), Historical Research MRes, Postgraduate Certificate, MSc Human Rights and Diplomacy MRes Humanities International Conflict and Cooperation (MSc), International Energy Law and Policy (LLM), MSc International Journalism Media Management MSc, Postgraduate Diploma, Media Research MRes, Postgraduate Diploma, Philosophy Postgraduate Diploma, MLitt, Public Policy (MPP), Publishing Studies (MLitt), Publishing Studies (MRes), Scottish Literature (MLitt), Strategic Communication & Public Relations (Joint Degree), MSc Strategic Public Relations (Online) Masters / MSc, Postgraduate Diploma, Postgraduate Certificate Strategic Public Relations & Communication Management Postgraduate Certificate, Postgraduate Diploma, MSc, MSc Television Content Development and Production The Gothic Imagination (MLitt), Translation Studies with TESOL (MSc Postgraduate Diploma, Postgraduate Certificate) MSc Translation and Conference Interpreting

Faculty of Natural Sciences;
www.stir.ac.uk/natural-sciences/
Undergraduate degrees in Animal Biology, Applied Biological Sciences, Applied Computing, Applied Mathematics, Aquaculture, Biology, Business Computing, Cell Biology, Computing Science, Conservation Biology and Management, Ecology, Environmental Geography, Environmental Geography and Outdoor Education, Environmental Science, Environmental Science (Integrated Masters), Environmental Science and Outdoor Education, Marine Biology, Mathematics, Psychology, Software Engineering

Postgraduate courses: Aquatic Pathobiology MSc Postgraduate Diploma, Postgraduate Certificate, Aquatic Veterinary Studies MSc, Big Data MSc, Professional Doctorate Big Data Science, MSc Earth and Planetary Observation MSc Environmental Management MSc, Environmental Management (Conservation) Postgraduate Certificate, Postgraduate Diploma, MSc, Environmental Management (Energy) MSc, Postgraduate Diploma, Postgraduate Certificate, MSc Financial Technology (FinTech) Health Psychology MSc, Postgraduate Certificate, Postgraduate Diploma, Professional Doctorate, Human Animal Interaction MA, MSc, Postgraduate Certificate, Postgraduate Diploma, MSc Financial Technology (FinTech), Psychological Research Methods (Autism Research) MSc, Postgraduate Certificate, Postgraduate Diploma, Psychological Research Methods (Bilingualism Research) MSc, Postgraduate Certificate, Postgraduate Diploma, Psychological Research Methods (Child Development) MSc, Postgraduate Certificate, Postgraduate Diploma, Psychological Research Methods (Cognition and Neuropsychology) MSc, Postgraduate Diploma, Postgraduate Certificate, Psychological Research Methods (Evolutionary Psychology) MSc, MSc Psychological Research Methods (General) MSc, Postgraduate Diploma, Postgraduate Certificate Postgraduate Certificate, Postgraduate Diploma, Psychological Research Methods (Perception and Action) MSc, Postgraduate Certificate, Postgraduate Diploma, Psychological Research Methods (Psychology of Faces) MSc, Postgraduate Certificate, Postgraduate Diploma, Psychological Therapy in Primary Care MSc, MSc Psychology (accredited conversion course), MSc Sustainable Aquaculture

The Faculty of Social Sciences;
www.stir.ac.uk/social-sciences/
Criminology and Social Policy BA(Hons), Criminology and Sociology BA(Hons), Education (Primary) BA(Hons), BSc(Hons), Education (Secondary) BA(Hons), BSc(Hons), In-service BA – Teaching Qualification in Further Education (TQFE), Pre-Service BA – Teaching Qualification in Further

Education (TQFE) Social Work BA(Hons), Sociology and Social Policy BA(Hons)
Postgraduate courses: MSc Applied Professional Studies Applied Social Research (Criminology) MSc, Postgraduate Diploma, Applied Social Research (MRes), Applied Social Research (MSc), Applied Social Research (Social Statistics and Social Research) (MSc), Applied Social Research Doctorate, Criminological Research (MRes), MSc Criminology Dementia Studies Postgraduate Certificate, Postgraduate Diploma, MSc, Doctorate in Education (EdD), Education Studies and TESOL Postgraduate Certificate, Postgraduate Diploma, MSc, Educational Leadership (Specialist Qualification for Headship) MSc, Postgraduate Diploma, Postgraduate Certificate, Educational Research Postgraduate Certificate, Postgraduate Diploma, MRes, Housing Studies MSc, Postgraduate Diploma, Postgraduate Certificate, Management and English Language Teaching MSc, Postgraduate Diploma, Postgraduate Certificate, PhD TESOL Research, Professional Education and Leadership MSc, Postgraduate Certificate, Postgraduate Diploma, Social Enterprise MSc, Postgraduate Diploma, Postgraduate Certificate, Social Work Studies Postgraduate Diploma, MSc, Teaching English to Speakers of Other Languages (TESOL) (Online) MSc, Postgraduate Certificate, Postgraduate Diploma, PhD TESOL Research, Teaching Qualification in Further Education (TQFE) – In-service Postgraduate Certificate, Teaching Qualification in Further Education (TQFE) – Pre-service Postgraduate Diploma, TESOL – Teaching English to Speakers of Other Languages Postgraduate Certificate, Postgraduate Diploma, MSc

Stirling Management School;
www.stir.ac.uk/management/
Accountancy BAcc(Hons), Accountancy and Finance BAcc(Hons), Business Studies BA(Hons), Economics BA(Hons), Finance BA(Hons), Human Resource Management BA(Hons), Management BSc, BSc(Hons), Marketing BA, BA(Hons), Professional Accountancy BA(Hons), Retail Marketing BA, BA(Hons), Sport Business Management BA(Hons), Sustainable Events Management BA(Hons)

Postgraduate courses: Banking and Finance MSc, Postgraduate Diploma, Postgraduate Certificate, Behavioural Science for Management MSc, Postgraduate Diploma, Business and Management MSc, MBM, Data Science for Business MSc, Postgraduate Diploma, Postgraduate Certificate, DBA Doctor of Business Administration, Economics for Business and Policy MSc, Finance MSc, Postgraduate Certificate, Postgraduate Diploma, MSc Human Resource Management, Masters / MSc, Postgraduate Diploma, Postgraduate Certificate International Accounting and Finance MSc, Postgraduate Diploma, Postgraduate Certificate, International Business MSc, Postgraduate Diploma, Investment Analysis Postgraduate Certificate, Postgraduate Diploma, MSc, MSc Management (Muscat) Masters / MSc Marketing, Masters / MSc, Postgraduate Diploma, Postgraduate Certificate MBA Master of Business Administration, Master of Research in Business and Management Masters / MRes, Postgraduate Diploma, Postgraduate Certificate Strategic Sustainable Business MSc

Faculty of Health Sciences and Sport ;
www.stir.ac.uk/health-sciences-sport/
Nursing – Adult BSc, Nursing – Adult BSc(Hons), Nursing – Mental Health BSc, Nursing – Mental Health (Honours) BSc(Hons), Sport and Exercise Science BSc(Hons), Sports Studies BA(Hons)
Postgraduate courses: Advancing Practice MSc, Postgraduate Diploma, Postgraduate Certificate, Clinical Doctorates Doctorate, MSc, Postgraduate Diploma, Early Years Practice Health Visiting MSc, Postgraduate Diploma, Global Issues in Gerontology and Ageing MSc, Postgraduate Diploma, Postgraduate Certificate, Health Research (Online) MRes, Postgraduate Diploma, Postgraduate Certificate, Performance Coaching MSc, Postgraduate Diploma, Postgraduate Certificate, Psychology of Sport (Accredited) MSc, Postgraduate Diploma, Postgraduate Certificate, Public Health MPH, Postgraduate Certificate, Postgraduate Diploma, MSc Sport Management MSc, Postgraduate Diploma, Postgraduate Certificate Sport Nutrition MSc

STOCKPORT COLLEGE
www.stockport.ac.uk

BA(Hons) Contemporary Creative Practice – Top Up from Foundation Degree, BA(Hons) Childhood Studies, BA(Hons) Contemporary Creative Practice – Top Up, BA(Hons) Contemporary Photography,

HNC/D Building Services Engineering HNC/D Computing, HNC Construction (Civil Engineering), HNC/D Construction & the Built Environment, BTEC HNC Creative Media Production, HNC Electrical Engineering, HNC Mechanical Engineering Foundation Degree Early Years Practice, Foundation Degree Graphic Arts and Design, Foundation Degree

in Education and Learning Support, Foundation Degree in Illustration, Foundation Degree Professional Practice In Health & Social Care – Assistant Practitioner, Foundation Degree Sports Coaching, Foundation Degree Working with Children/Young People, PGCE Post 16 Education and Training

UNIVERSITY OF STRATHCLYDE
www.strath.ac.uk

Faculty of Engineering;
www.strath.ac.uk/engineering/
studywithus/undergraduate/

Department of Architecture
BSc Architectural Studies
Postgraduate courses: MArch/PgDip Advanced Architectural Design, MSc/PgDip/PgCert Advanced Construction Technologies & BIM, March Architectural Design (International), MSc/PgDip/PgCert Architectural Design for the Conservation of Built Heritage, MSc/ PgDip/ PgCert Sustainable Engineering: Architecture & Ecology, MSc/PgDip/PgCert Urban Design, PhD/ MPhil/ MRes Architecture

Biomedical Engineering
BEng Biomedical Engineering, MEng Biomedical Engineering, BSc Prosthetics & Orthotics
Postgraduate courses: MSc/PgDip/PgCert Biofluid Mechanics, MSc/MEng Biomedical Engineering, MSc Prosthetics & Orthotics, MSc/ PgDip/PgCert Prosthetics &/or Orthotics Rehabilitation Studies

Chemical & Process Engineering
BEng Chemical Engineering, MEng Chemical Engineering
Postgraduate courses: MSc/PgDip/PgCert Advanced Chemical & Process Engineering, MSc Chemical Technology & Management, MSc Energy Systems Innovation, MSc Sustainable Engineering: Chemical Processing, MSc Process Technology and Management

Civil and Environmental Engineering
BEng/ MEng Civil and Environmental Engineering, BEng/ MEng Civil and Engineering
Postgraduate: MSc Civil and Engineering (with optional specialist streams), MSc Civil and Engineering with Industry, MRes Climate Change Adaption, MSc Environmental Engineering, MSc Environmental Entrepreneurship, MRes Geoenvironmental

Engineering, MSc Hydrogeology, MRes Integrated Pollution Prevention & Control, MSc Sustainability & Environmental Studies

Design, Manufacture & Engineering Management
BEng/ MEng Manufacturing Engineering with Management, BSc Product Design & Innovation, BEng Product Design Engineering, MEng Product Design Engineering, BEng Sports Engineering, MEng Sports Engineering
Postgraduate courses: MSc/PgDip/PgCert Advanced Manufacture: Technology & Systems, MSc/PgDip/ PgCert Design Engineering, MSc/ PgDip Design Engineering with Advanced Product Development, MSc/ PgDip Design Engineering with Sustainability, MSc/PgDip Digital Manufacturing, MSc Engineering Management for Process Excellence, MSc Global Innovation Management, MSc/PgDip/PgCert Mechatronics & Automation, MSc/PgDip/PgCert Product Design, MSc/PgDip/ PgCert Supply Chain & Logistics Management, MSc/ PgDip Supply Chain and Procurement Management, MSc/ PgDip Supply Chain & Sustainability Management, EngD/MSc/ PgDip/PgCert Systems Engineering Management

Electronic & Electrical Engineering
BEng Electrical & Mechanical Engineering, MEng Electrical & Mechanical Engineering / with International Study, MEng Electrical Energy Systems, MEng Electronic & Digital Systems, BEng Electronic and Electrical Engineering, MEng Electronic & Electrical Engineering / with International Study, MEng Electronic & Electrical Engineering with Business Studies
Postgraduate courses: MSc 5G Advanced Communications, MSc Advanced Electrical Power Engineering, MSc Autonomous Robotic Intelligent Systems, MSc Electrical Power and Energy Systems, MSc Electronic & Electrical Engineering, MSc Machine

Learning & Deep Learning, MSc Smart Grids, MSc Wind Energy Systems

Mechanical & Aerospace Engineering

BEng in Aero-Mechanical Engineering, BEng in Mechanical Engineering, BEng/MEng, Mechanical Engineering with International Study, MEng Aero-Mechanical Engineering, MEng Mechanical Engineering, MEng Mechanical Engineering with Aeronautics, MEng Mechanical Engineering with Financial Management, MEng Mechanical Engineering with International Study, MEng Mechanical Engineering with Materials Engineering

Postgraduate courses: MSc/PgDip/PgCert Advanced Mechanical Engineering, MSc Advanced Mechanical Engineering with Aerospace, MSc Advanced Mechanical Engineering with Energy Systems, MSc Advanced Mechanical Engineering with Materials, MSc Advanced Mechanical Engineering with Power Plant Technologies, MSc Satellite Applications (with Data Science), MSc/PgDip/PgCert Sustainable Engineering: Renewable Energy Systems & the Environment

Naval Architecture, Ocean & Marine Engineering

BEng Naval Architecture & Marine Engineering, MEng Naval Architecture & Marine Engineering, BEng Naval Architecture with High Performance Marine Vehicles, MEng Naval Architecture with High Performance Marine Vehicles, BEng Naval Architecture with Ocean Engineering, MEng Naval Architecture with Ocean Engineering

Postgraduate courses: MSc Advanced Naval Architecture, MSc/ PgDip Marine Engineering, MSc/ PgDip Offshore Floating Systems, MSc/ PgDip Ship & Offshore Structures, MSc Ship & Offshore Technology, MSc/ PgDip Subsea & Pipeline Engineering, MSc/ PgDip Sustainable Engineering: Marine Technology, MSc/ PgDip Sustainable Engineering: Offshore Renewable Energy, MSc/ PgDip Technical Ship Management

Faculty of Humanities & Social Sciences; www.strath.ac.uk/humanities/

School of Education

Childhood Practice BA, BA Education & Social Services, Education & Sport BA, Primary Education BA

Postgraduate courses: PGCAP Academic Practice, Applied Educational & Social research MSc, Autism MEd, Autism MSc, Early Years Pedagogue Med, Education Studies MSc/ MEd, Educational Leadership MEd, Gaelic Immersion for Teachers PgDip, Knowledge Exchange PGCKE, Learning & Teaching in Higher Education PGC LTHE, PGCE (International) PGCert, Primary Education PGDE Professional Practice Med, Researcher Development PGCRD, Safety and Risk Management MSc/PgDip/ PgCert, Secondary Education (Art & Design/ Biology with Science/ Business Education/ Chemistry with Science/ Computing Science/ English/ Gaelic/ Geography/ History/ Home Economics/ Mathematics/ Modern Languages/ Modern Studies/ Physical Education/ Physics with Science/ Psychology/ Religious Moral Education/ Technological Education) PGDE, MSc TESOL & Intercultural Communication

School of Government & Public Policy

Behavioural Aspects of Commerce BA(Hons), English & Creative Writing & Politics & International Relations BA, English Politics & International Relations BA, French & Politics & International Relations BA, History & Politics & International Relations BA, Law & Politics & International Relations BA, Philosophy, Politics & Economics BA, Politics & International Relations BA, Politics & International Relations & Social Policy BA, Politics & International Relations & Economics BA, Politics & International Relations & Education BA, Politics & International Relations & Human Resource Management BA, Politics & International Relations & Journalism, Media & Communication BA, Politics & International Relations & Psychology BA, Politics & International Relations & Spanish BA

Postgraduate courses: MSc Applied Gender Studies, MSc Data Science for Politics & Policymaking, MSc/ PgDip Diplomacy & International Security, European Politics MSc, International Relations MSc, International Relations, Law & Security MSc/LLM, Political Research MSc, Politics MSc, Public Policy MSc

School of Humanities

English (BA), English & Creative Writing BA, English & Education BA, English & French BA, English & History BA, English & Human Resource Management BA, English & Italian BA, English & Journalism & Creative Writing BA, English & Law BA, English & Politics BA, English & Psychology BA, English & Spanish BA, Journalism, Media & Communications & Economics (BA), Journalism, Media & Communications & Education (BA), Journalism, Media & Communications & Human Resource Management (BA), Journalism, Media & Communications & Law (BA), Journalism, Media & Communications &

Spanish (BA), History (BA), History & Economics BA, History & Education BA, History & Human Resource Management BA, History & Journalism & Creative Writing BA, History & Law BA, History & Politics BA, History & Psychology BA, History & Spanish BA, History & French BA, BA in Journalism & Creative Writing, BA French, English & Creative Writing & French BA, English & French BA, French & Economics BA, French & Education BA, French & History BA, French & Hospitality & Tourism BA, French & Human Resource Management BA, French & Journalism, Media & Communication BA, French & Law BA, French & Marketing BA, French & Politics & International Relations BA, French & Psychology BA, French & Social Policy BA, French & Spanish BA, Law with French LLB, BA Spanish, English & Creative Writing & Spanish BA, English & Spanish BA, French & Spanish, History & Spanish BA, Journalism, Media & Communication & Spanish, Law & Spanish BA, Law with Spanish LLB, Politics & International Relations & Spanish BA, Psychology & Spanish BA, Social Policy & Spanish BA, Spanish & Education BA, Spanish & Hospitality & Tourism BA, Spanish & Human Resource Management, Spanish & Marketing BA, English & Creative Writing & Journalism, Media & Communication BA, English & Journalism, Media & Communication BA, French & Journalism, Media & Communication BA, History & Journalism, Media & Communication BA, Intercultural Communications for Global Business BA, Journalism, Media & Communication & Economics BA, Journalism, Media & Communication & Education BA, Journalism, Media & Communication & Human Resource Management BA, Journalism, Media & Communication & Law BA, Journalism, Media & Communication & Social Policy BA, Journalism, Media & Communication & Spanish BA, Journalism, Media & Communications & Psychology BA, Politics & International Relations & Journalism, Media & Communication BA

Postgraduate courses: MSc Applied Gender Studies, Digital Journalism (MLitt/PgDip), Media & Communication (MLitt), HistoricalStudies (MSc), Health History (MSc), MRes/MPhil in Modern Languages, Interdisciplinary English Studies (MLitt), TESOL & Intercultural Communication (MSc), Creative Writing (MLitt), Interdisciplinary English Studies (MLitt), Diplomacy and International Security (MSc), Business Translation & Interpreting MSc/ PgDip, Secondary Education Modern Languages PGDE, Modern Languages PhD/ MPhil/ MRes,

Law School

LLB Scots Law, LLB Law (Scots & English), LLB English Law, Clinical LLB, LLB Scots & English Law (Clinical), Graduate Entry LLB Scots Law, Graduate Entry LLB (Scots & English Law), Part-time LLB, LLB Law with French, LLB Law with Spanish

Postgraduate courses: LLM/PgDip/PgCert Construction Law, LLM/MSc Criminal Justice & Penal Change, MSc/ PgDip Diplomacy & International Security, LLM/PgDip/PgCert Global Environmental Law & Governance, LLM/PgDip/PgCert Human Rights Law, LLM/PgDip/PgCert International Commercial Law, MSC/LLM International Relations, Law & Security, LLM/PgDip/PgCert Internet Law & Policy/ IT Telecommunications Law, LLM/PgDip/PgCert Law, LLM Law & Finance, LLM/MSc/PgDip/PgCert Mediation & Conflict Resolution, Diploma Professional Legal Practice

Psychological Sciences & Health

BA Psychology, BSc Psychology & Counselling, Behavioural Aspects of Commerce BA(Hons) Economics & Psychology BA, English & Creative Writing & Psychology BA, English & Psychology BA, French & Psychology BA, History & Psychology BA, Human Resource Management & Psychology BA, Journalism, Media & Communications & Psychology BA, Law & Psychology BA, Marketing & Psychology BA, Politics & International Relations & Psychology BA, Psychology BA, Psychology & Counselling BSc, Psychology & Economics BA, Psychology & Education BA, Psychology & Human Resource Management BA, Psychology & Mathematics BA, Psychology & Social Policy BA, Psychology & Spanish BA, Psychology & Sport BA, Speech & Language Pathology BSc, Sport & Physical Activity BSc

Postgraduate courses: Clinical Health Psychology MSc, Psychology with a specialisation in Business MSc, Research Methods in Psychology MSc. Secondary Education: Psychology PGDE, Speech & Language Therapy PhD/ MPhil, Physical Activity in Non-Communicable Disease Prevention & Control MSc, Physical Activity for Health PhD/ MPhil

School of Social Work & Social Policy

BA(Hons) Social Work

Postgraduate courses: Postgraduate Diploma/Master, in Social Work (MSW), MSc Advanced Residential, Childcare, MSc Child & Youth Care Studies by, Distance Learning, Mental Health Social Work PgCert

Faculty of Science; *www.strath.ac.uk/ science/*

Chemistry

MSci Applied Chemistry and Chemical Engineering, MChem Chemistry, MChem Chemistry with Drug, Discovery, MChem Chemistry with Teaching, MChem Forensic and Analytical Chemistry

Postgraduate courses: MSc Chemical Technology & Management, MSc Forensic Science, MPhil/ PhD Chemistry

Computer & Information Science

BEng/MEng Computer & Electronic Systems, BSc/ MEng Computer Science, BSc(Hons) Data Analytics, BSc Mathematics and Computer Science, BSc Software Engineering

Postgraduate courses: MSc Advanced Computer, Science, MSc Advanced Computer Science with Big, Data, MSc Advanced Software Engineering, MSc Artificial Intelligence & Applications, MSc/, PgDip Data Analytics, MSc Data Science for Politics and Policymaking, MSc Digital Health Systems, MSc Enterprise Information Systems, MSc Information, & Library Studies, MSc Information, Management, MSc Machine Learning & Deep Learning, MSc Software Development

Mathematics & Statistics

BA Accounting & Mathematics & Statistics, BA Business Analysis & Technology & Mathematics & Statistics, BA Economics, Mathematics and Statistics, BA Finance, Mathematics and Statistics, BSc Mathematics & Computer Science, BSc Mathematics & Physics, BSc Mathematics with Teaching, BSc Mathematics, Statistics & Accounting, BSc Mathematics, Statistics & Business Analysis, BSc Mathematics, Statistics & Economics, BSc Mathematics, Statistics & Finance, BA Psychology & Mathematics, BSc(Hons) Data Analytics, BSc/MMath Mathematics, BSc Mathematics, Statistics & Accounting

Postgraduate courses: MSc Actuarial Science, PGDE Secondary Education: Mathematics, PhD/ MPhil/ MRes Mathematics & Statistics, MSc Quantitative Finance, MSc Applied Statistics in Health Sciences, MSc Applied Mathematical Sciences, MSc Data Analytics

Physics

BSc/MPhys Physics, MPhys Physics with Advanced Research, BSc Physics with Teaching, BSc(Hons) Mathematics & Physics

Postgraduate courses: MSc Advanced Physics, MSc Applied Physics, MSc Nanoscience, MSc Optical Technologies

Strathclyde Institute of Pharmacy & Biomedical Sciences

Biochemistry MSci, Biochemistry BSc, BSc Biochemistry & Immunology, BSc Biochemistry & Microbiology, BSc Biochemistry & Pharmacology, BSc Biomedical Science, BSc Biomolecular Sciences, MSci Immunology, BSc Immunology & Microbiology, BSc Immunology & Pharmacology, MSci Microbiology, BSc Microbiology, MSci Pharmacology, BSc Pharmacology, BSc Pharmacology & Microbiology, MPharm Pharmacy

Postgraduate courses: MSc Advanced Biochemistry, MSc Advanced Drug Delivery, MSc Advanced Immunology, MSc Advanced Pharmacology, MSc Advanced Clinical Pharmacy Practice, MSc Advanced Pharmaceutical Manufacturing, MSc Biomedical Sciences, MSc Cancer Therapies, MSc Clinical Pharmacy, MSc Industrial Biotechnology, MSc Molecular Microbiology, MSc Pharmaceutical Analysis MSc / PgDip/ PgCert, MSc Pharmaceutical Quality & Good Manufacturing Practice, Practice Certificate Pharmacist Independent Prescribing – Full Course

Strathclyde Business School; www.strath.ac.uk/business

BA degrees in Accounting, Business Analysis & Technology, Business Enterprise, Business Management Economics, Finance, Hospitality & Tourism Management, Human Resource Management, International Business Management, Marketing BBA Business Administration, MBus International Business with a Modern Language

Postgraduate courses: Accounting & Finance, Economics, Economics & Finance, Finance, Finance & Management, Financial Technology, International Accounting & Finance, International Banking & Finance, Investment & Finance, Quantative Finance, Applied Economics, Global Energy Management, Business Analysis & Consulting, Data Analytics, International Master Project Management, Global Master in Industrial Management, Operational Research, Digital Marketing Management, Innovation & Marketing Management, International Marketing, Tourism marketing Management, International Management, Masters of Business Management (MBM), Project Mangement & Innovation, Masters of Business Administration (MBA), Human Resource Management, International Human Resource Management Entrepreneurship, Innovation & Technology, Entrepreneurial Management & Leadership, Management Science, Marketing, Strategy & Organisation, Strathclyde MBA

UNIVERSITY OF SUFFOLK
www.uos.ac.uk

School of Engineering, Arts, Science and Technology

BA(Hons) Architecture, BSc(Hons) Biomedical Science, BSc(Hons) Biomedical Science with Foundation Year, BSc(Hons) Bioscience, BSc(Hons) Bioscience (with Foundation Year), BA(Hons) Computer Games Design, BSc(Hons) Computer Games Programming, BSc(Hons) Cyber Security, BSc(Hons) Cyber Security Technical Professional, BA(Hons) Digital Film Production, Professional Degree Apprenticeship Network Engineering, Professional Degree Apprenticeship Software Engineering, BA(Hons) Film Studies, BA(Hons) Fine Art, MSc Games Development, BA(Hons) Graphic Design, BA(Hons) Graphic Design (Graphic Illustration), BSc(Hons) Mobile and Web Development, BSc(Hons) Network Engineering, FdSc Network Engineering, BSc(Hons) Network Engineering (Progression Route), BSc(Hons) Nutrition and Human Health, BSc(Hons) Nutrition and Human Health (with Foundation Year), BA(Hons) Photography, BA(Hons) Screenwriting, BSc(Hons) Software Engineering, FdSc Software Engineering, BSc(Hons) Software Engineering (Progression Route), BSc(Hons) Wildlife, Ecology and Conservation Science

Postgraduate: MSc Games Development, MSc Regenerative Medicine

School of Social Sciences and Humanities

BSc(Hons) Child Development and Developmental Therapies, BA(Hons) Childhood and Family Studies, BSc(Hons) Criminology, BSc(Hons) Criminology and Law, BSc(Hons) Criminology and Sociology, BA(Hons) Early Childhood Studies, BA(Hons) Early Learning (Progression Route), FdA Early Years Practice, BA(Hons) Early and Primary Education Studies, BA(Hons) English Literature with Creative Writing, BA(Hons) English Literature with Language, BA(Hons) History, BA(Hons) Human Geography, BA(Hons) Human Geography with Sociology, LLB(Hons) Law, LLB(Hons) Law with Business Management, LLB(Hons) Law with Criminology, LLB(Hons) Law with Politics, LLB(Hons) Law with Sociology, BA(Hons) Politics, BA(Hons) Politics and Economics, BA(Hons) Politics and History, BA(Hons) Politics and Sociology, BSc(Hons) Psychology, BSc(Hons) Psychology and Criminology, BSc(Hons) Psychology and Early Childhood Studies, BSc(Hons) Psychology and Sociology, BSc(Hons) Psychology with Business Management, BA(Hons) Social Work, BSc(Hons) Sociology, BA(Hons) Special Educational Needs and Disability Studies

Postgraduate: MSc Applications of Psychology, MA Childhood Studies, MSc Cognitive Behaviour Therapy and Counselling, MA Criminology: Crime & Victimisation, MA/PgDip/PGCert Education Studies, PGCert Pedagogy in Practice, Work & Social Policy PhD/MPhil

School of Health and Sports Sciences

BSc(Hons) Sport Performance Analysis, BSc(Hons) Sport and Performance Psychology, BSc(Hons) Sport and Exercise Science, BSc(Hons) Strength and Conditioning, BSc(Hons) Primary Care Nursing (District Nursing)

Postgraduate: MSc Advanced Clinical Practice, PGCert Advanced Practice and Reporting in Computed Tomography Colonography (CTC), PGCert/PGDip Enhanced Clinical Practice, PGDip Primary Care Nursing (District Nursing), PGDip Primary Care Nursing (General Practice Nursing), MSc Public Health Nursing, PGDip Specialist Community Public Health Nursing

Suffolk Business School

BA(Hons) Accounting and Financial Management, BA(Hons) Business Management, BSc(Hons) Computing and Business Management, BA(Hons) Event Management, BA(Hons) Event and Tourism Management, BA(Hons) Marketing and Public Relations, BA(Hons) Tourism Management

Postgraduate: MSc Business and Management, Postgraduate Diploma in Human Resource Management, MSc Human Resource Management, MA/ PgDip/ PGCert in Professional Practice in Heritage Management, Master of Business Administration (MBA), Senior Leader Master's Degree Apprenticeship (Master of Business Administration)

UNIVERSITY OF SUNDERLAND
www.sunderland.ac.uk

Computing

BSc(Hons) Web and Mobile Development, BSc(Hons) Computer Science, BSc(Hons) Cybersecurity and Digital Forensics, BSc(Hons) Game Development, BSc(Hons) Business Technology, BSc(Hons) Networks and Cybersecurity, BSc(Hons) Web and Mobile Development with Integrated Foundation Year, BSc(Hons) Computer Science with Integrated Foundation Year, BSc(Hons) Networks and Cybersecurity with Integrated Foundation Year, BSc(Hons) Game Development with Integrated Foundation Year, BSc(Hons) Cybersecurity and Digital Forensics with Integrated Foundation Year, BSc(Hons) Business Technology with Integrated Foundation Year, BSc(Hons) Applied Business Computing (Top-Up), BSc(Hons) Computer Systems Engineering (Top-Up), BSc(Hons) Network Systems (Top-Up)
Postgraduate: HND Internet of Things, MSc Business Technology Management, MSc Data Science, MSc Cybersecurity MSc Computing, MSc Computer Networks and Cybersecurity, MPhil Master of Philosophy, PhD Doctor of Philosophy, DProf Professional Doctorate, PhD by Existing Published or Creative Work, Higher Doctorate

Engineering

BEng(Hons) Mechanical Engineering, BEng(Hons) Automotive Engineering, BEng(Hons) Electronic and Electrical Engineering, BEng(Hons) Manufacturing Engineering, MEng Mechanical Engineering, MEng Manufacturing Engineering, MEng Electronic and Electrical Engineering, BEng(Hons) Mechanical Engineering with Integrated Foundation Year, BEng(Hons) Automotive Engineering with Integrated Foundation Year, BEng(Hons) Manufacturing Engineering with Integrated Foundation Year, BEng(Hons) Electronic and Electrical Engineering with Integrated Foundation Year, BEng(Hons) Manufacturing Engineering (Top-Up), BEng(Hons) Electronic and Electrical Engineering (Top-Up), FdSc Power Engineering,
Postgraduate: MSc Advanced Maintenance Engineering, MSc Electronic Engineering, MSc Mechanical Engineering, MSc Engineering Management, MSc Manufacturing Engineering, MSc Project Management, MPhil Master of Philosophy, PhD Doctor of Philosophy, DProf Professional Doctorate, PhD by

Existing Published or Creative Work, Higher Doctorate

Medicine

Postgraduate: MBChB Medicine

Nursing

BSc(Hons) Learning Disability Nursing Practice, BSc(Hons) Mental Health Nursing Practice, BSc(Hons) Adult Nursing Practice, BSc(Hons) Nursing (Top-Up), BSc(Hons) Practice Development (Top-Up)
Postgraduate: MSc Nursing, MPhil Master of Philosophy, PhD Doctor of Philosophy, DProf Professional Doctorate, PhD by Existing Published or Creative Work, Higher Doctorate

Pharmacy, Pharmaceutical and Cosmetic Sciences

(MPharm) Pharmacy, BSc(Hons) Biochemistry, BSc(Hons) Medicinal Chemistry, BSc(Hons) Biopharmaceutical Science, BSc(Hons) Cosmetic Science
Postgraduate: MSc Cosmetic Science, MSc Clinical Pharmacy, MSc Drug Discovery and Development, MSc Pharmaceutical and Biopharmaceutical Formulations, PgDip/MSc Pharmaceutical Sciences for the Overseas Pharmacist Assessment Programme, Master of Philosophy, PhD Doctor of Philosophy, DProf Professional Doctorate, PhD by Existing Published or Creative Work, Higher Doctorate

Health & Clinical Sciences

BSc(Hons) Biomedical Science, BSc(Hons) Healthcare Sciences: Physiological Sciences/Life Sciences, BSc(Hons) Physiological Sciences, BSc(Hons) Practice Development (Top-Up)
Postgraduate: MPhil Master of Philosophy, PhD Doctor of Philosophy, DProf Professional Doctorate, PhD by Existing Published or Creative Work, Higher Doctorate

Public and Allied Health

BSc(Hons) Physiotherapy, BSc(Hons) Occupational Therapy, BSc(Hons) Paramedic Science and out of Hospital Care, BSc(Hons) Public Health, BSc(Hons) Public Health with Integrated Foundation Year
Postgraduate: MSc Workplace Wellbeing, Health and Safety, PgD/MSc Workplace Wellbeing, Health and Safety (Independent Distance Learning), PgDip/MSc Environment, Health and Safety (Independent

Distance Learning), MSc Environment, Health and Safety, MSc Public Health, Master of Philosophy, PhD Doctor of Philosophy, DProf Professional Doctorate, PhD by Existing Published or Creative Work, Higher Doctorate

Psychology

BSc(Hons) Forensic Psychology, BSc(Hons) Forensic Psychology with Integrated Foundation Year, BSc(Hons) Psychology with Clinical Skills, BSc(Hons) Psychology with Clinical Skills with Integrated Foundation Year, BSc(Hons) Psychology, BSc(Hons) Psychology with Integrated Foundation Year, BSc(Hons) Psychology with Counselling, BSc(Hons) Psychology with Counselling with Integrated Foundation Year, BA(Hons) Counselling (Top-Up), FdA Counselling, MSc Psychology

Postgraduate: MSc Psychological Research Methods, Master of Philosophy, PhD Doctor of Philosophy, DProf Professional Doctorate, PhD by Existing Published or Creative Work, Higher Doctorate

Sport & Exercise Sciences

BSc(Hons) Nutrition, Exercise and Health, BSc(Hons) Sports Coaching, BSc(Hons) Sport and Exercise Sciences, BA(Hons) Physical Education and Youth Sport, BA(Hons) Physical Education and Youth Sport with Integrated Foundation Year, BSc(Hons) Nutrition, Exercise and Health with Integrated Foundation Year, BSc(Hons) Sports Coaching with Integrated Foundation Year, BSc(Hons) Sport and Exercise Sciences with Integrated Foundation Year, FdSc (Foundation Degree) Exercise, Health and Fitness, FdSc (Foundation Degree) Sports Coaching

Postgraduate: MSc Psychology, MSc Sport and Exercise Sciences, Master of Philosophy, PhD Doctor of Philosophy, DProf Professional Doctorate, PhD by Existing Published or Creative Work, Higher Doctorate

Arts

BA(Hons) Photography, Video and Digital Imaging, BA(Hons) Fine Art, BA(Hons) Artist Designer Maker: Glass and Ceramics, BA(Hons) Photography, Video and Digital Imaging with Integrated Foundation Year, BA(Hons) Fine Art with Integrated Foundation Year, BA(Hons) Artist Designer Maker: Glass and Ceramics with Integrated Foundation Year, (Foundation Degree) Applied Fine Art Practice, BA(Hons) Mass Communications (Top-Up)

Postgraduate courses: MA Photography, MA Fine Art, MA Glass and Ceramics, MPhil Master of Philosophy, PhD Doctor of Philosophy, DProf

Professional Doctorate, PhD by Existing Published or Creative Work, Higher Doctorate

Journalism & PR

BA(Hons) Social Media Management, BA(Hons) Social Media Management with Integrated Foundation Year, BA(Hons) Fashion Journalism, BA(Hons) Fashion Journalism with Integrated Foundation Year, BA(Hons) Sports Journalism, BA(Hons) Sports Journalism with Integrated Foundation Year, BA(Hons) Journalism, BA(Hons) Journalism with Integrated Foundation Year

Postgraduate: MA Journalism, MA Public Relations, MA Sports Journalism, MA Magazine Journalism, MPhil Master of Philosophy, PhD Doctor of Philosophy, DProf Professional Doctorate, PhD by Existing Published or Creative Work, Higher Doctorate

Design

BA(Hons) Graphic Design, BA(Hons) Fashion Design and Promotion, BA(Hons) Illustration and Design, BA(Hons) Animation and Games Art, BA(Hons) Fashion Product and Promotion via Study Centres, Graphic Design (Top-Up) via Study Centres BA(Hons), BA(Hons) Advertising and Design Via Study Centres, BA(Hons) Animation and Games Art with Integrated Foundation Year, BA(Hons) Fashion Design and Promotion with Integrated Foundation Year, BA(Hons) Graphic Design with Integrated Foundation Year, BA(Hons) Illustration and Design with Integrated Foundation Year

Postgraduate: MA Design, MPhil Master of Philosophy, PhD Doctor of Philosophy, DProf Professional Doctorate, PhD by Existing Published or Creative Work, Higher Doctorate

Media

BA(Hons) Film Production, BA(Hons) Film Production with Integrated Foundation Year, BA(Hons) Media Production, BA(Hons) Media Production with Integrated Foundation Year, BA(Hons) Film and Media, BA(Hons) Film and Media with Integrated Foundation Year, BA(Hons) Media, Culture and Communication, BA(Hons) Media, Culture and Communication with Integrated Foundation Year, BA(Hons) Screen Performance, BA(Hons) Screen Performance Integrated Foundation Year, BA(Hons) Mass Communications (Top-Up)

Postgraduate: MA Radio, MA Media Production (Film and TV), MA Film and Cultural Studies, MA Media and Cultural Studies (Dissertation stage only), MPhil Master of Philosophy, PhD Doctor of

Philosophy, DProf Professional Doctorate, PhD by Existing Published or Creative Work, Higher Doctorate

Performing Arts

BA(Hons) Performing Arts, BA(Hons) Performing Arts with Integrated Foundation Year, BA(Hons) Professional Dance, BA(Hons) Screen Performance, BA(Hons) Screen Performance Integrated Foundation Year, BA(Hons) Music (Top-Up), (Foundation Degree) Applied Music Practice

Postgraduate: MA Advanced Dance Performance, Master of Philosophy, PhD Doctor of Philosophy, DProf Professional Doctorate, PhD by Existing Published or Creative Work, Higher Doctorate

Business & Management

BSc(Hons) Management, BA(Hons) International Business, BA(Hons) International Business with Integrated Foundation Year, BA(Hons) Business and Management, BA(Hons) Business and Management with Integrated Foundation Year, BA(Hons) Business and Financial Management, BA(Hons) Business and Financial Management with Integrated Foundation Year, BA(Hons) Business and Marketing Management, BA(Hons) Business and Marketing Management with Integrated Foundation Year, BA(Hons) Business and Human Resource Management, BA(Hons) Business and Human Resource Management with Integrated Foundation Year, BA(Hons) Business and Economics, BA(Hons) Business and Economics with Integrated Foundation Year, BA(Hons) Accounting and Finance (with Professional Exemptions), BA(Hons) Business Management (Top-Up), BA(Hons) Business and Marketing (Top-Up), BA(Hons) Accounting and Financial Management (Top-Up), BA(Hons) Banking and Finance (Top-Up), BA(Hons) Applied Management, BA(Hons) Applied Investigation

Postgraduate courses: MBA Master of Business Administration with Placement, MBA Master of Business Administration, MBA Master of Business Administration (with PgCert), MBA Master of Business Administration (Cybersecurity), MBA Master of Business Administration (Marketing), MBA Master of Business Administration (Finance), MBA Master of Business Administration (Human Resource Management), MBA Master of Business Administration (Enterprise and Innovation), MBA Master of Business Administration (Supply Chain Management), MBA Master of Business Administration (Hospitality Management), MSc International Business Management, MA Marketing, MA Integrated Marketing Communications, MSc Digital Marketing and Analytics, MSc Finance and Management, MSc Human Resource Management (CIPD Accredited), MA/MSc Extended Award, MA Investigative Management, MBA Global Business/General Management Dual Award, MPhil Master of Philosophy, DProf Professional Doctorate, PhD Doctor of Philosophy, Higher Doctorate, PhD by Existing Published or Creative Work

Law

LLB(Hons) Law, LLB(Hons) Law with Integrated Foundation Year

Postgraduate: LLM Legal Practice, LLM Criminal Law and Procedure, LLM Law, LLM International Human Rights, LLM Commercial Law and International Trade, MPhil Master of Philosophy, PhD Doctor of Philosophy, DProf Professional Doctorate, PhD by Existing Published or Creative Work, Higher Doctorate

Tourism, Hospitality and Events

BSc(Hons) Tourism and Aviation Management, BSc(Hons) Tourism and Aviation Management with Integrated Foundation Year, BSc(Hons) Tourism Management, BA(Hons) Events Management, BSc(Hons) International Tourism and Hospitality Management, BSc(Hons) Tourism Management with Integrated Foundation Year, BSc(Hons) International Tourism and Hospitality Management with Integrated Foundation Year, BA(Hons) Events Management with Integrated Foundation Year, BSc(Hons) International Tourism and Hospitality Management (Top-Up)

Postgraduate: MSc Tourism and Events, MSc Tourism and Hospitality, MSc Tourism and Aviation, Master of Philosophy, PhD Doctor of Philosophy, DProf Professional Doctorate, PhD by Existing Published or Creative Work, Higher Doctorate

Teacher Training & Education

BA(Hons) Education Studies, BA(Hons) Primary Education with QTS, BA(Hons) Education Studies, BSc(Hons) Physics with Mathematics Education (11-16 years) with QTS, BSc(Hons) Mathematics Education (11-16 years) with QTS, BA(Hons) Childhood Studies, Certificate in Post Compulsory Education (PCET) in-service

Postgraduate: PGCE Secondary Religious Education (11-16) with QTS, PGCE Science with Physics Secondary Education, MA Teaching English to Speakers of Other Languages (TESOL) (Independent Distance Learning), MA Education (Full Time),

PGCE Primary Education, PGCE Post Compulsory Education and Training (PCET) Postgraduate Certificate, PGCE English Secondary Education, PGCE Geography Secondary Education, PGCE Science with Biology Secondary Education, PGCE Computer Science Secondary Education, PGCE Science with Chemistry Secondary Education, PGCE Mathematics Education – 1 Year with QTS, PgCert National Awards for Special Education Needs Coordination, PGCE Education, PgCert Leading Provision and Practice for Children with Special Educational Needs and Disabilities (Independent Distance Learning), PGCE Early Years Teaching, Subject Knowledge Enhancement (SKE) Mathematics/ Science Education (Chemistry, Physics, Biology)/ Computer Science, ProfGCE Post Compulsory Education and Training (PCET) Pre-Service, PGCE Post Compulsory Education and Training (PCET) Pre-Service, MA Education, MPhil Master of Philosophy, PhD Doctor of Philosophy, DProf Professional Doctorate, PhD by Existing Published or Creative Work, Higher Doctorate, PGCE Secondary History Education (11-16) with QTS

English

BA(Hons) English, BA(Hons) English with Integrated Foundation Year
Postgraduate: MA English Studies, MPhil Master of Philosophy, PhD Doctor of Philosophy, DProf Professional Doctorate, PhD by Existing Published or Creative Work, Higher Doctorate

History

BA(Hons) History, BA(Hons) History with Integrated Foundation Year, BA(Hons) Politics and History, BA(Hons) Politics and History with Integrated Foundation Year

Postgraduate: MA Historical Research, MPhil Master of Philosophy, PhD Doctor of Philosophy, DProf Professional Doctorate, PhD by Existing Published or Creative Work, Higher Doctorate

Languages

Postgraduate: MA Teaching English to Speakers of Other Languages (TESOL), MPhil Master of Philosophy, PhD Doctor of Philosophy, DProf Professional Doctorate, PhD by Existing Published or Creative Work, Higher Doctorate

Social Sciences

BSc(Hons) Sociology, BSc(Hons) Health and Social Care, BA(Hons) Community and Youth Work Studies, BA(Hons) Social Work, BSc(Hons) Criminology, BA(Hons) Childhood Studies, BSc(Hons) Sociology with Integrated Foundation Year, BSc(Hons) Health and Social Care with Integrated Foundation Year, BSc(Hons) Criminology with Integrated Foundation Year, BA(Hons) Childhood Studies (0-11 years) with Integrated Foundation Year, BA(Hons) Community and Youth Work Studies with Integrated Foundation Year, BA(Hons) Childhood and Society Studies (Top-Up), (Foundation Degree) Education and Care, (Foundation Degree) Health and Social Care, BA(Hons) Social Work, BA(Hons) Community and Youth Work Studies, BSc(Hons) Health and Social Care
Postgraduate: MSc Inequality and Society, MA Social Work, MSc Practice Development, Master of Philosophy, PhD Doctor of Philosophy, DProf Professional Doctorate, PhD by Existing Published or Creative Work, Higher Doctorate

---

SUNDERLAND COLLEGE
www.sunderlandcollege.ac.uk

Applied Music Practice, Counselling, Education & Care, & Fitness, Post Compulsory Education & Training; FdA, FdSc, BSc

---

UNIVERSITY OF SURREY
www.surrey.ac.uk

Accounting & Finance

Accounting and Finance BSc(Hons), Economics and Finance BSc(Hons), Accounting and Finance

Postgraduate: MSc, Economics and Finance MSc, International Corporate Finance MSc, International Financial Management MSc, Investment Management MSc

Biosciences and medicine

Biochemistry BSc(Hons)/MSci(Hons), Biological Sciences BSc(Hons), Biomedical Science BSc(Hons), Food Science and Nutrition BSc(Hons), Microbiology BSc(Hons), Nutrition BSc(Hons), Nutrition and Dietetics BSc(Hons), Sport and Exercise Science BSc(Hons), Veterinary Biosciences BSc(Hons)

Postgraduate: Medical Microbiology MSc, Medical Microbiology (EuroMasters) MSc, Medical Physics MSc, Veterinary Microbiology MSc

Business, marketing and management

Business and Retail Management BSc(Hons), Business Economics BSc(Hons), Business Management BSc(Hons), Business Management (Entrepreneurship) BSc(Hons), Business Management (HRM) BSc(Hons), Business Management (Marketing) BSc(Hons), Business Management and French BSc(Hons), Business Management and Spanish BSc(Hons), International Business Management BSc(Hons)

Postgraduate: Business Analytics MSc, Communication and International Marketing MA, Digital Marketing and Channel Management MSc, Entrepreneurship & Innovation Management MSc, Human Resources Management MSc, International Business Management MSc, International Financial Management MSc, International Marketing MSc, Investment Management MSc, Management MSc, Management Education PGCert, Master of Business Administration MBA, Occupational and Organizational Psychology MSc, Strategic Marketing MSc, Management and Business PhD

Chemical and process engineering

Chemical and Petroleum Engineering BEng(Hons)/MEng, Chemical Engineering BEng(Hons)/MEng

Postgraduate: Batteries, Fuel Cells and Energy Storage Systems MSc, Information and Process Systems Engineering MSc, Petroleum Refining Systems Engineering MSc, Process Systems Engineering MSc, Renewable Energy Systems Engineering MSc, Chemical and Process Engineering Research PhD

Chemistry

Chemistry BSc(Hons) / MChem, Chemistry with Forensic Investigation BSc(Hons)/MChem, Medicinal Chemistry BSc(Hons)/MChem

Postgraduate: Chemistry PhD

Civil and environmental engineering

Civil Engineering BEng(Hons)/MEng

Postgraduate: Advanced Geotechnical Engineering MSc, Bridge Engineering MSc, Civil Engineering MSc, Infrastructure Engineering and Management MSc, Structural Engineering MSc, Water and Environmental Engineering MSc, Civil and Environmental Engineering PhD

Computer games, media and film production

Film and Video Production Technology BSc(Hons)

Postgraduate: Digital Media Arts PhD

Computer science

Computer Science BSc(Hons), Computer Science BSc(Hons)

Postgraduate: Data Science MSc, Information Security MSc, Computer Science PhD

Criminology

Criminology BSc(Hons), Criminology and Sociology BSc(Hons), Law with Criminology LLB(Hons), Sociology BSc(Hons)

Postgraduate: Criminology MSc, Criminology (Corporate Crime and Corporate Responsibility) MSc Criminology (Cybercrime and Cybersecurity) MSc

Economics

Business Economics BSc(Hons), Economics BSc(Hons), Economics and Finance BSc(Hons), Economics and Mathematics BSc(Hons), Politics and Economics BSc(Hons)

Postgraduate: Business Economics and Finance MSc, Economics MSc, Economics MA, Economics MRes, Economics and Finance MSc, International Economics, Finance and Development MSc, Economics PhD

Electrical & Electronic Engineering

Computer and Internet Engineering BEng(Hons)/MEng, Electrical and Electronic Engineering BEng(Hons)/MEng, Electronic Engineering BEng(Hons)/MEng, Electronic Engineering with Computer Systems BEng(Hons)/MEng, Electronic Engineering with Nanotechnology BEng(Hons)/MEng, Electronic Engineering with Space Systems BEng(Hons)/MEng

Postgraduate: 5G and Future Generation Communication Systems MSc, Communications Networks and Software MSc, Computer Vision, Robotics and Machine Learning MSc, Electronic Engineering MSc, Electronic Engineering (EuroMasters) MSc, Medical Imaging MSc, Mobile and Satellite Communications MSc, Mobile Media Communications MSc, Nanotechnology and Renewable Energy MSc, RF and Microwave Engineering MSc, Satellite Communications Engineering MSc, Space Engineering MSc, Advanced Technology Institute PhD Information and Communication Systems PhD, Space Engineering PhD Vision, Speech and Signal Processing PhD

English literature and creative writing

English Literature BA(Hons), English Literature and French BA(Hons), English Literature and Spanish BA(Hons), English Literature with Creative Writing BA(Hons), English Literature with Film Studies BA(Hons), English Literature with German BA(Hons), English Literature with Politics BA(Hons), English Literature with Sociology BA(Hons)

Postgraduate: Creative Writing MA, English Literature MA, Creative Writing PhD, English Literature PhD

Environment and sustainability

Postgraduate: Corporate Environmental Management MSc, Environmental Psychology MSc, Environmental Strategy MSc, Sustainable Development MSc, Water and Environmental Engineering MSc, Environment and Sustainability PhD, Practitioner Doctorate in Sustainability PhD/EngD

Food, nutrition and dietetics

Food Science and Nutrition BSc(Hons), Nutrition BSc(Hons), Nutrition and Dietetics BSc(Hons)

Postgraduate: Human Nutrition MSc, Nutritional Medicine MSc

Health sciences, nursing and midwifery

Healthcare Practice BSc(Hons), Midwifery (Registered Midwife) BSc(Hons), Nursing Studies (Registered Nurse Adult Nursing) BSc(Hons), Nursing Studies (Registered Nurse Children's Nursing) BSc(Hons), Nursing Studies (Registered Nurse Mental Health Nursing) BSc(Hons), Paramedic Science BSc(Hons)

Postgraduate: Advanced Clinical Practice MSc, Advanced Practice (Primary and Community Care) PGCert, Advanced Practice (Public Health Practice) PGCert, Education for Health Professionals PGDip, Education for Health Professionals MA, Education for Health Professionals PGCert, Healthcare Practice MSc, Leadership in Healthcare MSc, Nursing Studies (Registered Nurse – Adult Nursing) PGDip, Nursing Studies (Registered Nurse – Mental Health) PGDip, Physician Associate Studies PGDip, Primary and Community Care (Community Children's Nursing) (SPQ) MSc, Primary and Community Care (District Nursing) (SPQ) MSc, Primary and Community Care (General Practice Nursing) (SPQ) MSc, Public Health Practice (SCPHN) (Health Visiting) MSc, Public Health Practice (SCPHN) (School Nursing) MSc, Health Sciences PhD

Higher Education

Postgraduate: Higher Education MA/PhD

Hospitality, events, tourism and transport

International Event Management BSc(Hons), International Hospitality and Tourism Management BSc(Hons), International Hospitality Management BSc(Hons), International Tourism Management BSc(Hons), International Tourism Management with Transport BSc(Hons)

Postgraduate: Air Transport Management MSc, International Events Management MSc, International Hospitality Management (EuroMasters) MSc, International Hotel Management MSc, International Tourism Management MSc, Strategic Hotel Management MSc, Strategic Tourism Management and Marketing MSc, Hospitality and Tourism Management PhD

Languages, communication, translation and interpreting

Business Management and French BSc(Hons), Business Management and Spanish BSc(Hons), English Literature and French BA(Hons), English Literature and Spanish BA(Hons), English Literature with German BA(Hons), Modern Languages (French and Spanish) BA(Hons), Modern Languages (French with German) BA(Hons), Modern Languages (Spanish with German) BA(Hons)

Postgraduate: Communication and International Marketing MA, Interpreting MA, Interpreting (Chinese Pathway) MA, Teaching English to Speakers of Other Languages (TESOL) MA, Translation MA, Translation and Interpreting MA, Translation and Interpreting Studies MRes, Film Studies PhD, Linguistics PhD, Literary and Cultural Studies PhD, Translation and Interpreting PhD

Law

Law LLB(Hons), Law with Criminology LLB(Hons), Law with International Relations LLB(Hons)

Postgraduate: Law PhD

Mathematics

Economics and Mathematics BSc(Hons), Financial Mathematics BSc(Hons), Mathematics BSc(Hons)/MMath, Mathematics and Physics BSc(Hons)/MPhys/MMath, Mathematics with Music BSc(Hons), Mathematics with Statistics BSc(Hons)/MMath

Postgraduate: Mathematics MSc, Mathematics PhD

Mechanical engineering sciences

Aerospace Engineering BEng(Hons)/MEng, Automotive Engineering BEng(Hons)/MEng, Biomedical

Engineering BEng(Hons)/MEng, Mechanical Engineering BEng(Hons)/MEng

Postgraduate: Biomedical Engineering MSc, Aerodynamic and Environmental Flow PhD, Automotive Engineering PhD, Biomedical Engineering PhD, Engineering Materials PhD, Micro- and NanoMaterials and Technologies EngD

Music and sound recording

Creative Music Technology BMus(Hons), Music BMus(Hons), Music and Sound Recording (Tonmeister) BSc(Hons)/BMus(Hons)

Postgraduate: Music (Composition) MMus, Music (Conducting) MMus, Music (Creative Practice) MMus, Music (Musicology) MMus, Music (Performance) MMus, Music PhD, Sound Recording PhD

Physics

Mathematics and Physics BSc(Hons)/MPhys/MMath, Physics BSc(Hons)/MPhys, Physics with Astronomy BSc(Hons)/MPhys, Physics with Nuclear Astrophysics BSc(Hons)/MPhys, Physics with Quantum Technologies BSc(Hons)/MPhys

Postgraduate: Medical Physics MSc, Nuclear Science and Applications MSc, Physics MSc, Radiation and Environmental Protection MSc, Physics PhD

Politics and international relations

English Literature with Politics BA(Hons), International Relations BSc(Hons), Politics BSc(Hons), Politics and Economics BSc(Hons), Politics and Sociology BSc(Hons), Public Affairs MPA

Postgraduate: International Relations MSc, International Relations (International Intervention) MSc, Public Affairs MSc, Politics PhD

Psychology

Advanced Practice in Psychological Wellbeing Grad Cert, Psychology BSc(Hons)

Postgraduate: Advanced Practice in Psychological Wellbeing PGCert, Developmental Psychology in Research and Practice MSc, Environmental Psychology MSc, Health Psychology MSc, Psychological Intervention (CBT) PGDip, Psychology (Conversion) MSc, Research Methods in Psychology MSc, Social Psychology MSc, Clinical Psychology PsychD, Health Psychology PhD, Psychology PhD

Sociology

Criminology BSc(Hons), Criminology and Sociology BSc(Hons), English Literature with Sociology BA(Hons), Media and Communication BSc(Hons), Politics and Sociology BSc(Hons), Sociology BSc(Hons)

Postgraduate: Criminology MSc, Criminology (Corporate Crime and Corporate Responsibility) MSc, Criminology (Cybercrime and Cybersecurity) MSc, Social Research Methods MSc, Sociology PhD

Sport and Exercise Sciences

Sport and Exercise Science BSc(Hons)

Theatre and performing arts

Acting BA(Hons), Actor-Musician BA(Hons), Musical Theatre BA(Hons), Theatre BA(Hons), Theatre Production BA(Hons)

Postgraduate: Acting MA, Acting MFA, Musical Theatre MA, Musical Theatre MFA, Stage and Production Management MA, Theatre MA, Dance PhD Theatre PhD

Veterinary medicine and science

Veterinary Biosciences BSc(Hons), Veterinary Medicine and Science BVMSci(Hons), Veterinary Microbiology MSc, Veterinary Medicine and Science PhD

FARNBOROUGH COLLEGE OF TECHNOLOGY
www.farn-ct.ac.uk

Business & Psychology, Business Management/ & Computing, Therapeutic Counselling, Computing, Criminology, Early Childhood Studies/Early Years Practice/Learning, Criminology & Sociology, Early Years Education and Practice, Early Years Care and Education, Electronic Engineering, English Literature & Criminology/Sociology/Psyhcology/ Modern Historygraphic Design, Health Care Practice, Hospitality Management, HR Management, Photography, Media Production Film/ Documentary/ Radio/ TV/ Top-up Professional Film Production, Modern History with Criminology/ Psychology/ Sociology, Psychology & Criminology, Sports Science/Human Performance, Sports Coaching, Software Engineering; BA(Hons), BSc(Hons), FdA, FdSc, FdEng, PGEd

NESCOT (NORTH EAST SURREY COLLEGE OF TECHNOLOGY)
www.nescot.ac.uk

Animal Management, Business & Accounting, Computing & IT, Counselling, Creative Media, Early Years and Healthcare Play, Environmental Health (Food Premises), Osteopathic Medicine, Performing Arts, Sports Therapy and Sports Coaching, Teacher Training and Education

ST MARYS UNIVERSITY
www.smuc.ac.uk

Acting BA(Hons) Acting (with a Foundation Year) BA(Hons), Applied Physics BSc(Hons), Applied Sport and Exercise, Business Law BA(Hons), Business Management BA(Hons), Business Management (with a Foundation Year) BA(Hons), Business Management and Entrepreneurship BA(Hons), Chelsea Football Club Foundation Coaching and Development FdSc, Business Management and Entrepreneurship (with a Foundation Year) BA(Hons), Business Management and Finance BA(Hons), Business Management and Finance (with a Foundation Year) BA(Hons), Chelsea Football Club Foundation Coaching and Development (Top-up) BSc(Hons), Communications and Marketing BA(Hons), Communications and Marketing (with a Foundation Year) BA(Hons), Data Analytics and Marketing BA(Hons), Communications, Data Analytics and Marketing (with a Foundation Year) BA(Hons), Communications, Design and Marketing BA(Hons), Communications, Design and Marketing (with a Foundation Year) BA(Hons), Communications, Media and Marketing BA(Hons), Communications, Media and Marketing (with a Foundation Year) BA(Hons), Criminology and Sociology BSc(Hons), Criminology and Sociology (with a Foundation Year) BSc(Hons), Creative and Professional Writing BA(Hons), Creative and Professional Writing (with a Foundation Year) BA(Hons), Creative Media BA(Hons), Drama and Creative Writing BA(Hons), Drama and Education BA(Hons), Education and Social Science BA(Hons), Education and Social Science (with a Foundation Year) BA(Hons), Education in Context FdA, English and Drama BA(Hons), English and Drama (with a Foundation Year) BA(Hons), English Language and Literature BA(Hons), English Literature BA(Hons), English Literature (with a Foundation Year) BA(Hons), Film and Digital Production BA(Hons), Film and Screen Media BA(Hons), Film and Screen Media (with a Foundation Year) BA(Hons), Health and Exercise Science BSc(Hons), History BA(Hons), History (with a Foundation Year) BA(Hons) International Business Management BA(Hons), International Business Management (with a Foundation Year) BA(Hons), Law LLB(Hons), Law (with a Foundation Year) LLB(Hons), Law with Criminology LLB(Hons), Law with Criminology (with a Foundation Year) LLB(Hons), Nutrition BSc(Hons), Nutrition (with a Foundation Year) BSc(Hons), Pastoral Ministry FdA, Physical Education, Sport and Youth Development BA(Hons), Physical Education, Sport and Youth Development (with a Foundation Year) BA(Hons), Politics and Communications BA(Hons), Politics and International Relations BA(Hons), Politics and International Relations (with a Foundation Year) BA(Hons), Politics, Policy and Public Management BA(Hons), Practitioners in Healthcare Ethics, Theology and Care FdA, Primary Education (Work-Based Route) BA(Hons), Primary Education with QTS BA(Hons), Primary Education with QTS (with a Foundation Year) BA(Hons), Primary Education with QTS (Work-Based Route) BA(Hons), Psychology BSc(Hons), Psychology (with a Foundation Year) BSc(Hons), Sport and Exercise Nutrition BSc(Hons), Sport and Exercise Nutrition (with a Foundation Year) BSc(Hons), Sport Psychology BSc(Hons), Sport Psychology (with a Foundation Year) BSc(Hons), Sport Rehabilitation BSc(Hons), Sport Rehabilitation (with a Foundation Year) BSc(Hons), Sport Science BSc(Hons), Sport Science (with a Foundation Year) BSc(Hons), Sports Coaching FdSc, Sports Coaching Science BSc(Hons), Sports Coaching Science (with a Foundation Year) BSc(Hons), Sports Communications and Marketing BA(Hons), Sports Communications and Marketing (with a Foundation Year) BA(Hons), Sports Management BA(Hons), Sports Management (with a Foundation Year) BA(Hons), Strength and Conditioning Science (with a Foundation Year) BSc(Hons), Technical Theatre BA(Hons), Technical Theatre (with a Foundation Year) BA(Hons), Theology, Religion, and Ethics BA(Hons), Theology, Religion, and Ethics (with a Foundation Year) BA(Hons), Tourism BA(Hons), Tourism

Management BA(Hons),Youth Ministry and School Chaplaincy FdA

Postgraduate: Physiology MSc, PGDip, PGCert, Applied Sport Psychology MSc, PGDip, PGCert, Applied Sports Nutrition MSc, PGDip, PGCert, Bioethics and Medical Law MA, PGDip, PGCert, Catholic School Leadership: Principles & Practice MA, Catholic Social Teaching MA, PGDip, PGCert, Charity Management MA, PGDip, PGCert, Christian Spirituality MA, PGDip, PGCert, Chronic Disease Management MSc, PGDip, PGCert, Communications, Creative Writing: First Novel MA, Diplomacy and International Relations MA, PGDip, PGCert, Education, Culture and Society MA, PGDip, PGCert Education: Leading Innovation and Change MA, PGDip, PGCert, Education: Pedagogical Leadership in Physical Education and Sport MA, PGDip, PGCert, Education: Pedagogy MA, PGDip, PGCert, Human Nutrition MSc, PGDip, PGCert, Human Trafficking, Migration and Organised Crime MA, PGCert, PGDip, International and European Business Law LLM, International Business Law LLM, International

Business Management MSc, PGDip, PGCert, International Sports Journalism MA, PGDip, PGCert, London Theatre MA, PGDip, PDCert, Master's in Research: Sport, Health and Applied Science MRes, Mountbatten Institute, International Business Practice MBA (validated by St. Mary's), Nutrition and Genetics MSc, Performance Football Coaching (Distance Learning) MSc, PGDip, PGCert, Physiotherapy (Pre-Registration) MSc, Playwriting MA, PGDip, PGCert, Primary PGCE, Psychology of Mental Health MSc PGDip, PGCert, Public History MA, PGDip, PGCert, Secondary English PGCE, Secondary Geography PGCE, Secondary History PGCE, Secondary Mathematics PGCE, Secondary Modern Foreign Languages (MFL) PGCE, Secondary Physical Education (PE) PGCE, Secondary Religious Education (RE) PGCE, Secondary Science PGCE, Sport Rehabilitation (Pre-Registration) MSc, PGDip, PGCert, Sports Journalism MA, PGDip, PGCert, Strength and Conditioning (Distance Learning) MSc, PGDip, PGCert, Theatre Directing MA, PGDip, PGCert, Theology MA, PGDip, PGCert

UNIVERSITY OF SUSSEX
www.sussex.ac.uk

School of Business, Management and Economics; www.sussex.ac.uk/bmec/

Department of Business and Management

Accounting and finance
Accounting and Finance BSc, Accounting and Finance (with a professional placement year) BSc, Finance BSc, Finance and Business BSc, Finance and Technology BSc, Finance and Technology (with a professional placement year), Finance (with a professional placement year) BSc

Business and Management
Business and Management Studies BSc, Business and Management Studies (with a professional placement year) BSc, International Business BSc, International Business (with a professional placement year) BSc, Marketing and Management BSc, Marketing and Management (with a professional placement year) BSc, Marketing and Management with Psychology BSc, Marketing and Management with Psychology (with a professional placement year) BSc

Postgraduate courses: Master of Business Administration-the Sussex MBA, Banking and Finance MSc, Entrepreneurship and Innovation MSc, Fintec Financial Risk and Investment Analysis MSc, Global

Supply Chain and Logistics Management MSc, Human Resource Management MSc, International Accounting and Corporate Governance MSc, International Management MSc, International Marketing MSc, Management MSc, Management and Finance MSc, Marketing and Consumer Psychology MSc Strategic Innovation Management MSc, Project Management MSc, Strategic Innovation Management MSc, International Marketing MSc, Science, Technology and Energy Policy, Science and Technology Policy MSc, Energy Policy MSc, Energy Policy MSc (online), Accounting PhD, Finance PhD, Management PhD, Department of Economics 2019 PhD programmes, Economics PhD, Science Policy Research Unit (SPRU) 2019 PhD programmes, Science and Technology Policy Studies PhD, Technology and Innovation Management PhD

Department of Economics
Economics BA, Economics (with a professional placement year) BA, Economics BSc, Economics (with a professional placement year) BSc, Economics and Finance BSc, Economics and International Development BA, Economics and International

Relations BA, Economics and Management Studies BSc, Economics and Politics BA

Postgraduate courses: Economics MSc, International Business Economics MSc, International Finance and Economics MSc Economics, finance and accounting MSc, Accounting and Finance MSc

Science Policy Research Unit

Energy Policy MSc, Project Management MSc, Science and Technology Policy MSc, Strategic Innovation Management MSc, Sustainable Development MSc

School of Education and Social Work; www.sussex.ac.uk/esw/

Department of Education and Teaching

Childhood and Youth: Theory and Practice BA, Primary and Early Years Education BA, Psychology with Education BSc

Postgraduate courses: Childhood and Youth Studies MA, Early Years in Education MA, Education MA, Education (Developing Research Leadership in Schools) PGCert English Language Teaching PGDip English Language Teaching MA International Education and Development MA, Media Studies PGCE, Primary PGCE, Secondary Classics PGCE, Secondary Drama PGCE, Secondary English PGCE, Secondary Geography PGCE, Secondary History PGCE, Secondary Mathematics PGCE, Secondary Modern Foreign Languages PGCE, Secondary Music PGCE, Secondary Psychology PGCE, Secondary Science PGCE, Education PhD Physics with Education MSc, Secondary Art and Design PGCE, Secondary Business Studies PGCE, Secondary Computer Science PGCE, Secondary Design Technology PGCE, Secondary English and Drama PGCE, Secondary English and Media Studies PGCE, Secondary Physical Education PGCE, Secondary Religious Education PGCE, Childhood and Youth PhD, Education PhD, International Education and Development PhD

Department of Social Work and Social Care

Social Work BA, Childhood and Youth: Theory and Practice BA

Postgraduate courses: Social Work MA, Childhood and Youth Studies MA, Wellbeing MRes, Social Work & Social Care PhD

School of Engineering and Informatics; www.sussex.ac.uk/ei/

Department of Engineering and Design

Engineering

Automotive Engineering BEng, Automotive Engineering MEng, Automotive Engineering (with an industrial placement year) BEng, Automotive Engineering (with an industrial placement year) MEng, Electrical and Electronic Engineering BEng, Electrical and Electronic Engineering MEng, Electrical and Electronic Engineering (with an industrial placement year) BEng, Electrical and Electronic Engineering (with an industrial placement year) MEng, Mechanical Engineering BEng, Mechanical Engineering MEng, Mechanical Engineering (with an industrial placement year) BEng, Mechanical Engineering (with an industrial placement year) MEng

Postgraduate courses: Advanced Mechanical Engineering MSc, 5G Mobile Communications and Intelligent Embedded Systems (with an industrial placement year) MSc, 5G Mobile Communications and Intelligent Embedded Systems MSc, Digital Signal and Image Processing MSc, Engineering Business Management MSc, Robotics and Autonomous Systems MSc, Robotics and Autonomous Systems (with a Masters industrial placement) MSc, Robotics and Autonomous Systems (with an industrial placement year) MSc, PhD study

Product Design

Product Design BSc, Product Design (with an industrial placement year) BSc

Informatics

Computer Science BSc, Computer Science MComp, Computer Science (with an industrial placement year) BSc, Computer Science (with an industrial placement year) MComp, Computer Science and Artificial Intelligence BSc, Computer Science and Artificial Intelligence (with an industrial placement year) BSc, Computing for Business and Management BSc, Computing for Business and Management (with an industrial placement year) BSc, Computing for Digital Media BSc, Computing for Digital Media (with an industrial placement year) BSc, Games and Multimedia Environments (GAME) BSc, Games and Multimedia Environments (GAME) (with an industrial placement year) BSc

Postgraduate courses: Advanced Computer Science MSc, Computing with Digital Media MSc, Human-Computer Interaction MSc, Information Technology with Business and Management MSc, Intelligent and Adaptive Systems MSc, Management of Information

Technology MSc, Cognitive Science PhD, Informatics PhD

School of English; www.sussex.ac.uk/english/

American Studies and English (with a study abroad year) BA, Drama and English BA, Drama and Film Studies BA, Drama with a Language BA, Drama, Theatre and Performance BA, English and Art History BA, English and Film Studies BA, English and History BA, English and Media Studies BA, English BA, English Language and Linguistics BA, English Language and Literature BA, Philosophy and English BA

Postgraduate courses: Masters in Literature, Theory and Culture, Modern and Contemporary Literature, Applied Linguistics, Creative and Critical Writing, Sexual Dissidence, PhD study

School of Global Studies; www.sussex.ac.uk/global/

Department of Anthropology
www.sussex.ac.uk/anthropology/

Anthropology BA, Anthropology and Cultural Studies BA, Anthropology and History BA, Anthropology and International Development BA, Anthropology with a Language BA, Geography and Anthropology BA, Geography and Anthropology MArts, International Relations and Anthropology BA
Postgraduate courses: Anthropology of Development and Social Transformation MA, Social Research Methods MSc, PhD studies

Department of Geography
www.sussex.ac.uk/geography/

Geography BA, Geography BSc, Geography and Anthropology BA, Geography and International Development BA, Geography with a Language BA
Postgraduate courses: Climate Change, Development and Policy MSc, Migration and Global Development MA, Social Research Methods MSc, African Studies PhD, Geography PhD, Migration Studies PhD

Department of International Development
www.sussex.ac.uk/development/

Anthropology and International Development BA, Economics and International Development BA, Geography and International Development BA, International Development BA, International Development with a Language BA, International Relations and Development BA, Sociology and International Development BA

Postgraduate courses: Africa and Development MA Anthropology of Development and Social Transformation MA Climate Change, Development and Policy MSc Conflict, Security and Development MA, Development Studies MA, Environment, Development and Policy MA, Food & Development MA Gender and Development MA, Gender, Violence and Conflict MA, Globalisation, Business and Development MA, Governance and Development MA, Human Rights MA, International Education and Development MA, Media Practice for Development and Social Change MA, Migration and Global Development MA Migration Studies MA, Poverty and Development MA, Sexual Dissidence MA, Social Anthropology MA, Social Development MA, Social Research Methods MSc, Development Studies (IDS) PhD, Human Rights PhD African Studies PhD International Development (Global Studies) PhD Migration Studies PhD Social Anthropology PhD

Department of International Relations
www.sussex.ac.uk/ir/

Economics and International Relations BA, Geography and International Relations BA, International Relations BA, International Relations and a Language (with a study abroad year) BA, International Relations and Anthropology BA, International Relations and Development BA, International Relations and Sociology BA, International Relations with a Language BA, Law with International Relations LLB, Politics and International Relations BA
Postgraduate courses: Conflict, Security and Development MA, Geopolitics and Grand Strategy MA, Global Political Economy MA, International Relations MA, International Security MA, Social Research Methods MSc, International Relations PhD

School of History, Art History and Philosophy; www.sussex.ac.uk/hahp/

Department of History

American Studies and History (with a study abroad year) BA, Anthropology and History BA, English and History BA, English and History (with a study abroad year) BA, History BA, History and Film Studies BA, History and Philosophy BA, History and Politics BA, History and Sociology BA
Postgraduate courses: Contemporary History MA, Intellectual History MA, Contemporary History PhD, History PhD, Intellectual History PhD

Department of Art History

Art History BA, Art History (with a professional placement year) BA, Art History and Film Studies BA, English and Art History BA, English and Art History (with a study abroad year) BA

Postgraduate courses: Art History MA, Art History and Museum Curating MA, Art History and Museum Curating with Photography MA Art History PhD Photography: History, Theory, Practice MA, Heritage MA

Department of Philosophy

History and Philosophy BA, Philosophy BA, Philosophy and English BA, Philosophy and Sociology BA, Politics and Philosophy BA, Philosophy, Politics and Economics (PPE) BA

Postgraduate courses: Literature and Philosophy MA, Philosophy MA, Social and Political Thought MA, Philosophy PhD, Social and Political Thought PhD

Sussex Centre for American Studies

American Studies (with a study abroad year) BA, American Studies and English (with a study abroad year) BA, American Studies and Film Studies (with a study abroad year) BA, American Studies and History (with a study abroad year) BA, American Studies and Politics (with a study abroad year) BA, Law with American Studies (with a study abroad year) LLB

Postgraduate courses: Critical American Studies MA, American History PhD, American Literature PhD

School of Law, Politics and Sociology; www.sussex.ac.uk/lps/

Department of Law

Law LLB, Law (Graduate Entry) LLB, Law with a Language LLB, Law with a Language (with a study abroad year) LLB, Law with American Studies (with a study abroad year) LLB, Law with Business and Management LLB, Law with Criminology LLB, Law with International Relations LLB, Law with Media LLB, Law with Politics LLB

Postgraduate courses: Corruption, Law and Governance (delivered in Qatar) LLM, Criminal Law and Criminal Justice LLM, Criminology and Criminal Justice MA, Graduate Diploma in Law/Common Professional Examination (CPE) Dip(Grad), Information Technology and Intellectual Property Law LLM, International Commercial and Trade Law LLM, International Criminal Law LLM, International Financial Law LLM, International Human Rights Law LLM, International Law LLM, International Trade Law LLM, Law LLM, Social Research Methods MSc, Law Studies PhD

Department of Politics

American Studies and Politics (with a study abroad year) BA, Economics and Politics BA, History and Politics BA, Law with Politics LLB, Philosophy, Politics and Economics (PPE) BA, Politics BA, Politics and International Relations BA, Politics and Philosophy BA, Politics and Sociology BA

Postgraduate courses: Corruption and Governance MA, Social Research Methods MSc, Contemporary European Studies PhD, Politics PhD

Department of Sociology

Sociology

History and Sociology BA, International Relations and Sociology BA, Philosophy and Sociology BA, Politics and Sociology BA, Sociology BA, Sociology and Cultural Studies BA, Sociology and International Development BA, Sociology and Media Studies BA, Sociology with a Language BA

Postgraduate courses: Criminology and Criminal Justice MA, Gender Studies MA, Social Research Methods MSc, Sociology PhD, Gender Studies (Social Sciences) PhD

Criminology

Criminology BA, Law with Criminology LLB, Criminology and Sociology BA, Psychology with Criminology BSc

School of Life Sciences; www.sussex.ac.uk/lifesci/

Biochemistry and Biomedicine

Biochemistry BSc, Biochemistry MSci, Biochemistry (with an industrial placement year) BSc, Biomedical Science BSc, Biomedical Science MSci, Biomedical Science (research placement) MSci, Genetics BSc, Genetics MSci

Postgraduate courses: Genetic Manipulation and Molecular Cell Biology MSc, Cancer Cell Biology MSc, Biochemistry PhD

Chemistry

BSc/MChem Chemistry Chemistry (with an industrial placement year) MChem Chemistry with Summer Research Placements MChem

Postgraduate courses: Chemistry PhD

Evolution, Behaviour and Environment

Biology BSc, Biology MSci, Ecology, Conservation and Environment BSc, Ecology, Conservation and

Environment MSci, Genetics BSc, Genetics MSci, Zoology BSc, Zoology MSci

Postgraduate courses: Animal Behaviour MRes, Conservation Biology MRes, Evolutionary Biology MRes, Global Biodiversity Conservation MSc, Biology PhD

Neuroscience

Medical Neuroscience BSc, Medical Neuroscience MSci, Neuroscience BSc, Neuroscience MSci, Neuroscience with Cognitive Science BSc, Neuroscience with Cognitive Science MSci, Psychology with Neuroscience BSc

Postgraduate courses: Neuroscience MRes, Neuroscience MSc, Neuroscience PhD, Sussex Neuroscience 4-Year PhD Programme

School of Mathematical and Physical Sciences; www.sussex.ac.uk/mps/

Department of Mathematics

Mathematics BSc, Mathematics MMath, Mathematics (research placement) MMath, Mathematics with Economics BSc, Mathematics with Economics MMath, Mathematics with Finance BSc, Mathematics with Finance MMath

Postgraduate courses: Corporate and Financial Risk Management MSc, Data Science MSc, Financial Mathematics MSc, Mathematics MSc, Mathematics PhD

Department of Physics and Astronomy

Astrophysics MPhys, Physics BSc, Physics MPhys, Physics (research placement) MPhys, Physics (with an industrial placement year) BSc, Physics (with an industrial placement year) MPhys, Physics with Astrophysics BSc, Physics with Astrophysics MPhys, Theoretical Physics BSc, Theoretical Physics MPhys

Postgraduate courses: Astronomy MSc, Cosmology MSc, Particle Physics MSc, Physics MSc, Physics with Education MSc Quantum Technology MSc Secondary Science with Physics PGCE, Astronomy PhD, Physics PhD

School of Media, Film and Music www.sussex.ac.uk/mfm/

Cultural Studies

Anthropology and Cultural Studies BA, Media and Cultural Studies BA, Sociology and Cultural Studies BA

Postgraduate courses: Cultural and Creative Industries MA Media and Cultural Studies MA, Gender Studies (Humanities) PhD

Film Studies

American Studies and Film Studies (with a study abroad year) BA, Art History and Film Studies BA, Drama and Film Studies BA, Drama and Film Studies (with a study abroad year) BA English and Film Studies BA, Film Studies BA, Filmmaking BA, Media Production BA

Postgraduate courses: Film Studies MA, Film Studies PhD

Journalism

Journalism BA

Postgraduate courses: International Journalism MA, Journalism and Documentary Practice MA, Journalism and Media Studies MA, Journalism Studies PhD

Media and Communications

English and Media Studies BA, English and Media Studies (with a study abroad year) BA, Global Media and Communications (with a study abroad year) BA, Law with Media LLB, Media and Communications BA, Media and Communications (with a partnership year in Hong Kong) BA-2020 entry Media and Cultural Studies BA, Sociology and Media Studies BA

Postgraduate courses: Digital Media MA, Gender and Media MA, Media and Cultural Studies MA, Digital Media PhD, Media and Communications PhD

Media Practice

Filmmaking BA, Media Production BA

Postgraduate courses: Digital Documentary MA, Filmmaking MA, Media Practice for Development and Social Change MA, Media, Film and Music by Published Works PhD, Creative and Critical Practice PhD

Music

Music BA, Music Technology BA

Postgraduate courses: Music and Sonic Media MA, Music PhD, Musical Composition PhD, Music Theatre PhD

School of Psychology; www.sussex.ac.uk/psychology/

Marketing and Management with Psychology BSc, Marketing and Management with Psychology (with a professional placement year) BSc, Psychology BSc, Psychology (with a professional placement year) BSc, Psychology with Business and Management BSc,

Psychology with Clinical Approaches BSc, Psychology with Cognitive Science BSc, Psychology with Criminology BSc, Psychology with Economics BSc, Psychology with Education BSc, Psychology with Neuroscience BSc

Postgraduate courses: Applied Social Psychology MSc, Cognitive Neuroscience MSc, Experimental Psychology MSc, Foundations of Clinical Psychology and Mental Health MSc, Low-Intensity Psychological Interventions for Children and Young People PGCert, Mental Health Practice PGCert, Psychological Methods MRes, Psychological Therapy PGDip, Psychology PhD

Brighton and Sussex Medical School;
www.bsms.ac.uk/index.aspx

Bachelor of Medicine Bachelor of Surgery (BM BS)

Postgraduate courses: Anaesthesia and Perioperative Medicine, Cardiology, Clinical Professional Studies Clinical Radiology, Clinical Education, Dementia Studies, Diabetes in Primary Care, Global health, Global Pharmacy, Internal Medicine, Healthcare Leadership and Commissioning, Medical Education, Medical Research, Paediatrics and Child Health, Physician Associate Studies, Psychiatry, Public Health Simulation in Clinical Practice, Surgical Studies

SWANSEA UNIVERSITY
www.swansea.ac.uk

College of Arts & Humanities;
www.swansea.ac.uk/undergraduate/
courses/artsandhumanities/

Department of Adult Continuing Education

BA Humanities

American Studies

BA American Studies, BA American Studies and English Literature, BA American Studies and Geography, BA American Studies and History, BA American Studies and International Relations with a Year Abroad, BA American Studies and Politics, LLB Law and American Studies, BA American Studies with Foundation Year

Classics, Ancient History and Egyptology

BA Ancient History, BA Classical Civilisation, BA Classics, BA Egyptology, BA Ancient History and English Literature, BA Ancient History and French with a Year Abroad, BA Ancient History and German with a Year Abroad, BA Ancient History and Greek, BA Ancient History and History, BA Ancient History and Latin, BA Ancient History and Politics, BA Ancient History and Spanish with a Year Abroad, BA Ancient and Medieval History, BA Classical Civilisation and English Literature, BA Classical Civilisation and French with a Year Abroad, BA Classical Civilisation and German with a Year Abroad, BA Classical Civilisation and Greek, BA Classical Civilisation and Latin, BA Classical Civilisation and Medieval Studies, BA Egyptology and Ancient History, BA Egyptology and Classical Civilisation, BA(Hons) Classical Civilisation with Foundation Year, BA(Hons) Classics with Foundation Year,

BA(Hons) Egyptology with Foundation Year, BA(Hons) Ancient History with Foundation Year

Postgraduate: Ancient Egyptian Culture, Ancient History and Classical Culture, Ancient Narrative Literature, Classics

Department of Welsh

BA Welsh – First Language, BA Welsh – Second Language, BA Welsh with a year in industry, BA Welsh (second language) with a year in industry, BA Welsh: Language, Law and Policy, First Language Joint Honours Degree Courses, BA Welsh and French, BA Welsh and English Literature (1st Language), BA Welsh and German, BA Welsh and History, BA Welsh and Media, BA Welsh and Politics, BA Welsh and Spanish, LLB Law and Welsh, Second Language Joint Honours Degree Courses, BA Welsh and English Literature, BA Welsh and French, BA Welsh and German, BA Welsh and History, BA Welsh and Media Studies, BA Welsh and Politics, BA Welsh and Spanish, LLB Law and Welsh

Education

BA Education, BA Education with Foundation Year, BA Early Childhood Studies, BA Early Childhood Studies with Early Years Practitioner Status, BA Early Childhood Studies with Early Years Practitioner Status with a Foundation Year, BSc Education and Computing, BSc Education and Mathematics, BSc Education and Psychology, BA Education and Welsh

English Language and TESOL

BA English Language, BA English Language and TESOL, BA English Language and English Literature, BA English Language and Media, BA English Language and French with a Year Abroad, BA

English Language and German with a Year Abroad, BA English Language and Spanish with a Year Abroad, BSc Applied Linguistics and English Language, BA TESOL and English Literature, BA TESOL and French with a Year Abroad, BA TESOL and German with a year abroad, BA TESOL and Spanish with a Year Abroad, BA TESOL and English Literature with a Year Abroad, BA(Hons) English Language with Foundation Year,

Postgraduate: MA English Literature, Chinese-English Translation & Language Teaching, Teaching English to Speakers of Other Languages (TESOL)

English Literature and Creative Writing

BA English Literature, BA English Literature and Ancient History, BA English Literature and American Studies, BA English Literature and Classical Civilisation, BA English Literature and English Language, BA English Literature and French with a Year Abroad, BA English with Gender, BA English Literature and German with a Year Abroad, BA English Literature and History, BA English Literature and Italian with a Year Abroad, BA English Literature and Media, BA English Literature and Medieval Studies, BA English Literature and Politics, BA English Literature and Spanish with a Year Abroad, BA English Literature and Welsh (First language), BA English Literature and Welsh (second language), BA TESOL and English Literature with a Year Abroad, BA(Hons) English Literature with Foundation Year, BA(Hons) English Literature and Creative Writing with Foundation Year,

Postgraduate: Creative Writing, MA Creative Writing (Extended), English Literature, Welsh Writing in English

History and Medieval Studies

BA History, BA Medieval Studies, BA(Hons) History with Foundation Year, LLB Law and History, BA History and Social Policy, BA Modern History and International Relations, BA Italian and History with a Year Abroad, BA History and Welsh (second language), BA History and Welsh (first language), BA History and Spanish with a Year Abroad, BA History and Politics, BA History and Medieval Studies, BA History and German with a Year Abroad, BA History and French with a Year Abroad, BA History and Italian with a year abroad, BA History and English Literature, BA History and Ancient History, BA History and American Studies, BA Ancient and Medieval History, BA Medieval Studies and Classical Civilisation, BA Medieval Studies and English Literature, BA Medieval Studies and History, BA

Medieval Studies and History with a Year Abroad, BA Medieval Studies with Foundation Year

Postgraduate: Early Modern History, History, Medieval Studies, Modern History, Public History and Heritage, Public History and Heritage (extended)

Media, Communication and Public Relations

BA Media and Communication, BA Public Relations and Media, BA Cymraeg, Cyfryngau a Chysylltiadau Cyhoeddus, BA Media and English Literature, BA Media and Welsh, BA English Language and Media, BA Media and French with a Year Abroad, BA Media and German with a Year Abroad, BA Media and Spanish with a Year Abroad, BA Media and Communication with Foundation Year, BA Public Relations and Media with Foundation Year,

Postgraduate: Communication, Media Practice and PR, International Journalism, Digital Media, Erasmus Mundus Journalism, Media and Globalisation

Modern Languages, Translation and Interpreting

BA Modern Languages with a year abroad (French, German, Mandarin and Spanish), BA Modern Languages, Translation and Interpreting with a year abroad, BA English-Chinese Translation and Interpreting, BA Ancient History and French with a Year Abroad, BA Ancient History and German with a Year Abroad, BA Ancient History and Spanish with a Year Abroad, BA Classical Civilisation and French with a Year Abroad, BA Classical Civilisation and German with a Year Abroad, BA English Language and Spanish with a Year Abroad, BA English Language and German with a Year Abroad, BA English Language and French with a Year Abroad, BA TESOL and Spanish with a Year Abroad, BA TESOL and German with a year abroad, BA TESOL and French with a Year Abroad, BA English Literature and French with a Year Abroad, BA English Literature and German with a Year Abroad, BA English Literature and Spanish with a Year Abroad, BA History and French with a Year Abroad, BA History and German with a Year Abroad, BA History and Spanish with a Year Abroad, BA Media and French with a Year Abroad, BA Media and German with a Year Abroad, BA Media and Spanish with a Year Abroad, BA Politics and French, BA Politics and German, BA Politics and Spanish, Law and Spanish, LLB(Hons)

Postgraduate: Professional Translation, Professional Translation (Extended), Translation and Interpreting, Translation and Interpreting (Extended), Postgraduate Certificate in Translation Technology

Political and Cultural Studies

BA Politics, BA International Relations, BA Philosophy, Philosophy, Politics and Economics, BA International Relations and American Studies, BA International, Relations (with French), BA International Relations (with German), BA International Relations and Modern History, BA International Relations (with Spanish), BA Politics and American Studies, BA Politics and Ancient History, BA Politics and English Literature, BA Politics and French, BA Politics and German, BA Politics and History, BA Politics and Social Policy, BA Politics and Spanish, BA Politics and Welsh (first language), BA Politics and Welsh (second language), LLB Law and Politics, BA Politics with Foundation Year, BA International Relations with Foundation Year

Postgraduate: Development and Human Rights, International Relations, MA International Relations (Extended), International Security & Development, MA International Security and Development (Extended), Politics, Public Policy, MA Public Policy (Extended)

War and Society

BA War and Society BA(Hons) War and Society with Foundation Year

Postgraduate: War and Society

College of Engineering

Aerospace

BEng Aerospace Engineering, MEng Aerospace Engineering, BEng Aerospace Engineering (with a Year abroad/ in Industry), MEng Aerospace Engineering (with a Yeara broad/in Industry)

Chemical

BEng Chemical Engineering, MEng Chemical Engineering, BEng Chemical Engineering (with a Year abroad/in Industry), MEng Chemical Engineering (with a Year abroad/in Industry)

Civil

BEng Civil Engineering, MEng Civil Engineering, BEng Civil Engineering (with a Year in Industry), MEng Civil Engineering (with a Year in Industry)

Electronic and Electrical

BEng Electronic and Electrical Engineering, MEng Electronic and Electrical Engineering, BEng Electronic and Electrical Engineering (with a year abroad or industry), MEng Electronic and Electrical Engineering (with a year in Europe, N. America, Australia or industry)

Foundation Year

Engineering Foundation Year, Aerospace Engineering Foundation Year, Chemical Engineering Foundation Year, Civil Engineering Foundation Year, Electrical and Electronic Engineering Foundation Year, Materials Science and Engineering Foundation Year, Mechanical Engineering Foundation Year, Medical Engineering Foundation Year

Materials

BEng Materials Science and Engineering, MEng Materials Science and Engineering, BEng Materials Science and Engineering (with a Year abroad/in Industry), MEng Materials Science and Engineering (with a Year abroad/ in Industry)

Mechanical

BEng Mechanical Engineering, MEng Mechanical Engineering, BEng Mechanical Engineering (with a Year abroad/in Industry), MEng Mechanical Engineering (with a Year abroad/in Industry)

Medical

BEng Medical Engineering, MEng Medical Engineering, BEng Medical Engineering (with a Year abroad/ in Industry), MEng Medical Engineering (with a Year abroad/in Industry)

Postgraduate: Aerospace Engineering, MSc Chemical Engineering, MSc Civil Engineering, MSc Communications Engineering, MSc Computational Mechanics, MSc Computer Modelling and Finite Elements in Engineering Mechanics, MSc Electronic and Electrical Engineering, MSc Engineering Leadership and Management, MSc Materials Engineering, MSc Mechanical Engineering, MSc Nanoscience to Nanotechnology, MSc Power Engineering and Sustainable Energy, MSc Sports Ethics and Integrity, MA Structural Engineering, MSc Sustainable Engineering Management for International Development, MSc

College of Human and Health Sciences

Healthcare Science

Healthcare Science (Audiology), BSc(Hons), Healthcare Science (Cardiac Physiology), BSc(Hons), Healthcare Science (Nuclear Medicine), BSc(Hons), Healthcare Science (Neurophysiology), BSc(Hons), Healthcare Science (Radiotherapy Physics), BSc(Hons), Healthcare Science (Radiation Physics), BSc(Hons), Healthcare Science (Respiratory and Sleep Physiology), BSc(Hons)

Nursing and Midwifery

Adult Nursing, Swansea BSc(Hons), Adult Nursing (Carmarthen campus) BSc(Hons), Child Nursing BSc(Hons), Mental Health Nursing, Swansea BSc(Hons), Maternity Care CertHE, Maternity Care (part-time) CertHE, Midwifery BMid

Osteopathy

Osteopathy, M.Ost

Paramedic Science

Paramedic Science, DipHE

Psychology

Criminology & Psychology BSc(Hons), Psychology, BSc(Hons) Education and Psychology, BSc(Hons) Sociology and Psychology, BSc(Hons) Education and Psychology BSc(Hons), Sociology and Psychology BSc(Hons)

Society and Wellbeing

Health and Social Care, BSc(Hons), Criminology & Social Policy, BSc, History and Social Policy, BA Politics & Social Policy, BA, Social Policy, BSc(Hons), Social Sciences, BSc(Hons), Sociology, BSc(Hons) Sociology and Social Policy, BSc(Hons) Social Work, BSc(Hons)

Postgraduate courses: MSc/PGCert/PGDip Gerontology and Ageing Studies, MA/PGDip/PGCert Childhood Studies, MA/PGDip/PGCert Developmental and Therapeutic Play, PGCert Enhanced Neonatal Care, MSc/PGDip/PGCert Child Public Health, MA/PGDip/PGCert Education for Health Professions, MSc/ PGDip Advanced Practice in Health Care, MSc/ PGDip/PGCert Advanced Specialist Blood Transfusion Practice, PGCert Approved Mental Health Professional, PGCert Blood Component Transfusion, MSc/PgD/PgC Community and Primary Health Care Practice, MSc/PGDip/PGCert Enhanced Professional Practice, MSc/PGDip Enhanced Professional Midwifery Practice, MSc Long Term and Chronic Conditions Management, PGCert Non-Medical Prescribing for Nurses and Midwives, PGCert Non-Medical Prescribing for Allied Health Professionals, PGCert Non-Medical Prescribing for Pharmacists, MSc Nursing Pre-Registration (Adult), MSc Nursing Pre-Registration (Child), MSc Nursing Pre-Registration (Mental Health), MSc/PgD Public Health & Health Promotion, MSc Social Work, MSc Health Care Management, MSc Abnormal and Clinical Psychology, MSc Research Methods in Psychology and Cognitive Neuroscience, MSc Research Methods in Psychology, MSc Social Research Methods, MPhil and PhDs

Hillary Rodham Clinton School of Law; *www.swansea.ac.uk/law*

BSc Criminology & Criminal Justice, BSc Criminology & Psychology, BSc Criminology & Social Policy, LLB Law and Criminology, LLB Single Honours Law, LLB Law (Crime and Criminal Justice), LLB Business Law, LLB Law Senior Status, Joint Honours Law Degrees: LLB Law and American Studies LLB Law and Criminology LLB Law and History LLB Law and Politics LLB Law and Spanish LLB law and Welsh Postgraduate courses: MA Applied Criminal Justice & Criminology, MA Global Challenges: Law, Policy and Practice MA Cyber Crime & Terrorism LLM in LegalTech LLM in Human Rights, LLM Intellectual Property & Commercial Practice, LLM in International Commercial Law, LLM in International Commercial and Maritime Law, LLM in International Maritime Law, LLM in International Trade Law, LLM in Legal Practice and Advanced Drafting, LLM in Oil, Gas and Renewable Energy Law, Law PhD/MPhil

College of Science www.swansea.ac.uk/ *science*

Department of biosciences

BSc Biology, BSc Biological Sciences (with deferred specialisation), BSc Marine Biology, BSc Zoology, BSc Biology (with Integrated Foundation), BSc Biology with a Year in Industry, BSc Marine Biology with a Year in Industry, BSc Zoology with a Year in Industry;

Postgraduate courses: MSc Environmental Biology: Conservation and Resource Management MRes Biosciences, PhD/MPhil Biological Sciences

Department of Computer Science

BSc Computer Science, MSci Computer Science, BSc Software Engineering, MEng Computing, BSc Computer Science (including Foundation Year), BSc Computer Science with a Year in Industry/abroad BSc Software Engineering with a Year in Industry/abroad MEng Computing with a Year in Industry, MSci Computer Science with a Year in Industry/abroad BSc Education and Computing

Postgraduate courses: MSc Computer Science, MSc Advanced Computer Science, MSc Advanced Software Technology, MSc High Performance and Scientific Computing, MSc Data Science, MSc Computer Science: Informatique (Swansea route), MSc Computer Science: Informatique (Grenoble route), MSc by Research in Human Computer Interaction, MSc by Research in Theoretical Computer Science, MSc by Research in Visual and Interactive Computing, MRes Computing and Future Interaction Technologies, MRes Visual Computing, MRes Logic and Computation, PhD/MPhil/ MSc by Research in Computer Science

Department of Chemistry

BSc Chemistry, BSc Chemistry with a Foundation Year/ Year Abroad/ Year in Industry, MChem Chemistry

Postgraduate research degrees also available

Department of Geography

BA Geography, BSc Geography, BA Human Geography, BSc Physical Geography, BSc Geography (with Integrated Foundation), BSc Physical Earth Science, BSc Geography and Geo-Informatics

Postgraduate courses: MSc Environmental Dynamics and Climate Change, MSc Geographic Information and Climate Change, MSc by Research in Earth Observation, MSc by Research in Environmental Dynamics, MSc by Research in Glaciology, MSc by Research in Global Environmental Modelling, MSc by Research in Global Migration, MSc by Research in Media Geographies, MSc by Research in Social Theory and Space, MSc by Research in Urban Studies, PhD/MPhil Human Geography, PhD/MPhil Physical Geography

Department of Mathematics

MMath Mathematics, BSc Mathematics, BSc Pure Mathematics, BSc Applied Mathematics, BSc Mathematics (with Integrated Foundation), BSc Mathematics with a Year in Industry, BSc Mathematics for Finance with a Year in Industry, BSc Mathematics and Sport and Exercise Science BSc Education and Mathematics

Postgraduate courses: MSc Maths & Computing for Finance, MSc Mathematics, MRes Stochastic Processes: Theory and Application, PhD/MSc by Research in Mathematics MPhil Mathematics

Department of Physics

BSc Physics, BSc Physics (with Integrated Foundation), BSc with a Year Abroad, BSc Theoretical Physics, BSc Physics with Particle Physics and Cosmology, BSc Physics with a Year in Industry, BSc Theoretical Physics with a Year in Industry, MPhys Physics, MPhys with a Year Abroad, MPhys Theoretical Physics, MPhys Theoretical Physics with a Year in Industry, MPhys Physics with a Year in Industry

Postgraduate courses: MSc by Research Degrees Applied Physics and Materials Theoretical Physics Experimental Physics PhDs and MPhils available

Swansea University Medical School

BSc Applied Medical Sciences, BSc Applied Medical Sciences (with a Foundation Year), Biochemistry BSc, Genetics BSc, MSci Biochemistry, MSci Genetics, BSc Medical Biochemistry, BSc Medical Genetics, BSc Biochemistry and Genetics, MSci Medical Biochemistry, MSci Medical Genetics, MSci Biochemistry and Genetics Medical Pharmacology, BSc(Hons) BSc Population Health and Medical Sciences Medicine (Graduate Entry), MBBCh

Postgraduate courses: PG Dip Physician Associate Studies, MSc Nanomedicine, MSc Clinical Science (Medical Physics), Diabetes Practice, MSc/PGDip/PGCert Genomic Medicine, MSc/PGDip/PGCert MSc Medical Radiation Physics, MSc Health Informatics, MSc Applied Analytical Science(LCMS), MSc Health Data Science, MSc Leadership for the Health Professions, MSc Medical Education, MRes Applied Analytical Science (LCMS), MRes Health Informatics, MRes Life Science and Healthcare Enterprise, MRes Medicine and Life Sciences, DProf/MRes Research in Health Professions Education; Postgraduate research degrees available

School of Management; www.swansea.ac.uk/som

Accounting and Finance

BSc Accounting & Finance, BSc Accounting, BSc Finance

Postgraduate courses: MSc Accounting & Finance, MSc Finance and Big Data Analytics MSc Financial Management, MSc Finance, MSc International Banking & Finance, MSc Investment Management, MSc Strategic Accounting

Business

BSc Business Management BSc Business Management with a Foundation Year BSc Business Management (Business Analytics) BSc Business Management (Business Analytics) with a Foundation Year BSc Business Management (e-business) BSc Business Management (e-business) with a Foundation Year BSc Business Management (Entrepreneurship) BSc Business Management (Entrepreneurship) with a Foundation Year BSc Business Management (Finance) BSc Business Management (Finance) with a Foundation Year BSc Business Management (Human Resource Management) BSc Business Management (Human Resource Management) with a Foundation Year BSc Business Management (Management Consulting) BSc Business Management (Management Consulting) with a Foundation Year BSc Business Management (Marketing) BSc Business Management (Marketing) with a Foundation Year BSc Business Management (Operations and Supply Management) BSc Business Management (Operations and Supply

Management) with a Foundation Year BSc Business Management (Tourism) BSc Business Management (Tourism) with a Foundation Year
Postgraduate: MSc Management MSc Management (Business Analytics) MSc Management (E-Business) MSc Management (Entrepreneurship) MSc Management (Finance) MSc Management (Human Resource Management) MSc Management (International Management) MSc Management (Marketing) MSc Management (Operations and Supply Management) MSc Management (Tourism) MSc by Research Business Management PhD/MPhil

Economics

BSc Economics, with a Foundation Year/Year in Industry/Year Abroad BSc Economics and Business, with a Foundation Year/Year in Industry/Year Abroad BSc Economics and Finance; with a Foundation Year/Year in Industry/Year Abroad
Postgraduate degrees: MSc Economics, MSc Economics & Finance Economics PhD/MPhil

Marketing

BSc Business Management (Marketing), BSc Business Management (Marketing) with a Foundation Year BSc Marketing
Postgraduate courses: MSc Management (Marketing), PhD, MSc Strategic Marketing

UNIVERSITY OF TEESSIDE
www.tees.ac.uk

School of Computing and Digital Technologies; www.tees.ac.uk/schools/scm/

Arts

BA(Hons) Comics, Graphic Novels, Contemporary Fashion, FdA Design For the Creative Industries, BA(Hons) Fashion Design, BA(Hons) Fashion Enterprise, BA(Hons) Fine Arts, BA(Hons) Graphic Design, BA(Hons) Interior Design, BA(Hons) Textile Design, BA(Hons) Product Design and Innovation
Postgraduate courses in MA Fine Art, MA Digital Arts And Design, MA Future Design

Computer Animation and Visual Effects

2D Animation BA(Hons), Computer Animation BA(Hons), Computer Animation and Visual Effects BA(Hons), Computer Character Animation BA(Hons), Technical Direction for Visual Effects BSc(Hons), Visual Effects BA(Hons), Visual Effects MComp(Hons)
Postgraduate courses: Computer Animation and Visual Effects MA

Computer Games

Computer Games Animation BA(Hons), Computer Games Art BA(Hons), Computer Games Design BA(Hons), Computer Games Design MComp(Hons), Computer Games Programming BSc(Hons), Computer Games Programming MComp(Hons), Concept Art BA(Hons), Indie Games Development BA(Hons), Technical Game Development BSc(Hons)
Postgraduate courses: Concept Art for Games and Animation MA, Games Development MA

Computing and the Web

Computer Science BSc(Hons), Computer Science MComp(Hons), Computing BSc(Hons), Computing FdSc, Computing (Networking) FdSc, Cybersecurity and Networks BSc(Hons), Health Informatics BSc(Hons), Information Technology (IT) BSc(Hons), Web Production BSc(Hons)
Postgraduate courses: Computer Security and Networks MSc, Computing MSc, IT Project Management MSc

Media and Communications

Broadcast Media Production BA(Hons), Film and Television Production BA(Hons), Journalism BA(Hons), Media and communications BA(Hons), Music technology BSc(Hons), Public Relations and Digital Communications BA(Hons), Sport Journalism BA(Hons)
Postgraduate courses: Digital Media and Communications MA, Journalism MA, Multimedia Journalism MA, Multimedia Public Relations MA

Producing for Film and Television

2D Animation and Stop Motion – BA(Hons), Computer Animation – BA(Hons), Computer Character Animation – BA(Hons), VFX Technology – BSc(Hons), Visual Effects – BA(Hons), Visual Effects – MComp(Hons), 2D and 3D Games Art – BA(Hons), Computer Games Art – BA(Hons), Computer Games Design – BA(Hons), Computer Games Design – MComp(Hons), Computer Games Programming – BSc(Hons), Computer Games Programming – MComp(Hons), Indie Games Development –

BA(Hons), Tabletop Game Design – BA(Hons), Technical Game Development – BSc(Hons), Computer Science – BSc(Hons), Computer Science – MComp(Hons), Computer Science with Artificial Intelligence – BSc(Hons), Computer Science with Industry Experience – BSc(Hons), Computing – BSc(Hons), Computing – FdSc, Computing (Digital Consultancy) (2 year Accelerated) – BSc(Hons), Computing with Industry Experience – BSc(Hons), Cybersecurity and Networks – BSc(Hons), Cybersecurity and Networks with Industry Experience – BSc(Hons), Data Analytics and Business Intelligence – BSc(Hons), Data Analytics and Business Intelligence with Industry Experience – BSc(Hons), Digital and Technology Solutions (Web Engineering) – Degree Apprenticeship, Information Technology – BSc(Hons), Information Technology with Industry Experience – BSc(Hons), Web Production – BSc(Hons), Broadcast Media Production – BA(Hons), Film and Television Production – BA(Hons), Journalism – BA(Hons), Journalism (Games) – BA(Hons), Journalism (Music and Events) – BA(Hons), Media and Communications – BA(Hons), Music Technology – BSc(Hons), Public Relations and Digital Communications – BA(Hons), Sport Journalism – BA(Hons), Comics and Graphic Novels – BA(Hons), Concept Art – BA(Hons), Fine Art – BA(Hons), Performing Arts – FdA, Performing Arts (Top-up) – BA(Hons), Photography – BA(Hons)

Postgraduate courses: 2D Animation and Stop Motion – MA, Animation – MA, Technical Direction for Visual Effects – MSc, Visual Effects, 3D Games Art – MA, Games Design – MA, Artificial Intelligence – MSc, Artificial Intelligence with Data Analytics – MSc, Computer Science – Mres, Computer Science – MSc, Computing – MSc, Cybersecurity – MSc, Cybersecurity (Online) – MSc, Data Science – MSc, IT Project Management – MSc, Digital Media and Communications – MA, Esports – MA, Immersive Events – MA, Multimedia Public Relations – MA, Producing for Film and Television – MA, Comics and Graphic Novels – MA, Concept Art – MA, Fine Art – MA, Illustration – MA, Photography – MA

School of Health and Social care; www.tees.ac.uk/Undergraduate_courses/ Health_Social_Care/

Dental Hygiene and Dental Therapy BSc(Hons), Dental Nurse Practice Cert HE, Diagnostic Radiography BSc(Hons), Health Informatics – BSc(Hons), Midwifery BSc(Hons), Nursing Studies (Adult) BSc(Hons), Nursing Studies (Child) BSc(Hons), Nursing Studies (Learning Disabilities) BSc(Hons), Nursing Studies (Mental Health), BSc(Hons), Occupational Therapy BSc(Hons), Operating Department Practice Studies BSc(Hons), Paramedic Practice BSc(Hons), Physiotherapy BSc(Hons), Health and Social Care Top-Up – BSc(Hons), Integrated Care Studies BSc(Hons), Operating Department Practice BSc(Hons), Paramedic Science (Top-up) BSc(Hons), Specialist Community Public Health Nursing (Health Visiting) BSc(Hons), Specialist Community Public Health Nursing (Occupational Health) BSc(Hons), Specialist Community Public Health Nursing (School Nursing) BSc(Hons), Specialist Practice in District Nursing BSc(Hons)

Postgraduate courses: Advanced Clinical Practice MSc, Clinical Research MRes, Clinical Research and Evidence based Medicine PgCert, Cognitive Behavioural Therapy MSc, Cognitive Behavioural Therapy PgDip, Diagnostic Radiography (Pre-registration) PgDip/ MSc, Dietetics – MSc, Evidence-based Practice MSc, Forensic Radiography PgCert/MSc, General and Oncoplastic Breast Surgery MCh, Global Leadership in Management & Healthcare – MSc, Health and Social Care Sciences (Generic pathway) MSc, Human Factors and Patient Safety – MSc, Low Intensity Assessment and Intervention Skills for Psychological Wellbeing Practice PgCert, Master of Public Health MPH, Medical Ultrasound MSc, Medical Ultrasound PgCert, Medical Ultrasound PgDip, Midwifery Studies (Pre-registration) PgDip, Occupational Therapy (Pre-registration) PgDip/MSc, Orthopaedics, Physiotherapy (Pre-registration) MSc, Public Health (DrPH), Specialist Community Public Health Nursing (Health Visiting) MSc, Specialist Community Public Health Nursing (Health Visiting) PgDip, Specialist Community Public Health Nursing (Occupational Health Nursing) PgDip, Specialist Community Public Health Nursing (School Nursing) MSc, Specialist Community Public Health Nursing (School Nursing) PgDip, Specialist Practice in District Nursing PgDip/MSc, Specialist Practice in District Nursing Professional Graduate Certificate, Surgical Gastroenterology and Minimally Invasive Surgery MCh, Vascular and Endovascular Surgery – MCh

Science & Engineering; www.tees.ac.uk/ schools/sse

Crime scene & Forensic science

Computer and Digital Forensics BSc(Hons), Crime Scene Science BSc(Hons), Forensic Science BSc(Hons)

Postgraduate courses: Crime Intelligence and Data Analytics PgDip/MSc, Crime Intelligence and Data Analytics with Advanced Practice MSc, Digital Forensics and Cyber Investigations – MSc, Forensic Science PgDip/MSc, Forensic Science with Advanced Practice MSc

Design

Design for the Creative Industries – FdA, Fashion – BA(Hons), Fashion (with Foundation Year) – BA(Hons), Fashion Buying and Merchandising – BA(Hons), Fashion Buying and Merchandising (with Foundation Year) – BA(Hons), Fashion Communication and Promotion – BA(Hons), Fashion Communication and Promotion (with Foundation Year) – BA(Hons), Graphic Design and Illustration – BA(Hons), Graphic Design and Illustration (with Foundation Year) – BA(Hons), Graphic Design with Marketing – BA(Hons), Graphic Design with Marketing (with Foundation Year) – BA(Hons), Interior Architecture and Design – BA(Hons), Interior Architecture and Design (with Foundation Year) – BA(Hons) – Interior Design BA(Hons), Interior Design (with Foundation Year) – BA(Hons), Product Design and Creative Innovation – BA(Hons), Product Design and Creative Innovation (with Foundation Year) – BA(Hons), Product Design Engineering – BSc(Hons), Product Design Engineering (with Foundation Year) – BSc(Hons)

ostgraduate courses: Design – MA, Design (with Advanced Practice) – MA, Engineering Design and Manufacture – MSc, Engineering Design and Manufacture (with Advanced Practice) – MSc, Visual Communication – MA, Visual Communication (with Advanced Practice) – MA

Engineering

Aerospace Engineering BEng(Hons), Aerospace Engineering MEng(Hons), Aerospace Engineering with Industry BEng(Hons), Aerospace Engineering with Industry MEng(Hons), Chemical Engineering BEng(Hons), Chemical Engineering MEng(Hons), Chemical Engineering with Industry BEng(Hons), Chemical Engineering with Industry MEng(Hons), Civil Engineering BEng(Hons), Civil Engineering MEng(Hons), Civil Engineering with Industry BEng(Hons), Civil Engineering with Industry MEng(Hons), Control/Technical Support Engineer Degree Apprenticeship, Electrical and Electronic Engineering BEng(Hons), Electrical and Electronic Engineering MEng(Hons), Electrical and Electronic Engineering with Industry BEng(Hons), Electrical and Electronic Engineering with Industry MEng(Hons), Electrical/Electronic Technical Support Engineer Degree

Apprenticeship, Embedded Electronic Systems Design and Development Engineer Degree Apprenticeship, Instrumentation and Control Engineering BEng(Hons), Instrumentation and Control Engineering MEng(Hons), Instrumentation and Control Engineering with Industry BEng(Hons), Instrumentation and Control Engineering with Industry MEng(Hons), Manufacturing Engineer Degree Apprenticeship, Mechanical Engineering BEng(Hons), Mechanical Engineering MEng(Hons), Mechanical Engineering with Industry BEng(Hons), Mechanical Engineering with Industry MEng(Hons), Product Design and Development Engineer Degree Apprenticeship

Postgraduate courses: Aerospace Engineering MSc, Aerospace Engineering with Advanced Practice MSc, Chemical Engineering MSc, Chemical Engineering with Advanced Practice MSc, Civil and Structural Engineering PgDip/MSc, Civil and Structural Engineering with Advanced Practice MSc, Electrical Power and Energy Systems PgDip/MS, Electrical Power and Energy Systems with Advanced Practice MSc, Food Processing Engineering PgDip/MSc, Food Processing Engineering with Advanced Practice MSc, Instrumentation and Control Engineering PgDip/MSc, Instrumentation and Control Engineering with Advanced Practice MSc, Mechanical Engineering PgDip/MSc, Mechanical Engineering with Advanced Practice MSc, Oil and Gas Management PgDip/MSc, Oil and Gas Management with Advanced Practice MSc, Petroleum Engineering PgDip/MSc, Petroleum Engineering with Advanced Practice MSc, Project Management PgDip/MSca, Project Management with Advanced Practice MSc

Mathematics

Financial Mathematics BSc(Hons), Mathematics BSc(Hons)

Life and Physical Sciences

Animal Science and Welfare BSc(Hons), Biochemistry BSc(Hons), Biological Sciences BSc(Hons), Biomedical Science BSc(Hons), Chemistry BSc(Hons), Environmental Science BSc(Hons), Food and Nutrition BSc(Hons), Food Science and Engineering BSc(Hons), Geography BSc, Geology BSc, Health Sciences BSc(Hons), Human Biology BSc(Hons), Laboratory Scientist Degree Apprenticeship, Pharmaceutical Science BSc(Hons), Pre-Medical Science Cert HE, Pre-Veterinary Science Cert HE

Postgraduate courses: Advanced Biomedical Science MSc, Bioinformatics MSc, Bioinformatics with Advanced Practice MSc, Biological Sciences MRes, Energy and Environmental Management PgDip/MSc, Energy and Environmental Management with

Advanced Practice MSc, Food Science and Biotechnology PgDip/MSc, Food Science and Biotechnology with Advanced Practice MSc, Microbiology MSc, Microbiology with Advanced Practice MSc

Home Design, Construction & the Built Environment
Construction Management- BSc(Hons), Construction Management (with Foundation Year) – BSc(Hons), Innovative Home Design and Construction – BSc(Hons), Innovative Home Design and Construction (with Foundation Year) – BSc(Hons)
Postgraduate courses: Advanced Home Futures MSc

School of Social Sciences, Humanities & Law; www.tees.ac.uk/schools/ssshl/
Criminology and Sociology
Criminology BSc(Hons), Criminology and Sociology BSc(Hons), Criminology with Law BSc(Hons), Criminology with Psychology BSc(Hons), Criminology with Youth Studies BSc(Hons), International Foundation Year (Social Sciences and Law), Sociology BSc(Hons)
Postgraduate courses: Criminology MSc, Social Research Methods (Criminology or Social Policy) MSc

Education, Early Childhood and Youth
Childhood and Youth Studies BA(Hons), Childhood Studies (Top-up Online) BA(Hons), Early Childhood Studies BA(Hons), Early Years Sector Endorsed FdA, Education and Training BA(Hons), Education and Training Certificate in Education, Education and Training (Supporting Teaching and Learning) BA(Hons), Education Studies BA(Hons), Supporting Teaching and Learning FdA, Teaching English to Speakers of Other Languages (TESOL) BA(Hons),- WorkingWith Children and Young People FdA,- Working with Children and Young People (Topup) BA(Hons), Young Children and Early Childhood (Top-up) BA(Hons)
Postgraduate courses: Applied Education Leadership PgCert, Education Doctorate, Education MA, Education (Early Childhood Studies) MA, Education (Educational Leadership) MA Education (TESOL) MA, Education (Trauma Informed Practice) MA, Education and Training Professional Graduate Certificate in Education, Education and Training with Literacy/ Numeracy/ SEND PGCE Learning and Teaching in HE PgCert, PGCEi, TESOL MA

English
Creative Writing BA(Hons), English Studies BA(Hons), English Studies with Creative Writing BA(Hons)

Postgraduate courses: Creative Writing MA, Creative Writing (Distance Learning) MA Creative Writing and Wellbeing MA, English MA

History
History BA(Hons), History MA, Politics BA(Hons)

Law, Policing and Investigation
Crime and Investigation BSc(Hons), International Foundation Year (Social Sciences and Law), Law LLB(Hons), Law with Business Management LLB(Hons), Law with policing LLB(Hons), Law, Criminology and Criminal Justice LLB(Hons), Police Studies (Top-up) BSc(Hons), Policing BSc(Hons); Professional Policing BSc(Hons), Public Services FdA
Postgraduate courses: Criminal Investigation MSc, LLM Master of Laws, LLM (Applied) Master of Laws

Psychology
Counselling FdA, Forensic Psychology BSc(Hons), Psychology BSc(Hons), Psychology and Clinical Skills BSc(Hons), Psychology and Counselling BSc(Hons), Psychology and Criminology BSc(Hons), Therapeutic Counselling (Top-up) BA(Hons)
Postgraduate courses: Clinical Psychology Doctorate, Psychology Doctorate, Forensic Psychology MSc, Health Psychology and Clinical Skills MSc, Psychology (Graduate Conversion) Diploma, Psychology (Top-up) Doctorate

Social Work
Social Work BA(Hons) and MA

Sport and Exercise
Applied Sport and Exercise (Top-up) BSc(Hons), Sport and Exercise Science BSc(Hons), Sports Therapy and Rehabilitation BSc(Hons); Sport & Fitness FdSc, Sports Coaching and Exercise FdSc
Postgraduate courses: Sport & Exercise Science MSc, Sports Physiotherapy MSc, Sports Rehabilitation MSc, Sport and Exercise MSc, Sports Rehabilitation MSc

Teesside University Business School
Accounting and Finance BA(Hons), Airline and Airport Management (Top-up) BA(Hons), Aviation and Tourism FdA, Business and Cybersecurity BA(Hons) and Cybersecurity BA(Hons), Business and Data Management BA(Hons), Business and Games Design BA(Hons), Business Management BA(Hons), Business with Accountancy BA(Hons), Business with Enterprise Top-up BA(Hons), Business & Games Design BA(Hons), Business Finance and Accounting (Top-up), Business Management FdA, Business Management BA(Hons), Business with Accountancy BA(Hons), Business Enterprise and Innovation BA(Hons), Business with Fashion

BA(Hons), Business with Marketing BA(Hons), Chartered Manager Degree Apprenticeship Linked to BA(Hons) Management Practice, Economics BA(Hons), Human Resource Management BA(Hons), International Business BA(Hons), International Business Management (Top-up) BA(Hons), International Business with Human Resource Management (Top-up) BA(Hons), International Business with Marketing (Top-up) BA(Hons), International Tourism Management (Top-up) BA(Hons) Management Practice BA(Hons), Marketing BA(Hons) Project Management BA(Hons) Sports Management and Marketing BA(Hons), Team Entrepreneurship BA(Hons) Tourism Management BA(Hons)

Postgraduate courses: Accounting and Finance MSc, Business Administration (DBA) Doctorate, Human Resource Management MA, Human Resource Management (Applied) MA, International Management MSc, International Management PgDip, International Management (Accountancy) MSc, International Management (Applied) MSc, International Management (Digital Business) MSc, International Management (Human Resource Management) MSc, International Management (Marketing Management) MSc, International Management (Operations) MSc, Master of Business Administration MBA, Master of Business Administration (Applied) MBA Master of Business Administration (Senior Leader Master's Degree Apprenticeship) MBA

MIMA School of Art

Fine Art BA(Hons), Fine Art MA and PhD

TRINITY COLLEGE LONDON
www.trinitycollege.co.uk

Dance, Drama & Speech, Music, Performing & Teaching, Rock & Pop, DaDa, English Language, Teaching English; PGDip, Music Diplomas, Teaching Diplomas

---

UNIVERSITY OF ULSTER
www.ulster.ac.uk

Faculty of Arts, Humanities and Social Sciences; www.ulster.ac.uk/faculties/ arts-humanities-and-social-sciences

Belfast School of Art www.ulster.ac.uk/ faculties/arts-humanities-and- socialsciences/schools/art

BDes(Hons) Animation BS(Hons) Art & Design Foundation year for Specialist degrees BA(Hons) Fine Art, BDes(Hons) Graphic Design and Illustration, BDes Interaction Design BA(Hons) Photography with Video, BDes(Hons) Product Design, BA(Hons) Textile Art, Design and Fashion

Postgraduate courses: MA Animation, MFA Games Design MSc, Arts Therapies: Art Therapy; Music Therapy, MFA Design, MFA Photography Fashion and Textile Retail Management – View the Fashion and Textile Retail Management course page

School of Arts and Humanities, www.ulster.ac.uk/faculties/ artshumanities-and-social-sciences/ schools/arts-and-humanities

Cinematic Arts – BSc(Hons), Drama – BA(Hons) (Modular), English – BA(Hons) (Modular), History – BA(Hons) (Modular), Irish Language and Literature – BA(Hons) (Modular), Irish Studies – AdvCert, Journalism with History – BA(Hons), Music – BMus(Hons), plus a range of joint honours degrees available

Postgraduate courses: MA Contemporary Performance Practices, Creative Musicianship – Mmus, Cultural Heritage and Museum Studies – MA, English Literature – MA, History – PgDip/MA, Irish History and Politics – PgDip/MA, Irish Language Translation, Interpreting and Professional Language Skills – MA, Museum Practice and Management – PgDip/MA

School of Communication and Media

BSc(Hons) Communication and Counselling Studies, – View the Communication and Counselling Studies course page Communication Management and Public Relations – BSc(Hons), Communication, Advertising and Marketing – BSc(Hons), Counselling – Professional Development – BSc(Hons), Interactive Media – BA(Hons), BA(Hons) Journalism – View the Journalism course page Journalism with Education – BA(Hons), Journalism with English – BA(Hons), Journalism with History – BA(Hons) Language and Linguistics – BSc(Hons), BA(Hons) Screen Production – View the Screen Production course page Postgraduate courses in Communication and Public Relations – PgDip/MSc, Counselling Studies and Therapeutic Communication – PgDip/MSc English Language and Linguistics – PgDip/MSc, Journalism – MA; PhDs MA International Journalism: Hostile Environment Reporting, MSc Linguistics and TESOL

School of Education
Education with Specialisms – PgDip/MEd, Headship – PgDip, Library and Information Management – PgDip/MSc, Middle, Leadership – PgCert, PGCE Art and Design, PGCE Further Education, PGCE English with Drama and Media Studies, PGCE Geography, PGCE History, PGCE Home Economics, PGCE Music PGCE Physical Education, PGCE Primary Education, PGCE Technology and Design, Teaching of English to Speakers of Other Languages – MA

School of Law
Law – LLB Hons (Modular), Law with Accounting – LLB(Hons), Law with Criminology – LLB(Hons), Law with Irish – LLB(Hons), Law with Marketing – LLB(Hons), Law with Politics – LLB(Hons)
Postgraduate courses in Access to Justice – LLM Employment Law and Practice – PgCert, Gender, Conflict and Human Rights – LLM, Human Rights Law and Transitional Justice – LLM International Commercial Law – LLM

School of Sociology and Applied Social Studies
Community Development – BSc(Hons), Community Youth Work – BSc(Hons), Criminology and Criminal Justice – BSc(Hons), Health and Social Care Policy – BSc(Hons), Politics – BSc(Hons), Politics with Criminology – BSc(Hons), Social Policy – BSc(Hons) (Modular), Social Policy with Criminology / Sociology – BSc(Hons), Social Work (3 year full-time course) – BSc(Hons), Sociology – BSc(Hons); Sociology with Criminology/ Politics BSc(Hons)
Postgraduate courses in PgDip/MSc Community Youth Work Peace and Conflict Studies – PgDip/

MSc, Public Administration – MPA, Social Policy – MSc, PgDip/MSc Community Youth Work

Faculty of Computing, Engineering and the Built Environment; www.ulster.ac.uk/faculties/computing-engineering-andthe-built-environment

Belfast School of Architecture and the Built Environment
Architectural Engineering – BEng(Hons), Architectural Technology and Management – BSc(Hons), Architecture – BA(Hons), Building Surveying – BSc(Hons), Civil Engineering – BEng(Hons)/MEng(Hons), Civil Engineering (Geoinformatics) – BSc(Hons), Construction Engineering and Management – BSc(Hons), Energy – BSc(Hons), Environmental Health – BSc(Hons), Planning, Regeneration and Development – MSci(Hons), Quantity Surveying and Commercial Management – BSc(Hons), Real Estate – BSc(Hons), Safety Engineering and Disaster Management – MEng(Hons)
Postgraduate courses: Civil and Infrastructure Engineering – PgDip/MSc Construction Business and Leadership (with management specialisms) – PgCert/PgDip/MSc, Energy Storage – MSc Fire Safety Engineering – PgDip/ MSc, Infrastructure Engineering – PgDip/MSc, Real Estate – PgCert/PgDip/MSc, Renewable Energy and Energy Management – PgDip/MSc

School of Computing, Engineering and Intelligent Systems
Artificial Intelligence – BEng Hons, Computer Science – BSc(Hons) (Modular), Computer Science (Software Systems Development) – BSc(Hons), Electrical and Electronic Engineering – BEng(Hons), Electronics and Embedded Systems – BEng(Hons) Information Technologies – BSc(Hons), Mechanical and Manufacturing Engineering – BEng(Hons), Renewable Energy Engineering – BEng(Hons)
Postgraduate courses: Data Science – MSc, Professional Software Development – MSc, MPhil and PhD

School of Computing
Computing Science – BSc(Hons), Computing Technologies – BSc(Hons), Interactive Computing – BSc(Hons), Software Engineering – BEng(Hons), Internet of Things – MSc

School of Engineering
Biomedical Engineering – BSc(Hons), Electronic Engineering – BEng(Hons), Electronic Engineering German Masters Degree – MEng(Hons), Engineering

Management – BEng(Hons), Mechanical Engineering – MEng(Hons), Mechatronic Engineering – BEng(Hons), Mechatronic Engineering German Masters Degree – MEng(Hons), Technology with Design – BSc(Hons)

Postgraduate courses: Advanced Composites and Polymers – PgDip, Advanced Composites and Polymers – MSc, Biomedical Engineering – PgDip, Biomedical Engineering – MSc, Manufacturing Management – PgDip

Faculty of Life & Health Sciences; www.ulster.ac.uk/faculties/life-andhealth-sciences

School of Biomedical Sciences

Biology – BSc(Hons), Biomedical Science – BSc(Hons), Applied Biomedical Science with DPP (Pathology) – BSc(Hons), Biomedical Science with DPP/DIAS – BSc(Hons), Biotechnology – BSc(Hons), Dietetics – BSc(Hons), Food and Nutrition – BSc(Hons), Human Nutrition – BSc(Hons), Optometry – BSc(Hons)/ MOptom Hons, Stratified Medicine – BSc(Hons)

Postgraduate courses: Biotechnology Research – MSc, Dietetics – MSc, Food Regulatory Affairs – PgCert/PgDip/MSc, Food and Nutrition – PgCert/PgDip/MSc, Human Nutrition – MSc, Physician Associate Studies – PgDip/MSc, Medicine – Stratified or Personalised – MSc, Stem Cell Biology – PgCert, Theory of Independent Prescribing for Optometrists – PgCert, Veterinary Public Health – PgCert; PhDs

School of Geography and Environmental Sciences

Environmental Science – BSc(Hons) (Modular), Environmental Science with Education – BSc(Hons), Environmental Science with Psychology – BSc(Hons), Geography – BSc(Hons) (Modular), Geography with Education – BSc(Hons), Geography with Psychology – BSc(Hons)

Postgraduate courses: Environmental Management – PgDip/ MSc, Environmental Management and Geographic Information Systems – PgDip/MSc, Environmental Toxicology and Pollution Monitoring – PgDip/MSc, Geographic Information Systems – PgDip/MSc

School of Health Sciences

Diagnostic Radiography & Imaging – BSc(Hons), Health Physiology / Healthcare Science – BSc(Hons), Occupational Therapy – BSc(Hons), Physiotherapy – BSc(Hons), Podiatry – BSc(Hons), Radiotherapy and Oncology – BSc(Hons), Speech and Language Therapy – BSc(Hons)

Postgraduate courses: Advancing Practice – PgCert/PgDip/MSc, Lower Limb Preservation in Diabetes – PgCert/PgDip/MSc, Medicines Management – PgCert, Professional Development in Physiotherapy – MSc, Sensory Integration – PgCert/PgDip/MSc

School of Nursing

Nursing (Adult) – BSc(Hons), Specialist Nursing (with pathways) – BSc(Hons), Applied Health Studies – BSc(Hons), Developing Practice in Healthcare – BSc(Hons), Health and Wellbeing – BSc(Hons) BSc(Hons), Nursing (Mental Health) – BSc(Hons), Specialist Community Public Health Nursing – BSc(Hons), Health Promotion and Public Health – PgCert/PgDip/MSc, Health and Wellbeing – PgDip/MSc, Nursing – PgCert/PgDip/ MSc, Specialist Community Public Health Nursing – PgDip, Palliative Care – PgDip/MSc; PhDs Specialist Nursing (with pathways) – PgDip, Applied Health Studies – PgCert/PgDip/MSc, PgDip/MSc Developing Practice in Healthcare – PgDip/MSc, PgCert Education for Healthcare Professionals – PGCert, Non Medical Prescribing – PGCert

School of Pharmacy and Pharmaceutical Sciences

Pharmaceutical Bioscience – MSci(Hons), Pharmacy – MPharm(Hons)

Postgraduate courses in Pharmaceutical Sciences - PgDip/MSc, Pharmacy Management – PgDip

School of Psychology

Psychology – BSc(Hons) (Modular), Social Psychology – BSc(Hons)

Postgraduate courses in Applied Psychology (Mental Health and Psychological Therapies) – MSc, Family Therapy and Systemic Practice – PgCert, Health Psychology – MSc; PhD Quantitative Methods for the Behavioural and Social Sciences – PGCert Applied Behaviour Analysis – MSc

School of Sport

Sport Studies – BSc(Hons), Sport and Exercise Sciences – BSc(Hons), Sport, Physical Activity and Health – BSc(Hons), Sports Coaching and Performance – BSc(Hons) Sport Studies – BSc(Hons), Football Coaching and Business Management BSc(Hons)

Postgraduate courses in Sport and Exercise Medicine – PgDip/ MSc, Sport and Exercise Psychology – MSc, Sports Coaching and Performance – MSc MSc, Sport and Exercise Medicine – PgDip/ MSc, Sport and

Exercise Nutrition – PgDip/MSc Strength & Conditioning – MSc

Ulster University Business School; www.ulster.ac.uk/faculties/ ulsteruniversity-business-school

Department of Accounting Finance and Economics

Accounting (Pathways) – BSc(Hons), Accounting and Law – BSc(Hons), Business Economics – BSc(Hons), Economics – BSc(Hons), Finance and Investment Management – BSc(Hons); Business Technology – BSc, Accounting & Management – BSc

Postgraduate courses in Accounting – GradDip, Advanced Accounting – MSc

Department of Hospitality and Tourism Management

Consumer Management and Food Innovation – BSc(Hons), Culinary Arts Management – BSc(Hons), International Hospitality Management – BSc(Hons), International Travel and Tourism Management – BSc(Hons), Leisure and Events Management – BSc(Hons); Consumer Management and Food Innovation – BSc(Hons), Culinary Arts Management – BSc(Hons)

Postgraduate courses in International Event Management – MSc, International Hospitality Management – MSc, International Tourism Management – MSc

Department of Global Business and Enterprise

Accounting and Marketing – BSc(Hons), Accounting and Law BSc(Hons) Accounting with Specialisms – BSC(Hons), Business Economics BSc(Hons) Businesss Information Systems – BSC(Hons), Business Studies with computing – BSc(Hons), Business Studies with Drama – BSc(Hons), Business Studies with Irish – BSc(Hons) Business Studies with Specialisms – BSC(Hons)

Department of Management Leadership and Marketing

Business Studies – BSc(Hons), Human Resource Management – BSc(Hons), Management and Leadership Development – BSc(Hons), Marketing – BSc(Hons)

Postgraduate courses in Business Development and Innovation – MSc, MBA (Master of Business Administration) – MBA, Executive MBA – MBA Management – MSc, Management and Corporate Governance – MSc, Marketing – MSc, Marketing with Advanced Practice – MSc Sport Management – MSc

UNIVERSITY OF WALES TRINITY SAINT DAVID
www.uwtsd.ac.uk

Faculty of Architecture, Computing & Engineering; www.uwtsd.ac.uk/face

School of Applied Computing

BCs/HND/HNC and Four-year courses in Computing, Computing (Business Information Systems) Computing (Computer Networks and Cybersecurity) Computing (Data and Information Systems) Computing (Games Development) Computing (Software Engineering) Computing (Web Development) BEng Electrical and Electronic Engineering, HND/HNC Electronics Engineering, Foundation Year in STEM (1 year) Digital Degree Apprenticeships, Applied Computing (MSc, PgDip, PgCert) Computer Networks and Cyber Security (MSc, PgDip, PgCert) Web and Software Development (MSc, PgDip, PgCert)

School of Architecture, Built & Natural Environment

BSc Architecture, BSc/HND Architectural Technology, Building Surveying, Civil Engineering and Environmental Management, Project & Construction Management, Quantity Surveying: Environmental Conservation, Certificate of Higher Education in STEM

Postgraduate courses: MSc Sustainable Construction, MSc Property and Facilities Management MSc Environmental Conservation & Management

School of Engineering

BSc/HND Automotive Engineering, BEng and MEng Automotive Engineering

Energy and Environmental

MEng/ BEng Energy and Environmental Engineering

Logistics

BSc/HND Logistics and Supply Chain Management, Logistics and Transport, Motorsport Management

Mechanical and Manufacturing Engineering

BEng/MEng Mechanical and Manufacturing Engineering, Mechanical and Manufacturing Engineering

Four-Year Foundation Entry, Mechanical Engineering, Mechanical Engineering Four-Year Foundation Entry, BEng Manufacturing and Systems Engineering
Postgraduate courses: MSc Engineering Project Management, MSc Lean and Agile Manufacturing, MSc Logistics, MSc Non-destructive Testing and Evaluation, MSc Engineering Product Design, MSc Mechanical Engineering

Motorcycle
MEng/ BEng Fd Motorcycle Engineering

Motorsport
MEng/ BEng/ Fd/ BSc/ HND Motorsport Engineering, BSc/ HND Motorsport Management

Natural Environments
BSc/HND Environmental Conservation
Postgraduate course: MSc Environmental Conservation and Management

Swansea College of Art ; www.uwtsd.ac.uk/art-design

Advertising and Brand Design
BA / MDes Advertising and Brand Design

Automotive Design
Automotive & Transport Design (MDes, BA)

Computer Animation
Computer Animation (MArts, BA)

Film & TV
Film & TV (MArts, BA)

Design Crafts
Design Crafts (MDes, BA)

Fine Art
BA / MArts Fine Art: Studio, Site & Context

Games Design
Computer Games Design (MArts, BA)

Glass
Glass (MDes, BA, CertHE)

Graphic Design
Graphic Design (MDes, BA)

Illustration
Illustration (MDes, BA)

Music
Creative Music Technology and Music (MMusTech, BA) BA Music (Performance and Production)

Performing Arts
Applied Drama: Education, Wellbeing, Community (BA, CertHE)

Photography
Photojournalism & Documentary Photography (MArts, BA) Photography in the Arts (MArts, BA)

Product Design
Product Design (MDes, BSc, BA)

Surface Pattern Design and Glass

Faculty of Business and Management ; www.uwtsd.ac.uk/ businessmanagement/

Swansea Business School
BA(Hons) Accounting, BA(Hons) Business and Finance, BA(Hons) Business Management, BA(Hons) Human Resource Management, BA(Hons) International Business, BA(Hons) Marketing Management, BA(Hons) Law and Business, HND Business Management, HND Business and Finance, Fda Business and Finance
Postgraduate courses: MBA, E-MBA, MSc Financial Management, MA Human Resource Management, MSc Trading and Financial Markets, CIPD Postgraduate Diploma in Human Resource Management, CIPD Intermediate Certificate in Human Resource Management, CIM Postgraduate Diploma in Marketing

Carmarthen Business School
BA Business and Management, BA Rural Enterprise Management, BA Cultural Industries Management
Postgraduate courses: MBA General Management, MA Technology Enhanced Learning

Sport, Health and Outdoor Education: Carmethen
BSc Sport and Exercise Science, BSc Sport and Exercise Science (Sports Nutrition), BSc Sport and Exercise Science (Personal Training), BSc Sport and Exercise Science (Outdoor Fitness), BSc Sport and Exercise Science (Clinical Exercise Physiology), BSc Sport Therapy, BSc Public Health, BSc Health, Nutrition and Lifestyle, BA Outdoor Adventure Education, BA Physical Education, Dip HE Nursing Studies and Health; MA Outdoor Education, MA Physical Education

Sport, Health and Public Services: Swansea
BA Public Services | HND Public Services, BSc Policing, BSc Policing & Criminology, BA Law & Business, BA Law & Public Services, BA Law &

Criminology, BA Law & Policing, BSc Health and Social Care, HND Health and Social Care, BSc Health Management, HND Health Management, BSc Health and Care of Children and Young People, FdSc Health and Care of Children and Young People, DipHE Nursing Studies & Health, BA International Sports Management, BA Sports Management, FDA Sports Management, HND Sports Management, BA Stadium and Sports Facility Management, BA Watersports Management

Swansea School of Tourism & Hospitality

BA and HNDs in Events Management, International Travel and Tourism Management, Leisure Management, Tourism Management, International Hotel Management; Postgraduate courses in MA International Tourism Management

Faculty of Education and Communities; www.uwtsd.ac.uk/education-andcommunities/

School of Early Years

Foundation Degree Early Childhood, BA Early Years Education & Care, BA Early Years Education & Care – 2 Years, BA Early Years Education & Care (Early Years Practitioner), BA Early Years Education & Care (Early Years Practitioner) – 2 Years, Integrated Masters Early Years Education & Care, Integrated Masters Early Years Education & Care (Early Years Practitioner)
Postgraduate courses: MA/Postgraduate Diploma Early Years Education & Care

School of Psychology

BSc Applied Psychology, BSc Psychology (BPS accredited), BA Counselling Studies and Psychology (BPS accredited), BA Education Studies and Psychology (BPS accredited), BSc Mental Health, MSc Applied Social and Health Psychology

School of Social Justice and Inclusion

Carmarthen: Certificate of Higher Education in Advocacy, Certificate of Higher Education in Playwork, Certificate of Higher Education Young Peoples Health and Wellbeing, Certificate of Higher Education Health and Wellbeing for Carers, Certificate of Higher Education Workplace Health and Wellbeing, Foundation Degree Inclusive Education, BA Social Studies: Additional Needs, BA Social Studies: Advocacy, BA Social Studies: Communities, Families and Individuals, BA Social Studies: Health and Social Care, BA Youth and Community Work, BA Gwaith Ieuenctid a Chymuned, BA Education Studies: Primary, BA Astudiaethau Addysg Gynradd
Postgraduate courses: Integrated Masters in Social Studies: Additional Needs, Integrated Masters in Social Studies: Advocacy, Integrated Masters in Social Studies: Communities, Families and Individuals, Integrated Masters in Social Studies: Health and Social Care, MA Youth Work, MA Equality and Diversity in Society, Graduate Certificate in Additional Learning Needs; Swansea: BA Counselling Skill and Interdisciplinary Studies, BA Counselling Studies and Psychology, BA Humanistic Counselling, Integrated Masters in Humanistic Counselling, Graduate Certificate in Counselling Skills, MA Psychotherapeutic Practice: Emotion-Focused Therapy, Foundation Degree in Inclusive Education, BA Education Studies, BA Education Studies: Additional Learning Needs & Inclusion, BA Education Studies: Contemporary Learners & Learning, BA Education Studies: International Perspectives, BA Humanities with Education Studies

SWWCentre of Teacher Education

BA Primary Education with QTS, BA Addysg Gynradd gyda SAC, PGCE Primary with QTS, PGCE Secondary Art & Design with QTS, PGCE Secondary Computing and ICT with QTS, PGCE Secondary Business Studies with QTS, PGCE Secondary Maths 11-18 with QTS, PGCE Secondary Maths 11-16 with ICT and QTS, PGCE Secondary Biology with QTS, PGCE Secondary Design and Technology with QTS, PGCE Secondary Geography with QTS, PGCE Secondary Physics with QTS, PGCE Secondary Science 11-16 with QTS, PGCE Secondary English with QTS, PGCE Secondary History with QTS, PGCE Secondary Modern Foreign Languages with QTS, PGCE Secondary Religious Education with QTS, PGCE Secondary Welsh with QTS, PGCE Secondary Chemistry with QTS

Faculty of Humanities & Performing Arts; www.uwtsd.ac.uk/faculty-ofhumanities-performingarts

Anthropology

BA Anthropology, BA Applied Anthropology, BA Archaeology and Anthropology

School of Archaeology

History and Anthropology BA Anthropology with Applied Psychology, BA Anthropology with Education Studies, BA Anthropology with Heritage Management

Postgraduate courses: MA Cultural Astronomy and Astrology, MA Ecology and Spirituality, MA Engaged Anthropology, MRes Anthropology, MRes Cultural Astronomy and Astrology

Ancient World

BA Ancient and Medieval History, BA Ancient Civilisations, BA Ancient History, BA Ancient History and Archaeology, BA Ancient History with Ancient Egyptian Culture, BA Ancient History with Ancient Egyptian Culture, BA Ancient History with Ancient Egyptian Culture, BA Ancient History with Education Studies, BA Ancient History with Heritage Management, BA Ancient History with Latin, BA Ancient History, Anthropology, Education Studies, BA Ancient History, Archaeology, Education Studies, BA Ancient History, Classical Studies, Education Studies, BA Ancient History, History, Education Studies, BA Ancient History, Religious Studies, Education Studies, BA Classical Civilisation, BA Classical Civilisation, BA Classical Studies, BA Classical Studies with Ancient Egyptian Culture, BA Classical Studies with Ancient Egyptian Culture, BA Classical Studies with Ancient Egyptian Culture, BA Classical Studies with Greek, BA Classical Studies with Heritage Management, BA Classical Studies with Latin, BA Classical Studies, Ancient History, Education Studies, BA Classical Studies, Anthropology, Education Studies, BA Classical Studies, Archaeology, Education Studies, BA Classical Studies, English, Education Studies, BA Classical Studies, History, Education Studies, BA Classical Studies, Religious Studies, Education Studies, BA Classics, BA Conflict and War

Postgraduate courses: MA Ancient History, MA Ancient Religions, MA Classical Studies, MA Classics, MRes Ancient History, MRes Classical Studies

Performing Arts

BA(Hons) Acting, BA(Hons) Dance, BA(Hons) Theatre Design and Production, BA(Hons) Applied Drama, BA(Hons) Performing Arts (Contemporary Performance), BA Perfformio

Archaeology

BA Archaeology, BA Archaeology and Anthropology, BA Archaeology of Egypt and the Near East, BA Archaeology Professional Practice, BA Nautical Archaeology, BA Environmental Archaeology, MArts Archaeology, BA Archaeology with Ancient Egyptian Culture, BA Archaeology with Education Studies, BA Archaeology with Forensic Studies, BA Archaeology with Heritage Management

Postgraduate courses: MA Landscape Management and Environmental Archaeology, MRes Landscape and Environmental Archaeology

Chinese Studies

BA Chinese Studies, BA Chinese Civilisation and Anthropology, BA Chinese Civilisation and English, BA Chinese Civilisation and Medieval Studies, BA Chinese Civilisation and Philosophy, BA Chinese Civilisation and Religious Studies

English & Creative Writing

BA English, BA Creative Writing

Postgraduate courses: MA Creative and Script Writing, MA Creative Writing, MA Modern Literature, MA Medieval and Early Modern Literature, MRes Contemporary Literature, MRes Early Modern Literature, MRes Medieval Literature

Environment & Ecology

BA Philosophy, Politics and Economics, BA Political Ecology, BA Political Ecology with Humanitarianism and Law

Heritage

BA Heritage Studies, BA Heritage Studies with Museums & Archives, BA Heritage Studies with Nautical Archaeology

Postgraduate courses: MA Heritage Practice, MA Heritage Tourism

International Development, Humanitarianism & Law

BA International Development, Humanitarianism and Law

Modern History & Medieval Studies

BA Ancient and Medieval History, BA Celtic Studies, BA Chinese Civilisation and Medieval Studies, BA Chinese Studies and Medieval Studies, BA History, BA History and Ancient History, BA History and Anthropology, BA History and Archaeology, BA History and English, BA History and Theology, BA History with Education Studies, BA Medieval Studies, BA Medieval Studies and Anthropology, BA Medieval Studies and Archaeology, BA Medieval Studies and Classical Studies, BA Medieval Studies and English, BA Medieval Studies and History, BA Medieval Studies and History, BA Medieval Studies and Modern Historical Studies, BA Medieval Studies and Modern Historical Studies, BA Medieval Studies with Latin, BA Modern Historical Studies, BA Philosophy and History, BA Philosophy and Medieval Studies, MArts History

Postgraduate courses: MA Heritage Practice, MA Local History, MA Medieval Studies, MRes Heritage Practice, MRes Medieval Studies

Philosophy

BA Philosophy, BA Ethical and Political Studies, MArts Philosophical Studies
Postgraduate courses: MA Ecology and Spirituality, MA Philosophy, MA Philosophy and Religion: Eastern and Western Thought, Master of Philosophy (MPhil), MRes Philosophy

Politics & Economics

BA Philosophy, Politics and Economics

Religion

Carmarthen: BA Religious Studies, BA Astudiaethau Crefyddol, BA Religious Studies and Islamic Studies;

Lampeter: BA Religious Studies, MArts Religious Studies, MArts Theology

The School of Performing Arts

BA Theology and Classical Studies, BA Theology and History, BA Theology and Philosophy, BA Theology and Heritage Studies, BA Theology with Heritage Management, BA Theology with Education Studies
Postgraduate courses: MA Biblical Interpretation, MA Islamic Studies, MA Study of Religions, MTh Christian Theology, MTh Church History, MRes Biblical Interpretation, MRes Islamic Studies, MRes Religious Experience, MRes Study of Religions; MPhil/PhD

Welsh International Academy of Voice

MA in Advanced Vocal Studies, Post Graduate Diploma in Advanced Pianoforte Studies

UNIVERSITY OF WARWICK
www.warwick.ac.uk

Centre for Applied Linguistics

Undergraduate degrees in English Language and Linguistics, Language, Culture and Communication with Year Abroad, Linguistics with Arabic, Linguistics with Chinese, Linguistics with French, Linguistics with German, Linguistics with Italian, Linguistics with Japanese, Linguistics with Portuguese, Linguistics with Russian, Linguistics with Spanish
Postgraduate courses: MA TESOL MRes Applied Linguistics MSc Intercultural Communication for Business and the Professions MPhil/PhD in Discourse Studies, MPhil/ PhD in Intercultural Communication, MPhil/PhD in English Language Teaching, MPhil/ PhD in English Language teaching and Applied Linguistics

Warwick Business School

Undergraduate degrees in Accounting and Finance, Accounting and Finance (with foundation year), International Business with French, International Business with German, International Business with Italian, International Business with Spanish, International Management, Management, Management (with foundation year)
Postgraduate courses: MSc Business with Accounting & Finance MSc Business with Consulting MSc Business with Marketing MSc Business with Operations Management MSc International Business MSc Business Analytics MSc Management MSc Human

Resource Management & Employment Relations MSc Management of Information Systems & Digital Innovation MSc Marketing & Strategy MSc Finance MSc Accounting & Finance MSc Finance & Economics MSc Financial Mathematics MSc Business & Finance MSc Global Central Banking & Financial Regulation MBA PhD

Department of Chemistry

Undergraduate degrees in Chemistry, Chemistry (MChem), Chemistry with Medicinal Chemistry, Chemistry with Medicinal Chemistry (MChem)/ (MBio), Chemistry with Industrial Placement (MChem), Chemistry with International Placement (MChem)
Postgraduate courses: MSc in Chemistry Masters degrees in: Polymer Chemistry Diamond Science & Technology, PhD in Chemistry, PhD in Chemistry with Industrial Collaboration Polymer Science Analytical Science & Instrumentation Analytical and Polymer Science Molecular Analytical Science (CDT students only) Chemistry with Scientific Writing Scientific Research and Communications

Department of Classics and Ancient History

Undergraduate degrees in Ancient History and Classical Archaeology, Ancient History and Classical Archaeology with Study in Europe, Classical

Civilisation, Classical Civilisation with Study in Europe, Classics, Classics (Ancient Greek) with Study in Europe, Classics (Latin) with Study in Europe, Classics and English, Italian and Classics Postgraduate courses: MA in Ancient Visual and Material Culture MA in the Visual and Material Culture of Ancient Rome MA in the Visual and Material Culture of Ancient Greece MA in Ancient Literature and Thought MRes in Classics and Ancient history, MPhil in Classics and Ancient History, PhD in Classics and Ancient History

Department of Computer Science
Undergraduate degrees in Computer Science, Computer Science (MEng), Computer and Business Studies, Computer Systems Engineering, Computer Systems Engineering (MEng), Discrete Mathematics, Discrete Mathematics (MEng), Data Science, Computer Science with Business Studies
Postgraduate courses: MSc Computer Science, MSc Data Analytics, PhD Computer Science

School for Cross-Faculty Studies
BASc Global Sustainable Development (Single Honours) BASc Global Sustainable Development (Joint Honours)

Centre for Cultural and Media Policy Studies
BA(Hons) Media and Creative Industries MA in Arts, Enterprise and Development MA in Creative and Media Enterprises MA in Global Media and Communication MA in International Cultural Policy and Management PhD in Cultural Policy Studies / PhD in Creative Industries / PhD in Media and Communication

Department of Economics
Undergraduate degrees in Economics, Economics and Industrial Organization, Economics, Politics and International Studies, Languages and Economics
Postgraduate courses: MRes/PhD Economics MSc Economics, Economics and Financial Economics, Behavioural and Economic Science, Finance and Economics

Centre for Education Studies
Postgraduate courses: MA Global Education and International Development MA Islamic Education: Theory and Practice MA Psychology and Education MA Drama and English Language Teaching MA Drama and Theatre Education MA Education MA

Educational Leadership and Management MA Educational Innovation MA Childhood in Society MA Religions and Education by distance learning Postgraduate Award in Islamic Education Postgraduate Award in Foundation Research Methods Postgraduate Award in Leading Education Change and Improvement

School of Engineering
Undergraduate degrees Automotive Engineering (BEng), Biomedical Systems Engineering (BEng), Biomedical Systems Engineering (MEng) Civil Engineering (BEng), Computer Systems Engineering Electrical and Electronic Engineering (BEng), Electronic Engineering (BEng), Engineering (BEng), Engineering Business Management (BEng), Manufacturing and Mechanical Engineering (BEng), Mechanical Engineering (BEng), Systems Engineering (BEng)
Postgraduate courses: MEng Advanced Mechanical Engineering MPhil/PhD in Engineering, EngD/EngD(Int) Engineering, Communcations & Information Engineering, Energy and Power Engineering Sustainable Energy Technologies Tunnelling and Underground Space Humanitarian Engineering

Department of English and Comparative Literary Studies
Undergraduate degrees in English Literature, English Literature and Creative Writing, English and Theatre Studies (QW34), English and History
Postgraduate courses: MPhil/PhD in English and Comparative Literary Studies, MPhil/PhD in Translation Studies, MPhil/PhD Writing

Department of Film and Television Studies
Undergraduate degrees in Film Studies, Film and Literature

Department of Global Sustainable Development
Undergraduate degrees in Global Sustainable Development, Economic Studies and Global Sustainable Development, Global Sustainable Development and Business Studies, History and Global Sustainable Development, Life Sciences and Global Sustainable Development, Philosophy and Global Sustainable Development, Politics, International Studies and Global Sustainable Development, Psychology and Global Sustainable Development, Sociology and Global Sustainable Development, Theatre and

Performance Studies and Global Sustainable Development

Department of History

Undergraduate degrees in History, History and Philosophy, History and Politics, History and Sociology, English and History, French and History, German and History, Hispanic Studies and History, History and Italian, History and Global Sustainable Development

Postgraduate courses: MA Early Modern History, Modern History, History of Medicine, Global History MPhil/PhD History

Department of History of Art

Undergraduate degrees in History of Art, History of Art with Italian

Postgraduate courses: MA History of Art and Visual Studies, History of Art PGDip MPhil History of Art, PhD History of Art

School of Law

Undergraduate degrees in Law (3 years), Law (4 years), Law (4 years – Study Abroad in English), Law and Business Studies, Law and Sociology (4 years), Law with French Law (4 years), Law with German Law (4 years), Law with Humanities, Law with Social Sciences, Politics, Philosophy and Law

Postgraduate courses: LLM International Commercial Law/ Economic Law/ Corporate Governance and Financial Regulation/ Development Law and Human Rights, LLM Advanced Legal Studies, PhD/ MRes MPhil/PhD Law, LLM

Department of Liberal Arts

Undergraduate degree in Liberal Arts

School of Life Sciences

Undergraduate degrees in Biochemistry, Biochemistry (MBio), Biological Sciences, Biological Sciences (MBio), Biomedical Science, Biomedical Science (MBio)

Postgraduate courses: MSc Biotechnology, Bioprocessing and Business Management MSc Environmental Bioscience in a Changing Climate MSc Food Security MSc Medical Biotechnology and Business Management MSc Sustainable Crop Production: Agronomy for the 21st Century Masters Level and Professional Short Courses

Warwick Manufacturing Group

BSc Cyber Security BSc(Hons) Digital Healthcare Science MSc Engineering Business Management MSc International Technology Management MSc Management for Business Excellence MSc Programme and Project Management MSc Supply Chain and Logistics Management MSc e-Business Management MSc Innovation and Entrepreneurship MSc International Trade, Strategy and Operations MSc Service Management and Design MSc Healthcare Operational Management MSc Cyber Security and Management MSc Cyber Security Engineering MSc Manufacturing Systems Engineering and Management MSc Sustainable Automotive Engineering MSc Smart, Connected and Autonomous Vehicles

Warwick Mathematics Institute

Mathematics (BSc), Master of Mathematics (MMath), Mathematics and Business Studies BSc, Mathematics and Economics BSc

Postgraduate courses: PhD/MPhils in Mathematics, Statistics Master of Advanced Study in Mathematical Sciences (MASt) MSc in Mathematics MSc in Interdisciplinary Mathematics MSc in Financial Mathematics PhD in Mathematics Offering an advanced research training in mathematics of high quality, and preparing doctoral students for their future careers, PhD in Interdisciplinary Mathematics, MSc/PhD in Mathematics for Real-World Systems (MathSys)

Warwick Medical School

MSci Integrated Science, BSc Health and Medical Sciences, MB ChB (Bachelor of Medicine and Surgery), Advanced Clinical Practice for Health Care Professionals MSc/Postgraduate Diploma/Postgraduate Certificate Advanced Critical Care Practice MSc/ Postgraduate Diploma/Postgraduate Certificate, Diabetes MSc, Diabetes (Paediatrics) MSc, Health Research MSc/Postgraduate Diploma/Postgraduate Certificate, Interdisciplinary Biomedical Research MSc, Medical Education Masters (MMedEd) Orthodontics MSc Public Health (MPH) Masters

School of Modern Languages and Cultures

Undergraduate degrees in Modern Languages (BA), Modern Languages and Economics, Modern Languages and Linguistics, Modern Languages with Linguistics, French Studies, German Studies, Hispanic Studies, Italian Studies Degrees with Arabic, Chinese, Japanese, Portuguese, or Russian International Business with French Linguistics with French

International Business with German Linguistics with German International Business with Spanish Linguistics with Spanish International Business with Italian History of Art with Italian Linguistics with Italian Postgraduate courses: MA/MRes/MPhil/PhD in French, German, Hispanic and Italian studies PhD in Translation and Transcultural Studies MA for Research in French and Francophone Studies MA in European Gothic and Romantic Studies MA in Translation and Cultures

MORSE

Undergraduate degrees in MMORSE (Mathematics, Operational Research, Statistics and Economics), MORSE (Mathematics, Operational Research, Statistics and Economics)

Department of Philosophy

Undergraduate degrees in Philosophy (V500), Philosophy and Literature, Philosophy with Psychology, Mathematics and Philosophy, Philosophy, Literature and Classics (BA) Philosophy, Politics and Economics (PPE) (BA/BSc) Politics, Philosophy and Law (PPL) (BA) History and Philosophy (BA) Philosophy and Global Sustainable Development (BASc) MA Continental Philosophy MA Philosophy and the Arts Philosophy and Literature PhD
Postgraduate courses: MA/MPhil/PhD in Philosophy

Department of Physics

Undergraduate degrees in Physics, Physics (BSc/MPhys), Physics and Business Studies, Mathematics and Physics, Mathematics and Physics (BSc/MPhys), Physics with Astrophysics BSc and MPhys
Postgraduate courses: MPhil/PhD in Physics

Department of Politics and International Studies

Undergraduate degrees in Politics, Politics and International Studies, Politics, International Studies and Chinese, Politics, International Studies and French, Politics, International Studies and German, Politic, International Studies and Hispanic Studies, Politics, International Studies and Italian, Politics, International Studies and Quantitative Methods, Politics and Sociology
Postgraduate courses: MA Political and Legal Theory, Politics, Big Data and Quantitative Methods, US Foreign Policy, Public Policy, International Politics and Europe/ East Asia, International Security, International Political Economy, International Relations PhD in Politics and International Studies

Department of Psychology

Undergraduate degrees in Psychology, Psychology with Linguistics, Psychology with Education
Postgraduate courses: MSc/MPhil/ PhD in Psychology MSc in Behavioural and Data Science MSc in Behavioural and Economic Science MSc in Clinical Applications of Psychology MSc Psychological Research

Department of Sociology

Undergraduate degrees in Sociology, Sociology and Quantitative Methods, Sociology and Criminology Sociology with Specialism in Gender Studies Sociology with Specialism in Race and Global Politics Sociology with Specialism in Social and Political Thought Sociology with Specialism in Research Methods Sociology with Specialism in Social Inequalities and Public Policy Sociology with Specialism in Technologies and Markets, BA Programmes Sociology 2019/20, Sociology and Quantitative Methods 2019/20, Sociology and Criminology (BA) 2020/21, Sociology with Specialism 2019/20, Sociology with Specialism in Gender Studies 2019/20, Sociology with Specialism in Race and Global Politics 2019/20, Sociology with Specialism in Social and Political Thought 2019/20, Sociology with Specialism in Research Methods 2019/20, Sociology with Specialism in Social Inequalities and Public Policy 2019/20, Sociology with Specialism in Technologies and Markets 2019/20, Combinations (Joint Honours) Sociology and Global Sustainable Development History and Sociology Politics and Sociology Law and Sociology (Qualifying Law Degree)
Postgraduate courses: MA Social Research Social and Political Thought Gender and International Development MSc Quantitative Social Research PhD in Sociology, Women's and Gender Studies

Department of Statistics

Undergraduate degrees in Data Science, Mathematics and Statistics, Mathematics and Statistics (MMathStat), MORSE (MMORSE)
Postgraduate courses: PhD/MPhil in Statistics, Mathematics and Statistics, MSc Financial Mathematics

School of Theatre and Performance Studies

Undergraduate degree in Theatre and Performance Studies, English and Theatre Studies French and Theatre Studies German and Theatre Studies Italian and Theatre Studies Hispanic Studies and Theatre

Studies Theatre and Performance Studies with Global Sustainable Development
Postgraduate courses: MA/MPhil/PhD in Theatre and Performance Studies

The Yesu Persaud Centre for Caribbean Studies
MRes in Caribbean Studies, MPhil/PhD in Caribbean Studies

UNIVERSITY OF WEST OF SCOTLAND
www.uws.ac.uk

School of Business and Enterprise; www.uws.ac.uk/schools/businessschool/
BAcc & BAcc(Hons) Accounting, BA & BA(Hons) Business, BA & BA(Hons) Business & Finance, BA & BA(Hons) Business & Human Resource Management, BA & BA(Hons) Business & Marketing, CertHE Business with English, CertHE Business with English Language (London), BA & BA(Hons) Events Management, BA & BA(Hons) International Business (Accelerated), BA & BA(Hons) Law, BA & BA(Hons) Law & Business, BA & BA(Hons) Tourism Management (3rd Year Entry)
Postgraduate courses: MSc Digital Marketing, Doctor of Business Administration, MSc Finance and Accounting with CIMA MSc Financial Accounting, MSc Human Resource Management, MSc International Events Management, MSc International Management, MSc International Marketing Management, MSc Logistics and Supply Chain, Master of Business Administration MSc Leadership & Mangement

School of Education; www.uws.ac.uk/schools/school-of-education/courses/
BSc(Hons) Chemistry with Education BA & BA(Hons) Childhood Studies (2nd year entry), BA & BA(Hons) Community Education, Digital Learning Design CertHE BA & BA(Hons) Education, BA & BA(Hons) English as a Second Language (3rd or 4th year entry), Physics with Education, BSc(Hons)
Postgraduate courses: Academic Practice PGCert MEd Artist Teacher, PGCert MEd Artist Teacher, PGCert Digital Learning Design CertHE, MEd Early years, MEd Enhanced Educational Practice, MEd Higher Education Practice, MSc Inclusive Education, MEd Leadership for Learning, MSc Mental Health and Education, PGCert Primary Physical Education, PGDiploma in education (Primary/Secondary), MEd Teaching of English to Speakers of other Languages (TESOL)

School of Computing, Engineering and Physical Sciences www.uws.ac.uk/about-uws/academic-schools/school-of-computing-engineering-physical-sciences/
BEng & BEng(Hons) Aircraft Engineering, BSc & BSc(Hons) Business Technology, BEng & BEng(Hons) Chemical Engineering, BEng & BEng(Hons) Civil Engineering, BSc & BSc(Hons) Computer Animation Arts, BSc & BSc(Hons) Computer Games Development, BSc & BSc(Hons) Computer Games Technology, BSc & BSc(Hons) Computer Networking, BSc & BSc(Hons) Computer-Aided Design (3rd Year entry), BSc & BSc(Hons) Computing Science, BSc(Hons) Cyber Security, BEng(Hons) Engineering Design and Manufacture (Graduate Apprenticeship), BEng & BEng(Hons) Engineering Management (2nd Year and 3rd Year Entry), BSc(Hons) IT: Software Development (Graduate Apprenticeship), BEng(Hons) Mechanical Engineering, BSc & BSc(Hons) Music Technology, BSc & BSc(Hons) Physics, BSc(Hons) Physics with Education, BSc & BSc(Hons) Physics with Nuclear Technology, BSc & BSc(Hons) Web and Mobile Development; BSc Chemistry, BSc Chemistry with Education, BSc Forensic Science and BSc Mathematics with Education
Postgraduate courses: MSc Advanced Computer Systems Development, MSc Advanced Computing, MSc Advanced Thin Film Technologies, MSc Big Data, MSc Chemical Engineering, MSc Civil Engineering, MSc Construction Management and Digital Engineering, MSc e-Health, MSc Engineering Management, MSc Information and Network Security, MSc Information Technology, MSc Internet of Things, MSc Mechanical Engineering, MSc Cyber Security, MSc Project Management, MSc Quality Management, MSc Waste & Resource Management, MSc Formulation, MSc Mobile Web Development

School of Health and Life Sciences
www.uws.ac.uk/about-uws/academic-schools/school-of-health-life-sciences/

BSc Adult Nursing, BA & BA(Hons) Integrated Health and Social Care (2nd Year Entry), BA & BA(Hons) Integrated Health and Social Care with Administration (2nd Year Entry), Maternity Care Assistant CertHE BSc Mental Health Nursing, BSc Midwifery, BSc(Hons) Nursing Studies (3rd Year Entry), BSc Professional Health Studies (3rd Year Entry), BSc(Hons)Professional Health Studies (Part-Time)

Postgraduate courses: MSc Advancing Practice, PGCert Child Protection, MSc Cognitive Behavioural Therapy, Graduate Dip. District Nurse, MSc Forensic Mental Health, MSc Gerontology, MSc Health Studies, MSc Health Studies (Family health), Graduate Cert. Health Visiting, Graduate Cert. Manging Respiratory Disorders, MSc Mental Health Nursing, MSc Mental Health Practice, MSc Midwifery, Graduate Cert. Neonatal Nursing, Graduate Dip. Palliative Care, Graduate Cert. Personality Disorder, Graduate Dip. School Nursing, Graduate Cert. Sexual and Reproductive Health, Graduate Cert. Unscheduled Care, MSc Vulnerability Specialist Community Public Health Nursing – Health Visiting/ Occupational Health/ School Nursing PGDip, MSc Nursing, Sport Coaching MSc BA & BA(Hons) Journalism (with option in Sport), BSc(Hons) Applied Biomedical Science, BSc & BSc(Hons) Applied Bioscience, BSc & BSc(Hons) Applied Bioscience and Zoology, BSc & BSc(Hons) Applied Bioscience with Forensic Investigation (3rd year entry), BSc & BSc(Hons) Biomedical Science – Applied Biomedical Science, BSc & BSc(Hons) Chemistry, BSc & BSc(Hons) Environmental Health, BSc & BSc(Hons) Occupational Safety and Health, BSc & BSc(Hons) Pharmacy Science and Health, BSc & BSc(Hons) Sport and Exercise Science, BSc & BSc(Hons) Sport Coaching, BSc & BSc(Hons) Sport Development, BA(hons) Sport Coaching and Development

School of Media, Culture and Society ;
www.uws.ac.uk/schools/school-ofmedia-culture-and-society

BA & BA(Hons) Broadcast Production TV and Radio, BA & BA(Hons) Commercial Music, BA Commercial Sound Production (3rd year entry), BA & BA(Hons) Criminal Justice/Criminal Justice (Policing), BA & BA(Hons) Digital Art and Design (3rd Year Entry), BA & BA(Hons) Filmmaking and Screen Writing, BA & BA(Hons) Performance with performance/ contemporary theatre/ screen acting BSc & BSc(Hons) Psychology, BA(Hons) Social and Creative Transformations, BA(Hons) Criminal Justice / BA(Hons) Criminal Justice (Policing) BA & BA(Hons) Social Science, BA(Hons) Social Work, BA & BA(Hons) Society, Politics and Policy, BA & BA(Hons) Technical Theatre & Production (3rd year entry)

Postgraduate courses: MA Broadcast Journalism, MA Creative Media Practice, MA Cultural Diplomacy, MA Cultural Diplomacy and International Events, MA Cultural Diplomacy and International Music MA Filmmaking, MA Music with songwriting/ sound production/ industries, MPA Master in Public Administration (MPA), MSc Applied Social Science, MSc Career Guidance and Development, MSc Contemporary Drug and Alcohol Studies, MSc Policy Analysis and Global Governance, MSc Psychology, MSc Social Work, PGCert Child Protection

THE UNIVERSITY OF WESTMINSTER
www.westminster.ac.uk

College of Design, Creative and Digital Industries

School of Architecture and Cities

Architectural Technology BSc(Hons), Architecture and Environmental Design BSc(Hons), Architecture BA(Hons), Designing Cities: Planning and Architecture, BA(Hons), Interior Architecture BA(Hons)

Postgraduate courses: Architecture and Environmental Design MSc, Architecture MA, Interior Design MA, Master of Architecture (MArch) (RIBA pt II), Urban Design MA, Urban Design Postgraduate Diploma, BA, BSc, MA, PGCert, PGDip

School of Planning, Housing and Urban Design

Designing Cities: Planning and Architecture BA(Hons), Property and Planning BSc(Hons)

Postgraduate courses: Energy and Environmental Change MA, International Planning and Sustainable Development MA, Urban and Regional Planning

411

MA, Urban Design MA, Urban Design Postgraduate Diploma BA(Hons), MA, PGDip

Tourism and Events

Tourism and Events Management BA(Hons), Tourism Planning and Management BA(Hons), Tourism with Business BA(Hons)

Postgraduate courses: Events MA, Tourism Management MA, PhD and MPhil study

Transport and Logistics

Postgraduate courses: Air Transport Planning and Management MSc, Logistics and Supply Chain Management MSc, Transport Planning and Management MSc

School of Computing Science and Engineering

Business Information Systems Data Science and Analytics Digital Media Development

Postgraduate courses: Big Data Technologies, Business Intelligence and Analytics BSc, MSc

Computer and Network Engineering

Computer Network Security Computer Systems Engineering BSc, PhD, MPhil, DProf and MRes

Computer Science and Software Engineering

Computer Science, Data Science and Analytics, Software Engineering

Postgraduate courses: Software Engineering Advanced Software Engineering Cyber Security and Forensics Data, Culture and Society BEng, BSc, MSc, MA, PhD, MPhil, DProf and MRes

Digital Media and Games Computing

Computer Games Development, Digital Media Development

Postgraduate courses: Interactive Media Practice BSc, MA, PhD, MPhil, DProf and MRes

Westminster School of Arts

Art and Design

Animation BA(Hons), Animation BA(Hons), Fine Art Mixed Media BA(Hons), Fine Art Mixed Media BA(Hons), Graphic Communication Design BA(Hons), Illustration and Visual Communication BA(Hons)

Postgraduate courses: Creative Practice MRes, Interactive Media Practice MA

Fashion

Fashion Buying Management BA(Hons), Fashion Design BA(Hons), Fashion Marketing and Promotion BA(Hons), Fashion Merchandise Management BA(Hons)

Postgraduate courses: Fashion Business Management MA, Menswear MA

Music

Music Production, Performance and Enterprise BMus Honours

Postgraduate courses: Audio Production MA, Music Business Management MA

Photography

Contemporary Media Practice BA(Hons), Photography BA(Hons)

Postgraduate courses: Documentary Photography and Photojournalism MA, Photography Arts MA

Television, Film and Moving Image

Animation BA(Hons), Contemporary Media Practice BA(Hons), Film BA(Hons), Television Production BA(Hons)

Postgraduate courses: Film, Television and Moving Image MA

School of Media and Communication

Jounalism, Digital Media and PR

Digital Media and Communication BA(Hons), Journalism BA(Hons), Public Relations and Advertising BA(Hons), Radio and Digital Production BA(Hons), Television Production BA(Hons)

Postgraduate courses: Communication MA Data, Culture and Society MA Digital and Interactive Storytelling LAB MA Diversity and the Media MA Global Media Business MA Global Media MA International Media Business MA Media and Development MA Media Management MA Media, Campaigning and Social Change MA Multimedia Journalism (Broadcast) MA Multimedia Journalism (Print & Online) MA Public Relations MA Social Media, Culture and Society MA

Journalism and Mass Communication

Digital Media and Communication BA(Hons), Journalism BA(Hons), Public Relations and Advertising BA(Hons), Radio and Digital Production BA(Hons), Television Production BA(Hons)

Postgraduate courses: Communication MA, Communication Policy MA, Digital and Interactive Storytelling LAB MA, Diversity and the Media MA, Global Media Business MA, Global Media MA, International Media Business MA, Media and Development MA, Media Management MA, Media, Campaigning and Social Change MA, Media, Campaigning and Social

Change PG Diploma, Multimedia Journalism (Broadcast) MA, Multimedia Journalism (Broadcast) PG Diploma, Multimedia Journalism (Print & Online) MA, Multimedia Journalism (Print & Online) PG Diploma, Public Relations MA, Social Media, Culture and Society MA

School of Life Sciences

Biomedical Sciences

Biomedical Sciences BSc(Hons), Biomedical Sciences with Foundation BSc(Hons), Applied Biomedical Sciences BSc(Hons)
Postgraduate courses: Biomedical Sciences (Cancer Biology) MSc, Biomedical Sciences (Cellular Pathology) MSc, Biomedical Sciences (Clinical Biochemistry) MSc, Biomedical Sciences (Haematology) MSc, Biomedical Sciences (Immunology) MSc, Biomedical Sciences (Medical Microbiology) MSc, Biomedical Sciences (Medical Molecular Biology) MSc, Biomedical Sciences MSc, PhD, MPhil, DProf and MRes study

Biosciences

Biochemistry BSc(Hons), Biochemistry with Foundation BSc(Hons), Biological Sciences BSc(Hons), Biological Sciences with Foundation BSc(Hons), Pharmacology & Physiology BSc(Hons), Pharmacology and Physiology with Foundation BSc(Hons)
Postgraduate courses: Applied Biotechnology MSc, PhD, MPhil, DProf and MRes study

Business Information Systems

Business Information Systems BSc(Hons), Business Information Systems with Foundation BSc(Hons), Digital Media Development BSc(Hons)
Postgraduate courses: Business Intelligence and Analytics MSc, Business Systems Design and Integration MSc, Big Data Technologies MSc, PhD, MPhil, DProf and MRes study

Computer and Network Engineering

Computer Network Security/with foundation, Computer Systems Engineering/with foundation
Postgraduate courses: Computer Networks and Communications, Computer Networks with Cloud Technologies/with Security, BSc(Hons), DProf, MSc, MPhil, MRes, PhD

Computer Science and Software Engineering

Computer Science/with foundation) BSC Honours, Software Engineering MEng, Software Engineering with Foundation BEng

Postgraduate courses: Computer Networks with Cloud Technologies MSc, Computer Networks with Communications MSc, Computer Networks with Security MSc, PhD, MPhil, DProf and MRes study

Electronic Engineering

Postgraduate courses: Electrical Engineering for Modern Sustainable Transport Systems MSc, Electronics with Embedded Systems MSc, Electronics with Medical Instrumentation MSc, Electronics with Robotic and Control Systems MSc, Electronics with System-on-Chip Technologies MSc, Telecommunications with Digital Signal Processing MSc, Telecommunications with Satellite and Broadband Technologies MSc, Telecommunications with Wireless Technologies MSc, PhD, MPhil, DProf and MRes study

Multimedia and Games Computing

Computer Games Development BSc(Hons), Computer Games Development with Foundation BSc(Hons), Digital Media Development BSc(Hons), Digital Media Development with Foundation BSc(Hons)
Postgraduate courses: Interaction Design and Computing MSc, Interactive Media Practice MA, PhD, MPhil, DProf and MRes study

Nutrition

Human Nutrition BSc(Hons), Human Nutrition with Foundation BSc(Hons)
Postgraduate courses: Global Public Health Nutrition MSc, Sport and Exercise Nutrition MSc, PhD, MPhil, DProf and MRes study
College of Liberal Arts and Sciences

School of Social Sciences

Psychology

Cognitive and Clinical Neuroscience BSc(Hons), Psychology BSc(Hons), Psychology and Counselling BSc(Hons)
Postgraduate courses: Business Psychology MSc, Health Psychology MSc, Psychology MSc, PhD, MPhil, DProf and MRes study

Criminology

Criminology BA(Hons), Sociology and Criminology BA(Hons)
Postgraduate courses: PhD, MPhil, DProf and MRes study

English

Arabic and English Language BA(Hons), Arabic and English Literature BA(Hons), Chinese and English Language BA(Hons), Chinese and English Literature

BA(Hons), Creative Writing and English Language BA(Hons), Creative Writing and English Literature BA(Hons), English Language and Linguistics BA(Hons), English Literature and History BA(Hons), English Literature and Language BA(Hons), English Literature BA(Hons), French and English Language BA(Hons), French and English Literature BA(Hons), Spanish and English Language BA(Hons), Spanish and English Literature BA(Hons)

Postgraduate courses: Creative Writing: Writing the City MA, Creative Writing: Writing the City MA (January), Cultural and Critical Studies MA, Cultural and Critical Studies MA (January), English Language and Linguistics MA, English Language and Linguistics MA (January), English Language and Literature MA (January), English Language and Literature MA, English Literature: Modern and Contemporary Fictions MA, English Literature: Modern and Contemporary Fictions MA (January), Teaching English to Speakers of Other Languages MA (January), Teaching English to Speakers of Other Languages MA, PhD, MPhil, DProf and MRes study

History

English Literature and History BA(Hons), History and Politics BA(Hons), History BA(Hons), PhD, MPhil, DProf and MRes study

Languages

Arabic and English Language BA(Hons), Arabic and English Literature BA(Hons), Arabic and International Relations BA(Hons), Arabic and Linguistics BA(Hons), Chinese and English Language BA(Hons), Chinese and English Literature BA(Hons), Chinese and International Relations BA(Hons), Chinese and Linguistics BA(Hons), French and English Language BA(Hons), French and English Literature BA(Hons), French and International Relations BA(Hons), French and Linguistics BA(Hons), French and Spanish BA(Hons), Modern Languages: Arabic and Global Communication BA(Hons), Modern Languages: Chinese and Global Communication BA(Hons), Modern Languages: French and Global Communication BA(Hons), Modern Languages: Spanish and Global Communication BA(Hons), Spanish and English Language BA(Hons), Spanish and English Literature BA(Hons), Spanish and International Relations BA(Hons), Spanish and Linguistics BA(Hons), Translation Studies (French) BA(Hons), Translation Studies (Spanish) BA(Hons)

Postgraduate courses: International Liaison and Communication MA, International Liaison and Communication MA (January), Specialised Translation MA, Translating Cultures MRes, Translation and Interpreting MA (January), Translation and Interpreting MA, PhD, MPhil, DProf and MRes study

Linguistics

Arabic and Linguistics BA(Hons), Chinese and Linguistics BA(Hons), English Language and Linguistics BA(Hons), French and Linguistics BA(Hons), Spanish and Linguistics BA(Hons)

Postgraduate courses: Teaching English to Speakers of Other Languages MA, Teaching English to Speakers of Other Languages MA (January), PhD, MPhil, DProf and MRes study

Politics and International Relations

Arabic and International Relations BA(Hons), Chinese and International Relations BA(Hons), French and International Relations BA(Hons), History and Politics BA(Hons), International Relations and Development BA(Hons), International Relations BA(Hons), Politics and International Relations BA(Hons), Politics BA(Hons), Spanish and International Relations BA(Hons)

Postgraduate courses: Energy and Environmental Change MA (January), Energy and Environmental Change MA, International Relations and Democratic Politics MA (January), International Relations and Democratic Politics MA, International Relations and Security MA (January), International Relations and Security MA, International Relations MA (January), International Relations MA, PhD, MPhil, DProf and MRes study

Sociology

Sociology and Criminology BA(Hons), Sociology BA(Hons), PhD, MPhil, DProf and MRes study

School of Humanities

Visual Culture

Art and Visual Culture MA, Art and Visual Culture MA (January), Cultural and Critical Studies MA, Cultural and Critical Studies MA (January), Museums, Galleries and Contemporary Culture MA, Museums, Galleries and Contemporary Culture MA (January), PhD, MPhil, DProf and MRes study

Westminster Business School; www.westminster.ac.uk/about-us/faculties/westminster-business-school

School of Finance and Accounting

Accounting BSc(Hons), Business Economics BSc(Hons), Business Management (Accounting)

BA(Hons), Business Management (Economics) BA(Hons), Business Management (Finance) BA(Hons), Finance BSc(Hons)

Postgraduate courses: Finance and Accounting MSc, Finance and Accounting MSc (January), Finance, Banking and Insurance MSc, Global Finance MSc, International Economic Policy & Analysis MSc, Investment and Risk Finance MSc (January), Investment and Risk Finance MSc, PhD, MPhil, DProf and MRes study

School of Applied Mangement

Project Management

Arabic and International Business BA(Hons), Business Management (Accounting) BA(Hons), Business Management (Digital Business) BA(Hons), Business Management (Economics) BA(Hons), Business Management (Entrepreneurship) BA(Hons), Business Management (Finance) BA(Hons), Business Management (Human Resource Management) BA(Hons), Business Management (Marketing) BA(Hons), Business Management BA(Hons), Business Management with Foundation BA(Hons), Chinese and International Business BA(Hons), French and International Business BA(Hons), Human Resource Management BA(Hons), International Business BA(Hons), International Marketing BA(Hons), Marketing Communications BA(Hons), Marketing Management BA(Hons), Spanish and International Business BA(Hons)

Postgraduate courses: Digital Business MSc Entrepreneurship, Innovation and Enterprise Development MSc Human Resource Management MA (January), Human Resource Management MA International Business and Management MA/MSc (January), International Business and Management MA/MSc International Development Management MSc International Human Resource Management MA Management MA Management MA (January), Marketing Communications MA (January), Marketing Communications MA Marketing Management MA/MSc (January), Marketing Management MA/MSc Project Management MSc Purchasing and Supply Chain Management MSc Purchasing and Supply Chain Management MSc

Property and Construction Management

Architectural Technology BSc(Hons), Building Surveying BSc(Hons), Construction Management BSc(Hons), Property and Planning BSc(Hons), Quantity Surveying and Commercial Management BSc(Hons), Real Estate BSc(Hons)

Postgraduate courses: Building Information Management MSc Building Information Management

Postgraduate Diploma Construction Commercial Management MSc Construction Project Management MSc Property Finance MSc Property Finance Postgraduate Diploma Real Estate Development MSc PhD, MPhil, DProf and MRes study

Business and Management

School of Finance and Accounting

Accounting BSc(Hons), Business Economics BSc(Hons), Business Management (Accounting) BA(Hons), Business Management (Economics) BA(Hons), Business Management (Finance) BA(Hons), Finance BSc(Hons)

Postgraduate courses: Economic Policy and Analysis MSc Finance (Banking) MSc Finance (International Finance) MSc Finance and Accounting MSc (January), Finance and Accounting MSc Investment and Risk Finance MSc (January), Investment and Risk Finance MSc PhD, MPhil, DProf and MRes

School of Organisations, Economy and Society

Human Resource Management

Business Management (Human Resource Management) BA(Hons), Human Resource Management BA(Hons)

Postgraduate courses: Human Resource Management MA, Human Resource Management MA (January), International Human Resource Management MA, PhD, MPhil, DProf and MRes study

International Business

Arabic and International Business BA(Hons), Business Management (Accounting) BA(Hons), Business Management (Digital Business) BA(Hons), Business Management (Economics) BA(Hons), Business Management (Entrepreneurship) BA(Hons), Business Management (Finance) BA(Hons), Business Management (Human Resource Management) BA(Hons), Business Management (Marketing) BA(Hons), Business Management BA(Hons), Business Management with Foundation BA(Hons), Chinese and International Business BA(Hons), French and International Business BA(Hons), Human Resource Management BA(Hons), International Business BA(Hons), International Marketing BA(Hons), Marketing Communications BA(Hons), Marketing Management BA(Hons), Spanish and International Business BA(Hons)

Postgraduate courses: Digital Business MSc Entrepreneurship, Innovation and Enterprise Development MSc Human Resource Management MA Human Resource Management MA (January),

International Business and Management MA/MSc (January), International Business and Management MA/MSc International Development Management MSc International Human Resource Management MA Management MA (January), Management MA Marketing Communications MA (January), Marketing Communications MA Marketing Management MA/MSc (January), Marketing Management MA/MSc Project Management MSc Purchasing and Supply Chain Management MSc (January), Purchasing and Supply Chain Management MSc PhD, MPhil, DProf and MRes

School of Management and Marketing

Management & Leadership Development

Arabic and International Business BA(Hons), Business Management (Accounting) BA(Hons), Business Management (Digital Business) BA(Hons), Business Management (Economics) BA(Hons), Business Management (Entrepreneurship) BA(Hons), Business Management (Finance) BA(Hons), Business Management (Human Resource Management) BA(Hons), Business Management (Marketing) BA(Hons), Business Management BA(Hons), Business Management with Foundation BA(Hons), Chinese and International Business BA(Hons), French and International Business BA(Hons), Human Resource Management BA(Hons), International Business BA(Hons), International Marketing BA(Hons), Marketing Communications BA(Hons), Marketing Management BA(Hons), Spanish and International Business BA(Hons)

Postgraduate courses: Digital Business MSc Entrepreneurship, Innovation and Enterprise Development MSc Human Resource Management MA (January), Human Resource Management MA International Business and Management MA/MSc (January), International Business and Management MA/MSc International Development Management MSc International Human Resource Management MA Management MA (January), Management MA Marketing Communications MA (January), Marketing Communications MA Marketing Management MA/

MSc (January), Marketing Management MA/MSc Project Management MSc Purchasing and Supply Chain Management MSc (January), Purchasing and Supply Chain Management MSc PhD, MPhil, DProf and MRes

Marketing Management

Business Management (Marketing) BA(Hons), International Marketing BA(Hons), Marketing Communications BA(Hons), Marketing Management BA(Hons)

Postgraduate courses: Marketing Communications MA Marketing Communications MA (January), Marketing Management MA/MSc Marketing Management MA/MSc (January), PhD, MPhil, DProf and MRes Business Management (Marketing) BA(Hons), International Marketing BA(Hons)

Postgraduate courses: Marketing Communications MA, Marketing Communications MA (January), Marketing Management MA/MSc, Marketing Management MA/MSc, PhD, MPhil, DProf and MRes study

Westminster Law School; www.westminster.ac.uk/about-us/faculties/law

Law

European Legal Studies LLB Honours, Law LLB Honours, Law with French Law LLB Honours, MLaw (Integrated Masters of Law)

Postgraduate courses: Corporate Finance Law LLM (January), Energy and Environmental Change MA, Energy and Environmental Change MA (January), Entertainment Law LLM (January), Entertainment Law LLM, Graduate Diploma in Law, International and Commercial Dispute Resolution Law LLM, International and Commercial Dispute Resolution Law LLM (January), International Commercial Law LLM (January), International Commercial Law LLM, International Law LLM, International Law LLM (January), Legal Practice LLM, Religion, Law and Society MA/LLM

THE UNIVERSITY OF WINCHESTER
www.winchester.ac.uk

Faculty of Arts; www.winchester.ac.uk/ aboutus/Universitystructure/arts/Pages/ faculty_of_arts.aspx

English, Creative Writing and American Studies

BA(Hons) American Studies, BA(Hons) American Studies & History/film BA(Hons) Creative Writing, Creative and professional writing/ drama/ English literature BA(Hons) English Literature / with education studies/ film/ history/ creative writing/ english language BA(Hons) English Language Studies, BA(Hons) English with American Literature, BSc(Hons) Modern English literature English / with Linguistics Forensic Linguistics (with optional sandwich year) (subject to validation)

Postgraduate courses: MA Creative and Critical Writing, MA Writing for Children, MA English Literature,, MA English language and linguistics

Performing Arts

BA(Hons) Creative Writing and Drama, BA(Hons) Drama, BA(Hons) Musical Theatre, BA(Hons) Performing Arts, BA(Hons) Theatre Production (Arts and Stage Management), BA(Hons) Music and Sound Production, BA(Hons) Music Production and Performance (Popular Music), BA(Hons) Liberal Arts and Drama

Postgraduate courses: MA Cultural and Arts Management, Doctor of Creative Arts (Performing Arts)

School of Media and Film

BA Broadcast Television and Media Production, BA Creative Screen Production, BA Film and American Studies, BA Film Production, BA Film Studies, BA Film Studies and Production, BA Film Studies and Screenwriting, BA Journalism, BA Media and Audio Communication, BA Media and Communication, BA Media, Communication and Advertising, BA Media, Communication and Journalism, BA Media, Communication and Social Media, BA Music and Sound Production

Faculty of Business, Lawand Sport ; www.winchester.ac.uk/aboutus/ Universitystructure/BLS/Pages/ FacultyofBusiness/LawandSport.aspx

Winchester Business School

FdA Business Management for Information Technology, BA(Hons) Fashion: Media and Marketing, BA(Hons) Accounting and Finance, BA(Hons) Accounting and Management, BA(Hons) Business Management (top up), BA(Hons) Business Management for Information Technology, BA(Hons) Business Management with Enterprise and Innovation, BA(Hons) Business Management, BA(Hons) Event Management, BA(Hons) Marketing, BSc(Hons) Information Systems Management, FdSc Information Systems Management, MAcc(Hons) Accounting and Finance, MAcc(Hons) Accounting and Management

Postgraduate courses: MSc Project Management, (DBA) Doctor of Business Administration, Executive MBA, MA Applied Global Practice (Management), MSc Accounting and Finance, MSc Applied Global Practice (Management), MSc Insight Management, MSc International Business, MSc Marketing Innovation

Law

LLB(Hons) Law, BA(Hons) Law, LLM Medical Law and Ethics

Sport and Exercise

BSc Sport and Exercise Science, MSci Sport and Exercise Science, BSc Sport Psychology and Coaching, BSc Sports Coaching, BA Sports Business and Marketing, BA Sports Studies, BSc Strength, Conditioning and Fitness

Postgraduate courses: MSc Applied Sport & Exercise Science, MSc Sport and Exercise Psychology, MRes Sport and Exercise

Faculty of Education, Health and Social Care; www.winchester.ac.uk/aboutus/ Universitystructure /BLS/Pages/ FacultyofEducation/ HealthandSocialCare.aspx

Education Studies and Liberal Arts

BA(Hons) Education Studies, BA(Hons) Education Studies (Early Childhood), BA(Hons) Education

Studies (Special and Inclusive Education), BA(Hons) Modern Liberal Arts

Postgraduate courses: MA Philosophy of Education, MA Modern Liberal Arts, MEd Stud(Hons) Education Studies, MEd Stud(- Hons) Education Studies (Early Childhood), MEd Stud(Hons) Education Studies (Special and Inclusive Education)

Teacher Development

BEd(Hons) Primary Education with Recommendation of Qualified Teacher Status 3 Years, BEd(Hons) Primary Education with Recommendation of Qualified Teacher Status 4 Years, MEd(Hons) Primary Education with Recommendation of Qualified Teacher Status 4 Years

Postgraduate courses: Doctor of Education, MA Education, Masters in Research, PGCE in Primary Education (3-7 full time and 5-11 full and part time), PGCE Secondary Religious Education, Postgraduate Early Years ITT, School Direct Route

Interprofessional Studies

BA Childhood, Youth and Community Studies, BSc Health, Community and Social Care Studies, BA Childhood Studies (top-up), BSc(Hons) Social Work

Postgraduate courses: Mid-Wessex GP Education, PGCert and MSc Delivery of Primary Health Care, MA Medical Education, MSc Social Work

Faculty of Humanities and Social Sciences; www.winchester.ac.uk/ aboutus/Universitystructure/HSS/ Pages/FacultyofHumanitiesand SocialSciences.aspx

Applied Social Sciences

BA(Hons) Criminology, BA(Hons) Criminology and Sociology, BA(Hons) Forensic Studies, BSc(Hons) Geography

Postgraduate courses: MSc in Applied Criminology

Archaeology and Anthropology

BA(Hons) Anthropology, BSc(Hons) Archaeology, BA(Hons) Archaeology, BSc(Hons) Archaeological Practice, BSc(Hons) Archaeological Practice with Professional Placement, BA(Hons) History and Archaeology, BA(Hons) Ancient, Classical and Medieval Studies, BA(Hons) Classical Studies

Postgraduate courses: MA Cultural Heritage and Resource Management, MSc Human Osteology and Funerary Studies, MRes Archaeology, MRes Human Bioarchaeology

History

BA(Hons) History, BA(Hons) History and the Medieval World, BA(Hons) History and the Modern World

Postgraduate courses: MA History

Politics and Society

BA(Hons) Animal Welfare and Society, BA(Hons) Politics and Global Studies, BA(Hons) Philosophy, Politics and Economics, BA(Hons) Global History and Politics, BA(Hons) Sociology

Postgraduate course: MSc Animal Welfare Science, Ethics and Law

Psychology

BSc(Hons) Psychology (single/combined honours), BSc(Hons) Psychology and Cognition (single honours), BSc(Hons) Psychology and Child Development (single honours), BSc(Hons) Psychological Science (single honours), BSc(Hons) Social Psychology

Postgraduate courses: MSc Forensic Psychology (BPS-accredited); MPhil and PhD study in a range of subjects

Theology, Religion and Philosophy

BA(Hons) Philosophy, Religion and Ethics, BA(Hons) Theology, Religion and Ethics, BA(Hons) Philosophy, Politics and Economics

Postgraduate courses: MA Reconciliation, MA Reconciliation and Peacebuilding

UNIVERSITY OF WOLVERHAMPTON
www.wlv.ac.uk

Faculty of Arts; www.wlv.ac.uk/about-us/our-schools-and-institutes/faculty-of-arts

Wolverhampton School of Art

Animation, Fashion, Computer Games Design, Film and Televsion Production, Furniture Design, Glass and Ceramics, Illustration, Media, Media Film and Television Studies, Textiles and Surface Pattermn, Painting and Printmaking, Sports Journalism, (FD) Interactve Medial and Computer Games Development, Fine Art; Interior Design; Photography; Product Design

Postgrad: Design and Applied Arts; Fine Art; Digital and Visual Communications; Animation, Contemporary Media, Film and Screen, Film and Television Production, Public Relations and Corporate Communication, Research in Art and Design MA

School of Humanities
English
English & Deaf Studies/Education Studies/Film Studies/History/Philosophy
Postgrad: English; BA(Hons), MA
Creative and Professional Writing
Creative and Professional Writing and English/Film Studies/Media Philosophy; BA(Hons) English Language; English Language and Creative and Professional Writing/Linguistics/Media and Communication Studies/Media and Cultural Studies; BA(Hons)
Linguistics
Linguistics and English Language/Deaf Studies, Linguistics and TESOL
Postgrad: Language and Information Processing; BA(Hons), MA
Philosophy
Philosophy and Creative Professional Writing/English/Film Studies/Law/Politics/Religious Studies/Sociology
Postgrad: Human Sciences; BA(Hons), MRes
Religious Studies
Religious Studies and Education Studies/Philosophy/Sociology; BA(Hons)
Postgrad: Popular Culture Computational Linguistics, English, Research in Humanities, Sikh Studies, Practical Corpus Linguistics for ELT, Lexicography and Translation BA(Hons), MA

School of Performing Arts
Acting Dance Dance Science and Performance Dance and Drama; Drama; Drama with QTS Drama and Musical Theatre; Music; Music for Education and Community Practice Music Technology, Musical Theatre, Music Technology and Popular Music, Popular Music, Sound Production
Postgrad: Contemporary Theatre and Performance, Musical Theatre, Research in Performing arts, Research in Music Technology Dance; Dance Science; Music; Audio Technology; BA(Hons), BMus(Hons), MA, MMus, MSc

Faculty of Education, Health and Wellbeing; www.wlv.ac.uk/about-us/our-schools and-institutes/faculty-ofeducation-health-and-wellbeing

Institute of Education
Chemistry or Computer Science or Mathematics with Education; Early Childhood Studies; Young People, Family and Community Studies; Childhood and Family Studies and Education Studies/Social Policy/Sociology/Special Educational Needs, Disability, Inclusion; Childhood Studies with early Years Teacher Status; Education; Education (Learning Education with Progression); Education Studies; Education Studies and English; Early Years Primary; Early Years Services; Primary Education; Special Educational Needs, Disability, Inclusion Studies; Special Educational Needs, Disability, Inclusion Studies and Education Studies; Supporting Children in Primary Education
Postgrad: Education; Secondary Education Higher Education and Professional Practice; PGCE; Graduate Employment Based Route to EYTS Professional Graduate Certificate Post-Compulsory Education; Professional Practice and Lifelong Education; BA(Hons), BA (PCE), EYTS, BEd(Hons), BSc(Hons), CertED, PGCert, DEd, EDD, PGCE, PhD, FdA

Institute of Health
Developing Palliative and End of Life Care Practice; Emergency Practitioner (top-up); Nursing (Adult/Children's/Mental Health/Community Health/Learning Disabilities); Health Visiting, District Nursing, School Nursing, Practice Nursing, Prescribing for Practice Non-Medical Prescribing (V150), Extended/Supplementary Non-Medical Prescribing (V300) – Level 6, Advanced University Diploma General Practice Nursing Health and Social Care Practice/Top-Up/Restraint Reduction; Health and Wellbeing (Learning, Education and Progression); Health Studies (Top-Up); Lymphoedema Care; Nursing Studies Fast Track/Topup/ Subject-Specific Pathways (Acute Care/Care of the Older Person/Critical Care/Mental Health and Psychological Interventions/Orthopaedic Care/Renal Care); Midwifery; Palliative and End-of-Life Care/for Adults with Life-Limiting Illness/for Adults with Progressive Life-Limiting Illness; Paramedic Science; Podiatry; Special Educational Needs, Inclusion and Childhood and Family Studies Emergency Practitioner Physiotherapy, Podiatry
Postgrad: Adult / Mental Health Nursing; Health Visiting District Nursing School Nursing Practice Nursing Extended/Supplementary Non-Medical

Prescribing (V300) – Level 7 Advanced Clinical Practice; Advanced Practice for Allied Health Professionals (Diabetology/Musculoskeletal Disorders); Commissioning for Health and Social Care; Education for Health Social Care and Allied Professionals; Emergency Planning, Resilience and Response; Health and Social Care; Health and Wellbeing; Health and Wellbeing Top-up; Leadership and Management in Specialist Practice Perspectives of Child Development Safeguarding Children, Young People and Families Developing Skills in Primary Care Developing Health Assessment and Examination Skills within Clinical Practice (Previously 6NH019) 6NH050 Examining Public Health in Specialist Practice (Previously 6NH025) Supporting and Managing Patients with Complex Needs Working with Children and Adolescents Healthcare Leadership; Medical Education; Mental Health; Mental Health Nursing; Midwifery Studies; Nursing; Physician Associate Studies; Return to Nursing; Service Improvement; Specialist Clinical Nursing; Specialist Community Public Health Nursing (Health Visiting) BA(Hons), BNurs(Hons), BSc, BSc(Hons), MNurs, MAN, MMHN, MSc, PGCert, PGDip, ProfDoc

Institute of Human Sciences
Psychology; Psychology (Counselling Psychology/ Criminal Behaviour)
Postgrad: Counselling Psychology; Forensic and Investigative Psychology; Psychology; Psychology (Forensic/Occupational); BSc(Hons), PGCert, MSci(Hons), PhD, ProfDoc
Exercise and Health; Physical Education; Sport and Sports Studies and Development Sport and Exercise; Sports Coaching Practice; Sports Coaching Practice (Football/Martial Arts); Strength and Conditioning; Youth Sport; Exercise Science
Postgrad: Sport and Exercise Science; FDSc BA(Hons); BSc(Hons); MRes; MSci(Hons); PhD

Institute of Community and Society
Health Studies; Health Studies (top-up); Health and Social Care; Public Health; Social Care; Social Care and Criminology and Criminal Justice/Deaf Studies/ Health Studies/Sociology/Social Policy; Social Care (Learning, Education and Progression); Social Work; Social Work Studies; Specialist Social Work Studies; Standalone Modules: Becoming/ Developing Skills as a Social Work Practice Educator, Decision Making and Interventions with Adults, Qualifying as a Best Interests Assessor

Postgrad: Health and Social Care; Health and Wellbeing; Master of Public Health; Mental Health Practice for Approved Mental Health Professions; Standalone Modules: Becoming/ Developing Skills as a Social Work Practice Educator, Consolidating Critical Reflective Practice, Developing Critical Approaches to Decision Making, Decision Making and Interventions with Adults BSc(Hons), FD, MA/ MSc, MPH, PGCert, PGDip

Faculty of Science & Engineering; www.wlv.ac.uk/about-us/our-schoolsand-institutes/faculty-of-science-andengineering

School of Architecture & Built Environment
Architecture; Architectural Design Technology; Architectural Studies Building Surveying; Building Studies Civil Engineering; Civil and Transportation Engineering, Construction and the Built Environment Constructional Management; Environmental Health; Geography, Urban Environments and Climate Change / with QTS; Infrastructure Engineering and Management; Property Management and Real Estate Quantity Surveying
Postgrad: Built Environment Building Information Modelling; Civil Engineering; Civil Engineering Management; Construction Law Dispute and Resolution; Construction Programme and Project Management; Oil and Gas Management, Demolition Management HND, HNC, Fd BSc(Hons), BEng(Hons), MSc, PGCert, PhD

School of Sciences
Biology
]BSc(Hons) Animal Behaviour and Wildlife Conservation, BSc(Hons) Animal Behaviour and Wildlife Conservation with Sandwich Placement, MSci in Animal Behaviour and Wildlife Conservation, HND Animal Behaviour and Wildlife Conservation, HND Applied Biology, BSc(Hons) Biochemistry, BSc(Hons) Biochemistry with Sandwich Placement, BSc(Hons) Biological Sciences, BSc(Hons) Biological Sciences with Sandwich Placement, BSc(Hons) Genetics and Molecular Biology, BSc(Hons) Genetics and Molecular Biology with Sandwich Placement, BSc(Hons) Microbiology and Biotechnology, BSc(Hons) Microbiology and Biotechnology with Sandwich Placement, Foundation Routes, BSc(Hons) Biological Sciences with Foundation Year, HND Biomedical Science, BSc(Hons) Biomedical Science, BSc(Hons) Biomedical Science with Sandwich Placement, BSc(Hons) Healthcare Science (Physiological

Sciences), BSc(Hons) Medical Physiology and Diagnostics, BSc(Hons) Medical Science and Clinical Practice, Foundation Routes, Biomedical Science with Foundation Year, Fd (Science) Healthcare Science (Biomedical Science) (Spefically for Current NHS Employees) Animal Behaviour and Wildlife Conservation; Biochemistry; Biological Sciences; Biotechnology; Genetics and Molecular Biology; Microbiology; Molecular Bioscience

Chemistry
HND Chemistry, BSc(Hons) Chemistry, BSc(Hons) Chemistry with Sandwich Placement, BSc(Hons) Chemistry with Secondary Education (QTS), BSc(Hons) Chemistry with Pharmaceutical Science, BSc(Hons) Chemistry with Chemical Engineering, BSc(Hons) Chemistry with Chemical Engineering with Sandwich Placement, BSc(Hons) Chemical Engineering with Pharmaceutical Science, BSc(Hons) Chemical Engineering with Pharmaceutical Science with Sandwich Placement, BSc(Hons) Chemical Engineering with Chemistry, BSc(Hons) Chemical Engineering with Chemistry with Sandwich Placement, Master of Chemistry (MChem) – 4 Year Integrated Degree Chemistry, Chemistry with Secondary Education (QTS)

Forensic Science
Forensic Science with Policing

Physics
BSc(Hons) Physics, BSc(Hons) Physics with Secondary Education (QTS), BSc(Hons) Mathematics with Physics
Postgrad: Biomedical Science, MSc Biomedical Science, MSc Biomedical Science (Cellular Pathology), MSc Biomedical Science (Clinical Biochemistry), MSc Biomedical Science (Haematology), MSc Biomedical Science (Medical Microbiology), Doctor of Biomedical Science, Biological Sciences, MSc Applied Microbiology and Biotechnology, MSc Molecular Biology with Bioinformatics, Chemistry, MSc Chemistry, MSc Instrumental Chemical Analysis, Forensic, MSc Forensic Genetics and Human Identification, MSc Fire Scene Investigation, Wildlife, MSc in Wildlife Conservation HND BSc(Hons), MSc, MSci

School of Engineering

Aerospace Engineering
BEng(Hons) Aerospace Engineering, MEng(Hons) Aerospace Engineering

Automotive Engineering
BEng(Hons) Automotive Engineering MEng(Hons) Automotive Engineering

Chemical Engineering
BEng(Hons) Chemical Engineering, BSc(Hons) Chemical Engineering with Chemistry, BSc(Hons) Chemical Engineering with Pharmaceutical Science, Electronic and Telecommunications Engineering, BEng(Hons) Electronic and Telecommunications Engineering, MEng(Hons) Electronic and Telecommunications Engineering, Mechanical Engineering, BEng(Hons) Mechanical Engineering, MEng(Hons) Mechanical Engineering

Mechatronics Engineering
BEng(Hons) Mechatronics Engineering, MEng(Hons) Mechatronics Engineering

Motorsport Engineering
BEng(Hons) Motorsport Engineering, MEng(Hons) Motorsport Engineering

Foundation Routes
BEng(Hons) Aerospace Engineering with Foundation Year, BEng(Hons) Chemical Engineering with Foundation Year, BEng(Hons) Mechanical Engineering with Foundation Year, BEng(Hons) Electronics and Telecommunications Engineering with Foundation Year, BEng(Hons) Motorsport Engineering with Foundation Year, BEng(Hons) Manufacturing Engineering
Postgrad: MSc Manufacturing Engineering, MSc Advanced Technology Management (Engineering Analysis)

School of Mathematics & Computer Science
BSc Cyber Security, BSc(Hons) Computer Networking, BSc(Hons) Computer Science, BSc(Hons) Computing and Information Technology, BSc(Hons) Computer Science (Games Development), BSc(Hons) Computer Science (Software Engineering), BSc(Hons) Computer Science with Secondary Education (QTS), BSc(Hons) Data Science, BSc(Hons) Business Intelligence, BSc(Hons) Cloud Computing, HND Computing, BSc(Hons) Computing Software Development (Top-up), BSc(Hons) Management of IT (Top-up), BSc(Hons) Computer Networks (Top up), BSc(Hons) Computer Security (Top-Up), HND Information Technology, Fd (Science) Computing
Postgrad: MSc Web and Mobile Application Development, MSc Human Computer Interaction, MSc Cyber Security/ with digital forensics, MSc Cybersecurity and Digital Forensics, MPHIL/PhD Postgraduate research in Computer Science, MPHIL/PhD Postgraduate research in Computing and Mathematics by Distance Learning, MSc Computer Science with Professional Practice (International Applicants Only) Fd, HND BSc(Hons), MSc, PGCert

School of Pharmacy

Pharmaceutical Science; Pharmacology; Pharmacy
Postgrad: Pharmaceutical Science Independent Prescribing; BSc(Hons), MPharm, MSc

School of Medicine and Clinical Practice

BSc in Medical Sciences and Clinical Practice
Postgrad: MSc Clinical Practice Physician Associate
PG Diploma

*Faculty of Social Sciences;
www.wlv.ac.uk/about-us/our-schoolsand-institutions/faculty-of-socialsciences*

The Wolverhampton Business School

Business, Business Management, Finance, Accounting Systems and Economics: BA(Hons) Accounting and Finance, BA(Hons) Economics
Human Resources and Leadership: BA(Hons) Human Resource Management
Marketing, Innovation, Leisure and Enterprise: BA(Hons) Event and Venue Management, BA(Hons) International Hospitality Management, BA(Hons) Marketing Management, BA(Hons) Tourism Management
Postgrad: Master of Business Administration (MBA), Master of Business Administration (International Development), International Masters of Business Administration (IMBA), MSc Finance and Accounting, MSc Healthcare Leadership, MSc Human Resource Development and Organisational Change (CIPD accredited), MSc Human Resource Development and Organisational Change (CIPD accredited) Top-Up, MA Human Resource Management (CIPD accredited), MA Human Resource Management (Top Up), MSc Innovation and Entrepreneurship, MSc Innovation and Entrepreneurship at University Centre Stafford (Beaconside), MSc International Banking and Finance, MSc International Business Management, MSc Professional Accounting and Finance, MSc Leadership and Management, MSc Marketing Management, MA Hospitality and Event Management, Master of Business Administration (Extended), Master of Business Administration (International Development) Extended, International Masters of Business Administration (IMBA) Extended, MSc Finance and Accounting (Extended), MA Human Resource Management (Extended), MSc Innovation and Entrepreneurship (Extended), MSc International Banking and Finance (Extended), MSc International Business Management (Extended), MSc Professional Accounting and Finance (Extended), MSc Leadership

and Management (Extended), MSc Marketing Management (Extended)
Diplomas and Certificates: Postgraduate Certificate Coaching and Mentoring, Diploma in Management Studies, Postgraduate Certificate in Management Studies, Postgraduate Diploma Human Resource Development and Organisational Change (CIPD accredited), Postgraduate Diploma Human Resource Management (CIPD accredited), Postgraduate Certificate Medical Education, PG Certificate Hospitality and Event Management, PG Certificate Leadership
Professional courses: CIM Professional Certificate in Marketing, CIM Professional Diploma in Marketing, HND, Fd, BA(Hons), PGCert, PGDip, MSc, MA CIM

Wolverhampton Law School; Law, Accounting and Law, Business and Law

LLB(Hons) Law, BA(Hons) Accounting and Law, BA(Hons) Business and Law, BA(Hons) Human Resource Management and Law, Law with Criminology and Criminal Justice/ Social Policy/ Philosophy
Postgrad: LLM (Law), LLM (Common Professional Examination), LLM CPE by Distance Learning, Legal Practice Course (LPC), LLM Legal Practice Course (LPC), LLM Professional Practice (Top up), LLM International Corporate and Financial Law, LLM International Business Law, LLM Law and Human Resource Management
Professional Course: CILEx (Chartered Institute of Legal Executives), LLB, LLM, CILEx

School of Sociology, History & Political Studies

BA(Hons) Sociology, BA(Hons) Criminology, Criminal Justice & Sociology, BA(Hons) Sociology and History, BA(Hons) Sociology and Politics, BA(Hons) Sociology and Social Policy, BA(Hons) Philosophy and Sociology and BA(Hons) Religious Studies and Sociology., BA(Hons) Social Care and Sociology, BA(Hons) Childhood and Family Studies and Sociology., BA(Hons) Social Policy, BA(Hons) Sociology and Social Policy, BA(Hons) Politics and Social Policy, BA(Hons) Criminology, Criminal Justice and Social Policy, BA(Hons) Social Policy and Law, BA(Hons) Criminology and Criminal Justice, BA(Hons) Criminology and Criminal Justice and Law, BA(Hons) Criminology and Criminal Justice and Sociology, BA(Hons) Criminology and Criminal Justice and Social Policy, BA(Hons) Criminology and Criminal Justice and Social Care

History

BA(Hons) Politics and History, BA(Hons) Politics and Media, BA(Hons) Politics and Philosophy, BA(Hons)

Politics and Social Policy, BA(Hons) Politics and War Studies, BA(Hons) Sociology and Politics, BA(Hons) War Studies, BA(Hons) History and War Studies, BA(Hons) Politics and War Studies, BA(Hons) War Studies and Philosophy, BSc(Hons) Armed Forces, BSc(Hons) Aviation Fire and Rescue (distance learning), BSc(Hons) Fire and Rescue, BSc(Hons) Policing and Intelligence, BA(Hons) Professional Policing

Postgrad: MA in the History of the First World War, MA Second World War: Conflict, Societies, Holocaust, MA Military History by Distance Learning (fully online course), MA in Twentieth Century Britain, MA Military History by Distance Learning, MA History of the First World War, MA Second World War Studies: Conflict, Societies, Holocaust, MA Air, Space and Cyber Power Studies by Distance Learning

UNIVERSITY OF WORCESTER
www.worc.ac.uk

School of Arts; www.worc.ac.uk/about/academic-schools/school-of-the-arts/home.aspx

Animation (Joint Honours), Animation & Film Production BA(Hons), Animation & Game Art/ Graphic Design/ Illustration/ Screenwriting BA(Hons), Art & Design MPhil/ PhD, Creative Media & Film Production/ Graphic Design/ Journalism/ Media & Culture, Creative Media MA/ MPhil/ PhD, Creative Writing and Illustration/ Screenwriting BA(Hons), Dance HND, Design MRes, Drama and Performance and English Literature/ Film Studies/ Screenwriting BA(Hons), Drama & Performance BA(Hons)/ MPhil/ PhD, Drama with Psychology BA(Hons), English Literature and Journalism BA(Hons), Film Production and Screenwriting BA(Hons), Film Production BA(Hons), Fine Art BA(Hons)/ MRes, Fine Art and Illustration/ Psychology BA(Hons), Game Art BA(Hons), Graphic Design and Illustration BA(Hons), Graphic Design BA(Hons), Illustration BA(Hons), Journalism and Media Culture/ Politics/ Screenwriting BA(Hons), Journalism BA(Hons), Product Design BA(Hons), Screenwriting (Joint Honours), Theatre and Performance MRes, Touring Theatre MTheatre

School of Education; www.worc.ac.uk/discover/institute-of-education

BA(Hons)/ FdA Birth and Beyond Collaborative Working with Children, Young People & Families FdA, Diploma in Education and Training, Doctor of Education EdD, Early Childhood (Professional Practice) BA(Hons), Early Years Foundation Degree (Flexible and Distributed Learning Pathway), Early Years Foundation Degree, Early Years Professional FdA Education Studies BA(Hons), Education studies with English Language BA(Hons) Education Studies degrees, Education MA/PGDip/PGCert, Inclusive Education FdA Integrated Working with Children & Families BA(Hons) Top-up Degree, Leading Early Years Practice PGCert, Learning Support FdA, Learning and Development from Early Years to Adolescence (0-19) FdA, Learning and Teaching in Higher Education PG Cert, MA / PG Dip / MA / PG Dip / PG Cert Education (Special and Inclusive Education), Primary (QTS), PGCE – Primary Mathematics, PGCE – Primary Physical Education, PGCE – School Direct Primary, PGCE – School Direct Secondary, PGCE – Secondary with Business with Economics, ICT, Design and technology (food), English, Geography, History, Mathematics, Modern languages, PE, Psychology, RE, Biology, Chemistry, Physics Primary Initial Teacher Education (with QTS) BA(Hons), Primary and Outdoor Education BA(Hons Outdoor Education MA), Professional Practice BA(Hons) Top-up Degree, Religion, Philosophy & Values in Education BA(Hons), Special Educational Needs, Disabilities and Inclusion BA(Hons), Sports Coaching and Physical Education FdSc Subject Knowledge Enhancement, Teaching and Learning FdA, University Diploma in Private Tutoring

School of Allied Health and Community www.worc.ac.uk/discover/institute-ofhealth-and-society.html

Advancing Practice MSc, Animal Biology MPhil/ PhD, Allied Health Studies and Social Care BA(Hons) Top up MPhil/ PhD, Applied Criminology BA(Hons), Applied Health & Social Science BA(Hons) Top-up Degree, Birth and Beyond BA(Hons), Birth and Beyond FdA, Business Psychology BSc(Hons), Child & Adolescent Mental Health FdSc, Child and Adolescent Mental Health BSc(Hons) Top-up Degree, Counselling FdSc, Dementia Studies MPhil/PhD, EMDR Therapy MSc, Health and Social Care FdSc, Health and Wellbeing in Society FdSc Integrative

Counselling BA(Hons), Integrative Counselling FdA, Mental Health FdSc, Mental Health and Wellbeing of Children and Young People FdSc Nutritional Therapy PGDip / MSc, Occupational Therapy BSc(Hons), Occupational Therapy MPhil/PhD, Paramedic Science BSc, Paramedic Science BSc Top-up Degree Physician Associate MSc, Physiotherapy BSc(Hons), Public Health MSc, Social Work & Social Policy MPhil/PhD, Social Work BA(Hons), Social Work MA (Subject to approval), Supervision PGCert Understanding Domestic and Sexual Violence MA /PG Cert/ PG Dip

School of Humanities www.worc.ac.uk/about/academic-schools/school-of-humanities/school-of-humanities.aspx

Creative Media and Film Production/ Culture BA(Hons) Creative Writing Joint Honours, Creative Writing and English Language/ Literature/HIstory/ Illustration/Screenwriting BA(Hons) Criminology BA(Hons), Criminology and Psychology/Sociology BA/ BSc Criminology with Policing BA(Hons), Drama & Performance and English Literature/Film Studies BA(Hons) degrees, Education Studies and English Language/Literature/Sociology BA(Hons) English Language degrees, English Literature BA(Hons), English Literature and Language MPhil/ PhD, English Literature degrees, Employment Law LLM, Film Studies BA(Hons)/MPhil/PhD, Film Studies and Media & Culture/Screen writing BAHons History BA(Hons)/MA, History and Journalism/ Politics/Sociology History MPhil/PhD/MRes, Journalism and Media Culture/Politics BA(Hons), Law LLB(Hons), Law with Criminology LLB(Hons), Law with Forensic Psychology LLB(Hons), Media & Culture BA(Hons), Media & Culture degrees, Media and Cultural Studies MPhil/PhD, Politics (Joint Honours), Politics and Sociology BA(Hons), Psychology and Sociology BA/BSc(Hons), Religion, Philosophy & Values in Education and Sociology BA(Hons) Sociology BA(Hons), Sociology MPhil/PhD/MRes, Sociology degrees

School of Law www.worcester.ac.uk/about/academic-schools/school-of-humanities/school-of-law.aspx

Law LLB Hons, Law with Criminology/ Psychology LLB Hons, Legal Practice LLM Top Up

School of Psychology www.worc.ac.uk/about/academic-schools/school-of-psychology/home.aspx

Business Psychology BSc(Hons), Clinical Psychology BSc(Hons), Counselling MSc, Counselling Psychology BSc(Hons), Criminology and Psychology BSc(Hons), Criminology MPhil/ MRes, Education Studies and Psychology BSc(Hons), Fine Art with Psychology BA(Hons), Forensic Psychology BSc(Hons), Human Biology and Psychology BSc(Hons), Human Nutrition and Psychology BSc(Hons), Occupational/ Business Psychology MSc, Positive Psychology Coaching PG Cert, Psychology and Religion, Philosophy and Values in Education BA/ BSc(Hons), Psychology and Sociology BA/ BSc(Hons), Psychology BSc(Hons)/ MPhil/ PhD/ MSc, Sport and Exercise Psychology BSc(Hons)

School of Science and the Environment www.worc.ac.uk/about/academic-schools/school-of-science-and-the-environment/home.aspx

Animal Biology BSc(Hons), Animal Biology MBiol (Integrated Masters), Animal Biology MPhil/PhD, Animal Biology degrees, Archaeological Landscapes MA, Archaeology & Heritage Studies degrees, Archaeology MPhil/PhD, Archaeology MRes, Archaeology and Heritage Studies BA(Hons), Atmospheric Sciences MPhil/PhD, Biochemistry BSc(Hons), Biochemistry MBiol (Integrated Masters) Biochemistry MPhil/PhD, Biological Sciences degrees, Biology BSc(Hons), Biology MBiol (Integrated Masters), Biology MRes, Biology and Ecology BSc(Hons) Biomedical Science BSc(Hons), Dental Technology FdSc Ecology BSc(Hons), Ecology MPhil/PhD, Ecology and Environmental Management MRes, Ecology degrees, Environmental Science BSc(Hons), Environmental Science degrees, Environmental Studies/Science MPhil/PhD, Forensic and Applied Biology BSc(Hons), Geography BSc(Hons), Geography with teaching BSc(Hons), Geography degrees, Human Biology BSc(Hons), Human Biology MBiol (Integrated Masters), Human Biology MPhil/ PhD, Human Biology degrees, Human Geography BA(Hons), Human Geography MPhil/PhD, Human Geography degrees, Human Nutrition BSc(Hons), Human Nutrition degrees, Mathematics BSc(Hons), Mathematics MPhil/PhD, Mathematics and Computer Science BSc(Hons), Mathematics degrees, Pharmacology BSc(Hons) Physical Geography BSc(Hons), Physical Geography MPhil/PhD, Physical Geography degrees, Plant Biology MPhil/PhD, River Science MRes

School of Sport & Exercise Science; www.worc.ac.uk/about/academic-schools/school-of-sport-and-exercise-science/home.aspx

Adapted Sport MSc Applied Sport Science MSc, Applied Sports Performance Analysis MSc, Dance and Applied Practice BA(Hons), Football Business Management and Coaching FdSc, International Sport Management MSc, Outdoor Adventure Leadership & Management BSc(Hons), Outdoor Education MA, Physical Education BSc(Hons), Physical Education and Dance BA(Hons), Physical Education and Outdoor Education/Sports Coaching Science BSc(Hons), Physical Education degrees, Socio-Cultural Studies of Sport and Exercise MRes, Sport and Community FdA Sport & Exercise Science BSc(Hons), Sport & Exercise Science MPhil/PhD, Sport Business Management BA(Hons), Sport MSc Sport Development & Coaching BA(Hons), Sport, Coaching & Physical Education, Sports Coaching MSc, Sports Coaching Science BSc(Hons), Sports Coaching Science degrees, Sports Coaching Science with Disability Sport BSc(Hons), Sports Therapy BSc(Hons)

Three Counties School of Nursing and Midwifery

Advancing Practice MSc, Midwifery BSc(Hons), Midwifery MPhil/ PhD, Nursing Associate FdSc, Public Health MSc, Return to Nursing Practice

Worcester Business School; www.worc.ac.uk/discover/worcesterbusines-school

Accounting and Finance BA(Hons), Business & Accountancy BA(Hons), Business & Digital Communications BA(Hons), Business & Enterprise BA(Hons), Business & Finance BA(Hons), Business & Human Resource Management BA(Hons), Business & Marketing BA(Hons), Business Information Technology BSc(Hons), Business MPhil/PhD, Business Management BA(Hons) Top-Up, Business Management BA(Hons), Business Management HND, Business Management degrees, Business Studies BA(Hons), Business, Economics & Finance BA(Hons), Chartered Manager Degree Apprenticeship Computer Games Design & Development BSc(Hons), Computing and Education Studies BSc(Hons), Computing MPhil/PhD, Computing degrees, Doctor of Business Administration DBA, Human Resource Management MA, Human Resource Management MSc International Business Management BA(Hons), International Finance BA(Hons) top-up, International Management MSc, Leadership and Management FdA/BA(Hons), MBA – Master of Business Administration, MBA in Executive Leadership & Management (Part-Time), Marketing BA(Hons), Marketing Marketing, Advertising and Public Relations BA(Hons), University Diploma in Leadership and Management (UDLM), Senior Leaders Masters Degree Apprenticeship, Operations/ Departmental Management Higher Apprenticeship

UNIVERSITY OF YORK
www.york.ac.uk

Dept of Archaeology; www.york.ac.uk/archaeology

BA and BSc archaeology; BA archaeology and heritage; BA historical archaeology; BSc bioarchaeology

Postgrad: MSc Digital Archaeology MSc Bioarchaeology; MA Conservation Studies; MA in Cultural Heritage Management, MSc Digital Heritage; MA/MSc early Prehistory and Human Origins; MA/MSc Funerary Archaeology; MA/ MSc Material Culture and Experimental Archaeology; MA Historical Archaeology; Zooarchaeology; the Archaeology of Buildings; Conservation Studies; Cultural Heritage Management; Field Archaeology; Historical Archaeology; Medieval Archaeology; Prehistoric Landscape Archaeology; Mesolithic Studies MA English Buildings History by Distance Learning (with the Centre for Lifelong Learning); MA Stained Glass Conservation and Heritage Management (with the Department of History of Art); MSc Human Anatomy and Evolution (with Hull York Medical School)

Dept of Biology; www.york.ac.uk/biology

Biology; Biochemistry; Biomedical Sciences; Biotechnology & Microbiology; Ecology; Genetics; Molecular Cell Biology; Industrial Biotechnology (MSc only); BSc, MPhil, MRes, MSc, PhD, MBiol

Dept of Chemistry; www.york.ac.uk/chemistry

Chemistry; Chemistry, Green Principles and Sustainable Processes; Chemistry, the Atmosphere and the Environment Chemistry, Biological and Medicinal Chemistry; Molecular Medicine; Biodiversity, Ecology and Ecosystems; Industrial Biotechnology BSc, MChem, MPhil, MSc, PhD

Dept of Computer Science; www.cs.york.ac.uk

Computer Science; Computer Science with Artificial Intelligence; Computer Science and Mathematics
Postgraduate: Computer Science with Cyber Security; Doctorate in Intelligent Games and Game Intelligence; Humancentred Interactive Technologies; Safety Critical Systems Engineering; System Safety Engineering with Automotive Applications; Social Media & Interactive Technology; Computer Science with Data Analytics BEng, BSc, MEng, MMath, MPhil, MSc, PGCert, PGDip

Dept of Economics & Related Studies; www.york.ac.uk/economics

Economics; Economics and Finance; Economics and Econometrics; Economics, Econometrics and Finance; Economics and Mathematics; Economics and Philosophy; Economics and Politics; Mathematics and Finance; Philosophy, Politics and Economics
Postgrad: Development Economics and Emerging Markets; Econometrics and Economics; Economics; Economics and Finance; Economics and Public Policy; Finance and Econometrics; Financial Engineering; Health Economics; Project Analysis, Finance and Investment; BA, BSc, MPhil, MSc, PGCert, PGDip, PhD

Dept of Education; www.york.ac.uk/education

Education; English in Education; Sociology and Education; Psychology in Education, PGCE (English, History, Maths, Foreign Languages, Sciences, Teacher Training)
Postgraduate Courses: Applied Linguistics; Applied Linguistics for ELT; Applied Linguistics for Language Teaching; Global & International Citizenship Education; Science Education; Social Justice and Education; Teaching English to Speakers of Other Languages; Teaching English to Young Learners; BA, MA, MPhil, PhD, PGCE

Dept of Electronic Engineering www.york.ac.uk/electronics

Electronic Engineering; Electronic and Communication Engineering; Electronic and Computer Engineering; Electronic Engineering with Nanotechnology; Electronic Engineering with Business Management; Music Technology Systems; Engineering; Medical Engineering; Micro-Mechanical Engineering; Robotic Engineering
Postgraduate Courses: Audio and Music Technology; Communications Engineering; Digital Systems Engineering; Electronic Engineering; Embedded Wireless Systems; Engineering Management; Intelligent Robotics; Music Technology; Nanoscale BEng, MEng, MSc, MPhil, PhD

Centre for Eighteenth Century Studies; www.york.ac.uk/eighteenth-centurystudies

MA in Eighteenth Century Studies; MA

Dept of English & Related Literature; www.york.ac.uk/english

English; English/History; English/History of Art; English/Linguistics; English/Philosophy; English/Politics
Postgraduate Courses: Culture & Thought After 1945, Eighteenth Century Studies; English Literary Studies; Film and Literature; Global Literature and Cultures; Literature of the Romantic Period, 1775-1832; Medical History and Humanities; Medieval Literatures & Languages, Modern and Contemporary Literature and Culture; Poetry and Poetics, Renaissance Literature, 1500-1700; Victorian Literature and Culture; BA, MA, MPhil, PhD

Dept of Environment and Geography; www.york.ac.uk/environment

Environment, Economics and Ecology; Environmental Geography; Environmental Science; Human Geography and Environment; BSc, MEnv
Postgraduate Courses: Environmental Economics & Environmental Management; Environmental Science and Management; Marine Environmental Management; Corporate Social Responsibility and Environmental Management; MPhil, MSc, PhD

Centre for Health Economics; www.york.ac.uk/che

Economic Evaluation of Health Technologies; Economic evaluation for Health Technology Assessment, Health Econometrics & Data; Health Economics; Health Economics for Healthcare Professionals; Health Policy, Mental Health Policy; MSc, PhD

Dept of Health Sciences; www.york.ac.uk/ healthsciences

Biomedical Sciences; Nursing; Nursing (Adult); Nursing (Child); Nursing (Learning Disability); Nursing (Mental Health); Midwifery

Postgraduate: Advanced Clinical Practice Applied Health Research, Health Research and Statistics; International Humanitarian Affairs; Public Health; BA, BSc, DipHE, MPhil, MSc, PGCert, PGDip, PhD, MPH, FD, MNursing, Dip

Dept of History; www.york.ac.uk/history

History; History/Economics; History/English; History/ French; History/Philosophy; History/Politics; History of Art

Postgrad: Contemporary History and International Politics; Culture and Thought After 1945; Early Modern History; Eighteenth Century Studies; Medical History and Humanities; Medieval History; Medieval Studies; Modern History; Public History; Renaissance and Early Modern Studies, Women's Studies; Eighteenth Century Studies A, MA, MPhil, PhD, PGDip

Dept of History of Art; www.york.ac.uk/ history-of-art

History of art, English/History of Art; History/ History of Art; Curating and Art History

Postgrad: History of Art; History of Art (Architectural History and Theory); History of Art (British art); History of Art (Medieval Art and Medievalisms); History of Art (Modern and Contemporary Art); History of Art (Sculpture Studies); Stained Glass Conservation & Heritage Management; BA, MA, MPhil, PhD

Hull YorkMedical School; www.hyms.ac.uk

Undergraduate Qualifying Medical Courses

Postgraduate: Pharmacology and Drug Development Biomedical Sciences; Clinical Anatomy; Clinical Anatomy and Education; Human Sciences, Medical Sciences; Medicine; Public Health; Health Professions Education; Human Anatomy and Evolution; Physicians Associate Studies; MBBS, MSc, PGCert, MD, PhD, MPhil, BSc

Centre for Applied Human Rights; www.york.ac.uk/cahr

Applied Human Rights, International Human Rights Law & Practice; LLM, MA, PhD, PGCert

Dept of Language & Linguistic Science; www.york.ac.uk/language

Studying two Languages: French and German/ Italian/Spanish; German and Italian/Spanish; Italian and Spanish; Studying one Language and Linguistics: French/German/Italian/Spanish; Linguistics with French/German/Italian/Spanish; History/French; French/Philosophy; German/Philosophy; Studying English, English Language & Linguistics; English/ Linguistics; Studying Linguistics: Linguistics; Philosophy/Linguistics

Postgraduate Courses: Linguistics; Comparative Syntax and Semantics; Forensic Speech Science; Language and Communication; Language Variation and Change; Linguistics by Research; Phonetics and Phonology; Phonological Development, Psycholinguistics; Sociolinguistics; BA, MA, MPhil, MSc, PhD

York Law School; www.york.ac.uk/law

Law; Law Senior Status International Corporate & Commercial Law, International Human Rights Law & Practice; Law by Research; Legal & Political Theory; Art Law; Professional Practice (Corporate Commercial) LLB, LLM, MPhil, PhD, MA

York Management School; www.york.ac.uk/management

Business and Management/ with a Year in Industry/ Abroad Accounting, Business Finance/ with a Year in Industry/ Abroad and Management; Actuarial Science/ with a Year Abroad/ in Industry; Marketing; Finance Operations Research, Management and Statistics/ with a Year Abroad/ in Industry

Postgraduate Courses: Accounting and Financial Management; Global Marketing; Human Resource Management; International Business; International Strategic Mangement; International Business and Strategic Management; Management; Management with Business Finance; Leadership and Management with Innovation/ Finance/ International Business; BA, BSc, MA, MPhil, MRes, MSc, PhD

Dept of Mathematics; www.york.ac.uk/ maths/

Mathematics / with a Year in Industry/ Europe; Actuarial Science; Mathematics with Actuarial Science/ Computer Science/Economics/Physics/Statistics/ Finance/Philosophy/Linguistics; Natural Sciences; Finance, Operations Research, Management and Statistics

Postgrad: Mathematical Sciences; Financial Engineering, Mathematical Finance (Distance Learning also Available); Statistics & Computational Finance; BA,

BSc, MMath, MPhil, MRes, MSc, PGCert, PGDip, PhD

Centre for Modern Studies; www.york.ac.uk/modernstudies
Culture & Thought after 1945; MA

Dept of Music; www.york.ac.uk/music
Music; Music with Composition/ English Church music, Music Psychology, Musicology/ Performance Practice/ Piano Studies/ Solo Voice Ensemble/ Vocal Studies and Sound Recording

Postgraduate Courses: Music; Music by Thesis/ Research/ Composition/ Performance; Community Music; Music Education; Music Production, Music Technology/ by Research BA, MA, MPhil, PhD, PGDip/Cert

Dept of Philosophy; www.york.ac.uk/philosophy
Philosophy, Philosophy with Economics/Politics/Politics & Economics/Mathematics & Physics/Neuroscience/ Social & Political Sciences/English/French/German/ History/ Mathematics/Linguistics/Sociology/Physics; BA, BSc

Postgraduate: PPE with Economics and Development/ Philosophy/ Politics; Politics and Development; Political Economy; Philosophy and Public Affairs; Political Research; Economics; Philosophy; Politics BA, BSc, GradDip, MA, MPhil, PhD

Dept of Physics; www.york.ac.uk/physics
Physics; Physics with Astrophysics/Mathematics/Philosophy; Theoretical Physics

Postgraduate: Physics/ by Research; Plasma Science in Fusion Energy; BA, BSc, MMath, MPhys, MSc, PhD

Dept of Politics; www.york.ac.uk/politics
Politics with a Year in Industry; Politics with International Relations/English/ History/Economics/ Philosophy ; Politics, Philosophy and Economics; Social and Political Sciences; International Relations with a Year in Industry

Postgraduate Courses: Politics; Conflict, Governance & Development; Environment and Politics; Social Research; Applied Human Rights; International Political Economy; International Relations; Public Administration; Public Administration & Public Policy/International Development; Postwar Recovery Studies; Global Development BA, MA, MSc, PhD MPA

Dept of Psychology; www.york.ac.uk/psychology
Psychology; Neuroscience

Postgraduate Courses: Cognitive Neuroscience and Neuroimaging, Forensic Psychology Studies; Development, Disorders and Clinical Practice; Developmental Cognitive Neuroscience; Research in Psychology; BSc, MPsych, MPhil, MRes, MSc, PhD

Dept of Social Policy & SocialWork; www.york.ac.uk/spsw
Applied Social Science; Social Policy (Children & Young People/Crime & Criminal Justice); Criminology; Social and Political Sciences; Social Work

Postgraduate Courses: Comparative and International Social Policy; Comparative Applied Social and Public Policy; Global Crime and Justice; Global Social Policy; Master of Public Administration; Master of Public Administration, International Development; Public Policy and Management; Public Policy and Management (Online); Social and Public Policy (Online); Social Policy; Social Work/ Practice (Think Ahead); Practice Education in Social Work BA, MA, MPA, MPhil, MRes, PhD MSocW

Dept of Sociology; www.york.ac.uk/sociology
Postgrad: Sociology by Research, Language and Communication, Bioscience and Society Sociology, Sociology with Criminology/ Social Psychology, Sociology/Education, Philosophy/Sociology, Social and Political Sciences/ with Philosophy; Criminology Postgraduate; Criminology/ and Social Research, Culture, Society and Globalization, Social Media and Social Research, Social Media and Management, Social Media and Interactive Technologies; BA, MA, MPhil, MSc, PhD

Dept of Theatre, Film & Television; www.york.ac.uk/tftv
Business of the Creative Industries; Interactive Media; Theatre Writing, Directing & Performance; Film & Television Production

Postgraduate Courses: Playwriting; Theatre-Making; Film and Television Production with Cinematography/ Directing/ Producing/ Sound/ Visual Effects Screenwriting/ Filmmaking/ Theatre by Research; Theatre, Film, Television and Interactive Media/ Creative Practice by Research BA, BSc, MA, MSc, PhD

Part 5

Qualifications Awarded by Professional and Trade Associations

THE FUNCTIONS OF PROFESSIONAL ASSOCIATIONS

Qualifications

Some associations qualify individuals to act in a certain professional capacity. They also try to safeguard high standards of professional conduct. Few associations have complete control over the profession with which they are concerned. Some professions are regulated by the law, and their associations act as the central registration authority. Entry to others is directly controlled by associations that alone award the requisite qualifications. If a profession is required to be registered by the law and is controlled by the representative council, a practitioner found guilty by his or her council of misconduct may be suspended from practice or completely debarred by the removal of his or her name from the register of qualified practitioners. In other professions, the consequence of misdemeanour may not be so serious, because the profession does not exercise the same degree of control.

The professions registered by statute, and therefore subject to restrictions on entry and loss of either privileges or the right to practise on erasure, are listed in Table 5.1. Certain other professions are closed.

Table 5.1 Professions registered by statute

Profession	Statutory committee controlling professional conduct
Architects	Architects Registration Board
Dentists	General Dental Council
Doctors	General Medical Council
Professions supplementary to medicine: art therapists, biomedical scientists, chiropodists/podiatrists, clinical scientists, dieticians, hearing aid dispensers, occupational therapists, operating department practitioners, orthoptists, paramedics, physiotherapists, practitioner psychologists, prosthetists/orthotists, radiographers, speech and language therapists and social workers	Health and Care Professions Council (HCPC)
Nurses and midwives	Nursing and Midwifery Council
Opticians and optometrists	General Optical Council
Osteopaths	General Osteopathic Council
Patent attorneys	Chartered Institute of Patent Attorneys
Pharmacists, pharmacy technicians	General Pharmaceutical Council
Teachers	The National College for Teaching and Leadership

Study

Some associations give their members an opportunity to keep abreast of a particular discipline or to undertake further study in it. Such associations are especially numerous in medicine, science and applied science. Many qualifying associations also provide an information and study service for their members. Some of the more famous learned societies, for example, The Royal Society, confer added status upon distinguished practitioners by electing them to membership or honorary membership.

Protection of Members' Interests

Some associations exist mainly to look after the professional interests of individual practitioners and the group.

MEMBERSHIP OF PROFESSIONAL ASSOCIATIONS

Qualifying associations

The principal function of qualifying associations is to examine and qualify people who wish to become practitioners in the field with which they are concerned. As already indicated, some regulate professional conduct and many offer opportunities for further study. Membership is divided into grades, usually classified as corporate and non-corporate. Non-corporate members are those not yet admitted to full membership, mainly students; they are divided from corporate membership by barriers of age and levels of responsibility and experience. The principal requirement for admission to membership is the knowledge and ability to pass the association's exams; candidates may be exempted from the association's exams if they have acceptable alternative qualifications.

Non-corporate or affiliated members

Non-corporate members are those who are as yet unqualified or only partly qualified. They are accorded limited rights and privileges, but may not vote at meetings of the corporate body. Most associations have a student membership grade. Students are those who are preparing for the exams that qualify them for admission to corporate membership. Some associations have licentiate and graduate membership grades, which are senior to the student grade. Graduates are those who have passed the qualifying exams but lack other requirements, such as age and experience, for admission to corporate membership.

Corporate or full members

Corporate members are the fully qualified constituent members of incorporated associations. They are accorded full rights and privileges and may vote at meetings of the corporate body. Corporate membership is often divided into two grades: a senior grade of members or fellows and a general grade of associate members or associates.

Honorary members

Some associations have a special class of honorary members or fellows for distinguished members or individuals who have made an outstanding contribution to the profession in question.

Examinations and requirements

Professionals normally become corporate members by exam or exemption, with or without additional requirements. Many final professional exams are of degree standard, and a number of professional qualifications are accepted by employers as evidence of competence at operational level. Ongoing professional development is encouraged by most associations to ensure members' skills and knowledge are up to date and relevant.

The transition from the general grade of membership to the senior can be automatic in some associations (for instance, on reaching a prescribed age), but in others the higher grade is reached only after the submission of evidence of research or progress in the profession.

Qualifying exams are usually conducted in two or more stages. The first stage leads to an Intermediate or Part I qualification, the second leads to a Final or Part II or Part III qualification, which is about the standard of a degree.

Gaining professional qualifications

Prospective students can study by any of the following means:

- correspondence courses (distance learning and/or online support);

- personal attendance at the schools maintained by some associations (e.g. the Architectural Association School of Architecture),
- courses at further and higher education institutions.

ACCOUNTANCY
Membership of Professional Institutions and Associations

ASSOCIATION OF ACCOUNTING TECHNICIANS

140 Aldersgate Street
London EC1A 4HY
Tel: +44 (0)20 3735 2434
Fax: 020 7397 3009
E-mail: aat@aat.org.uk
Website: www.aat.org.uk

AAT is the UK's leading qualification and membership body for accounting professionals. We have over 125,000 members including students, people working in accountancy and self-employed business owners, in more than 90 countries worldwide. Established in 1980 to ensure consistent training and regulation for accounting staff, our qualifications provide a progression route to CIMA, CIPFA, ICAS, ICAEW and ACCA.

MEMBERSHIP
Student Member
Affiliate Member
Full Member (MAAT)
Fellow Member (FMAAT)

QUALIFICATION/EXAMINATIONS
AAT Accounting Qualifications
Entry Award in Accounting (AAT Access)
Entry Certificate in Accounting
Introductory Certificate in Accounting
Introductory Diploma in Accounting and Business

(16–19-year-olds)
Intermediate Diploma in Accounting
Advanced Diploma in Accounting
Advanced Certificate in Taxation and Ethics
AAT Bookkeeping
Introductory Award in Bookkeeping
Intermediate Certificate in Bookkeeping
Advanced Certificate in Bookkeeping and Ethics
AAT Computerised Accounting
Introductory Award in Computerised Accounting
Intermediate Award in Computerised Accounting
Advanced Certificate in Computerised Accounting and Ethics
AAT Small Business Courses
Introductory Award in Accounting Skills to Run Your Business
AAT Essentials (One day courses)

DESIGNATORY LETTERS
MAAT and FMAAT

ASSOCIATION OF CHARITY INDEPENDENT EXAMINERS

19 Windsor Place Edinburgh EH15 2AJ
Edinburgh EH15 2AJ
Tel: 0131 659 9751
E-mail: info@acie.org.uk
Website: www.acie.org.uk

ACIE provides support, training, conferences, resources and qualifications for independent examiners of charity accounts throughout the UK (*subscriptions apply*). Further information at the website: **www.acie.org.uk**

MEMBERSHIP
Affiliate
Full Member (*with category of either Associate or Fellow*)

QUALIFICATION/EXAMINATIONS
Associate (*limited re: size and type of charity by one of several authorisation bands – see website*): ACIE

Fellow (*all UK charities eligible for IE*): FCIE

DESIGNATORY LETTERS
ACIE, FCIE

CHARTERED INSTITUTE OF INTERNAL AUDITORS

13 Abbeville Mews
88 Clapham Park Road
London SW4 7BX
Tel: 020 7498 0101
Fax: 020 7978 2492
E-mail: membership@iia.org.uk
Website: www.iia.org.uk

The Chartered Institute of Internal Auditors (IIA) is the only professional body in the UK and Ireland focused exclusively on internal auditing and we are passionate about supporting, promoting and training the professionals who work in it. Every year we help internal auditors at every stage of their career with training, qualifications and technical resources.

MEMBERSHIP
Student Member
Affiliate Member
Voting Member (PIIA, CMIIA)

Head of Internal Audit Service Member
Fellow (FIIA, CFIIA)

QUALIFICATION/EXAMINATIONS
IIA Certificate in Internal Audit and Business Risk (IA Cert)
IIA Diploma (PIIA)
IIA Advanced Diploma (CMIIA)
IT Auditing Certificate

DESIGNATORY LETTERS
IA Cert, PIIA, CMIIA, FIIA, CFIIA

CIMA – THE CHARTERED INSTITUTE OF MANAGEMENT ACCOUNTANTS

The Helicon
One South Place
London EC2M 2RB
Tel: 020 8849 2251
E-mail: cima.contact@cimaglobal.com
Website: www.cimaglobal.com

CIMA is the employers' choice when recruiting financially qualified business leaders.

The Chartered Institute of Management Accountants, founded in 1919, is the world's leading and largest professional body of Management Accountants, with 183,000 members and students operating at the heart of business in 168 countries. CIMA works closely with employers and sponsors leading-edge research, constantly updating its qualification, professional experience requirements and continuing professional development to ensure it remains the most relevant international accountancy qualification for business.

MEMBERSHIP
Member
Associate (ACMA)
Fellow (FCMA)

QUALIFICATION/EXAMINATIONS
Certificate in Business Accounting
CIMA Professional
Certificate in Islamic Finance

Diploma in Islamic Finance

DESIGNATORY LETTERS
ACMA, FCMA

ICAEW (THE INSTITUTE OF CHARTERED ACCOUNTANTS IN ENGLAND AND WALES)

Metropolitan House
321 Avebury Boulevard
Milton Keynes MK9 2FZ
Tel: 01908 248 250
E-mail: careers@icaew.com
Website: https://careers.icaew.com/

ICAEW is a world leading professional membership organisation that promotes, develops and supports over 140,000 chartered accountants worldwide. We provide qualifications and professional development, share our knowledge, insight and technical expertise, and protect the quality and integrity of the accountancy and finance profession.

MEMBERSHIP
ACA (Associate of the Institute of Chartered Accountants in England and Wales)
FCA (Fellow Chartered Accountant)

QUALIFICATION/EXAMINATIONS
The ICAEW chartered accountancy qualification, the ACA, is one of the most advanced learning and professional development programmes available. It has integrated components which give an in-depth understanding across accountancy, finance and business. Combined they help build the technical knowledge, professional skills and practical experience needed to become an ICAEW Chartered Accountant. There is more than one way to start the ACA, find out more at icaew.com/careers

The ICAEW Certificate in Finance, Accounting and Business (ICAEW CFAB) provides fundamental knowledge and skills in finance, accounting and business. ICAEW CFAB consists of the same six exam modules as the first level of the ACA qualification. It can be studied as a stand-alone qualification or as an entry route to the ACA. There are no entry requirements and it is achievable in as little as 12 months through online learning, self-study or classroom tuition. Find out more at icaew.com/cfab

DESIGNATORY LETTERS
ACA, FCA

ICAS (INSTITUTE OF CHARTERED ACCOUNTANTS OF SCOTLAND)

CA House
21 Haymarket Yards
Edinburgh EH12 5BH
Tel: 0131 347 0100
E-mail: enquiries@icas.com
Website: icas.com

ICAS is a professional body for more than 20,000 world class business men and women who work in the UK and in more than 100 countries around the world. Our members have all achieved the internationally recognised and respected CA qualification (Chartered Accountant). We are an educator, examiner, regulator, and thought leader.

MEMBERSHIP
To qualify as a CA, trainees must enter and complete a training contract with an ICAS authorised employer for a prescribed period, normally three years. They must achieve relevant work experience requirements and key competencies, study for and pass three stages of examinations and complete a course and assignment in Business Ethics. For further information please see the ICAS website.

QUALIFICATION/EXAMINATIONS

The CA qualification syllabus contains ten subjects leading to three stages of exams.

Test of Competence (TC) contains five subjects: Financial Accounting, Principles of Auditing and Reporting, Finance, Business Management, Business Law.

Test of Professional Skills (TPS): Taxation, Advanced Finance, Financial Reporting, Assurance and Business Systems.

Test of Professional Expertise (TPE) contains a multidisciplinary case study designed to apply theoretical knowledge and practical skills to a real-life situation.

In addition to including ethics within the three levels, Business Ethics forms a standalone subject and assessment.

DESIGNATORY LETTERS
CA

INSTITUTE OF FINANCIAL ACCOUNTANTS

CS111, Clerkenwell Workshops,
27-31 Clerkenwell Close
Farringdon
London EC1R 0AT
Tel: +44 (0)20 3567 5999
E-mail: mail@ifa.org.uk
Website: www.ifa.org.uk

The IFA was established in 1916 and is the oldest body of non-Chartered Accountants in the world. We represent members and students in more than 80 countries, providing qualifications for those wishing to work in financial management and accountancy, and CPD for qualified Financial Accountants, particularly in SMEs.

MEMBERSHIP
Associate (AFA/MIPA)
Fellow (FFA/FIPA)
Associate Tax Adviser (ATA)
Fellow Tax Adviser (FTA)

QUALIFICATION/EXAMINATIONS
IFA Admission to Membership Programme (AMP)

INTERNATIONAL ASSOCIATION OF BOOKKEEPERS

Suite 5
20 Churchill Square
Kings Hill
West Malling
Kent ME19 4YU
Tel: +44 (0)1732 897750
Fax: +44 (0)1732 897751
E-mail: mail@iab.org.uk
Website: www.iab.org.uk

The IAB specializes in providing high-quality, accredited and regulated financial and business qualifications. We continue to be the leading international membership body for professional bookkeepers. Established in 1973, we now have many thousands of students and members worldwide.

MEMBERSHIP
Associate (AIAB)
Member (MIAB)
Fellow (FIAB)

QUALIFICATION/EXAMINATIONS
Level 1 Award in Bookkeeping 601/9065/6
Level 1 Award in Computerised Bookkeeping 601/9050/4

Level 2 Certificate in Bookkeeping 601/9061/9

Level 2 Certificate in Computerised Bookkeeping 601/9052/8

Level 3 Certificate in Bookkeeping and Accounting 601/9058/9

Level 3 Certificate in Computerised Bookkeeping and Accounting 601/9055/3

Level 1 Award in Computerised Payroll 601/9040/1

Level 1 Award in Payroll 601/9039/5

Level 1 Award in Payroll for Business 603/3022/3

Level 1 Certificate in Bookkeeping and Payroll 603/3010/7

Level 2 Award in Computerised Payroll 601/9041/3

Level 2 Certificate in Payroll 601/9046/2

Level 3 Certificate in Computerised Payroll Administration 601/9048/6

Level 3 Certificate in Payroll Administration 601/9047/4

Level 1 Award in Computerised Accounting for Business 603/2736/4

Level 2 Certificate in Computerised Accounting for Business 603/2735/2

Level 3 Certificate in Computerised Accounting for Business 603/2737/6

Level 3 Diploma in Accounting and Cash Management 603/2755/8

Level 4 Certificate in International Accounting Standards and IFRS 603/3017/X

THE ASSOCIATION OF CHARTERED CERTIFIED ACCOUNTANTS

ACCA UK
The Adelphi
1-11 John Adam Street
London WC2N 6AU
Tel: 0141 582 2000
Fax: 020 7059 5050
E-mail: info@accaglobal.com
Website: www.accaglobal.com

We believe that accountancy is vital for economies to grow and prosper, which is why we work all over the world to build the profession and make society fairer and more transparent.

We have more than 208,000 fully qualified members and 503,000 students worldwide. They're among the world's best-qualified and most highly sought-after accountants – and they work in every sector you can imagine.

MEMBERSHIP
Associate (ACCA)
Fellow (FCCA)

QUALIFICATION/EXAMINATIONS
ACCA Qualification
Foundation level qualifications

Oxford Brookes BSc degree
University of London MSc in Professional Accountancy
Oxford Brookes Global MBA
CertIFR – Certificate in International Financial Reporting
DIPIFR – Diploma in International Financial Reporting
CertIA – Certificate in International Auditing
Certificate in International Public Sector Accounting Standards
Certificate in Business Valuations

DESIGNATORY LETTERS
ACCA, FCCA

THE ASSOCIATION OF CORPORATE TREASURERS

69 Leadenhall Street
London EC3A 2BG
Tel: 020 7847 2540
E-mail: customer@treasurers.org
Website: www.treasurers.org

The Association of Corporate Treasurers (ACT) is the only professional treasury body with a Royal Charter. We set the global benchmark for treasury excellence and lead the profession through our internationally recognised qualifications, by defining standards and by championing continuing professional development. We are the authentic voice of the treasury profession representing the interests of the real economy and educating, supporting and leading the treasurers of today and tomorrow.

MEMBERSHIP
eAffiliate Member
Student Member
Affiliate Member
Associate Member

Fellowship
Business Member

QUALIFICATION/EXAMINATIONS
Treasury qualifications
Certificate in Treasury Fundamentals
Certificate in Treasury
Diploma in Treasury Management
Advanced Diploma in Treasury Management
Cash management qualifications
Award in Cash Management Fundamentals
Certificate in International Cash Management

DESIGNATORY LETTERS
CertTF, CertT, AMCT, FCT, AwardCMF, CertICM,

THE ASSOCIATION OF INTERNATIONAL ACCOUNTANTS

Staithes 3
The Watermark
Metro Riverside
Newcastle upon Tyne
Tyne & Wear NE11 9SN
Tel: 0191 493 0277
Fax: 0191 493 0278
E-mail: aia@aiaworldwide.com
Website: www.aiaworldwide.com

AIA was founded in 1928 as a global accountancy body and has recognition as a Recognised Qualifying Body for statutory auditors, supervisory status for its members in the Money Laundering Regulations 2007 and an Awarding Body in the UK. AIA is a Prescribed Body in ROI and is recognised worldwide.

MEMBERSHIP
Student Member
Academic Member
Associate (AAIA)
Fellow (FAIA)
Honorary Member
Retired Member

QUALIFICATION/EXAMINATIONS
Professional Accountancy Qualification
Recognised Professional Qualification (Statutory Audit)
QCF Level 5 Certificate in Accountancy
QCF Level 6 Diploma in Accountancy
QCF Level 7 Diploma in Professional Accountancy
Auditing Diploma
IFRS Diploma
Management Accounting & Costing Diploma
IFRS for SMEs Certificate

DESIGNATORY LETTERS
AAIA, FAIA

THE CHARTERED INSTITUTE OF PUBLIC FINANCE AND ACCOUNTANCY (CIPFA)

77 Mansell Street
London E1 8AN
Tel: 020 7543 5600
Fax: 020 7543 5700
E-mail: students@cipfa.org.uk
Website: www.cipfa.org.uk

The Chartered Institute of Public Finance and Accountancy (CIPFA) is *the* professional body for people in public finance. Our 14,000 members work throughout the public services and as the only UK professional accountancy body to specialise in public services, CIPFA's qualifications are the foundation for a career in public finance.

MEMBERSHIP
Affiliate
Associate
Full Member

QUALIFICATION/EXAMINATIONS
CIPFA Professional Qualification
Professional Qualification in Public & Corporate Accounting
Integrated Qualification for Auditors
Certificate in International Public Sector Financial Reporting
Certificate in International Public Sector Accounting Standards
Certificate in Financial Reporting for Academies

DESIGNATORY LETTERS
CPFA, CPFA Affil

THE INSTITUTE OF CERTIFIED BOOKKEEPERS

122-126 Tooley Street
London SE1 2TU
Tel: 0203 405 4000
E-mail: info@bookkeepers.org.uk
Website: www.bookkeepers.org.uk

The ICB is the largest bookkeeping institute in the world. We promote and maintain the standards of bookkeeping as a profession through the establishment of relevant qualifications and the award of grades of membership that recognise academic attainment, working experience and competence.

MEMBERSHIP
Registered Student
Affiliate
Associate Member (AICB)
Member (MICB)
Fellow (FICB)

QUALIFICATION/EXAMINATIONS
Core qualifications:
Level 2 Certificate in Bookkeeping
Level 3 Certificate in Bookkeeping and Accounts

Level 4 Certificate in Advanced Bookkeeping and Accounts

Optional Qualifications
Level 3 Diploma in Payroll Management
Level 3 Diploma in Self Assessment Tax
Level 3 Diploma in Costing and Budgeting

Level IV Diploma in Advanced Bookkeeping and Accounting Level 4 Certificate in Preparing and Submitting Final Accounts for a micro-entity under FRS105
Level 4 Certificate in Drafting Financial Statements
Level 4 Certificate in Management Accounting

DESIGNATORY LETTERS
AICB, MICB, FICB

ACOUSTICS
Membership of Professional Institutions and Associations

INSTITUTE OF ACOUSTICS

Silbury Court
406 Silbury Blvd
Milton Keynes
Buckinghamshire MK9 2AF
Tel: +44 (0) 300 999 9675
E-mail: ioa@ioa.org.uk
Website: www.ioa.org.uk

The IOA is the UK's professional body for those working in acoustics, noise and vibration, and has more than 3,000 members in research, educational, environmental, government and industrial organisations. It offers professionally recognized courses and is licensed by the Engineering Research Council to offer registration at Chartered and Incorporated Engineer levels.

MEMBERSHIP
Chartered Engineer (CEng)
SponsorStudent
Affiliate
Technician Member (TechIOA)
Associate Member (AMIOA)
Member (MIOA)
Fellow (FIOA)
Honorary Fellow (HonFIOA)

Incorporated Engineer (IEng)

QUALIFICATION/EXAMINATIONS

Certificate of Competence in Environmental Noise Measurement
Certificate of Competence in Workplace Noise Risk Assessment
Certificate Course in the Management of Occupational Exposure to Hand–Arm Vibration
Certificate Course in Building Acoustics Measurements
Diploma in Acoustics and Noise Control

DESIGNATORY LETTERS
TechIOA, AMIOA, MIOA, FIOA, HonFIOA, IEng, CEng

ADVERTISING AND PUBLIC RELATIONS
Membership of Professional Institutions and Associations

CHARTERED INSTITUTE OF PUBLIC RELATIONS

4th Floor, 85 Tottenham Court Road
Fitzrovia
London W1T 4TQ
Tel: 020 7631 6900
Fax: 020 7631 6944
E-mail: info@cipr.co.uk
Website: www.cipr.co.uk

The CIPR advances professionalism in public relations by making its members accountable to their employers and the public through a code of conduct and searchable public register, setting standards through training, qualifications, awards and the production of best practice and skills guidance.

MEMBERSHIP
Student

Affiliate
Associate (ACIPR)
Member (MCIPR)
Fellow (FCIPR)
Global Affiliate

QUALIFICATION/EXAMINATIONS
Foundation Award in Public Relations
Advanced Certificate
Diploma

DESIGNATORY LETTERS
ACIPR, MCIPR, FCIPR

INSTITUTE OF PRACTITIONERS IN ADVERTISING

44 Belgrave Square
London SW1X 8QS
Tel: 020 7235 7020
Fax: 020 7245 9904
E-mail: webhelpdesk@ipa.co.uk
Website: www.ipa.co.uk

The IPA is widely recognised as the world's most influential professional body for practitioners in advertising and marketing communications. It has a well-earned reputation for thought leadership, best practice and continuous professional development and also provides core support and advisory services for its corporate and individual members. Based in the United Kingdom for 100+ years, IPA programmes can be found in more than 60 countries worldwide.

MEMBERSHIP
Agency Membership
Personal Member (MIPA)
Fellow/Honorary Fellow (FIPA)

QUALIFICATION/EXAMINATIONS
The IPA Foundation Certificate
TV Production Knowledge
Digital Performance Certificate
LegRegs
Commercial Certificate
Production Certificate Qualification
Digital Performance Certificate
Strategic Bootcamp
Fundamentals of Branding
Production Lite
Foundation Certificate
HR Knowledge
Advanced Business Acumen
Advanced Leadership and Delegation
Advanced Certificate
Applied Behavioural Economics
Train the Trainer
Excellence Diploma
Eff Test Certificate
Excellence Diploma
How to be Human
IPA Leadership Programme
Eff Essentials

INSTITUTE OF PROMOTIONAL MARKETING

193-197 High Holborn
London WC1V 7BD
Tel: 020 3848 0444
E-mail: training@theipm.org.uk
Website: www.theipm.org.uk

The Institute of Promotional Marketing represents promoters, agencies and service partners engaged in promotional marketing in the UK by protecting, promoting and progressing effective sales promotion across all media channels through its education, legal advice, awards, and other products and services.

MEMBERSHIP
Corporate Member

IPM Foundation Certificate
IPM Incentive & Motivation Diploma

IPM Diploma
Legal Code Certification (LCC)

LONDON SCHOOL OF PUBLIC RELATIONS

118A Kensington Church Street
London W8 4BH
Tel: 020 7221 3399
E-mail: info@lspr-education.com
Website: www.lspr-education.com

Established in 1992, the London School of Public Relations (LSPR) provides up-to-date pracitical, hands-on training courses for those wishing to enter public relations as a career or for those already in a PR or communications role. They are suitable for anyone who needs up-to-date practical training awarded with a professional development qualification.

LSPR provides the following courses:

DIPLOMA:
- PR & Reputation Management – 5 day course
  ADVANCED CERTIFICATES:
- Business Strategy for PR – 2 day course
- Branding -2 day course
- Corporate Social Responsibility & Sustainability – 2 day course
- Risk & Crisis Management – 2 day course
  CERTIFICATES:
- Business Writing – 1 day workshop
- Copy Editing – 1 day course
- Impression Management (Personal Branding) – 1 day course
- On Camera – Media Handeling – 1 day
- Press Release Writing – 1 day course
- Presentation Skills – 1 day course

Our Diploma, *PR & Reputation Management*, is awarded to delegates upon successful completion of a 5 day full-time intensive course: Monday–Friday.

The Advanced Certificate courses run for 2 days.

Certificate courses are intensive short workshops run for 1 day on Thursday or Friday (Presentation Skills and Press Release Writing)

All the courses are also offered in-house for clients.

LSPR training programmes are approved and recognised by Continuous Professional Development (CPD).

LSPR operates globally with headquarters in London and international partners, in association with PR bodies and agencies.

MEMBERSHIP
Continuous Professional Development (CPD)

QUALIFICATION/EXAMINATIONS
- Diploma: In class assessment and a Final project
- Advanced Certificates: In class critical thinking exercises
- Certificates: Attendance based and in class presentations and group work

AGRICULTURE AND HORTICULTURE
Membership of Professional Institutions and Associations

INSTITUTE OF HORTICULTURE

Chartered Institute of Horticulture
BGA House
Nottingham Road
Louth
Lincolnshire LN11 OWB
Tel: 03330 050 181
E-mail: cih@horticulture.org.uk
Website: www.horticulture.org.uk

We are the professional voice for horticulture, uniting a growing profession. The Chartered Institute of Horticulture is open to any professional within the horticultural industry, from those at the beginning of their education or career, to those already well established within the field.

MEMBERSHIP
Student Member, Associate, Member, Fellow, Chartered

DESIGNATORY LETTERS
ACI Hort, MCI Hort, FCI Hort, CIHort

ROYAL HORTICULTURAL SOCIETY

80 Vincent Square
London SW1P 2PE
Tel: 020 3176 5800
E-mail: qualifications@rhs.org.uk
Website: www.rhs.org.uk

The Royal Horticultural Society is a recognized awarding body offering a range of qualifications in horticultural knowledge and skills. Part-time courses leading to RHS qualifications are offered by approved centres throughout the UK and Ireland, and by distance-learning providers. The RHS School of Horticulture provides courses in practical horticultural skills.

QUALIFICATION/EXAMINATIONS
RHS Level 1 Introductory Award in Practical HorticultureRHS Level 1 Award in Practical Horticulture
RHS Level 2 Certificate in the Principles of Plant Growth, Propagation and Development
RHS Level 2 Certificate in the Principles of Garden Planning, Establishment and Maintenance
RHS Level 2 Certificate in the Principles of Horticulture
RHS Level 2 Certificate in Practical Horticulture
RHS Level 2 Diploma in the Principles and Practices of Horticulture
RHS Level 3 Certificate in the Principles of Plant Growth, Health and Applied Propagation
RHS Level 3 Certificate in the Principles of Garden Planning, Construction and Planting
RHS Level 3 Certificate in Practical Horticulture
RHS Level 3 Diploma in the Principles and Practices of Horticulture

THE ROYAL BOTANIC GARDEN EDINBURGH

20A Inverleith Row
Edinburgh EH3 5LR
Tel: 01312 482909
Fax: 01312 482901
E-mail: education@rbge.org.uk
Website: www.rbge.org.uk

The RBGE was founded in the 17th century as a physic garden, growing medicinal plants. Now it extends over four gardens boasting a rich living collection of plants, and is a world-renowned centre for plant science and education.

QUALIFICATION/EXAMINATIONS
Certificate in Botanic Illustration (Online)
Certificate in Botanic Illustration
Certificate in Herbology
Certificate in the Principles of Horticulture (RHS Level 2) Attended/Distance

Certificate in the Principles of Horticulture (RHS Level 3) via Distance Learning
Certificate in Practical Field Botany
Certificate in Practical Horticulture
Diploma in Botanical Illustration (Attended and Distance)
Diploma in Garden Design
Diploma in Garden History
Diploma in Herbology
HND/BSc in Horticulture with Plantsmanship
MSc in The Biodiversity and Taxonomy of Plants

AMBULANCE SERVICE
Membership of Professional Institutions and Associations

AMBULANCE SERVICE INSTITUTE

Suite 183
Maddison House
226 High Street
Croydon CR9 1DF
Tel: +44 (0) 131 248 2909

The ASI is a non-union, non-political, independent institute whose membership is dedicated to raising the standards and quality of ambulance provision and thereby improving the professionalism and quality of care available to patients. Membership is open to non-NHS personnel as well as to employees of NHS Ambulance Services.

MEMBERSHIP
Student
Member (MASI)
Licentiate (LASI)
Associate (AASI)

Graduate (GASI)
Fellow (FASI)

QUALIFICATION/EXAMINATIONS
The Institute offers professional examinations and qualifications in the areas of Pre-Hospital Care, Control and Communications, and Management, for those who desire a career in the ambulance service.

DESIGNATORY LETTERS
MASI, LASI, AASI, GASI, FASI

ARBITRATION

Membership of Professional Institutions and Associations

THE CHARTERED INSTITUTE OF ARBITRATORS

12 Bloomsbury Square
London WC1A 2LP
Tel: 020 7421 7447
E-mail: info@ciarb.org
Website: www.ciarb.org

CIArb is an international centre of excellence for the practice and profession of alternative dispute resolution (ADR).

Our growing membership of 15,000 is based across 133 countries and supported by an international network of 39 branches.

CIArb provides education and training for arbitrators, mediators and adjudicators. It also acts as a global hub for practitioners, policy makers, academics and those in business, supporting the global promotion, facilitation and development of all ADR methods.

MEMBERSHIP
Student
Associate (ACIArb)
Member (MCIArb)
Fellow (FCIArb)
Corporate

QUALIFICATION/EXAMINATIONS
Arbitration pathway
Adjudication pathway
Mediation pathway

DESIGNATORY LETTERS
ACIArb, MCIArb, FCIArb

ARCHAEOLOGY

Membership of Professional Institutions and Associations

CHARTERED INSTITUTE FOR ARCHAEOLOGISTS

Power Steele Building
Wessex Hall
Whiteknights Road, Earley
Reading
Berkshire RG6 6DE
Tel: 0118 966 2841
E-mail: admin@archaeologists.net
Website: www.archaeologists.net

CIfA is the leading professional body representing archaeologists working in the UK and overseas.

Many different people are employed in conserving, managing and understanding the historic environment. Seeking the advice and guidance of a professional archaeologist ensures you receive the best possible service.

Our members are professionally accredited and skilled in the study and care of the historic environment. They sign up to a rigorous Code of conduct, professional development (CPD) schemes and complaints procedures to uphold competence and standards in archaeology.

CIfA champions professionalism in archaeology, which is good for practitioners, clients and protects the public. We do this by setting standards, improving careers and promoting best practice.

MEMBERSHIP
Student

Affiliate

Practitioner (PCIfA)

Associate (ACIfA)

Member (MCIfA)

Registered Organisation

ARCHITECTURE

Membership of Professional Institutions and Associations

ARCHITECTS REGISTRATION BOARD (ARB)

8 Weymouth Street

London W1W 5BU

Tel: 020 7580 5861

Fax: 020 7436 5269

E-mail: info@arb.org.uk

Website: www.arb.org.uk

The Architects Registration Board (ARB) is the regulatory body for architects in the UK. Only individuals registered with ARB can use the title 'architect'. Applicants to the register must hold ARB-prescribed qualifications and/or examinations (or have successfully been granted equivalence for non-UK qualifications by ARB) along with at least 2 years' practical experience working under the supervision of an architect.

CHARTERED INSTITUTE OF ARCHITECTURAL TECHNOLOGISTS (CIAT)

397 City Road

London EC1V 1NH

Tel: 020 7278 2206

Fax: 020 7837 3194

E-mail: info@ciat.org.uk

Website: www.ciat.org.uk

CIAT represents professionals working and studying in the field of Architectural Technology. We are internationally recognised as the qualifying body for Chartered Architectural Technologists (MCIAT) and Architectural Technicians (TCIAT).

MEMBERSHIP

Student member

Profile candidate

Associate (ACIAT)

Architectural Technician (TCIAT)

Chartered Architectural Technologist (MCIAT)

Honorary Member (HonMCIAT)

DESIGNATORY LETTERS

ACIAT, TCIAT, MCIAT

ROYAL INSTITUTE OF BRITISH ARCHITECTS

66 Portland Place
London W1B 1AD
Tel: 020 7580 5533
E-mail: info@riba.org
Website: www.architecture.com

The Royal Institute of British Architects is the UK membership body for architecture and the architectural profession. We provide support for our 41,000 members worldwide in the form of training, technical services, publications and events, and set standards for the education of architects, both in the UK and overseas. We also work with government to improve the design quality of public buildings, new homes and new communities.

MEMBERSHIP
Student Member
Affiliate Member
Associate Member
Chartered Member
Fellow Member
Chartered Practice

QUALIFICATION/EXAMINATIONS
The RIBA Studio Examination in Architecture Part 1 and Part 2 (distance learning)

ART AND DESIGN
Membership of Professional Institutions and Associations

BRITISH ASSOCIATION OF ART THERAPISTS

Claremont
24–27 White Lion Street
London N1 9PD
Tel: 020 7686 4216
E-mail: info@baat.org
Website: www.baat.org

The British Association of Art Therapists (BAAT) is the professional organisation for art therapists in the UK. It works to promote art therapy and provides professional support and advice to its members. The BAAT represents art therapy within national organisations and has a growing international profile.

The BAAT provides information to members of the public about art therapy Careers & Training and maintains a list of State Registered Art Therapists in private practice.

MEMBERSHIP
Trainee Member
Associate Member
Full Member

QUALIFICATION/EXAMINATIONS
The BAAT organises a programme of CPD courses for Art Therapists. For details see the website.

D&AD

64 Cheshire Street
London E2 6EH
Tel: 020 7840 1111
E-mail: info@dandad.co.uk
Website: www.dandad.org

Founded in 1962, D&AD is a professional association and educational charity with a membership of more than 2,000, working on behalf of the design and advertising communities. Our mission is to set creative standards, educate and inspire the next creative generation, and promote the importance of good design and advertising to business as a whole.

MEMBERSHIP
Awarded
Full
Education Network

SOCIETY OF DESIGNER CRAFTSMEN (SDC)

24 Rivington Street
London EC2A 3DU
Tel: 020 7739 3663
E-mail: info@societyofdesignercraftsmen.org.uk
Website: www.societyofdesignercraftsmen.org.uk

The Society, which was founded in 1887 as the Arts and Crafts Exhibition Society, is the largest and oldest multi-craft society in the UK. Our aim is to emphasize designer-making where innovation, originality and quality are important; we provide promotional services and exhibiting opportunities to members.

MEMBERSHIP
Associate
Licentiate (LSDC)
Member (MSDC)

Fellow (FSDC)

QUALIFICATION/EXAMINATIONS
Membership is by direct application by an individual craftsman and assessment is on quality of craftsmanship and design.
New graduates can be assessed at New Designers or College degree show following graduation.
Application forms and criteria are on our website.

DESIGNATORY LETTERS
LSDC, MSDC, FSDC

THE BRITISH ASSOCIATION OF PAINTINGS CONSERVATOR-RESTORERS (BAPCR)

Rose Green
Broomham Lane
Whitesmith
East Sussex BN8 6JQ
Tel: 07989 559346
E-mail: BAPCRsecretary@gmail.com
Website: www.bapcr.org.uk

The British Association of Paintings Conservator-Restorers promotes the practice of paintings conservation in the United Kingdom and around the world.

Established in 1943, we are the oldest dedicated professional organisation for all conservator-restorers of paintings in the UK.

Our members are skilled professionals working in private practice or established institutions.

MEMBERSHIP
Associate (Student)
Associate
Fellow

THE CHARTERED SOCIETY OF DESIGNERS

1 Cedar Court
Royal Oak Yard
Bermondsey Street
London SE1 3GA
Tel: 020 7357 8088
E-mail: info@csd.org.uk
Website: www.csd.org.uk

The internationally recognised body for the design profession, providing support and guidance for designers at every stage of their career.

We champion professional design practice.

We do this by offering a range of programmes, initiatives and guidance to support our members, designers and those studying and teaching design. This in turn delivers benefit to the wider public including: clients, consumers, other organisations and government, allowing us to fulfill our remit as a Registered Charity.

MEMBERSHIP
Student Member
Associate (Assoc. CSD)
Member (MCSD)
Chartered Designer
Fellow (FCSD)
Affiliate Member
Affiliate Fellow

DESIGNATORY LETTERS
MCSD, FCSD

ASTRONOMY AND SPACE SCIENCE
Membership of Professional Institutions and Associations

THE BRITISH INTERPLANETARY SOCIETY

Arthur C Clarke House
27/29 South Lambeth Road
London SW8 1SZ
Tel: 020 7735 3160
E-mail: info@bis-space.com
Website: www.bis-space.com

The BIS was formed in 1933 and has been at the forefront of actively promoting new ideas on space exploration at technical, educational and popular levels for 80 years. We serve the interests of those professionally involved with space, promote fundamental space research, technology and applications, encourage technical and scientific space studies, and undertake educational activities on space topics.

MEMBERSHIP
Member
Fellow (FBIS)

DESIGNATORY LETTERS
FBIS

AVIATION
Membership of Professional Institutions and Associations

THE GUILD OF AIR PILOTS AND AIR NAVIGATORS

Cobham House
9 Warwick Court
London WC1R 5DJ
Tel: 020 7404 4032
Fax: 020 7404 4035
E-mail: via website, or office@airpilots.org
Website: www.gapan.org

The Guild, an active Livery Company of the City of London, represents pilot and navigator interests within all areas of aviation. Most of our members are, or have been, professional licence holders, or hold a private licence. Our aims include promoting the highest standards of air safety, liaising with all authorities connected with licensing, training and legislation, providing advice and facilitating exchange of information.

MEMBERSHIP
Associate
Freeman
Upper Freeman

QUALIFICATION/EXAMINATIONS
Master Air Pilot Certificate
Master Air Navigator Certificate
Master Rearcrew Certificate

THE GUILD OF AIR TRAFFIC CONTROL OFFICERS

Membership Services
4 St Mary's Road
Bingham
Nottingham
Nottinghamshire NG13 8DW
Tel: +44 (0) 1949 876405
Fax: +44 (0) 1949 876405
E-mail: info@gatco.org
Website: www.gatco.org

Founded in 1954, GATCO is an independent professional organisation that exists to promote the highest standards in all aspects of Air Traffic Management. It is dedicated to the safety of all who travel by air.

MEMBERSHIP
Student Member
ATM Support Member
Non-Operational Member
Retired Member

FISO Member
ABM(W) Member
ATCO Abroad Member
ATCO UK Member
Corporate Member

QUALIFICATION/EXAMINATIONS
Qualifying criteria apply to all membership categories. Further information should be sought from GATCO Ltd, Membership Services.

AWARDS
Membership of Professional Institutions and Associations

CONFEDERATION OF PROFESSIONAL AWARDING BODIES (COPAB)

40 Archdale Road
East Dulwich
London SE22 9HJ
Tel: 0208 693 0555
Fax: 0208 693 0555
E-mail: secretary@copab.net
Website: www.copab.net

Confederation of Professional Awarding Bodies represents educational, vocational, technical and scientific fields world-wide. COPAB will works in partnership with colleges, universities, consultancies and all types of businesses to provide a coherent business and professional education to fulfil identified needs.

MEMBERSHIP
Member (MCOPAB)
Affiliate (ACOPAB)

DESIGNATORY LETTERS
MCOPAB, ACOPAB

BANKING
Membership of Professional Institutions and Associations

THE CHARTERED INSTITUTE OF BANKERS IN SCOTLAND

Drumsheugh House
38B Drumsheugh Gardens
Edinburgh EH3 7SW
Tel: 0131 473 7777
E-mail: info@charteredbanker.com
Website: www.charteredbanker.com

The Chartered Institute of Bankers in Scotland provides world-class professional qualifications for both the UK and international markets. Our vision for the financial services industry is one of professionalism. We are the only organisation in the world entitled to award the designation 'Chartered Banker' to its members.

MEMBERSHIP
Affiliate
Student
Associate (ACIBS)
Certificated
Member (MCIBS)
Fellow (FCIBS)
International

QUALIFICATION/EXAMINATIONS
Professional Banker Diploma
Green Finance Certificate
Associate Chartered Banker Diploma
Professional Banker Certificate
Certificate in Offshore Banking Practice
Certificate in Complaint Handling
Certificate in Credit Union Principles and Practice
Chartered Banker MBA
Professional Conversion Programme
ACIBS/ACIB Conversion Programme
IIBF Professional Conversion Programme

DESIGNATORY LETTERS
ACIBS, MCIBS, FCIBS, MBA

THE LONDON INSTITUTE OF BANKING & FINANCE

8th Floor
Peninsular House
36 Monument Street
London EC3R 8LJ
Tel: 0207 4447111
Fax: 0207 4447115
E-mail: customerservices@libf.ac.uk
Website: www.libf.ac.uk

We exist to advance banking and finance by providing outstanding education and thinking; equipping individuals with the knowledge to achieve what they want in their career.

And because we've been at the heart of the sector since 1879, we create connections and build partnerships that make banking and finance more accessible.

MEMBERSHIP
Member

Student Member
Associate
Fellow
Chartered Associate
Chartered Fellow

QUALIFICATION/EXAMINATIONS
Offering a wide range of qualifications for those employed or aspiring to a career in the financial services industry. For details see www.libf.ac.uk

BEAUTY THERAPY AND BEAUTY CULTURE
Membership of Professional Institutions and Associations

BRITISH ASSOCIATION OF BEAUTY THERAPY AND COSMETOLOGY LTD

BABTAC Limited
Ambrose House, Meteor Court
Barnett Way
Barnwood
Gloucester GL4 3GG
Tel: 0845 250 7277
Fax: 01452 611599
E-mail: info@babtac.com
Website: www.babtac.com

BABTAC was formed in 1977 and is a non-profit-making organisation for beauticians and therapists in the UK. Members work to a rigorous code of ethics and good practice, both in terms of the treatments and therapies they offer and the way they conduct their relationships with their clients. CIBTAC, an international, educational awarding body that works closely with BABTAC, offers over 30 internationally recognized diplomas in beauty and complementary therapies to accredited colleges and students in the UK and abroad.

MEMBERSHIP
Student Member
Associate Member
Full Therapist Member
Full Hairdresser Member
Salon and Spa Member
International Member

QUALIFICATION/EXAMINATIONS
BABTAC offers a programme of short courses. For details see the BABTAC website. For CIBTAC diplomas see www.cibtac.com/courses_home.htm

BRITISH INSTITUTE AND ASSOCIATION OF ELECTROLYSIS LTD

Kitts
Weavering Street
Bearstead
Maidstone
Kent ME14 5JJ
Tel: 07547 355034
E-mail: sec@electrolysis.co.uk
Website: www.electrolysis.co.uk

The BIAE is a non-profit-making organisation that demands a high standard of skill and ethical conduct from its members, who are spread throughout the UK and overseas. Candidate Electrolysists must complete the rigorous assessments, both theoretical and practical, of the BIAE Examining Board before being accepted onto the Register.

MEMBERSHIP
Member

FEDERATION OF HOLISTIC THERAPISTS

18 Shakespeare Business Centre
Hathaway Close
Eastleigh
Hampshire SO50 4SR
Tel: 023 8062 4350
Fax: 023 8062 4396
E-mail: info@fht.org.uk
Website: www.fht.org.uk

The FHT is the leading and largest professional beauty, sports and complementary therapist association in the UK, which has been representing the interests of holistic therapists since 1962. The FHT leads the industry by offering its members a Code of Conduct and Professional Practice, public liability insurance, access to regulation, a robust CPD programme with auditing, class-leading journal, local therapist network, and comprehensive business and public affairs updates.

MEMBERSHIP
Student
Affiliate
Associate
Member
Ireland
International

QUALIFICATION/EXAMINATIONS
Please see the FHT's website.

DESIGNATORY LETTERS
MFHT, FFHT, AFHT, AfFHT

ITEC

2nd Floor, Chiswick Gate
598–608 Chiswick High Road
London W4 5RT
Tel: 020 8994 4141
Fax: 020 8994 7880
E-mail: info@itecworld.co.uk
Website: www.itecworld.co.uk

ITEC is a leading international specialist examination board, providing high quality qualifications specialising in: Beauty & Spa Therapy, Hairdressing, Complementary Therapies, Sports & Fitness and Customer Service.

QUALIFICATION/EXAMINATIONS
Beauty & Spa Therapies
Hairdressing
Complementary Therapies
Sports & Fitness
Customer Service

BIOLOGICAL SCIENCES
Membership of Professional Institutions and Associations

INSTITUTE OF BIOMEDICAL SCIENCE

12 Coldbath Square
London EC1R 5HL
Tel: 020 7713 0214
Fax: 020 7837 9658
E-mail: mail@ibms.org
Website: www.ibms.org

Advancing knowledge and setting standards in biomedical science With over 20,000 members in 61 countries, the Institute of Biomedical Science (IBMS) is the leading professional body for scientists, support staff and students in the field of biomedical science.

MEMBERSHIP
eStudent
Associate
Licentiate (LIBMS)
Member (MIBMS)
Fellow (FIBMS)
Company Member

QUALIFICATION/EXAMINATIONS
Certificate of Achievement Part I and II
Certificate of Competence (also required for registration with the Health and Care Professions Council (HCPC))
Specialist Diploma in:
Cellular Pathology, Clinical Biochemistry, Clinical

Immunology, Cytopathology, Haematology & Transfusion Science, Histocompatibility & Immunogenetics (developed in conjunction with BSHI), Medical Microbiology, Transfusion Science, Virology
Diploma of Biomedical Science
Diploma of Specialist Practice
Higher Specialist Diploma in:
Cellular Pathology, Clinical Chemistry, Cytopathology, Haematology, Immunology, Histocompatibility & Immunogenetics (developed in conjunction with BSHI), Medical Microbiology, Transfusion Science, Virology
Diploma of Higher Specialist Practice
Complementary qualifications/examinations related to areas of scientific expertise (available to Members and/or Fellows)
Certificates and Diplomas of Expert Practice
Advanced Specialist Diplomas

DESIGNATORY LETTERS
LIBMS, MIBMS, FIBMS

ROYAL SOCIETY OF BIOLOGY

1 Naoroji Street
London WC1X 0GB
E-mail: membership@rsb.org.uk
Website: www.rsb.org.uk

The Royal Society of Biology is a single unified voice for biology: advising Government and influencing policy; advancing education and professional development; supporting our members, and engaging and encouraging public interest in the life sciences. The Society represents a diverse membership of individuals, learned societies and other organisations.

MEMBERSHIP
Associate Member (AMRSB)
Member (MRSB)
Fellow (FRSB)
Affiliate
Student

BioNet

QUALIFICATION/EXAMINATIONS
Chartered Biologist (CBiol)
Licenced by the Science Council to provide:
Registered Scientist (RSci)
Registered Science Technician (RSciTech)
Chartered Scientist (CSci)
Chartered Science Teacher (CSciTeach)

DESIGNATORY LETTERS
AMRSB, MRSB, FRSB, CBiol, CSci, CSciTeach, RSci, RSciTech

BREWING
Membership of Professional Institutions and Associations

INSTITUTE OF BREWING & DISTILLING

44A Curlew Street
Butler's Wharf
London SE1 2ND
Tel: 020 7499 8144
Fax: 020 7499 1156
E-mail: enquiries@ibd.org.uk
Website: www.ibd.org.uk

The IBD is a members' organisation dedicated to the education and training needs of brewers and distillers and those in related industries. We do this by offering a range of internationally recognized qualifications and the training to support them, through either direct instruction or distance learning.

MEMBERSHIP
Standard
Student
Introductory
Member in Retirement
Life Member
Fellow
Honorary Member/Honorary Fellow

QUALIFICATION/EXAMINATIONS
Certificate in the Fundamentals of Brewing and Packaging
Certificate in the Fundamentals of Distilling
Diploma in Beverage Packaging
General Certificate in Distilling
Diploma in Brewing
Diploma in Distilling
Master Brewer

DESIGNATORY LETTERS
Dipl.Brew, Dipl.Distil, Dipl.Pack, MBrew, FIBD, Hon FIBD

BUILDING

Membership of Professional Institutions and Associations

INSTITUTE OF ASPHALT TECHNOLOGY

PO Box 15690
BATHGATE EH48 9BT
Tel: 01360440682
E-mail: info@instituteofasphalt.org
Website: www.instituteofasphalt.org

The IAT is the UK's professional body for persons working in asphalt technology and those interested in aspects of the manufacture, placing, technology and uses of materials containing asphalt or bitumen. A fully audited CPD system for members has been available since 1994 and is now also offered in computerized format for ease of data entry and auditing, via members' own PCs.

MEMBERSHIP
Student

Technician (Tech.IAT)
Affiliate (AIAT)
Associate Member (AMIAT)
Member (MIAT)
Fellow (FIAT)
Honorary Fellow (Hon FIAT)

DESIGNATORY LETTERS
Tech.IAT, AIAT, AMIAT, MIAT, FIAT, Hon.FIAT

THE CHARTERED INSTITUTE OF BUILDING

1 Arlington Square
Downshire Way
Bracknell
Berkshire RG12 1WA
Tel: 01344 630700
Fax: 01344 306430
E-mail: reception@ciob.org.uk
Website: www.ciob.org

The CIOB is the international voice of the construction industry. CIOB members are largely Construction Managers engaged in managing the development, conservation and improvement of the built environment, with a common commitment to achieving and maintaining the highest possible standards.

MEMBERSHIP
Applicant
Student
Chartered
Fellowship

QUALIFICATION/EXAMINATIONS
• CIOB Level 3 Certificate in Supervising Construction Works to Existing Buildings and Structures(Ofqual accredited)

• CIOB Level 3 Diploma in Site Construction Supervisory Studies (Ofqual accredited)
• CIOB Level 4 Certificate in Construction Site Management (Ofqual accredited)
• CIOB Level 4 Diploma in Construction Site Management (Ofqual accredited)
• CIOB Level 4 Graduate Conversion Certificate (Ofqual accredited)

DESIGNATORY LETTERS
ACIOB, ICIOB, MCIOB, FCIOB, CENV

THE INSTITUTE OF CARPENTERS

32 High Street
Wendover
Buckinghamshire HP22 6EA
Tel: 0844 879 7696
E-mail: info@instituteofcarpenters.com
Website: www.instituteofcarpenters.com

The IOC was founded in 1890 to oversee training for carpenters and joiners and maintain high professional standards at a time when many feared that traditional skills were being lost. Today, while remaining committed to our original aims, we embrace many other wood craftsmen, such as shopfitters, furniture and cabinetmakers, boat builders (woodworking skills), structural post & beam carpenters (heavy structural timber framers), wheelwrights, wood carvers and wood turners, and offer professional status to those holding recognized qualifications.

MEMBERSHIP
Student
Mature Student
Affiliate
Licentiate (LIOC)
Member (MIOC)
Fellow (FIOC)
College

THE INSTITUTE OF CLERKS OF WORKS AND CONSTRUCTION INSPECTORATE OF GREAT BRITAIN INC

28 Commerce Road
Lynch Wood
Peterborough PE2 6LR
Tel: 01733 405160
Fax: 01733 405161
E-mail: info@icwci.org
Website: www.icwci.org

The ICWCI is the professional body that supports quality construction through inspection. As a membership organisation, we provide a support network of meeting centres, technical advice, publications and events to help keep our members up to date with the ever-changing construction industry.

MEMBERSHIP
Student
Licentiate (LICWCI)
Member (MICWCI)
Fellow (FICWCI)
Life Member
Honorary Member

DESIGNATORY LETTERS
LICWCI, MICWCI, FICWCI

BUSINESS STUDIES
Membership of Professional Institutions and Associations

ASSOCIATION OF BUSINESS RECOVERY PROFESSIONALS (R3)

8th Floor
120 Aldersgate Street
London EC1A 4JQ
Tel: 020 7566 4200
Fax: 020 7566 4224
E-mail: association@r3.org.uk
Website: www.r3.org.uk

The Association of Business Recovery Professionals (known by its brand name 'R3') is the leading professional association for insolvency, business recovery and turnaround specialists in the UK. A not-for-profit organisation, it promotes best practice for professionals working with financially troubled individuals and businesses, and provides a forum for debate on key issues facing the profession.

MEMBERSHIP
New Professional (Student) Member

New Professional (Networking) Member
Associate Member (AABRP)
Full Member (MABRP)
Fellow (FABRP)

QUALIFICATION/EXAMINATIONS
R3 provides comprehensive Continuing Professional Education in the field of Insolvency and Restructuring. For details of courses see R3's website.

DESIGNATORY LETTERS
AABRP, MABRP, FABRP

INSTITUTE OF ASSESSORS AND INTERNAL VERIFIERS

26 Gilbert House
Old Coach Room
Runcorn WA7 1NJ
Tel: 07884 245 319
E-mail: office@iavltd.co.uk
Website: www.iavltd.co.uk

The IAV is the professional organisation representing assessors and internal verifiers in the UK in vocational training and assessment.

THE ACADEMY OF EXECUTIVES & ADMINISTRATORS

Office 13275
PO Box 4336
Manchester
United Kingdom M61 0BW
Tel: 01386 277973
E-mail: info@academyofexecutivesandadministrators.org.uk
Website: www.academyofexecutivesandadministrators.org.uk

The Academy of Executives & Administrators was founded in 2002 to give professional status and recognition to the knowledge and skills of executives and administrators. We encourage excellence and flexibility in the changing environment of executive and administrative roles, and support lifelong learning to help members fulfil their career ambitions.

MEMBERSHIP
Student Member (StudAEA)

Associate Member (AMAEA)
Member (MAEA)
Fellow (FAEA)
Companion (CAEA)

QUALIFICATION/EXAMINATIONS
Certified Administration PractitionerCertified Executive Practitioner

THE ACADEMY OF MULTI-SKILLS, UK

6/F Berkeley Square House
Berkeley Square
London
UK W1J6BR
Tel: 00 44 (0) 709 201 29
E-mail: info@academyofmulti-skillsuk.org
Website: www.academyofmulti-skillsuk.org

The Academy of Multi-Skills was founded in 1995 to give professional recognition to multi-skilled personnel, skilled trades, crafts and professions. The Academy encourages a positive and energetic attitude to the challenges of careers that require diversity, creativity and intellect, and recognizes the valuable contribution that these skills provide to society.

MEMBERSHIP
Student Member   GBP 100 Stud AMS (Cert MS)
Associate GBP 200 AMAMS (Dip MS)
Full Member GBP 250 MAMS (Dip MS)
Fellow GBP 300 FAMS (Dip MS)

Doctorate Fellow GBP 3,000 DFAMS
Company GBP 750 COAMS

QUALIFICATION/EXAMINATIONS
Professional Doctorate Diploma for Executives – Equivalent to Doctorate Degree (Level 8)Level 7 Advanced Professional Diploma (Equivalent to Masters Degree)
Level 6 Professional Diploma (Equivalent to Bachelors Degree)

DESIGNATORY LETTERS
Stud AMS, AMAMS, MAMS, FAMS, DFAMS, COAMS

THE FACULTY OF SECRETARIES AND ADMINISTRATORS LIMITED

The Association of Corporate Secretaries
Brightstowe
Catteshall Lane
Godalming
Surrey GU7 1LL
Tel: 0871 288 6935
Fax: 0871 288 6935
E-mail: admin@facultyofsecretaries.org.uk
Website: www.facultyofsecretaries.co.uk

The Faculty is a professional body for corporate secretaries whose qualified designation is that of Certified Public or Corporate Secretary and since 1930 has led in promoting good, fair and liberal governance.

The Faculty kitemark embeds concepts of reasonableness and care for others in an organisation's operation and decision taking.

MEMBERSHIP
Membership Fellows (FFCS)
Associates (AFCS)
Member (MACS)
Ordinary Member
Student Member
Licentiate (LFCS)
Corporate

QUALIFICATION/EXAMINATIONS
Part 1 The Generic Business Assessment to ONC/D Level
Part 2 Professional Papers in Company Secretarial Practice, Company Law and Management, Secretarial and Administrative Practice, Commercial Law, Ethics Equality and Justice, Data Protection and Freedom of Information.
Part 3 Professional Meetings Law and Procedure, Company Taxation, Accountancy and Finance, Company Law, Current Affairs Equality and Justice.
Assessment of Senior Personnel for direct entry now involves a viva voce interview and rated questions on corporate secretaryship as well as exemptions based on an agreed list of qualifications and a declaration of working with the general ethos of the faculty.

Single subject examinations are available and a programme for the assessment of in-house courses for company secretaries, directors and trustees. The Faculty gives credit for approved attendance at Directory of Social Change, Institute of Directors and other recognised bodies', courses on governance, leadership and management where it is clear they are beneficial to the development of caring, fair and liberal governance. The Faculty supports the aims and objectives of 'The Commonwealth' and seeks to ensure a fit with the syllabi of related bodies in Commonwealth countries.

The Society of Teachers in Business Education monitors this interview process.

The Kitemark is an assessment which an organisation can go through to establish good and liberal governance and has formats for private, public and voluntary sector organisations.

The former designations of Certified Book-keeper and Certified Company Accountant at Licentiate Level are not now directly offered although records of equivalence and Licentiate graduation on these are kept and entry to the main qualification grades is done on an 'on-a-par' basis. The Faculty continues to support the promotion of English as a Foreign Language in conjunction with The Society of Teachers in Business Education and other national bodies and delivers courses as a body on the UK Register of training providers seeking to work with local bodies who are also so registered.

DESIGNATORY LETTERS
FCCS, FFCS, AFCS, LFCS, MACS

THE INSTITUTE OF CHARTERED SECRETARIES AND ADMINISTRATORS

Saffron House
6-10 Kirby Street
London EC1N 8TS
Tel: 020 7580 4741
Website: www.icsa.org.uk

The Institute of Chartered Secretaries and Administrators is the international qualifying and membership body for the Chartered Secretary profession. With a global community of 37,000 members we provide Chartered Membership, training and a professional qualifying scheme to set you on the path to a diverse, challenging and rewarding career.

MEMBERSHIP
Student
Affiliate
Graduate (GradICSA)
Associate (ACIS)
Fellow (FCIS)
Chartered

QUALIFICATION/EXAMINATIONS
• Chartered Qualification:
• The Foundation Programme
ICSA qualifying programme

Fast Track professional route
Short course qualifications: International Finance and AdministrationLevel 5 Certificate in Fund Administration Specialist governance qualifications: Certificate in Corporate GovernanceAdvanced Certificate in Corporate GovernanceCertificate in Employee Share Plans
Certificate in Company Secretarial Practice and Share Registration PracticeCertificate in Company Secretarial Law and Practice (Ireland)
Charity:Certificate in Charity Law and Governance Diploma in Charity Management Education:Certificate in Academy Governance Health:Advanced Certificate in Health Service Governance
Sports:Certificate in Sports Governance Executive Education:Governance Leadership Programme
DESIGNATORY LETTERS
GradICSA, ACIS, FCIS

CATERING AND INSTITUTIONAL MANAGEMENT
Membership of Professional Institutions and Associations

BII

Infor House
1 Lakeside Road
Farnborough
Surrey GU14 6XP
Tel: 01276 684449
E-mail: enquiries@bii.org
Website: www.bii.org

Founded in 1981, BII is the professional body for the licensed retail sector with a remit to raise standards throughout the industry. BIIAB, the wholly owned awarding body of BII, does this through offering qualifications specifically tailored to, and designed in conjunction with, the industry.

MEMBERSHIP
There is a wide range of membership grades available, from those who have just started their careers in licensed retailing to those who have been in the industry for many years. The grade of membership awarded depends on both experience and qualifications and is determined by a points system. Member of the Hotel Catering and Management Association, HCIMA.

QUALIFICATION/EXAMINATIONS

Qualifications for licensing

Award for Designated Premises Supervisors (Level 2)

Award for Licensing Practitioners (Alcohol) (Level 2)

Award for Personal Licence Holders (Level 2)

Award for Upskilling Door Supervisors (Level 2)

Award for Upskilling Door Supervisors (Scotland)

Award in Door Supervision (Level 2)

Award in Door Supervision (Scotland)

Award in Door Supervision (Northern Ireland)

Award in CCTV Operations (Public Space Surveillance) (Scotland)

Award in Crime Scene Preservation (Level 2)

Award in Drug Awareness for Licensed Hospitality Staff (Level 2)

Award in Fire Safety (Level 2)

Scottish Certificate for Licensees (Drugs Awareness)

Award in Isle of Man Licensing Law

Award in Jersey Licensing Law

Qualifications for new licensed retail managers

Award in Licensed Retailing (Level 2)

Award in Beer and Cellar Quality (Cask and Keg) (Level 2)

Award in Beer and Cellar Quality (Keg) (Level 2)

Scottish Certificate in Licensed Retailing

Qualifications for staff development

Award in Kitchen Management (Level 3)

Award in Introduction to Employment in the Hospitality Industry (Level 1)

Professional Barperson's Qualification

Award in Conflict Management for Licensed Premises Staff (Level 2)

Award in Customer Service Excellence (Licensed Hospitality)

Award in Food Safety in Catering (Level 2)

Award in Health and Safety in the Workplace (Level 2)

Isle of Man Security Staff Qualification

Qualifications for management development

Award in Licensed Hospitality Operations (Level 2)

Certificate in Licensed Hospitality Operations (Level 2)

Certificate in Licensed Hospitality Skills (Level 2)

Award in Hospitality Business Management (Level 3)

Certificate in Hospitality Business Management (Level 3)

Certificate in Multiple Licensed Premises Management (Level 4)

Qualifications for personal and social responsibility

Award in Alcohol Awareness (Level 1)

Award in Assessment of Licensed Premises (Social Responsibility) (Level 2)

Award in Assessment of Licensed Premises (Social Responsibility) (Scotland)

GUILD OF INTERNATIONAL PROFESSIONAL TOASTMASTERS

Life President: Ivor Spencer

22 Great Mead

Denmead

Waterlooville

Hampshire PO7 6HH

Tel: 07802 250477

E-mail: info@guildoftoastmasters.co.uk

Website: www.guildoftoastmasters.co.uk

The Guild of Professional Toastmasters was established over 30 years ago to improve standards in the profession and support its members. A 5-day course is offered to prospective members, who may apply for membership upon successful completion of the course. Applications are considered by the Fellows of the Guild.

MEMBERSHIP

Fellow (FGIntPT)

DESIGNATORY LETTERS

FGIntPT

INSTITUTE OF HOSPITALITY

Counting House
14 Palmerston Road
Sutton
Surrey SM1 4QL
Tel: 020 8661 4900
Fax: 020 8661 4901
E-mail: Info@instituteofhospitality.org
Website: www.instituteofhospitality.org

The Institute of Hospitality is the international professional body for managers and leaders in hospitality, leisure and tourism. We offer professional qualifications through our partners CTH Awards, accredit academic programmes of study, endorse training courses providing professional development opportunities ranging from daily operational duties to board level strategy.

Uniting Professionals, Promoting Excellence, Facilitating Learning

MEMBERSHIP
Student Member
Affiliate
Associate (AIH)
Member (MIH)
Fellow (FIH)

QUALIFICATION/EXAMINATIONS
Institute of Hospitality Level 3 Diploma in Hospitality and Toursim Management (VRQ)
Institute of Hospitality Level 4 Diploma in Advanced Hospitality and Tourism Management (VRQ)
Institute of Hospitality Level 2 Award in Professional Cookery in Health and Social Care

DESIGNATORY LETTERS
AIH, MIH, FIH

CHEMISTRY
Membership of Professional Institutions and Associations

SOCIETY OF COSMETIC SCIENTISTS

Suite 109
Christchurch House
40 Upper George Street
Luton
Bedfordshire LU1 2RS
Tel: 01582 726661
Fax: 01582 405217
E-mail: gem.bektas@scs.org.uk
Website: www.scs.org.uk

The main object of the Society, which was formed in 1948, is to advance the science of cosmetics. We endeavour to do this by attracting highly qualified scientists with both academic and industrial experience in cosmetics or a related science to our membership of around 900 members, and by means of our publications, educational programmes and scientific meetings.

MEMBERSHIP
Student
Affiliate
Associate Member
Member – B Grade
Member – A Grade
Honorary Member

QUALIFICATION/EXAMINATIONS
SCS Diploma in Cosmetic Science
Principles and Practice of Cosmetic Science (PPCS)

THE OIL AND COLOUR CHEMISTS' ASSOCIATION

4th Floor
Clayton House
59 Piccadilly
Manchester M1 2AQ
Tel: 0161 933 7280
E-mail: admin@occa.org.uk
Website: www.occa.org.uk

OCCA, founded in 1918, is a learned society comprising individual qualified persons employed in, or associated with, the worldwide surface coatings industries. Most of our members work in a technical capacity, but there are commercial and other senior personnel from throughout the surface coating industries. The word 'oil' in our title refers to vegetable oils, which once formed a major part of surface coatings' formulations.

MEMBERSHIP
Student Member
Honorary Member
Licentiate (LTSC)
Associate (ATSC)
Fellow (FTSC)
Retired Member

DESIGNATORY LETTERS
LTSC, ATSC, FTSC

THE ROYAL SOCIETY OF CHEMISTRY

Thomas Graham House
Science Park
Milton Road
Cambridge CB4 0WF
Tel: 01223 420066
Fax: 01223 423623
E-mail: membership@rsc.org
Website: www.rsc.org

The Royal Society of Chemistry has over 54,000 members and an international publishing and knowledge business we are the UK's professional body for chemical scientists, supporting and representing our members and bringing together chemical scientists from all over the world.

MEMBERSHIP
Affiliate
Associate Member (AMRSC)
Member (MRSC)
Fellow (FRSC)

QUALIFICATION/EXAMINATIONS
Registered Science Technician (RSciTech)
Registered Scientist (RSci)
Mastership in Chemical Analysis (MChemA)
Chartered Chemist (CChem)
Chartered Scientist (CSci)
Chartered Science Teacher (CSciTeach)
Chareterd Environmentalist (CEnv)

DESIGNATORY LETTERS
AMRSC, MRSC, FRSC, CChem

CHIROPODY
Membership of Professional Institutions and Associations

BRITISH CHIROPODY AND PODIATRY ASSOCIATION

The New Hall
149 Bath Road
Maidenhead
Berkshire SL6 4LA
Tel: 01628 632440
E-mail: membership@bcha-uk.org
Website: www.bcha-uk.org

The BChA, formed in 1959, is the largest professional organisation in the UK representing the interests of independent private chiropodists / podiatrists. Since 2005 we have added foothealth practitioners to include our 7,000 members, most of whom work mainly in private practice. Those who are registered with the Health Professions Council may work in the NHS or in education.

MEMBERSHIP
Member (MSSCh & MBChA) – Podiatrists

Fellow (FSSCh) – Podiatrist
Associate members are foothealth practitioners trained by The SMAE Institute.

QUALIFICATION/EXAMINATIONS
Diploma in Podiatric Medicine (DipPodMed)
Foothealth practitioners carry the qualification – MAFHP

DESIGNATORY LETTERS
MSSCh, MBChA, FSSCh and MAFHP

THE COLLEGE OF PODIATRY

Quartz House, 207 Providence Square
Mill Street
London SE1 2EW
Tel: 020 7234 8620
E-mail: reception@scpod.org
Website: www.scpod.org

The SCP is the professional body and trade union for registered podiatrists. Membership is restricted to those qualified for registration and the Society represents around 10,000 NHS podiatrists, private practitioners and students. We monitor standards of undergraduate education and provide opportunities for CPD for our members.

MEMBERSHIP
Member (MChS)
Associate

DESIGNATORY LETTERS
MChS

THE INSTITUTE OF CHIROPODISTS AND PODIATRISTS

150 Lord Street
Southport
Merseyside PR9 0NP
Tel: 01704 546141
E-mail: secretary@iocp.org.uk
Website: www.iocp.org.uk

The Institute serves members throughout the whole of the profession of podiatry and podiatric medicine. Its members include chiropodists, podiatrists and podiatric surgeons, employed and self-employed at all levels of practice. The Institute certificate of membership is proof that members undertake to adhere to a strict code of ethics and professional conduct and that they have access to some of the UK's most innovative continuing professional development training.

The Institute is a democratic organisation with the election of officers both local and national being decided bi-annually by members. All members therefore play an active role in their own affairs. For more than 60 years the Institute has followed an independent line at the forefront of the profession it serves, for the progress and well-being of both the profession and the public.

The IOCP represents all levels of the profession and our CPD is open to both members and non-members, as by elevating professional standards we aim to improve public safety. We have branches throughout the UK and the Republic of Ireland, and members overseas, and hold lectures, seminars and workshops to enable members to keep up to date.

MEMBERSHIP
Full Member
Student
Associate/Member of The College of Foot health

QUALIFICATION/EXAMINATIONS
MInstChP – Full Member
AInstFHP – Associate
MCFH – Member of The College of Foot Health

CHIROPRACTIC
Membership of Professional Institutions and Associations

MCTIMONEY CHIROPRACTIC ASSOCIATION

Crowmarsh Gifford
Wallingford
Oxfordshire OX10 8DJ
Tel: 01491 739120
E-mail: admin@mctimoney-chiropractic.org
Website: https://www.mctimoney-chiropractic.org/home.aspx

The McTimoney Chiropractic Association is a professional association for Chiropractors, who in the UK are registered with the General Chiropractic Council.

MEMBERSHIP
Provisional Member

Full Member
Fellow

DESIGNATORY LETTERS
MMCA

SCOTTISH CHIROPRACTIC ASSOCIATION

The Old Barn
Houston Road
Houston
Renfrewshire PA6 7BH
Tel: 0141 404 0260
E-mail: admin@sca-chiropractic.org
Website: www.sca-chiropractic.org

The SCA was formed in 1979 and now has more than 60 members practising in Scotland and over 120 associated members elsewhere in the UK and abroad. Our aims are to enhance the chiropractic profession in the UK, maintain high standards of professional practice, and provide advice and support to our members.

MEMBERSHIP
Member

UNITED CHIROPRACTIC ASSOCIATION

Unit 57
Basepoint Business Centre
Metcalf Way
Crawley
West Sussex RH11 7XX
Tel: +44 (0)1293 817 175
E-mail: membership@united-chiropractic.org
Website: www.united-chiropractic.org

The UCA is a UK-based organisation for qualified, professional, principal-based chiropractors, associates and students. Full membership is open to qualified, GCC-registered chiropractors from any recognized school of chiropractic.

MEMBERSHIP
Student
1st Year Graduate
2nd Year Graduate
Full Member

THE CHURCHES
Membership of Professional Institutions and Associations

ADMINISTRATION MANAGER

Church Street
Jump
Barnsley
South Yorkshire S74 0HZ
Tel: 441226891608
E-mail: admin@thewru.co.uk
Website: www.thewru.com

The Wesleyan Reform Union has no training college of its own and encourages candidates for its Ministry to enter a Bible College for 2 or 3 years. All candidates are, however, under the personal supervision of a Union Tutor, who directs a Biblical Studies & Training Department offering fairly extensive courses. Candidates attend Headquarters once a year for an oral exam in Theology conducted by the Tutor in the presence of the Union Examination Committee; they also take written exams.

BRISTOL BAPTIST COLLEGE

The Promenade
Clifton Down
Clifton
Bristol BS8 3NJ
Tel: 0117 946 7050
Fax: 0117 946 7787
E-mail: reception@bristol-baptist.ac.uk
Website: www.bristol-baptist.ac.uk

The central aim of the College is to train men and women for ministry in the Church and in the world. We do this by enabling critical reflection upon the Bible and Christian theological tradition and on the contexts from which we come and within which we are placed.

QUALIFICATION/EXAMINATIONS
Certificate in Theological Studies
Diploma in Theological Studies
BA in Theological Studies
MA in Christian Theology
(all validated by the University of Bristol)

METHODIST CHURCH IN IRELAND

9 Lennoxvale
Belfast
Co. Antrim BT9 5BY
Tel: 028 9076 7969
Fax: 028 9023 9467
E-mail: secretary@irishmethodist.org
Website: www.irishmethodist.org

MEMBERSHIP
Candidates for training must normally have the standard of general education for university entrance. They must be accredited Local Preachers of the Methodist Church, and are examined by written papers in Biblical Studies and Theology and by oral aptitude and personality tests. After admission to training, candidates normally spend 3 years at Edgehill Theological College, Belfast, studying for a diploma or degree of Queen's University, Belfast, in New Testament Greek, Hebrew, the English Bible, Theology, Church History, Pastoral Psychology, or Homiletics. This is followed by 3 years as a probationer Minister working under a superintendent Minister. During probation the candidate continues study within a tutorial system and is examined by continuous assessment.

SCOTTISH EPISCOPAL INSTITUTE

Forbes House
21 Grosvenor Crescent
Edinburgh EH12 5EE
Tel: 0131 225 6357
E-mail: institute@scotland.anglican.org
Website: www.scotland.anglican.org/sei/

Candidates are trained for lay and ordained, stipendiary and non-stipendiary ministries in the Scottish Episcopal Church and the United Reformed Church.

The curriculum is delivered centrally through residential sessions and seminar teaching. A Mixed Mode pathway is also available. The Diploma of Higher Education in Theology, Ministry and Mission and the BA in Theology, Ministry and Mission courses run by the Institute are validated by Common Awards/Durham University. Some students undertake degree programmes in parallel with their formation through Scottish Universities.

THE CHURCH IN WALES

St Michael's College
Llandaff
Cardiff CF5 2YJ
Tel: 029 205 63379
Fax: 029 208 38008
Website: www.stmichaels.ac.uk

The Church in Wales expects candidates for ordination and reader ministry to satisfy the requirements of recognized theological courses. University graduates usually spend at least 2 years full time (or its part time equivalent) at a theological college or course, and will be encouraged to study for a postgraduate degree.

Non-theological graduates are encouraged to study for a university degree, diploma or certificate in Theology, depending on their age and the ministry for which they are being trained. Non-graduate candidates must have at least 5 passes at GCSE and normally study for a university certificate or diploma in Theology or a degree in Theology if they have obtained the necessary grades at A level. These requirements may be modified in the case of older candidates.

THE CHURCH OF ENGLAND

Ministry Division of The Archbishops' Council
Church House
Great Smith Street
London SW1P 3AZ
Tel: 020 7898 1397
E-mail: keith.beech-gruneberg@churchofengland.org
Website: www.churchofengland.org/ministry-division www.aet-lambeth.org/

The Church of England's Ministry Division oversees training for ordination and licensed lay ministry/Reader ministry including the Common Awards created by the Church and validated by Durham University.

In addition, The Archbishop's Examination in Theology offers means of study at research degree level.

QUALIFICATION/EXAMINATIONS
Awards validated by Durham University:
Foundation Award in Theology, Ministry and Mission
Certificate of Higher Education in Theology, Ministry and Mission

Certificate of Higher Education in Christian Ministry and Mission (180 credits)
Diploma of Higher Education in Theology, Ministry and Mission
BA in Theology, Ministry and Mission
Graduate Certificate in Theology, Ministry and Mission
Graduate Diploma in Theology, Ministry and Mission
Postgraduate Certificate in Theology, Ministry and Mission
Postgraduate Diploma in Theology, Ministry and Mission
MA in Theology, Ministry and Mission
Archbishop's Examination:
Master of Philosophy
Doctor of Philosophy

THE CHURCH OF SCOTLAND

Church of Scotland Offices
121 George Street
Edinburgh EH2 4YN
Tel: 0131 225 5722
Website: www.churchofscotland.org.uk

The vision of The Church of Scotland is to be a church which seeks to inspire the people of Scotland and beyond with the Good News of Jesus Christ through enthusiastic worshipping, witnessing, nurturing and serving communities.

THE METHODIST CHURCH

Formation in Ministry Office (Initial Development of Ministries)
25 Marylebone Road
London NW1 5JR
Tel: 020 7486 5502
E-mail: enquiries@methodistchurch.org.uk
Website: www.methodist.org.uk

Candidates for Diaconal or Presbyteral Ministry in the Methodist Church must have been members of the Methodist Church at least 2 years and are expected to offer at least 10 years of ministerial service. The first stage of preparation is Foundation Training, which requires 1 year (FT) or 2 years (PT) to complete, during which a person may apply to become a candidate for ordained ministry. The process of selection takes 6 months. To enter into training for Presbyteral Ministry, a candidate must be a trained Local Preacher, which involves taking the Methodist Local Preachers' Training Course, Faith & Worship. Deacons become members of the Methodist Diaconal and are not required to be preachers. Accepted candidates for either order receive 1 or 2 years of further theological training, which in most cases leads to a degree or diploma in Theology or Ministry. Upon completion of training, a candidate serves as a Methodist Minister for 2 years on probation before ordination. For Presbyters, the appointment may be to an itinerant appointment (stipendiary) or to a local appointment (usually non-stipendiary) or as licensed to minister in secular employment. Deacons are always itinerant.

THE MORAVIAN CHURCH IN GREAT BRITAIN AND IRELAND

Moravian Church House
5–7 Muswell Hill
London N10 3TJ
Tel: 020 8883 3409
Fax: 020 8365 3371
E-mail: office@moravian.org.uk
Website: www.moravian.org.uk

Candidates for Moravian Church Service must be members of the Moravian Church and would normally have completed the Lay Training Course and have the support of their local church committee. They should make an initial application to the Provincial Board of the Moravian Church. Their qualifications are examined by the Church Service Advisory Board, which reports on them to the Provincial Board, with whom the final decision rests. Normally the standard of education required for the work of the Ministry is a university Divinity degree or Certificate together with a thorough acquaintance with the history, principles and methods of the Moravian Church. Candidates receive guidance for the Ministry during a period of supervised service under the direction of experienced Ministers. A class of non-stipendiary Ministers has been established for those who wish to serve on a non-maintained basis. Training varies according to candidates' needs. In all cases applications should be made to the address given above.

THE PRESBYTERIAN CHURCH IN IRELAND

The Director of Ministerial Studies
Union Theological College
108 Botanic Avenue
Belfast BT7 1JT
Tel: 02890 205088
Fax: 02890 205099

Qualifications required: Under 30 – a non-theological degree; over 30 but under 40 (as reckoned on 1 October following application) – either a non-theological degree or 2 years, non-graduating Arts or 4 modules of PT BD study or 6 modules of PT study in Humanities acceptable to the Board of Studies; over 40 – not normally accepted, except in exceptional circumstances, where candidate is already possessed of good educational background and/or professional experience.

THE PRESBYTERIAN CHURCH OF WALES

Tabernacle Chapel
81 Merthyr Road
Whitchurch
Cardiff CF14 1DD
Tel: 02920 627465
Fax: 02920 616188
E-mail: swyddfa.office@ebcpcw.org.uk
Website: www.ebcpcw.org.uk

The Presbyterian Church of Wales (PCW) is a Protestant non-conformist denomination. Ordination is dependent on successful application through the local church and Presbytery to the Candidates and Training Department.

MEMBERSHIP
Ministers are ordained to the full-time, part-time or non-stipendiary ministry.

QUALIFICATION/EXAMINATIONS
Pastoral Studies course

THE ROMAN CATHOLIC CHURCH

Candidates for the priesthood in the RC Church attend a residential seminary course of at least 6 years. Among subjects studied are Philosophy, Psychology, Dogmatic and Moral Theology, Scripture, Church History, Canon Law, Liturgy, Catechetics, Communications and Pastoral Theology. Each college/seminary has its own arrangements for the university education of its students. Those who do not attend university take a final internal exam.

THE SALVATION ARMY

UK Headquarters
101 Newington Causeway
London SE1 6BN
Tel: 020 7367 4500
E-mail: info@salvationarmy.org.uk
Website: www.salvationarmy.org.uk

Salvation Army officers engaged in FT service are ordained ministers of religion, and are commissioned following a 2-year period of residential training at the William Booth College, Denmark Hill, London SE5 8BQ. This course – an HE Diploma in Salvation Army Officer Training – may now be undertaken by distance learning, or a mixture of residential and distance learning. Officers may be appointed to corps (church) work, to social services centres (for which additional professional qualifications are required) or to administrative posts.

THE SCOTTISH UNITED REFORMED AND CONGREGATIONAL COLLEGE

113 West Regent Street
Glasgow G2 2RU
Tel: 0141 248 5382
E-mail: scottishcollege@urcscotland.org.uk
Website: www.scottishcollege.org.uk

The College is recognised as a resource centre for learning by the General Assembly of the United Reformed Church, and is one of the institutions engaged in initial ministerial education. It is in close partnership with URC National Synod of Scotland, the Scottish Episcopal Institute and the University of Glasgow.

QUALIFICATION/EXAMINATIONS
The College awards only its own certificate, which is part of the process of accreditation as ministers of the United Reformed Church. Students, however, are normally concurrently matriculated for a degree, usually in Theology or Religious Studies, at a university.

THE UNITARIAN AND FREE CHRISTIAN CHURCHES

Essex Hall
1-6 Essex Street
London WC2R 3HY
Tel: 020 7240 2384
E-mail: info@unitarian.org.uk
Website: www.unitarian.org.uk

Candidates accepted for training for the ministry in the Unitarian and Free Christian Churches take courses of training either at Manchester Academy & Harris College, Oxford (2 to 4 years' study for an Oxford degree in Theology/or Theology & Philosophy or an Oxford Certificate in Theology/Religious Studies), or at the Unitarian College (Luther King House, Brighton Grove, Rusholme, Manchester; an individually designed contextual theology course of the Partnership for Theological Education which may lead to a degree or other academic qualification validated by Chester or Manchester University). Alternative arrangements can be made for candidates wishing to study through the Welsh language. Placement work and Unitarian studies are also integral to ministerial preparation. Training normally takes 2 or more years.

THE UNITED REFORMED CHURCH

Church House
86 Tavistock Place
London WC1H 9RT
Tel: 020 7916 2020
Fax: 020 7916 2021
E-mail: urc@urc.org.uk
Website: www.urc.org.uk

Candidates for **Ministry of Word and Sacraments** must have been a member of the URC for at least 2 years. and complete a candidating process. Most then take a 3- or 4-year course of part-time or full-time academic study alongside a minimum of 800 hours of pastoral placements. The minimum required outcome is a Diploma of Higher Education, in Theology. **Church-related Community Workers** strengthen the local church's mission through community development. Candidates are required to obtain at least a Diploma in Theology and a Diploma in Community Work before being commissioned.

Lay Preacher's Certificate: The qualifying course for this takes 3 years in local groups, residential weekends, and practical work in churches.

UNITED FREE CHURCH OF SCOTLAND

11 Newton Place
Glasgow G3 7PR
Tel: 01413 323435
E-mail: office@ufcos.org.uk
Website: www.ufcos.org.uk

The United Free Church of Scotland is a small presbyterian denomination which came into being in 1929. Those seeking to become involved in ministry should normally have been members of the denomination for at least a year. They will require to undertake a suitable course including Biblical and Theological Studies as well as practical studies and experience appropriate to the type of ministry for which they are preparing.

CINEMA, FILM AND TELEVISION
Membership of Professional Institutions and Associations

INTERNATIONAL MOVING IMAGE SOCIETY (IMIS)

Pinewood Studios
Pinewood Road
Iver Heath
Buckinghamshire SL0 0NH
Tel: 01753 656656
E-mail: info@societyinmotion.com
Website: www.societyinmotion.com

The IMIS, formerly the BKSTS, was founded in 1931 to inspire, train, educate and connect all members of the media industry around the world. IMIS provides a series of lectures, training, and networking events as well as offering affordable membership rates.

473

MEMBERSHIP
Student Member
Associate Member
Full Member (MBKS)
Emeritus Member
Fellow (FBKS)

QUALIFICATION/EXAMINATIONS
For Full Membership:

Age 23 or over
5 years of experience in the industry
Submission of CV/Resume
(2) References

DESIGNATORY LETTERS
MBKS, FBKS

LONDON FILM SCHOOL

24 Shelton Street
Covent Garden
London WC2H 9UB
Tel: 020 7836 9642
E-mail: info@lfs.org.uk
Website: https://lfs.org.uk

LFS is the oldest film school in the UK and recognised by Screenskills as a Centre of Excellence. Since 1956 we have trained thousands of directors, cinematographeres, editors and film professionals from around the world. LFS is a registered charity with Greg Dyke as Chairman.

MEMBERSHIP
CILECT, NAHEMI, GEECT, GuildHE

QUALIFICATION/EXAMINATIONS
MA in Filmmaking (validated by University of Warwick)
MA in Screenwriting (validated by University of Warwick)
MA International Film Business and PhD (validated by University of Exeter)
PhD Film by Practice (validated by University of Exeter)

THE NATIONAL FILM AND TELEVISION SCHOOL

Beaconsfield Studios
Station Road
Beaconsfield
Buckinghamshire HP9 1LG
Tel: 01494 671234
Fax: 01494 674042
E-mail: info@nfts.co.uk
Website: www.nfts.co.uk

Creative Skillset Film Academy, the UK's leading film and television school, offers full-time MA and Diploma courses in all the key film and television disciplines, from Animation to VFX. Purpose-built studios include two film stages, a large television studio, and post-production facilities rivalling those of many professional companies.

QUALIFICATION/EXAMINATIONS
Diploma (in 1 of 8 disciplines)
MA in Film and Television (specializing in 1 of 13 disciplines)

CLEANING, LAUNDRY AND DRY CLEANING

Membership of Professional Institutions and Associations

BRITISH INSTITUTE OF CLEANING SCIENCE

9 Premier Court
Boarden Close
Moulton Park
Northampton
Northants NN3 6LF
Tel: 01604 678710
Fax: 01604 645988
E-mail: info@bics.org.uk
Website: www.bics.org.uk

The British Institute of Cleaning Science is the largest independent professional and educational body within the cleaning industry.

Our mission is to raise the standards of education and to build awareness of the cleaning industry, through professional standards and accredited training.

MEMBERSHIP

- **Student Membership** – free of charge for any individual undertaking a qualification relating to the cleaning industry.
- **PBICSc** – For individuals who have undertaken their BICSc Licence to Practice and hold a valid card, we offer the first year of PBICSc Membership free of charge.
- **ABICSc** – For individuals who hold a valid BICSc Licence to Practice and 5 or more skills from our Cleaning Professionals Skills Suite and have been in the industry for one or more years.

- **MBICSc** – For individuals who hold or have previously held a BICSc Licence to Practice or hold 12 BICSc CPD (Continuous Professional Development) points and have been a manager or supervisor in the industry for five or more years.
- **LBICSc** – For Licensed Assessors who hold a valid Licence to Practice, at least 7 more skills from our Cleaning Professionals Skills Suite, completed the Assessor Course and have been approved as an Assessor.
- **FBICSc** – Fellow of BICSc, we may award this to individuals for exceptional service to the Institute, or to the industry as a whole.

QUALIFICATION/EXAMINATIONS
The Cleaning Professional's Skills Suite (CPSS)
Car Valeting Training
On Premises Laundry Training
Health and Safety Workshop
Train the Trainer Course
Other cleaning qualifications are also available

THE GUILD OF CLEANERS AND LAUNDERERS

56 Maple Drive
Larkhall
South Lanarkshire ML9 2AR
Tel: 01698 322669
E-mail: enquiries@gcl.org.uk
Website: www.gcl.org.uk

The Guild, formed in 1949, is a technical and professional society whose aim is to further knowledge and skill in all branches of the industry. We keep our members up to date through lectures, seminars and written reports, exchange information of mutual benefit with other organisations in the industry, and voice our opinion in relevant forums.

MEMBERSHIP
Ordinary
Associate
Advanced
Fellow
Corporate
Honorary
Junior

QUALIFICATION/EXAMINATIONS
See https://gcl.org.uk/guild-qualifications/ for qualifications and examinations.

DESIGNATORY LETTERS
AGCL, AdGCL, LGCL, FGCL

COLOUR TECHNOLOGY
Membership of Professional Institutions and Associations

PAINTING AND DECORATING ASSOCIATION

32 Coton Road
Nuneaton
Warwickshire CV11 5TW
Tel: 024 7635 3776
Fax: 024 7635 4513
E-mail: info@paintingdecoratingassociation.co.uk
Website: www.paintingdecoratingassociation.co.uk

The PDA is a registered trade and employers' organisation, catering exclusively for the needs of professional painting and decorating trade employers. The Association conducts no examinations, but all membership applications are scrutinized at branch level to ensure that only bona fide firms that agree to abide by our code of conduct are admitted.

MEMBERSHIP
Full Member
Associate

THE SOCIETY OF DYERS AND COLOURISTS

Perkin House
82 Grattan Road
Bradford BD1 2LU
Tel: 01274 725138
E-mail: info@sdc.org.uk
Website: www.sdc.org.uk

An educational charity, professional body and chartered society, serving globally all aspects of the coloration industries including the textile supply chain through the knowledgeable and enthusiastic involvement of its professional members and industry partners. Recognized as the authority for colour science and technology, delivering high-quality international qualifications and training programmes.

MEMBERSHIP
Individual Voting Member, Individual Non-voting Member, Individual Student Member, College Member, Company Member

QUALIFICATION/EXAMINATIONS
Fellowship (FSDC), Associateship (ASDC), Licentiateship (LSDC), Chartered Colourist (CCol), Textile Coloration Certificate, Foundation Textile Coloration Certificate.

DESIGNATORY LETTERS
FSDC, ASDC, LSDC, CCol

COMMUNICATIONS AND MEDIA
Membership of Professional Institutions and Associations

THE PICTURE RESEARCH ASSOCIATION

c/o 10 Marrick House
Mortimer Crescent
London NW6 5NY
Tel: 0771403017
E-mail: chair@picture-research.org.uk
Website: www.picture-research.org.uk

The PRA, founded in 1977, is a professional organisation for picture researchers, picture editors and anyone specifically involved in the research, management and supply of visual material to the media industry. Our aims are to provide information and give support to our members, and to promote their interests and specific skills to potential employers.

MEMBERSHIP
Full Membership/Image buyers, Picture Researchers, Picture Editors
Sponsors – Image agency providers

QUALIFICATION/EXAMINATIONS
To qualify as a member of the Association you will need a minimum of 2 years experienceas a qualified picture researcher/picture editor, eg you were involved in the online search of images, working to a specific brief or project.

You would have supplied both digital or analogue files for reproduction. You would also be required to have knowledge and experience of fee negotiations, clearances, copyright and licensing of photographic images from a selection of photographic sources and collections. Proof of your experience will be required. Sponsors: A full- or part-time employee of a picture library, picture agency or image archive who is directly involved in the supply of images to the media in general.

COMPUTING AND INFORMATION TECHNOLOGY
Membership of Professional Institutions and Associations

ASSOCIATION OF COMPUTER PROFESSIONALS

ACP
Chilverbridge House
Arlington
East Sussex BN26 6SB
Tel: 01323 871874
Fax: 01323 871875

The ACP is an independent professional examining body, founded in 1984 to set and maintain standards of education that reflect the constantly changing requirements of the computer industry, both in the UK and overseas. We do so through the provision of course syllabuses and examinations to our carefully vetted training centres around the world.

MEMBERSHIP
Student
Practitioner
Graduate (GradACP)
Licentiate (LACP)
Associate (AACP)
Member (MACP)
Fellow (FACP)

QUALIFICATION/EXAMINATIONS
Please see the ACP's website for details of certificates and diplomas.

DESIGNATORY LETTERS
GradACP, LACP, AACP, MACP, FACP

BCS, THE CHARTERED INSTITUTE FOR IT

1st Floor, Block D
North Star House
North Star Avenue
Swindon
Wiltshire SN2 1FA
Tel: 01793 417417
Fax: 01793 417444
E-mail: customerservices@bcs.uk
Website: www.bcs.org

We promote wider social and economic progress through the advancement of information technology science and practice. We bring together industry, academics, practitioners and government to share knowledge, promote new thinking, inform the design of new curricula, shape public policy and inform the public.

Our vision is to be a world-class organisation for IT. Our 75,000 strong membership includes practitioners, businesses, academics and students in the UK and internationally. We deliver a range of professional development tools for practitioners and employees. A leading IT qualification body, we offer a range of widely recognised qualifications.

MEMBERSHIP
Memberships:
Associate Member (AMBCS)
Professional Member (MBCS)
Chartered IT Professional (CITP)
Fellowship (FBCS)
Student
Apprentice
Affiliate

QUALIFICATION/EXAMINATIONS
IT User Qualifications
- Computer and Online Basics – Understand the basics of how to use a computer
- Digital Skills – Develop skills for our digital world
- ECDL – Develop skills using office-based software
- e-safety – The online safety qualification for Schools
- ITQ – The flexible IT qualification – Create your own qualification, or use one of our tailor-made solutions

Higher Education Qualifications
- BCS Level 4 Certificate in IT/100/6190/2
- BCS Level 5 Diploma in IT/100/6190/3
- BCS Level 6 Professional Graduate Diploma in IT/100/6191/5

Professional Certification
- Agile and Agile Scrum
- Artificial Intelligence
- Business analysis
- DevOps
- GDPR and Data Protection
- Information Security and CCP Scheme
- IT Asset Management
- IT Service Management
- Openstack Software
- Project and Program Management
- Software Testing
- Solution Development and Architecture
- User Experience

Apprenticeships
- Data Analyst
- IS Business Analyst
- Cyber Intrusion Analyst
- Cyber Security Technologist
- Infrastructure Technician
- Unified Communications Technician
- Unified Troubleshooter
- Network Engineer
- Software Development Technician
- Software Developer
- Software Tester
- Digital Marketer
- IT Technical Salesperson

See the BCS website for details of other qualifications.

INSTITUTE FOR THE MANAGEMENT OF INFORMATION SYSTEMS

BCS Swindon (HQ)
First Floor, Block D
North Star House
North Star Avenue
Swindon SN2 1FA
Tel: +44 (0)1793 417417
Fax: 0845 850 0007
E-mail: imis@bcs.org
Website: www.imis.org.uk

IMIS is one of the leading professional associations in the IT sector. A registered charity, it plays a prominent role in fostering greater understanding of IS management, in working to enhance the status of those engaged in the profession, and in promoting higher standards through better education and training worldwide.

MEMBERSHIP
Student Member
Practitioner Member
Licentiate Member (LIMIS)

Associate Member (AIMIS)
Full Member (MIMIS)
Fellow (FIMIS)

QUALIFICATION/EXAMINATIONS
Foundation
Diploma
Higher Diploma

DESIGNATORY LETTERS
LIMIS, AIMIS, MIMIS, FIMIS

INSTITUTION OF ANALYSTS AND PROGRAMMERS

Boundary House
Boston Road
London W7 2QE
Tel: 020 8004 9085
E-mail: admin@iap.org.uk
Website: www.iap.org.uk

The IAP is a professional organisation for people who work in the development, installation and testing of business systems and computer software. Our aim is to promote high standards of competence and conduct among our members, to encourage them to develop their skills and progress their career, and to facilitate the advancement and spreading of knowledge within the profession.

MEMBERSHIP
Licentiate
Graduate (GradIAP)
Associate Member (AMIAP)
Member (MIAP)
Fellow (FIAP)

DESIGNATORY LETTERS
GradIAP, AIAP, MIAP, FIAP

COUNSELLING

Membership of Professional Institutions and Associations

COUNSELLING LTD

Registered Office
5 Pear Tree Walk
Wakefield
West Yorkshire WF2 0HW
E-mail: via website
Website: www.counselling.ltd.uk

Counselling, a registered charity founded in 1998, is a membership organisation for counsellors and psychotherapists in the UK that has established a network of about 2,700 affiliated CCC-registered counsellors, many of whom are able to provide occasional free or discounted face-to-face counselling with clients on low incomes.

MEMBERSHIP
Affiliate

CSCT COUNSELLING TRAINING

7 Seal Close
Sutton Coldfield
West Midlands B76 1FJ
Tel: 0121 321 1941
E-mail: info@counsellingtraining.com
Website: www.counselling-training.com

CSCT has been producing counselling training courses for over 25 years, during which time we have trained over 50,000 students. Our courses are offered PT via a network of colleges and private providers throughout the UK. Our training materials are written to the specifications of the appropriate awarding body and we provide 24-hour e-mail and telephone support from Client Services and the Academic Team.

QUALIFICATION/EXAMINATIONS
Please see the CSCT's website.

CREDIT MANAGEMENT
Membership of Professional Institutions and Associations

CHARTERED INSTITUTE OF CREDIT MANAGEMENT

The Water Mill
Station Road
South Luffenham
Oakham
Leicestershire LE15 8NB
Tel: 01780 722900
Fax: 01780 721333
E-mail: info@cicm.com
Website: www.cicm.com

CICM is the largest recognised professional body in the world for the credit management community. Representing all areas of credit and collections, CICM is the trusted leader and expert providing its members with support, resources, advice, accredited qualifications and career development opportunities as well as a networking and interactive community.

MEMBERSHIP
Studying Member (non professional grade)
Affiliate (non professional grade)
Associate Member (ACICM)
Graduate Member (MCICM(Grad))
Member (MCICM)
Fellow (FCICM)

QUALIFICATION/EXAMINATIONS
Level 2 Certificate in Credit and Collections
Level 2 Diploma in Credit and Collections
Level 3 Diploma in Credit and Collections
Level 5 Diploma in Credit and Collections
Level 2 and 3 Certificates in Money and Debt Advice
Level 2 and 3 Diplomas in Money and Debt Advice
Level 4 Diploma in High Court Enforcement

DESIGNATORY LETTERS
ACICM, MCICM(Grad), MCICM, FCICM

DANCING
Membership of Professional Institutions and Associations

BRITISH BALLET ORGANISATION

Ensign House
Battersea Reach
Juniper Drive
London SW18 1TA
Tel: 020 8748 1241
E-mail: info@bbo.org.uk
Website: www.bbo.org.uk

The BBO, founded in 1930, is an awarding body offering teacher training and examinations in classical ballet, tap, modern dance and jazz. We have schools throughout the UK and in several other countries.

MEMBERSHIP
Student Member
Associate Member
Registered Teacher
Friend

QUALIFICATION/EXAMINATIONS
Please see the BBO website for details.

IMPERIAL SOCIETY OF TEACHERS OF DANCING

Imperial House
22/26 Paul Street
London EC2A 4QE
Tel: +44 (0)20 7377 1577
Fax: +44 (0)20 7247 8829
E-mail: via website
Website: www.istd.org

The ISTD is a registered educational charity and examinations board. We aim to promote knowledge of dance, to maintain and improve teaching standards, and to qualify (by examination) teachers of dancing. Our dance techniques cover more than 12 different genres and are taught by more than 7,500 members by our members worldwide.

MEMBERSHIP
A range of 9 categories from Student to Life Membership.

QUALIFICATION/EXAMINATIONS
Please see our website www.istd.org or www.dance-teachers.org

DESIGNATORY LETTERS
ISTD

INTERNATIONAL DANCE TEACHERS' ASSOCIATION LIMITED

International House
76 Bennett Road
Brighton BN2 5JL
Tel: 01273 685652
Fax: 01273 674388
E-mail: via website
Website: www.idta.co.uk

The IDTA is one of the world's largest dance examination boards, with more than 7,000 members in 55 countries. Our aims are to promote knowledge and foster the art of dance in all its forms, to maintain and improve dancing standards, and to offer a comprehensive range of professional qualifications in all dance genres.

MEMBERSHIP
Associate (AIDTA)
Licentiate (LIDTA)
Fellow (FIDTA)

DESIGNATORY LETTERS
AIDTA, LIDTA, FIDTA

THE BENESH INSTITUTE

36 Battersea Square
London SW11 3RA
Tel: 020 7326 8035

The Benesh Institute is the international centre for Benesh Movement Notation (BMN) founded in 1962 to promote, develop and offer education in BMN. We also function as an examining body and professional centre, and are responsible for coordinating technical developments. Since 1997 The Benesh Institute has been incorporated within the Royal Academy of Dance.

QUALIFICATION/EXAMINATIONS
Certificate in Benesh Movement Notation (CBMN) (validated by the Royal Academy of Dance)

Diploma for Professional Benesh Movement Notators (DPBMN) (validated by the Royal Academy of Dance)

Associate of the Institute of Choreology (AI Chor)

DENTISTRY
Membership of Professional Institutions and Associations

BRITISH ASSOCIATION OF CLINICAL DENTAL TECHNOLOGY

44–46 Wollaton Road
Beeston
Nottingham N69 2NR
Tel: 0115 957 5370
Fax: 0115 925 4800

The CDTA provides political and educational representation for its members, who are registered with the General Dental Council and trained in designing, creating, constructing, repairing and rebasing removable appliances to ensure optimal fit, maximum comfort and general wellbeing of patients. We are committed to team dentistry and ensure that our members work to the highest professional standards.

MEMBERSHIP
Full Membership
In training Membership
Practice Membership
Multi Practice Membership

BRITISH ASSOCIATION OF DENTAL NURSES

Room 200
Hillhouse International Business Centre
Thornton-Cleveleys
Lancashire FY5 4QD
Tel: 01253 338360
E-mail: conference@badn.org.uk
Website: www.badn.org.uk

BADN is the UK's only professional association for dental nurses. Membership is open to all dental nurses, working in all areas of dentistry. Benefits of membership include access to quarterly digital British Dental Nurses' Journal, verifiable CPD, free legal helpline and a wide range of special offers and discounts.

MEMBERSHIP
Associate Member (overseas, former, retired)

Full Member (Registered Dental Nurses) – with or without indemnity cover. Special rates for part time and maternity.
Student Member (student dental nurses on, or awaiting a place on, an approved training course leading to a registerable qualification)
Fellow (BADN member for at least 10 years with additional qualifications – conditions apply)

DESIGNATORY LETTERS
FBADN (Fellows only)

BRITISH SOCIETY OF DENTAL HYGIENE AND THERAPY

First Floor
10-12 Albert Street
Rugby
Warwickshire CV21 2RS
Tel: 01788 575050
E-mail: enquiries@bsdht.org.uk
Website: www.bsdht.org.uk

The BSDHT is the only nationally recognised body that represents Dental Hygienists and Dental Therapists. Join the UK's largest professional body for practising dental hygienists and dental therapists and students of the profession. We represent your interests, influence positive change for the industry and provide information to the public. See more at: www.bsdht.org.uk. We have a membership of more than 3,500, and look after their interests by liaising with the Department of Health, General Dental Council, British Dental Association and other organisations.

MEMBERSHIP
Member
Student
Associate

DENTAL TECHNOLOGISTS ASSOCIATION

PO Box 1318
Cheltenham GL50 9EA
Tel: 01242 461931
E-mail: via website, or info@dta-uk.org
Website: www.dta-uk.org

The DTA is an organisation that supports the development of the dental technology profession by encouraging and promoting education, including CPD, and for the exchange of views between dental technicians. We advise, develop and support dental technicians and maintain links with the government, other dental organisations, service providers and the public.

MEMBERSHIP
Member

GENERAL DENTAL COUNCIL

37 Wimpole Street
London W1G 8DQ
Tel: +44 (0) 20 7167 6000
E-mail: information@gdc-uk.org
Website: www.gdc-uk.org

The GDC regulates dental professionals in the UK. All dentists, clinical dental technicians, dental hygienists, dental nurses, dental technicians, dental therapists and orthodontic therapists must be registered with the GDC in order to work in the UK.

THE BRITISH DENTAL ASSOCIATION

64 Wimpole Street
London W1G 8YS
Tel: 020 7935 0875
Fax: 020 7487 5232
E-mail: enquiries@bda.org
Website: www.bda.org

The BDA, which was founded in 1880, is the professional association and trade union for dentists in the UK. Our aims are to advance the science, arts and ethics of dentistry, improve the UK's oral health, and promote the interests of our members. Membership, which is voluntary, stands at around 18,000, mostly in general practice.

MEMBERSHIP
Essential
Extra
Expert

DIETETICS
Membership of Professional Institutions and Associations

THE BRITISH DIETETIC ASSOCIATION

5th Floor
Charles House
148–49 Great Charles Street Queensway
Birmingham B3 3HT
Tel: 0121 200 8080
E-mail: info@bda.uk.com
Website: www.bda.uk.com

The BDA, established in 1936, is the UK's leading professional association and trade union for dietitians. Our aims are to advance the science and practice of dietetics and associated subjects, to promote education and training in the science and practice of dietetics and associated subjects, and to regulate relations between our 8,500+ members and their employers.

MEMBERSHIP
Full Member
Associate Member
Affiliate Member
Alliance Member
Student Member
International Member

DISTRIBUTION

Membership of Professional Institutions and Associations

THE CHARTERED INSTITUTE OF LOGISTICS AND TRANSPORT (UK)

Earlstrees Court
Earlstrees Road
Corby
Northamptonshire NN17 4AX
Tel: 01536 740106
Fax: 01536 740101
E-mail: membership@ciltuk.org.uk
Website: www.ciltuk.org.uk

The Chartered Institute of Logistics and Transport is the membership organisation for professionals involved in the movement of goods and people and their associated supply chains.

Members are involved in the management and design of infrastructure, systems, processes and information flows and in the management and development of effective organisations.

MEMBERSHIP
Learner Affiliate
Student
Apprentice
e-Member
Affiliate
Member (MILT)
Chartered Member (CMILT)
Chartered Fellow (FCILT)

QUALIFICATION/EXAMINATIONS
Regulated qualifications cover areas within the Institute's nine Professional Sectors: Logistics & Supply Chain, Transport Planning, Rail, Active Travel & Planning, Bus & Coach, Ports Maritime & Waterways, Freight Forwarding, Aviation and Operations Management.

Regulated qualifications meet the regulatory requirements for the design, delivery, assessment and award of units and qualifications, and are regulated by Ofqual and/or Qualifications Wales/CCEA Accreditation, if appropriate.
Level 1 – Award
Level 2 – Award, Certificate, Diploma
Level 3 – Award, Certificate
Level 4 – Certificate
Level 5 – Award, Certificate, Diploma, Professional Diploma
Level 6 – Advanced Diploma

Non-Regulated Programmes
Humanitarian Logistics (3 programmes)
Supply Chain Practitioner Award (Foundation, Professional and Master programmes)
Certificate of Customs Competency
Certified European Logistician (Junior, Senior, Master programmes)
Certified DOPsys (Delivery, Offload and Position System) (Technician, Team Leader, Project Manager)

DESIGNATORY LETTERS
MILT, CMILT, FCILT

DRAMATIC AND PERFORMING ARTS
Membership of Professional Institutions and Associations

EQUITY

Guild House
Upper St Martins Lane
London WC2H 9EG
Tel: 020 7379 6000
E-mail: info@equity.org.uk
Website: www.equity.org.uk

Equity is the UK trade union representing professional performers and other creative workers from across the entertainment, creative and cultural industries. The main function of Equity is to negotiate minimum terms and conditions of employment for its members and to represent its members' interests to the government and other bodies. We also provide a wide range of services and support for members.

MEMBERSHIP
Student Member
Graduate Member
Full Member
Long Service Member

FEDERATION OF DRAMA SCHOOLS

c/o Liverpool Institute For Performing Arts
Mount Street,
Liverpool L1 9HF
E-mail: info@federationofdramaschools.co.uk
Website: www.federationofdramaschools.co.uk

FDS membership identifies the leading providers of UK performing arts conservatoire training. FDS aims to ensure that all graduates from member schools are equipped to engage with, and make a lasting contribution to, a highly demanding industry. Membership provides a quality training hallmark that is widely recognised by industry stakeholders.

THE BRITISH (THEATRICAL) ARTS

12 Deveron Way
Rise Park
Romford
Essex RM1 4UL
Tel: 01708 756263
E-mail: sally.chennelle1@ntlworld.com
Website: www.britisharts.org

The British Arts is a non-profit-making organisation dedicated to maintaining and where necessary raising the standard of the teaching of Performing Arts subjects. We work to encourage a strong technical foundation combined with an understanding of professional theatrical presentation and conduct exams in Dramatic Art, Classical & Stage Ballet, Mime, Tap, Musical Theatre and Modern Dance.

MEMBERSHIP
Student Member

Companion
Associate (Teaching and Non-teaching)
Member (Teaching and Non-teaching)
Advanced Teacher Member

Fellow

QUALIFICATION/EXAMINATIONS
Please see the British Arts website for full details.

DRIVING INSTRUCTORS
Membership of Professional Institutions and Associations

REGISTER OF APPROVED DRIVING INSTRUCTORS

The Axis Building
112 Upper Parliament Street
Nottingham NG1 6LP
Tel: 0300 200 1122
E-mail: ADIReg@dvsa.gov.uk

The Register of Approved Driving Instructors (ADI) and the licensing scheme for trainee instructors (PDI) are administered under the provisions of the Road Traffic Act 1988 by the Department for Transport (DfT). It is an offence for anyone to give professional instruction (that is instruction paid for by or in respect of the pupil) in driving a motor car unless: (a) his or her name is on the Register of Approved Driving Instructors; or (b) he or she holds a 'trainee's licence to give instruction' issued by the Registrar.

QUALIFICATION/EXAMINATIONS
Please see the GOV.UK website (www.gov.uk/apply-to-become-a-driving-instructor) for details of the qualifying examinations.

EMBALMING
Membership of Professional Institutions and Associations

INTERNATIONAL EXAMINATIONS BOARD OF EMBALMERS

146 Alexandra Road
Great Wakering
Essex SS3 0GW
Tel: 01702 218907
E-mail: admin@iebe.co.uk

The Board examines candidates who wish to become qualified members of the British Institute of Embalmers (qv), which is not itself an examining body but can provide information packs (also available from the above address) that contain lists of approved schools and accredited tutors.

THE BRITISH INSTITUTE OF EMBALMERS

Anubis House
21c Station Road
Knowle
Solihull
West Midlands B93 0HL
Tel: 01564 778991
Fax: 01564 770812
E-mail: enquiry@bioe.co.uk
Website: www.bioe.co.uk

The BIE, founded in 1927, is an organisation for professional embalmers. Its objectives include supporting and protecting the status, character and interests of embalmers, promoting the efficient tuition of persons seeking to become embalmers, and encouraging the study and practice of improved methods of embalming.

MEMBERSHIP
Member (MBIE)
Fellow (FBIE)

DESIGNATORY LETTERS
MBIE, FBIE

EMPLOYMENT AND CAREERS SERVICES
Membership of Professional Institutions and Associations

CAREER DEVELOPMENT INSTITUTE

Ground Floor
Copthall House
1 New Road
Stourbridge
West Midlands DY8 1PH
Tel: 01384 376464
E-mail: hq@thecdi.net
Website: www.thecdi.net

The CDI is the largest UK-wide professional and membership body for career development professionals. Our aim is to support members and promote access to high-quality career development services, delivered by professionally qualified staff working within an appropriate ethical framework. Suitably qualified members can join the UK Register of Career Development Professionals.

MEMBERSHIP
Student Member
Full Member
Registered Member
Retired Member
International Digital Member
Affiliate Organisation
School Affiliate

QUALIFICATION/EXAMINATIONS
Qualification in Career Development (QCD)
Qualification in Career Guidance (QCG)
Qualification in Career Guidance and Development (QCGD)
CDI Certificate in Career Guidance Theory (CCGT)
CDI Certificate in Careers Leadership (CCL)
QCF Level 6 Diploma in Career Guidance and Development
CDI Certificate for Careers Assistants

RECRUITMENT AND EMPLOYMENT CONFEDERATION

Dorset House
First Floor
27–45 Stamford Street
London SE1 9NT
Tel: 020 7009 2100
Fax: 020 7935 4112
Website: www.rec.uk.com

The Institute of Recruitment Professionals (IRP) is the representative body for individual recruiters and resourcing specialists. We represent over 10,500 individual members who deliver the UK's recruitment services.

The IRP helps recruiters from private, public and in-house sectors demonstrate their commitment to best practice, world-class recruitment standards and the best possible services to clients and candidates. Becoming a member of the IRP helps you demonstrate commitment, professionalism and added value to your clients and candidates.

Whether you are just starting out, running a fast growing business, looking for a change in direction or just wanting to develop your experience, membership of the IRP will provide you with the very best platform to make recruitment your career of choice.

MEMBERSHIP
Affiliate (AIRP)
Member (MIRP)
Fellow (FIRP)

QUALIFICATION/EXAMINATIONS
Level 5 Diploma in Recruitment Leadership
Level 4 Diploma iN Recruitment Management
Level 3 Certificate in Recruitment Practice
Level 3 Certificate in In-house Recruitment
Level 2 Certificate in Recruitment Resourcing

DESIGNATORY LETTERS
AIRP, MIRP, FIRP

ENGINEERING, AERONAUTICAL
Membership of Professional Institutions and Associations

ROYAL AERONAUTICAL SOCIETY

4 Hamilton Place
Hyde Park Corner
London W1J 7BQ
Tel: 020 7670 4300
E-mail: raes@aerosociety.com
Website: www.aerosociety.com

The RAeS, founded in 1866 to further the science of aeronautics, is a multidisciplinary professional institution dedicated to the global aerospace community. We work on our members' behalf to promote the highest professional standards in all aerospace disciplines, to provide specialist information and act as a central forum for the exchange of ideas, and to play a leading role in influencing opinion on aviation matters.

MEMBERSHIP
Student Affiliate
Affiliate
Associate (ARAeS)
Associate Member (AMRAeS)
Member (MRAeS)
Companion (CRAeS)
Fellow (FRAeS)
Apprentice

ENGINEERING, AGRICULTURAL
Membership of Professional Institutions and Associations

BRITISH AGRICULTURAL AND GARDEN MACHINERY ASSOCIATION

225 Bristol Road
Edgbaston
Birmingham B5 7UB
Tel: 0800 028 0245
E-mail: info@bagma.com
Website: www.bagma.com

BAGMA is the trade association representing agricultural and garden machinery dealers in the UK. We have some 850 dealer members and 75 affiliated suppliers and allied industry companies. We offer a range of training and assessment courses through our online learning package and at approved Training and Assessment Centres.

QUALIFICATION/EXAMINATIONS
Please see the BAGMA website.

THE INSTITUTION OF AGRICULTURAL ENGINEERS

The Bullock Building (53)
University Way
Cranfield
Bedford
Bedfordshire MK43 0GH
Tel: 01234 750876
E-mail: secretary@iagre.org
Website: www.iagre.org

The Institution of Agricultural Engineers is the professional body for engineers, scientists, technologists and managers in agriculture and environment, agri-technology and allied landbased industries, including forestry, food engineering and technology, amenity, renewable energy, horticulture. Bringing together academics, practitioners and industry sharing knowledge and promoting professionalism in advancement and application of technology.

MEMBERSHIP
Student
Affiliate (AIAgrE)
Technician (TIAgrE)
Associate Member (AMIAgrE)
Member (MIAgrE)
Fellow (FIAgrE)
Honorary Fellow

QUALIFICATION/EXAMINATIONS
Chartered Engineer (CEng), Chartered Environmentalist (CEnv), Incorporated Engineer (IEng), Engineering Technician (EngTech)

DESIGNATORY LETTERS
AIAgrE, TIAgrE, AMIAgrE, MIAgrE, FIAgrE

ENGINEERING, AUTOMOBILE
Membership of Professional Institutions and Associations

INSTITUTE OF AUTOMOTIVE ENGINEER ASSESSORS

Pennyroyal Court
Station Road
Tring
Hertfordshire HP23 5QY
Tel: 01296 642895
Fax: 01296 640044
E-mail: sally@theiaea.org
Website: www.iaea-online.org

The IAEA, a Professional Affiliate of the Engineering Council, was founded in 1932 and now represents more than 1,400 automotive engineer assessors responsible for activities such as vehicle damage assessment, accident reconstruction, investigation of mechanical failures, electrical failures and vehicle fires, providing expert witness testimony, repair assessment, car fleet surveys, and conciliation and arbitration.

MEMBERSHIP
Affiliate
Associate (A.Inst.AEA)
Member (M.Inst.AEA)
Fellow (F.Inst.AEA)

QUALIFICATION/EXAMINATIONS
Basic Principles of Maths & Physics Application to Accident Reconstruction
Motor Vehicle Legislation as related to Insurance Principles
Principles and Practice of Vehicle Damage Assessment
Motor Insurance
Automotive Technology

DESIGNATORY LETTERS
A.Inst.AEA, M.Inst.AEA, F.Inst.AEA

THE INSTITUTE OF THE MOTOR INDUSTRY

Fanshaws
Brickendon
Hertford SG13 8PQ
Tel: 01992 511521
Fax: 01992 511548
E-mail: comms@theimi.org.uk
Website: https://www.theimi.org.uk/

The IMI is the professional body for individuals working in the motor industry and the authoritative source of industry careers information, standards, qualifications and accreditations. It is an awarding organisation, with over 350 regulated qualifications, 25 accreditations and quality assured programmes, delivered at 600 training providers across the UK.

MEMBERSHIP
Student
Affiliate
Associate
Member
Fellow

QUALIFICATION/EXAMINATIONS
Please see https://www.theimi.org.uk/learning-and-development for qualifications.

DESIGNATORY LETTERS
AffIMI, AMIMI, MIMI, FIMI, AAE, CAE

ENGINEERING, BUILDING SERVICES
Membership of Professional Institutions and Associations

THE CHARTERED INSTITUTION OF BUILDING SERVICES ENGINEERS

222 Balham High Road
London SW12 9BS
Tel: 020 8675 5211
Fax: 020 8675 5449
E-mail: membership@cibse.org
Website: www.cibse.org

CIBSE is the professional body for people involved in the design, construction, operation and maintenance of the engineering elements of a building other than its structure and enables it to operate efficiently by saving energy and contributing to a low carbon built environment. This includes heating, ventilation, air conditioning, electrical services, lighting etc.

MEMBERSHIP
Student Affiliate
Affiliate
Graduate
Licentiate (LCIBSE)
Associate (ACIBSE)
Member (MCIBSE)

Fellow (FCIBSE)
CIBSE is a licensed institution of the Engineering Council. This means that, as well as joining CIBSE, you will be Registered as a Chartered Engineer (CEng), Incorporated Engineer (IEng) or Engineering Technician (EngTech) when you have reached the appropriate level of qualification and professional skill.

QUALIFICATION/EXAMINATIONS
Please see the CIBSE website for more information www.cibse.org

DESIGNATORY LETTERS
LCIBSE, ACIBSE, MCIBSE, FCIBSE

ENGINEERING, CHEMICAL
Membership of Professional Institutions and Associations

THE INSTITUTION OF CHEMICAL ENGINEERS

Davis Building
Railway Terrace
Rugby
Warwickshire CV21 3HQ
Tel: 01788 578214
Fax: 01788 560833
E-mail: membersupport@icheme.org
Website: www.icheme.org

Founded in 1922, the Institution of Chemical Engineers (IChemE) embraces over 37,000 members in more than 100 countries. We are a multi-national institution with primary offices in the UK and Australia. IChemE sets the standards for chemical and process safety engineering professionals and uses members' collective knowledge to function as a respected learned society. We advance the contribution of chemical engineering for the good of society.

MEMBERSHIP
Student
Affiliate
Associate Fellow

Technican Member
Associate Member (AMIChemE)
Member (MIChemE)
Fellow (FIChemE)
Chartered Chemical Engineer (CEng MIChemE)
Chartered Engineer (CEng)
Chartered Scientist (CSci)
Chartered Environmentalist (CEnv)
Professoinal Process Safety Engineer
   Registered Professional Engineer Queensland (RPEQ)

European Engineer (EUR ING)
Incorporated Engineer (IEng)
Engineering Technician (EngTech)
Registered Science Technician (RSciTech)

DESIGNATORY LETTERS
AMIChemE, MIChemE, FIChemE, CEng, MIChemE, TIChemE, CEng, EUR ING, IEng, CSci, CEnv, AFIChemE, RSciTech

ENGINEERING, CIVIL
Membership of Professional Institutions and Associations

INSTITUTION OF CIVIL ENGINEERS

1 Great George Street
Westminster
London SW1P 3AA
Tel: 020 7222 7722
E-mail: via website
Website: www.ice.org.uk

ICE is an international organisation with over 90,000 members that promotes civil engineering around the world. Our purpose is to qualify professionals engaged in civil engineering, provide knowledge and best practice to all engaged in infrastructure, and advise policy makers on opportunites, issues and trends in the built environment.

MEMBERSHIP
Student

Graduate (GMICE)
Technician Member (MICE)
Member (MICE)
Associate Member (AMICE)
Fellow (FICE)

QUALIFICATION/EXAMINATIONS
EngTech, IEng, CEng, CEnv

ENGINEERING, ELECTRICAL, ELECTRONIC AND MANUFACTURING
Membership of Professional Institutions and Associations

INSTITUTION OF LIGHTING PROFESSIONALS

Regent House
Regent Place
Rugby
Warwickshire CV21 2PN
Tel: 01788 576492
E-mail: info@theilp.org.uk
Website: www.theilp.org.uk

The ILP is a professional lighting association with about 2,000 members, including lighting designers, consultants and engineers. We are dedicated to excellence in lighting and to raising awareness about the important contribution of lighting in road safety, crime prevention and the environment. We support members by providing technical advice and encourage their CPD through our monthly journal and by holding a wide range of conferences, regional meetings, seminars and courses.

MEMBERSHIP
Apprentice
Student
Affiliate

Associate Member (AMILP)
Member (MILP)
Fellow (FILP)
Corporate Member
Premier Corporate Member
Engineering Technician (EngTech)
Incorporated Engineer (IEng)
Chartered Engineer (CEng)

QUALIFICATION/EXAMINATIONS
Exterior Lighting Diploma
LET Diploma in Lighting

DESIGNATORY LETTERS
AMILP, MILP, FILP, EngTech, IEng, CEng

THE INSTITUTION OF ENGINEERING AND TECHNOLOGY

Michael Faraday House
Stevenage
Hertfordshire SG1 2AY
Tel: 01438 313311
Fax: 01438 765526
E-mail: postmaster@theiet.org
Website: www.theiet.org

The IET is working to engineer a better world through our mission to inspire, inform and influence the global engineering community, supporting technology innovation to meet the needs of society. The IET has over 169,000 members in over 150 countries, with offices in Europe, North America, South Asia and Asia-Pacific.

MEMBERSHIP
Student
Associate

Member (MIET)
Fellow (FIET)
Honorary Fellow
ICT Technician (ICTTech)
Engineering Technician (EngTech)
Incorporated Engineer (IEng)
Chartered Engineer (CEng)

DESIGNATORY LETTERS
FIET, ICTTech, EngTech, IEng, CEng, MIET

ENGINEERING, ENERGY
Membership of Professional Institutions and Associations

ENERGY INSTITUTE

61 New Cavendish Street
London W1G 7AR
Tel: 020 7467 7100
E-mail: info@energyinst.org
Website: www.energyinst.org

The EI is the chartered professional membership body for the energy industry, providing learning and networking opportunities, professional recognition and energy knowledge resources for individuals and companies worldwide. We offer professional qualifications including Chartered, Incorporated and Engineering Technician status for engineers, as well as Chartered Energy Manager and Chartered Environmentalist.

MEMBERSHIP
Student Member
Associate Member (AMEI)
Affiliate
Technician Member (TMEI)
Member (MEI)
Fellow (FEI)

QUALIFICATION/EXAMINATIONS
Engineering Technician (EngTech)
Incorporated Engineer (IEng)
Chartered Engineer (CEng)
Chartered Environmentalist (CEnv)
Chartered Energy Manager (exclusive EI title)
Chartered Energy Engineer (exclusive EI title)
Chartered Petroleum Engineer (exclusive EI title)

DESIGNATORY LETTERS
AMEI, TMEI, MEI, FEI, EngTech, IEng, CEng, CEnv

ENGINEERING, ENVIRONMENTAL
Membership of Professional Institutions and Associations

INSTITUTE OF ENVIRONMENTAL MANAGEMENT AND ASSESSMENT

Saracen House
Lincoln LN6 7AS
Tel: 01522 540069
E-mail: info@iema.net
Website: www.iema.net

The IEMA is a not-for-profit membership organisation that provides recognition and support to environmental professionals and promotes sustainable development through improved environmental practice and performance. We have about 15,000 individual and corporate members in 87 countries, in the public, private and non-governmental sectors

MEMBERSHIP
Student Member
Affiliate Member
Graduate Member
Associate (AIEMA)
Practitioner (PIEMA)
Full (MIEMA)
Fellow (FIEMA)

QUALIFICATION/EXAMINATIONS
Foundation Certificate in Environmental Management
Associate Certificate in Environmental Management
Diploma

AIEMA, MIEMA, FIEMA, PIEMA, GradIEMA

THE CHARTERED INSTITUTION OF WATER AND ENVIRONMENTAL MANAGEMENT

106-109 Saffron Hill
London EC1N 8QS
Tel: 020 7831 3110
Fax: 020 7405 4967
E-mail: frontofhouse@ciwem.org
Website: www.ciwem.org

Founded in 1895, CIWEM is an independent professional body and registered charity with 12,000 members that advances the science and practice of water and environmental management for a clean, green and sustainable world by promoting environmental excellence and professional development and training, supplying independent advice and evidence-based opinion, and providing a forum for debate through conferences, technical meetings and its publications.

MEMBERSHIP
Apprentice
Graduate
Student
Non-chartered
Technician
Chartered
Fellow

QUALIFICATION/EXAMINATIONS
CIWEM provide a variety of online technical training courses, some of which are currently supported by the likes of Ellen MacArthur Foundation, Exeter and Brunel Universities. CIWEM accredits university courses at 12 leading institutions and offers a range of membership levels to suit and support all career stages.

DESIGNATORY LETTERS
GradCIWEM, MCIWEM, C.WEM MCIWEM, FCI-WEM C.WEM

THE SOCIETY OF ENVIRONMENTAL ENGINEERS

22 Greencoat Place
London SW1P 1PR
Tel: 0207 630 2132
E-mail: membership@environmental.org.uk
Website: www.environmental.org.uk

The SEE, founded in 1959, is a professional society that promotes awareness of the discipline of environmental engineering (the measurement, modelling, control and simulation of all types of environment). We provide members with information, training and representation within this field and encourage communication and good practice in quality, reliability, and cost-effective product development and manufacture.

MEMBERSHIP
Student
Associate
Member
Engineering Technician (EngTech)
Incorporated Engineer (IEng)
Chartered Engineer (CEng)
Chartered Environmentalist (CEnv)

DESIGNATORY LETTERS
MSEE, FSEE, CEnv,EngTech, IEng, CEng

ENGINEERING, FIRE
Membership of Professional Institutions and Associations

ASSOCIATION OF PRINCIPAL FIRE OFFICERS

9–11 Pebble Close
Amington
Tamworth
Staffordshire B77 4RD
Tel: 01827 302300
Fax: 01827 302399
E-mail: enquiries@apfo.org.uk
Website: www.apfo.org.uk

The APFO is the staff association of the most senior Fire Officers in the UK. Our objectives are: to represent and promote the interests of members in conditions of service and legal and employment matters; to negotiate and promote the settlement of disputes involving members; to provide assistance to members and their dependants in exceptional circumstances; and to provide support to members in matters concerning employment or a work-related injury.

MEMBERSHIP
Associate Member
Lifetime Past Member

CHIEF FIRE OFFICERS' ASSOCIATION

9–11 Pebble Close
Amington
Tamworth
Staffordshire B77 4RD
Tel: 0121 380 7311
Website: www.cfoa.org.uk

The CFOA is a professional membership association of the most senior fire officers in the UK. We provide independent advice to the government, local authorities and others. Our aim is to reduce loss of life, personal injury and damage to property by improving the quality of fire fighting, rescue, fire protection and fire prevention in the UK.

MEMBERSHIP
Member

THE INSTITUTION OF FIRE ENGINEERS

IFE House
64–66 Cygnet Court
Timothy's Bridge Road
Stratford-upon-Avon CV37 9NW
Tel: 01789 261 463
Fax: 01789 296 426
E-mail: info@ife.org.uk
Website: www.ife.org.uk

The IFE, founded in 1918, is a non-profit-making professional body for fire professionals and 10,000 members worldwide. Our aim is to encourage and improve the science and practice of fire extinction, fire prevention and fire engineering, to enhance technical networks, and to give advice and support to our members for the benefit of the community at large.

MEMBERSHIP
Student
Affiliate Member
Technician (TIFireE)
Graduate (GIFireE)
Associate (AIFireE)
Member (MIFireE)
Fellow (FIFireE)
Engineering Technician (EngTech)
Incorporated Engineer (IEng)
Chartered Engineer (CEng)
Affiliate Organisation

QUALIFICATION/EXAMINATIONS
IFE Level 2 Certificate in Fire Science, Operations and Safety

IFE Level 3 Certificate in Fire Science, Operations, Fire Safety and Management

IFE Level 3 Diploma in Fire Science and Fire Safety

IFE Level 4 Certificate in Fire Science and Fire Safety

IFE Level 3 Certificate for Operational Supervisory Managers in Fire and Rescue Services

IFE Level 5 Award in Fire Investigation: Theory and Practice

IFE Level 5 Diploma in Fire Engineering Design

IFE Level 3 Certificate in Passive Fire Protection

DESIGNATORY LETTERS
TIFireE, GIFireE, AIFireE, MIFireE, FIFireE, EngTech, IEng, CEng

ENGINEERING, GAS
Membership of Professional Institutions and Associations

THE INSTITUTION OF GAS ENGINEERS AND MANAGERS

IGEM House
High Street
Kegworth
Derbyshire DE74 2DA
Tel: +44 (0)1509 678 150
E-mail: general@igem.org.uk
Website: www.igem.org.uk

IGEM is licensed by EC(UK) and serves a wide range of professionals in the UK and international gas industry through membership and technical standards, having a diverse membership ranging from university students to qualified professionals. Anyone working or interested in the gas industry can form positive connections to enhance their career through IGEM.

MEMBERSHIP
Student/Apprentice Member
Graduates
Installers:
Licensed Gas Technician
Gas Technician

Engineers and Technicians:
Fellow
Incorporated Engineer
Engineering Technician
Engineering Associate

Managers:
Member Manager
Management Associate
Associate (AIGEM)
Associate Member (AMIGEM)
Graduate Member (GradIGEM)
Member Manager (MIGEM)
Technician Member (Eng Tech (MIGEM))

Incorporated Member (I Eng (MIGEM))
Chartered Member (C Eng (MIGEM))
Fellow (C Eng (FIGEM))

ENGINEERING, GENERAL
Membership of Professional Institutions and Associations

ASSOCIATION OF COST ENGINEERS

Administration Office
Lea House
5 Middlewich Road
Sandbach
Cheshire CW11 1XL
Tel: 01270 764798
Fax: 01270 766180
E-mail: enquiries@acoste.org.uk
Website: www.acoste.org.uk

The ACostE represents the professional interests of those with responsibility for the prediction, planning and control of resources for engineering, manufacturing and construction. As a Professional Affiliate of The Engineering Council, we can propose suitably qualified members for the award of the titles of Chartered Engineer (CEng) and Incorporated Engineer (IEng).

MEMBERSHIP
Student
Associate (AA Cost E)
Companion (Companion A Cost E)
Graduate (Grad A Cost E)
Member (MA Cost E)
Fellow (FA Cost E)
Honorary Fellow (Hon FA Cost E)
Certified Cost Engineer (CCE)
Engineering Technician (EngTech)
Incorporated Engineer (IEng)
Chartered Engineer (CEng)

QUALIFICATION/EXAMINATIONS
Level 2 DiplomaProject Control, Estimating, Planning and Cost Engineering

Level 3 Diploma listing:• Commercial Support
• Cost Engineering (Cost Control) – e.g. likely to appeal to Construction / Petro-Chemical applicants.
• Cost Engineering (Cost Planning) – e.g. likely to appeal to Manufacturing industry applicants.
• Estimating
• Planning
• Project Control
Level 5 Diploma listing:• Commercial Support
• Cost Engineering (Cost Control) – e.g. likely to appeal to Construction / Petro-Chemical applicants.
• Cost Engineering (Cost Planning) – e.g. likely to appeal to Manufacturing industry applicants.
• Estimating
• Planning
• Project Control (Cost)
• Project Control (Schedule)
• Project Control

DESIGNATORY LETTERS
AA Cost E, Companion A Cost E, Grad A Cost E, MA Cost E, FA Cost E, CCE, EngTech, IEng, CEng

ENGINEERING COUNCIL

Woolgate Exchange, 25 Basinghall Street
London
London EC2V 5HA
Tel: +44 (0) 20 3206 0500
Fax: 020 3206 0501
Website: www.engc.org.uk

The Engineering Council holds the national registers of Engineering Technicians (EngTech), Incorporated Engineers (IEng), Chartered Engineers (CEng) and Information and Communications Technology Technicians (ICTTech). We set and maintain internationally recognised standards of competence and ethics, ensuring that employers, government and society can have confidence in registrants' skills and commitment.

DESIGNATORY LETTERS
EngTech, IEng, CEng, ICTTech

INSTITUTE OF MEASUREMENT AND CONTROL

297 Euston Road
London NW1 3AD
Tel: 020 7387 4949
E-mail: membership@instmc.org
Website: www.instmc.org

The IMC is a multidisciplinary body that brings together thinkers and practitioners from the many disciplines that have a common interest in measurement and control. Our object is to promote for the public benefit, by all available means, the general advancement of the science and practice of measurement and control technology and its application.

MEMBERSHIP
Student Member
Affiliate Member
Associate Member
Member (MInstMC)
Fellow (FInstMC)
Honorary Fellow (HonFInstMC)

SEMTA

Unit 2, The Orient Centre
Greycaine Road
Watford
Watford
Hertfordshire WD24 7GP
Tel: 0845 643 9001
E-mail: Customerservices@semta.org.uk
Website: www.semta.org.uk

Semta is a not-for-profit skills support organisation. It works with employers in the aerospace, automotive, electrical, electronics, marine, mechanical, metals and science & bioscience sectors to ascertain their current and future skills needs and provide short and long-term solutions to meet those needs.

WOMEN'S ENGINEERING SOCIETY

Michael Faraday House
Six Hills Way
Stevenage
Herts SG1 2AY
Tel: 01438 765506
E-mail: info@wes.org.uk
Website: www.wes.org.uk

The WES, founded in 1919, is a professional, not-for-profit network of women engineers, scientists and technologists, who offer inspiration, support and professional development. Working in partnership, we campaign to encourage women to participate and achieve as engineers, scientists and as leaders.

MEMBERSHIP
Student Member

Associate
Full Member (MWES)
Fellow
Company Member

DESIGNATORY LETTERS
WES

ENGINEERING, MARINE
Membership of Professional Institutions and Associations

THE INSTITUTE OF MARINE ENGINEERING, SCIENCE AND TECHNOLOGY

1 Birdcage Walk
London SW1H 9JJ
Tel: +44 (0)20 7382 2600
E-mail: info@imarest.org
Website: www.imarest.org

The IMarEST, established in 1889, is the leading international membership body and learned society for marine professionals and has more than 15,000 members worldwide. We have a strong international presence, with a network of 50 international branches, affiliations with major marine societies around the world, representation on the key marine technical committees and non-governmental status at the International Maritime Organisation.

MEMBERSHIP
Affiliate
Student (SIMarEST)
Associate Member (AMIMarEST)
Member (MIMarEST
Fellow (FIMarEST)

DESIGNATORY LETTERS
SIMarEST, AMIMarEST, MIMarEST, FIMarEST

ENGINEERING, MECHANICAL
Membership of Professional Institutions and Associations

INSTITUTION OF MECHANICAL ENGINEERS

1 Birdcage Walk
Westminster
London SW1H 9JJ
Tel: 020 7222 7899
E-mail: enquiries@imeche.org
Website: www.imeche.org

The IMechE is a professional engineering body with about 80,000 members. Our aims are to promote sustainable energy and engineering sustainable supply, economic growth while mitigating and adapting to climate change and the depletion of natural resources, and safe, efficient transport systems to ensure less congestion and emissions, and to inspire, prepare and support tomorrow's engineers so we can respond to society's changes.

MEMBERSHIP
Affiliate

Associate Member (AMIMechE)
Member (MIMechE)
Fellow (FIMechE)
Engineering Technician (EngTech)
Incorporated Engineer (IEng)
Chartered Engineer (CEng)

DESIGNATORY LETTERS
AMIMechE, MIMechE, FIMechE, EngTech, IEng, CEng

ENGINEERING, MINING
Membership of Professional Institutions and Associations

INSTITUTE OF EXPLOSIVES ENGINEERS

Ground Floor, Unit 1
Greyfriars Business Park
Frank Foley Way
Stafford
Staffordshire ST16 2ST
Tel: 01785 594136
E-mail: vicki.hall@iexpe.org
Website: www.iexpe.org

The Institute of Explosives Engineers promotes the occupational competency, education and professional standing of those who work with explosives and provides consultative facilities for organisations and government departments within the explosives field.

MEMBERSHIP
Student
Associate (AIExpE)
Technical
Member (MIExpE)

Fellow (FIExpE)
Company
Company Affiliate
Retired

QUALIFICATION/EXAMINATIONS
CEng, IEng, Eng Tech

DESIGNATORY LETTERS
AIExpE, MIExpE, FIExpE

THE INSTITUTE OF MATERIALS, MINERALS AND MINING (IOM³)

297 Euston Road
London NW1 3AD
Tel: 020 7451 7300
E-mail: via website
Website: www.iom3.org

IOM³ is a major UK engineering institution whose activities encompass the whole materials cycle, from exploration and extraction, through characterization, processing, forming, finishing and application, to product recycling and land reuse. We promote and develop all aspects of materials science and engineering, geology, mining and associated technologies, mineral and petroleum engineering and extraction metallurgy, as a leading authority in the worldwide materials and mining community.

MEMBERSHIP
Student
Affiliate
Member (MIMMM)
Fellow (FIMMM)
Associate (AIMMM)
Technician (Eng Tech)

DESIGNATORY LETTERS
MIMMM, FIMMM, AIMMM, Eng Tech

THE INSTITUTE OF QUARRYING

McPherson House
8a Regan Way
Chetwynd Business Park
Chilwell
Nottingham NG9 6RZ
Tel: 0115 972 9995
E-mail: mail@quarrying.org
Website: www.quarrying.org

The Institute of Quarrying, which dates from 1917, is the international professional body for quarrying, construction materials and related extractive and processing industries, and has 6,000 members in some 50 countries. Our aim is to improve all aspects of operational performance through education and training at every level.

MEMBERSHIP
Student
Associate

Technical Member (TMIQ)
Member (MIQ)
Fellow (FIQ)

QUALIFICATION/EXAMINATIONS
Diploma in Quarry Technology
IQ Professional Examination
Introduction to Aggregates, Crushing and Screening

DESIGNATORY LETTERS
TMIQ, MIQ, FIQ

ENGINEERING, NUCLEAR
Membership of Professional Institutions and Associations

THE NUCLEAR INSTITUTE

18 King William Street
London EC4N 7BP
Tel: 020 7816 2600
E-mail: admin@nuclearinst.com
Website: www.nuclearinst.com

The NI (a Nominated Body of the UK Engineering and Science Councils) is the only professional membership body for the Nuclear Sector. We organise lectures, seminars and events at a regional and national level, have a vibrant young generation network and provide opportunities for career development and networking.

MEMBERSHIP
Student Member
Learned Member
Graduate Member
Technician Member (TNucI)
Associate Member (AMNucI)
Member (MNucI)
Fellow (FNucI)

New Structure from Jan 2016:
Affiliate (formerly Student)
Associate (formerly Learned and Graduate Members)
Member (MNucI)(incorporating Member, Associate Member and Technician Member)
Fellows (FNucI)
*Member and Fellow Grades require interview to assess competency and professional standards against The Nuclear Deltaxxx

QUALIFICATION/EXAMINATIONS
The Nuclear Deltaxxx

DESIGNATORY LETTERS
MNucI, FNucI

ENGINEERING, REFRACTORIES
Membership of Professional Institutions and Associations

INSTITUTE OF REFRACTORIES ENGINEERING

575 Trentham Road
Burton
Stoke on Trent
Staffs ST3 3BN
Tel: 01782 310 234
Fax: 01782 310 234
E-mail: secretary@ireng.org
Website: www.ireng.org

The IRE is a non-profit-making organisation dedicated to fostering the science, technology and skills of refractories engineering and to serving the needs of refractories engineers worldwide. Our members have a background in R&D, design, engineering, manufacturing and installation contracting in the iron & steel, cement, non-ferrous, glass, chemical/petrochemical incineration, power generation, ceramics/bricks and similar industries.

MEMBERSHIP
Student
Associate Member (AMI Ref Eng)
Member (MI Ref Eng)
Fellow (FI Ref Eng)

DESIGNATORY LETTERS
AMI Ref Eng, MI Ref Eng, FI Ref Eng

ENGINEERING, REFRIGERATION
Membership of Professional Institutions and Associations

THE INSTITUTE OF REFRIGERATION

Kelvin House
76 Mill Lane
Carshalton
Surrey SM5 2JR
Tel: 020 8647 7033
E-mail: ior@ior.org.uk
Website: www.ior.org.uk

The IOR is the professional body for the refrigeration, air conditioning and heat pump industries. It promotes the technical advancement and perfection of refrigeration, air conditioning and heat pumps, and the minimization of its effects on the environment, encourage the extension of refrigeration, air conditioning and heat pump services for the benefit of the community, and provides advice, CPD and support to interested individuals.

MEMBERSHIP
Technician
Associate
Member
Affiliate
Student
Student and Pre-Associate
Fellow

QUALIFICATION/EXAMINATIONS
REAL Zero CPD, REAL Skills Europe CPD, REAL Alternative
Engineering Council Registration

DESIGNATORY LETTERS
AMInstR, TMInstR, MInstR, FInstR

ENGINEERING, ROAD, RAIL AND TRANSPORT
Membership of Professional Institutions and Associations

INSTITUTE OF HIGHWAY ENGINEERS

Floor 32-34
286 Euston Road
London NW1 3DP
Tel: 020 3551 5681
E-mail: info@theihe.org
Website: www.theihe.org

The IHE is the main professional body for highway and traffic professionals. We are run by engineers for engineers and technicians, and work to keep the standards of the profession high, to safeguard the interests of our members, and to ensure that their contribution is recognised.

MEMBERSHIP
Student Member
Apprentice Member (AppIHE)
Affiliate Member
Associate Member (AMIHE)
Member (MIHE)
Fellow (FIHE)

QUALIFICATION/EXAMINATIONS
Prof Cert/Diploma in Traffic Signing and Road Markings
Prof Cert/Diploma in Traffic Signal Control
Prof Cert/Diploma in Highway Development Management
Prof Cert in Highway Maintenance

Prof Cert/Diploma for Winter Services Decision Makers and Managers
Prof Cert/Diploma in Road Safety Engineering
Prof Cert/Diploma in Transport Development Management

Prof Cert in Temporary Traffic Management
Prof Cert/Diploma in Asset Management

DESIGNATORY LETTERS
AMIHE, MIHE, FIHE, EngTech, IEng, CEng

INSTITUTION OF RAILWAY SIGNAL ENGINEERS

4th Floor
1 Birdcage Walk
Westminster
London SW1H 9JJ
Tel: 020 7808 1180
Fax: 020 7808 1196
E-mail: hq@irse.org
Website: www.irse.org

The Institution of Railway Signal Engineers, known more usually as the IRSE, is an international organisation, active throughout the world. It is the professional institution for all those engaged or interested in railway signalling and telecommunications and allied disciplines. Membership is open to anyone engaged or interested in the management, planning, design, installation, telecommunications or associated equipment.

MEMBERSHIP
Student

Associate
Accredited Technician
Associate Member
Member
Fellow
Companion

QUALIFICATION/EXAMINATIONS
Professional Examination

DESIGNATORY LETTERS
AMIRSE, MIRSE, FIRSE, CompIRSE

SOCIETY OF OPERATIONS ENGINEERS

22 Greencoat Place
London SW1P 1PR
Tel: 020 7630 1111
Fax: 020 7630 6677
E-mail: soe@soe.org.uk
Website: www.soe.org.uk

SOE is a professional membership organisation representing more than 16,000 individuals and companies in the engineering industry. It was formed in 2000 by the merger of the Institute of Road Transport Engineers (IRTE) and the Institution of Plant Engineers (IPlantE). The Society's third Professional Sector, the Bureau of Engineer Surveyors (BES), joined in 2004.

MEMBERSHIP
Associate Member (AMSOE)
Member (MSOE)
Fellow (FSOE)
Engineering Technician (EngTech)
Incorporated Engineer (IEng)
Chartered Engineer (CEng)

THE CHARTERED INSTITUTION OF HIGHWAYS AND TRANSPORTATION

119 Britannia Walk
London N1 7JE
Tel: 020 7336 1555
Fax: 020 7336 1556
E-mail: info@ciht.org.uk
Website: www.ciht.org.uk

The CIHT is a learned society and membership organisation concerned with the planning, design, construction, maintenance and operation of land-based transport systems and infrastructure. CIHT provides professional development and networking opportunities to members, with routes to qualifications, cutting-edge technical conferences and exciting social events.

MEMBERSHIP
Apprentice
Student
Graduate
Associate Member (AMCIHT)
Member (MCIHT)
Fellow (FCIHT)

QUALIFICATION/EXAMINATIONS
Transport Planning Professional (TPP) status (awarded jointly with the Transport Planning Society (TPS))

DESIGNATORY LETTERS
AMCIHT, MCIHT, FCIHT

ENGINEERING, SHEET METAL
Membership of Professional Institutions and Associations

INSTITUTE OF SHEET METAL ENGINEERING

102 Richmond Drive
Perton
Wolverhampton
West Midlands WV6 7UQ
Tel: 07891 499146
E-mail: ismesec@googlemail.com
Website: www.isme.org.uk

The ISME is a learned body with individual membership open to those employed in the sheet metal and associated industries and corporate membership open to relevant companies. Our aims are to promote the science of working and using sheet metal by providing opportunities for the exchange of ideas and information, and to encourage the professional development of our members.

MEMBERSHIP
Student Member
Member (MISME)
Fellow (FISME)
Corporate Member

DESIGNATORY LETTERS
MISME, FISME

ENGINEERING, STRUCTURAL
Membership of Professional Institutions and Associations

THE INSTITUTION OF STRUCTURAL ENGINEERS

47–58 Bastwick Street
London EC1V 3PS
Tel: 020 7235 4535
Fax: 020 7235 4294
E-mail: membership@istructe.org
Website: www.istructe.org

The Institution of Structural Engineers, founded in 1908, is the world's largest membership organisation dedicated to the art and science of structural engineering. Our aims include: maintaining professional standards for structural engineering; ensuring continued technical excellence; advancing safety, creativity and innovation; and promoting a sustainable approach to both the structural engineering profession and the built environment.

MEMBERSHIP
Student
Graduate
Technician (TIStructE)
Associate Member (AMIStructE)
Associate (AIStructE)
Chartered Member (MIStructE)
Fellow (FIStructE)

DESIGNATORY LETTERS
TIStructE, AMIStructE, AIStructE, MIStructE, FIStructE

ENGINEERING, WATER
Membership of Professional Institutions and Associations

INSTITUTE OF WATER

4 Carlton Court
Team Valley
Gateshead
Tyne and Wear NE11 0AZ
Tel: 0191 422 0088
Fax: 0191 422 0087
E-mail: info@instituteofwater.org.uk
Website: www.instituteofwater.org.uk

The IW is the only institute concerned with the UK water industry. Our aim is to promote high standards of integrity, conduct and ethics, and to provide our members with an opportunity for CPD and growth through sharing knowledge, experience and networking opportunities.

MEMBERSHIP
Student Member
Associate Member
Technician Member
Corporate Member
Company Affiliate

DESIGNATORY LETTERS
EngTech, IEng, CEng, CEnv

ENGINEERING DESIGN
Membership of Professional Institutions and Associations

THE INSTITUTION OF ENGINEERING DESIGNERS

Courtleigh
Westbury Leigh
Westbury
Wiltshire BA13 3TA
Tel: 01373 822801
Fax: 01373 858085
E-mail: via website
Website: https://www.institution-engineering-designers.org.uk/

Established in 1945, the IED represents 4,000 members worldwide working in engineering design, product design and CAD. Benefits include a bimonthly journal, access to an extensive library, legal advice helpline, local branch activities, and guidance and support to registration with the EC(UK) for suitably qualified members.

MEMBERSHIP
IED membership has two divisions: Engineering Design, and Product Design and Technology.

Each division has a range of membership grades: Student Member (StudIED), Graduate/Diplomate Member (GradIED/DipIED), Competent Draughting Associate (CDAIED), Associate (AIED), Member (MIED), Fellow (FIED), Affiliate

QUALIFICATION/EXAMINATIONS
Registration with EC(UK) for suitably qualified members

DESIGNATORY LETTERS
AIED, MIED, FIED

ENVIRONMENTAL SCIENCES
Membership of Professional Institutions and Associations

CHARTERED INSTITUTE OF ECOLOGY AND ENVIRONMENTAL MANAGEMENT

43 Southgate Street
Winchester
Hampshire SO23 9EH
Tel: 01962 868626
E-mail: enquiries@cieem.net
Website: https://www.cieem.net/

Founded in 1991 to advance the science, technology and practice of ecology, environmental management and sustainable development to further conservation and the enhancement of biodiversity through education, training, study and research. CIEEM now has more than 5,000 members drawn from local authorities, government agencies, industry, environmental consultancy, teaching/research and NGOs.

MEMBERSHIP
Student Member
Qualifying Member
Graduate Member (Grad CIEEM)
Associate Member (ACIEEM)
Full Member (MCIEEM)
Fellow (FCIEEM)

DESIGNATORY LETTERS
Grad CIEEM, ACIEEM, MCIEEM, FCIEEM

EXPORT

Membership of Professional Institutions and Associations

THE INSTITUTE OF EXPORT AND INTERNATIONAL TRADE

Export House
Minerva Business Park
Lynch Wood
Peterborough PE2 6FT
Tel: 01733 404400
E-mail: via website
Website: www.export.org.uk

Established since 1935 offering training and professional qualifications to those working within international trade. We are the only professional institute in the UK offering qualifications ranging from the new 14–19 Diploma up to a level 5 Diploma as well as standard and bespoke training courses for individuals and companies.

MEMBERSHIP
Affiliate
Student
Associate
Member MIEx (Grad)
Member MIEx
Fellow
Business

QUALIFICATION/EXAMINATIONS
Young International Trader (Level 1)
International Trade and Logistics Operations (Level 2)
Certificate in International Trade (Level 3)
Diploma in International Trade (Level 4)
Diploma in International Trade (Level 5)
Diploma in World Customers Compliance & regulations (Level 5)
Foundation Degree in International Trade (Level 5)
BSc(Hons) Management Practice – International Trade (Level 6)
MSc in International Trade, Startegy and Operations (Level 7)

FISHERIES MANAGEMENT

Membership of Professional Institutions and Associations

INSTITUTE OF FISHERIES MANAGEMENT

PO Box 679
Hull
East Yorkshire HU5 9AX
Tel: 0845 388 7012
E-mail: info@ifm.org.uk
Website: www.ifm.org.uk

The Institute of Fisheries Management is an international organisation of persons sharing a common interest in the modern and sustainable management of recreational and commercial fisheries. It is a non-profit-making body and is a constituent body of the Society for the Environment.

MEMBERSHIP
Subscriber
Student Member
Associate Member (AMIFM)
Affiliate Member (AMIFM)
Registered Member (MIFM)
Fellow (FIFM)
Honorary Fellow (Hon FIFM)

Corporate Member
Honorary Member (Hon MIFM)

Award
Short courses in a range of specialist subjects.

QUALIFICATION/EXAMINATIONS
Certificate
Diploma

DESIGNATORY LETTERS
AMIFM, MIFM, FIFM, Hon FIFM, Hon MIFM

FLORISTRY
Membership of Professional Institutions and Associations

BRITISH FLORIST ASSOCIATION

PO Box 365
Worksop S80 9EF
E-mail: via website
Website: https://www.bfaflorist.org/default.aspx

The Institute of Professional Florists was founded in 2015 as part of the British Florist Association to uphold the professional status of Florists in the UK and to ensure we maintain consistent high standards within the Industry. Working in close partnership with Colleges, Training Providers and Awarding Bodies, to enable us to uphold this commitment and we also ensure that our members continue their professional development throughout their career.

We provide help, advice and information to our more than 1,000 members, who include business owners, florists, training providers, and students.

MEMBERSHIP
Student
Member
Senior Member
Academic Member
Licentiate
Fellow
Academic Member
Academic Fellow

FOOD SCIENCE AND NUTRITION
Membership of Professional Institutions and Associations

INSTITUTE OF FOOD SCIENCE AND TECHNOLOGY

5 Cambridge Court
210 Shepherds Bush Road
London W6 7NJ
Tel: 020 7603 6316
E-mail: info@ifst.org
Website: www.ifst.org

IFST is the leading independent qualifying body for food professionals in Europe and the only professional body in the UK concerned with all aspects of food science and technology. As a registered charity we are independent of government, industry, lobby or special interest groups.

MEMBERSHIP
Associate
Member (MIFST)
Fellow (FIFST)

DESIGNATORY LETTERS
MIFST, FIFST, CSci, RSci, RSciTech

FORESTRY AND ARBORICULTURE
Membership of Professional Institutions and Associations

INSTITUTE OF CHARTERED FORESTERS

59 George Street
Edinburgh EH2 2JG
Tel: 0131 240 1425
Fax: 0131 240 1424
E-mail: icf@charteredforesters.org
Website: www.charteredforesters.org

The Intstitute of Chartered Foresters is the Royal Chartered body for foresters and arboriculturists in the UK. We have over 1,800 members, to whom we offer advice, guidance and support. We also strive to foster a greater public understanding and awareness of the profession, as the environment and its management become more relevant to everyone.

MEMBERSHIP
Student Member

Supporter
Associate Member
Professional Member (MICFor)
Fellow (FICFor)

QUALIFICATION/EXAMINATIONS
Professional Membership

DESIGNATORY LETTERS
MICFor & FICFor

THE ARBORICULTURAL ASSOCIATION

The Malthouse
Stroud Green
Standish
Stonehouse
Gloucestershire GL10 3DL
Tel: 01242 522152
Fax: 01242 577766
E-mail: admin@trees.org.uk
Website: www.trees.org.uk

The Arboricultural Association, founded in 1964, is the leading body in the UK for the amenity tree care professional in either civic or commercial employment at craft, technical, supervisory, managerial or consultancy level. There are currently over 2,000 members of The Arboricultural Association in a variety of membership classes.

MEMBERSHIP
Student Member
Ordinary Member
Associate Member

Technician Member
Professional Member
Fellow
Professional Retired
Fellow Retired
Corporate Member

QUALIFICATION/EXAMINATIONS
Arboricultural Association Approved Contractor
Arboricultural Association Registered Consultant

DESIGNATORY LETTERS
TechArborA, MArborA, FArborA

THE ROYAL FORESTRY SOCIETY

The Hay Barns
Home Farm Drive
Upton Estate
Banbury OX15 6HU
Tel: 01295 678588
Fax: 01295 670798
E-mail: rfshq@rfs.org.uk
Website: www.rfs.org.uk

The RFS was founded in 1882 and now has over 3,600 members. We are an educational charity dedicated to promoting the wise management of trees and woodlands, and to increasing understanding of forestry. We publish a popular journal, the *Quarterly Journal of Forestry,* arrange outdoor meetings, organise woodland study tours in the UK and overseas, run courses in forestry and arboriculture, and manage model woodlands.

MEMBERSHIP
Individual Member
Corporate Member
Student Member

QUALIFICATION/EXAMINATIONS
RFS Certificate in Arboriculture (Level 2) – Individual award

Royal Forestry Society Certification Scheme:
Level 2 or higher theory award in either forestry or an alligned discipline + a suite of 8 practical NPTC/Lantra modules.
Allows the recipient to use the Post nominal – RFS Cert Arb. or RFS Cert For.

DESIGNATORY LETTERS
RFS Cert Arb, RFS Cert For

FOUNDRY TECHNOLOGY AND PATTERN MAKING
Membership of Professional Institutions and Associations

THE INSTITUTE OF CAST METALS ENGINEERS

National Foundry Training Centre
ECMS
Tipton Road
Tipton
West Midlands DY4 7UW
Tel: 0121 752 1810
E-mail: info@icme.org.uk
Website: www.icme.org.uk

ICME is the Institute of Cast Metals Engineers, the Institute for all individuals involved in the castings industry and associated industries.
Our members include foundrymen, design engineers, metallurgists, moulders, patternmakers, CAD technicians, methods engineers, researchers, students and suppliers to the industry. The aim of the institute is to bring together people from all sectors and levels, to offer help and advice, technical support and professional development opportunities, helping our members make the most of their careers in the castings industry.

MEMBERSHIP
Student
Member (MICME)
Professional Member (Prof MICME)
Fellow (FICME)
Retired Member

DESIGNATORY LETTERS
MICME, Prof MICME, FICME, EngTech, IEng, CEng, EurIng

FREIGHT FORWARDING
Membership of Professional Institutions and Associations

BRITISH INTERNATIONAL FREIGHT ASSOCIATION (BIFA)

Redfern House
Browells Lane
Feltham
Middlesex TW13 7EP
Tel: 020 8844 2266
E-mail: bifa@bifa.org
Website: www.bifa.org

BIFA is the principal trade association providing representation, training and support to British companies engaged in the international movement of freight to and from the UK by air, rail, road and sea. It is a not-for-profit organisation. Members are encouraged to contribute to the running of the Association.

MEMBERSHIP
Associate Member
Trade Member

FUNDRAISING
Membership of Professional Institutions and Associations

THE INSTITUTE OF FUNDRAISING

Institute of Fundraising
Charter House
13 – 15 Carteret Street
London SW1H 9DJ
Tel: 020 7840 1000
E-mail: info@institute-of-fundraising.org.uk
Website: www.institute-of-fundraising.org.uk

The Institute of Fundraising is the professional body for fundraisers in the UK, representing over 6,000 individual fundraisers and 600 organisations. We provide professional support, act as a voice for fundraisers and promote best practice. We offer professional qualifications and training, and the annual three-day IoF Fundraising Convention is the largest fundraising conference of its type in Europe.

MEMBERSHIP
Associate
Full Member (MInstF)
Fully Certificated Member MInstF(Cert)
Diploma Qualified Member MInstF(Dip)
Advanced Diploma Qualified Member MInstF(AdvDip)
Organisational Member

QUALIFICATION/EXAMINATIONS
Certificate in Fundraising
Diploma in Fundraising
Advanced Diploma in Fundraising

DESIGNATORY LETTERS
MInstF, MInstF(Cert), MInstF(Dip), MinstF(AdvDip), FInstF, FInstF(Cert), FInstF(Dip), FInstF(AdvDip)

FUNERAL DIRECTING, BURIAL AND CREMATION ADMINISTRATION

Membership of Professional Institutions and Associations

NATIONAL ASSOCIATION OF FUNERAL DIRECTORS

618 Warwick Road
Solihull
West Midlands B91 1AA
Tel: 0845 230 1343
Fax: 0121 711 1351
E-mail: info@nafd.org.uk
Website: www.nafd.org.uk

The NAFD, founded in 1905, is an independent trade association whose members include more than 3,200 funeral homes throughout the UK, suppliers to the profession, and overseas funeral directing businesses. We provide support to our members and offer informed opinion to government.

MEMBERSHIP
Funeral Director (Category A) Member
Supplier (Category B) Member
Overseas Member

QUALIFICATION/EXAMINATIONS
Diploma in Funeral Arranging and Administration (Dip.FAA)
Diploma in Funeral Directing (Dip.FD)

NATIONAL ASSOCIATION OF MEMORIAL MASONS

1 Castle Mews
Rugby
Warwickshire CV21 2AL
Tel: 01788 542264
Fax: 01788 542276
E-mail: enquiries@namm.org.uk
Website: www.namm.org.uk

The NAMM was formed in 1907 to promote excellence and craftsmanship within the memorial masonry trade. Our services to members include training, business advice, technical advice, promotion, a legal helpline, a conciliation and arbitration service, trade exhibitions and a conference. We protect members' interests through representation to the British Standards Institution (BSI) and the Burial & Cemeteries Advisory Group (BCAG).

MEMBERSHIP
Individual Associate Member
Affiliate Member
Full Retail and Wholesale Members
Company Associate Member
Corporate Associate Member
Overseas Member
Overseas Affiliate Member

QUALIFICATION/EXAMINATIONS
NAMM – Memorial Masonry – Certificate of Competence for fixing of lawn type memorials – NPTC City & Guilds
NAMM – Memorial Inspection – Safety Inspection and Assessment of Memorials (SIAM) – NPTC City & Guilds

THE INSTITUTE OF BURIAL AND CREMATION AUTHORITIES

ICCM National Office & Training Centre
City of London Cemetery
Aldersbrook Road
Manor Park
London E12 5DQ
Tel: 020 8989 4661
Fax: 020 8989 6112
E-mail: iccmjulie@gmail.com
Website: www.iccm-uk.com

Accredited education and training opportunities for those working in cemeteries and cremators.

Best practice guidance and policy for burial and cremation authorities.

MEMBERSHIP
Member (MICCM)
Associate Member (AICCM)
Fellow (FICCM)
Corporate
Associate Corporate

QUALIFICATION/EXAMINATIONS
Diploma – Fully Accredited NHC in Cemetery & Crematorium Management and the Management of Natural Burial Grounds
Cemetery Operatives Training Scheme – A comprehensive suite of City & Guilds accredited qualifications
Crematorium Technicians Training Scheme – BTEC accredited qualifications for crematory staff

DESIGNATORY LETTERS
MICCM, AICCM, FICCM

FURNISHING AND FURNITURE
Membership of Professional Institutions and Associations

FLOORING INDUSTRY TRAINING ASSOCIATION

Unit 23 Eldon Business Park
Eldon Road
Chilwell
Nottingham NG96DZ
Tel: 0115 9506836
Fax: 0115 941 2238
E-mail: info@fita.co.uk
Website: www.fita.co.uk

FITA was set up and is fully supported by the CFA and the NICF to provide training for the floor-covering industry. We have two fully equipped training centres in Loughborough and Kirkaldy, where the majority of our courses run. We also offer tailor-made courses to suit individual specifications and requirements.

QUALIFICATION/EXAMINATIONS
Co-founded by the Contract Flooring Association (CFA) and the National Institute of Carpet and

Floorlayers (NICF) to proved specialist training for the floorcovering industry. FITA is an independent, not-for-profit organisation – by industry, for industry. We have two specialist training centres at Loughborough and Kirkcaldy with fully equipped practical and lecture areas.

DEDICATED TO TRAINING THE 'FITA WAY'
On every training course, you'll always hear our instructors talk about the 'FITA Way'. Simply put, it's

our philosophy. Following British Standards and current industry best practices, utilising the latest products, tools and techniques, we believe our method of teaching gives you the best opportunity to learn new skills, develop existing ones, improve confidence, gain a competitive edge and invest in the future.

Whether you're just starting out or need additional training to go one step further, our courses (aimed at both domestic and commercial markets) are taught by season professionals with specialist knowledge of the flooring industry.

FITA instructors have all passed assessments and knowledge exams and are supported on courses by technicians with specialist knowledge from the trade. FITA also enjoys the support of a considerable number of suppliers who freely donate materials, accessories and tools.

Fully trained staff are an asset to any company. The outlay for training courses far outweighs the initial cost.

Please be sure to book early to reserve your place on a course. Go to our Course Dates page for details of our latest courses and the training centres where they are being held.

Training courses
Carpet Fitting
Domestic Sheet Vinyl Fitting
Subfloor Preparation
Commercial Vinyl Fitting
Cost Effective Estimating and Planning
Linoleum Installation
Laminate and Wood Fitting
Moisture – Preventing floor failures
Resilient / Luxury Vinyl Tile Fitting
Wood Fitting
Wood Sanding and Finishing

NATIONAL INSTITUTE OF CARPET AND FLOORLAYERS

Unit 23, Eldon Business Park
Eldon Road
Chilwell
Nottingham NG9 6DZ
Tel: 0115 9583077
Fax: 0115 9412238
E-mail: info@nicfltd.org.uk
Website: www.nicfltd.org.uk

The NICF furthers the interests of its members by promoting excellence in the field of carpet and floorlaying and providing a range of benefits, products and services.

MEMBERSHIP
Master Fitter Member
Fitter Member

Trainee Fitter Member
Retailer Member
Associate Member
Patron Member

QUALIFICATION/EXAMINATIONS
Fitter qualification assessment
Master Fitter qualification assessment

GEMMOLOGY AND JEWELLERY
Membership of Professional Institutions and Associations

GEM-A

21 Ely Place
London EC1N 6TD
Tel: 020 7404 3334
Fax: 020 7404 8843
E-mail: information@gem-a.com
Website: www.gem-a.com

Gem-A, The Gemmological Association of Great Britain, is the world's longest established provider of gem and jewellery education. Our prestigious Gemmology and Diamond Diplomas are globally recognised as qualifications of the highest status. In addition to our educational programmes we also provide membership, including the world-famous FGA and DGA Memberships.

MEMBERSHIP
Associate
Fellow (FGA)

Diamond Member (DGA)
Corporate Member
Gold Corporate Member

QUALIFICATION/EXAMINATIONS
Foundation Certificate in Gemmology
Diploma in Gemmology
Diamond Diploma

DESIGNATORY LETTERS
FGA, DGA

THE NATIONAL ASSOCIATION OF JEWELLERS

Federation House
10 Vyse Street
Birmingham B18 6LT
Tel: 0121 237 1110
E-mail: info@naj.co.uk
Website: www.naj.co.uk

The NAJ serves and supports the jewellery industry of Great Britain and Ireland. We promote high professional standards among our members, who must adhere to a code of professional practice. In return, we offer them advice, support and learning and development in the form of distance learning courses and short courses.

MEMBERSHIP
Alumni Member

Allied Member
Affiliate Member
Ordinary Member

QUALIFICATION/EXAMINATIONS
JET Certirficate
JET Diploma
JET Management
JET Business Development
CAT

GENEALOGY
Membership of Professional Institutions and Associations

SOCIETY OF GENEALOGISTS

14 Charterhouse Buildings
Goswell Road
London EC1M 7BA
Tel: 020 7251 8799
Fax: 020 7250 1800
E-mail: info@sog.org.uk
Website: www.sog.org.uk

The Society (founded 1911) is the National Family History Centre. A registered educational charity, it was founded to encourage and foster the study, science and knowledge of genealogy. This it does chiefly through its library, publications and extensive education programme of courses and events. It currently does not hold exams.

MEMBERSHIP
Associate
Member
Fellow (FSG)
Honorary Fellow (FSG Hon)

DESIGNATORY LETTERS
FSG, FSG Hon

THE HERALDRY SOCIETY

53 Hitchin Street
Baldock
Herts SG7 6AQ
Tel: 01462 892062
E-mail: membership@theheraldrysociety.com
Website: www.theheraldrysociety.com

The Heraldry Society is a registered charity that aims to encourage interest in heraldry through publications, lectures, visits and related activities. Members receive *The Heraldry Gazette*, which contains heraldic news and comments, and Society information quarterly and also the Coat of Arms, our scholarly journal. We maintain contact with heraldic societies in many parts of the UK and abroad.

MEMBERSHIP
Associate Member
Ordinary Member

Fellow (FHS)
Honorary Fellow (Hon FHS)

QUALIFICATION/EXAMINATIONS
Elementary Certificate
Intermediate Certificate
Advanced Certificate
Diploma (DipHS)

DESIGNATORY LETTERS
FHS, Hon FHS

THE INSTITUTE OF HERALDIC AND GENEALOGICAL STUDIES

79–82 Northgate
Canterbury
Kent CT1 1BA
Tel: 01227 768664
Fax: 01227 765617
E-mail: registrar@ihgs.ac.uk
Website: www.ihgs.ac.uk

The IHGS, founded in 1961, is an independent educational charitable trust that offers a wide range of courses on family history, heraldry and related historical subjects, and has an extensive library, archive and research facilities. We also offer a genealogical and heraldic research service.

MEMBERSHIP
Fellow
Associate Member
Graduate Member

QUALIFICATION/EXAMINATIONS
Correspondence Course in Genealogy
Correspondence Course in Heraldry
Online Course in Genealogy

Higher Certificate in Genealogy
Diploma in Genealogy
Licentiateship in Heraldry and Genealogy
Online Course in Heraldry
Elementary online course in Genealogy
Intermediate online course in Genealogy
Advanced online course in Genealogy
Elementary Certificate in Genealogy
Intermediate Certificate in Genealogy
Advanced Certificate in Genealogy
Elementary Certificate in Heraldry
Intermediate Certificate in Heraldry

DESIGNATORY LETTERS
Dip Gen, LHG, FHG

GEOGRAPHY
Membership of Professional Institutions and Associations

ROYAL GEOGRAPHICAL SOCIETY (WITH THE INSTITUTE OF BRITISH GEOGRAPHERS)

1 Kensington Gore
London SW7 2AR
Tel: 020 7591 3000
Fax: 020 7591 3001
E-mail: via website, or enquiries@rgs.org
Website: www.rgs.org

The RGS-IBG is the learned society and professional body for geography. We aim to foster an understanding and informed enjoyment of our world: developing, supporting and promoting geographical research, expeditions and fieldwork, education, public engagement, and providing geography input to policy.

MEMBERSHIP
Young Geographer

Member
Postgraduate Fellow
Fellow
Chartered Geographer (CGeog)
Corporate Member

DESIGNATORY LETTERS
FRGS, CGeog

GEOLOGY
Membership of Professional Institutions and Associations

THE GEOLOGICAL SOCIETY

Burlington House
Piccadilly
London W1J 0BG
Tel: 020 7434 9944
Fax: 020 7439 8975
E-mail: via website
Website: www.geolsoc.org.uk

The Geological Society, founded in 1807, is the UK's national organisation for professional Earth scientists. The normal grade of membership is Fellow. Students may become Candidate Fellows. Members of the public not eligible for any other status may join as Friends.

MEMBERSHIP
Junior

Candidate Fellow
Fellow
Chartered Geologist
European Geologist
Chartered Scientist

DESIGNATORY LETTERS
FGS, CGeol

GLASS TECHNOLOGY
Membership of Professional Institutions and Associations

BRITISH SOCIETY OF SCIENTIFIC GLASSBLOWERS

Glassblowing Department
S.U.E.R.C
Scottish Enterprise Technology Park Rankine Avenue
East Kilbride
Lanarkshire G75 0QF
Tel: 01355 270150
Fax: 01355 229898
E-mail: Robert.McLeod@glasgow.ac.uk
Website: www.bssg.co.uk

The Society was founded in 1960 for the benefit of those engaged in Scientific Glassblowing and its associated professions, and to uphold and further the status of Scientific Glassblowers. We welcome written submissions to our quarterly journal, which is circulated to members.

MEMBERSHIP
Associate
Student Member
Fellow
Full Member

Master
Honorary Member
Retired Member
Overseas Member

QUALIFICATION/EXAMINATIONS
Introduction to Elementary Scientific Glassblowing.
Hand Burner Glassworking.
Scientific Glassblowing Stage One and Two
Lathe Glassworking Stage One and Advanced.
Standard of Competance.

DESIGNATORY LETTERS
Master MBSSG, Fellow FBSSG

SOCIETY OF GLASS TECHNOLOGY

9 Churchill Way
Chapeltown
Sheffield
South Yorkshire S35 2PY
Tel: 0114 2634455
E-mail: info@sgt.org
Website: www.sgt.org

The objects of the Society of Glass Technology are to encourage and advance the study of the history, art, science, design, manufacture, after treatment, distribution and end use of glass of any and every kind.

MEMBERSHIP
Personal Member
Fellow (FSGT)
Fellow Emeritus
Honorary Fellow (HonFSGT)
Centenary Honorary Fellow (CentHonFSGT) only three and only in 2016, our centenary year.

Corporate Member

QUALIFICATION/EXAMINATIONS
Peer review by the Board of Fellows.
2016 was the SGT centenary and three Centenary Honorary Fellows were created. These are in addition to the limit of 12 for Honorary Fellows. Decided by the Board of Fellows as normal.

DESIGNATORY LETTERS
FSGT, HonFSGT

HAIRDRESSING
Membership of Professional Institutions and Associations

HABIA

First Floor
Styrupp Gold and Country Club
Main Streer
Styrupp DN11 8NB
Tel: 0845 2 306080
E-mail: info@habia.org
Website: www.habia.org

Habia is the government-appointed standards-setting body for hair, beauty, nails, spa therapy, barbering and African-type hair, and creates the standards that form the basis of all qualifications, including NVQs, SVQs, apprenticeships, diplomas and foundation degrees, as well as industry codes of practice.

MEMBERSHIP
Habia offers a membership programme for training providers (Habia Members) and a wider, free membership for industry professionals and educators.

THE GUILD OF HAIRDRESSERS

Archway House
Barnsley S71 1AQ
Tel: 01226 786555
Fax: 01226 208300

The Guild of Hairdressers dates back to 1340, when it was part of the Guild of Barbers and Surgeons. Then in the late 16th century, when the surgeons split off, it became the Guild of Hairdressers, Wigmakers and Perfumers. Today it still exists for the benefit of its members, who adhere to a code of ethics and to whom it provides help and advice.

HEALTH AND HEALTH SERVICES
Membership of Professional Institutions and Associations

BRITISH OCCUPATIONAL HYGIENE SOCIETY (BOHS)

5/6 Melbourne Business Court
Millennium Way
Pride Park
Derby DE24 8LZ
Tel: 01332 298101
E-mail: admin@bohs.org
Website: www.bohs.org

BOHS is the Chartered Society for Worker Health Protection – one of the largest occupational hygiene societies in Europe and the only professional society representing qualified occupational hygienists in the UK. BOHS provides internationally recognised qualifications, scientific conferences and membership services, and has 1,400+ members in 56 countries.

MEMBERSHIP
Individual
Student
Affiliate (Corporate)
Retired

Faculty of Occupational Hygiene:
Associate (AFOH)
Licentiate (LFOH)
Chartered Member (CMFOH)
Specialist Member (MFOH(S))
Chartered Fellow (CFFOH)

Faculty of Asbestos Assessment and Management:
Technician (TFAAM)
Associate (AFAAM)

Licentiate (LFAAM)
Member (MFAAM)

QUALIFICATION/EXAMINATIONS
Since 1953, BOHS has been the only organisation dedicated to occupational hygiene, and to be awarded a Royal Charter – in recognition of its unique and pre-eminent role as the leading authority in occupational disease prevention. This also means that BOHS is the only occupational hygiene organisation to offer the opportunity to achieve 'Chartered Occupational Hygienist' status, via its professional development route: the BOHS Faculty of Occupational Hygiene sets, develops and maintains the professional standards of occupational hygienists. It is also an internationally recognised, and the only UK-based, examining board for qualifications in occupational hygiene. BOHS qualifications are widely regarded as the industry standard, and are recognised by HSE, UKAS and IOHA, and by national and international institutions, organisations and employers.

DESIGNATORY LETTERS
AFOH, LFOH, CMFOH, CFFOH, TFAAM, AFAAM, LFAAM, MFAAM

CHARTERED INSTITUTE OF ENVIRONMENTAL HEALTH

Chadwick Court
15 Hatfields
London SE1 8DJ
Tel: 020 7827 5800
Fax: 020 7806 0666
E-mail: via website
Website: www.cieh.org

The CIEH is an Awarding Organisation providing Ofqual regulated qualifications in Food Safety, Health & Safety, First Aid, Environmental Protection and Fire Safety.

MEMBERSHIP
Affiliate
Associate
Member
Fellow

QUALIFICATION/EXAMINATIONS
The CIEH offers a range of Ofqual-regulated qualifications at four levels in health and safety, food safety, environmental protection, fire safety and education and training.

CHARTERED INSTITUTE OF ERGONOMICS & HUMAN FACTORS

Edmund House
12-22 Newhall St
Birmingham B3 3AS
Tel: 07736 893350
E-mail: ciehf@ergonomics.org.uk
Website: www.ergonomics.org.uk

The Chartered Institute of Ergonomics & Human Factors, founded in 1949, is a UK-based professional society for ergonomists worldwide. We encourage and maintain high standards of professional practice through education, accreditation and development, promote the interests of our members across government, academia, business and industry, and raise awareness of ergonomics in general.

MEMBERSHIP
Student Member
Associate Member
Graduate Member
Registered Member
Fellow
Technical Member
Retired Member
Corporate Member

QUALIFICATION/EXAMINATIONS
Chartered Ergonomist & Human Factors Specialist

DESIGNATORY LETTERS
C.ErgHF

INSTITUTE OF HEALTH PROMOTION AND EDUCATION

PO Box 7409,
LICHFIELD WS14 4LS
Tel: c/o 01438 840040
E-mail: admin@ihpe.org.uk
Website: www.ihpe.org.uk

The IHPE was established 50 years ago to bring together professionals with a common interest in health education and promotion to share their experience, ideas and information. Our members come from a diverse range of backgrounds, including nursing, midwifery, health visiting, medicine, dentistry, public health, stress management, psychology and teaching.

MEMBERSHIP
Student Member

Associate Member (AIHPE)
Full Member (MIHPE)
Fellow (FIHPE)
Corporate Member

DESIGNATORY LETTERS
MIHPE, AIHPE, FIHPE

INSTITUTE OF HEALTH RECORDS AND INFORMATION MANAGEMENT

Marshall House
Heanor Gate Road
Heanor
Derbyshire DE75 7RG
Tel: 01773 713927
Fax: 01773 713927
E-mail: office@ihrim.co.uk, or email via website
Website: www.ihrim.co.uk

IHRIM was founded in 1948, primarily as an educational body, to provide qualifications as well as career and professional assistance to members. We encourage professionalism and high standards among our members who work in the fields of health records, information management, clinical coding and information governance.

MEMBERSHIP
Student
Affiliate
Licentiate
Certificated Member (CHRIM)
Accredited Clinical Coder (ACC)

Associate (AHRIM)
Fellow (FHRIM)
Corporate Affiliate

QUALIFICATION/EXAMINATIONS
Certificate of Technical Competence
Foundation exam
Certificate exam
Diploma exam
National Clinical Coding Qualification

DESIGNATORY LETTERS
CHRIM, ACC, AHRIM, FHRIM

INSTITUTE OF HEALTHCARE ENGINEERING AND ESTATE MANAGEMENT

2 Abingdon House
Cumberland Business Centre
Northumberland Road
Portsmouth PO5 1DS
Tel: 023 92 823186
Fax: 023 92 815927
E-mail: office@iheem.org.uk
Website: www.iheem.org.uk

The Institute of Healthcare Engineering and Estate Management (IHEEM) is a Professional Engineering Institute, a specialist institute for the Healthcare Estates Sector.

The Institute counts among its members employees of both public and private healthcare providers, as well as those employed in private sector engineering and consultancy firms and practices.

MEMBERSHIP
Graduate (GIHEEM)
Craftsperson (CPIHEEM)

Associate Member (AMIHEEM)
Technician (TIHEEM)
Member (MIHEEM)
Fellow (FIHEEM)

DESIGNATORY LETTERS
GIHEEM, CPIHEEM, AMIHEEM, TIHEEM,
MIHEEM, FIIIEEM

INSTITUTE OF HEALTHCARE MANAGEMENT

33 Cavendish Square
London W1G 0PW
Tel: 0207 182 4066
E-mail: contact@ihm.org.uk
Website: www.ihm.org.uk

The IHM is the professional organisation for managers throughout healthcare, including the NHS, independent providers, healthcare consultants and the armed forces. Our focus is on improving patient/user care by publishing standards of management practice, promoting the IHM Code (which covers behavioural and ethical aspects of management practice) and establishing a CPD framework for our members.

MEMBERSHIP
Student Member
Associate Member

Full Member (MIHM)

QUALIFICATION/EXAMINATIONS
Certificate in Health Management Studies (CertHMS)
Certificate in Health Services Management (CertHSM)
Certificate in Managing Health Services (CertMHS)
Certificate in Managing Health & Social Care (CertMHSC)
Diploma in Health Services Management (DipHSM)

DESIGNATORY LETTERS
MIHM, FIHM, CIHM

ROYAL SOCIETY FOR PUBLIC HEALTH (RSPH)

John Snow House
59 Mansell Street
London E1 8AN
Tel: 020 7265 7300
Fax: 020 7265 7301
E-mail: info@rsph.org.uk
Website: www.rsph.org.uk

RSPH is an independent health education charity, dedicated to protecting and promoting the public's health and wellbeing. As an awarding body, it offers a wide range of Ofqual-recognised vocational qualifications in the fields of food safety and nutrition, hygiene, health and safety, pest control, health promotion and the built environment.

MEMBERSHIP
Student

Associate (AMRSPH)
Member (MRSPH)
Fellow (FRSPH)

QUALIFICATION/EXAMINATIONS
Visit www.rsph.org.uk/qualifications for more information.

DESIGNATORY LETTERS
AMRSPH, MRSPH, FRSPH

HORSES AND HORSE RIDING

Membership of Professional Institutions and Associations

EQUESTRIAN QUALIFICATIONS GB LTD

Equestrian House
Abbey Park
Stareton Lane
Kenilworth
Warwickshire CV8 2XZ
Tel: 02476 840544
E-mail: enquiries@eql.org.uk
Website: www.equestrian-qualifications.org.uk

EQL offers vocational and work-based qualifications for the Equestrian Industry. We work in partnership with a variety of organisations to develop and award qualifications for grooms, stable managers, riding and coaches. Our qualifications include British Horse Society qualifications, Work Based Diplomas, Scottish Vocational Qualifications and Equestrian Tourism qualifications.

QUALIFICATION/EXAMINATIONS
Our Awards include:
Horse Knowledge and Care – Level 1 to Level 4

Riding Exams – Level 1 to Level 4
Coaching and Teaching – Level 3 to Level 5
Work Based Diplomas (WBD)
Scottish Vocational Qualifications (SVQ)

The BHS also offers higher level qualifications for BHS Instructor and Fellowship of the BHS, as well as those for the recreational horse owner.

EQL website: www.equestrian-qualifications.org.uk
BHS website: www.bhs.org.uk

HOUSING

Membership of Professional Institutions and Associations

THE CHARTERED INSTITUTE OF HOUSING

Octavia House
Westwood Way
Coventry CV4 8JP
Tel: 024 7685 1700
E-mail: membership.services@cih.org
Website: www.cih.org

The CIH is the professional body for people involved in housing and communities. We are a registered charity and not-for-profit organisation. We have a diverse and growing membership of over 22,000 people – both in the public and private sectors – living and working in over 20 countries on five continents across the world.

MEMBERSHIP
Offering two grades of membership we look to support members at all stages of their career:

CIH Member
CIH Chartered Member
Visit www.cih.org/membership to find out more about CIH membership.

QUALIFICATION/EXAMINATIONS
Certificate Courses
The CIH offers a range of certificated courses at Levels 2, 3, 4 and 5+ delivered at various centres across the UK. They are also available by online learning.

Professional Qualifications

The CIH Professional Qualification can be achieved at either undergraduate or postgraduate level, FT or PT.

Please see the CIH's website for details.

DESIGNATORY LETTERS

CIH Members: CIH Member or CIHM, CIH Chartered Members: CIH Chartered Member or CIHCM (existing Fellows can continue to use FCIH and Honorary Members can use (Hon).

INDEXING
Membership of Professional Institutions and Associations

SOCIETY OF INDEXERS

Woodbourn Business Centre
10 Jessell Street
Sheffield S9 3HY
Tel: 01142 449561
E-mail: admin@indexers.org.uk
Website: www.indexers.org.uk

The Society of Indexers is the professional body for indexing in the UK and Ireland, and exists to promote indexing, the quality of indexes and the profession of indexing. We offer information to publishers and other organisations on commissioning indexes and our online directory 'Indexers Available' provides an up-to-date guide to indexers currently working in a wide range of fields.

MEMBERSHIP
Student Member

Member
Professional Member (MSocInd)
Advanced Professional Member (MSocInd(Adv))
Fellow (FSocInd)

QUALIFICATION/EXAMINATIONS
Indexing course
Advanced Test

DESIGNATORY LETTERS
MSocInd, MSocInd(Adv), FSocInd

INDUSTRIAL SAFETY
Membership of Professional Institutions and Associations

BRITISH SAFETY COUNCIL

70 Chancellors Road
Hammersmith
London W6 9RS
Tel: +44 (0)20 3510 8355
E-mail: info@britsafe.org
Website: www.britsafe.org

The British Safety Council is one of the world's leading health and safety organisations. Our mission is to keep people healthy and safe at work. Our range of charitable initiatives is supported by a broad mix of commercial activities centred on membership, training, auditing and qualifications.

MEMBERSHIP
UK Core Member
UK Full Member
International Member

QUALIFICATION/EXAMINATIONS
Entry Level Award in Workplace Hazard Awareness

Level 1 Award in Health and Safety in the Workplace

Level 1 Award in Health and Safety in a Construction Environment

Level 1 Award in Environmental Sustainability

Level 2 Award in Health and Safety in the Workplace

Level 2 Award in Health and Safety in Health and Social Care

Level 2 Award in Principles of Risk Assessment

Level 2 Award in Principles of COSHH

Level 2 Award in Principles of Fire Safety

Level 2 Award in Principles of Manual Handling

Level 2 Award in Contact Dermatitis Prevention

Level 2 Award in Risk Assessment

Level 2 Award in COSHH Risk Assessment

Level 2 Award in DSE Risk Assessment

Level 2 Award in Fire Risk Assessment

Level 2 Award in Manual Handling Risk Assessment

Level 2 Award in Supervising Staff Safely

Level 2 Award in Environmental Sustainability

Level 2 Award in Safe Driving at Work

Level 2 Award in Food Safety in Catering

Level 2 Award in Food Safety for Retail

Level 2 Award in Food Safety for Manufacturing

Level 3 Award in Emergency First Aid at Work

Level 3 Award in Supervising Food Safety in Catering

Level 3 Award in Food Safety Supervision for Retail

Level 3 Award in Food Safety Supervision for Manufacturing

Level 3 Certificate in Occupational Safety and Health

Level 3 Award in Emergency First Aid at Work

Level 3 Award in First Aid at Work

Level 3 Award in Paediatric First Aid

Level 6 Diploma in Occupational Safety and Health

INTERNATIONAL INSTITUTE OF RISK AND SAFETY MANAGEMENT

Suite 7a
77 Fulham Palace Road
London W6 8JA
Tel: 020 8741 9100
Fax: 020 8741 1349
E-mail: info@iirsm.org
Website: www.iirsm.org

The IIRSM is a professional body for health & safety practitioners and specialists in associated professions. Our aim is to advance professional standards in accident prevention and occupational health throughout the world. We have more than 8,100 members, in the UK and over 70 other countries, to whom we provide support and offer advice via a technical helpline.

MEMBERSHIP
Student

Affiliate
Associate (AIIRSM)
Member (MIIRSM)
Specialist Member (SIIRSM)
Fellow (FIIRSM)
Specialist Fellow (SFIIRSM)

DESIGNATORY LETTERS
AIIRSM, MIIRSM, SIIRSM, FIIRSM, SFIIRSM

NEBOSH (THE NATIONAL EXAMINATION BOARD IN OCCUPATIONAL SAFETY AND HEALTH)

Dominus Way
Meridian Business Park
Leicester LE19 1QW
Tel: (+44) 116 263 4700
Fax: (+44) 116 282 4000
E-mail: info@nebosh.org.uk
Website: www.nebosh.org.uk

NEBOSH offers globally recognized qualifications designed to meet the health, safety, environmental and risk management needs of all places of work. Courses leading to NEBOSH qualifications attract around 50,000 candidates annually and are offered by over 600 course providers, with exams taken in over 120 countries around the world.

MEMBERSHIP

NEBOSH's National General Certificate, National Certificate in Fire Safety and Risk Management, National Certificate in Construction Health and Safety, and the International General Certificate are all accepted as meeting the academic requirements to apply for Technical Membership (Tech IOSH) of the Institution of Occupational Safety and Health (IOSH).

In partnership with the Association for Project Safety (APS) the NEBOSH National and International Certificates in Construction Health and Safety meet the headline entrance criteria requirements for Construction Safety Associate membership (AaPS).

In addition holders of either the NEBOSH National or International Diploma in Occupational Health and Safety and either the NEBOSH National or International Certificate in Construction Health and Safety meet the headline qualification entrance criteria requirements for Registered Construction Safety Practitioner (RMaPS).

NEBOSH environmental management qualifications are now being accepted by CIWEM (The Chartered Institution of Water and Environmental Management) as meeting its membership requirements.

The NEBOSH Certificate in Environmental Management will be accepted for its new Technician Membership grade entitling the use of post-nominal designation (TechCIWEM).

The NEBOSH National Diploma in Environmental Management fulfils the qualification requirements for non-chartered Member of CIWEM (MCIWEM). Progression on to chartered membership is a further opportunity.

The NEBOSH Certificate in Environmental Management meets the academic criteria to gain the globally recognised IEMA Associate (AIEMA) membership, whilst holders of the NEBOSH National Diploma in Environmental Management will be eligible to apply for IEMA Practitioner (PIEMA) level membership.

NEBOSH's National Diploma and International Diploma are accepted as meeting the requirements to apply for Graduate Membership (Grad IOSH) of the Institution of Occupational Safety and Health (IOSH).

A NEBOSH Diploma provides a sound basis for progression to MSc level: a number of UK universities offer MSc programmes that accept the National Diploma as a full or partial entry requirement.

The new Masters Degrees are open to holders of a NEBOSH Diploma who wish to further their career in Health and Safety and/or Environment. It will be delivered by distance learning through research directly relevant to the candidate's own work.

QUALIFICATION/EXAMINATIONS

NEBOSH Environmental Awareness at Work Qualification
NEBOSH Health and Safety at Work Qualification
NEBOSH Health, Safety and Environment in the Process Industries Qualification
NEBOSH National Certificate in Construction Health and Safety
NEBOSH Certificate in Environmental Management
NEBOSH National Certificate in Fire Safety and Risk Management
NEBOSH National General Certificate in Occupational Health and Safety

NEBOSH International General Certificate in Occupational Health and Safety

NEBOSH International Technical Certificate in Oil and Gas Operational Safety

NEBOSH National Certificate in the Management of Health and Well-being at Work

NEBOSH International Certificate in Construction Health and Safety

NEBOSH International Certificate in Fire Safety and Risk Management

NEBOSH HSE Certificate in Process Safety Management

NEBOSH HSE Certificate in Health and Safety Leadership Excellence

NEBOSH National Diploma in Environmental Management

NEBOSH National Diploma in Occupational Health and Safety

NEBOSH International Diploma in Occupational Health and Safety

NEBOSH International Diploma in Environmental Management

Masters programmes in partnership with the University of Hull

MRes in Occupational Health and Safety Management

MRes in Occupational Health, Safety and Environmental Management

MRes in Environmental Management

MSc in Occupational Health and Safety Management

MSc in Occupational Health, Safety and Environmental Management

MSc in Environmental Management

NEBOSH Diploma in Regulatory Health and Safety – developed for the Health and Safety Executive for all new UK HSE Inspectors

DESIGNATORY LETTERS

DipNEBOSH, EnvDipNEBOSH

THE INSTITUTION OF OCCUPATIONAL SAFETY AND HEALTH

The Grange
Highfield Drive
Wigston
Leicestershire LE18 1NN
Tel: 0116 257 3100
Fax: 0116 257 3101
E-mail: membership@iosh.co.uk
Website: www.iosh.co.uk

Our membership totals over 46,000 – we are the focal point for health and safety professionals working in a diverse range of organisations.

Founded in 1945 IOSH is an independent, not-for-profit organisation setting professional standards, supporting and developing members, and providing authoritative advice and guidance on health and safety issues.

MEMBERSHIP
Affiliate Member
Associate Member
Technical Member (Tech IOSH)

Graduate Member (Grad IOSH)
Chartered Member (CMIOSH)
Chartered Fellow (CFIOSH)

QUALIFICATION/EXAMINATIONS
For qualifications that meet our academic requirements for our designatory categories of membership please see the IOSH website: https://www.iosh.co.uk/Membership/About-membership/Qualifications.aspx

DESIGNATORY LETTERS
AIOSH, Tech IOSH, Grad IOSH, CMIOSH, CFIOSH

INSURANCE AND ACTUARIAL WORK
Membership of Professional Institutions and Associations

ASSOCIATION OF AVERAGE ADJUSTERS

c/o Charles Taylor Insurance Services Limited
Lloyds Chambers
1 Portsoken Street
London E1 8BT
Tel: (+44) 191 349 8810
E-mail: via website
Website: www.average-adjusters.com

The AAA was founded in 1869 to promote correct principles in the adjustment of marine insurance claims and general average, uniformity of practice among average adjusters and the maintenance of good professional conduct. It ensures the independence and impartiality of its members by imposing a strict code of conduct and has close links with other international associations and insurance markets.

MEMBERSHIP
Fellow of the Association of Average Adjusters

Senior Associate
Associate
Subscriber
Representative Member

QUALIFICATION/EXAMINATIONS
The Association's examination consists of 6 modules. Passes in Modules A1 and either A2 or A3 are required for Associateship, passes in Modules F3, F4, F5 and F6 for Fellowship. For details see the Association's website.

INSTITUTE AND FACULTY OF ACTUARIES

7th Floor
Holburn Gate
326-330 High Holborn
London WC1V 7PP
Tel: 020 7632 2100
Fax: 020 7632 2111
E-mail: faculty@actuaries.org.uk
Website: www.actuaries.org.uk

Actuaries are experts in assessing the financial impact of tomorrow's uncertain events. They enable financial decisions to be made with more confidence by analysing the past, modelling the future, assessing the risks involved, and communicating what the results mean in financial terms.

MEMBERSHIP
Student Member
Affiliate Member
Associate (AFA or AIA)

Fellow (FFA or FIA)
Chartered Enterprise Risk Actuary (CERA)
Certified Actuarial Analyst (CAA)
Honorary Fellowship

QUALIFICATION/EXAMINATIONS
Please see https://www.actuaries.org.uk/studying

DESIGNATORY LETTERS
AFA, AIA, FFA, FIA Insurance and Actuarial Work

THE CHARTERED INSTITUTE OF LOSS ADJUSTERS

20 Ironmonger Lane
London EC2V 8EP
Tel: +44(0)20 3861 5720
E-mail: info@cila.co.uk
Website: www.cila.co.uk

The CILA, which was founded in 1941, is the professional body representing the claims specialists who investigate, negotiate and agree the conclusion of insurance and other claims on behalf of insurers and policyholders. We safeguard the interests of our members and maintain the high standards of the profession by requiring them to abide by our code of professional conduct.

MEMBERSHIP
Student Member
Ordinary Member
Certificate Member (Cert CILA)
Diploma
Advanced

Associate (ACILA)
Certified
Fellow (FCILA)
Retired

QUALIFICATION/EXAMINATIONS
Certificate
Diploma
Advanced Diploma
Associate
Fellow
MSC Professional Development

DESIGNATORY LETTERS
Cert CILA, Dip CILA, ACILA, FCILA, MSc

THE CHARTERED INSURANCE INSTITUTE

42–48 High Road
South Woodford
London E18 2JP
Tel: 020 8989 8464
Fax: 020 8530 3052
E-mail: customer.serv@cii.co.uk
Website: www.cii.co.uk

The CII is the premier professional body for those working in the insurance and financial services industry. We are dedicated to promoting higher standards of competence and integrity through the provision of relevant qualifications for employees at all levels across all sectors of the industry.

MEMBERSHIP
Ordinary Member
SMP Ordinary Member
Discover Member

Certificate Member
Fellowship Member
Diploma Member
Chartered Member
Advanced Diploma Member

QUALIFICATION/EXAMINATIONS
Please see https://www.cii.co.uk/qualifications/

DESIGNATORY LETTERS
ACII, FCII

JOURNALISM
Membership of Professional Institutions and Associations

NATIONAL COUNCIL FOR THE TRAINING OF JOURNALISTS

The New Granary
Station Road
Newport
Saffron Walden
Essex CB11 3PL
Tel: 01799 544014
Fax: 01799 544015
E-mail: info@nctj.com
Website: www.nctj.com

The NCTJ provides a range of multimedia journalism training products and services in the UK, including: accredited courses; apprenticeships; qualifications and examinations; awards; careers information; distance learning; short courses and CPD; information and research; publications and events. We play an influential role in all areas of journalism education and training.

QUALIFICATION/EXAMINATIONS
Certificate in Foundation Journalism
Diploma in Journalism
Junior journalist apprenticeship
National Qualification in Journalism (NQJ)
Shorthand

THE CHARTERED INSTITUTE OF JOURNALISTS

2 Dock Offices
Surrey Quays Road
London SE16 2XU
Tel: 020 7252 1187
Fax: 020 7232 2302
E-mail: memberservices@cioj.co.uk
Website: www.cioj.co.uk

The CIoJ, which dates back to 1884, is a professional body and trade union for journalists. We expect our members to uphold high standards in the way they work and to adhere to a strict code of conduct, and in return we champion journalistic freedom, protect their interests in the workplace and campaign for better working conditions.

MEMBERSHIP
Student Member
Affiliate Member
Trainee Member
Full Member
International Member

DESIGNATORY LETTERS
MCIJ – Member, FCIJ – Fellow

LAND AND PROPERTY
Membership of Professional Institutions and Associations

RICS (ROYAL INSTITUTION OF CHARTERED SURVEYORS)

Parliament Square
London SW1P 3AD
Tel: 024 7686 8555
Fax: 020 7334 3811
E-mail: contactrics@rics.org
Website: www.rics.org/careers

RICS, an independent, not-for-profit organisation, has around 100,000 qualified members and more than 50,000 students and trainees in some 140 countries, and provides the world's leading professional qualification in land, property, construction and associated environmental issues. We accredit over 600 courses at leading universities worldwide and provide impartial, authoritative advice on key issues for business, society and governments.

MEMBERSHIP
Student
Associate (AssocRICS)
Member (MRICS)
Fellow (FRICS)

DESIGNATORY LETTERS
AssocRICS, MRICS, FRICS

THE INSTITUTE OF REVENUES, RATING AND VALUATION

Northumberland House
5th Floor
303–306 High Holborn
London WC1V 7JZ
Tel: 020 7831 3505
Fax: 020 7831 2048
E-mail: education@irrv.org.uk
Website: www.irrv.org.uk

The Institute offers professional and technical qualifications for all those whose professional work is concerned with local authority revenues (council tax and business rates); welfare benefits; benefit fraud investigation; valuation for rating and appeals procedures. Our qualifications are widely recognised throughout the profession.

MEMBERSHIP
Student Member
Apprentice Member
Affiliate Member
Graduate Member
Technician Member (Tech IRRV)
Corporate Member (IRRV)
Diploma Member (IRRV Dip)
Honours Member (IRRV Hons)

Honorary Member
Fellow (FIRRV)
Retired

QUALIFICATION/EXAMINATIONS
Level 3 Certificate in Local Taxation and Benefits
Level 3 Local Taxation & Benefits (RQF)
Certificate in Local Taxation, Revenues and Welfare Benefits
Level 4 Revenues and Welfare Benefits Practitioner
Apprenticeship
Professional Diploma in Local Taxation and Benefits
Honours

DESIGNATORY LETTERS
Tech IRRV, IRRV, IRRV (Dip), IRRV(Hons), FIRRV

THE NATIONAL FEDERATION OF PROPERTY PROFESSIONALS AWARDING BODY

Arbon House
6 Tournament Court
Edgehill Drive
Warwick CV34 6LG
Tel: 0845 250 6008
Fax: 01926 417789
E-mail: quals@nfopp.co.uk
Website: www.nfopp-awardingbody.co.uk

The **NFOPP Awarding Body** is committed to raising standards within agency through the provision of accredited, nationally recognized qualifications. We are recognized by the Qualifications and Examinations Regulator (Ofqual) and Welsh Government and we have to follow strict guidelines and maintain quality standards in the provision of all our qualifications.

MEMBERSHIP
For membership details of the following organisations please refer to the relevant website:
APIP: www.apip.co.uk
ARLA: www.arla.co.uk
ICBA: www.icba.uk.com
NAEA: www.naea.co.uk
NAVA: www.nava.org.uk

QUALIFICATION/EXAMINATIONS
NFoPP **Level 2 Award** in Introduction to Residential Property Management Practice (QCF)
NFoPP **Level 3 Technical Award** in Commercial Property Agency (QCF)

NFoPP **Level 3 Technical Award** in Real Property Auctioneering (QCF)
NFoPP **Level 3 Technical Award** in Residential Letting and Property Management (QCF)
NFoPP **Level 3 Technical Award** in Residential Letting and Property Management Northern Ireland (QCF)
NFoPP **Level 3 Technical Award** in Sale of Residential Property (QCF)
NFoPP **Level 3 Technical Award** in Chattels Auctioneering (QCF)
NFoPP **Level 3 Technical Award** in Residential Inventory Management & Practice (QCF)
NFoPP **Level 4 Certificate** in Residential Letting & Property Management (QCF)
NFoPP **Level 4 Certificate** in Sale of Residential Property (QCF)
NFoPP **Level 4 Certificate** in Commercial Property Agency (QCF)
NFoPP **Level 6 Technical Award** in Sale of Residential Property Scotland (SCQF)
NFoPP **Level 6 Technical Award** in Residential Letting & Property Management Scotland (SCQF)

THE PROPERTY CONSULTANTS SOCIETY

Basement Office
Surrey Court
1 Surrey Street
Arundel
West Sussex BN18 9DT
Tel: 01903 883787
E-mail: info@propertyconsultantssociety.org
Website: www.propertyconsultantssociety.org

The Property Consultants Society is a non-profit-making organisation that offers advice to qualified surveyors, architects, valuers, auctioneers, land and estate agents, master builders, construction engineers, accountants and members of the legal profession to help them to undertake their property consultancy in a competent, legitimate and publicly acceptable way.

MEMBERSHIP
Student (SPCS)
Licentiate (LPCS)
Associate (APCS)
Fellow (FPCS)

Honorary Member

DESIGNATORY LETTERS
SPCS, LPCS, APCS, FPCS

UNIVERSITY COLLEGE OF ESTATE MANAGEMENT

Horizons
60 Queen's Road
Reading RG1 4BS
Tel: +44 (0)118 467 2100
Fax: 0118 921 4620
E-mail: enquiries@cem.ac.uk
Website: www.ucem.ac.uk

The College of Estate Management is the leading provider of supported distance learning for real estate and construction professionals. We have been playing a key role in the property world for over 90 years. At any one time we have over 4,000 students based all over the world.

QUALIFICATION/EXAMINATIONS
BCSC Diploma in Shopping Centre Management
BSc(Hons) Building Surveying
BSc(Hons) Construction Management
BSc(Hons) Estate Management

BSc(Hons) Property Management
BSc(Hons) Quantity Surveying
Postgraduate Diploma/MSc Conservation of the Historic Environment
Postgraduate Diploma/MSc Surveying
MBA Real Estate and Construction Management
Postgraduate Diploma/MSc Facilities Management
Postgraduate Diploma/MSc Property Investment
RICS Professional Membership Graduate Route – Adaptation 1

LANDSCAPE ARCHITECTURE
Membership of Professional Institutions and Associations

LANDSCAPE INSTITUTE

Charles Darwin House
107 Grays Inn Road
London WC1X 8TZ
Tel: 020 7685 2640
E-mail: membership@landscapeinstitute.org
Website: www.landscapeinstitute.org

The Landscape Institute (LI) is the chartered body for the landscape profession. It is an educational charity that promotes the art and science of landscape practice.

The LI's aim, through the work of its members is to protect, conserve and enhance the natural and built environment for the public benefit.

The LI provides a professional home for all landscape practitioners including landscape scientists, landscape planners, landscape architects, landscape managers and urban designers.

MEMBERSHIP
Affiliate Member
Student Member
Licentiate Member
Chartered Member (CMLI)
Fellow (FLI)

Academic Member (AMLI)
Academic Fellow (AFLI)

DESIGNATORY LETTERS
CMLI, FLI

QUALIFICATION/EXAMINATIONS
Pathway to Chartership oral examination conferring
chartered professional status (CMLI)

LANGUAGES, LINGUISTICS AND TRANSLATION
Membership of Professional Institutions and Associations

CIOL – THE CHARTERED INSTITUTE OF LINGUISTS

7th Floor
167 Fleet Street
London EC4A 2EA
Tel: 020 7940 3100
E-mail: info@ciol.org.uk
Website: www.ciol.org.uk

CIOL, founded in 1910, is the UK's leading language assessment and professional body and the only specialist language awarding organisation recognised by Ofqual. CIOL has over 7,000 language professionals as members of whom over 500 are now Chartered. Our purpose is to represent, accredit, support and develop professional linguists and promote the learning and use of modern languages. We set the professional standards for translating and interpreting, aim to improve the status of all language professionals and assure rigorous professional integrity.

MEMBERSHIP
Student Affiliate
IoLET Affiliate
Career Affiliate
Associate (ACIL)
Member (MCIL)
Fellow (FCIL)
Chartered Linguist (CL)

QUALIFICATION/EXAMINATIONS
Diploma in Translation (Level 7)
Diploma in Public Service Interpreting (DPSI) (Level 6)
Diploma in Police Interpreting (Level 6)
CBS Police (Level 3)
Certificate in Languages for Business (Level 2)

DESIGNATORY LETTERS
ACIL, MCIL, FCIL, CL

INSTITUTE OF TRANSLATION & INTERPRETING

Milton Keynes Business Centre
Foxhunter Drive
Linford Wood
Milton Keynes MK14 6GD
Tel: 01908 325250
Fax: 01908 325259
E-mail: info@iti.org.uk
Website: www.iti.org.uk

The Institute of Translation & Interpreting is one of the primary sources of information on these services to government, industry, the media and the general public. We promote the highest standards, providing guidance to those entering the profession and advice to those who offer language services and to their customers.

MEMBERSHIP
Student
Affiliate
Associate (AITI)
Academic
Supporter
Qualified Member (MITI)

Fellow

QUALIFICATION/EXAMINATIONS
Applicants for qualified membership must take an exam (translators) or attend an interview (interpreters).

THE GREEK INSTITUTE

29 Onslow Gardens
London N21 1DY
Tel: 020 8360 7968
Fax: 020 8360 7968
E-mail: info@greekinstitute.co.uk
Website: www.greekinstitute.co.uk

The Greek Institute, which was founded in 1969, is a non-profit-making cultural organisation that promotes Modern Greek studies and culture through lectures, publications, literary competitions, Greek cultural evenings and the award of Certificates and a Diploma which are recognized by many UK universities as equivalent to GCSE and GCE A level Modern Greek.

MEMBERSHIP
Member
Associate (AGI)
Fellow (FGI)

QUALIFICATION/EXAMINATIONS
Certificate in Greek Conversation – Basic Stage: Levels 1 and 2
Certificate in Greek Conversation – Intermediate Stage: Levels 3 and 4
Certificate in Greek Conversation – Higher Stage: Levels 5 and 6
Preliminary Certificate
Intermediate Certificate
Advanced Certificate
Diploma in Greek Translation (DipGrTrans)

DESIGNATORY LETTERS
AGI, FGI

LAW

ENGLAND AND WALES

MAGISTRATES

The President of the Courts of England and Wales, The Lord Chief Justice, is head of the Judiciary. He is responsible for the welfare, training and deployment of magistrates, for approving the names of the candidates recommended for appointment and for disciplinary action, short of removal. He also has responsibility for the protection of judicial independence and for working to ensure that the magistracy reflects the diversity of society as a whole.

There are key qualities that a magistrate must possess: good character, understanding and effective communication, social awareness, maturity and a sense of fairness, sound judgement, commitment and reliability. Magistrates do not sit exams nor do they have to be legally qualified.

Before sitting in court, magistrates must undertake some basic training, which includes structured observations in court. This covers practice and procedure in court, structured decision making, sentencing, and so on. New magistrates are assigned a mentor for the first year or so. Core training also involves visits to penal institutions to equip magistrates with the key knowledge they need. Consolidation training takes place at the end of the first year; this is designed to help magistrates plan for their ongoing development and prepare for their first appraisal which takes place about 12 to 18 months after appointment. Magistrates only sit in adult courts when first appointed. Having got that experience they may apply to sit in youth courts and family courts and have to undertake more training before they can sit.

Ongoing training and development includes appraisals which take place every three years, continuation training which takes place once every three years, usually before appraisals, update training on new legislation and procedures and threshold training which accompanies each development in a magistrate's role.

The Magistrates Association has more information about magistrates (www.magistrates-association.org. uk).

JUDGES

All judicial office holders are Her Majesty's Judges and as such all appointments are made by the Queen or her Ministers. All candidates for judicial appointment in England and Wales have been selected by the independent Judicial Appointments Commission (JAC, website: https://www.judicialappointments. gov.uk), which passes its recommendations to the Lord Chancellor for approval. The key statutory responsibilities of the JAC are to select candidates solely on merit; to select only people of good character; to have regard to the need to encourage diversity in the range of people available for selection for appointments.

Once the JAC's selections have been received, the actual appointments are made in slightly different ways depending on the type of post. The Lord Chancellor appoints Deputy District Judges and most members of tribunals. The 30,000 unpaid magistrates who are selected by local Advisory Committees, not by the JAC, are also appointed by The Lord Chancellor. The Queen appoints High Court and Circuit Judges, Masters, Registrars and District Judges, District Judges (Magistrates Courts) and Recorders on the advice of the Lord Chancellor. A special panel convened by the JAC appoints the Lord Chief Justice. The Queen appoints Heads of Division, Court of Appeal judges and senior judges with lengthy judicial experience, on the recommendation of a selection panel convened by the JAC. Scotland and Northern Ireland have their own separate court systems, with their own arrangements for appointing members of the judiciary.

The Supreme Court (http://supremecourt.uk) has jurisdiction over the whole of the UK, so its Justices are not selected by the JAC, which is an England and Wales body. Rather, a special committee is set up, which is made up of the three judicial appointments bodies from around the UK (England and Wales, Scotland and Northern Ireland), who recommend a name to Ministers. The Queen appoints the Justices on the basis of advice from the Prime Minister.

Candidates for appointment as Justices of the Supreme Court must have held high judicial office for two years or must have been practising barristers or solicitors of the senior courts for at least 15 years (www.supremecourt.uk/faqs.html#1d). More information about judges can be found at the Courts and Tribunals Judiciary website: www.judiciary.gov. uk

OFFICERS OF THE COURT

Officers of the Court include judicial and administrative staff; the former include Masters and Registrars, the latter secretaries and clerks to the judges and the staff who administer the court service. Details are given in *The English Legal System*, 17th edition, 2016–17 (Routledge). Qualifications for the judicial offices vary somewhat, but most appointments are limited to established barristers and solicitors.

THE LEGAL PROFESSION

The legal profession consists of two branches. Each performs distinct duties, although there is a degree of overlap in some aspects of their work.

Solicitors undertake all ordinary legal business for their clients (with whom they are in direct contact). They may also appear on behalf of a client in the magistrates and county courts and tribunals, and with specialist training are able to represent them in the higher courts (Crown Court, High Court and Court of Appeal). The website for the Law Society contains further information (www.lawsociety.org. uk).

Barristers (known collectively as the Bar and collectively and individually as Counsel) advise on legal problems submitted by solicitors and conduct cases in court when instructed by a solicitor; only barristers or qualified solicitor advocates may represent clients in the higher courts. More information on barristers can be found on The Bar Council website (www.barcouncil.org.uk).

LEGAL EXECUTIVES

Both graduates and non-graduates can work in a legal office with the option of qualifying as a solicitor through further vocational training. Chartered Legal Executive lawyers are 'authorised persons' undertaking 'reserved legal activities' alongside, for example, solicitors and barristers. As a general rule, a Chartered Legal Executive lawyer is able to undertake all the same work that may be undertaken by a solicitor, with some conditions. The Chartered Institute of Legal Executives website has information on becoming a legal executive and the work they can undertake (www.cilex.org.uk).

CORONERS

Coroners must be barristers, solicitors or legally qualified medical practitioners of not less than five years standing. They are appointed by local authorities. There are approximately 95 coroner areas in England and Wales; each area is locally funded and resourced by local authorities. Coroners are independent judicial officers. When not engaged in coronal duties, coroners (apart from whole-time coroners) continue in their legal or medical practices. The Chief Coroner is head of the coroner system, assuming overall responsibility and providing national leadership for coroners in England and Wales. He oversees the implementation of the Coroner and Justice Act 2009. Further information from the Coroners Society of England and Wales, website: www.coronersociety.org.uk and the Crown Prosecution Service website: www.cps.gov.uk/legal/a_to_c/coroners/#a02.

BARRISTERS

Qualification as a barrister at the Bar of England and Wales

There are three stages that must be completed to qualify as a barrister. The academic stage consists of an undergraduate degree in law or in any other subject with a minimum of a 2:2. For those with an undergraduate degree in a subject other than law a one-year conversion course (CPE/GDL) must be completed.

Before commencing the vocational stage candidates must join one of the four Inns and then undertake the Bar Professional Training Course (BPTC), which is either one year full time or two years part time. The main skills taught on the BPTC are: casework skills, legal research, fact management, general written skills including opinion-writing (that is, giving written advice) and drafting, management and interpersonal skills including conference skills (interviewing clients), resolution of disputes out of court (ReDOC) and advocacy (court or tribunal appearances). The main areas of legal knowledge taught on the BPTC are: civil litigation, evidence and remedies, criminal litigation, evidence and sentencing, professional ethics, and two optional subjects or

one double optional subject selected from a choice of at least six.

Three centralised assessments are set by a Central Examinations Board, which is comprised of experienced legal practitioners and academics appointed by the Bar Standards Board (BSB). The subjects that are centrally assessed are Civil Litigation, Evidence and Remedies, Criminal Litigation, Evidence and Sentencing and Professional Ethics. Applicants will also have to take the Bar Course Aptitude Test. It aims to test critical thinking and reasoning, but does not test legal knowledge. Practice tests are available on the BSB website. The Aptitude Test will ensure that those undertaking the BPTC have the required skills to succeed.

Once the BPCT has been successfully completed candidates are called to the Bar by their Inn. The Pupillage Stage consists of one year spent in an authorized pupillage training organisation. Pupillage is divided into two parts: the non-practising six months (also known as the first six) and the practising six months (also known as the second six).

To find out more about all three stages of qualification as a barrister visit www.barcouncil.org.uk and www.barstandardsboard.org.uk

SOLICITORS

Qualification as a solicitor in England and Wales

To practise as a solicitor in England and Wales a person must have been admitted as a solicitor, his or her name having been entered on the Roll of Solicitors, and must hold a practising certificate issued by The Solicitors Regulation Authority (SRA) (Solicitors Regulation Authority, The Cube, 199 Wharfside Street, Birmingham B1 1RN; Tel: 0370 606 2555; www.sra.org.uk).

The SRA is the independent regulatory body of the Law Society of England and Wales. People will be admitted as solicitors only if they have passed the appropriate academic and vocational course and have completed a training contract and Professional Skills course, or have transferred from another jurisdiction or the Bar. The SRA controls the training of solicitors. Most solicitors become members of the Law Society, but membership is not compulsory. Intending solicitors other than Fellows of the Chartered Institute of Legal Executives (CILEx), Justices Clerk's Assistants and qualified lawyers from overseas, are required to serve a period of training with a practising solicitor after they have completed the legal practice course.

All new entrants to the profession are required to complete a Disclosure and Barring Service (DBS) standard disclosure prior to admission. Candidates wishing to start training must enrol as a student with the SRA and satisfy it that they have successfully completed the academic stage of training and there are no issues that may call their character and suitability into question.

It is not necessary for the first degree to be in law as about 20 per cent of solicitors qualify via the non-law graduate route. The key stages of this are:

- degree in any subject;
- Common Professional Examination/Graduate Diploma in Law;
- Legal Practice course;
- practice-based training incorporating the Professional Skills course;
- admission to the roll of solicitors.

THE COMMON PROFESSIONAL EXAMINATION (CPE) OR GRADUATE DIPLOMA IN LAW (GDL)

The seven taught modules are the foundation subjects prescribed by the Joint Academic Stage Board on behalf of the Law Society and General Council of the Bar: Criminal Law, Contract Law, the Law of Tort, Equity and Trusts, Public Law, European Union Law and Property Law. For an up-to-date list of course providers for the CPE, use the training provider search in the student section on the SRA website: www.sra.org.uk

THE LEGAL PRACTICE COURSE

Stage 1 covers core practice areas: Litigation, Property Law and Practice (PLP), Business Law and Practice (BLP); Course Skills: Research, Writing, Drafting, Interviewing and Advising, and Advocacy (these skills form an integral part of the compulsory and elective subjects) and also Professional Conduct and Regulation, Taxation and Wills and Administration of Estates. Stage 2 covers three vocational electives chosen from a range of corporate client or private client topics (the range of electives available can differ from institution to institution). An up-to-date list of course providers for the LPC is available using the training provider search in the student section on the SRA website: www.sra.org.uk

TRAINING CONTRACT

The training contract to be served by all intending solicitors, other than Fellows of the Institute of Legal Executives and Justices Clerk's Assistants, is usually two years full time or a part-time study training contract that normally lasts between three and four years. During this period the trainee works and is studying the last two years of a part-time qualifying law degree, the part-time Common Professional Examination course and/or the part-time Legal Practice Course.

The law graduate who holds a qualifying law degree must complete the Legal Practice course at a recognized institution, and then serve under the training contract, usually for two years. The non-law graduate must first pass the Common Professional Exam (CPE) or the Postgraduate Diploma in Law, having attended either a one-year full-time or two-year part-time preparatory course. He or she may then serve under the training contract for two years after completion of a Legal Practice Course. A Professional Skills course must be attended and successfully completed during the training contract.

Fellows of the Institute of Chartered Legal Executives (CILEx) may obtain partial or full exemptions from the CPE and Justices Clerk's Assistants courses by virtue of similar subjects passed in their Fellowship exams or the Diploma in Magisterial Law. After passing or being exempted from the CPE, the Fellow/Justices Clerk's Assistant may be exempt from serving under a training contract following successful completion of a Legal Practice Course. A Professional Skills course must be taken prior to application for admission.

THE PROFESSIONAL SKILLS COURSE

The aim of the Professional Skills course is to build on the foundations laid in the Legal Practice Course so as to develop a trainee's professional skills. Providers of the course, trainees and their employers are encouraged to regard the course as the first stage of a trainee's lifetime professional development.

Built upon the Legal Practice Course, the course provides training in three subject areas: financial and business skills; advocacy and communication skills; client care and professional standards. Elective topics will also be chosen, which fall within one or more of these three core areas. All trainees have to complete all sections of the course satisfactorily before being admitted. The course consists of face-to-face instruction on the core subjects, for a minimum of 18 hours each for financial and business skills and advocacy and communication skills, and a minimum of 12 hours for client care and professional standards. The elective topics require a minimum total of 24 hours, of which a minimum of 12 hours must be face-to-face. The instruction must be completed during the training contract. The PSC is offered by accredited external course providers.

APPRENTICESHIPS

Legal apprenticeships have been introduced as alternative way to gain legal qualifications. While working for an employer, an apprentice can qualify as a solicitor, a legal executive or a paralegal. During the apprenticeship a combination of classroom and work-based learning is undertaken and the apprentice receives a salary. The minimum entry requirements can be found on the Law Society's website: www.lawsociety.org.uk. The apprenticeship lasts from five to six years. The apprentice is assessed by timed examination and a work-based assessment. The apprentice then takes a standardised practical legal exam in the last six months of the apprenticeship in order to qualify. Further information is available on the SRA's website and www.getingofar.gov.uk

QUALIFIED LAWYERS FROM OTHER JURISDICTIONS

Lawyers from certain foreign jurisdictions can apply for admission under the Qualified Lawyers Transfer Scheme Regulations 2011. They need to obtain a QLTS Certificate of Eligibility, but may be entitled to exemption from some or all of the QLTS assessments if they are:

- a lawyer qualified in the EEA/EU/Switzerland and seeking to qualify via Directive 2005/36/EC (recognition of professional qualifications)
- a lawyer qualified in Northern Ireland or Scotland
- a barrister who has qualified in England and Wales who has completed a pupillage.

The Solicitors Regulation Authority has appointed Kaplan QLTS as the assessment organisation for the operation of the assessments (http://qlts.kaplan.co.uk) and the assessments are only available at Kaplan QLTS. The assessments are usually only available twice a year and take place in London. The email address for queries regarding eligibility is contact-centre@sra.org.uk.

EU, Northern Irish and Scottish lawyers and barristers qualified in England and Wales follow a different transfer process and should get in touch with the SRA Contact Centre for further information. SRA Contact Centre Tel: 0370 606 2555 (International callers: +44 (0)121 329 6800); Website: www.sra.org.uk/contact-us

All international applicants must satisfy the requirements and pass the QLTS Assessments. The Assessments are in two parts: Part 1 is a multiple choice test designed to test Part A of the SRA's Day One Outcomes, namely the knowledge of law expected of a newly qualified solicitor of England and Wales and consists of 180 questions; Part 2, is an Objective Structured Clinical Examination (OSCE). For the OSCE, candidates are examined in the skills of interviewing, advocacy/oral presentations, legal research, legal drafting and legal writing in business, civil and criminal litigation, property and probate.

EEA, Northern Irish and Scottish lawyers, and barristers qualified in England and Wales will be individually assessed against the Day One Outcomes. All transferees are required to prove their character and suitability to be a solicitor by taking the SRA Suitability Test. Candidates who have passed the LPC can get exemption from the Part 1 (MCT) assessment.

Prospective candidates wanting more information on QLTS can consult the website www.sra.org.uk/solicitors/qlts/key-features.page for guidance, or contact the SRA on 0370 606 2555 (International callers: +44(0)121 329 6800); Website: www.sra.org.uk/contact-us

SCOTLAND

The Court of Session, High Court of Justiciary, Sheriff Courts and Justice of the Peace Courts are administered by the Scottish Court service, an Executive Agency of the Scottish Government. For further information on Scottish Courts go to www.scotcourts.gov.uk

THE LEGAL PROFESSION

The profession consists of solicitors and advocates.

Qualification as a Solicitor in Scotland

Solicitors in Scotland have their names inserted in a Roll of Solicitors and are granted annual Certificates entitling them to practise by The Law Society of Scotland, contact details: Atria One, 144 Morrison Street, Edinburgh EH3 8EX; Tel: 0131 226 7411; e-mail: lawscot@lawscot.org.uk; website: www.lawscot.org.uk; Education and Careers e-mail: careers@lawscot.org.uk.

For any queries relating to qualifying as a solicitor in Scotland, including LLB/diploma providers, diploma validity, traineeships, admission as a solicitor, entrance certificates and training contracts, alternative routes to qualification and requalifying into Scotland, contact legaleduc@lawscot.org.uk.

A Certificate is granted to candidates who have passed approved exams, completed a term of practical training and been admitted as solicitors.

THE QUALIFYING EXAMINATIONS

The standard route to qualification is the LLB (the Ordinary degree is a three-year course, the Honours is four years) followed by the Diploma in Professional Legal Practice (Professional Education and Training Stage 1: PEAT 1) and then the traineeship, the period of paid in-office training working towards the standard of the qualified solicitor (Professional Education and Training Stage 2: PEAT 2). Outcomes in professionalism, professional ethics and standards, professional communication and business, commercial, financial and practice awareness apply across both PEAT 1 and 2, linking them and providing real clarity across the two stages.

All trainees are required to undertake Trainee Continuing Professional Development (TCPD). All solicitors are required to undertake CPD for a minimum of 20 hours each year. To support solicitors in their CPD activities, the Society provides basic templates, which can be completed online, to assist with identifying training needs, recording CPD undertaken and evaluating the outcome of the training. A wide range of activities are acceptable as CPD, including structured and formalized one-to-one training, coaching and online training.

An alternate route to qualifying as a solicitor in Scotland is by a combination of the Law Society's own examinations and three years pre-Diploma training. To be eligible to sit the Law Society's examinations, non-law graduates must find full-time employment as a pre-Diploma trainee with a qualified solicitor practising in Scotland. A pre-Diploma training contract lasts for three years. During the period of the training contract, a pre-Diploma trainee will study for the Law Society's examinations. The two routes to qualification (degree and Law Society exams) merge at this point as all intending solicitors are required to complete the Diploma in Professional Legal Practice. Upon successful completion of the Diploma the graduate will enter into a two-year post-Diploma training contract with a qualified solicitor practising in Scotland.

Transfer tests are in place for solicitors from England, Wales, Northern Ireland and other parts of the European Union who wish to requalify as Scottish solicitors.

Qualification as an advocate in Scotland

Barristers in Scotland are called Advocates. Scottish Advocates are not only members of the Faculty of Advocates but also members of the College of Justice and officers of the Court. The procedure for the admission of Intrants is subject in part to the control of the Court and in part to the control of the Faculty; the Court is responsible for most of the formal procedures and the Faculty for the exams and periods of professional training. To become an Intrant, applicants must produce evidence that they hold one of the following standard of degree: a degree with Honours, Second Class (Division 2) or above, in Scottish Law at a Scottish university, or a degree in Scottish Law at a Scottish university together with a degree with Honours, Second Class (Division 2) or above, in another subject at a UK university or an ordinary degree with distinction in Scottish Law at a Scottish university. A Diploma in Legal Practice from a Scottish University is also required, although in exceptional cases this requirement may be waived.

In order to go through the various stages of qualification and training, applicants must matriculate as intrants to the Faculty. Matriculation involves making an application to the Court of Session and to the Faculty.

An Intrant must also comply with the professional training required by the Faculty, which consists of a period of 21 months training in a solicitors office (although the Faculty recommends a traineeship of 24 months). Subject-for-subject exemptions are granted to Intrants who have passed exams at this standard in the course of a curriculum for a law degree at a Scottish university. Every Intrant must pass or be exempted from exams in the compulsory subjects and two optional subjects. In addition, and prior to the commencement of pupillage (also known as devilling) every Intrant must sit the Faculty's entrant examination in Evidence, Practice and Procedure. If successfully passed, the Intrant can then commence his or her pupillage.

During the first five or six weeks of pupillage pupils undertake the Foundation course. After about three months of work with their devil master, the pupils will participate in the February Skills course, comprising a series of performance workshops involving the use of documents in evidence, the conduct of a procedure roll discussion, workshops on judicial review, section 275 applications and working with expert evidence. Shortly before admission, the pupils attend the May Preparation for Practice course, covering workshops on vulnerable witnesses, longer motions, reclaiming motions, negotiation and mediation, as well as carrying out civil and criminal appeals before a serving judge.

Intrants who have passed all the necessary exams and undergone the necessary professional training as well as successfully completing their pupillage may apply to be admitted to membership of the Faculty and are admitted at a public meeting of the Faculty. Once admitted, Intrants are introduced to the Court by the Dean of Faculty, make a Declaration of Allegiance to the Sovereign in open Court and are then admitted by the Court to the public office of Advocate. For further information on becoming an advocate contact Faculty of Advocates, Parliament House, Edinburgh EH1 1RF; Tel: 0131 226 5071; e-mail: admissions@advocates.org.uk; website: www.advocates.org.uk

NORTHERN IRELAND

As in England and Wales, the superior courts are the Supreme Court, Court of Appeal, the High Court and the Crown Court. The latter is an exclusively criminal court. The Court of Appeal hears appeals on points of law in civil and criminal cases from all courts. Appeals lie from the Court of Appeal to the Supreme Court.

Inferior Courts: as in England and Wales, the county courts are principally civil courts, but in Northern Ireland they also hear appeals from conviction in the Magistrates Courts for summary offences.

Magistrates Courts: these deal principally with minor criminal offences (summary offences) and are presided over by Resident Magistrates (stipendiaries). Resident Magistrates are appointed by the Crown on the advice of the Lord Chancellor.

Coroners: coroners in Northern Ireland must be barristers or solicitors who have practised for not less than five years. They are appointed by the Lord Chancellor.

THE LEGAL PROFESSION

The legal profession in Northern Ireland consists of barristers and solicitors belonging to professional bodies organised on similar lines to those in England and Wales.

Qualification as a barrister in Northern Ireland

The path to becoming a barrister in Northern Ireland will differ depending on where you study, qualify and complete your pupillage training. There are different pathways for those who have trained as barristers in Northern Ireland, the Republic of Ireland or England and Wales. A different procedure exists for solicitors who wish to requalify as barristers or those who wish to transfer from European jurisdictions. Full information can be found at www.barofni.com/page/becoming-a-barrister

To qualify to practise as a barrister in Northern Ireland a candidate who has trained in Northern Ireland must have a recognized law degree of 2.1 honours standard or higher, or equivalent. The candidate must then complete the Bar Post-Graduate Diploma in Professional Legal Studies at the Institute of Professional Legal Studies, Queen's University, Belfast (IPLS). Finally the candidate must call to the Bar of Northern Ireland and complete a 12-month pupillage. Enquiries about the Bar can be made to the Bar Council Office, The Bar Library, 91 Chichester Street, Belfast BT1 3JQ; Tel: 028 9024 1523; website: www.barofni.com).

Qualification as a solicitor in Northern Ireland

The solicitors' professional body in Northern Ireland is the Law Society of Northern Ireland (Law Society House, 96 Victoria Street, Belfast BT1 3GN; Tel: 028 9023 1614; e-mail: enquiry@lawsoc-ni.org; website: www.lawsoc-ni.org). It has overall responsibility for education and admission to the profession.

Admission to training is generally dependent upon possession of a recognized law degree from a university. Law graduates must attend a two-year vocational apprenticeship course at the Institute of Professional Legal Studies, The Queen's University of Belfast, 10 Lennoxvale, Belfast, BT9 5BY; Tel: 028 9097 5567; e-mail: iplsenquiries@qub.ac.uk. On completion of the two-year apprenticeship newly qualified solicitors receive restricted practising certificates, which means that although they are fully qualified they cannot practise on their own account or in partnership for at least two more years.

Non-law graduates must satisfy the Society that they possess an acceptable degree in a discipline other than law and have attained a satisfactory level of legal knowledge in areas such as: Constitutional Law, Law of Tort, Law of Contract, Criminal Law,

Equity, Land Law and Law of Evidence; that they have been offered a place in the Institute; and that they have obtained a Master (a solicitor with whom the applicant proposes to serve his or her apprenticeship).

Membership of Professional Institutions and Associations

CHARTERED INSTITUTE OF LEGAL EXECUTIVES (CILEX)

Kempston Manor
Kempston
Bedford MK42 7AB
Tel: 01234 845777
E-mail: membership@cilex.org.uk
Website: www.cilex.org.uk

The Chartered Institute of Legal Executives (CILEx) is the professional association which represents 20,000 Chartered Legal Executive lawyers, paralegals and other legal practitioners. Our role is to enhance the position and standing of Chartered Legal Executive lawyers in the legal profession. For more than 50 years, we have been offering unparalleled access to a flexible career in law. We work closely with Government and the Ministry of Justice and are recognised in England and Wales as one of the three core approved regulators of the legal profession alongside barristers and solicitors.

MEMBERSHIP
Student Member
Affiliate Member
Associate Member (ACILEx)
Graduate Member (GCILEx)
Chartered Legal Executive Lawyer (FCILEx)

QUALIFICATION/EXAMINATIONS
Level 1 Award/Certificate/Diploma in Legal Studies
Level 2 Award/Certificate/Diploma in Legal Studies
Level 2 Certificate/Diploma for Legal Secretaries
Level 3 Certificate/Diploma for Legal Secretaries
Level 3 Professional Diploma in Law and Practice
Level 3 Certificate in Law and Practice
Level 3 Certificate in Civil Litigation
Level 3 Certificate in Family Practice
Level 3 Certificate in Employment Practice
Level 3 Certificate in Private Client Practice
Level 3 Certificate in Property
Level 3 Diploma in Providing Legal Services
Level 4 Diploma in Commercial Litigation
Level 4 Diploma in Debt Recovery and Insolvency
Level 4 Diploma in Personal Injury Litigation
Level 4 Diploma in Providing Legal Services
Level 4 Extended Diploma in Personal Injury Litigation
Level 6 Certificate in Law
Level 6 Higher Diploma in Law and Practice
Graduate Fast-track Diploma (Level 6)

DESIGNATORY LETTERS
ACILEx, GCILEx, FCILEx

COUNCIL FOR LICENSED CONVEYANCERS

WeWork
131 Finsbury Pavement
London EC2A 1NT
Tel: 020 3859 0904
E-mail: clc@clc-uk.org
Website: www.clc-uk.org

The CLC was established under the provisions of the Administration of Justice Act 1985 as the Regulatory Body for Licensed Conveyancers. Our purpose is to set entry standards and regulate the profession of

Licensed Conveyancers effectively. CLC regulates Probate services provided by its licensed practitioners. CLC is an authorised regulator for ABS.

MEMBERSHIP
Student
Licensed Conveyancer
Probate Practitioner

Conveyancing Technician
Probate Technician

QUALIFICATION/EXAMINATIONS
Level 4 Diploma (Technician)
Level 6 Diploma (Licensed Conveyancer/Probate Practitioner)

ILFM (THE INSTITUTE OF LEGAL FINANCE AND MANAGEMENT)

2nd Floor
Marlowe House
109 Station Road
Sidcup
Kent DA15 7ET
Tel: 020 8302 2867
E-mail: info@ilfm.org.uk
Website: www.ilfm.org.uk

The ILFM is a not-for-profit professional institute dedicated to the education and support of legal finance and management professionals working within the legal sector. We encourage development by providing educational courses, member forum, recognised professional qualifications, training workshops, conferences and our bi-monthly magazine, Legal Abacus.

MEMBERSHIP
Member
Diploma Member – ILFM (Dip)
Associate Member – AILFM
Fellow Member – FILFM
Affiliated Professional Member

QUALIFICATION/EXAMINATIONS
Diploma – ILFM (Dip)
Certificate D1: Bookkeeping for Legal Finance Professionals
Certificate D2: Legal Finance Compliance & Accounts Rules
Associate – AILFM
Certificate A1: Accounting for Legal Finance Professionals
Certificate A2: Financial Management
Certificate A3: Legal Practice Management
Certificate A4: Tax for Legal Finance Professionals

DESIGNATORY LETTERS
ILFM(Dip), AILFM, FILFM, HonFILFM

LAW SOCIETY OF SCOTLAND

Atria One
144 Morrison Street
Edinburgh EH3 8EX
Tel: 0131 226 7411
Fax: 0131 225 2934
E-mail: careers@lawscot.org.uk
Website: www.lawscot.org.uk

The Law Society of Scotland is the professional body for Scottish solicitors. We set the route to qualification, regulate the profession to assure compliance and public trust and support our members with guidance, training and policy work. We work with schools and universities, running a variety of programmes to ensure we attract and accommodate aspiring solicitors from all communities and support them with their career choices.

All practising solicitors in Scotland must be members of the Society and must hold a current Practising Certificate which is renewed annually.

Students studying the LLB or Diploma can become Student Associates free of charge. We also run an Accredited Paralegal scheme.

QUALIFICATION/EXAMINATIONS
Please see the Qualifying and Education section of our website for detailed information. Any individual wishing to become a solicitor must follow an accredited route, which will usually involve undertaking an LLB degree in Scots Law followed by the Diploma in Professional Legal Practice, then a traineeship.

DESIGNATORY LETTERS
LLB/DipLP/NP

THE ACADEMY OF EXPERTS

3 Gray's Inn Square
Gray's Inn
London WC1R 5AH
Tel: 020 7430 0333
Fax: 020 7430 0666
E-mail: admin@academy-experts.org
Website: www.academy-experts.org

The Academy of Experts, multidisciplinary body established in 1987 to establish and promote high objective standards for those acting as expert witnesses. We act as an accrediting and professional body, offering training, technical guidance and representation. In addition we promote cost-efficient dispute resolution, maintaining a register of qualified dispute resolvers.

MEMBERSHIP
Associate Member
Associate Member (AMAE)
Full Member (MAE)
Fellow (FAE)
Practising Corporate Member
Dispute Resolver Member

QUALIFICATION/EXAMINATIONS
There are examinations for upgrade.

DESIGNATORY LETTERS
AMAE, MAE, FAE, QDR

LEISURE AND RECREATION MANAGEMENT
Membership of Professional Institutions and Associations

CHARTERED INSTITUTE FOR THE MANAGEMENT OF SPORT AND PHYSICAL ACTIVITY (CIMSPA)

Sportpark Loughborough University
3 Oakwood Drive
Loughborough
Leicestershire LE11 3QF
Tel: 01509 226474
Fax: 01509 226475
E-mail: info@cimspa.co.uk
Website: www.cimspa.co.uk

CIMSPA is the membership body for sport and physical activity professionals. We promote high standards and provide CPD as well as a wide range of training courses to our members in-house and at venues across the UK. We also work hard to influence government policy on behalf of our members.

MEMBERSHIP
Student affiliate
Student
Practitioner (exercise & fitness)
Associate (leisure operations)
Affiliate (leisure operations)
Affiliate (exercise & fitness)
Coach Advanced Practitioner
Coach Practitioner
Coaching Assistant Practitioner
Member
Chartered fellow
Chartered member

QUALIFICATION/EXAMINATIONS
National Pool Plant Operators Certificate
National Pool Plant Foundation Certificate
National Spa Pool Operators Certificate
Supervisory Management Certificate
Fitness Management Certificate
Health and Safety Management Certificate
Higher Professional Diploma in Sport and Recreation Management

Online Continuing Professional Development (CPD) (Entrance and Supervisory Level)
Online Continuing Professional Development (CPD) (Management Level)
Certificate in Leisure Operations (QCF) (1st4sport Level 2)
NVQ Award in Mechanical Ride Operation (QCF) (1st4sport Level 2)
NVQ Certificate in Active Leisure, Learning and Well-being Operational Services (QCF) (1st4sport Level 2)
Certificate in Leisure Management (QCF) (1st4sport Level 3)
NVQ Diploma in Leisure Management (QCF) (1st4sport Level 3)
NVQ Diploma in Sports Development (QCF) (1st4sport Level 3)
Award in Introductory Work in the Outdoors (QCF) (1st4sport Level 2)
NVQ Diploma in Outdoor Programmes (QCF) (1st4sport Level 3)
Award in Coordinating Sports Volunteers (QCF) (1st4sport Level 3)
Certificate in Managing Sports Volunteers (QCF) (1st4sport Level 3)

DESIGNATORY LETTERS
NPPO, RoPPPS, CPD, QCF

INSTITUTE OF GROUNDSMANSHIP

28 Stratford Office Village
Walker Avenue
Wolverton Mill East
Milton Keynes MK12 5TW
Tel: 01908 312511
Fax: 01908 311140
E-mail: iog@iog.org
Website: www.iog.org

The Institute of Groundsmanship is the only membership organisation supporting the whole of the grounds care industry. Serving the industry for more than 80 years, we provide a range of quality products, services and events including education, training and membership services, the national SALTEX exhibition, local information days, an annual conference and awards programme.

MEMBERSHIP
Student Member
Facility/Organisation Member
E-Member
Individual Member
Corporate and Corporate PLUS Member

QUALIFICATION/EXAMINATIONS
For details see: www.iog.org/training-training-courses.asp

IOG Learning – Qualifications

- Level 2 IOG Technical Awards in Turf Surface Maintenance
- • Level 2 IOG Technical Certificate in Turf Surface Maintenance
- • Level 3 IOG Supervisory Management
- • Level 3 IOG Technical Awards in Turf Surface Management
- • Level 3 IOG Technical Diploma in Turf Surface Management
- • Level 4 IOG Certificate in Sustainable Turf Management
- • Level 4 IOG Professional Certificate in Turf Surface Management
- • Level 5 IOG Professional Diploma in Turf Surface Management

- • Level 6 IOG Professional Certificate in Turf Surface Consulting
-
- **IOG Learning – Training**
-
- **Cricket**
- • Level 1 Cricket Pitches: In Season
- • Level 1 Cricket Pitches: Renovation
- • Level 2 Cricket Pitches: Applied Turf Culture
- • Level 3 Cricket Pitches: Advanced Turf Culture
- **Winter Pitches** (Football and Rugby)
- • Level 1 Winter Pitches: In Season (Maintenance)
- • Level 1 Winter Pitches: Renovation
- • Level 2 Winter Pitches: Applied Turf Culture
- • Level 3 Winter Pitches: Advanced Turf Culture
- **Bowling Green**
- • Level 1 Bowling Greens: Annual Maintenance
- • Level 2 Bowling Greens: Applied Turf Culture
- • Level 3 Bowling Greens: Advanced Turf Culture
- **Racecourses**
- • Level 1 Racecourse: Turf Maintenance
- • Level 2 Racecourse: Turf Management
- • Level 3 Racecourse: Management Skills
- **Artificial and 3G**
- • Level 2 Effective Maintenance of 3G Pitches
- • Level 2 Effective Maintenance of Artificial Surfaces
- • Level 2 Effective Maintenance of Reinforced Pitches
- • Level 1 Warm Season Grasses
- **General Grounds**
- • Level 2 Grounds: Maintenance and Management
- • Level 3 Grounds: Management

LIBRARIANSHIP AND INFORMATION WORK
Membership of Professional Institutions and Associations

CILIP, THE LIBRARY AND INFORMATION ASSOCIATION

7 Ridgmount Street
London WC1E 7AE
Tel: 020 7255 0500
Fax: 020 7255 0501
E-mail: memberservices@cilip.org.uk
Website: www.cilip.org.uk

CILIP is the leading voice for the information, knowledge management, and library profession. Our goal is to put information skills and professional values at the heart of a democratic, equal and prosperous society.

MEMBERSHIP
Member, Student, Registered Professional (ACLIP, MCLIP, FCLIP, Supplier Partner, Employer Partner, Learning Partner

QUALIFICATION/EXAMINATIONS
Application for levels of professional registration is through the submission of a portfolio of evidence meeting published criteria. Please contact the Institute for further information.

DESIGNATORY LETTERS
ACLIP, MCLIP, FCLIP

MANAGEMENT
Membership of Professional Institutions and Associations

ASSOCIATION FOR PROJECT MANAGEMENT

Ibis House
Regent Park
Summerleys Road
Princes Risborough
Buckinghamshire HP27 9LE
Tel: 0845 458 1944
E-mail: via website
Website: www.apm.org.uk

The association is a registered charity with over 19,500 individual and 500 corporate members making it the largest professional body of its kind in Europe. APM's mission statement is 'to develop and promote the professional disciplines of project and programme management for the public benefit'.

MEMBERSHIP
Student Member
Associate Member
Full Member (MAPM)
Fellow (FAPM)

Corporate Member
Honorary Member/ Fellow (HonFAPM)

QUALIFICATION/EXAMINATIONS
Project Fundamentals Qualification (PFQ)
Project Management Qualification (PMQ)
Project Management Qualification (PMQ) for PRINCE2 Practitioners
Practitioner Qualification (PQ)
Project Professional Qualification (PPQ)
Risk level 1
Risk level 2

Pan sector standard:
Registered Project Professional (RPP)
Chartered Project Professional (ChPP)
Higher Apprenticeship:
Level 4 Associate Project Manager Apprenticeship

The Level 6 Project Manager Degree Apprenticeship

DESIGNATORY LETTERS
MAPM, FAPM, HonFAPM, RPP, ChPP

ASSOCIATION OF CERTIFIED COMMERCIAL DIPLOMATS (ACCD)

Commercial Diplomats Regulation Authority
ACCD Global Headquarters
Central Administration Office
PO Box 50561, Canary Wharf
London E16 3WY
Tel: +44(0)8445 864249
E-mail: enquiries@chartereddiplomats.org.uk
Website: www.commercialdiplomats.org.uk

Association of Certified Commercial Diplomats plays an important role in the development, advancement, standardization, accreditation and better Regulation of Commercial Diplomats and Commercial Diplomatic Practice, and in advocating Responsible Commercial Diplomacy. The organisation was established as the independent regulation authority, and extra-territorial body for Commercial Diplomats and Institutions of Commercial Diplomacy. The umbrella of ACCD covers ambassadors, representatives of government, trade commissioners, facilitators, advisors and negotiators, arbitrators, negotiators of IIAs, policy-makers and government officials, involved in international trade, investment and commercial policy issues, vis a vis Commercial Service Officers, Trade or Commercial Counsellors, IIA experts, academia, private sector & NGO representatives, officials in government ministries, parastatals, corporations, academic, public and private institutions worldwide. ACCD's principal objectives are to advocate Responsible Commercial Diplomacy, strengthen Commercial Diplomatic Integrity, and provide accreditation and better regulation. Also, to advance the interests of members and practitioners as qualified, certified and competent Commercial Diplomats. As the global voice of Responsible Commercial Diplomacy, ACCD has overall responsibility, including the setting of policy and guidelines, as well as the qualification and accreditation procedures for the commercial diplomatic profession. ACCD is non-partisan, not-for-profit, independent of government, and uniquely the professional accreditation and regulatory body for Commercial Diplomats.

MEMBERSHIP
REGULATED MEMBERSHIP
Affiliated Professional Associate
Associate
Member
Fellow

QUALIFICATION/EXAMINATIONS
ACCD REGULATED ADVANCED AND POST QUALIFICATION EXAMINATIONS AND QUALIFICATIONS
Certificate of Competency
Advanced Certificate of Competency
Master Certificate of Competency
Advanced Master Certificate of Competency*
ACCD REGULATED ACCREDITATIONS
Associate Expert (AE)
Qualified Advocate (QA)
Qualified Policy Advocate (QPA)
Qualified Certified Diplomat (QCD)
Chartered Diplomat (C. Dipl)

DESIGNATORY LETTERS
ACDipl, MCDipl, FCDipl, AE, QA, (QPA), QCD, C. Dipl

AUA

AUA National Office
University of Manchester
Sackville Street Building
Manchester M1 3WE
Tel: 0161 275 2063
Fax: 0161 275 2036
E-mail: aua@aua.ac.uk
Website: www.aua.ac.uk

As a member-led organisation with over 3,500 members, AUA promotes best practice in higher education management and exists to advance and promote professional recognition and development of those who work in higher and further education by encouraging and fostering sound methods of leadership, management and administration, through a range of professional development initiatives.

AUA members are individually and collectively committed to:

- the continuous development of their own and others' professional knowledge, skills and practices;
- actively championing equality of educational and professional opportunity;
- the advancement of higher education through the robust application of professional knowledge, skills and practices;
- the highest standards of fair, ethical and transparent professional behaviours.

AUA is at the forefront of professional development in higher education and has developed a sector-wide framework to support the development of professional services colleagues. Through continuing professional development, individuals, teams and institutions can foster skills and behaviours associated with the profession. AUA also holds the largest professional development annual conference in the UK higher education calendar.

MEMBERSHIP
Member (MAUA)
Retired / Student Member (MAUA)

QUALIFICATION/EXAMINATIONS
Postgraduate Certificate in Higher Education Administration, Management and Leadership (PG Cert)
A self-directed, independent, work-based learning programme for higher education professionals working within UK higher education administration.

BUSINESS MANAGEMENT ASSOCIATION

North House
5 Parkins Close
Colliers End
Ware
Hertfordshire SG11 1ED

The Business Management Association is a professional body for business owners and managers. We promote the aims and interests of the small business sector internationally, provide information and advice to our members, encourage networking between members, and seek to provide members with advanced knowledge, skill and qualifications in several aspects of management.

MEMBERSHIP
Affiliate (AffBMA)
Associate (ABMA)
Member (MBMA)
Fellow (FBMA)
Companion (CBMA)
Certified Manager (CertMgr)
Certified Master of Management (CMMgt)
Certified Master of Business Administration (CMBA)
Certified Doctor of Business Administration (CDBA)

DIPLOMATIC ACADEMY OF EUROPE AND THE ATLANTIC

ACCD Global Headquarters
PO Box 50561, Canary Wharf
Greater London E16 3WY

Diplomatic Academy of Europe and the Atlantic is an authoritative knowledge-based international professional diplomatic institution whose activities include advanced research, training and development, provision of advanced mandatory qualifying and post-qualification commercial diplomatic training and capacity building, and contribution to responsible commercial diplomatic practice and service. The Diplomatic Academy is a key independent extra-territorial organisation established for the advancement of greater knowledge and skills in Commercial Diplomacy. DAEA offers a complete portfolio of specialized mandatory programmes on commercial diplomacy.

MEMBERSHIP
Fellow of the Diplomatic Academy (FDA)

QUALIFICATION/EXAMINATIONS
Certificate of Competency
Advanced Certificate of Competency
Master Certificate of Competency
Advanced Master Certificate of Competency

FACULTY OF PROFESSIONAL BUSINESS AND TECHNICAL MANAGEMENT

Office 13275
PO Box 4336
Manchester
United Kingdom M61 0BW
Tel: 01386 277973
E-mail: info@pbtm.org.uk
Website: www.pbtm.org.uk

FPBTM was founded in 1983 to forge the link between business and technology. We give professional recognition to the knowledge and skills of managers in business and technology, supporting lifelong learning to help members fulfil their career ambitions and develop their potential.

MEMBERSHIP
Student Member (SFPBTM)
Technician Member (TMFPBTM)
Associate Member (AMFPBTM)
Member (MFPBTM)
Fellow (FFPBTM)
Companion (CFPBTM)

INSTITUTE OF ADMINISTRATIVE MANAGEMENT

Grosvenor House
Suite 4.02
Central Park
Telford
Shropshire TF2 9TW
Tel: 01952 797396
E-mail: info@instam.org
Website: www.instam.org

The IAM is one of the oldest UK professional bodies, championing administration and management. It provides professional recognition, and professional development through CPD opportunities and qualifications. As part of the IQ group (IQ: Awarding Organisation & IQ Verify: UKAS Accredited Body), it is well equipped to aid businesses.

MEMBERSHIP
IAM Student
Non-IAM Student
Affiliate
Associate (AInstAM)
Member (MInstAM)
Fellow (FInstAM)
Honorary (HInstAM) – by invitation only
Companion (CInstAM) - by invitation only

QUALIFICATION/EXAMINATIONS
IQ IAM Level 2 Diploma in Business Administration
IQ IAM Level 2 Diploma in Team Leading
IQ Level 3 Award in Grant-funding Administration
IQ IAM Level 3 Award in Professional PA and Administration Skills
IQ IAM Level 3 Diploma in Business Administration
IQ IAM Level 3 Diploma in Business and Administrative Management
IQ Level 3 Diploma in Customer Service
IQ IAM Level 3 Diploma in Management
IQ IAM Level 4 Certificate in Office and Administration Management
IQ IAM Level 4 Certificate in Principles of Business Administration
IQ IAM Level 4 Diploma in Business and Administrative Management
IQ IAM Level 4 NVQ Diploma in Business Administration
IQ IAM Level 4 NVQ Diploma in Management
IQ IAM Level 5 Diploma in Business and Administrative Management
IQ IAM Level 5 NVQ Diploma in Management and Leadership
IQ IAM Level 6 Diploma in Business and Administrative Management

DESIGNATORY LETTERS
AInstAM, MInstAM, FInstAM, HInstAM, CInstAM

INSTITUTE OF CONSULTING

Management House
Cottingham Road
Corby NN17 1TT
Tel: 01536 207360
E-mail: membership@ibconsulting.org.uk
Website: www.iconsulting.org.uk

The Institute of Consulting was formed in 2007 by the merger of the Institute of Business Advisers and the Institute of Management Consultancy, and we are the professional body for business consultants and advisers. Our aim is to raise the standards of professional practice in support of better business performance.

MEMBERSHIP
Affiliate
Associate (AIBC)
Member (MIBC)
Fellow (FIBC)
Certified Business Advisor (CBA)
Certified Management Consultant (CMC)

Practice Member (corporate membership)

QUALIFICATION/EXAMINATIONS
Award in Professional Consulting (Level 5) (QCF)
Certificate in Professional Consulting (Level 5) (QCF)
Diploma in Professional Consulting (Level 5) (QCF)
Award in Business Support (Level 5) (QCF)
Certificate in Business Support (Level 5) (QCF)
Diploma in Business Support (Level 5) (QCF)

Award in Professional Consulting (Level 7) (QCF)
Certificate in Professional Consulting (Level 7) (QCF)
Diploma in Professional Consulting (Level 7) (QCF)
Certified Management Consultant Award (CMC)
Certified Business Advisor Award (CBA)

DESIGNATORY LETTERS
AIBC, MIBC, FIBC

INSTITUTE OF DIRECTORS

116 Pall Mall
London SW1Y 5ED
Tel: 020 7766 8866
E-mail: professionaldev@iod.com
Website: www.iod.com/development

The IoD represents professional leaders, with individual members ranging from entrepreneurs of start-up companies to CEOs of multinational organisations. The Institute's principal objectives are to advance the interests of its members as company directors, and to provide them with business facilities and a variety of services.

MEMBERSHIP
Student
Associate Member

Member (MIoD)
Fellow (FIoD)

QUALIFICATION/EXAMINATIONS
Certificate in Company Direction (CertIoD)
Diploma in Company Direction (DipIoD)
Chartered Director (C Dir)

DESIGNATORY LETTERS
MIoD, FIoD, C Dir

INSTITUTE OF LEADERSHIP & MANAGEMENT

Pacific House
Relay Point
Burntwood
Tamworth B77 5PA
Tel: 01543 266867
Fax: 01543 266893
E-mail: customer@i-l-m.com
Website: www.institutelm.com

The ILM supports, develops and informs leaders and managers at every stage of their career. With our broad range of industry-leading qualifications, membership services and learning resources, the ILM provides flexible development solutions that can be blended to meet the specific needs of employers and learners.

MEMBERSHIP
Studying Member
Professional Member

QUALIFICATION/EXAMINATIONS
Management
Principles of Team Leading including Foundation Award in Management Practice (Level 2)
Award, Certificate in Effective Team Member Skills (Level 2)

Award, Certificate in Leadership and Team Skills (Level 2)

NVQ Certificate in Team Leading (Level 2)

Certificate in Team Leading (Level 2)

NVQ Certificate in Management (Level 3)

Certificate in Effective Management (Level 3)

Certificate in Principles of Leadership and Management (Level 3)

Award, Certificate and Diploma in Leadership and Management (Level 4)

Diploma in Principles of Leadership and Management (Level 5)

NVQ Diploma in Management (Level 5)

Award in Management (Level 6)

NVQ Diploma in Management (Level 7)

Diploma in Strategic Leadership and Executive Management (Level 7)

Award, Certificate and Diploma in Executive Management (Level 7)

Leadership

Certificate in Leadership (Level 3)

Award in Leadership (Level 4)

Award, Certificate and Diploma in Strategic Leadership (Level 7)

Leadership and Management

Award, Certificate and Diploma in Leadership and Management (Level 3)

Award, Certificate and Diploma in Leadership and Management (Level 5)

Coaching and Mentoring

Certificate in Coaching and Mentoring (Level 3)

Certificate and Diploma in Coaching and Mentoring (Level 5)

Certificate and Diploma in Coaching Supervision (Level 7)

Certificate and Diploma in Executive Coaching and Leadership Mentoring (Level 7)

Specialist Management Qualifications

Environmental Management

Facilities Management

Equality and Diversity

Managing Volunteers

Sales Management

Waste Management

Business and Enterprise

Certificate in Enterprise (Level 2)

Award and Certificate in Enterprise and Entrepreneurship (Level 3)

Award in Management (Level 5)

Certificate and Diploma in Social Enterprise Support (Level 5)

Specialist Management Qualifications

Operational management

Service improvement

Waste management

Equality and diversity

Volunteer management

Management consultancy

Staff and organisational development

Quality improvement

Scottish Vocational Qualifications (SVQs)

SVQ 2 in Team Leading (Scottish Level 5)

SVQ 3 in Management (Scottish Level 7)

SVQ 4 in Management (Scottish Level 9)

SVQ 5 in Management (Scottish Level 11)

INSTITUTE OF MANAGEMENT SERVICES

Brooke House
24 Dam Street
Lichfield
Staffordshire WS13 6AA
Tel: 01543 266909
Fax: 01543 257848
E-mail: admin@ims-productivity.com
Website: www.ims-productivity.com

QUALIFICATION/EXAMINATIONS
IMS Certificate

DESIGNATORY LETTERS
AMS, MMS, FMS

INSTITUTE OF VALUE MANAGEMENT

PO Box 101
Ledbury
Herefordshire HR8 9JW
Tel: 01531 631444
E-mail: secretary@ivm.org.uk
Website: www.ivm.org.uk

The Institute aims to establish Value Management as an all-encompassing strategy for achieving value in every sector of the economy and to provide support in the innovative use of value management techniques.

MEMBERSHIP

Corporate – This grade is for organisations that use or promote value management and want to make a corporate statement to that effect. A Corporate Member may nominate up to 10 members of staff who will have full voting rights. Corporate members may use the designatory letters AIVM (or MIVM if they meet the requirements and make a successful application).

Student – This grade is for students studying full time for a UK qualification. Student members are not eligible to use any designatory letters.

Trainee – This grade is for individuals who have completed either an IVM accredited Foundation Course in Value Management in the previous 6 months or a Management of Value (MoV) Foundation Course in the previous 6 months. Trainee membership is limited to two years. Trainee Members are not eligible to use designatory letters.

Associate – This grade is open to individuals who have a demonstrable interest in Value Management and who either promote, use or are associated with Value Management. Associate Members may use the designatory letters AIVM.

Member – This grade is open to individuals who have considerable sector knowledge and skills in their profession and who meet at least one of the following requirements:

- Hold a QVA or CVA qualification
- Have successfully completed an IVM accredited VM2 Course

- Have successfully completed a Management of Value (MoV) Practitioner course
- Have a minimum of 3 years' experience working in a Value Management environment
- Hold a relevant professional qualification in Lean, Benefits or Project Management

Members may use the post nominals MIVM.

Fellow – Fellowship of the Institute of Value Management is the most senior grade available and is reserved for those who have reached the highest echelons in their career. It is open to those who meet at least one of the following requirements:

- Have demonstrated significant experience or contribution to the field of Value Management
- Hold a current PVM qualification

Fellows may use the post nominals FIVM.

QUALIFICATION/EXAMINATIONS

IVM Certification Board – The IVM's Certification Board is an independent body whose role is to implement and control the certification and training policies developed by the IVM and the European Governing Board (EGB), representing all the European value associations.

Certification Levels

There are three levels of recognised certification based on experience and knowledge:

- Qualified Value Associate (QVA) – (Europe)
- Professional in Value Management (PVM) – (Europe). This qualification signals competence to lead value studies in a variety of environments and contribute to the development of VM strategies.
- Trainer in Value Management (TVM) – (Europe). In order to develop competence to train to an appropriate standard, the qualification of Trainer in Value Management (TVM) has been introduced. This qualification is only available for PVMs with at least 2 years experience, who have completed an approved train the trainer course.

DESIGNATORY LETTERS
AIVM, MIVM, FIVM, HFIVM

INSTITUTE OF WORKPLACE AND FACILITIES MANAGEMENT

1st Floor South
Charringtons House
The Causeway
Bishops Stortford
Hertfordshire CM23 2ER
Tel: 01279 712651
E-mail: qualifications@iwfm.org.uk
Website: www.iwfm.org.uk

The IWFM is a community of over 17,000 workplace and facilities management professionals. We share best practice and knowledge with the profession and support our member's professional development through internationally recognised, regulated qualifications, short courses and training.

MEMBERSHIP
Affiliate
Associate (AIWFM)
Member (MIWFM)
Certified Member (CIWFM)
Fellow (FIWFM)
Corporate Member

QUALIFICATION/EXAMINATIONS
IWFM Level 2 Certificate in Facilities Services
IWFM Level 2 Certificate in Facilities Services Principles
IWFM Level 3 Award in Facilities Management
IWFM Level 3 Certificate in Facilities Management

IWFM Level 3 Certificate in Facilities Management Practice
IWFM Level 3 Diploma in Facilities Management
IWFM Level 4 Award in Facilities Management
IWFM Level 4 Certificate in Facilities Management
IWFM Level 4 Diploma in Facilities Management
IWFM Level 5 Award in Facilities Management
IWFM Level 5 Certificate in Facilities Management
IWFM Level 5 Diploma in Facilities Management
IWFM Level 6 Award in Facilities Management
IWFM Level 6 Certificate in Facilities Management
IWFM Level 6 Extended Diploma in Facilities Management
IWFM Level 7 Certificate in Facilities Management
IWFM Level 7 Extended Diploma in Facilities Management

DESIGNATORY LETTERS
AIWFM, MIWFM, CIWFM, FIWFM

INTERNATIONAL PROFESSIONAL MANAGERS ASSOCIATION

5 Starnes Court
Union Street
Maidstone
Kent ME14 1EB
Tel: 01622 672867
Fax: 01622 755149
E-mail: admin@ipma.co.uk
Website: www.ipma.co.uk

The IPMA is an international examining, licensing and regulatory professional body, which, through its qualifying examinations, enables practising managers to participate in and be part of the process of improving managerial performance and effectiveness in all areas of business, industry and public administration.

MEMBERSHIP
Graduate Member (GRD PMA)
Licentiate Member (LMPMA)
Certified Associate (AMPMA)
Certified Member (MPMA)
Certified Fellow (FPMA)

QUALIFICATION/EXAMINATIONS
Certified International Professional Manager (CIPM) examinations
Foundation: Economics, Legal Environment of Business, Information Communication and Technology, Business Management, Statistical Methods for Business, Principles of Finance

Intermediate: Business Marketing, Entrepreneurship, Corporate Law, Management Accounting, Advanced Management Practice, Managing People
Professional Level 1: Human Resource Management, Management Decision Making, Organisational Behaviour, Information Systems Management, Operations Management
Professional Level 2: Business Policy and Strategic Management, Corporate Finance and Risk Management, Organisation Change and Development, Multinational Business Management, Case Study and a Project

DESIGNATORY LETTERS
GRD PMA, LMPMA, AMPMA, MPMA, FPMA, CIPM

THE ASSOCIATION OF BUSINESS EXECUTIVES

5th Floor, CI Tower
St Georges Square
New Malden
Surrey KT3 4TE
Tel: 020 8329 2930
Fax: 020 8329 2945

ABE is a professional membership body and examination board. We develop business and management qualifications at Levels 4, 5, 6 & 7 on the QCF framework. ABE's range of OFQUAL accredited qualifications provide progression routes to degree and Master's programmes worldwide.

MEMBERSHIP
Affiliate Member
Student Member
Associate Member (AMABE)
Member (MABE)

QUALIFICATION/EXAMINATIONS
Diploma Levels 4, 5 and 6 in:

Business Management
Management of Information Systems (Pathway)
Financial Management (Pathway)
Human Resource Management
Marketing Management
Travel, Tourism and Hospitality Management
Diploma in Business Development (Level 7)
Diploma in Business Start-Up and Entrepreneurship (Level 4)

DESIGNATORY LETTERS
AMABE, MABE

THE CHARTERED MANAGEMENT INSTITUTE

Customer Service Department
Management House
Cottingham Road
Corby
Northants NN17 1TT
Tel: 01536 204222
Fax: 01536 201651
E-mail: enquiries@managers.org.uk
Website: www.managers.org.uk

CMI is the only chartered professional body in the UK dedicated to promoting the highest standards of management and leadership excellence. With a member community of 130,000, CMI gives managers and leaders, and their organisations, the skills they need to improve their performance and create an impact.

MEMBERSHIP
Affiliate
Associate (ACMI)
Member (MCMI)
Fellow (FCMI)
Foundation Chartered Manager (fCMgr)
Chartered Member (CMgr MCMI)
Chartered Fellow (CMgr FCMI)
Companion (CCMI)
Chartered Companion (CMgr CCMI)

QUALIFICATION/EXAMINATIONS
The breadth and depth of our management and leadership qualification portfolio is unmatched. We have over 60 individual qualifications ranging from team leading, to strategic management to coaching and mentoring to name a few.

To support your development we have a wide range of online and hardcopy resources and materials, including ManagementDirect and Pathways Workbooks. With CMI Membership you can also enjoy benefits of a Career Development Centre, mentoring and professional development.

We have a network of more than 500 Centres delivering our qualifications so you can always find somewhere to study that's convenient for you.

DESIGNATORY LETTERS
ACMI, MCMI, FCMI, fCMgr, CMgr MCMI, CMgr FCMI, CCMI, CMgr CCMI

THE INSTITUTE OF COMMERCIAL MANAGEMENT

ICM House
Yeoman Road
Ringwood
Hampshire BH24 3FA
Tel: 01202 490555
E-mail: info@icm.education
Website: www.icm.education

Established in 1979, the Institute is the leading professional body for Commercial and Business Development Managers. It provides examining and assessment services for those undertaking business and management studies and offers in excess of 200 qualifications. The Institute works with public and private sector education and training providers in more than 100 countries.

MEMBERSHIP
Student Membership and Professional Membership

QUALIFICATION/EXAMINATIONS
ICM Qualifications cover the following areas: Accounting & Finance; Business Studies; Commercial Management; Hospitality Management; Human Resource Development; Journalism; Management Studies; Maritime Management; Marketing Management; Retail Management; Sales Management; Travel & Tourism

THE INSTITUTE OF MANAGEMENT SPECIALISTS

Office 13275
PO Box 4336
Manchester
United Kingdom M61 0BW
Tel: 01386 277973
E-mail: info@instituteofmanagementspecialists.org.uk
Website: www.instituteofmanagementspecialists.org.uk

The Institute of Management Specialists was founded in 1971 to give professional recognition to the knowledge and skills of managers and specialists. The Institute encourages management excellence and specialist expertise, and supports lifelong learning to help members fulfil their career ambitions.

Specialised Manager Awards are available in a range of specialised areas and IMS offers a CPD (Continuous Professional Development) programme leading to Certified Specialist Manager status.

MEMBERSHIP
Student Member (StudIMS)

Associate Member (AMIMS)
Member (MIMS)
Fellow (FIMS)
Companion (CompIMS)

QUALIFICATION/EXAMINATIONS
Diploma of Management and Leadership
Advanced Diploma of Management and Leadership
Professional Diploma of Management and Leadership
Executive Diploma of Management and Leadership

THE OXBRIDGE: THE OXFORD AND CAMBRIDGE INTERNATIONAL PROFESSIONAL QUALIFICATIONS

Connaugh House
Benarth Road
Conwy
Wales LL32 8UB
Tel: +44 7502 471429
E-mail: admin@oxbridge-uk.org
Website: www.oxbridge-uk.org

We have a simple mission: to help learners make more of their lives through learning. Whether it's in the classroom or in the workplace, learning is the key to improving life chances. Oxbridge together leading names in education provide a blend of ssessment to make learning more engaging and effective.

MEMBERSHIP
Member
Awarded to persons who have less than 3 years' experience.
Certified Associate
This grade is awarded to those individuals who hold the relevant qualifications at undergraduate level and more than 3 years of experience in their profession.
Certified Fellow

This grade is awarded to those individuals who have achieved the relevant qualifications at postgraduate level and have more than 10 years of experience in their professions and are operating at a senior level.
Specialist Doctorate (Drs)
This grade is awarded to those individuals who have achieved the relevant qualifications at doctoral level and have more than 25 years of experience in their profession of expertise.
Specialist Doctorate of Oxbridge is granted by Executive Board approval after an oral defence. The Executive Board fellowship reviews are carried out every 3 months.
If you wish to be considered for any of the above membership awards please email to: admin@ox-bridge-uk.org

Membership Fees and Renewals

We welcome all new members to Oxbridge giving you immediate access to all the benefits of being an Oxbridge member for one year.

QUALIFICATION/EXAMINATIONS

THE OXBRIDGE QUALIFICATIONS

Oxbridge offers recognition, accreditation and validation of work-based learning assessments. An award gives a reliable indication of an individual learner's knowledge, skills or understanding and are only awarded to a learner who has demonstrated that they have a specified level of attainment through a reliable assessment method. A certificate naming the qualification is awarded to successful learners.

A qualification sets out what an individual need to know or be able to do in order to be given (awarded) that qualification. Most vocational qualifications are made up of a number of units of learning, each one covering a specific area or topic. In some qualifications, particularly the smaller ones, a learner may have to do all of the units to get the qualification. In the majority of vocational qualifications some of these units will be required units (mandatory) and there will be number of other units to choose from (optional).

Each unit has a number of statements that set out what the learner needs to know or be able to do. These are called the learning outcomes and they are checked (assessed) in a number of different ways. It might involve an on-line test, an observation of what the learner is doing, a written assignment, project work, an exam or compiling a portfolio of evidence demonstrating what the learning knows or can do.

Qualifications are respected by learners, employers, further and higher education and many others. Awarding bodies are responsible for ensuring that the quality of their qualifications is maintained at a high level.

Quality assurance is built in throughout the life of a qualification. As they are writing a qualification, an awarding body has to check it out with teachers, subject specialists, employers and others. Before it is sent to the regulator, the awarding body has to make sure that the qualification meets certain technical rules and employers and others support the qualification.

The assessments are crucial to the quality of the qualification and need to be rigorously checked. If the awarding body writes and arranges the assessment, for example an examination, they will have lots of internal checks. The examiners marking the exams will have their marking checked by senior subject experts and staff in the awarding body.

Most vocational qualifications are assessed by the staff in the school, college or training provider (i.e. the Centre) where a learner is studying. The awarding body will check that these assessment decisions are correct in a number of ways. One of the most common ways is for the awarding body to appoint a subject expert to visit the centre.

The qualifications award levels are as follows:

Level 1: Basic Certificate

Level 2: Intermediate Certificate

Level 3: Certificate

Level 4: Diploma

Level 5: Higher Diploma

Level 6: Graduate Diploma

Level 7: Postgraduate Diploma

Level 8: Doctorate Diploma

The good news is that, there are quite a number of these programs and on top of that, they are being offered as certificates, or diploma.

If you are looking to start a new career, further studies, or enhancing of your current job, below is a list of the work-based learnings to select from.

The assessment is carried out in the following areas:

Agriculture

Agriculture biotechnology

Plantation

Horticulture

Fisheries

Landscape horticulture

Agriculture business

Agriculture economic

AGRO forestry

AGRO tourism

Eco tourism

Vocational education

Early childhood education management

Entrepreneur development

Humana relations

Training and development

Business Administration Specialist

Teaching English to speakers of other Languages (TESOL)

Computer Specialist

Radiation Therapist

Nuclear Technician

Dental Hygienist

Fashion Designer

Nuclear Medicine Technologist

Commercial Pilot

Electrical and Electronics Repairman

Web Developer
Cardiovascular Technologist
Electrician
Landscape technician
HVAC Technician
Surgical Technologist
Medical Laboratory Technician
Bricklayer
Chemical Plant Operator
Derrickman
Executive Housekeeper
Hospitality management
Firefighter
Locomotive Engineer
Personal Trainer
Police Officer
Art/Design
Auto Repair Training
Automation control
AutoCAD
Aviation
Bookkeeping, Accounting and Auditing
Blacksmithing
Business and marketing management
Business and Office management
Carpentry
Catering and hotel management
Culling arts
Collision Repair
Computer networking management
Construction Management
Daycare management
Diesel Mechanics
Early Child Care Education
Engineering-Mechanical, Civil, Electric and Electronic, Chemical among others.
Food and Beverage Management
Hairstyling, Cosmetics and Beautification
Health care and social assistant
Home inspector
Interior Design
Industrial Maintenance
Massage Therapy
Medical Billing
Medical Transcription
Organisational/Leadership Skills
Project management
Paralegal Studies
Paramedic-EMT
Practical Nursing
Precision Manufacturing and Machining

Pharmacy Technician
Photography
Private investigator
Property Management
Psychology and Counselling
Real Estate Appraisal
Small Business Management
Small Engine Repair
Tax Preparation
Travel Agent
Truck driving
Veterinary Technician
Welding and Fabrication
Architectural and Structural CADD and Graphics Technician
Boilermaker
Construction Estimating
Construction Operations
Construction Supervision
Gas fitting
Heat and Frost Insulator
Hydronic Technician
Industrial Electrician
Ironworker – Reinforcing
Metal Fabricator
Piping foundation
Pump Maintenance
Roadworks Maintenance
Security Systems Technician
Sheet Metal Worker Foundation
Security Systems Technician
Telecommunications Technician
Wireless Communications Technician
CNC Machinist Technician
Fire Protection Inspection and Testing
Heating, Ventilation, Air Conditioning and Refrigeration Technician
Machinist
Millwright
Power and Process Engineering
Refrigeration Mechanic Foundation
Refrigeration Systems
Aircraft Gas Turbine Technician
Airport Operations
Logistic management operations

DESIGNATORY LETTERS
MOXBRIDGE (MEMBER), AOXBRIDGE (ASSOCIATE), FOXBRIDGE (FELLOE), DRS (SPECIALIST DOCTORATE)

THE SOCIETY OF BUSINESS PRACTITIONERS

PO Box 11
Sandbach
Cheshire CW11 3GE
Tel: 01270 526339
Fax: 01270 526339
E-mail: info@mamsasbp.org.uk
Website: www.mamsasbp.org.uk

SBP is an International Examination Board founded in 1956 by experienced educationalists and executives to fulfil a need to set standards in business practice achieved by examinations/assessments. Inexperienced and mature students should be able to follow careers in further education and/or be proficient in employment and receive the benefits of membership.

MEMBERSHIP
Student (StuSBP)
Member (MSBP)
Certified Professional Manager (CPMSBP)
Honorary Fellow
Professional Memberships *(Senior Professional Qualifications)*
Associateship (ASBP)
Licentiateship (LSBP)
Graduateship (GSBP)
Fellowship (FSBP)
These are certified competency-based Membership Awards open to persons occupied in business practice who are considered suitable by the Membership Committee.
CPD programmes are also offered for the Asia region.

QUALIFICATION/EXAMINATIONS
Diploma in Business Administration
Advanced Diploma in Business Administration
PGDip in Business Administration
PGDip in International Marketing
Diploma in Computer Studies
Advanced Diploma in Computer Studies
GradDip in IT & E-Commerce
GradDip in Entrepreneurship
Advanced Diploma in Accounting
Diploma & Advanced Diploma in Marketing Management (Joint Award with the Managing & Marketing Sales Association)

DESIGNATORY LETTERS
StuSBP, MSBP, CPMSBP, ASBP, LSBP, GSBP, FSBP

MANUFACTURING
Membership of Professional Institutions and Associations

THE INSTITUTE OF MANUFACTURING

OFFICE 13275
PO BOX 4336
MANCHESTER
United Kingdom M61 0BW
Tel: 01386 277973
E-mail: info@instituteofmanufacturing.org.uk
Website: www.instituteofmanufacturing.org.uk

The Institute of Manufacturing was founded in 1978 to give professional recognition to the knowledge and skills of people in all aspects of manufacturing. The Institute supports lifelong learning to help members fulfill their career ambitions and develop their potential.

Certified Manufacturing Practitioner award is available to recognise management knowledge with manufacturing experience.

MEMBERSHIP
Student Member (StudIManf)
Associate Member (AMIManf)
Member (MIManf)
Fellow (FIManf)
Companion (CompIManf)

QUALIFICATION/EXAMINATIONS
Diploma in Manufacturing Management
Advanced Diploma in Manufacturing Management
Professional Diploma Diploma in Manufacturing Management
Executive Diploma in Manufacturing Management
Certified Manufacturing Practitioner

MARKETING AND SALES
Membership of Professional Institutions and Associations

INSTITUTE OF SALES MANAGEMENT (ISM)

18 King William Street
London EC4N 7BP
Tel: 020 167 4790
E-mail: info@ismprofessional.com
Website: www.ismprofessional.com

Founded in 1911, the ISM is the worldwide representative body for sales people. To help members improve their skills set the ISMM provide qualifications, approved by Ofqual, the UK Government's regulatory body for education. Written by qualified and experienced sales professionals they cover the salesperson's career right up to sales director level.

MEMBERSHIP
Student
Associate
Executive
Leader
Master

QUALIFICATION/EXAMINATIONS
Level 1 Award in Selling Lawfully and Ethically
Level 1 Award in Understanding the Sales Cycle
Level 1 Award in Understanding Marketing
Level 1 Award in Communication Skills in Sales
Level 1 Award in Sales and Marketing
Level 2 Award in Understanding Laws and Ethics of Selling
Level 2 Award in Understanding Marketing
Level 2 Award in Understanding Buyer Behaviour
Level 2 Award in Sales Targets
Level 2 Award in Selling to Customers
Level 2 Award in Understanding Selling to Customers
Level 2 Award in Telesales
Level 2 Certificate in Sales and Marketing

Level 3 Award in Preparing and Delivering a Sales Presentation
Level 3 Award in Handling Objections, Negotiating and Closing Deals
Level 3 Award in Understanding Influences on Buyer Behaviour
Level 3 Award in Understanding customer segmentation and profiling
Level 3 Award in Understanding sales and marketing in organisations
Level 3 Award in Using market information for sales
Level 3 Award in Time and territory management for sales people
Level 3 Award in Planning for professional development
Level 3 Award in Prospecting for new business
Level 3 Award in Sales pipeline management
Level 3 Certificate in Sales and Marketing
Level 3 Diploma in Sales and Marketing
Level 4 Award in Managing responsible selling
Level 4 Award in Understanding segmentation, targeting and positioning
Level 4 Award in Managing a sales team
Level 4 Award in Operational sales planning
Level 4 Award in Sales negotiations
Level 4 Award in Analysing the marketing environment
Level 4 Award in Finance for sales managers
Level 4 Award in Writing and delivering a sales proposal

Level 4 Certificate in Sales and Marketing Management
Level 4 Diploma in Sales and Marketing Management
Level 5 Award in Understanding and developing customer accounts
Level 5 Award in Understanding the integrated functions of sales and marketing
Level 5 Award in Sales forecasts and target setting
Level 5 Award in Leading a team
Level 5 Award in Motivation and compensation for sales teams
Level 5 Award in Coaching and mentoring
Level 5 Award in Designing, planning and managing sales territories
Level 5 Award in Analysing the financial potential and performance of customer accounts
Level 5 Award in Relationship management for account managers
Level 5 Award in Bid and tender management for account managers

Level 5 Award in Developing a product portfolio
Level 5 Certificate in Sales and Account Management
Level 5 Diploma in Sales and Account Management
Level 6 Award in Leading a culture for responsible selling
Level 6 Award in Leadership and management in sales
Level 6 Award in Planning and implementing sales and marketing strategy
Level 6 Award in Salesforce organisation
Level 6 Award in Sales forecasting and budgeting
Level 6 Award in Developing strategic relationships with major customers
Level 6 Award in Managing sales-related change
Level 6 Award in Developing and using customer insight
Level 6 Certificate in Strategic Sales Management
Level 6 Diploma in Strategic Sales Management

DESIGNATORY LETTERS
AInstSMM, MInstSMM, FInstSMM

MANAGING AND MARKETING SALES ASSOCIATION EXAMINATION BOARD

PO Box 11
Sandbach
Cheshire CW11 3GE
Tel: 01270 526339
Fax: 01270 526339
E-mail: info@mamsasbp.org.uk
Website: www.mamsasbp.org.uk

MAMSA is an international Examination Board offering qualifications in Sales, Marketing and Management and its senior specialist Diploma in Marketing Strategy. The importance of 'Customer Service' is emphasized throughout all the programmes.

MEMBERSHIP
Graduate (GradMAMSA)
Graduate Affiliate (GradAfMAMSA)
Professional (MMAMSA)
Fellow (FMAMSA)

QUALIFICATION/EXAMINATIONS
Standard Diploma in Salesmanship

Certificate in Sales Marketing
Higher Diploma in Marketing
Advanced Diploma in Sales Management
Certificate in Marketing Strategy
Diploma in Marketing Strategy & Management (Hypothesis/Thesis)
Diploma in Sales and Marketing Practices (Joint Award with the Society of Business Practitioners)
A CPD programme is also offered

DESIGNATORY LETTERS
GradMAMSA, GradAfMAMSA, MMAMSA, FMAMSA

MRS (THE MARKET RESEARCH SOCIETY)

The Old Trading House
15 Northburgh Street
London EC1V 0JR
Tel: 020 7490 4911
Fax: 020 7490 0608
E-mail: profdevelopment@mrs.org.uk
Website: www.mrs.org.uk

The Market Research Society (MRS) is the UK Professional Body for research, insight and analytics. We recognise 5,000 individual members and over 500 accredited Company Partners in over 50 countries. MRS supports the sector with specialist training and qualifications, membership, company accreditation, cutting-edge conferences, awards and advice on best practice.

MEMBERSHIP
Student Member
Member (MMRS)
Certified Member (CMRS)

Fellow (FMRS)
Honorary Fellow (Hon. FMRS)

QUALIFICATION/EXAMINATIONS
MRS Certificate in Market and Social Research
MRS Certificate in Interviewing Skills
MRS Advanced Certificate in Market and Social Research Practice
MRS Diploma in Market and Social Research Practice

DESIGNATORY LETTERS
MMRS, CMRS, FMRS, Hon. FMRS

THE CHARTERED INSTITUTE OF MARKETING

Moor Hall
Cookham
Maidenhead
Berkshire SL6 9QH
Tel: 01628 427500
Fax: 01628 427158
E-mail: qualifications@cim.co.uk
Website: www.cim.co.uk

The Chartered Institute of Marketing is the leading international professional marketing body, with 47,000 members worldwide. We aim to improve the skills of marketing practitioners, enabling them to deliver exceptional results for their organisation. Qualifications from Introductory to Chartered postgraduate level are offered to anyone wanting to develop their career in marketing.

MEMBERSHIP
Affiliate (Studying/Professional)
Associate (ACIM)
Member (MCIM)

Fellow (FCIM)

QUALIFICATION/EXAMINATIONS
Foundation Certificate in Marketing
Certificate in Professional Marketing
Diploma in Professional Marketing
Digital Diploma in Professional Marketing
Postgraduate Diploma in Professional Marketing
CIM Marketing Leadership Programme

DESIGNATORY LETTERS
ACIM, MCIM, FCIM

THE INSTITUTE OF DIRECT AND DIGITAL MARKETING

DMA House
70 Margaret St
London W1W 8SS
Tel: 020 8614 0255
E-mail: ask@theidm.com
Website: www.theidm.com

For more than 30 years the IDM has existed to support, encourage and improve marketing performance from your first steps on the career ladder, right to the very top. We've become the trusted training partner for hundreds of leading brands from over 30 countries and have trained over 100,000 delegates. Now, as part of the DMA Group, we are the largest marketing association in Europe.

From foundation to advanced level, we have the cutting-edge content, world-class tutors and advanced delivery platforms that will help you prepare for your future.

MEMBERSHIP
Associate Member
Member
Fellow

QUALIFICATION/EXAMINATIONS
Professional Diploma in Digital Marketing
Professional Diploma in Digital Marketing with B2B

Professional Diploma in Direct and Digital
Professional Diploma in Direct and Digital Marketing with B2B
Postgraduate Diploma in Digital Marketing
Postgraduate Diploma in Digital Marketing with B2B
Postgraduate Diploma in Direct and Digital Marketing
Postgraduate Diploma in Direct and Digital Marketing with B2B
Professional Certificate in Social Media
Professional Certificate in Email Marketing
Professional Certificate in Search Marketing
Professional Certificate in Content Marketing
Award in Digital Copywriting
Award in Data Fundamentals
Award in Direct and Digital Marketing
Award in Digital Marketing
Award in General Data Protection Regulation (GDPR)
Award in Direct Mail

MARTIAL ARTS
Membership of Professional Institutions and Associations

INSTITUTE OF MARTIAL ARTS AND SCIENCES

1 Henrietta Street
Bolton
Lancashire BL3 4HL
Tel: 07792 214993
E-mail: admin@instituteofmartialartsandsciences.com
Website: www.instituteofmartialartsandsciences.com

The IMAS is a professional institute for martial artists, dedicated to education and research in the martial arts and offering memberships, accredited training and qualifications, and university degrees in martial arts studies. IMAS publishes a quarterly, peer reviewed journal, and an annual yearbook containing its research articles.

MEMBERSHIP
Affiliate
Student
Associate (AIMAS)
Member (MIMAS)
Fellow (FIMAS)

QUALIFICATION/EXAMINATIONS
Accredited teacher training in partnership with the
Teaching and Learning Academy (AMTLA/MTLA/
FTLA)
Specialist courses for police/security professionals
Higher Educational opportunities include: Graduate
of the Institute of Martial Arts and Sciences (Grad.

IMAS); Post graduate studies available through our
partner insitutes

DESIGNATORY LETTERS
Grad.IMAS, MA, MSc,

MASSAGE AND ALLIED THERAPIES
Membership of Professional Institutions and Associations

BRITISH MEDICAL ACUPUNCTURE SOCIETY

BMAS House
3 Winnington Court
Winnington Street
Northwich
Cheshire CW8 1AQ
Tel: 01606 786782
Fax: 01606 786783
E-mail: admin@medical-acupuncture.co.uk
Website: www.medical-acupuncture.co.uk

The BMAS was formed in 1980 as an association of
medical practitioners interested in acupuncture and
we now have a membership of more than 2,500
registered doctors and allied health professionals
who practise acupuncture alongside more conven-
tional techniques. We believe that acupuncture has an
important role to play in healthcare and promote its
use as a therapy following orthodox medical diagnosis by suitably trained practitioners. We run
training programmes in the UK for doctors, dentists
and other healthcare professionals.

MEMBERSHIP
Member
Accredited Member
Dental/Veterinary Member
Retired Member
Affiliated
Overseas Member
Honorary

QUALIFICATION/EXAMINATIONS
Certificate of Basic Competence (CoBC)
Diploma of Medical Acupuncture (DipMedAc)

LCSP REGISTER OF REMEDIAL MASSEURS AND MANIPULATIVE THERAPISTS

38A High Street
Lowestoft
Suffolk NR32 1HY
Tel: 01502 563344
Fax: 01502 582220
E-mail: admin@lcsp.uk.com
Website: www.lcsp.uk.com

The Register accepts practitioners who currently
work in Massage, Sports / Remedial Massage or
Manipulative Therapy. Applicants must have

completed a course of education at an establishment
whose training meets or exceeds the National
Occupational Standards. The Register offers heavily

discounted comprehensive medical malpractice insurance, business support, regular communications and CPD.

MEMBERSHIP
Student Member
Associate Member (LCSP (Assoc))

Full Member (LCSP (Phys))
Affiliate
Fellow (FLCSP)
Honorary Member

DESIGNATORY LETTERS
LCSP (Assoc), LCSP (Phys), FLCSP

NORTHERN INSTITUTE OF MASSAGE LTD

14- 16 St Mary's Place
Bury
Greater Manchester BL9 0DZ
Tel: 0161 797 1800

The NIM was founded in 1924 and offers professional training in Remedial Massage, Advanced Remedial Massage, and Manipulative Therapy. We also offer a number of CPD seminars and short courses to supplement our main training programme. Research is carried out mostly by therapists on patients from their own clinics or by students completing university courses.

QUALIFICATION/EXAMINATIONS
Courses offered in:
Remedial massage
Advanced Remedial Massage
Manipulative Therapy Diploma

SOCIETY OF HOMEOPATHS

11 Brookfield Duncan Close
Moulton Park
Northampton NN3 6WL
Tel: 01604 817890
E-mail: info@homeopathy-soh.org
Website: www.homeopathy-soh.org

The Society of Homeopaths was established in 1978 and is now the largest organisation registering professional homeopaths in Europe. Our vision is 'homeopathy for all' and we aim to achieve this both by supporting our members and by raising the profile of homeopathy in general.

MEMBERSHIP
Subscriber
Student Member
Student Clinical Member
Registered Member (RSHom)

DESIGNATORY LETTERS
RSHom

MATHEMATICS
Membership of Professional Institutions and Associations

EDINBURGH MATHEMATICAL SOCIETY

School of Mathematics, Edinburgh University
James Clerk Maxwell Building
Mayfield Road
Edinburgh EH9 3JZ
Tel: 01316 505060
Fax: 01316 506553
E-mail: queries@maths.ed.ac.uk
Website: www.maths.ed.ac.uk

The EMS, founded in 1883, is the principal mathematical society for the academic community in Scotland as well as mathematicians in industry and commerce. We organise meetings, publish a journal and support mathematical activities through various funds.

MEMBERSHIP
Ordinary Member
Reciprocal Member
Honorary Member

THE INSTITUTE OF MATHEMATICS AND ITS APPLICATIONS

Catherine Richards House
16 Nelson Street
Southend-on-Sea
Essex SS1 1EF
Tel: 01702 354020
Fax: 01702 354111
E-mail: post@ima.org.uk
Website: www.ima.org.uk

The IMA, founded in 1964, is the UK's learned society for mathematics and its applications. We promote mathematical research, education and careers, and the use of mathematics in business, industry and commerce. In 1990 the Institute was incorporated by Royal Charter and subsequently granted the right to award the status of Chartered Mathematician, Chartered Scientist and Chartered Mathematics Teacher.

MEMBERSHIP
Student

Affiliate
Associate Member (AMIMA)
Member (MIMA)
Fellow (FIMA)
Chartered Mathematician (CMath)

DESIGNATORY LETTERS
AMIMA, MIMA, FIMA, CMath, CMathTeach, CSci

THE MATHEMATICAL ASSOCIATION

259 London Road
Leicester LE2 3BE
Tel: 01162 210013
Fax: 01162 122835
E-mail: office@m-a.org.uk
Website: www.m-a.org.uk

The MA dates from 1871 and aims to support and improve the teaching and learning of mathematics and its applications, and provide opportunities for communication and collaboration between teachers and students of mathematics. We publish a number of books, journals and magazines, hold an annual conference and regional meetings, and organise CPD events. We also confer with government re the curriculum and assessment.

MEMBERSHIP
Personal Member
Institutional Member
Trainee/NQT Member

MEDICAL HERBALISM
Membership of Professional Institutions and Associations

THE NATIONAL INSTITUTE OF MEDICAL HERBALISTS

Clover House
James Court
South Street
Exeter
Devon EX1 1EE
Tel: 01392 426022
Fax: 01392 498963
E-mail: info@nimh.org.uk
Website: www.nimh.org.uk

The NIMH is the UK's leading professional organisation of qualified medical herbal practitioners. We maintain high standards of practice and patient care, and work to promote the benefits of western herbal medicine. We provide codes of conduct, ethics and practice, and represent the profession, patients and the public through participation in external processes.

MEMBERSHIP
Member (MNIMH) Membership is open to graduates holding a BSc(Hons) degree in Herbal Medicine from Lincoln College or University of Westminster. There is also a student affiliate membership scheme for those who are undergraduates of either of the above schools. We are also able to offer a distance learning course through Heartwood and a diploma in Herbal Medicine from the School of Herbal Medicine in Somerset. All the above courses allow memberhsip to the NIMH.

QUALIFICATION/EXAMINATIONS
The NIMH has historically managed its own accreditation process, with universities currently offering a BSc(Hons) degree in Herbal Medicine at Lincoln College and University of Westminster.
From 2011 accreditation of the above courses transferred to The European Herbal and Traditional Medicine Practitioners Association (EHTPA), as an umbrella body of Professional Herbal Medicine Associations, although graduates will continue to be eligible to apply for NIMH membership.

DESIGNATORY LETTERS
MNIMH, FNIMH

MEDICAL SECRETARIES
Membership of Professional Institutions and Associations

ASSOCIATION OF MEDICAL SECRETARIES, PRACTICE MANAGERS, ADMINISTRATORS AND RECEPTIONISTS

Tavistock House North
Tavistock Square
London WC1H 9LN
Tel: 020 7387 6005
Fax: 020 7388 2648
E-mail: info@amspar.co.uk
Website: www.amspar.com

AMSPAR is a professional membership and educational organisation. We work with City & Guilds to provide non-clinical qualifications for health administration within the UK qualification frameworks. We aim to promote quality and coherence in the delivery of qualifications, and encourage and support standards of excellence in the pursuit of continuous professional development and lifelong learning.

MEMBERSHIP
Associate Member (AAMS)
Member (MAMS)
Fellow (FAMS)

QUALIFICATION/EXAMINATIONS
The Level 5 Diploma in Primary Care & Health Management
The Level 5 Certificate in Primary Care & Health Management
The Level 3 Diploma for Medical Secretaries
The Level 3 Certificate in Medical Administration
The Level 3 Certificate in Medical Terminology
The Level 3 Award in Legal Aspects of Medical Administration
The Level 3 Award in Medical Principles for the Administrator
The Level 3 Award in Medical Word Processing
The Level 3 Award in Production of Medical Documents from Recorded Speech
The Level 2 Diploma in Medical Administration
The Level 2 Certificate in Medical Administration
The Level 2 Award in Medical Terminology
The Level 2 Award in Working in the NHS
The Level 2 Award in Medical Word Processing
The Level 2 Award in Production of Medical Documents from Recorded Speech
The Level 3 Advanced Technical Diploma in Medical Administration
The Level 2 Technical Certificate in Medical Administrative Support

DESIGNATORY LETTERS
AAMS, MAMS, FAMS

MEDICINE

A student who wishes to qualify as a doctor in the UK must first obtain a primary qualification. Medical students in the UK typically study for five years to receive their medical degrees or for four years on a graduate-entry accelerated course. There are also courses offered for candidates with non-science subjects to offer at A level (or equivalent) that include the pre-medical year. The pre-medical year is a preliminary course in chemistry, physics and biology and lasts normally 30 weeks. Each medical school sets its own entry requirements, and may require applicants to complete clinical aptitude tests.

After graduation, a trainee doctor will enter the two-year Foundation Programme. There is a national application process for entry to the F1 year, but trainees successfully completing this year move into F2 without having to compete for a place. The trainee is provisionally registered with a licence to practise with the General Medical Council (GMC) while completing the first year and full registration is awarded upon completion of year one.

The F1 year aims to provide experience in a broad range of settings prior to full GMC registration. Regular work-based assessments take place, and trainees must maintain a national learning portfolio in order to progress.

The F2 year usually consists of four varied three-month placements giving trainees the opportunity to try a number of different specialities before making a decision about which specialty training programme they would like to pursue. More information can be found at www.nhscareers.nhs.uk

The GMC is charged with the responsibility under the Medical Act 1983 of keeping a register of all duly qualified medical practitioners. General Medical Council, Regent's Place, 350 Euston Road, London NW1 3JN; Tel: 0161 923 6602; e-mail: gmc@gmc-uk. org; website: www.gmc-uk.org. For information on how to apply to join the register, see www.gmc-uk. org/doctors/applications.asp

PRIMARY QUALIFICATIONS

The GMC decides which universities are entitled to issue medical degrees. Qualifying examinations are examinations held for the granting of one or more primary medical qualifications (PMQs) by any one of the bodies or combinations of bodies in the United Kingdom that are included in a list maintained by the GMC and published on the GMC's website (www. gmc-uk.org/education/undergraduate/awarding_bodies.asp).

LICENSING AND REVALIDATION

Doctors must be registered with a licence to practise with the General Medical Council (GMC) and hold a licence to practise medicine in the UK. The licence to practise gives a doctor the legal authority to undertake certain activities in the UK, for example prescribing, signing death or cremation certificates and holding certain medical posts (such as working as a doctor in the NHS). Any person whose fitness to practise is not impaired and who a) holds one or more primary United Kingdom qualifications and has satisfactorily completed an acceptable programme for provisionally registered doctors; or b) being a national of any relevant European State, holds one or more primary European qualifications, is entitled to be registered as a fully registered medical practitioner. Doctors who do not work in the UK, or who do not undertake any activities for which a licence is required, do not need to hold a licence to practise and can continue to be registered without a licence.

Revalidation ensures that all licensed doctors demonstrate on an ongoing basis that they are up to date and fit to practise in their chosen field and able to provide a good level of care. Licensed doctors have to revalidate, usually every five years, by having regular appraisals based on the GMC's core guidance for doctors, *Good Medical Practice*.

Membership of Professional Institutions and Associations

COLLEGE OF OPERATING DEPARTMENT PRACTITIONERS

130 Euston Road
London NW1 2AY
Tel: 0870 121 5414
E-mail: office@codp.org
Website: www.codp.org.uk

The CODP is the professional body for Operating Department Practitioners, now part of the Science, technical and Therapy occupational group within UNISON. It is a membership, not-for-profit organisation that sets standards of education for the pre-registration aspect of the profession and promotes the enhancement of knowledge and skills, in the context of the multidisciplinary team, through regional, national and international networks.

MEMBERSHIP
Student Member
Association Member
Full College Member

ROYAL COLLEGE OF GENERAL PRACTITIONERS

30 Euston Square
London NW1 2FB
Tel: 020 3188 7400
Fax: 020 3188 7401
E-mail: info@rcgp.org.uk
Website: www.rcgp.org.uk

The aims of the College are to encourage, foster and maintain the highest possible standards in general medical practice. Full entry to the College is by MRCGP exam undertaken whilst in training for general practice, or by membership by assessment (MAP) in the case of qualified GPs.

MEMBERSHIP
Associate in Training
Associate

Member (MRCGP)
Fellow (FRCGP)
International Member (MRCGP[INT])

QUALIFICATION/EXAMINATIONS
Assessment for Membership of the RCGP (MRCGP)

DESIGNATORY LETTERS
MRCGP, FRCGP

ROYAL COLLEGE OF OBSTETRICIANS AND GYNAECOLOGISTS

27 Sussex Place
London NW1 4RG
Tel: 020 7772 6200
E-mail: via website, https://www.rcog.org.uk/en/contact-us/
Website: www.rcog.org.uk

The RCOG encourages the study and advancement of the science and practice of obstetrics and gynaecology. We do this through postgraduate medical education and training development, and the publication of clinical guidelines and reports on aspects of the specialty and service provision. The RCOG International Office works with other international organisations to help lower maternal morbidity and mortality in under-resourced countries.

MEMBERSHIP
Fellow

Member
Associate
Affiliate
Trainee

QUALIFICATION/EXAMINATIONS
MRCOG (Membership Exam)
DRCOG (Diploma)

DESIGNATORY LETTERS
MRCOG, FRCOG, DRCOG

ROYAL SOCIETY OF MEDICINE

1 Wimpole Street
London W1G 0AE
Tel: 020 7290 2900
Fax: 020 7290 2992
E-mail: membership@rsm.ac.uk
Website: www.rsm.ac.uk

The RSM, founded in 1805, is a medical charity that promotes the exchange of information and ideas in medical science. We provide a broad range of educational activities and opportunities for doctors, dentists, veterinary surgeons, students of these disciplines and allied healthcare professionals.

MEMBERSHIP
Student

Associate
Fellow

QUALIFICATION/EXAMINATIONS
NONE

DESIGNATORY LETTERS
N/A

THE FEDERATION OF ROYAL COLLEGES OF PHYSICIANS OF THE UNITED KINGDOM

MRCP(UK)
11 St Andrews Place
Regent's Park
London NW1 4LE
Tel: +44 (0)20 3075 1548
E-mail: via website, https://www.mrcpuk.org/contact-us
Website: www.mrcpuk.org

The Federation is a partnership between the Royal College of Physicians of Edinburgh, the Royal College of Physicians and Surgeons of Glasgow and the Royal College of Physicians of London. Working together, the colleges develop and deliver membership and specialty examinations that are recognized around the world as quality benchmarks.

MEMBERSHIP
Membership of the Royal Colleges of Physicians (MRCP(UK)): Once candidates have successfully completed their final part of the examination they must then submit and complete the Form of Faith as a testimonial for election to membership.

QUALIFICATION/EXAMINATIONS
The Federation is responsible for a portfolio of examinations: MRCP(UK) Diploma (Membership of the Royal Colleges of Physicians of the United Kingdom): Candidates for the MRCP(UK) Diploma may enter through the Royal College of Physicians of Edinburgh, the Royal College of Physicians and

Surgeons of Glasgow, the Royal College of Physicians of London, via the online application system. There are three components to the MRCP(UK) Diploma. The part 1 and part 2 examinations have a two-paper format. Each paper is 3 hours in duration and contains 100 multiple choice questions in one from five (best of five) format, where a candidate chooses the best answer from five possible answers. The questions will usually have a clinical scenario, may include the results of investigations and, in the part 2 examination, may be illustrated. The part 2 clinical examination (PACES) consists of five clinical stations, each assessed by two independent examiners. Candidates will start at any one of the five stations, and then move round the carousel of stations at 20-minute intervals until they have completed the cycle. There is a 5-minute period between each station. Candidates may apply to sit the MRCP(UK) part 1 examination provided they graduated at least 12 months in advance of the examination dat, and have had at least 12 months' experience in medical employment. Candidates who have passed the part 1 examination can proceed to complete the remaining components. The MRCP(UK) Examination provides valid, reliable evidence of attainment in knowledge, clinical skills and behaviour, and is a mandatory component of assessment for Core Medical Training (CMT). The Specialty Certificate Examinations (SCEs): The Federation of Royal Colleges of Physicians of the UK, in association with Specialist Societies, delivers Specialty Certificate Examinations. The aim of these national assessments is to ensure that trainees have sufficient knowledge of their specialty to practise safely and competently as consultants. The Specialty Certificate Examination is delivered in computer-based format (referred to as CBT) at Pearson VUE test centres. SCEs have a two-paper format, with each paper containing 100 multiple choice questions in 'best of five' format. A Specialty Certificate Examination is a compulsory component of assessment for Certificate of Completion of Training (CCT) for all UK trainees in the following specialties: Acute Medicine, Dermatology; Endocrinology and Diabetes; Gastroenterology; Geriatric Medicine; Medical Oncology; Nephrology; Neurology; Palliative Medicine; Respiratory Medicine and Rheumatology.

DESIGNATORY LETTERS
MRCP(UK)

THE INSTITUTE OF CLINICAL RESEARCH

Suite 10, Cedar Court
Grove Park
White Waltham Road
Maidenhead
Tel: 0845 521 0056
E-mail: info@icr-global.org
Website: www.icr-global.org

The ICR was founded in 1978 and is now the largest professional clinical research body in Europe and India. Our aim is to promote knowledge and understanding by engaging with the healthcare community and the general public, to support and facilitate communication between our members, and to provide opportunities for learning and development to enhance professional competence.

MEMBERSHIP
Affiliate

Registered Member (RICR)
Professional Member (MICR)
Fellow (FICR)
Honorary Fellow (Hon FICR)

QUALIFICATION/EXAMINATIONS
Please see the ICR's website http://www.icr-global.org/training/examinations/

DESIGNATORY LETTERS
RICR, MICR, FICR, HonFICR

THE ROYAL COLLEGE OF ANAESTHETISTS

Churchill House
35 Red Lion Square
London WC1R 4SG
Tel: 020 7092 1500
E-mail: info@rcoa.ac.uk
Website: www.rcoa.ac.uk

The RCoA, which dates from 1948, is the professional body responsible for the specialty of anaesthesia throughout the UK. Our principal responsibility is to ensure the quality of patient care through the maintenance of standards in anaesthesia, pain medicine and critical care. We set and run examinations, and provide CPD for all practising anaesthetists.

MEMBERSHIP
Honorary Fellow (FRCA)
Fellow (FRCA)
Fellow ad Eundem (FRCA)
Associate Fellow
Senior Fellows and Members Club
Member (MRCA)
Associate Member
Anaesthetist in Training

Affiliates
Foundation Years Doctor
Medical Student

QUALIFICATION/EXAMINATIONS
FRCA Examinations (FRCA)

DESIGNATORY LETTERS
MRCA, FRCA

THE ROYAL COLLEGE OF PATHOLOGISTS

6 Alie Street
London E1 8QT
Tel: 020 7451 6700
E-mail: exams@rcpath.org
Website: www.rcpath.org

The College aims to advance the science and practice of pathology, to provide public education, to promote research in pathology and to disseminate the results.

MEMBERSHIP
Affiliate Member
Diplomate Member (DipRCPath)
Fellow (FRCPath)

QUALIFICATION/EXAMINATIONS
Training programmes are approved for all pathology specialities and sub-specialities. The exact examination arrangements vary for each speciality but they will all involve a Part 1 and a Part 2 which include, inter alia, written, practical and oral components. In addition the College offers a Diploma in Dermatopathology and a Diploma in Forensic Pathology and a Certificate in Autopsy, Cervical Cytology, Infection, and Medical Genetics. Further details may be obtained from the Examinations Department or the College's website.

DESIGNATORY LETTERS
DipRCPath, FRCPath

THE ROYAL COLLEGE OF PHYSICIANS AND SURGEONS OF GLASGOW

232–242 St Vincent Street
Glasgow G2 5RJ
Tel: 0141 2216072
Fax: 0141 2211804
E-mail: exams@rcpsg.ac.uk
Website: www.rcpsg.ac.uk

The Royal College of Physicians and Surgeons of Glasgow (RCPSG) welcomes professionals from a diverse range of disciplines. At present, our collegiate body includes Physicians, Surgeons, professionals in Dentistry, Travel Medicine, Podiatric Medicine and other professions allied to medicine. The College aims to provide career support to our membership through education, training, professional development, examinations and assessment, whilst acting as a charity and leading voice on health issues in order to set the highest standards of health care.

MEMBERSHIP
Fellow FRCP (Glasg)/ FRCS (Glasg)/ FDS RCPS (Glasg)/ FFTM RCPS (Glasg)/ FFPM RCPS (Glasg)
Member MRCPS (Glasg)/ MFDS RCPS (Glasg)/ MRCS (Glasg)/ MRCS(ENT) (Glasg)/ MFTM RCPS (Glasg)/ MFPM RCPS(Glasg)

Associate Member
Affiliate Member
Student Member

QUALIFICATION/EXAMINATIONS
Diploma in Otolaryngology – Head and Neck Surgery (DOHNS)
Diploma in Travel Medicine (DipTravMed)
Diploma in Expedition and Wilderness Medicine
Postgraduate Diploma in Clinical Education
Diploma of Membership of the Royal Colleges of Physicians of the United Kingdom (MRCP(UK))
Diploma of Membership of the Royal College of Surgeons (MRCS(Glasg))
Diploma of Membership of the Royal College of Surgeons (MRCS(ENT)(Glasg))
Diploma of Membership of the Faculty of Dental Surgery (MFDS RCPS (Glasg))
Diploma of Membership in (dental specialty) (M(dental specialty) RCPS (Glasg)
Diploma of Membership of the Faculty of Travel Medicine (MFTM RCPS (Glasg))

Diploma of Membership of the Faculty of Podiatric Medicine (MFPM RCPS (Glasg))
Diploma of Fellowship of the Royal College of Physicians and Surgeons of Glasgow in Ophthalmology (FRCS(Glasg))
Diploma of Fellowship of the Royal College of Physicians and Surgeons of Glasgow (FDS (dental specialty) RCPS (Glasg))
Diploma of Fellowship of the Royal College of Physicians and Surgeons of Glasgow (FRCSGlasg (surgical specialty))
Diploma of Fellowship of the Faculty of Travel Medicine (FFTM RCPS (Glasg))
Diploma of Fellowship of the Faculty of Podiatric Medicine (FFPM RCPS (Glasg))

DESIGNATORY LETTERS
AFTM RCPS(Glasg), MFDS RCPS(Glasg), MFTM RCPS(Glasg), MRCP(UK), MRCS(Glasg), MRCS(ENT)(Glasg), MRCPS(Glasg), MFPM RCPS(Glasg), M(dental specialty) RCPS(Glasg)/ FRCP(Glasg)/ FRCS(Glasg)/ FRCSGlasg(surgical specialty)/ FDS RCPS(Glasg)/ FRCS(Urol)(Glasg), FF

THE ROYAL COLLEGE OF PHYSICIANS OF EDINBURGH

9 Queen Street
Edinburgh EH2 1JQ
Tel: 01312 257324
E-mail: l.thompson@rcpe.ac.uk
Website: www.rcpe.ac.uk

The RCPE promotes the highest standards in internal medicine in the UK and internationally. Along with our sister Colleges in Glasgow and London we oversee the membership examination of the Royal Colleges of Physicians, MRCP(UK), enabling doctors to enter higher specialist training, leading eventually to a Certificate of Completion of Specialist Training (CCST).

MEMBERSHIP
Student & Foundation
Associate

Collegiate Member (MRCPE)
Fellow (FRCPE)
Retired
Refugee Doctor

QUALIFICATION/EXAMINATIONS
MRCP(UK)
Specialty Certificate Examinations

DESIGNATORY LETTERS
MRCPE, FRCPE

THE ROYAL COLLEGE OF PHYSICIANS OF LONDON

11 St Andrews Place
Regent's Park
London NW1 4LE
Tel: +44 (0)20 3075 1649
E-mail: via website – https://www.rcplondon.ac.uk/contact
Website: www.rcplondon.ac.uk

The Royal College of Physicians of London offers a Diploma in Geriatric Medicine (DGM) Examination and a Diploma in Tropical Medicine and Hygiene, run in conjunction with the London School of Tropical Medicine and Hygiene.

MEMBERSHIP

The Royal College of Physicians of London runs the MRCP(UK) Examination which is the MRCP(UK) membership examination. As the examination is run in conjunction with two other Royal Colleges of Physicians, this examination and the membership qualification MRCP(UK) are listed in this directory under *The Federation of Royal Colleges of Physicians.*

QUALIFICATION/EXAMINATIONS

Diploma in Geriatric Medicine The Diploma in Geriatric Medicine is designed to give recognition of competence in the provision of care of older people to General Practitioner vocational trainees, staff physicians and others working in non-consultant career posts in Departments of Geriatric Medicine, and other doctors with interests in or responsibilities for the care of older people.

The Diploma in Geriatric Medicine is available to all registered doctors. It is not primarily directed towards career geriatricians, but is generally to family doctors, psycho-geriatricians and indeed any doctor involved in the care of older people.

The Diploma in Geriatric Medicine is in two parts, the first of which is a written examination of multiple choice (best of 5) questions, lasting 2 hours and 30 minutes normally held twice a year at the Royal College of Physicians of London.

The second part is a Clinical Examination also held twice a year at various clinical centres in England and Wales. The clinical examination is a four-station standardized examination similar to an Objective Standard Clinical Examination (OSCE).

Diploma in Tropical Medicine and Hygiene The Diploma in Tropical Medicine and Hygiene is intended to test the knowledge required of physicians who wish to practise medicine effectively in developing countries.

Candidates for the Diploma in Tropical Medicine & Hygiene must hold a primary medical qualification recognized by the Royal College of Physicians of London.

The Royal College of Physicians of London will accept applications from candidates who are in the process of completing, or have completed within the last 5 years, the Tropical Medicine courses in London, Liverpool, Sheffield and Glasgow, which are recognized as appropriate training centres for the examination. The examination is held once a year over 2 days (unless required for a viva) and is conducted in the following sections: A **Practical Section** lasting 2 hours and 30 minutes consists of a mixture of microscopy specimens, including 20 'spot' questions that are set up on a microscope for identification. Other specimens require the candidate to use the microscopes themself. They are mainly parasitological and may include faecal, blood and haematological preparations together with some entomological specimens. A **Written Section** (3 hours and 20 minutes in total) consists of three papers. The **Clinical Paper** (1 hour) contains 18 compulsory questions. The first 16 are based on clinical pictures – usually of patients with abnormal physical signs; but occasionally laboratory slides, X-rays, or epidemiological data may be shown. There will be 2 or 3 questions on each, asking (for example) identification, diagnosis, further investigation, treatment etc. Each of these 16 questions is worth a maximum of 5 marks. The last 2 questions (17 and 18) are brief clinical cases, with 2 or 3 questions (again concentrating on diagnosis or differential diagnosis, investigation and treatment). The **Multiple Choice Question Paper** (1 hour and 20 minutes) consists of 40 multiple choice questions designed to test the knowledge of tropical medicine and hygiene over a wide area. The **Preventative Medicine Paper** (1 hour including 5 minutes reading time) consists of 10 questions of which the candidate must choose 5. Each question may have several parts, covering all aspects of preventative medicine and international community health in a tropical context.

There is also an **Oral ('Viva') Examination** for borderline candidates. The examination is conducted by two examiners. The first part of the examination (10 minutes) is a discussion of an illustrated clinical case history, which candidates are allowed to study for 10 minutes before the examination. The second part of the examination (10 minutes) consists of more general questions.

DESIGNATORY LETTERS
MRCP

THE ROYAL COLLEGE OF PSYCHIATRISTS

21 Prescot Street
London E1 8BB
Tel: 020 7235 2351
Fax: 020 3701 2761
E-mail: via website https://www.rcpsych.ac.uk/about-us/contact-us
Website: www.rcpsych.ac.uk

The RCPsych is the professional and educational body for psychiatrists in the UK and Ireland. We are committed to improving the understanding of psychiatry and mental health, and are at the forefront in setting and achieving the highest standards through education, training and research. We actively promote psychiatry as a career, and provide guidance and support to our members and associates.

MEMBERSHIP
Pre-Membership Psychiatric Trainee
Affiliate
Specialist Associate
Member (MRCPsych)
Fellow (FRCPsych)
International Associate
Student Associate
Foundation Doctor Associate

QUALIFICATION/EXAMINATIONS
MRCPsych qualifying exams
Paper A – The Scientific and Theoretical Basis of Psychiatry
Paper B – Critical Review and the Clinical Topics in Psychiatry
CASC – Clinical Assessment of Skills and Competencies

DESIGNATORY LETTERS
MRCPsych, FRCPsych

THE ROYAL COLLEGE OF RADIOLOGISTS

63 Lincoln's Inn Fields
London WC2A 3JW
Tel: 020 7405 1282
E-mail: enquiries@rcr.ac.uk
Website: www.rcr.ac.uk

The Royal College of Radiologists (RCR) leads, supports and educates in medical imaging and cancer treatment. RCR sets and maintains the standards for entry to, and practice in, the specialties of clinical oncology and clinical radiology and shapes their future development for the benefit of patients. The College works to advance the science and practice of radiology and oncology. It furthers public awareness and education, and promotes study and research through setting professional standards of practice. It also sets the curriculum for the two specialties ensuring that high educational standards are met in the interests of safe and responsible practice.

MEMBERSHIP
Associate
Trainee
Member
Fellow (FRCR)

Honorary Member/Fellow (Hon MRCR/Hon FRCR)

QUALIFICATION/EXAMINATIONS
First FRCR Examination
Final FRCR Examination

Diploma in Dental and Maxillofacial Radiology (DDMFR)

DESIGNATORY LETTERS
FRCR, Hon MRCR, Hon FRCR

THE ROYAL COLLEGE OF SURGEONS OF EDINBURGH

Nicolson Street
Edinburgh EH8 9DW
Tel: 0131 527 1600
Fax: 0131 557 6406
E-mail: mail@rcsed.ac.uk
Website: www.rcsed.ac.uk85-89 Colmore Row Birmingham B3 2BB

The Royal College of Surgeons of Edinburgh, which dates from 1505, is dedicated to the maintenance and promotion of the highest standards of surgical practice, through education, training and rigorous examination, and its liaison with external medical bodies. Today, with more than 20,000 Fellows and Members, we pride ourselves also on our innovation and adaptability.

MEMBERSHIP
Affiliate

Associate
Member (MRCSEd)
Fellow (FRCSEd)

QUALIFICATION/EXAMINATIONS
Please see the Royal College of Surgeons of Edinburgh website.

DESIGNATORY LETTERS
MRCSEd, FRCSEd

THE ROYAL COLLEGE OF SURGEONS OF ENGLAND

35–43 Lincoln's Inn Fields
London WC2A 3PE
Tel: 020 7405 6700
Fax: 020 7869 6740
E-mail: membership@rcseng.ac.uk
Website: www.rcseng.ac.uk

The Royal College of Surgeons of England is committed to enabling surgeons to achieve and maintain the highest standards of surgical practice and patient care. We examine trainees, supervise the training of and provide support and advice for surgeons, promote and support surgical research in the UK, and liaise with the DoH, health authorities, Trusts and hospitals in the UK and other medical and academic organisations worldwide.

MEMBERSHIP
Affiliate
Associate
Fellow *ad eundem*
Membership *ad eundem*
Specialty Membership

QUALIFICATION/EXAMINATIONS
Please see the Royal College of Surgeons of England website.

THE WORSHIPFUL SOCIETY OF APOTHECARIES OF LONDON

Apothecaries' Hall
Black Friars Lane
London EC4V 6EJ
Tel: 020 7236 1189
Fax: 020 7329 3177
E-mail: via website
Website: www.apothecaries.org

The Society was incorporated by Royal Charter in 1617 and allowed to prepare and sell drugs for medicinal purposes, laying the foundations of the pharmaceutical industry. Apothecaries were permitted to prescribe medicines, becoming the forerunners of today's GPs. The Society is now a teaching and examining body for postgraduate medical eduication.

MEMBERSHIP
Member of Yeomanry

QUALIFICATION/EXAMINATIONS
PGDip in Forensic Medical Sciences (DipFMS)
PGDip in Genitourinary Medicine (Dip GU Med)
PGDip in the History of Medicine (DHMSA)
PGDip in HIV Medicine (Dip HIV Med)
PGDip in the Medical Care of Catastrophes (DMCC)
PGDip in Medical Jurisprudence (Pathology) (DMJ[Path])
PGDip in the Philosophy of Medicine (DPMSA)

METALLURGY
Membership of Professional Institutions and Associations

INSTITUTE OF CORROSION

Barratt House
Kingsthorpe Road
Northampton NN2 6EZ
Tel: 01604 438222
E-mail: admin@icorr.org
Website: www.icorr.org

The Institute of Corrosion has since 1959 been serving the corrosion science, technology and engineering community in the fight against corrosion, which costs the UK around 4 per cent of GNP per annum. We promote the establishment and promotion of sound corrosion management practice, the advancement of cost-effective corrosion control measures, and a sustained effort to raise corrosion awareness at all stages of design, fabrication and operation.

MEMBERSHIP
Student Member
Ordinary Member
Professional Member (MICorr)
Company membership

Chartered Scientist (CSci)

QUALIFICATION/EXAMINATIONS
Cathodic Protection Technician (Level 1)
Senior Cathodic Protection Technician (Level 2)
Senior Cathodic Protection Engineer (Level 3)
Painting Inspector (ICorr Levels 1, 2 and 3)
Coating Inspector (ICorr Levels 1, 2 and 3)
FireProofing Inspector Level 2
Insulation Inspector Level 2
Hot Dip Galvanizing Inspector Level 2

DESIGNATORY LETTERS
TICorr, MICorr, FICorr, EngTech, IEng, CEng

THE INSTITUTE OF METAL FINISHING

Exeter House
48 Holloway Head
Birmingham B1 1NQ
Tel: 01216 227387
E-mail: info@materialsfinishing.org
Website: www.uk-finishing.org.uk

The IMF, founded in 1925, provides a focus for surface engineering and finishing activities worldwide through the fulfilment of technical, educational and professional needs at all levels for individuals and companies involved in the coatings industry. We promote R&D within the industry and CPD for our members, cooperate with other institutes, and liaise with legislative bodies to influence decision making.

MEMBERSHIP
Student
Affiliate
Associate (AssocIMF)
Technician (TechIMF)

Licentiate (LIMF)
Member (MIMF)
Fellow (FIMF)
Engineering Technician (EngTech)
Sustaining Member (company)

QUALIFICATION/EXAMINATIONS
Foundation Certificate
Technician Certificate
Advanced Technician Certificate

DESIGNATORY LETTERS
AssocIMF, TechIMF, LIMF, MIMF, FIMF, EngTech

METEOROLOGY AND CLIMATOLOGY
Membership of Professional Institutions and Associations

MET OFFICE COLLEGE

Met Office
Fitzroy Road
Exeter
Devon EX1 3PB
Tel: 01392 885680
Fax: 01392 885681
E-mail: enquiries@metoffice.gov.uk
Website: https://college.metoffice.gov.uk/

The Meteorological Office College is part of the Met Office and is located in Exeter, Devon. We provide meteorological training for our own staff and to meteorological services worldwide, as places become available on a fee-paying basis.

QUALIFICATION/EXAMINATIONS
Level 3 Diploma in Meteorological Observing (QCF)

Level 4 Certificate for a Meteorological Forecasting Technician (QCF)
Level 5 Diploma in Meteorological Forecasting (QCF)
Level 5 Award in Meteorological Briefing (QCF)
Level 5 Certificate in Meteorological Broadcasting (QCF)
Level 6 Diploma in Flood Forecasting (QCF)

ROYAL METEOROLOGICAL SOCIETY

104 Oxford Road
Reading RG1 7LL
Tel: +44 (0)118 2080 142
E-mail: via website, https://www.rmets.org/contact-us
Website: www.rmets.org

The RMetS is the learned and professional society for anyone whose profession or interests are connected with weather and climate. It administers the NVQs of the profession and is the accreditation body for the status of Chartered Meteorologist. Its principal aim is the advancement of the understanding of weather and climate for the benefit of everyone.

MEMBERSHIP
Associate Fellow
Fellow (FRMetS)
Chartered Meteorologist (CMet)
Registered Meteorologist

DESIGNATORY LETTERS
FRMetS, CMet

MICROSCOPY
Membership of Professional Institutions and Associations

THE ROYAL MICROSCOPICAL SOCIETY

37/38 St Clements
Oxford OX4 1AJ
Tel: 01865 254760
Fax: 01865 791237
E-mail: info@rms.org.uk
Website: www.rms.org.uk

The RMS, which dates from 1839, is an international scientific society dedicated to advancing the science of microscopy and the interests of its 1,400 members, who range from individuals interested in microscopy to scientists and company members representing manufacturers and suppliers of microscopes, other equipment and services.

MEMBERSHIP
Ordinary Member

Concessionary
Student
Fellow (FRMS)
Corporate

QUALIFICATION/EXAMINATIONS
RMS Diploma

DESIGNATORY LETTERS
FRMS

MUSEUM AND RELATED WORK
Membership of Professional Institutions and Associations

MUSEUMS ASSOCIATION

42 Clerkenwell Close
London EC1R 0AZ
Tel: 020 7566 7800
E-mail: info@museumsassociation.org
Website: www.museumsassociation.org

The MA is the oldest museums association in the world, set up in 1889 to guard the interests of museums and galleries. Today, we have 5,200 individual members, 600 institutional members and 250 corporate members. Our aim is to enhance the value of museums to society by sharing knowledge, developing skills, inspiring innovation and providing leadership.

MEMBERSHIP
Student
Volunteer
Professional Member
Associate (AMA)
Corporate Member
Institutional Member

DESIGNATORY LETTERS
AMA

MUSIC
Membership of Professional Institutions and Associations

ABRSM (ASSOCIATED BOARD OF THE ROYAL SCHOOLS OF MUSIC)

4 London Wall Place
London EC2Y 5AU
Tel: 020 7636 5400
E-mail: via website: gb.abrsm.org/en/contact-us/
Website: www.abrsm.org

ABRSM's mission is to motivate musical achievement. We aim to support the development of learners and teachers in music education worldwide and to celebrate their achievements. We do this through authoritative and internationally recognized assessments, publications and professional development support for teachers, and through charitable donations.

MEMBERSHIP
Licentiate (LRSM)
Fellow (FRSM)

QUALIFICATION/EXAMINATIONS
Certificate of Teaching (CT ABRSM)
Diploma in Instrumental/Vocal Teaching (DipABRSM)
Diploma in Music Direction (DipABRSM)
Diploma in Music Performance (DipABRSM)

Please see the ABRSM website for details of other examinations and awards.

DESIGNATORY LETTERS
CT ABRSM, DipABRSM, LRSM, FRSM

INCORPORATED SOCIETY OF MUSICIANS

4–5 Inverness Mews
London W2 3JQ
Tel: 020 7221 3499
Fax: 020 7243 3437
E-mail: membership@ism.org
Website: www.ism.org

The Incorporated Society of Musicians (ISM) is the UK's professional body for musicians and a nationally recognised subject association for music. Since 1882 we have been promoting the importance of music and protecting the rights of those working within music. We are a wholly independent organisation supporting nearly 9,500 members.

MEMBERSHIP
Student member
Full member
Corporate member
Graduate member
Friend of the ISM Trust

MUSICAL INSTRUMENT TECHNOLOGY
Membership of Professional Institutions and Associations

PIANOFORTE TUNERS' ASSOCIATION

PO Box 230
Hailsham
East Sussex BN27 9EA
Tel: 0845 602 8796
Fax: 0845 602 8796
E-mail: secretary@pianotuner.org.uk
Website: www.pianotuner.org.uk

The PTA is a professional body committed to improving standards, and applicants for membership must pass a theoretical and practical examination to prove their ability as a qualified piano tuner or technician. We publish a regular newsletter and hold an Annual Convention and General Meeting in different towns around Britain, to which members and aspiring non-members are invited.

MEMBERSHIP
Student
Patron
Associate
Member
Apprentice

THE INCORPORATED SOCIETY OF ORGAN BUILDERS

The Tower
7 Lower Port View
SALTASH
Cornwall PL12 4BY
Tel: 01752-842027
Fax: 01752-842027
E-mail: via website, http://www.isob.co.uk/contact/
Website: www.isob.co.uk

The ISOB was founded in 1947 to advance the science and practice of organ building, to provide a central organisation for organ builders, and to provide for the better definition and protection of the profession by a system of examinations and the issue of certificates and distinctions. We hold regular meetings and conferences around the UK and overseas.

MEMBERSHIP
Student Member

Ordinary Member (MISOB)
Associate Member (AISOB)
Fellow (FISOB)
Counsellor (CISOB)
Companion

DESIGNATORY LETTERS
MISOB, AISOB, FISOB, CISOB

NAVAL ARCHITECTURE
Membership of Professional Institutions and Associations

THE ROYAL INSTITUTION OF NAVAL ARCHITECTS

8–9 Northumberland Street
London WC2N 5DA
Tel: 020 7235 4622
Fax: 020 7259 5912
E-mail: membership@rina.org.uk
Website: www.rina.org.uk

The RINA is an internationally renowned professional institution whose members are involved at all levels in the design, construction, maintenance and operation of marine vessels and structures. Our members are widely represented in industry, universities and colleges, and maritime organisations in over 90 countries.

MEMBERSHIP
Junior Member

Student Member
Associate (AssocRINA)
Associate Member (AMRINA)
Member (MRINA)
Fellow (FRINA)

DESIGNATORY LETTERS
AssocRINA, AMRINA, MRINA, FRINA

NAVIGATION, SEAMANSHIP AND MARINE QUALIFICATIONS
Membership of Professional Institutions and Associations

THE NAUTICAL INSTITUTE

202 Lambeth Road
London SE1 7LQ
Tel: 020 7928 1351
Fax: 020 7401 2817
E-mail: sec@nautinst.org
Website: www.nautinst.org

The Nautical Institute is the international representative body for maritime professionals involved in the control of sea-going ships with an interest in nautical matters. It provides a wide range of services to enhance the professional standing and knowledge of members who are drawn from all sectors of the maritime world.

MEMBERSHIP
Honorary Fellow
Fellow (FNI)
Associate Fellow (AFNI)
Member (MNI)
Associate Member (AMNI)

QUALIFICATION/EXAMINATIONS
Harbour Master's Certificate
Pilotage Certificate
Command Diploma
International Sail Endorsement Scheme
Ice Navigator Scheme
Navigation Assessor Certificate
Incident Investigation Certificate
Navigation Assessors Certificate

DESIGNATORY LETTERS
FNI, AFNI, MNI, AMNI

THE ROYAL INSTITUTE OF NAVIGATION

1 Kensington Gore
London SW7 2AT
Tel: 020 7591 3134
E-mail: admin@rin.org.uk
Website: www.rin.org.uk

The RIN is a learned society with charitable status. Our aims are: to unite those with a professional or personal interest in any aspect of navigation in one unique body; to further the development of navigation in every sphere; and to increase public awareness of both the art and science of navigation, how it has shaped the past, how it impacts our world today, and how it will affect the future.

MEMBERSHIP
Junior Associate
Student
Associate
Ordinary Member (MRIN)
Associate Fellow (AFRIN)

Affiliated Club
Corporate
Small Business
Affiliate College or University
Corporate Member
Small Business

QUALIFICATION/EXAMINATIONS
Chartered Engineer (CEng)
Incorpoirated Engineer (IEng)
Engineering Technician (EngTech)

DESIGNATORY LETTERS
MRIN, AFRIN, FRIN

NON-DESTRUCTIVE TESTING
Membership of Professional Institutions and Associations

THE BRITISH INSTITUTE OF NON-DESTRUCTIVE TESTING

Midsummer House
Riverside Way
Bedford Road
Northampton NN1 5NX
Tel: 01604 438300
Fax: 01604 438301
E-mail: info@bindt.org
Website: www.bindt.org

The BINDT was formed in 1976 from the merger of the Society of Non-Destructive Examination (SONDE) and the Society of Industrial Radiology and Allied Methods of Non-Destructive Testing, later renamed the NDT Society of Great Britain (NDTS), both formed in 1954. Our aim is to promote and advance the science and practice of non-destructive testing, condition monitoring, diagnostic engineering and all other materials and quality testing disciplines.

MEMBERSHIP
Affiliate Member

Associate Member (AMInstNDT)
Member (MInstNDT)
Fellow (FInstNDT)
Corporate Member (organisations)

QUALIFICATION/EXAMINATIONS
See website: www.bindt.org/education-and-training/education-and-training/

DESIGNATORY LETTERS
AMInstNDT, MInstNDT, FInstNDT, EngTech, IEng, CEng

NURSERY NURSING
Membership of Professional Institutions and Associations

COUNCIL FOR AWARDS IN CHILDREN'S CARE AND EDUCATION

Q6 Quorum Business park
Benton lane
Newcastle upon Tyne NE12 8BT
Tel: 0345 347 2123
E-mail: info@cache.org.uk
Website: www.cache.org.uk

CACHE is an Awarding Body that designs courses and qualifications in the care and education of children and young people. Our courses, which are widely available, range from entry level to advanced qualifications for sector professionals. We regularly lobby the government and other agencies to raise the quality and professionalism of child care.

QUALIFICATION/EXAMINATIONS
Please see the CACHE website: www.cache.org.uk/our-qualifications-and-services

NURSING AND MIDWIFERY
Membership of Professional Institutions and Associations

THE NURSING & MIDWIFERY COUNCIL

23 Portland Place
London W1B 1PZ
Tel: 020 7333 9333
E-mail: UKenquiries@nmc-uk.org
Website: www.nmc-uk.org

We are the nursing and midwifery regulator for England, Wales, Scotland, Northern Ireland and the Islands. We exist to safeguard the health and well-being of the public.

MEMBERSHIP
Registration by relevant professional qualification.

OCCUPATIONAL THERAPY
Membership of Professional Institutions and Associations

ROYAL COLLEGE OF OCCUPATIONAL THERAPISTS

106–114 Borough High Street
Southwark
London SE1 1LB
Tel: 020 7357 6480
Fax: 020 7450 2299
E-mail: membership.department@rcot.co.uk
Website: www.rcot.org.uk

The Royal College of Occupational Therapists is the professional body for occupational therapy in the UK. The College has over 33,000 members and represents the profession nationally and internationally. RCOT accredits pre-registration occupational therapy degree programmes in 31 UK Universities.

MEMBERSHIP
Student Member
Associate
Discounted Associate
Professional Member
Discounted Professional Member
Self-employed Member
Retired Member
Overseas Member

QUALIFICATION/EXAMINATIONS
BA(Hons)
PG Dip
MSc

DESIGNATORY LETTERS
MRCOT

OPTICIANS (DISPENSING)

Dispensing opticians must be registered with the General Optical Council (GOC, 10 Old Bailey, London EC4M 7NG; Tel: 020 7580 3898; e-mail: goc@optical.org; website: www.optical.org). The GOC publishes registers of all optometrists, dispensing opticians, student opticians and optical businesses that are qualified and fit to practise, train or carry on business.

Qualification takes three years in total, and can be completed by combining a distance learning course or day release while working as a trainee under the supervision of a qualified and GOC-registered optician. Alternatively students can do a two-year full-time course followed by one year of supervised practice with a qualified and registered optician. The GOC has approved training courses in dispensing optics at the following institutions in the UK: Anglia Ruskin University, Association of British Dispensing Opticians (ABDO) College (Distance Learning Institute), Bradford College, City and Islington College, City University and Glasgow Caledonian University. All routes are assessed by final ABDO examinations. On successful completion of training you must register with the GOC in order to practise in the UK. Once qualified, you will need to undertake a minimum amount of continuing education and training to remain on the register. All registered dispensing opticians have to renew their registration each year: this is called 'retention'.

The approved training course for the contact lens specialty is run by ABDO College and City and Islington College. For further information contact the ABDO College (Tel: 01227 738 829 option 1; email: info@abdocollege.org.uk) or City and Islington College (Tel: 020 7700 9200; email: courseinfo@candi.ac.uk).

If you qualify as a dispensing optician and have worked in practice as a qualified dispensing optician for at least two years, the University of Bradford offers a career progression course that enables you to graduate with a degree in optometry by undertaking 6 months of distance-learning followed by 12 months of study at the University (Tel: 01274 236296; email: admissions-life@bradford. ac.uk).

Continuing education and training is a statutory requirement for all fully-qualified dispensing opticians. The CET scheme is a points-based scheme that runs over a three-year cycle. All full registrants must earn a minimum number of CET points by the end of each cycle to stay on the registers.

Nationals of EU/EEA countries who have gained optical quailfications in an EU/EEA country can apply to another EU/EEA country to have their qualifications recognised.

ENTRY REQUIREMENTS

Requirements vary according to the college or university, but typically five GCSEs at Grade C or above, to include Mathematics, English and Science and perhaps two or three A Levels at a minimum of a Grade D or equivalent are required. Relevant work experience will also be considered.

For further details contact the admissions tutor or check the website of the university you wish to apply to.

Membership of Professional Institutions and Associations

ASSOCIATION OF BRITISH DISPENSING OPTICIANS

199 Gloucester Terrace
London W2 6LD
Tel: 020 7298 5100
E-mail: general@abdolondon.org.uk
Website: www.abdo.org.uk

The ABDO is the qualifying body for dispensing opticians in the UK. Our aims are to advance the science and art of dispensing optics, to further the education and training of dispensing opticians, and to support and promote the interests of the profession.

MEMBERSHIP
Student Member
Associate Member
Full Member
Full (overseas)
Fellow (FBDO)

Elder

QUALIFICATION/EXAMINATIONS
Certificate in Contact Lens Practice (Level 6)
Diploma in The Assessment & Management of Low Vision (Level 6)
Diploma in Ophthalmic Dispensing (Level 6)
Diploma in Advanced Contact Lens Practice (Level 7)
Diploma in Spectacle Lens Design (Level 7)

DESIGNATORY LETTERS
FBDO

ASSOCIATION OF CONTACT LENS MANUFACTURERS

PO Box 735
Devizes
Wiltshire SN10 3TQ
Tel: 01380 860418
E-mail: secgen@aclm.org.uk
Website: www.aclm.org.uk

The ACLM was founded in 1962 to publicize the work of UK contact lens manufacturers, to develop new products and to raise standards. Today we represent the manufacturers of the vast majority of prescription contact lenses and lens care products sold in the UK, and provide a cohesive voice for our members.

MEMBERSHIP

UK based contact lens, care product and material manufacturers, distributors and consultants

OPTOMETRY

Careers in optometry are overseen by the General Optical Council (10 Old Bailey, London EC4M 7NG; Tel: 020 7580 3898; e-mail: goc@optical.org; website: www.optical.org). You can study for an undergraduate optometry degree from one of nine GOC-approved institutions in the UK: Anglia Ruskin University, Aston University, the University of Bradford, Cardiff University, City University, Glasgow Caledonian University, Plymouth University, the University of Manchester and the University of Ulster.

LENGTH OF COURSE

Usually four years in total (five in Scotland): a full-time three-year (four-year in Scotland) degree course, followed by one year's salaried pre-registration training with a practice under the guidance of a GOC-registered optometrist. This includes a series of assessments, set by the College of Optometry, or the University of Manchester, throughout the placement. Trainees must have gained a degree in Optometry at 2:2 or above and have a valid Certificate of Clinical Competency in order to enter a pre-registration placement. Trainees whose certificate has expired or who fail to achieve a 2:2 in their degree must successfully complete the GOC's Optometry Progression Scheme before entering a pre-registration placement.

ENTRY REQUIREMENTS

You will normally need five GCSEs (or equivalent) at grade C or above, one of which should be English; often maths and physics or double science are also required. You will normally be required to have three A Level passes/approximately 320 UCAS tariff points from the following subjects: physics, biology, chemistry or mathematics. Requirements vary between universities, so be sure to check the university's prospectus and/or consult the relevant admission tutors.

REGISTRATION

On successful completion of the pre-registration period of training, which includes work-based assessment and a final assessment on the Stage 2 core competencies for optometry, the qualified optometrist must register with the GOC in order to practise.

Nationals of EU/EEA countries who have gained optical qualifications in an EU/EEA country can apply to another EU/EEA country to have their qualifications recognised. For people who gained their qualification outside the EU/EEA the requirements for registration as an optometrist in the UK are detailed on the GOC website.

Membership of Professional Institutions and Associations

ASSOCIATION OF OPTOMETRISTS

2 Woodbridge Street
London EC1R 0DG
Tel: 020 7549 2000
Fax: 020 7251 8315
E-mail: postbox@aop.org.uk
Website: www.aop.org.uk

The AOP serves its members by promoting and protecting them, providing them with relevant services, representing and supporting them, enhancing their professional and business effectiveness, and expanding the role of optometry in primary and secondary eyecare.

MEMBERSHIP
Student and pre-registration Member
Honorary Member
Dispensing opticians
Full Member
Overseas member
Lay practice owner

ORTHOPTICS

Membership of Professional Institutions and Associations

BRITISH AND IRISH ORTHOPTIC SOCIETY

3rd Floor
Interchange Place
151-165 Edmund Street
Birmingham B3 2TA
Tel: +44 (0)121 728 5633
E-mail: bios@orthoptics.org.uk
Website: www.orthoptics.org.uk

Orthoptists diagnose and treat problems with visual development and binocular vision (how the eyes work together as a pair), and eye movement disorders. They are experts in childhood vision screening. Most orthoptists in the UK work in the Ophthalmology Clinics of acute hospitals, treating patients with stroke, glaucoma, reading difficulties, neurological disorders, low vision and other conditions.

MEMBERSHIP
Full

Full (Republic of ireland)
Academic / non-taxpayer
Overseas
Non-practising
Associate

QUALIFICATION/EXAMINATIONS
Degrees in orthoptics are offered by Liverpool University (www.liv.ac.uk), Sheffield University (www.sheffield.ac.uk) and Glasgow Caledonian University (www.gcu.ac.uk)

OSTEOPATHY AND NATUROPATHY
Membership of Professional Institutions and Associations

INSTITUTE OF OSTEOPATHY

3 Park Terrace
Manor Road
Luton
Bedfordshire LU1 3HN
Tel: 01582 488455
E-mail: enquiries@iosteopathy.org
Website: www.iosteopathy.org

The Institute of Osteopathy provides opportunities for individual and professional development in osteopathic practice and promote the highest standards of osteopathic education and research.

MEMBERSHIP
Student Member
1st/2nd/3rd/4th Year Graduate Member
Full Member
Overseas Member

PATENT AGENCY
Membership of Professional Institutions and Associations

THE CHARTERED INSTITUTE OF PATENT ATTORNEYS

2nd floor, Halton House
20-23 Holborn
London EC1N 2JD
Tel: 020 7405 9450
Fax: 020 7430 0471
E-mail: mail@cipa.org.uk
Website: www.cipa.org.uk

CIPA is the professional, training and examining body for patent attorneys in the UK. From 2010 the IP Regulation Board, an independent body within the CIPA, sets the standards for regulation of the profession. Trainees, all technical graduates, also study for the qualification to practise before the European Patent Office.

MEMBERSHIP
Student
Associate

Fellow
British Overseas
Foreign

QUALIFICATION/EXAMINATIONS
Qualifying examination for registration as a Patent Attorney

DESIGNATORY LETTERS
RPA, CPA

PENSION MANAGEMENT
Membership of Professional Institutions and Associations

THE PENSIONS MANAGEMENT INSTITUTE

Floor 20, Tower 42
25 Old Broad street
London EC2N 1HQ
Tel: 020 7247 1452
Fax: 020 7375 0603
E-mail: via website
Website: www.pensions-pmi.org.uk

The Pensions Management Institute is the professional body that promotes standards of excellence and lifetime learning for pensions professionals and trustees through its qualifications, membership and ongoing support services. For further details please visit our website.

MEMBERSHIP
Student Membership
Certificate Membership
Diploma Membership
Associate Membership
Fellowship
Affiliate Membership
Trustee Group Membership
PMI Accredited Adviser
PMI Automatic Enrolment Accredited CPD programme

QUALIFICATION/EXAMINATIONS
Award in Pensions Essentials (APE)
Certificate in Pensions Essentials (CPE)
Certificate in Pension Calculations (CPC)
Certificate in Pensions Administration (CPA)
Diploma in Pensions Administration (DPA)
Retirement Provision Certificate (RPC)
Certificate in Pensions Automatic Enrolment (CPAE)
Diploma in Retirement Provision (DRP)
Diploma in Employee Benefits and Retirement Savings (DEBRS)
Diploma in International Employee Benefits (DipIEB)
Diploma in Regulated Retirement Advice (DRRA)
Advanced Diploma in Retirement Provision (ADRP)
Awards in Pensions Trusteeship (APT)

DESIGNATORY LETTERS
CertPMI, DipPMI, APMI, FPMI

PERSONNEL MANAGEMENT
Membership of Professional Institutions and Associations

CHARTERED INSTITUTE OF PERSONNEL AND DEVELOPMENT

151 The Broadway
Wimbledon
London SW19 1JQ
Tel: +44(0)20 8612 6200
E-mail: email via website, https://www.cipd.co.uk/about/contact
Website: www.cipd.co.uk

The CIPD is the world's largest Chartered HR and development professional body. With 135,000 members across 120 countries it supports and develops those responsible for the management and development of people within organisations.

MEMBERSHIP
Affiliate Member
Student Member
Associate Member (Assoc CIPD)
Chartered Member (MCIPD)
Chartered Fellow (FCIPD)

Academic Member

For further information see: www.cipd.co.uk/membership

QUALIFICATION/EXAMINATIONS

CIPD qualifications are available at three levels:
Level 3 Foundation
Level 5 Intermediate
Level 7 Advanced
In three different sizes:

Awards
Certificates
Diplomas
For more information and to find out where to study CIPD qualifications visit: www.cipd.co.uk/qualifications

DESIGNATORY LETTERS

Assoc CIPD, Chartered MCIPD, Chartered FCIPD, CCIPD

THE INSTITUTE OF CONTINUING PROFESSIONAL DEVELOPMENT

Royal Institute of Chartered Surveyors
Parliament Square
London SW1P 3AD
Tel: 020 7695 1673
E-mail: info@cpdinstitute.org
Website: www.cpdinstitute.org

The Institute of Continuing Professional Development is part of the Continuing Professional Development Foundation, an educational charitable trust providing high-quality and broad-ranging CPD since 1981. We serve the public interest by helping to raise the effectiveness of professionals through the promotion of CPD as an important and integral element of lifelong learning.

MEMBERSHIP

Member (MInstCPD)
Fellow (FInstCPD)

DESIGNATORY LETTERS

MInstCPD, FInstCPD

UK EMPLOYEE ASSISTANCE PROFESSIONALS ASSOCIATION

PO Box 291
York YO42 9BB
E-mail: info@eapa.org.uk
Website: www.eapa.org.uk

The UK Employee Assistance Professionals Association represents the interests of professionals concerned with employee assistance, psychological health and wellbeing in the UK. Members include external and internal EAP providers, purchasers, counsellors, consultants and trainers.

MEMBERSHIP

- Registered Provider
- Non Registered Provider
- Consultant Associate Member
- Associate Member
- Individual Member
- Student Member

PHARMACY
Membership of Professional Institutions and Associations

GENERAL PHARMACEUTICAL COUNCIL

25 Canada Square
London E14 5LQ
Tel: 020 3713 8000
Fax: 020 7735 7629
E-mail: info@pharmacyregulation.org
Website: www.pharmacyregulation.org

The General Pharmaceutical Council, which dates from 1841, is the professional body for pharmacists and pharmacy technicians in England, Scotland and Wales. Our primary objectives are to lead, regulate, develop and represent the profession. We promote advancement of the science and practice of pharmacy, and pharmaceutical education and knowledge, and liaise with government and other bodies in the interests of our members.

MEMBERSHIP
Pharmacy Technician
Pharmacist
Student

QUALIFICATION/EXAMINATIONS
Membership by relevant porofessional qualification.

DESIGNATORY LETTERS
MRPharmS, FRPharmS

THE PHARMACEUTICAL SOCIETY OF NORTHERN IRELAND

73 University Street
Belfast BT7 1HL
Tel: 028 9032 6927
Fax: 028 9043 9919
E-mail: info@psni.org.uk
Website: www.psni.org.uk

The Pharmaceutical Society of Northern Ireland, founded in 1925, is the regulatory and professional body for pharmacists in Northern Ireland. It maintains a register of more than 2,000 pharmacists and over 500 pharmacy premises, and sets and promotes the standards for pharmacists' admission to and remaining on the register, thereby protecting public safety.

MEMBERSHIP
Trainee
Member

QUALIFICATION/EXAMINATIONS
Registration Examination

PHOTOGRAPHY
Membership of Professional Institutions and Associations

ASSOCIATION OF PHOTOGRAPHERS (AOP)

Somerset House
South Wing
Strand
London WC2R 1LA
Tel: 020 7739 6669
E-mail: info@aophoto.co.uk
Website: www.the-aop.org

The AOP was founded in 1968 to promote the highest standards throughout the industry and to improve the rights of all professional photographers based in the UK. Our membership currently comprises 1,800 photographers and photographic assistants, and we are supported by photographers' agents, printers, and manufacturers and suppliers of photographic equipment.

MEMBERSHIP
Student Member
Assistant Member
Photographer (full) Member
Agent Member
College Member
Affiliated Company

BRITISH INSTITUTE OF PROFESSIONAL PHOTOGRAPHY

The Artistry House
16 Winckley Square
Preston PR1 3JJ
E-mail: admin@bipp.com
Website: www.bipp.com

The BIPP is the qualifying body for professional photographers in the UK. We provide support, training and qualifications for photographers across all types of photography, and organise a number of regional activities and events. A not-for-profit orga-nisation, we ensure that professional standards are met and maintained.

MEMBERSHIP
Open to full- or part-time professional photogra-phers. Join as a Provisional member (for a maximum of 1 year) and work towards gaining a professional qualification. Friends' & Student membership is also available.

QUALIFICATION/EXAMINATIONS
Three tiers of qualification:
Licentiateship (LBIPP)
Associateship (ABIPP)
Fellowship (FBIPP)

DESIGNATORY LETTERS
LBIPP, ABIPP, FBIPP

MASTER PHOTOGRAPHERS ASSOCIATION

Jubilee House
1 Chancery Lane
Darlington
Co Durham DL1 5QP
Tel: 01325 356555
Fax: 01325 357813
E-mail: membership@thempa.com
Website: www.thempa.com

The MPA was founded in 1952 and is now the UK's only organisation for FT, qualified professional photographers. We have more than 2,000 members, who enjoy a range of benefits, including education, qualifications, informative regional meetings, business building promotions and marketing support, and abide by the Association's Code of Conduct.

MEMBERSHIP
Licentiate (LMPA)
Associate (AMPA)
Fellow (FMPA)

QUALIFICATION/EXAMINATIONS
The Diploma in Photographic Practice (DipPP) is recognized by SkillSet, as a benchmark competence mapped to the Photo Imaging National Standards: it is available to all qualified members and is an assessment process of professional photographic business and personal skills.

DESIGNATORY LETTERS
LMPA, AMPA, FMPA, DipPP

THE ROYAL PHOTOGRAPHIC SOCIETY

RPS House
337 Paintworks
Arnos Vale
Bristol BS4 3AR
Tel: 01225 325733
E-mail: available via website, http://rps.org/contact
Website: www.rps.org

The RPS was founded in 1853. It is an educational charity and membership organisaton with the aim of promoting photography and supporting photographers. It realises these through exhibitions, workshops and courses and a distinctions and qualifications programme. Membership is open to anyone. It acts as an advocate on behalf of photographers and photography with the media and government.

MEMBERSHIP
Member
Family
Student
65 and over
25 and under
Disabled
Overseas

QUALIFICATION/EXAMINATIONS
Licentiate (LRPS)
Associate (ARPS)
Fellowship (FRPS)
Qualified Imaging Scientist and Licentiate (QIS LRPS)
Graduate Imaging Scientist and Associate (GIS ARPS)
Accredited Imaging Scientist and Associate (AIS ARPS)
Accredited Senior Imaging Scientist and Fellow (ASIS FRPS)
Qualified in Imaging in the Creative Industries (QICI & LRPS)
Graduate in Imaging in the Creative Industries (GICI & ARPS)

| Accredited in Imaging in the Creative Industries (AICI & ARPS) | Creative Industries Qualification |
| Accredited Senior in Imaging in the Creative Industries (ASICI FRPS) | *DESIGNATORY LETTERS*
LRPS, ARPS, FRPS |

PHYSICS

Membership of Professional Institutions and Associations

INSTITUTE OF PHYSICS AND ENGINEERING IN MEDICINE

Fairmount House
230 Tadcaster Road
York YO24 1ES
Tel: 01904 610821
Fax: 01904 612279
E-mail: office@ipem.org.uk
Website: www.ipem.ac.uk

The IPEM is dedicated to bringing together physical science, engineering and clinical professionals in academia, healthcare services and industry to share knowledge, advance science and technology, and inform and educate the public, with the purpose of improving the understanding, detection and treatment of disease and the management of patients.

MEMBERSHIP
Affiliate
Associate
Full Member
Corporate Member (MIPEM)
Fellow (FIPEM)
International
RCP Affiliate / Associate

DESIGNATORY LETTERS
MedMIPEM, MedFIPEM, IIPEM, MIPEM, FIPEM

THE INSTITUTE OF PHYSICS

37 Caledonian Road
London N1 9BU
Tel: 020 7470 4800
Fax: 020 7470 4848
E-mail: membership@iop.org
Website: www.iop.org

The Institute of Physics is the professional body and learned society for physics in the UK and Ireland. We inspire people to develop their knowledge, understanding and enjoyment of physics. We are a world-leading science publisher and are proud to be a trusted and valued voice for the physics community

MEMBERSHIP
Associate Member; Member (MInstP); Fellow (FInstP); and Honorary Fellow (Hon.FInstP â by invitation only)

DESIGNATORY LETTERS
MInstP, FInstP, Hon.FInstP, CPhys, RSciTech, RSci, EngTech, IEng and CEng

PHYSIOTHERAPY
Membership of Professional Institutions and Associations

THE CHARTERED SOCIETY OF PHYSIOTHERAPY

14 Bedford Row
London WC1R 4ED
Tel: 0207 306 6666
E-mail: via website: www.csp.org.uk/contact_us
Website: www.csp.org.uk

The CSP is the professional, educational and trade union body for the UK's 52,000 chartered physiotherapists, physiotherapy students and assistants. In order to become a member of the CSP it is necessary to have undertaken a qualification recognized by the Health and Care Professions Council (HCPC) – see: www.hcpc-uk.org

MEMBERSHIP
Associate
Member (MCSP)

DESIGNATORY LETTERS
MCSP

PLUMBING
Membership of Professional Institutions and Associations

CHARTERED INSTITUTE OF PLUMBING AND HEATING ENGINEERING

64 Station Lane
Hornchurch
Essex RM12 6NB
Tel: 01708 472791
Fax: 01708 448987
E-mail: info@ciphe.org.uk
Website: www.ciphe.org.uk

The CIPHE, founded in 1906, is the professional body for the UK plumbing and heating industry. Our membership of around 7500 is made up of individuals from a wide range of backgrounds and includes trainees, specifiers, designers, public health engineers, lecturers, trainers, consultants and practitioners, as well as manufacturers and distributors.

MEMBERSHIP
Trainee or Apprentice
Affiliate
Companion (CompCIPHE)
Associate (ACIPHE)
Member (MCIPHE)
Fellow (FCIPHE)

QUALIFICATION/EXAMINATIONS
Membership is based on qualifications and experience in each category. There is also the opportunity to register through the CIPHE for registration with the Engineering Council at EngTech, IEng or CEng level. The prestigious awards of Apprentice, Journeyman and Master Plumber Certificate (awarded jointly with the Worshipful Company of Plumbers and the City & Guilds of London Institute) are also available.
Guidance and advice is always available whether you are considering a career in the plumbing and heating industry or you are a plumbing or heating professional seeking advice on career progression.

DESIGNATORY LETTERS
CompCIPHE, ACIPHE, MCIPHE, FCIPHE

PRINTING

Membership of Professional Institutions and Associations

PROSKILLS UK

Unit 24 East Central
127 Olympic Avenue
Milton Park
Abingdon
Oxfordshire OX14 4SA
Tel: 01235 833844
E-mail: info@proskills.co.uk
Website: www.proskills.co.uk

Proskills UK is the bridge between employers and government on skills and training. Employer-led representing key industries including: Building Products, Coatings, Furniture, Furnishings & Interiors, Glass & Related Industries, Health and Safety Paper, Printing and Wood industries, which make up a third of the UK manufacturing sector. We help to raise the profile of the sector, set the skills standards and qualifications and ensure that the skills and funding system delivers against the current and future needs of the industries.

QUALIFICATION/EXAMINATIONS
Please see the Proskills UK website.

THE INSTITUTE OF PAPER, PRINTING AND PUBLISHING (IP3)

Claremont House
70–72 Alma Road
Windsor
Berks SL4 3EZ
Tel: 0870 330 8625
Fax: 0870 330 8615
E-mail: info@ip3.org.uk
Website: www.ip3.org.uk

IP3 is the professional body representing the interests of individuals within the paper, printing and publishing sector. It was formed in 2005 from the merger of the Institute of Paper, the Institute of Printing and the Institute of Publishing, and brought together more than 2,000 members and a wealth of knowledge.

MEMBERSHIP
Student

Associate (AIP3)
Member (MIP3)
Fellow (FIP3)

QUALIFICATION/EXAMINATIONS
Certificate

DESIGNATORY LETTERS
AIP3, MIP3, FIP3

PROFESSIONAL INVESTIGATION
Membership of Professional Institutions and Associations

THE INSTITUTE OF PROFESSIONAL INVESTIGATORS

Jubilee House
3 The Drive
Brentwood
Essex CM13 3FR
Tel: 0870 330 8622
Fax: 0870 330 8612
E-mail: admin@ipi.org.uk
Website: www.ipi.org.uk

The IPI was founded in 1976 as a professional body, catering primarily for the work and educational needs of professional investigators of all types and all specializations. We encourage members' CPD and require them to adhere to the Institute's strict code of ethics, and we promote the recognition of professional investigation as a profession by government, legislative bodies and the public.

MEMBERSHIP
Associate
Member (MIPI)
Student
Fellow (FIPI)

Retiree

QUALIFICATION/EXAMINATIONS
The Institute provides an interactive online IPI Level 3 Professional Invesigator's course for students and others interested in becoming part of the investigative industry; this course also provides a refresher course for those who need to update their specialization and/or interest in other areas of investigative work.

DESIGNATORY LETTERS
MIPI, FIPI

PSYCHOANALYSIS
Membership of Professional Institutions and Associations

THE BRITISH PSYCHOANALYTICAL SOCIETY

Byron House
112a Shirland Road
London W9 2BT
Tel: 020 7563 5000
Fax: 020 7563 5001
E-mail: admin@iopa.org.uk
Website: www.psychoanalysis.org.uk

The British Psychoanalytical Society has c500 members and c60 candidates for membership. Our aims include: to support the development of psychoanalytical knowledge as a general theory of mind, to further the clinical and scientific standards of psychoanalysis, and to train high-quality psychoanalytical professionals in sufficient numbers to develop the profession.

MEMBERSHIP
Associate Member
Full Member
Fellow

QUALIFICATION/EXAMINATIONS
See website: www.psychoanalysis.org.uk/education/training-with-the-institute-of-psychoanalysis

PSYCHOLOGY
Membership of Professional Institutions and Associations

BRITISH PSYCHOLOGICAL SOCIETY

St Andrews House
48 Princess Road East
Leicester LE1 7DR
Tel: 0116 254 9568
Fax: 0116 227 1314
E-mail: enquiries@bps.org.uk
Website: www.bps.org.uk

Psychology is the scientific study of people, the mind and behaviour. The British Psychological Society is the representative body for psychology and psychologists in the UK. We are responsible for the development, promotion and application of psychology for the public good.

MEMBERSHIP
Student Member
Graduate Member (MBPsS)
Associate Fellow (AFBPsS)
Fellow (FBPsS)
Honorary Fellow (HonFBPsS)
Affiliate
Chartered Membership (CPsychol)
Subscriber
e-Subscriber

QUALIFICATION/EXAMINATIONS
Statement of Equivalence in Clinical Psychology (SoE)
Qualification in Educational Psychology (Scotland) (Stage 2)
Qualification in Forensic Psychology (Stage 2) (QFP)
Qualification in Clinical Neuropsychology (QiCN)
Qualification in Counselling Psychology (QCoP)
Qualification in Health Psychology (Stage 2)
Qualification in Occupational Psychology (QOccPsych)
Qualification in Sport & Exercise Psychology (QSEP)

DESIGNATORY LETTERS
MBPsS, AFBPsS, FBPsS, CPsychol, HonMBPsS, HonFBPsS, SoE

PSYCHOTHERAPY
Membership of Professional Institutions and Associations

ASSOCIATION OF CHILD PSYCHOTHERAPISTS

CAN Borough
7-14 Great Dover Street
London SE1 4YR
Tel: 020 7922 7751
E-mail: admin@childpsychotherapy.org.uk
Website: www.childpsychotherapy.org.uk

The ACP is the main professional body for psychoanalytic child and adolescent psychotherapists in the UK. Our members work with children and young people as well as their parents, families and wider networks, treating a wide range of difficulties ranging from problems with sleeping and bed-wetting to eating disorders, self-harm, depression and anxiety.

MEMBERSHIP
Member

BRITISH ASSOCIATION FOR COUNSELLING AND PSYCHOTHERAPY

BACP House
15 St John's Business Park
Lutterworth
Leicestershire LE17 4HB
Tel: 01455 883300
E-mail: bacp@bacp.co.uk
Website: www.bacp.co.uk

BACP is the largest and broadest body within the sector and participates in the development of counselling and psychotherapy at an international level. Our work with large and small organisations ranges from advising schools on how to set up a counselling service to assisting the NHS on service provision, working with voluntary agencies and supporting independent practitioners.

MEMBERSHIP
Student member
Individual Member
Registered Member (MBACP)
Accredited member
Senior Accredited Member (Snr Accred)
Retired member
Organisational member

QUALIFICATION/EXAMINATIONS
We run workshops for members and accredit individual counsellors/psychotherapists, supervisors, counselling services and training courses. For details see our website.

DESIGNATORY LETTERS
MBACP, MBACP (Accred), Snr Accred

BRITISH ASSOCIATION FOR THE PERSON CENTRED APPROACH

BAPCA
PO Box 143
Ross-on-Wye
Herefordshire HR9 9AH
Tel: 01600 891508
E-mail: via website
Website: www.bapca.org.uk

The BAPCA was founded in 1989 as a non-religious, non-profit-making organisation with the aim of advancing education in Client-Centred Psychotherapy and Counselling and the Person-Centred Approach through its publications and website, and cooperation with other national and international organisations with similar goals.

MEMBERSHIP
Individual Member
Joint Member
International Member
Institutional Member

BRITISH PSYCHOTHERAPY FOUNDATION

37 Mapesbury Road
London NW2 4HJ
Tel: 020 8452 9823
E-mail: enquiries@bpf-psychotherapy.org.uk
Website: www.britishpsychotherapyfoundation.org.uk

The BAP is one of the longest established and largest independent providers of Jungian analytic and psychoanalytic psychotherapy for adults and children in the UK. We have been training psychoanalytic and Jungian psychotherapists for nearly 60 years, and our members work in the NHS, the corporate and voluntary sectors and as private practitioners.

MEMBERSHIP
Member

QUALIFICATION/EXAMINATIONS
Certificate/Diploma/MSc in Psychodynamics of Human Development (jointly with Birkbeck College, University of London)
DPsych in Child and Adolescent Psychotherapy (jointly with Birkbeck College, University of London)

NATIONAL COLLEGE OF HYPNOSIS AND PSYCHOTHERAPY

23-24 Great James Street
London WC1N 3ES
Tel: 0207 831 8801 or 0345 257 8735
E-mail: enquiries@nchp.org.uk
Website: www.hypnotherapyuk.net

The NCHP is a not-for-profit organisation founded in 1977 and now offers accredited hypnotherapy training, hypnosis training and psychotherapy training at weekends in Leicester, London, Manchester and Oxford. We also provide a programme of 1- and 2-day workshops and seminars, and (where appropriate) distance-learning courses.

QUALIFICATION/EXAMINATIONS
Foundation Course
Certificate in Hypno-Psychotherapy (CHP(NC))
Diploma in Hypno-Psychotherapy (DHP(NC))
Advanced Diploma in Hypno-Psychotherapy (ADHP(NC))

NATIONAL COUNCIL OF PSYCHOTHERAPISTS

First Floor, East Suite
The Waterfront
Salts Mill Road
Shipley
West Yorkshire BD17 7TD
Tel: 01274 028685
E-mail: info@thencp.org
Website: www.thencp.org

The National Council is a registering and accrediting body for psychotherapists, counsellors and coaches within the UK and also, through the International Council, the rest of the world.

Members can join the Council regardless of which discipline and where they completed their training.

MEMBERSHIP
Accredited Member (MNCP Accred)

Member (MNCP)
Fellow (FNCP)
Student membership
International membership

DESIGNATORY LETTERS
ANCP, LNCP, MNCP, FNCP

THE FOUNDATION FOR PSYCHOTHERAPY AND COUNSELLING

5 Maidstone Buildings Mews
72–76 Borough High Street
London SE1 1GN
Tel: 0207 378 7392
E-mail: office@thefpc.org.uk
Website: www.thefpc.org.uk

The Foundation for Psychotherapy and Counselling was formed during the 1970s as the graduate body of WPF Therapy (the largest charitable provider of counselling and psychotherapy in England) and now has some 700 fully trained and qualified members, most of whom are in private practice.

MEMBERSHIP
Member

THE NATIONAL REGISTER OF HYPNOTHERAPISTS AND PSYCHOTHERAPISTS

86 Wateringpool lane
Lostock Hall
Preston
Lancashire PR5 5UA
Tel: 0161 635 3530
E-mail: admin@nrhp.co.uk
Website: www.nrhp.co.uk

NRHP (est 1985) – a professional association of qualified hypno-psychotherapists who trained with a UKCP-accredited training organisation. Members are required to adhere to a code of ethics and carry appropriate insurance. We publish a Directory of Practitioners and offer a public referral service via our website and office. Member of the UKCP.

MEMBERSHIP
Student

Associate 1 (NRHP(Assoc 1))
Associate 2 (NRHP(Assoc 2))
Associate 3 (NRHP(Assoc 3))
Full Member (MNRHP)
Fellow (FNRHP)

DESIGNATORY LETTERS
NRHP(Assoc 1), NRHP(Assoc 2), NRHP(Assoc 3), MNRHP, FNRHP

UK COUNCIL FOR PSYCHOTHERAPY (UKCP)

America House
2 America Square
London EC3N 2LU
Tel: 020 7014 9955
E-mail: Via website: www.psychotherapy.org.uk/contact-us/
Website: www.psychotherapy.org.uk

UKCP is the leading professional body for the education, training, accreditation and regulation of psychotherapists and psychotherapeutic counsellors. Our register is accredited by the government's Professional Standards Authority. As part of our commitment to protecting the public, we work to improve access to psychotherapy, to support and disseminate research, to improve standards and to respond effectively to complaints against our members.

MEMBERSHIP
Student
Trainee
Full clinical
Full non-clinical

Retired
Organisational
Non-clinical affiliate
Affiliate organisational

PURCHASING AND SUPPLY

Membership of Professional Institutions and Associations

THE CHARTERED INSTITUTE OF PROCUREMENT & SUPPLY

Easton House
Easton on the Hill
Stamford
Lincolnshire PE9 3NZ
Tel: 01780 756777
Fax: 01780 751610
E-mail: press@cips.org
Website: www.cips.org

The Chartered Institute of Procurement & Supply (CIPS) is the world's largest procurement and supply professional organisation. It is the worldwide centre of excellence on purchasing and supply management issues. CIPS has a global community of 200,000 in 180 different countries, including senior business people, high-ranking civil servants and leading academics. The activities of purchasing and supply chain professionals have a major impact on the profitability and efficiency of all types of organisation and CIPS offers corporate solutions packages to improve business profitability.

MEMBERSHIP
Student Member

Affiliate
Certificate Member
Diploma Member
Associate Member
Full Member (MCIPS)
Fellow (FCIPS)
Chartered Professional in Procurement and Supply management

QUALIFICATION/EXAMINATIONS
Please see website: www.cips.org

DESIGNATORY LETTERS
MCIPS, FCIPS, Chartered Professional in procurement and supply management

QUALITY ASSURANCE
Membership of Professional Institutions and Associations

THE CHARTERED QUALITY INSTITUTE

2nd Floor
10 Furnival street
London EC4A 1AB
Tel: 020 7245 6722
E-mail: membership@quality.org
Website: www.quality.org

The CQI is the chartered body for quality management professionals. Established in 1919, we gained a Royal Charter in 2006 and became the CQI shortly afterwards. Our vision is to place quality at the heart of every organisation; we promote the benefits of quality management to industry, disseminate quality knowledge and resources, provide qualifications and training, and assess quality competence.

MEMBERSHIP
Student
Associate Member (ACQI)
Practitioner (PCQI)
Member, Chartered Quality Professional (MCQI, CQP)
Fellow, Chartered Quality Professional (FCQI, CQP)

QUALIFICATION/EXAMINATIONS
Level 3 Certificate in Quality Management (QCF)
Level 5 Certificate in Systems Management (QCF)
Level 5 Certificate in Assuring Service & Product Quality (QCF)
Level 5 Certificate in Managing Supply Chain Quality (QCF)
Level 5 Certificate in Quality Improvement for Business (QCF)
Level 5 Certificate in Quality Management Systems Audit (QCF)
Level 5 Diploma in Quality Management (QCF)

DESIGNATORY LETTERS
MCQI, CQP; FCQI, CQP

RADIOGRAPHY
Membership of Professional Institutions and Associations

THE SOCIETY OF RADIOGRAPHERS

207 Providence Square
Mill Street
London SE1 2EW
Tel: 020 7740 7200
Fax: 020 7740 7233
E-mail: via website: www.sor.org/about-us/contact-us
Website: www.sor.org

The Society of Radiographers, founded in 1920, represents diagnostic and therapeutic radiographers in the UK. Associated professionals working in medical imaging, radiation therapy and oncology are also welcome. It is responsible for their professional, educational, public and workplace interests. Together with the College of Radiographers, our charitable subsidiary, our efforts are directed towards education, research and other activities in support of the science and practice of radiography.

MEMBERSHIP
We have a range of membership options, including student, associate professional, healthcare support worker and assistant practitioner, retired and international membership options. See www.sor.org/being-member/join-us

RETAIL
Membership of Professional Institutions and Associations

INSTITUTE OF MASTERS OF WINE

6 Riverlight Quay
Kirtling Street
London SW11 8EA
Tel: 020 7383 9130
Fax: 020 7383 9139
E-mail: info@mastersofwine.org
Website: www.mastersofwine.org

The Institute of Masters of Wine is a membership body that represents the interests of its members (Masters of Wine), administers the MW Examination, and runs an education programme in preparation for the examination. We also hold a number of events throughout the year, including seminars and tastings, master classes, discussions and, every 4 years, a symposium, most of which are open to the public.

MEMBERSHIP
Master of Wine (MW)

QUALIFICATION/EXAMINATIONS
Master of Wine Examination

DESIGNATORY LETTERS
MW

THE BRITISH ANTIQUE DEALERS' ASSOCIATION

20 Rutland Gate
London SW7 1BD
Tel: 020 7589 4128
Fax: 020 7581 9083
E-mail: info@bada.org
Website: www.bada.org

BADA, which was founded in 1918, is the trade association for antique dealers in Britain. Our vetted members are elected for their high business standards and expertise, and adhere to a strict code of practice; we provide safeguards for members of the public who deal with our members, including independent arbitration if a dispute arises.

MEMBERSHIP
Member

THE GUILD OF ARCHITECTURAL IRONMONGERS

BPF House
6 Bath Place
Rivington Street
London EC2A 3JE
Tel: +44 (0)207 033 2480
E-mail: info@gai.org.uk
Website: www.gai.org.uk

The GAI represents the interests of architectural ironmongers and manufacturers of architectural ironmongery. This includes all door hardware and the saftey standards and regualtion concerning doors. We develop, promote and protect standards of integrity and excellence, and encourage academic study relating to the industry, operating an Institute for individual members to facilitate their continuous professional development. We liaise with various bodies on matters affecting the industry.

MEMBERSHIP
Affiliate Member
Associate Member
Full Member
Registered Architectural Ironmonger (Reg AI)

QUALIFICATION/EXAMINATIONS
The GAI provides a 3-year incremental training programme. Students are examined each year and must pass each stage in turn before progressing to the next. A Certificate is awarded to successful students each year, culminating in the GAI Diploma (Dip GAI) on successful completion of year 3.

DESIGNATORY LETTERS
Reg AI

THE INSTITUTE OF BUILDERS MERCHANTS

209 Watling Street
Dartford
Kent DA2 6EG
Tel: 01623 628441
E-mail: admin@iobm.co.uk
Website: www.iobm.co.uk

To improve through seminars and website articles, the technical and general knowledge of persons engaged in builders' merchants; to verify management training courses with providers; to acknowledge personal achievements and award diplomas, certificates and other distinctions; to encourage the need for knowledge, integrity and efficiency in the builders' merchants industry.

MEMBERSHIP
Student
Associate
Member
Supplier Partner

QUALIFICATION/EXAMINATIONS
University Degree
The Institute of Builders Merchants Business Studies Course
The Builders Merchants Federation Diploma in Merchanting
Higher National Certificate (HNC) in Business Studies
Higher National Diploma (HND) in Business Studies
NVQ Level 4
Company management programmes as approved by the Board of Governors

THE SOCIETY OF SHOE FITTERS

c/o The Anchorage
28 Admirals Walk
Hingham
Norfolk NR9 4JL
Tel: 01953 851171
E-mail: secretary@shoefitters-uk.org
Website: www.shoefitters-uk.org

The Society of Shoe Fitters estd. in 1959 is now a registered charity to assist the public and industry with enquiries. The Footwear & Fitting course teaches professional shoe fitting plus instore training and Entrance Application for experienced shoe fitters. Provides National Shoe Fitting Week and lobbies government.

MEMBERSHIP
Student Member
Associate Member

Member (MSSF)
Fellow (FSSF)
Associate Member (corporate membership)

QUALIFICATION/EXAMINATIONS
One-day on-site courses – certificate only

Five-month course leading to membership qualification
Entrance Examination and Entrance Application for experienced shoe fitters leading to qualification

DESIGNATORY LETTERS
MSSF, FSSF

SECURITY

Membership of Professional Institutions and Associations

THE SECURITY INSTITUTE

1 The Courtyard
Caldecote
Warwickshire CV10 0AS
E-mail: info@security-institute.org
Website: www.security-institute.org

The Security Institute promotes professionalism in the security world through its professional grades of membership, and encourages a proper understanding of the value of the security function by management. Membership can be an employment prerequisite, and successful students of the Certificate, Diploma and Advance Diploma enjoy enhanced credibility and automatic membership.

MEMBERSHIP
Non Professional grades of membership:
Student
Affiliate
Professional grades offered on following validation:

Associate (ASyI)
Member (MSyI)
Fellow (FSyI)
Chartered Security Professional (CSyP)

QUALIFICATION/EXAMINATIONS
Certificate in Security Management (Level 3)
Diploma in Security Management (Level 5)
Advanced Diploma in Security Management (Level 7)

DESIGNATORY LETTERS
ASyI, MSyI, FSyI, CSyP

SOCIAL WORK AND PROBATION

SOCIAL WORK
Social work is a career for people who like people and much of a social worker's time is spent working in the community, helping support and protect people who are vulnerable and at risk. They work with people who are experiencing social and emotional problems and their families if they are affected. They may help people who use services to claim benefits, plan budgets, obtain legal advice or deal with other local authority departments. Social workers undertake assessment in relation to childcare, mental health and criminal justice. Depending on individual needs, a social worker may arrange services such as home care assistance or hospital treatment

HEALTH AND CARE PROFESSIONS COUNCIL
The role of the Health and Care Professions Council (HCPC) is to protect the public. It does this by developing and monitoring strategy and policy for the HCPC, and ensuring that the organisation fulfils its functions under the Health and Social Work Professions Order 2001. The Council has 12 members made up of 6 registrant and 6 lay members. The HCPC also runs committees to help the Council with its work. Four statutory committees have been set up to establish and monitor standards of education and training and to deal with fitness to practise issues. In addition, the Council has established two non-statutory committees to provide it with advice and guidance on specific issues.

The HCPC is a regulator and keeps a register of health and care professionals who meet their standards for their training, professional skills, behaviour and health. It is an offence for someone to claim they are registered with the HCPC when they are not or to use a protected title they are not entitled to use. Each of the professions regulated by the HCPC have at least one professional title that must be registered.

The HCPC accredits universities that offer social work qualifications at both qualifying and post-qualifying levels, and quality-assures all social work courses.

EDUCATION AND TRAINING

Social workers need a breadth of skills, as they will act as an adviser, advocate, counsellor and listener. There are various routes to becoming a social worker, but you will need to gain a professional qualification in social work (usually at degree level) either on a full-time or part-time basis. This is offered at under-graduate and postgraduate masters level. It is also possible to take a degree course combining social work with mental health or learning disability nursing. To find HCPC-approved degree courses visit www.hcpc-uk.org/education/programmes/register

Students following a social work course may be eligible for a bursary from the Department of Health. For further information visit the NHS Business Authority website: www.nhsbsa.nhs.uk/837.aspx and the Gov.UK website: www.gov.uk/social-work-bursaries

REGISTRATION

Social work regulation in the UK is covered by the HCPC in England, The Care Council for Wales in Wales, the Scottish Social Services Council (SSSC) in Scotland and the Northern Ireland Social Care Council (NISCC) in Northern Ireland. It is possible to register with more than one regulator.

For further details, contact The Health and Care Professions Council, Park House, 184 Kennington Park Road, London SE11 4BU; Tel: 0300 500 6184; Fax: 020 7820 9684; e-mail: via website; website: www.hcpc-uk.org

For information about social work training and registration in Scotland, contact Scottish Social Services Council, Compass House, 11 Riverside Drive, Dundee DD1 4NY; Tel: 0345 6030 891; website: www.sssc.uk.com (online contact form).

For information about social work training and registration in Wales, contact Care Council for Wales, South Gate House, Wood Street, Cardiff CF10 1EW; Tel: 0300 3033 444; e-mail: info@ccwales.org.uk; website: www.ccwales.org.uk

For information about social work training and registration in Northern Ireland, contact Northern Ireland Social Care Council, 7th Floor, Millennium House, 19--25 Great Victoria Street, Belfast BT2 7AQ; Tel: 028 9536 2600; e-mail: info@niscc.hscni.net; website: www.niscc.info

Membership of Professional Institutions and Associations

THE BRITISH ASSOCIATION OF SOCIAL WORKERS

16 Kent Street
Birmingham B5 6RD
Tel: 0121 6223911
Fax: 0121 6224860
E-mail: via website
Website: www.basw.co.uk

The BASW is the largest professional association representing social work and social workers in the UK. Whether you are qualified or not, experienced or just entering the profession, we are here to help, support, advise and campaign on your behalf.

MEMBERSHIP
Student Member
Employed Member (2 categories)

Retired Member
Indeopendent Member
Unemployed / unpaid
Overseas Member

QUALIFICATION/EXAMINATIONS
Professional Capabilities Framework (PCF) – 9 levels
Professional development and education (ProfDE)

SOCIOLOGY
Membership of Professional Institutions and Associations

BRITISH SOCIOLOGICAL ASSOCIATION

Chancery Court
Belmont Business Park
Belmont
Durham DH1 1TW
Tel: 0191 383 0839
Fax: 0191 383 0782
E-mail: enquiries@britsoc.org.uk
Website: www.britsoc.co.uk

The BSA was founded in 1951 to promote sociology in the UK. Our members include researchers, teachers, students and practitioners in a variety of fields. We provide a network of communication to all who are concerned with the promotion and use of sociology and sociological research.

MEMBERSHIP
UK Member
UK Teacher
UK Concessionary
Non-UK Concessionary
Non-UK Member
Non-UK Teacher

SPEECH AND LANGUAGE THERAPY
Membership of Professional Institutions and Associations

ROYAL COLLEGE OF SPEECH AND LANGUAGE THERAPISTS

2 White Hart Yard
London SE1 1NX
Tel: 020 7378 1200
E-mail: via website
Website: www.rcslt.org

The RCSLT is the professional body for speech and language therapists and support workers. We set, promote and maintain high standards in education, clinical practice and ethical conduct. Our national campaigning work aims to improve services for people with speech, language, communication and swallowing needs and to influence health, education and social care policies.

MEMBERSHIP
Student Member

Newly Qualified Member – practisiong / non-practising
Full Member
Overseas
Returner
Retired
Assistant
Fellow (FRCSLT)
Honorary Fellow (Hon FRCSLT)

DESIGNATORY LETTERS
FRCSLT, Hon FRCSLT

SPORTS SCIENCE
Membership of Professional Institutions and Associations

LONDON SCHOOL OF SOFT TISSUE THERAPY

28 Station Parade
Willesden Green
London NW2 4NX
Tel: 020 8452 8855
Fax: 020 8452 4524
E-mail: via website
Website: www.lssm.com

This is a BTEC level 5 qualification which is equivalent to a university under-graduate level of education. It has to provide you with a very high level of skill and knowledge to enable you to become a professional clinical therapist who can effectively assess and treat injuries.

Please see our website for more information www. lssm.com

MEMBERSHIP
Member

QUALIFICATION/EXAMINATIONS
Introductory Massage Workshop
Professional Diploma in Clinical Soft Tissue Therapy (BTEC Level 5)
Myofascial Release
CPD courses

STATISTICS
Membership of Professional Institutions and Associations

THE ROYAL STATISTICAL SOCIETY

12 Errol Street
London EC1Y 8LX
Tel: 020 7638 8998
E-mail: rss@rss.org.uk
Website: www.rss.org.uk

The RSS is the learned society and professional body for statistics and statisticians in the UK. We have over 7,000 members worldwide, and are active in a wide range of areas both directly and indirectly relating to the study and application of statistics.

MEMBERSHIP
Fellow
Professional
Corporate

e-Student
e-Teacher

QUALIFICATION/EXAMINATIONS
Chartered Statistician
Graduate Statistician
Cahertered Scientist

DESIGNATORY LETTERS
GradStat, CStat

STOCKBROKING AND SECURITIES
Membership of Professional Institutions and Associations

CFA SOCIETY OF THE UK

4th Floor
Minster House
42 Mincing Lane
London EC3R 7AE
Tel: +44 (0)20 7648 6200
E-mail: info@cfauk.org
Website: www.cfauk.org

Founded in 1955, CFA UK represents around 12,000 investment professionals and comprises part of the worldwide network of member societies of CFA Institute (the global, not-for-profit association of investment professionals that awards the CFA designation).

CFA UK is the awarding body for the Investment Management Certificate (IMC), the UK's leading entry level qualification for investment professionals. We also support the CFA Program and the Investment Foundations Program, which are awarded by CFA Institute. CFA UK supports the ASIP designation that was awarded to those passing the Associate examinations of the IIMR.

MEMBERSHIP
IMC Member
CFA Candidate Member
Affiliate Member
Regular Member

QUALIFICATION/EXAMINATIONS
Investment Management Certificate (IMC)

SURGICAL, DENTAL AND CARDIOLOGICAL TECHNICIANS
Membership of Professional Institutions and Associations

THE BRITISH INSTITUTE OF DENTAL AND SURGICAL TECHNOLOGISTS

44-46 Wollaston Road
Beeston
Nottingham NG9 2NR
Tel: 0115 9683 182
E-mail: secretary@bidst.org
Website: www.bidst.org

The BIDST has been established for over 70 years and exists to provide a vehicle for the continuing education of technicians within the spheres of dental and surgical technology. It is our aim to make membership of the British Institute of Dental and Surgical Technologists an aspiration for all technicians, raising standards and portraying an image of professionalism which professional technicians deserve.

MEMBERSHIP
Affiliate (Overseas)
Affiliate (DCP)
Affiliate (Student)
Associate
Member
Fellow
Licentiate

DESIGNATORY LETTERS
LBIDST, FBIDST

SURVEYING
Membership of Professional Institutions and Associations

CHARTERED ASSOCIATION OF BUILDING ENGINEERS

Lutyens House
Billing Brook Road
Weston Favell
Northampton
Northamptonshire NN3 8NW
Tel: 44 (0)1604 404 121
E-mail: via website
Website: www.cbuilde.com

Formed in 1925 as the Incorporated Association of Architects and Surveyors, the Chartered Association of Building Engineers (CABE) is a leading body for professionals specialising in the design, construction, evaluation and maintenance of buildings. Its members practise across the United Kingdom, mainland Europe and around the World, and work in both the private and public sectors. The CABE provides the prime qualification of Building Engineer, a title that exactly reflects the professional expertise of members.

MEMBERSHIP
Student
Technician
Training Affiliate
Academic Affiliate
Associate Member (ABEng)
Graduate Member (GradBEng)
Corporate Member (MBEng)
Corporate Fellow (FBEng)
Honorary Fellow (HonFBEng)

QUALIFICATION/EXAMINATIONS
For a full listed of accredited courses, please see https://www.cbuilde.com/careers/accredited-universities/list-of-accredited-universities/

DESIGNATORY LETTERS
ACABE, Grad CABE, C. Build E MCABE, C. Build E FCABE

SWIMMING INSTRUCTION
Membership of Professional Institutions and Associations

THE SWIMMING TEACHERS' ASSOCIATION

Anchor House
Birch Street
Walsall
West Midlands WS2 8HZ
Tel: 01922 645097
E-mail: via website
Website: www.sta.co.uk

Today with more than 10,000 members, the Swimming Teachers' Association (STA) is an independent swimming teaching and lifesaving organisation, and delivers the highest quality training across four key business areas – Swimming Teaching, Lifesaving, First Aid and Leisure Management.

MEMBERSHIP
Member

QUALIFICATION/EXAMINATIONS
For full list of qualifications, please see https://www.safetytrainingawards.co.uk/qualifications/

TAXATION
Membership of Professional Institutions and Associations

SOCIETY OF TRUST & ESTATE PRACTITIONERS (STEP)

Artillery House (South)
11–19 Artillery Row
London SW1P 1RT
Tel: +44 (0)20 3752 3700
E-mail: step@step.org
Website: www.step.org

STEP is a global professional body, comprising lawyers, accountants, financial advisors and other practitioners that help families plan for their futures.

STEP provides confidence to families by setting standards, training and educating members, and upholding those standards.

Full STEP members, known as 'TEPs', are internationally recognised as experts in their field.

MEMBERSHIP
TEP, Full membership (top level)

Associate (mid level)
Affiliate (entry level)

QUALIFICATION/EXAMINATIONS
For a full list of qualifications, please see https://www.step.org/qualifications/qualifications-membership-framework

DESIGNATORY LETTERS
TEP

THE ASSOCIATION OF TAXATION TECHNICIANS

30 Monck Street
London SW1P 2AP
Tel: 020 7340 0551
E-mail: info@att.org.uk
Website: www.att.org.uk

The primary charitable objective of the Association of Taxation Technicians is to promote education and the study of tax administration and practice. One of our key aims is to provide an appropriate qualification for individuals who undertake tax compliance work. Drawing on our members' practical experience and knowledge, we contribute to consultations on the development of the UK tax system and seek to ensure that, for the general public, it is workable and as fair as possible.

MEMBERSHIP
Member

QUALIFICATION/EXAMINATIONS
Certificate of Competency
Foundation Qualification
VAT Compliance Diploma (non-UK)
ATT Trailblazer Apprenticeship
ATT

DESIGNATORY LETTERS
ATT

THE CHARTERED INSTITUTE OF TAXATION

30 Monck Street
London SW1P 2AP
Tel: 020 7340 0550
E-mail: via website
Website: www.tax.org.uk

The CIOT is the leading body in the UK for taxation professionals dealing with all aspects of taxation. Our primary purpose is to promote education in taxation. One of our key aims is to achieve a more efficient and less complex tax system for all. Our comments and recommendations on tax issues are made solely in order to achieve this aim; we are an entirely apolitical organisation.

MEMBERSHIP
Member (CTA)

QUALIFICATION/EXAMINATIONS
Chartered Tax Adviser (CTA) examination
Level 7 Apprenticeship
ATT CTA Tax Pathway
ACA CTA Joint Pathway

DESIGNATORY LETTERS
CTA, ADIT, ATT CTA, ACA CTA

TEACHING/EDUCATION

Initial qualifications in the UK

QUALIFIED TEACHER STATUS

To obtain a teaching appointment as a qualified teacher in maintained schools and non-maintained special schools in England and Wales, it is necessary to have Qualified Teacher Status (QTS). To be qualified, teachers must have satisfactorily completed an approved course of initial teacher training (ITT), and to be able to teach in maintained schools in England must have successfully completed their induction period (there are similar arrangements for teaching in Scotland, Wales and Northern Ireland). The National College for Teaching and Leadership (NCTL), an executive agency of the Department for Education, is the awarding body for QTS (See note on page 610 about the NCTL being replaced by **Department for Education and Teaching Regulation Agency**).

Qualified Teacher Learning and Skills

Qualified Teacher Learning and Skills (QTLS) status is recognised in law as equal to QTS for teaching in schools. The Society for Education and Training (SET) provides QTLS which you can gain by successfully completing professional formation -- a process that enables you to demonstrate the ability to use effectively the skills and knowledge acquired whilst training to be a teacher and also the application of the occupational standards required of a teacher.

To apply for QTLS, you need an initial teacher training qualification at Level 5, for example, equivalent to the Diploma to Teach in the Lifelong Learning Sector (DTLLS) or Diploma in Education and Training (DET). You are also required to demonstrate numeracy and literacy qualifications at (or above) Level 2.

The Society for Education and Training also offers a recognition route to QTLS for members with substantial teaching experience but who do not hold a recognised teaching qualification. Visit the SET website for more information: https://set.et-foundation.co.uk. The Society for Education and Training, 157-197 Buckingham Palace Road, London, SW1W 9SP; telephone: 0800 093 9111 (free) or 020 3092 5001 (local call); email: membership.enquiries@etfoundation.co.uk.

Teacher training courses

Initial teacher training courses in England and Wales are provided by accredited training providers mainly through university departments of education. Courses available include Bachelor of Arts or Bachelor of Science with QTS, Bachelor of Education (BEd) for undergraduates, and Postgraduate Certificates of Education (PGCEs) for graduates.

Undergraduate training courses generally take three or four years full time, or four to six years part time. However, if you have undergraduate credits from previous study you may be able to complete a course in two years. A PGCE generally lasts one year full time, or up to two years part time.

There are also some employment-based routes into teaching. The School Direct Programme allows schools to recruit trainees with the expectation that they will go on to work in the school or group of schools in which they have been trained, though there is no guarantee of employment. There are more than 100 schools offering places. Courses generally last for one year full time.

School Direct offers two separate training options: the School Direct Training Programme and the School Direct Training Programme (salaried). The School Direct Training Programme (salaried) is open to graduates with three or more years' career experience (there may be exceptions for some subjects). Trainees will be employed as unqualified teachers with a salary subsidised by The National College for Teaching and Leadership. Trainees on a School Direct Training Programme will have to pay tuition fees to cover the cost of the course, but home and EU trainees will be eligible for a tuition fee loan to cover these costs and you might be eligible for funding through training bursaries or scholarships. For more information, see The National College for Teaching and Leadership, School Direct (https://www.gov.uk/government/organisations/national-college-for-teaching-and-leadership). With School Direct, you are selected for training by a school or group of schools in partnership with a university or SCITT.

School-centred initial teacher training (SCITT) is training in a school environment for those with a UK degree or an equivalent qualification. SCITT programmes are designed and delivered by groups of neighbouring schools and colleges; they are usually full time for one year. Taught by experienced, practising teachers, and often tailored towards local teaching needs, all SCITT courses lead to QTS. Many, though not all, will also award you a PGCE validated by a higher education institution. There are consortia of schools and colleges running SCITT courses all over England. These groups provide all kinds of SCITT, covering primary, middle years and the full range of secondary subjects. Application for SCITT courses is usually through UCAS (www.ucas.com/ucas/teacher-training).

Teach First offers a two-year Leadership Development Programme for those interested in an employment-based route into teaching. Teach First enables graduates with a 2:1 or a First to spend two years working in secondary and primary schools in low income communities while earning a full-time salary. It offers the programme in different regions in the UK. During the application process you will be able to state your local area preference but they recommend that you be open minded about local area and understand that they will prioritise the needs of the schools and their children over the preferences of applicants. A PGCE is awarded on completion of the course. Candidates have to demonstrate a high proficiency in eight core competencies throughout this process to ensure they can achieve real impact for pupils: Humility, respect and empathy, interaction, leadership, planning and organising, problem solving, resilience, self-evaluation, and knowledge of Teach First and their academic subjects. Visit the Teach First website for further information: www.teachfirst.org.uk.

There are also other ways into teaching, including Troops to Teachers, Researchers in Schools and Assessment Only. Further details can be found at https://getintoteaching.education.gov.uk/explore-my-options/teacher-training-routes.

The qualification of Professional Graduate Diploma in Education (PGDE) is a one-year postgraduate degree course leading to registration as a primary or secondary school teacher in Scotland (see www.teachinscotland.org). Alternatively it is possible to undertake a four-year undergraduate degree course in education. In Scotland there are seven universities that offer teacher training courses: University of Aberdeen, University of Dundee, University of Edinburgh, University of Stirling, University of Glasgow, University of Strathclyde and University of the West of Scotland. For more information on how to apply for a teaching course in Scotland contact the Universities and Colleges Admissions System (UCAS), Tel: 0371 468 0469, www.ucas.com/ucas/teacher-training. The General Teaching Council for Scotland is also a useful source of information: www.gtcs.org.uk.

The Education Workforce Council (EWC) is the independent regulator in Wales for teachers in maintained schools, Further Education teachers and learning support staff in both school and FE settings. Contact details: EWC 9th Floor Eastgate House, 35--43 Newport Road, Cardiff, CF24 0AB; Tel: 029 20460099; Fax: 029 20475850; e-mail: information@ewc.wales; website: www.ewc.wales. EWC is responsible for administering the award of Qualified Teacher Status (QTS) in Wales, on behalf of the Welsh Government. The main ways to gain QTS in Wales are completion of a course of teacher training at an accredited institution in Wales (see www.teachertrai-ningcymru.org/home) or completion of employment-based training under the Graduate Teacher Programme (GTP). GTP programmes in Wales are managed and delivered by three regional centres of teacher training and education on behalf of the Welsh Government.

Initial Teacher Education (ITE) in Northern Ireland consists of the Postgraduate Certificate of Education course, approved by the Department of Education Northern Ireland, or a four-year BEd(Hons) course, which leads to recognition as a schoolteacher in Northern Ireland (see www.education-ni.gov.uk).

Qualifications for admission to training

Higher education institutions offering undergraduate ITT or ITE courses will set admissions criteria, typically two good A levels (or equivalent qualifications). Entrants to PGCE and other graduate training courses will require a relevant UK Bachelor's degree or a recognized equivalent and be expected to demonstrate a standard equivalent to GCSE grade C in English and mathematics (in Wales grade B, or equivalent is required), and additionally a standard equivalent to GCSE grade C in a science subject for those wishing to train to teach primary school children. Trainees who have undertaken their initial teacher training in England must pass professional skills tests in numeracy and literacy before starting the course. These tests cover core skills that teachers need in their jobs and QTS cannot be awarded until they are passed. If you are undertaking initial teacher training in Wales, you are not required to complete the skills tests in order to be awarded QTS.

There are various funding options available to support you throughout your teacher training. These include tax-free scholarships and bursaries. Your eligibility for financial support, and the amount you can expect to receive, generally depends on the subject you choose to teach, the class of your degree, and sometimes other qualifications and experience are taken into account too.

The National College for Teaching and Leadership

The National College for Teaching and Leadership was an executive agency, sponsored by the Department for Education (DfE). It existed from 29 March 2013 to 31 March 2018. It was the body responsible for ITT in England and the award of QTS. It had two key aims: improving the quality of the education workforce; and helping schools to help each other to improve. NCTL works with schools to develop an education system supported locally by partnerships and led by the best head teachers. Note that the NCTL has been repurposed and no longer exists. It has been replaced by **Department for Education and Teaching Regulation Agency**. Regulation of the teaching profession, including misconduct hearings, continue to be handled by an executive agency of the Department for Education, the Teaching Regulation Agency (TRA). The Teaching Regulation Agency started operation on 1 April 2018. All other NCTL functions have been moved into the Department for Education. You can find out more by visiting https://www.gov.uk/government/organisations/national-college-for-teaching-and-leadership.

General Teaching Councils

General Teaching Councils exist in Wales (EWC), Scotland (GTCS) and Northern Ireland (GTCNI). These councils hold registers of qualified teachers and also act as disciplinary bodies. You can find out more from their respective websites: EWC: www.ewc.wales; GTCS: www.gtcs.org.uk; GTCNI: www.gtcni.org.uk

Applications

Applications for undergraduate and postgraduate courses are made through UCAS. For courses in Northern Ireland visit the Department for Education on Northern Ireland's website (www.education-ni.gov.uk). You can find out more about training to teach from the following websites: UCAS: www.ucas.com; and https://getintoteaching.education.gov.uk for queries relating to becoming a teacher, initial teacher training, recruitment opportunities or provision of relevant training.

TECHNICAL COMMUNICATIONS
Membership of Professional Institutions and Associations

THE INSTITUTE OF SCIENTIFIC AND TECHNICAL COMMUNICATORS (ISTC LTD)

Unit 19
Omega Business Village
Thurston Road
Northallerton DL6 2NJ
Tel: 020 8253 4506
E-mail: istc@istc.org.uk
Website: www.istc.org.uk

The ISTC is a non-profit-making organisation and the largest UK body representing professional communicators and information designers. Our aims include improving standards of scientific and technical communication, promoting scientific and technical communication as a career, supporting our members, and consulting, cooperating and collaborating with other bodies that share our ideals.

MEMBERSHIP
Student
Associate
Junior
Member (MISTC)
Fellow (FISTC)
Business Affiliate

DESIGNATORY LETTERS
MISTC, FISTC

TEXTILES
Membership of Professional Institutions and Associations

THE TEXTILE INSTITUTE

8th Floor St James' Buildings
79 Oxford Street
Manchester M1 6FQ
Tel: 0161 2371188
Fax: 0161 2361991
E-mail: tiihq@textileinst.org.uk
Website: www.textileinstitute.org

The Textile Institute covers all disciplines – from technology and production to design, development and marketing – relating to fibres, fabrics, clothing, footwear, and interior and technical textiles.

MEMBERSHIP
Individual: Standard
Individual: Association
Individual: Graduate
Individual: Retired
Individual: Student
Individual: Unwaged
Individual: Corporate Student
Corporate

QUALIFICATION/EXAMINATIONS
Licentiateship (LTI)
Associateship (CText ATI)
Fellowship (CText FTI)

DESIGNATORY LETTERS
LTI, CText ATI, CText FTI

TIMBER TECHNOLOGY
Membership of Professional Institutions and Associations

WOOD TECHNOLOGY SOCIETY

The Boilerhouse
Springfield Business Park
Caunt Road
Grantham
Lincs NG31 7FZ
Tel: 01476 513880
Fax: 01476 513899
E-mail: via website
Website: www.iom3.org/content/wood-technology

The Wood Technology Society (IWSc – a Division of the Institute of Materials, Minerals and Mining), formerly the Institute of Wood Science, is the professional body for the timber and allied industries. We promote and encourage a better understanding of timber, wood-based materials and associated timber processes, and are the UK examining body, awarding qualifications at Foundation, Certificate and Diploma level.

MEMBERSHIP
Student Member
Affiliate Member
Technician (EngTech)
Fellow (FIMMM)
Professional Member (MIMMM)
Graduate (Grad IMMM)
Corporate Member

QUALIFICATION/EXAMINATIONS
Level 2 Award in Timber and Panel Products (QCF)
Certificate
Diploma

DESIGNATORY LETTERS
TIWSc, LIWSc, MIWSc, FIWSc

TOWN AND COUNTRY PLANNING
Membership of Professional Institutions and Associations

ROYAL TOWN PLANNING INSTITUTE

41 Botolph Lane
London EC3R 8DL
Tel: 020 7929 9494
E-mail: education@rtpi.org.uk
Website: www.rtpi.org.uk

The RTPI is the largest professional institute for planners in Europe, with over 25,000 members. As well as promoting spatial planning, we develop and shape policy affecting the built environment, work to raise professional standards and support members through their education, training and career development.

MEMBERSHIP
Chartered Town Planner (MRTPI)
Fellow (FRTPI)
Associate Member (AssocRTPI)
Legal Associate (LARTPI)
Licentiate Member
Student Member
Retired Member
Affiliate
Honorary Member

QUALIFICATION/EXAMINATIONS
QUALIFICATION/EXAMINATIONS

From January 2017 all routes to become a Chartered Town Planner are competency based and applicants must submit an Assessment of Professional Competence.

There are a range of educational pathways to Chartered Membership although the majority of applicants will have studied an accredited planning degree. Please see www.rtpi.org.uk/findacourse for a list of accredited training providers.

DESIGNATORY LETTERS
MRTPI, FRTPI, LARTPI, AssocRTPI

TRADING STANDARDS
Membership of Professional Institutions and Associations

CHARTERED TRADING STANDARDS INSTITUTE

1 Sylvan Court
Sylvan Way
Southfields Business Park
Basildon
Essex SS15 6TH
Tel: 01268 582200
E-mail: institute@tsi.org.uk
Website: www.tradingstandards.uk

CTSI represents trading standards professionals working in the UK and overseas – in local authorities, business and consumer sectors and central government.

CTSI exists to:
- promote and protect the success of a modern vibrant economy, and
- safeguard the health, safety and wellbeing of citizens by enhancing the professionalism of its members.

MEMBERSHIP
Retired
Full
Associate
Fee Paying Student
Free Student
Affiliate
International

QUALIFICATION/EXAMINATIONS
The Trading Standards Qualifications Framework consists of:
Certificate of Competence
Core Skills in Consumer Affairs and Trading Standards
Module Certificate in Consumer Affairs and Trading Standards
Diploma in Consumer Affairs and Trading Standards
Higher Certificate in Consumer Affairs and Trading Standards
Higher Diploma in Consumer Affairs and Trading Standards

DESIGNATORY LETTERS
ACTSI, MCTSI, CTSP, FCTSI

TRANSPORT

Membership of Professional Institutions and Associations

INSTITUTE OF TRANSPORT ADMINISTRATION

The Old Studio
25 Greenfield Road
Westoning
Bedfordshire MK45 5JD
Tel: 01525 634940
E-mail: director@iota.org.uk
Website: www.iota.org.uk

The Institute of Transport Administration (the Institute) is a registered Friendly Society regulated by the Financial Services Authority whose objectives are defined as: *"For the purpose of promoting education pursuant to the special authority of 10th June 1967. Given under section (7) of the Friendly Societies Act, 1974.)'*

It is a professional membership organisation representing individuals from companies within all spheres of the transport industry in both the United Kingdom and overseas. It supports and encourages efficient transport best practice and is committed to the growth and development of its members through sharing specialist knowledge and the provision and promotion of educational programmes.

MEMBERSHIP
Student (StInstTA)

Graduate (GradInstTA)
Associate (AInstTA)
Honorary Member
Associate Member (AMInstTA)
Member (MInstTA)
Fellow (FInstTA)

QUALIFICATION/EXAMINATIONS
Transport Manager Refresher (TMR), Operator Licence Awareness training (OLAT)
Management CPC
Certificate in Transport Management (CTM)
Driver CPC

DESIGNATORY LETTERS
TMR, OLAT, CPC, CTM

THE INSTITUTE OF TRAFFIC ACCIDENT INVESTIGATORS

Column House
London Road
Shrewsbury
Shropshire SY2 6NN
Tel: 08456 212066
E-mail: admin@itai.org
Website: www.itai.org

The aim of the Institute is to promote road safety for the benefit of the public by improving the technical and general knowledge and skills of persons involved in the field of investigating road traffic collisions. It promotes the free and open exchange of knowledge and provides a forum for communication, education and representation, through all of which it aims to enhance expertise.

It also seeks, through the collective knowledge of its members to improve the standards of safety of vehicles and roads of all kinds.

The Institute is committed to promoting a professional approach to traffic accident investigation by encouraging honesty and integrity among investigators.

MEMBERSHIP
Affiliate

Associate (AMITAI)
Member (MITAI)
Retired
Student

TRAVEL AND TOURISM

Membership of Professional Institutions and Associations

CONFEDERATION OF TOURISM AND HOSPITALITY (CTH)

37 Duke Street
London W1U 1LN
Tel: 020 7258 9850
Fax: 020 7258 9869
E-mail: info@cthawards.com
Website: www.cthawards.com

The Confederation of Tourism and Hospitality (otherwise known as CTH) is an awarding body approved by Ofqual, and registered on the QCA's National Qualifications Framework. We were established in 1982 to provide recognized standards of management and vocational training appropriate to the needs of the hotel, travel and culinary industries, via our syllabuses, examinations and awards.

MEMBERSHIP
Student Member

QUALIFICATION/EXAMINATIONS
CTH Level 1 Award, Certificate & Diploma in English for Tourism & Hospitality
CTH (IoH) Level 2 Specialist Award for Chefs in Health & Social Care
CTH (IoH) Level 3 Diploma in Hospitality & Tourism Management
CTH (IoH) Level 4 Diploma in Advanced Hospitality & Tourism Management
CTH Level 3 Foundation Diploma in Tourism and Hospitality
CTH Level 4 Diploma in Hospitality Management
CTH Level 4 Diploma in Tourism Management
CTH Level 5 Advanced Diploma in Hospitality Management
CTH Level 5 Advanced Diploma in Tourism Management
CTH Level 6 Professional Diploma in Hospitality and Tourism Management
CTH Level 7 Executive Diploma in Hospitality and Tourism Management
CTH Level 2 Award in Culinary Skills
CTH Level 2 Award in Vegetarian Culinary Skills
CTH Level 2 Certificate in Culinary Skills
CTH Level 2 Diploma in Culinary Skills
CTH Level 3 Certificate in Professional Cookery
CTH Level 3 Extended Certificate in Professional Cookery
CTH Level 3 Diploma in Professional Cookery – Kitchen & Larder
CTH Level 3 Diploma in Professional Cookery – Confectionary and Pattisserie
CTH Level 4 Diploma in Professional Culinary Arts
CTH Level 5 Advanced Diploma in Culinary and Hospitality Management

INSTITUTE OF TRAVEL AND TOURISM

PO Box 217
Ware
Hertfordshire SG12 8WY
Tel: 0844 4995 653
Fax: 0844 4995 654
E-mail: admin@itt.co.uk
Website: www.itt.co.uk

The ITT, founded in 1956, is a professional membership body for individuals employed in the travel and tourism industry. We provide support and guidance for our members throughout their career and offer them CPD and training to maintain standards for the benefit of the industry as a whole.

MEMBERSHIP
Student Member
Introductory Member
Member
Fellow
Fellow (FInstTT)
University/College Member
Group Member
Corporate Member
Retired Member

DESIGNATORY LETTERS
F Inst TT

THE TOURISM MANAGEMENT INSTITUTE

c/o Hon Secretary, Dr Cathy Guthrie, FTMI
18 Cuninghill Avenue
Inverurie
Aberdeenshire AB51 3TZ
Tel: 01467 620769
E-mail: secretary@tmi.org.uk
Website: www.tmi.org.uk

TMI is the professional body for tourism destination managers. Its network of 250+ members shares information via website, conferences, e-mails and newsletters. The TMI CPD programme aims to support destination management professionals throughout their career. TMI HE Course Recognition gives students & lecturers assurance of industry engagement, relevance and employability.

MEMBERSHIP
Student
Affiliate
Associate (ATMI)
Member (MTMI)
Fellow (FTMI)

DESIGNATORY LETTERS
ATMI, MTMI, FTMI

THE TOURISM SOCIETY

South Bank University
103 Borough Road
London SE1 0AA
Tel: 0203 696 8330
E-mail: admin@tourismsociety.org
Website: www.tourismsociety.org

Founded in 1977, the Tourism Society is where individuals from across all sectors of the Visitor Economy come together (online and offline) for discussion, debate, to share views and knowledge, and to network. For forty years it has had a strong voice in driving the development and wider recognition of tourism and its economic and social benefits, both in the UK and further afield. It is a founder member of the Tourism Alliance, and contributes actively to Government policy formulation, through the submission of position papers.

MEMBERSHIP
Student
Full Member (MTS)
Fellow (FTS)
Overseas/Retired Member
Group Member
Corporate Member
Graduate

DESIGNATORY LETTERS
MTS, FTS

VETERINARY SCIENCE
Membership of Professional Institutions and Associations

BRITISH VETERINARY ASSOCIATION

7 Mansfield Street
London W1G 9NQ
Tel: 020 7636 6541
Fax: 020 7908 6349
E-mail: bvahq@bva.co.uk
Website: www.bva.co.uk

BVA is the national representative body for the veterinary profession in the UK

We are the only UK veterinary association that looks after the interests of all vets in all disciplines. Our members are at the heart of everything we do, and with the power of more than 17,000 members behind us, we're able to provide a voice to represent members and services to support them.

MEMBERSHIP
Standard
Concessions
Joint
Student
Associate
Young Vet
Group

ROYAL COLLEGE OF VETERINARY SURGEONS

Belgravia House
62–64 Horseferry Road
London SW1P 2AF
Tel: 020 7222 2001
Fax: 020 7222 2004
E-mail: info@rcvs.org.uk
Website: www.rcvs.org.uk

The RCVS is the regulatory body for veterinary surgeons and veterinary nurses in the UK. We aim to enhance society through improved animal health and welfare. We do this by setting, upholding and advancing the educational, ethical and clinical standards of veterinary surgeons and veterinary nurses.

MEMBERSHIP
Member (MRCVS)

Fellow (FRCVS)
Registered veterinary nurse (RVN)

QUALIFICATION/EXAMINATIONS
Certificate in Advanced Veterinary Practice (CertAVP)
Diploma in Advanced Veterinary Nursing (DipAVN)

DESIGNATORY LETTERS
MRCVS, FRCVS, RVN

SOCIETY OF PRACTISING VETERINARY SURGEONS

Unit 19a
Hatton Country World
Hatton
Warwick CV35 8XA
Tel: 01926 840318
E-mail: office@spvs.org.uk
Website: www.spvs.org.uk

SPVS is the division of the BVA with a primary focus on matters concerning vets in practice and the practices where they work.The Society is a not-for-profit organisation run by a Board elected by the members. We have administrative offices in Warwick run by our permanent full and part-time staff.

The Society is financed by member subscriptions, with help from some of the events we organise and occasional support from generous sponsors.

MEMBERSHIP
Full
Additional
Member plus CPD for support staff
Part time
Student Recent Graduate
Retired

WASTES MANAGEMENT
Membership of Professional Institutions and Associations

CHARTERED INSTITUTION OF WASTES MANAGEMENT

7-9 St Peter's Gardens
St Peter's Gardens
Marefair
Northampton NN1 1SX
Tel: 01604 620426
E-mail: membership@ciwm.co.uk
Website: www.ciwm.co.uk

The CIWM represents more than 6,000 waste management professionals – predominantly in the UK but also overseas. We promote education, training and research in the scientific, technical and practical aspects of waste management for the safe-guarding of the environment, and set and strive to maintain high standards for individuals working in the waste management industry.

MEMBERSHIP
Student
Affiliate
Associate
Chartered

Fellow
Graduate
Licentiate
Technician

QUALIFICATION/EXAMINATIONS
CIWM Training Services specializes in developing and providing waste management training for individuals and organisations. Each year we organise more than 70 courses. For details see the website.

DESIGNATORY LETTERS
TechMCIWM, AssocMCIWM, GradMCIWM, LCIWM, MCIWM, FCIWM

WATCH AND CLOCK MAKING AND REPAIRING
Membership of Professional Institutions and Associations

THE BRITISH HOROLOGICAL INSTITUTE LIMITED

Upton Hall
Upton
Newark
Nottinghamshire NG23 5TE
Tel: 01636 813795
Fax: 01636 812258
E-mail: via website
Website: www.bhi.co.uk

The BHI, which was formed in 1858 to promote horology, is a professional body with about 3,000 members worldwide. We provide education and specialist training, set recognized standards of excellence in workmanship and professional conduct, and support our members in their work, making, repairing and servicing clocks and watches.

MEMBERSHIP
Associate
Member (MBHI)
Fellow (FBHI)

QUALIFICATION/EXAMINATIONS
Diploma in Clock and Watch Servicing (Level 3)

Diploma in the Servicing and Repair of Clocks / Watches (Level 4)

Diploma in the Repair, Restoration and Conservation of Clocks / Watches (Level 5)

DESIGNATORY LETTERS
MBHI, FBHI

WELDING

Membership of Professional Institutions and Associations

THE WELDING INSTITUTE

Granta Park
Great Abington
Cambridge CB21 6AL
Tel: 01223 899000
E-mail: via website
Website: www.theweldinginstitute.com

The Welding Institute is the preferred engineering institution for welding and joining professionals. We are committed to promoting the importance of welding/materials joining technology, given its importance as a key industrial technology governing the reliability and safety of many products, and to the advancement of education, training and CPD for our members.

MEMBERSHIP
Associate (AWeldI)

Technician (TechWeldI)
Member (MWeldI)
Fellow (FWeldI)
Engineering Technician (EngTech)
Incorporated Engineer (IEng)
Chartered Engineer (CEng)

DESIGNATORY LETTERS
AWeldI, TechWeldI, MWeldI, FWeldI, EngTech, IEng, CEng

WELFARE

Membership of Professional Institutions and Associations

INSTITUTE OF WELFARE

PO Box 5570
Stourbridge DY8 9BA
Tel: 0800 0 32 37 25
Website: www.instituteofwelfare.com

The Institute of Welfare was founded in 1945 and exists to promote the highest possible standards in the delivery of welfare to those who need it. We make representations to government, undertake research on welfare issues, encourage and facilitate the exchange of information, and provide opportunities for those engaged in welfare work to pursue CPD.

MEMBERSHIP
Affiliate Member

Member (MIW)
Fellow (FIW)
Companion (CIW)

DESIGNATORY LETTERS
MIW, FIW, CIW

Part 6

Bodies Accrediting Independent Institutions

THE BRITISH ACCREDITATION COUNCIL FOR INDEPENDENT FURTHER AND HIGHER EDUCATION (BAC)

BAC is a registered charity that was established in 1984 to act as the national accrediting body for independent further and higher education. It is independent of both government and of the colleges it accredits.

A college that is accredited by BAC undergoes a thorough inspection every three or four years, with an interim visit in the middle of the accreditation cycle. BAC accreditation is not only available to colleges in the United Kingdom, there are now accredited colleges in 11 countries around the world. At present BAC accredits or approves 201 colleges in the United Kingdom and 25 overseas. Lists of accredited colleges are published each year; full details can be viewed on the BAC website (www.the-bac.org).

BAC has a close relationship with the accreditation scheme operated by Accreditation UK (in the field of English as a Foreign Language) and is a member of ENQA, the European Association for Quality Assurance in Higher Education. It maintains close links with The British Council, UK Council for International Student Affairs (UKCISA), UK NARIC, OFQUAL and the Federation of Awarding Bodies (FAB) and The Accreditation Body for Language Services (ABLS). In 2015 it was admitted onto the European Quality Assurance Register for Higher Education (EQAR).

Accreditation by BAC is recognized by the UK Visas and Immigration (UKVI) department of the Home Office as a qualifying requirement for institutions to enrol visa students.

Contact details for BAC are: BAC, Ground Floor, 14 Devonshire Square, London, EC2M 4YT; Tel: 0300 330 1400; Fax: 0300 330 1401; e-mail: info@the-bac.org; website: www.the-bac.org

THE BRITISH COUNCIL

The British Council runs the Accreditation UK scheme in partnership with English UK for the inspection and accreditation of organizations that provide courses in English as a Foreign Language (EFL) in Britain. The British Council aims to make quality language materials available to learners and teachers all over the world, and they offer over three million UK examinations worldwide, helping people gain access to trusted qualifications to support their career and study prospects.

Under the terms of the scheme, institutions are inspected rigorously every four years in the areas of management, resources and environment, teaching and learning, welfare and student services and care of under 18s. The scheme also includes a system of random spot-checking. The management and policy of the scheme are conducted by an independent board while a separate independent committee reviews inspectors' reports.

The majority of recognized schools are also members of English UK, which insists on British Council accreditation as a criterion for membership. In addition, all English UK members, of which there are around 450, are required to abide by the Association's Code of Practice and Regulations. English UK exists to raise the high standards of its members even further through conferences, training courses and publications. The association also represents the interests of members and students to government bodies, and promotes international student mobility.

Further information on the Accreditation UK scheme may be obtained from the Accreditation Unit, British Council, Bridgewater House, 58 Whitworth Street, Manchester M1 6BB;

Tel: 0161 957 7755; or use the online enquiry form at www.britishcouncil.org/contact; website: www.britishcouncil.org/education/accreditation

Further information on English UK may be obtained from English UK, 219 St John Street, London EC1V 4LY; Tel: 020 7608 7960; Fax: 020 7608 7961; e-mail: info@englishuk.com; website: www.englishuk.com

THE OPEN AND DISTANCE LEARNING QUALITY COUNCIL (ODLQC)

ODLQC was established in 1968 as the Council for the Accreditation of Correspondence Colleges, a joint initiative of the then Labour government and representatives of the sector. It is the principal accrediting body for a wide variety of providers of open and distance learning (ODL) in the UK, from commercial colleges to professional and public-sector institutions. Now independent, it nevertheless continues to have the informal support of government. ODLQC promotes quality by:

- establishing standards of education and training in ODL;
- recognizing good quality provision, wherever it occurs;
- supporting and protecting the interests of learners;
- encouraging the improvement of existing methods and the development of new ones;
- linking ODL with other forms of education and training;
- promoting wider recognition of the value of ODL.

Accreditation includes a rigorous assessment of educational provision, covering materials, tutorial support, publicity, contractual arrangements with learners and general administrative procedures, each of which is measured against the Council's published benchmark standards. If accredited, the provider is monitored on a regular basis and reassessed at least once every three years.

The Council promotes those colleges that it accredits, which are by definition quality providers of ODL, and acts as an honest broker in matching accredited colleges to potential markets. A list of accredited providers is included on the Council's website: www.odlqc.org.uk. The Council also seeks to protect the interests of learners by promoting the importance of accreditation, and by offering advice and support directly to learners. At the same time, knowledge of good practice is disseminated more widely, and quality encouraged wherever ODL occurs.

The Council consists of members drawn from professional and public bodies involved in education, as well as representatives of accredited providers, and has strong links with other bodies in the sector, both in the UK and abroad.

All enquiries should be through the contact form on the website: www.odlqc.org.uk

THE COUNCIL FOR INDEPENDENT EDUCATION (CIFE)

CIFE was founded in 1973 to promote strict adherence by independent sixth-form and tutorial colleges to the highest standards of academic and professional integrity and to provide an inspection service for these colleges. All member colleges must be accredited by the British Accreditation Council for Independent Further and Higher Education (BAC), and/or the Independent Schools Inspectorate (ISI). CIFE colleges all undergo regular inspection by the Department for Education.

They are also inspected either by the British Accreditation Council, the Independent Schools Inspectorate, or both. Ofsted (Office for Standards in Education) check college-provided accommodation and student welfare. Candidate membership is available for up to three years for colleges that are seeking BAC or ISI accreditation and otherwise satisfy CIFE's exacting membership criteria. All colleges must also abide by stringent codes of conduct and practice; the character and presentation of their published exam results are subject to regulation, and the accuracy of the information must be validated by BAC as academic auditor to CIFE. Full members are subject to reinspection by their accrediting bodies. There are 19 colleges in full or candidate membership of CIFE at present, spread throughout England but with concentrations in London and Oxford.

CIFE colleges offer a wide range of GCSE, A and AS level courses. In addition, some CIFE colleges offer English language tuition for students from overseas, and degree-level tuition. Most colleges also provide A level and GCSE revision courses during the Easter holidays. Further information on CIFE may be obtained from the CIFE website: www.cife.org.uk; Tel: 020 8767 8666; e-mail: enquiries@cife.org.uk

Part 7

Study Associations and the 'Learned Societies'

Study associations consist of people who wish to increase their knowledge of a particular subject or range of subjects; they may be professionals or amateurs. Some associations consist almost entirely of specialists (e.g. the Royal Statistical Society); others (e.g. the Royal Geographical Society and the Zoological Society of London) have a more general membership. The learned societies usually have two grades of membership: fellows and members. Some also admit group members (such as schools or libraries), known as corporate members, and junior associate, corresponding and overseas members, who pay lower subscriptions. Some also elect honorary fellows or members. The members of some societies may use designatory letters, but this does not mean that the holder is 'qualified' in the same sense as a doctor or a chartered accountant.

Membership of some learned societies is by election and is commonly accepted as distinguishing the candidate by admission to an exclusive group. Candidates may be selected in respect of pre-eminence in their subject or in the public service. The chief associations of this type are the Royal Society (founded in 1660 and granted Royal Charters in 1662 and 1663), the Royal Academy of Arts (founded in 1768) and the British Academy (granted the Royal Charter in 1902).

The Royal Society (www.royalsociety.org) was established to improve 'natural knowledge' and is mainly concerned with pure and applied science and technology. Election to Fellowship (FRS) is regarded as one of the highest distinctions. The society elects Fellows, Foreign Members, Royal Fellows and Honorary Fellows. The Royal Academy (www.royalacademy.org.uk) was established to cultivate and improve the arts of painting, sculpture and architecture. There are two main grades of membership: Academicians (RAs) (including Senior Academicians) and the Honorary RAs, Honorary Fellows and Honorary Members. The British Academy (www.britac.ac.uk) is the UK's national academy for the humanities and the social sciences. It is the counterpart to the Royal Society that exists to serve the natural sciences. The Academy has Fellows (FBA), Corresponding Fellows and a small number of Honorary Fellows.

A list of learned societies and study associations can be found below.

OCCUPATIONAL ASSOCIATIONS

The occupational associations do not qualify practitioners but organize them. Some coordinate the activities of specialists and others promote the individual and collective interests of professionals working in a wider area. Both types also seek to safeguard the public interest and to offer an educational service to their members. The latter type of association is especially numerous among teachers (e.g. the National Union of Teachers (NUT), the Educational Institute of Scotland (EIS), NASWUT (the National Association of Schoolmasters/Union of Women Teachers) and the National Association of Head Teachers (NAHT)), and is represented in the medical profession by the British Medical Association.

LIST OF STUDY ASSOCIATIONS AND LEARNED SOCIETIES

This list largely excludes qualifying bodies, which are covered in Part 5. The date on the left is that of foundation or adoption of title.

Agriculture and related subjects

1926	Agricultural Economics Society (AES)	1839	Royal Agricultural Society of England (now part of Innovation for Agriculture)
1952	British Agricultural History Society		
1945	British Grassland Society		
1944	British Society of Animal Science (BSAS)	1882	Royal Forestry Society
		1784	Royal Highland and Agricultural Society of Scotland (RHASS)
1947	British Society of Soil Science		
1921	Commonwealth Forestry Association (CFA)	1804	Royal Horticultural Society (RHS)
		1854	Royal Scottish Forestry Society
1927	Herb Society of Great Britain	1904	Royal Welsh Agricultural Society (RWAS)
1925	Institute of Chartered Foresters (ICF)		
1938	Institution of Agricultural Engineers (IAgrE)	1943	Society of Dairy Technology
		1945	The Soil Association
1947	International Fertiliser Society (IFS)		

Anthropology and related subjects

1963	African Studies Association of the UK (ASAUK)	1972	Japan Foundation
		1891	Japan Society
1979	Association for the Study of Modern and Contemporary France	1843	Royal Anthropological Institute of Great Britain and Ireland (the RAI)
1982	Association for the Study of Modern Italy	1823	Royal Asiatic Society of Great Britain and Ireland
1946	Association of Social Anthropologists of the UK and Commonwealth	1868	Royal Commonwealth Society (RCS)
		1901	Royal Society for Asian Affairs (RSAA)
1985	British Association for Irish Studies (BAIS)		
		1936	Saltire Society
1974	British Association for Japanese Studies	1977	Society for Caribbean Studies (SCS)
		1964	Society for Latin American Studies (SLAS)
1972	British Association for South Asian Studies (BASAS)		
		1969	Society for Libyan Studies
1961	British Institute of Persian Studies (BIPS)	1983	Society for the Promotion of Byzantine Studies
1973	British Society for Middle Eastern Studies (BRISMES)	1879	Society for the Promotion of Hellenic Studies
1981	European Association for Jewish Studies (EAJS)	1910	Society for the Promotion of Roman Studies
1878	Folklore Society	1969	University Association for Contemporary European Studies (UACES)
1943	Hispanic and Luso Brazilian Council (Canning House)		
1974	International Association for the Study of German Politics (IASGP)	1892	Viking Society for Northern Research

Archaeology and related subjects

1924	Ancient Monuments Society	1948	British Institute at Ankara (BIAA)
1979	Association for Environmental Archaeology (AEA)	1846	Cambrian Archaeological Association
		1944	Council for British Archaeology
1843	British Archaeological Association (BAA)	1838	Ecclesiological Society
		1882	Egypt Exploration Society
1996	British Epigraphy Society		

1855	London and Middlesex Archaeological Society (LAMAS)	1843	Royal Archaeological Institute
1865	Palestine Exploration Fund (PEF)	1967	Society for Post-Medieval Archaeology (SPMA)
1908	Prehistoric Society		

Art and Design

1974	Association of Art Historians (AAH)	1754	Royal Society for the Encouragement of Arts, Manufactures and Commerce (RSA)
1910	Contemporary Art Society		
1915	Design and Industries Association		
1950	International Institute for Conservation of Historic and Artistic Works	1904	Royal Society of British Sculptors
		1904	Royal Society of Marine Artists (RSMA)
1888	National Society for Education in Art and Design (NSEAD)	1895	Royal Society of Miniature Painters, Sculptors and Gravers
1898	Pastel Society	1884	Royal Society of Painter-Printmakers
1768	Royal Academy of Arts	1891	Royal Society of Portrait Painters
1814	Royal Birmingham Society of Artists (RBSA)	1804	Royal Watercolour Society
		1919	Society of Graphic Fine Art (SGFA)
1883	Royal Institute of Oil-Painters (ROI)	1952	Society of Portrait Sculptors
1831	Royal Institute of Painters in Watercolours	1952	United Society of Artists
		1955	William Morris Society
1826	Royal Scottish Academy of Art and Architecture		

Biology and related subjects

1936	Association for the Study of Animal Behaviour (ASAB)	1931	Society for Applied Microbiology (SfAM)
1904	Association of Applied Biologists (AAB)	1911	The Biochemical Society
		1913	The British Ecological Society (BES)
1968	Biomedical Engineering Society (BMES)	1896	The British Mycological Society
		1858	The British Ornithologists' Union (BOU)
1836	Botanical Society of Scotland		
1836	Botanical Society of the British Isles (BSBI)	1959	The British Society for Cell Biology (BSCB)
1896	British Bryological Society (BBS)	1933	The British Trust for Ornithology (BTO)
1929	Freshwater Biological Association (FBA)		
		1937	The Systematics Association
1889	Marine Biological Association (MBA)	1826	Zoological Society of London (ZSL)
1833	Royal Entomological Society		

Chemistry

1918	Oil and Colour Chemists' Association (OCCA)	1881	Society of Chemical Industry (SCI)
		1897	Society of Leather Technologists and Chemists (SLTC)
1980	Royal Society of Chemistry (RSC)		

Economics, Statistics and related subjects

1992	Chartered Association of Business Schools	1902	Royal Economic Society (RES)
1927	Economic History Society	1834	Royal Statistical Society (RSS)
1955	Institute of Economic Affairs (IEA)	1897	Scottish Economic Society (SES)

Engineering and related subjects

1997	Chartered Institute of Ergonomics and Human Factors	1866	Royal Aeronautical Society
1966	Concrete Society	1916	Royal Incorporation of Architects in Scotland (RIAS)
1946	Forum for the Built Environment (fbe) (formerly the Faculty of Building)	1860	Royal Institution of Naval Architects (RINA)
1997	Faculty of Party Wall Surveyors	1916	Society of Automotive Engineers (SAE)
1978	Institute of Concrete Technology (ICT)	1958	Society of Environmental Engineers
2006	Institution of Engineering and Technology (IET)	2003	The Energy Institute (EI)
1976	Royal Academy of Engineering (RAEng)	1899	Town and Country Planning Association (TCPA)

Geography, Geology and related subjects

1963	British Cartographic Society (BCS)	1971	Institution of Environmental Sciences (IES)
1949	British Geotechnical Society (BGA)	1876	Mineralogical Society of Great Britain and Ireland
1940	British Society of Rheology (BSR)	1847	Palaeontographical Society
1923	English Place-Name Society (EPNS) (University of Nottingham)	1957	Paleontological Association
1931	Gemmological Association of Great Britain (Gem-A)	1830	Royal Geographical Society (RGS)
1893	Geographical Association (GA)	1997	Royal Institute of Navigation (RIN)
1807	Geological Society of London	1884	Royal Scottish Geographical Society (RSGS)
1858	Geologists' Association (GA)		
1846	Hakluyt Society		

History and related subjects

1902	British Academy	1961	Institute of Heraldic and Genealogical Studies (IHGS)
1952	British Agricultural History Society (BAHS)	1921	Institute of Historical Research (IHR)
1888	British Record Society	1893	Jewish Historical Society of England
1932	British Records Association (BRA)	1964	London Record Society
1947	British Society for the History of Science (BSHS)	1920	Newcomen Society for the Study of the History of Engineering and Technology
1988	Centre for Metropolitan History (CMH)	1921	Oriental Ceramic Society (OCS)
1864	Early English Texts Society (EETS)	1868	Royal Historical Society (RHS)
1964	Furniture History Society (FHS)	1836	Royal Numismatic Society
1869	Harleian Society	1869	Royal Philatelic Society, London (RPSL)
1885	Huguenot Society of Great Britain and Ireland	1953	Scottish Genealogy Society
		1886	Scottish History Society

1897	Scottish Record Society	1707	Society of Antiquaries of London
1976	Social History Society	1780	Society of Antiquaries of Scotland
1921	Society for Army Historical Research	1956	Society of Architectural Historians in Great Britain (SAHGB)
1910	Society for Nautical Research		
1967	Society for Renaissance Studies	1911	Society of Genealogists
1970	Society for the Social History of Medicine (SSHM)	1906	The Historical Association
		1958	Victorian Society

Languages

1883	Alliance Française	1910	Chartered Institute of Linguists (CIOL)
1891	An Comunn Gaidhealach		
1981	Association for French Language Studies (AFLS)	1991	Instituto Cervantes
		1964	National Association for the Teaching of English (NATE)
1932	Association for German Studies in Great Britain and Ireland (AGS)		
		1993	University Council of Modern Languages (UCML)
1990	Association for Language Learning (ALL)		
		1988	Women in German Studies (WIGS)

Law

1958	British Institute of International and Comparative Law (BIICL)	1920	Royal Institute of International Affairs (Chatham House)
1972	Intellectual Property Bar Association	1965	Scottish Law Commission
1922	Law Society of Northern Ireland	1887	Selden Society (Queen Mary University)
1949	Law Society of Scotland		

Literature and Arts

1959	Yr Academi Gymreig (The Welsh Academy)	1904	Classical Association
		2009	Deans and Leaders of Arts, Social Sciences and Humanities (DASSH-UK)
1973	Alliance of Literary Societies (ALS)		
1969	Art Libraries Society (ARLIS/UK & Ireland)	1902	Dickens Fellowship
		1890	Edinburgh Bibliographical Society
1970	Association for Scottish Literary Studies (ASLS)	1906	English Association (University of Leicester)
1989	Association of Independent Libraries (AIL)	1886	Francis Bacon Society Inc
1892	Bibliographical Society	1960	H. G. Wells Society
1992	British Association for Information and Library Education and Research (BAILER)	1997	Historical Novel Society
		1973	Joseph Conrad Society
		1997	Leeds Philosophical and Literary Society
1975	British Comparative Literature Association (BCLA)		
		1906	Malone Society
1933	British Film Institute (BFI)	1781	Manchester Literary and Philosophical Society
1960	British Society of Aesthetics (BSA)		
1893	Bronte Society	1995	Philip Larkin Society
1949	Cambridge Bibliographical Society	1842	Philological Society
1935	Charles Lamb Society (CLB)		

1909	Poetry Society	2004	Society of College, National and University Libraries (SCONUL)
1820	Royal Society of Literature		
1884	Society of Authors	1968	Thomas Hardy Society

Management

| 1986 | British Academy of Management (BAM) |

Mathematics and Physics

1924	Astronomical Society of Edinburgh (ASE)	1927	British Institute of Radiology (BIR)
		1933	British Interplanetary Society (BIS)
1890	British Astronomical Association (BAA)	1871	Mathematical Association (MA)
		1820	Royal Astronomical Society (RAS)
1966	British Biophysical Society (BBS)	1850	Royal Meteorological Society (RMetS)

Medicine (including Psychology)

1887	Anatomical Society (AS)	1948	British Geriatrics Society (BGS)
1957	Association for Child and Adolescent Mental Health (ACAMH)	1832	British Medical Association (BMA)
		1950	British Neuropathological Society (BNS)
1957	Association for the Study of Medical Education (ASME)	1953	British Occupational Hygiene Society (BOHS)
1932	Association of Anaesthetists of GB and Ireland (AAGBI)	1965	British Orthodontic Society (BOS)
1933	Association of British Neurologists (ABN)	1918	British Orthopaedic Association (BOA)
1953	Association of Clinical Biochemistry and Laboratory Medicine (ACB)	1901	British Psychological Society (BPS)
		1948	British Society for Allergy and Clinical Immunology (BSACI)
1927	Association of Clinical Pathologists (ACP)	2011	British Association for Cytopathology (BAC)
1920	Association of Surgeons of GB and Ireland (ASGBI)	1937	British Society of Gastroenterology (BSG)
1971	BASO – The Association for Cancer Surgery	1960	British Society for Haematology (BSH)
1959	British Academy for Forensic Science (BAFS)	1947	British Society for Research on Ageing (BSRA)
2003	British Association for Sexual Health and HIV (BASHH)	1945	British Thoracic Society (BTS)
		2014	Chartered Institute of Ergonomics and Human Factors
1977	British Association of Clinical Anatomists (BACA)	1959	Chartered Society of Forensic Sciences
1950	British Association of Forensic Medicine (BAFM)	1934	Diabetes UK
		1946	Experimental Psychology Society (EPS)
1962	British Association of Oral Surgeons (BAOS)	1950	Faculty of Homeopathy
2008	British Association of Otohinolaryngology (ENT UK)	1819	Hunterian Society
		2014	Institute of Osteopathy (iO)
1954	British Association of Paediatric Surgeons (BAPS)	1924	Institute of Psychoanalysis
		1969	Institute of Occupational Medicine (IOM)
1945	British Association of Urological Surgeons (BAUS)		

1964	Institute of Pharmacy Management (IPM)	2008	Royal Society for Public Health (RSPH)
1773	Medical Society of London	1805	Royal Society of Medicine (RSM)
1901	Medico-Legal Society	1907	Royal Society of Tropical Medicine and Hygiene (RSTMH)
1941	Nutrition Society		
1906	Pathological Society of Great Britain and Ireland	1946	Society for Endocrinology
		1950	Society for Reproduction and Fertility (SRF)
1875	Royal Environmental Health Institute of Scotland (REHIS)	1884	Society for the Study of Addiction (SSA)
1734	Royal Medical Society		
1931	Royal Pharmaceutical Society of Great Britain (RPS)	1926	Society of British Neurological Surgeons

Music

1977	Alkan Society	1888	Plainsong and Medieval Music Society (PMMS)
1979	British Music Society		
1971	Chopin Society	1874	Royal Musical Association (RMA)
1932	English Folk Dance and Song Society (efdss)	1955	Welsh Music Guild
1882	Incorporated Society of Musicians (ISM)		

Philosophy

1880	Aristotelian Society	1781	Manchester Literary and Philosophical Society
1984	British Society for the History of Philosophy (BSHP)		
		1913	Philosophical Society of England
1819	Cambridge Philosophical Society	1925	Royal Institute of Philosophy
1990	Friedrich Nietzsche Society (FNS)	1802	Royal Philosophical Society of Glasgow
1979	Hegel Society of Great Britain (HSGB)		

Politics

1975	British International Studies Association (BISA)	1987	Institute of Welsh Affairs
		1974	International Association for the Study of German Politics (ISAGP)
1951	David Davies Memorial Institute of International Studies (Aberystwyth University)		
		1950	Political Studies Association (PSA)
		1868	Royal Commonwealth Society
1884	Electoral Reform Society (ERS)	1920	Royal Institute of International Affairs (Chatham House)
1945	Federal Trust for Education and Research		

Science general

1831	British Science Association (BSA)	1799	Royal Institution of Great Britain (Ri)
1947	British Society for the History of Science (BSHS)	1660	Royal Society
		1783	Royal Society of Edinburgh
1960	British Society for the Philosophy of Science (BSPS)		

Theology and Religious Studies

1908	Baptist Historical Society	1981	European Association for Jewish Studies (EAJS)
1954	British Association for the Study of Religions (BASR)	1903	Friends Historical Society
1904	Canterbury and York Society	1972	United Reformed Church History Society (Westminster College)
1904	Catholic Record Society		
1961	Ecclesiastical History Society (EHS)	1893	Wesley Historical Society

General Index

Note: In addition to the abbreviations listed at the beginning of the book, the following are used throughout the index; FE – Further Education; HE – Higher Education. Universities are listed under locations eg: Aberdeen, University of